T0180315

Lecture Notes in Computer Science 13111

More information about this subseries at https://link.springer.com/bookseries/7407

Teddy Mantoro · Minho Lee ·
Media Anugerah Ayu · Kok Wai Wong ·
Achmad Nizar Hidayanto (Eds.)

Neural
Information Processing

28th International Conference, ICONIP 2021
Sanur, Bali, Indonesia, December 8–12, 2021
Proceedings, Part IV

Springer

Editors
Teddy Mantoro 🆔
Sampoerna University
Jakarta, Indonesia

Minho Lee 🆔
Kyungpook National University
Daegu, Korea (Republic of)

Media Anugerah Ayu 🆔
Sampoerna University
Jakarta, Indonesia

Kok Wai Wong 🆔
Murdoch University
Murdoch, WA, Australia

Achmad Nizar Hidayanto 🆔
Universitas Indonesia
Depok, Indonesia

ISSN 0302-9743   ISSN 1611-3349   (electronic)
Lecture Notes in Computer Science
ISBN 978-3-030-92272-6   ISBN 978-3-030-92273-3   (eBook)
https://doi.org/10.1007/978-3-030-92273-3

LNCS Sublibrary: SL1 – Theoretical Computer Science and General Issues

This Springer imprint is published by the registered company Springer Nature Switzerland AG
The registered company address is: Gewerbestrasse 11, 6330 Cham, Switzerland

Preface

Welcome to the proceedings of the 28th International Conference on Neural Information Processing (ICONIP 2021) of the Asia-Pacific Neural Network Society (APNNS), held virtually from Indonesia during December 8–12, 2021.

The mission of the Asia-Pacific Neural Network Society is to promote active interactions among researchers, scientists, and industry professionals who are working in neural networks and related fields in the Asia-Pacific region. APNNS has Governing Board Members from 13 countries/regions – Australia, China, Hong Kong, India, Japan, Malaysia, New Zealand, Singapore, South Korea, Qatar, Taiwan, Thailand, and Turkey. The society's flagship annual conference is the International Conference of Neural Information Processing (ICONIP).

The ICONIP conference aims to provide a leading international forum for researchers, scientists, and industry professionals who are working in neuroscience, neural networks, deep learning, and related fields to share their new ideas, progress, and achievements. Due to the current COVID-19 pandemic, ICONIP 2021, which was planned to be held in Bali, Indonesia, was organized as a fully virtual conference.

The proceedings of ICONIP 2021 consists of a four-volume set, LNCS 13108–13111, which includes 226 papers selected from 1093 submissions, representing an acceptance rate of 20.86% and reflecting the increasingly high quality of research in neural networks and related areas in the Asia-Pacific. The conference had four main themes, i.e., "Theory and Algorithms," "Cognitive Neurosciences," "Human Centred Computing," and "Applications."

The four volumes are organized in topical sections which comprise the four main themes mentioned previously and the topics covered in three special sessions. Another topic is from a workshop on Artificial Intelligence and Cyber Security which was held in conjunction with ICONIP 2021. Thus, in total, eight different topics were accommodated at the conference. The topics were also the names of the 20-minute presentation sessions at ICONIP 2021. The eight topics in the conference were: Theory and Algorithms; Cognitive Neurosciences; Human Centred Computing; Applications; Artificial Intelligence and Cybersecurity; Advances in Deep and Shallow Machine Learning Algorithms for Biomedical Data and Imaging; Reliable, Robust, and Secure Machine Learning Algorithms; and Theory and Applications of Natural Computing Paradigms.

Our great appreciation goes to the Program Committee members and the reviewers who devoted their time and effort to our rigorous peer-review process. Their insightful reviews and timely feedback ensured the high quality of the papers accepted for publication. Finally, thank you to all the authors of papers, presenters, and participants at the conference. Your support and engagement made it all worthwhile.

December 2021

Teddy Mantoro
Minho Lee
Media A. Ayu
Kok Wai Wong
Achmad Nizar Hidayanto

Organization

Honorary Chairs

Jonathan Chan — King Mongkut's University of Technology Thonburi, Thailand

Lance Fung — Murdoch University, Australia

General Chairs

Teddy Mantoro — Sampoerna University, Indonesia
Minho Lee — Kyungpook National University, South Korea

Program Chairs

Media A. Ayu — Sampoerna University, Indonesia
Kok Wai Wong — Murdoch University, Australia
Achmad Nizar — Universitas Indonesia, Indonesia

Local Arrangements Chairs

Linawati — Universitas Udayana, Indonesia
W. G. Ariastina — Universitas Udayana, Indonesia

Finance Chairs

Kurnianingsih — Politeknik Negeri Semarang, Indonesia
Kazushi Ikeda — Nara Institute of Science and Technology, Japan

Special Sessions Chairs

Sunu Wibirama — Universitas Gadjah Mada, Indonesia
Paul Pang — Federation University Australia, Australia
Noor Akhmad Setiawan — Universitas Gadjah Mada, Indonesia

Tutorial Chairs

Suryono — Universitas Diponegoro, Indonesia
Muhammad Agni Catur Bhakti — Sampoerna University, Indonesia

Proceedings Chairs

Adi Wibowo   Universitas Diponegoro, Indonesia
Sung Bae Cho   Yonsei University, South Korea

Publicity Chairs

Dwiza Riana   Universitas Nusa Mandiri, Indonesia
M. Tanveer   Indian Institute of Technology, Indore, India

Program Committee

Abdulrazak Alhababi   Universiti Malaysia Sarawak, Malaysia
Abhijit Adhikary   Australian National University, Australia
Achmad Nizar Hidayanto   University of Indonesia, Indonesia
Adamu Abubakar Ibrahim   International Islamic University Malaysia, Malaysia
Adi Wibowo   Diponegoro University, Indonesia
Adnan Mahmood   Macquarie University, Australia
Afiyati Amaluddin   Mercu Buana University, Indonesia
Ahmed Alharbi   RMIT University, Australia
Akeem Olowolayemo   International Islamic University Malaysia, Malaysia
Akira Hirose   University of Tokyo, Japan
Aleksandra Nowak   Jagiellonian University, Poland
Ali Haidar   University of New South Wales, Australia
Ali Mehrabi   Western Sydney University, Australia
Al-Jadir   Murdoch University, Australia
Ana Flavia Reis   Federal Technological University of Paraná, Brazil
Anaissi Ali   University of Sydney, Australia
Andrew Beng Jin Teoh   Yonsei University, South Korea
Andrew Chiou   Central Queensland University, Australia
Aneesh Chivukula   University of Technology Sydney, Australia
Aneesh Krishna   Curtin University, Australia
Anna Zhu   Wuhan University of Technology, China
Anto Satriyo Nugroho   Agency for Assessment and Application of
                            Technology, Indonesia
Anupiya Nugaliyadde   Sri Lanka Institute of Information Technology,
                            Sri Lanka
Anwesha Law   Indian Statistical Institute, India
Aprinaldi Mantau   Kyushu Institute of Technology, Japan
Ari Wibisono   Universitas Indonesia, Indonesia
Arief Ramadhan   Bina Nusantara University, Indonesia
Arit Thammano   King Mongkut's Institute of Technology Ladkrabang,
                            Thailand
Arpit Garg   University of Adelaide, Australia
Aryal Sunil   Deakin University, Australia
Ashkan Farhangi   University of Central Florida, USA

Atul Negi	University of Hyderabad, India
Barawi Mohamad Hardyman	Universiti Malaysia Sarawak, Malaysia
Bayu Distiawan	Universitas Indonesia, Indonesia
Bharat Richhariya	IISc Bangalore, India
Bin Pan	Nankai University, China
Bingshu Wang	Northwestern Polytechnical University, Taicang, China
Bonaventure C. Molokwu	University of Windsor, Canada
Bo-Qun Ma	Ant Financial
Bunthit Watanapa	King Mongkut's University of Technology Thonburi, Thailand
Chang-Dong Wang	Sun Yat-sen University, China
Chattrakul Sombattheera	Mahasarakham University, Thailand
Chee Siong Teh	Universiti Malaysia Sarawak, Malaysia
Chen Wei Chén	Chongqing Jiaotong University, China
Chengwei Wu	Harbin Institute of Technology, China
Chern Hong Lim	Monash University, Australia
Chih-Chieh Hung	National Chung Hsing University, Taiwan
Chiranjibi Sitaula	Deakin University, Australia
Chi-Sing Leung	City University of Hong Kong, Hong Kong
Choo Jun Tan	Wawasan Open University, Malaysia
Christoph Bergmeir	Monash University, Australia
Christophe Guyeux	University of Franche-Comté, France
Chuan Chen	Sun Yat-sen University, China
Chuanqi Tan	BIT, China
Chu-Kiong Loo	University of Malaya, Malaysia
Chun Che Fung	Murdoch University, Australia
Colin Samplawski	University of Massachusetts Amherst, USA
Congbo Ma	University of Adelaide, Australia
Cuiyun Gao	Chinese University of Hong Kong, Hong Kong
Cutifa Safitri	Universiti Teknologi Malaysia, Malaysia
Daisuke Miyamoto	University of Tokyo, Japan
Dan Popescu	Politehnica University of Bucharest
David Bong	Universiti Malaysia Sarawak, Malaysia
David Iclanzan	Sapientia Hungarian Science University of Transylvania, Romania
Debasmit Das	IIT Roorkee, India
Dengya Zhu	Curtin University, Australia
Derwin Suhartono	Bina Nusantara University, Indonesia
Devi Fitrianah	Universitas Mercu Buana, Indonesia
Deyu Zhou	Southeast University, China
Dhimas Arief Dharmawan	Universitas Indonesia, Indonesia
Dianhui Wang	La Trobe University, Australia
Dini Handayani	Taylors University, Malaysia
Dipanjyoti Paul	Indian Institute of Technology, Patna, India
Dong Chen	Wuhan University, China

He Chen   Nankai University, China
He Huang   Soochow University, China
Hea Choon Ngo   Universiti Teknikal Malaysia Melaka, Malaysia
Heba El-Fiqi   UNSW Canberra, Australia
Heru Praptono   Bank Indonesia/Universitas Indonesia, Indonesia
Hideitsu Hino   Institute of Statistical Mathematics, Japan
Hidemasa Takao   University of Tokyo, Japan
Hiroaki Inoue   Kobe University, Japan
Hiroaki Kudo   Nagoya University, Japan
Hiromu Monai   Ochanomizu University, Japan
Hiroshi Sakamoto   Kyushu Institute of Technology, Japan
Hisashi Koga   University of Electro-Communications, Japan
Hiu-Hin Tam   City University of Hong Kong, Hong Kong
Hongbing Xia   Beijing Normal University, China
Hongtao Liu   Tianjin University, China
Hongtao Lu   Shanghai Jiao Tong University, China
Hua Zuo   University of Technology Sydney, Australia
Hualou Liang   Drexel University, USA
Huang Chaoran   University of New South Wales, Australia
Huang Shudong   Sichuan University, China
Huawen Liu   University of Texas at San Antonio, USA
Hui Xue   Southeast University, China
Hui Yan   Shanghai Jiao Tong University, China
Hyeyoung Park   Kyungpook National University, South Korea
Hyun-Chul Kim   Kyungpook National University, South Korea
Iksoo Shin   University of Science and Technology, South Korea
Indrabayu Indrabayu   Universitas Hasanuddin, Indonesia
Iqbal Gondal   RMIT University, Australia
Iuliana Georgescu   University of Bucharest, Romania
Iwan Syarif   PENS, Indonesia
J. Kokila   Indian Institute of Information Technology, Allahabad,
                           India
J. Manuel Moreno   Universitat Politècnica de Catalunya, Spain
Jagdish C. Patra   Swinburne University of Technology, Australia
Jean-Francois Couchot   University of Franche-Comté, France
Jelita Asian   STKIP Surya, Indonesia
Jennifer C. Dela Cruz   Mapua University, Philippines
Jérémie Sublime   ISEP, France
Jiahuan Lei   Meituan, China
Jialiang Zhang   Alibaba, China
Jiaming Xu   Institute of Automation, Chinese Academy of Sciences
Jianbo Ning   University of Science and Technology Beijing, China
Jianyi Yang   Nankai University, China
Jiasen Wang   City University of Hong Kong, Hong Kong
Jiawei Fan   Australian National University, Australia
Jiawei Li   Tsinghua University, China

Kok Wai Wong	Murdoch University, Australia
Kitsuchart Pasupa	King Mongkut's Institute of Technology Ladkrabang, Thailand
Kittichai Lavangnananda	King Mongkut's University of Technology Thonburi, Thailand
Koutsakis Polychronis	Murdoch University, Australia
Kui Ding	Nanjing Normal University, China
Kun Zhang	Carnegie Mellon University, USA
Kuntpong Woraratpanya	King Mongkut's Institute of Technology Ladkrabang, Thailand
Kurnianingsih Kurnianingsih	Politeknik Negeri Semarang, Indonesia
Kusrini	Universitas AMIKOM Yogyakarta, Indonesia
Kyle Harrison	UNSW Canberra, Australia
Laga Hamid	Murdoch University, Australia
Lei Wang	Beihang University, China
Leonardo Franco	Universidad de Málaga, Spain
Li Guo	University of Macau, China
Li Yun	Nanjing University of Posts and Telecommunications, China
Libo Wang	Xiamen University of Technology, China
Lie Meng Pang	Southern University of Science and Technology, China
Liew Alan Wee-Chung	Griffith University, Australia
Lingzhi Hu	Beijing University of Technology, China
Linjing Liu	City University of Hong Kong, Hong Kong
Lisi Chen	Hong Kong Baptist University, Hong Kong
Long Cheng	Institute of Automation, Chinese Academy of Sciences, China
Lukman Hakim	Hiroshima University, Japan
M. Tanveer	Indian Institute of Technology, Indore, India
Ma Wanli	University of Canberra, Australia
Man Fai Leung	Hong Kong Metropolitan University, Hong Kong
Maram Mahmoud A. Monshi	Beijing Institute of Technology, China
Marcin Wozniak	Silesian University of Technology, Poland
Marco Anisetti	Università degli Studi di Milano, Italy
Maria Susan Anggreainy	Bina Nusantara University, Indonesia
Mark Abernethy	Murdoch University, Australia
Mark Elshaw	Coventry University, UK
Maruno Yuki	Kyoto Women's University, Japan
Masafumi Hagiwara	Keio University, Japan
Masataka Kawai	NRI SecureTechnologies, Ltd., Japan
Media Ayu	Sampoerna University, Indonesia
Mehdi Neshat	University of Adelaide, Australia
Meng Wang	Southeast University, China
Mengmeng Li	Zhengzhou University, China

Miaohua Zhang	Griffith University, Australia
Mingbo Zhao	Donghua University, China
Mingcong Deng	Tokyo University of Agriculture and Technology, Japan
Minghao Yang	Institute of Automation, Chinese Academy of Sciences, China
Minho Lee	Kyungpook National University, South Korea
Mofei Song	Southeast University, China
Mohammad Faizal Ahmad Fauzi	Multimedia University, Malaysia
Mohsen Marjani	Taylor's University, Malaysia
Mubasher Baig	National University of Computer and Emerging Sciences, Lahore, Pakistan
Muhammad Anwar Ma'Sum	Universitas Indonesia, Indonesia
Muhammad Asim Ali	Shaheed Zulfikar Ali Bhutto Institute of Science and Technology, Pakistan
Muhammad Fawad Akbar Khan	University of Engineering and Technology Peshawar, Pakistan
Muhammad Febrian Rachmadi	Universitas Indonesia, Indonesia
Muhammad Haris	Universitas Nusa Mandiri, Indonesia
Muhammad Haroon Shakeel	Lahore University of Management Sciences, Pakistan
Muhammad Hilman	Universitas Indonesia, Indonesia
Muhammad Ramzan	Saudi Electronic University, Saudi Arabia
Muideen Adegoke	City University of Hong Kong, Hong Kong
Mulin Chen	Northwestern Polytechnical University, China
Murtaza Taj	Lahore University of Management Sciences, Pakistan
Mutsumi Kimura	Ryukoku University, Japan
Naoki Masuyama	Osaka Prefecture University, Japan
Naoyuki Sato	Future University Hakodate, Japan
Nat Dilokthanakul	Vidyasirimedhi Institute of Science and Technology, Thailand
Nguyen Dang	University of Canberra, Australia
Nhi N. Y. Vo	University of Technology Sydney, Australia
Nick Nikzad	Griffith University, Australia
Ning Boda	Swinburne University of Technology, Australia
Nobuhiko Wagatsuma	Tokyo Denki University, Japan
Nobuhiko Yamaguchi	Saga University, Japan
Noor Akhmad Setiawan	Universitas Gadjah Mada, Indonesia
Norbert Jankowski	Nicolaus Copernicus University, Poland
Norikazu Takahashi	Okayama University, Japan
Noriyasu Homma	Tohoku University, Japan
Normaziah A. Aziz	International Islamic University Malaysia, Malaysia
Olarik Surinta	Mahasarakham University, Thailand

Olutomilayo Olayemi Petinrin	Kings University, Nigeria
Ooi Shih Yin	Multimedia University, Malaysia
Osamu Araki	Tokyo University of Science, Japan
Ozlem Faydasicok	Istanbul University, Turkey
Parisa Rastin	University of Lorraine, France
Paul S. Pang	Federation University Australia, Australia
Pedro Antonio Gutierrez	Universidad de Cordoba, Spain
Pengyu Sun	Microsoft
Piotr Duda	Institute of Computational Intelligence/Czestochowa University of Technology, Poland
Prabath Abeysekara	RMIT University, Australia
Pui Huang Leong	Tunku Abdul Rahman University College, Malaysia
Qian Li	Chinese Academy of Sciences, China
Qiang Xiao	Huazhong University of Science and Technology, China
Qiangfu Zhao	University of Aizu, Japan
Qianli Ma	South China University of Technology, China
Qing Xu	Tianjin University, China
Qing Zhang	Meituan, China
Qinglai Wei	Institute of Automation, Chinese Academy of Sciences, China
Qingrong Cheng	Fudan University, China
Qiufeng Wang	Xi'an Jiaotong-Liverpool University, China
Qiulei Dong	Institute of Automation, Chinese Academy of Sciences, China
Qiuye Wu	Guangdong University of Technology, China
Rafal Scherer	Częstochowa University of Technology, Poland
Rahmadya Handayanto	Universitas Islam 45 Bekasi, Indonesia
Rahmat Budiarto	Albaha University, Saudi Arabia
Raja Kumar	Taylor's University, Malaysia
Rammohan Mallipeddi	Kyungpook National University, South Korea
Rana Md Mashud	CSIRO, Australia
Rapeeporn Chamchong	Mahasarakham University, Thailand
Raphael Couturier	Université Bourgogne Franche-Comté, France
Ratchakoon Pruengkarn	Dhurakij Pundit University, Thailand
Reem Mohamed	Mansoura University, Egypt
Rhee Man Kil	Sungkyunkwan University, South Korea
Rim Haidar	University of Sydney, Australia
Rizal Fathoni Aji	Universitas Indonesia, Indonesia
Rukshima Dabare	Murdoch University, Australia
Ruting Cheng	University of Science and Technology Beijing, China
Ruxandra Liana Costea	Polytechnic University of Bucharest, Romania
Saaveethya Sivakumar	Curtin University Malaysia, Malaysia
Sabrina Fariza	Central Queensland University, Australia
Sahand Vahidnia	University of New South Wales, Australia

Saifur Rahaman	City University of Hong Kong, Hong Kong
Sajib Mistry	Curtin University, Australia
Sajib Saha	CSIRO, Australia
Sajid Anwar	Institute of Management Sciences Peshawar, Pakistan
Sakchai Muangsrinoon	Walailak University, Thailand
Salomon Michel	Université Bourgogne Franche-Comté, France
Sandeep Parameswaran	Myntra Designs Pvt. Ltd., India
Sangtae Ahn	Kyungpook National University, South Korea
Sang-Woo Ban	Dongguk University, South Korea
Sangwook Kim	Kobe University, Japan
Sanparith Marukatat	NECTEC, Thailand
Saptakatha Adak	Indian Institute of Technology, Madras, India
Seiichi Ozawa	Kobe University, Japan
Selvarajah Thuseethan	Sabaragamuwa University of Sri Lanka, Sri Lanka
Seong-Bae Park	Kyung Hee University, South Korea
Shan Zhong	Changshu Institute of Technology, China
Shankai Yan	National Institutes of Health, USA
Sheeraz Akram	University of Pittsburgh, USA
Shenglan Liu	Dalian University of Technology, China
Shenglin Zhao	Zhejiang University, China
Shing Chiang Tan	Multimedia University, Malaysia
Shixiong Zhang	Xidian University, China
Shreya Chawla	Australian National University, Australia
Shri Rai	Murdoch University, Australia
Shuchao Pang	Jilin University, China/Macquarie University, Australia
Shuichi Kurogi	Kyushu Institute of Technology, Japan
Siddharth Sachan	Australian National University, Australia
Sirui Li	Murdoch University, Australia
Sonali Agarwal	Indian Institute of Information Technology, Allahabad, India
Sonya Coleman	University of Ulster, UK
Stavros Ntalampiras	University of Milan, Italy
Su Lei	University of Science and Technology Beijing, China
Sung-Bae Cho	Yonsei University, South Korea
Sunu Wibirama	Universitas Gadjah Mada, Indonesia
Susumu Kuroyanagi	Nagoya Institute of Technology, Japan
Sutharshan Rajasegarar	Deakin University, Australia
Takako Hashimoto	Chiba University of Commerce, Japan
Takashi Omori	Tamagawa University, Japan
Tao Ban	National Institute of Information and Communications Technology, Japan
Tao Li	Peking University, China
Tao Xiang	Chongqing University, China
Teddy Mantoro	Sampoerna University, Indonesia
Tedjo Darmanto	STMIK AMIK Bandung, Indonesia
Teijiro Isokawa	University of Hyogo, Japan

Thanh Tam Nguyen	Leibniz University Hannover, Germany
Thanh Tung Khuat	University of Technology Sydney, Australia
Thaweesak Khongtuk	Rajamangala University of Technology Suvarnabhumi, Thailand
Tianlin Zhang	University of Chinese Academy of Sciences, China
Timothy McIntosh	Massey University, New Zealand
Toan Nguyen Thanh	Ho Chi Minh City University of Technology, Vietnam
Todsanai Chumwatana	Murdoch University, Australia
Tom Gedeon	Australian National University, Australia
Tomas Maul	University of Nottingham, Malaysia
Tomohiro Shibata	Kyushu Institute of Technology, Japan
Tomoyuki Kaneko	University of Tokyo, Japan
Toshiaki Omori	Kobe University, Japan
Toshiyuki Yamane	IBM, Japan
Uday Kiran	University of Tokyo, Japan
Udom Silparcha	King Mongkut's University of Technology Thonburi, Thailand
Umar Aditiawarman	Universitas Nusa Putra, Indonesia
Upeka Somaratne	Murdoch University, Australia
Usman Naseem	University of Sydney, Australia
Ven Jyn Kok	National University of Malaysia, Malaysia
Wachira Yangyuen	Rajamangala University of Technology Srivijaya, Thailand
Wai-Keung Fung	Robert Gordon University, UK
Wang Yaqing	Baidu Research, Hong Kong
Wang Yu-Kai	University of Technology Sydney, Australia
Wei Jin	Michigan State University, USA
Wei Yanling	TU Berlin, Germany
Weibin Wu	City University of Hong Kong, Hong Kong
Weifeng Liu	China University of Petroleum, China
Weijie Xiang	University of Science and Technology Beijing, China
Wei-Long Zheng	Massachusetts General Hospital, Harvard Medical School, USA
Weiqun Wang	Institute of Automation, Chinese Academy of Sciences, China
Wen Luo	Nanjing Normal University, China
Wen Yu	Cinvestav, Mexico
Weng Kin Lai	Tunku Abdul Rahman University College, Malaysia
Wenqiang Liu	Southwest Jiaotong University, China
Wentao Wang	Michigan State University, USA
Wenwei Gu	Chinese University of Hong Kong, Hong Kong
Wenxin Yu	Southwest University of Science and Technology, China
Widodo Budiharto	Bina Nusantara University, Indonesia
Wisnu Ananta Kusuma	Institut Pertanian Bogor, Indonesia
Worapat Paireekreng	Dhurakij Pundit University, Thailand

Xiang Chen	George Mason University, USA
Xiao Jian Tan	Tunku Abdul Rahman University College, Malaysia
Xiao Liang	Nankai University, China
Xiaocong Chen	University of New South Wales, Australia
Xiaodong Yue	Shanghai University, China
Xiaoqing Lyu	Peking University, China
Xiaoyang Liu	Huazhong University of Science and Technology, China
Xiaoyang Tan	Nanjing University of Aeronautics and Astronautics, China
Xiao-Yu Tang	Zhejiang University, China
Xin Liu	Huaqiao University, China
Xin Wang	Southwest University, China
Xin Xu	Beijing University of Technology, China
Xingjian Chen	City University of Hong Kong, Hong Kong
Xinyi Le	Shanghai Jiao Tong University, China
Xinyu Shi	University of Science and Technology Beijing, China
Xiwen Bao	Chongqing Jiaotong University, China
Xu Bin	Northwestern Polytechnical University, China
Xu Chen	Shanghai Jiao Tong University, China
Xuan-Son Vu	Umeå University, Sweden
Xuanying Zhu	Australian National University, Australia
Yanling Zhang	University of Science and Technology Beijing, China
Yang Li	East China Normal University, China
Yantao Li	Chongqing University, China
Yanyan Hu	University of Science and Technology Beijing, China
Yao Lu	Beijing Institute of Technology, China
Yasuharu Koike	Tokyo Institute of Technology, Japan
Ya-Wen Teng	Academia Sinica, Taiwan
Yaxin Li	Michigan State University, USA
Yifan Xu	Huazhong University of Science and Technology, China
Yihsin Ho	Takushoku University, Japan
Yilun Jin	Hong Kong University of Science and Technology, Hong Kong
Yiming Li	Tsinghua University, China
Ying Xiao	University of Birmingham, UK
Yingjiang Zhou	Nanjing University of Posts and Telecommunications, China
Yong Peng	Hangzhou Dianzi University, China
Yonghao Ma	University of Science and Technology Beijing, China
Yoshikazu Washizawa	University of Electro-Communications, Japan
Yoshimitsu Kuroki	Kurume National College of Technology, Japan
Young Ju Rho	Korea Polytechnic University, South Korea
Youngjoo Seo	Ecole Polytechnique Fédérale de Lausanne, Switzerland

Contents – Part IV

Applications

Deep Supervised Hashing by Classification for Image Retrieval   3
Xiao Luo, Yuhang Guo, Zeyu Ma, Huasong Zhong, Tao Li, Wei Ju,
Chong Chen, and Minghua Deng

Towards Human-Level Performance in Solving Double Dummy
Bridge Problem.   15
Szymon Kowalik and Jacek Mańdziuk

Coarse-to-Fine Visual Place Recognition   28
Junkun Qi, Rui Wang, Chuan Wang, and Xiaochun Cao

BFConv: Improving Convolutional Neural Networks
with Butterfly Convolution.   40
Dengjie Yang, Xuehui Yu, Yi Sun, Fuzhen Zhuang, Qing He,
and Shiwei Ye

Integrating Rich Utterance Features for Emotion Recognition
in Multi-party Conversations   51
Yang Sun, Nan Yu, and Guohong Fu

Vehicle Image Generation Going Well with the Surroundings.   63
Jeesoo Kim, Jangho Kim, Jaeyoung Yoo, Daesik Kim, and Nojun Kwak

Scale Invariant Domain Generalization Image Recapture Detection   75
Jinian Luo, Jie Guo, Weidong Qiu, Zheng Huang, and Hong Hui

Tile2Vec with Predicting Noise for Land Cover Classification   87
Marshal Arijona Sinaga, Fadel Muhammad Ali,
and Aniati Murni Arymurthy

A Joint Representation Learning Approach for Social Media Tag
Recommendation   100
Xiangyu Li and Weizheng Chen

Identity-Based Data Augmentation via Progressive Sampling for One-Shot
Person Re-identification.   113
Runxuan Si, Shaowu Yang, Jing Zhao, Haoang Chi, and Yuhua Tang

Feature Fusion Learning Based on LSTM and CNN Networks for Trend
Analysis of Limit Order Books.   125
Xuerui Lv and Li Zhang

WikiFlash: Generating Flashcards from Wikipedia Articles.   138
   Yuang Cheng, Yue Ding, Sebastien Foucher, Damián Pascual,
   Oliver Richter, Martin Volk, and Roger Wattenhofer

Video Face Recognition with Audio-Visual Aggregation Network.   150
   Qinbo Li, Qing Wan, Sang-Heon Lee, and Yoonsuck Choe

WaveFuse: A Unified Unsupervised Framework for Image Fusion
with Discrete Wavelet Transform   162
   Shaolei Liu, Manning Wang, and Zhijian Song

Manipulation-Invariant Fingerprints for Cross-Dataset Deepfake Detection . . .   175
   Zuoyan Li, Wenyuan Yang, Ruixin Liu, and Yuesheng Zhu

Low-Resource Neural Machine Translation Using Fast
Meta-learning Method   188
   Nier Wu, Hongxu Hou, Wei Zheng, and Shuo Sun

Efficient, Low-Cost, Real-Time Video Super-Resolution Network.   200
   Guanqun Liu, Xin Wang, Daren Zha, Lei Wang, and Lin Zhao

On the Unreasonable Effectiveness of Centroids in Image Retrieval.   212
   Mikołaj Wieczorek, Barbara Rychalska, and Jacek Dąbrowski

Few-Shot Classification with Multi-task Self-supervised Learning   224
   Fan Shi, Rui Wang, Sanyi Zhang, and Xiaochun Cao

Self-supervised Compressed Video Action Recognition
via Temporal-Consistent Sampling   237
   Pan Chen, Shaohui Lin, Yongxiang Zhang, Jiachen Xu, Xin Tan,
   and Lizhuang Ma

Stack-VAE Network for Zero-Shot Learning   250
   Jinghao Xie, Jigang Wu, Tianyou Liang, and Min Meng

TRUFM: a Transformer-Guided Framework for Fine-Grained Urban
Flow Inference   262
   Xinchi Zhou, Dongzhan Zhou, and Lingbo Liu

Saliency Detection Framework Based on Deep Enhanced
Attention Network.   274
   Xing Sheng, Zhuoran Zheng, Qiong Wu, Chunmeng Kang,
   Yunliang Zhuang, Lei Lyu, and Chen Lyu

SynthTriplet GAN: Synthetic Query Expansion for Multimodal Retrieval. . . .   287
   Ivona Tautkute and Tomasz Trzciński

SS-CCN: Scale Self-guided Crowd Counting Network.   299
   Jinfang Zheng, Jinyang Xie, Chen Lyu, and Lei Lyu

QS-Hyper: A Quality-Sensitive Hyper Network for the No-Reference
Image Quality Assessment   311
    Xuewen Zhang, Yunye Zhang, Wenxin Yu, Liang Nie, Ning Jiang,
    and Jun Gong

An Efficient Manifold Density Estimator for All Recommendation Systems . . .   323
    Jacek Dąbrowski, Barbara Rychalska, Michał Daniluk, Dominika Basaj,
    Konrad Gołuchowski, Piotr Bąbel, Andrzej Michałowski,
    and Adam Jakubowski

Cleora: A Simple, Strong and Scalable Graph Embedding Scheme   338
    Barbara Rychalska, Piotr Bąbel, Konrad Gołuchowski,
    Andrzej Michałowski, Jacek Dąbrowski, and Przemysław Biecek

STA3DCNN: Spatial-Temporal Attention 3D Convolutional Neural
Network for Citywide Crowd Flow Prediction   353
    Gaozhong Tang, Zhiheng Zhou, and Bo Li

Learning Pre-grasp Pushing Manipulation of Wide and Flat Objects Using
Binary Masks   366
    Jiaxi Wu, Shanlin Zhong, and Yinlin Li

Multi-DIP: A General Framework for Unsupervised Multi-degraded Image
Restoration   378
    Qiansong Wang, Xiao Hu, Haiying Wang, Aidong Men,
    and Zhuqing Jiang

Multi-Attention Network for Arbitrary Style Transfer   390
    Sihui Hua and Dongdong Zhang

Image Brightness Adjustment with Unpaired Training   402
    Chaojian Liu, Hong Chen, and Aidong Men

Self-supervised Image-to-Text and Text-to-Image Synthesis   415
    Anindya Sundar Das and Sriparna Saha

TextCut: A Multi-region Replacement Data Augmentation Approach
for Text Imbalance Classification   427
    Wanrong Jiang, Ya Chen, Hao Fu, and Guiquan Liu

A Multi-task Model for Sentiment Aided Cyberbullying Detection
in Code-Mixed Indian Languages   440
    Krishanu Maity and Sriparna Saha

A Transformer-Based Model for Low-Resource Event Detection   452
    Yanxia Qin, Jingjing Ding, Yiping Sun, and Xiangwu Ding

Malicious Domain Detection on Imbalanced Data with Deep
Reinforcement Learning.   464
   Fangfang Yuan, Teng Tian, Yanmin Shang, Yuhai Lu, Yanbing Liu,
   and Jianlong Tan

Designing and Searching for Lightweight Monocular Depth Network   477
   Jinfeng Liu, Lingtong Kong, and Jie Yang

Improving Question Answering over Knowledge Graphs Using Graph
Summarization   489
   Sirui Li, Kok Wai Wong, Chun Che Fung, and Dengya Zhu

Multi-stage Hybrid Attentive Networks for Knowledge-Driven Stock
Movement Prediction.   501
   Jiaying Gong and Hoda Eldardiry

End-to-End Edge Detection via Improved Transformer Model   514
   Yi Gao, Chenwei Tang, Jiulin Lang, and Jiancheng Lv

Isn't It Ironic, Don't You Think?   526
   Saichethan Miriyala Reddy and Swati Agarwal

Neural Local and Global Contexts Learning for Word Sense
Disambiguation.   537
   Fumiyo Fukumoto, Taishin Mishima, Jiyi Li, and Yoshimi Suzuki

Towards Better Dermoscopic Image Feature Representation Learning
for Melanoma Classification.   550
   ChengHui Yu, MingKang Tang, ShengGe Yang, MingQing Wang,
   Zhe Xu, JiangPeng Yan, HanMo Chen, Yu Yang, Xiao-Jun Zeng,
   and Xiu Li

Paraphrase Identification with Neural Elaboration Relation Learning   562
   Sheng Xu, Fumiyo Fukumoto, Jiyi Li, and Yoshimi Suzuki

Hybrid DE-MLP-Based Modeling Technique for Prediction of Alloying
Element Proportions and Process Parameters   574
   Ravindra V. Savangouder, Jagdish C. Patra, and Suresh Palanisamy

A Mutual Information-Based Disentanglement Framework
for Cross-Modal Retrieval   585
   Han Wu, Xiaowang Zhang, Jiachen Tian, Shaojuan Wu, Chunliu Dou,
   Yue Sun, and Zhiyong Feng

AGRP: A Fused Aspect-Graph Neural Network for Rating Prediction   597
   Cong Huang, Huiping Lin, and Yuhan Xiao

Classmates Enhanced Diversity-Self-Attention Network for Dropout
Prediction in MOOCs 609
    Dongen Wu, Pengyi Hao, Yuxiang Zheng, Tianxing Han, and Cong Bai

A Hierarchical Graph-Based Neural Network for Malware Classification 621
    Shuai Wang, Yuran Zhao, Gongshen Liu, and Bo Su

A Visual Feature Detection Algorithm Inspired by Spatio-Temporal
Properties of Visual Neurons 634
    Eisaku Horiguchi and Hirotsugu Okuno

Knowledge Distillation Method for Surface Defect Detection 644
    Jiulin Lang, Chenwei Tang, Yi Gao, and Jiancheng Lv

Adaptive Selection of Classifiers for Person Recognition by Iris Pattern
and Periocular Image. 656
    Keita Ogawa and Keisuke Kameyama

Multi-Perspective Interactive Model for Chinese Sentence
Semantic Matching 668
    Baoshuo Kan, Wenpeng Lu, Fangfang Li, Hao Wu, Pengyu Zhao,
    and Xu Zhang

An Effective Implicit Multi-interest Interaction Network
for Recommendation 680
    Wei Yang, Xinxin Fan, Yiqun Chen, Feimo Li, and Hongxing Chang

Author Index 693

Applications

Deep Supervised Hashing
by Classification for Image Retrieval

Xiao Luo[1,2], Yuhang Guo[1], Zeyu Ma[3], Huasong Zhong[2], Tao Li[1], Wei Ju[4], Chong Chen[2], and Minghua Deng[1(✉)]

[1] School of Mathematical Sciences, Peking University, Beijing, China
{xiaoluo,yuhangguo,li_tao,dengmh}@pku.edu.cn
[2] Damo Academy, Alibaba Group, Hangzhou, China
{huasong.zhs,cheung.cc}@alibaba-inc.com
[3] School of Computer Science and Technology, Harbin Institute of Technology, Shenzhen, China
zeyu.ma@stu.hit.edu.cn
[4] Department of Computer Science and Technology, Peking University, Beijing, China
juwei@pku.edu.cn

Abstract. Hashing has been widely used to approximate the nearest neighbor search for image retrieval due to its high computation efficiency and low storage requirement. With the development of deep learning, a series of deep supervised methods were proposed for end-to-end binary code learning. However, the similarity between each pair of images is simply defined by whether they belong to the same class or contain common objects, which ignores the heterogeneity within the class. Therefore, those existing methods have not fully addressed the problem and their results are far from satisfactory. Besides, it is difficult and impractical to apply those methods to large-scale datasets. In this paper, we propose a brand new perspective to look into the nature of deep supervised hashing and show that classification models can be directly utilized to generate hashing codes. We also provide a new deep hashing architecture called **D**eep **S**upervised **H**ashing by **C**lassification (DSHC) which takes advantage of both inter-class and intra-class heterogeneity. Experiments on benchmark datasets show that our method outperforms the state-of-the-art supervised hashing methods on accuracy and efficiency.

Keywords: Learning to hash · Supervised learning · Deep hashing

1 Introduction

In recent years, hundreds of thousands of images are generated in the real world every day, making it extremely difficult to find the relevant images. Due to the effectiveness of deep convolution neural networks, images either in the

---

X. Luo, Y. Guo and Z. Ma—Contribute equally to this work. The work was done when Xiao Luo interned in Damo Academy, Alibaba Group.

T. Mantoro et al. (Eds.): ICONIP 2021, LNCS 13111, pp. 3–14, 2021.
https://doi.org/10.1007/978-3-030-92273-3_1

database or the query image can be well represented by real-valued features. Therefore image retrieval can be addressed as an approximating nearest neighbor (ANN) searching problem for the sake of computational efficiency and high retrieval quantity. Compared to the traditional content-based methods, hashing methods has shown its superiority for data compression, which transforms high-dimensional media data into the generated binary representation [4,11]. There are a number of learning-to-hashing methods for efficient ANN searching [14], which mainly fall into unsupervised methods [4,13] and supervised methods [11,12]. As the development of deep learning, deep hashing methods have prevailed and shown competitive performance for their ability to learn image representation [7]. By transferring deep representation learned by deep neural networks, effective hash codes are obtained by controlling the loss function. Specifically, they can learn similar-preserving representations and control quantization error for continuous representation by converting into binary codes. These methods can also be divided into three schemes, pairwise label based methods [1,9], triplet label based methods [24] and point-wise classification schemes [10,21], respectively. It's noticed that the above schemes can be mixed and utilized together [8]. Recently, several methods have added label information into their models and achieved great success [8].

Although these existing methods have achieved considerable progress, two significant drawbacks have not been fully addressed yet. The supervised hashing methods are usually guided by a similarity matrix S, while the definition of S is quite simple. Specifically, $s_{ij} = 1$ if image i and image j belong to the same class or contain common objects, and $s_{ij} = 0$ otherwise. Definitely, this way of definition is reasonable in a sense since images of the same category are considered to be the same. However, there are usually many sub-classes in the same class, and there should be some differences between different sub-classes. If all the sub-classes are forced to be regarded as the same, the obtained hash codes will be very unstable [15], so that the extension results on the test set will be poor. Therefore, the existing methods do not fully proceed from the perspective of image retrieval, and thus leading to unsatisfied retrieval accuracy. On the other hand, we notice that the schemes mentioned above often include complex pairwise loss functions, which means training on large datasets is difficult. Therefore, VGG-Net [16] is often used in deep supervised hashing task for the sake of speeding. If deeper models like ResNet are used [5], we need to replace the loss function of deep hashing with simpler forms such as those in the classification problem.

To address the two disadvantages mentioned above, we investigate the relationship between deep supervised hashing and classification problems. It turns out that high-quality binary codes can be generated by deep classification models. For single-label datasets, we can construct the mapping relationship between the classification result and the hash code in some ways, making the hamming distance between different classes of hash codes relatively large, while the hamming distance between the subclasses of the same class relatively small. For multi-label datasets, it is very natural to regard the predicted multi-shot labels as the final hash codes, since the dissimilarity of two images is well captured by the hamming distance. Following this idea, we proposed Deep Supervised Hashing by Classification (DSHC), a novel deep hashing model that can generate effective and concentrated hash codes to enable effective and efficient image retrieval. The main contributions of DSHC are outlined as follows:

- DSHC is an end-to-end hash codes generation framework containing three main components: 1) a standard deep convolutional neural network (CNN) such as ResNet101 or ResNeXt, 2) a novel classification loss based on cross-entropy that helps to divide the origin classed into several sub-classes by their features and 3) a heuristic mapping from sub-labels to hash codes making the hash codes of the sub-classed with the same label approach in Hamming space.
- To the best of our knowledge, DSHC is the first method that addresses deep supervised hashing as a classification problem and looks into the heterogeneity within the class.
- Comprehensive empirical evidence and analysis show that the proposed DSHC can generate compact binary codes and obtain state-of-the-art results on both CIFAR-10 and NUS-WIDE image retrieval benchmarks.

2 Related Work

Existing hashing methods can be divided into two categories: unsupervised hashing and supervised hashing methods. We can refer to [14] for a comprehensive survey. In unsupervised hashing methods, data points are encoded to binary codes by training from unlabeled data. Typical methods are based on reconstruction error minimization or graph learning [4,19]. Supervised hashing further makes use of supervised information such as pair-wise similarity and label information to generate compact and discriminative hash codes. Across similar pairs of data points, nonlinear or discrete binary hash codes are generated by minimizing the Hamming distances and vice versa across dissimilar pairs [11,15].

Deep hash learning demonstrates their superiority over shallow learning methods in the field of image retrieval through powerful representations. Specifically, Deep Supervised Discrete Hashing [8] combines CNN model with a probability model to preserve pairwise similarity and regress labels using hash codes simultaneously. Deep Hashing Network [25] proposes the first end-to-end framework which jointly preserves pairwise similarity and reduces the quantization error between data points and binary codes. To satisfy Hamming space retrieval, DPSH [9] introduces a novel cross-entropy loss for similarity-preserving and the quantization loss for controlling hashing quality. However, these methods are difficult to apply to large-scale datasets that ignore heterogeneity within classes. Recently, [22] uses a self-learning strategy and improves the performance.

Image Classification Tasks including single-label and multi-label have been made impressive progress by using deep convolutional neural networks. Single-label image classification, paying attention to assign a label from a predefined set to an image, has been extensively studied. The performance of single-label image classification has surpassed human in ImageNet dataset [5]. However, multi-label image classification is a more practical and general problem, because the majority of images in the real-world contain more than one object from different categories.

A simple and straightforward way for multi-label image classification is training an independent binary classifier for each class. However, this method does not consider the relationship among classes! Indeed, the relationship between different labels can be considered by graph neural networks [2]. Additionally, Wang et al. [17] adopted recurrent neural network (RNN) to encode labels into embedded label vectors, which can employ the correlation between labels. Recently, the attention mechanism and label balancing have been introduced to discover the label correlation for multi-label image classification. Different from other hash methods, this paper treats the generation of hash codes as a classification task.

3   Approach

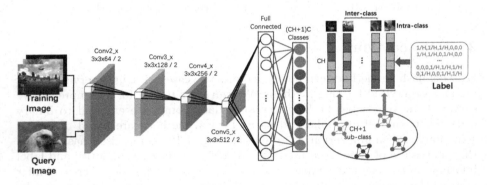

Fig. 1. Overview of our proposed method: The CNN layers perform feature extracting followed by fully connected layer with soft-max to output $(CH+1)C$ sub-classes. There are $(CH+1)$ sub-class contained for each class. And each sub-class will be mapped into a hash code with length CH. The multi-hot labels are employed to optimize the network. (Best viewed in color) (Color figure online)

3.1   Problem Formulation

In the problem of image retrieval, given a dataset $\mathcal{O} = \{o_i\}_{i=1}^n$, $o_i = (x_i, l_i)$, in which x_i is the feature of the i-th image, and $l_i = [l_{i1}, \cdots, l_{iC}]$ is the label annotation assigned to the i-th image, in which C is the number of classes. The similarity label $s_{ij} = 1$ implies the i-th image and the j-th image are similar, otherwise $s_{ij} = 0$. The similar pairs are constructed by the image labels, i.e. two images will be considered similar if they have at least one common label. The goal of deep hashing is to learn a non-linear hash function: $f : o \rightarrow h \in \{-1, 1\}^L$, encoding each sample o into compact L- bit hash code h where original similarities between sample pairs are well preserved. For computational consideration, the distance between different hash codes is Hamming distance, which can be formulated as

$$\text{dis}_H(\boldsymbol{h}_i, \boldsymbol{h}_j) = \frac{1}{2}(L - \langle \boldsymbol{h}_i, \boldsymbol{h}_j \rangle)$$

where $<, >$ denotes the inner product of hash codes.

3.2 Mapping Sub-classes to Hash Codes

As mentioned in the introduction, we would like to construct a mapping from sub-classes to hash codes, such that the hamming distances in the same class are relatively smaller than those between classes. Suppose we have C classes and each class can be divided into m sub-classes. And for j-th sub-class of i-th class, it has a unique hash code mapping p_{ij}. Then we define

$$D_{inter} = \sum_{i_1} \sum_{i_2 \neq i_1} (\sum_{j_1} \sum_{j_2} dist_H(p_{i_1 j_1}, p_{i_2 j_2}))$$
$$D_{intra} = \sum_{i} \sum_{j_1} \sum_{j_2} dist_H(p_{ij_1}, p_{ij_2})$$

as the total inter-class and intra-class distances respectively. Given the code length L, we aim to find $C \times m$ hash codes such that

$$D_{intra} - D_{inter} \tag{1}$$

is minimized. However, finding the global optimization of the objective function 1 is NP-hard, so we proposed a space partition based method to get an approximate solution of it.

As shown in Fig. 1, suppose the hamming space with dimension L is well separated into m sub-spaces, each sub-space corresponding to a class. For each subspace i, suppose there is a center point p_i, which can be viewed as the benchmark code of class i. Then for each subclass of class i, we just substitute one position of p_i, thus every sub-class is mapped to a unique hash code eventually. It is easy to check that all hamming distances in the same class are smaller than or equal to 2. So we can get high-quality hash codes if the hamming distances between center points are much larger than 2.

The most critical step is to construct the center points that are well separated. To make this purpose, we proposed two methods named Center Point-Based Construction (CPBC) and K-means Based Construction (KBC). The idea of CPBC is simple but effective. Specifically, assume each class has a sub-hash code with a length of H, and the total code length is CH. For a center point p_i, the i-th sub-hash code(length H) is all set to be 1 and other sub-hash codes are -1. Then all the center points can be determined, while the Hamming distance between any two of them is equal to $2H$. We can see that hash codes generated by CPBC are generally well separated through T-SNE clustering (see Fig. 2). For CPBC, we have to choose a relatively big H to get high-quality center points. KBC is proposed to generate relatively shorter but high-quality center points. First, we choose C initial points with a given hash code length L, and all the 2^L points are clustered into C groups by K-means. Then the resulted in C clustering centroids are viewed as C center points. Since each cluster contains many more points than the number of subclasses, all subclasses are only mapping to a small ball centered in the corresponding center point. Theoretically, KPC needs a shorter hash code than CPBC, but we found that the effect is difficult to guarantee in the numeric experiments. So we always use CPBC when comparing with other methods.

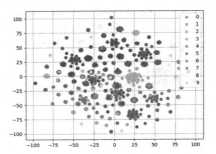

Fig. 2. T-SNE clustering visualization of hash codes generated by CPBC with CIFAR10 data set. Axes represent the first two dimensions of t-SNE embedding.

3.3   Loss Function

Our model converts learning to hash into a classification problem by introducing multiple subclasses for each superclass. To learn a novel function that maps each subclass to a unique hash code, all we need is to determine which subclass each image belongs to. In this section, we will see that the first loss is the cross-entropy loss for a single-label dataset, while the second loss is the binary cross-entropy and soft-margin loss for a multi-label dataset.

For the single-label image classification, the cross-entropy loss is usually employed [5]. Suppose there are C classes in the training dataset and sub-hash code with length H for each class, the whole length of the hash code is CH. In intra-class, one of the hash codes can be replaced to generate CH sub-classes. Thus $(CH + 1)C$ classes will be contained in the soft-max output. Correspondingly, the one-hot ground truth will be converted into the multi-hot, in which the $(CH + 1)$ label points are assigned to $1/H$ or otherwise set to 0. Here we use $1/H$ instead of $1/(CH + 1)$ for computation. Formally, the loss function is:

$$L_{ce} = - \sum_{c=1}^{(CH+1)C} y_c \log(p_c), \qquad (2)$$

where $y_c \in \{0, 1/H\}$ is the ground truth and p_c is the predicted probability distribution. Due to considering the robustness of the model, the top-K prediction probabilities are chosen to generate the corresponding hash codes. And the final hash code can be calculated by the average of K hash codes.

As for the multi-label image classification, the labels are multi-hot values which are contained in the ground truth so that they can be utilized to express the hash code directly. There are relatively large Hamming distances between intra-class and relatively small Hamming distances within inter-class. Besides, our method can explore the correlation between classes rather than predict correctly as long as one label is matched. Since the loss with soft margin is introduced to address the multi-label classification task, the loss is computed as:

$$
\begin{aligned}
L_{x,y} = &-\sum_{i=1}^{N} y_i \log((1 + \exp(-x_i))^{-1}) \\
&+ (1 - y_i) \log((1 + \exp(x_i))^{-1}),
\end{aligned}
\tag{3}
$$

where $y_i \in \{1, -1\}$ express positive or negative class. x_i and N are the predicted probability and the batch size of data in the training phase, respectively.

4 Experiments

The performance of our proposed approach is evaluated on two public benchmark datasets: CIFAR-10 [6] and NUS-WIDE [3] comparing with state-of-the-art methods.

4.1 Datasets and Settings

CIFAR-10. CIFAR-10 is a dataset containing 10 object categories, each with 6000 images (resolution of 32×32). We sampled $1,000$ images per class ($10,000$ images in total) as the query set and the remaining $50,000$ images were utilized as the training set and database for retrieval.

NUS-WIDE. NUS-WIDE is a public multi-label image dataset consisting of $269,648$ images. Each image is manually annotated using some of the 81 ground truth concepts for evaluating retrieval models. Following [8], we picked a subset of $195,834$ images associated with 21 most frequent labels. We randomly sampled $2,100$ images as query sets and the remaining images were treated as the training set.

The retrieval quality is evaluated by the following four evaluation metrics: Mean Average Precision(MAP), Precision-Recall curves, Precision curves concerning hamming radius, and Recall curves for hamming radius. We measure the goodness of the result by comprehensively calculating MAP. For NUS-WIDE, for each bit, the distance needs to be different when the values are all 1s or all 0s when calculating the distance between two images. As a result, we convert -1 to 0 in hash codes and the distance between two images is still in the form of Equation in Sect 3.1.

Our methods are compared with a list of classical or state-of-the-art supervised methods, including DSDH [8], DPSH [9], VDSH [23], DTSH [18], RMLH

[20] and unsupervised hashing methods including SH [19], ITQ [4]. For CIFAR10, we utilize ResNet50 and replace the last layers with the corresponding number of nodes, with the learning rate 0.1. We also rerun the source code of DPSH and DSDH. The number of total epochs is 160 since we found all models can fit very well afterward. For NUS-WIDE, we utilize ResNet 101 and the learning rate is set to 0.1 which decreases every 6 epochs.

4.2   Performance

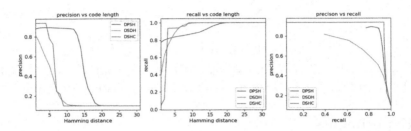

Fig. 3. Precision curves, Recall curves respect to hamming radius and Precision-Recall curves when code length is 30. In the first two figures, the x axis represents the Hamming distance (radius), and the y axis represents the average precision and recall. The last figure is the curve of precision and recall.

Table 1 shows the results of different hashing methods on two benchmark data sets when the code length is about 32 and 24, respectively. Here, for our method, the code length is a little smaller than 32, but they are comparable because the last two or three bits can be filled with zero for all images. Figure 3 and Table 1 shows the Precision-Recall curves, Precision curves, and Recall curves respectively for different methods (code length of 30 and 60 bits).

We find that on the two benchmark datasets, DSHC outperforms all the compared baseline methods. What's more, unsupervised traditional hashing methods show poor performances, which implies that labels and the strong representation ability of deep learning are significant for learning to the hash. Compared with DSDH which regresses the labels with hash codes, our method directly utilizes the labels to produce sub-labels, showing superiority from the increment of performance. Compared with DPSH, our model is based on it a deeper model such as ResNet50 for the sake of getting rid of the pairwise loss whose computation cost increases greatly. As shown in Table 2, our method takes the advantage of a deeper model like ResNet but with less training time, which implies it can easily extend to large-scale image datasets. Figure 3 shows that when code length varies from 60 to 30, the performance of our method is stable while those of DPSH and DSDH are sensitive to the code length. Besides, when the code length is 60, the average recall for the code distance 0 in our model is about 0.024 while the value of DPSH is about 0.724. In other words, most images with the same labels

Table 1. MAP for different methods on CIFAR10 dataset and NUS-WIDE dataset. The MAP for the NUS-WIDE dataset is calculated based on the top 50000 returned neighbors. We re-run the source codes of DSDH and DPSH with code length 30, shown in the brackets while other results are from their papers.

Method	Published year	CIFAR10		NUS-WIDE	
		MAP	Length(bits)	MAP	Length(bits)
DSHC	Ours	**0.9431**	30	**0.844**	21
RMLH	2019	0.816	32	0.823	32
DSDH*	2017	0.939(0.802)	32(30)	0.814	24
DPSH*	2016	0.781(0.887)	32(30)	0.722	24
DTSH	2016	0.925	32	0.776	24
VDSH	2017	0.844	32	0.564	24
ITQ	2012	0.172	32	0.468	24
SH	2009	0.126	32	0.406	24

in DPSH are projected into the same hash codes while our method can retrieval the most similar images within the class.

Table 2. MAP for different methods on CIFAR10 dataset (60-bit hash codes)

Method	MAP	Runtime (Last Ten epochs)
DSHC	**0.9437**	409.27
DPSH	0.8990	600.30
DSDH	0.8786	**352.64**

Since NUS-WIDE is annotated with multi-labels, we directly use the classification binary output as hash codes. The results show that this kind of hash code works quite well and performs much better than other methods. A reasonable explanation is that the binary classification output has already captured the intra-class heterogeneity of the dataset. What's more, the multi-labeled classification model considers the relationship between sub-labels while most deep hash methods only consider the similarity between the two images.

4.3   Results with Different Code Length

We also compare the performance of our model with different code lengths. Taking the CIFAR10 dataset, for instance, the result is shown in Table 3. When a short hash code is used, CPBC is not able to partition the space well, resulting in poor performance. When the hash code length is large enough (e.g. above 30), the MAP of our model is quite stable. Under the condition of a complex dataset, more hash bits will be needed for acceptable performance. It is worth noting that the length of the hash code does not influence the running time.

Table 3. MAP and Runtime (Last Ten epochs) for different length

Length	MAP	Runtime
10	0.3599	**408.21**
20	0.8264	427.09
30	0.9431	420.92
60	**0.9437**	409.27

4.4 Comparison Between CPBC and KBC

As mentioned above, the performance of our method is difficult to guarantee when the hash code length is small (e.g., 10). However, if KBC is used to obtain the centroids, its performance is acceptable even if the hash code length is as small as 10, while CPBC is difficult to separate the Hamming space well. As shown in Table 4, when the hash code length is set to 10, 950 points out of 1024 points in the KBC model are filtered, while the model using CPBC leaves 110 points. The model using KBC performs much better than CPBC, which means that the model using KBC can successfully select several groups with larger distances in Hamming space. However, when the hash code length is large enough, it is recommended to use the CPBC model for simplification.

Table 4. MAP@5000 for CPBC and KBC methods

Length	Method	MAP@5000	Number of sub-classes
10	CPBC	0.5238	110
10	KBC	**0.8980**	74(filter 950)

5 Discussion

From the results, our classification method shows superior performance compared to state-of-the-art methods when the labels of the images are known. Also, it can handle large-scale datasets without dealing with pairwise losses, thus speeding up the computation. More importantly, when the classification output is directly transformed into hash codes in NUS-WIDE, this suggests that the classification model may be the key to deep supervised hashing.

Sometimes, similarity information is the only supervised information. We have two methods to obtain the labels of images. First, if the real model is simple, we can find images that contain only one label and get the exact specific label from the similarity. Second, if the real model is complex, we can construct a similarity graph based on the information and then derive the final labels by graph clustering (e.g., Markov clustering). From the clustering results, we can derive the label for each image. However, the results are limited by the performance of clustering, which is difficult to promise.

6   Conclusion

In this paper, we investigate the relationship between deep supervised hashing and classification problems and find that high-quality hash codes can be generated by deep classification models. We propose a new supervised hashing method named DSHC, which consists of a classification module and a transformation module, and exploits inter-and intra-class heterogeneity. Based on the performance of several benchmark datasets, DSHC proves to be a promising approach. Further research can focus on designing an efficient ANN search algorithm based on hash codes generated by DSHC.

Acknowledgements. This work was supported by The National Key Research and Development Program of China (No. 2016YFA0502303) and the National Natural Science Foundation of China (No. 31871342).

References

1. Cao, Z., Long, M., Wang, J., Yu, P.S.: Hashnet: deep learning to hash by continuation. In: Proceedings of the IEEE International Conference on Computer Vision, pp. 5608–5617 (2017)
2. Chen, T., Xu, M., Hui, X., Wu, H., Lin, L.: Learning semantic-specific graph representation for multi-label image recognition. In: Proceedings of the IEEE International Conference on Computer Vision, pp. 522–531 (2019)
3. Chua, T.S., Tang, J., Hong, R., Li, H., Luo, Z., Zheng, Y.: Nus-wide: a real-world web image database from national university of Singapore. In: Proceedings of the ACM International Conference on Image and Video Retrieval, p. 48. ACM (2009)
4. Gong, Y., Lazebnik, S., Gordo, A., Perronnin, F.: Iterative quantization: a procrustean approach to learning binary codes for large-scale image retrieval. IEEE Trans. Pattern Anal. Mach. Intell. **35**(12), 2916–2929 (2012)
5. He, K., Zhang, X., Ren, S., Sun, J.: Deep residual learning for image recognition. In: Proceedings of the IEEE Conference on Computer Vision and Pattern Recognition, pp. 770–778 (2016)
6. Krizhevsky, A., et al.: Learning multiple layers of features from tiny images (2009)
7. Lai, H., Pan, Y., Liu, Y., Yan, S.: Simultaneous feature learning and hash coding with deep neural networks. In: Proceedings of the IEEE Conference on Computer Vision and Pattern Recognition, pp. 3270–3278 (2015)
8. Li, Q., Sun, Z., He, R., Tan, T.: Deep supervised discrete hashing. In: Advances in Neural Information Processing Systems, pp. 2482–2491 (2017)
9. Li, W.J., Wang, S., Kang, W.C.: Feature learning based deep supervised hashing with pairwise labels. In: Proceedings of the Twenty-Fifth International Joint Conference on Artificial Intelligence, pp. 1711–1717. AAAI Press (2016)

10. Lin, K., Yang, H.F., Hsiao, J.H., Chen, C.S.: Deep learning of binary hash codes for fast image retrieval. In: Proceedings of the IEEE Conference on Computer Vision and Pattern Recognition Workshops, pp. 27–35 (2015)
11. Liu, W., Wang, J., Ji, R., Jiang, Y.G., Chang, S.F.: Supervised hashing with kernels. In: 2012 IEEE Conference on Computer Vision and Pattern Recognition, pp. 2074–2081. IEEE (2012)
12. Liu, X., He, J., Deng, C., Lang, B.: Collaborative hashing. In: Proceedings of the IEEE Conference on Computer Vision and Pattern Recognition, pp. 2139–2146 (2014)
13. Liu, X., He, J., Lang, B., Chang, S.F.: Hash bit selection: a unified solution for selection problems in hashing. In: Proceedings of the IEEE Conference on Computer Vision and Pattern Recognition, pp. 1570–1577 (2013)
14. Luo, X., et al.: A survey on deep hashing methods. arXiv preprint arXiv:2003.03369 (2020)
15. Luo, X., et al.: Cimon: towards high-quality hash codes. In: IJCAI (2021)
16. Simonyan, K., Zisserman, A.: Very deep convolutional networks for large-scale image recognition. arXiv preprint arXiv:1409.1556 (2014)
17. Wang, J., Yang, Y., Mao, J., Huang, Z., Huang, C., Xu, W.: CNN-RNN: a unified framework for multi-label image classification. In: Proceedings of the IEEE Conference on Computer Vision and Pattern Recognition, pp. 2285–2294 (2016)
18. Wang, X., Shi, Y., Kitani, K.M.: Deep supervised hashing with triplet labels. In: Lai, S.-H., Lepetit, V., Nishino, K., Sato, Y. (eds.) ACCV 2016. LNCS, vol. 10111, pp. 70–84. Springer, Cham (2017). https://doi.org/10.1007/978-3-319-54181-5_5
19. Weiss, Y., Torralba, A., Fergus, R.: Spectral hashing. In: Advances in Neural Information Processing Systems, pp. 1753–1760 (2009)
20. Wu, L., Fang, Y., Ling, H., Chen, J., Li, P.: Robust mutual learning hashing. In: 2019 IEEE International Conference on Image Processing (ICIP), pp. 2219–2223. IEEE (2019)
21. Yang, H.F., Lin, K., Chen, C.S.: Supervised learning of semantics-preserving hashing via deep neural networks for large-scale image search. arXiv preprint arXiv:1507.00101 1(2), 3 (2015)
22. Zhan, J., Mo, Z., Zhu, Y.: Deep self-learning hashing for image retrieval. In: 2020 IEEE International Conference on Image Processing (ICIP), pp. 1556–1560. IEEE (2020)
23. Zhang, Z., Chen, Y., Saligrama, V.: Efficient training of very deep neural networks for supervised hashing. In: Proceedings of the IEEE Conference on Computer Vision and Pattern Recognition, pp. 1487–1495 (2016)
24. Zhao, F., Huang, Y., Wang, L., Tan, T.: Deep semantic ranking based hashing for multi-label image retrieval. In: Proceedings of the IEEE Conference on Computer Vision and Pattern Recognition, pp. 1556–1564 (2015)
25. Zhu, H., Long, M., Wang, J., Cao, Y.: Deep hashing network for efficient similarity retrieval. In: Thirtieth AAAI Conference on Artificial Intelligence (2016)

Towards Human-Level Performance in Solving Double Dummy Bridge Problem

Szymon Kowalik📷 and Jacek Mańdziuk$^{(\boxtimes)}$📷

Faculty of Mathematics and Information Science, Warsaw University of Technology,
Koszykowa 75, 00-662 Warsaw, Poland
mandziuk@mini.pw.edu.pl

Abstract. Double Dummy Bridge Problem (DDBP) is a hard classification problem that consists in estimating the number of tricks to be taken by N-S pair during a bridge game. In this paper we propose a new approach to DDBP which utilizes convolutional neural networks (CNNs) and a dedicated matrix representation of the problem, suitable for the CNN application. Following previous studies on the application of neural networks to DDBP, we take a knowledge-free approach, i.e. the CNN models are trained with no use of any expert knowledge or explicitly indicated bridge rules. As a result, two models are derived: a baseline CNN model and its ensemble refinement. The results are compared with two former neural network approaches, showing significant superiority of the CNN-based solution. Depending on the type DDBP deal, i.e. trump or notrump, our approach either outperforms or is slightly inferior to the outcomes of human bridge grandmasters solving DDBP. This state-of-the-art performance is complemented in the paper with an analysis of the internal structure (weight patterns) of the trained CNNs, which partly explains the underlying classification process.

Keywords: Deep learning · Convolutional neural network · Double dummy bridge problem · Classification

1 Introduction

The Game of Bridge. Contract bridge (or simply bridge) - one of the most popular classic card games - is an interesting Artificial Intelligence (AI) challenge. Among others, incomplete information about game state and cooperation of players in pairs can be pointed out as demanding aspects of this game. Creating a master-level bridge program is therefore a difficult task.

Formally, bridge is a trick-taking card game for four players. It begins by dealing a standard 52-card deck to the players. Each card has its value (from lowest to highest: 2, 3, ..., 10, J - *Jack*, Q - *Queen*, K - *King*, A - *Ace*) and suit (♠ - *spades*, ♡ - *hearts*, ♢ - *diamonds*, ♣ - *clubs*). The players are forming two pairs playing against each other. They are marked according to their positions

© Springer Nature Switzerland AG 2021
T. Mantoro et al. (Eds.): ICONIP 2021, LNCS 13111, pp. 15–27, 2021.
https://doi.org/10.1007/978-3-030-92273-3_2

at the table: N - North and S - South (first pair); E - East and W - West (second pair). Following bridge related literature, we will refer to the set of 13 cards possessed by a given player as his/her *hand*.

A bridge game begins with a bidding phase that aims at establishing a contract which is defined as the number of tricks to be taken by the partners (within a pair) assuming a given *trump* (TR) suit or its absence - the so-called *notrump* (NT) contract. After an auction the trick-taking part of game begins (aka play phase). Each *trick* consists of four cards - one played by each player. The player with the highest card takes the trick. However, any card in TR suit is considered to be higher than any card in other suits. The team that made the highest bid during auction tries to win at least as many tricks as it was declared in the contract, otherwise - it loses. More detailed bridge rules can be found in [16].

Definition and Significance of Double Dummy Bridge Problem (DDBP). The key issue during a bidding phase is to identify opponents' and partner's hands and determine the highest possible contract based on this knowledge. Experienced bridge players are able to deduce a partial distribution of cards among players based on the course of bidding. This allows to estimate the most probable variants of card locations, evaluate them and determine the optimal contract.

As proposed in [11], a similar approach can be imitated by a bridge playing program. To this end the DDBP was defined as an auxiliary problem. DDBP consists in answering the question of *"How many tricks can be taken by N-S pair assuming that location of each card is known and each player plays in an optimal way?"*. Please note that considering possible locations of certain key cards mentioned above is equivalent to solving a number of DDBP instances related to their possible distributions. This observation led to a simulation-based bidding approach that considers numerous possible cards distributions and their DDBP outcomes. Such an approach was successfully implemented in a bridge-playing program utilizing the DDBP solver [6].

The assumptions made in DDBP make the problem deterministic. However, as indicated below in Sect. 2, DDBP proven to be a demanding machine learning challenge due to its high complexity and strong sensitivity to even subtle changes in input data. For example, swapping two seemingly minor cards can result in a significant change in the DDBP outcome [18].

Contribution. The main contribution of this work is threefold. Firstly, we verify the suitability of CNNs to solving complex, combinatorial problem known as the DDBP. Secondly, we compare the efficacy of CNN DDBP solver with shallower neural network architectures considered in the past - a multilayer perceptron (MLP) and its combination with an autoencoder (MLP-AE). Thirdly, we demonstrate the state-of-the-art AI performance in solving DDBP, which in certain problem settings outperforms the results of top human bridge players, while in other settings narrows the gap between humans and AI.

2   Related Literature

Fast DDBP solver relying on the so-called partition search [5] is a core element of
Ginsberg's Intelligent Bridgeplayer (GIB) program [6]. GIB was solving DDBP
to find an optimal contract based on Monte Carlo (MC) simulation of various
possible double dummy distributions of the key cards among four players. The
program was twice winning a title of the World Computer Bridge Champion in
the late 1990s [7]. The approach was further developed in [1] leading to significant
reductions of the search tree and computation time.

Despite over 20 years of research, bridge-playing programs based on this idea
still determine the state-of-the-art.[1] Recent research also focused on a bidding
phase using deep learning techniques and double dummy analysis [20,21]. In
parallel, the use the Recursive Monte Carlo method instead of MC search (which
tends to stuck in local extremes [2]) was also proposed.

When it comes to DDBP itself, several neural network approaches to solving
this problem were considered over the years. The key ones, from the perspective
of this study, are briefly summarized below. The main rationale behind their
usage is an extremely fast inference phase of neural models. Once trained, the
network is capable to solve millions of deals in a fraction of time required by
exact methods, e.g. partition search [5].

Multilayer Perceptron (MLP) approach to DDBP was initially proposed
in [17], further developed in several subsequent papers and summarized in [18],
where results of a direct comparison with human grandmasters solving DDBP
task within 30 s time per instance were presented.

One of the critical factors in this research was effective representation of a
hand in the input layer. Furthermore, it was noticed that TR and NT deals
are significantly different, thus require separate training in order to achieve the
best fit of each resulting model. Additionally, it was observed that the most
effective approach in TR contracts is to assume one particular TR suit in all
deals (without loss of generality - a spade suit ♠). Deals with other TR suit can
be considered by simply mapping a real TR suit to ♠.

The results obtained with MLP, presented in the top row of Table 1, indicate high model performance which, however, demonstrates certain difficulties
in determining the exact number of tricks. It is also apparent that the case of
NT contracts is more difficult than the case of TR contracts. This discrepancy
is caused by the way in which neural networks solve DDBP, i.e. basing solely on
the analysis of the distribution of cards among players. Professional players, on
the other hand, in addition to statistical hand analysis also benefit from mental
simulation of the play phase based on their experience, which is of particular
importance in NT deals [13].

---

[1] The 2019 World Computer Bridge Champion, Micro Bridge (http://www.osk.3web.
ne.jp/~mcbridge/index.html), uses MC simulations and DDBP solver.

Autoencoder (AE-MLP). DDBP was revisited in [14] with the use of MLP combined with a shallow autoencoder. The model consists of two parts - pretrained encoding layers that provide an efficient representation of the problem and fully connected layers responsible for further inference. Please consult [14] for the details. The efficacy of AE-MLP is similar to that of MLP (see Table 1).

Table 1. Summary of literature results in comparison with the results of human professional bridge players (bottom row) achieved in experiments described in [13]. For each combination of model and contract type three error measures are presented, from left to right referred to as (acc_2 | acc_1 | acc_0) that indicate the percentage of deals in which the error did not exceed two, one and zero tricks (exact result), respectively. This notation was proposed in [18] and is followed in this paper for the sake of comparability.

Model	NT Contracts	TR Contracts
MLP	97.34|84.31|37.80	99.88|96.48|53.11
AE-MLP	96.63|86.18|41.73	99.72|95.33|51.28
Human grandmasters	94.74|88.30|73.68	88.34|81.63|53.06

3   Proposed CNN-Based Approach to DDBP

3.1   Effective DDBP Coding

The key concept contributing to the overall efficacy of the proposed solution is innovative, CNN-plausible problem representation. It extends the idea proposed in the Poker-CNN model [19] and relies on the following assumptions [9]: (a) each card is represented by fixed matrix element; (b) spatial arrangement of matrix elements reflect certain relations between them (e.g. neighbouring elements correspond to cards of similar strength); (c) channels refer to players or suits. Initial tests showed that the first option - assigning channels to players - is more advantageous, thus it has been utilized in presented experiments.

Several DDBP encodings were proposed and tested until selecting the most effective variant, presented in Fig. 1. The encoding matrix consists of 13 columns assigned to cards' ranks and 12 rows corresponding to suits. Four channels are used, one per each player. The matrix has three parts, four rows each:

In rows 1–4 the binary coding is used. Each matrix element has a value of 1 for a hand containing a card in the corresponding rank and suit, or 0 otherwise.

Rows 5–8 are structured in a similar manner with positive values corresponding to the rank of the card to which they refer to. Each cell of this matrix fragment can thus take one of 14 values uniformly distributed in the range ⟨0, 1⟩, the lowest of which - 0 - represents the absence of a given card. The stronger the card, the higher the number representing it.

Coding in rows 9–12 is derived from rows 5–8 by shifting positive values to the left, replacing zero values. So in this case, the location of the value in the column is not related to the card rank. It is only represented by a numeric value.

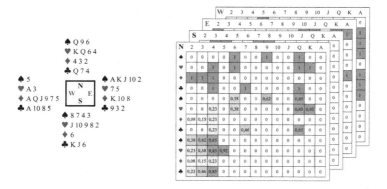

Fig. 1. Example of the DDBP encoding. It refers to the deal presented in the left part of the figure. Channels are illustrated as layers. In the upper left corner of each layer, the corresponding player is indicated.

Unlike in the previous approaches with MLP [18] and AE-MLP [14] the key aspect of proposed coding is data redundancy. Presentation of the same information in different ways facilitates more complex reasoning process (compared to previous architectures) implemented in the CNN model.

3.2   Baseline CNN-Based DDBP Solver

Our CNN model relies on AlexNet [10], but is heavily adapted to the considered problem. Figure 2 presents the model architecture and Table 2 its hyperparemeter values. The input layer is fed with matrices containing the DDBP instance, encoded in a way described in Sect. 3.1. The output layer consists of 14 neurons, each corresponding to one of the possible DDBP outcomes.

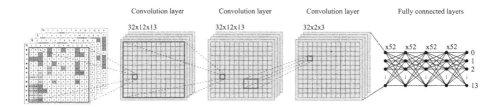

Fig. 2. Baseline CNN model architecture used in the experiments - TR contract variant.

The model is composed of 3 or 4 convolutional layers - depending on the variant (specialized for TR or NT contracts, respectively). The first two convolutional layers use filters of the same size as the input data. This approach is intended to support feature extraction with respect to the full problem knowledge (e.g. suits length determination or individual cards strength identification).

This is not a typical approach for CNNs, but in this case it turns out to be valid (as confirmed by the results). A possible explanation is attributed to the fact that the input data is also not structured in a typical way. Full knowledge of the problem seems to be much more important in this case than in image analysis - a typical CNNs domain of application - that relies on detecting patterns in chunks of the input data.

Deeper convolutional layers serve just this purpose: the filters used there have a significantly smaller size (2×3) and extract local, non-obvious features. All convolutional layers include zero-padding to keep the matrix size equal at their input and output. In Fig. 2, zero-padding is omitted for the sake of clarity of the presentation. The use of pooling layers was abandoned as they cause a reduction in the size of the problem representation, which is relatively small in terms of CNNs. Consequently, in preliminary tests we observed that the networks containing pooling layers perform visibly worse than networks without these layers. Typically for CNNs, convolutional layers are followed by fully connected layer (cf. Table 2).

Table 2. Baseline model hyperparameters values.

Hyperparameter	Value	
	NT Contracts	*TR Contracts*
Convolutional layers		
Number of layers	4	3
Filter sizes in successive layers	$(12 \times 13), (12 \times 13),$ $(2 \times 3), (2 \times 3)$	$(12 \times 13), (12 \times 13),$ (2×3)
Number of filters	32	
Activation function	SELU	
Fully connected layers		
Number of layers	4 and output layer	
Number of neurons in successive layers	$52, 52, 26, 26, 14$	$52, 52, 52, 52, 14$
Activation function	ELU	Softplus

3.3 Ensemble of Classifiers

We also attempted to increase classification accuracy by using an ensemble of classifiers consisting of 10 independently trained instances of the above-described baseline CNN model. Two different types of training set construction for each component model were considered: (1) all instances of the baseline model were *trained on the full training set* (the differences between the models were caused by random weight initialization); (2) *bagging* [3].

Additionally, the influence of the voting method on the ensemble results was also investigated. Two approaches were tested: (1) *hard (majority) voting*, where each individual model votes for the class and the ensemble result is determined by a majority vote, and (2) *soft voting* involving the summation of the probabilities assigned to each class by individual classifiers - the class with the highest sum becomes the ensemble outcome [8].

4   Experimental Evaluation

The Dataset. Using the GIB program, M.L. Ginsberg generated a library of DDBP solutions [4], hereafter referred to as the GIB library. The set consists of exact problem solutions for over 700 000 randomly generated bridge deals. For each deal, the number of tricks to be taken by N-S pair under the DDBP assumptions was calculated. It is given for all combinations of the TR suit and a player making an opening lead, which gives a total of 20 values for a single deal.

The GIB library has been used in all previous research on neural networks in DDBP referenced in this paper. For the sake of results comparability we follow the training/test set construction proposed in previous works [15,18]. Namely, deals numbered from 1 to 100 000 form a *training set* and deals numbered from 600 001 to 700 000 form a *test set*. Additionally, a *validation set* consisting of deals numbered from 500 001 to 600 000 is used.

Baseline Model Tuning. We adopted the following tuning methodology [9]. First, several hyperparameters were simultaneously tuned to discover their impact on model quality. Once a significant hyperparameter was detected, a second phase aimed at finding its optimal value proceeded. It was discovered using the best model configuration so far. This process was repeated until getting a model that no longer showed significant performance improvement by further tuning. The greatest impact on the performance of the trained model comes from the size of the filters in the convolutional layers and the number of these layers.

4.1   Results

Baseline Model. For each of the two deal types (TR/NT) 10 independent experiments were performed. The aggregated results are presented in Table 3.

Table 3. The average out-of-sample results obtained in 10 tests of the baseline model (Mean) vs the state-of-the-art results (SOTA). Higher outcomes are bolded.

	NT Contracts	TR Contracts
Mean	**98.03 | 93.17 | 57.24**	**99.89 | 97.84 | 58.42**
St. dev.	00.18 | 00.44 | 00.89	00.02 | 00.21 | 00.90
SOTA	96.63 | 86.18 | 41.73	99.88 | 96.48 | 53.11

The first observation is the superiority of the CNN model over state-of-the-art (SOTA) literature results. It is worth noting that in case of NT contracts - the more challenging variant - the improvement is significant: 15 p.p. with respect to accuracy measure (acc_0). Actually, the CNN model yields very similar acc_0 results for NT (average 57.24%) and TR (average 58.42%) contracts. However, the difference between these variants is clearly evident when one compares the percentage of deals where the estimation error did not exceed one or two tricks (acc_1 and acc_2, resp.). This confirms higher level of complexity in the case of NT contracts, which manifests in higher errors. The proposed solution is stable - the standard deviation of accuracy (acc_0) does not exceed 1 p.p., and is naturally even lower for acc_1 and acc_2.

In summary, the baseline model is a strong estimator of the number of tricks to be taken by the N-S pair and provides a promising starting point for the ensemble approach discussed below.

Ensemble of Classifiers. Table 4 presents the results of an ensemble of classifiers built on 10 instances of the baseline model. According to the assumptions described in Sect. 3.3, four variants were considered.

Table 4. Out-of-sample results of four variants of classifier ensembles. Each ensemble is built on 10 instances of the baseline CNN model. The best results are bolded. The average results of the 10 baseline models (Mean) and the best literature results (SOTA) are outperformed by the best ensemble variant (Full/Soft). Compared to results of professional players, the Full/Soft variant is inferior only in acc_0 measure for NT deals.

Training set	Voting	NT Contracts	TR Contracts
Full	Hard	98.55 | 95.16 | 63.46	99.93 | 98.79 | 63.62
Full	Soft	**98.61 | 95.39** | 64.13	**99.94 | 98.83 | 63.83**
Bagging	Hard	98.08 | 93.68 | 58.40	99.91 | 98.27 | 60.37
Bagging	Soft	98.15 | 94.03 | 59.08	99.91 | 98.38 | 60.87
Mean		98.03 | 93.17 | 57.24	99.89 | 97.84 | 58.42
SOTA		96.63 | 86.18 | 41.73	99.88 | 96.48 | 53.11
Human grandmasters		94.74 | 88.30 | **73.68**	88.34 | 81.63 | 53.06

In all cases, the results improved significantly over a single instance of the baseline model. It is worth observing that ensembles composed of models trained on the full training set perform better than those using bagging. This implies that the size of training set is crucial for the discussed problem and using only 2/3 of the original set deteriorates model quality. Moreover, visible improvement in ensemble performance over a single model confirms the non-trivial nature of DDBP as already noted in previous research [18].

The voting method has less influence on the results, nevertheless it is possible to indicate that soft voting performs better than hard voting in both regarded cases considering all measures. Therefore, one can conclude that *even if the model outputs an incorrect result, it assigns a relatively high probability to the correct number of tricks to be taken by N-S pair.*

Even though the ensemble performance improvement relative to a single model was certainly expected, its degree is surprisingly large. The accuracy (acc_0) increases by more than 5 p.p. (to 63%) and almost 7 p.p. (to 64%) for TR and NT contracts, resp. *In the latter case the results excelled human grandmaster scores by 10 p.p.* This also resulted in an outperforming the TR model by the NT one with respect to the acc_0, which is reported for the first time in the literature.

4.2   Analysis of Weight Structures of Trained Baseline CNN Models

Following previous studies, an analysis of weight structures of trained baseline models was performed in attempt to *explain the model performance*. In particular, the first convolutional layer filters, in both TR and NT models were examined after training. The goal of this process is to relate patterns found in these filters to the common bridge knowledge. An intriguing research question is whether the knowledge gained by CNN models during training will be in line with human expert knowledge. Attention was given to finding analogous patterns to those identified in previous neural network studies [12,15] as well as new, *previously unobserved ones - specific to CNN-based approach.*

As a general remark, it is worth emphasizing that the analyzed filters are applied multiple times to the matrix representing DDBP, each time with different offsets. Consequently, the structure of the filters should not be expected to explicitly correspond to the selected DDBP coding, thus the search for patterns should rather focus on the spatial relationships between the filter weights.

The contents of the exemplary filters are shown in Fig. 3. At first glance one can see that filter elements form mainly two types of patterns - *vertical stripes* and *horizontal stripes*. A *stripe* is defined as a row or column (or part thereof) that contains mostly elements with absolute values significantly higher than its surroundings and/or elements with values of the same sign. It can be deduced that vertical stripes are used to detect cards of certain ranks, while the horizontal ones have to do with suits. More detailed information on the identified patterns is highlighted below. These patterns have been identified in networks specialized in processing both TR and NT contracts.

Patterns consistent with observations from previous studies:

Vertical stripes on the right side of the filters (e.g. filter #2). Due to their location, it can be hypothesized that they are responsible for identifying cards of the highest rank, aka *honors*. Their importance (i.e. frequency of occurrence and distinctness) is greater for NT contracts than for TR ones, which is in line with the expert knowledge - having high-ranked cards is more important in NT deals [16].

A single vertical stripe in the far right column (e.g. #20). This pattern is presumably used to identify Aces - the strongest cards in a deck whose significance is widely supported by the expert knowledge.

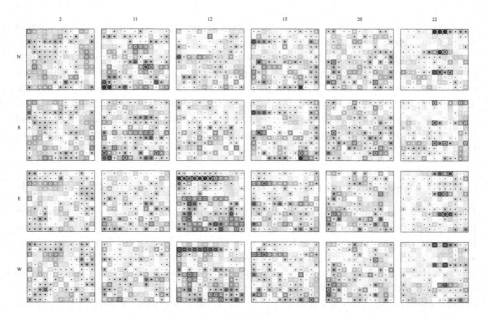

Fig. 3. Visualization of example filters in the first convolutional layer - a variant of TR contract network. The absolute value of each matrix element (filter weight) is represented by the cell color intensity and the circle radius. Positive value is indicated by red cell and black circle, negative value is marked with blue cell and white circle. (Color figure online)

Long horizontal stripes whose weights approximate the card hierarchy (e.g. #12). For TR deals, the hierarchy is reversed, which can be interpreted as detecting unfavorable patterns for a given pair of players that may have a positive effect on their opponents situation.

Long horizontal stripes with relatively low absolute values, but clearly distinguishable along the entire filter length, occurring only in the case of TR contracts (e.g. #15). They can be used to detect all cards of a particular suit in a hand, which is a crucial information for such deals.
Newly observed patterns:

Horizontal stripes repeatable every 4 rows (e.g. #22). This is in line with the structure of the input data. Correlations between various representations of the same information have been correctly detected.

Accumulation of relevant elements in the lower left corner of the filter (e.g. #11). These patterns refer to elements in the last four rows of the DDBP coding. As described in Sect. 3.1, for these elements, the location in the columns does not matter, and all non-zero values are shifted left. The presence of such pattern suggests that the network captured the high significance of the data in this part of the matrix during training.

Associating the sign of filter elements' values to players (e.g. #15). Elements of the pattern have the same sign for players within one pair and the opposite sign for players within the other pair. Hence, the network identifies the positive impact of certain card combinations on the situation of one pair and, at the same time, its negative impact for the other pair.

The above overview demonstrates that *despite knowledge-free training regime* CNNs are able to infer extensive knowledge about the game of bridge, consistent with expert experience. Most of the patterns found in previously applied neural models were also identified in our experiments. Additionally, some new patterns, arising mainly from a new way of data representation and processing, were discovered. What is more, several patterns described above can be often found within a single filter (e.g. #2). At the same time - in contrast to previous models - no filters with structures appearing to be fully random were discovered. These observations, together with excellent performance of the baseline model, suggest that deep CNNs are able to infer much more information about the DDBP than shallower MLP and AE-MLP models.

5 Conclusions and Future Work

In this paper a new approach to solving DDBP relying on CNNs was proposed. The results outperform those of the previous SOTA reference models, i.e. MLP and AE-MLP, by a significant margin. Hence, the primary conclusion of this research is that deep convolutional networks are very well suited to modeling the DDBP.

The experiments confirm the previous conclusion regarding the difference between NT and TR contracts. Despite similar accuracy (acc_0) in these two variants, it is shown that if the prediction is incorrect, the error is statistically greater for NT deals than for TR ones. What is more, a model specialized for NT contracts requires a more complex architecture in order to obtain best results, which further confirms the more challenging nature of this DDBP variant.

The internal structure analysis of the trained networks identified patterns with similar roles as those found in the MLP and AE-MLP models, albeit in the case of CNNs they are, in general, less straightforward and harder to explain. This is due to the fact that deeper networks are capable of making more complex inference, which positively influences the quality of the model but negatively impacts its interpretability.

Application of an ensemble of classifiers yielded significant improvement over the performance of a baseline model. The range of the advancement of results is yet another indication of high complexity of the considered problem.

Finally, a comparison of results presented in Table 4 reveals that proposed solution outperforms the results of top human players (bridge grandmasters) in TR deals. It is, however, still inferior in NT contracts, albeit in the exact measure (acc_0) only.

Acknowledgements. Studies were funded by BIOTECHMED-1 project granted by Warsaw University of Technology under the program Excellence Initiative: Research University (ID-UB).

References

1. Beling, P.: Partition search revisited. IEEE Trans. Comput. Intell. AI Games **9**(1), 76–87 (2017)
2. Bouzy, B., Rimbaud, A., Ventos, V.: Recursive Monte Carlo search for bridge card play. In: 2020 IEEE Conference on Games (CoG), pp. 229–236 (2020)
3. Breiman, L.: Bagging predictors. Mach. Learn. **24**(2), 123–140 (1996)
4. Ginsberg, M.L.: Library of double-dummy results. http://www.cirl.uoregon.edu/ginsberg/gibresearch.html
5. Ginsberg, M.L.: Partition search. In: Shrobe, H., Senator, T. (eds.) Proceedings of the Thirteenth National Conference on Artificial Intelligence and the Eighth Innovative Applications of Artificial Intelligence Conference, vol. 2. pp. 228–233. AAAI Press, Menlo Park (1996)
6. Ginsberg, M.L.: GIB: Steps toward an expert-level bridge-playing program. In: Proceedings of the Sixteenth International Joint Conference on Artificial Intelligence (IJCAI 1999), pp. 584–589 (1999)
7. Ginsberg, M.L.: GIB: imperfect information in a computationally challenging game. J. Artif. Intell. Res. **14**, 303–358 (2001)
8. Kim, J., Choi, S.: Automated machine learning for soft voting in an ensemble of tree-based classifiers. In: ICML Workshop on Automatic Machine Learning (AutoML), Stockholm, Sweden (2018)
9. Kowalik, Sz.: Deep learning in Double Dummy Bridge Problem. Master's thesis, Warsaw University of Technology, Warsaw, Poland (2021)
10. Krizhevsky, A., Sutskever, I., Hinton, G.E.: Imagenet classification with deep convolutional neural networks. In: Proceedings of the 25th International Conference on Neural Information Processing Systems, NIPS 2012, vol. 1, pp. 1097–1105. Curran Associates Inc., Red Hook (2012)
11. Levy, D.N.: The million pound bridge program. In: Levy, D., Beal, D. (eds.) Heuristic Programming in Artificial Intelligence: The First Computer Olympiad, pp. 95–103. Ellis Horwood, Chichester (1989)
12. Mańdziuk, J., Mossakowski, K.: Looking inside neural networks trained to solve double-dummy bridge problems. In: 5th Game-On International Conference on Computer Games: Artificial Intelligence, Design and Education (CGAIDE 2004), Reading, UK, pp. 182–186 (2004)
13. Mańdziuk, J., Mossakowski, K.: Neural networks compete with expert human players in solving the double dummy bridge problem. In: 2009 IEEE Symposium on Computational Intelligence and Games, pp. 117–124, September 2009
14. Mańdziuk, J., Suchan, J.: Solving the double dummy bridge problem with shallow autoencoders. In: Cheng, L., Leung, A.C.S., Ozawa, S. (eds.) ICONIP 2018. LNCS, vol. 11304, pp. 268–280. Springer, Cham (2018). https://doi.org/10.1007/978-3-030-04212-7_23
15. Mańdziuk, J., Suchan, J.: Who should bid higher, NS or WE, in a given bridge deal? In: 2019 International Joint Conference on Neural Networks, pp. 1–8 (2019)
16. Manley, B., Horton, M., Greenberg-Yarbro, T., Rigal, B. (eds.): The Official Encyclopedia of Bridge, 7th edn. American Contract Bridge League Inc (2011)

17. Mossakowski, K., Mańdziuk, J.: Artificial neural networks for solving double dummy bridge problems. In: Rutkowski, L., Siekmann, J.H., Tadeusiewicz, R., Zadeh, L.A. (eds.) ICAISC 2004. LNCS (LNAI), vol. 3070, pp. 915–921. Springer, Heidelberg (2004). https://doi.org/10.1007/978-3-540-24844-6_142
18. Mossakowski, K., Mańdziuk, J.: Learning without human expertise: a case study of the double dummy bridge problem. IEEE Trans. Neural Netw. **20**(2), 278–299 (2009)
19. Yakovenko, N., Cao, L., Raffel, C., Fan, J.: Poker-CNN: a pattern learning strategy for making draws and bets in poker games using convolutional networks. In: Proceedings of the AAAI Conference on Artificial Intelligence (AAAI 2016), pp. 360–367 (2016)
20. Yeh, C.K., Hsieh, C.Y., Lin, H.T.: Automatic bridge bidding using deep reinforcement learning. IEEE Trans. Games **10**(4), 365–377 (2018)
21. Zhang, X., Liu, W., Yang, F.: A neural model for automatic bidding of contract bridge. In: 2020 IEEE 22nd International Conference on High Performance Computing and Communications; IEEE 18th International Conference on Smart City; IEEE 6th International Conference on Data Science and Systems (HPCC/SmartCity/DSS), pp. 999–1005 (2020)

Coarse-to-Fine Visual Place Recognition

Junkun Qi[1,3], Rui Wang[1,2,3(✉)], Chuan Wang[1,3], and Xiaochun Cao[1,3]

[1] State Key Laboratory of Information Security, Institute of Information Engineering, Chinese Academy of Sciences, Beijing, China
{qijunkun,wangrui,wangchuan,caoxiaochun}@iie.ac.cn
[2] Zhejiang Lab, Hangzhou, China
[3] School of Cyber Security, University of Chinese Academy of Sciences, Beijing, China

Abstract. Visual Place Recognition (VPR) aims to locate one or more images depicting the same place in the geotagged database with a given query and is typically conducted as an image retrieval task. Currently, global-based and local-based descriptors are two mainstream representations to solve VPR. However, they still struggle against viewpoint change, confusion from similar patterns in different places, or high computation complexity. In this paper, we propose a progressive Coarse-To-Fine (CTF-VPR) framework, which has a strong ability on handling irrelevant matches and controlling time consumption. It employs global descriptors to discover visually similar references and local descriptors to filter those with similar but irrelative patterns. Besides, a region-specific representing format called regional descriptor is introduced with region augmentation and increases the possibilities of positive references with partially relevant areas via region refinement. Furthermore, during the spatial verification, we provide the Spatial Deviation Index (SDI) considering coordinate deviation to evaluate the consistency of matches. It discards exhaustive and iterative search and reduces the time consumption hundreds of times. The proposed CTF-VPR outperforms existing approaches by 2%–3% recalls on Pitts250k and Tokyo24/7 benchmarks.

Keywords: Visual place recognition · Coarse-to-fine · Multi-scale descriptors

1 Introduction

Visual place recognition (VPR) seeks to locate one or more images depicting the same place in the geotagged database with a given query [1,11,13]. It has been employed on a range of potential applications, as the prior information or key components, including Simultaneous Localization And Mapping (SLAM) [12,21]

This work is supported in part by the National Natural Science Foundation of China Under Grants No. U20B2066, the Open Research Projects of Zhejiang Lab (Grant No. 2021KB0AB01), and the National Key R&D Program of China (Grant No. 2020AAA0109304).

T. Mantoro et al. (Eds.): ICONIP 2021, LNCS 13111, pp. 28–39, 2021.
https://doi.org/10.1007/978-3-030-92273-3_3

  (a) Query 1   (b) Positive of (a)   (c) Query 2   (d) Negative of (c)

Fig. 1. Examples of challenges in VPR. (a) and (b) show the same place, where the scene visible in the query is merely within the green box in its positive counterpart. (c) and (d) show different places with visually similar patterns. (Color figure online)

and Augmented Reality (AR) [5,20], thus plays an important role in the fields of computer vision [1,8,13] and robotics [12,19,21].

In practice, VPR encounters many inherent challenges due to occlusions and changes in condition (e.g., season and illumination) and viewpoint (e.g., translation and rotation). These challenges bring large visual and content variations therefore leading to irrelevant matching between the query and positive references. As shown in Fig. 1(a) and 1(b), the two images depict the same place but their similarities are low owing to the irrelevant regions caused by viewpoint change. Besides, similar patterns such as building facades, fences or road markings always exist in different scenes and are notoriously difficult for discovering the true correspondences. As shown in Fig. 1(c) and 1(d), there are similar patterns between the two different scenes, making it difficult to distinguish them.

VPR is typically conducted as an image retrieval task [1,11,13] and solved based on two mainstream representation methods: those based on global descriptors [1,11,16,17,25] and local descriptors [4,13,22]. Global descriptor methods embed the integral image into a single vector and select database images based on the pairwise descriptor distances. These compact global descriptors are typically efficient and robust to changes in appearance and illumination, since they are directly optimized for VPR. However, they still suffer from viewpoint change and similar patterns of different places. Local descriptor approaches encode an image into a series of vectors, each of which depicts a local patch of the image. These local descriptors are then used to perform feature matching followed by spatial (geometric) verification. Through spatial prioritization, these methods are less susceptible to irrelevant regions and similar patterns but cannot avoid struggling with computation complexity. Although integrating the benefits of both descriptors is straightforward, little research [13] has been attempted and obtains limited efficiency and effectiveness. The novel Coarse-To-Fine (CTF-VPR) approach not only combines the advantages of global and local descriptors but also makes up for their shortcomings.

To achieve this goal, firstly, we designs a progressive coarse-to-fine framework that estimates the similarity score between an image pair. It employs global descriptors to discover condition-related candidates (e.g., images with similar appearance, illumination, and etc.) and local descriptors to filter candidates without relative patterns. Besides, to fully utilize the content information and eliminate irrelevant areas, we introduce a region-specific representing format called regional descriptor, which focuses on parts of the image. It possesses rich regional representation ability and is utilized with region refinement to mitigate the impact of irrelevant areas. Furthermore, to distinguish images with similar but irrelative patterns and reduce time consumption, we provide the Spatial Deviation Index (SDI), which only concerns the coordinate deviation of local matches and discarding time-consuming steps. The provided SDI effectively filters similar but irrelative patterns and enables fast spatial verification, holding the performance with tolerance.

We conduct extensive experiments on well-known VPR benchmarks [32,33] to verify the proposed CTF-VPR approach. CTF-VPR outperforms existing global-descriptor-oriented methods by a large margin (2%–6% recall improvement). It also shows superiority to approaches based on local descriptors (up to a recall increase of 4%), where CTF-VPR not only brings a boost in recalls but also runs hundreds of times faster.

2   Related Work

Visual place recognition can be mainly grouped into direct 2D-3D registration-based [14,28–30] and image-retrieval-based [1,11,13,25] methods. In this paper, we mainly focus on the latter ones and review the development of VPR as well as Image Retrieval (IR) in this section.

Global Descriptors. IR and VPR have long been studied since the era of hand-crafted features. BoW [6], VLAD [2,15], and etc. [23] are typical global descriptors. With the flourishing development of deep learning, CNN-based features have been exploited. NetVLAD [1] proposed a generalized VLAD layer to aggregate deep feature maps for VPR. GeM [25] proposed a generalized mean pooling layer to get compact image representations for IR.

Based on NetVLAD, CRN [16] proposed a context-aware feature reweighting mechanism to highlight regions of interest. SARE [17] proposed a new loss function by modeling similarities as probability distributions to learn better image features. SFRS [11] emphasized the importance of hard positives and exploited these samples through image-to-region similarities and self-distillation. APGeM [26] equipped GeM pooling with a listwise ranking loss for an optimal mean average precision.

These compact global descriptors are directly optimized for IR or VPR and typically robust to condition change. However, they are sensitive to viewpoint change and similar patterns of different places.

Local Descriptors. SIFT [18], SURF [3], and etc. [24] are typically hand-crafted local descriptors to represent images. For CNN-based features, LIFT [34] introduced a deep network architecture implementing detection, orientation estimation, and feature description. DELF [22] adopted an attention mechanism to select key points and local descriptors from deep feature maps. SuperPoint [7] presented a self-supervised framework for interest point detectors and descriptors aiming at multiple-view geometry problems. D2Net [9] adopted a single

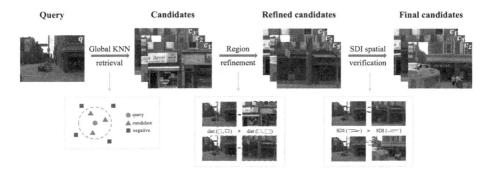

Fig. 2. Framework of CTF-VPR. Global KNN first retrieves several reference images as candidates (only three of them are illustrated for simplicity). These candidates are then sequentially re-ranked by region refinement and SDI spatial verification to obtain the final results.

CNN model simultaneously as a dense feature descriptor and a feature detector for more stable key points.

These local descriptors are typically cross-matched followed by geometric verification with RANSAC [10]. Recently, SuperGlue [27] also predicts matches using Graph Neural Networks (GNNs) and SuperPoint features. Through spatial prioritization, these methods are less susceptible to the aforementioned problems but have a very high time complexity due to time-consuming RANSAC or GNNs.

Joint Global and Local Descriptors. It is straightforward to integrate the benefits of the global and local descriptors, where the local descriptors are used to rearrange the top-ranking reference images retrieved by global ones.

Besides extracting these representations separately using the above methods, efforts have been exerted to encapsulate them in a single model. DELG [4] equipped GeM with the DELF's attention mechanism to extract global and local descriptors simultaneously for IR. Patch-NetVLAD [13] extended NetVLAD and derived additional patch-level local descriptors from VLAD residuals for VPR. Despite the progress, limited efficiency is obtained.

In this paper, we propose a novel coarse-to-fine approach for VPR to combine the advantages of global and local descriptors and make up for their shortcomings, mitigating the aforementioned problems with acceptable retrieval time.

3   Methods

As illustrated in Fig. 2, our CTF-VPR framework consists of three components: global K-Nearest Neighbor (KNN) retrieval to obtain top k_1 image candidates, region refinement to increase the possibilities of positive candidates with partial relevance, and spatial verification via SDI to efficiently eliminate results covering similar patterns but different places.

3.1 Global KNN Retrieval

Given the query q and the reference database, we first extract image feature representations from a pre-trained Convolutional Neural Network (CNN). Then the similarity estimation progress is provided based on representations between the query and images in the database. Subsequently, the KNN-based retrieval is performed to obtain top k_1 similar references that form a candidate set. Detailed steps are illustrated as follows.

For an image I, we extract the deep feature map $\boldsymbol{F}$ from the CNN as $\boldsymbol{F} \in \mathbb{R}^{N \times D}$, where $N = H \times W$ and H, W, D are the height, width, and the number of channels, respectively. Then we aggregate $\boldsymbol{F}$ into compact global descriptors via NetVLAD [1] as:

$$\boldsymbol{f}^g = f_{proj}(f_{VLAD}(\boldsymbol{F})), \tag{1}$$

where $f_{VLAD} : \mathbb{R}^{N \times D} \to \mathbb{R}^{M \times D}$ is the VLAD aggregation operation, $f_{proj} : \mathbb{R}^{M \times D} \to \mathbb{R}^{D^g}$ is a set of normalization and dimension reduction operations, and M is the number of learned cluster centers. By weighting the residuals between each feature $\boldsymbol{f}_i \in \boldsymbol{F}$ and M cluster centers with soft assignments, f_{VLAD} aggregates them into a compact matrix representation with shape $M \times D$. f_{proj} then normalizes and vectorizes this matrix followed by Principal Component Analysis (PCA) to reduce feature dimension and produce global feature descriptor $\boldsymbol{f}^g \in \mathbb{R}^{D^g}$, where $D^g \ll M \cdot D$.

With the obtained query and reference image features, we compute the Euclidean distances between query q and each reference c, represented as $\mathrm{d}(q,c) = \left\| \boldsymbol{f}_q^g - \boldsymbol{f}_c^g \right\|_2$. Then we rank the references based on the computed distances and select k_1 references with KNN strategy, comprising the coarse candidate set $\mathcal{C} = \{c_i\}_{i=1}^{k_1}$.

3.2 Region Refinement

In practice, candidates retrieved by global representations mostly cover scenes with similar appearances but suffer from irrelevant matching caused by occlusions and viewpoint change. In this section we introduce a region refinement module incorporating with region-specific representing format to increase the possibilities of candidates with partially relevant areas.

Firstly, we construct region-specific representation based on heuristically cropped areas from the image. For simplicity, we carry out region cropping on the feature map instead of the image. As illustrated in Fig. 3, we fix the area ratio of the target region to the image feature map as γ and crop it in two ways. The one crops the long side to γ times the original with fixed short side, e.g., the red dashed box. We crop the image along each short side and obtain two interest regions. The other crops both sides to $\sqrt{\gamma}$ times the original, as the green dashed box shows. It is conducted at four corners of the image, leading to another four interest regions. With the cropped regions, deep features of each region are aggregated in the same way presented in Sect. 3.1. Six regional descriptors $\boldsymbol{f}_1^r, \ldots, \boldsymbol{f}_6^r \in \mathbb{R}^{D^g}$ are derived to indicate different parts of the image. Noticing that to avoid neglecting key contents during region cropping, we limit

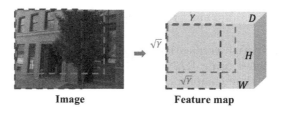

Image   **Feature map**

Fig. 3. Two ways of region cropping, i.e., red and green boxes. (Color figure online)

the interest region to larger than half and set a greater area ratio for the query than the candidates, i.e., $0.5 \leq \gamma_c \leq \gamma_q \leq 1$.

To refine and update the candidates with region-specific descriptors, we evaluate the distances of both regional and global descriptors between each pairwise query-candidate images. Then the distance between each pair $d(q,c)$ is updated with the minimal distance as:

$$d(q,c) = \min_{f \in \{f^g, f_1^r, \cdots, f_6^r\}} \left\| f_q - f_c \right\|_2. \tag{2}$$

In this way, the most relevant contents between the query and the candidates are identified. We thus rearrange elements in candidate set $\mathcal{C}$ according to the updated distances and select top k_2 candidates as the refined set $\mathcal{C}_r$.

3.3   SDI Spatial Verification

Thanks to the region refinement module, we alleviate the problem of irrelevant areas between the query and positive references and get candidate set $\mathcal{C}_r$ containing k_2 reference images. However, distinguishing negative references holding similar patterns is still difficult based on current framework. To deal with the problem caused by similar patterns, we perform feature matching using local descriptors, and propose fast SDI verification for efficiency.

Firstly, we intend to locate some small patches of the image. We also conduct the operation on the feature map due to simplicity. We fix the patch size as $p \times p$ and ignore those on the edge smaller than $p \times p$. Each patch corresponds to a key point and consists of neighborhoods of the key point. Deep features within the patch are aggregated into a local descriptor. Considering that the number of local descriptors is much larger than that of global ones, we set a shorter length D^l for them when applying PCA, where $D^l \ll D^g$. The obtained local descriptors are denoted as $\{f_i^l\}_{i=1}^{N^l}$. For simplicity, we ignore local indication of local descriptor f^l in the following illustration in this subsection.

As the candidates have been elaborately re-ranked during region refinement, it is sufficient to conduct matching and verification on a small number of them, i.e., $k_2 \ll k_1$, benefiting time consumption. For a query-candidate pair, f_i^q and f_j^c are matched if and only if they are the mutual nearest neighbors to each other. We utilize exhaustive comparison between the query and candidate local descriptor sets and formulate the set of mutual nearest neighbor matches $\mathcal{P}$ as:

$$\mathcal{P} = \{(i,j) : i = \arg\min_{i'} \left\| \boldsymbol{f}_{i'}^q - \boldsymbol{f}_j^c \right\|_2, j = \arg\min_{j'} \left\| \boldsymbol{f}_i^q - \boldsymbol{f}_{j'}^c \right\|_2 \}. \tag{3}$$

Subsequently, spatial verification is performed by fitting a homography among all the matches using RANSAC [10]. However, it is an iterative algorithm and has high time complexity. Thus, we propose a fast verification approach using Spatial Deviation Index (SDI) while still preserve the performance to some extent. SDI is obtained as follows.

Given the matching pairs and their corresponding key point coordinates (x, y), we calculate the differences between the coordinates of the query and the candidate for each match (i, j) as $\Delta x = (x_i)_q - (x_j)_c$ and $\Delta y = (y_i)_q - (y_j)_c$. Horizontal and vertical coordinate differences make up two sets, denoted as $\mathcal{D}_x(q,c)$ and $\mathcal{D}_y(q,c)$, respectively. SDI of the matches is then defined as:

$$\mathrm{SDI}(q,c) = \frac{N_q^l}{N^s} \cdot \Big(\sigma\big(\mathcal{D}_x(q,c)\big) + \sigma\big(\mathcal{D}_y(q,c)\big) \Big). \tag{4}$$

where N_q^l is the number of local descriptors of the query, N^s is the number of matches, and $\sigma(\cdot)$ is the standard derivation of a set. A smaller SDI indicates larger number of matches and smaller coordinate difference derivation, implying a better matching between the query and the candidate. We hence re-rank these k_2 images for the second time according to their SDIs and treated them as the final results.

4   Experiments

4.1   Experimental Setup

Dataset We evaluate our method on two leading benchmarks: Pittsburgh [33] and Tokyo24/7 [32]. Pittsburgh contains queries and images projected from large-scale panoramic images taken at different times. The full Pittsburgh dataset is called Pitts250k for short and its subset Pitts30k is also commonly used. Images in Tokyo24/7 are collected from Google Street Views except that the queries are taken using mobile phones with various illumination conditions.

Evaluation. A query place is deemed correctly recognized if at least one of the top N retrieved reference images is within 25 m from it. Recall@N is then applied to evaluate the performance. For evaluation settings such as image resolution and spatial non-maximal suppression, we follow SFRS [11].

Implementation. We use the same architecture as NetVLAD [1], i.e., VGG16 [31] backbone and NetVLAD layer with 64 cluster centers, and adopt the pretrained models from SFRS which are trained on Pitts30k.

As conventionally, we re-rank the top $k_1 = 100$ candidates from coarse global retrieval results. For the second rearrangement, we match only $k_2 = 10$ top candidates. When aggregating deep features, we set the dimensions of global and local descriptors as $D_g = 4096$ and $D_l = 128$, respectively. The corresponding PCA parameters are trained on the training set of Pitts30k. To assign area ratios

Table 1. Recalls of different methods. * indicates our default settings.

Methods	Recall@1/5/10 (%)	
	Pitts250k	Tokyo24/7
NetVLAD [1]	86.0/93.2/95.1	73.3/82.9/86.0
SARE [17]	89.0/95.5/96.8	79.7/86.7/90.5
SFRS [11]	90.7/96.4/97.6	85.4/91.1/93.3
SuperPoint [7]	88.7/95.1/96.4	88.2/90.2/90.2
Patch-NetVLAD [13]	89.7/95.6/96.7	86.0/88.6/90.5
Ours (RR only)	91.1/96.5/**97.7**	87.0/92.4/**93.7**
Ours (RR+SV) *	**92.6/97.2/97.7**	**91.1/93.7/93.7**

and patch sizes, we conduct experiments on the validation set of Pitts30k. We first fix γ_q as 1 and take one γ_c every 0.5 from 0.5 to 1, from which the best $\gamma_c = 0.65$ is chosen. Then we fix γ_c as 0.65 and take one γ_q every 0.5 from 0.65 to 1, during which the best $\gamma_q = 0.75$ is selected. The patch size is obtained by searching from $\{3,5,7\}$ and $p = 5$ is finally fetched.

It is noted that all the parameters mentioned above are fixed throughout the evaluation process and no fine-tuning is performed when tested on other datasets.

4.2   Comparison with SOTAs

We compare with several benchmark VPR approaches: NetVLAD [1], SARE [17], SFRS [11], SuperPoint [7] and Patch-NetVLAD [13]. The first three methods are based on global descriptors. SuperPoint is local-descriptor-oriented and Patch-NetVLAD derives both representations jointly. For SuperPoint, we first retrieve coarse candidates based on NetVLAD and then re-rank the top 100 of them with SuperPoint descriptors and SuperGlue [27] matching, as did in [13]. For Patch-NetVLAD, the number of reference images to be rearranged is also 100 for the sake of fairness. The comparison results are presented in Table 1.

We observe that superior performance is obtained merely based on the region refinement module. As listed in Table 1, Region Refinement (RR in the Table) brings a remarkable recall improvement from 0.4% to 1.6%. It outperforms all global-descriptor-based approaches and shows comparable performance to the methods based on local descriptors. This benefits from explicitly identifying the relevant regions between the query and the reference images and extracting corresponding regional features. In this way, we increase the similarities between the query and the hard positives with irrelevant regions and thus rank them higher. Several qualitative examples are shown at the top of Fig. 4.

Further, following the SDI Spatial Verification (SV in the Table), we leads to an additional boost in recalls from 1.5% to 4.1%, as shown in the last row in Table 1. With spatial verification, the visually similar images of different places are distinguished from the real positives and thus are ranked lower. Several

(a) Query   (b) KNN   (c) RR

(d) Query   (e) RR   (f) SV

Fig. 4. Top 1 candidate recognized by different methods. Images in red boxes are wrongly retrieved. The dashed (blue and green) boxes indicate the most relevant regions identified by RR. SV distinguishes negative reference images with similar patterns from the real positives. (Color figure online)

examples are illustrated at the bottom of Fig. 4. Besides, our proposed SDI verification efficiently accelerates the verification process. As shown in Table 2, our method is hundreds of times faster than SuperPoint and Patch-NetVLAD.

4.3   Parameter Analysis

To characterize the properties of our CTF-VPR, we conduct detailed parameter analysis in this section.

We first try to use different area ratios during region refinement and list the recalls in Table 3. As shows, conducting region cropping both for the query and the reference images leads to better results. Applying region refinement with other ratios also brings (even greater) performance improvements. It is noted that the default area ratios are derived based on the validation set of Pitts30k and kept unchanged for other evaluations.

Table 2. Balance between recalls and average retrieval time per query on Tokyo24/7. * indicates our default settings.

Methods	Recall@1/5/10 (%)	Time (ms)
SFRS [11]	85.4/91.1/93.3	**6.391**
Ours (RR only)	87.0/92.4/**93.7**	10.53
SuperPoint [7]	88.2/90.2/90.2	∼6000
Patch-NetVLAD [13]	86.0/88.6/90.5	∼5600
Ours (RR+F-SV-5)	91.1/92.4/**93.7**	**23.39**
Ours (RR+F-SV-10)*	91.1/**93.7**/93.7	35.50
Ours (RR+R-SV-5)	90.5/92.4/**93.7**	70.46
Ours (RR+R-SV-10)	**91.4/93.7/93.7**	163.0

Table 3. Recalls of region refinement with different area ratios on Tokyo24/7. ___ indicates our default settings.

γ_q	γ_c	Recall@1/5/10 (%)	γ_q	γ_c	Recall@1/5/10 (%)
1.00	0.60	85.7/91.1/92.7	0.65	0.65	**87.9/93.0/94.6**
	0.65	86.7/90.8/92.7	0.70		87.3/**93.0**/94.0
	0.70	86.0/91.1/93.7	0.75		87.0/92.4/93.7
	0.75	86.7/91.4/93.3	0.80		87.0/93.0/93.3

Next, we test at different settings for spatial verification. By default, we calculate SDI for top $k_2 = 10$ candidates known as fast spatial verification (denoted as F-SV-10). We emphasize that a smaller k_2 is enough to get satisfactory results for our method but rises a larger increment on speed, as shown in Table 2. This demonstrates the stability of our proposed CTF-VPR framework. Besides, we compare the time consumption with RANSAC verification (denoted as R-SV-k_2). The results are listed in Table 2. Compared with RANSAC, SDI obtains obvious acceleration (3–5 times faster) with a little performance drop.

5   Conclusions

In this paper, we propose a progressive coarse-to-fine strategy for effective visual place recognition called CTF-VPR. Specifically, we first use KNN search based on global descriptors to capture references depicting similar visual scenes. Then regional descriptors are derived and effectively increase the possibilities of positive references with partially relevant areas via region refinement. Finally, local feature matching is adopted based on patch-level descriptors to distinguish different places covering similar patterns, in which SDI is provided for fast spatial verification. SDI-based verification not only provides accurate matching estimation but also accelerates the speed in a large amount.

References

1. Arandjelovic, R., Gronat, P., Torii, A., Pajdla, T., Sivic, J.: Netvlad: CNN architecture for weakly supervised place recognition. In: Proceedings of the IEEE Conference on Computer Vision and Pattern Recognition, pp. 5297–5307 (2016)
2. Arandjelovic, R., Zisserman, A.: All about VLAD. In: Proceedings of the IEEE conference on Computer Vision and Pattern Recognition, pp. 1578–1585 (2013)
3. Bay, H., Ess, A., Tuytelaars, T., Van Gool, L.: Speeded-up robust features (surf). Comput. Vis. Image Underst. **110**(3), 346–359 (2008)
4. Cao, B., Araujo, A., Sim, J.: Unifying deep local and global features for image search. In: European Conference on Computer Vision (2020)
5. Castle, R., Klein, G., Murray, D.W.: Video-rate localization in multiple maps for wearable augmented reality. In: 2008 12th IEEE International Symposium on Wearable Computers, pp. 15–22. IEEE (2008)
6. Csurka, G., Dance, C., Fan, L., Willamowski, J., Bray, C.: Visual categorization with bags of keypoints. In: Workshop on Statistical Learning in Computer Vision, ECCV, pp. 1–22, Prague (2004)
7. DeTone, D., Malisiewicz, T., Rabinovich, A.: Superpoint: self-supervised interest point detection and description. In: 2018 IEEE/CVF Conference on Computer Vision and Pattern Recognition Workshops, pp. 337–33712 (2018)
8. Doan, A.D., Latif, Y., Chin, T.J., Liu, Y., Do, T.T., Reid, I.: Scalable place recognition under appearance change for autonomous driving. In: Proceedings of the IEEE/CVF International Conference on Computer Vision (2019)
9. Dusmanu, M., et al.: D2-net: A trainable CNN for joint description and detection of local features. In: 2019 IEEE Conference on Computer Vision and Pattern Recognition (2019)
10. Fischler, M.A., Bolles, R.C.: Random sample consensus: a paradigm for model fitting with applications to image analysis and automated cartography. Commun. ACM **24**(6), 381–395 (1981)
11. Ge, Y., Wang, H., Zhu, F., Zhao, R., Li, H.: Self-supervising fine-grained region similarities for large-scale image localization. In: European Conference on Computer Vision (2020)
12. Häne, C., Heng, L., Lee, G.H., Fraundorfer, F., Furgale, P., Sattler, T., Pollefeys, M.: 3d visual perception for self-driving cars using a multi-camera system: calibration, mapping, localization, and obstacle detection. Image Vis. Comput. **68**, 14–27 (2017)
13. Hausler, S., Garg, S., Xu, M., Milford, M., Fischer, T.: Patch-NetVLAD: multi-scale fusion of locally-global descriptors for place recognition. In: Proceedings of the IEEE Conference on Computer Vision and Pattern Recognition (2021)
14. Irschara, A., Zach, C., Frahm, J.M., Bischof, H.: From structure-from-motion point clouds to fast location recognition. In: 2009 IEEE Conference on Computer Vision and Pattern Recognition, pp. 2599–2606. IEEE (2009)
15. Jégou, H., Douze, M., Schmid, C., Pérez, P.: Aggregating local descriptors into a compact image representation. In: 2010 IEEE Computer Society Conference on Computer Vision and Pattern Recognition, pp. 3304–3311 (2010)
16. Kim, H.J., Dunn, E., Frahm, J.M.: Learned contextual feature reweighting for image geo-localization. In: 2017 IEEE Conference on Computer Vision and Pattern Recognition, pp. 3251–3260 (2017)
17. Liu, L., Li, H., Dai, Y.: Stochastic attraction-repulsion embedding for large scale image localization. In: Proceedings of the IEEE International Conference on Computer Vision, pp. 2570–2579 (2019)

18. Lowe, D.G.: Distinctive image features from scale-invariant keypoints. Int. J. Comput. Vis. **60**(2), 91–110 (2004)
19. Lowry, S., Sünderhauf, N., Newman, P., Leonard, J.J., Cox, D., Corke, P., Milford, M.J.: Visual place recognition: a survey. IEEE Trans. Rob. **32**(1), 1–19 (2016)
20. Middelberg, S., Sattler, T., Untzelmann, O., Kobbelt, L.: Scalable 6-DOF localization on mobile devices. In: Fleet, D., Pajdla, T., Schiele, B., Tuytelaars, T. (eds.) ECCV 2014. LNCS, vol. 8690, pp. 268–283. Springer, Cham (2014). https://doi.org/10.1007/978-3-319-10605-2_18
21. Mur-Artal, R., Montiel, J.M.M., Tardos, J.D.: ORB-SLAM: a versatile and accurate monocular slam system. IEEE Trans. Rob. **31**(5), 1147–1163 (2015)
22. Noh, H., Araujo, A., Sim, J., Weyand, T., Han, B.: Large-scale image retrieval with attentive deep local features. In: Proceedings of the IEEE International Conference on Computer Vision, pp. 3456–3465 (2017)
23. Perronnin, F., Liu, Y., Sánchez, J., Poirier, H.: Large-scale image retrieval with compressed fisher vectors. In: 2010 IEEE Computer Society Conference on Computer Vision and Pattern Recognition, pp. 3384–3391. IEEE (2010)
24. Philbin, J., Chum, O., Isard, M., Sivic, J., Zisserman, A.: Object retrieval with large vocabularies and fast spatial matching. In: 2007 IEEE Conference on Computer Vision and Pattern Recognition, pp. 1–8. IEEE (2007)
25. Radenović, F., Tolias, G., Chum, O.: Fine-tuning CNN image retrieval with no human annotation. IEEE Trans. Pattern Anal. Mach. Intell. **41**(7), 1655–1668 (2018)
26. Revaud, J., Almazán, J., Rezende, R.S., Souza, C.R.: Learning with average precision: training image retrieval with a listwise loss. In: Proceedings of the IEEE/CVF International Conference on Computer Vision, pp. 5107–5116 (2019)
27. Sarlin, P.E., DeTone, D., Malisiewicz, T., Rabinovich, A.: SuperGlue: learning feature matching with graph neural networks. In: 2020 IEEE Conference on Computer Vision and Pattern Recognition (2020)
28. Sattler, T., Leibe, B., Kobbelt, L.: Fast image-based localization using direct 2D-to-3D matching. In: 2011 International Conference on Computer Vision, pp. 667–674. IEEE (2011)
29. Sattler, T., Weyand, T., Leibe, B., Kobbelt, L.: Image retrieval for image-based localization revisited. In: 2012 British Machine Vision Conference, p. 4 (2012)
30. Schonberger, J.L., Frahm, J.M.: Structure-from-motion revisited. In: Proceedings of the IEEE Conference on Computer Vision and Pattern Recognition, pp. 4104–4113 (2016)
31. Simonyan, K., Zisserman, A.: Very deep convolutional networks for large-scale image recognition. In: International Conference on Learning Representations (2015)
32. Torii, A., Arandjelović, R., Sivic, J., Okutomi, M., Pajdla, T.: 24/7 place recognition by view synthesis. In: 2015 IEEE Conference on Computer Vision and Pattern Recognition, pp. 1808–1817 (2015)
33. Torii, A., Sivic, J., Okutomi, M., Pajdla, T.: Visual place recognition with repetitive structures. IEEE Trans. Pattern Anal. Mach. Intell. **37**(11), 2346–2359 (2015)
34. Yi, K.M., Trulls, E., Lepetit, V., Fua, P.: LIFT: learned invariant feature transform. In: Leibe, B., Matas, J., Sebe, N., Welling, M. (eds.) ECCV 2016. LNCS, vol. 9910, pp. 467–483. Springer, Cham (2016). https://doi.org/10.1007/978-3-319-46466-4_28

BFConv: Improving Convolutional Neural Networks with Butterfly Convolution

Dengjie Yang[1], Xuehui Yu[1], Yi Sun[2], Fuzhen Zhuang[3], Qing He[3], and Shiwei Ye[1(✉)]

[1] School of Electronic, Electrical and Communication Engineering, University of Chinese Academy of Sciences, Beijing 100049, China
{yangdengjie20,yuxuehui17}@mails.ucas.ac.cn, shwye@ucas.ac.cn
[2] School of Microelectronics, University of Chinese Academy of Sciences, Beijing 100049, China
sunyi@ucas.ac.cn
[3] Institute of Computing Technology, Chinese Academy of Sciences, Beijing 100086, China
{zhuangfuzhen,heqing}@ict.ac.cn

Abstract. Convolutional neural network (CNN) is a basic neural network widely used in vision tasks. Many CNNs alleviate the redundancy in feature maps to reduce model complexity. Inspired by digital signal processing theories, this paper reviews discrete fourier transform (DFT), finding its similarities with standard convolution. In particular, DFT has a fast algorithm called FFT, which sparks our thinking: can we learn from the idea of FFT to realize a more efficient convolution filter? Based on the butterfly operation of FFT, we propose a novel butterfly convolution (BFConv). In addition, we illustrate that group weight sharing convolution is a basic unit of BFConv. Compared with the traditional group convolution structure, BFConv constructs group residual-like connections and increases the range of receptive fields for each sub-feature layer. Without changing the network architecture, we integrate BFConv into ResNet-50, ShuffleNet and VGG-16. Experimental results on CIFAR-10 and ImageNet demonstrate the above BFConv-equipped networks reduce parameters and computation, achieving similar or higher accuracy. Remarkably, when ResNet-50 embedded BFConv reaches nearly half of the compression ratio of the model, it performs favorably against its state-of-the-art competitors.

Keywords: Convolutional neural network · FFT · Butterfly convolution · Group Weight sharing convolution

1 Introduction

Due to the powerful feature transformation ability of convolutional neural network (CNN), it has made remarkable achievements in computer vision. The success of the residual network (ResNet) [7] has demonstrated the great potential of deep CNNs and attracted extensive attention from researchers. However,

T. Mantoro et al. (Eds.): ICONIP 2021, LNCS 13111, pp. 40–50, 2021.
https://doi.org/10.1007/978-3-030-92273-3_4

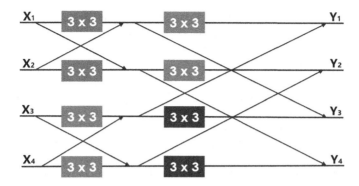

Fig. 1. Schematic illustration of the proposed butterfly convolution. As can be seen, in butterfly convolution, the original input is split into four portions, each of which undergoes a series of corresponding convolution operations. Convolution blocks with the same color represent shared weight parameters. Note that we omit BN and ReLU operations after each convolution for notational convenience. More details about butterfly convolution can be found in Sect. 3.3. (Color figure online)

the gradual improvement of accuracy is often at the cost of increasing the complexity of the model, which brings the risk of model degradation. Hence, a lot of work and efforts are trying to reduce the number of parameters and computation, while ensuring that the performance of the model does not decrease significantly.

In this case, how to design an efficient convolution filter has become a problem worthy of further discussion. Convolution is the basic operation unit of CNN. Through a series of convolution and nonlinear activation operations, CNN can generate image representation that captures abstract features and covers the global theoretical receptive field. For each convolution layer, the convolution kernel can capture specific types of features in the input. Group-wise convolution [19] divides the input into multiple groups according to the channel. Depth-wise convolution [22] performs a separate convolution operation on each input channel. Point-wise convolution [4] is to use a 1×1 size convolution kernel to calculate point by point on the feature map. It is a tendency to make full use of group-wise convolution, depth-wise convolution and point-wise convolution. The ingenious permutation and combination of these three schemes result in many efficient models, such as ResNext [15], ShuffleNet [11] and Xception [13]. Effective practice of the above networks indicates that the redundancy of inter-channel connections can be reasonably reduced, or that the effect of dense convolution kernel can be compared with the combination of some sparse kernels.

Furthermore, it is a consensus that there are plenty of pattern similarities in the output feature maps of the convolution layer. The practical idea of this natural phenomenon is to delete redundant feature maps, so as to reduce unnecessary convolution operations. However, because of the communication among layers, it is limited to locate redundant channels. Although the channel attention mechanisms [1,8,9,17] evaluate the importance score of each channel, the process of channel pruning leads to excessive manual work. In order to avoid struggling in such obstacles, we hope to process feature maps in a more elegant way, with the goal of reducing the number of parameters and computation without performance loss.

Our work is inspired by digital signal processing, many theories of which are of guiding significance to the study of CNN. Firstly, we analyze the similarities and differences between DFT and convolution operation from the perspective of mathematical definition. Subsequently, as shown in Fig. 1, we propose a novel BFConv based on the butterfly operation of FFT. Notably, we indicate that group weight sharing convolution is the basis of BFConv. We have proved their effectiveness through a large number of experiments. In general, the contributions of this paper are as follows:

1) We introduce a lightweight yet effective convolution filter, BFConv, which generates from butterfly operation of FFT and applies group weight sharing convolution to multiple sub-features.
2) Experimental results on ImageNet demonstrate ResNet-50 embedded BFConv has lower model complexity than most of the state-of-the-art model compression approaches while achieving higher performance.

2   Related Work

2.1   Efficient and Compact Model Design

Over the years, researchers have carried out active explorations and experiments on the depth, width and scale of CNN, making great progress in efficient and compact model design. The popular and efficient convolution filters are group-wise convolution [19], depth-wise convolution [22] and point-wise convolution [4]. Most of the recent architectures, such as GoogelNets [4,14,20,23] and MobileNets [3,10,12], adopt a combination of these convolution filters to make the model efficient. Furthermore, several novel convolution filters have also been proposed.

HetConv [16] contains a heterogeneous convolution kernel (for example, a few kernels have a size of 3×3, others may be 1×1) to reduce the computation of the existing model with the same accuracy as the original model. Inspired by the elastic collision model in physics, the "Inter-layer Collision" structure [21] is presented to capture more fine-grained features. Our proposed BFConv is constructed in the way of butterfly operation to save parameters and computation.

2.2   Feature Maps Redundancy

Although a well-trained deep CNN has good feature extraction capabilities for the input, output feature maps of its convolutional layer contain a lot of redundant information. Through the experiment of feature maps visualization, Ghost-Net [24] reveals that there are similarities between some feature maps, so redundant feature maps can be generated in a cheaper way. SPConv [27] rethinks the problem of the redundancy in vanilla convolution and then splits the input channels into two groups for different processing. In addition, orthogonal to channel redundancy, OctConv [18] explores and alleviates redundancy on the spatial dimension of features maps. Compared with the above-mentioned soft operations, channel-based pruning methods [26,31,33] cut off the entire weight channel of low importance, thereby compressing the model without causing loss of accuracy as much as possible. All these redundancies imply that we can reduce the number of parameters through parameter sharing.

2.3   Frequency Domain Learning

Mainstream CNNs mainly operate on the input in the spatial domain. Specifically, some substantive work focuses on the organic combination of frequency domain and deep learning. A phenomenon frequency principle (F-Principle) is proposed in [2], which concludes that deep CNN is good at capturing low-frequency components, while controlling high-frequency components in a small range and capturing high-frequency components. [5] transforms the original input image from the spatial domain to the frequency domain by discrete cosine transform (DCT) and uses DCT coefficients as network input. Based on [5], [6] extends the application scene from image classification to instance segmentation. Combining mathematical methods such as fourier transform, discretization and low-pass filter, if we interpret or apply CNNs from the perspective of the frequency domain, we may have surprising discoveries. Significantly, it is also our work strategy.

3   Method

In this section, we first analyze the similarities and differences between DFT and convolution. Secondly, we introduce the butterfly operation, which is the basic operating unit of FFT. Then we show how to build BFConv from butterfly operation. Finally, BFConv with cross-channel information interaction capability and group weight sharing convolution are proposed.

3.1   DFT and Convolution Operation

DFT is an important mathematical analysis method in digital signal processing. $x(n)$ is defined as a 1-D discrete real sequence of length N, and its DFT is expressed as follows:

$$X(k) = \sum_{n=0}^{N-1} x(n)e^{-j\frac{2\pi kn}{N}} = \sum_{n=0}^{N-1} x(n)W_N^{kn} \tag{1}$$

The 1×1 convolution (the same number of input and output points) is represented as follows:

$$X(k) = \sum_{n=0}^{N-1} x(n)W_k^n \tag{2}$$

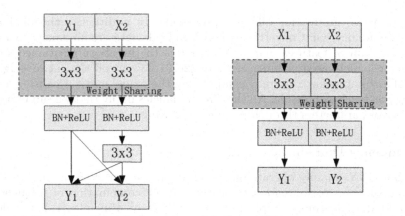

(a) Butterfly Convolution-v1   (b) Group Weight Sharing Convolution

Fig. 2. The initial butterfly convolution and group weight sharing convolution. (a) is the initial version of butterfly convolution (Butterfly Convolution-v1), constructed from butterfly operation. (b) is group weight sharing convolution with a group number of 2. More details can be seen in Sect. 3.2.

According to the above two equations, we can find that the form of DFT and 1×1 convolution is similar, both of which are weighted summation operations on the input. Moreover, they can be regarded as a process of feature transformation. DFT is from the time domain to the frequency domain, while 1×1 convolution is from one real number domain to another real number domain. On the other hand, there are many differences between DFT and convolution. The weight coefficients of DFT are regular and fixed with the determination of k and n. However, the weight coefficients of convolution are constantly updated with the back propagation process of network training. Similarly, for 2-D images, 2-D DFT and 3×3 convolution can be compared in this way. We know that DFT has a fast calculation method FFT, which effectively reduces the amount of calculation and improves the calculation efficiency. It can not help but trigger our thinking: can we learn from the idea of FFT to achieve a more efficient convolution filter? The answer is self-evident.

3.2   From Butterfly Operation to Butterfly Convolution

Butterfly operation is the basic operating unit of DFT. The entire FFT is composed of several levels of iterative butterfly operations. Butterfly operation is described as:

$$Y(K) = \begin{cases} X_1(K) + W_N^k X_2(K) & k = 0, 1, ..., \frac{N}{2} - 1 \\ X_1(K) - W_N^k X_2(K) & k = \frac{N}{2}, \frac{N}{2} + 1, ..., N - 1 \end{cases} \tag{3}$$

It can be seen from the above equation that the DFT of an N-point sequence $(X(k))$ can be formed by combining the DFT of two $\frac{N}{2}$-point sequences $(X_1(K)$

and $X_2(K)$). The input of $X_1(K)$ and $X_2(K)$ is the original input sequence divided by even-numbered points and odd-numbered points, respectively. In particular, the weight coefficients of the corresponding positions of $X_1(K)$ and $X_2(K)$ are the same. Next, we construct BFConv according to the definition of butterfly operation. As exhibited in Fig. 2(a), an input X is split into two groups (X_1 and X_2) according to the original order of the channels. Then, X_1 and X_2 generate $X_1(K)$ and $X_2(K)$ by two weight-sharing convolutions (3×3 kernel size), respectively. Besides, performing a convolution (3×3 kernel size) on $X_2(K)$ to get $W_N^k X_2(K)$. Finally, through addition and subtraction, we obtain Y_1 and Y_2, which are concatenated together as the output Y.

3.3 Enhanced Butterfly Convolution

BFConv is characterized by the weight sharing of the convolution kernel. It means that two sets of inputs use two convolution kernels that share the same parameters. Therefore, as illustrated in Fig. 2(b), we point out group weight sharing convolution is the basic operating unit of BFConv. Furthermore, the introduction of $W_N^k X_2(K)$ increases the receptive field of local information to a certain extent, which is conducive to better feature extraction. In order to further fuse information on different scales, we propose an enhanced BFConv. Unless otherwise specified, BFConv mentioned in this paper refers to the enhanced BFConv. According to the signal flow diagram of the 4-point FFT algorithm with 2-based decimated in time, we design BFConv.

As shown in Fig. 1, BFConv is composed of four group weight sharing convolutions and multiple skip connections, which constructs hierarchical residual-like connection. In our method, we consider a simple case where the number of input and output channels of the convolutional layer is equal. Given a set of nonlinear functions $F = [F_1, F_2, F_3, F_4]$, four components of F are corresponding to blue, orange, green and purple 3×3 convolution blocks. For notational convenience, each F_i represents Conv-BN-ReLU operation. BFConv transforms input $X = [X_1, X_2, X_3, X_4] \in \mathbb{R}^{H \times W \times C}$ to output $Y = [Y_1, Y_2, Y_3, Y_4] \in \mathbb{R}^{H \times W \times C}$ through the combination of F_i. It is worth noting that X_i is obtained by dividing X into four groups according to channels, and the dimensions of X_i and Y_i are the same. Y_1 is represented as follows:

$$Y_1 = F_3(F_1(X_1) + X_2) + F_2(X_3) + X_4 \qquad (4)$$

And so on, we can get Y_2, Y_3 and Y_4. After that, Y_1, Y_2, Y_3 and Y_4 are concatenated in the channel dimension as the final output.

4 Experiments

In this section, we exhaustively evaluate the effect of our proposed method for image classification task. Experimental results on CIFAR-10 [28] and ImageNet [30] benchmarks verify the validity of our method.

4.1 Implementation Details

We implement our method using the public PyTorch framework. For a fair comparison, we adopt ResNet-50 [7], ShuffleNet [11] and VGG-16 [25], and only replace partial convolutions of these networks. Meanwhile, the number of input channels of the convolution layer is adjusted appropriately. In detail, we have the scale(s for short) that is the number of groups and refer to the width(w for short) as the number of channels in each group. When applying ResNet-50 to CIFAR-10 dataset, due to the small input image size, in order to avoid excessive downsampling, we change the size of the first convolution kernel from 7×7 to 3×3 and remove the max-pooling layer. For ShuffleNet, we substitute for the second group convolution of ShuffleNet-Unit. For VGG-16, we replace standard 3×3 convolutions between the third and fourth downsampling.

On the one hand, we evaluate the performance of our proposed BFConv and group weight sharing convolution on CIFAR-10 dataset. In the training phase, each image is zero-padded with 4 pixels then randomly cropped to the original size. We train networks using stochastic gradient descent (SGD) for 200 epochs with mini-batch size of 128 on a single GPU, weight decay of 0.0001 and momentum of 0.9. The initial learning rate is set to 0.1, which is divided by 10 at 100 and 150 epochs. Evaluation is performed on the original images.

Each input image is randomly cropped to 224×224 with random horizontal flipping. We optimize network parameters using SGD with weight decay of 0.0001, momentum of 0.9 and mini-batch size of 256 on four 2080 GPUs. All the models are trained 100 epochs. The learning rate is initially set to 0.1 and decreased by a factor of 10 after every 30 epochs. When testing on the validation set, we first resize the shorter side of an input image to 256 and then use a center crop of 224×224 for evaluation.

4.2 Results on CIFAR-10

Group Convolution vs. Group Weight Sharing Convolution. On the CIFAR-10 dataset, we first compare the performance differences between group convolution (GConv) and group weight sharing convolution (GWSConv). In Table 1, we can observe that ResNet-50-GWSConv ($24w \times 4s$) saves 20.5% of the parameters than ResNet-50-GConv ($24w \times 4s$) and achieves similar accuracy. Under the setting of 39w and 2s, ResNet-50-GWSConv has the same parameter compression effect. For ShuffleNet, as it is a lightweight network, the channel width is slightly expanded in the process of using GWSConv, which brings a few increase in FLOPs, but it achieves a dynamic balance with the reduction of parameters. Specifically, ShuffleNet-GWSConv (4s) and ShuffleNet-GConv (2s) can compress 28.7% and 18.1% of parameters, respectively.

Butterfly Convolution vs. Group Weight Sharing Convolution. BFConv, with cross-group information fusion, enhances the receptive field of local information, obtaining stronger feature expression ability than GWSConv. Table 2 shows the performance comparison of BFConv and GWSConv. We can

Table 1. Comparison of group convolution and group weight sharing convolution. Top-1 Acc means Top-1 accuracy (%).

Model	Setting	Params	FLOPs	Top-1 Acc
ResNet-50 [7]	64w	23.52M	1.31G	94.74
ResNet-50-GConv	24w × 4s	23.25M	1.32G	94.89
ResNet-50-GWSConv	24w × 4s	**18.48M**	1.32G	94.95
ResNet-50-GConv	39w × 2s	22.66M	1.27G	94.87
ResNet-50-GWSConv	39w × 2s	**18.46M**	1.27G	94.82
ShuffleNet-GConv	4s	902.88K	43.40M	91.97
ShuffleNet-GWSConv	4s	**644.18K**	48.89M	92.06
ShuffleNet-GConv	2s	950.46K	45.44M	92.34
ShuffleNet-GWSConv	2s	**778.62K**	49.56M	92.52

see that ResNet-50-BFConv-v1, ResNet50-GWSConv and ResNet50-BFConv reduce the number of parameters by 20.0%, 21.3% and 29.9%, respectively, achieving similar or higher classification accuracy than ResNet-50. In addition, compared with VGG-16, VGG16-BFConv-v1 and VGG16-GWSConv, VGG16-BFConv reduces the number of parameters by 32.0%, 32.3% and 44.3%, respectively, without loss of classification accuracy. Therefore, BFConv requires fewer parameters and FLOPs than GWSConv, while obtaining similar accuracy.

Table 2. Comparison of butterfly convolution and group weight sharing convolution. Here - denotes no special setting.

Model	Setting	Params	FLOPs	Top-1 Acc
ResNet-50 [7]	64w	23.52M	1.31G	94.74
ResNet-50-BFConv-v1	36w × 2s	18.81M	1.38G	94.89
ResNet-50-GWSConv	24w × 4s	18.48M	1.32G	94.95
ResNet-50-BFConv	19w × 4s	**16.49M**	**1.11G**	94.99
VGG-16 [25]	–	14.72M	314.03M	93.42
VGG-16-BFConv-v1	–	10.01M	314.09M	93.50
VGG-16-GWSConv	4s	9.97M	342.58M	93.52
VGG-16-BFConv	–	**8.20M**	**307.15M**	93.56

4.3   Results on ImageNet

We next conduct several experiments on ImageNet dataset. ResNet-50 has about 25.56M parameters and 4.11G FLOPs with a Top-1 accuracy of 76.42% and a Top-5 accuracy of 93.04%. We equip ResNet-50 with GConv, GWSConv and BFConv to obtain compact models and compare the results with recent state-of-the-art methods.

Table 3. Comparison of state-of-the-art methods for compressing ResNet-50 on ImageNet dataset. - represents no reported results available.

Model	Params	FLOPs	Top-1 Acc	Top-5 Acc
ResNet-50 [7]	25.56M	4.11G	76.42	93.04
ResNet-50-OctConv-2s [18]	25.56M	2.40G	76.40	93.14
ResNet-50-HetConv-P4 [16]	–	2.85G	75.95	92.99
ResNet-50-SPConv-α1/2 [27]	18.34M	2.97G	76.26	93.05
ResNet-50-GConv	20.49M	4.10G	76.55	93.14
ResNet-50-GWSConv-24w-4s	20.50M	4.10G	76.60	93.17
ResNet-50-BFConv-19w-4s(Ours)	**18.52M**	**3.52G**	**76.79**	**93.37**
Compress the model further				
ResNet-50-Thinet [26]	16.90M	2.60G	72.10	90.30
ResNet-50-NISP-B [29]	14.40M	2.30G	–	90.80
ResNet-50-Versatile [33]	11.00M	3.00G	74.50	91.80
ResNet-50-SSS [31]	–	2.80G	74.20	91.90
ResNet-50-Ghost-2s [24]	13.00M	2.20G	75.00	92.30
ResNet-50-BFConv-12w-4s(Ours)	12.90M	**2.19G**	**75.50**	**92.62**

From the results in Table 3, we can find that our ResNet-50-BFConv-19w-4s obtains a 27.5% drop in parameters and a 14.4% drop in FLOPs, with slightly improved over the original ResNet-50 in accuracy. Additionally, ResNet-50-GConv and ResNet-50-GWSConv-24w-4s also have the same model compression effect. Compared methods [16,18,27] with similar or more parameters have lower performance than ours. When we further compress the model with a compression ratio close to 50%, compared with recent state-of-the-art methods including Thinet [26], NISP [29], Versatile [33], Sparse structure selection (SSS) [31] and Ghost [24], our method can obtain significantly better performance in both Top-1 and Top-5 accuracy.

In order to validate the effectiveness of BFConv more intuitively, we sample some images from ImageNet val split. Grad-CAM [32] is used to visualize their heatmaps on ResNet-50, ResNet-50-GWSConv-24w-4s and ResNet-50-BFConv-19w-4s. As shown in Fig. 3, compared with ResNet-50 and ResNet-50-GWSConv-24w-4s, ResNet-50-BFConv-19w-4s has similar or slightly higher ability to capture the target regions. Therefore, ResNet-50 embedded BFConv is able to achieve or outperform the performance of the original ResNet-50 with fewer parameters and FLOPs.

Input Image   ResNet-50   GWSConv   BFConv   Input Image   ResNet-50   GWSConv   BFConv

Fig. 3. Sample visualization on ImageNet val split generated by Grad-CAM. All target layer selected is "layer4.2". GWSConv and BFConv represent ResNet-50-GWSConv-24w-4s and ResNet-50-BFConv-19w-4s, respectively.

5 Conclusion

In this paper, we present a novel efficient convolution filter BFConv to compress parameters and FLOPs without losing the representation power of convolutional neural networks. Our proposed BFConv inherits the advantages of group weight sharing and residual connection. We replace some vanilla convolutions with BFConv in ResNet-50, ShuffleNet and VGG-16. Extensive image classification results on CIFAR-10 and ImageNet benchmarks demonstrate the effectiveness of BFConv.

References

1. Hu, J., Shen, L., Sun, G.: Squeeze-and-excitation networks. In: CVPR (2018)
2. Xu, Z.-Q.J., Zhang, Y., Xiao, Y.: Training behavior of deep neural network in frequency domain. In: Gedeon, T., Wong, K.W., Lee, M. (eds.) ICONIP 2019. LNCS, vol. 11953, pp. 264–274. Springer, Cham (2019). https://doi.org/10.1007/978-3-030-36708-4_22
3. Howard, A.G., et al.: Mobilenets: efficient convolutional neural networks for mobile vision applications. arXiv:1704.04861 (2017)
4. Szegedy, C., et al.: Going deeper with convolutions. In: CVPR (2015)
5. Gueguen, L., Sergeev, A., Kadlec, B., Liu, R., Yosinski, J.: Faster neural networks straight from JPEG. In: NeurIPS (2018)
6. Xu, K., Qin, M., Sun, F., Wang, Y., Chen, Y., Ren, F.: Learning in the frequency domain. In: CVPR (2020)
7. He, K., Zhang, X., Ren, S., Sun, J.: Deep residual learning for image recognition. In: CVPR (2016)
8. Zhang, Q., Yang, Y.: SA-Net: shuffle attention for deep convolutional neural networks. In: ICASSP (2021)
9. Wang, Q., Wu, B., Zhu, P., Li, P., Zuo, W., Hu, Q.: ECA-Net: efficient channel attention for deep convolutional neural networks. In: CVPR (2020)
10. Sandler, M., Howard, A., Zhu, M., Zhmoginov, A., Chen, L.-C.: MobileNetV2: inverted residuals and linear bottlenecks. In: CVPR (2018)
11. Zhang, X., Zhou, X., Lin, M., Sun, J.: ShuffleNet: an extremely efficient convolutional neural network for mobile devices. In: CVPR (2018)

12. Howard, A., Sandler, M., Chu, G., Chen, L.-C., Chen, B., Tan, M.: Searching for MobileNetV3. In: CVPR (2019)
13. Chollet, F.: Xception: deep learning with depthwise separable convolutions. In: CVPR (2017)
14. Ioffe, S., Szegedy, C.: Batch normalization: accelerating deep network training by reducing internal covariate shift. In: ICML (2015)
15. Xie, S., Girshick, R., Dollar, P., Tu, Z., He, K.: Aggregated residual transformations for deep neural networks. In: CVPR (2017)
16. Singh, P., Verma, V.K., Rai, P., Namboodiri, V.P.: Hetconv: Heterogeneous kernel-based convolutions for deep CNNs. In: CVPR (2019)
17. Hou, Q., Zhou, D., Feng, J.: Coordinate attention for efficient mobile network design. In: CVPR (2021)
18. Chen, Y., et al.: Drop an Octave: reducing spatial redundancy in convolutional neural networks with octave convolution. In: ICCV (2019)
19. Krizhevsky, A., Sutskever, I., Hinton, G.E.: ImageNet classification with deep convolutional neural networks. In: NeurIPS (2012)
20. Szegedy, C., Vanhoucke, V., Ioffe, S., Shlens, J., Wojna, Z.: Rethinking the inception architecture for computer vision. In: CVPR (2016)
21. An, J., Liu, F., Zhao, J., Shen, F.: IC networks: remodeling the basic unit for convolutional neural networks. arXiv:2102.03495 (2021)
22. Vanhoucke, V.: Learning visual representations at scale. In: ICLR (Invited Talk) (2014)
23. Szegedy, C., Ioffe, S., Vanhoucke, V., Alemi, A.: Inception-v4, inception-ResNet and the impact of residual connections on learning. In: AAAI (2017)
24. Han, K., Wang, Y., Tian, Q., Guo, J., Xu, C., Xu, C.: Ghostnet: more features from cheap operations. In: CVPR (2020)
25. Simonyan, K., Zisserman, A.: Very deep convolutional networks for large-scale image recognition. In: ICLR (2015)
26. Luo, J.-H., Wu, J., Lin, W.: ThiNet: a filter level pruning method for deep neural network compression. In: ICCV (2017)
27. Zhang, Q., et al.: Split to be slim: an overlooked redundancy in vanilla convolution. In: IJCAI (2020)
28. Krizhevsky, A., Hinton, G.: Learning multiple layers of features from tiny images. Technical report, Citeseer (2009)
29. Yu, R., et al.: NISP: pruning networks using neuron importance score propagation. In: CVPR (2018)
30. Deng, J., Dong, W., Socher, R., Li, L.-J., Li, K., Fei-Fei, L.: ImageNet: a large-scale hierarchical image database. In: CVPR (2009)
31. Huang, Z., Wang, N.: Data-driven sparse structure selection for deep neural networks. In: Ferrari, V., Hebert, M., Sminchisescu, C., Weiss, Y. (eds.) ECCV 2018. LNCS, vol. 11220, pp. 317–334. Springer, Cham (2018). https://doi.org/10.1007/978-3-030-01270-0_19
32. Selvaraju, R.R., Cogswell, M., Das, A., Vedantam, R., Parikh, D., Batra, D.: Grad-CAM: visual explanations from deep networks via gradient-based localization. In: ICCV (2017)
33. Wang, Y., Xu, C., Xu, C., Xu, C., Tao, D.: Learning versatile filters for efficient convolutional neural networks. In: NeurIPS (2018)

Integrating Rich Utterance Features for Emotion Recognition in Multi-party Conversations

Yang Sun[1], Nan Yu[1], and Guohong Fu[1,2(✉)]

[1] School of Computer Science and Technology, Soochow University, Suzhou, China
{ysun23,nyu}@stu.suda.edu.cn, ghfu@suda.edu.cn
[2] Institute of Artificial Intelligence, Soochow University, Suzhou, China

Abstract. Emotion recognition in multi-party conversations is a challenging task in natural language processing as it requires modeling the conversational context, the speaker-specific information, and the interaction within a conversation. To this end, we propose a graph-based multi-task learning network to integrate these utterance features for emotion recognition in multi-party conversations. First, we represent each utterance and each speaker as a node in a graph. In particular, we use three types of edges to connect these nodes to incorporate rich utterance features. Finally, we exploit link prediction as an auxiliary task to enhance the emotional consistency of extracted speaker-specific features. To verify the effectiveness of our strategy, we conduct experiments on two multi-party conversation corpora. Experimental results demonstrate an improvement of 1–2% in F1-score over multiple baselines.

Keywords: Conversational emotion recognition · Graph neural network · Multi-task learning

1 Introduction

Emotion recognition has remained an active research topic for decades in natural language processing (NLP) [2,10]. In the literature, emotion recognition has mainly focused on non-conversational text, such as sentence-level text [14] and document-level text [24]. However, the recent proliferation of open conversational data on social media platforms has attracted increasing attention towards emotion recognition in multi-party conversations (ERMC) [7,8]. Similar to text sentiment analysis, ERMC is a task to determine the emotion of each utterance within a conversation and plays an important role in many NLP applications, such as opinion mining over chat history [3], social media analysis in Facebook, YouTube, Twitter, etc. [16], and creating empathetic dialogue systems [6]. Due to the emotional dynamics in conversations [20], ERMC primarily depends on not only the utterance itself and its context but also the speaker-specific information and the interaction underlying a conversation [13,16,18,19].

Many approaches have been proposed for ERMC with a focus on conversational context representation and speaker-specific modeling. While earlier works

© Springer Nature Switzerland AG 2021
T. Mantoro et al. (Eds.): ICONIP 2021, LNCS 13111, pp. 51–62, 2021.
https://doi.org/10.1007/978-3-030-92273-3_5

for ERMC exploit Recurrent Neural Networks (RNNs) to capture sequential context features of conversations [16,18], recent studies explore different techniques such as Transformer [28] and pre-training language model [13] to capture speaker-specific information.

Besides contextual and speaker-specific information, modeling the interaction within a conversation is also pivotal for ERMC [20]. To model the interaction, [6] proposed a graph-based method and achieved promising results, which encodes utterances with a directed graph according to their relative positions within a certain window. However, this graph structure is hard to represent conversational context and extract speaker-specific information.

To integrate the aforementioned three types of utterance features, we propose a graph-based multi-task learning network. First, we represent each utterance and each speaker as a node in a heterogeneous graph. In particular, we use three types of undirected edges to connect different pairs of nodes. Each type of edge represents one of the utterance features. Therefore, ERMC can be reformulated as a task of node classification in the graph. Specifically, we exploit link prediction as an auxiliary task to enhance the emotional consistency of the extracted speaker-sensitive features. Link prediction (LP) is to represent the likelihood of connectivity between an utterance node and a speaker node. In summary, we make the following contributions:

- We propose a graph-based multi-task learning network for emotion recognition in multi-party conversation (ERMC).
- We devise three types of edges to integrate rich utterance features in the graph. Specifically, we exploit link prediction as an auxiliary task to enhance the emotional consistency of extracted speaker-sensitive features.
- Experimental results on two benchmark datasets demonstrate that our method obtains an improvement of 1–2% in F1-score over multiple baselines.

2   Related Works

Emotion recognition has become increasingly popular in the natural language processing community with a focus on exploring various types of features for different-level emotion classification, such as sentence-level [14] and document-level [24].

2.1   Emotion Recognition in Multi-party Conversations

Recently, ERMC has become a new trend due to the emergence of publicly available conversational datasets collected from scripted situations, such as movies and TV-shows [19,27]. Along with these datasets, many deep learning methods are applied to model the conversational context. As an early work, [18] propose Long Short-Term Memory (LSTM) [9] network to capture contextual information for sentiment classification. Later, [16] model the emotional dynamics for each target utterance by employing attention mechanisms to pool information from the global context. [28] propose a Knowledge-Enriched Transformer that learns structured conversation representations by hierarchical self-attention and external commonsense knowledge. [6] encode utterances with a graph and successfully model the interaction within a conversation. Recently, [13] exploit speaker identification as an auxiliary task to capture speaker-specific features and obtain state-of-the-art results. Compared to existing methods, we are the first to integrate rich utterance features in a graph.

2.2   Graph Neural Networks

Graphs are good at representing complex relationships and interdependence between objects from non-Euclidean domains and have received growing attention [25]. Recently, [12] present a simplified graph neural network model, called graph convolutional network (GCN). Then, GCN has been applied in several NLP tasks to encode the syntactic structure of sentences, such as semantic role labeling [17] and emotion recognition [6]. Our graph model is inspired by the graph relational modeling work introduced in [21].

2.3   Multi-task Learning Methods

Multi-Task Learning (MTL) [4] is a machine learning approach that is capable of exploiting potential shared features across multiple relevant tasks simultaneously. Considerable research efforts have been devoted to applying MTL in the NLP community [1,15,26]. Since speaker-specific features play an important role in ERMC, we apply link prediction as an auxiliary task to enhance the emotional consistency of the extracted speaker-sensitive features.

3   Methodology

3.1   Problem Definition

Suppose there are N constituent utterances $u_1, u_2, \ldots, u_N$ from a conversation with $X(X \geqslant 2)$ speakers $s_1, s_2, \ldots, s_X$, where utterance u_i is uttered by speaker $S_{m(u_i)}$, and the function m maps an utterance into its corresponding speaker, the goal of ERMC is to predict the emotion label for each utterance.

3.2   Model Overview

As illustrated in Fig. 1, the proposed framework consists of three main components, namely an encoder, a graph modeling module and a multi-task decoder. In the following sections, we explain each component in detail.

First, we use pre-trained BERT [5] to extract context-independent utterance-level feature vectors. Then, we build a graph to integrate rich utterance features. Finally, the output feature vectors from the graph are used to recognize emotions for utterances. Meanwhile, we exploit link prediction as an auxiliary task.

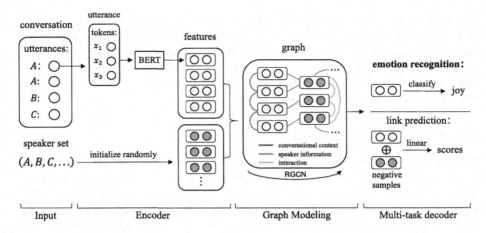

Fig. 1. Overview of the proposed graph-based multi-task learning network for ERMC

3.3   Encoder

Similar to most existing studies, the input of our model is a sequence of utterances from a multi-party conversation. Earlier works adopt the Convolution Neural Network (CNN) [10] to encode utterances into context-independent feature vectors. To compare with the latest model [13], we use the BERT model to extract feature vectors for the utterances. Let an utterance u consists of a sequence of tokens $x_1, x_2, \ldots, x_N$. First, a special token $[CLS]$ is appended at the beginning of the utterance to create the input sequence for the model: $[CLS], x_1, x_2, \ldots, x_N$. Then, we pass the $[CLS]$ appended utterances to BERT and extract out activations from the final four layers corresponding to the $[CLS]$ token. Finally, these four vectors are averaged to obtain the feature vector.

3.4   Graph Modeling

Graphs neural networks are good at representing complex relationships and interdependence between objects [25]. In our method, we devise three types of edges to integrate rich utterance features in the graph.

Graph Construction. First, we introduce the following notation: an entire conversation corpus is constructed as a large undirected heterogeneous graph $G = (\mathcal{V}, \mathcal{E}, \mathcal{R})$ with vertices/nodes $v_i \in \mathcal{V}$, labeled edges (relations) $e_{ij} \in \mathcal{E}$ where r_{ij} is the relation type of the edge between v_i and v_j, and all edge weights are set to be 1. Concretely, all utterances and all speakers are considered as two types of nodes (v_u and v_s) respectively.

Node Representations. For the utterance nodes, we use the encoded feature vectors $\mathbf{v}_u \in \mathbb{R}^d$ of dimension d as their representations. While for the speaker nodes, we randomly initialize the vectors of different speakers $\mathbf{v}_s \in \mathbb{R}^d$ of the same dimension d.

Edges. As shown in Fig. 1, we devise three types of edges to connect different pairs of nodes: (*i*) For the conversational context, each utterance node is connected with the utterance nodes of the past and future; (*ii*) For the speaker-specific information, we connect each utterance node with its corresponding speaker node; (*iii*) To model the interaction, each speaker node has edges with other speaker nodes within the same conversation. The maximum number of edges between two speaker nodes is set to be 1, avoiding duplicate edges.

Feature Transformation. The utterance-level feature vectors $\mathbf{v}_i^{(0)} \in \mathbb{R}^d$ are initially context and speaker independent. To aggregate the local neighborhood information and transform the encoded features, we use the RGCNs [21]. For a single-layer RGCN, the new d-dimensional feature vector $\mathbf{h}_i^{(1)} \in \mathbb{R}^d$ is computed as:

$$\mathbf{h}_i^1 = ReLU(\mathbf{W}_0^{(1)}\mathbf{v}_i^{(0)} + \sum_{r \in R}\sum_{j \in N_i^r}\frac{1}{c_{i,r}}\mathbf{W}_r^{(1)}\mathbf{v}_j^{(0)}) \tag{1}$$

where N_i^r represents the neighboring indices of node v_i under relation $r \in R$. And $c_{i,r}$ which is set in advance ($c_{i,r} = |N_i^r|$) is a problem specific normalization constant. $\mathbf{W}_r^{(1)} \in \mathbb{R}^{d \times d'}$ and $\mathbf{W}_0^{(1)} \in \mathbb{R}^{d \times d'}$ are trainable parameters, only edges of the same relation type r are associated with the same projection weight $\mathbf{W}_r^{(1)}$. As for a multi-layer RGCN, the utterance node features are updated by the following formula:

$$\mathbf{h}_i^{l+1} = ReLU(\mathbf{W}_0^{(l+1)}\mathbf{h}_i^{(l)} + \sum_{r \in R}\sum_{j \in N_i^r}\frac{1}{c_{i,r}}\mathbf{W}_r^{(l+1)}\mathbf{h}_j^{(l)}) \tag{2}$$

where l denotes the layer number. In our approach, we employ RGCNs with L layers to incorporate rich utterance features in multi-party conversations.

3.5   Emotion Recognition

After feature transformation, we consider the final layer node vectors $\mathbf{h}_i^{(L)} \in \mathbb{R}^d$ as the utterance representation. Then, the feature vectors are fed into a softmax classifier:

$$\mathbf{P}_i = softmax(\mathbf{W}_{smax}\mathbf{h}_i^{(L)}) \tag{3}$$

where $\mathbf{W}_{smax} \in \mathbb{R}^{d \times Z}$ is the trainable parameter and Z is the number of emotion labels. To train the model, we choose the cross-entropy loss function:

$$\mathcal{L}_{ERMC} = -\sum_{v \in y_\mathcal{V}}\sum_{z=1}^{Z}Y_{vz}\ln P_{vz} \tag{4}$$

where $y_\mathcal{V}$ is the set of node indices that have labels and Y is the label indicator matrix.

3.6   Link Prediction

In the graph structure, we devise a labeled edge $(v_u, r, v_s) \in \mathcal{E}$ to extract speaker-specific information. Link Prediction (LP) is to represent the likelihood of connectivity between v_u and v_s. In our method, the likelihood $f(v_u, v_s)$ is computed as:

$$f(v_u, v_s) = \mathbf{W}_{LP}[\mathbf{h}_{v_u}^{(L)}; \mathbf{h}_{v_s}^{(L)}] \tag{5}$$

where $\mathbf{W}_{LP} \in \mathbb{R}^{2d \times 1}$ is a trainable parameter, $\mathbf{h}_{v_u}^{(L)} \in \mathbb{R}^d$ and $\mathbf{h}_{v_s}^{(L)} \in \mathbb{R}^d$ represent the feature vectors of utterance nodes and speaker nodes respectively.

Inspired by [21], we train the model with negative sampling. For each observed example, we sample I negative ones. In particular, We sample by randomly corrupting the speaker node of each positive example and further choose margin loss to push the model to score observable edges higher than the negative ones:

$$\mathcal{L}_{LP} = \sum_{v_s' \sim P_n(v_s)} max(0, 1 - f(v_u, v_s) + f(v_u, v_s')) \tag{6}$$

where $n = 1, 2, \ldots, I$. Given an edge connecting v_u and v_s, v_s' is a sampled node from an arbitrary noise distribution $v_s' \sim P_n(v_s)$.

3.7   Multi-task Training

For the multi-task learning of two tasks, we sum the losses of the two individual tasks together as the joint objective:

$$\mathcal{L}_{Multi} = \alpha \cdot \mathcal{L}_{ERMC} + (1 - \alpha) \cdot \mathcal{L}_{LP} \tag{7}$$

where α is a constant hyper-parameter.

4   Experiments

4.1   Datasets

We evaluate our model on two benchmark datasets – MELD [19] and EmoryNLP [27]. All these datasets contain multi-modal information for utterances of each conversation, while in this work we only focus on the textual information. Table 1 shows the corpus statistics.

MELD [19]: A multi-party conversation corpus collected from the TV show *Friends*, in which each utterance is annotated as one of the seven emotion classes, namely *neutral, surprise, fear, sadness, joy, disgust,* and *anger.*

EmoryNLP [27]: A multi-party conversation corpus that is also collected from the TV show Friends but is different from MELD in the choice of scenes and emotion labels which include *neutral, joyful, peaceful, powerful, scared, mad,* and *sad.*

Table 1. Statistics of the datasets

Dataset	Conversations train/val/test	Utterances train/val/test	Speakers train/val/test
MELD	1028/114/280	9989/1109/2610	260/47/100
EmoryNLP	659/89/79	7551/954/984	225/42/45

4.2 Implementation Details

We use pre-trained BERT-Base to encode utterances and adopt Adam [11] as the optimizer during training with an initial learning rate of 1e-4 and L2 weight decay of 1e-5 for two datasets. The dimensions of $\mathbf{h}_i^l$ is set to be 128. The dropout [22] is set to be 0.5. For each observed example, we sample 2 negative ones. In addition, the number of RGCN layers L is set to be 2 unless otherwise stated. We train all models for a maximum of 200 epochs and stop training if the validation loss does not decrease for 20 consecutive epochs. We report the results of our model in experiments based on the average score of 5 random runs on the test set.

4.3 Baselines and SOTA

To evaluate the effectiveness of our model, we compare it with the following baseline approaches for ERC. These approaches also focus on textual information only.

- c-LSTM [18]: Contextual utterance representations are generated by using a Bi-directional LSTM network.
- DialogueRNN [16]: It is a recurrent network that uses three GRUs to track individual speaker states, global context, and emotional states within conversations.
- DialogueGCN [6]: First, pre-trained utterance-level features are fed into a bidirectional GRU to capture contextual information. After that, a GCN is applied to generating relative interaction features between utterances. Finally, these features are concatenated for the final classification.
- KET [28]: Enriched by the external commonsense knowledge, KET employs the Transformer encoder and decoder [23] for ERMC.
- GRU-SI [13]: It is a GRU-based multi-task learning framework where features extracted from BERT are used for emotion recognition and speaker identification.
- BERT-DialogueGCN: A variation of [6] where the CNN-based utterance-level feature vectors are replaced by our BERT-based encoder. We consider this model as our strong baseline.
- ERMC-RGCN: A variation of our approach where the link prediction decoder is removed.

Table 2. Overall performance on MELD and EmoryNLP

Model	MELD		EmoryNLP	
	Acc.	F1	Acc.	F1
c-LSTM [18]	57.52	56.44	33.82	32.89
DialogueRNN [16]	58.27	57.61	32.38	31.27
DialogueGCN [6]	59.54	58.10	–	–
KET [28]	59.11	58.18	35.77	34.39
GRU-SI [13]	61.93	60.69	36.08	34.54
BERT-DialogueGCN	62.91	61.15	36.15	34.57
ERMC-RGCN	63.52	62.09	36.89	35.31
ERMC-RGCN+LP	**64.10**	**62.57**	**37.35**	**35.72**

4.4   Comparison with Baselines

We first compare our proposed ERMC-RGCN+LP framework (LP stands for the link prediction task) with the aforementioned baselines. We report results with an average of 5 runs and use the weighted average accuracy and F1 to evaluate our model. The comparative experimental results are shown in Table 2.

As can be seen from Table 2, our models consistently outperform the baseline approaches under discussion. In particular, our proposed ERMC-RGCN achieves new state-of-the-art F1-score of 62.57% and accuracy of 64.10% on MELD, which are around 1% better than the strong baseline. We attribute this gap in performance to the nature of conversations. There are many utterances, like "oh", "yeah", and "no", that can express different emotions depending on the context and speaker-specific information within conversations. In these cases, our model integrates rich utterance features that contribute to emotion recognition. Moreover, the average conversation length in EmoryNLP is 12 utterances, with many conversations having more than 5 participants, which makes context and speaker modeling difficult. As a result, the improvement in EmoryNLP is not as contrasting as that in MELD.

In addition, compared to ERMC-RGCN, exploiting LP as an auxiliary task leads to F1 improvement of 0.48% and 0.41% on two datasets. Each speaker has a specific personality and characteristic of uttering which has a significant impact on emotional expression [20]. The LP task enhances the emotional consistency of the extracted speaker-specific features and releases more ability in improving the performance.

4.5   Ablation Study

We conduct ablation experiments in detail to comprehensively study the effectiveness of integrating rich utterance features. The results are listed in Table 3. By eliminating the interaction edges (connecting speaker nodes from the same conversations), our model falls by around 0.5% on two datasets. This phenomenon is in tune with DialogueGCN [6] that modeling the interaction benefits

Table 3. Results of ablation study on two datasets

Context edges	Speaker edges	Interaction edges	Average F1-score	
			MELD	EmoryNLP
✓	✓	✓	62.09	35.31
✓	✓	✗	61.56	34.87
✓	✗	✗	60.46	33.95
✗	✓	✗	36.02	21.77
✗	✓	✓	36.08	22.22

emotion recognition in multi-party conversations. And on this basis, the model shows a 1.1% decline on MELD by excluding the speaker edges (connecting each utterance node and its speaker node). As discussed before, speaker-specific information helps to recognize the emotions of some short utterances. Further, we remove the context edges (connecting two utterance nodes), as we can see, resulting in very poor F_1 scores on MELD and EmoryNLP. The main reason may be that our approach generates speaker-specific features in the process of propagating contextual and sequential information. Thus, without the context edges, neither the speaker edges nor the interaction edges will work.

4.6 Impact of Multi-layer RGCNs

Table 4. Performance with different numbers of RGCN layers

RGCN layers' number	Average F1-score	
	MELD	EmoryNLP
Layer = 1	61.92	34.64
Layer = 2	**63.47**	**36.76**
Layer = 3	52.88	32.62
Layer = 4	35.27	22.58

To illustrate the impact of different numbers of RGCN layers, we conduct experiments to compare the performance on the development sections of the two datasets. Experimental results are offered in Table 4. It shows that, whether on MELD or EmoryNLP, as the number of RGCN layers increases, the performance of our proposed approach first rises and then decreases. While using a two-layer RGCN, the method yields the best results both on the two datasets. On MELD, the model drops a lot (more than 10%) when using 3 and 4 layers of RGCN. This is mainly because simply stacking multiple RGCN layers leads to the complex back-propagation and the common vanishing gradient problem. On EmoryNLP, the model shows a more slight decline by using 3 layers of RGCN. These indicate that the RGCN structure with more than two layers is not good choice for our approach.

4.7   Impact of Different Loss Weights

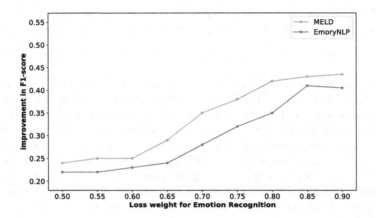

Fig. 2. Performance with different loss weights

In this section, we explore how the auxiliary task boosts the performance of our model. Since the loss weight α is a constant hyper-parameter in our method, we conduct experiments on the development datasets and report results with an average of 5 runs. Higher loss weights for emotion recognition indicate that we bias the model to prefer task-specific representations. As shown in Fig. 2, exploiting link prediction as an auxiliary task leads to improvements of 0.22%–0.46% on two datasets. We can see from Fig. 2 that the improvement in F1-score on MELD continues to rise with the increase of loss weight. Especially, the improvement shows a slight decline on EmoryNLP when the loss weight is more than 0.85. In short, increasing the loss weight for emotion recognition is beneficial to improve the performance of our model, but the specific amplitude and trend are slightly different in different datasets.

5   Conclusion

In this work, we propose a graph-based multi-task learning network for emotion recognition in multi-party conversations. To explore richer features for ERMC, we represent each utterance and each speaker as a node in a heterogeneous graph and employ three types of edges to integrate rich utterance features within multi-party conversations. As such, we reformulate emotion recognition as a task of node classification in the graph. Furthermore, we exploit the link prediction task to enhance the representations of speaker nodes. We conduct experiments on two benchmark datasets to verify the effectiveness of the proposed method. Results show that integrating rich utterance features brings improvement for ERMC. And the link prediction boosts the performance, achieving new SOTA results in the literature.

We would like to improve the representations of the utterances by incorporating multi-modal information in our future work. Since our method uses the whole conversation, we will study its performance on more natural conversation datasets without future utterances.

Acknowledgments. This work was supported by National Natural Science Foundation of China under grants 62076173 and 61672211.

References

1. Akhtar, M.S., Chauhan, D.S., Ghosal, D., Poria, S., Ekbal, A., Bhattacharyya, P.: Multi-task learning for multi-modal emotion recognition and sentiment analysis. In: Proceedings of NAACL-HLT, pp. 370–379 (2019)
2. Busso, C., et al.: IEMOCAP: interactive emotional dyadic motion capture database. Lang. Resour. Eval. **42**(4), 335 (2008)
3. Cambria, E., Poria, S., Gelbukh, A., Thelwall, M.: Sentiment analysis is a big suitcase. IEEE Intell. Syst. **32**(6), 74–80 (2017)
4. Caruana, R.: Multitask learning. Mach. Learn. **28**(1), 41–75 (1997)
5. Devlin, J., Chang, M.W., Lee, K., Toutanova, K.: BERT: pre-training of deep bidirectional transformers for language understanding. In: Proceedings of NAACL-HLT, pp. 4171–4186 (2019)
6. Ghosal, D., Majumder, N., Poria, S., Chhaya, N., Gelbukh, A.: DialogueGCN: a graph convolutional neural network for emotion recognition in conversation. In: Proceedings of EMNLP-IJCNLP, pp. 154–164 (2019)
7. Hazarika, D., Poria, S., Mihalcea, R., Cambria, E., Zimmermann, R.: ICON: interactive conversational memory network for multimodal emotion detection. In: Proceedings of EMNLP, pp. 2594–2604 (2018)
8. Hazarika, D., Poria, S., Zadeh, A., Cambria, E., Morency, L.P., Zimmermann, R.: Conversational memory network for emotion recognition in dyadic dialogue videos. In: Proceedings of NAACL-HLT, vol. 2018, p. 2122. NIH Public Access (2018)
9. Hochreiter, S., Schmidhuber, J.: Long short-term memory. Neural Comput. **9**(8), 1735–1780 (1997)
10. Kim, Y.: Convolutional neural networks for sentence classification. In: Proceedings of EMNLP, pp. 1746–1751 (2014)
11. Kingma, D.P., Ba, J.: Adam: a method for stochastic optimization. In: International Conference on Learning Representations (2015)
12. Kipf, T.N., Welling, M.: Semi-supervised classification with graph convolutional networks. In: International Conference on Learning Representations (2017)
13. Li, J., Zhang, M., Ji, D., Liu, Y.: Multi-task learning with auxiliary speaker identification for conversational emotion recognition. arXiv e-prints pp. arXiv-2003 (2020)
14. Li, S., Huang, L., Wang, R., Zhou, G.: Sentence-level emotion classification with label and context dependence. In: Proceedings of ACL-IJCNLP (Volume 1: Long Papers), pp. 1045–1053 (2015)

15. Liu, P., Qiu, X., Huang, X.J.: Adversarial multi-task learning for text classification. In: Proceedings of ACL, pp. 1–10 (2017)
16. Majumder, N., Poria, S., Hazarika, D., Mihalcea, R., Gelbukh, A., Cambria, E.: DialogueRNN: an attentive RNN for emotion detection in conversations. In: Proceedings of AAAI, vol. 33, pp. 6818–6825 (2019)
17. Marcheggiani, D., Titov, I.: Encoding sentences with graph convolutional networks for semantic role labeling. In: Proceedings of EMNLP, pp. 1506–1515 (2017)
18. Poria, S., Cambria, E., Hazarika, D., Majumder, N., Zadeh, A., Morency, L.P.: Context-dependent sentiment analysis in user-generated videos. In: Proceedings of ACL, pp. 873–883 (2017)
19. Poria, S., Hazarika, D., Majumder, N., Naik, G., Cambria, E., Mihalcea, R.: MELD: a multimodal multi-party dataset for emotion recognition in conversations. In: Proceedings of ACL, pp. 527–536 (2019)
20. Poria, S., Majumder, N., Mihalcea, R., Hovy, E.: Emotion recognition in conversation: research challenges, datasets, and recent advances. IEEE Access **7**, 100943–100953 (2019)
21. Schlichtkrull, M., Kipf, T.N., Bloem, P., van den Berg, R., Titov, I., Welling, M., et al.: Modeling relational data with graph convolutional networks. In: Gangemi, A. (ed.) ESWC 2018. LNCS, vol. 10843, pp. 593–607. Springer, Cham (2018). https://doi.org/10.1007/978-3-319-93417-4_38
22. Srivastava, N., Hinton, G., Krizhevsky, A., Sutskever, I., Salakhutdinov, R.: Dropout: a simple way to prevent neural networks from overfitting. J. Mach. Learn. Res. **15**(1), 1929–1958 (2014)
23. Vaswani, A., et al.: Attention is all you need. In: Advances in Neural Information Processing Systems, pp. 5998–6008 (2017)
24. Wang, J., Yu, L.C., Lai, K.R., Zhang, X.: Dimensional sentiment analysis using a regional CNN-LSTM model. In: Proceedings of ACL (Volume 2: Short Papers), pp. 225–230 (2016)
25. Wu, Z., Pan, S., Chen, F., Long, G., Zhang, C., Philip, S.Y.: A comprehensive survey on graph neural networks. IEEE Trans. Neural Netw. Learn. Syst. (2020)
26. Xiao, L., Zhang, H., Chen, W.: Gated multi-task network for text classification. In: Proceedings of NAACL-HLT, pp. 726–731 (2018)
27. Zahiri, S.M., Choi, J.D.: Emotion detection on TV show transcripts with sequence-based convolutional neural networks. In: The Workshops of AAAI, pp. 44–52 (2018)
28. Zhong, P., Wang, D., Miao, C.: Knowledge-enriched transformer for emotion detection in textual conversations. In: Proceedings of EMNLP-IJCNLP, pp. 165–176 (2019)

Vehicle Image Generation Going Well with the Surroundings

Jeesoo Kim[1], Jangho Kim[1], Jaeyoung Yoo[2], Daesik Kim[2],
and Nojun Kwak[1(✉)]

[1] Graduate School of Convergence Science and Technology,
Seoul National University, Suwon 16229, Republic of Korea
{kimjiss0305,kjh91,nojunk}@snu.ac.kr
[2] Naver Webtoon, Seongnam, Republic of Korea
{yoojy31,daesik.kim}@webtoonscorp.com

Abstract. In spite of the advancement of generative models, there have been few studies generating objects in uncontrolled real-world environments. In this paper, we propose an approach for vehicle image generation in real-world scenes. Using a subnetwork based on a precedent work of image completion, our model makes the shape of an object. Details of objects are trained by additional colorization and refinement subnetworks, resulting in a better quality of generated objects. Unlike many other works, our method does not require any segmentation layout but still makes a plausible vehicle in an image. We evaluate our method by using images from Berkeley Deep Drive (BDD) and Cityscape datasets, which are widely used for object detection and image segmentation problems. The adequacy of the generated images by the proposed method has also been evaluated using a widely utilized object detection algorithm and the FID score.

Keywords: Generative model · Image completion · Image generation

1 Introduction

Most of the recent advances of object generation models [1,6] often implicitly assume some rules when learning a domain such as aligned components and fixed location of an object. To compose an image and arrange objects in a non-trivial location, several works have used the semantic layout to transform it into an image of a real scene. One of the frequently used datasets in this task is *Cityscape* [3] which includes road scene images with pixel-wise annotations. Many researchers have made remarkable progress and succeeded to generate a realistic synthetic image using a semantic layout [2,10,13]. Using these techniques, Hong *et al.* [8] has proposed a method that can generate an object in an arbitrary location assigned by a user using a semantic layout. However, training a model and synthesizing an image using the semantic layout is an inefficient

---

J. Kim and J. Kim—Equally contributed.

© Springer Nature Switzerland AG 2021
T. Mantoro et al. (Eds.): ICONIP 2021, LNCS 13111, pp. 63–74, 2021.
https://doi.org/10.1007/978-3-030-92273-3_6

method since making a pixel-wise annotation requires a lot of time and human effort. Demand for an inexpensive annotation in computer vision tasks is being raised steadily and one example is the weakly supervised object localization which tries to localize images only using image-level labels [17].

Meanwhile, image completion is the task of filling a missing area in an image. Research using convolutional neural networks(CNN) has made a breakthrough in this field by making the models learn features around the deleted area [9,12]. Based on the clues given around the deleted area such as the corners of the table or the bottom side of the window of a house, models are able to complete the image naturally. However, with no other condition given, generating an object is impossible if no clue is given outside the deleted area. Also, they usually fail to complete some complicated texture such as the face of a human or a portion of animals. Training these models with a single object category, they are capable of making the coarse outline of the object but lack details when not enough clues from its surroundings are given. Since the appearance of the objects in image inpainting problems is not consistent like the images of *MNIST* or *Celeb*, image inpainting methods highly rely on the reconstruction loss rather than the adversarial loss which makes the object sharper. For this reason, the existing inpainting methods are very hard to generate a sharp image with an object inside.

In this paper, we propose a method to generate vehicles in given locations, which understands typical appearances of vehicles but with various orientations and colors. With a box given at an appropriate location with an appropriate size, our model can generate learned objects inside. The generated cars suit the surrounding background and even complete occluding objects ahead. Note that all we need to generate an object is just a box annotation while many other works in image translation require a segmented target map to transform it into a realistic image. Our proposed method simply needs a rectangular-shaped mask to generate a vehicle, regardless of the location it is placed. For this purpose, we utilize Berkeley Deep Drive (BDD) dataset [14] which contains box annotations around the objects in the images. It is widely used for the tasks of object detection and image segmentation. By training the car areas annotated in the BDD dataset, we can generate a vehicle that goes well with its surroundings in an arbitrary location. The contributions of this paper are as the followings:

- We propose a method that generates a vehicle object in an image that goes well with the background.
- Unlike other methods using pixel-wise annotated information, only box annotations are used as a given knowledge.
- Our method is capable of generating vehicles over an empty road image as well as substituting the existing vehicles.

2 Related Works

In order to synthesize a lifelike image, many researchers utilized label maps or contours as a guide to generate a real image. Isola *et al.* [10] proposed a method to transform any kind of blueprint into the desired output using GAN. Chen *et al.* [2] adopted a feature learning method by defining layer-wise losses. This enabled transforming a high-resolution semantic layout into an actual image. Patch-based methods such as the work of Wang *et al.* [13] enabled high-quality image translation with an image size more than 512×512. Generating objects in locations decided by a user has been possible in the work of Hong *et al.* [8] using generative adversarial network. However, input layouts used in all of these methods are expensive to prepare in real-world since they should be annotated pixel-wise, which requires much more cost than just annotating bounding boxes.

Studies trying to generate more complicated context using clues in the image have been proposed recently. Image completion is the task of filling an appropriate image segment into a vacated region of a real-world image. The model must learn to paint the image through the blank area. For example, in an image of a building, the corner of a window is removed and then the model must fill it up with glass and bricks aside. Coming to an image of a human face, one of the eyes or the nose is erased and the network recovers it in a natural form.

The Context Encoder (CE), an early work of image completion using a neural network [12], has been proposed for this problem. Using a channel-wise fully connected layer between an encoder and a decoder, CE roughly generates pixels in the image using the encoder features. The work of Iizuka *et al.* [9] has approached this problem using dilated convolutions and a specific type of discriminator. The dilated convolution acts just the same as the original convolution except that the filter is applied to the feature skipping a few pixels or more. This derives the expansion of the receptive field without loss of resolution. Although both approaches can recover the missing parts of an image, it is impossible to generate a whole object. Even if trained only with a particular object, the result still suffers from poor performance. This is because the model bumbles among many choices of how the object will be generated. Since the completion model can predict the shape and surrounding context roughly, we use it as a primary module of our method.

3   Approach

In this paper, we assume that every object can be expressed using two traits, shape and texture. Our method consists of two consecutive networks learning each of these properties (Fig. 1).

3.1   ShapeNet

As we assume that the segmentation layout is not given, we adopt an image completion model which understands the surrounding texture around the erased area. The architecture used in our ShapeNet (Snet) is the same as the work of Iizuka *et al.* [9]. Snet maintains the feature resolution at a certain level rather than going down to a vector-level representation, which is just a quarter of the original image size in our case. For the image completion task, the information

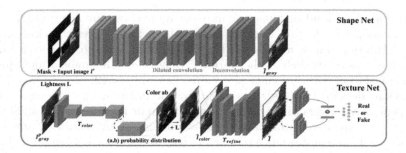

Fig. 1. Overall architecture. The top-side of the figure shows the Snet and the bottom-side shows the Tnet which is composed of T_{color} and T_{refine}. Transposed convolutional layers are used to recover the resolution of $\hat{I}_{color}$.

from the features nearby is more important. Therefore, decreasing the resolution only to half is adequate to fill the blank area. Also, to extend the receptive field of the features in each layer, dilated convolution [15] is used in the middle of the network. In this way, the network can reflect the information not only from the pixels adjacent to the blank area but also from those far away. This highly encourages the network to decide how the object should be placed and how the occluding object should be completed. At the end of the Snet, the network reconstructs the gray-scaled image of the original input so that the model concentrates on constructing the pose and shape of the generated object, not the color or details of the context. The detailed procedure of Snet can be summarized as follows:

$$\hat{I}_{gray} = S([I'; M]). \tag{1}$$

Here, I' represents the image of which an area corresponding to the mask M has been removed and $S(\cdot)$ denotes the Snet. Note that the mask M is not a segmentation layout but a rectangular binary map which corresponds to the bounding box of the object. The encoding step includes 2 steps of downsampling and 4 types of dilated convolution (rate = 1, 2, 4, 8). The decoding step upsamples the features into the original scale using transposed convolutional layers. Pixels outside the generated region are preserved as we do not wish any change outside of the box. After the Snet generates an image, only the region inside the box is combined with the stored background pixels. By doing this, only the change that occurred inside of the box is taken into consideration. The Snet is trained to minimize the L_1 distance between the synthesized grayscale image $\hat{I}_{gray}$ and the original gray scale image I_{gray} as in (2). The Snet is trained individually beforehand.

$$L_S = \|I_{gray} - \hat{I}_{gray}\|_1. \tag{2}$$

3.2   TextureNet

Complicated visual properties of real objects often disrupt the learning of generative models. In the problem settings of this paper, the overall structure and the detailed texture including colors can be difficult to depict by a single generator. When it comes to generating a car, details such as headlights, taillights, or the windshield of a car may vary a lot. If the Snet makes a rough sketch, the TextureNet (Tnet) adds details by painting colors on the sketched grayscale image and refines it. We have adopted the architecture in [16] which was used for a colorization task. The Tnet can be summarized as follows:

$$\hat{I}_{color} = T_{color}(I_{gray}^p, I') \tag{3}$$

$$\hat{I} = T_{refine}(\hat{I}_{color}) \tag{4}$$

$$L_T = CrossEntropy(I, \hat{I}_{color}) + \lambda\|I - \hat{I}\|_1. \tag{5}$$

Tnet is divided into two components: $T_{color}(\cdot)$ which paints colors on the gray patch image $\hat{I}_{gray}^p$ and paste it back to the masked image I', and $T_{refine}(\cdot)$ which corrects the details of the colorized image $\hat{I}_{color}$ as in (3) and (4), respectively. After the T_{color} classifies the color classes of all pixels, the colorized image of $\hat{I}_{gray}$ is pasted back to I, which produces $\hat{I}_{color}$. We crop the patch image $I_{gray}^p = Crop(I_{gray}, M)$ where the object is to be generated since the remaining region does not need any colorization nor manipulation. In the Tnet, T_{color} in (3) learns the color distribution of cars in detail. As in [16], T_{color} predicts the values of each pixel in the CIELab color space. Since the grayscale image corresponds to the lightness L, the model should predict the remaining a and b values. A pretrained VGG-19 network is used to extract features from the gray image. After that, a 1×1 convolution filter outputs a tensor with a depth of 313. Dividing the ab color space into 313 bins, the T_{color} turns the colorization problem into a classification problem which is much easier than directly generating images having various occlusions and a wide color variation. The cost is calculated by the cross-entropy function between the output and the Lab-encoded ground-truth values as in the first term of (5). The color is painted solely on the patch image, which can be awkward when the patch is pasted back to the original image. Therefore, we use an additional network module T_{refine} that encourages the object to get along with the surroundings of the image. Using the same structure with the Snet highly sharpens the blurry results of colorized images and adaptively optimizes the colors of the neighboring objects such as occluding cars, road segments or parts of buildings. This module is trained adversarially using a global-local discriminator along with a reconstruction L1-loss as shown by the second term in (5). The value of λ is set to be 0.5 in our work. The colorization network offers important clues for the refinement network such as the location of taillights and the rear window, helping the refinement network concentrate on polishing the details.

3.3 Global-Local Discriminator

A global-local context discriminator is used to train our model in the same way as in [9]. The overall discriminator D consists of one global discriminator D_{global} and one local discriminator D_{local}. The global discriminator takes the entire

Fig. 2. Results from our method and the baseline [9]. From top to bottom, 1) completed gray-scaled results of Snet, 2) results colorized by T_{color}, 3) final results of Tnet after refinement, and 4, 5) results of the baselines. Compared to the results of the baselines, our model depicts the details better since the refine module of Tnet can produce elaborate outputs. To present how well our method performs by itself, no post-processing is applied to all results.

image I (real) or $\hat{I}$ (generated) as an input and the local discriminator takes the patch image I_p or $\hat{I}_p$ inside the annotated box from the respective image I or $\hat{I}$. The size of the patch image is normalized to 64×64 by ROI-pooling. Each discriminator is followed by a fully connected layer. After that, both features are concatenated into a single vector and then processed by a single fully connected layer. A sigmoid output produces an outcome which is trained to correctly decide whether the given image is real or completed by the model. This encourages the model to depict sophisticated details of the object. The discriminator D and T_{refine} are trained in an adversarial way as follows:

$$
\min_{T_{refine}} \max_{D} \quad (\mathbb{E}_{I_p, I \sim P_{data}}[\log(D(I_p, I))]
$$
$$
+ \mathbb{E}_{\hat{I}_{color} \sim P_{T_{color}(I_{gray})}}[1 - \log(D(\hat{I}_p, \hat{I}))]) \tag{6}
$$

We may consider the colorized image input $\hat{I}_{color}$ from the T_{color} as a noise. This allows our model to be trained adversarially.

4 Experiments

4.1 Vehicle Generation Subject to the Surroundings

Among various objects, we have chosen to specifically concentrate on the car which has more clear visibility compared to other objects in the data. BDD100K is a dataset including videos filmed by running cars [14]. After resizing the resolution to 320×180 for the stable training, boxes sized under 10 pixels either

Fig. 3. Generating vehicles on empty roads. Target regions where the vehicles are to be generated are marked by red rectangles in the first row. With proper boxes given, both the baselines and our method draw vehicles inside. (Color figure online)

Fig. 4. Our results generated over the *Cityscape* dataset. The red arrows indicate where the vehicles are generated. (Color figure online)

horizontally or vertically are excluded in the training since they are so small that it is hard to acknowledge them as cars, which makes it meaningless to generate them. Also, a large vacated area is known to be hard to fill by the image completion frameworks. Therefore, we exclude boxes bigger than 64×50 since both the baseline and our method show poor results on them. We evaluated our trained model by generating vehicles on test images of BDD100K dataset. Since there is no other research generating an object in a given position only using the box annotation, we set the research of [9,11] used in the image completion problem as the baseline models. As the image completion problem is quite similar to our problem, the baseline holds the capacity to generate objects if trained properly. Instead of vacating a random region of the image, we only deleted the region where a vehicle exists and regenerated a new vehicle. As the baseline models only witness particular appearances, this makes them possible to generate an object, though they fail to express the details of objects as explained in this paper.

Some results of [9] are shown in the fourth row of Fig. 2. Cars generated at the center of the images mostly show their backside since most of the cars are running forward. For the boxes located between the road and the sidewalk, the cars are generated slightly askew as the camera usually shoots them in the diagonal direction. The overall appearances of all results resemble the real vehicles but the details such as taillights and wheels lack delicacy. Despite using the global-local discriminator described in Sect. 3.3, the baseline model generates blurry results. Excessive abuse of adversarial loss easily corrupts the model and impedes the training, which is why we mitigated the problem by our method. Results from the work of [11], the last row in Fig. 2, are considerably poor compared to other methods. Using the perceptual loss introduced by Gatys *et al.* [5], the model produces reasonable background segments and makes an appropriate outline of a vehicle. However, the texture inside is quite noisy, which seems to draw cars inside a car, which are hard to be perceived as cars. The third row of Fig. 2 shows some results of our method. In our method, the outline of vehicles is clearly visible and parts such as the taillights and wheels are described delicately. Also, the texture around the generated car suits the surrounding background. The paved roads are naturally connected at the bottom side with shadows shaded by the body of the vehicle. Furthermore, the model can recognize a building or a bush behind and reflect it in the background. Especially, for the cars tailing back aside from the road, the generation of an occluding car ahead is possible (see the third column in Fig. 2).

Although not presented in this paper, we also have tried to use the refine network module (T_{refine}) directly after the Snet producing colorized images instead of black and white images. However, the adversarial loss easily corrupts the model making the images unrecognizable. In Fig. 2, the results of Snet (the first row) and Iizuka *et al.* (the fourth row) are similarly blurry and incomplete. Adding clues of texture by colorization (the second row) highly helps the training of T_{refine} in which the adversarial loss is dominant. Also, while T_{color} focuses on painting the vehicle regardless of its surroundings, T_{refine} makes up for the inconsistent surroundings.

4.2   Vehicle Generation on an Empty Road

After training the model, we experimented with the situation in which our model generates cars at given locations where no car existed in the original images, which is the eventual objective of this paper. Images of the road with no cars on it are chosen, which would have been never used in training since it has no annotation box on it. Figure 3 shows the results of how well our method generates objects on empty roads where we asked it to. Given a reasonable location, the model is capable of generating a car with a random context. Especially, our method shows a remarkable performance when it comes to generating a car parking alongside the road.

4.3   Vehicle Generation on Cityscape Dataset

To show that our method is not restricted to the dataset it is trained on, we apply our network trained by BDD to generate cars on images from the *Cityscape* dataset [3]. Since, both of the datasets contain road scene images in the view of the drivers, the perspective and overall aspects are quite similar except that BDD is taken in the U.S.A and *Cityscape* in Germany. Figure 4 shows the results of our model applied to the *Cityscape* dataset. Without the red arrow indicating the generated vehicle, it is difficult to recognize which one is the generated vehicle at one glance.

Ours   **Baseline**

Fig. 5. Detection results of generated objects. Boxes in purple show the detection result of SSD. The top row shows the generated sample that our method succeeded to deceive the detector to perceive it as a vehicle while the baseline failed and the second row shows the case where both methods deceived the detector in spite of the poor quality of the baseline. In spite of our far better quality, SSD occasionally detects the deformed results of the baseline as a car. (Color figure online)

4.4 Effectiveness of Using Texture Net

Bringing the global-local discriminator to the end of Snet and changing the output dimension to RGB channels is equivalent to the work of [9]. Though we have shown the qualitative improvement in the figures above, we report an additional numerical comparison to prove the effectiveness of Tnet. For a fair evaluation of how much our TextureNet contributes to the training, we apply the Single Shot multibox Detector (SSD) [18], a widely used object detection algorithm, to the images generated by our method and the baseline [9]. Vehicles from the original images are substituted by both methods. If objects are generated properly, the detector should be able to locate them in the image, meaning that the generated objects are assumed to be sampled from the data distribution it is trained.

Table 1. Object detection score (recall in %) when Tnet is additionally used (Ours) or not (Baseline). Single Shot multibox Detector(SSD) [18] is used to evaluate how well the objects are generated. Weights of SSD are pre-trained using PascalVOC dataset. We only report the recall score at the target region since vehicles outside are not under consideration.

Method	Confidence threshold	
	0.12	0.3
Original BDD	87.42	78.59
Baseline (Iizuka *et al.*)	63.35	50.23
Ours	**73.12**	**60.24**

Table 2. The FID scores of the methods used in this paper. Only the generated region is used for the evaluation since the rest of the area is not synthesized.

Method	FID score
Iizuka *et al.*	112.3
Liu *et al.*	50.54
Ours	41.04

Our model and the baseline [9] have been trained using the training data in BDD100K and the evaluation has been carried out with the validation data. Since only the object to be generated is under consideration, vehicles detected outside the generated region are ignored. Therefore, we only evaluate the recall of SSD, which is the ratio of whether the detector finds the generated object or not. In the dataset, there are a total of 6,020 vehicles to recall that satisfy our size constraints. Since the detector is trained using PascalVOC dataset [4], it is fair enough to compare the baseline and our method applied to BDD100K dataset.

Table 1 shows the recall scores of SSD on BDD dataset. For the original BDD images, SSD detects vehicles in the box area at a rate of 78.59% using the confidence threshold of 0.3 and 87.42% using the confidence threshold of 0.12 as shown in Table 1. In both class confidence score thresholds, our method highly precedes the baseline by about 10% points. Additionally, we analyze the detection result of which the threshold is 0.12. Samples, which our method successfully makes the detector perceive as vehicles while the baseline fails to, occupy 17.24% while the opposite case records 7.47%. One example of this case is shown in the top row of Fig. 5. Meanwhile, though both methods successfully deceive the detector in many cases, quite a lot of samples generated by the baseline suffer from a qualitatively poor performance. This case is presented in the bottom row of Fig. 5. Considering that some ambiguous results from the baseline are occasionally detected by the detector, we expect that the performance of our method would be rated higher if evaluated by a qualitative metric.

4.5   Measuring Generation Quality

Frechet inception distance (FID) score [7] is a measure frequently used to evaluate the generation quality of generative models. Using a pre-trained Inception-V3, FID compares the statistics of generated images to the real ones.

In Table 2, we assess the quality of images generated by each method. Images from [9] roughly have the appearance of vehicles but record the worst FID score. This attributes to the abstractly depicted context of each vehicle. The work of Liu *et al.* shows an intermediate level of FID score. Though the silhouette of the generated sample resembles the vehicle, the texture inside is rather a noise which causes an increase in the FID score. Our method has the lowest FID score, which means that our method generates samples that have the most similar distribution to that of real samples.

Fig. 6. Failure cases. On the first row lie some single channel outputs of Snet and on the second row lie the corresponding 3-channel outputs of Tnet.

5 Discussion

The object detection dataset includes annotations indicating the location where the car exists, not where the car *may* be. This enforces us to give the model a box at a reasonable position manually. Although the most important merit of our method is that we only use a box annotation to generate a vehicle, the necessity of giving a box candidate still remains. For example, with a box given upon a building, the model would still try to generate a car even if it is nonsense. With a highly predictive scene understanding model that can suggest the location where the vehicle may be, we expect a fully automated vehicle image augmentation would be possible. Also, wide boxes, which correspond to the cars near the camera, usually fail to be filled, which is the drawback of the image completion models. A portion of the car may lie outside the camera angle and this will go against the overall aspect of trained objects. Some of the failure examples are given in Fig. 6.

6 Conclusion

We tackled a problem to generate vehicles at designated locations over images of real scenes. To solve this problem, we used an architecture composed of two subnetworks which generate the shape and the texture of the vehicle respectively. The Snet roughly completes the shape of the car according to the surroundings while the Tnet decides the details of the generated vehicle resulting in a better generating performance. Consequently, our method can generate objects going well with the surroundings in arbitrary locations. This is highly expected to be foundation research for image augmentation research.

Acknowledgements. This work was supported by the National Research Foundation of Korea (NRF) grant funded by the Korea government (2021R1A2C3006659).

References

1. Berthelot, D., Schumm, T., Metz, L.: BEGAN: boundary equilibrium generative adversarial networks. arXiv preprint arXiv:1703.10717 (2017)

2. Chen, Q., Koltun, V.: Photographic image synthesis with cascaded refinement networks. In: The IEEE International Conference on Computer Vision (ICCV), vol. 1 (2017)
3. Cordts, M., et al.: The cityscapes dataset for semantic urban scene understanding. In: Proceedings of the IEEE Conference on Computer Vision and Pattern Recognition, pp. 3213–3223 (2016)
4. Everingham, M., Van Gool, L., Williams, C.K., Winn, J., Zisserman, A.: The PASCAL visual object classes (VOC) challenge. Int. J. Comput. Vis. **88**(2), 303–338 (2010)
5. Gatys, L.A., Ecker, A.S., Bethge, M.: A neural algorithm of artistic style. arXiv preprint arXiv:1508.06576 (2015)
6. Gulrajani, I., Ahmed, F., Arjovsky, M., Dumoulin, V., Courville, A.C.: Improved training of Wasserstein GANs. In: Advances in Neural Information Processing Systems, pp. 5767–5777 (2017)
7. Heusel, M., Ramsauer, H., Unterthiner, T., Nessler, B., Hochreiter, S.: GANs trained by a two time-scale update rule converge to a local Nash equilibrium. In: Advances in Neural Information Processing Systems, pp. 6626–6637 (2017)
8. Hong, S., Yan, X., Huang, T., Lee, H.: Learning hierarchical semantic image manipulation through structured representations. arXiv preprint arXiv:1808.07535(2018)
9. Iizuka, S., Simo-Serra, E., Ishikawa, H.: Globally and locally consistent image completion. ACM Trans. Graph. (TOG) **36**(4), 107 (2017)
10. Isola, P., Zhu, J.Y., Zhou, T., Efros, A.A.: Image-to-image translation with conditional adversarial networks. arXiv preprint (2017)
11. Liu, G., Reda, F.A., Shih, K.J., Wang, T.-C., Tao, A., Catanzaro, B.: Image inpainting for irregular holes using partial convolutions. In: Ferrari, V., Hebert, M., Sminchisescu, C., Weiss, Y. (eds.) ECCV 2018. LNCS, vol. 11215, pp. 89–105. Springer, Cham (2018). https://doi.org/10.1007/978-3-030-01252-6_6
12. Pathak, D., Krahenbuhl, P., Donahue, J., Darrell, T., Efros, A.A.: Context encoders: feature learning by inpainting. In: Proceedings of the IEEE Conference on Computer Vision and Pattern Recognition, pp. 2536–2544 (2016)
13. Wang, C., Zheng, H., Yu, Z., Zheng, Z., Gu, Z., Zheng, B.: Discriminative region proposal adversarial networks for high-quality image-to-image translation. arXiv preprint arXiv:1711.09554 (2017)
14. Xu, H., Gao, Y., Yu, F., Darrell, T.: End-to-end learning of driving models from large-scale video datasets. arXiv preprint (2017)
15. Yu, F., Koltun, V.: Multi-scale context aggregation by dilated convolutions. arXiv preprint arXiv:1511.07122 (2015)
16. Zhang, R., Isola, P., Efros, A.A.: Colorful image colorization. In: Leibe, B., Matas, J., Sebe, N., Welling, M. (eds.) ECCV 2016. LNCS, vol. 9907, pp. 649–666. Springer, Cham (2016). https://doi.org/10.1007/978-3-319-46487-9_40
17. Zhou, B., Khosla, A., Lapedriza, A., Oliva, A., Torralba, A.: Learning deep features for discriminative localization. In: Proceedings of the IEEE Conference on Computer Vision and Pattern Recognition, pp. 2921–2929 (2016)
18. Liu, W., et al.: SSD: single shot multibox detector. In: Leibe, B., Matas, J., Sebe, N., Welling, M. (eds.) ECCV 2016. LNCS, vol. 9905, pp. 21–37. Springer, Cham (2016). https://doi.org/10.1007/978-3-319-46448-0_2

Scale Invariant Domain Generalization Image Recapture Detection

Jinian Luo[1], Jie Guo[2(✉)], Weidong Qiu[2], Zheng Huang[2], and Hong Hui[1]

[1] Institute of Cyber Science and Technology, Shanghai Jiao Tong University,
800 Dongchuan Road, Shanghai 200240, People's Republic of China
{jinianluo,huih}@sjtu.edu.cn
[2] School of Cyber Science and Engineering, Shanghai Jiao Tong University,
800 Dongchuan Road, Shanghai 200240, People's Republic of China
{guojie,qiuwd,huang-zheng}@sjtu.edu.cn

Abstract. Recapturing and rebroadcasting of images are common attack methods in insurance frauds and face identification spoofing, and an increasing number of detection techniques were introduced to handle this problem. However, most of them ignored the domain generalization scenario and scale variances, with an inferior performance on domain shift situations, and normally were exacerbated by intra-domain and inter-domain scale variances. In this paper, we propose a scale alignment domain generalization framework (SADG) to address these challenges. First, an adversarial domain discriminator is exploited to minimize the discrepancies of image representation distributions among different domains. Meanwhile, we exploit triplet loss as a local constraint to achieve a clearer decision boundary. Moreover, a scale alignment loss is introduced as a global relationship regularization to force the image representations of the same class across different scales to be undistinguishable. Experimental results on four databases and comparison with state-of-the-art approaches show that better performance can be achieved using our framework.

Keywords: Image processing and computer vision · Recapture detection · Domain generalization · Scale variance

1 Introduction

Digital images can now be easily obtained by cameras and distributed over the Internet. Modifications including recapturing are direct threats to image credibility at present. Thus, images as evidence require rigorous validation on the originality to be dependable testimonies [2]. According to [4], human beings have difficulty discminating between recaptured and original images. To this end, recapture detection forensics are required to exclude recapture frauds. In recapture detection tasks, wavelets statistical distributions [2,7,21], texture distribution [4] are exploited as detection features. According to [13], texture distribution is considered to be a solid method in this task. Physical traits, such as specularity, blurriness and chromaticity [9,14,15] are also considered as an effective discriminative cue. DCT coefficients [24,26], quality [27] and gray level co-occurance matrix (GLCM) [3] are also modeled. Besides, neural network

© Springer Nature Switzerland AG 2021
T. Mantoro et al. (Eds.): ICONIP 2021, LNCS 13111, pp. 75–86, 2021.
https://doi.org/10.1007/978-3-030-92273-3_7

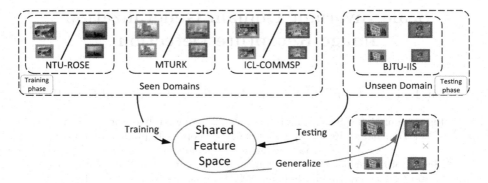

Fig. 1. Introduction to cross domain recapture detection. Our SADG method aims to learn a shared feature space which is robust with domain shift and scale variances scenarios. Images with green boarders are single captured and images with red boarders are recaptured. The upper row of images in each domain are of smaller scales and the lower row represents larger scales. (Color figure online)

methods [1,5,13,25] are proposed to further enhance the detection accuracy. However, after compression on a recaptured image, the consequent deformation of texture feature patterns decreases the classification accuracy [10,17,19]. Besides, in order to build a robust recapture detection system, different datasets are collected for model training, which causes domain shift effects on properties of input images, including scale, illumination and color [23]. Therefore, the distribution biases introduced by the dataset collection process is a practical challenge in recapture detection tasks. All of the above methods achieve successful performance only on single domain scenarios. Therefore, as is illustrated in Fig. 1, cross domain recapture detection task is proposed to learn a shared feature space which preserves the most generalized classification cues and is robust with intra-domain and inter-domain scale variances.

Domain generalization (DG) methods are direct solutions for this task. Here a domain $\mathbb{D} = \{\mathcal{X}, \mathbb{P}^X\}$ is defined by a feature space $\mathcal{X}$ and a marginal distribution $\mathbb{P}^X$ [18], and each single database is considered an independent domain in this paper. In a similar task, face-antispoofing, DG methods such as MADDG [20] and SSDG [12] achieve promising performance in multi-domain scenarios. However, these DG methods are highly customized and consequently not applicable for recapture detection. Firstly, the recaptured images are only obtained from screens, thus recaptured features can be aggregated in feature space across different domains. Furthermore, the global relationship [6] such as scale variances can be exploited to enhance the discriminability of the representations.

In this paper, as is illustrated in the left part of Fig. 1, the shared feature space is learned from source domains. This paper makes the following contributions: (1) We introduce a competition between feature generator and domain discriminator for domain generalization; (2) In training phase the scale alignment(SA) operations are performed in each category across all source domains to aggregate the embedded features of different scale levels but the same cap-

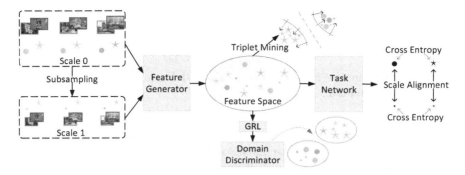

Fig. 2. Overview of the proposed method. Dots and stars represent single captured and recaptured images respectively. Symbols of three different colors represent different domains. Red border represents recaptured images, green border represents single captured images. Scale 1 represents larger scales and scale 0 represents smaller scales.

ture category; (3) To improve the local representation compactness and further enhance the discriminability of generalized features, a triplet mining strategy is incorporated in the framework.

2 Method

2.1 Overview

This framework consists of three modules, i.e. (1) a domain discriminator competing with feature generator; (2) a global scale alignment loss on the classification outputs of large and small scales, alongside the cross-entropy loss; (3) a triplet loss applied to the feature space as a local constraint. Details are described in the following sections.

2.2 Adversarial Learning

Suppose we have N domains $\mathcal{D} = \{\mathbb{D}_1, \mathbb{D}_2, ..., \mathbb{D}_N\}$ and corresponding labels $\mathcal{Y} = \{\mathbf{Y}_1, \mathbf{Y}_2, ..., \mathbf{Y}_N\}$. There are $C = 2$ categories in each domain, where $Y = 0/1$ represents single capture/recapture. Our goal is to generalize from $\mathcal{D}$ and $\mathcal{Y}$ to unseen target domain $\mathbb{D}_{N+1}$. Here labels in target domain are not necessary for practical purposes. In recapture detection tasks, we postulate that common discriminative cues exist in both categories in sight of the identical nature of data collection in each domain and each class. To this end, we introduce adversarial learning method to the embedded feature space to exploit generalized differentiation information and minimize distribution bias of any specific source domain.

For a feature generator G, network input $\mathbf{X}_r$ (recaptured images) and $\mathbf{X}_s$ (single captured images) are transformed into embedded features $\mathbf{F}_r$ and $\mathbf{F}_s$:

$$\mathbf{F}_r = G(\mathbf{X}_r), \ \mathbf{F}_s = G(\mathbf{X}_s) \tag{1}$$

A domain discriminator D is applied on $\mathbf{F}_r$ and $\mathbf{F}_s$ to determine their corresponding source domain:

$$d_r = D(\mathbf{F}_r), \ d_s = D(\mathbf{F}_s) \tag{2}$$

There is a competition between domain discriminator D and feature generator G, where G is trained to fool D to make domain label indistinguishable from the shared discriminative feature space. Domain discriminator and feature generator are trained simultaneously and adversarially across all of source domains and categories in the training phase. Furthermore, in order to optimize domain discriminator and feature generator in the same backpropagation step, a gradient reverse layer(GRL) [8,12] is inserted between them. The task of domain discriminator is effectively a multiclass classification, thus we utilize cross-entropy loss to measure the performance of G and D:

$$\min_D \max_G \mathcal{L}_{Ada}(X, Y_D; G, D) = -\mathbb{E}_{x,y \sim X, Y_D} \sum_{n=1}^{N} \mathbb{1}[n = y] \log D(G(x)) \tag{3}$$

where Y_D is a set of domain labels.

2.3   Scale Alignment Clustering

Images from different domains or even the same domain have different scales [17], which adversely affects the generalization performance. Inspired by the global class alignment objective in MASF [6], we propose to introduce a scale alignment objective to the distribution of classification outputs and structure the feature space by an explicit regularization. Our preliminary experiments demonstrated that scale relationship is better represented in the classification outputs than in the feature space, therefore, scale alignment is performed on task network outputs, which is different from [6]. For each class c, the concept of scale is modeled by $\mathbf{s}_c^{(jl)}$ for large scale and $\mathbf{s}_c^{(js)}$ for small scale:

$$\mathbf{s}_c^{(jl)} = T(G(\mathbf{x}_c^{(jl)})), \ \mathbf{s}_c^{(js)} = T(G(\mathbf{x}_c^{(js)})) \tag{4}$$

where T and G represents task network and feature generator, and j is the index of the image from the synthesized training dataset. We define scale alignment loss on the distribution of $\mathbf{s}_c^{(jl)}$ and $\mathbf{s}_c^{(js)}$:

$$\min_{G, T} \mathcal{L}_{SA}(G, T; \mathbb{D}_r, \mathbb{D}_s) = \frac{1}{C} \sum_{c=1}^{C} \frac{1}{N} \sum_{j=1}^{N} \frac{1}{2} [D_{KL}(\mathbf{s}_c^{(jl)} \parallel \mathbf{s}_c^{(js)}) \tag{5}$$

$$+ \ D_{KL}(\mathbf{s}_c^{(js)} \parallel \mathbf{s}_c^{(jl)})]$$

where $D_{KL}(\mathbf{p}\|\mathbf{q}) = \sum_r p_r \log \frac{p_r}{q_r}$ and symmetric Kullback-Leibler (KL) divergence is $\frac{1}{2}[D_{KL}(\mathbf{p}\|\mathbf{q}) + D_{KL}(\mathbf{q}\|\mathbf{p})]$. The discrepency between distributions of $\mathbf{s}_c^{(jl)}$ and $\mathbf{s}_c^{(js)}$ are measured by symmetric KL divergence across two classes.

2.4   Triplet Mining

To hold local feature compactness [6] in the feature space, we insert a triplet loss to aggregate intra-class samples and separate inter-class samples for a clearer decision boundary. Triplet mining is also introduced by Jia et al. [12] and Shao et al. [20] with a view to structure the feature space. However, in recapture detection context, images are recaptured only from screens, thus in contrast we enforce feature compactness in both classes regardless of domain or scale. Specifically, we assume there are three source domains in training phase. In a triplet mining procedure, recaptured and single captured images are recollected from all source domains.

The two objectives in triplet mining are: pull apart recapture samples from single capture samples, and aggregate each class respectively. In the backpropagation step, feature generator G is optimized by:

$$
\min_{G} \quad \mathcal{L}_{DA\_Trip}(G;\ \mathbf{X}_r,\ \mathbf{X}_s) \ =
$$

$$
\sum_{\substack{\forall y_a = y_p, y_a \neq y_n \\ i = j}} [\| G(x_i^a) - G(x_j^p)\|_2^2 \ - \ \| G(x_i^a) - G(x_j^n)\|_2^2 \ + \alpha]_+ \qquad (6)
$$

$$
+ \sum_{\substack{\forall y_a = y_p, y_a \neq y_n \\ i \neq j}} [\| G(x_i^a) - G(x_j^p)\|_2^2 \ - \ \| G(x_i^a) - G(x_j^n)\|_2^2 \ + \alpha]_+
$$

where G denotes the feature generator, superscripts a and n represents different classes and a and p samples stem from the same class. Subscripts i and j indicates there is no restriction on domain or scale of samples. α represents a pre-defined positive parameter. Finally, samples from different domains or scales but the same category are forced to be more compact in the feature space.

2.5   Scale Invariant Domain Generalization

We formulate the integrated framework into an optimization objective as follow:

$$
\mathcal{L}_{SADG} = \mathcal{L}_{Cls} + \lambda_1 \mathcal{L}_{Ada} + \lambda_2 \mathcal{L}_{DA\_Trip} + \lambda_3 \mathcal{L}_{SA} \qquad (7)
$$

where $\mathcal{L}_{Cls}$ is a task-specific loss function. Because recapture detection is a classification task, the framework is optimized by cross-entropy loss, denoted by $\mathcal{L}_{Cls}$. λ_1, λ_2 and λ_3 are pre-defined parameters to balance four losses. As is illustrated in Fig. 2, this framework is trained in an end-to-end manner in the training phase. After training, G achieves a more generalized feature space, which is robust with domain shift and scale variances.

3   Experiments

3.1   Experimentsal Settings

Dataset. Four recapture detection datasets are collected to simulate real- life scenarios and evaluate our proposed method against other baseline methods.

Table 1. Four experimental datasets.

Dataset	Recapture device count	Recaptured image count	Single captured image count
B	2	706	636
I	8	1440	905
M	119	1369	1368
N	9	2776	2712

Our selected datasets are BJTU-IIS [15] (B for short), ICL-COMMSP [16,22] (I for short), mturk [1] (M for short) and NTU-ROSE [4,11] (N for short), and the number of recapture/single capture images and recapture devices are shown in Table 1. These datasets are collected for different purposes, specifically, B is for evaluation on high resolution images; images in I are controlled by distance between camera and screen; images in N are captured in a lighting controlled room; and for M, the aim was to crowd-source the collection of images. The contents, illumination, scales and resolution of pictures are different across datasets or within a single dataset.

Implementation Details. Our work is implemented using Pytorch as a framework. The images are cropped $256 \times 256 \times 3$ off, in a RGB color space. ResNet-18 is exploited as backbone of feature generator. In order to achieve a better generalization performance, the Adam optimizer learning rate is set to 1e-4, and batch size is 8 for each domain. So the total batch size is 24 in a 3 source domains case, and 16 in a limited source experiment. We set the hyperparameters λ_1, λ_2 and λ_3 in Eq. 7 to be 0.1, 0.2 and 0.1, respectively. Each time one domain is chosen as target, and remaining three domains are source domains. Thus, there are four experimental tasks in total.

3.2 Experimental Comparison

Baseline Methods. We compare our proposed SADG framework with several state-of-the-art recapture detection methods, multi-scale learning methods and domain generalization algorithms: **Multi-scale LBP(MS-LBP)** [4], **Choi-CNN** [5], **Multi-scale CNN (MS-CNN)** [17], **mturk** [1], **MADDG** [20], **SSDG** [12]. The MS-LBP and MS-CNN are multi-scale methods, Choi-CNN and mturk are deep learning methods for recapture detection. MADDG and SSDG are two algorithms for face anti-spoofing task, and we compare these two methods with SADG because no recapture detection methods pay attention to domain generalization to our best knowledge.

Comparison Results. As is shown in Table 2 and 3, our algorithm outperforms all compared state-of-the-art methods except the HTER in experiment I&M&N

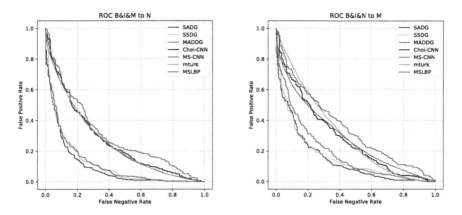

Fig. 3. ROC curves for two recapture detection domain generalization experiments.

to B, with only 0.01% behind SSDG. By subsampling, the scale variances are amplified in target domains. From these two tables, we can see that scale variances are crucial to detection performance. In the second column of Table 1, the recapture device counts are significantly different. Furthermore, the variation of scale and resolution are larger in M than in B, and thus all of the methods performs better in experiment I&M&N to B than in experiment B&I&N to M, but SADG is better than all other methods, which demonstrates the effectiveness of our scale alignment loss and domain generalization strategy. As is shown in Fig. 3 and Fig. 4, when compared with traditional methods, the proposed method performs better because other methods pay no attention on domain shift and cannot achieve a generalized feature space. Moreover, although SSDG and MADDG are domain generalization methods, neither of them focuses on the scale variances, either within a single domain or among different domains. The domain shift affects introduced by scale variances can be addressed by adversarial learning, but scale variances also exists in a single domain. This was resolved by global alignment and clustering operations of SADG in a pairwise manner.

Table 2. Comparison with state-of-the-art methods on four recapture detection domain generalization experiments with original and subsampled scales.

Method	B&I&M to N		B&I&N to M		B&M&N to I		I&M&N to B	
	HTER (%)	AUC (%)	HTER (%)	AUC (%)	HTER (%)	AUC (%)	HTER (%)	AUC (%)
MS-LBP [4]	33.07	69.85	39.50	65.09	35.86	81.08	20.56	87.25
Choi-CNN [5]	24.87	73.60	47.70	71.60	37.99	87.20	30.39	73.47
MS-CNN [17]	32.50	74.43	28.59	70.90	38.91	72.35	15.00	85.72
mturk [1]	32.81	74.41	35.16	69.32	36.88	73.72	18.25	85.88
MADDG [20]	19.74	88.39	26.15	81.72	20.40	87.64	18.25	89.40
SSDG [12]	20.06	88.41	22.37	83.67	18.43	90.59	**15.12**	90.48
Ours (**SADG**)	**15.95**	**90.28**	**22.20**	**85.60**	**15.93**	**92.03**	15.13	**91.65**

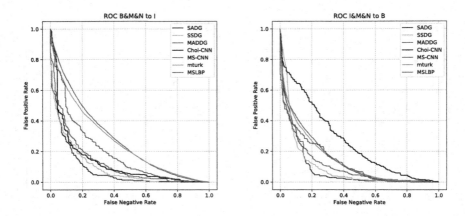

Fig. 4. ROC curves for two recapture detection domain generalization experiments.

Table 3. Comparison with state-of-the-art methods on domain generalization experiments with original scale.

Method	B&I&M to N		B&I&N to M		B&M&N to I		I&M&N to B	
	HTER (%)	AUC (%)	HTER (%)	AUC (%)	HTER (%)	AUC (%)	HTER (%)	AUC (%)
MADDG [20]	18.75	90.06	10.85	96.09	14.64	93.32	12.99	94.17
SSDG [12]	16.61	91.58	12.66	94.93	12.17	93.84	11.02	94.85
Ours (**SADG**)	**16.45**	**91.42**	**10.03**	**96.14**	**11.18**	**95.28**	**8.55**	**94.85**

3.3   Discussion

Ablation Study. Because every component, adversarial learning, triplet mining and scale alignment clustering in SADG framework are independent from domain settings, we conduct ablation study on the aforementioned four sets of domain generalization experiments, eliminating effects of one component each time. **SADG wo/ad** denotes the SADG framework without adversarial learning, where we disengage GRL and domain discriminator from the backpropagation procedure. This specific network does not explicitly exploit the shared information in feature space. **SADG wo/trip** denotes the SADG framework without triplet mining, where the effects of triplet loss are canceled. In this case, the framework does not utilize local clustering objective as a regularization. **SADG wo/sa** denotes the SADG framework without scale alignment clustering, where the global relationship alignment between different scales are removed from feature space.

Table 4 shows the performance of every incomplete SADG framework degrades on each set of domain generalization experiments. As expected, this result verifies that each component in SADG advances the performance simultaneously by global and local alignment and clustering operations, and that the intact version of proposed scheme achieves the finest performance.

Table 4. Ablation study on the effectiveness of three components in the framework.

Method	B&I&M to N		B&I&N to M		B&M&N to I		I&M&N to B	
	HTER(%)	AUC (%)	HTER (%)	AUC (%)	HTER (%)	AUC (%)	HTER (%)	AUC (%)
SADG wo/ad	21.05	87.73	25.49	82.16	23.87	83.23	15.46	**92.66**
SADG wo/trip	24.18	83.17	25.16	82.92	23.84	85.58	16.77	91.63
SADG wo/sa	18.75	88.27	23.25	84.15	17.59	90.69	15.46	91.88
Ours (**SADG**)	**15.95**	**90.28**	**22.20**	**85.60**	**15.93**	**92.03**	**15.13**	91.65

Table 5. Comparison with other scale alignment strategies on domain generalization.

Method	B&I&M to N		B&I&N to M		B&M&N to I		I&M&N to B	
	HTER (%)	AUC (%)	HTER (%)	AUC (%)	HTER (%)	AUC (%)	HTER (%)	AUC (%)
Feature-SADG	18.43	85.98	23.68	83.16	16.93	91.44	**15.12**	**91.87**
Task-SADG	16.94	87.76	23.85	83.37	16.45	91.15	17.43	87.39
Ours (**SADG**)	**15.95**	**90.28**	**22.20**	**85.60**	**15.93**	**92.03**	15.13	91.65

Stages Comparison. According to MASF [6], the concept of a class is represented by the average of embedded features in the feature space. However, our preliminary experiments indicated that KL divergence output alignment strategy is better in scale alignment. There is also an average strategy deployed on task network classification score. We conduct an extensive study on these different strategies. The first strategy is a feature scale alignment. Following the work of [6], the large (l) scale concept of class c is:

$$\bar{\mathbf{z}}_c^{(l)} = \frac{1}{N_l^{(c)}} \sum_{n:y_n^{(l)}=c} G(x_n^{(l)}) \tag{8}$$

where G is the feature generator. And we can define soft label distribution and loss as such:

$$s_c^{(l)} = softmax(T(\bar{\mathbf{z}}_c^{(l)})) \tag{9}$$

$$\mathcal{L}_{SA} = \frac{1}{C} \sum_{c=1}^{C} \frac{1}{2} [D_{KL}(s_c^{(l)} \| s_c^{(s)}) + D_{KL}(s_c^{(s)} \| s_c^{(l)})] \tag{10}$$

where l and s indicate large scale and small scale respectively. The second strategy is a task network classification score alignment. The average classification score of large scale and scale alignment loss as such:

$$\bar{s}_c^{(l)} = \frac{1}{N} \sum_{j=1}^{N} s_c^{(jl)} \tag{11}$$

$$\mathcal{L}'_{SA} = \frac{1}{C} \sum_{c=1}^{C} \frac{1}{2} [D_{KL}(\bar{s}_c^{(l)} \| \bar{s}_c^{(s)}) + D_{KL}(\bar{s}_c^{(s)} \| \bar{s}_c^{(l)})] \tag{12}$$

The third strategy is the KL divergence output alignment described in Eqs. 4 and 5. Here the KL divergence is calculated in a pairwise manner.

Table 5 shows that the last strategy outperforms the other two strategies except for the I&M&N to B experiment, where the proposed method is 0.01% behind the feature scale alignment method. Therefore, our KL divergence alignment strategy is the robustest method.

Table 6. Comparison with state-of-the-art methods on limited source domains for recapture detection.

Method	M&N to B		M&N to I	
	HTER (%)	AUC (%)	HTER (%)	AUC (%)
MS-LBP [4]	24.83	83.15	36.33	81.58
Choi-CNN [5]	45.70	81.30	48.05	72.24
MS-CNN [17]	24.34	83.48	30.13	76.95
SSDG [12]	22.03	85.38	23.93	84.08
Ours (**SADG**)	**18.56**	**88.81**	**22.94**	**84.31**

Limited Source Domains. We further conduct experimental comparison in a limited source scenario (e.g. only two source domains are available), which is a normal case in real-life practices. The scale variance between mturk (M for short) and NTU-ROSE (N for short) is more significant than that of the other two domains, thus we choose M and N as source domains and the remaining two as target domains. In Table 6, our proposed method outperforms other methods significantly. When compared with Table 2, our proposed method performs better by exploiting the scale variance information. Therefore, our method achieves more generalized feature space even in a extremely limited source scenario.

3.4   Conclusion

To address two challenges, scale variances and domain shift, we propose a scale alignment domain generalization framework (SADG). Different from existing recapture detection methods, our SADG framework exploits generalized discriminative information in shared feature space. Moreover, we apply global and local regularization on the embedded features. Specifically, the global relationship between different scales is aligned and utilized for optimization. Meanwhile, triplet loss is also incorporated as a further constraint for class clustering and a clearer decision boundary. Extensive experiments on public databases validate the effectiveness of our proposed method and prove that our SADG framework achieves state-of-the-art results in domain generalization recapture detection.

Acknowledgements. Portions of the research in this paper used the ROSE Recaptured Image Dataset made available by the ROSE Lab at the Nanyang Technological University, Singapore.

References

1. Agarwal, S., Fan, W., Farid, H.: A diverse large-scale dataset for evaluating rebroadcast attacks. In: 2018 IEEE International Conference on Acoustics, Speech and Signal Processing (ICASSP), pp. 1997–2001. IEEE (2018)
2. Anjum, A., Islam, S.: Recapture detection technique based on edge-types by analysing high-frequency components in digital images acquired through LCD screens. Multimedia Tools Appl., 1–21 (2019)
3. Awati, C., Alzende, N.H.: Classification of singly captured and recaptured images using sparse dictionaries. Int. J. 5(7) (2017)
4. Cao, H., Kot, A.C.: Identification of recaptured photographs on LCD screens. In: 2010 IEEE International Conference on Acoustics, Speech and Signal Processing, pp. 1790–1793. IEEE (2010)
5. Choi, H.-Y., Jang, H.-U., Son, J., Kim, D., Lee, H.-K.: Content recapture detection based on convolutional neural networks. In: Kim, K., Joukov, N. (eds.) ICISA 2017. LNEE, vol. 424, pp. 339–346. Springer, Singapore (2017). https://doi.org/10.1007/978-981-10-4154-9_40
6. Dou, Q., Castro, D.C., Kamnitsas, K., Glocker, B.: Domain generalization via model-agnostic learning of semantic features. In: Advances in Neural Information Processing Systems (NeurIPS), vol. 32, Vancouver, BC, Canada (2019)
7. Farid, H., Lyu, S.: Higher-order wavelet statistics and their application to digital forensics. In: 2003 Conference on Computer Vision and Pattern Recognition Workshop, vol. 8, pp. 94–94. IEEE (2003)
8. Ganin, Y., Lempitsky, V.: Unsupervised domain adaptation by backpropagation. In: International Conference on Machine Learning, pp. 1180–1189. PMLR (2015)
9. Gao, X., Ng, T.T., Qiu, B., Chang, S.F.: Single-view recaptured image detection based on physics-based features. In: 2010 IEEE International Conference on Multimedia and Expo, pp. 1469–1474. IEEE (2010)
10. Gluckman, J.: Scale variant image pyramids. In: 2006 IEEE Computer Society Conference on Computer Vision and Pattern Recognition (CVPR 2006), vol. 1, pp. 1069–1075. IEEE (2006)
11. Hong, C.: Statistical image source model identification and forgery detection. Ph.D. thesis, Nanyang Technological University (2011)
12. Jia, Y., Zhang, J., Shan, S., Chen, X.: Single-side domain generalization for face anti-spoofing. In: Proceedings of the IEEE/CVF Conference on Computer Vision and Pattern Recognition, pp. 8484–8493 (2020)
13. Li, H., Wang, S., Kot, A.C.: Image recapture detection with convolutional and recurrent neural networks. Electron. Imaging **2017**(7), 87–91 (2017)
14. Li, J., Wu, G.: Image recapture detection through residual-based local descriptors and machine learning. In: Sun, X., Chao, H.-C., You, X., Bertino, E. (eds.) ICCCS 2017. LNCS, vol. 10603, pp. 653–660. Springer, Cham (2017). https://doi.org/10.1007/978-3-319-68542-7_56
15. Li, R., Ni, R., Zhao, Y.: An effective detection method based on physical traits of recaptured images on LCD screens. In: Shi, Y.-Q., Kim, H.J., Pérez-González, F., Echizen, I. (eds.) IWDW 2015. LNCS, vol. 9569, pp. 107–116. Springer, Cham (2016). https://doi.org/10.1007/978-3-319-31960-5_10
16. Muammar, H., Dragotti, P.L.: An investigation into aliasing in images recaptured from an LCD monitor using a digital camera. In: 2013 IEEE International Conference on Acoustics, Speech and Signal Processing, pp. 2242–2246. IEEE (2013)

17. Noord, N.V., Postma, E.: Learning scale-variant and scale-invariant features for deep image classification. Pattern Recogn. **61**, 583–592 (2017)
18. Pan, S.J., Yang, Q.: A survey on transfer learning. IEEE Trans. Knowl. Data Eng. **22**(10), 1345–1359 (2010)
19. Park, D., Ramanan, D., Fowlkes, C.: Multiresolution models for object detection. In: Daniilidis, K., Maragos, P., Paragios, N. (eds.) ECCV 2010. LNCS, vol. 6314, pp. 241–254. Springer, Heidelberg (2010). https://doi.org/10.1007/978-3-642-15561-1_18
20. Shao, R., Lan, X., Li, J., Yuen, P.C.: Multi-adversarial discriminative deep domain generalization for face presentation attack detection. In: Proceedings of the IEEE/CVF Conference on Computer Vision and Pattern Recognition, pp. 10023–10031 (2019)
21. Sun, Y., Shen, X., Lv, Y., Liu, C.: Recaptured image forensics algorithm based on multi-resolution wavelet transformation and noise analysis. Int. J. Pattern Recognit. Artif. Intell. **32**(02), 1854003 (2018)
22. Thongkamwitoon, T., Muammar, H., Dragotti, P.L.: An image recapture detection algorithm based on learning dictionaries of edge profiles. IEEE Trans. Inf. Forensics Secur. **10**(5), 953–968 (2015)
23. Torralba, A., Efros, A.A.: Unbiased look at dataset bias. In: CVPR 2011, pp. 1521–1528. IEEE (2011)
24. Yang, P., Li, R., Ni, R., Zhao, Y.: Recaptured image forensics based on quality aware and histogram feature. In: Kraetzer, C., Shi, Y.-Q., Dittmann, J., Kim, H.J. (eds.) IWDW 2017. LNCS, vol. 10431, pp. 31–41. Springer, Cham (2017). https://doi.org/10.1007/978-3-319-64185-0_3
25. Yang, P., Ni, R., Zhao, Y.: Recapture image forensics based on Laplacian convolutional neural networks. In: Shi, Y.Q., Kim, H.J., Perez-Gonzalez, F., Liu, F. (eds.) IWDW 2016. LNCS, vol. 10082, pp. 119–128. Springer, Cham (2017). https://doi.org/10.1007/978-3-319-53465-7_9
26. Yin, J., Fang, Y.: Markov-based image forensics for photographic copying from printed picture. In: Proceedings of the 20th ACM International Conference on Multimedia, pp. 1113–1116 (2012)
27. Zhu, N., Li, Z.: Recaptured image detection through enhanced residual-based correlation coefficients. In: Sun, X., Pan, Z., Bertino, E. (eds.) ICCCS 2018. LNCS, vol. 11068, pp. 624–634. Springer, Cham (2018). https://doi.org/10.1007/978-3-030-00021-9_55

Tile2Vec with Predicting Noise for Land Cover Classification

Marshal Arijona Sinaga[(✉)], Fadel Muhammad Ali,
and Aniati Murni Arymurthy

Faculty of Computer Science University of Indonesia, Depok, Indonesia
{marshal.arijona01,fadel.muhammad01}@ui.ac.id,
aniati@cs.ui.ac.id

Abstract. Tile2vec has proven to be a good representation learning model in the remote sensing field. The success of the model depends on $l2$-norm regularization. However, $l2$-norm regularization has the main drawback that affects the regularization. We propose to replace the $l2$-norm with regularization with predicting noise framework. We then develop an algorithm to integrate the framework. We evaluate the model by using it as a feature extractor on the land cover classification task. The result shows that our proposed model outperforms all the baseline models.

Keywords: Tile2vec · Predicting noise · Representation learning · Land cover classification · Remote sensing · Deep learning

1 Introduction

The rapid development of deep learning has helped the remote sensing community to analyze the enormous geospatial data streams. We use the analyses to interpret the earth's surface, such as land-use change detection and land cover classification [25, 26]. However, most deep-learning-based remote sensing analysis lean extensively on the supervised learning approach, which requires a plenteous dataset with annotated labels [13]. Furthermore, remote sensing suffers from data scarcity, where there are lots of data available but not enough labels to train with supervised approach [14]. This problem hinders the researchers from analyzing downstream tasks such as classification or detection with deep learning.

Alternative methods have been proposed to tackle the necessity of the label while training deep learning models. Most methods rely on a representation learning model which transforms the data into a low-dimensional representation (can also be referred to as feature or embedding) that is useful for any downstream tasks [14, 16, 17]. One of the most successful approach for remote sensing tasks is Tile2Vec [14]. Tile2vec was inspired by word embedding model in natural language processing like Word2Vec [18] and GLoVe [21]. The model extends the idea by chunking an image into several tiles at first. Subsequently, the model learns the vector representation for each tile such that a tile that is a neighbor of another tile have a similar vector representation. In addition, Tile2vec has

© Springer Nature Switzerland AG 2021
T. Mantoro et al. (Eds.): ICONIP 2021, LNCS 13111, pp. 87–99, 2021.
https://doi.org/10.1007/978-3-030-92273-3_8

l^2-norm regularization on its objective function. The norm aims to impose the representation's distribution to follow a hypersphere [14]. Such circumstance will give a meaning for a relative distance between two vector representations.

However, $l2-$norm regularization tends to shrink the less contributed variables towards but not precisely to zero [20]. This condition leads to such a less impactful regularization. Meanwhile, an unsupervised learning model was proposed by matching a set of fixed target representations with the data representations [3] (later, we call the model as noise as target (NAT)). The target representations are generated from a low-dimensional space. Intuitively, the proposed model imposes the data representation's distribution to be matched with the target representation's distribution [3]. Note that the notion is the same with $l2$-norm regularization when we choose $l2$-hypersphere as the target representation's distribution. The model works well to capture data representation as it reduces the representation collapse [3].

In this paper, we propose an improvement of Tile2Vec by replacing the l^2-norm penalty with NAT. We call the proposed model as Tile2Vec with predicting noise. We then develop an algorithm that offers the model two options to utilize the tile embeddings: sampling-based and non-sampling-based. Later, we evaluate the model on a land cover classification task. The results are compared with the baseline and the other state-of-the-art models.

This paper is presented as follows. The first section discusses the background of the research, which is rooted in Tile2vec and NAT. Section 2 reviews several representation learning models that relate to this research. We then elaborate the Tile2vec with predicting noise in Sect. 3. In Sect. 4, we run several experiments to examine the proposed model. Finally, we give a summary of the research and the future works in Sect. 5.

2   Related Works

At first, we review state-of-the-art representation learning on the image domain. Later, we discuss unsupervised learning with predicting noise and representation learning models in the remote sensing field.

Autoencoder. Autoencoder has two networks, encoder and decoder [9]. Encoder infers the latent representations of the high-dimensional data. Meanwhile, the decoder transforms the latent representations back to the high-dimensional data. The latent representations are responsibly capturing the distribution of high-dimensional data. There are several paradigms to develop an autoencoder. Variational autoencoder (VAE) treats the encoder and decoder as directed probabilistic models with stochastic variational inference [15]. Denoising autoencoder developed a robust representation learning model by reconstructing the data injected by noise [27]. Autoencoders have been used to decode transformation operations applied to high-dimensional data [22,29]. Such autoencoder extract latent representations that are equivariant toward transformation operations.

Generative Adversarial Network (GAN). A generative adversarial network (GAN) is a deep generative model trained in a mini-max framework [10]. GAN consists of two networks: generator and discriminator. Generator acts to generate high dimensional data by transforming vector noises sampled from a prior distribution (mostly standard normal distribution). The discriminator is responsibly predicting whether a sample is coming from the data distribution or the generator. The goal of the discriminator is to maximize the accuracy of predicting the origin of the data samples. On the other hand, the generator aims to generate data that follow data distribution to drop the accuracy of the discriminator. [23] proposed rigorous steps to train GAN as GAN has two main problems: mode collapse and vanishing gradient [1]. Another work proposed a new criterion based on Lipschitz function to ensure the convergence of the training [2].

Self-supervised-Learning. Self-supervised learning utilizes the parts of input as the learning signals to build a representation model. Conducted researches used various parts as the learning signals. [5] partition the image into several patches. The model then uses relative positions of two sampled patches. [19] shuffle the patches of images and use the model to solve them. Later researches extend the concept by introducing positive samples and negative samples as part of the learning signals [4,11]. Such a concept is called contrastive learning.

Bojanowski et al., 2019 proposed an unsupervised learning model which utilizes a predefined target sampled from a low-dimensional distribution [3]. Theoretically, the model optimizes the earth mover distance between vector representation's distribution and predefined target distribution [24]. Before the statement, the model has two optimization problems. The first optimization is to the parameters of the encoder. The second optimization is to find the assignment between the vector representation and the predefined targets. The first optimization uses stochastic gradient descent. The latter optimization uses a stochastic Hungarian algorithm.

Several representation learning models in remote sensing are built upon word embedding models such as Word2vec [18] and GLoVE [21]. The model works by partitioning the geospatial data into smaller pieces. The model then extracts the representation of each piece. The pieces which are the neighbor of a particular piece will have similar representations. One of the models is Tile2vec which partitions the National Agriculture Imagery Program (NAIP) data into triplets of tiles [14]. Each triplet consists of three tiles: anchor tile, neighbor tile, and distant tile. Tile2vec aims to pull the anchor representation close to the neighbor representation and pull the anchor representation away from the distant representation. The model uses the metric loss to meet the requirement. There are also similar works with a slight difference [7,8,28].

3   Proposed Method

We first recall the Tile2vec model. The model extracts the representation at the atomic level by partitioning geospatial images into tiles [14]. We then compose the tiles as a triplet matrix $(\boldsymbol{T}_a, \boldsymbol{T}_n, \boldsymbol{T}_d)$. $\boldsymbol{T}_a, \boldsymbol{T}_n, \boldsymbol{T}_d$ denote anchor, neighbor, ans distant tiles, respectively. Let $(\boldsymbol{T}_a^{(i)}, \boldsymbol{T}_n^{(i)}, \boldsymbol{T}_d^{(i)})$, $i \in \{1, ..., n\}$ be a triplet at index-i^{th}. The tile $\boldsymbol{T}_n^{(i)}$ lies around the region of $\boldsymbol{T}_a^{(i)}$. Oppositely, The tile $\boldsymbol{T}_d^{(i)}$ lies outside the region of $\boldsymbol{T}_a^{(i)}$. $\boldsymbol{T}_d^{(i)}$ can also come from different geospatial images. Figure 1 shows the illustration of triplet of tiles in Tile2vec model.

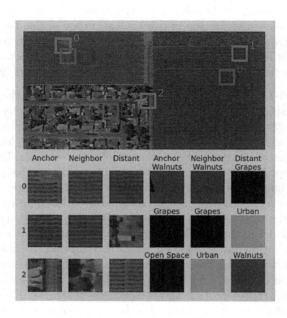

Fig. 1. The Illustration of triplet of tiles in Tile2vec model. Neighbor tile lies around the anchor tile while the distant tile lies away from the anchor tile [14].

The model aims to extract similar representations between $\boldsymbol{T}_a^{(i)}$ and $\boldsymbol{T}_n^{(i)}$ and extract contrast representations between $\boldsymbol{T}_a^{(i)}$ and $\boldsymbol{T}_d^{(i)}$. For n triplets, Tile2vec minimizes the triplet loss:

$$\min_\theta \frac{1}{n} \sum_{i=1}^{n} L(\boldsymbol{T}_a^{(i)}, \boldsymbol{T}_n^{(i)}, \boldsymbol{T}_d^{(i)}) + \lambda \left(\|\boldsymbol{Z}_a^{(i)}\|_2 + \|\boldsymbol{Z}_n^{(i)}\|_2 + \|\boldsymbol{Z}_d^{(i)}\|_2 \right) \quad (1)$$

where

$$L(\boldsymbol{T}_a^{(i)}, \boldsymbol{T}_n^{(i)}, \boldsymbol{T}_d^{(i)}) = [\|f_\theta(\boldsymbol{T}_a^{(i)}) - f_\theta(\boldsymbol{T}_n^{(i)})\|_2 - \|f_\theta(\boldsymbol{T}_a^{(i)}) - f_\theta(\boldsymbol{T}_d^{(i)})\|_2 + m]_+ \quad (2)$$

with $\boldsymbol{Z}_a^{(i)}, \boldsymbol{Z}_n^{(i)}, \boldsymbol{Z}_d^{(i)} = f_\theta(\boldsymbol{T}_a^{(i)}), f_\theta(\boldsymbol{T}_n^{(i)}), f_\theta(\boldsymbol{T}_d^{(i)}) \in \mathbb{R}^d$ and $m > 0$. f_θ denotes an encoder parameterized by θ. Note that in the criterion above, the rectifier function helps to restrict the distant between $\boldsymbol{T}_a$ and $\boldsymbol{T}_d$. The $l2$-norm constraint the triplet loss not collapsing towards zero.

3.1   Model

Recall that [3] uses predefined target U, which is matched with the data representation. The matching is achieved by minimizing $l2$-distance between data representation $g_\omega(X)$ and predefined target U with respect to ω and U:

$$\min_\omega \quad \min_U \frac{1}{s} \sum_{i=1}^{s} \|g_\omega(X)^{(i)} - U^{(i)}\|_2 \tag{3}$$

with s denotes the number of data X. Unfortunately, we cannot directly optimize the function since it will lead to feature collapse [3]. Instead, we decompose U into $U = M Q$, with $M = \{0, 1\}^{(3s \times k)}$ such that $M\, 1_k \leq 1_s$ and $M^T\, 1_s = 1_k$. We can choose Q as elements of the canonical basis of $\mathbb{R}^d$ or samples from $l2$-sphere [3]. Suppose we choose to sample from standard $l2-$sphere distribution. Then, we have $Q^{(i)} = V^{(i)} \oslash \|V\|$ where $V = \{v \sim \mathcal{N}(0, 1)\}^{s \times d}$. We then rewrite the optimization problem as:

$$\max_\omega \quad \max_P \operatorname{Tr}(M Q g_\omega(X)^T) \tag{4}$$

with Tr is a matrix trace operation.

Tile2vec with Predicting Noise. We replace the $l2$-norm regularization by using the NAT loss function. Let $Y = PC$ be the predefined targets with $P = \{0, 1\}^{(3n \times 3n)}$ such that $P\, 1_{3n} \leq 1_{3n}$ and $P^T\, 1_{3n} = 1_{3n}$. We also have $O^{(i)} = O^{(i)} \oslash \|O\|$ where $O = \{o \sim \mathcal{N}(0, 1)\}^{3n \times d}$. By replacing the second term of Objective 1 with Objective 3, we get:

$$\min_\theta \min_Y \frac{1}{n} \sum_{i=1}^{n} L(t_a^{(i)}, t_n^{(i)}, t_d^{(i)}) + \frac{1}{3n} \sum_{i=1}^{3n} \|Z^{(i)} - Y^{(i)}\|_2 \tag{5}$$

with $Z = \operatorname{concat}((Z_a, Z_n, Z_d), axis = 0)$. Note that we get Z by stack Z_a, Z_n, and Z_d horizontally. We set P to be $3n \times 3n$ and O to be $3n \times d$ since each triplet consists of 3 tiles. Convince that the purpose of the model is the same with Tile2vec. Next, we elaborate on the training steps of the proposed algorithm since Objective 5 is not complete yet, due to the decomposition of Y.

3.2   Training Algorithm

We propose an algorithm to train Tile2vec with predicting noise. Recall in Objective 5, we have $Y = PC$. Note that matrix P acts as the index which pointing the assignment between each element of Z into each element of Y. We want a configuration of P such that the second term of Objective 5 is minimum.

Therefore, we have two optimization problems. The first optimization is the triplet loss to θ. The second optimization is to choose P^* such that the second term is minimum. The first optimization is trivial by using stochastic gradient descent. We optimize the latter optimization problem by applying the same method as [3], by using a stochastic Hungarian algorithm (since we work with mini-batch). The algorithm performs an ordinary Hungarian algorithm for each mini-batch b. Suppose mini-batch b consists of E data. Stochastic Hungarian algorithm then optimizes the $E \times E$ sub-matrix of P. We obtain the sub-matrix by restricting the K data on the mini-batch and their corresponding targets. This algorithm is computationally more efficient but less accurate than the Hungarian algorithm [3].

We offer two approaches to train Tile2vec with predicting noise. The first approach is to assign all of T_a, T_n, T_d into predefined targets. Suppose that we have K triplets in one mini-batch. Thus, we have $3K$ of predefined targets since each triplet consists of 3 tiles. We call this approach Tile2vec with non-sampling noise. Another approach is to choose one of three tiles (anchor or neighbor or distant) from each triplet in a mini-batch. Given K triplets in one mini-batch, we have K predefined targets. We call the latter approach as Tile2vec with sampling noise. Sampling technique reduces the computation time linearly. Figure 2 shows the illustration of both approaches.

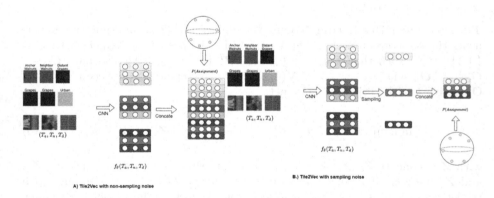

Fig. 2. a.) Illustration of Tile2vec with non-sampling noise. We assign all three representations of each triplet into predefined targets. **b.)** Illustration of Tile2vec with sampling noise. We only assign one of the tiles from each triplet into predefined targets. The color contrast shows the similarity level of the representations.

To wrap up the prior concepts, we propose an algorithm to train Tile2vec with predicting noise. Algorithm 1 shows the algorithm to train Tile2vec with predicting noise.

Algorithm 1: Stochastic Optimization for Tile2Vec with predicting noise.

Require: T batch of images; $\alpha > 0$;

for $t = 1, 2, ..., T$ **do**

> obtain batch b and representation target $Y^{(b)}$;
>
> compute $\boldsymbol{Z}_a^{(b)} = f_\theta((\boldsymbol{T}_a)^{(b)})$;
>
> compute $\boldsymbol{Z}_n^{(b)} = f_\theta((\boldsymbol{T}_n)^{(b)})$;
>
> compute $\boldsymbol{Z}_d^{(b)} = f_\theta((\boldsymbol{T}_d)^{(b)})$;
>
> compute metric loss $L(\boldsymbol{Z}_a^{(b)}, \boldsymbol{Z}_n^{(b)}, \boldsymbol{Z}_d^{(b)})$;
>
> horizontal-concat-z $\leftarrow$ concatenate$((\boldsymbol{Z}_a^{(b)}, \boldsymbol{Z}_n^{(b)}, \boldsymbol{Z}_d^{(b)}), axis = 0)$;
>
> vertical-concat-z $\leftarrow$ concatenate$((\boldsymbol{Z}_a^{(b)}, \boldsymbol{Z}_n^{(b)}, \boldsymbol{Z}_d^{(b)}), axis = 1)$;
>
> **if** *sampling* **then**
>
> > $\boldsymbol{Z}^{(b)} = $ [sampling one from $\boldsymbol{Z}_{a-i}^{(b)}$ or $\boldsymbol{Z}_{n-i}^{(b)}$ or $\boldsymbol{Z}_{d-i}^{(b)}$ for each tuple $(\boldsymbol{Z}_{a-i}^{(b)}, \boldsymbol{Z}_{n-i}^{(b)}, \boldsymbol{Z}_{d-i}^{(b)})$ in vertical-concat-z] ;
>
> **end**
>
> **else**
>
> > $\boldsymbol{Z}^{(b)} = $ horizontal-concat-z ;
>
> **end**
>
> compute noise loss $NL = \frac{1}{n}\|\boldsymbol{Z}^{(b)} - \boldsymbol{Y}^{(b)}\|_2$;
>
> compute $\boldsymbol{P}^*$ by minimizing NL w.r.t $\boldsymbol{P}$;
>
> compute $\nabla_\theta(NL + L(\boldsymbol{Z}_a^{(b)}, \boldsymbol{Z}_n^{(b)}, \boldsymbol{Z}_d^{(b)}))$ with $\boldsymbol{P}^*$;
>
> update $\boldsymbol{\theta} \leftarrow \boldsymbol{\theta} - \alpha\nabla_\theta(NL + L(\boldsymbol{Z}_a^{(b)}, \boldsymbol{Z}_n^{(b)}, \boldsymbol{Z}_d^{(b)}))$;

end

Here, we slightly abuse the indexing notation. The upper-script index shows the batch index and the sub-script index shows the index of the data on a particular mini-batch.

3.3   Implementation Details

We implement Tile2vec with predicting noise by using convolutional neural network. All of the details are described below.

Features. We train the tile2vec with predicting noise on unlabeled geospatial images. Subsequently, we apply the trained model as a feature extractor for the land cover classification task. The output of the encoder is set as the input for the classification task.

Architecture. We use the same architecture as Tile2vec [14]. We call the network the encoder. The encoder adopts Resnet-18 architecture [12] with slight differences. We do not use additional multi-perceptron layers on top of the encoder. Instead, we flatten the features from the last layer of the encoder network. The encoder uses the same parameters to encode anchor, neighbor, and distant tiles (sometimes we call it siamese network). The details can be found in Appendix A.

Optimization. We optimize the encoder with stochastic gradient descent. Later, we use Adam as the optimizer. We set 15 triplets per mini-batch and train the models for 50 epochs. All of the hyperparameters follow the Tile2vec's settings [14]. For the optimization of assignment P, we update it for every three epochs, following [3].

4   Experiments

We evaluate the Tile2vec with predicting noise on land cover classification task after training the model. Furthermore, we analyze the performance of the model.

4.1   Dataset

We use the modified USDA **National Agriculture Imagery Program** (NAIP) dataset to train the Tile2vec with predicting noise. The dataset was obtained from the Tile2vec repository [6]. It consists of 100000 triplets of aerial imagery tiles with four spectral bands: red (R), green (G), blue (B), and infrared (N) [14]. Each tile sized 50×50 pixels.

For the land cover classification task, we use the modified **Cropland Data Layer** (CDL). This dataset is a raster geo-referenced land cover map collected by USDA for the USA's continental [14]. We obtain the data from the Tile2vec repository as well [6]. The dataset consists of 1000 images sized 50×50 pixels. In total, the dataset has 28 labels. We use 800 of data to train the classifiers and 200 of data to evaluate them.

4.2   Land Cover Classification

We use Tile2vec with predicting noise as a feature extractor for several classifiers, including linear regression, random forest, and multi-layer-perceptrons (MLP). After finish the training, we freeze the parameters of the model. Later, the model extracts the representation for each instance of the CDL dataset. The classifiers use those representations for training and evaluation. We also compare the model with Tile2vec, autoencoder, PCA, ICA, and K-Means. Table 1 provides the average of classification accuracies for each representation model. The averages are obtained after running ten consecutive predictions.

The result shows that both approaches of Tile2vec with predicting noise outperform other models on each classifier. On the other hand, K-Means achieve the lowest performance on linear regression and random forest. Tile2vec with non-sampling noise surpasses Tile2vec with sampling noise on each classifier. Even so, Tile2vec with sampling noise has a shorter training time.

4.3   Representation Space

We also analyze the representation embedding to investigate the Tile2vec with predicting noise. First we visualize the representation of 1000 CDL dataset. We apply t-SNE [9] to visualize them. Figure 3 provides the visualization.

Table 1. The comparison of Tile2vec with predicting noise with other representation models. We compare each model on land cover classification task with various classifiers.

Model	Linear regression	Random forest	MLP
Tile2Vec with non-sampling noise	**0.6960 ± 0.0301**	**0.7120 ± 0.0407**	**0.696 ± 0.0241**
Tile2Vec with sampling noise	0.6930 ± 0.0326	0.7080 ± 0.0222	0.6735 ± 0.0261
Tile2Vec	0.6705 ± 0.02603	0.7045 ± 0.0292	0.661 ± 0.0223
Autoencoder	0.5380 ± 0.0323	0.6550 ± 0.0247	0.6345 ± 0.0131
PCA	0.5730 ± 0.0329	0.6160 ± 0.0273	0.5845 ± 0.0289
ICA	0.5685 ± 0.0287	0.6380 ± 0.0436	0.5725 ± 0.0393
K-Means	0.5785 ± 0.0293	0.5925 ± 0.0343	0.6045 ± 0.0246

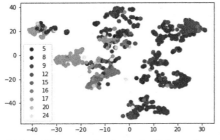
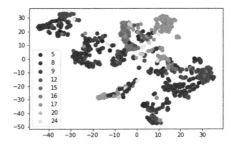

A.) Embedding space visualization by Tile2vec with non-sampling noise

B.) Embedding space visualization by Tile2vec with sampling noise

Fig. 3. Left: t-SNE of CDL dataset representation by Tile2vec with non-sampling noise. Right: t-SNE of CDL dataset representation by Tile2vec with sampling noise.

We observe that most of the representations on both models are clustered based on their class. Furthermore, Tile2vec with sampling noise produces a sparser t-SNE between classes. We infer that the sparsity of the sampling approach gives less certainty about the class of the data.

Furthermore, we also investigate how well the Tile2vec with predicting noise can capture the similarity. First, we sample 1000 NAIP instances. Then, we take 5 of them. For each selected tile, we pick the top 5 tiles which have the most similar representation. We compute the euclidean distance between two representations to measure the similarity. Figure 4 provides five samples of tiles and their neighborhood.

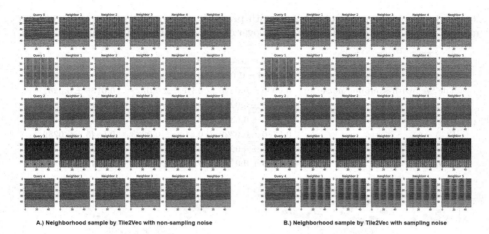

A.) Neighborhood sample by Tile2Vec with non-sampling noise   B.) Neighborhood sample by Tile2Vec with sampling noise

Fig. 4. Left: neighbors of 5 sampled tiles on Tile2vec with non-sampling noise. Right: neighbors of 5 sampled tiles on Tile2vec with sampling noise. The most left tile on each row is the sampled tile, and the rest of the row is the neighbors.

It can be observed that for each sampled tile, the neighbors have a very similar texture. Therefore, we infer that Tile2vec with predicting noise can encode the neighborhood factor on its produced representation.

5   Conclusion

This paper presents the improvement of Tile2vec. Tile2vec has proven to be a good representation model for remote sensing data. The success of Tile2vec depends on the $l2$-norm regularization. However, $l2$-norm has a less impactful regularization due to its nature. To improve the regularization, we propose to replace the $l2$-norm regularization with predicting noise framework. We assign the tiles representation into predefined targets, which are sampled from the $l2$-sphere. The regularization constrains the tile's representation to follow the $l2$-sphere. Later, the model is called Tile2vec with predicting noise. We also propose an algorithm to train the proposed model by introducing the method, sampling-based and non-sampling-based. The proposed model is built upon the deep learning framework. We then evaluate the model on the land cover classification task. The result shows that both Tile2vec with non-sampling noise and Tile2vec with sampling-noise outperform other representation models. Finally, we infer that Tile2vec with predicting noise encodes the neighborhood factor into the produced representation. These results can give the direction of the utilization of Tile2vec with predicting noise in many more remote sensing applications in the future.

A Model's Architecture

The model adopts Resnet18 architecture with slight differences. Each row describes a residual block with particular kernels except the first row. All blocks set padding as 1.

Encoder	Note
Conv(kernels=64, size=3, stride=1), B-Norm, ReLU	1 Block
Conv(kernels=64, size=3, stride=1), B-Norm, ReLU Conv(kernels=64, size=3, stride=1), B-Norm, ReLU	2 Blocks
Conv(kernels=128, size=3, stride=2), B-Norm, ReLU Conv(kernels=128, size=3, stride=1), B-Norm, ReLU	2 Blocks
Conv(kernels=256, size=3, stride=2), B-Norm, ReLU Conv(kernels=256, size=3, stride=1), B-Norm, ReLU	2 Blocks
Conv(kernels=512, size=3, stride=2), B-Norm, ReLU Conv(kernels=512, size=3, stride=1), Batch Norm, ReLU	2 Blocks
Conv(kernels=z, size=3, stride=2), Batch Norm, ReLU Conv(kernels=z, size=3, stride=1), Batch Norm, ReLU	2 Blocks

B Hyperparameters

Parameter	Value
Learning rate	0.02
α	1.0
Representation dimension	512
m	0.1

References

1. Arjovsky, M., Bottou, L.: Towards principled methods for training generative adversarial networks. arXiv preprint arXiv:1701.04862 (2017)
2. Arjovsky, M., Chintala, S., Bottou, L.: Wasserstein generative adversarial networks. In: International Conference on Machine Learning, pp. 214–223. PMLR, July 2017
3. Bojanowski, P., Joulin, A.: Unsupervised learning by predicting noise. In: International Conference on Machine Learning, pp. 517–526. PMLR, July 2017

4. Chen, T., Kornblith, S., Norouzi, M., Hinton, G.: A simple framework for contrastive learning of visual representations. In: International Conference on Machine Learning, pp. 1597–1607. PMLR, November 2020

5. Doersch, C., Gupta, A., Efros, A.A.: Unsupervised visual representation learning by context prediction. In: Proceedings of the IEEE international Conference on Computer Vision, pp. 1422–1430 (2015)

6. Ermon: tile2vec. https://github.com/ermongroup/tile2vec (2019). Accessed 24 June 2021

7. Fried, O., Avidan, S., Cohen-Or, D.: Patch2vec: globally consistent image patch representation. In: Computer Graphics Forum, vol. 36, no. 7, pp. 183–194, October 2017

8. Gao, S., Yan, B.: Place2vec: visualizing and reasoning about place type similarity and relatedness by learning context embeddings. In: Adjunct Proceedings of the 14th International Conference on Location Based Services, pp. 225–226. ETH Zurich, January 2018

9. Goodfellow, I., Bengio, Y., Courville, A., Bengio, Y.: Deep Learning, vol. 1, no. 2. MIT Press, Cambridge (2016)

10. Goodfellow, I.J., et al.: Generative adversarial networks. arXiv preprint arXiv:1406.2661 (2014)

11. Grill, J.B., et al.: Bootstrap your own latent: a new approach to self-supervised learning. arXiv preprint arXiv:2006.07733 (2020)

12. He, K., Zhang, X., Ren, S., Sun, J.: Deep residual learning for image recognition. In: Proceedings of the IEEE Conference on Computer Vision and Pattern Recognition, pp. 770–778 (2016)

13. Helber, P., Bischke, B., Dengel, A., Borth, D.: Eurosat: a novel dataset and deep learning benchmark for land use and land cover classification. IEEE J. Sel. Top. Appl. Earth Obs. Remote Sens. **12**(7), 2217–2226 (2019)

14. Jean, N., Wang, S., Samar, A., Azzari, G., Lobell, D., Ermon, S.: Tile2vec: unsupervised representation learning for spatially distributed data. In: Proceedings of the AAAI Conference on Artificial Intelligence, vol. 33, no. 01, pp. 3967–3974, July 2019

15. Kingma, D.P., Welling, M.: Auto-encoding variational bayes. arXiv preprint arXiv:1312.6114 (2013)

16. Lin, D., Fu, K., Wang, Y., Xu, G., Sun, X.: MARTA GANs: unsupervised representation learning for remote sensing image classification. IEEE Geosci. Remote Sens. Lett. **14**(11), 2092–2096 (2017)

17. Lu, X., Zheng, X., Yuan, Y.: Remote sensing scene classification by unsupervised representation learning. IEEE Trans. Geosci. Remote Sens. **55**(9), 5148–5157 (2017)

18. Mikolov, T., Chen, K., Corrado, G., Dean, J.: Efficient estimation of word representations in vector space. arXiv preprint arXiv:1301.3781 (2013)

19. Noroozi, M., Favaro, P.: Unsupervised learning of visual representations by solving jigsaw puzzles. In: Leibe, B., Matas, J., Sebe, N., Welling, M. (eds.) ECCV 2016. LNCS, vol. 9910, pp. 69–84. Springer, Cham (2016). https://doi.org/10.1007/978-3-319-46466-4_5

20. Parr, T.: 3 The difference between L1 and L2 regularization. https://explained.ai/regularization/L1vsL2.html#sec:3.2. Accessed 22 June 2021

21. Pennington, J., Socher, R., Manning, C.D.: Glove: global vectors for word representation. In: Proceedings of the 2014 Conference on Empirical Methods in Natural Language Processing (EMNLP), pp. 1532–1543, October 2014

22. Qi, G.J., Zhang, L., Chen, C.W., Tian, Q.: AVT: unsupervised learning of transformation equivariant representations by autoencoding variational transformations. In: Proceedings of the IEEE/CVF International Conference on Computer Vision, pp. 8130–8139 (2019)

23. Radford, A., Metz, L., Chintala, S.: Unsupervised representation learning with deep convolutional generative adversarial networks. arXiv preprint arXiv:1511.06434 (2015)

24. Rubner, Y., Tomasi, C., Guibas, L.J.: A metric for distributions with applications to image databases. In: Sixth International Conference on Computer Vision (IEEE Cat. No. 98CH36271), pp. 59–66. IEEE, January 1998

25. Vali, A., Comai, S., Matteucci, M.: Deep learning for land use and land cover classification based on hyperspectral and multispectral earth observation data: a review. Remote Sens. **12**(15), 2495 (2020)

26. Varghese, A., Gubbi, J., Ramaswamy, A., Balamuralidhar, P.: ChangeNet: a deep learning architecture for visual change detection. In Proceedings of the European Conference on Computer Vision (ECCV) Workshops, pp. 0–0 (2018)

27. Vincent, P., Larochelle, H., Bengio, Y., Manzagol, P.A.: Extracting and composing robust features with denoising autoencoders. In: Proceedings of the 25th International Conference on Machine Learning, pp. 1096–1103, July 2008

28. Wang, Z., Li, H., Rajagopal, R.: Urban2Vec: incorporating street view imagery and pois for multi-modal urban neighborhood embedding. In: Proceedings of the AAAI Conference on Artificial Intelligence, vol. 34, no. 01, pp. 1013–1020, April 2020

29. Zhang, L., Qi, G.J., Wang, L., Luo, J.: Aet vs. aed: unsupervised representation learning by auto-encoding transformations rather than data. In: Proceedings of the IEEE/CVF Conference on Computer Vision and Pattern Recognition, pp. 2547–2555 (2019)

A Joint Representation Learning Approach for Social Media Tag Recommendation

Xiangyu Li[1(✉)] and Weizheng Chen[2(✉)]

[1] School of Software Engineering, Beijing Jiaotong University, Beijing, China
lixiangyu@bjtu.edu.cn
[2] Beijing, China

Abstract. In this paper, we analyze the mutual relationship between social media text and tags and explore how to integrate sematic information for tag recommendation. Our key motivation is to jointly map all words, tags and posts to vectors in a same hidden semantic space by modeling the syntagmatic and paradigmatic information simultaneously. We propose two novel distributed representation learning models for tagged documents: Tag Representation Learning (TRL) and Tag and Word Representation Learning (TWRL). The first models the immediate relationship between tags and words. The second one adds a skip-gram output layer to the first model, in order to enhance the semantic relationship among words. Extensive experiments are conducted on large scale datasets crawled from Twitter and Sina Weibo. By simulating two typical recommendation tasks, we discover that both models mentioned above outperform other competitive baselines remarkably.

Keywords: Representation learning · Tag recommendation · Social media

1 Introduction

The fact that social media has been developing rapidly provides people with lots of chance and challenge on many research fields, such as advertisement [1], human behavior [2], etc. As a component of social media, tag, aka hashtag, is a kind of meta data which assists users in finding specific topics. Users can label each of their posts with tags to represent the post's topic, so that they can be discovered by other users easily. Moreover, quite a few researches have taken tags into consideration to improve the performance of various systems, such as sentiment analysis [3], entity recognition [21], etc.

Although tags play important roles in social media, most posts are not labeled with any tag [7]. Thus, researches have been conducted on recommending tags for social media text in two typical application scenarios:

– **Tag Prediction** [10]: Predict tags for a future post when it is ready to be published by the user. In this case, the recommendation system can help enhance users' experience by helping them publish labeled posts.

W.Chen—Independent Researcher.

© Springer Nature Switzerland AG 2021
T. Mantoro et al. (Eds.): ICONIP 2021, LNCS 13111, pp. 100–112, 2021.
https://doi.org/10.1007/978-3-030-92273-3_9

- **Tag Annotation** [15]: Annotate tags for those unlabeled posts in social media, in order to provide more high-quality labeled data for other related researches on social media.

Most traditional and representative related works are based on topic models or statistical machine translation (SMT). However, topic models build ties among words and tags by only utilizing document-level syntagmatic relations at high abstract level of topics, which usually leads to common but not precise tags in recommendation. Similarly, SMT methods consider the co-occurrences among words and tags, which could not model accurate semantic relations. It still remains to be a difficult problem for three reasons. First, noisiness, the randomness of human behavior brings big noise to posts and tags in social media [4], which makes them hard to understand without adequate background knowledge. Second, shortness, most posts in social media are so short that features among them are not easy to be captured. Third, data in social media is large in volume. It's a challenge to make full use of those data rapidly.

During the past few years, distributed representation learning has made great progress in natural language processing, due to its efficiency, robustness and scalability. As a fundamental model for untagged texts, Word2Vec [17] has been adopted in content-based recommendation task [8], which shows promising performance. But its performance is limited by only using the paradigmatic information in a local sliding window [20] whose size is usually set to 5. In practice, a user can put the tags at any positions of a post. As shown in Table 1, we show a real tweet which has two tags at the end of the post.

Table 1. Example of a typical tweet with two tags.

Just had a great meal and tasted my first Lebanese wine. #food #wine
contexts of #food in Word2Vec when the window size is 5

If we treat the words and the tags equally and feed this post to Word2Vec, the meaning of a tag will be determined by its surrounding words in the local window. However, this goes against the fact that the tags are depend on the full text of the post. In this case, the words "meal", "great", "had" all have some relationships with the tag "#food" which is not captured in Word2Vec. Note that it is not reasonable to increase the size of the window to a larger value since many unrelated word pairs will reduce the quality of the word vectors significantly. To model such syntagmatic information, our first assumption is that **the context of a tag is all the words in its corresponding post**.

We also find that the tags appears in the same post have related semantics, such as "#food" and "#wine". Thus for simplicity of modeling, our second assumption is that **the tags in a same post contribute equally to the generative process of the words**.

Based on the aforementioned intuitions, we argue that the semantic relationships among words, tags and posts can be modeled to enhance tag recommendation for social media text. Our motivation lies in representing any semantic entity as a distributed vector, and the distance between those vectors indicates the semantic closeness between what they represent. We first present a neural network model, TRL, which uses the averaged tag vectors to predict all the word context vectors in a post. Furthermore, by modeling the syntagmatic and paradigmatic [13] information simultaneously, we propose TWRL, which can project the tags and the words into a same semantic space. Finally, the post vectors can be inferred after the model is trained. For each unlabeled post, we recommend tags whose vectors are nearest to the post's distributed vector.

In summary, our major contributions are as follows:

1. We present two new representation learning models for tagged text, which can map all words, tags and posts to vectors in a same hidden sematic space.
2. Experiments are conducted on two famous social media datasets, Twitter and Sina Weibo, respectively. We discover that our models outperform baselines significantly.

2   Related Work

There have been quite a few researches on tag recommendation for social media text.

- **Topic Model** [5] can be used to discover abstract topics within corpus. Intuitively, tag is a kind of description on its post's topic, so it seems that there is a clear relationship between topic and tag. Several researches [12,15,19] have tried to make use of topic model in social media tag recommendation. Most of them evaluate each tag given post by $\Pr(tag|post) = \sum_{topic} \Pr(tag|topic) \Pr(topic|post)$. Despite the correspondence between the concepts of topic and tag, topic model is not convincing enough, due to its awkwardness on short text training. Moreover, the complexity of this model grows rapidly as the number of topics increases, so that it's not suitable for large number of topics.
- **Statistical Machine Translation (SMT)** [11] takes posts as a language, while tags as another language. IBM Model 1 is the most popular SMT model, which focuses on translating from posts to tags word by word. Quite a few tag recommendation researches [6,9,14] have been conducted based on this model. Many such models evaluate each tag given post by $\Pr(tag|post) = \sum_{word} \Pr(tag|word) \Pr(word|post)$. Most of them have achieved better performance than previous works. Nevertheless, we believe that the loss of semantic information between words limits the improvement of SMT.

3   Our Approaches

In this section, we propose two models based on neural network, which learn distributed representation for each tag. We first introduce notions briefly. Assuming a tagged text corpus D which consists of $|D|$ documents, we use V and H

to represent the word vocabulary and tag vocabulary respectively. Each tag t_i ($1 \leq i \leq |H|$) is associated with an input vector $\mathbf{v_i}$. Each word w_i ($1 \leq i \leq |V|$) is associated with an input vector $\mathbf{u_i}$ and a context vector $\mathbf{u_i}'$.

3.1 TRL Model

According to the document-level relationship between tags and words, we first propose TRL model. Given that a post d_k is made up of n_k words, $w_1^k, w_1^k, \ldots, w_{n_k}^k$, and labeled with m_k tags, $t_1^k, t_2^k, \ldots, t_{m_k}^k$, TRL model takes its tags as the input of a 3-layer neural network, and its words as the output.

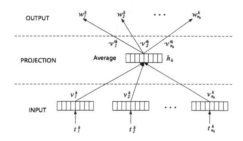

Fig. 1. TRL model

As shown in Fig. 1, TRL model contains the following 3 layers:

- **INPUT**: Each tag, t_i^k is represented as a vector $\mathbf{v}_i^k \in \mathbb{R}^L$ by looking up the tag vector table.
- **PROJECTION**: According to the assumption that the tags contributes equally to the generation of each word, the average of input tag vectors is taken as the hidden layer vector $\mathbf{h}_k$:

$$\mathbf{h_k} = \frac{1}{m} \sum_{i=1}^{m} \mathbf{v_i^k}. \tag{1}$$

- **OUTPUT**: Finally, the probability of each word's occurrence is predicted with $\mathbf{h}_k$ by softmax as follow:

$$p\left(w_i^k \mid \mathbf{h}_k\right) = \frac{\exp\left(\mathbf{u}_i'^k \cdot \mathbf{h}_k\right)}{\sum_{j=1}^{|V|} \exp\left(\mathbf{u}_j' \cdot \mathbf{h}_k\right)}. \tag{2}$$

In TRL model, the log likelihood of generating post d_k's words given tags is shown as follows:

$$\mathcal{L}_{TRL}(d_k)$$
$$= \log p\left(w_1^k, \cdots, w_{n_k}^k \mid t_1^k, \cdots, t_{m_k}^k\right)$$
$$= \sum_{w_i^k \in d_k} \log p\left(w_i^k \mid \mathbf{h}_k\right). \tag{3}$$

Thus the overall objective loss of TRL on D is defined as follow:

$$\mathcal{O}_{TRL}(D) = -\sum_{k=1}^{|D|} \mathcal{L}_{TRL}(d_k). \tag{4}$$

In order to train TRL model, we can minimize Eq. 4 by using stochastic gradient descent. TRL model is set up by considering the immediate relationship between tags and words in each post. It simulates human associates content when seeing tags.

3.2 TWRL Model

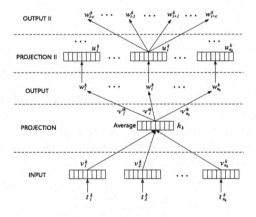

Fig. 2. TWRL model

There isn't immediate connection among words in TRL model, which means that most semantic relationships among words may be lost. Thus, we propose TRWL model to enhance the quality of tag vectors. As shown in Fig. 2, TWRL model contains 2 parts and 5 layers. The first part is exactly a 3-layer TRL model, while the second part is a Skip-gram model for each word. The second part contains following two layers:

- **PROJECTION II**: Each word w_i^k is projected as a input word vector $\mathbf{u_i^k} \in \mathbb{R}^L$ by looking up the input word vector table..

- **OUTPUT II**: Finally, the probability of each neighboring word w_j^k's occurrence near by w_i^k is estimated by softmax which is similar to Eq. 2 by replacing the appropriate variables.

The log likelihood of each word for skip-gram model is defined as follows:

$$
\begin{aligned}
\mathcal{L}_{sg}\left(w_i^k\right) \\
= \log p\left(w_{i-c}^k, \cdots, w_{i-1}^k, w_{i+1}^k, \cdots, w_{i+c}^k \mid w_i^k\right) \\
= \sum_{\substack{i-c \leq j \leq i+c \\ j \neq i}} \log p\left(w_j^k \mid w_i^k\right),
\end{aligned}
\tag{5}
$$

where c is the size of the sliding window. Finally, the whole log likelihood of a post d_k is as follows.

$$
\mathcal{L}_{TWRL}\left(d_k\right) = \mathcal{L}_{TRL}\left(d_k\right) + \sum_{w_i^k \in d_k} \mathcal{L}_{sg}\left(w_i^k\right).
\tag{6}
$$

In a similar way, the overall objective loss of TWRL on D is defined as follows:

$$
\mathcal{O}_{TWRL}\left(D\right) = -\sum_{k=1}^{|D|} \mathcal{L}_{TWRL}\left(d_k\right).
\tag{7}
$$

It is necessary to distinguish the difference between our TWRL model and the HDC model [20]. HDC is designed to learn document vectors and word vectors from the untagged texts. And TWRL learns tag vectors and word vectors from the more complicated tagged texts. But TWRL also can be applied to the untagged texts. For an untagged text corpus which consists of many documents, we can assume that each document has a unique tag whose vector equals the vector of the document. Therefore, HDC can be seen as a special case of TWRL.

3.3   Hierarchical Softmax

It is extremely time consuming to compute softmax functions defined in TRL and TWRL, because they need to iterate over the whole word vocabulary. In order to make the training process more efficient, we apply hierarchical softmax [16] to our models. We built a Huffman tree for words. Each leaf of the tree corresponds to a word. Thus, the probability of a word's occurrence is the probability of routing from root to the word's leaf on the Huffman tree. After applying hierarchical softmax, we decrease the time complexity of computing softmax function from $O\left(|V|\right)$ to $O\left(\log |V|\right)$.

3.4   Recommend Tags for an Unlabeled Post

After our models are trained, we can get each tag's distributed vector. Like Word2Vec, the distance between tag's vectors correspond to the semantic distance between tags.

We recommend tags for an unlabeled post by the following steps.

1. Set up a virtual tag and initialize its distributed vector randomly. This virtual tag vector is regarded as the post vector.
2. Fix all weights in model, and run the training process to update the virtual tag's vector.
3. Select top-K tags to recommend, which are nearest to the virtual tag in the measurement of cosine similarity.

4   Experiments

4.1   Datasets and Experiment Configurations

High-volume tagged posts are crawled for our experiments from 2 famous online social media, Twitter and Sina Weibo. In our dataset, each tweet(post) contains 13.2 words and 1.3 tags on average, while each weibo(post) contains 26 words and 1.1 tags on average.

In tag prediction task, the training data and the test data are in chronological order. For Twitter, posts published between Nov 16, 2009 and Nov 19, 2009 are used for training. And posts published on Nov 20, 2009 are used as test data. Tags whose frequency are less than 10 are removed. Finally, we get 367,684 posts for training and 64,352 posts for test. The vocabulary size of words and tags are 169,602 and 6,355 respectively. For Weibo, posts published on Sep 12, 2013 are used for training. And posts published on Sep 13, 2013 are used as test data. Finally, we get 242,015 posts for training and 239,739 posts for test. The vocabulary size of words and tags in Weibo are 254,018 and 3,038 respectively.

In tag annotation task, the training data and the test data used in tag prediction task are mixed first. Then we random sample 80% posts for training in Twitter and 50% posts for training in Weibo. The rest are used for test.

We adopt same parameter settings for TRL and TWRL. The size of all representation vectors $L = 300$, the number of iterations over all posts $I = 50$. The length c of the sliding window in TWRL is 5. $Precision@K$ and $Recall@K$ are used as evaluation metrics in following experiments.

4.2   Baseline Methods

- PMI [6]. An effective recommendation model which utilizes the mutual information to the estimate translation probabilities between words and tags. We use the code provided by [6].
- Word2vec [17]. A popular neural language model which learns distributed representations for words. Here, we treat tags and words equally and feed the original posts which contain words and tags to Word2Vec to learn word vectors and tags vectors simultaneously. For an unlabeled post, we use the average vector of all words occurs in it as document vector. Then we recommend top-K nearest tags. For Word2Vec, The number of iterations $I = 50$, the size of vectors $L = 300$, the length of the sliding window $c = 5$.

- TAGLDA [18]. A probabilistic topic model which models the generative process of words and tags in a document. We set the number of topics $K = 50$. The two hyperparameters $\alpha = \frac{50}{K}$, $\beta = 0.01$.
- NaiveBayes. We treat the tag recommendation task as a classification problem and use NaiveBayes algorithm as classifier.

4.3   Tag Recommendation

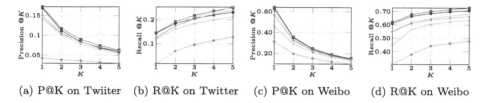

(a) P@K on Twiiter   (b) R@K on Twitter   (c) P@K on Weibo   (d) R@K on Weibo

Fig. 3. Precision, Recall in tag prediction task: TRL ➝, Word2Vec ➝, TWRL ➝, PMI ➝, TAGLDA ➝, NaiveBayes ➝

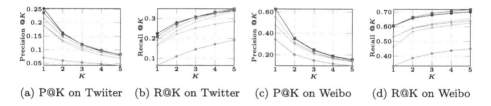

(a) P@K on Twiiter   (b) R@K on Twitter   (c) P@K on Weibo   (d) R@K on Weibo

Fig. 4. Precision, Recall in tag annotation task: TRL ➝, Word2Vec ➝, TWRL ➝, PMI ➝, TAGLDA ➝, NaiveBayes ➝

By ranging the number of recommended tags for one post from 1 to 5, the performances of different models in tag prediction task and tag annotation task are reported in Figs. 3 and 4. We have the following observations:

(1) TRL and TWRL consistently outperform all baseline methods in both two scenarios, which proves the superiority of the proposed methods. For tag prediction task, as shown in Fig. 3, compared with the most competitive PMI method, TWRL achieves nearly 6.6% improvement in the measure of Precision@1 and 7.4% improvement in the measure of Recall@1 on Weibo. In the case of Twitter, the improvement of TWRL over PMI is 3.2% and 3.3% respectively. For tag annotation task, the improvement of TWRL are very similar.

(2) TWRL performs better than TRL in most situations except in tag annotation task on Twitter. There are two reasons that account for this phenomenon. First, tags with high frequency in test data may occur very few
times in training data in tag prediction task, TWRL has stronger ability to
predict these tags than TRL by the benefit of modeling word co-occurrence
patterns. But in tag annotation task, TWRL loses this advantage because
the distribution of tags in training and test data are approximately equal.
Second, most tweets are very short, which further restricts the ability of
TWRL.
(3) Word2Vec only consider the co-occurrence of tags and words in a local window to learn tag representations. But a tag is indeed associated with the
full text of a post. Through modeling document-level co-occurrence of words
and tags, our models perform much better than Word2Vec.

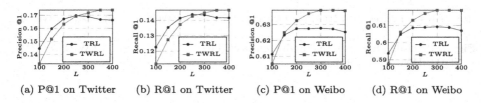

(a) P@1 on Twitter   (b) R@1 on Twitter   (c) P@1 on Weibo   (d) R@1 on Weibo

Fig. 5. Parameter sensitivity w.r.t dimension L

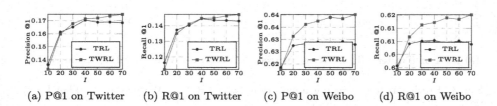

(a) P@1 on Twitter   (b) R@1 on Twitter   (c) P@1 on Weibo   (d) R@1 on Weibo

Fig. 6. Parameter sensitivity w.r.t iteration I

4.4   Parameter Sensitivity

We conduct parameter sensitivity analysis to explore the recommendation performance of TRL and TWRL w.r.t. the vector size L and the iteration number
I. Here, we take tag prediction task as example and report $P@1$ and $R@1$.

As shown in Fig. 5, TRL exceeds TWRL when L is not large enough. With
growing L, the performance of TWRL continues to increase and tends to be
stable finally. But TRL is less stable than TWRL when L is larger than 300,
which indicates that the tag vectors learned by TWRL are more informative.

As shown in Fig. 6, TRL has faster convergence than TWRL since TWRL
has more complicated structure and more parameters to learn. Nevertheless,
approximate optimal performance can be acquired by setting $I = 50$.

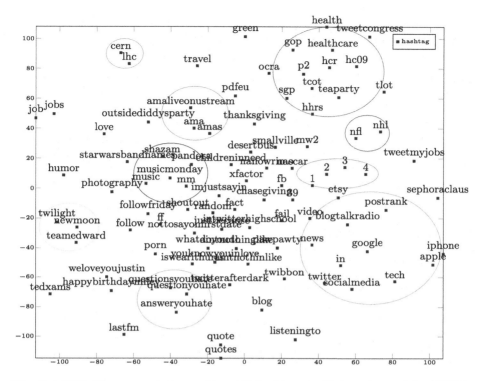

Fig. 7. t-SNE 2D representations of top-100 hashtags in Twitter learned by TWRL. We use colored ellipses to indicate hashtags related to a certain topic.

4.5   Case Study

To explore the semantic correlations among tag vectors, word vectors and document vectors learned or inferred in TWRL, we provide two case studies here.

Table 2. Top-5 most similar tags or words of "#healthcare" and "healthcare".

#healthcare		healthcare	
#hcr, #killbill, #tcot, #obamacare, #handsoff	hc, bill, Reid, Senate, Dems	#healthcare, #hcr, #tcot, #killbill, #obamacare	hc, health, reform, Senate, care

We find that "Health Care Reform in the United States" is a popular political topic on Twitter in 2009. Thus after selecting a representative tag "#healthcare" and a representative word "healthcare", we show their top-5 most similar tags and words in Table 2. We distinguish tags and words by "#" symbol. We can observe that the retrieved tags and words are highly related to the query.

In Table 3, top-3 recommended tags for two selected posts are listed. The recommended tags are highly related to the original posts. By encoding different entities into the same sematic space, we believe these vectors would be helpful to many text mining tasks, such as document retrieval.

Table 3. Top-3 recommended tags for selected posts. The groundtruth is emphasized in bold type.

Posts	Recommended tags
iPhone cleared for sale in South Korea	#iphone, **#apple**, #south
Do you think health care will pass this year?	#healthcare, #hcr, **#hcr09**

4.6   Tag Visualization

To visually display the sematic character of tag vectors, we create 2D representations of top-100 hashtags on Twitter by utilizing t-SNE package [22] as dimensionality reduction tool.

As shown in Fig. 7, we can find out many clusters made up of tags which have relevant semantics. For example, tags related to "Health Care Reform" are distributed in the red ellipse; tags related to the "music" topic are in the blue ellipse; tags related to social media and technology are in the green ellipse.

5   Conclusion

In this paper, we propose two novel models to learn distributed representations for tags, words and documents in the same semantic space for the tagged social media text. The key idea is to model the tag-word and the word-word co-occurrence relationships simultaneously. Experiments carried on two large scale real social media datasets demonstrate the superiority of our models over several competitive baselines in tag recommendation task.

Acknowledgments. This work is supported by Fundamental Research Funds for the Central Universities [2019RC045]. We thank the anonymous reviewers for their comments.

References

1. Zhao, X., Zheng, X., Yang, X., Liu, X., Tang, J.: Jointly learning to recommend and advertise. In: Proceedings of the 26th ACM SIGKDD International Conference on Knowledge Discovery & Data Mining, pp. 3319–3327 (2020)
2. Xu, S., Zhou, A.: Hashtag homophily in twitter network: examining a controversial cause-related marketing campaign. Comput. Hum. Behav. **102**, 87–96 (2020)
3. Singh, L.G., Anil, A., Singh, S.R.: She: sentiment hashtag embedding through multitask learning. IEEE Trans. Comput. Soc. Sys. **7**(2), 417–424 (2020)

4. Baldwin, T., Cook, P., Lui, M., MacKinlay, A., Wang, L.: How noisy social media text, how diffrnt social media sources? In: Proceedings of the Sixth International Joint Conference on Natural Language Processing, pp. 356–364 (2013)
5. Blei, D.M.: Probabilistic topic models. Commun. ACM **55**(4), 77–84 (2012)
6. Chen, X., Liu, Z., Sun, M.: Estimating translation probabilities for social tag suggestion. Expert Sys. Appl. **42**(4), 1950–1959 (2015)
7. Cunha, E., et al.: Analyzing the dynamic evolution of hashtags on twitter: a language-based approach. In: Proceedings of the Workshop on Languages in Social Media, pp. 58–65. Association for Computational Linguistics (2011)
8. Dey, K., Shrivastava, R., Kaushik, S., Subramaniam, L.V.: Emtagger: a word embedding based novel method for hashtag recommendation on twitter. In: 2017 IEEE International Conference on Data Mining Workshops (ICDMW), pp. 1025–1032. IEEE (2017)
9. Ding, Z., Qiu, X., Zhang, Q., Huang, X.: Learning topical translation model for microblog hashtag suggestion. In: Twenty-third International Joint Conference on Artificial Intelligence (2013)
10. Harvey, M., Crestani, F.: Long time, no tweets! time-aware personalised hashtag suggestion. In: Hanbury, A., Kazai, G., Rauber, A., Fuhr, N. (eds.) ECIR 2015. LNCS, vol. 9022, pp. 581–592. Springer, Cham (2015). https://doi.org/10.1007/978-3-319-16354-3_65
11. Koehn, P.: Statistical Machine Translation. Cambridge University Press, Cambridge (2009)
12. Kou, F.F., et al.: Hashtag recommendation based on multi-features of microblogs. J. Comput. Sci. Technol. **33**(4), 711–726 (2018)
13. Lapesa, G., Evert, S., Im Walde, S.S.: Contrasting syntagmatic and paradigmatic relations: insights from distributional semantic models. In: Proceedings of the Third Joint Conference on Lexical and Computational Semantics (* SEM 2014), pp. 160–170 (2014)
14. Liu, Z., Chen, X., Sun, M.: A simple word trigger method for social tag suggestion. In Proceedings of the Conference on Empirical Methods in Natural Language Processing, EMNLP 2011, Stroudsburg, PA, USA, pp. 1577–1588. Association for Computational Linguistics (2011)
15. Ma, Z., Sun, A., Yuan, Q., Cong, G.: Tagging your tweets: a probabilistic modeling of hashtag annotation in twitter. In: Proceedings of the 23rd ACM International Conference on Conference on Information and Knowledge Management, pp. 999–1008 (2014)
16. Mikolov, T., Deoras, A., Povey, D., Burget, L., Černocký, J.: Strategies for training large scale neural network language models. In: Automatic Speech Recognition and Understanding (ASRU), 2011 IEEE Workshop on, pp. 196–201. IEEE (2011)
17. Mikolov, T., Sutskever, I., Chen, K., Corrado, G.S., Dean, J.: Distributed representations of words and phrases and their compositionality. In: Advances in Neural Information Processing Systems 26: 27th Annual Conference on Neural Information Processing Systems 2013. Proceedings of a meeting held 5–8, December 2013, Lake Tahoe, Nevada, United States, pp. 3111–3119 (2013)
18. Ramage, D., Heymann, P., Manning, C.D., Garcia-Molina, H.: Clustering the tagged web. In: Proceedings of the Second ACM International Conference on Web Search and Data Mining, pp. 54–63. ACM (2009)
19. Si, X., Sun, M.: Tag-lda for scalable real-time tag recommendation. J. Comput. Inf. Sys. **6**(1), 23–31 (2009)

20. Sun, F., Guo, J., Lan, Y., Xu, J., Cheng, X.: Learning word representations by jointly modeling syntagmatic and paradigmatic relations. In: Proceedings of the Annual Meeting of the Association for Computational Linguistics (2015)
21. Tran, V.C., Hwang, D., Jung, J.J.: Semi-supervised approach based on co-occurrence coefficient for named entity recognition on twitter. In: Information and Computer Science (NICS), 2015 2nd National Foundation for Science and Technology Development Conference, pp. 141–146. IEEE (2015)
22. Van Der Maaten, L.: Accelerating t-sne using tree-based algorithms. J. Mach. Learn. Res. 15(1), 3221–3245 (2014)
23. Zangerle, E., Gassler, W., Specht, G.: Recommending#-tags in twitter. In: Proceedings of the Workshop on Semantic Adaptive Social Web (SASWeb 2011). CEUR Workshop Proceedings, vol. 730, pp. 67–78 (2011)

Identity-Based Data Augmentation via Progressive Sampling for One-Shot Person Re-identification

Runxuan Si, Shaowu Yang$^{(\boxtimes)}$, Jing Zhao, Haoang Chi, and Yuhua Tang

State Key Laboratory of High Performance Computing, College of Computer,
National University of Defense Technology, Changsha, China
shaowu.yang@nudt.edu.cn

Abstract. One-shot person re-identification (Re-ID) is a hot spot nowadays, where there is only one labeled image along with many unlabeled images for each identity. Due to the short of labeled training images, it's hard to catch up with performance under full supervision. In this paper, we propose a progressive method with identity-based data augmentation to improve lack of supervision information, which takes advantage of information of each identity to generate high-quality images. Specifically, with a certain image-to-image translation model, images are decoupled into content and style codes, where the images holding the features of identity well and injected in the style codes exclusive to the identity can be obtained by labeled images through the process of recombination. A progressive data augmentation method for one-shot labeled samples is also designed to optimize the sampling accuracy of pseudo labeled images, which contributes to our identity-based data augmentation process. The experimental results show that our method represents new state-of-the-art one-shot Re-ID work.

Keywords: Identity-based · GAN · Progressive · Re-ID · One-shot

1 Introduction

Person re-identification has become the hottest research fields due to its important status in the public safety field. As a cross-camera retrieval task, the Re-ID task tries to retrieve the same person for a query person from the dataset with different cameras and views. Recently, some methods [9] have led to impressive success in supervised domains. However, it is labor intensive to annotate all kinds of data. Therefore, some researchers start to study few-shot learning methods to take full advantage of labeled data.

Recently, the task of Re-ID focuses on model learning with data augmentation, semi-supervised learning [5] and so on. Specially, GAN is the most popular tool with the researchers for the data augmentation. For example, CamStyle Adaptation [15] learns image-to-image translation processes with CycleGAN [16]. Nevertheless, above unsupervised method introduces noise due to paying little attention to the identity information, which affects the performance of Re-ID.

© Springer Nature Switzerland AG 2021
T. Mantoro et al. (Eds.): ICONIP 2021, LNCS 13111, pp. 113–124, 2021.
https://doi.org/10.1007/978-3-030-92273-3_10

To provide a more cost-effective solution to real-world re-ID problems, where cross-camera annotation requires a lot of annotation work, one-shot Re-ID is proposed. The one-shot Re-ID task can be divided into video-based and image-based Re-ID. For video-based person re-identification, EUG [12] achieves significant progress via one labeled tracklet for each person with a progressive sampling strategy. During the progressive training process, unlabeled data in the dataset will be gradually assigned pseudo labels. However, when this method transfers to the image-based Re-ID task, where each identity owns only one labeled example, the performance shows a significant degradation. In this paper, we experiment with the one-shot image-based Re-ID setting, which lacks more annotated information compared with the video-based Re-ID methods. Although Progressive Pseudo Label Sampling (PPLS) [7] has made success for one-example Re-ID, image quality can be further improved considering the data augmentation with CycleGAN.

Inspired by the idea of supervised learning, we choose a GAN model which can make full use of the identity information of each labeled image to generate high-quality images for the Re-ID task. In this paper, we propose an identity-based data augmentation method for one-example Re-ID. Firstly, we choose Multimodal Unsupervised Image-to-image Translation (MUNIT) [6] which can decouple an image into content and style space to do data augmentation. Secondly, we use the progressive learning method to obtain pseudo-labeled samples that reach the optimal iteration, which can balance the number of samples and sampling accuracy. After each iteration, we generate fake images for one-shot labeled samples to build new identity centers for further training. Finally, we take the image with the same identity as a reference to generate a fake image for each picture in our labeled dataset and follow the progressive learning method to train our dataset after our identity-based data augmentation. We conduct our experiments on three large-scale datasets, demonstrating that we get better performance compared with state-of-the-art performance.

In summary, the main contributions of our proposed approach can be summarized as follows:

(1) We identify the efficiency of our identity-based data augmentation method, where content and style codes are decoupled from images and recombined to generate new images. In this way, features of the identity maintain well and styles from other samples are introduced in the generated images. So the basic generated picture quality holds when taking style from a different identity as reference. Our data augmentation mode can make full use of information of labeled samples to generate high-quality images.

(2) We propose a one-shot data augmentation mechanism for the progressive learning process. During the progressive training stage, we generate fake images for one-shot labeled samples and replace the one-shot image features with the feature centers for sample mining reference. The features of the one-shot images and corresponding fake images describe the characteristics of people better than only the one-shot images, which improves the accuracy of labeled samples mined. This mechanism paves the way for good performance

in the Re-ID task. Especially on Market-1501, the improvement can reach as large as 5.5% without modifying the structure of the model or attaching any auxiliary task.

2 Related Work

2.1 Generative Adversarial Networks

In recent years, Generative Adversarial Networks (GANs) has been applied in quite a lot of fields, such as style transfer, image generation, image-to-image translation and so on. Without having paired samples, CycleGAN [16] learns the joint distribution for image-to-image translation. Furthermore, StarGAN [1] learns the mapping between multiple domains with only one generator. Star-GANv2 [2] introduces latent codes and style codes to optimize generated images at the base of StarGAN. However, the new images from StarGANv2 may be disturbed by much noise because the background is not decoupled. To keep the identity characteristics well, MUNIT [6] is proposed to separate and recombine the content and style codes of images.

2.2 Deep Learning Methods in Re-ID

With the rapid development of the Convolutional Neural Network, pretty of methods based on deep learning methods make significant contributions to the Re-ID task on fully-supervised and semi-supervised domains. A lot of research for fully-supervised learning has made great performance and even has reached the application level. Pose-driven Deep Convolutional (PDC) [10] generates images from different views via the human position which makes full use of information from person key-points.

In the area of semi-supervised Re-ID, transfer learning becomes the mainstream. Li et al. [8] introduces a pre-trained tracking model as the auxiliary task to improve the effect of transfer learning. For a special domain of semi-supervised Re-ID, the one-example task, EUG [5] designs a progressive learning framework which exploits the unlabeled data gradually. PPLS [7] proposes a triplet loss specially for one-example Re-ID with a progressive learning method.

Even if large scale datasets are available, the overfitting problem still happens as a result of lacking enough training samples. Zhong et al. [15] designs a camera style transferred data augmentation method to get images with different camera styles. Via StarGAN, SP-StarGAN [3] achieves the camera style data augmentation with only one generator.

3 Methodologies

The overview of our framework is shown in Fig. 1. Algorithm 1 describes our method. We first briefly look back at the model of MUNIT in Sect. 3.1 and the PPLS method in Sect. 3.2 respectively. Then we introduce the module of mining labeled samples for data augmentation in Sect. 3.3. Finally, we describe the identity-based data augmentation method in Sect. 3.4.

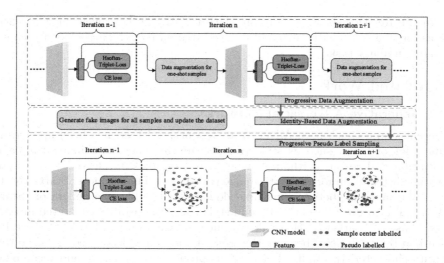

Fig. 1. Framework of our method. The process includes three steps. Firstly, generate fake images for one-shot samples via progressive sample mining. Secondly, use labeled samples for data augmentation. Lastly, train the CNN model with our updated dataset through progressive learning.

Algorithm 1: Progressive learning with identity-based data augmentation

---

Input: Dataset with both labeled (one-shot) and unlabeled images
Output: Generated fake images for all samples through real and pseudo labels

1 Pre-train the GAN model for the dataset;
2 Initialize model with one-shot labeled data;
3 **while** *the accuracy and number of labeled samples still need to search an optimal balance* **do**
4   Load the newest model;
5   Get the distance matrix;
6   Mine labeled images based on distance matrix;
7   Generate fake images for the one-shot labeled samples through mined samples;
8   Update the labeled dataset with fake images;
9   Reload ImageNet pre-trained model;
10   **while** *model in this selection iteration needs further training* **do**
11   **for** *images from labeled data* **do**
12   Build triplets for labeled samples via the matrix;
13   Get the loss for samples;
14   Update the model by minimizing the loss;
15   **end**
16   **end**
17 **end**
18 Generate fake images for all labeled samples through real and pseudo labels;
19 Randomly select images for unlabeled samples to generate fake images;
20 Train the new dataset with the progressive learning method;

3.1 MUNIT Review

In MUNIT, the image representation is decomposed into a content code which is domain-invariant, and a style code which captures domain-specific properties. Then through recombining the content code with a style code sampled from the style space of the target domain, an image with a specific style can be generated. For MUNIT, each model consists of an encoder E_i and a decoder G_i for each domain X_i (i = 1, 2). And two discriminators D_1 and D_2 are introduced to distinguish whether images are translated from another domain. The encoders, decoders, and discriminators are jointly trained to optimize the whole model. More details about MUNIT can be accessed in [6].

3.2 Progressive Pseudo Label Sampling (PPLS)

In PPLS, Softmax loss is used for classification loss and defined as:

$$L_{softmax} = -\sum_{i=1}^{B}\sum_{j=1}^{S} \frac{e^{f(W_{y_{i_j}};\phi(\theta;x_{i_j}))}}{\sum_{k=1}^{C} e^{f(W_k;\phi(\theta;x_{i_j}))}} \tag{1}$$

where y_{i_j} represents the label of x_{i_j}, W_k is the weight parameter and B is the number of randomly sampled labeled images and S is the number of pseudo labels selected corresponding to the sampled labeled samples. C means the number of cameras and $\phi(\theta;x)$ represents the feature representation.

Considering the noise of pseudo labels during sampling process, PPLS introduces HSoften-Triplet-Loss (HTL) to reduce the negative influence of noise from pseudo labels. HTL is defined as follows:

$$L_{Hsoft} = -\sum_{i=1}^{B}\sum_{j=1}^{S}[(\left\|\phi(\theta;x_{i_j}) - \hat{\phi}(\theta;x_i)\right\|_2)$$
$$- \min_{\substack{n=1\ldots B(n\neq i)\\m=1\ldots S}}(\left\|\phi(\theta;x_{i_j}) - \phi(\theta;x_{n_m})\right\|_2) + \alpha] \tag{2}$$

The overall loss function is expressed as:

$$L_{Overall} = L_{Softmax} + \lambda L_{HSoft} \tag{3}$$

where λ is the hyper-parameter for the relative importance of HTL. Different from EUG, the sampling method of PPLS forms a positive and negative pair of samples for each class, which can be used for HTL during the training stage.

3.3 Progressive Data Augmentation

PPLS takes one-shot image features as the reference for image mining. However, due to short of labeled samples and deviation of one-shot image features, the accuracy of basic progressive mining samples is relatively low. In this work, a progressive data augmentation mechanism is proposed for one-shot images during the training stage to improve the accuracy of mined labeled samples. Figure 2 shows the core idea of the process. As for our Re-ID model, we follow the training strategy in [13] and use ResNet-50 as the backbone. As Algorithm 1 showed, the Re-ID model is firstly trained with one-shot labeled samples to update the model. When the model trains well in its selection iteration, the latest model is loaded to mine labeled images based on distance matrix. Now pseudo labeled samples are captured. Fake images for one-shot samples are generated via pseudo labeled samples to make full use of the space features of all labeled samples. In this part, MUNIT is the tool to generate images for each one-shot labeled sample through pseudo labeled samples which owning the same identity and different cameras compared to the one-shot images. During the progressive learning process, the strategy in [7] is followed to use the feature centers of people under different cameras to take place of the one-shot image features for training the Re-ID model. Then this process is repeated until the accuracy and number of labeled samples mined reaches an optimal balance. The balance is assessed through the performance of the final dataset with fake images in the Re-ID task. It is worth noting that we take incremental data augmentation for one-shot samples which can make sure pseudo samples are referenced with a high level of precision. This is because although sampling accuracy declines gradually, the incremental method still preserves samples with high confidence.

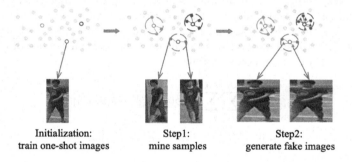

Initialization: Step1:   Step2:
train one-shot images   mine samples   generate fake images

Fig. 2. An illustration of the data augmentation procedure for one-shot samples. The hollow point, solid point and solid triangle denote labeled samples, unlabeled samples and fake images respectively.

3.4   Identity-Based Data Augmentation

After the process of progressive data augmentation, MUNIT is used to decompose an image with the pseudo label into content and style space. In this way, features such as the gesture and shape of a person keeps well, and styles like the background and colors of clothes are introduced. Moreover, by observing the Re-ID dataset, we find that the person features belonging to a same identity resemble, but differ a lot under different identities. This inspires us to extract the styles from other images of a person to generate fake images for the person.

Figure 3 shows our idea and an example of transferred images on Market-1501. In Fig. 3 (a), two images with the same identity are captured from different cameras. Then an image with another style for each picture is generated. Considering the process of data augmentation, fake images with different styles maintaining the features of identity well play a great role in the task of Re-ID. Firstly, the characteristic of identity features maintaining well explicitly reduces the interference of environmental noise in contrast to the methods of data augmentation without labeled samples as reference. Secondly, images generated through introducing style codes from different samples have style diversity to further relieve the overfitting problem of model training. The above two advantages greatly improve the performance of Re-ID. To make a fair comparison, we generate fake images with styles of all other cameras for each picture through pseudo labeled samples like [7] did. The example is depicted in Fig. 3 (b). Furthermore, because only part of the unlabeled samples are mined, images are randomly selected from the dataset as the reference to generate fake images with specific camera styles for unlabeled samples. Although random samples and wrong labeled samples referred bring some degree of interference, generated images can maintain a relatively satisfying performance due to the content codes from the original images. Finally, we obtain a dataset with generated samples generated from all other cameras for each original image.

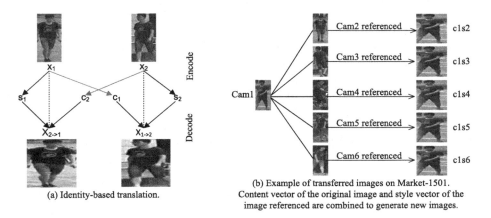

(a) Identity-based translation.

(b) Example of transferred images on Market-1501. Content vector of the original image and style vector of the image referenced are combined to generate new images.

Fig. 3. Identity-based data augmentation with labeled samples. (a) Images are encoded to a content and style space. To generate identity x_1 with style x_2, we recombine content of x_1 and style of x_2 via the decoder. (b) Cam1 represents the original real picture taken by camera 1 of the identity, and cls2 means that camera 2 shooting style generated image of the identity in camera 1. For a fair comparison with CycleGAN, an image is translated to styles in other cameras.

4   Experiments

4.1   Datasets

As shown in Table 1, three widely-used datasets including Market-1501, CUHK03 and DukeMTMC-reID are evaluated. The mean Average Precision (mAP) and the Cumulative Match Characteristic (CMC) curve are used to evaluate the performance. In our task, Rank-1, Rank-5 and Rank-10 are selected to represent the CMC curve.

Table 1. Statistics of the datasets used in our experiments

Dataset	Train IDs	Train images	Test IDs	Query images	Cameras	Total images
Market-1501	751	12,936	750	3,368	6	32,217
DukeMTMC-reID	702	16,522	702	2,228	8	36,441
CUHK03-Detected	767	7,365	700	1,400	Pairs	14,096
CUHK03-labeled	767	7,368	700	1,400	Pairs	14,096

4.2   Experiment Settings

Identity-Based Data Augmentation Model. Referring to MUNIT, components of the GAN model remain unchanged. The training set for each dataset is copied to build a pair of domains provided for the GAN model. During training, input images are resized to 128×128. To make the generated images preserve the domain-invariant characteristics (e.g., poses) of the input images, the cycle consistency loss is added for $\lambda_{cyc} = 10$. Batch size is set to 1. During the test stage, labeled images from the progressive learning method are referred to generate images for each picture and the output images are resized to 256×256. During the process of data augmentation, L is the number of cameras and we generate L-1 (7 for DukeMTMC-reID, 5 for Market-1501 and 1 for CUHK03) extra fake images for each image.

Deep Person Re-ID Network. ResNet-50 pre-trained on the ImageNet dataset is chosen as the backbone for our Re-ID model without any auxiliary module. The number of output channels in the final layer is up to classes of the person identities which correspond to 751, 702, 767 for Market-1501 dataset, DukeMTMC-reID dataset and CUHK03 dataset respectively. The dropout rate is 0.5.

Adam is used with the momentum of 0.7. The margin hyper-parameter α is 0.3. During the training process, batch size B is 16 and the number of pseudo labeled images S is 6.

4.3   Comparison with State-of-the-Arts Methods

We compare our method with state-of-the-art methods for Re-ID in this section. Some latest methods with transfer learning strategy are introduced for comparison, considering that relatively few people study one-shot Re-ID. The one-shot methods include EUG and PPLS. Methods with transfer learning strategy include, SPGAN [4], TJ-AIDL [11] and ECN [14].

Table 2. Comparison with state-of-the-art methods on Market1501 and DukeMTMC-ReID

Methods	Labels	Market-1501				DukeMTMC-reID			
		rank-1	rank-5	rank-10	mAP	rank-1	rank-5	rank-10	mAP
SPGAN [4]	Transfer	51.5	70.1	76.8	22.8	41.1	56.6	63.0	22.3
TJ-AIDL [11]	Transfer	56.7	75.0	81.8	27.4	45.3	59.8	66.3	24.7
ECN [14]	Transfer	75.1	87.6	91.6	43.0	63.3	75.8	80.4	40.4
EUG [5]	One-shot	55.8	72.3	78.4	26.2	48.8	63.4	68.4	28.5
PPLS [7]	One-shot	74.6	86.3	90.1	42.7	64.6	75.2	79.1	40.3
Ours	One-shot	76.9	89.3	92.5	48.2	65.0	76.2	79.8	40.8

Table 3. Comparison with PPLS on CUHK03-Detected and CUHK03-labeled

Methods	Labels	CUHK03-Detected				CUHK03-labeled			
		rank-1	rank-5	rank-10	mAP	rank-1	rank-5	rank-10	mAP
PPLS [7]	One-shot	12.1	21.8	28.3	12.1	12.8	22.4	29.9	12.6
Ours	One-shot	12.8	24.6	32.0	12.6	14.6	23.6	30.7	13.7

As shown in Table 2, our method achieves the best performance on both Market1501 (mAP of 48.2%) and DukeMTMC-ReID (mAP of 40.8%) among one-shot learning strategies. We improve the accuracy of mAP by 5.5 on Market1501 and by 0.5 on DukeMTMC-ReID compared with state-of-the-art method, PPLS. We notice that our method improves little on DukeMTMC-ReID. The reason can be concluded as follows. Persons from DukeMTMC-ReID may wear clothes of different colors while people from Market-1501 wear the same clothes among different camera views. This characteristic will result in style interference for the generated images. To verify our idea, we test our method on CUHK03-Detected and CUHK03-labeled, which can ensure that everyone dresses consistently among different cameras. The result is depicted in Table 3. We improves the accuracy of mAP by 0.5 on CUHK03-Detected and by 1.1 on CUHK03-labeled, which proves our idea on the two relatively small scale datasets. As for comparison with transfer learning models, our method also achieves satisfying results, which shows the efficiency of our method.

4.4   Ablation Study

Influence of Different Structures. We conduct the ablation study on Market1501, DukeMTMC-ReID. We disable some components or replace parts of our method by inferior counterparts to make sure the impact of each component. Firstly, we train the Re-ID model on HSoften-Triplet-Loss (HTL) without any data augmentation. Then we generate fake images with CycleGAN to update the dataset and also train the model relying on HTL. Finally, we replace CycleGAN with our identity-based augmentation method and train the model with the same loss function. The one-shot baseline is to directly train the model with only one-shot labeled images. Table 4 show the results of our experiments. Compared with the one-shot baselines, the PPLS method without data augmentation improves mAP by 36.5 on the Market1501, 35.5 on the DukeMTMC-ReID, showing the contribution of the basic method. After our identity-based data augmentation, we improve the performance of mAP, reaching 7.9 on Market1501, 1.6 on DukeMTMC-ReID compared with the PPLS baseline. By introducing our identity-based data augmentation, the final method achieves a satisfactory performance for one-shot Re-ID against previous state-of-the-art method, PPLS.

Table 4. Ablation study on Market1501 and DukeMTMC-ReID

Methods	Market1501				DukeMTMC-ReID			
	rank-1	rank-5	rank-10	mAP	rank-1	rank-5	rank-10	mAP
Full-labeled baseline	93.1	97.7	98.5	81.5	85.2	93.3	95.3	71.2
One-shot baseline	9.8	20.2	27.6	3.8	8.5	16.7	21.1	3.7
PLS + HTL	69.1	82.7	86.9	40.3	62.2	73.2	78.1	39.2
PLS+HTL+CycleGAN	74.6	86.4	90.1	42.7	64.6	75.2	79.1	40.3
Ours	76.9	89.3	92.5	48.2	65.0	76.2	79.8	40.8

Ablation Study on the GAN Categories. To prove the significance of our identity-based method instead of the GAN categories, we conduct experiments by choosing different GAN models. Modes of the GAN models can be classified into two types. The first type is generating fake images through injecting gaussian noise into the generator. Secondly, GAN models generate images through capturing information from the referred images. In Table 5, we can find that our identity-based data augmentation gets the optimal performance. This attributes to the high-quality images generated through our method. Although StarGANv2 can achieve good results in face generation, Re-ID datasets introduce too much noise from the background with reference-guided method which does not decouple the content and style of the picture. Because StarGANv2 train the model with latent code and referred images simultaneously, latent-guided method also gets poor performance. When randomly choosing pseudo labeled images with our identity-based GAN model, we may get an image which holds identity features well but style features poor. In this situation, the mAP drops by 2.8 on the Market-1501 dataset.

Table 5. Ablation study on GAN categories

GAN categories	Modes	Market-1501			
		rank-1	rank-5	rank-10	mAP
StarGAN	Noise	73.4	85.6	89.6	40.8
CycleGAN	Noise	74.6	86.3	90.1	42.7
Latent-guided StarGANv2	Noise	56.9	72.5	78.3	26.1
Reference-guided StarGANv2	Images	55.6	71.8	78.1	25.8
Identity-based GAN(random)	Images	76.0	87.9	91.1	45.4
Ours	Images	76.9	89.3	92.5	48.2

5 Conclusion

In this work, we propose an identity-based data augmentation method, which can generate high-quality images for one-shot Re-ID through labeled images belonging to the identity. To relieve the interference of the wrong pseudo labeled samples, a progressive data augmentation method for one-shot images is designed to balance well between the number and accuracy of samples explored. However, because MUNIT simply decouples the image into content and style space, the quality of generated images will be disturbed by complex environment factors like diverse scenes in the DukeMTMC-reID dataset. In the future, we plan to design a fine-grained GAN model to further make full use of identity information, while reducing the interference of environmental noise as much as possible to improve the performance of Re-ID.

Acknowledgments. This work was partially supported by the National Natural Science Foundation of China (No. 61803375 and 91948303), and the National Key Research and Program of China (No. 2017YFB1001900 and 2017YFB1301104).

References

1. Choi, Y., Choi, M., Kim, M., Ha, J.W., Kim, S., Choo, J.: Stargan: unified generative adversarial networks for multi-domain image-to-image translation. In: Proceedings of the IEEE Conference on Computer Vision and Pattern Recognition, pp. 8789–8797 (2018)
2. Choi, Y., Uh, Y., Yoo, J., Ha, J.W.: Stargan v2: diverse image synthesis for multiple domains. In: Proceedings of the IEEE/CVF Conference on Computer Vision and Pattern Recognition, pp. 8188–8197 (2020)
3. Chung, D., Delp, E.J.: Camera-aware image-to-image translation using similarity preserving stargan for person re-identification. In: Proceedings of the IEEE/CVF Conference on Computer Vision and Pattern Recognition Workshops (2019)
4. Deng, W., Zheng, L., Ye, Q., Kang, G., Yang, Y., Jiao, J.: Image-image domain adaptation with preserved self-similarity and domain-dissimilarity for person re-identification. In: Proceedings of the IEEE Conference on Computer Vision and Pattern Recognition, pp. 994–1003 (2018)

5. Hu, M., Zeng, K., Wang, Y., Guo, Y.: Threshold-based hierarchical clustering for person re-identification. Entropy **23**(5), 522 (2021). WOS:000653870600001
6. Huang, X., Liu, M.Y., Belongie, S., Kautz, J.: Multimodal unsupervised image-to-image translation. In: Proceedings of the European Conference on Computer Vision (ECCV), pp. 172–189 (2018)
7. Li, H., Xiao, J., Sun, M., Lim, E.G., Zhao, Y.: Progressive sample mining and representation learning for one-shot person re-identification. Pattern Recogn. **110**, 107614 (2021)
8. Li, M., Zhu, X., Gong, S.: Unsupervised tracklet person re-identification. CoRR abs/1903.00535 (2019)
9. Ma, L., Zhang, X., Lan, L., Huang, X., Luo, Z.: Ranking-embedded transfer canonical correlation analysis for person re-identification. In: 2018 International Joint Conference on Neural Networks (IJCNN), pp. 1–8. IEEE (2018). WOS:000585967403027
10. Su, C., Li, J., Zhang, S., Xing, J., Gao, W., Tian, Q.: Pose-driven deep convolutional model for person re-identification. In: Proceedings of the IEEE International Conference on Computer Vision, pp. 3960–3969 (2017)
11. Wang, J., Zhu, X., Gong, S., Li, W.: Transferable joint attribute-identity deep learning for unsupervised person re-identification. In: Proceedings of the IEEE Conference on Computer Vision and Pattern Recognition, pp. 2275–2284 (2018)
12. Wu, Y., Lin, Y., Dong, X., Yan, Y., Ouyang, W., Yang, Y.: Exploit the unknown gradually: one-shot video-based person re-identification by stepwise learning. In: Proceedings of the IEEE Conference on Computer Vision and Pattern Recognition, pp. 5177–5186 (2018)
13. Zheng, L., Yang, Y., Hauptmann, A.G.: Person re-identification: past, present and future. CoRR abs/1610.02984 (2016)
14. Zhong, Z., Zheng, L., Luo, Z., Li, S., Yang, Y.: Invariance matters: exemplar memory for domain adaptive person re-identification. In: Proceedings of the IEEE/CVF Conference on Computer Vision and Pattern Recognition, pp. 598–607 (2019)
15. Zhong, Z., Zheng, L., Zheng, Z., Li, S., Yang, Y.: Camera style adaptation for person re-identification. In: Proceedings of the IEEE Conference on Computer Vision and Pattern Recognition, pp. 5157–5166 (2018)
16. Zhu, J.Y., Park, T., Isola, P., Efros, A.A.: Unpaired image-to-image translation using cycle-consistent adversarial networks. In: Proceedings of the IEEE International Conference on Computer Vision, pp. 2223–2232 (2017)

Feature Fusion Learning Based on LSTM and CNN Networks for Trend Analysis of Limit Order Books

Xuerui Lv and Li Zhang[✉][ID]

School of Computer Science and Technology, Soochow University, Suzhou, China
20194227038@stu.suda.edu.cn, zhangliml@suda.edu.cn

Abstract. In recent years, deep learning has been successfully applied to analyzing financial time series. In this paper, we propose a novel feature fusion learning (FFL) method to analyze the trend of high-frequency limit order books (LOBs). The proposed FFL method combines a convolutional neural network (CNN) and two long short-term memory (LSTM) models. The CNN module uses a kind of up-sampling techniques to enhance basic features and the two LSTM modules can extract time-related information from time-insensitive and time-sensitive features. In addition, two fusion rules (majority voting and weighted summation) are designed to fuse different feature models. Experiments are conducted on the benchmark dataset FI-2010. Experimental results show that FFL can go beyond the performance of every sub-model and outperform the state-of-the-art model on the prediction performance of LOBs.

Keywords: Feature fusion learning · Limit order books · Long short-term memory · Convolutional neural network

1 Introduction

The financial market can reflect not only the macroeconomy of a country, but also the future economic trends of listed companies and commodities, which is a complex and changeable market. Stock, one of the most popular securities in the financial market, produces large amounts of high-frequency data, such as historical tick charts, minute charts, and limit order books (LOBs). Owing to containing multi-level bid and ask orders of investors at a time point, LOBs can reflect the expectations of investors on the underlying asset, the interaction situation between the market and investors, and the overall trend of the short-term

This work was supported in part by the Natural Science Foundation of the Jiangsu Higher Education Institutions of China under Grant No. 19KJA550002, by the Six Talent Peak Project of Jiangsu Province of China under Grant No. XYDXX-054, by the Priority Academic Program Development of Jiangsu Higher Education Institutions, and by the Collaborative Innovation Center of Novel Software Technology and Industrialization.

T. Mantoro et al. (Eds.): ICONIP 2021, LNCS 13111, pp. 125–137, 2021.
https://doi.org/10.1007/978-3-030-92273-3_11

in the future. Therefore, the future trends of financial markets are predictable to some extent [1] and LOBs are suitable for analyzing the financial market.

On account of the noise and nonlinearity of the financial market, the analysis and prediction of LOBs is a very challenging task in the financial field. Moreover, it is vital for investors to forecast the price trends of financial assets, because they can appropriately reduce the risk of decision-making by identifying future trends. Some scholars have introduced various mathematical models into the research of high-frequency LOBs, and their main application models can be roughly divided into three aspects: statistical models [1,2], traditional learning models [3] and deep learning models [4–8].

Statistical models can eliminate the instability and noise of some financial time series, like ridge regression (RR) [1] and multilinear discriminant analysis (MDA) [2]. However, statistical models are so strict and rigid that they cannot capture the latent characteristics under a large number of assumptions. Some traditional learning methods can solve the aforementioned limitations and capture the dynamic changes of LOBs. For example, multi-class support vector machines (SVMs) were proposed to capture the dynamics of LOBs [3,9]. But these methods cannot achieve great robustness and generalization for LOBs. Deep learning has been widely used to predict the movement of financial time-series, such as the volatility and price prediction of financial assets [10,11], and LOBs analysis [5–8]. However, it is hardly ever considered time factors in deep learning methods when analyzing LOBs. Tran et al. [8] introduced the temporal correlation layer to detect temporal information, but they only used the basic features.

In order to introduce time-related information in deep learning methods, we propose a feature fusion learning (FFL) method to deal with basic features and time-related features at the same time. First, FFL extracts three kinds of features from LOBs: basic features, time-insensitive, and time-sensitive features that were first designed for SVM [1]. Then, we adopt the appropriate model for each type of feature. A convolutional neural network (CNN) can study the potential characteristics of LOBs that can be treated as many images with overlaps. A long short-term memory (LSTM) network can well describe the temporal correlation of the sequence data. FFL uses the combination of one CNN and two LSTMs to analyze financial time series. The contributions of our paper can be summarized as follows:

- Time-related features are introduced to deep learning models. These features contain imbalance information of the feature distribution of LOBs and time-sensitive information.
- A novel FFL model is proposed for analyzing the fluctuation of LOBs by using one CNN on basic features and two LSTM networks on time-insensitive features and time-sensitive features.
- To fuse features, we design two combination rules: majority voting and weighted summation. Experimental results show that the rule of weighted summation achieves better prediction performance.

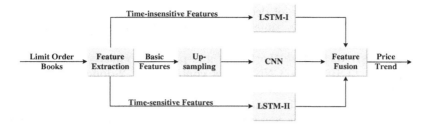

Fig. 1. The architecture of the proposed feature fusion

2   Related Work

Financial time series analysis is to study the future movement of financial assets using the historical time series. The financial assets contain tradable securities, like stock, futures, and commodities. Under the same macro environment, the analysis and prediction of these assets have some similarities that are complex and non-stationary time series with strong randomness [12].

The time series used for forecasting the stock trend can be divided into several types: tick data, candlestick chart data, and limit order books. Tokuoka and Yamawaki [13] extracted trading strategies from the tick data of eight stocks based on genetic algorithm. Most of the existing methods use the candlestick chart data (opening price, closing price, highest price, lowest price, volume). Zhou et al. [14] used LSTM and CNNs based on a generic framework for predicting the trend of stock price. They evaluated the performance on the candlestick chart with one-minute intervals and compared it with three statistical methods.

Methods used to forecast the trend of LOBs can be divided into three types: statistical methods, traditional machine learning methods, and deep learning methods. Ntakaris et al. [1] provided a public benchmark dataset FI-2010 that includes high-frequency LOBs data for the trend analysis in stock markets. In this dataset, the up, down, or constant movements are taken into consideration. Tran et al. [2] proposed a weighted multichannel time-series regression (WMTR) method to detect the latent features of LOBs and predict the movement on FI-2010. They compared WMTR with MDA and the neural bag-of-features (N-BoF) network on the same benchmark dataset and showed that WMTR outperforms vector-based algorithms.

Kercheval and Zhang [3] believed that the statistical methods are not suitable for the trend analysis of LOBs. They pointed out the statistical characteristics of LOBs are always dynamic and changeable and the prediction results of the model are limited by the preconditions, while machine learning methods have relatively few constraints, and can capture the dynamic changes of high-frequency LOBs and predict the future direction. Ntakaris et al. [1] proposed two baseline machine learning approaches: the single-layer-feedforward network (SLFN) and ridge regression to extract potential features from time-series data.

Recently, the emergence of deep learning significantly improves the prediction performance of financial time series. The common structures of deep learning contain CNNs and recurrent neural network (RNN). Tsantekidis et al. [6] proposed a CNN to analyze the future mid-price movements from large-scale high-frequency LOBs. This CNN model contains one 2-dimensional convolutional layer, three 1-dimensional convolutional layers, and two fully connected layers. The design of CNN is so simple that it ignores the multi-level characteristic of LOBs. This network has a significant improvement compared to linear SVMs and MLPs. As a classical model commonly used in time series, LSTM naturally can recognize the trend of LOBs [15]. Tsantekidis et al. [9] found that a temporally aware normalization scheme is appropriate for LOBs and applied LSTM to LOBs. However, this LSTM model only contains one LSTM layer, which results in a poor outcome. Zhang et al. [7] developed a deep CNNs for LOBs (DeepLOB) and thought that it was crucial to consider the levels of LOBs [7]. DeepLOB combines the level structure of LOBs and the shape of convolutional kernels, where the convolutional layers can learn the relationship between prices and volumes of one level. According to their experimental results, Zhang et al. denied the positive effect of pooling layers and deleted the pooling layers from DeepLOB. Besides, DeepLOB takes into account the basic features and ignores the other features about LOBs.

3   Methodology

In this paper, we propose the FFL model that consists of three sub-models: one CNN and two LSTMs. The framework of FFL is shown in Fig. 1. The LOB data is used as the input of FFL. Through the module of feature extraction, basic features, time-sensitive features, and time-insensitive features are obtained, where the basic features are first processed by the up-sampling layer and then input to the CNN sub-model, and the time-insensitive and time-sensitive features are input into LSTM-I and LSTM-II sub-models, respectively. The outputs of the three parts are fused to generate the price trend. In the following, we describe FFL in detail from four main steps.

3.1   Limit Order Book

An n-level LOB at time t for each stock contains limit orders that can be submitted to an exchange by investors when they would like to trade. A limit order contains a security symbol, order direction, limit price, and volume. Limit orders have two types: bid orders and ask orders, where bid orders are also called buy orders and ask orders are called sell orders. These orders would be sorted according to the commission prices before generating an LOB that has n bid orders and n ask orders. The lowest price of ask orders and the highest price of bid orders are the $1st$-level limit orders. A limit order might be executed quickly when it became the $1st$-level prices of an LOB. It also might be cancelled by traders at any time. LOBs only have several prices and volumes, so it is necessary to perform feature extraction for LOBs.

3.2 Feature Extraction

Let $\{(\mathbf{v}_t^B, u_t)\}_{t=1}^N$ be the set of original LOB samples for training, where N is the total number of training samples, $u_t \in \{Up, Down, Constant\}$ is the trend of $\mathbf{v}_t^B$ at time $(t+H)$, H is the future time period, and $\mathbf{v}_t^B \in \mathbb{R}^{4n}$ is the sample with basic features at time t and can be defined as [3]:

$$\mathbf{v}_t^B = [P_{t_1}^{bid}, V_{t_1}^{bid}, P_{t_1}^{ask}, V_{t_1}^{ask}, \cdots, P_{t_n}^{bid}, V_{t_n}^{bid}, P_{t_n}^{ask}, V_{t_n}^{ask}]^T,$$

where n denotes the levels of LOBs, $P_{t_i}^{bid}$ and $V_{t_i}^{bid}$ denote the price and volume of the i-th level bid order at time t, $P_{t_i}^{ask}$ and $V_{t_i}^{ask}$ denote the price and volume of the i-th level ask order at time t.

The goal of the feature extraction module is to generate time-related features and process them and basic features as image-like data. Ntakaris et al. [1] provided a way for calculating more time-related features based on the scheme in [3].

Following the way in [1], we extract more $(8n+24)$ time-related features from LOBs. Hence, we have $(12n + 24)$-dimensional features in total. Without loss of generality, let $\{(\mathbf{v}_t, u_t)\}_{t=1}^N$ be the new set of training samples, where

$$\mathbf{v}_t = [(\mathbf{v}_t^B)^T, (\mathbf{v}_t^I)^T, (\mathbf{v}_t^S)^T]^T \tag{1}$$

$\mathbf{v}_t^I \in \mathbb{R}^{(4n+8)}$ is the time-insensitive features and $\mathbf{v}_t^S \in \mathbb{R}^{(4n+16)}$ is the time-sensitive features. We normalize the set $\{(\mathbf{v}_t)\}_{t=1}^N$ by using z-score.

In the t-th LOB sample, $\mathbf{v}_t^B$ contains n-level limit orders, $\mathbf{v}_t^I$ indicates the state of the LOBs and past information, including the bid-ask spread, the corresponding mid-price of each level, as well as the accumulated differences of price and volume between ask and bid sides. These features in $\mathbf{v}_t^I$ express the distribution state of the limit order book. They themselves are not involved in factors that change with time. Therefore, these features are called time-insensitive features. $\mathbf{v}_t^S$ takes time into account, including the change rate of stock price and volume at each level, the average strength of different orders. The rate of change is obtained by calculating the derivative of price and volume to time and the average strength of different orders is calculated according to the change of time. All features in $\mathbf{v}_t^S$ express the sensitivity of entrusted price, volume, and orders over time, so these features are called time-sensitive features.

The price trend of future time $(t + H)$ corresponding to time t is closely related to a series of historical LOBs data. Therefore, we can obtain matrix data by merging the samples in the time period $(t - \Delta T_i + 1) \sim t, i = 1, 2, 3$, which is very similar to images, where ΔT_i is the past time span used to predict. Let $\mathbf{x}_t^*$ be the corresponding image-like sample of $\mathbf{v}_t$ for three kinds of features, where $* \in \{B, I, S\}$. Thus, we have

$$\mathbf{x}_t^B = [\mathbf{v}_{t-\Delta T_i+1}^B, \mathbf{v}_{t-\Delta T_i+2}^B, ..., \mathbf{v}_t^B]^T, i = 1, 2, 3 \tag{2}$$

$$\mathbf{x}_t^I = [\mathbf{v}_{t-\Delta T_i+1}^I, \mathbf{v}_{t-\Delta T_i+2}^I, ..., \mathbf{v}_t^I]^T, i = 1, 2, 3 \tag{3}$$

$$\mathbf{x}_t^S = [\mathbf{v}_{t-\Delta T_i+1}^S, \mathbf{v}_{t-\Delta T_i+2}^S, ..., \mathbf{v}_t^S]^T, i = 1, 2, 3 \tag{4}$$

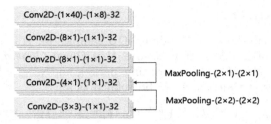

Fig. 2. Configurations of CNN sub-model, where Conv2D-$(m_1 \times m_2)$-$(m_3 \times m_4)$-m_5 denotes the 2D-convolutional layer with a filter size of $m_1 \times m_2$, a stride size of $m_3 \times m_4$ and m_5 output channels, MaxPooling-$(a_1 \times a_2)$-$(a_3 \times a_4)$ denotes the maximum pooling layer with a filter size of $a_1 \times a_2$ and a stride size of $a_3 \times a_4$

where $\mathbf{x}_t^B \in \mathbb{R}^{\Delta T_1 \times 4n}$, $\mathbf{x}_t^I \in \mathbb{R}^{\Delta T_2 \times (4n+8)}$, or $\mathbf{x}_t^S \in \mathbb{R}^{\Delta T_3 \times (4n+16)}$, which are image-like samples of basic, time-insensitive, or time-sensitive features at time t. Let the set of image-like samples be $\{(\mathbf{x}_t^*, \mathbf{y}_t)\}_{t=1}^N$, where $\mathbf{y}_t$ is the label vector of $\mathbf{x}_t^*$ that indicates the future trend of volatility. The label vector $\mathbf{y}_t \in \mathbb{R}^3$ is defined based on u_t:

$$
\mathbf{y}_t = \begin{cases} [1,0,0]^T, & \text{if } u_t = Up \\ [0,1,0]^T, & \text{if } u_t = Down \\ [0,0,1]^T, & \text{otherwise} \end{cases} \tag{5}
$$

Now, we choose three appropriate models for training these features: a CNN sub-model for $\mathbf{x}_t^B$, two LSTM sub-models for $\mathbf{x}_t^I$ and $\mathbf{x}_t^S$.

3.3   CNN Sub-model

Before we input $\mathbf{x}_t^B$ into CNN, we use the up-sampling layer to process the basic features. The goal of using up-sampling is to enlarge the information in $\mathbf{x}_t^B$. Through the up-sampling layer, the input information is doubled and the same values in the input feature map are mapped and filled into a corresponding area of the output feature map. The output of the up-sampling layer is the input of CNN module. The detailed structure of CNN according to the actual meaning and structure of LOBs is shown in Fig. 2, including five 2D-convolutional (Conv2D) layers and two maximum pooling (MaxPooling) layers.

Every level LOB has 4 features that contain prices and volumes of bid order and ask order. The first convolutional layer with a stride size of 1×8 moves 8 steps each time in the feature dimension. The layer has a filter size of 1×40, which can learn the relationship between adjacent 5-level LOBs in each time series. The local relationship of samples between several time steps is learned by the next four convolutional layers with different sizes of filters at the time dimension.

The two maximum pooling layers can simplify the network complexity through compressed features and prevent overfitting and improve network performance. The first maximum pooling layer does not reduce the feature information of LOBs, but compress the length of the time window. The second one is a common maximum pooling layer. At the end of convolutional layers, there are two fully connected layers.

3.4 LSTM Sub-models

LSTM is a variant of RNN [16], which can learn long-term dependent information and solve the issue of overfitting. An LSTM unit contains three gates: a forget gate, an input gate, an output gate, and a cell, which help the unit to remove or add information. The forget gate determines the information that could be discarded from the unit, the input gate determines the information that could be saved, the output gate provides the output information, and the cell saves the status information of the unit.

LSTM can effectively learn long-term and short-term dependencies through storage units and gates, and add the concept of time to its network structure, making it suitable to analyze time-series data. In our model, there are two LSTM sub-models for processing time-insensitive features $\mathbf{x}_t^I$ and time-sensitive features $\mathbf{x}_t^S$. We denote LSTM-I and LSTM-II for $\mathbf{x}_t^I$ and $\mathbf{x}_t^S$, respectively.

3.5 Feature Fusion Learning

It is necessary to combine the outputs of three sub-models to generate a final output. In this paper, we design two later fusion schemes for FFL: majority voting and weighted summation.

In majority voting, it is assumed that the category with the most votes is the winner. Three individual sub-models directly output their price trends when applying the majority voting rule. The only fuzzy case is that three sub-models have totally different outputs. In other words, each price trend has one vote. In this case, we take *"Constant"* as the final price trend.

For applying weighted summation, individual sub-models output probabilities of price trends. We need to set weights for three sub-models in advance and integrate probabilities of price trends by weights. The final price trend is determined by the highest integrated probability of price trend.

4 Experiments

In this section, we perform comprehensive experiments to validate the effectiveness of the proposed FFL model. We first investigate the settings of some parameters and then conduct experiments on sub-models to compare with other models.

4.1 Dataset and Experimental Settings

We validate the effectiveness of FFL on the FI-2010 dataset [1] that contains approximately $4,000,000$ time series samples of 10 weekdays from the Nasdaq

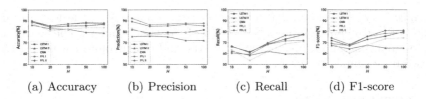

(a) Accuracy   (b) Precision   (c) Recall   (d) F1-score

Fig. 3. Comparison of FFL with sub-models on Setup1 under different indexes

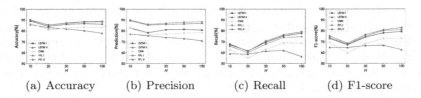

(a) Accuracy   (b) Precision   (c) Recall   (d) F1-score

Fig. 4. Comparison of FFL with sub-models on Setup2 under different indexes

Nordic stock market. The trading period can be divided into auction period and non-auction period. The opening price and the closing price are determined by the auction period so that the auction period is a period of non-routine transactions. This dataset provides ten folds for training, validating, and testing. We utilize two ways (Setup1 and Setup2) of dividing data in this dataset without the auction period. In Setup1, the training set contains data of nine days and the test set contains data of one day. In Setup2, the training set contains data of seven days and the test set contains data of three days. The price trend in different future horizons $H \in \{10, 20, 30, 50, 100\}$ is divided into three classes: Up, Down, and Constant. We use the FI-2010 standardized by z-score to assess our FFL model.

FFL is implemented in Python and trained by Keras [17], which is a modularity and extensibility Python library. The activation function of the hidden layer in CNN is ReLU. The number of output neurons in LSTMs is set to 16 and 32 for time-insensitive and time-sensitive features, respectively. We use $\Delta T_1 = 100$, $\Delta T_2 = 10$, $\Delta T_3 = 10$ according to the experience. In both CNN and LSTMs, we use the dropout layer with a fixed rate of 0.5 to avoid overfitting. In the training, we use Adam for optimization with the learning rate of 0.01 and epsilon of 0.9 at the start. The activation function used in the final layer of all sub-models is Softmax for classification. Our model is trained with a batch size of 64 for a total of 200 epochs. The cross-entropy loss function is used in FFL.

Our FFL model is evaluated by four metrics: precision, recall, F1-score and accuracy. We report the evaluation merits by averaging the values of three categories. We first conduct experiments on Setup1 and Setup2 using sub-models of LSTM I, LSTM II, and CNN in the FFL model. Then, we use two fusion schemes to construct the integrated model FFL. For short, we denote FFL with the majority voting as FFL I, and with weighted summation as FFL II.

Table 1. Comparison of the existing models on Setup1

Method	Precision (%)	Recall (%)	F1-Score (%)	Accuracy (%)
Prediction horizon $H = 10$				
SLFN [1]	51.20	36.60	32.70	64.30
MDA [2]	44.21	60.07	46.06	71.92
TABL(C) [8]	72.03	74.06	72.84	78.01
MCSDA [18]	46.11	48.00	46.72	83.66
N-BoF [19]	42.28	61.41	41.63	62.70
T-LoBoF [20]	47.80	68.25	51.58	–
DeepLOB [7]	78.47	**78.91**	**77.66**	78.91
FFL II	**89.33**	66.67	74.24	**89.88**
Prediction horizon $H = 50$				
SLFN [1]	46.80	46.40	45.90	47.30
MDA [2]	–	–	–	–
TABL(C) [8]	74.58	74.27	74.32	74.81
MCSDA [18]	–	–	–	–
N-BoF [19]	47.20	58.17	46.15	56.52
T-LoBoF [20]	51.56	65.81	53.73	–
DeepLOB [7]	75.10	75.01	74.96	75.01
FFL II	**86.67**	**76.67**	**80.96**	**88.46**
Prediction Horizon $H = 100$				
SLFN [1]	45.30	43.20	41.00	47.70
MDA [2]	–	–	–	–
TABL(C) [8]	73.51	73.80	73.52	74.07
MCSDA [18]	–	–	–	–
N-BoF [19]	47.27	54.99	46.86	56.43
T-LoBoF [20]	–	–	–	–
DeepLOB [7]	76.77	76.66	76.58	76.66
FFL II	**85.33**	**77.67**	**81.14**	**87.86**

Empirically, the weights of FFL II are 0.4 (LSTM-I), 0.2 (CNN), and 0.4 (LSTM-II), respectively.

As shown in Fig. 3, we observe LSTM-I obtains the best F1-score 73.55% among three sub-models. We also see that the two ensemble models both improve the performance of sub-models and demonstrate that FFL-II provides 6.33% and 2.52% higher in precision and F1-score than the best sub-model, respectively.

4.2 Experimental Results

From Fig. 4, we can see that LSTM-I has the best F1-score between three sub-models. Compared with the three sub-models, FFL I and FFL II have achieved

Table 2. Comparison of different models on Setup2

Method	Precision (%)	Recall (%)	F1-Score (%)	Accuracy (%)
Prediction horizon $H = 10$				
SVM [9]	44.92	39.62	35.88	–
MLP [9]	60.78	47.81	48.27	–
LSTM [9]	75.92	60.77	66.33	–
LSTM-I	82.67	67.33	73.04	89.11
CNN-I [6]	65.54	50.98	55.21	–
CNN-II [21]	45.00	56.00	44.00	–
CNN	82.67	62.67	69.41	87.28
DeepLOB [7]	84.00	**84.47**	**83.40**	84.47
FFL II	**89.33**	68.00	75.31	**90.21**
Prediction horizon $H = 20$				
SVM [9]	47.77	45.08	43.20	–
MLP [9]	65.20	51.33	51.12	–
LSTM [9]	70.52	59.60	62.37	–
LSTM-I	78.33	61.67	67.18	84.25
CNN-I [6]	67.38	54.79	59.17	–
CNN-II [21]	–	–	–	–
CNN	76.67	55.33	59.66	81.02
DeepLOB [7]	74.06	**74.85**	**72.82**	74.85
FFL II	**85.33**	61.33	68.54	**85.48**
Prediction Horizon $H = 50$				
SVM [9]	60.30	46.05	49.42	–
MLP [9]	67.14	55.21	55.95	–
LSTM [9]	68.50	60.03	61.43	–
LSTM-I	81.33	75.33	77.93	86.64
CNN-I [6]	67.12	55.58	59.44	–
CNN-II [21]	47.00	56.00	47.00	–
CNN	78.00	69.00	72.95	83.40
DeepLOB [7]	80.38	**80.51**	80.35	80.51
FFL II	**86.33**	76.33	**80.66**	**88.47**

better performance in accuracy, precision, and F1-score. Therefore, FFL is helpful for improving the generalization of the model. The majority voting scheme is inferior to the weighted sum scheme that can improve every index of sub-models.

Further, we compare the performance of FFL II with other representative classifiers on both Setup1 and Setup2.

For Setup1, the compared methods include SLFN [1], MDA [2], the multilinear class-specific discriminant analysis (MCSDA) [18], N-BoF [19], the temporal logistic bag-of-features (T-LoBoF) [20], the temporal attention-augmented bilinear layer (TABL) [8], and DeepLOB [7]. Experimental results are shown in Table 1, where "−" denotes that the result is not provided by the corresponding method. When $H = 10$, FFL-II is inferior only to DeepLOB on both recall and F1-score. For $H = 50$ and $H = 100$, we observe that the model of FFL-II is much better than all compared methods on all indexes. For example, FFL-II achieves the best F1-score 80.96% and DeepLOB provides the second best 74.96%. FFL-II is higher in F1-score than DeepLOB by 6%. With the increase of H, the F1-score of FFL increases, which indicates that our model has the long-term dependence.

For Setup2, the compared methods contain SVMs [9], multilayer perceptrons (MLP) [9], LSTM [9], CNN-I [6], CNN-II [21] and DeepLOB [7]. As shown in Table 2, we observe that deep learning methods are much better than conventional machine learning (SVMs). The result of the sub-model LSTM-I shows some improvements over LSTM [9]. The sub-model CNN also outperforms CNN-I and CNN-II by about 9.40% and 25.68% in terms of F1-score. Compared with the state-of-the-art model DeepLOB, FFL II achieves improvements in precision and accuracy. The F1-score of FFL II (80.66%) is higher than that of DeepLOB (80.35%) when $H = 50$.

In summary, our proposed sub-models with different kinds of features are better than the existing simple deep learning methods. The fusion of three sub-models integrates their merits and improves the performance of sub-models. In addition, the performance of FFL-II on the FI-2010 dataset is improved significantly over other models under the same circumstances.

5   Conclusion

This paper proposes an FFL model for LOBs, which strengthens the attention to time information according to the structure of LOBs. FFL extracts basic, time-insensitive, and time-sensitive features and feeds them into CNN and LSTMs sub-models. The structure of the FFL model is designed based on the practical significance of LOBs. Two fusion methods are used by combining the outputs of three sub-models. Experimental results on the FI-2010 dataset show that FFL can improve the interpretability and generalization on future trend analysis of LOBs.

However, FFL is not so good on Setup2, the proportion of the three types of samples is extremely imbalanced. The number of majority samples is four times that of minority samples. We think that the imbalance situation leads to poor performance of FFL. To further improve the performance of FFL, we plan to solve the issue of class imbalance in future work and design more efficient schemes to fuse these features of LOBs.

References

1. Ntakaris, A., Magrisv, M., Kanniainen, J., et al.: Benchmark dataset for mid-price forecasting of limit order book data with machine learning methods. J. Forecast. **37**, 852–866 (2018)
2. Tran, D.T., Magris, M., Kanniainen, J., et al.: Tensor representation in high-frequency financial data for price change prediction. In: 2017 IEEE Symposium Series on Computational Intelligence, pp. 1–7. IEEE (2017)
3. Kercheval, A.N., Zhang, Y.: Modelling high frequency limit order book dynamics with support vector machines. Quant. Finan. **15**, 1315–1329 (2015)
4. Daiya, D., Wu, M., Lin, C.: Stock movement prediction that integrates heterogeneous data sources using dilated causal convolution networks with attention. In: 2020 IEEE International Conference on Acoustics, Speech and Signal Processing (ICASSP), pp. 8359–8363 (2020)
5. Sirignano, J.A.: Deep learning for limit order books. Quant. Finan Intell. **19**, 549–570 (2019)
6. Tsantekidis, A., Passalis, N., Tefas, A., et al.: Forecasting stock prices from the limit order book using convolutional neural networks. In: 2017 IEEE 19th Conference on Business Informatics (CBI), pp. 7–12 (2017)
7. Zhang, Z., Zohren, S., Roberts, S.: DeepLOB: deep convolutional neural networks for limit order books. IEEE Trans. Signal Process. **11**, 3001–3012 (2019)
8. Tran, D.T., Iosifidis, A., Kanniainen, J., et al.: Temporal attention-augmented bilinear network for financial time-series data analysis. IEEE Trans. Neural Netw. Learn. Syst. **5**, 1407–1418 (2018)
9. Tsantekidis, A., Passalis, N., Tefas, A., et al.: Using deep learning to detect price change indications in financial markets. In: 25th European Signal Processing Conference (EUSIPCO), pp. 2511–2515 (2017)
10. Kelotra, A., Pandey, P.: Stock market prediction using optimized Deep-ConvLSTM model. Big Data. **8**, 5–24 (2020)
11. Ai, X.W., Hu, T., Bi, G.P., et al.: Discovery of jump breaks in joint volatility for volume and price of high-frequency trading data in China. In: International Conference on Knowledge Science, Engineering and Management, pp. 174–182 (2017)
12. Barbulescu, A., Bautu, E.: A hybrid approach for modeling financial time series. Int. Arab J. Inf. Technol. **9**, 327–335 (2012)
13. Tokuoka, S., Yamawaki, M.T.: Trend predictions of tick-wise stock prices by means of technical indicators selected by genetic algorithm. Artif. Life Robot. **12**, 180–183 (2008)
14. Zhou, X., Pan, Z., Hu, G., et al.: Stock market prediction on high-frequency data using generative adversarial nets. Math. Probl. Eng. **2018**, 1–11 (2018)
15. Hochreiter, S., Schmidhuber, J.: Long short-term memory. Neural Comput. **9**, 1735–1780 (1997)
16. Gers, F.A., Schraudolph, N.N., Schmidhuber, J.: Learning precise timing with LSTM recurrent networks. J. Mach. Learn. Res. **3**, 115–143 (2002)
17. Chollet F.: Deep Learning with Python. Manning Publications Company, Shelter Island (2018)
18. Tran, D.T., Gabbouj, M., Iosifidis, A.: Multilinear class-specific discriminant analysis. Pattern Recogn. Lett. **100**, 131–136 (2019)
19. Passalis N., Tsantekidis A., Tefas A., et al.: Time-series classification using neural bag-of-features. In: 2017 25th European Signal Processing Conference (EUSIPCO), pp. 301–305 (2017)

20. Passalis, N., Tefas, A., Kanniainen, J., et al.: Deep temporal logistic bag-of-features for forecasting high frequency limit order book time series. In: 2019 IEEE International Conference on Acoustics, Speech and Signal Processing (ICASSP), pp. 7545–7549 (2019)
21. Tsantekidis, A., Passalis, N., Tefas, A., et al.: Using deep learning for price prediction by exploiting stationary limit order book features. Appl. Soft Comput. **93**(106401), 1–10 (2020)

WikiFlash: Generating Flashcards from Wikipedia Articles

Yuang Cheng[1], Yue Ding[1], Sebastien Foucher[2], Damián Pascual[2(✉)],
Oliver Richter[2(✉)], Martin Volk[1], and Roger Wattenhofer[2]

[1] University of Zurich, Zürich, Switzerland
{yuang.cheng,yue.ding}@uzh.ch, volk@cl.uzh.ch
[2] ETH Zurich, Zürich, Switzerland
{sfoucher,dpascual,orichter,wattenhofer}@ethz.ch

Abstract. Flashcards, or any sort of question-answer pairs, are a fundamental tool in education. However, the creation of question-answer pairs is a tedious job which often defers independent learners from properly studying a topic. We seek to provide a tool to automatically generate flashcards from Wikipedia articles to make independent education more attractive to a broader audience. We investigate different state-of-the-art natural language processing models and propose a pipeline to generate flashcards with different levels of detail from any given article. We evaluate the proposed pipeline based on its computing time and the number of generated and filtered questions, given the proposed filtering method. In a user study, we find that the generated flashcards are evaluated as helpful. Further, users evaluated the quality of human created flashcards that are available open source as comparable to or only slightly better than the automatically generated cards (Our application is available at: flashcard.ethz.ch).

Keywords: Question-answer extraction · Personalized education · Natural language processing

1 Introduction

The recent development of artificial intelligence make available a new set of tools that can be exploited to advance the field of personalized education. In the last years, we have seen how, thanks to new deep learning methods, machines have attained super-human performance in a large number of language-related tasks [33]. These methods can accelerate the development of personalized education by automatically generating instructional material. Generating instructional materials manually is a costly task that requires instructors to select and cure large amounts of information. With a growing internet, an ever-increasing (and overwhelming) amount of information and data is available. However, it is challenging for a person to learn in a systematic manner from this information.

Authors in alphabetical order.

© Springer Nature Switzerland AG 2021
T. Mantoro et al. (Eds.): ICONIP 2021, LNCS 13111, pp. 138–149, 2021.
https://doi.org/10.1007/978-3-030-92273-3_12

To improve human learning, it is necessary to structure the information into instructional materials that select the most relevant points and guide learning. Automatically generating these materials can widely accelerate human learning while giving each person the freedom to learn any arbitrary topic of her interest.

A well-known and effective format for instructional materials are flashcards [30]. Flashcards are small cards (physical or virtual) with a question written on the front face and the answer to that question written on the back face. Flashcards stimulate learning by hiding the answer that the student is trying to learn. A big advantage of flashcards is that they are topic-independent, i.e., flashcards can be used to learn anything: languages, history, mathematics... Nevertheless, a large number of flashcards is necessary to cover a given topic or subtopic, and preparing good flashcards requires good summarization skills, all of which makes the process of manually producing flashcards challenging and time consuming.

In this work, we present a system for automatically generating flashcards about any arbitrary topic. We leverage recent advances in language processing, in particular transformer-based models [32], to extract questions and answers from input text. We implement our system as a web application that takes as input the title of a Wikipedia article and outputs flashcards for that article. We evaluate the application, profiling generation time and the number of flashcards produced. Furthermore, we run a user study to assess the quality of our automatically generated cards in comparison to human-created cards. The results show that the quality of our automatically generated cards is similar to the quality of cards generated by humans. Our system has the flexibility of generating instructional materials (in the form of flashcards) for any topic a student may be interested in, beyond standard curricula. We build our system as a web application that serves as both, a proof-of-concept of how current technologies allow automatic generation of materials for learning, as well as a first step towards a completely functional tool to enhance learning anywhere and about anything.

2   Related Work

Automatic question generation for educational purposes is a growing research area with many works focusing on assessment and template based question generation [13]. In a recent trend, data driven approaches that use neural networks became more prominent in many natural language processing tasks, including question generation [21]. These data driven approaches might struggle to extract questions that require several steps of reasoning as in the LearningQ dataset [6]. However, for flashcard generation, simple factoid questions are often preferred. We therefore focus on models that perform well on the Wikipedia based SQuADv1 dataset [24], which was originally developed for question answering models but can be re-purposed for context based question generation.

On this dataset, transformer based approaches for question generation [3, 5, 7, 12, 19] are currently preforming best in terms of n-gram similarity metrics such as ROUGE-L [17]. This is likely due to the fact that these models benefit from large scale unsupervised pretraining. Our implementation is based on the publicly available code of [22], which follows ideas from [5,19] and [1] and achieves results not far behind the state-of-the-art [3].

As a pre-processing step, text summarization can be used to reduce the text from which questions are to be generated. Automatically summarizing text is the focus of a large body of research and a number of datasets exist that are used to benchmark progress [11,26,28]. There are two types of summarization: extractive [36], the summary consist of sentences copied from the original text; and abstractive [10], the sentences do not coincide with the original text but the meaning does. Abstractive summarization is both, more natural and harder. Recently proposed models [16,23,34,35] have achieved new state-of-the-art results as measured by ROUGE-L score. Here, we leverage this progress and use abstractive summarization for content selection before question generation.

The general idea of filtering questions in a post-processing step has been explored in different settings [1,4,14,18,20]. Using a question-answering system to filter questions where the answers do not align, was proposed by [1] to create a synthetic data corpus for pretraining a question-answering model. We use this approach in our system with slight adjustments. Compared to their approach of filtering all questions where answers do not align, we relax the filtering by allowing for questions where the extracted answers and the answers produced by the question-answer model yield a sufficient overlap.

The main contribution of this work is an end-to-end application that allows for flashcard generation based on a Wikipedia article freely chosen by the users. Our work thereby differs from the work of [8] that created a fixed size corpus for scientific investigation. Also, despite the existence of many applications that allow for the design and/or studying of flashcards, we only encountered one working application which allows for automated flashcard creation [9]. This application uses a key-phrase based system for the creation of flashcards in the biological and medical domain. In contrast, our approach does not rely on key phrases and is therefore applicable to a much wider range of topics.

3 Method

Generating meaningful flashcards from an arbitrary piece of text is not a trivial problem. Currently, there does not exist a single model that can alone perform this task. We therefore divide the flashcard generation process into four subtasks that cover more general and well-studied problems that can be individually addressed by state-of-the-art models. In particular, we build a pipeline consisting of four stages: summarization, answer identification, question generation and question answering. Figure 1 shows a depiction of this pipeline.

Summarization. By definition, a summary contains the most relevant information for a general understanding of the corresponding text. Thus, generating flashcards from a summary reduces the level of detail in the resulting flashcards, in comparison to using the original text as input. A summarization stage gives the user the freedom of deciding between two levels of detail for the information

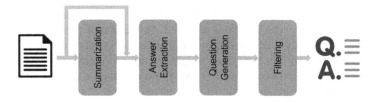

Fig. 1. Pipeline of the flashcard generation system. The summarization step is optional.

contained in the flashcards. If more detailed flashcards are preferred, the summarization step is skipped and the input text is passed directly to the next step of the pipeline. Otherwise, a summary is generated from the input text and fed into the next stage.

Answer Extraction. After the optional summarization step, we proceed to generate flashcards by identifying potential answers in the text. To this end, we use a model for answer extraction, which receives as input a piece of text and finds words or groups of words that can be answers to questions. These answers, together with the original text, are passed as input to the next stage.

Question Generation. In this stage we use an answer-aware question generation model to generate answer specific-questions. This way, the output of this stage is the set of question-answer tuples that we need for flashcards. However, the question-answer tuples generated at this point tend to include some questions that either make no sense or are incorrect. Therefore, we include a final step in our pipeline to filter out unusable questions.

Filtering. To filter out erroneous questions, we use a model for question answering. For each question-answer tuple we provide this model with the question and the paragraph where the answer can be found. If the answer provided by the question-answering model overlaps enough with the answer from which the question was generated, then the question-answer tuple is accepted, otherwise it is discarded.

4   Implementation

We implement our flashcard generation pipeline as a web application. The interface of our application is simple and intuitive. The main screen displays the existing flashcard decks and their status, e.g., "Generating", "Complete", as well as a button to add a new deck. When clicking on this button the user is prompted a screen where they should provide a title of a Wikipedia article they want flashcards from. Given this title, the application suggests a number of actual Wikipedia articles; this way, if the article name is redundant, i.e., there are more than one article with the same name, disambiguation results are suggested. Once the Wikipedia article is selected, the user can define which sections of the article they want flashcards from, and whether summarization should be applied or not. Finally, the user can choose the name of the generated deck, by default the name of the corresponding Wikipedia article is given.

Regarding, the implementation of each stage of our system, we use the following models to build the pipeline:

Summarization. We use DistilBART for summarization [16,29], pre-trained on the CNN/DailyMail summarization dataset [11]. The maximum input length of this model is 1024 tokens, which is less than a long Wikipedia article. To circumvent this issue, our summaries are generated paragraph-wise.

Answer Extraction. We use T5 fine-tuned on the SQuADv1 dataset for answer extraction [22,23]. At inference time, for each paragraph we highlight one sentence at a time and feed it together with the rest of the paragraph to the model. The model extracts answers from the highlighted sentence leveraging the additional context information contained in the rest of the paragraph. To stay within the admitted input size of the model, we clip the paragraphs to 512 tokens.

Question Generation. Here we use T5 fine-tuned on the SQuADv1 dataset for answer-aware question generation [22,23]. For each extracted answer, we append the corresponding paragraph as context and feed it to the model. Again, to not exceed the maximum input size we clip the input to a length of 512 tokens.

Filtering. For filtering we use DistilBERT fine-tuned using a second step of knowledge distillation on the SQuADv1 dataset for question answering [27,31]. Similar to the previous steps, we feed the model at inference time with each of the generated questions together with their corresponding paragraphs. We calculate an overlap score between the answer obtained in the answer extraction step and the answer produced by this question-answering model. The overlap score we calculate here is the ratio of identical bigrams over the total number of bigrams. Questions with an overlap score below 0.75 are discarded. Duplicates and questions whose answer is the title of the article are also discarded.

For each of the stages of our system, many different models exist in the literature. We selected each specific model based on their fitness to the task (i.e., models that are trained on Wikipedia based data-sets) as well as their availability as open source implementation.

Once a deck is generated, the user can interact with the flahscards in two different ways: 1) in grid view, 2) in study mode. In grid view, all the cards of the deck are displayed in a grid, showing the question faces. When the mouse is placed over the question, the card flips showing the answer to that question. In study mode, one question is presented at a time and after clicking the answer is revealed. In this mode the user can edit the card as well as give feedback about it, choosing from

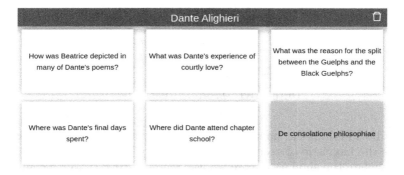

Fig. 2. Grid view for the topic *Dante Alighieri*. The white squares contain the questions and the yellow square is the answer to *"What Boethius work did Dante read?"*. (Color figure online)

four options: *"The answer does not fit the question"*, *"The answer is wrong"*, *"The answer is trivial"* and *"Other"* (where the user can input their own text). Finally, after the answer is shown, the user is asked to label the difficulty of the card choosing from five possibilities, from *"Too easy"* to *"Too hard"* or alternatively, as *"Not interested"*. These feature may be used in future work for designing algorithms that decide the optimal card ordering for human learning. Figure 2 shows an example of generated cards displayed in grid view.

To make our cards usable beyond our web application, we provide the option of exporting the generated cards as text file that can be imported into Anki. Anki is a popular framework for flashcard-based learning with a large community of users that share their own flashcard decks as well as a number of commercial applications for smart-phones and web to help learning. This way, our generated flashcards are compatible with existing commercial applications and the users can choose the learning platform they prefer.

5   Evaluation

In this section we evaluate objective parameters of our flashcard generation pipeline, such as compute time or number of questions generated. Conversely, in Sect. 6 we evaluate the subjective quality of the generated cards through a user study. We divide our objective evaluation in two parts: 1) summarization step and 2) question generation and filtering step.

5.1   Summarization

Since we do not have reference summaries of the pieces of text that we are aiming to summarize, we cannot rely on the ROUGE score, which is the most common metric for summary quality. Instead, we calculate two values, similarity and error rate, that do not require a reference summary. The similarity score gives us a

Table 1. Comparison of T5, BART and DistilBART summarization.

Model	Similarity	Error rate
T5	0.912	0.129
BART	0.947	0.057
DistilBART	0.937	0.052

notion of how faithful the summary is to the original text, while the error rate quantifies the linguistic correctness of the summary.

To calculate the similarity score we use Sentence-BERT [25] to compute an embedding of each sentence in the original text and in the summary. Then, we calculate a context vector for the original text by adding up all of its sentence embeddings. We do the same for the summarized text. This results in two context vectors, one representing the original text and one representing the summary. Our similarity score is the cosine similarity of these two vectors. The error rate is the percentage of erroneous tokens. To calculate it, we determine the number of wrong tokens using *LanguageTool* [15] and divide this number by the total number of tokens. If a sentence has no end-of-sentence token, it is considered incomplete and an error is added to the count.

To determine which model to use in the summarization step, we compare three state-of-the-art models: T5, BART, and DistilBART (the distilled version of BART). In Table 1 we compare the models in terms of similarity and error rate scores over the introduction of 256 Wikipedia articles. These articles were randomly selected based on the requirement that their introductions have more than 200 tokens. BART presents the highest similarity score and Distil-BART the lowest error rate. This result is in line with the fact that BART obtains higher ROUGE score than T5 in summarization benchmarks such as CNN/DailyMail [16,23].

Since we are implementing our system as a web application, we need to consider computation time: to improve user experience we are interested in reducing as much as possible the time needed for the system to generate the cards. Using the same set of 256 Wikipedia articles we calculate the average time it takes for BART and DistilBART to summarize the introductions, when running on a 24 GB Nvidia Titan RTX GPU. While BART needs on average 6.1 s per article, DistilBART requires only 3.7 s, i.e., DistilBART is 1.64 faster. While the absolute difference in computation time might seem small, we note that the computation time scales linearly with the article length, as articles are fed one paragraph at a time. We therefore choose DistilBART for the summarization step of our system, as the total speed up is significant and obtains a similarity score and an error rate comparable to BART.

5.2   Question Generation and Filtering

We study the performance of the question generation and filtering stage of our pipeline in terms of computing time and questions generated. We use 1024 randomly selected articles from Wikipedia with more than 200 tokens and analyse

Table 2. Average number of questions generated and kept after filtering.

		Time	Number of Questions	Questions after filter
Original	Per section	14.3 s	10.4	8.7
	Per article	240.5 s	178.4	148.2
Summary	Per section	9.3 s	8.6	7.2
	Per article	151.2 s	144.0	120.5

the number of questions generated. In Table 2, we report the average number of flashcards generated and the average number of flashcards kept after the filtering stage.

We see that even after applying our filtering step the number of questions kept, i.e., questions that meet a minimal quality requirement, is relatively large. In particular, generating 148.2 questions on average for a Wikipedia article implies that a student can access a significant amount of information from the cards. Furthermore, from the results we see that summarization helps in reducing the number of questions that are discarded.

From the results presented in this section, we cannot assess the quality and usefulness of the generated cards, since this is a feature that depends on human perception. However, we can visually examine some examples of flashcards to have a notion of what kind of question-answer pairs our model generates. Table 3 shows the first four question-answer tuples generated for the article *Animal Farm* (novel by George Orwell) for the summary of the introduction. From the examples we see that generally, the generated cards are grammatically correct and contain meaningful information. However, to evaluate flashcard quality in a more rigorous manner, in the next section we conduct a user study.

Table 3. Flashcards from the Wikipedia article on *Animal Farm* by George Orwell.

Question	Answer
Who did George Orwell write a letter to about Animal Farm?	Yvonne Davet
Who do the farm animals rebel against?	Human farmer
When was Animal Farm written?	Between November 1943 and February 1944
What are two other variations of the title of Animal Farm?	A Satire and A Contemporary Satire

6   User Study

Given the strong perceptual component of flashcards, the best way of evaluating the quality of automatically generated cards is with a user study. In this study, we are interested in determining three aspects: usefulness for learning, linguistic

Table 4. Questions in the user study

Question	Scale
1) *Is this card helpful for people who are studying this topic?*	$0 - 3$
2) *The text on the card makes sense to me.*	$0 - 3$
3) *Is the answer to this question correct?*	$0 - 1$

comprehensibility and content correctness. In our user study, we ask about this three aspects and define a four-point scale for helpfulness and comprehensibility (strongly disagree, disagree, agree and strongly agree), and a binary scale for perceived content correctness ("I think the answer is incorrect", "I think the answer is correct/I do not know"). Table 4 displays the detail of the questions asked in the study. During the study, the user is shown one card at a time and has to answer the three questions before the next card is displayed.

The study consisted of 50 cards, from which 25 are generated by our automatic flashcard generation system, and the other 25 are created by humans. We obtain the human-created cards from flashcard decks that are freely available online in Anki format [2]. At the beginning of the study, the user can choose between two topics, History and Geography; this gives the user the possibility of deciding the topic she is most familiar with, or interested in. We chose History and Geography as representative topics since they consist of factual knowledge, which is often studied with flashcards. The human-created cards for History were taken from decks with titles: "Christianity" and "French Revolution", while our cards were generated from the Wikipedia article "French Revolution" and the history section of the article "Germany". For Geography, the topics were "India", "Physical Geography" and "General Geography" for the human-created cards; and our cards were generated from the article "Atmosphere", and the geography section of the articles "India" and "China". For each category, we randomly chose 25 cards from the generated cards and mixed them with 25 randomly chosen cards from the human-created decks. The origin of the flashcards, i.e., whether they are automatically generated or human created, was not revealed to the participants. 50 participants from Amazon Mechanical Turks took part in the study. Data from participants which completed the study in less than 1,000 seconds was discarded. From the remaining, 21 participants selected the category history and 27 geography. Figure 3 show the results of our user study. The maximum score for helpfulness and comprehensibility is 3 and minimum is 0; and for correctness maximum is 1 and minimum is 0.

The results show that in the case of geography there is no statistically meaningful difference between human-created and our cards for either of the three aspects. For history, the difference for helpfulness and comprehensibility is statistically significant ($p < 0.01$), with human cards being marginally better than our cards. Neither category revealed a statistically significant difference in perceived correctness. Upon further investigation we found that the difference in the history category is mainly due to three automatically generated flashcards

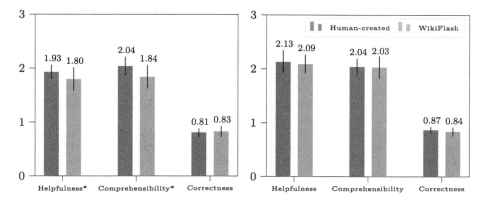

Fig. 3. Results of the user study. **Left:** Category history. Statistically significant differences ($p < 0.01$) are marked with an asterisk. **Right:** Category geography. The differences are not statistically significant.

which are too ambiguous. We intend to improve our generation and filtering procedure in future work based on this insight.

Overall, this study demonstrates that the quality of our automatically generated cards is close to the quality of cards created by humans. This result validates our system and evidences its potential for enhancing personalized learning.

7   Discussion

In this work, we have presented a system for flashcard generation from raw text. Our system builds on recent advances in natural language processing, in particular on summarization, answer extraction, question generation and question answering. We thereby base our work on recent ideas on combining different models for question-answer generation and filtering. We have implemented our system as a web application that generates flashcards from Wikipedia articles with four different levels of detail. Our user study shows that the quality of the cards generated by our application is comparable, or only slightly worse, than human-created flashcards. Our work makes available a valuable tool for personalized education. By speeding up and automatizing flashcard generation, we give students the flexibility to decide which topics to learn, beyond standard curricula. Moreover, our work can be extended and combined with existing curricula by mapping course concepts to Wikipedia pages. A usage of knowledge graphs can also be envisioned to link a user to adjacent topics for an automatically generated curriculum. We will explore these ideas in future work. We believe that in the near future tools and applications such as the one presented here will play a major role in enhancing autonomous and personalized learning. Although our application is already functional, there is still a lot of room for improvement and we plan to develop it further in order to improve computing efficiency and user experience.

References

1. Alberti, C., Andor, D., Pitler, E., Devlin, J., Collins, M.: Synthetic QA corpora generation with roundtrip consistency. In: Proceedings of the 57th Conference of the Association for Computational Linguistics, ACL (2019)
2. AnkiWeb. Shared decks - ankiweb (2020)
3. Bao, H., et al.: UniLMv2: pseudo-masked language models for unified language model pre-training. CoRR, abs/2002.12804 (2020)
4. Blšták, M., Rozinajová, V.: Automatic question generation based on analysis of sentence structure. In: Sojka, P., Horák, A., Kopeček, I., Pala, K. (eds.) TSD 2016. LNCS (LNAI), vol. 9924, pp. 223–230. Springer, Cham (2016). https://doi.org/10.1007/978-3-319-45510-5_26
5. Chan, Y.-H., Fan, Y.-C.: A recurrent BERT-based model for question generation. In: Proceedings of the 2nd Workshop on Machine Reading for Question Answering, MRQA@EMNLP (2019)
6. Chen, G., Yang, J., Hauff, C., Houben, G.-J.: LearningQ: a large-scale dataset for educational question generation. In: Proceedings of the Twelfth International Conference on Web and Social Media, ICWSM (2018)
7. Dong, L., et al.: Unified language model pre-training for natural language understanding and generation. In: Annual Conference on Neural Information Processing Systems, NeurIPS (2019)
8. Du, X., Cardie, C.: Harvesting paragraph-level question-answer pairs from Wikipedia. In: Proceedings of the 56th Annual Meeting of the Association for Computational Linguistics (2018)
9. The Examiners. theexaminers (2020)
10. Gupta, S., Gupta, S.K.: Abstractive summarization: an overview of the state of the art. Expert Syst. Appl. **121**, 49–65 (2019)
11. Hermann, K.M.: Teaching machines to read and comprehend. In: Advances in Neural Information Processing Systems (2015)
12. Kriangchaivech, K., Wangperawong, A.: Question generation by transformers (2019)
13. Kurdi, G., Leo, J., Parsia, B., Sattler, U., Al-Emari, S.: A systematic review of automatic question generation for educational purposes. Int. J. Artif. Intell. Educ. **30**(1), 121–204 (2020)
14. Kwankajornkiet, C., Suchato, A., Punyabukkana, P.: Automatic multiple-choice question generation from Thai text. In: 2016 13th International Joint Conference on Computer Science and Software Engineering (JCSSE), pp. 1–6 (2016)
15. LanguageTool. Languagetool (2020)
16. Lewis, M., et al.: BART: denoising sequence-to-sequence pre-training for natural language generation, translation, and comprehension. In: Proceedings of the 58th Annual Meeting of the Association for Computational Linguistics, ACL (2020)
17. Lin, C.-Y.: ROUGE: a package for automatic evaluation of summaries. In: Text Summarization Branches Out, pp. 74–81 (2004)
18. Liu, M., Rus, V., Liu, L.: Automatic Chinese factual question generation. IEEE Trans. Learn. Technol. **10**(2), 194–204 (2017)
19. Lopez, L.E., Cruz, D.K., Cruz, J.C.B., Cheng, C.: Transformer-based end-to-end question generation. CoRR, abs/2005.01107 (2020)
20. Niraula, N.B., Rus, V.: Judging the quality of automatically generated gap-fill question using active learning. In: Proceedings of the Tenth Workshop on Innovative Use of NLP for Building Educational Applications (2015)

21. Pan, L., Lei, W., Chua, T.-S., Kan, M.-Y.: Recent advances in neural question generation. arXiv preprint arXiv:1905.08949 (2019)
22. Patil, S.: Question generation using transformers (2020)
23. Raffel, C.: Exploring the limits of transfer learning with a unified text-to-text transformer. arXiv preprint arXiv:1910.10683 (2019)
24. Rajpurkar, P., Zhang, J., Lopyrev, K., Liang, P.: Squad: 100, 000+ questions for machine comprehension of text. In: Proceedings of the 2016 Conference on Empirical Methods in Natural Language Processing, EMNLP (2016)
25. Reimers, N., Gurevych, I.: Sentence-BERT: sentence embeddings using Siamese BERT-networks. In: Proceedings of the 2019 Conference on Empirical Methods in Natural Language Processing and the 9th International Joint Conference on Natural Language Processing, EMNLP-IJCNLP (2019)
26. Rush, A.M., Chopra, S., Weston, J.: A neural attention model for abstractive sentence summarization. In: Proceedings of the 2015 Conference on Empirical Methods in Natural Language Processing, EMNLP (2015)
27. Sanh, V., Debut, L., Chaumond, J., Wolf, T.: DistilBERT, a distilled version of BERT: smaller, faster, cheaper and lighter (2020)
28. See, A., Liu, P.J., Manning, C.D.: Get to the point: summarization with pointer-generator networks. In: Proceedings of the 55th Annual Meeting of the Association for Computational Linguistics, pp. 1073–1083 (2017)
29. Shleifer, S.: Distilbart model (2020)
30. Thalheimer, W.: The learning benefits of questions. Work Learning Research (2003)
31. HuggingFace Transformers. Question answering using distilbert (2020)
32. Vaswani, A., et al.: Attention is all you need. In: Advances in Neural Information Processing Systems (2017)
33. Wang, A., et al.: Superglue: a stickier benchmark for general-purpose language understanding systems. In: Advances in Neural Information Processing Systems (2019)
34. Yan, Y., et al.: Prophetnet: predicting future n-gram for sequence-to-sequence pre-training. CoRR, abs/2001.04063 (2020)
35. Zhang, J., Zhao, Y., Saleh, M., Liu, P.J.: PEGASUS: pre-training with extracted gap-sentences for abstractive summarization. CoRR, abs/1912.08777 (2019)
36. Zhong, M., Liu, P., Wang, D., Qiu, X., Huang, X.: Searching for effective neural extractive summarization: what works and what's next. In: Proceedings of the 57th Conference of the Association for Computational Linguistics, ACL (2019)

Video Face Recognition with Audio-Visual Aggregation Network

Qinbo Li[1]([✉]), Qing Wan[1], Sang-Heon Lee[2], and Yoonsuck Choe[1]

[1] Texas A&M University, College Station, USA
lee@tamu.edu
[2] DGIST, Daegu, Korea

Abstract. With the continuing improvement in deep learning methods in recent years, face recognition performance is starting to surpass human performance. However, current state-of-the-art approaches are usually trained on high-quality still images and do not work well in unconstrained video face recognition. We propose to use audio information in the video to aid in the face recognition task with mixed quality inputs. We introduce an Audio-Visual Aggregation Network (AVAN) to aggregate multiple facial and voice information to improve face recognition performance. To effectively train and evaluate our approach, we constructed an Audio-Visual Face Recognition dataset. Empirical results show that our approach significantly improves the face recognition accuracy on unconstrained videos.

Keywords: Video face recognition · Multimodal learning · Attention

1 Introduction

Face recognition has received considerable attention in the past decades. With the rise of Deep Convolutional Neural Network (DCNN) and large-scale face recognition datasets such as MS-Celeb-1M [10] and MegaFace [14], face recognition performance has started to exceed human performance. However, directly using the representations learned from still images does not work well on unconstrained videos.

In this paper, we propose to utilize the audio information from the video to aid in the face recognition task, as describes in Fig. 1. Our motivation is to use the audio information to increase the face recognition performance when the subject speaks in the video where the video quality is low. We collected and curated a large dataset of unconstrained videos where the subject is actively speaking. To the best of our knowledge, this is the first dataset of this kind. We also propose an Audio-Visual Aggregation Network (AVAN) to aggregate visual embeddings and audio embeddings to improve video face recognition performance.

While it is not new to use an attention module to aggregate visual embeddings, we believe that we are the first to introduce attention to aggregate speaker embeddings. AVAN then learns to aggregate the fused visual embedding and fused audio

© Springer Nature Switzerland AG 2021
T. Mantoro et al. (Eds.): ICONIP 2021, LNCS 13111, pp. 150–161, 2021.
https://doi.org/10.1007/978-3-030-92273-3_13

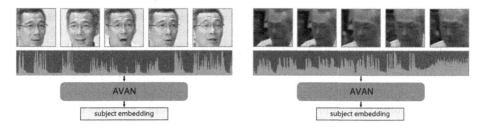

Fig. 1. The Audio-Visual Aggregation Network (AVAN) uses both the visual information and the audio information to generate a feature embedding for the subject.

embedding to generate the final embedding for the subject. Experiments show that our approach improves face recognition performance significantly.

Overall, our contributions are as follows: (1) We propose an approach to aggregate visual embeddings and audio embeddings respectively, and aggregate the resulting embeddings into the final embedding. (2) To effectively train and evaluate our approach, we constructed a large speech-video-matched audio-visual person recognition dataset, which is a first of its kind. (3) Experiments show that our approach significantly improves person recognition accuracy.

2 Related Works

Recently, convolutional neural networks (CNNs) have been used successfully in face recognition. However, large intra-class variations existing in face recognition reduce the effectiveness of softmax. To address this issue, L-Softmax [18] is the first one to encourage intra-class compactness and inter-class separability. FaceNet [24] and Triplet Network [11] use the triplet loss. SphereFace [17] and Additive Margin [28] proposed a training loss based on trigonometric functions to learn angle dis/similarities existing in the face features. These angular-based loss functions were further improved in CosFace [29] and ArcFace [6] to enhance the CNN's ability to learn geometric attributes from face images. Besides, adding an exclusive regularization term [34] could also extend the angular distance and tell apart differences in the identities.

Major categories of methods on video face recognition tasks can be classified into geometry-based methods and deep-learning-based methods. Conventionally, geometry-based methods include learning on a Euclidean metric [8] or learning on a Riemannian metric [27].

Deep learning methods [23,35] intend to distill an embedding by aggregating frames from a video sequence, with the knowledge acquired from trainable convolutional kernels, so that they are more discriminable. Applying attention algorithms could efficiently improve a CNN's performance on a video [31]. Other models like RNNs also have been found to be experimentally effective in video face recognition [9].

There are several papers on combined audio-video face recognition from the conventional machine learning perspective [1,5,26]. However, few studies [25] explore this area using deep learning methods. One of the potential reasons might be the lack of a comprehensive audio- and video-labeled dataset.

Audio-visual resources related to different tasks are abundant (not addressing face recognition). These include a lip-reading dataset [2] that decodes text from video frames containing a speakers mouth movement, an audio-video fusion dataset [12] that presents a deep learning approach to connect audio with the face in unstructured video to better identify multiple speakers, and speech separation [7] that proposes an audio-visual model to isolate a single speech signal from a mixture of sounds.

3   Existing Datasets and Their Limitations

Table 1. Comparison of different face recognition datasets. **AVFR** is the dataset we collected. Note that the video-based data sets are significantly smaller in size than the image-based ones.

Image datasets	Identity	Images	Labeled face	Labeled audio	Video datasets	Identity	Videos	Labeled face	Labeled audio
LFW	5,749	13,233	Yes	NA	YTF	1,595	3,425	Yes	No
AgeDB	568	16,488	Yes	NA	PaSC	2,802	265	Yes	No
CASIA	10k	500k	Yes	NA	UMD	3,107	22,075	Yes	No
MS1MV2	85K	5.8M	Yes	NA	iQIYI-VID	4,934	172,835	No	No
MegaFace	690K	1M	Yes	NA	IJB-C	3,531	11,779	No	No
					VoxCeleb	7,363	172,976	Yes	Yes
					AVFR	1,000	5,534	Yes	Yes

The success of image-based face recognition is largely because of large-scale face recognition datasets. Examples include the Labeled Faces in the Wild (LFW) [13], AgeDB [21], CASIA-WebFace [32], MS-Celeb-1M [10], MegaFace [14], etc. The LFW dataset focuses on an unconstrained face recognition task. It contains 13,233 images of 5,749 people. AgeDB manually collected images in the wild annotated with accurate age. The CASIA-WebFace dataset semi-automatically collected 500K images of 10K celebrities from the Internet. The MS-Celeb-1M is one of the largest datasets that contains about 10M images from 100K people (now discontinued due to concerns). The MegaFace dataset collected 1M images of 690K subjects from Flickr.

The YouTube Face dataset (YTF) [30] contains 3,425 videos of 1,595 subjects collected from Youtube, significantly smaller than image datasets. The Point and Shoot Face Recognition dataset (PaSC) [4] collected various videos concerning the distance to the camera, alternative sensors, frontal versus not-frontal views, and varying locations. UMD Face dataset [3] consists of still images as well as video frames. In terms of the video frames, the UMD Face dataset is one of the largest video face recognition datasets. However, it is currently unavailable.

IJB-C dataset [20] contains 11k videos from 3,531 subjects. However, the faces in the video frames of IJB-C dataset are not labeled.

The iQIYI-VID dataset [19] is a multi-modal person identification dataset. Each sample of the videos in this dataset contains an entire body with face and audio. However, it does not guarantee an active speaker in the video or the subject being the main speaker.

Our goal is to collect a video face recognition dataset where every subject actively speaks, and the audio information can be combined to improve face recognition accuracy. The YTF, PaSC, and UMD Face datasets only contain video frames without audio. Although IJB-C and iQIYI-VID datasets contain audio, they do not label the audio such that there is an active speaker or the active speaker is the subject. The VoxCeleb dataset and our AVFR dataset are the only two datasets with correlated audio and visual information. However, the VoxCeleb dataset is not suitable to be used in a low-quality video face recognition task. Because the VoxCeleb dataset is collected in a fully automatic way, one crucial step is to use CNN to detect celebrity faces. Compared with the VoxCeleb dataset, our AVFR dataset is collected in a semi-automatic manner, so that our AVFR dataset contains many low-quality videos, for example, the video on column 2 row 3 in Fig. 2. A relevant dataset is the AV Speech dataset. Instead of face recognition, it is proposed for isolating a single speech signal from a mixture of sounds. It contains around 300K video clips with labeled faces, and there is an active speaker in each video clip. However, all the video clips for one subject comes from the same video. Therefore, there is not enough intra-class variance for each class.

To overcome these shortcomings, we collected and curated a large video face recognition dataset, the Audio-Visual Face Recognition dataset (AVFR). See Sect. 4.1 for details. Table 1 summarizes the related face recognition datasets compared to our dataset.

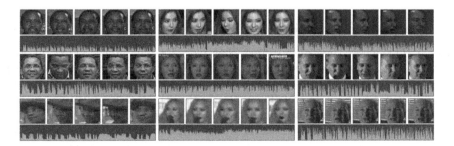

Fig. 2. We selected some examples from our AVFR dataset. Each column shows three videos from the same subject. As it is can be seen, the intra-class variance is very large. The variance comes from lighting, head pose, age, occlusion, makeup, watermark, and so on. Our dataset also covers videos with different quality. The low quality videos are due to low resolution, or the camera being far from the subject.

4   Approach

4.1   Collection of the AVFR Dataset

Our AVFR dataset contains around 5.5K unconstrained videos of 1K subjects. In the following, "subject" means the main speaker in the videos. Our goal is to collect a large video dataset, where each subject has multiple videos, and the subject is the main speaker in each video. We started by creating a list of 2,801 celebrities, covering different ages, gender, occupations, nationality, and so on. Then, we searched and downloaded 40 videos from YouTube for each subject. In this step, we downloaded 58,270 videos of the 2,801 subjects in total.

We added the search terms "speech" and "interview" in addition to the subject's name to search for the videos. However, this did not guarantee that the results satisfy our requirements. There were many videos whose subjects are not speaking or not the main speakers, or even some of the subjects are not in the video. Therefore, we selected the video clips where the subject is present and actively speaking in the next step.

We extracted MFCC with a sampling rate of 2 s and generated audio embeddings for each audio clip to aid in this labeling process. Next, we used k-means to cluster the audio clips into two categories: one is the subject's audio, and the other is not. We then manually selected the audio clips that belong to the subject. In this step, we selected 5,534 videos from 1,000 subjects.

Note that even when the subject is the main speaker in the video, there could still be other video subjects. Therefore, we also labeled the face of the subject in the video. We used a facial landmark detection approach, MTCNN [33], to detect faces from the videos. We detected faces one frame per second and then manually labeled the face belonging to the target subject. The detected face image was then resized to 112×112. In total, we detected 230,718 face images. Figure 2 shows some examples from our AVFR dataset. We will release our AVFR dataset upon publication of this paper.

4.2   Embedding: Overview

Given a video where the target subject is actively speaking in the video, our goal is to generate a feature embedding for use in identity recognition. Our approach first generates visual feature embeddings for each video frame and audio feature embeddings for each audio clip. Then, we use the attention module to aggregate the visual embeddings and audio embeddings, respectively. The attention module for the visual embeddings and audio embeddings share the same architecture but do not share the weights. Finally, we add a fully connected layer to fuse the visual embedding and audio embedding. Figure 3 illustrates our overall system architecture.

4.3   Audio and Visual Embeddings

We use pre-trained CNNs to generate audio embeddings from audio clips and visual embeddings from video frames. These CNNs are trained on large-scale

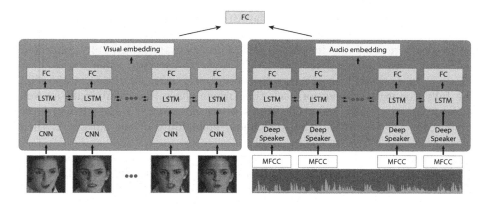

Fig. 3. This figure shows the overall architecture of our approach. We use both the video frames and audio as input to generate the embedding for the subject. Next, we use pre-trained CNNs to calculate visual embeddings from video frames and audio embeddings from audio clips. We then use the attention module to aggregate the visual embeddings and audio embeddings.

image face recognition dataset and speaker recognition dataset. These datasets are usually much larger than the video face recognition datasets.

To generate visual embeddings, we first use MTCNN [33] to detect a face from the video frame and then use the similarity transformation with the facial landmarks generated by the MTCNN. The face images are then resized into 112 × 112. The visual embedding CNN is trained on the MS1MV2 dataset with the ArcFace loss. The visual embedding network will generate visual embeddings $VF = \{vf_1, vf_2, ..., vf_N\}$, where N is the number of frames. Next, we use the pre-trained DeepSpeaker [16] model to generate the audio embeddings. The DeepSpeaker model is trained on the LibriSpeech dataset with Triplet loss. The raw audio is converted into MFCC with a sampling interval of 2 s. Next, the audio embedding network will generate audio embeddings $AF = \{af_1, af_2, ..., af_M\}$, where M equals the length of the 2-second audio clips.

4.4   Audio-Visual Attention Module

From the previous step, we generated the visual and audio embeddings. However, simple pooling does not work due to the various forms of noise and varying audio/visual quality. Therefore, we propose to use an attention module to generate weights to aggregate the visual embeddings and the audio embeddings. Similar to Gong et al.'s [9] method, we use RNN to generate the attention weights to aggregate embeddings. While it is not new to use an attention mechanism to aggregate facial embeddings, to the best of our knowledge, we are the first to introduce using an attention mechanism to aggregate speaker embeddings.

The architecture of the attention module is shown in Fig. 3. Both attention modules share the same architecture, so we use the audio embedding attention module as an example to describe the attention module. We use the feature embeddings $AF = \{af_1, af_2, ..., af_M\}$ generated from DeepSpeaker as input to the attention module. A bidirectional LSTM processes the input. Fully connected layers follow the output from the LSTM layer to generate value scores $V = \{v_1, v_2, ..., v_m\}$, where v_i represents the importance value for the i_{th} audio clip. The fully connected layers for each time frame share the architecture as well as the weights. Finally, the value scores V are normalized by a softmax layer to generate the weight w. The final audio embedding of the subject is then calculated as $e_a = \sum_i^M w_i \cdot af_i$.

Algorithm 1 describes our audio attention module. The visual attention module is very similar to the audio attention module, so it is not repeated here (the only difference is that the MFCC feature is not used, and instead of DeepSpeaker, ArcFace is used for the embedding of individual images).

We use the triplet loss to train the attention module: $L = \sum_i^N (\|e_i^a - e_i^p\|^2 - \|e_i^a - e_i^n\|^2 + m)$ where e_i^a is the embedding of the anchor sample, e_i^p is the embedding of the positive sample, and e_i^n is the embedding of the negative sample. The parameter m represents the margin penalty (in our experiment, we set it to be 3).

After the visual embeddings and the audio embeddings are aggregated, we can concatenate the embeddings to represent the subject. We further add fully connected layers for the face verification task to generate weights to concatenate the embeddings: $E = w \cdot e_v + (1 - w) \cdot e_a$.

Unlike the attention module that takes a single subject's embeddings as input, this fully connected layer takes embeddings of a pair of subjects as input, and the two subjects share the generated weight. Our intuition is that using visual embeddings only has a higher performance than using audio embeddings only, because speaker recognition is generally a more challenging task than face recognition. However, when the image quality of the video is deficient, the audio information is more reliable than the visual information. Therefore, the final fully connected layers can adjust the weights for the visual embeddings and the audio embeddings. However, our experiment shows that the last fully connected layer does not improve the performance (see Sect. 5).

5 Experiments and Results

We implemented our approach in PyTorch [22]. The DCNN for visual embeddings outputs 512-D embeddings, and the DeepSpeaker model also outputs 512-D embeddings. We used the single layer bi-LSTM with 128 hidden units, followed by a single fully connected layer to output the value score, and then a softmax layer for the attention module. The attention module for visual embedding and audio embedding share the same architecture. To train our model, we used the Adam optimizer [15] with default parameters. We set the learning rate as 2×10^{-4} and batch size as 32.

Algorithm 1: Pseudo-code of audio attention

Input: The extracted audio track from the video
$mfcc$ =extract_mfcc($audio$)
$embeddings$ =DeepSpeaker($mfcc$)
$hidden$ =initialize_hidden($batch\_size$)
$lstm\_outs, hidden$ =lstm($embeddings, hidden$)
$v = []$
for $lstm\_output$ in $lstm\_outs$:
    v_i =fc($lstm\_output$)
    $v.append(v\_i)$
w =softmax(v)
$output$ =sum($w \times embeddings, dim = 1$)
Output: The aggregated audio embedding

The network is trained with an Nvidia GTX 1080Ti GPU with 11 GB of memory. We randomly split our AVFR dataset into 90% of data for the training set and 10% of the data for the test set.

We evaluated our approach with the standard face verification task and compared our approach with three baseline methods as described below:

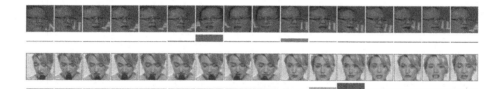

Fig. 4. This figure shows a qualitative evaluation of our visual attention module. As it can be seen, our model assigns high weights (tall red bars) for the high-quality frames, and low weights for the low-quality frames due to the undesired head pose, occlusion, etc. (Color figure online)

- **ArcFace** [6] only uses the video frames to generate feature embedding for the video. It is a pre-trained ResNet-50 network, trained on MS1MV2 dataset with ArcFace loss. It generates a 512-D embedding for each video frame. Then, we use mean fusion on all the video frames to get the final embedding for the video.
- **DeepSpeaker** [16] only uses the audio to generate feature embedding for the video. It is a pre-trained DCNN trained on the LibriSpeech dataset with triplet loss. It generates a 512-D embedding for each audio clip. Then, we use mean fusion on all the audio clips to get the final embedding for the video.
- **ArcFace+DeepSpeaker** uses ArcFace to generate a 512-D embedding from the video frames and uses DeepSpeaker to generate a 512-D embedding from

the audio. Then, it simply concatenates these two embeddings into a 1024-D embedding.

- **Ours-Visual (ArcFace + Attention)** uses ArcFace to generate 512-D embedding for each video frame. Then, it uses the attention module discussed in Sect. 4 to fuse the embeddings to generate the final embedding for the video.
- **Ours-Audio (DeepSpeaker + Attention)** uses DeepSpeaker to generate 512-D embedding for each audio clip. Then, it uses the attention module (Sect. 4) to fuse the embeddings.
- **AVAN** is our approach, as discussed in Sect. 4.

We run 10-fold cross-validation and report the True Acceptance Rate (TAR) when False Acceptance Rate (FAR) equals 0.1 and 0.01, and the best accuracy. Table 2 shows that our method outperforms the competition.

Table 2. We compare our approach with ArcFace [6] and DeepSpeaker [16] on the standard face verification task. We report the best accuracy and TAR when FAR = 0.1 and 0.01. We ran all experiments 5 times and reported the average value and std. As it can be seen, our approach (AVAN) outperforms other approaches significantly.

Method	Input Type	TAR@FAR= 0.1	TAR@FAR= 0.01	Accuracy
ArcFace [6]	Image	95.53 ± 0.68	90.76 ± 0.87	94.89 ± 0.64
DeepSpeaker [16]	Audio	86.23 ± 0.77	56.29 ± 5.54	87.47 ± 0.42
ArcFace+DeepSpk	Image+Audio	97.79 ± 0.77	93.02 ± 1.17	95.97 ± 0.43
Ours-Visual	Image	95.93 ± 0.94	92.47 ± 0.63	95.63 ± 0.47
Ours-Audio	Audio	86.83 ± 0.94	46.85 ± 5.19	88.12 ± 0.51
AVAN (Full model)	Image+Audio	$\mathbf{98.90 \pm 0.40}$	$\mathbf{95.12 \pm 0.98}$	$\mathbf{96.99 \pm 0.29}$

Figure 4 shows a qualitative evaluation of our visual attention module. The height of the bar graph is proportional to the weights assigned by our model (also, red = high, blue = low). We can see that our model assigns low weights for the low-quality frames.

For example, in the first row of Fig. 4, the head pose of the subject in the beginning and ending are not facing the camera. In the second row, the head pose in the beginning frames are also not desirable, and there are occlusions in these frames. In both cases our model assigns lower weight to these frames.

Another finding is that the attention module usually assigns high weights for some high-quality frames instead of distributing the weights to all the high-quality frames. As a result, we think it is easier for the model to learn to identify some of the highest quality frames instead of finding all of them and assigning average weights for them.

Figure 5 shows a qualitative evaluation of our audio attention module. The meaning of the bar graph is the same as in Fig. 4. It is noteworthy that audio is the only input at this stage. The reason that we include the video frames with the audio in the figure is to better explain the content of the audio. In the top row of Fig. 5, the video begins with background music, followed by the speech given by the subject. Our model assigns very low weights to the beginning of the audio.

In the second example, the video starts with the subject's speech, and then the audience applauds. Then the subject speak for 2 s, and the audience starts to laugh while the subject is speaking. Finally, the video ends with the subject's speech without noise. Our model assigns very high weights for the beginning of the audio, low weights for the middle of the audio, and some weights for the end of the audio.

Fig. 5. A qualitative evaluation of our audio attention module. In the first example, the video begins with background music. In the second example, there is background noise such as applause and laughter from the audience interleaved with the subject's speech. Our attention module assigns low weights when the quality of the audio is low.

We further add fully connected layers for the face verification task to fuse the visual embedding and audio embedding aggregated by the attention modules (Sect. 4). Our intuition is that the model can learn to adjust the weight based on the quality of the video frames to improve the accuracy. However, our experiments show that it does not improve the performance: the model simply assigns 0.5 to both the visual embedding and the audio embedding. We think this is because our dataset is not large enough to enable the model to learn such knowledge. We leave this as one of our future works.

6   Discussion and Conclusion

The main contributions of this work are two-fold: (1) we collected and curated a matched-video-speech audio-visual data set for video face recognition, which can serve as a valuable resource for the research community, and (2) we showed that attention-based fusion for each visual and audio embeddings, followed by an audio-visual fusion, again using attention, leads to superior performance compared to recognition based on vision or audio separately and without attention.

Acknowledgments. This work was supported by was supported by the DGIST R&D Program, funded by the Korean Ministry of Science and ICT (21-IT-02).

References

1. Albiol, A., Torres, L., Delp, E.J.: Fully automatic face recognition system using a combined audio-visual approach. IEE Proc.-Vis. Image Sign. Process. **152**(3), 318–326 (2005)
2. Assael, Y.M., Shillingford, B., Whiteson, S., De Freitas, N.: Lipnet: End-to-end sentence-level lipreading. arXiv preprint arXiv:1611.01599 (2016)
3. Bansal, A., Nanduri, A., Castillo, C.D., Ranjan, R., Chellappa, R.: Umdfaces: an annotated face dataset for training deep networks. In: 2017 IEEE International Joint Conference on Biometrics (IJCB), pp. 464–473. IEEE (2017)
4. Beveridge, J.R., et al.: The challenge of face recognition from digital point-and-shoot cameras. In: 2013 IEEE Sixth International Conference on Biometrics: Theory, Applications and Systems (BTAS), pp. 1–8. IEEE (2013)
5. Choudhury, T., Clarkson, B., Jebara, T., Pentland, A.: Multimodal person recognition using unconstrained audio and video. In: Proceedings, International Conference on Audio-and Video-Based Person Authentication, pp. 176–181. Citeseer (1999)
6. Deng, J., Guo, J., Xue, N., Zafeiriou, S.: Arcface: additive angular margin loss for deep face recognition. In: Proceedings of the IEEE Conference on Computer Vision and Pattern Recognition, pp. 4690–4699 (2019)
7. Ephrat, A., et al.: Looking to listen at the cocktail party: a speaker-independent audio-visual model for speech separation. arXiv preprint arXiv:1804.03619 (2018)
8. Goldberger, J., Hinton, G.E., Roweis, S., Salakhutdinov, R.R.: Neighbourhood components analysis. Adv. Neural Inform. Process. Syst. **17**, 513–520 (2004)
9. Gong, S., Shi, Y., Jain, A.K.: Recurrent embedding aggregation network for video face recognition. arXiv preprint arXiv:1904.12019 (2019)
10. Guo, Y., Zhang, L., Hu, Y., He, X., Gao, J.: MS-Celeb-1M: a dataset and benchmark for large-scale face recognition. In: Leibe, B., Matas, J., Sebe, N., Welling, M. (eds.) ECCV 2016. LNCS, vol. 9907, pp. 87–102. Springer, Cham (2016). https://doi.org/10.1007/978-3-319-46487-9_6
11. Hoffer, E., Ailon, N.: Deep metric learning using triplet network. In: Feragen, A., Pelillo, M., Loog, M. (eds.) SIMBAD 2015. LNCS, vol. 9370, pp. 84–92. Springer, Cham (2015). https://doi.org/10.1007/978-3-319-24261-3_7
12. Hoover, K., Chaudhuri, S., Pantofaru, C., Slaney, M., Sturdy, I.: Putting a face to the voice: Fusing audio and visual signals across a video to determine speakers. arXiv preprint arXiv:1706.00079 (2017)
13. Huang, G.B., Mattar, M., Berg, T., Learned-Miller, E.: Labeled faces in the wild: A database forstudying face recognition in unconstrained environments (2008)
14. Kemelmacher-Shlizerman, I., Seitz, S.M., Miller, D., Brossard, E.: The megaface benchmark: 1 million faces for recognition at scale. In: Proceedings of the IEEE Conference On Computer Vision and Pattern Recognition, pp. 4873–4882 (2016)
15. Kingma, D.P., Ba, J.: Adam: a method for stochastic optimization. In: International Conference on Learning Representations (ICLR) (2015)
16. Li, C., et al.: Deep speaker: an end-to-end neural speaker embedding system. arXiv preprint arXiv:1705.02304 650 (2017)
17. Liu, W., Wen, Y., Yu, Z., Li, M., Raj, B., Song, L.: Sphereface: deep hypersphere embedding for face recognition. In: Proceedings of the IEEE Conference on Computer Vision and Pattern Recognition, pp. 212–220 (2017)
18. Liu, W., Wen, Y., Yu, Z., Yang, M.: Large-margin softmax loss for convolutional neural networks. In: ICML, vol. 2, p. 7 (2016)

19. Liu, Y., et al.: iqiyi-vid: A large dataset for multi-modal person identification. arXiv preprint arXiv:1811.07548 (2018)
20. Maze, B., et al.: Iarpa janus benchmark-c: Face dataset and protocol. In: 2018 International Conference on Biometrics (ICB), pp. 158–165. IEEE (2018)
21. Moschoglou, S., Papaioannou, A., Sagonas, C., Deng, J., Kotsia, I., Zafeiriou, S.: Agedb: the first manually collected, in-the-wild age database. In: Proceedings of the IEEE Conference on Computer Vision and Pattern Recognition Workshops, pp. 51–59 (2017)
22. Paszke, A., et al.: Pytorch: an imperative style, high-performance deep learning library. In: Advances in Neural Information Processing Systems, pp. 8024–8035 (2019)
23. Rao, Y., Lin, J., Lu, J., Zhou, J.: Learning discriminative aggregation network for video-based face recognition. In: Proceedings of the IEEE International Conference on Computer Vision, pp. 3781–3790 (2017)
24. Schroff, F., Kalenichenko, D., Philbin, J.: Facenet: a unified embedding for face recognition and clustering. In: Proceedings of the IEEE Conference on Computer Vision and Pattern Recognition, pp. 815–823 (2015)
25. Sell, G., Duh, K., Snyder, D., Etter, D., Garcia-Romero, D.: Audio-visual person recognition in multimedia data from the iarpa janus program. In: 2018 IEEE International Conference on Acoustics, Speech and Signal Processing (ICASSP), pp. 3031–3035. IEEE (2018)
26. Tang, X., Li, Z.: Audio-guided video-based face recognition. IEEE Trans. Circ. Syst. Video Technol. **19**(7), 955–964 (2009)
27. Tuzel, O., Porikli, F., Meer, P.: Pedestrian detection via classification on riemannian manifolds. IEEE Trans. Pattern Anal. Mach. Intell. **30**(10), 1713–1727 (2008)
28. Wang, F., Cheng, J., Liu, W., Liu, H.: Additive margin softmax for face verification. IEEE Sign. Process. Lett. **25**(7), 926–930 (2018)
29. Wang, H., et al.: Cosface: large margin cosine loss for deep face recognition. In: Proceedings of the IEEE Conference on Computer Vision and Pattern Recognition, pp. 5265–5274 (2018)
30. Wolf, L., Hassner, T., Maoz, I.: Face recognition in unconstrained videos with matched background similarity. In: CVPR 2011, pp. 529–534. IEEE (2011)
31. Yang, J., et al.: Neural aggregation network for video face recognition. In: Proceedings of the IEEE Conference on Computer Vision and Pattern Recognition, pp. 4362–4371 (2017)
32. Yi, D., Lei, Z., Liao, S., Li, S.Z.: Learning face representation from scratch. arXiv preprint arXiv:1411.7923 (2014)
33. Zhang, K., Zhang, Z., Li, Z., Qiao, Y.: Joint face detection and alignment using multitask cascaded convolutional networks. IEEE Sign. Process. Lett. **23**(10), 1499–1503 (2016)
34. Zhao, K., Xu, J., Cheng, M.M.: Regularface: deep face recognition via exclusive regularization. In: Proceedings of the IEEE Conference on Computer Vision and Pattern Recognition, pp. 1136–1144 (2019)
35. Zheng, J., Ranjan, R., Chen, C.H., Chen, J.C., Castillo, C.D., Chellappa, R.: An automatic system for unconstrained video-based face recognition. IEEE Trans. Bio. Behav. Identity Sci. **2**(3), 194–209 (2020)

WaveFuse: A Unified Unsupervised Framework for Image Fusion with Discrete Wavelet Transform

Shaolei Liu[1,2], Manning Wang[1,2(✉)], and Zhijian Song[1,2(✉)]

[1] Digital Medical Research Center, School of Basic Medical Science,
Fudan University, Shanghai, China
{slliu,mnwang,zjsong}@fudan.edu.cn
[2] Shanghai Key Laboratory of Medical Image Computing and Computer Assited
Intervention, Shanghai, China

Abstract. We propose an unsupervised image fusion architecture for multiple application scenarios based on the combination of multi-scale discrete wavelet transform through regional energy and deep learning. To our best knowledge, this is the first time that a conventional frequency method has been combined with deep learning for feature maps fusion. The useful information of feature maps can be utilized adequately through multi-scale discrete wavelet transform in our proposed method. Compared with other state-of-the-art fusion methods, the proposed algorithm exhibits better fusion performance in both subjective and objective evaluation. Moreover, it's worth mentioning that comparable fusion performance trained in COCO dataset can be obtained by training with a much smaller dataset with only hundreds of images chosen randomly from COCO. Hence, the training time is shortened substantially, leading to the improvement of the model's performance both in practicality and training efficiency.

Keywords: Multi-scene image fusion · Unsupervised learning · Discrete wavelet transform · Regional energy

1 Introduction

Image fusion is the technique of integrating complementary information from multiple images obtained by different sensors of the same scene, so as to improve the richness of the information contained in one image [3]. Image fusion can compensate for the limitation of single imaging sensors, and this technique has developed rapidly in recent years because of the wide availability of different kinds of imaging devices [3]. For example, in medical imaging applications, images of different modalities can be fused to achieve more reliable and precise medical diagnosis [23]. In military surveillance applications, image fusion integrates information from different electromagnetic spectrums (such as visible and infrared bands) to achieve night vision [10].

© Springer Nature Switzerland AG 2021
T. Mantoro et al. (Eds.): ICONIP 2021, LNCS 13111, pp. 162–174, 2021.
https://doi.org/10.1007/978-3-030-92273-3_14

The extraction of feature maps and the selection of fusion rules are the two key factors determining the quality of the fused image [15], and most studies focus on proposing new methods based on these two factors. Before the overwhelming application of deep learning in image processing, many conventional approaches were used in feature extraction for image fusion, which can be divided into two categories: transform domain algorithms and spatial domain algorithms [10]. In transform domain algorithms, the source images are transformed to a specific transform domain, such as the frequency domain, where the feature maps are represented by the decomposition coefficients of the specific transform domain. In feature maps fusion, max-rule and averaging are commonly used for high and low frequency bands, respectively, and then the fused image is reconstructed by the inverse transform from the fused feature maps [1, 6]. Unlike transform domain algorithms, spatial domain algorithms employ the original pixel of source images as feature maps and directly calculate the weighted average of the source images to obtain the final fused image without dedicated feature maps extraction, where the weights are selected according to image blocks [11] or gradient information [9]. Consequently, the conventional approaches can be regarded as designing some hand-crafted filters to process the source images, and it is difficult for them to adapt to images of different scenes or parts with different visual cues in one image.

Nowadays, deep learning has been the state-of-the-art solution in most tasks in the fields of image processing and computer vision. Recently, deep learning has also been used in image fusion and achieved higher quality than conventional methods. For example, CNN can be used to automatically extract useful features and can learn the direct mapping from source images to feature maps. In recent image fusion research based on deep learning [2, 7, 8, 15, 16, 20, 23], fusion using learned features through CNN achieved higher quality than conventional fusion approaches. According to the different fusion framework utilized, deep learning based methods can be divided into the following three categories: CNN based methods [8, 14, 15, 29], encoder-decoder based methods [7, 20, 23, 27] and generative adversarial network (GAN) based methods [18]. CNN based methods merely apply several convolutional layers to obtain the weight map for source images. Encoder-decoder based methods introduce encoder-decoder architecture to extract deep features, and the deep features are fused by weighted average or concatenation. Furthermore, GAN based methods leverage conditional GAN to generate the fused image, where the concatenated source images are directly input to the generator. In these studies, the feature maps obtained through deep learning are usually simply fused by weighted averaging, and we will show that this is not optimal. More importantly, the neural networks used in these studies [7, 8, 15, 20, 23] usually need to be trained on large image dataset, which is time consuming.

In this paper, we propose an image fusion algorithm by combining the deep learning based approaches with conventional transform domain based approaches. Concretely, we first train an encoder-decoder network and extract feature maps from the source images by the encoder. Inspired by the multi-scale transform [10], discrete wavelet transform (DWT) is utilized to transform the feature maps into the wavelet domain, and adaptive fusion rules are used at low and high frequencies, thus making the beat use of the information of feature maps. Finally, inverse wavelet transform is used to reconstruct the fused feature map, which is decoded by the decoder to obtain the final fused image. Experiments show that with the additional processing of the feature maps by DWT, the quality of the fused image is remarkably improved. To the best of our knowledge, this is the first time to adopt conventional transform domain approaches to fuse the feature maps obtained from deep learning approaches.

The main contributions are summarized as follows:

(1) A generalized and effective unsupervised image fusion framework is proposed based on the combination of multi-scale discrete wavelet transform and deep learning.
(2) With multi-scale decomposition in DWT, the useful information of feature maps can be fully utilized. Moreover, a region-based fusion rule is adopted to capture more detail information. Extensive experiments demonstrate the superiority of our network over the state-of-the-art fusion methods.
(3) Our network can be trained in a smaller dataset with low computational cost to achieve comparable fusion performance compared with existing deep learning based methods trained on full COCO dataset. Our experiments show that the quality of the fused images and the training efficiency are improved sharply.

2   Proposed Method

2.1   Network Architecture

WaveFuse is a typical encoder-decoder architecture, consisting of three components: an encoder, a DWT-based fusion part and a decoder. As shown in Fig. 1(b), the inputs of the network are spatially aligned source images I_k, where $k = 1,2$ is used to index the images. Feature maps F_k are obtained by extracting features from the input source images I_k through the encoder. The feature maps F_k are first transformed into the wavelet domain, and an adaptive fusion rule is used to obtain the fused feature maps F'. Finally, the fused feature maps are input into the decoder to obtain the final fused image I_F. The encoder is composed of three ConvBlocks, where two CNNs and a Relu layer are included. The kernel size of CNNs are all 3×3. After encoding, 48D feature maps are obtained for fusion. In the DWT-based fusion part, to take 1 layer wavelet decomposition and one dimension of the feature maps F_k for example, the feature maps are decomposed to different wavelet components C_k, including one low-frequency component C_{kL}, namely L_{1k} and three high-frequency components C_{kH}: horizontal component H_{1k}, vertical component V_{1k} and diagonal component D_{1k}, respectively. Different fusion rules are employed for different components to obtain the fused wavelet components F, where the low-frequency component L_2 is obtained from the fusion of L_{11} and L_{12}, and the high-frequency components

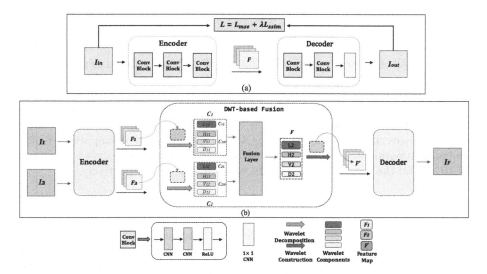

Fig. 1. (a) The framework of the training process. (b) Architecture of the proposed WaveFuse image fusion network. The feature maps learned by the encoder from the input images are processed by multi-scale discrete wavelet transform, and finally the fused feature maps are utilized to the fused image reconstruction by the decoder.

H_2, V_2 and D_2 are obtained from the fusion of H_{1k}, V_{1k} and D_{1k}, respectively. Finally, the fused low-frequency component and high-frequency components are integrated by wavelet reconstruction to obtain the final fused feature map F'. The decoder is mainly composed of two ConvBlocks and one 1×1 CNN, where the fused image is finally reconstructed.

2.2 Loss Function

The loss function L used to train the encoder and the decoder in WaveFuse is a weighted combination of pixel loss L_p and structural similarity loss L_{ssim} with a weight λ , where λ is assigned as 1000 according to [7]. The loss function L, pixel loss L_p and structural similarity loss L_{ssim} are defined as follows:

$$L = L_p + \lambda L_{ssim}, \tag{1}$$

$$Lp = ||I_{out} - I_{in}||_2, \tag{2}$$

$$L_{ssim} = 1 - SSIM(I_{out}, I_{in}), \tag{3}$$

where I_{in} and I_{out} represent the input image to the encoder and the output image of the decoder, respectively. The structural similarity (SSIM) is a widely used perceptual image quality metric, which combines the three components of luminance, structure and contrast to comprehensively measure image quality [25].

2.3 Training

We trained our network shown in Fig. 1(a) using COCO [12] containing 70,000 images, and all of them were resized to 256×256 and transformed to gray images. The batch size and epochs were set as 64 and 50, respectively. Learning rate was 1×10^{-4}. The proposed method was implemented on Pytorch 1.1.0 with Adam as the optimizer and a NVIDIA GTX 2080 Ti GPU for training. In our practical training process, we found that using comparatively small dataset, containing 300–700 images chosen randomly from COCO, still achieved a comparable fusion quality. The parameters for small dataset are as follows: learning rate was set as 1×10^{-4}, and the batch size and epochs were 16 and 100, respectively.

2.4 Fusion Rule

The selection of fusion rules largely determines the quality of fused images [15]. Existing image fusion algorithms based on deep learning usually calculate the sum of the feature maps directly, leaving the information of feature maps not fully mined.

In our method, two complementary fusion rules based on DWT are adopted for wavelet components C_k transformed by feature maps F_k, including adaptive rule based on regional energy [26] and *l1-Norm* rule [7], and the fused wavelet components are denoted as F_r and F_{l1}, respectively. In adaptive rule based on regional energy, different fusion rules are employed for different frequency components, that is, the low-frequency components C_{kL} adopts an adaptive weighted averaging algorithm based on regional energy, and for the high-frequency components C_{kH}, the one with larger variance between C_{1H} and C_{2H} will be selected as the fused high-frequency components. Due to the page limitation, the detailed description and futher equations can be found in [13]. Additionally, to preserve more structural information and make our fused image more natural, we apply *l1-Norm* rule [7] to our fusion part, where both low and high frequency components are fused by the same rule to obtain global and general fused wavelet components.

3 Experimental Results and Analysis

In this section, to validate the effectiveness and generalization of our WaveFuse, we first compare it with several state-of-the-art methods on four fusion tasks, including mult-exposure (ME), multi-modal medical (MED), multi-focus (MF) and infrared and visible (IV) image fusion. There are 20 pairs of images in each scenario, and all the images are from publicly available datasets [7,15,18,22]. For quantitative comparison, we use nine metrics to evaluate the fusion results. Then, we evaluate the fusion performance of the proposed method trained with small datasets. Finally, we also conduct the fine-tuning experiments on wavelet parameters for the further improvement of fusion performance.

3.1 Compared Methods and Quantitative Metrics

WaveFuse is compared against nine representative peer methods including discrete wavelet transform (DWT) [6], cross bilateral filter method (CBF) [5], convolutional sparse representation (ConvSR) [17], GAN-based fusion algorithm (FusionGAN) [18], DenseFuse [7] IFCNN [29], and U2Fusion [27]. All the nine comparative methods were implemented based on public available codes, where the parameters were set according to the original papers.

The commonly used evaluation methods can be classified into two categories: subjective evaluation and objective evaluation. Subjective evaluation is susceptible to human factors, such as eyesight, subjective preference and individual emotion. Furthermore, no prominent difference among the fusion results can be observed in most cases based on subjective evaluation. In contrast, objective evaluation is a relatively accurate and quantitative method on the basis of mathematical and statistical models. Therefore, in order to compare fairly and comprehensively with other fusion methods, we choose the following nine metrics:EN [21], cross entropy(CE), FMI_pixel [4], FMI_dct [4], FMI_w [4], Q^{NICE} [24]), $Q^{AB/F}$ [28], variance(VARI) and subjective similarity (MS-SSIM [19]). Each of them reflects different image quality aspects , and the larger the nine quality metrics are, the better the fusion results will be.

3.2 Comparison to Other Methods

Table 1. Quantitative comparison of WaveFuse with existing multi-scene image fusion methods. Red ones are the best results, and blue ones mark the second results. For all metrics, larger is better.

ME	EN	CE	FMI_pixel	FMI_dct	FMI_w	Q^{NICE}	$Q^{AB/F}$	VARI	MS-SSIM
U2Fusion	6.9525	4.7649	0.8529	0.4005	0.4411	0.8146	0.4319	41.5841	0.9349
IFCNN	6.5269	2.1552	0.8590	0.4580	0.4892	0.8134	0.4788	34.4859	0.9478
Wavefuse	6.9224	4.7309	0.8661	0.4941	0.5265	0.8240	0.5149	39.8423	0.9582
MED	EN	CE	FMI_pixel	FMI_dct	FMI_w	Q^{NICE}	$Q^{AB/F}$	VARI	MS-SSIM
U2Fusion	5.1257	7.5716	0.8430	0.2876	0.3471	0.8067	0.2879	57.8377	0.8980
IFCNN	5.0101	1.2406	0.8581	0.3611	0.4450	0.8075	0.3240	73.6683	0.9434
Wavefuse	5.2814	7.8243	0.8650	0.4052	0.3848	0.8094	0.3265	67.0572	0.9007
MF	EN	CE	FMI_pixel	FMI_dct	FMI_w	Q^{NICE}	$Q^{AB/F}$	VARI	MS-SSIM
U2Fusion	7.4552	0.3424	0.8706	0.4018	0.4653	0.8269	0.6586	55.5703	0.9574
IFCNN	7.2756	0.0558	0.8903	0.4687	0.5389	0.8356	0.7447	48.6216	0.9947
Wavefuse	7.3681	0.3483	0.8912	0.5041	0.5619	0.8368	0.7743	51.7256	0.9896
IV	EN	CE	FMI_pixel	FMI_dct	FMI_w	Q^{NICE}	$Q^{AB/F}$	VARI	MS-SSIM
U2Fusion	6.9092	1.1991	0.8795	0.3158	0.3546	0.8055	0.4775	37.1806	0.9196
IFCNN	6.5600	1.3125	0.8850	0.3450	0.3912	0.8062	0.5456	30.5133	0.8883
Wavefuse	6.8877	1.4285	0.8892	0.3702	0.4202	0.8084	0.5525	39.3585	0.8770

Subjective Evaluation. Examples of the original image pairs and the fusion results obtained by each comparative method for the four scenarios are shown in Fig. 2.

Multi-scene Image Fusion: We first compare the proposed WaveFuse with existing multi-scene image fusion algorithms U2Fusion [27] and IFCNN [29] in all the four different fusion scenarios, and the results of the objective metrics are shown in Table 1. From Table 1, we can see that WaveFuse achieves the best results in almost all scenarios. In some scenarios that it does not achieve the highest metric, our method is still close to the highest one.

Multi-exposure Image Fusion: The multi-exposure image fusion aims to combine different exposures to generate better subjective images in both dark and bright regions. From Fig. 2 (c1-j1, c2-j2), we can observe that CBF and ConvSR generate many artifacts. JSRSD, DWT, DeepFuse and IFCNN suffer from low brightness and blurred details. U2Fusion and WaveFuse achieve better fusion reluslts considerding both dark and bright factors.

Multi-modal Medical Image Fusion: Multi-modal medical image fusion can offer more accurate and effective information for biomedical research and clinical applications. Better multi-modal medical fused image should provide combined features sufficiently and preserve both significant textural features. As shown in Fig. 2 (c3-j3, c4-j4), JSR, JSRSD and ConvSR shows obvious artifacts in the whole image. DWT and CBF fail to preserve the crucial features of the source images. U2Fusion shows better visual results than the above-mentioned methods. However, DenseFuse still weakens the details and brightness. Information-rich fused images can be obtained by IFCNN. In contrast, our method preserves the details and edge information of both source images, which is more in line with the perception characteristics of the human vision compared to other fusion methods.

Multi-focus Image Fusion: The multi-focus image fusion aims to reconstruct a fully focused image from partly focused images of the same scene. From Fig. 2 (c5-j5, c6-j6), we can observe that JSR and JSRSD shows obvious blurred artifacts. DWT shows low brightness in the fusion results. Other compared methods perform well.

Infrared/Visible Image Fusion: Visible images can capture more detail information compared to infrared images. However, the interested objects can not be easily observed in visible image especially when it is under low contrast circumstance and the light is insufficient. Infrared images can provide thermal radiation information, making it easy to detect the salient object even in complex background. Thus, the fused image can provide more complementary information. Figure 2 (c7-j7, c8-j8) show fusion results of infrared and visible images with the comparison methods. JSR, JSRSD and FusionGAN exhibit significant artifacts., and U2Fusion shows unclear salient objects. The results in DWT, DenseFuse and IFCNN weaken the contrast. We can see that, WaveFuse preserves more details in high contrast and brightness.

Objective Evaluation. From Fig. 2, we can observe that the fusion results of CBF and ConvSR in multi-exposure images, the fusion results of CBF, JSR,

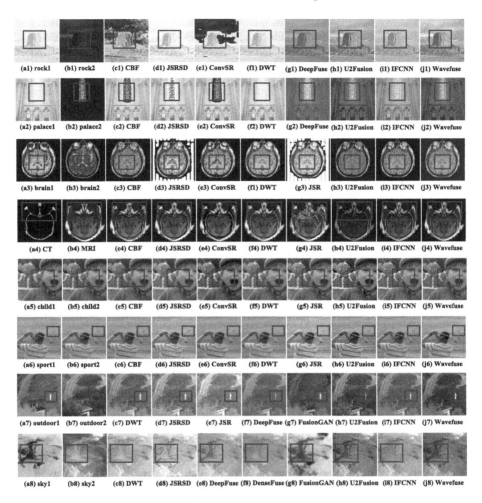

Fig. 2. Fusion results by different methods. (a1)-(b1),(a2)-(b2) are two pairs of multi-exposure source images and (c1)-(j1),(c2)-(j2) are the fusion results of them by different methods; (a3)-(b3),(a4)-(b4) are two pairs of multi-modal medical source images and (c3)-(j3),(c4)-(j4) are the fusion results of them by different methods; (a5)-(b5),(a6)-(b6) are two pairs of multi-focus source images and (c5)-(j5),(c6)-(j6) are the fusion results of them by different methods; (a7)-(b7),(a8)-(b8) are two pairs of infrared and visible source images and (c7)-(j7),(c8)-(j8) are the fusion results of them by different methods;

JSRSD and ConvSR in multi-modal medical images and the fusion results of JSRSD in multi-focus images contain poor visual effects owing to considerable artificial noise, and in this case their objective quality metrics will not be calculated for the quantitative evaluation.

Table 2. The average values of fusion quality metrics for fused images of four different scenarios. Red ones are the best results, and blue ones mark the second results. For all metrics, larger is better.

ME	EN	CE	FMI_pixel	FMI_dct	FMI_w	Q^{NICE}	$Q^{AB/F}$	VARI	MS-SSIM
DWT	5.9089	0.7402	0.8510	0.3592	0.3826	0.8165	0.4603	33.8954	0.8936
JSRSD	6.4366	1.4055	0.8533	0.2649	0.3026	0.8150	0.4257	36.3555	0.9001
DeepFuse	6.5352	0.8456	0.8556	0.4360	0.4462	0.8163	0.4573	30.7345	0.9115
U2Fusion	6.9525	4.7649	0.8529	0.4005	0.4411	0.8146	0.4319	41.5841	0.9349
IFCNN	6.5269	2.1552	0.8590	0.4580	0.4892	0.8134	0.4788	34.4859	0.9478
WaveFuse	6.9224	4.7309	0.8661	0.4941	0.5265	0.8240	0.5149	39.8423	0.9582
MED	EN	CE	FMI_pixel	FMI_dct	FMI_w	Q^{NICE}	$Q^{AB/F}$	VARI	MS-SSIM
DWT	5.1344	1.1957	0.8522	0.2472	0.3730	0.8090	0.3171	82.7802	0.8974
U2Fusion	5.1257	7.5716	0.8430	0.2876	0.3471	0.8067	0.2879	57.8377	0.8980
IFCNN	5.0101	1.2406	0.8581	0.3611	0.4450	0.8075	0.3240	73.6683	0.9434
WaveFuse	5.2814	7.8243	0.8650	0.4052	0.3848	0.8094	0.3265	67.0572	0.9007
MF	EN	CE	FMI_pixel	FMI_dct	FMI_w	Q^{NICE}	$Q^{AB/F}$	VARI	MS-SSIM
DWT	7.2436	0.0406	0.8811	0.3716	0.4908	**0.8360**	0.7530	46.9477	0.9706
DeepFuse	7.2488	0.4975	0.8791	0.4340	0.4868	0.8292	0.7361	47.8298	0.9812
U2Fusion	7.4552	0.3424	0.8706	0.4018	0.4653	0.8269	0.6586	55.5703	0.9574
IFCNN	7.2756	0.0558	0.8903	0.4687	0.5389	0.8356	0.7447	48.6216	0.9947
WaveFuse	7.3681	0.3483	0.8912	0.5041	0.5619	0.8368	0.7743	51.7256	0.9896
IV	EN	CE	FMI_pixel	FMI_dct	FMI_w	Q^{NICE}	$Q^{AB/F}$	VARI	MS-SSIM
DWT	6.6684	0.9913	0.8799	0.2244	0.3117	0.8009	0.5416	34.9068	0.7703
JSRSD	6.7557	1.3340	0.8482	0.1439	0.1924	0.8056	0.3976	36.1247	0.7636
DeepFuse	6.1759	1.0604	0.8799	0.3346	0.3718	0.8051	0.5044	22.9167	0.8473
DenseFuse	6.3550	1.0577	0.8909	0.3592	0.4157	0.8083	0.5458	27.8602	0.8131
FusionGAN	6.6208	2.3257	0.8729	0.2334	0.2937	0.8080	0.3266	40.1621	0.3963
U2Fusion	6.9092	1.1991	0.8795	0.3158	0.3546	0.8055	0.4775	37.1806	0.9196
IFCNN	6.5600	1.3125	0.8850	0.3450	0.3912	0.8062	0.5456	30.5133	0.8883
WaveFuse	6.8877	1.4285	0.8892	0.3702	0.4202	0.8084	0.5525	39.3585	0.8770

Table 2 shows the average values of the fusion quality metrics among four different fusion tasks by different fusion methods. In multi-exposure image fusion, our method ranks first in FMI_pixel, FMI_dct, FMI_w, Q^{NICE}, $Q^{AB/F}$ and MS-SSIM, and ranks second in EN, CE and VARI. In multi-modl medical image fusion, our method ranks first in EN, CE, FMI_pixel, FMI_dct, Q^{NICE} and $Q^{AB/F}$, and ranks second in FMI_w and MS-SSIM. In multi-focus image fusion, our method ranks first in FMI_pixel, FMI_dct, FMI_w, Q^{NICE} and $Q^{AB/F}$, and ranks second in EN, CE, VARI and MS-SSIM . In the infrared and visible image fusion, our method obtains the highest metrics in FMI_dct, FMI_w, Q^{NICE} and $Q^{AB/F}$, and ranks second in EN, FMI_pixel and VARI. Furthermore, from the value of the last row among three image fusion task in Overall, compared with other peer methods, our proposed method achieves the highest values in most fusion quality metrics and the second in the remaining metrics.

3.3   Comparison of Using Different Training Dataset

In order to further demonstrate the effectiveness and robustness of our network, we conducted experiments on another three different training minisets: MINI1-MINI3, each of which contains 0.5%, 1% and 2% images respectively chosen randomly from COCO, and the fusion results difference can be found among the subjective fused images, we compared the objective fusion results of WaveFuse on COCO and MINI1-MINI3. The fusion performance was compared and analyzed by the averaged fusion quality metrics. In WaveFuse, higher performance is even achieved by training on minisets. Due to page limitation, further details can be found in [13].

Furthermore, we can observe that WaveFuse is trained on minisets within one hour, where the GPU memory utilization is just 4085 MB, so it can be trained with lower computational cost compared with that trained in COCO (7.78h and 17345 MB). Accordingly, we can learn that our proposed network is robust both to the size of the training dataset and to the selection of training images.

3.4   Ablation Studies

- **DWT-based feature fusion.** In this section, we attempt to explain why DWT-based feature fusion module can improve fusion performance. DWT has been a poweful multi-sacle analysis tool in signal and image processing since it was proposed. DWT transforms the images into different low and high frequencies, where low frequencies represent contour and edge information and high frequencies represent detailed texture information [6]. In this way, DWT-based fusion methods first transform the images into low and high frequencies, and then fuse them in the wavelet domain, achieving promising fusion results. Inspired by DWT methods, we apply DWT-based fusion module to deep feature fusion extracted by deep-learning models, so as to fully utilize the information contained in deep features. We conducted the ablation study about DWT-based feature fusion module, and the results is shown in Table 3. As we can see, when we apply the module, the fusion performance is indeed improved largely.

Table 3. Ablation study on the DWT-based feature fusion module. Red ones are the best results. For all metrics, larger is better.

		EN	CE	FMI_pixel	FMI_dct	FMI_w	Q^{NICE}	$Q^{A/BF}$	VARI	MS-SSIM
ME	BaseLine	6.8230	4.9708	0.8473	0.2500	0.2875	0.8153	0.4451	37.5291	0.9566
	WaveFuse	6.9224	4.7309	0.8661	0.4941	0.5265	0.8240	0.5149	39.8423	0.9582
MED	BaseLine	5.5631	7.8961	0.8505	0.2098	0.2274	0.8078	0.2911	66.7267	0.8970
	WaveFuse	5.2814	7.8243	0.8650	0.4052	0.3848	0.8094	0.3265	67.0572	0.9007
MF	BaseLine	7.3759	0.3276	0.8663	0.2686	0.3314	0.8290	0.6821	51.0500	0.9812
	WaveFuse	7.3679	0.3498	0.8909	0.5028	0.5609	0.8368	0.7746	51.6778	0.9889
IV	baseline	6.7367	1.4337	0.8776	0.1919	0.2443	0.8054	0.5036	33.1956	0.9182
	WaveFuse	6.7805	1.4595	0.8891	0.3853	0.4122	0.8057	0.5449	34.2832	0.9268

- **Experiments on Different Wavelet Decomposition Layers and Different Wavelet Bases.** In wavelet transform, the number of decomposition layers and the selection of different wavelet bases could exert great impacts on the effectiveness of wavelet transform. We also conducted the ablation study on different settings. Due to the page limitation, we just give our final conclusion, when the number of decomposition layers and the wavelet base are set as 2 and *db1* respectively, we achieve the best fusion results. More details can be found in [13].

4   Conclusions

In this paper, we propose a novel image fusion method through the combination of a multi-scale discrete wavelet transform based on regional energy and deep learning. To our best knowledge, this is the first time that a conventional technique is integrated for feature maps fusion in the pipeline of deep learning based image fusion methods, and we think there are still a lot of possibilities to explore in this direction.

Our network consists of three parts: an encoder, a DWT-based fusion part and a decoder. The features of the input image are extracted by the encoder, then we use the adaptive fusion rule at the fusion layer to obtain the fused features, and finally reconstruct the fused image through the decoder. Compared with existing fusion algorithms, our proposed method achieves better performance. Additionally, our network has strong universality and can be applied to various image fusion scenarios. At the same time, our network can be trained in smaller datasets to obtain the comparable fusion results trained in large datasets with shorter training time and higher efficiency, alleviating the dependence on large datasets. Extensive experiments on different wavelet decomposition layers and bases demonstrate the possibility of further improvement of our method.

References

1. Da Cunha, A.L., Zhou, J., Do, M.N.: The nonsubsampled contourlet transform: theory, design, and applications. IEEE Trans. Image Process. **15**(10), 3089–3101 (2006)
2. Du, C., Gao, S.: Image segmentation-based multi-focus image fusion through multi-scale convolutional neural network. IEEE Access **5**, 15750–15761 (2017)
3. Goshtasby, A.A., Nikolov, S.: Image fusion: advances in the state of the art. Inform. Fus. **2**(8), 114–118 (2007)
4. Haghighat, M., Razian, M.A.: Fast-fmi: non-reference image fusion metric. In: 2014 IEEE 8th International Conference on Application of Information and Communication Technologies (AICT), pp. 1–3. IEEE (2014)
5. Shreyamsha Kumar, B.K.: Image fusion based on pixel significance using cross bilateral filter. Sign. Image Video Process. **9**(5), 1193–1204 (2013). https://doi.org/10.1007/s11760-013-0556-9
6. Li, H., Manjunath, B., Mitra, S.K.: Multisensor image fusion using the wavelet transform. Graph. Models Image Process. **57**(3), 235–245 (1995)
7. Li, H., Wu, X.J.: Densefuse: a fusion approach to infrared and visible images. IEEE Trans. Image Process. **28**(5), 2614–2623 (2018)
8. Li, H., Wu, X.J., Durrani, T.S.: Infrared and visible image fusion with resnet and zero-phase component analysis. Infrared Phys. Technol. **102**, 103039 (2019)

9. Li, S., Kang, X.: Fast multi-exposure image fusion with median filter and recursive filter. IEEE Trans. Consum. Electron. **58**(2), 626–632 (2012)

10. Li, S., Kang, X., Fang, L., Hu, J., Yin, H.: Pixel-level image fusion: a survey of the state of the art. Inform. Fus. **33**, 100–112 (2017)

11. Li, S., Kwok, J.T., Wang, Y.: Combination of images with diverse focuses using the spatial frequency. Inform. Fus. **2**(3), 169–176 (2001)

12. Lin, T.-Y., et al.: Microsoft COCO: common objects in context. In: Fleet, D., Pajdla, T., Schiele, B., Tuytelaars, T. (eds.) ECCV 2014. LNCS, vol. 8693, pp. 740–755. Springer, Cham (2014). https://doi.org/10.1007/978-3-319-10602-1_48

13. Liu, S.: Fusion rule description (2021). https://github.com/slliuEric/WaveFuse_code

14. Liu, Y., Chen, X., Cheng, J., Peng, H.: A medical image fusion method based on convolutional neural networks. In: 2017 20th International Conference on Information Fusion (Fusion), pp. 1–7. IEEE (2017)

15. Liu, Y., Chen, X., Peng, H., Wang, Z.: Multi-focus image fusion with a deep convolutional neural network. Inform. Fus. **36**, 191–207 (2017)

16. Liu, Y., Chen, X., Wang, Z., Wang, Z.J., Ward, R.K., Wang, X.: Deep learning for pixel-level image fusion: recent advances and future prospects. Inform. Fus. **42**, 158–173 (2018)

17. Liu, Y., Chen, X., Ward, R.K., Wang, Z.J.: Image fusion with convolutional sparse representation. IEEE Sign. Process. Lett. **23**(12), 1882–1886 (2016)

18. Ma, J., Yu, W., Liang, P., Li, C., Jiang, J.: Fusiongan: a generative adversarial network for infrared and visible image fusion. Inform. Fus. **48**, 11–26 (2019)

19. Ma, K., Zeng, K., Wang, Z.: Perceptual quality assessment for multi-exposure image fusion. IEEE Trans. Image Process. **24**(11), 3345–3356 (2015)

20. Prabhakar, K.R., Srikar, V.S., Babu, R.V.: Deepfuse: a deep unsupervised approach for exposure fusion with extreme exposure image pairs. In: ICCV, pp. 4724–4732 (2017)

21. Roberts, J.W., Van Aardt, J.A., Ahmed, F.B.: Assessment of image fusion procedures using entropy, image quality, and multispectral classification. J. Appl. Remote Sens. **2**(1), 023522 (2008)

22. Sheikh, H.R., Bovik, A.C.: Image information and visual quality. IEEE Trans. Image Process. **15**(2), 430–444 (2006)

23. Song, X., Wu, X.-J., Li, H.: MSDNet for medical image fusion. In: Zhao, Y., Barnes, N., Chen, B., Westermann, R., Kong, X., Lin, C. (eds.) ICIG 2019. LNCS, vol. 11902, pp. 278–288. Springer, Cham (2019). https://doi.org/10.1007/978-3-030-34110-7_24

24. Wang, Q., Shen, Y.: Performances evaluation of image fusion techniques based on nonlinear correlation measurement. In: Proceedings of the 21st IEEE Instrumentation and Measurement Technology Conference (IEEE Cat. No. 04CH37510), vol. 1, pp. 472–475. IEEE (2004)

25. Wang, Z., Bovik, A.C., Sheikh, H.R., Simoncelli, E.P.: Image quality assessment: from error visibility to structural similarity. IEEE Trans. Image Process. **13**(4), 600–612 (2004)

26. Xiao-hua, S., Yang, G.S., Zhang, H.l.: Improved on the approach of image fusion based on region-energy. Journal of Projectiles, Rockets, Missiles and Guidance, vol. 4 (2006)

27. Xu, H., Ma, J., Jiang, J., Guo, X., Ling, H.: U2fusion: A unified unsupervised image fusion network. IEEE Transactions on Pattern Analysis and Machine Intelligence (2020)

28. Xydeas, C., Petrovic, V.: Objective image fusion performance measure. Electron. Lett. **36**(4), 308–309 (2000)
29. Zhang, Y., Liu, Y., Sun, P., Yan, H., Zhao, X., Zhang, L.: Ifcnn: a general image fusion framework based on convolutional neural network. Inform. Fus. **54**, 99–118 (2020)

Manipulation-Invariant Fingerprints for Cross-Dataset Deepfake Detection

Zuoyan Li, Wenyuan Yang, Ruixin Liu, and Yuesheng Zhu[✉]

Shenzhen Graduate School, Peking University, Beijing, China
{lizuoyan,wyyang,anne_xin,zhuys}@pku.edu.cn

Abstract. Most of the current deepfake detection methods make efforts to learn the classifiers on the manipulated face dataset forged by a single manipulation method. However, these classifiers lack the generalization capacity to other kinds of manipulated face images, limiting their applications in real-world scenarios. In this paper, we find common detectable fingerprints for face images manipulated by different forgery methods through mapping images into a fingerprint space. Such fingerprints are called manipulation-invariant fingerprints, which would allow a classifier to generalize to face datasets forged by other methods. Therefore, a mask drop regularized unsupervised domain adaptation (MDRUDA) method is proposed for cross-dataset deepfake detection through building up the manipulation-invariant fingerprints. Specifically, a feature generator and a discriminator are trained adversarially to align the fingerprint distributions from face images forged by different methods, building up the manipulation-fingerprints that could train a more generalized classifier. We impose a mask drop regularization on the discriminator and the classifier to enrich the fingerprint space and further boost generalization ability. Experiments on public deepfake datasets show that our approach can gain significantly better generalization capability in cross-datasets scenarios, compared with prior works.

Keywords: Deepfake detection · Digital forensics · Face manipulation

1 Introduction

With the rapid development of facial manipulation technology directed by the DeepFakes[1] technique, the visual discrepancies between the facial area of real and synthetic images become invisible for humans. However, it may be abused to spread political chaos, misinformation, and porn. To mitigate the adverse impact and benefit both public security and privacy, it is of great significance to develop deepfake detection technology. Although deepfake detection methods [4, 14, 19] have made progress, most of the current approaches lack the generalization capability to the face data manipulated by unseen manipulation methods as they are tied to the face dataset forged by a specific facial manipulation method. Even worse, if the manipulation technology updates, such manipulation-specific

---

[1] https://www.github.com/deepfakes/faceswap.

© Springer Nature Switzerland AG 2021
T. Mantoro et al. (Eds.): ICONIP 2021, LNCS 13111, pp. 175–187, 2021.
https://doi.org/10.1007/978-3-030-92273-3_15

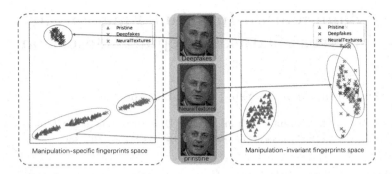

Fig. 1. A t-SNE visualization of DeepFakes and NeuralTextures forged images in two fingerprint spaces, i.e., manipulation-specific fingerprint space (left) and manipulation-invariant fingerprint space (right).

classifier may obtain near-chance performance. Some recent works have noticed this problem. Face X-ray [10] present a novel image presentation used to make a classifier more generalized only under the assumption that the face manipulation methods share a standard step. [25] attempts to find the forgery cues to improve the generalization performance. However, its generalization capability is limited as they rely on the generated facial forgeries for supervision. Thus, our work aims to find an approach that can easily generalize to manipulated images forged by other methods without being restricted by supervision.

So, it is worth asking whether manipulated face images contain common artifacts that do not rely on specific forgeries, e.g., some kind of detectable fingerprints which allow a classifier to generalize to manipulated images forged by other methods. In a related field, we find that [26] points out that GANs leave stable fingerprints in their generated images, which are distinct across different GAN-generated images, and [23] shows that CNN-generated images can exhibit a generalization ability cross datasets. That is, there are common detectable fingerprints in different CNN-generated data, helping classifiers generalize to images generated by diverse CNN-based models. Such fingerprints are for generative models related to our goal but not the same, as those models generate all the pixels of an image while the manipulated face image retains pristine pixels introducing a more complex problem.

In this paper, we focus on the common detectable fingerprints in deepfakes for making the classifier more generalized. Firstly, we define a fingerprint space where the features of images are easily identified as real or fake, and the detectable features are defined as fingerprints for corresponding face images. As a t-SNE [13] visualization of feature distributions shown in Fig. 1, we use a learning-based method to map two kinds of manipulated images e.g., NeuralTextures [21] and DeepFakes into fingerprint spaces, i.e., manipulation-specific space fingerprint space and manipulation-invariant fingerprint space. In the former, feature distributions are predictive for their corresponding forgeries. We define the features as manipulation-specific fingerprints. In the latter, feature distributions are closer and predictive for the fakeness of images without relying on a specific manipulation method. We define the features as manipulation-invariant fingerprints. That is, manipulation-specific and manipulation-invariant fingerprints exist in fingerprint spaces. It is possible to find a way to build up manipulation-invariant fingerprints and use them to make a more generalized classifier because of the existence of manipulation-invariant fingerprints.

With the above thoughts in mind, we cast the cross-dataset deepfake detection task to an unsupervised domain adaptation problem to build up the manipulation-invariant fingerprints for forged face images. Thus, we propose a mask drop regularized domain adaptation method for cross-dataset deepfake detection. A feature generator is trained competing with a discriminator to align the fingerprint distributions from datasets forged by different manipulation methods, making fingerprints more generic. Thus, the fingerprints tend to be invariant rather than specific. Moreover, the classifier is trained to identify whether a face image is forged and directs the generator to learn detectable fingerprints. To enrich the intrinsic structures of the fingerprint space and further boost the generalization, we propose a mask drop regularization applied to the classifier and the discriminator on the feature level.

We conduct extensive experiments on FaceForensics++ [19], Celeb-DF [12], and DFDC datasets [6]. The promising results exhibit that our method could enhance the generalization capacity of the standard deepfakes detection model. The major contributions of this work are summarized as follows:

- We cast the cross-dataset deepfake detection task into an unsupervised domain adaptation problem, which builds up manipulation-invariant fingerprints between the source dataset and the unlabeled target dataset in an unsupervised fashion to learn a generalized classifier.
- We propose a mask drop regularization on the feature level, which could enrich the intrinsic structures of the fingerprint space and further boost generalization ability.
- We quantitatively and qualitatively evaluate our method and its efficacy. Our experiments present that the existence of manipulation-invariant fingerprints in forged images, allowing a classifier to generalize to face images forged by other manipulation methods.

2   Related Work

In the infancy of deepfake detection, works focus on the apparent artifacts left by manipulation models, such as eye blinking frequency, blurry teeth, the inconsistency around faces, and so forth. Regarding deepfakes, [11] monitored irregular eye blinking patterns. In [17,19], It was shown that CNNs outperform traditional image forensic methods on compressed digital images. The authors [15] use DNNs to extract and compare clues corresponding to the perceived emotions from the two audiovisual modes in the video, and judge whether the input video is forged or not. DeepRhythm [18] aims to monitor the heartbeat rhythms and uses dual-spatial-temporal attention to adapt different type of fake faces.

To bridge the generalization gap, LAE [8] uses a pixel-wise mask to regularize local interpretation to enforce the model to learn intrinsic representation from the forgery region, instead of capturing artifacts in the training set and learning superficial correlations to perform detection. FT-res [3] FT proposes a new representation learning method to improve transfer performance with zero- and few-shot training for different generation methods. X. Wang et al., [24] design auxiliary supervision to guide the network to learn generalized cues. Face X-ray [10] observes most face forgery methods share a common step and tries to locate the forgery boundary with well generalization performance.

3   PROPOSED Methods

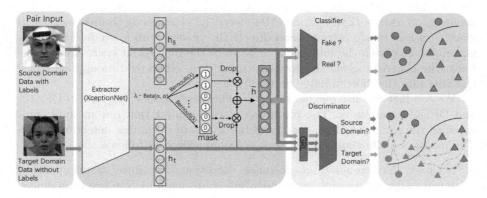

Fig. 2. Overview of Mask drop regularized unsupervised domain adaptation method.

In this paper, we propose a mask drop regularized unsupervised domain adaptation method for cross-dataset deepfake detection. Consider this task as following settings, given a labeled face dataset containing fake and real face images, which denoted by $\mathcal{X}_s = \{(x_s^i, y_s^i)\}$, where $i = 1, 2, ..., n_s$, n_s is the number of samples in $\mathcal{X}_s$ and x_s^i is a sample with label y_s^i. y_s^i is a binary label, which 0 indicates real samples and 1 for fake samples. We train on $\mathcal{X}_s$ and then test on a dataset forged by other methods, which denoted as $\mathcal{X}_t = \{x_t^j\}$, where $j = 1, 2, ..., n_t$, n_t is number of samples in $\mathcal{X}_t$, and x_t^j is a sample without label. In our method, $\mathcal{X}_s$ and $\mathcal{X}_t$ are defined as the source dataset and the target dataset respectively. Fake faces in two datasets are produced by different manipulation methods. In such a scenario, standard supervised deepfake detection methods are not competent to generalize from $\mathcal{X}_s$ to $\mathcal{X}_t$. Therefore, our goal is to utilize the labeled dataset $\mathcal{X}_s$ and the unlabeled dataset $\mathcal{X}_t$ to learn a predictive model $f : \mathcal{X} \mapsto \mathcal{Y}$ which can generalize well to $\mathcal{X}_t$. Our method is shown in Fig. 2. A feature generator G maps images into a fingerprint space H and is trained adversarially with a discriminator D to align fingerprint distributions from $\mathcal{X}_s$ and $\mathcal{X}_t$, making fingerprints generic. A classifier C is trained on $\mathcal{X}_s$ via learning the generic fingerprint distributions and constructs a more generalized classification boundary. We construct a virtual fingerprint with a non-linear combination of two fingerprints from different datasets to enrich the fingerprint space.

3.1 Unsupervised Domain Adaptation for Cross-Dataset Deepfake Detection

The unsupervised domain adaptation consists of three parts: a feature extractor G, a category classifier C and a domain discriminator D. Generator $G : \mathcal{X} \mapsto R^m$ maps both $\mathcal{X}_s$ and $\mathcal{X}_t$ to a latent space $\mathcal{H} = G(\mathcal{X}) \in R^m$, m is the dimension of $\mathcal{H}$. A category classifier $C : \mathcal{H} \mapsto \mathcal{Y}$ maps the features $\mathbf{h} \in \mathcal{H}$ into the label space $\mathcal{Y}$. A domain discriminator $D : \mathcal{H} \mapsto [0, 1]$ distinguishes the source domain data and the target domain data with label 0 and 1, respectively. The generator G is trained competitively with the domain discriminator D to bridge the divergence between the source manipulated face dataset and the target one, building up manipulation-invariant fingerprints. The process can be formulated as follows:

$$\min_G \max_D \quad \mathcal{L}_{Clf}(G, C) + \beta \mathcal{L}_{Adv}(G, D) \tag{1}$$

$$\mathcal{L}_{Clf}(G, C) = E_{(\mathbf{x}_s, y_s) \sim \mathcal{X}_s} \ell \left(C \left(G \left(\mathbf{x}_s \right) \right), y_s \right) \tag{2}$$

$$\mathcal{L}_{Ada}(G, D) = E_{\mathbf{x}_s \sim \mathcal{X}_s} \log D \left(G \left(\mathbf{x}_s \right) \right) + E_{\mathbf{x}_t \sim \mathcal{X}_t} \log \left(1 - D \left(G \left(\mathbf{x}_t \right) \right) \right) \tag{3}$$

where $\ell(\cdot, \cdot)$ is the binary cross-entropy loss.

For the purpose of optimizing the generator and the discriminator simultaneously, we integrate a gradient reverse layer (GRL) [9] between the generator and the discriminator, which multiplies the gradient of the adversarial loss by $-\rho$ during backward propagation. We follow the setting of ρ in [9] where $\rho = \frac{2}{1 + \exp(-10t)} - 1$ and $t = \frac{iters_{curr}}{iters_{total}}$.

3.2 Mask Drop Regularization

Samples from the source and target datasets alone are not sufficient for invariant fingerprints building in the fingerprint space. To alleviate this issue, we propose a mask drop regularized learning method (MDR) based on adversarial domain adaptation on the feature level, motivated by [1,27]. We construct a virtual fingerprint with a non-linear combination of pairs of a source fingerprint and a target fingerprint then feed it into the classifier and the discriminator. This combination plays a crucial role in reducing the domain discrepancy for unsupervised domain adaptation and enriches the intrinsic structures of fingerprint spaces, further boosting generalization.

Mask Drop. Firstly, we generate a mask $\mathbf{\Lambda} \in R^m$, and define the lth element of the mask as $\Lambda^{(l)} \in \mathbf{\Lambda}$, where $\Lambda^{(l)} \sim Bernoulli(\lambda)$, and $\lambda \sim Beta(\alpha, \alpha)$. α is a hyper-parameter. Then, the mask is applied to construct a virtual feature vector $\mathbf{h} \in R^m$ with non-linear combination of pairs of $(\mathbf{h}_s, \mathbf{h}_t)$ through randomly masking and dropping the elements of feature vector, where $\mathbf{h}_s = G(\mathbf{x}_s), \mathbf{h}_t = G(\mathbf{x}_t)$, for any given inputs pairs of $(\mathbf{x}_s, \mathbf{x}_t)$:

$$\mathbf{h} = M \left(\mathbf{h}_s, \mathbf{h}_t \right) = \mathbf{\Lambda} \otimes \mathbf{h}_s + (1 - \mathbf{\Lambda}) \otimes \mathbf{h}_t \tag{4}$$

where $\otimes$ denotes element-wise product.

Regularization on Category and Domain. We utilize the virtual feature $\mathbf{h}$ which contains a subset of elements of $\mathbf{h}_s$ and a subset of elements of $\mathbf{h}_t$ to regularize both on category classifier and domain discriminator. For category regularization, we only use the virtual feature vector and the label in the source domain to enforce robust prediction as the target domain data are unlabeled:

$$
\begin{aligned}
\mathcal{L}_{Clf}^{MDR}(G,C) = \\
\lambda E_{(\mathbf{x}_s,y_s)\sim\mathcal{X}_s,(\mathcal{X}_t)\sim\mathcal{X}_t} \ell\left(C\left(M(G(\mathbf{x}_s),G(\mathbf{x}_t))\right), y_s\right)
\end{aligned}
\tag{5}
$$

And the domain regularization can be defined as follows:

$$
\min_{D}\max_{G}\mathcal{L}_{Ada}^{MDR}(G,D)
\tag{6}
$$

$$
\begin{aligned}
\mathcal{L}_{Ada}^{MDR}(G,D) = \lambda E_{\mathbf{x}_s\sim\mathcal{X}_s,\mathbf{x}_t\sim\mathcal{X}_t} \log D(M(G(\mathbf{x}_s),G(\mathbf{x}_t))) \\
+ (1-\lambda) E_{\mathbf{x}_s\sim\mathcal{X}_s,\mathbf{x}_t\sim\mathcal{X}_t} \log\left(1 - D(M(G(\mathbf{x}_s),G(\mathbf{x}_t)))\right)
\end{aligned}
\tag{7}
$$

3.3   Loss Function

Integrating all modules in question, the loss function of the proposed drop regularized unsupervised domain adaptation method is:

$$
\mathcal{L}_{MDRUDA} = \mathcal{L}_{Clf} + \beta\mathcal{L}_{Ada} + \gamma_1\mathcal{L}_{Clf}^{MDR} + \gamma_2\mathcal{L}_{Ada}^{MDR}
\tag{8}
$$

where β, γ_2 and γ_2 are the hyperparameters for trading off different losses.

4   Experiments

4.1   Datasets

FaceForensics++ (FF++) [19] is a forged facial video dataset consisting of 1000 original videos that have been forged with four face manipulation methods: DeepFakes (DF), Face2Face (F2F) [22], FaceSwap[2] (FS), and NeuralTextures (NT) [21]. Deepfake Detection Challenge (DFDC) [6] is a video dataset, with over 100,000 total videos sourced from 3,426 actors, produced with several Deepfake, GAN-based, and non-learned methods. Celeb-DF [12] is a deepfake dataset including 408 real videos and 795 fake video with higher visual quality. In our experiments, we adopt FF++ [19] for training. To evaluate the generalization of our method, we use the following datasets: 1)FF++ [19] that contains four types of facial forgeries; 2) DFDC [6]; 3) Celeb-DF [12].

4.2   Implementation Detail

Training Details. RetinaFace algorithm [5] was adopted for face detection and face alignment to perform the data pre-processing. All the detected faces were normalized to $299 \times 299 \times 3$ as the input of the network, and we did not adopt

---

[2] www.github.com/MarekKowalski/FaceSwap.

any data augmentation while training our model for directly evaluating the efficacy of our method. We sampled 40 frames per video in FF++ and 32 frames per video in others. Xception [2] is imposed as the standard model and our backbone. The Adam optimizer with an initial learning rate of 0.0002 is used for the optimization. Models are trained in 20 epochs with 2x2080ti GPUs and 32 GB memory. α is a hyperparameter that controls the selection of λ. β, γ_1 and γ_2 are hyperparameters that balance different losses. In our experiments, β was set to 0.1. The values of α, γ_1 and γ_2 had influences on the adaptation performance, so they were selected via tuning on the unlabeled test data for different tasks. α was set to 0.2 or 0.5. γ_1 and γ_2 were chosen from $\{0.1, 0.01\}$ and $\{0.01, 0.001\}$.

Evaluation Metrics. To get a comprehensive performance evaluation of our method, we use the Accuracy (ACC), Area Under Curve (AUC), Average Precision (AP), Equal Error Rate (EER) as evaluation metrics.

4.3   Cross-Dataset Experimental Results

Table 1. Generalization ability evaluation. BI is an extra dataset in [10].

Model	Source	Target dataset AUC			
		DF	F2F	FS	NT
Xception [19]	DF	99.38	75.05	49.13	80.39
X. Wang [24]	DF	99.26	98.05	97.13	-
Face X-ray [10]	DF	99.17	94.14	75.34	93.85
	DF+BI	99.12	97.64	98.00	**97.77**
Ours	DF	99.99	**99.67**	**99.92**	97.57
Xception [19]	F2F	87.56	99.53	65.23	65.90
X. Wang [24]	F2F	98.53	99.99	78.63	-
Face X-ray [10]	F2F	98.52	99.06	72.69	91.49
	F2F+BI	99.03	99.31	98.64	**98.14**
Ours	F2F	**99.96**	99.65	**99.99**	97.15
Xception [19]	FS	70.12	61.70	99.36	65.90
X. Wang [24]	FS	99.98	99.64	**1.00**	-
Face X-ray [10]	FS	93.77	92.29	99.20	86.63
	FS+BI	99.10	98.16	99.09	**96.66**
Ours	FS	**99.64**	**99.91**	1.00	96.18
Xception [19]	NT	93.09	84.82	47.98	99.50
X. Wang [24]	NT	-	-	-	-
Face X-ray [10]	NT	99.14	98.43	70.56	98.93
	NT+BI	99.27	98.43	97.85	99.27
Ours	NT	**99.56**	**99.60**	**99.65**	99.04

Overfiting of The Standard Classifier. As we can see in Table 1, the standard classifier Xception relies on specific fingerprints for forged images and lacks generalization ability.

The Generalization Ability of Our Method. We then evaluated the generalization of our method. For a fair comparison, we used the same network architecture with Xception, which was pretrained on imageNet [20]. As shown in Table 1, the generalization of the standard model with our method got enhancement surprisingly. And we got better performance on most of the datasets than the state-of-the-art generalized classifier Face X-ray, except on the NT dataset. Note that we directly cite the numbers from the original paper [10] for a fair comparison. We think it is because the discrepancies among the distributions of NT and other manipulated data are too large, but the gap between the distribution of real faces and fake faces in NT is relatively small. Moreover, the large scale of self-supervised training dataset [10] is another factor.

Table 2. Benchmark results in terms of ACC, AUC, AP and EER for our framework, the baseline Xception [19] and Face X-ray [10]. * indicates the number is from [10].

Method	Source	Target dataset							
		Celeb-DF				DFDC			
		ACC	AUC	AP	EER	ACC	AUC	AP	EER
Xception	FF++	35.71	36.92	55.60	64.40	51.57	64.85	62.30	39.00
Face X-ray	BI	-	*74.76	*68.99	*31.16	50.36	60.27	60.48	45.00
	BI and FF++	-	*80.58	*73.33	*26.70	-	-	-	-
Ours	DF	**83.67**	91.04	93.86	17.20	**63.53**	**68.12**	**65.14**	**36.67**
	F2F	80.61	89.47	93.53	19.40	58.80	63.39	60.82	40.87
	FS	77.55	**91.98**	**94.73**	**16.40**	59.50	62.50	59.48	40.73
	NT	75.51	84.41	88.56	19.40	60.97	63.69	60.71	39.63

Benchmark Results on Unseen Datasets. We evaluated our method on popular benchmark datasets. We showed the forgery detection results in terms of ACC, AUC, AP, and EER. Table 2 exhibits the results of the baseline, Face X-ray [10] and our method on public large scale datasets, i.e., DFDC and Celeb-DF. Note that, as the DFDC preview dataset's [7] inaccessibility, we reproduced Face X-ray then tested on the DFDC dataset. Here, we compared our method with the baseline Xception and the state-of-the-art detector Face X-ray. The generalization results show that our method is better than both Face X-ray and the baseline. It was worth noting that our method obtained better performance on Celeb-DF, just using a subset of FF++ as the training set, such like DF, F2F, FS, and NT. In this case, the Face X-ray uses millions of images as its training set, on the contrary, ours is less. Our method's performance in generalizing to DFDC is not as good as Celeb-DF, since fake faces in DFDC could be either a face swap or voice swap (or both) claimed by Facebook, and videos in DFDC are suffered from varieties transforms. There may be two faces in a frame, which one face may be fake and another may be real. This will influence our method.

Table 3. Detection accuracy comparison with recent methods.

Model	Source		Detection accuracy	
	F2F	FS	F2F	FS
LAE	yes	no	90.93	63.15
FT-res	yes	4 images	94.47	72.57
MTDS	yes	no	92.77	54.07
Face X-ray	yes	no	**97.73**	85.69
Ours	yes	no	96.61	**88.82**

Comparison with Recent Works. Two methodologies have evolved from recent research works. One is focusing on direct artifacts left by manipulation methods. Another one is making efforts to learn intrinsic representation. One of representative work of the former is face X-ray [10], which try to locate the blending boundary introduced by blend procedure. For the latter, there are two works FT-res [3] and LAE [8], as well as a MTDS [16] learning detection and localization simultaneously. We presented comparisons with such works of two methodologies in Table 3, where the 'yes' indicates the dataset is labeled, 'no' indicates the dataset is unlabeled, and '4 images' indicates that there are 4 labeled images from the corresponding dataset. It shows our method outperforms recent works.

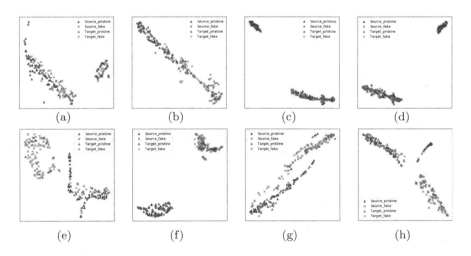

(a)   (b)   (c)   (d)

(e)   (f)   (g)   (h)

Fig. 3. The effect of adaptation on the distribution of the extracted features (best viewed in color). Blue points correspond to the source domain examples, while red ones correspond to the target domain.

T-SNE Visualization. To validate our method's generalization ability and observe manipulation-invariant fingerprints, we used t-SNE projection to visualize feature distributions at different points of our method and of Xception, as shown in Fig. 3, while color-coding the domains. We randomly sampled 50 positive samples and 50 negative samples in each case. All of the experiments were only trained on DF. Experiments in the first row of Fig. 3 are trained with XceptionNet [19], then tested on Celeb-DF, F2F, NT and FS corresponding to Fig. 3(a), 3(c) and 3(d) respectively. Experiments in the second row of Fig. 3 are trained with our proposed method, then tested on Celeb-DF, F2F, NT and FS. The corresponding results are shown in Figure 3(e), 3(f), 3(g) and 3(h). We mapped the input data into the fingerprint space with a trained extractor. We can see mostly all feature distributions of training data are discriminative with both two methods. However, the first row exhibited that feature distributions of unseen data were not discriminative with the baseline Xception [19], as the model relied on training manipulated images and learned a specific kind of fingerprints for DF. With our method, the feature distributions of unseen data were more generic and discriminative for different kinds of forged images, shown in Figure 3(e), 3(f), 3(g) and 3(h).

Table 4. Comparison results of our method with different scales of the target dataset.

Source	Target	Scale of target dataset	ACC	AUC	AP	EER
DF	FS	10%	89.33	95.24	96.15	11.19
		50%	87.74	95.87	96.69	9.82
		100%	**89.60**	**97.35**	**98.32**	**9.68**

4.4 Influence of Target Dataset's Scale

We wonder how the scale of the target dataset influences our method. So, we evaluated the impact of the number of samples in the target dataset on our method, as shown in Table 4. We use ACC, AUC, AP and EER to evaluate the performance on frame level. Specifically, when the source data set is DF and the target data set is FS, we train our model on DF and different numbers of FS, and evaluate generalization on the same FS test set. We use 3 different scales of FS dataset, which contain 10%, 50%, and 100% number of the original FS in FF++ [19]. Experimental results show that the number of target datasets will affect the effectiveness of our method. For example, a larger number of samples increases generalization, on the contrary, it decreases generalization. Compared with the original dataset, even if only 10% of the original FS data set can be obtained, the AUC is reduced by 2.11%, the EER is increased by 1.51%, and the AP is reduced by 2.17%.

Table 5. Ablation study on FF++ dataset.

Method	Source	Target dataset											
		DF			FF			FS			NT		
		ACC	AUC	EER	ACC	AUC	EER	ACC	AUC	EER	ACC	AUC	EER
w/o MDR	DF	99.57	99.96	0.42	92.48	98.66	4.82	89.25	95.00	19.35	88.24	92.49	11.59
Ours		99.39	99.91	0.61	**95.42**	**99.13**	**4.20**	89.60	**97.35**	**9.68**	**89.23**	**95.79**	**10.23**
w/o MDR	FF	**97.43**	**99.78**	2.54	98.26	98.93	2.13	91.49	95.87	8.23	84.27	93.95	12.79
Ours		96.26	99.67	**2.03**	98.66	99.16	1.67	**92.74**	**98.64**	**5.49**	**86.67**	**95.53**	**9.82**
w/o MDR	FS	95.27	98.90	4.36	92.54	97.71	5.56	98.13	99.68	2.08	81.34	89.43	16.19
Ours		**96.61**	**99.09**	**3.10**	**94.98**	**98.17**	**5.06**	99.03	99.60	0.94	**87.58**	**93.58**	**13.06**
w/o MDR	NT	92.87	**98.57**	6.17	93.16	96.83	7.16	89.28	95.04	11.46	96.13	98.14	4.64
Ours		**93.74**	98.13	**5.76**	**93.68**	**97.30**	**6.12**	**91.67**	**98.16**	**6.82**	95.69	98.30	4.85

4.5 Effectiveness of MDR

To further improve the generalization ability, we propose the mask drop regularization (MDR), which enriches intrinsic structures of the fingerprint space. For evaluating the effectiveness of MDR, we conduct and evaluate all of experiments on the frame level in terms of ACC, AUC, and EER. We used Xception [2] as our backbone network and set the unsupervised domain adaption with GAN [9] as our baseline. We conduct ablation experiments on FF++ dataset, as shown in Table 5. Compared with baseline, the enhancement in terms of ACC varies from +0.98% (FS to DF) to +4.14% (FS to NT). And increase +0.19% (FS to DF) and +4.15% (FS to NT) for AUC. In terms of EER, the values vary from −0.51% (FF to DF) to −3.13% (FS to NT). But there are some cases where the performance of baseline is better.

5 Conclusion

In this work, we propose a mask drop regularized unsupervised domain adaptation method (MDRUDA) for cross-dataset deepfake detection, based on the existence of manipulation-invariant fingerprints in different kinds of manipulated face images. We enhance the standard detector's generalization capacity using manipulation-invariant fingerprints in cross-dataset scenarios, built up by an adversarial scheme that trains a generator and a discriminator to align fingerprint distributions. We then propose mask drop regularization on the feature level to boost generalization ability further. Extensive experiments have been performed to demonstrate the generalization ability of MDRUDA, showing that our method is capable of accurately distinguishing unseen forged images and t-SNE visualization results show that our method can build up the manipulation-invariant and detectable fingerprints of different forged faces. Such fingerprints allow a classifier to generalize to face images forged by other manipulation methods, which is helpful for practical deepfake detection applications.

Acknowledgments. This work was supported in part by the National Innovation 2030 Major S&T Project of China under Grant 2020AAA0104203, and in part by the Nature Science Foundation of China under Grant 62006007.

References

1. Berthelot, D., Raffel, C., Roy, A., Goodfellow, I.J.: Understanding and improving interpolation in autoencoders via an adversarial regularizer. In: ICLR (Poster). OpenReview.net (2019)
2. Chollet, F.: Xception: deep learning with depthwise separable convolutions. In: Proceedings of the IEEE Conference on Computer Vision and Pattern Recognition, pp. 1251–1258 (2017)
3. Cozzolino, D., Thies, J., Rössler, A., Riess, C., Nießner, M., Verdoliva, L.: Forensictransfer: weakly-supervised domain adaptation for forgery detection. arXiv preprint arXiv:1812.02510 (2018)
4. Dang, H., Liu, F., Stehouwer, J., Liu, X., Jain, A.K.: On the detection of digital face manipulation. In: Proceedings of the IEEE/CVF Conference on Computer Vision and Pattern Recognition, pp. 5781–5790 (2020)
5. Deng, J., Guo, J., Zhou, Y., Yu, J., Kotsia, I., Zafeiriou, S.: Retinaface: Single-stage dense face localisation in the wild. arXiv preprint arXiv:1905.00641 (2019)
6. Dolhansky, B., et al.: The deepfake detection challenge dataset. arXiv preprint arXiv:2006.07397 (2020)
7. Dolhansky, B., Howes, R., Pflaum, B., Baram, N., Ferrer, C.C.: The deepfake detection challenge (DFDC) preview dataset. arXiv preprint arXiv:1910.08854 (2019)
8. Du, M., Pentyala, S., Li, Y., Hu, X.: Towards generalizable deepfake detection with locality-aware autoencoder. In: Proceedings of the 29th ACM International Conference on Information & Knowledge Management, pp. 325–334 (2020)
9. Ganin, Y., et al.: Domain-adversarial training of neural networks. J. Mach. Learn. Res. **17**(1), 2030–2096 (2016)
10. Li, L., et al.: Face X-ray for more general face forgery detection. In: Proceedings of the IEEE/CVF Conference on Computer Vision and Pattern Recognition, pp. 5001–5010 (2020)
11. Li, Y., Chang, M.C., Lyu, S.: In ICTU oculi: exposing AI created fake videos by detecting eye blinking. In: 2018 IEEE International Workshop on Information Forensics and Security (WIFS), pp. 1–7. IEEE (2018)
12. Li, Y., Yang, X., Sun, P., Qi, H., Lyu, S.: Celeb-DF: a new dataset for deepfake forensics. arXiv preprint arXiv:1909.12962 (2019)
13. van der Maaten, L., Hinton, G.: Visualizing data using t-SNE. J. Mach. Learn. Res. **9**(Nov), 2579–2605 (2008)
14. Masi, I., Killekar, A., Mascarenhas, R.M., Gurudatt, S.P., AbdAlmageed, W.: Two-branch recurrent network for isolating deepfakes in videos. In: Vedaldi, A., Bischof, H., Brox, T., Frahm, J.-M. (eds.) ECCV 2020. LNCS, vol. 12352, pp. 667–684. Springer, Cham (2020). https://doi.org/10.1007/978-3-030-58571-6_39
15. Mittal, T., Bhattacharya, U., Chandra, R., Bera, A., Manocha, D.: Emotions don't lie: an audio-visual deepfake detection method using affective cues. In: ACM Multimedia, pp. 2823–2832. ACM (2020)
16. Nguyen, H.H., Fang, F., Yamagishi, J., Echizen, I.: Multi-task learning for detecting and segmenting manipulated facial images and videos. arXiv preprint arXiv:1906.06876 (2019)

17. Nguyen, H.H., Yamagishi, J., Echizen, I.: Capsule-forensics: Using capsule networks to detect forged images and videos. In: ICASSP 2019–2019 IEEE International Conference on Acoustics, Speech and Signal Processing (ICASSP), pp. 2307–2311. IEEE (2019)
18. Qi, H., et al.: Deeprhythm: exposing deepfakes with attentional visual heartbeat rhythms. In: ACM Multimedia, pp. 4318–4327. ACM (2020)
19. Rossler, A., Cozzolino, D., Verdoliva, L., Riess, C., Thies, J., Nießner, M.: Face-forensics++: learning to detect manipulated facial images. In: Proceedings of the IEEE International Conference on Computer Vision, pp. 1–11 (2019)
20. Russakovsky, O., Deng, J., Su, H., Krause, J., Satheesh, S., Ma, S., Huang, Z., Karpathy, A., Khosla, A., Bernstein, M., et al.: ImageNet large scale visual recognition challenge. Int. J. Comput. Vision 115(3), 211–252 (2015)
21. Thies, J., Zollhöfer, M., Nießner, M.: Deferred neural rendering: Image synthesis using neural textures. ACM Trans. Graph. (TOG) 38(4), 1–12 (2019)
22. Thies, J., Zollhofer, M., Stamminger, M., Theobalt, C., Nießner, M.: Face2face: real-time face capture and reenactment of RGB videos. In: Proceedings of the IEEE Conference on Computer Vision and Pattern Recognition, pp. 2387–2395 (2016)
23. Wang, S.Y., Wang, O., Zhang, R., Owens, A., Efros, A.A.: CNN-generated images are surprisingly easy to spot... for now. In: Proceedings of the IEEE Conference on Computer Vision and Pattern Recognition, vol. 7 (2020)
24. Wang, X., Yao, T., Ding, S., Ma, L.: Face manipulation detection via auxiliary supervision. In: Yang, H., Pasupa, K., Leung, A.C.-S., Kwok, J.T., Chan, J.H., King, I. (eds.) ICONIP 2020. LNCS, vol. 12532, pp. 313–324. Springer, Cham (2020). https://doi.org/10.1007/978-3-030-63830-6_27
25. Xuan, X., Peng, B., Wang, W., Dong, J.: On the generalization of GAN image forensics. In: Sun, Z., He, R., Feng, J., Shan, S., Guo, Z. (eds.) CCBR 2019. LNCS, vol. 11818, pp. 134–141. Springer, Cham (2019). https://doi.org/10.1007/978-3-030-31456-9_15
26. Yu, N., Davis, L.S., Fritz, M.: Attributing fake images to GANs: Learning and analyzing GAN fingerprints. In: Proceedings of the IEEE International Conference on Computer Vision, pp. 7556–7566 (2019)
27. Zhang, H., Cisse, M., Dauphin, Y.N., Lopez-Paz, D.: Mixup: beyond empirical risk minimization. arXiv preprint arXiv:1710.09412 (2017)

Low-Resource Neural Machine Translation Using Fast Meta-learning Method

Nier Wu, Hongxu Hou$^{(\boxtimes)}$, Wei Zheng, and Shuo Sun

College of Computer Science-College of Software,
Inner Mongolia University, Hohhot, China
cshhx@imu.edu.cn

Abstract. Data sparsity is fundamental reason that affects the quality of low-resource neural machine translation models (NMT), although transfer learning methods can alleviate data sparsity by introducing external knowledge. However, the pre-trained model parameters are only suitable for the current task set, which does not ensure better performance improvement in downstream tasks. Although meta-learning methods have better potential, while meta-parameters are determined by the second-order gradient term corresponding to a specific task, which directly leads to the consumption of computing resources. In addition, the integration and unified representation of external knowledge is also the main factor to improve performance. Therefore, we proposed a fast meta-learning method using multiple-aligned word embedding representation, which can map all languages to the word embedding space of the target language without seed dictionary. Meanwhile, we update the meta-parameters by calculating the cumulative gradient on different tasks to replace the second-order term in the ordinary meta-learning method, which not only pays attention to the potential but also improves the calculation efficiency. We conducted experiments on three low-resource translation tasks of the CCMT2019 data set and found that our method significantly improves the model quality compared with traditional methods, which fully reflects the effectiveness of the proposed method.

Keywords: Meta-learning · Machine translation · Low-resource

1 Introduction

Common methods to deal with data sparsity mainly include unsupervised learning methods and knowledge transfer methods. The unsupervised learning training process using the back-translation mainly improves the model quality by minimizing the cosine distance between the source monolingual word embedding and the source monolingual word embedding after round-trip translation. Generally, some destabilization are introduced into the model by adding adversarial samples in the training set, the model is forced to adapt to various noise signals to improve robustness. However, due to the lack of supervision signal,

T. Mantoro et al. (Eds.): ICONIP 2021, LNCS 13111, pp. 188–199, 2021.
https://doi.org/10.1007/978-3-030-92273-3_16

the effect of the model is often lower than that of the model based on supervised learning. Transfer learning method [10] enables the model to quickly adapt to low-resource tasks (also known as fine-tuning) by pre-training the model in high-resource language pairs, then freezing some parameters and updating only output layer parameters. It adopts the prior knowledge of the resource-rich language pairs to assist the generation of the low-resource tasks [2].

As a type of transfer learning, meta-learning is essentially a process of learn to learn. This is a model-agnostic method, that is, the learned parameters do not depend on any specific tasks, so that it can be well extended to new tasks never encountered during training phase. At present, parameter optimization based meta-learning method and model-based meta-learning method can be well applied to machine translation, text generation and other tasks. [9] proposed a meta-learning method leveraging multiple domain data for low-resource machine translation. They found that the performance of machine translation is affected by the size of training sets in some domains, so they utilized a new word transition technique for fast domain adaptation. Meanwhile, they also proposed a meta-learning training policy to alternately update model parameters and meta-parameters to improve model quality. [6] proposed to apply model-agnostic meta-learning algorithm (MAML) [4] to low-resource neural machine translation, and construct the translation problem as a meta-learning problem. They trained an excellent initial parameter, and then constructed a vocabulary for all languages. Then they trained the translation model of low-resource languages based on the initial parameters. [8] proposed an unsupervised word-level translation model to obtain cross-lingual word embedding for multi-language representation. Although the meta-learning method has better potential and robustness to new tasks than the transfer learning method, the meta-parameters are limited by the second-order term of the specific task, and the resource consumption increases exponentially. Therefore, we proposed a fast meta-learning policy to replace the original MAML algorithm. The specific process is as follows.

- We presented a cross-lingual word embedding representation for integrating multilingual knowledge, mapping multiple languages to the word embedding space of the target language (Chinese) to achieve word alignment.
- We proposed a method that can quickly update meta-parameters, also known as Reptile meta-learning method, without performing quadratic gradient calculations on specific tasks to guide the gradient direction of meta-parameters. It can not only improve the computational efficiency, but also ensure the robustness of the model.

2 Background

Neural Machine Translation. The neural machine translation model consists of encoder and decoder. The encoder encodes the source language $X = x_1, ..., x_n$ into a set of vectors with fixed dimensions, and the decoder predicts the current target token y_t based on the translated tokens $y_{0:t-1}$ and the source language X, see Eq. 1.

$$p(Y|X;\theta) = \prod_{t=1}^{T+1} p(y_t|y_{0:t-1}, x_{1:T'};\theta) \qquad (1)$$

At present, the encoder mainly includes sequential (Recurrent neural network, RNN) and non-sequential structures (Convolutional neural network, CNN), and the decoder usually adopts autoregressive mode (RNN) to avoid information leakage. With the efficient feature extraction ability of self-attention, the NMT model based on Transformer gradually shows significant performance.

NMT Model with Low Resources. The common method to solve the problem of data sparsity is to use external knowledge. At present, the effective methods are unsupervised learning method and transfer learning method. For unsupervised learning, both data enhancement [1] and dual-learning [7] can improve the robustness of the model by expanding the corpus and adapting to noise. For transfer learning method, the common practice is to pre-training the model on the resource-rich corpus, and fine-tuning the low-resource tasks based on the pre-trained parameters [3,5].

Meta-learning is similar to transfer learning, which is divided into two steps: task-specific parameter update and meta-parameter update. The parameter update process of task-specific task is consistent with the above, that is, the model samples a group of resource-rich tasks $T^1, ..., T^k$ and estimates the parameters through the maximum likelihood estimation method (MLE). Meta-parameter updating is to calculate the second-order gradient of each task through the MAML algorithm, and then update the meta-parameters through the second-order gradient, so that it can adapt to low-resource tasks after a few steps of training, see Eq. 2.

$$\theta^* = Learn(T^0; MetaLearn(T^1, ..., T^K)) \qquad (2)$$

According to the above process, we summarize the task-specific learning process for maximizing the logarithmic posterior probability of model parameters for a low-resource task T^0 with a given data set D_T. See Eq. 3.

$$Learn(D_T, \theta^0) = \underset{\theta}{argmax} \sum_{(X,Y) \in D_T} logp(Y|X;\theta) - \beta \left\| \theta - \theta^0 \right\|^2 \qquad (3)$$

where X and Y represent the source language and target language data sets, respectively. We introduced a constraint condition to prevent the updated parameters θ^0 from being too far away from the meta-parameter θ. β indicates the hyper-parameter which is used to adjust the weight of the constraint condition to improve the generalization of the model. See Eq. 4 for loss function.

$$Loss(\theta) = E_k E_{D_{T^k}, D'_{T^k}} \left[\sum_{(X,Y) \in D_{T^k}} logp(Y|X; Learn(D_{T^k}, \theta)) \right] \qquad (4)$$

3   Our Approach

This paper mainly introduces a cross-lingual word embedding representation method for integrating multilingual knowledge and a NMT method using Reptile meta-learning training policy. The model structure is shown in Fig. 2.

3.1   Cross-Lingual Word Embedding

In general, the lexical spaces of languages are independent of each other, and mapping the vocabulary of all languages to the same vector space is a prerequisite for knowledge transfer. However, the general method is to use the seed dictionary as the supervision signal to minimize the cosine distance of semantically equivalent words in the two languages. Finally, the 2-norm loss is used to construct the optimal assignment matrix Q, see Eq. 5.

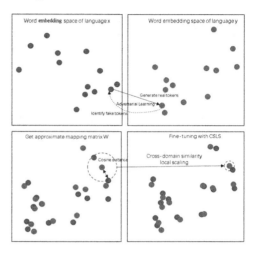

$$M = argmin_Q \sum_i \|X - QY_i\|^2$$

(5)

Fig. 1. Cross-lingual word embedding representation.

where X indicates mapped language, Y_i indicates target language. For low-resource tasks, since there is no seed dictionary as a supervised signal to optimize the mapping matrix. Therefore, we use the adversarial learning method to obtain an approximate mapping matrix W assisted by word frequency information, then optimize W by fine-tuning. Specifically, we train a discriminator to distinguish between WX and Y, and also train a generator to deceive the discriminator so that it cannot distinguish whether the representation is obtained by sampling directly from Y or by mapping after sampling from X. Wherein the discriminator and the generator loss function as shown in Eq. 6 and 7.

$$L_D(\theta_D|W) = -\frac{1}{n}\sum_{i=1}^{n} logP_{\theta_D}(src=1|WX_i) - \frac{1}{m}\sum_{i=1}^{m} logP_{\theta_D}(src=0|Y_i) \quad (6)$$

$$L_D(W|\theta_D) = -\frac{1}{n}\sum_{i=1}^{n} logP_{\theta_D}(src=0|WX_i) - \frac{1}{m}\sum_{i=1}^{m} logP_{\theta_D}(src=1|Y_i) \quad (7)$$

However, the accuracy of the mapping matrix W obtained in the high frequency words is better than the low frequency words, so it is necessary to fine tune W.

In addition, the process of fine-tuning W is essentially a *Procrustes* problem, and we obtain an approximate value through singular value decomposition W^*. See Eq. 8.

$$W^* = \underset{W \in O_d(\mathbb{R})}{argmin} \|WX - Y\|_F, U\Sigma V^T = SVD(YX^T) \tag{8}$$

where $\mathbb{R}$ represents vector set. Then we select some high-frequency words and their nearest neighbors in another language to construct high-quality bilingual corpus to obtain the refined W. For the metric selection of nearest neighbor words distance, if cosine distance is used, it may lead to hubness: some words are neighbors of many words, while some words are not neighbors of any words. Therefore, in order to punish these hubness, we adopt cross-domain similarity local scaling (CSLS) distance as a measure. See Eq. 9.

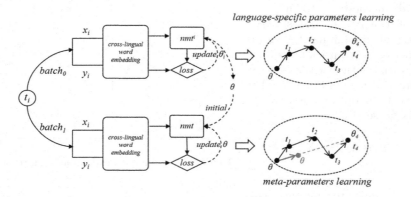

Fig. 2. In batch 0, the parameters of a specific task are learned and used it as initialization parameters for the next task. In batch 1, when the meta parameter is ready to be updated, there are two steps: 1. Utilize the cumulative gradient obtained by K-sampling as the direction of the meta-gradient. 2. The initial meta-parameters advance after 1 steps and update (about half the distance between the final task-specific model parameter and the meta-parameters).

$$CSLS(Wx_s, y_t) = 2cos(Wx_s, y_t) - \frac{1}{K}\sum_{y_t \in N_T(Wx_s)} cos(Wx_s, y_t) - r_S(y_t) \tag{9}$$

Where r_T represents the mean value of cosine similarity of K words closest to Wx_s in the target language, and r_S represents the mean of cosine similarity of K words closest to y_t in the source language.

3.2   Reptile Meta-learning Based NMT Method

Task-Specific Model Parameters. To improve the generalization of the model and make it better adapt various tasks, we first need to let the model learn the corresponding specific tasks. Like transfer learning methods, we need to learn model parameters from other high-resource language pairs. Given the training set $D_{train}^{(i)}$ and test set $D_{test}^{(i)})$ of the tasks t_i, we use the maximum likelihood estimation algorithm (MLE) to update the model parameters, and the specific process is shown in Eq. 10.

$$Learn(D_{train}^{(i)}; \theta') = \theta - \alpha \bigtriangledown_\theta Loss_{t_i}^{(0)}(nmt_\theta^i) \tag{10}$$

Where θ indicates model parameters, α is learning rate and nmt_θ^i indicates the corresponding model. $Loss_{t_i}^{(0)}$ indicates the loss in the 0-th batch data in task t_i.

Meta-parameter. In order to adapt the model parameters to various tasks, in each iteration step, there will be an initial parameter θ, using $D_{train}^{(i)}$ to update the gradient of K tasks and obtain new parameters θ^* corresponding to different tasks, and then using $D_{test}^{(i)})$ on K tasks to update the global initial parameter θ. The calculation process of task-specific model parameters θ^* and meta-parameters θ is shown in Eq. 11 and 12.

Table 1. Reptile meta-parameter update algorithm.

Algorithm
Require: $p(\tau)$: Distribution over tasks
Require: α, K:Step hyper-parameters
Initialisation: Random θ
For $i = 1, 2, ..., n$ **do**
sample tasks $\tau_i \sim p(\tau)$
For all τ_i **do**
Evaluate the update $\theta_i = \theta - \alpha \bigtriangledown_\theta Loss_{\tau_i}(\theta)$
k times
End for
update:$\theta = \theta + \frac{\alpha}{K} \sum_i^n (\theta_i - \theta)$
End for

$$\theta^* = \underset{\theta}{argmin} \sum_{t_i \sim p(t)} Loss_{t_i}^{(1)}(nmt_{\theta'}^i) \tag{11}$$

$$\theta \leftarrow \theta - \beta \bigtriangledown_\theta \sum_{t_i \sim p(t)} Loss_{t_i}^{(1)}(nmt_{\theta - \alpha \bigtriangledown_\theta Loss_{t_i}^{(0)}(nmt_\theta^i)}) \tag{12}$$

Meta-learning is regarded as a nested parameter update process. As shown in Eq. 13, after learning specific task parameters in the inner loop, the model samples new batches of data from the same data set in the outer loop to estimate the gradient. The meta-parameters are updated iteratively with the current gradient as the optimization direction. It can be seen that this method realizes the model parameter update at the cost of calculating the high-order gradient. Although it has potential for training the new task model, it consumes a lot of computing resources. Therefore, we adopt a Reptile meta-learning parameter updating method, and the specific process is shown in Table 1.

According to Table 1, for initial parameter θ, k-round stochastic gradient descent of $SGD(Loss(nmt_\theta^i), \theta, k)$ is carried out according to $Loss(nmt_\theta^i)$, and then the parameter vector is returned. The version with batch samples multiple tasks at a single step. The gradient of our method is defined as $(\theta - W)/s$, where s is the step size used by SGD.

4   Experiments

4.1   Experimental Datasets

Our experimental data set include four language pairs from the Europarl[1]: French-English (Fr-En), German-English (De-En), Italian-English (It-En) and Spanish-English (Es-En). It can be seen that all language pairs take English as the target language. For convenience, we build a pivot-based machine translation model to obtain the corresponding parallel corpus of European languages-Chinese: En-Zh, Fr-Zh, De-Zh, Es-Zh, It-Zh. In addition, it also includes three Asian language pairs: Korean-Chinese (Ko-Zh), Japanese-Chinese (Ja-Zh) and Vietnamese-Chinese

Table 2. The size of the training sample during meta-training and meta-test.

Corpus	sents.	src-tokens	trg-tokens
En-Zh	1.93M	3.22M	33.61M
Fr-Zh	2.77M	51.39M	50.2M
De-Zh	1.92M	44.55M	47.81M
Es-Zh	1.96M	51.58M	49.09M
It-Zh	1.91M	47.4M	49.67M
Ko-Zh	0.54M	10.82M	11.11M
Vt-Zh	0.8M	15.95M	16.3M
Ja-Zh	0.68M	10.17M	11.23M
Mo-Zh	0.26M	8.85M	9.39M
Ti-Zh	0.4M	9.12M	8.68M
Ug-Zh	0.46M	10.12M	11.29M

(Vt-Zh). Among them, the Korean-Chinese (Ko-Zh) language pairs is from the Korean parallel data set[2], and the Japanese-Chinese (Ja-Zh) language pairs is from the ASPEC-JC corpus, which is constructed through manual translation of Japanese scientific papers. Due to the lack of sufficient Vietnamese-Chinese (Vt-Zh) parallel corpus, we use crawler tools to obtain Vietnamese (Vt) text from Wikipedia, and use Google translator[3] to generate the corresponding Chinese (Zh) text[4]. For the low-resource neural machine translation tasks, we use three data set of Mongolian-Chinese (Mo-Zh), Uyghur-Chinese (Ug-Zh) and Tibetan-Chinese (Ti-Zh) in CCMT2019 corpus. The scale of all translation tasks is shown in Table 2.

---

[1] http://www.statmt.org/europarl.

[2] https://sites.google.com/site/koreanparalleldata.

[3] https://translate.google.cn/?sl=vi&tl=zh-CN&op=translate.

[4] The Vietnamese corpus has 0.8 million Vietnamese sentences and 10 million Vietnamese monosyllables.

4.2 Configuration and Benchmarks

Configuration. Our model is mainly constructed by Pytorch[5], which is a flexible neural network framework and our model is improved based on the Transformer model of the released Pytorch version[6]. Among them, the word embedding dimension is set to 300, the number of hidden layer nodes is set to 512, the number of hidden layers of encoder and decoder is set to 4, and the number of heads is set to 6. We set dropout rate to 0.2 to avoid over-fitting, and the batch size is set to 256. In addition, the beam search size of candidate set is set to 10. Because the word embedding space belongs to the unified word embedding space, it can encode any language. Therefore, we need to vectorize the vocabulary of multi-lingual. To improve the representation ability of word embedding, we adopt a dynamic word embedding representation method, we first employed FastText[7] to generate static monolingual word vector, and then use MUSE[8] or VECMAP[9] to generate cross-lingual word embedding representation. Meanwhile, we use ELMo[10] to obtain contextual dynamic word embedding to avoid the problem of ambiguous words. In test phase, we use beam search to find the best translated sentences. Decoding ends when every beam gives an ⟨*eos*⟩.

Table 3. Comparison of experimental results. Our model shows potential advantages in three different target tasks in a fully supervised environment.

Model	Mo-Zh	Ug-Zh	Ti-Zh
Tensor2Tensor	28.15	23.42	24.35
Transfer-NMT	28.58	24.39	25.27
Meta-NMT	29.95	25.52	26.73
R.Meta-NMT	**30.83**	**26.29**	**27.18**

Benchmarks. Our benchmarks includes: Tensor2Tensor[11], Tansfer-NMT[12], Meta-NMT[13] [6].

4.3 Result and Analysis

The translation quality of the proposed method in low-resource tasks is observed by comparing with various benchmarks. Meanwhile, we also use different data sets to conduct experiments to verify the degree of knowledge transfer. See Table 3 and 4. As shown in Table 3, compared with the classic benchmark (Tensor2Tensor), the BLEU scores of our method in the three low-resource tasks has increased by 2.68, 2.87, and 2.83 respectively. This fully demonstrates that the knowledge transfer method can effectively improve the quality of low-resource

---

[5] https://pytorch.org/.
[6] https://github.com/pytorch/fairseq.
[7] https://github.com/facebookresearch/fastText.
[8] https://github.com/facebookresearch/MUSE.
[9] https://github.com/artetxem/vecmap.
[10] https://github.com/DancingSoul/ELMo.
[11] https://github.com/tensorflow/tensor2tensor.
[12] https://github.com/ashwanitanwar/nmt-transfer-learning-xlm-r.
[13] https://github.com/MultiPath/MetaNMT.

Table 4. Low resource translation quality corresponding to various source datasets.

Meta-Train	Mo-Zh		Ug-Zh		Ti-Zh	
	none	finetune	none	finetune	none	finetune
It Es	9.98	14.61 ± .18	3.58	5.61 ± .18	4.41	4.51 ± .28
Fr En De	11.76	16.92 ± .3	4.05	7.25 ± .24	4.29	5.94 ± .15
European	14.53	19.08 ± .12	4.46	8.16 ± .08	5.17	6.91 ± .35
Ko	11.39	15.97 ± .25	6.39	10.38 ± .14	6.53	8.1 4± .16
Vt Ja	15.55	21.38 ± .11	7.11	9.57 ± .31	6.74	7.89 ± .15
Asia Languages	18.86	23.15 ± .29	10.76	11.41 ± .12	10.76	11.57 ± .10
All Languages	19.49	24.01 ± .27	11.12	12.56 ± .08	12.17	12.96 ± .19
Full Supervised	**31.76**		**27.1**		**28.35**	

tasks by introducing external knowledge. In addition, compared with the benchmark based on knowledge transfer method, the performance of our model has also been improved. In addition, compared with the benchmark based on knowledge transfer methods (Transfer-NMT and Meta-NMT), the performance of our model has also been improved. Among them, the method based on transfer learning pays more attention to the current task and lacks certain potential for new tasks, which makes the new task easy to lead to local optimal problems in the model fine-tuning phase.

Meta-NMT [6] used a MAML based meta-learning method (a method involving second-order gradient calculation), and employed a traditional cross-lingual word embedding representation as modeling unit, that is, queries and locates the position of low-resource language words in the unified word embedding space

Table 5. Time consumption.

Model	Time	Speedup
Meta-NMT	≈72 h	-
RMeta-NMT	≈40 h	1.8×

through the key-value network, without considering the hubness phenomenon. However, the method proposed in this paper has a certain improvement in word embedding representation and calculation efficiency due to the consideration of the above problems. Among them, the training time consumption of the two meta-learning based models is shown in Table 5.

As shown in Table 4, when we choose some large-scale languages (such as English, German, French, etc.) at the learning stage of specific tasks, the fine-tuned low-resource tasks have better translation quality than the models that choose small-scale language pairs. In addition, when we choose Asian language, the performance of the model is significantly improved compared with choosing European language. Therefore, we conclude that no matter which method is adopted, the translation performance will be improved when there have some implicit connection between the high-resource and low-resource languages. For example, it belongs to a unified language family or has similar orthographic and syntactic forms.

4.4 Ablation Experiments

In order to verify the effectiveness of our method, we conducted ablation experiments to observe the impact of cross-lingual word embedding method and Reptile meta-learning method on low-resource tasks. Among them, for cross-lingual word embed-

Table 6. Ablation experiments.

Model	Mo-Zh		Ug-Zh		Ti-Zh	
	Dev	Test	Dev	Test	Dev	Test
ML+CSM	28.78	28.16	24.2	23.35	25.77	25.28
ML+CSLS	30.34	29.99	28.53	25.72	29.01	27.14
RML+CSM	32.48	29.61	27.29	25.8	28.85	27.02
RML+CSLS	**34.35**	**31.16**	**29.25**	**27.17**	**31.21**	**28.18**

ding representation, our word embedding method based on cross-domain similarity local scaling (CSLS) is mainly compared with cross-lingual word embedding using cosine similarity measurement (CSM). For parameter update methods, we mainly compare with Gu's method (ML)[14]. See Table 6 for details.

We use the BPE method to tokenize the corpus. As shown in Table 6, when we choose the Gu's method to update the model parameters and use the CSLS-based cross-lingual word embedding representation, compared with the traditional CSM-based method, the BLEU scores on the test set are increased by 1.83, 2.37 and 1.86, respectively. It can be seen that our cross-lingual word embedding method has richer semantic representation

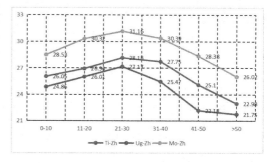

Fig. 3. BLEU scores for sentences of different lengths.

capabilities. In addition, compared with traditional meta-learning methods, our Reptile meta-learning parameter updating method (RML) also shows significant performance in low-resource translation tasks. When using the same experimental configuration, the quality of the model is improved by 1.17, 1.45 and 1.04 respectively compared with the traditional meta-learning method.

Figure 3 shows the translation performance of the model for sentences of different lengths. The BLEU scores was highest when the sentence length was about 25 words, and significantly decreased when the length was greater than 50 words.

---

[14] https://github.com/MultiPath/MetaNMT.

4.5 Case Analysis

Figure 4 shows an example generated using different models. It can be seen that the example translation obtained using the Tensor2Tensor model has a certain fluency and fidelity, and also handle the UNK problem well, but it lacks the ability to identify and translate named entities.

Source	ᠴᠣᠨᠠᠷ᠎ᠠ᠋ ᠢᠷᠦᠭᠡ ᠴᠣᠨᠠᠷ ᠦᠨ ᠴᠣᠣᠷᠬᠠᠨ ᠥᠷᠥᠭᠡ᠎ᠠ᠋ ᠰᠢᠨᠰᠬᠠᠨ᠎ᠠ᠋ ᠰᠢᠮᠨ᠎ᠠ᠋ ᠥ ᠢᠣᠷᠭᠣᠨ᠎ᠠ᠋ ᠥᠮᠣᠭ᠎ᠠ᠋〉 ··
Ref.	游览 了 包括 温莎 城堡 和汉普顿 皇宫 。
Tensor2Tensor	游览 包含 温特 古堡 和 皇宫 。
Transfer-NMT	游览 了 unk 城堡 和 unk 园林 。
Meta-NMT	游历 包括 unk 城堡 和汉普森 皇宫 。
RMeta-NMT	游览 了 温莎 城堡 和 英国 皇宫 。

Fig. 4. Translation analysis.

Although Transfer-NMT and Meta-NMT models can identify named entities well by introducing external knowledge, due to the inherent defects of cross-lingual word embedding, the models are not sufficient to deal with the UNK problem (low accuracy of cross-domain word alignment).

5 Conclusion

The paper proposed a Reptile meta-learning method that uses cross-domain similarity local scaling word embedding to optimize model parameters so that it can efficiently and accurately adapt to low-resource translation tasks. In future work, we will continue to study low-resource machine translation methods based on meta-learning to better deal with common problems in translation, such as data sparsity, out-of-vocabulary (OOV).

References

1. Abdulmumin, I., Galadanci, B.S., Isa, A.: Iterative batch back-translation for neural machine translation: a conceptual model. CoRR abs/2001.11327 (2020). https://arxiv.org/abs/2001.11327
2. Aji, A.F., Bogoychev, N., Heafield, K., Sennrich, R.: In neural machine translation, what does transfer learning transfer? In: Jurafsky, D., Chai, J., Schluter, N., Tetreault, J.R. (eds.) Proceedings of the 58th Annual Meeting of the Association for Computational Linguistics, ACL 2020, Online, 5–10 July 2020, pp. 7701–7710. Association for Computational Linguistics (2020). https://doi.org/10.18653/v1/2020.acl-main.688
3. Cheng, Y., Liu, Y., Yang, Q., Sun, M., Xu, W.: Neural machine translation with pivot languages. CoRR abs/1611.04928 (2016). http://arxiv.org/abs/1611.04928
4. Finn, C., Abbeel, P., Levine, S.: Model-agnostic meta-learning for fast adaptation of deep networks. In: Precup, D., Teh, Y.W. (eds.) Proceedings of the 34th International Conference on Machine Learning, ICML 2017, Sydney, NSW, Australia, 6–11 August 2017. Proceedings of Machine Learning Research, vol. 70, pp. 1126–1135. PMLR (2017).http://proceedings.mlr.press/v70/finn17a.html

5. Gu, J., Hassan, H., Devlin, J., Li, V.O.K.: Universal neural machine translation for extremely low resource languages. In: Walker, M.A., Ji, H., Stent, A. (eds.) Proceedings of the 2018 Conference of the North American Chapter of the Association for Computational Linguistics: Human Language Technologies, NAACL-HLT 2018, New Orleans, Louisiana, USA, 1–6 June 2018, Volume 1 (Long Papers), pp. 344–354. Association for Computational Linguistics (2018). https://doi.org/10.18653/v1/n18-1032

6. Gu, J., Wang, Y., Chen, Y., Li, V.O.K., Cho, K.: Meta-learning for low-resource neural machine translation. In: Riloff, E., Chiang, D., Hockenmaier, J., Tsujii, J. (eds.) Proceedings of the 2018 Conference on Empirical Methods in Natural Language Processing, Brussels, Belgium, 31 October–4 November 2018, pp. 3622–3631. Association for Computational Linguistics (2018). https://doi.org/10.18653/v1/d18-1398

7. He, D., et al.: Dual learning for machine translation. In: Lee, D.D., Sugiyama, M., von Luxburg, U., Guyon, I., Garnett, R. (eds.) Advances in Neural Information Processing Systems 29: Annual Conference on Neural Information Processing Systems 2016, 5–10 December 2016, Barcelona, Spain, pp. 820–828 (2016), https://proceedings.neurips.cc/paper/2016/hash/5b69b9cb83065d403869739ae7f0995e-Abstract.html

8. Lample, G., Conneau, A., Ranzato, M., Denoyer, L., Jégou, H.: Word translation without parallel data. In: 6th International Conference on Learning Representations, ICLR 2018, Vancouver, BC, Canada, 30 April–3 May 2018,Conference Track Proceedings. OpenReview.net (2018). https://openreview.net/forum?id=H196sainb

9. Li, R., Wang, X., Yu, H.: Metamt, a meta learning method leveraging multiple domain data for low resource machine translation. In: The Thirty-Fourth AAAI Conference on Artificial Intelligence, AAAI 2020, The Thirty-Second Innovative Applications of Artificial Intelligence Conference, IAAI 2020, The Tenth AAAI Symposium on Educational Advances in Artificial Intelligence, EAAI 2020, New York, NY, USA, 7–12 February 2020, pp. 8245–8252. AAAI Press (2020). https://aaai.org/ojs/index.php/AAAI/article/view/6339

10. Zoph, B., Yuret, D., May, J., Knight, K.: Transfer learning for low-resource neural machine translation. In: Su, J., Carreras, X., Duh, K. (eds.) Proceedings of the 2016 Conference on Empirical Methods in Natural Language Processing, EMNLP 2016, Austin, Texas, USA, 1–4 November 2016, pp. 1568–1575. The Association for Computational Linguistics (2016). https://doi.org/10.18653/v1/d16-1163

Efficient, Low-Cost, Real-Time Video Super-Resolution Network

Guanqun Liu[1,2] , Xin Wang[1(✉)] , Daren Zha[1], Lei Wang[1] ,
and Lin Zhao[1]

[1] Institute of Information Engineering, Chinese Academy of Sciences, Beijing, China
{liuguanqun,wangxin,zhadaren,wanglei,zhaolin1}@iie.ac.cn
[2] School of Cyber Security, University of Chinese Academy of Sciences,
Beijing, China

Abstract. Video Super-Resolution (VSR) task aims to reconstruct missing high-frequency information lost in degradation. Researchers have proposed many excellent models. However, these models require large memory and high computational cost. In this paper, we propose a novel VSR model called StudentVSR (StuVSR) which is a unidirectional recurrent network. To guarantee StuVSR can generate sufficient high-frequency information, we propose Inceptual Attention (IA) mechanism. Meanwhile, to compress the model size, we utilize the idea of knowledge distillation. We take an auto-encoder network as teacher and redesign the knowledge distillation mode. StuVSR employs extremely small parameters and accomplishes the VSR task in a rapid manner. StuVSR can generate 30-frame-per-second (FPS) 1080p-2k videos in real-time. We conduct comparison experiments to prove the superiority of StuVSR and StuVSR achieves the highest Peak Signal to Noise Ratio (PSNR) score among 16 state of the arts. We also explore the function of the inceptual attention and the knowledge distillation mode through ablation experiments. We will publish the codes at https://github.com/Dawn3474/StuVSR.

Keywords: Video super-resolution · Knowledge distillation · Attention mechanism

1 Introduction

Super-resolution (SR) aims to generate high-resolution (HR) images or frames from their degraded low-resolution (LR) counterparts and has been applied in many fields, such as object recognition [14], facial recognition [24], medical imaging /cite2013Cardiac and so on. SR is composed of Single Image Super-Resolution (SISR) and Video Super-Resolution (VSR). Compare to SISR focuses on the intrinsic properties of single image, VSR poses an extra challenge as it involves multiple high-related video frames and requires exploring additional properties between frames.

L. Wang—Supported by Institute of Information Engineering.

T. Mantoro et al. (Eds.): ICONIP 2021, LNCS 13111, pp. 200–211, 2021.
https://doi.org/10.1007/978-3-030-92273-3_17

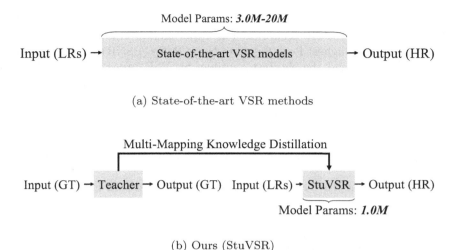

(b) Ours (StuVSR)

Fig. 1. Comparison of model scale. Figure 1a is the statistical results of the 16 state-of-the-art methods, and Fig. 1b is our StuVSR. GT represents ground truth. In inference, the teacher network is discarded, leaving the StuVSR to participate in the VSR calculation. StuVSR is 3–20 times lighter than existing VSR models.

Recently, researchers have proposed many outstanding VSR networks [1,4, 8,16,17,19]. Most VSR models consist of four modules: propagation, feature enhancement, upsampling, and reconstruction. For instance, RBPN [6] introduces sliding window for propagation, proposes multiple projections for feature enhancement, employs pixel-shuffle [17] for upsampling and a convolutional layer for reconstruction. Such designs are effective but inevitably increase the model size and redundant computation (see Fig. 1). In practice, completing VSR in real-time or embedding VSR in other tasks requires the VSR network to achieve excellent results with a small computational cost and short running time. Existing networks hardly meet this requirement.

In this paper, we propose a model called **StudentVSR** (StuVSR). Real-time processing requires the network to handle the situation where the number of input frames is unfixed and no future frames are given. Therefore, we adopt unidirectional recurrent network (RNN) as propagation. According to BasicVSR [2], unidirectional RNN is not the optimal choice. This requires our network to have a superior feature enhancement module. Inspired by the achievements of attention mechanism in SR field [26], we propose a novel attention mechanism called **Inceptual Attention** (IA) and embed it in the feature enhancement module. Furthermore, to achieve the goal of small computational cost and short running time, we borrow the idea of knowledge distillation. However, unlike traditional knowledge distillation, we set up a teacher network to handle image restoration that is different from the student network and propose multi-mapping knowledge distillation as a method of knowledge distillation.

To analyze the performance of our proposed framework, we compare StuVSR with state-of-the-art VSR networks. The experimental results show that our model achieves the highest Peak Signal to Noise Ratio (PSNR) with the smallest model parameters and the shortest runtime. StuVSR processes more than 30 frames per second on Nvidia Tesla T4. We also conduct the ablation experiment to explore the function of multi-mapping knowledge distillation and IA and the results show that these components have indispensable roles.

To summarize, our contributions are four-fold:

- We propose a novel VSR network called StuVSR, which processes videos in real-time.
- We propose a new attention mechanism to assist network in generating sufficient high-frequency information.
- We propose a new knowledge distillation mode to compress the model size.
- We conduct extensive comparison experiments to prove the superiority of our model and demonstrate the indispensable functions of components through ablation experiments.

2   Related Work

Video Super-Resolution. The superiority of the VSR mission lies in utilizing complementary information across frames. Most networks extract spatio-temporal information between frames and propagate it to the current frame. According to the mode of propagation, existing VSR approaches can be mainly divided into two frameworks - sliding-window and recurrent.

VESPCN [1] used a sliding window with a window size of 3. They utilized motion compensation between frames to align adjacent frames. The aligned frames are finally turned into an HR frame through convolutions and upsampling. TDAN [20] adopted deformable convolutions (DCNs) to implicitly extract the temporal information and perform spatial warping. EDVR [21] further used DCNs in a multi-scale manner to align more accurately. Other approaches adopted recurrent framework. FRVSR [16] propagated the previous HR frame unidirectionally and took the current LR frame as input. BasicVSR [2] explored the function of modules in VSR networks and found that bidirectional propagation is the optimal choice and proposed two baseline models BasicVSR and IconVSR. The parameters of these models range from 3.3M to 20.6M.

Knowledge Distillation. Hitton et al. [7] proposed knowledge distillation. Introducing the soft target related to the teacher network as part of the total loss can induce the training of the student network (simplified and low complexity) to realize the knowledge transfer. Knowledge distillation has been widely used in many fields.

Choi et al. [3] introduced knowledge distillation to object detection task. Peng et al. [15] used knowledge distillation for one-shot neural architecture search with the help of knowledge distillation, So et al. [18] managed to achieve the same quality with the original Transformer by using 37.6% fewer parameters.

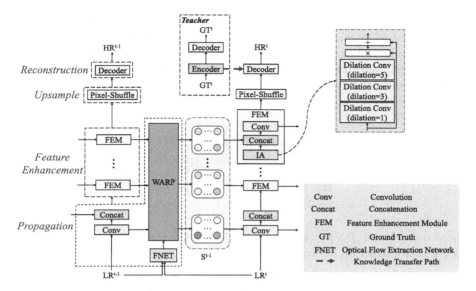

Fig. 2. Structure of StuVSR. StuVSR consists of four modules: propagation, feature enhancement, upsampling and reconstruction. StuVSR takes LR^t and the propagated S^{t-1} as input, produces current state S^t with feature enhancement, and generates output HR^t with upsampling and reconstruction.

For the sake of streamlining network parameters and generating sufficient high-frequency information, we redesign the knowledge distillation mode and propose a new attention mechanism. With the help of the above, StuVSR has outperformed state of the arts with only 1.0M parameters.

3 Model

Our proposed network **StudentVSR** (StuVSR) is illustrated in Fig. 2. The input is sequence of t LR frames $\{LR^0, ..., LR^{t-1}, LR^t\}$ where LR^t represents the current frame. StuVSR aims to output HR^t which is HR version of LR^t. We set StuVSR as student and take a well-trained auto-encoder network as teacher. StuVSR learn knowledge from teacher through our proposed multi-mapping distillation method.

3.1 StudentVSR

StuVSR has four modules: propagation, feature enhancement, upsampling and reconstruction. Our network takes the current layer's input LR^t and the previous layer's state S^{t-1} as input, produces current state S^t with k feature enhancement modules, and generates output HR^t with up-sampling and reconstruction module. The specific structure is shown as follow:

Propagation: StuVSR adopts unidirectional RNN for propagation. Given an input frame LR^t, a convolutional layer is first applied to extract its feature H_0^t. We choice optical flow as temporal information and extract it with a coarse-to-fine structure. According to BasicVSR [2], using temporal information to align features is better than images. We warp H_0^{t-1} and outputs of all feature enhancement modules $\{H_1^{t-1}, ..., H_k^{t-1}\}$ with optical flow and make up S^{t-1}. The specific equation is shown on Eq. 1.

$$
\begin{aligned}
op^{t-1,t} &= FNET(LR^{t-1}, LR^t) \\
\hat{H}_0^{t-1} &= Warp(op^{t-1,t}, H_0^{t-1}) \\
\hat{H}_k^{t-1} &= Warp(op^{t-1,t}, H_k^{t-1}) \\
S^{t-1} &= \{H_0^{t-1}, \hat{H}_1^{t-1}, ..., \hat{H}_k^{t-1}\}
\end{aligned}
\tag{1}
$$

where $op^{t-1,t}$ and $FNET$ denote optical flow between LR^{t-1} and LR^t and optical flow extraction network.

Feature Enhancement: This part has k feature enhancement modules and the modules are arranged in series. Furthermore, each feature enhancement module contains Inceptual Attention (IA) we proposed. IA uses three dilated convolutional layers as attention-map extraction function. The dilation settings are 1, 3, and 5. Compared with original convolution, dilation convolution uses the same amount of parameters but provides a larger receptive field. The extracted attention map helps the network concentrates on high-frequency information and improves the quality of the generated frame. The equation of IA is shown on Eq. 2.

$$
\begin{aligned}
Map &= \begin{cases} Att(concat(H_0^t, \hat{H}_0^{t-1})) & \text{if } i = 1 \\ Att(H_{i-1}^t) & otherwise \end{cases} \quad i \in [1, ..., k] \\
H_{IA,i}^t &= H_{i-1}^t + Map \times H_{i-1}^t
\end{aligned}
\tag{2}
$$

where Att, $concat$, and $H_{IA,i}^t$ represent attention-map extraction function, concatenation on channel dimension, and output of IA. The output of ith feature enhancement module is obtained by Eq. 3.

$$
H_i^t = Conv(concat(H_{IA,i}^t, \hat{H}_i^{t-1}))
\tag{3}
$$

where $Conv$ denotes convolution.

Upsampling and Reconstruction: After enhancement, H_k^t are used to generate HR frames through pixel-shuffling and decoder. The decoder consists of three convolutional layers.

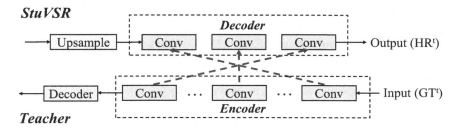

Fig. 3. Process of multi-mapping knowledge distillation. The red dotted lines represent the knowledge transfer paths. (Color figure online)

3.2   Teacher Network

To guide a student, teacher should be way ahead of student. Although state-of-the-art models have achieved great results, we hope that the trained student network can achieve higher PSNR score and generate clearer HR frames than any state-of-the-art models. When the teacher network and the student network deal with the same task, student hardly achieves better results with a shallower network model. We choose an auto-encoder structure instead of existing VSR model and take ground truth (GT) as input. Compared with existing VSR methods, an auto-encoder network that is trained to restore GT contains more prior knowledge.

A traditional auto-encoder network consists of convolutional layers, pooling layers, upsampling layers, and maybe fully connected layers. The pooling layer and the fully connected layer are introduced to extract the semantic representation of the image. However, we observed the intermediate representations of trained VSR networks and found that the trained VSR model focuses on the shallow features which are edge and color information of frames and pays less attention to semantic information. Therefore, our teacher network abandons the pooling layers, the fully connected layers, and the upsampling layers but employs several convolutional layers with leaky ReLU activation function.

3.3   Training

We first train the teacher network and then use the trained teacher network to guide StuVSR in a multi-mapping manner.

The teacher network is an auto-encoder structure and aims to restore image. The loss function is $L1$ distance between the generated frame and GT and is shown on Eq. 4.

$$L_{tea} = ||Tea(GT^t), GT^t)||_1 \tag{4}$$

where Tea and GT^t represent teacher network and GT of current frame.

Loss functions for StuVSR consist of a distillation loss and a reconstruction loss. The process of multi-mapping knowledge distillation is shown in Fig. 3. The distillation loss is Mean Squared Error (MSE) distance between intermediate representations of decoder in student network and encoder in teacher network. The loss function of multi-mapping knowledge distillation is computed in a layer-wise way and the specific equation is shown on Eq. 5.

$$g(l) = L' - (l \times round(\frac{L'}{L}))$$
$$L_{dis} = \sum_{l=0}^{L} ||H_l^{Stu}, H_{g(l)}^{tea}||_2$$

(5)

where L, L', $round$, H_l^{Stu}, and $H_{g(l)}^{tea}$ denote the number of layers in student decoder, the number of layers in teacher encoder, the rounding-off operation, output of the lth layer in student decoder, and output of the $g(l)^{th}$ layer in teacher encoder. StuVSR uses this knowledge distillation model to gradually learn the knowledge in the teacher network and generates better results. The reconstruction loss is L1 distance between generated HR frame and GT. The specific equation is shown on Eq. 6.

$$L_{rec} = ||Stu(LR^t), GT^t)||_1$$

(6)

where Stu denotes StuVSR. These two losses are combined with weighted sum. The loss function equation is shown on Eq. 7.

$$L_{stu} = L_{rec} + \alpha L_{dis}$$

(7)

where α is a hyper-parameter.

4 Experiment

4.1 Dataset and Experimental Details

We train StuVSR and teacher network on Vimeo90k [22] training set and evaluate StuVSR on Vimeo90k testing set and Vid4 dataset. We compare model parameters, running time, and Peak Signal to Noise Ratio (PSNR) score on these two datasets. We set Bicubic, VESPCN [1], SPMC [19], TOFlow [22], FRVSR [16], DUF [12], RBPN [6], EDVR-M [21], EDVR [21], PFNL [23], MuCAN [13], TGA [10], RLSP [5], RSDN [9], RRN [11], BasicVSR [2], and IconVSR [2] as baselines. All models are tested with 4 × downsampling using Bicubic degradation (BI) and Blur Downsampling degradation (BD). The operating equipment is Nvidia Tesla T4.

The num of feature enhancement modules in StuVSR is 4. The encoder and decoder in teacher have 9 and 5 convolutional layers with leaky ReLU activation function respectively. We adopt Adam optimizer. The initial learning rate of the student and teacher network is 1×10^{-4}. The total number of iteration is

Table 1. Quantitative comparison (PSNR). All results are calculated on Y-channel. The runtime is computed on an LR size of 180×320. A $4\times$ upsampling is performed following previous studies. Blanked entries correspond to codes not released and results not reported in previous works.

	Params (M)	Runtime (ms)	BI degradation		BD degradation	
			Vimeo90K	Vid4	Vimeo90K	Vid4
Bicubic	–	–	31.32	23.78	31.30	21.80
VESPCN [1]	–	–	–	25.35	–	–
SPMC [19]	–	–	–	25.88	–	–
TOFlow [22]	–	–	33.08	25.89	34.62	–
FRVSR [16]	5.1	137	–	–	35.64	26.69
DUF [12]	5.8	974	–	–	36.87	27.38
RBPN [6]	12.2	1507	37.07	27.12	37.20	–
EDVR-M [21]	3.3	118	37.09	27.10	37.33	27.45
EDVR [21]	20.6	378	37.61	27.35	37.81	27.85
PFNL [23]	3.0	295	36.14	26.73	–	27.16
MuCAN [13]	–	–	37.32	–	–	–
TGA [10]	5.8	–	–	–	37.59	27.63
RLSP [5]	4.2	49	–	–	36.49	27.48
RSDN [9]	6.2	94	–	–	37.23	27.92
RRN [11]	3.4	45	–	–	–	27.69
BasicVSR [2]	6.3	63	37.18	27.24	37.53	27.96
IconVSR [2]	8.7	70	37.19	27.39	37.55	28.04
Ours (StuVSR)	**1.0**	**19**	**37.63**	**27.57**	**37.99**	**28.29**

600K. The optical flow extraction network in our student network is the same as RBPN [6]. When StuVSR processes the first frame I^0, the feature matrix in S^{-1} is a copy of the current layer's output. Hyper-parameter α in loss function of StuVSR is 1.5.

4.2 Comparisons with State-of-the-Art Methods

We conduct comparison experiments with 16 baseline models and show PSNR score, model parameters amount, and running time comparison results in Table 1. The visual effect comparison is provided in Fig. 4.

As shown in Table 1, our method outperforms state of the arts on Vimeo 90k and Vid4 datasets with the smallest model. In addition to improving the quality of restoration, our method also achieves high efficiency. Compared with the baseline model PFNL [23] with the smallest parameter amount, the parameter amount of our method is less than 1/3 of it, and the PSNR score is markedly improved by 0.94dB in BI environment. Compared with IconVSR [2], the baseline model with the highest PSNR score in the BI environment, our method has less than 1/8 of its parameters, and the PSNR score is markedly increased by 0.18 dB. The runtime of our method is less than 33ms, which means our method is capable of handling 30-frame-per-second (FPS) video in practice.

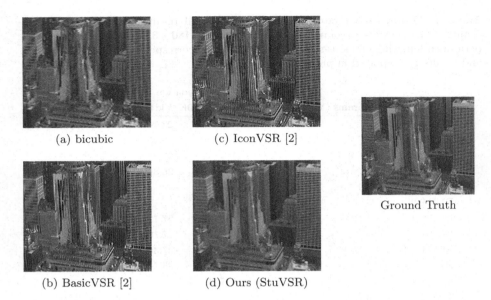

(a) bicubic   (c) IconVSR [2]

Ground Truth

(b) BasicVSR [2]   (d) Ours (StuVSR)

Fig. 4. Visual comparison. StuVSR has the least distortion.

5   Ablation Studies

To understand the functions of the proposed components, we not only explore their respective roles but also their interactions. Due to the limitation of the pages, we only show the experimental results on the Vid4 dataset in Fig. 5.

5.1   Studies on Feature Enhancement Module

In this experiment, We adjust the number of feature enhancement modules in StuVSR to 0, 1, and 8 as baselines. Each feature enhancement module will bring 0.18M parameters. As the number of feature enhancement modules increases, the number of network parameters is increasing and the PSNR score is getting higher.

In theory, feature enhance module can be increased without any upper limit. However, as the number increases, the performance gain of the network is getting smaller, the calculation cost is getting higher, and the running time is getting longer. Besides, As the resolution of the input video increases, the processing time of the network will increase inevitably. To allow the network to process videos with higher resolution in real-time while surpassing state of the arts, the number of feature enhancement modules in our final model is 4.

5.2   Studies on Multi-mapping Knowledge Distillation

To test the function of multi-mapping knowledge distillation, we remove the teacher network and let the student network learn by itself through the recon-

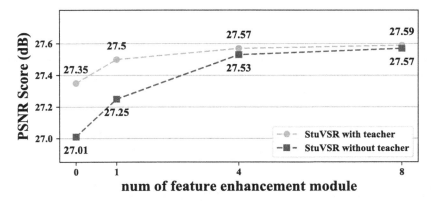

Fig. 5. Ablation studies of the components. The greater the number of feature enhancement modules, the stronger the ability of network to process VSR, and the less reliance on the teacher network.

struction loss. Through the observation of Fig. 5, we find that the role of multi-mapping knowledge distillation is inversely proportional to the number of feature enhancement modules. When the number of feature enhancement modules is low, multi-mapping knowledge distillation has greatly improved the performance of StuVSR.

6   Discussion and Future Work

Bidirectional propagation is better than unidirectional propagation [2]. However, bidirectional propagation takes all the video frames as input and requires large memory, which barely meet the requirement of real-time processing. Therefore, unidirectional propagation is the only choice, which leads to inherent shortcomings in using temporal information. This requires that our feature enhancement module be sufficiently excellent. General practice self-attention [25] can expand the receptive field of the convolutional neural networks (CNN) and allow CNN network to focus on the entire image. However, self-attention requires larger memory. Therefore, to achieve the same goal, we design three layers of different dilation convolutions with different dilation to extract the attention map. Experiments show that this structure well enhances the video features.

The weakness of our method lies in extracting suitable temporal information. During the training process, we observed the distance between the features aligned with temporal information and the features of the current frame. We found that the distance quickly stabilized to a relatively high degree. We tried to use this distance as a loss function to assist the network training, which achieved no improvement. Accurate alignment can improve the effectiveness of the network [2]. We hope to find an unsupervised method to capture the temporal information between frames more accurately.

7 Conclusion

This work devotes attention to design a network structure that can process video frames in real-time with a shallow network. We propose StuVSR, a simple and effective network. The proposed attention mechanism IA allows StuVSR to generate sufficient high-frequency information. Meanwhile, learning from an auto-encoder network in a multi-mapping manner, StuVSR surpasses state of the arts with an 8–20 times smaller network.

References

1. Caballero, J., et al.: Real-time video super-resolution with spatio-temporal networks and motion compensation. In: IEEE Conference on Computer Vision and Pattern Recognition, pp. 4778–4787 (2017)
2. Chan, K.C., Wang, X., Yu, K., Dong, C., Loy, C.C.: BasicVSR: the search for essential components in video super-resolution and beyond. In: IEEE Conference on Computer Vision and Pattern Recognition (2021)
3. Chen, G., Choi, W., Yu, X., Han, T., Chandraker, M.: Learning efficient object detection models with knowledge distillation. In: Neural Information Processing Systems, NIPS 2017, pp. 742–751. Curran Associates Inc., Red Hook (2017)
4. Ding, L., Wang, Z., Fan, Y., Liu, X., Huang, T.: Robust video super-resolution with learned temporal dynamics. In: IEEE International Conference on Computer Vision (2017)
5. Fuoli, D., Gu, S., Timofte, R.: Efficient video super-resolution through recurrent latent space propagation. In: IEEE International Conference on Computer Vision Workshop, pp. 3476–3485. IEEE (2019)
6. Haris, M., Shakhnarovich, G., Ukita, N.: Recurrent back-projection network for video super-resolution. In: IEEE Conference on Computer Vision and Pattern Recognition, pp. 3897–3906 (2019)
7. Hinton, G., Vinyals, O., Dean, J.: Distilling the knowledge in a neural network. Comput. Sci. **14**(7), 38–39 (2015)
8. Huang, Y., Wang, W., Wang, L.: Bidirectional recurrent convolutional networks for multi-frame super-resolution. In: Cortes, C., Lawrence, N., Lee, D., Sugiyama, M., Garnett, R. (eds.) Neural Information Processing Systems, vol. 28. Curran Associates, Inc. (2015)
9. Isobe, T., Jia, X., Gu, S., Li, S., Wang, S., Tian, Q.: Video super-resolution with recurrent structure-detail network. In: Vedaldi, A., Bischof, H., Brox, T., Frahm, J.-M. (eds.) ECCV 2020. LNCS, vol. 12357, pp. 645–660. Springer, Cham (2020). https://doi.org/10.1007/978-3-030-58610-2_38
10. Isobe, T., et al.: Video super-resolution with temporal group attention. In: IEEE Conference on Computer Vision and Pattern Recognition, pp. 8008–8017 (2020)
11. Isobe, T., Zhu, F., Jia, X., Wang, S.: Revisiting temporal modeling for video super-resolution. arXiv preprint arXiv:2008.05765 (2020)
12. Jo, Y., Oh, S.W., Kang, J., Kim, S.J.: Deep video super-resolution network using dynamic upsampling filters without explicit motion compensation. In: IEEE Conference on Computer Vision and Pattern Recognition, pp. 3224–3232 (2018)
13. Li, W., Tao, X., Guo, T., Qi, L., Lu, J., Jia, J.: MuCAN: multi-correspondence aggregation network for video super-resolution. In: Vedaldi, A., Bischof, H., Brox, T., Frahm, J.-M. (eds.) ECCV 2020. LNCS, vol. 12355, pp. 335–351. Springer, Cham (2020). https://doi.org/10.1007/978-3-030-58607-2_20

14. Noh, J., Bae, W., Lee, W., Seo, J., Kim, G.: Better to follow, follow to be better: towards precise supervision of feature super-resolution for small object detection. In: IEEE International Conference on Computer Vision, pp. 9725–9734 (2019)
15. Peng, H., Du, H., Yu, H., LI, Q., Liao, J., Fu, J.: Cream of the crop: distilling prioritized paths for one-shot neural architecture search. In: Larochelle, H., Ranzato, M., Hadsell, R., Balcan, M.F., Lin, H. (eds.) Neural Information Processing Systems, vol. 33, pp. 17955–17964. Curran Associates, Inc. (2020)
16. Sajjadi, M.S., Vemulapalli, R., Brown, M.: Frame-recurrent video super-resolution. In: IEEE Conference on Computer Vision and Pattern Recognition, pp. 6626–6634 (2018)
17. Shi, W., et al.: Real-time single image and video super-resolution using an efficient sub-pixel convolutional neural network. In: IEEE Conference on Computer Vision and Pattern Recognition, pp. 1874–1883 (2016). https://doi.org/10.1109/CVPR.2016.207
18. So, D., Le, Q., Liang, C.: The evolved transformer. In: International Conference on Machine Learning, pp. 5877–5886. PMLR (2019)
19. Tao, X., Gao, H., Liao, R., Wang, J., Jia, J.: Detail-revealing deep video super-resolution. IEEE Computer Society (2017)
20. Tian, Y., Zhang, Y., Fu, Y., Xu, C.: TDAN: temporally-deformable alignment network for video super-resolution. In: IEEE Conference on Computer Vision and Pattern Recognition, pp. 3360–3369 (2020)
21. Wang, X., Chan, K.C., Yu, K., Dong, C., Change Loy, C.: EDVR: video restoration with enhanced deformable convolutional networks. In: IEEE Conference on Computer Vision and Pattern Recognition Workshops, p. 0 (2019)
22. Xue, T., Chen, B., Wu, J., Wei, D., Freeman, W.T.: Video enhancement with task-oriented flow. Int. J. Comput. Vision 127(8), 1106–1125 (2019)
23. Yi, P., Wang, Z., Jiang, K., Jiang, J., Ma, J.: Progressive fusion video super-resolution network via exploiting non-local spatio-temporal correlations. In: IEEE International Conference on Computer Vision, pp. 3106–3115 (2019)
24. Zangeneh, E., Rahmati, M., Mohsenzadeh, Y.: Low resolution face recognition using a two-branch deep convolutional neural network architecture. Expert Syst. Appl. 139, 112854 (2020)
25. Zhang, H., Goodfellow, I., Metaxas, D., Odena, A.: Self-attention generative adversarial networks. In: International Conference on Machine Learning, pp. 7354–7363. PMLR (2019)
26. Zhang, Y., Li, K., Li, K., Wang, L., Zhong, B., Fu, Y.: Image super-resolution using very deep residual channel attention networks. In: Ferrari, V., Hebert, M., Sminchisescu, C., Weiss, Y. (eds.) ECCV 2018. LNCS, vol. 11211, pp. 294–310. Springer, Cham (2018). https://doi.org/10.1007/978-3-030-01234-2_18

On the Unreasonable Effectiveness of Centroids in Image Retrieval

Mikołaj Wieczorek[1,2(✉)], Barbara Rychalska[1,3], and Jacek Dąbrowski[1]

[1] Synerise, Cracow, Poland
mikolaj.wieczorek@synerise.com
[2] Faculty of Electronics and Information Technology,
Warsaw University of Technology, Warsaw, Poland
[3] Faculty of Mathematics and Information Science,
Warsaw University of Technology, Warsaw, Poland

Abstract. Image retrieval task consists of finding similar images to a query image from a set of gallery (database) images. Such systems are used in various applications e.g. person re-identification (ReID) or visual product search. Despite active development of retrieval models it still remains a challenging task mainly due to large intra-class variance caused by changes in view angle, lighting, background clutter or occlusion, while inter-class variance may be relatively low. A large portion of current research focuses on creating more robust features and modifying objective functions, usually based on Triplet Loss. Some works experiment with using centroid/proxy representation of a class to alleviate problems with computing speed and hard samples mining used with Triplet Loss. However, these approaches are used for training alone and discarded during the retrieval stage. In this paper we propose to use the mean centroid representation both during training and retrieval. Such an aggregated representation is more robust to outliers and assures more stable features. As each class is represented by a single embedding - the class centroid - both retrieval time and storage requirements are reduced significantly. Aggregating multiple embeddings results in a significant reduction of the search space due to lowering the number of candidate target vectors, which makes the method especially suitable for production deployments. Comprehensive experiments conducted on two ReID and Fashion Retrieval datasets demonstrate effectiveness of our method, which outperforms the current state-of-the-art. We propose centroid training and retrieval as a viable method for both Fashion Retrieval and ReID applications. Our code is available at https://github.com/mikwieczorek/centroids-reid.

Keywords: Clothes retrieval · Fashion retrieval · Person re-identification · Deep learning in fashion · Centroid triplet loss

1 Introduction

Instance retrieval is a problem of matching an object from a query image to objects represented by images from a gallery set. Applications of retrieval

---

M. Wieczorek and B. Rychalska–Equal contribution.

© Springer Nature Switzerland AG 2021
T. Mantoro et al. (Eds.): ICONIP 2021, LNCS 13111, pp. 212–223, 2021.
https://doi.org/10.1007/978-3-030-92273-3_18

systems span person/vehicle re-identification, face recognition, video surveillance, explicit content filtering, medical diagnosis and fashion retrieval.

Most existing instance retrieval solutions use Deep Metric Learning methodology [1,4,6,7,13,15], in which a deep learning model is trained to transform images to a vector representation, so that samples from the same class are close to each other. At the retrieval stage, the query embedding is scored against all gallery embeddings and the most similar ones are returned. Until recently, a lot of works used classification loss for the training of retrieval models [8,14,16,19]. Currently most works use comparative/ranking losses and the Triplet Loss is one of the most widely used approaches. However, state-of-the-art solutions often combine a comparative loss with auxiliary losses such as classification or center loss [3,7,12,13,15].

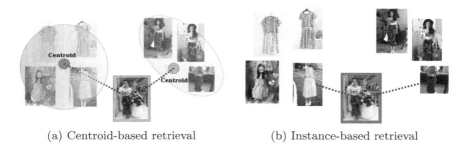

(a) Centroid-based retrieval   (b) Instance-based retrieval

Fig. 1. Comparison of centroid-based and instance-based retrieval. Dashed lines indicate distance between the query image (coloured frame) and the nearest neighbour from each class. a) The centroid is calculated as the mean of all samples (shaded images) belonging to each class. The query is assigned the class of the nearest centroid, which is the correct "gold" class. b) The distance is calculated between all samples and the query. It is erroneously assigned the "blue" class, as the blue-class sample is its nearest neighbour (Color figure online)

Even though Triplet Loss is superior to most other approaches, it has problems that were indicated by numerous works [2,15,17,20]: 1) Hard negative sampling is the dominant approach in creating training batches containing only informative triplets in a batch, but it may lead to bad local minima and prevent the model from achieving top performance [2,17]; 2) Hard negative sampling is computationally expensive, as the distance needs to be calculated between all samples in the batch [2,15]; 3) Triplet Loss is prone to outliers and noisy labels due to hard negative sampling and the nature of point-to-point losses [15,17].

To alleviate problems stemming from the point-to-point nature of Triplet Loss, changes to point-to-set/point-to-centroid formulations were proposed, where the distances are measured between a sample and a prototype/centroid representing a class. Centroids are aggregations of each item's multiple representations. A centroid approach results in one embedding per item, decreasing both memory and storage requirements. There are a number of approaches investigating the prototype/centroid formulation and their main advantages are as follows: 1) Lower computational cost [2,15], of even linear complexity instead of cubic [2]; 2) Higher robustness to outliers and noisy labels [15,17]; 3) Faster training [11]; 4) Comparable or better performance than the standard point-to-point triplet loss [3,11,15].

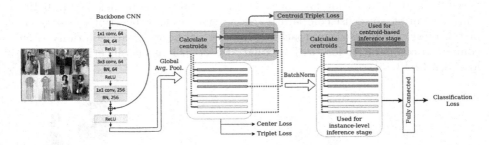

Fig. 2. Architecture of our CTL-Model. Parts added over [13] are marked in red (Color figure online)

We propose to go a step further and use the centroid-based approach for both training and inference, with applications to fashion retrieval and person re-identification. We implement our centroid-based model by augmenting the current state-of-the-art model in fashion retrieval [13] with a new loss function we call Centroid Triplet Loss. The baseline model has a number of losses optimized simultaneously, which account for various aspects of the retrieval problem. An additional centroid-based loss can thus be easily added in order to amend one of the recurring problems: lack of robustness against variability in object galleries. Centroids are computed with simple averaging of image representations. We show that this straightforward model amendment allows to lower the latency of requests and decrease infrastructure costs, at the same time producing new state-of-the-art results in various evaluation protocols, datasets and domains. We also discuss why such formulation of the retrieval problem is viable and advantageous compared to standard image-based approaches.

The contributions of this work are fourfold:

- We introduce the Centroid Triplet Loss - a new loss function for instance retrieval tasks
- We propose to use class centroids as representations during retrieval.
- We show through thorough experiments that the centroid-based approach establishes new state-of-the-art results across different datasets and domains (fashion retrieval and person re-identification).
- We show that the centroid-based approach for retrieval tasks brings significant inference speed-ups and storage savings compared to the standard instance-level approach.

2   Proposed Method

The image retrieval task aims to find the most similar object to the query image. In both fashion retrieval and person re-identification it is usually done on an instance-level basis: each query image is scored against all images from the gallery. If an object has several images assigned (e.g. photos from multiple viewpoints, under variable lighting conditions), then each image is treated separately. As a result, the same object may occur multiple times in the ranking result. Such a protocol can be beneficial as it allows to match images that were taken in similar circumstances, with similar angle, depicting the same part of the object or a close-up detail. On the other hand, the advantage can easily turn disadvantageous as a photo of a detail of a completely different object may be similar to the details in the query image, causing a false match.

We propose to use an aggregated item representation using all available samples. This approach results in a robust representation which is less susceptible to a single-image false matches. Using aggregated representations, each item is represented by a single embedding, leading to a significantly reduced search space - saving memory and reducing retrieval times significantly. Apart from being more computationally efficient during retrieval, the centroid-based approach also improves retrieval results compared to non-centroid-based approaches.

Note that training the model in a centroid-based setting does not restrict the evaluation protocol to centroid-only evaluation, but also improves results in the *typical* setting of instance-level evaluation.

2.1   Centroid Triplet Loss

Triplet Loss originally works on an anchor image A, a positive (same class) example P and a negative example belonging to another class N. The objective is to minimize the distance between $A - P$, while push away the N sample. The loss function is formulated as follows:

$$\mathcal{L}_{triplet} = \left[\|f(A) - f(P)\|_2^2 - \|f(A) - f(N)\|_2^2 + \alpha \right]_+ \qquad (1)$$

where $[z]_+ = max(z, 0)$, f denotes embedding function learned during training stage and α is a margin parameter.

We propose the *Centroid Triplet Loss (CTL)*. Instead of comparing the distance of an anchor image A to positive and negative instances, CTL measures the distance between A and class centroids c_P and c_N representing either the same class as the anchor or a different class respectively. CTL is therefore formulated as:

$$\mathcal{L}_{triplet} = \left[\|f(A) - c_P\|_2^2 - \|f(A) - c_N\|_2^2 + \alpha_c \right]_+ \qquad (2)$$

2.2   Aggregating Item Representations

During training stage each mini-batch contains P distinct item classes with M samples per class, resulting in batch size of $P \times M$. Let S_k denote a set of samples for class k in the mini-batch such that $\mathcal{S}_k = \{x_1, ..., x_M\}$ where x_i represents an embedding of i-th sample, such that $x_i \in R^D$, with D being the sample representation size. For effective training, each sample from $\mathcal{S}_k$ is used as a query q_k and the rest $M - 1$ samples are used to build a prototype centroid c_{k_p}, which can be expressed as:

$$c_{k_p} = \frac{1}{|\mathcal{S}_k \setminus \{q_k\}|} \sum_{x_i \in \mathcal{S}_k \setminus \{q_k\}} f(x_i) \tag{3}$$

where f represents the neural network encoding images to D dimensional embedding space.

During evaluation query images are supplied from the query set $\mathcal{Q}$, and centroids for each class k are precalculated before the retrieval takes place. To construct these centroids we use all embeddings from the gallery set $\mathcal{G}_k$ for class k. The centroid of each class $c_k \in R^D$ is calculated as the mean of all embeddings belonging to the given class:

$$c_k = \frac{1}{|\mathcal{G}_k|} \sum_{x_i \in \mathcal{G}_k} f(x_i) \tag{4}$$

We apply centroid computation and CTL to the fashion retrieval state-of-the-art model described in [13]. This model embeds images with a baseline CNN model (using variations of the ResNet architecture) and passes them through a simple feed-forward architecture with average pooling and batch normalization. Three separate loss functions are computed at various stages of forward propagation. We add centroid computation for training just after embedding with the CNN. Centroids for inference are computed in the next step (after batch normalization) for consistency with the original model. The resulting architecture is displayed in Fig. 2. Note that our centroid-based training and evaluation method can be also transplanted to other models, as CTL can be computed next to other existing loss functions.

3   Experiments

3.1   Datasets

DeepFashion (Fashion Retrieval). The dataset was introduced by [6] an contains over 800,000 images, which are spread across several fashion related tasks. The data we used is a *Consumer-to-shop Clothes Retrieval* subset that contains 33,881 unique clothing products and 239,557 images.

Street2Shop (Fashion Retrieval). The dataset contains over 400,000 shop photos and 20,357 street photos. In total there are 204,795 distinct clothing items in the dataset. It is one of the first modern large-scale fashion dataset and was introduced by [5].

Table 1. Fashion Retrieval Results. S or L in the model name indicates input image size, either Small (256×128) or Large (320×320). R50 or R50IBN suffix indicates which backbone CNN was used, Resnet50 or Resnet50-IBN-A respectively. 'CE' at the end of model name denotes Centroid-based Evaluation

Dataset	Model	mAP	Acc@1	Acc@10	Acc@20	Acc@50
DeepFashion	SOTA (S-R50) [13]	0.324	0.281	0.583	0.655	0.742
	CTL-S-R50	0.344	**0.298**	0.612	0.685	0.770
	CTL-S-R50 **CE**	**0.404**	0.294	**0.613**	**0.689**	**0.774**
	SOTA (L-R50IBN) [13]	0.430	**0.378**	0.711	0.772	0.841
	CTL-L-R50IBN	0.431	0.376	0.711	0.776	0.847
	CTL-L-R50IBN **CE**	**0.492**	0.373	**0.712**	**0.777**	**0.850**
Street2Shop	SOTA (S-R50) [13]	0.320	0.366	0.611	0.606	–
	CTL-S-R50	0.353	0.418	0.594	0.643	0.702
	CTL-S-R50 **CE**	**0.498**	**0.432**	**0.619**	**0.660**	**0.721**
	SOTA (L-R50IBN) [13]	0.468	**0.537**	0.698	0.736	–
	CTL-L-R50IBN	0.459	0.533	0.689	0.728	0.782
	CTL-L-R50IBN **CE**	**0.598**	**0.537**	**0.709**	**0.750**	**0.792**

Market1501 (Person Re-identification). Introduced in [18] in 2015, it contains 1501 classes/ identities scattered across 32,668 bounding boxes and captured by 6 cameras at Tsinghua University. 751 classes are used for training, and 750 with distractors are used for evaluation.

DukeMTMC-reID (Person Re-identification). It is a subset of DukeMTMC dataset [9]. It contains 1,404 classes/identities, 702 are used for training and 702 along with 408 distractor identities are used for evaluation.

3.2   Implementation Details

We implement our centroid-based solution on top of the current fashion retrieval state-of-the-art model [13], which itself is based on a top-scoring ReID model [7]. We train our model on various Resnet-based backbones pretrained on ImageNet, and report results for Fashion Retrieval and Person Re-Identification tasks. We evaluate the model both in centroid-based and instance-based setting. Instance-based setting means that pairs of images are evaluated, identically as in the evaluation setting of [13]. We use the same training protocol presented in the aforementioned papers (e.g. random erasing augmentation, label smoothing), without introducing any additional steps.

Feature Extractor. We test two CNNs: Resnet-50 and Resnet50-IBN-A to compare our results on those two networks. Like [7,13], we use $stride = 1$ for the last convolutional layer and Resnet-50 native 2048 dimensional embedding size.

Loss Functions. [7,13] use a loss function consisting of three parts: (1) Triplet loss calculated on the raw embeddings, (2) Center Loss [12] as an auxiliary loss,

(3) classification loss computed on batch-normalized embeddings. To train our model based on centroids we use the same three losses and add CTL, which is computed between query vectors and class centroids. Center Loss was weighted by a factor of $5e^{-4}$, all other losses were assigned a weight of 1.

Our Fashion Retrieval parameter configuration is identical as in [13]. We use Adam optimizer with base learning rate of $1e^{-4}$ and multistep learning rate scheduler, decreasing the learning rate by a factor of 10 after 40th and 70th epoch. Like in [7,13] the Center Loss was optimized separately by SGD optimizer with $lr = 0.5$. Each model was trained 3 times, for 120 epochs each. For Person Re-Identification, the configuration is identical as in [7]. The base learning rate is $3.5e^{-4}$, decayed at 40th and 70th epoch. The models were trained for 120 epochs each.

Resampling. For Triplet Loss it is important to have enough positive samples per class, but some classes may have few samples. Therefore it is a common practice to define a target sample size M and resample class instances if $|\mathcal{S}_k| < M$, resulting in repeated images in the mini-batch. We empirically verify that in our scenario it is beneficial to omit the resampling procedure. As resampling introduces noise to class centroids, we use only the unique class instances which are available.

Retrieval Procedure. We follow [7,13] in utilizing batch-normalized vectors during inference stage. Likewise, we use cosine similarity as the distance measure. For the ReID datasets we use a cross-view matching setting, which is used in other ReID papers [7,10]. This protocol ensures that for each query its gallery samples that were captured by the same camera are excluded during retrieval.

3.3 Fashion Retrieval Results

We present the evaluation results for fashion retrieval in Table 1. We evaluate two models: SOTA denotes the model presented in [13], and CTL - our centroid-based model. Each model was evaluated in two modes: 1) standard instance-level evaluation on per-image basis (for both SOTA and CTL models), and 2) centroid-based evaluation, (denoted by CE in Table 1): evaluation of CTL model on per-object basis, where all images from each class were used to build the class centorid and retrieval was done in centroid domain.

Our CTL model performs better than the current state-of-the-art in most metrics across all tested datasets. Especially noticeable is the surge in mAP metric, which can be explained by the fact that usage of centroids reduces the search space. The reduction of the search space with centroid-based evaluation is coupled with reduction of the number of positive instances (from several to just one). Accuracy@K metrics on the other hand are not influenced by the change of search space.

3.4 Person ReID Results

We present the evaluation results for person re-identification in Table 2. Similarly as in fashion retrieval, we evaluate the following models: SOTA denotes

Table 2. Person Re-Identification Results. 'CE' at the end of model name denotes Centroid-based Evaluation. 'RK' indicates that re-ranking was used for post-processing of the results

Dataset	Model	mAP	Acc@1	Acc@5	Acc@10
Market1501	SOTA **RK** [10]	0.955	0.980	0.989	0.991
	CTL-S-R50	0.857	0.941	0.982	0.989
	CTL-S-R50 **CE**	**0.986**	**0.984**	**0.990**	**0.996**
Duke-MTMC-ReID	SOTA **RK** [10]	0.927	0.945	0.968	0.971
	CTL-S-R50	0.749	0.856	0.936	0.959
	CTL-S-R50 **CE**	**0.969**	**0.962**	**0.986**	**0.989**

the current state-of-the-art in ReID [10], and CTL - our centroid-based model. We only report centroid-based evaluation results for CTL-model, as previous methods often restrict the search space arbitrarily. For example, [10] reduce the search space during retrieval with spatial and temporal constraints to decrease the number of candidates by eliminating cases where the person could not have possibly moved by a certain distance in the given time. Their approach requires extra information in the dataset and world knowledge necessary to construct the filtering rules, apart from just image understanding. Despite reliance on image matching alone, our centroid-based search space reduction achieves nearly the same or even better results across all metric on both datasets, outperforming [10] across most metrics and establishing the new state-of-the-art results.

3.5 Centroid-Based Retrieval and the Number of Instances

One of the aspects of using centroid-based retrieval concerns the number of instances used to build centroid representation and its influence on the retrieval results. Comparison of the improvement of the results for fashion and person-reidentification datasets may be regarded as an implicit ablation study of the aforementioned aspect. For *DeepFashion* and *Street2Shop* , where most items have 1–3 images in the gallery set, the centroid-based retrieval brings only a limited uplift in performance (see Table 1). However, while the performance level is preserved, the storage and latency for centroid variant are reduced significantly (see Table 3). On the other hand, for *Market1501* and *Duke-MTMC-ReID*, which have 15–20 images per person, centroids brought significant improvements across all metrics allowing to achieve SOTA results on both datasets (see Table 2).

Based on the results we conjecture that the centroid-based retrieval is especially beneficial for settings where there are many images per product/person in the gallery set. This is especially true in application for e-commerce retailers, as there are often numerous images of a product available. Moreover, apart from improved performance, centroid-based retrieval allows to reduce storage and speed-up the search process. Finally, even for limited number of images per product the centroid-based retrieval preserves the standard level of performance while reducing storage and latency.

3.6   Instance-Based vs Centroid-Based Retrieval

In Fig. 3 we show an example of a difference between standard instance-based and our centroid-based retrieval using Market1501 data. In the Fig. 3a multiple positive true matches are returned in the top-10 results, as multiple instances of the same person are in the gallery set. However, two last queries were not matched correctly at Rank-1. Centroid-based retrieval on the other hand have only one possible true positive match per person, as all person's embeddings were used to create the centroid representing the person. What is also important, two mismatched queries in instance-based retrieval, were correctly matched at Rank-1 when using centroids approach. Is worth to note that the number of candidates for Market1501 in instance-based retrieval is around 16,000, while for centroid the number is reduced to 750, thus, reducing latency and storage requirements while improving quality of the results.

3.7   Memory Usage and Inference Times

To test memory and computation efficiency of our centroid-based method compared to standard image-based retrieval, we compare the wall-clock time taken for evaluating all test datasets and the storage required for saving all embeddings. Table 3 shows the statistics for all datasets for instance-level and centroid-based scenarios. It can be seen that the centroid-based approach significantly reduces both retrieval time and the disk space required to store the embeddings. The reduction is caused by the fact that there are often several images per class, thus representing a whole group of object images with a centroid reduces the number of vectors necessary for a successful retrieval to one.

Table 3. Comparison of storage and time requirements between instance and centroid-based models across tested datasets

Dataset	Mode	# in gallery	Embeddings filesize (MB)	Total eval time (s)
Deep Fashion	Instances	22k	175	81.35
	Centroids	16k	130	59.83
Street2Shop	Instances	350k	2700	512.30
	Centroids	190k	1500	146.28
Market1501	Instances	16k	120	4.75
	Centroids	0.75k	6	0.26
Duke-MTMC	Instances	17k	140	3.61
	Centroids	1.1k	9	0.37

(a) Instance-based retrieval

(b) Centroid-based retrieval

Fig. 3. Comparison of instance-based retrieval and centroid-based retrieval on Market1501 dataset. Both samples were produced by the same model CTL-S, yet for Fig. 3a standard retrieval using instances was used, while for Fig. 3b we used our centroids approach. First column of images with black border denotes query image. Green border is a true positive match and red border indicates false positive match. For centroid-based approach only one true positive match is possible, as each person is represented by a single centroid (Color figure online)

4   Conclusions

We introduce Centroid Triplet Loss - a new loss function for instance retrieval tasks. We empirically confirm that it significantly improves the accuracy of retrieval models. In addition to the new loss function, we propose the usage of class centroids during retrieval inference, further improving the accuracy metrics on retrieval tasks. Our methods are evaluated on four datasets from two different domains: Person Re-identification and Fashion Retrieval, and establish new state-of-the-art results on all datasets. In addition to accuracy improvements, we show that centroid-based inference leads to very significant computation speedups and lowering of memory requirements. The combination of increased accuracy with faster inference and lower resource requirements make our method especially useful in applied industrial settings for instance retrieval.

Acknowledgements. Barbara Rychalska was supported by grant no 2018/31/N/ST6/02273 funded by National Science Centre, Poland.

References

1. Diao, H., Zhang, Y., Ma, L., Lu, H.: Similarity reasoning and filtration for image-text matching. ArXiv abs/2101.01368 (2021)
2. Do, T.T., Tran, T., Reid, I.D., Kumar, B.V., Hoang, T., Carneiro, G.: A theoretically sound upper bound on the triplet loss for improving the efficiency of deep distance metric learning. In: 2019 IEEE/CVF Conference on Computer Vision and Pattern Recognition (CVPR), pp. 10396–10405 (2019)
3. Fortiz, M.A.L., Damen, D., Mayol-Cuevas, W.: Centroids triplet network and temporally-consistent embeddings for in-situ object recognition. In: 2020 IEEE/RSJ International Conference on Intelligent Robots and Systems (IROS), pp. 10796–10802 (2020)
4. Jun, H., Ko, B., Kim, Y., Kim, I., Kim, J.: Combination of multiple global descriptors for image retrieval. ArXiv abs/1903.10663 (2019)
5. Kiapour, M.H., Han, X., Lazebnik, S., Berg, A.C., Berg, T.L.: Where to buy it: matching street clothing photos in online shops. In: 2015 IEEE International Conference on Computer Vision (ICCV), pp. 3343–3351 (2015)
6. Liu, Z., Luo, P., Qiu, S., Wang, X., Tang, X.: DeepFashion: powering robust clothes recognition and retrieval with rich annotations. In: 2016 IEEE Conference on Computer Vision and Pattern Recognition (CVPR), pp. 1096–1104 (2016)
7. Luo, H., et al.: A strong baseline and batch normalization neck for deep person re-identification. IEEE Trans. Multimedia **22**, 2597–2609 (2020)
8. Noh, H., de Araújo, A.F., Sim, J., Weyand, T., Han, B.: Large-scale image retrieval with attentive deep local features. In: 2017 IEEE International Conference on Computer Vision (ICCV), pp. 3476–3485 (2017)
9. Ristani, E., Solera, F., Zou, R., Cucchiara, R., Tomasi, C.: Performance measures and a data set for multi-target, multi-camera tracking. In: Hua, G., Jégou, H. (eds.) ECCV 2016. LNCS, vol. 9914, pp. 17–35. Springer, Cham (2016). https://doi.org/10.1007/978-3-319-48881-3_2
10. Wang, G., Lai, J., Huang, P., Xie, X.: Spatial-temporal person re-identification. In: Proceedings of the AAAI Conference on Artificial Intelligence, pp. 8933–8940 (2019)

11. Wang, J., Wang, K.C., Law, M.T., Rudzicz, F., Brudno, M.: Centroid-based deep metric learning for speaker recognition. In: ICASSP 2019–2019 IEEE International Conference on Acoustics, Speech and Signal Processing (ICASSP), pp. 3652–3656 (2019)
12. Wen, Y., Zhang, K., Li, Z., Qiao, Yu.: A discriminative feature learning approach for deep face recognition. In: Leibe, B., Matas, J., Sebe, N., Welling, M. (eds.) ECCV 2016. LNCS, vol. 9911, pp. 499–515. Springer, Cham (2016). https://doi.org/10.1007/978-3-319-46478-7_31
13. Wieczorek, M., Michalowski, A., Wroblewska, A., Dabrowski, J.: A strong baseline for fashion retrieval with person re-identification models. In: Communications in Computer and Information Science, vol. 1332, pp. 294–301 (2020). https://doi.org/10.1007/978-3-030-63820-7_33
14. Xiao, T., Li, H., Ouyang, W., Wang, X.: Learning deep feature representations with domain guided dropout for person re-identification. In: Proceedings of the IEEE Computer Society Conference on Computer Vision and Pattern Recognition (2016). https://doi.org/10.1109/CVPR.2016.140
15. Yuan, Y., Chen, W., Yang, Y., Wang, Z.: In defense of the triplet loss again: learning robust person re-identification with fast approximated triplet loss and label distillation. In: 2020 IEEE/CVF Conference on Computer Vision and Pattern Recognition Workshops (CVPRW), pp. 1454–1463 (2020)
16. Zhai, A., Wu, H.Y.: Classification is a strong baseline for deep metric learning. In: BMVC (2019)
17. Zhang, Z., Lan, C., Zeng, W., Chen, Z., Chang, S.F.: Rethinking classification loss designs for person re-identification with a unified view. ArXiv abs/2006.04991 (2020)
18. Zheng, L., Shen, L., Tian, L., Wang, S., Wang, J., Tian, Q.: Scalable person re-identification: a benchmark. In: 2015 IEEE International Conference on Computer Vision (ICCV), pp. 1116–1124 (2015)
19. Zhou, K., Yang, Y., Cavallaro, A., Xiang, T.: Omni-scale feature learning for person re-identification. In: 2019 IEEE/CVF International Conference on Computer Vision (ICCV), pp. 3701–3711 (2019)
20. Zhou, S., Wang, J., Wang, J., Gong, Y., Zheng, N.: Point to set similarity based deep feature learning for person re-identification. In: 2017 IEEE Conference on Computer Vision and Pattern Recognition (CVPR), pp. 5028–5037 (2017)

Few-Shot Classification with Multi-task Self-supervised Learning

Fan Shi[1,3], Rui Wang[1,2,3]($\boxtimes$), Sanyi Zhang[1,3], and Xiaochun Cao[1,3]

[1] State Key Laboratory of Information Security, Institute of Information Engineering, Chinese Academy of Sciences, Beijing 100093, China
{shifan,wangrui,zhangsanyi,caoxiaochun}@iie.ac.cn
[2] Zhejiang Lab, Hangzhou, China
[3] School of Cyber Security, University of Chinese Academy of Sciences, Beijing 100049, China

Abstract. Few-shot learning aims to mitigate the need for large-scale annotated data in the real world. The focus of few-shot learning is how to quickly adapt to unseen tasks, which heavily depends on outstanding feature extraction ability. Motivated by the success of self-supervised learning, we propose a novel multi-task self-supervised learning framework for few-shot learning. To alleviate the deficiency of annotated samples in few-shot classification tasks, we introduce and analyze three different aspects, *i.e.*, data augmentation, feature discrimination, and generalization, to improve the ability of feature learning. The proposed method achieves clear classification boundaries for different categories and shows promising generalization ability. Experimental results demonstrate that our method outperforms the state-of-the-arts on four few-shot classification benchmarks.

Keywords: Few-shot learning · Self-supervised · Contrastive learning · image classification · Multi-task

1 Introduction

With the development of deep learning, deeper and wider models have been proposed, along with more learnable parameters. In terms of image recognition, large-scale annotated datasets [3] make it possible to train robust deep networks, which leads to the trend of data-driven learning methods. However, these data-driven ones face a series of challenges when directly applied to real-world applications. On the one hand, the process of annotating and cleaning data is time-consuming and labor-intensive. On the other hand, data is insufficient in some specific scenarios and hard to collect, such as rare cases in the medical scene

This work is supported in part by the National Natural Science Foundation of China Under Grants No. U20B2066, the Open Research Projects of Zhejiang Lab (No. 2021KB0AB01), and the National Key R&D Program of China (Grant No. 2020AAA0109304).

T. Mantoro et al. (Eds.): ICONIP 2021, LNCS 13111, pp. 224–236, 2021.
https://doi.org/10.1007/978-3-030-92273-3_19

and scarce species in the wild. To address these challenges, few-shot learning has been proposed and widely researched [6,26,27,29] to learn from insufficient samples. The goal of the few-shot learning is to learn quickly from few support samples (*e.g.*, only 1 or 5 examples per class) and generalize to query samples successfully.

The key idea of few-shot learning is how to quickly adapt to unseen tasks, which attracts much attention in recent years. Specifically, meta-learning [6] has been proposed, which aims at learning to learn. It is a task-level method aiming to learn a base-learner, which can adapt quickly to new tasks with few samples. According to recent research [20,26], it is the learned feature representation rather than the meta-learning algorithm that is responsible for fast adaptation. As a result, how to obtain a suitable feature extractor, which can transfer knowledge from the pre-trained network to unseen tasks, plays an important role in few-shot learning. However, it is hard to directly train a robust feature extractor considering the limitation of annotated samples. Thus, exploring feature learning in a self-supervised manner will be useful to improve the ability of the few-shot learning.

Motivated by the success of self-supervised learning [5,8,19], in this paper, we propose a novel multi-task self-supervised learning framework for the few-shot classification task. To mitigate the need for annotated samples in few-shot learning tasks, we introduce and analyze three different aspects, *i.e.*, data augmentation, feature discrimination, and generalization, to improve the ability of feature learning. For the data augmentation factor, self-supervised learning has been certificated that it is an effective method for feature extraction without labels. It first defines some annotation-free tasks, such as pixel prediction [19] and position rearrangement [5]. Then it forces the feature extractor to learn more information by exploring the predefined tasks. In our work, we introduce image rotation [8] to augment the training samples and the rotation prediction task to enhance the feature learning ability. However, only utilizing the data augmentation mechanism is not enough to train a robust feature extractor. Thus, we improve the robustness of the model by taking account of the feature discrimination factor. Contrastive learning [2,9] has led to great progress in unsupervised classification tasks. To be specific, the inputs derived from the same samples are pulled close in the embedding space, and vice versa. Given the data limitation in few-shot learning, exploring contrastive learning in the fully supervised setting [12] is beneficial to feature embedding. It can achieve a clear classification boundary for different categories by introducing the supervised class information. Further, we also consider the feature generalization factor that guarantees the representation ability in novel class. It seems intuitive that two structurally identical networks tend to share similar representations for the same input image. Thus, mutual learning is utilized as a regularization task to improve the generalization performance of the framework.

We formulate these three different self-supervised tasks into a unified framework to improve the performance of the few-shot classification. Extensive experiments demonstrate that the proposed method outperforms the state-of-the-art methods on four few-shot classification benchmarks, *i.e.*, miniImageNet [27], tieredImageNet [22], CIFAR-FS [1], and FC-100 [18]. The main contributions of our work can be summarized as follows:

- We propose a novel multi-task self-supervised learning framework for the few-shot classification, which makes full use of the self-supervised mechanism to extend and enrich the limited labeled images.
- Three constructive clues, *i.e.*, data augmentation, feature discrimination, and generalization, are explored to solve the limitation of annotated samples in few-shot learning tasks. Data augmentation is used to diversify training samples. Feature discrimination is explored to improve the representation ability as well as to achieve a clear classification boundary for different categories. Feature generalization is also utilized to boost the generalization ability of the network.
- Experiments are conducted on four popular few-shot classification benchmarks and we achieve state-of-the-art performance on them.

2   Related Work

Few-Shot Learning: Few-shot classification tasks involve training a model with base classes and then adapting the model to novel classes using only few samples. Great efforts have been made in few-shot learning in recent years. One dominant method is meta-learning, including optimization-based [6,24] and metric-based [23,25,27] meta-learning. Optimization-based methods aim to learn the update rule of model parameters instead of a single model, forcing the model to search for the optimal initialization of the model parameters which can quickly adapt to new tasks with few samples. [24] achieves the balance between the representation ability and meta-learning ability through fixing the pre-trained feature extractor and only updating part of parameters. Metric-based methods focus on how to get a transferable distance metric to measure the similarity between different samples. MatchingNet [27] leverages two networks for the support set and query set respectively and utilizes cosine similarity as the metric to predict the unlabeled samples. ProtoNet [23] implies that each category has its prototype representation, namely the mean embedding of each category. The Euclidean distance between query sets and prototype representations in the embedding space can measure their similarity. RelationNet [25] designs a CNN-based distance module to replace the non-parametric distance function with a parametric relation module. Recent studies suggest that feature reuse is more important than rapid learning for the fast adaption in meta-learning [20]. As a result, a suitable feature extractor is the main challenge of few-shot learning.

Self-supervised Learning: In terms of improving the representation ability of feature extractor, self-supervised learning is widespreadly studied, enabling the network to learn more information through pretext tasks. As a result, it mitigates the need for large-scale annotated data in unsupervised learning as well as few-shot learning [7,14,21]. To be specific, self-supervised learning provides surrogate supervision for representation learning through predefining some annotation-free tasks, including predicting the angle of rotated images [8], the relative position of image patches [5], and the missing parts of images [19].

Supervised Contrastive Learning: Contrastive learning [2,9] treats images derived from the same images as positive pairs, which leads to the state-of-the-art performance in unsupervised image classification tasks. Supervised contrastive learning [12] is structurally similar to [2], while it treats images within the same class as positive pairs. In the training procedure of supervised contrastive learning, the features of positive pairs are pulled together in embedding space while the negative pairs are pushed apart from each other simultaneously.

Deep Mutual Learning: Knowledge distillation [11] is a common and effective technique for model compression and knowledge transfer, composed of a deeper teacher network and a shallower student network. During the training procedure, knowledge is transferred from teacher to student by forcing the student to output the same distribution as the teacher. Self-distillation [17,21,30] is a variant of knowledge distillation, aiming to improve transferability rather than compressing models, in which the student and teacher models are structurally identical and trained in sequence. In mutual learning [32], two networks are trained simultaneously and the Kullback Leibler divergence is adopted to make their prediction matched.

3   Our Approach

In this section, we first describe the problem setting and preliminary in Sect. 3.1, then we introduce the proposed multi-task self-supervised learning framework for the few-shot classification task. As shown in Fig. 2, our model is composed of multiple self-supervised learning tasks which takes three different perspectives into account, *i.e.*, 1) data augmentation (Sect. 3.2), 2) feature discrimination (Sect. 3.3), and 3) feature generalization (Sect. 3.4). With 1), we augment the number of the training samples by rotating input images and enhance the feature learning ability via an auxiliary rotation prediction task. With 2), the feature discrimination ability is improved through supervised contrastive learning. With 3), mutual learning is utilized to further boost the feature generalization. Finally, we provide a self-driven few-shot classification framework based on joint self-supervised learning, which works in an end-to-end manner.

3.1   Problem Formulation

As shown in Fig. 1, few-shot learning contains two phases, *i.e.*, training on base classes and testing on novel classes. In the training phase, the base class training set is defined as $D_{train} = \{(x, y)\}$, where x is the input image and y is the one-hot encoded label belonging to N_b base classes. In the testing phase, the novel

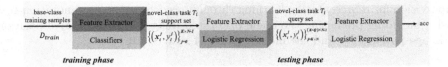

Fig. 1. The pipeline for the training and testing phase in our approach. The training of the feature extractor is described in the part of Sect. 3. The testing phase includes training the linear classifier model and inference. Input data are along with arrows. Modules in deeper colors are updated in their corresponding phases.

class testing set is similarly defined as $D_{test} = \{(x, y)\}$ with a total of N_n novel classes, from which we sample several tasks for evaluation. Each task contains N novel classes with K samples for training the linear classification model and Q samples for final evaluation. It is denoted as the N-way, K-shot setting for few-shot learning. We follow [26] to use logistic regression as the linear model to train the support set with $N \times K$ samples in the first part of the testing phase. The pre-trained feature extractor and linear model are then evaluated on the $N \times Q$ query set in the second part. The pipeline of the training and testing phase is shown in Fig. 1.

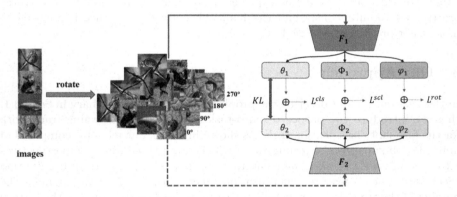

Fig. 2. Network architecture for the training phase. Training set is augmented into 4 copies by rotation, and then encoded into the feature space through two structurally same feature extractor F_1 and F_2. The symbol $\oplus$ represents the sum of the two outputs. The output feature representation of the two feature extractors are provided to three classifiers respectively to further improve their representation ability.

The framework in the training phase is shown in Fig. 2. The network contains one main image classification task and three auxiliary self-supervised tasks. The input images are firstly augmented by the image rotation operation. Then the images are fed into two structurally same feature extractors F_1 and F_2 to obtain the feature representations. The base classifier f_θ is adopted to address the main classification task equipped with the standard cross-entropy loss. Through data augmentation, the trained data D_{train} will be replaced with D^*. The classification learning aim is to minimize the following loss through iteratively updating the parameters of F_i and f_{θ_i}:

$$L_i^{cls} = E_{(x,y)\in D^*}\left[L\left(f_{\theta_i}\left(F_i\left(x\right)\right), y\right)\right], \tag{1}$$

where L represents the standard cross-entropy loss.

In addition, three auxiliary self-supervised tasks are also introduced to enhance the feature learning ability, which will be introduced in Sect. 3.2, 3.3 and 3.4, respectively. In total, the proposed network is in a multi-task way. While in the testing phase, the feature extractors are frozen, we just train the linear classifier for final evaluation.

3.2 Self-supervised Learning

Considering the limited annotated data for training in the few-shot classification task, we utilize an annotation-free self-supervised mechanism to enrich the scale and diversity of training samples. In this way, we can not only augment data but also improve the ability of feature learning. In our work, we choose image rotation to augment the training data and introduce the rotation prediction as the self-supervised pretext task. The advantage of the image rotation operation lies in that while we rotate the image, the label can keep constant. To be specific, we generate four rotated copies for each input image, which are rotated among four rotations in $C_r = \{0°, 90°, 180°, 270°\}$. The augmented dataset $D^* = \{(x^r, y)\}$, where $r = 0, 1, 2, 3$, is reconstructed, substituting for the original training set D_{train}. After mapped into the embedding space by the feature extractor F_i, the input image gets its feature representation $F_i(x^r)$. Then, the rotation classifier is employed to predict the rotation type r using a fully-connection layer f_{φ_i}, which is a simple four-class classification task without additional annotation. The self-supervised loss of image rotation is given by:

$$L_i^{rot} = \frac{1}{|C_r|} \sum_{x\in D_{train}} \sum_{r\in C_r} L\left(f_{\varphi_i}\left(F_i\left(x^r\right), r\right)\right), \tag{2}$$

where $|C_r|$ denotes the cardinality of C_r and L is the standard cross entropy loss.

3.3 Supervised Contrastive Learning

To achieve a clear classification boundary for different categories, supervised contrastive learning is introduced to improve the feature discrimination ability. The aim of supervised contrastive learning is to pull samples within the same class close in the embedding space and simultaneously push samples of different classes apart from each other [12]. Specifically, we construct a projection network with the multi-layer perception. It maps encoded features by the feature extractor F_i to a projection space first, and then normalizes the output to lie on the unit hypersphere, where inner product can be used as a metric to measure distance of features. Despite the supervision comes from labels, we also utilize data augmentation as contrastive learning in the unsupervised way to boost the strength of network. For a batch of n randomly sampled data $\{x_k, y_k\}$, $k = 1, .., n$. The corresponding batch for training contains $4n$ samples, which has been augmented through the image rotation operation. The loss for supervised contrastive learning is as follows:

$$L_i^{scl} = E_{(x,y) \in D^*} \frac{1}{|S(x)|} \sum_{\tilde{x} \in S(x)} \log \frac{\exp(h_i(x) \cdot h_i(\tilde{x})/\tau)}{\sum_{\bar{x} \in B(x)} \exp(h_i(x) \cdot h_i(\bar{x})/\tau)}, \qquad (3)$$

where $h_i(x) = f_{\Phi_i}(F_i(x))$, the symbol $\cdot$ denotes the inner product, τ is a scalar temperature parameter. As x serves as the anchor, $S(x)$ contains all positive samples in the augmented batch, and $B(x)$ contains samples in the augmented batch distinct from x.

3.4   Deep Mutual Learning

Although we have owned good feature learning ability by the self-supervised data augmentation and supervised contrastive learning, the feature generalization ability is also limited while applied it in the real world. Thus, we use deep mutual learning instead of sequent self-distillation as a knowledge distillation method in our framework. Specifically, two structurally identical models, *i.e.*, F_1 and F_2, are constructed and trained independently. And then we connect the output logits which are responsible for knowledge transfer. Considering classification is the main task of our network, we only minimize the Kullback Leibler (KL) divergence for the soft output of the supervised classifier f_θ. Since KL divergence is asymmetrical, we compute KL divergence twice by exchange the position of the pair, similar to JS divergence. The learning objective for mutual learning includes two KL divergence parts is denoted as follows:

$$L^{kl} = \frac{1}{2} E_{x \in D^*} [KL(f_{\theta_1}(F_1(x)), f_{\theta_2}(F_2(x)))$$
$$+ KL(f_{\theta_2}(F_2(x)), f_{\theta_1}(F_1(x)))]. \qquad (4)$$

3.5   Overall Objective

Finally, three different types of self-supervised learning tasks and the standard image classification task are combined in a unified framework and optimized in an end-to-end manner. The overall objective of our approach is formulated by combining three afore-mentioned losses with different weights, as follows:

$$L^{total} = \frac{1}{2} \sum_{i=1}^{2} [\alpha L_i^{cls} + \beta L_i^{rot} + \gamma L_i^{scl}] + \eta L^{kl}, \qquad (5)$$

where α, β, γ, η correspond to the weight of classification loss, self-supervised learning loss, supervised contrastive learning and mutual learning, respectively.

4   Experiment

Dataset. We conduct our experiments on four widely-used few-shot classification benchmarks: miniImageNet [27], tieredImageNet [22], CIFAR-FS [1], and FC100 [18]. The first two datasets are derivatives of the ImageNet dataset [3] while the last two datasets are subsets of CIFAR-100. The miniImageNet dataset [27] consists of 100 classes sampled from the original ImageNet dataset for few-shot learning, which are split into three groups, 64 classes as base classes for training, 16 classes for validation, and 20 classes for testing. Each class contains a total of 600 images of size 84×84. The tieredImageNet dataset [22] is a more challenging derivative than miniImageNet, which randomly picks 608 classes from the original ImageNet. The classes are then grouped into 34 high-level categories and we use 20/351, 6/97, and 8/160 categories/classes for training, validation, and testing. The CIFAR-FS dataset [1] consists of 100 classes with 64, 16, and 20 classes for training, validation, and testing. Each class contains 600 images of size 32×32 in total. The FC-100 dataset [18] is constructed similarly as tieredImageNet through grouping the 100 original classes into 20 high-level categories. The images are of size 32×32.

Implementation Details. Following recent works in few-shot learning [16,29, 31], we use the 12-layer ResNet as our backbone network for feature extraction. In terms of the three classifiers in the training phase, we utilize the fully connected network to train f_θ and f_φ, and multi-layer perception with a hidden layer to train f_Φ. Dropblock and feature normalization are also utilized in our method as [26]. We use 64 as the batch size in all datasets. Dataset augmentation is utilized besides image rotation as the self-supervised task, *e.g.* randomly cropping, randomly horizontal flipping, and color jittering. The temperatures for supervised contrastive learning and mutual learning are set as 0.5 and 4, respectively. We set the weights of losses in the overall objective as $\alpha = \beta = \gamma = \eta = 1$.

We use SGD optimizer with a momentum of 0.9, a weight decay of $5e - 4$, and an initial learning rate of 0.5 for all datasets. We train 90 epochs for CIFAR-FS, FC-100 and miniImageNet. The learning rate is decayed with a factor of 0.1 every 15 epochs after the first 50 epochs. We train 60 epochs for tieredImageNet, for which the learning rate is decayed every 10 epochs after the first 30 epochs.

4.1   Quantitative Results

We evaluate our experiments on 5-way, 1-shot and 5-shot classification settings. During the test phase, we train an N-way logistic regression classifier on the support set of each sampled task and evaluate the query set of size 15. A total of 600 tasks are sampled to calculate the mean accuracy in the four few-shot learning benchmarks.

Table 1. The 5-way, 1-shot and 5-shot classification accuracy (%) on the miniImageNet and tieredImageNet.

Method	Backbone	miniImageNet		tieredImageNet	
		1-shot	5-shot	1-shot	5-shot
MAML [6]	4CONV	48.70 ± 1.84	63.11 ± 0.92	51.67 ± 1.81	70.30 ± 1.75
MatchingNet [27]	4CONV	43.56 ± 0.84	55.31 ± 0.73	–	–
ProtoNet [23]	4CONV	49.42 ± 0.78	68.20 ± 0.66	–	–
MetaOptNet [16]	ResNet-12	62.64 ± 0.35	78.63 ± 0.68	65.99 ± 0.72	81.56 ± 0.53
MTL [24]	ResNet-12	61.20 ± 1.80	75.50 ± 0.80	65.60 ± 1.80	80.80 ± 0.80
Boosting [7]	WRN-28-10	63.77 ± 0.45	80.70 ± 0.33	70.53 ± 0.51	84.98 ± 0.36
Fine-tuning [4]	WRN-28-10	57.73 ± 0.62	78.17 ± 0.49	66.58 ± 0.70	85.55 ± 0.48
RFS-distill [26]	ResNet-12	64.82 ± 0.60	82.14 ± 0.43	71.52 ± 0.69	86.03 ± 0.49
DeepEMD [15]	ResNet-12	65.91 ± 0.82	82.41 ± 0.56	71.16 ± 0.87	86.03 ± 0.58
FEAT [29]	ResNet-12	66.78 ± 0.20	82.05 ± 0.14	70.80 ± 0.23	84.79 ± 0.16
FRN [28]	ResNet-12	66.45 ± 0.19	82.83 ± 0.13	71.16 ± 0.22	86.01 ± 0.15
Ours	ResNet-12	**67.12 ± 0.76**	**83.04 ± 0.55**	**73.02 ± 0.90**	**86.82 ± 0.54**

The overall comparisons with state-of-the-art methods on the miniImageNet, tieredImageNet, CIFAR-FS, and FC100 datasets are presented in Table 1 and Table 2, respectively. The experimental results demonstrate that our approach outperforms the feature embedding baseline [26] in both 1-shot and 5-shot settings on four few-shot classification datasets. Specifically, in the tough 1-shot setting, our method can obtain 2.3% and 2.53% accuracy improvement than RFS-distill [26] on the miniImageNet and CIFAR-FS datasets, respectively. In addition, our approach outperforms the state-of-the-art methods compared with both optimization-based [6,16,24] and metric-based methods [23,27]. It shows the significance of feature embedding in few-shot learning tasks. If we improve the feature embedding ability through multiple self-supervised learning tasks, our method obtains the best performance over all current state-of-the-art methods. It proves that improving the representation ability of the feature extractor through multi-task self-supervised learning benefits few-shot classification.

4.2   Ablation Study

To explain the significance of the three aspects of our approach, we conduct an ablation study on whether the image rotation task, supervised contrastive learning, and mutual learning are responsible for the improvement.

Table 3 shows the result of the ablation study on the miniImageNet dataset. In general, the self-supervised task of image rotation improves the performance by 2.42% and 2.04% in 1-shot and 5-shot settings, respectively (see last two rows). While we employ the mutual learning strategy, it can obtain a 2.23%

Table 2. The 5-way, 1-shot and 5-shot classification accuracy (%) on the CIFAR-FS and FC-100 dataset.

Method	Backbone	CIFAR-FS		FC-100	
		1-shot	5-shot	1-shot	5-shot
MAML [6]	4CONV	58.90 ± 1.90	71.50 ± 1.00	38.10 ± 1.70	50.40 ± 1.00
MetaOptNet [16]	ResNet-12	72.00 ± 0.70	84.20 ± 0.50	41.10 ± 0.60	55.50 ± 0.60
MTL [24]	ResNet-12	–	–	45.10 ± 1.80	57.60 ± 0.90
MABAS [13]	ResNet-12	73.51 ± 0.92	85.49 ± 0.68	42.31 ± 0.75	57.56 ± 0.78
TADAM [18]	ResNet-12	–	–	40.10 ± 0.40	56.10 ± 0.40
RFS-distill [26]	ResNet-12	73.90 ± 0.80	86.90 ± 0.50	44.60 ± 0.70	60.90 ± 0.60
Ours	ResNet-12	**76.43 ± 0.90**	**88.48 ± 0.58**	**45.80 ± 0.82**	**61.77 ± 0.76**

Table 3. Ablation study on miniImageNet. "ROT" means rotating images as a self-supervised task. "SCL" stands for constructing supervised contrastive loss for few-shot learning. "ML" indicates utilizing mutual learning strategy in the training phase.

ROT	SCL	ML	1-shot	5-shot
√	√		64.89 ± 0.82	81.94 ± 0.57
√		√	67.07 ± 0.85	82.85 ± 0.55
	√	√	64.70 ± 0.78	81.00 ± 0.53
√	√	√	**67.12 ± 0.76**	**83.04 ± 0.55**

improvement for the 1-shot setting and 1.1% gain for the 5-shot setting (see the second and the last rows). If we further adopt supervised contrastive learning, our method will lead to additional improvement in the accuracy score.

4.3 Qualitative Analysis

We visualize the feature embeddings on the miniImageNet dataset for few-shot learning through t-SNE [10]. As shown in Fig. 3, our method leads to more discriminative boundaries and more compact clusters compared with the baseline models [26] equipped with or without knowledge distillation (KD), when applied to unseen tasks. It suggests that our method benefits from combining three self-supervised tasks from three different perspectives. Thus, the proposed method owns better feature representation ability than the baseline models for few-shot classification tasks.

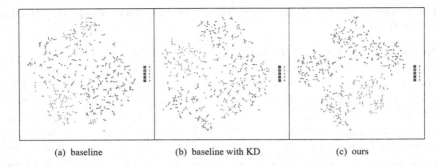

(a) baseline   (b) baseline with KD   (c) ours

Fig. 3. The t-SNE visualization of the feature embeddings on the miniImageNet dataset by randomly selecting 750 samples from five novel classes. (a) and (b) show the performance on the baseline without and with knowledge distillation (KD). (c) shows the feature embeddings with our full method.

5   Conclusion

In this paper, we propose a novel multi-task self-supervised learning method to mitigate the need for large-scale annotated data in the real world, which considers three aspects of data augmentation, feature discrimination, and generalization. The proposed method achieves clear classification boundaries and shows great generalization ability in few-shot learning. Experimental results demonstrate that our method outperforms current state-of-the-art methods on four few-shot classification benchmarks.

References

1. Bertinetto, L., Henriques, J.F., Torr, P.H.S., Vedaldi, A.: Meta-learning with differentiable closed-form solvers. ArXiv arxiv:1805.08136 (2019)
2. Chen, T., Kornblith, S., Norouzi, M., Hinton, G.E.: A simple framework for contrastive learning of visual representations. ArXiv arxiv:2002.05709 (2020)
3. Deng, J., Dong, W., Socher, R., Li, L.J., Li, K., Fei-Fei, L.: Imagenet: a large-scale hierarchical image database. In: CVPR (2009)
4. Dhillon, G.S., Chaudhari, P., Ravichandran, A., Soatto, S.: A baseline for few-shot image classification. arXiv (2019)
5. Doersch, C., Gupta, A., Efros, A.A.: Unsupervised visual representation learning by context prediction. In: 2015 IEEE International Conference on Computer Vision (ICCV), pp. 1422–1430 (2015)
6. Finn, C., Abbeel, P., Levine, S.: Model-agnostic meta-learning for fast adaptation of deep networks. In: ICML (2017)
7. Gidaris, S., Bursuc, A., Komodakis, N., Pérez, P., Cord, M.: Boosting few-shot visual learning with self-supervision. In: 2019 IEEE/CVF International Conference on Computer Vision (ICCV) (2019)

8. Gidaris, S., Singh, P., Komodakis, N.: Unsupervised representation learning by predicting image rotations. ArXiv arxiv:1803.07728 (2018)
9. He, K., Fan, H., Wu, Y., Xie, S., Girshick, R.: Momentum contrast for unsupervised visual representation learning. In: 2020 IEEE/CVF Conference on Computer Vision and Pattern Recognition (CVPR) (2020)
10. Hinton, G.E.: Visualizing high-dimensional data using t-SNE. Vigiliae Christianae **9**, 2579–2605 (2008)
11. Hinton, G.E., Vinyals, O., Dean, J.: Distilling the knowledge in a neural network. ArXiv arxiv:1503.02531 (2015)
12. Khosla, P., et al.: Supervised contrastive learning. ArXiv arxiv:2004.11362 (2020)
13. Koch, G., Zemel, R., Salakhutdinov, R.: Siamese neural networks for one-shot image recognition (2015)
14. Lee, H., Hwang, S.J., Shin, J.: Rethinking data augmentation: Self-supervision and self-distillation. ArXiv arxiv:1910.05872 (2019)
15. Zhang, C., Cai, Y., Lin, G., Shen, C.: DeepEMD: Differentiable Earth Mover's Distance for Few-Shot Learning (2020)
16. Lee, K., Maji, S., Ravichandran, A., Soatto, S.: Meta-learning with differentiable convex optimization. In: 2019 IEEE/CVF Conference on Computer Vision and Pattern Recognition (CVPR), pp. 10649–10657 (2019)
17. Mobahi, H., Farajtabar, M., Bartlett, P.: Self-distillation amplifies regularization in Hilbert space. ArXiv arxiv:2002.05715 (2020)
18. Oreshkin, B.N., Rodriguez, P., Lacoste, A.: Tadam: task dependent adaptive metric for improved few-shot learning. In: NeurIPS (2020)
19. Pathak, D., Krähenbühl, P., Donahue, J., Darrell, T., Efros, A.A.: Context encoders: feature learning by inpainting. In: 2016 IEEE Conference on Computer Vision and Pattern Recognition (CVPR), pp. 2536–2544 (2016)
20. Raghu, A., Raghu, M., Bengio, S., Vinyals, O.: Rapid learning or feature reuse? Towards understanding the effectiveness of MAML. ArXiv arxiv:1909.09157 (2020)
21. Rajasegaran, J., Khan, S., Hayat, M., Khan, F., Shah, M.: Self-supervised knowledge distillation for few-shot learning. ArXiv arxiv:2006.09785 (2020)
22. Ren, M., et al.: Meta-learning for semi-supervised few-shot classification. ArXiv arxiv:1803.00676 (2018)
23. Snell, J., Swersky, K., Zemel, R.: Prototypical networks for few-shot learning. In: NIPS (2017)
24. Sun, Q., Liu, Y., Chua, T.S., Schiele, B.: Meta-transfer learning for few-shot learning. In: 2019 IEEE/CVF Conference on Computer Vision and Pattern Recognition (CVPR) (2019)
25. Sung, F., Yang, Y., Zhang, L., Xiang, T., Torr, P.H.S., Hospedales, T.M.: Learning to compare: relation network for few-shot learning. In: 2018 IEEE/CVF Conference on Computer Vision and Pattern Recognition, pp. 1199–1208 (2018)
26. Tian, Y., Wang, Y., Krishnan, D., Tenenbaum, J., Isola, P.: Rethinking few-shot image classification: a good embedding is all you need? ArXiv arxiv:2003.11539 (2020)
27. Vinyals, O., Blundell, C., Lillicrap, T., Kavukcuoglu, K., Wierstra, D.: Matching networks for one shot learning. In: NIPS (2016)
28. Wertheimer, D., Tang, L., Hariharan, B.: Few-shot classification with feature map reconstruction networks. In: Proceedings of the IEEE/CVF Conference on Computer Vision and Pattern Recognition (CVPR) (2021)
29. Ye, H.J., Hu, H., Zhan, D.C., Sha, F.: Few-shot learning via embedding adaptation with set-to-set functions. In: 2020 IEEE/CVF Conference on Computer Vision and Pattern Recognition (CVPR) (2020)

30. Zhang, L., Song, J., Gao, A., Chen, J., Bao, C., Ma, K.: Be your own teacher: improve the performance of convolutional neural networks via self distillation (2019)
31. Zhang, M., Zhang, J., Lu, Z., Xiang, T., Ding, M., Huang, S.: IEPT: instance-level and episode-level pretext tasks for few-shot learning. In: ICLR (2021)
32. Zhang, Y., Xiang, T., Hospedales, T.M., Lu, H.: Deep mutual learning (2017)

Self-supervised Compressed Video Action Recognition via Temporal-Consistent Sampling

Pan Chen[1], Shaohui Lin[2(✉)], Yongxiang Zhang[2], Jiachen Xu[1], Xin Tan[1], and Lizhuang Ma[1,2(✉)]

[1] Shanghai Jiao Tong University, Shanghai, China
prilochen@sjtu.edu.cn, ma-lz@cs.sjtu.edu.cn
[2] East China Normal University, Shanghai, China
shlin@cs.ecnu.edu.cn

Abstract. Compressed video action recognition targets at classifying action class in compressed video, instead of decoded/standard video. It benefits from fast training and inference by reducing the utilization of redundant information. However, off-the-shelf methods still rely on heavy-cost labels for training. In this paper, we propose self-supervised compressed video action recognition method via Momentum contrast (MoCo) and temporal-consistent sampling. We leverage temporal-consistent sampling into MoCo to improve the ability of feature presentation on each input modality of compressed video. Modality-oriented fine-tuning is introduced to applying into the downstream compressed video action recognition.

Extensive experiments demonstrate the effectiveness of our method on different datasets with different backbones. Compared to SOTA self-supervised learning methods for decoded videos on HMDB51 dataset, our method achieves the highest accuracy of 57.8%.

Keywords: Action recognition · Compressed video · Contrastive learning · Temporal-consistent sampling

1 Introduction

As a popular vision analysis task, action recognition pertains to tell the action class observed in a video [13]. With the widely-used cameras in daily life, action recognition has played an essential role in many applications, *e.g.*, surveillance, human-computer interaction and robotics. Basically, action recognition methods aim to extract spatial and temporal information from input videos for classification. For example, two-stream frameworks [10,27,31] have been proposed to employ 2D CNNs to separately extract the appearance and temporal or motion information, which can be late merged for final prediction.

Supported by NSFC (No. 61972157), Shanghai Municipal Science and Technology Major Project (2021SHZDZX0102), Shanghai Science and Technology Commission (21511101200), Art major project of National Social Science Fund (I8ZD22).

© Springer Nature Switzerland AG 2021
T. Mantoro et al. (Eds.): ICONIP 2021, LNCS 13111, pp. 237–249, 2021.
https://doi.org/10.1007/978-3-030-92273-3_20

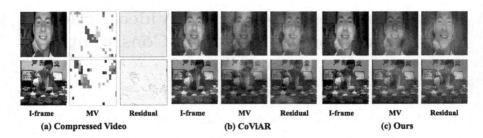

| I-frame | MV | Residual | I-frame | MV | Residual | I-frame | MV | Residual |
| (a) Compressed Video | | | (b) CoViAR | | | (c) Ours | | |

Fig. 1. Visualization comparison on three modalities using supervised CoViAR [32] and ours. Area marked as red indicate the network pays more attention on that region. (a) Three-modality input in compressed video. (b) Visualization of CoViAR. (c) Ours.

Several techniques have been also studied to learn temporal features, such as RNNs [7], temporal CNNs [20] and temporal shift module (TSM) [19]. Alternatively, 3D CNNS [13,24,29,30,34] have been proposed to directly model and extract the spatial-temporal information using 3D convolutions. However, both two-stream frameworks and 3D CNNs often perform on the standard/decoded videos (*i.e.* all RGB frames) for action recognition, which leads to expensively time-consuming processing without considering the redundancy of inner frames. Moreover, this redundancy affects CNNs to extract meaningful information and results in the slower training.

As a solution, several works directly work on compressed video domain and make use of motion information like motion vectors that are already stored in compressed videos. For example, CoViAR [32] exploits three 2D CNNs to extract appearance, motion and residual features on I-frame (*a.k.a.* RGB framework), motion vector and residual in compressed videos, respectively. The late fusion for these three features is further used to obtain the final results for action recognition.

With a generator network, DMC-Net [26] generates discriminative motion cue on the motion vector by optical flow supervision, helping the network to achieve better predictions. However, off-the-shelf compressed video action recognition methods follow the supervised learning paradigm to extract the effective features, which requires time-cost and labor-expensive labelling that restricts the extensive applications. Moreover, they are hard to focus attention on the area of action happening. As shown in Fig. 1, CoViAR [32] fails to focus attention on motion vector and residual of two given videos. This begs our rethinking: why not exploit label-free self-supervised methods to learn better feature representation for three-modality inputs, and focus on action happening area?

To answer the above question, we propose a novel contrastive learning structure inspired by MoCo [9], which utilizes each modalily information straightly on compressed video. MoCo creates different views on the same image by different augmentations (*e.g.* flipping, color jitter and greyscale) as positive pairs, which can be leveraged to successfully obtain feature representation of I-frame. However, it significantly decreases the ability of feature presentation for motion vector and residual. This is due to the corrupted spatial information by using random augmentation in MoCo. To this end, we further propose temporal-consistent sampling to construct the positive pairs by selecting two clips from different position of the same video in a probability manner, rather than the same input in MoCo. As such, it benefits from the strong discriminability and generalization ability for feature representation of motion vector and residual, which help the network to focus on the action happening area. Finally, modality-oriented fine-tuning is introduced to obtain final prediction by fusing three streams. We term our MoCo with temporal-consistent sampling as TCS-MoCo for compressed video action recognition.

In summary, the main contributions can be summarized as follows:

1. We introduce self-supervised learning into compressed video action recognition task. To the best of our knowledge, this is the first work to leverage self-supervision learning into compressed video action recognition.
2. An effective temporal-consistent sampling method is proposed to create positive pairs as the input of MoCo.
3. Extensive experiments on compressed video action recognition demonstrate the superior performance of our approach. On UCF101 [28] and HMDB51 [18] dataset, our TCS-MoCo achieves 84.3% and 57.8% accuracy, respectively. Furthermore, TCS-MoCo employs an effective self-supervised pre-training on compressed video, which helps the network focus on the action happening area showed by visualization.

2   Preliminaries

2.1   Compressed Videos

Compressed videos can be constructed by several video compression methods, such as, MPEG-4, H.264 and HEVC, which significantly reduce video storage and transmission. They only need to efficiently store several frames in whole video by reusing contents from other frames and store the difference, which is due to the redundancy where successive frames often have similar patterns/contents.

We take MPEG-4 for example, videos can be split into I-frames (intra-coded frames), P-frames (predictive frames) and B-frames (bi-directional frames).

I-frames are compressed regular frames containing RGB information. P-frames use motion vectors to track movement of image patches and use residual to correct the predicted frames, aiming to be closed to the original frames. B-frames can be seen as special P-frames, where motion vectors are computed bidirectionally and may reference a future frame as long as there are no circles [32]. In addition, GOP is an important and coarse unit in the compressed video, including only one I-frame, multiple P-frames and B-frames. The size of GOP is determined by the number of P-frames following one I-frame.

As original frames can be recovered by I-frames and P-frames, here we just focus on I-frames and P-frames for action recognition, like the previous works [11, 26,32]. The recurrence relation for reconstructing P-frames is

$$I_i^{(t)} = I_{i-\mathcal{T}_i^{(t)}}^{(t-1)} + \triangle_i^{(t)}, \tag{1}$$

for each pixel i at time t, where $I^{(t)}$, $\mathcal{T}^{(t)}$ and $\triangle^{(t)}$ denote RGB image, motion vector and residual at time t respectively.

| I-frame | MV | Residual | Accumulated MV | Accumulated Residual |

Fig. 2. Three modalities of compressed videos. Motion vectors are plotted in HSV space, where the H channel encodes the direction of motion, and the S channel shows the amplitude. I-frame and residual are plotted in RGB space.

Here P-frame just contain the difference between itself to the reference frame which might be a P-frame again. This chain continues back to a preceding I-frame. To break the recurrent dependency, CoViAR [32] propose a decoupled model which traces all motion vectors back to the reference I-frame and accumulates the residual, thus P-frames can recover its original RGB frames just depending on itself and the preceding I-frame. The sample of three modalities of compressed videos is shown in Fig. 2. This accumulation also provides more robust motion vector and residual information. In this paper, we also employ the decoupled model to obtain the reference I-frames and the corresponding accumulated motion vectors and residual as inputs.

2.2 Momentum Contrast

Momentum contrast (MoCo) is one of the most effective self-supervised learning methods, which builds constrative learning as dictionary look-up that minimizes the distance of visual representation between positive pairs and maximizes the distance of visual representation between negative ones. Specifically, with a query q, MoCo aims to find the most relevant (positive) key k^+ among all keys k from the keys of a dictionary K with N elements. InfoNCE [22], a contrastive loss function, is introduced to implement the constrative learning for MoCo by:

$$min_{\theta_q, \theta_k} \mathbb{E}_{x \sim p\chi} [-log \frac{e^{q \cdot k^+ / \tau}}{\sum_{i=0}^{N} e^{q \cdot k_i / \tau}}], \tag{2}$$

where θ_q ans θ_k are parameters of the query and key encoders, and τ is a temperature term [33]. x is input data for sampling and encoding to generate q and k. MoCo decouples the dictionary size from the mini-batch size by a queue-based dictionary [5]. After a look-up procedure, the current keys are enqueued and the oldest keys are dequeued.

For query encoder, MoCo directly updates the gradients via back-propagation, while the weights of key encoder are updated by momentum updates:

$$\theta_k \leftarrow m\theta_k + (1 - m)\theta_q, \tag{3}$$

where $m \in [0, 1)$ is a coefficient. Inspired by the effectiveness of MoCo, we build our action recognition framework applied into compressed videos rather than images.

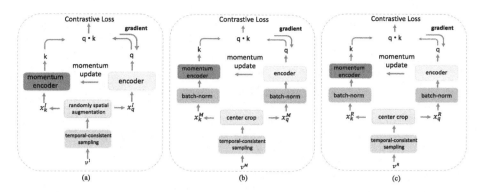

Fig. 3. The framework of TCS-MoCo. (a), (b) and (c) show the pre-training stage for I-frame, motion vector and residual, respectively.

3   Proposed Method

3.1   Representation Learning for Compressed Video Using MoCo

As described in Sect. 2, we employ MoCo to build feature representation learning framework for compressed videos.

In particular, we utilizes all three modalities in compressed videos (*i.e.* I-Frame, motion vector (MV) and residual) independently for parallel MoCo, which is shown in Fig. 3.

For feature representation learning of I-frames, we can simply sample two random "views" of the same I-frame under random data augmentation (including flipping, color jitter, greyscale) to form a positive pair, as the domain of I-frames is RGB that is similar to the original MoCo processing images. Therefore, we encode the augmented I-frames over query and key by query encoder f and key encoder h:

$$q = f(x_q, \theta_q), k^+ = h(x_k, \theta_k), \qquad (4)$$

where x_q and x_k are I-frames over query and key, respectively. Note that f and h have the same network structure but different parameters θ_q and θ_k. Then, we can formulate the contrastive loss via InfoNCE Loss [22] as:

$$L_q = -log \frac{exp(q \cdot k^+/\tau)}{\sum_{k \in K} exp(q \cdot k/\tau)}, \qquad (5)$$

where k^+ and q are the outputs of query and key encoders, which has the same I-frame as an input.

For training, parameter θ_q of query encoder are optimized via back-propagate by minimizing Eq. 5. Meanwhile, parameter θ_k of key encoder are momentum updated using Eq. 3. Key dictionary updating is implemented by putting the current key encoding features into dictionary and the oldest ones will be dequeued from dictionary.

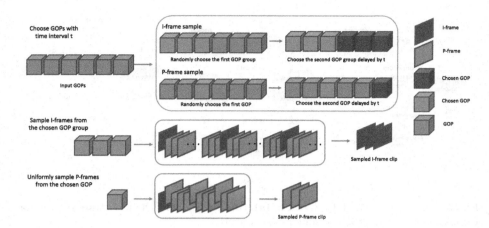

Fig. 4. The temporal-consistent sampling procedure. Clips length s is 3 and GOP size g is 12. Here time interval t is set to 3 for example.

However, applying MoCo into the inputs of MV and residual directly is not compatible, as motion vector and residual have their *intrinsic data representation*. On the one hand, the channel number of MV is 2, which is different to RGB channel number 3. On the other hand, random augmentation on motion vector and residual will corrupt internal rich spatial information, which leads to poor feature representation. To this end, we first set the input channel number in the first Conv layer of encoder to 2 for MV and also apply a Batch-Norm layer on MV and residual that reduces their imbalanced distribution. Then, we only use center crop for MV and residual to keep spatial information unchanged. Furthermore, temporal-consistent sampling is proposed to construct positive samples from different clips of the same video, which is described in the next subsection. Note that temporal-consistent sampling can also applied into I-frame for further improving the effectiveness of its feature representation.

3.2 Temporal-Consistent Sampling

In MoCo [10], different views (query and key) of a instance are generated from the same image with different potential augmentations.

As discussed in Sect. 3.1, it may be not effective applied into MV and residual. To obtain better feature representation of MV and residual, we propose temporal-consistent sampling to construct the positive pairs by selecting different clips from the same video in a probability manner.

Inspired by [24], our sampling idea lies in the assumption that larger temporal interval in two clips from the same video, larger probability of their distinct appearance. In particular, GOP is basic coarse unit in compressed videos and each GOP consists of one I-frame and several P-frames, which is described in Sect. 2. For I-frame, as a GOP can only provide an I-frame, we sample a clips with s I-frames by choosing s successive GOPs as a group. For P-frame, GOP size g of

MPEG-4 which we used is larger than clips length s, thus we uniformly sample a P-frame clips from a chosen GOP. Figure 4 shows our temporal-consistent sampling procedure. Given a compressed video with frame length T, we aim to sample two clips as different views of this video based on time interval t for I-frame and P-frame respectively. Firstly, we draw a time interval t from a distribution $P(t)$ over $[0, T/g]$. As longer distance between two clips makes they become more distinct [24], we choose a decreasing distribution:

$$P(t) = \frac{t}{\int_0^{T/g} t \cdot dt}. \tag{6}$$

For I-frame, we randomly choose a GOP group for the first clip sampling between $[0, T/g - t]$, then the second GOP group are delayed by t after the first. Each sampled I-frame clip consists of all I-frames from chosen GOP group. For MV and residual, as they are components of P-frames, sampling MV clips and residual clips is equivalent to sampling P-frame clips. The first GOP is randomly chosen between $[0, T/g - t]$, then the second GOP are delayed by t after the first. Two P-frame clips are generated by uniformly sampled from P-frames of two chosen GOPs.

3.3 Modality-Oriented Fine-Tuning

After the above pre-training process, we obtain feature representation of I-frame, MV and residual. We then fine-tune pre-trained models following CoViAR [32] training and testing settings. In particular, we use corresponding pre-trained model for each modality and take a final fusion of three predictions for action recognition by simply adding three prediction scores.

4 Experiments

4.1 Dataset

We pre-train our model on Kinetics400 dataset [14], and fine-tune on UCF101 [28] and HMDB51 [18] datasets. Kinetics400 dataset contains 400 classes. Each class has more than video number of 400 videos and the total number of videos is about 240k. UCF101 and HMDB51 datasets have 101 classes and 51 classes with the total video number of 13,320 and 6,766, respectively. They both can be divided into 3 splits and each split includes training set and testing set. We select HMDB51 split1 for ablation study, and select HMDB51 all three splits for efficiency analysis.

4.2 Implementation Details

Following CoviAR [32], we use ResNet-152 [10] as I-frame encoder and ResNet-18 as motion vector and residual encoders. For fair comparison, we also replace our backbones with R(2+1)D-18 networks [30] when comparing our model with

Table 1. Comparison with state-of-the-art methods

Method	Compressed video	Backbone	Pretrained	UCF101	HMDB51
Supervised					
I3D [3]	✗	–	ImageNet	84.5%	49.8%
C3D [29]	✗	–	ImageNet	82.3%	51.6%
ResNet3D-18 [30]	✗	–	ImageNet	85.8%	54.9%
S3D-G [34]	✗	–	ImageNet	86.6%	57.7%
CoViAR [32]	✔	ResNet152 (I), ResNet18 (P)	ImageNet	90.4%	59.1%
DMC-Net [26]	✔	ResNet152 (I), ResNet18 (P)	ImageNet	90.9%	62.8%
Self-supervised					
3D-RotNet [12]	✗	ResNet3D-18	Kinetics400	62.9%	33.7%
ST-Puzzle [15]	✗	ResNet3D-18	Kinetics400	63.9%	33.7%
DPC [8]	✗	ResNet3D-18	Kinetics400	75.7%	35.7%
SpeedNet [2]	✗	S3D-G	Kinetics400	81.8%	48.8%
XDC [1]	✗	R(2+1)D-18	Kinetics400	84.2%	47.1%
RSPNet [4]	✗	R(2+1)D-18	Kinetics400	81.1%	44.6%
VideoMoco [23]	✗	R(2+1)D-18	Kinetics400	78.7%	49.2%
TCLR [6]	✗	R(2+1)D-18	Kinetics400	84.3%	54.2%
TCS-MoCo (Ours)	✔	ResNet152 (I), ResNet18 (P)	Kinetics400	83.7%	50.1%
TCS-MoCo (Ours)	✔	R(2+1)D-18	Kinetics400	**84.3%**	**57.8%**

Table 2. Comparison with two re-implemented cross-modal methods

Method	I-frame	MV	Residual	Combine
AVID* [21]	24.2%	36.5%	32.3%	45.9%
MMV* [17]	28.5%	38.7%	**37.8%**	47.8%
TCS-MoCo (Ours)	**41.5%**	**39.5%**	37.3%	**52.2%**

other state-of-the-art methods. If not declared, ResNet2D backbones are used. In the pre-training stage, following MoCo [9], we use SGD as our optimizer with $1e-4$ weight decay. The learning rate is 0.03 and batch size is 128. For ResNet2D backbone, we set feature dimension to 128, except 1,024 in R(2+1)D backbone. The dictionary size is set to 65,536. The temperature τ in Eq. 5 is set to 0.07. The coefficient m in Eq. 3 is 0.999. During fine-tuning stage, we resize video clips into 340×256 then centrally crop them to 224×224. Learning rate is $1e-4$, and Adam [16] optimizer is adopted for optimization. We train 200 epochs in pre-training stage and 150 epochs in fine-tuning stage. MPEG-4 encoded videos are used as input data with GOP size of 12, *i.e.* 11 P-frames follow each I-frames averagely. During pre-training each clip contains 3 frames sampled from input videos. During fine-tuning stage, 3 frames and 25 frames are sampled respectively for training and testing, except 16 frames in the R(2+1)D backbone.

We select the fusion factor by 1:1:1 on I-frame, MV and residual to achieve the combined prediction, and select the classification accuracy as evaluation metric.

4.3   Comparison with State-of-the-Art Methods

We first compare our methods with several supervised methods for compressed video action recognition. As shown in Table 1, we achieve the best performance with 57.8% accuracy on HMDB51 dataset, compared to supervised methods like I3D, C3D, ResNet3D and S3D-G. Moreover, our method directly performs on the compressed video, while these supervised methods for the decoded video. Although CoViAR and DMC-Net achieves higher accuracy on UCF101 and HMDB51, they need large amount of ImageNet dataset labels to pre-train the model. Instead, our pre-training process is label-free that can be more flexible for action recognition. Moreover, DMC-Net requires additional optical flow as supervision, which significantly increases the computation and memory cost for the entire training. We also compare our method with other self-supervised learning methods pre-training on the same Kinetics400 dataset and performing on decoded videos. As shown in Table 1, we can see that our method achieves the highest accuracy than self-supervised methods. For example, our method using R(2+1)D backbone achieves 3.6% performance gains over the best baseline TCLR on HMDB51. This is due to the better feature representation learning obtained by using MoCo and temporal-consistent sampling in our method.

Table 3. Results of different pre-trained feature representation using all ResNet18.

Structure	I-frame	MV	Residual	Combine
Scratch	11.0%	33.7%	28.4%	41.1%
I-Transfer	**21.8%**	37.9%	35.4%	45.8%
MO-FT	**21.8%**	**38.3%**	**36.7%**	**47.1%**

Table 4. Results of different sampling strategies.

Method	I-frame	MV	Residual	Combine
RS-MoCo	35.4%	39.4%	36.2%	49.5%
TCS-MoCo (ours)	**41.5%**	**39.5%**	**37.3%**	**52.2%**

As I-frame, MV and residual can be regarded as different modality inputs, we consider to compare our method with cross-modal self-supervised methods for better effective evaluation. AVID [21] and MMV [17] are selected and re-implemented for compressed video, as they are SOTA cross-modal self-supervised methods on decoded video. AVID aims to learn audio-visual feature representation, while MMV for multimodal representation of audio, visual and language stream. When applied to compressed video, AVID takes I-frame and the concatenating of MV and residual as visual and audio input, respectively. MMV takes three modalities input in compressed video as the input of audio, visual and language, respectively. As shown in Table 2 on HMDB51 split1, our method achieves the best performance of 52.2% accuracy when combination three streams, compared to AVID and MMV.

4.4   Ablation Study

Effect of Temporal-Consistent Sampling. We compare temporal-consistent sampling with random sampling (RS) under the same MoCo framework. As shown in Table 4, temporal-consistent sampling significantly improves the performance of each modality input, as well as the combination result. Especially, TCS-Moco achieves 6.1% and 2.7% performance gains over RS-MoCo for I-frame prediction and combination prediction, respectively.

Table 5. Efficiency comparison of different methods on HMDB51 dataset.

Method	Backbone	Param	FLOPs	Time	Accuracy
DPC [8]	ResNet3D-18	33.3M	19.3G	96.9 ms	35.7%
RSPNet [4]	C3D	78.4M	38.5G	63.5 ms	44.6%
VideoMoCo [23]	R(2+1)D-18	31.5M	40.6G	98.0 ms	49.2%
TCS-MoCo (Ours)	ResNet152 (I), ResNet18 (P)	27.9M	4.2G	31.5 ms	50.1%

Effect of Pre-trained Feature Representation. To evaluate the effect of pre-trained feature representation on three-modality inputs, we use the same ResNet18 backbone for all three modalities (I-frame, MV and residual) for fair comparison. First, we directly train the three-stream model without pre-trained model, denoted as "Scratch". We also use TCS-MoCo to obtain the pre-trained model for I-frame, and then transfer it to MV and residual, denoted as "I-Transfer". Therefore, We can compare our method training three different streams with Modality-Oriented Fine-tuning (denoted as MO-FT) to scratch and I-Transfer. As shown in Table 3, our method achieves significant performance gains (both on each stream and combination result) over scratch and I-Transfer. For example, MO-FT achieves the highest combination accuracy of 47.1%, compared to 41.1% and 45.8% on scratch and I-Transfer respectively.

4.5   Efficiency Analysis

To evaluate the efficiency of our method, we compare TCS-MoCo with several self-supervised methods, such as DPC [8], VideoMoCo [23] and RSPNet [4]. The batch size is set to 1 for fair comparison on a RTX 2080Ti GPU. As shown in Table 5, our methods achieves highest accuracy on HMDB51 dataset with significant parameter and FLOPs reduction, and fastest inference time.

4.6   Visualization of Feature Maps

We visualize the last layer features of backbone as heat-map by grad-cam [25]. Taking motion vector for example, Fig. 5 shows the visual results of three action samples: Cartwheel, ApplyEyeMakeup and CuttingInKitchen generated by CoViAR [32], AVID [21], MMV [17] and ours. It can be seen that our learned features have the strongest ability in telling the action happening area.

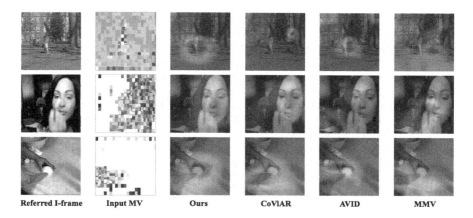

Referred I-frame   Input MV   Ours   CoViAR   AVID   MMV

Fig. 5. Attention visualization of four methods on MV.

5   Conclusion

In this paper, we propose a self-supervised compressed video action recognition method via Momentum contrast and temporal-consistent sampling. A temporal-consistent sampling strategy is applied to improve the feature representation ability of each modality of compressed video. Moreover, we introduce modality-oriented fine-tuning for performance improvement on action recognition task. Overall, our method achieves the highest accuracy of 57.8% on HMDB51 dataset compared to SOTA self-supervised learning methods for decoded videos.

References

1. Alwassel, H., Mahajan, D., Korbar, B., Torresani, L., Ghanem, B., Tran, D.: Self-supervised learning by cross-modal audio-video clustering. In: NeurIPS (2020)
2. Benaim, S., et al..: SpeedNet: learning the speediness in videos. In: CVPR (2020)
3. Carreira, J., Zisserman, A.: Quo Vadis, action recognition? A new model and the kinetics dataset. In: CVPR (2017)
4. Chen, P., et al.: RSPNet: relative speed perception for unsupervised video representation learning. In: AAAI (2021)
5. Chen, X., Fan, H., Girshick, R., He, K.: Improved baselines with momentum contrastive learning. arXiv:2003.04297 (2020)
6. Dave, I., Gupta, R., Rizve, M.N., Shah, M.: TCLR: temporal contrastive learning for video representation. arXiv:2101.07974 (2021)
7. Donahue, J., et al.: Long-term recurrent convolutional networks for visual recognition and description. TPAMI **39**(4), 677–691 (2017)
8. Han, T., Xie, W., Zisserman, A.: Video representation learning by dense predictive coding. In: ICCV Workshop (2019)
9. He, K., Fan, H., Wu, Y., Xie, S., Girshick, R.: Momentum contrast for unsupervised visual representation learning. In: CVPR (2020)
10. He, K., Zhang, X., Ren, S., Sun, J.: Deep residual learning for image recognition. In: CVPR (2016)

11. Huo, Y., et al.: Lightweight action recognition in compressed videos. In: Bartoli, A., Fusiello, A. (eds.) ECCV 2020. LNCS, vol. 12536, pp. 337–352. Springer, Cham (2020). https://doi.org/10.1007/978-3-030-66096-3_24

12. Jing, L., Yang, X., Liu, J., Tian, Y.: Self-supervised spatiotemporal feature learning via video rotation prediction. arXiv:1811.1138 (2019)

13. Kalfaoglu, M.E., Kalkan, S., Alatan, A.A.: Late temporal modeling in 3D CNN architectures with BERT for action recognition. In: Bartoli, A., Fusiello, A. (eds.) ECCV 2020. LNCS, vol. 12539, pp. 731–747. Springer, Cham (2020). https://doi.org/10.1007/978-3-030-68238-5_48

14. Kay, W., et al.: The kinetics human action video dataset. arXiv:1705.06950 (2017)

15. Kim, D., Cho, D., Kweon, I.S.: Self-supervised video representation learning with space-time cubic puzzles. In: AAAI (2019)

16. Kingma, D.P., Ba, J.: Adam: a method for stochastic optimization. In: ICLR (2015)

17. Komkov, S., Dzabraev, M., Petiushko, A.: Mutual modality learning for video action classification. arXiv:2011.02543 (2020)

18. Kuehne, H., Jhuang, H., Garrote, E., Poggio, T., Serre, T.: HMDB: a large video database for human motion recognition. In: ICCV (2011)

19. Lin, J., Gan, C., Han, S.: TSM: temporal shift module for efficient video understanding. In: ICCV (2019)

20. Ma, C.Y., Chen, M.H., Kira, Z., AlRegib, G.: TS-LSTM and temporal-inception: exploiting spatiotemporal dynamics for activity recognition. Sig. Process.: Image Commun. **71**, 76–87 (2019)

21. Morgado, P., Vasconcelos, N., Misra, I.: Audio-visual instance discrimination with cross-modal agreement. arXiv:2004.12943 (2020)

22. Oord, A.V.D., Li, Y., Vinyals, O.: Representation learning with contrastive predictive coding. arXiv:1807.03748 (2019)

23. Pan, T., Song, Y., Yang, T., Jiang, W., Liu, W.: VideoMoCo: contrastive video representation learning with temporally adversarial examples. arXiv:2103.05905 (2021)

24. Qian, R., et al.: Spatiotemporal contrastive video representation learning. arXiv:2008.03800 (2021)

25. Selvaraju, R.R., Cogswell, M., Das, A., Vedantam, R., Parikh, D., Batra, D.: Grad-CAM: visual explanations from deep networks via gradient-based localization. IJCV **128**(2), 336–359 (2019)

26. Shou, Z., et al.: DMC-Net: generating discriminative motion cues for fast compressed video action recognition. In: CVPR (2019)

27. Simonyan, K., Zisserman, A.: Two-stream convolutional networks for action recognition in videos. In: NeurIPS (2014)

28. Soomro, K., Zamir, A.R., Shah, M.: UCF101: a dataset of 101 human actions classes from videos in the wild. arXiv:1212.0402 (2012)

29. Tran, D., Bourdev, L., Fergus, R., Torresani, L., Paluri, M.: Learning spatiotemporal features with 3D convolutional networks. In: ICCV (2015)

30. Tran, D., Wang, H., Torresani, L., Ray, J., LeCun, Y., Paluri, M.: A closer look at spatiotemporal convolutions for action recognition. In: CVPR (2018)

31. Wang, L., et al.: Temporal segment networks: towards good practices for deep action recognition. In: Leibe, B., Matas, J., Sebe, N., Welling, M. (eds.) ECCV 2016. LNCS, vol. 9912, pp. 20–36. Springer, Cham (2016). https://doi.org/10.1007/978-3-319-46484-8_2

32. Wu, C.Y., Zaheer, M., Hu, H., Manmatha, R., Smola, A.J., Krähenbühl, P.: Compressed video action recognition. In: CVPR (2018)

33. Wu, Z., Xiong, Y., Yu, S.X., Lin, D.: Unsupervised feature learning via non-parametric instance discrimination. In: CVPR (2018)
34. Xie, S., Sun, C., Huang, J., Tu, Z., Murphy, K.: Rethinking spatiotemporal feature learning: speed-accuracy trade-offs in video classification. In: Ferrari, V., Hebert, M., Sminchisescu, C., Weiss, Y. (eds.) ECCV (2018)

Stack-VAE Network for Zero-Shot Learning

Jinghao Xie, Jigang Wu, Tianyou Liang, and Min Meng$^{(\boxtimes)}$ (iD)

Guangdong University of Technology, Guangzhou 510006, China

Abstract. Zero-shot learning aims to transfer knowledge from the seen classes to unseen ones through some high-level semantics (e.g., per-class attributes), enabling the learning model to recognize novel classes without retraining. Among them, the generative methods adopt the scheme that synthesizes samples for the unseen classes, thereby converting the task into a standard classification problem. However, most existing work inevitably suffers from the domain shift problem when only the seen classes are used for supervision. Furthermore, they can not fully leverage the semantic information in data synthesis due to the limited expressiveness of the generator. In this paper, we develop a novel network, named stack-VAE, to alleviate the above problems. The proposal mainly consists of a generative module and a feature core agent. Specifically, we design the generator based on hierarchical VAE, which exploits multi-layer Gaussian distribution to improve the expressiveness, thereby better mimicking the real data distribution of the unseen classes. Besides, we propose a feature core agent based objective, which is beneficial to mitigate seen class bias by enforcing the inter-class separability and reducing the intra-class scatter. Experimental results conducted on three widely used datasets, i.e., AWA2, SUN, CUB, show that the proposed network outperforms the baselines and achieves a new state-of-the-art.

Keywords: Zero-shot learning · Generalized zero-shot learning · Generative model · Object recognition

1 Introduction

With the ever-growing supply of data and demand of applications, collecting the labeled training samples is expensive and retraining a new model upon the occurrence of new classes each time is impractical. An interesting and effective method is zero-shot learning [12], which aims to learn a model that imitates the way human thinks, transferring the knowledge in the well-learnt domain to new ones. With this motivation, object classes are divided into two groups,

This work was supported in part by the National Natural Science Foundation of China under Grant 62172109 and Grant 62072118, in part by the Natural Science Foundation of Guangdong Province under Grant 2020A1515011361, and in part by the High-level Talents Programme of Guangdong Province under Grant 2017GC010556.

T. Mantoro et al. (Eds.): ICONIP 2021, LNCS 13111, pp. 250–261, 2021.
https://doi.org/10.1007/978-3-030-92273-3_21

one of which is accessible in the training phase, called the seen classes, while the other one is unavailable during training and thus referred to as the unseen classes. However, to transfer the knowledge from the seen classes to the unseen ones, some high-level semantic information, such as attributions, are assumed to be available. According to whether the seen classes are included for testing, the ZSL problem can be further divided into two settings: 1) Conventional Zero-Shot Learning (ZSL) and 2) Generalized Zero-Shot Learning (GZSL) [31].

Most of the early work can be categorized into the line of embedding model, which seeks to connect the visual space and semantic space by learning a mapping function [3,11,30,33]. However, these methods typically lead to the well-known hubness problem [22], which means that a small proportion of objects in the dataset, or hubs, may occur as the nearest neighbor of a large proportion of objects. What's worse, they suffer from the domain shift [4] due to the absence of unseen classes data during training, which is more severe in GZSL. A popular way to alleviate these two issues is the generative method [2,9,19,21,26], which uses the semantic embedding of invisible classes to synthesize corresponding visual features and then converts the problem into supervised learning. Although some progresses are achieved, these methods presented an obvious bias towards the seen classes. The primary reason is that naive deep generative methods, such as GAN and VAE, are prone to paying more attention on the easy samples. Therefore, the well-trained models tend to ignore the hard samples which overlap with samples belonging to different classes. Apart of that, they can't fully leverage the semantic information due to their limitation in expressiveness.

In this paper, we propose a new model, named stack-VAE, to address the above issues, which consists of two key components, i.e., a well designed hierarchical generative module and a novel feature core agent based objective. The overview of our stack-VAE is shown in Fig. 1. The first motivation is upgrading the generator. Inspired by the recent work on hierarchical VAEs [20,23,25], we adopt the design of hierarchical latent variable to improve the expressiveness of the generator for better modeling the unseen class distributions. Different from [25], our model gives up the output variable of the first hidden layer, due to the fact that the output variable is a global variable, which is not conducive to learning a meaningful hidden distribution. Besides, it is difficult to learn a meaningful hierarchy when there are too many layers of latent variables as mentioned in [23]. In addition, we optimize the inference process of hidden layer variables to make them more suitable for zero-shot learning. The second motivation is to improve the discriminative ability of the feature space. We observe that some estimated class centroids from data may be too close to or even overlap with others, especially when there are hard samples. Towards this goal, we introduce a feature core agent for each class. By utilizing a triplet-based objective, we simultaneously push the centroids of different classes away from each other and constrain the intra-class variance to explicitly enhance the discriminativeness. To the best of our knowledge, we are the first to incorporate hierarchical generator in ZSL and GZSL task.

The contributions in this paper are summarized as follows:

1. We design a novel generative module, which is more expressive for modeling the real visual distribution of the unseen classes. We also design an optimized inference process for it to suit zero-shot learning.
2. We introduce feature core agents that can be learned adaptively for seen classes and derive a loss function based on them, which can efficiently enhance the discriminativeness of the feature space, thereby alleviating the domain shift problem.
3. Extensive experiments and analyses conducted on three widely used benchmarks demonstrate the excellent performance and the insensitivity to hyperparameters of the proposed model.

2   Related Work

Embedding Method. In recent years, several related work have been developed to address (generalized) zero-shot learning. The early work, known as embedding method, focuses on learning the mapping between visual and semantic space under zero-shot learning settings. For example, DAP [11] and IAP [11] rely on the attributes within a two-stage approach to learn a mapping from visual to semantic domain. DeViSE [3] learns a linear mapping from visual space to semantic space by optimizing the pairwise ranking objective. Additionally, to make use of latent correlations between visual features and semantic attributes, some works [30,33] explore to learn a common space shared by image and semantic. These methods often suffer from the hubness problem, and will probably lead to a bias towards seen classes due to the inaccessibility to unseen classes data.

Generative Method. Recently, generative methods [2,9,13,14,16,21,26,27,30,32] obtain impressive results in (generalized) zero-shot learning. These works leverage a generative model such as GAN [6], VAE [10], or the hybrid of them to generate samples. Instead of directly learning the mapping between visual space and semantic space with seen class samples, generative methods convert the (generalized) zero-shot learning to a standard classification problem by synthesizing unseen class samples for training. For example, [26] presents a model which consists of a probabilistic encoder, decoder, and a regressor. Their model utilizes the encoder and decoder to form a VAE for image features generation. And they leverage regressor to retain the relationship between visual space and corresponding attribute space. Similarly, Cycle-WGAN [2] learns a GAN with an regressor, enforcing the consistency between the regressed attributes from synthesized visual representations and the original ones. CADA-VAE [21] mimics both the image features and class embeddings distribution via aligned variational autoencoders. To mitigate the prediction bias towards the seen classes in generalized zero-shot learning, [9] proposes the concept of Over-Complete Distribution (OCD) and trains the model in three stages. However, seen class bias is the direct consequence of the domain shift [4] between training and testing time. The primary reason is the deficiency of the generative module in expressiveness, making it fail to model the real unseen class feature distribution.

Hierarchical VAE. In order to improve the model's ability to generate discriminative information, we draw inspiration from the hierarchical VAEs. In works of deep hierarchical VAEs [20,23,25], they partition the latent variables z into disjoint groups $z = \{z_1, z_2, ..., z_L\}$. Then, its prior distribution can be expressed as $p(z) = \prod_l p(z_l|z_{<l})$. Disjoint groups enable the VAE to model the more complex distribution. [15] introduces a correlated variable as the conditional variable to guide the direction of feature generation and gives the complicated computation of KL divergence between different stacks. In [25], they propose NVAE, which can use normalizing flows to successfully generate high-quality images under challenging datasets. Besides, they promote the hierarchical structure in the encoder, which improves the model's use efficiency of visual features, and they optimize the calculation of KL divergence. Regarding its advantage in modeling complex distributions, hierarchical VAE is a better choice for the task of ZSL to mimic both visual features and semantic embedding.

3   Stack-VAE

3.1   Problem Setting

Let $C_s = \{c_1, c_2, ..., c_l\}$ denotes the set of seen classes, and $C_u = \{c_{l+1}, c_{l+2}, ..., c_{l+m}\}$ for the set of unseen classes, where l and m are the numbers of seen and unseen classes, respectively. The set of seen classes and unseen classes are disjoint, i.e., $C_s \cap C_u = \emptyset$. Given a set of seen class instances $S = \{(x_i, y_i)\}_{i=1}^{n_s}$, where $x_i \in X^s$ is the visual feature of the i-th instance and $y_i \in C_s$ is the corresponding class label, the goal of ZSL is to build a classifier for a set of unseen class instances $U = \{(x_i)\}_{i=1}^{n_u}$, where $x_i \in X^u$ is an unseen class sample. Although no labelled instance from those unseen classes is available, we assume that the attribute embeddings for all classes is provided, which can be denoted as $A = \{a_i\}_{i=1}^{l+m}$. In conventional ZSL setting, we apply the classifier on the unseen samples, i.e., $f_{ZSL} : X \to C^u$, while in GZSL setting, predictions are made for both seen and unseen samples, i.e., $f_{GZSL} : X \to C^s \bigcup C^u$.

3.2   Generative Module

We develop a stack-VAE network for (generalized) zero-shot learning, which consists of an encoder E and a generator (decoder) G. In general, the samples synthesized by the generator can well approximate the distribution of the seen classes. However, as mentioned in [9], the generated sample distribution of the unseen classes is too ideal to mimic the real one, where the classes are not so well-separated or even overlapping. Inspired by [20,23,25], we propose to infer the visual distribution by a stack of two latent variables $z = \{z_1, z_2\}$. Remind that the fundamental goal of ZSL is to transfer knowledge to the unseen classes through attributes, we design to involve them in both the encoder and generator. For the encoder, we rewrite the prior as $p_\phi(z_1|a)$ and $p_\phi(z_2|z_1, a)$, both assumed to be standard Gaussian distributions, and drive the posterior $p_E(z_1|x, a)$ and

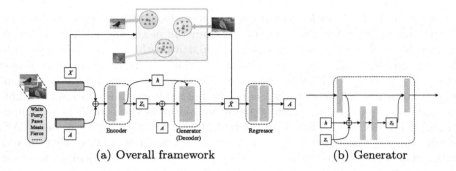

(a) Overall framework   (b) Generator

Fig. 1. The overview of our stack-VAE architecture. The generative module adopts the hierarchical latent variables design, with which its expressiveness can be greatly enhanced. Also, by incorporating the attributes in both the priors and the VAE architecture, the semantic information in attributes are expected to be well embodied in the synthesized sample features. In addition, a set of feature core agents are maintained to alleviate the seen class bias and improve the discriminativeness of the feature space.

$p_E(z_2|z_1, x, a)$ to approximate them. In addition, similar to [25], we draw a skip connection from h, the last hidden layer output of E, to the generator, improving the utilization efficiency of visual features and enhancing the association between semantic embedding and z_2. Note that, unlike [25], we do not feed the the output of other shallow hidden layers in E to the generator, because we empirically found that these connections will harm the performance. As for the decoder, we use mixed information and condition variables to reconstruct visual features. The fundamental loss function is given by:

$$L_{VAE} = -\mathbb{E}_{p_E(z_1, z_2|x, a), p(a|x)}[\log p_G(x|z, a)] + \mathrm{KL}(p_E(z_1|x, a)\|p_\phi(z_1|a)) \quad (1)$$

$$\text{s.t.} \quad \mathrm{KL}(p_E(z_2|z_1, x, a)\|p_\phi(z_2|z_1, a)) \leqslant b,$$

where b is a soft margin. The first term is the marginal likelihood and the second term is the KL divergence. We optimize the above terms similar to CVAE, driving the posterior $p_E(z|x, a)$ to be close to the prior $p_\phi(z|a)$. The KL divergence between $p_E(z_2|z_1, x, a)$ and $p_\phi(z_2|z_1, a)$ is analogous to the second term, which is used for driving the estimated posterior to be close to its prior with the autoregressive method. By constraining it not exceeding b, it can be expected that the semantic information in a can be well preserved in z_2, and thus embodied in the synthesized sample. Furthermore, it increases the expressiveness of the encoder and generator. Specifically, following [25], we similarly compute $p_\phi(z_2|z_1, a)$ and $p_E(z_2|z_1, x, a)$ as:

$$p_\phi(z_2|z_1, a) = N(\mu(z_1, a), \sigma(z_1, a)), \quad (2)$$

$$p_E(z_2|z_1, x, a) = N(\mu(z_1, a) + \Delta\mu(z_1, x, a), \sigma(z_1, a) \cdot \Delta\sigma(z_1, x, a)), \quad (3)$$

Therefore, the KL divergence can be calculated as:

$$\mathrm{KL}(p_E(z_2|z_1, x, a)\|p_\phi(z_2|z_1, a)) = \frac{1}{2}\left(\frac{\Delta\mu^2}{\sigma^2} + \Delta\sigma^2 - \log\Delta\sigma^2 - 1\right), \quad (4)$$

where for the brevity of notation, we drop the arguments of μ, $\Delta\mu$ to σ and $\Delta\sigma$.

Moreover, to stabilize the training and to ensure the cycle-consistency on the synthesized sample, we add a regressor R and the following regress loss [2,26]:

$$L_R = -\mathbb{E}_{p_G(\tilde{x}|a,z)}[\log p_R(a|\tilde{x})], \tag{5}$$

3.3 Feature Core Agent

To alleviate the bias towards seen classes, researchers have proposed to use one or more data centroid to prompt the generalization performance in GZSL [13,14,27]. Nonetheless, if the model meets the hard samples which overlap with another class, the data centroid will confuse the model. Inspired by [29], we address this issue by introducing the agent strategy that learns a feature core agent for each seen class. Then, we measure the difference between the cosine similarity of each input and the agent of all seen classes and integrate them in the triplet loss. With the occurrence of the agent, we don't need to consider the sampling of positive and negative examples. Let w^r be the r-th feature core agent of seen classes, x_i^r be the i-th sample from one batch belonging to class r, the objective is defined as below:

$$L_C' = \frac{1}{N}\sum_{i=1}^{N}\sum_{j=1,j\neq r}^{C_s} \max(0, \cos(x_i^r, w^r) - \cos(x_i^r, w^j) + m), \tag{6}$$

where $\cos(\cdot,\cdot)$ denotes cosine similarity, m is a margin, and N is batch size. Obviously, as the number of classes increases, it's difficult for a fixed hyperparameter margin to optimize the inter-class boundary value. Following [24], we rewrite the objective as:

$$L_C = \frac{1}{N}\sum_{i=1}^{N}\log[1 + \exp(-\gamma\alpha_r^p\beta_r^p)\sum_{j=1,j\neq r}^{C_s}\exp(\gamma\alpha_j^n\beta_j^n)], \tag{7}$$

with

$$\begin{cases} \alpha_r^p = \max(0, 1 + m - \cos(x_i^r, w^r)), \\ \alpha_k^n = \max(0, m + \cos(x_i^r, w^j)), \\ \beta_r^p = \cos(x_i^r, w^r) - 1 + m, \\ \beta_k^n = \cos(x_i^r, w^j) - m, \end{cases} \tag{8}$$

where γ is a scale factor which we set 80 as suggested in [24]. For brevity of expression, x_i can be a real data sample or synthesized sample in this module. This loss allows the similarity score between classes to choose the optimization weight according to its optimization state.

3.4 Overall Objective

Finally, the overall objective function for our stack-VAE is:

$$L_{stack-VAE} = L_{VAE} + \lambda_r L_R + \lambda_c L_C, \tag{9}$$

Table 1. Datasets statistics.

Dataset	Train-S	Test-S	Test-U	Total number	Attributes	Seen/Unseen classes
AWA2	23527	5882	7913	37322	85	40/10
CUB	7057	1764	2967	11788	312	150/50
SUN	10320	2580	1440	14340	102	645/72

where λ_r, λ_c, are treated as hyperparameters. After training the stack-VAE, we use the generator to synthesize features for unseen classes with their attributes, and use them together with the ones from seen classes to train a softmax classifier. As in [22], both features and predicted attributes from the regressor are fed as inputs for the classifier for (generalized) zero-shot learning.

4   Experiments

4.1   Datasets

Experiments are conducted on three popular datasets, i.e., AWA2 [31], CUB [28], and SUN [18]. AWA2 is a medium-scale coarse-grained animal dataset including 50 classes with 37, 322 images. Each class of AWA2 has a large number of samples, which is highly suitable for training ZSL. CUB contains 11, 788 fine-grained images of 200 bird species. Each class of CUB is carefully annotated with 312 attributes. SUN is a Scene benchmark containing 14, 204 images of 397 scene categories. The detailed statistics are listed in Table 1.

4.2   Evaluation Protocols

For fair comparison, we follow the evaluation protocol of Xian *et al.* [31], adopting its dataset features(ResNet [7]) and data splits. In ZSL setting, we report the average per-class top-1 accuracy, denoted as T1. In GZSL setting, we report the average per-class top-1 accuracy of seen classes and unseen classes, denoted as S and U respectively, and their harmonic mean $H = 2 \times S \times U/(S + U)$.

4.3   Implementation Details

In this work, we implement all three sub-networks, i.e. the E, G and the R, as MLP. Suppose the dimension of image features is d_1, and that of attributes is d_2. The encoder contains three layers, with dimension 4,096, $2 \times d_2$ and d_2, respectively. The generator is a two-branch structure with residual connection as shown in Fig. 1(b). The dimensions in the upper branch are 4,096 and d_2, while that of the lower branch are 4,096 and d_1. For the regessor, the length of the hidden layer is 4096, and the output dimension is d_2. All layers are activated with LReLU, except the output layer of the generator and regressor, for which we use sigmoid for activation instead. λ_r, λ_c are cross-validated from 0.01 to 10. As for m and b, we cross-validate them from 0.1 to 0.45.

Table 2. Performance comparison on CUB, AWA2, and SUN under the ZSL and GZSL settings. The best results are shown in boldface, and the second place are underlined.

Generative model	ZSL			GZSL								
	CUB	SUN	AWA2	CUB			SUN			AWA2		
	T1	T1	T1	U	S	H	U	S	H	U	S	H
f-CADA-VAE [8]	–	–	–	53.3	54.1	53.7	48.1	36.5	41.5	55.9	_78.2_	65.2
DE-VAE [16]	_63.1_	_64.0_	69.3	52.5	56.3	54.3	45.9	36.9	40.9	58.8	**78.9**	**67.4**
LsrGAN [27]	60.3	62.5	66.4	48.1	59.1	53.0	44.8	37.7	40.9	54.6	74.6	63.0
OCD-VAE [9]	60.3	63.5	**71.3**	44.8	**59.9**	51.3	44.8	**42.9**	_43.8_	59.5	73.4	65.7
AFC-GAN [14]	62.9	63.3	69.4	_53.5_	_59.7_	**56.4**	_49.1_	36.1	41.6	58.2	66.8	62.2
CADA-VAE [21]	60.4	61.8	64.0	51.6	53.5	52.4	47.2	35.7	40.6	55.8	75.0	63.9
f-CLSWGAN [32]	57.3	60.8	69.1	43.7	57.7	49.7	47.2	35.7	40.6	–	–	–
SE-ZSL/GZSL [26]	59.6	63.4	69.2	41.5	53.3	46.7	40.9	30.5	34.9	58.3	68.1	62.8
JGM-ZSL [5]	54.9	59.0	69.5	42.7	45.6	44.1	44.4	30.9	36.5	56.2	71.7	63.0
Cycle-WGAN [2]	58.6	59.9	66.8	47.9	59.3	53.0	47.2	33.8	39.4	_59.6_	63.4	59.8
stack-VAE	**63.8**	**66.7**	_70.0_	**55.0**	57.6	_56.3_	**52.0**	_38.0_	**43.9**	**61.0**	72.0	_66.0_

4.4 State-of-the-Art Comparison

The results on CUB, AWA2, and SUN are shown in Table 2, in which we select ten state-of-the-art methods published in recent two years for comparison. Specifically, the left part are the results of the ZSL setting, and the right part is for the GZSL. We mainly compare our method to OCD-VAE [9] and DE-VAE [16], as they're the two most competitive baselines.

In ZSL setting, the proposed method achieves the best results on CUB and SUN datasets, outperforming the closest competitor DE-VAE by 0.7% and 2.8%, respectively. While on the AWA2 dataset, OCD-VAE performs better than our method, which can be attributed to insufficient information on the semantic attributes of AWA2.

In GZSL setting, our network outperforms current state-of-the-art OCD-VAE with 5.0%, 0.1%, and 0.3% improvements on CUB, SUN, and AWA2, respectively. DEVAE reports the top harmonic mean with 67.4%, but our network achieves superior performance with 2.2%, 3.0% improvements on CUB and SUN. Although our network does not obtain the best results on the AWA2 dataset, the drop in performance is slight, comparing with other datasets. We suspect that this may be caused by the inconsistency in the distribution between semantic embedding and visual features, and we leave this and other above-mentioned issues for future exploration.

In general, across the three databases, the proposed model can achieve superior performance. It fully proves that our model can generate discriminative features, while effectively alleviating the bias problem.

Table 3. Ablation study on three datasets

	CUB	SUN	AWA2	CUB			SUN			AWA2		
	T1	T1	T1	U	S	H	U	S	H	U	S	H
Ours without L_C	62.98	66.74	69.99	53.63	59.13	56.24	51.53	38.02	43.76	60.92	**72.02**	66.01
Ours without hierarchical VAE	62.41	64.86	68.87	49.80	60.90	54.79	46.88	38.33	42.18	60.82	66.07	63.33
Ours without above all	62.52	65.21	68.84	48.32	**62.81**	54.62	46.39	**38.95**	42.35	60.96	65.72	63.25
Ours	**63.83**	**66.81**	**70.08**	**55.00**	57.60	**56.27**	**52.08**	37.98	**43.93**	**61.02**	71.95	**66.03**

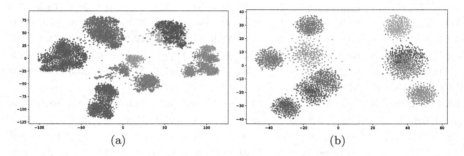

(a)   (b)

Fig. 2. Visualization of the synthetic visual feature distributions of unseen classes on AWA2 using T-SNE [17]. (a) is the ground-truth unseen distribution of unseen class samples, and (b) shows the distribution of 400 synthesized samples per class.

4.5   Ablation Study

To validate the effectiveness of our method, we introduce three variants of our model by removing the feature core agent module, substituting the hierarchical VAE with a regular one and a combination of them, respectively. The comparison results are listed in Table 3. By comparing the experimental results, we can observe that with the hierarchical VAE structure, the classification accuracy of the proposed model has been significantly improved. The feature core agent can balance the hierarchical VAE. The advantage is that the samples generated can achieve a better trade-off between the seen classes and the unseen classes. In general, our model can not only improve the expressiveness of the generative model, but also alleviate the bias problem. Figure 2 shows visualization of the synthetic visual feature distributions of unseen classes on AWA2.

4.6   Sensitivity Study

In this subsection, we analyze the model sensitivity to the parameters λ_r, λ_c m, and b on AWA2. We firstly set the λ_r, λ_c, m, and b as 0.01, 0.01, 0.3, and 0.1, respectively. Figure 3 presents the performance of ZSL with T1 and GZSL with H under different above parameters setting. As shown in Fig. 3(a), Fig. 3(c) and Fig. 3(d), we find little impact on the accuracy of ZSL under the different values of λ_r, m, and b. Moreover, the peak T1 accuracy 70.77% in Fig. 3(a) is even better than the result shown in Table 2. However, we can observe that λ_r takes a negative impact on the accuracy of GZSL as the value of λ_r becomes

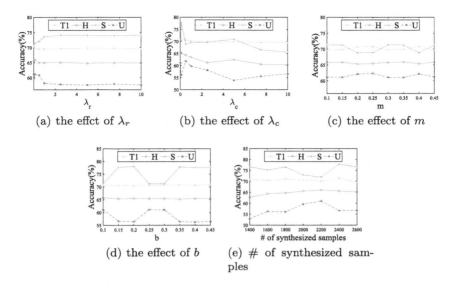

Fig. 3. Sensitivity study to different hyper-parameters.

larger. Comparing with the result of ZSL, this is not necessarily a drawback but a well-known trade-off [1] between seen classes and unseen classes. As show in Fig. 3(b), the bigger value of λ_c will seriously affect the harmonic mean, it means that the high weight of the feature core agent will affect the training of the generator module. To sum up, our model is robust to the hyper-parameters, and we choose 0.1, 0.01, 0.3, and 0.3 for our AWA2 result.

Figure 3(e) shows the evaluation of the number of synthesized samples for each unseen class. It's easy to find that the peak is the result which we have shown in Table 2. In conclusion, our stack-VAE successfully apply the hierarchical VAE to ZSL, and it can mitigate the bias effectively with the appropriate number of synthesized samples.

5   Conclusion

In this work, we propose a novel stack-VAE network for zero-shot learning and generalized zero-shot learning. To mitigate the bias towards seen classes, we design a generative module based on hierarchical VAE for synthesizing high-quality samples. Moreover, we propose a feature core agent loss that prompts the generative module to retain discriminative information effectively. By extensive experiments on three benchmark datasets, we show that the proposed network yields improved performance.

References

1. Chao, W.-L., Changpinyo, S., Gong, B., Sha, F.: An empirical study and analysis of generalized zero-shot learning for object recognition in the wild. In: Leibe, B., Matas, J., Sebe, N., Welling, M. (eds.) ECCV 2016. LNCS, vol. 9906, pp. 52–68. Springer, Cham (2016). https://doi.org/10.1007/978-3-319-46475-6_4
2. Felix, R., Kumar, B.G.V., Reid, I.D., Carneiro, G.: Multi-modal cycle-consistent generalized zero-shot learning. In: Proceedings of the European Conference on Computer Vision (ECCV), pp. 21–37 (2018)
3. Frome, A., et al.: DeViSE: a deep visual-semantic embedding model. In: Advances in Neural Information Processing Systems 26, vol. 26, pp. 2121–2129 (2013)
4. Fu, Y., Hospedales, T.M., Xiang, T., Gong, S.: Transductive multi-view zero-shot learning. IEEE Trans. Pattern Anal. Mach. Intell. **37**(11), 2332–2345 (2015)
5. Gao, R., Hou, X., Qin, J., Liu, L., Zhu, F., Zhang, Z.: A joint generative model for zero-shot learning. In: Proceedings of the European Conference on Computer Vision (ECCV), pp. 631–646 (2018)
6. Goodfellow, I., et al.: Generative adversarial nets. In: Advances in Neural Information Processing Systems 27, vol. 27, pp. 2672–2680 (2014)
7. He, K., Zhang, X., Ren, S., Sun, J.: Deep residual learning for image recognition. In: 2016 IEEE Conference on Computer Vision and Pattern Recognition (CVPR), pp. 770–778 (2016)
8. Huang, Y., Deng, Z., Wu, T.: Learning discriminative latent features for generalized zero-and few-shot learning. In: 2020 IEEE International Conference on Multimedia and Expo (ICME), pp. 1–6 (2020)
9. Keshari, R., Singh, R., Vatsa, M.: Generalized zero-shot learning via over-complete distribution. In: 2020 IEEE/CVF Conference on Computer Vision and Pattern Recognition (CVPR), pp. 13300–13308 (2020)
10. Kingma, D.P., Welling, M.: Auto-encoding variational Bayes. In: ICLR 2014: International Conference on Learning Representations (ICLR) 2014 (2014)
11. Lampert, C.H., Nickisch, H., Harmeling, S.: Attribute-based classification for zero-shot visual object categorization. IEEE Trans. Pattern Anal. Mach. Intell. **36**(3), 453–465 (2014)
12. Larochelle, H., Erhan, D., Bengio, Y.: Zero-data learning of new tasks. In: Proceedings of the AAAI Conference on Artificial Intelligence, vol. 2, pp. 646–651 (2008)
13. Li, J., Jing, M., Lu, K., Ding, Z., Zhu, L., Huang, Z.: Leveraging the invariant side of generative zero-shot learning. In: 2019 IEEE/CVF Conference on Computer Vision and Pattern Recognition (CVPR), pp. 7402–7411 (2019)
14. Li, J., Jing, M., Lu, K., Zhu, L., Yang, Y., Huang, Z.: Alleviating feature confusion for generative zero-shot learning. In: Proceedings of the 27th ACM International Conference on Multimedia, pp. 1587–1595 (2019)
15. Louizos, C., Swersky, K., Li, Y., Welling, M., Zemel, R.: The variational fair autoencoder. In: ICLR 2016: International Conference on Learning Representations 2016 (2016)
16. Ma, P., Hu, X.: A variational autoencoder with deep embedding model for generalized zero-shot learning. In: Proceedings of the AAAI Conference on Artificial Intelligence, pp. 11733–11740 (2020)
17. van der Maaten, L., Hinton, G.: Visualizing data using t-SNE. J. Mach. Learn. Res. **9**(86), 2579–2605 (2008)

18. Patterson, G., Hays, J.: Sun attribute database: discovering, annotating, and recognizing scene attributes. In: 2012 IEEE Conference on Computer Vision and Pattern Recognition, pp. 2751–2758 (2012)
19. Qin, P., Wang, X., Chen, W., Zhang, C., Xu, W., Wang, W.Y.: Generative adversarial zero-shot relational learning for knowledge graphs. In: Proceedings of the AAAI Conference on Artificial Intelligence, pp. 8673–8680 (2020)
20. Rezende, D.J., Mohamed, S., Wierstra, D.: Stochastic backpropagation and approximate inference in deep generative models. In: Proceedings of the 31st International Conference on Machine Learning, pp. 1278–1286 (2014)
21. Schonfeld, E., Ebrahimi, S., Sinha, S., Darrell, T., Akata, Z.: Generalized zero- and few-shot learning via aligned variational autoencoders. In: 2019 IEEE/CVF Conference on Computer Vision and Pattern Recognition (CVPR), pp. 8247–8255 (2019)
22. Shigeto, Y., Suzuki, I., Hara, K., Shimbo, M., Matsumoto, Y.: Ridge regression, hubness, and zero-shot learning. In: Proceedings of the 2015th European Conference on Machine Learning and Knowledge Discovery in Databases - Volume Part I, pp. 135–151 (2015)
23. Sønderby, C.K., Raiko, T., Maaløe, L., Sønderby, S.K., Winther, O.: Ladder variational autoencoders. In: 29th Annual Conference on Neural Information Processing Systems (NIPS 2016), vol. 29, pp. 3738–3746 (2016)
24. Sun, Y., et al.: Circle loss: a unified perspective of pair similarity optimization. In: 2020 IEEE/CVF Conference on Computer Vision and Pattern Recognition (CVPR), pp. 6398–6407 (2020)
25. Vahdat, A., Kautz, J.: NVAE: a deep hierarchical variational autoencoder. In: Advances in Neural Information Processing Systems, vol. 33 (2020)
26. Verma, V.K., Arora, G., Mishra, A., Rai, P.: Generalized zero-shot learning via synthesized examples. In: 2018 IEEE/CVF Conference on Computer Vision and Pattern Recognition, pp. 4281–4289 (2018)
27. Vyas, M.R., Venkateswara, H., Panchanathan, S.: Leveraging seen and unseen semantic relationships for generative zero-shot learning. In: Vedaldi, A., Bischof, H., Brox, T., Frahm, J.-M. (eds.) ECCV 2020. LNCS, vol. 12375, pp. 70–86. Springer, Cham (2020). https://doi.org/10.1007/978-3-030-58577-8_5
28. Wah, C., Branson, S., Welinder, P., Perona, P., Belongie, S.: The Caltech-UCSD birds-200-2011 dataset. California Institute of Technology (2011)
29. Wang, F., Xiang, X., Cheng, J., Yuille, A.L.: NormFace: L 2 hypersphere embedding for face verification. In: Proceedings of the 25th ACM International Conference on Multimedia, pp. 1041–1049 (2017)
30. Wei, K., Yang, M., Wang, H., Deng, C., Liu, X.: Adversarial fine-grained composition learning for unseen attribute-object recognition. In: 2019 IEEE/CVF International Conference on Computer Vision (ICCV), pp. 3741–3749 (2019)
31. Xian, Y., Lampert, C.H., Schiele, B., Akata, Z.: Zero-shot learning-a comprehensive evaluation of the good, the bad and the ugly. IEEE Trans. Pattern Anal. Mach. Intell. 41(9), 2251–2265 (2019)
32. Xian, Y., Lorenz, T., Schiele, B., Akata, Z.: Feature generating networks for zero-shot learning. In: 2018 IEEE/CVF Conference on Computer Vision and Pattern Recognition, pp. 5542–5551 (2018)
33. Zhang, Z., Saligrama, V.: Zero-shot learning via semantic similarity embedding. In: 2015 IEEE International Conference on Computer Vision (ICCV), pp. 4166–4174 (2015)

TRUFM: a Transformer-Guided Framework for Fine-Grained Urban Flow Inference

Xinchi Zhou[1], Dongzhan Zhou[1], and Lingbo Liu[2]([✉])

[1] The University of Sydney, Sydney, Australia
{xinchi.zhou1,d.zhou}@sydney.edu.au
[2] The Hong Kong Polytechnic University, Hung Hom, Hong Kong SAR
lingbo.liu@polyu.edu.hk

Abstract. Reconstructing the fine-grained urban flow from the coarse-grained counterpart is an essential component in intelligent transportation systems, as it can provide accurate traffic flow information under a reduced number of sensors. However, current models based on Convolutional Neural Networks (CNNs) mainly focus on the local pixel correlations and ignore the long-range dependencies. To this end, we propose a TRansformer-guided Urban Flow Magnifier (TRUFM) that incorporates the transformer module in the traffic flow analysis system, which naturally enjoys the advantage of modeling the global-scale correlations. By utilizing this superiority, our framework facilitates the joint inference of the flow distribution across the entire map and hence estimates more precise fine-grained traffic flow. Experimental results demonstrate the effectiveness of our TRUFM, which exceeds the current state-of-the-art methods on various datasets.

Keywords: Intelligent transportation systems · Urban flow inference · Neural network · Vision transformer

1 Introduction

With the expansion of city scales and the rapid growth of population, the deployment of intelligent transportation systems has become more important. In the entire system, the urban flow monitoring system serves as a crucial component, which provides essential information to alleviate the traffic congestion problem and further raise the management efficiency.

To achieve accurate flow monitoring, a large number of sensing devices need to be installed to capture the fine-grained traffic flow data across different urban areas. However, the deployment of these sensors will inevitably cause economic burdens, mainly due to the device installation and maintenance costs, as well as the corresponding energy consumption. Under this circumstance, it is ideal to build a framework that can provide fine-grained urban flow information while only utilizing data from a reduced number of sensors.

In this work, we focus on the task of predicting the fine-grained traffic flow from coarse-grained flow data, which are collected from fewer sensors. The

T. Mantoro et al. (Eds.): ICONIP 2021, LNCS 13111, pp. 262–273, 2021.
https://doi.org/10.1007/978-3-030-92273-3_22

previous works [17, 18] normally adopt deep convolution neural networks (DCNN) to accomplish the mapping from the traffic flow maps of coarse granularity to those of fine granularity and achieve impressive results. Despite their success, the CNN-based systems still exhibit a limitation in capturing long-range dependencies, which may hinder their global perception ability and further affect performance.

To tackle this problem, we propose a TRansformer-guided Urban Flow Magnifier (TRUFM), which adopts the vision transformer architecture [19, 20] to model the global-scale dependencies for the prediction of fine-grained traffic flow maps. We argue that the transformer module is effective in three folds: (1) The global self-attention mechanism in the transformer structure can promote cross-region interactions to jointly infer the traffic conditions, so as to achieve more precise fine-grained flow map generation. (2) The transformer stage enjoys a hierarchical structure that can acquire multi-scale semantic information, while also providing richer contextual signals and more details. (3) As shown in [17], the traffic condition is affected by multiple external factors such as weather and time span. Thus, we also incorporate the embeddings of these factors in the transformer module to enhance features at the long-range scale and better exploit the additional guidance. Experimental results demonstrate the effectiveness and robustness of our TRUFM, which surpasses the current state-of-the-art methods on datasets collected under various scenarios. Furthermore, we also conduct extensive ablation studies to analyze the specific impacts of the three aspects discussed above.

2 Related Work

Urban Flow Analysis. The urban flow analysis framework, as a crucial component in the intelligent transportation system, has attracted extensive attention from many researchers in recent years [1, 10, 13, 21, 22, 26]. Benefiting from its powerful representation capability, deep learning gradually becomes the most popular technology for urban flow analysis tasks. Zong et al. [15] utilize a super-resolution neural network to realize the mapping from the coarse inputs to the high-resolution targets. Liang et al. propose the UrbanFM framework [17], which leverages several external factors as additional guidance and adopts a distributional upsampling module to exert structural constraints. Ouyang et al. [18] apply a cascading strategy to the original UrbanFM system, where the coarse-grained flows are progressively upsampled. Despite the impressive developments, the current CNN-based methods only consider the correlations between local regions while our method further boosts the performances by incorporating the long-range dependencies.

Single-Image Super-Resolution. The objective of the single-image super-resolution (SISR) task is to reconstruct the high-resolution (HR) images from the low-resolution (LR) counterparts. Dong et al. [4] propose the first deep-learning based end-to-end mapping between the LR/HR images. Shi et al. [6] introduce an efficient sub-pixel convolution operation to upscale the LR feature maps to the HR outputs. The VDSR [9] framework extends the backbone network to 20 layers and SRResNet [14] improves the architecture by stacking the residual blocks [8]. The noticeable performance gains from the two methods demonstrate the necessity of deepening the neural networks. Although the traffic flow reconstruction task has some correlations with the image super-resolution task, it is not reasonable to directly utilize the off-the-shelf SISR algorithms, mainly due to the structural constraints in the coarse-grained traffic flow maps. Thus, fine-grained traffic flow estimation is still a challenging task.

Vision Transformers. The transformer architecture [12] has achieved great success in the NLP field, which also enlightens the explorations about its application to the computer vision field [23,30]. In contrast to CNNs, which focus on local correlations between elements, the transformer can capture long-range dependencies via the self-attention mechanism and hence provide the global-scale perception. The vision transformer architectures achieve on-par or even better performances in many fundamental vision tasks, such as image classification [19,24,25], object detection [20,27], low-level image processing [28,29], and so on. Inspired by these works, we apply the transformer module to perceive global perceptions over the urban flow distribution and construct more accurate fine-grained traffic flow maps. Moreover, as the pure transformer-based architectures may require either pre-training [19,28] on an additional large-scale dataset, or delicate training strategy [24], we choose to integrate the transformer structure to the original CNN-based framework, which will combine their advantages and achieve better performances without consuming significant extra training costs.

3   Methodology

3.1   Task Formulation

The goal of the fine-grained traffic flow prediction task is to reconstruct the high-resolution (fine granularity) flow map from the corresponding low-resolution (coarse granularity) flow map. For a given city, we evenly partition the target area into a $H \times W$ grid map according to the longitude and latitude. By recording the flow volume inside each grid region (h, w), the coarse-grained flow map $X \in \mathbb{R}^{H \times W}$ is obtained. To simulate the scene of a large number of sensors, we further divide each original grid into $K \times K$ non-overlapping subregions and count the traffic value inside the smaller area. In this way, we can acquire the flow map $Y \in \mathbb{R}^{KH \times KW}$ of fine granularity. Our objective is to find an optimal upscaling strategy to recover the fine-grained map Y from the coarse-grained map X.

3.2   TRUFM Pipeline

The overall framework of the TRUFM is illustrated in Fig. 1, which consists of three components: the backbone network for extracting features from the coarse-grained input flow map, the external factor network for learning representations

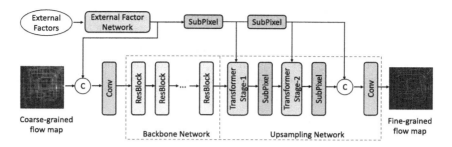

Fig. 1. Overview of the TRUFM pipeline, which incorporates the backbone network, the external factor network, and the upsampling network. ⓒ refers to the concatenation operation. We utilize a two-stage transformer architecture to capture the global-scale dependencies of multi-scale feature maps. The structure of the SubPixel block follows [17], which will enlarge the feature size by 2 times

from the external factors, and the upsampling network, which includes the hierarchical transformer modules.

We follow [17] to build the backbone network and the external factor network. The backbone network includes 16 residual blocks, where each residual block is composed of two convolution layers (kernel size 3×3), two BatchNorm layers [5], and one ReLU activation function. The external factor network consists of embedding layers to convert the external factors from distinct values to low-level vectors. As shown in Fig. 1, we first feed the input external factors into the external factor network and combine the low-level vectors to generate the external feature $\mathbf{f_e}$. Then the input coarse flow map $\mathbf{X} \in \mathbb{R}^{C_{in} \times H \times W}$ and the external feature $\mathbf{f_e}$ are concatenated along the channel dimension and pass through a convolution layer with 9×9 kernel size to produce the fused feature $\mathbf{f_{in}}$. Afterwards, $\mathbf{f_{in}}$ is fed into the backbone network to extract the higher-level semantic features $\mathbf{f_h} \in \mathbb{R}^{C \times H \times W}$ for the final upsampling operations.

In the upsampling network, we aim to expand the size of the coarse flow map $H \times W$ to the same as that of the fine-grained flow map, $KH \times KW$ (we omit the channel dimension for simplicity). If not specified, we set $K = 4$ as the default value. As shown in Fig. 1, the upscaling operation is accomplished by two SubPixel blocks, where each block will enlarge the feature size by 2 times. Please note that we place the transformer stages (details will be illustrated in Sect. 3.3) in front of the SubPixel blocks so that the network can capture the global dependencies before the size expansion. The two transformer stages enjoy the same structure but receive feature maps of different resolutions. In this way, the two-stage transformers create a hierarchical architecture that gets access to multi-scale contextual information. The structure of the SubPixel block is the same as [17], which is composed of a convolution layer, a BatchNorm operation, a PixelShuffle layer [6], and a ReLU activation function. To better exploit the external guidance, the enlarged feature will be integrated with the upsampled external feature in a similar way as the initial fusion. Finally, the fused feature passes through a convolution layer to reduce the channel from C to C_{in} and produces the predicted fine-grained flow map $\mathbf{Y^{pred}} \in \mathbb{R}^{C_{in} \times KH \times KW}$.

The whole pipeline is trained end-to-end in a fully-supervised mode. We adopt the pixel-wise L_2 loss between the predicted fine-grained flow map and the Ground-Truth fine-grained flow map as the supervision signal.

3.3   Transformer Stage

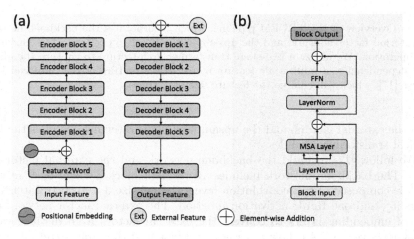

Fig. 2. Illustration of the transformer stage in the TRUFM pipeline (a) and the specific architecture of transformer block (b). The transformer stage employs an encoder-decoder structure, where the 'Feature2Word' layer refers to the process of vision word generation, while the 'Word2Feature' layer converts the vision word back to the 2D feature format via projection and reshape. Please note that the external feature will be added to the input of each decoder block while we only show the addition in the first block for simplicity

An overview of the transformer stage is depicted in Fig. 2(a), which also enjoys an encoder-decoder structure [20,28]. Before feeding the feature map $\mathbf{f_h}$ into the transformer encoder body, we first convert its format for the subsequent transformer processing. Specifically, we reshape and project the 2D spatial feature map to a 1D sequence of token embeddings (denoted as $\mathbf{f_p}$), which can be regarded as the 'vision words'. For the decoder, apart from the output from the encoder, we utilize the external feature as an additional input, which is also transferred to the vision word format (denoted as $\mathbf{f_{ext}}$) in the same way as $\mathbf{f_h}$. At the end of the transformer stage, we project and reshape the output feature back to the original format of $C \times H \times W$.

Generation of Vision Words. We divide the input feature map $\mathbf{f_h} \in \mathbb{R}^{C \times H \times W}$ into patches and flatten the patches to create the 'vision words'. The feature map is firstly reshaped to $\mathbb{R}^{L \times (P^2 C)}$, where P is the patch size and $L = HW/P^2$

refers to the sequence length. Then the reshaped feature map passes through a projection layer to reduce the embedding size from (P^2C) to D, which improves the computation efficiency. We also add a learnable positional encoding $\mathbf{E_p} \in \mathbb{R}^{1 \times D}$ to the input vision word sequence $\mathbf{f_p} \in \mathbb{R}^{L \times D}$ to maintain the position information.

Structure of the Transformer Block. Both the encoder and decoder structures are stacked by transformer blocks, which include a Multi-head Self-Attention (MSA) layer and a Feed-Forward Network (FFN), as shown in Fig. 2(b). The MSA layer splits the embedding dimension of the input sequence into n_h heads and performs the standard self-attention operation [12] in parallel on each head. These independent attention tensors are concatenated to produce the final output of the MSA layer. The FFN is composed of two fully connected layers with a GELU activation function in between. The LayerNorm operation [7] is applied before both the MSA layer and the FFN. The entire process for the encoder block is formulated in Eq. 1,

$$
\begin{aligned}
\mathbf{y_0} &= \mathbf{f_p} + \mathbf{E_p}, \\
\mathbf{y}_n' &= \mathrm{MSA}(\mathrm{LN}(\mathbf{y}_{n-1})) + \mathbf{y}_{n-1}, \\
\mathbf{y}_n &= \mathrm{FFN}(\mathrm{LN}(\mathbf{y}_n')) + \mathbf{y}_n', n = 1, ..., N
\end{aligned}
\tag{1}
$$

where N is the number of transformer blocks in the encoder, $\mathbf{y}_n$ represents the output of the nth encoder transformer block. The decoder block shares the same architecture as the encoder block, except that the input is enhanced by the external feature, as shown in Eq. 2,

$$
\begin{aligned}
\mathbf{z_0} &= \mathbf{y_N}, \quad \mathbf{z}_n^i = \mathbf{z}_{n-1} + \mathbf{f_{ext}} \\
\mathbf{z}_n' &= \mathrm{MSA}(\mathrm{LN}(\mathbf{z}_n^i)) + \mathbf{z}_n^i, \\
\mathbf{z}_n &= \mathrm{FFN}(\mathrm{LN}(\mathbf{z}_n')) + \mathbf{z}_n', n = 1, ..., N
\end{aligned}
\tag{2}
$$

where $\mathbf{f_{ext}}$ refers to the reshaped external feature, $\mathbf{z}_n^i$ and $\mathbf{z}_n$ stand for the input and output of the transformer decoder block, respectively.

4   Experiments

4.1   Experiment Configurations

Datasets. To verify the robustness of our framework, we validate the performance on two datasets, TaxiBJ-P1 and XiAn, which are collected in two cities with different traffic scenes. The TaxiBJ dataset was released by [17] and we utilize the P1 subset, which records the taxi flows in Beijing, China, from 07/01/2013 to 10/31/2013. The studied regions are divided into 32×32 grids to construct the coarse flow maps, while the resolution of the fine-grained flow maps is 128×128. The XiAn dataset was created based on the vehicle flow of Xian, China, which contains coarse-grained flow maps of 16×16 grids and fine-grained ones of 64×64

grids. The relatively sparse grids make the XiAn dataset more challenging. Both datasets are divided into the training/validation/testing splits, while we use the validation set to find the hyper-parameters for training and report the results on the testing set.

Implementation Details. The channel number C in the backbone network is 64 for all residual blocks. In each transformer stage, both the encoder and decoder structures are stacked by 5 transformer blocks. We set the patch size P of stage 1 and stage 2 to 4 and 8, respectively, keeping the sequence length L the same all the way. The embedding size D of vision words is 512, which is divided into 8 heads in the MSA layer (the dimension for each head is 64). The two fully connected layers in the FFN firstly expand the dimension to 1024 and then reduce it back to 512. We also apply 0.3 dropout ratio [2] to the FFN to prevent the network from over-fitting.

The proposed TRUFM is implemented with the PyTorch framework [16] on RTX 2080Ti. The whole pipeline is optimized via the Adam optimizer [3] with the (0.9, 0.999) beta parameters. The initial learning rate is 0.001, which is halved every 20 epochs. The entire system is trained for 60 epochs in total.

Evaluation Metrics. We evaluate the effectiveness of different methods on three metrics: Root Mean Square Error (RMSE), Mean Absolute Error (MAE), and Mean Absolute Percentage Error (MAPE). Following [17], the RMSE and MAE metrics are defined as followed: $\text{RMSE} = \sqrt{\frac{1}{S} \sum_{i=1}^{S} \left\| \mathbf{Y}_i^{\text{pred}} - \mathbf{Y}_i^{\text{GT}} \right\|_2}$, $\text{MAE} = \frac{1}{S} \sum_{i=1}^{S} \left\| \mathbf{Y}_i^{\text{pred}} - \mathbf{Y}_i^{\text{GT}} \right\|$, where S denotes the total number of samples, $\mathbf{Y}_i^{\text{pred}}$ and $\mathbf{Y}_i^{\text{GT}}$ represent the estimated and the Ground-Truth fine-grained traffic flow maps, respectively.

As for the MAPE side, we revise the original version in [17], which converts the mean percentage error from the pixel-wise level to the full image level. In this way, the revised MAPE is more robust for regions with low volumes and thus serves as a more reliable performance indicator. The specific formulation is depicted in Eq. 3.

$$\text{MAPE} = \frac{1}{S} \sum_{i=1}^{S} \frac{\left\| \mathbf{Y}_i^{\text{pred}} - \mathbf{Y}_i^{\text{GT}} \right\|}{\left\| \mathbf{Y}_i^{\text{GT}} \right\|} \tag{3}$$

4.2   Experiment Results

Table 1 display the performance comparison of TRUFM with existing baseline methods, which are summarized as followed. These competing algorithms include heuristic, image super-resolution, and climate statistical downscaling approaches.

- **Historical Average (HA)** computes the average value of the fine-grained maps in the training dataset.

Table 1. Performance comparison on the testing split of TaxiBJ-P1 and XiAn dataset. Lower is better for all metrics. Our TRUFM surpasses all baseline methods on all metrics, which demonstrate the importance of applying the long-range dependencies

	TaxiBJ-P1			XiAn		
	RMSE	MAE	MAPE	RMSE	MAE	MAPE
HA	9.998	4.204	0.398	54.909	21.897	3.185
SRCNN [4]	5.830	3.651	0.320	17.813	8.416	0.353
ESPCN [6]	4.187	2.489	0.216	18.316	8.788	0.373
DeepSD [11]	4.094	2.348	0.203	16.617	6.566	0.260
VDSR [9]	4.265	2.313	0.200	21.850	10.591	0.404
SRResNet [14]	4.210	2.510	0.219	16.946	6.988	0.277
UrbanFM [17]	4.079	2.100	0.181	17.406	6.285	0.239
TRUFM (Ours)	**3.934**	**1.970**	**0.169**	**16.109**	**5.779**	**0.218**

- **SRCNN** [4] introduces the neural network to the super-resolution field, which consists of three convolutional layers.
- **ESPCN** [6] adopts an efficient sub-pixel operation to upscale the low-resolution feature maps to the high-resolution outputs.
- **VDSR** [9] proposes an effective training strategy and thus extends the backbone depth to 20 layers.
- **SRResNet** [14] replaces the blocks of plain topology with the residual blocks so that more layers can be stacked to build a deeper network.
- **DeepSD** [11] stacks SRCNN blocks to reconstruct the high-resolution maps and achieves state-of-the-art in the climate scenario.
- **UrbanFM** [17] is the state-of-the-art method for the inference of fine-grained traffic maps from the coarse-grained inputs.

From the results, we can observe that the heuristic method HA simply provides the average value of the dataset, which can not adapt to different scenarios and shows trivial results. Due to the feature representation superiority of neural networks, the deep-learning based approaches such as SRCNN [4], ESPCN [6] exhibit better performances compared with HA. As the depth of the network increases, the advantages become more obvious, which can be seen from the results of DeepSD [11] and SRResNet [14]. Targeting the characteristics of the traffic flow maps, UrbanFM [17] outperforms the normal super-resolution approaches and becomes the current state-of-the-art. However, the existing deep-learning based methods possess fully convolutional architectures, which merely consider the local pixel correlations and ignore the long-range dependencies.

To this end, we introduce the transformer modules in the upsampling stage so that the global-scale correlations can be captured. Specifically, compared with the most competitive UrbanFM, our TRUFM reduces the RMSE by 0.145, MAE by 0.130, and MAPE by 0.012 on the TaxiBJ-P1 benchmark, while on the XiAn dataset, we obtain gains of 1.297, 0.506, and 0.021 on RMSE, MAE, and MAPE, respectively. The consistent improvements on all datasets and all metrics demonstrate the effectiveness of our approach.

4.3   Ablation Study

Comparison with CNNs. To verify that the improvements come from the collection of long-range dependencies instead of the increased network depth in the upsampling network, we replace the transformer blocks with the same amount of residual blocks (with the same structure as in the backbone network) and display the results in Table 2. We observe that adding convolution layers may bring some slight gains, but still inferior to the transformer counterpart, which reflects the importance of capturing the global-scale dependencies.

Table 2. Performance comparison between the residual and transformer blocks in the upsampling network on the testing split of the TaxiBJ-P1 dataset. Lower is better for all metrics. We can see that simply adding CNN layers will only bring slight improvements compared with the transformer counterpart

	RMSE	MAE	MAPE
UrbanFM [17]	4.079	2.100	0.181
w. CNN	4.069	2.074	0.179
w. transformer (ours)	**3.934**	**1.970**	**0.169**

Hierarchical Transformer. To explore the influence of input feature scales, we replace the two-stage transformer module as one-stage, that is, the transformer is placed at stage-1 *or* stage-2 (please refer to Fig. 1 for the detailed position information). The one-stage designs can only access features of a single scale and we use 'stage-1 & 2' to represent our original two-stage transformer architecture. The comparison of results is illustrated in Fig. 3(a), which indicates that the 'stage-1 & 2' transformer outperforms the single-level counterparts. Thus, it is beneficial to build a hierarchical transformer so that the multi-scale semantic information can be exploited. On the other hand, we also notice that all approaches employed with the transformer structure surpass the UrbanFM baseline, which indicates that the performance does not rely on a specific architecture design but adding the long-range dependencies is more important.

External Features in the Transformer. We make a comparison between *w.* and *w/o* utilizing the external features in the decoder structure and show the results in Fig. 3(b). We find that adopting the external features in the decoder structure will bring a 0.3% gain in MAPE to the system. There may be other solutions to perform the feature fusion in the decoder stage and we leave this exploration for future work.

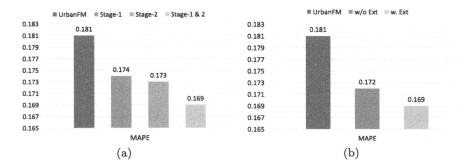

Fig. 3. Performance comparison for hierarchical structure effects (a) and external features in the transformer decoder (b)

5   Conclusion

In this work, we propose TRUFM, which incorporates the transformer architecture in the fine-grained urban flow estimation framework. Compared with the previous methods based on fully convolutional architectures, our TRUFM can capture the long-range dependencies within the flow map and hence facilitate the cross-region interactions to realize the joint inference of the traffic conditions. To further improve the performance, we employ a two-stage transformer and the hierarchical structure can process multi-scale feature maps. In this way, the system will obtain richer semantic information and thus estimate more accurate fine-grained traffic flow maps. Experimental results demonstrate that TRUFM surpasses the baseline methods by a noticeable margin under various scenarios, which verify the effectiveness of our approach.

Acknowledgement. We would like to thank Didi Chuxing for providing the trajectory data of XiAn, China.

References

1. Zheng, Y., et al.: Urban computing: concepts, methodologies, and applications. ACM Trans. Intell. Syst. Technol. (TIST) **5**(3), 1–55 (2014)
2. Srivastava, N., et al.: Dropout: a simple way to prevent neural networks from overfitting. J. Mach. Learn. Res. **15**(1), 1929–1958 (2014)
3. Kingma, D.P., Jimmy B.: Adam: a method for stochastic optimization. arXiv preprint arXiv:1412.6980 (2014)
4. Dong, C., et al.: Image super-resolution using deep convolutional networks. IEEE Trans. Pattern Anal. Mach. Intell. **38**(2), 295–307 (2015)
5. Ioffe, S., Szegedy, C.: Batch normalization: accelerating deep network training by reducing internal covariate shift. In: International Conference on Machine Learning, PMLR (2015)
6. Shi, W., et al.: Real-time single image and video super-resolution using an efficient sub-pixel convolutional neural network. In: Proceedings of the IEEE Conference on Computer Vision and Pattern Recognition (2016)

7. Ba, J.L., Jamie R.K., Hinton, G.E.: Layer normalization. arXiv preprint arXiv:1607.06450 (2016)
8. He, K., et al.: Deep residual learning for image recognition. In: Proceedings of the IEEE Conference on Computer Vision and Pattern Recognition (2016)
9. Kim, J., Jung K.L., Kyoung M.L.: Accurate image super-resolution using very deep convolutional networks. In: Proceedings of the IEEE Conference on Computer Vision and Pattern Recognition (2016)
10. Zhang, J., Zheng, Y., Qi, D.: Deep spatio-temporal residual networks for citywide crowd flows prediction. In: Thirty-First AAAI Conference on Artificial Intelligence (2017)
11. Vandal, T., et al.: DeepSD: generating high resolution climate change projections through single image super-resolution. In: Proceedings of the 23rd ACM SIGKDD International Conference on Knowledge Discovery and Data Mining (2017)
12. Vaswani, A., et al.: Attention is all you need. In: Advances in Neural Information Processing Systems (2017)
13. Yu, B., Yin, H., Zhu, Z.: Spatio-temporal graph convolutional networks: a deep learning framework for traffic forecasting. arXiv preprint arXiv:1709.04875 (2017)
14. Ledig, C., et al.: Photo-realistic single image super-resolution using a generative adversarial network. In: Proceedings of the IEEE Conference on Computer Vision and Pattern Recognition (2017)
15. Zong, Z., et al.: DeepDPM: dynamic population mapping via deep neural network. In: Proceedings of the AAAI Conference on Artificial Intelligence, vol. 33, no. 01 (2019)
16. Paszke, A., et al.: PyTorch: an imperative style, high-performance deep learning library. In: Advances in Neural Information Processing Systems, vol. 32, pp. 8026–8037 (2019)
17. Liang, Y., et al.: UrbanFM: inferring fine-grained urban flows. In: Proceedings of the 25th ACM SIGKDD International Conference on Knowledge Discovery & Data Mining (2019)
18. Ouyang, K., et al.: Fine-grained urban flow inference. IEEE Trans. Knowl. Data Eng., 1 (2020). https://doi.org/10.1109/TKDE.2020.3017104
19. Dosovitskiy, A., et al.: An image is worth 16×16 words: transformers for image recognition at scale. arXiv preprint arXiv:2010.11929 (2020)
20. Carion, N., Massa, F., Synnaeve, G., Usunier, N., Kirillov, A., Zagoruyko, S.: End-to-end object detection with transformers. In: Vedaldi, A., Bischof, H., Brox, T., Frahm, J.-M. (eds.) ECCV 2020. LNCS, vol. 12346, pp. 213–229. Springer, Cham (2020). https://doi.org/10.1007/978-3-030-58452-8_13
21. Tedjopurnomo, D.A., Bao, Z., Zheng, B., Choudhury, F., Qin, A.K.: A survey on modern deep neural network for traffic prediction: trends, methods and challenges. IEEE Trans. Knowl. Data Eng., 1 (2020). https://doi.org/10.1109/TKDE.2020.3001195
22. Yin, X., et al.: A comprehensive survey on traffic prediction. arXiv preprint arXiv:2004.08555 (2020)
23. Han, K., et al.: A survey on visual transformer. arXiv preprint arXiv:2012.12556 (2020)
24. Touvron, H., et al.: Training data-efficient image transformers & distillation through attention. In: International Conference on Machine Learning, PMLR (2021)
25. Wu, B., et al.: Visual transformers: token-based image representation and processing for computer vision. arXiv preprint arXiv:2006.03677 (2020)

26. Liu, L., et al.: Road network guided fine-grained urban traffic flow inference. arXiv preprint arXiv:2109.14251 (2021)
27. Zhu, X., et al.: Deformable DETR: deformable transformers for end-to-end object detection. arXiv preprint arXiv:2010.04159 (2020)
28. Chen, H., et al.: Pre-trained image processing transformer. In: Proceedings of the IEEE/CVF Conference on Computer Vision and Pattern Recognition (2021)
29. Jiang, Y., Chang, S., Wang, Z.: TransGAN: two transformers can make one strong GAN. arXiv preprint arXiv:2102.07074 (2021)
30. Khan, S., et al.: Transformers in vision: a survey. arXiv preprint arXiv:2101.01169 (2021)

Saliency Detection Framework Based on Deep Enhanced Attention Network

Xing Sheng[1], Zhuoran Zheng[2], Qiong Wu[1], Chunmeng Kang[1(✉)],
Yunliang Zhuang[1], Lei Lyu[1], and Chen Lyu[1(✉)]

[1] School of Information Science and Engineering, Shandong Normal University,
Jinan, China
lvchen@sdnu.edu.cn
[2] School of Computer Science and Engineering, Nanjing University of Science
and Technology, Nanjing, China

Abstract. In recent years, RGB-D based salient object detection has received increasing attention. Most of the previous models are based on early fusion and late fusion to fuse the input RGB-D images. Such an approach cannot effectively explore the complementary information on RGB-D images, and thus information loss and incomplete fusion can occur. To address these problems, we propose a novel framework for RGB-D salient object detection (DEANet). Our framework uses Siamese networks to extract features of RGB-D images to mine the similarity between the two modal data onto a shared-weight manner. Specifically, we propose the Channel-Spatial Fusion Block (CSF) for feature condensation of the extracted Depth features, which can capture the spatial and channel dependencies on RGB-D images from both spatial and dimensional perspectives, thus better mining the complementary information between the two modal images and enables the thoroughness and completeness of the features for which useful information is extracted. In addition, we propose an edge-optimization loss (EL) to obtain smoother salient object edges by supervising the edges of the objects. Comprehensive experiments on four popular evaluation metrics show that our DEANet is able to generate RGB-D saliency detectors with high robustness and generalization ability. In particular, DEANet outperforms thirteen current state-of-the-art methods in terms of four evaluation metrics on six challenging datasets.

Keywords: RGB-D saliency object detection · Channel-spatial fusion block · Edge optimization loss

1 Introduction

The purpose of salient object detection (SOD) is to represent the human visual attention mechanism in a model way, mining the most salient objects in data such as images or videos. In recent decades, a number of saliency detection models have been proposed, and the vast majority of them have been studied on the RGB images.

© Springer Nature Switzerland AG 2021
T. Mantoro et al. (Eds.): ICONIP 2021, LNCS 13111, pp. 274–286, 2021.
https://doi.org/10.1007/978-3-030-92273-3_23

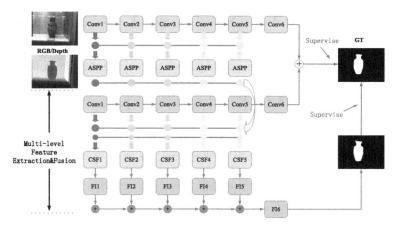

Fig. 1. The model diagram of DEANet framework for RGB-D saliency detection proposed in this paper. Among them, FI1∼FI6 are the feature integration modules, CSF is the dimensional-channel fusion module proposed in this paper, and ASPP [1] denotes the spatial pyramid pooling model. The details are detailed in Sect. 3.

With the advent of range sensors such as RGB-D (here RGB-D refers to the red, green and blue channels of color images plus aligned Depth images) cameras, stereo cameras and light detection and ranging (LIDAR) in recent years, it has become easy to collect paired RGB and Depth images. Most of the published literature is devoted to modeling on the basis of Depth images and then fusing the information from both modalities, the RGB and Depth. There are three mainstream feature fusion methods: early-fusion, middle-fusion and late-fusion (resultant fusion). The early-fusion approach cannot well explore the correlation information between RGB images and Depth images, which will result in missing and mismatching of key data. In the late-fusion approach, the high-level semantic information is usually lost after compression, and the features are not well fused with the Depth image. Unlike the above two methods, middle-fusion is widely used because it ensures that the features of both RGB and Depth images are extracted efficiently, and also enables cross-modal feature fusion through a well-designed network structure. Most of the existing middle-fusion methods first use convolutional neural networks (CNN) to extract RGB and Depth features, and then fuse them by element-wise addition or concatenating them. Such simple feature summation or concatenation only learns linear RGB and Depth images fusion features and cannot explore complex multimodal interactions. In addition, most of the existing models do not deeply optimize the image edges. This has negatively affected the smoothness of image edges of many state-of-the-art frameworks under the influence of poor-quality Depth images.

To solve the above problem, we propose a novel saliency detection framework, DEANet, as illustrated in Fig. 1. It first extracts the features of RGB and Depth inputs by a Siamese network [4], respectively. Then, DEANet performs subsequent feature extraction and concatenates the extracted RGB and

Depth features using the Atrous Spatial Pyramid Pooling (ASPP) module and Channel-Spatial Fusion Block (CSF) module, respectively, for the two types of features. Finally, DEANet uses the Feature Integration (FI) module (instead of the decoder module used in the existing model) to aggregate the connected features and use the edge optimization loss (EL) to optimize the predicted image edges during the training process. In summary, our DEANet has three main contributions:

· We introduce a CSF, which includes tandem dimensional attention and spatial attention, with dimensional attention focusing on the relationship between Depth features and spatial attention being able to uncover more valuable regions;
· We propose an edge-optimization loss function (EL), which can efficiently enhance the detection of object edges and improve the consistency of saliency images;
· Experimental evidences demonstrate that our method achieves the state-of-the-art performance on thirteen benchmarks.

2   Related Work

2.1   The RGB Salient Object Detection Methods

Early RGB saliency detection models usually utilize hand-set feature methods, including human intuition and heuristic priors, such as using chromaticity comparison [3], background comparison [31], and boundary point priors [14]. However, these methods rely too much on artificially designed prior information, are ineffective, and are very time-consuming. The study of saliency target detection has been greatly facilitated by the advent of deep neural networks. Unlike traditional methods, deep neural network-based methods can automatically learn the obtained multi-scale features and substantially improve the detection performance, such as detection speed and detection accuracy.

For example, Li et al. [16] first applied deep neural networks to saliency detection and proposed a deep convolutional neural network saliency detection model with multi-scale features. Liu et al. [20] proposed a deep convolutional network (DHSNet) that can fuse local contextual information and achieved better results. However, the method discussed above introduces a large number of underlying features, which poses difficulties in learning the best multiscale information about the whole network.

2.2   The RGB-D Salient Object Detection Methods

Traditional saliency detection methods of RGB-D also rely on manual features [2,34]. For example, Cong et al. [6] introduced Depth information into the graph construction and represented RGB as graphs. Further, the authors proposed a method to compute compact saliency graphs using RGB and Depth. The development of deep neural networks has likewise greatly advanced RGB-D SOD.

In order to effectively combine the saliency information about RGB and Depth, researchers have used new and different methods of the traditional approach. In the works [5,22], the Depth image is treated as a fourth channel (in addition to the RGB three channels) and directly connected in series with the input network (early fusion). However, such an approach ignores the differences and complementarities between RGB and Depth and does not explore the relationship between them well. In the works [12,29], the authors first extracted the features of RGB images and Depth images separately using two separate networks and then fused them into the final saliency map (late-fusion). However, this approach does not assume that there is a mutual relationship between RGB and Depth. Therefore, they do not extract the features shared between them well. In addition to the above two approaches, there are some approaches that use two branching networks to fuse the extracted features and then perform significance prediction on the fused features, which is called middle-fusion. Our proposed method belongs to the middle-fusion methods. Unlike other middle-fusion methods, we innovatively propose to use a Siamese network [4] architecture to share the network weights, which can make the model learning more efficient while reducing the model parameters.

3 Proposed Methods

3.1 Overview

In this section, we first go over the specifics of our proposed framework for SOD in Sec. 3.2. Then, we discuss our proposed attention-based block and its key components-CSF in Sec. 3.3. Next, We offer the FI module which can better incorporate the collected features in Sec. 3.4. Finally, we present an edge-optimization loss, which will provide cleaner image edges in Sect. 3.5.

3.2 The Overall Structure

As exhibited in Fig. 1, our DEANet using the Siamese network [4], which share the weights during the training process.

The input of the Siamese network [4] is RGB and its corresponding Depth. We first perform a normalization operation on them, and then we map the Depth images to three channels and input them into the Siamese network [4] separately. We use element-wise addition operation to process the features extracted from the sixth layer of RGB and Depth then process them by 1×1 convolutional layer alignment to generate an initial prediction map. We use the Ground Truth (GT) to supervise this phase of the training process. We refer to the loss generated in this phase as the bootstrap loss L_g, which enables the convolutional network to roughly localize the targets of the RGB and Depth.

After the above treatment, we arrived to the multi-scale feature extraction & fusion module. It exploits the features extracted by the convolution operations in a side-output manner: the RGB and Depth are passed through the ASPP [1]

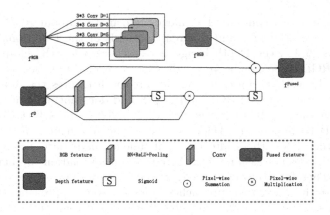

Fig. 2. Details of our proposed CSF Module

module and our proposed CSF module, respectively, to further extract features. And then they are concatenated to produce the final prediction map, subject to GT supervision. Specifically, the RGB input is subjected to a series of convolution operations, and we make use of the hierarchical features extracted from the first five layers in a similar way of the side output in [13]: they are passed through the ASPP [1] module to capture data onto larger sensory fields in order to extract more features from the image itself. Then, we feed the features from the side outputs of the first five layers of the Depth image into the CSF module and use the dimensional attention and spatial attention mechanisms to uncover the similarity information between the two modalities' information. Finally, we concat the feature maps of RGB and Depth and input the information of the fused two modalities, CSF1~CSF5, into FI1~FI5, respectively, for multi-scale feature fusion. In this way, similar features can be better mined.

3.3 CSF Module

Inspired by [30], we introduce a Depth enhancement unit to filter the redundant information about the Depth image and fuse the valid information from the RGB image and the Depth image.

Specifically, f_i^{RGB}, f_i^D denote the output from the ith side branch of the RGB and Depth, respectively. As demonstrated in Fig. 1, each Depth map sidebar output is followed by a Depth refinement unit to refine the features of the Depth input. This sidebar output preserves the edge information and semantic information in the feature maps, and can better support RGB and Depth input fusion. The two modal feature fusion processes are represented as follows:

$$f_i^m = f_i^{RGB} + F_{CSF}\left(f_i^D\right) \tag{1}$$

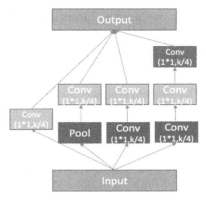

Fig. 3. The Inception v3 [28] structure of the FI module in Fig. 1, with all convolutional and maximum pooling layers in steps of 1, keeps the spatial feature size constant, unlike the original Inception v3 [28], which we have changed so that it has the same number of channels for input and output.

where f_i^m represents the fused multimodal features. As shown in Fig. 2, the Depth refinement unit contains dimensional attention and spatial attention operations, and the operations of the Depth refinement unit are defined as:

$$F_{CSF}\left(f_i^D\right) = S\left(C\left(f_i^D\right)\right) \tag{2}$$

where, $C(\cdot)$ and $S(\cdot)$ represent dimensional attention and spatial attention, respectively:

$$S(F) = \text{Sigmoid}\left(G\left(P_{\max}(F)\right)\right) \otimes F \oplus F \tag{3}$$

where G denotes the normalization, the convolution operation with 64 convolution kernels and the ReLU activation function, and $P_{\max}$ denotes the maximum pooling operation. The dimensional attention is defined as:

$$C(F) = \text{Conv}\left(\text{ReLU}\left(\text{Conv}\left(P_{\max}(F)\right)\right)\right) \otimes F \oplus F \tag{4}$$

where $\otimes$ represents element multiplication operations and $\oplus$ represents element addition operations. The spatial and dimensional attention mechanisms used in this paper are different from existing methods, such as [30]. While [30] uses both global average pooling operation and global maximum pooling operation for RGB and Depth, we use only a single global average pooling operation for feature condensation of Depth input, which can reduce the number of parameters, improve the learning efficiency and enhance the accuracy of prediction.

3.4   FI Module

The fused features of CSF1~CSF5 are fed to the FI module. Unlike previous decoders, an aggregation module receives as input the output of all levels deeper than itself. For this purpose, we use the Inception v3 [28] module presented in Fig. 3, which performs a multiscale convolution operation using filters of size 1×1, 3×3 and maximization, here k represents the number of channels of the input image.

We perform a 1×1 convolution on the final generated output FI6 to generate a final prediction map. This process is supervised by GT and the losses generated at this stage are denoted as L_f.

3.5 Loss Function

The overall loss function of our framework consists of the bootstrap loss and the final loss, the EL. The overall function is defined as:

$$L_{final} = L_f\left(S^f, G\right) + m \sum_{i \in \{rgb,d\}} L_g\left(S_i^c, G\right) + nL_{el} \tag{5}$$

where m and n are used as superparameters to adjust the weights between the three loss values, L_{el} denotes the edge optimization loss, and L_f and L_g adopt the widely used cross-entropy loss function:

$$\mathrm{L(S, G)} = -\sum_i \left[G_i \log\left(S_i\right) + (1 - G_i)\log\left(1 - S_i\right)\right] \tag{6}$$

where i denotes the pixel index, $S \in \left\{S_{rgb}^C, S_d^c, S^f\right\}$, S^f denotes the final prediction map, G denotes the GT, and S_i^c denotes the initial prediction image.

Edge-Optimization Loss Function. We design the edge optimization loss function to supervise the loss of the saliency fusion graph after the final fusion, which is defined as follows:

$$L_{el} = \frac{1}{N} \sum_{i=1}^{N} \left(\| \left(\mathrm{dx}\left(S_i^f\right) - \mathrm{dx}\left(Y_i\right)\right) \|_2^2 + \| \left(\mathrm{dy}\left(S_i^f\right) - \mathrm{dy}\left(Y_i\right)\right) \|_2^2\right) \tag{7}$$

where $\mathrm{dx}(\cdot)$, $\mathrm{dy}(\cdot)$ represent the gradients in the horizontal and vertical directions, respectively, to maximize the optimization of edge information by reducing the difference between the edges in the fused significant graph and the edges of the true values.

4   Experiments

4.1   Dataset

We conducted experiments on six publicly available SOD datasets: NJU2K [15] contains 1985 image pairs which collected from the Internet and 3D movies. NLPR [23] includes 1000 images made by Kinect. STERE [22] has 1000 images includes a variety of scenarios. RGBD135 [2] also named DES, contains 135 indoor images collected by Microsoft Kinect. LFSD [18] contains 100 pairs of images on Light Field, and SSD [17] includes 80 images picked up from three stereo movies.

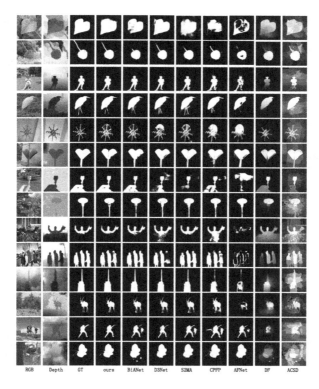

RGB   Depth   GT   ours   BiANet   D3Net   S2MA   CPFP   AFNet   DF   ACSD

Fig. 4. Comparisons of our proposed model with 7 SOTA methods.

4.2 Evaluation Metrics

For the evaluation, we used four widely adopted metrics, namely S_α [7,33], $E_\varphi^{\max}$ [2,8], maximum $F_\beta^{\max}$ [13,23], and MAE(M) [19,24]. The S-measure can evaluate the spatial structure similarities and the E-measure can jointly capture image level statistics and local pixel matching information. The F-measure can evaluate the overall performance. The MAE represents the mean absolute difference between the saliency map and GT map.

4.3 Comparison with State-of-the-art

As given in Table 1, We compared thirteen recent deep models on six datasets and retrained the above models using their default settings. Significant improvements were observed in all four metrics relative to existing and recently proposed techniques. This validates the effectiveness and generalization of our network. A significant plot of the predictions of our method and the comparison method is given in Fig. 4, which seems to be more effective against using Depth information on cross-modal fusion.

4.4 Ablation Study

The current model is called "DEANet(RGB-D+CSF+edge)", where RGB-D indicates that both RGB and Depth are input, edge indicates that the EL func-

Table 1. Quantitative comparison of models using S-measure (S_m), max F-measure $(maxF)$, max E-measure $(maxE_\xi)$ and MAE (M) scores on six public datasets. ↑ (↓) denotes that the higher (lower) the score, the better. The best score in each row is highlighted in boldface. From left to right: five models based on handcrafted features and eight CNNs-based models. The top three scores in each column are marked in **boldface**, red, and green fonts, respectively.

Dataset	Metric	Hand-crafted-features-Based Models					CNNs-Based Models								
		ACSD [15]	LBE [10]	DCMC [6]	MDSF [27]	SE [26]	DF [25]	AFNet [29]	CPFP [33]	MMRA [24]	JL-DCF [11]	S2MA [21]	D3Net [9]	BiANet [32]	DEANet ours
NJU2K [15]	S_α ↑	0.699	0.695	0.686	0.748	0.664	0.763	0.833	0.878	0.886	0.902	0.884	0.657	0.661	**0.917**
	$maxF$ ↑	0.711	0.748	0.715	0.775	0.748	0.804	0.844	0.837	0.872	0.885	0.865	0.589	0.594	**0.900**
	E_ξ ↑	0.803	0.803	0.799	0.868	0.813	0.864	0.876	0.895	0.908	0.913	0.896	0.752	0.753	**0.919**
	MAE ↓	0.202	0.153	0.172	0.157	0.169	0.141	0.077	0.053	0.051	0.041	0.053	0.167	0.167	**0.038**
NLPR [23]	S_α ↑	0.673	0.762	0.724	0.805	0.756	0.802	0.767	0.900	0.899	0.941	0.932	0.912	0.944	**0.959**
	$maxF$ ↑	0.607	0.745	0.648	0.793	0.713	0.778	0.704	0.844	0.854	0.904	0.881	0.897	0.909	**0.922**
	E_ξ ↑	0.78	0.855	0.793	0.885	0.847	0.880	0.860	0.939	0.941	0.968	0.955	0.944	0.97	**0.979**
	MAE ↓	0.179	0.081	0.117	0.095	0.091	0.085	0.069	0.032	0.031	0.017	0.025	0.030	0.012	**0.014**
STERE [22]	S_α ↑	0.692	0.660	0.731	0.728	0.708	0.757	0.820	0.879	0.886	0.903	0.890	0.892	0.898	**0.908**
	$maxF$ ↑	0.669	0.633	0.740	0.719	0.755	0.757	0.813	0.830	0.862	0.869	0.855	0.859	0.851	**0.877**
	E_ξ ↑	0.806	0.787	0.819	0.809	0.846	0.847	0.886	0.903	0.92	0.919	0.907	0.920	0.917	**0.921**
	MAE ↓	0.200	0.250	0.148	0.176	0.143	0.141	0.074	0.051	0.047	**0.040**	0.051	0.046	0.044	0.041
RGBD135 [2]	S_α ↑	0.728	0.703	0.707	0.741	0.741	0.752	0.536	0.872	0.901	0.931	0.577	0.572	0.573	**0.932**
	$maxF$ ↑	0.756	0.788	0.666	0.746	0.741	0.766	0.410	0.838	0.857	0.900	0.447	0.441	0.442	**0.907**
	E_ξ ↑	0.850	0.890	0.773	0.851	0.856	0.870	0.747	0.922	0.945	**0.969**	0.755	0.759	0.755	0.968
	MAE ↓	0.169	0.208	0.111	0.122	0.090	0.093	0.137	0.037	0.029	**0.020**	0.134	0.133	0.133	0.021
LFSD [18]	S_α ↑	0.727	0.729	0.746	0.694	0.692	0.783	0.695	0.828	0.847	**0.861**	0.533	0.825	0.845	0.855
	$maxF$ ↑	0.763	0.722	0.813	0.779	0.786	0.813	0.699	0.813	0.849	0.854	0.497	0.805	0.840	**0.855**
	E_ξ ↑	0.829	0.797	0.849	0.819	0.832	0.857	0.773	0.867	**0.899**	0.882	0.652	0.853	0.876	0.885
	MAE ↓	0.195	0.214	0.162	0.197	0.174	0.146	0.147	0.088	0.075	**0.070**	0.265	0.095	0.085	0.075
SSD [17]	S_α ↑	0.675	0.621	0.704	0.673	0.675	0.747	0.703	0.807	0.857	-	0.868	0.857	0.861	**0.87**
	$maxF$ ↑	0.682	0.619	0.711	0.703	0.710	0.735	0.673	0.726	0.821	-	0.815	0.814	0.810	**0.830**
	E_ξ ↑	0.785	0.736	0.786	0.779	0.800	0.828	0.799	0.832	0.892	-	0.891	0.897	0.891	**0.901**
	MAE ↓	0.203	0.278	0.169	0.192	0.165	0.142	0.124	0.082	0.058	-	0.052	0.058	0.054	**0.051**

tion is used, and CSF indicates the Depth refinement module; The second model is called "D(CSF+Depth+edge)", which means only the Depth data is input; The third model is called "w/o edge(CSF+RGB-D)", which means no EL function; The fourth model is called "RGB(CSF+RGB+edge)", which means only RGB data is used; The fifth model is called "VGG16", which replaces the frame with VGG16; The sixth model is called "w/o CSF(Depth+RGB+edge)", which means no CSF block.

Table 2 shows the quantitative comparison of various evaluation metrics. The following conclusions can be drawn:

ResNet and VGG16. From the comparison between DEANet and DEANet-VGG16, it is known that the ResNet backbone network is superior compared to the VGG-16 backbone network.

Effectiveness of the EL Function. Except on the RGBD135 [2] dataset, the other five datasets perform better after using the EL function. The reason is that the quality of the Depth images of this dataset is much lower than the

Table 2. Quantitative evaluation results of ablation tests described in Sect. 4.4, using S-measure (S_m), max F-measure ($maxF$), max E-measure ($maxE_\xi$) and MAE (M) scores on six public datasets. ↑ (↓) denotes that the higher (lower) the score, the better. The best score in each row is highlighted in **boldface**. From left to right: w/o edge, RGB, D, VGG16, CSF, DEANet.

Dataset	Metric	A	B	C	D	E	F
NJU2K [15]	S_α ↑	0.916	0.829	0.757	0.866	0.915	**0.917**
	$maxF$ ↑	0.895	0.738	0.702	0.837	0.897	**0.900**
	E_ξ ↑	0.915	0.829	0.811	0.894	0.918	**0.919**
	MAE ↓	0.038	0.111	0.131	0.066	0.038	**0.038**
NLPR [23]	S_α ↑	0.957	0.848	0.838	0.893	**0.959**	0.959
	$maxF$ ↑	**0.922**	0.687	0.721	0.833	0.918	**0.922**
	E_ξ ↑	0.975	0.831	0.866	0.933	0.977	**0.979**
	MAE ↓	**0.014**	0.077	0.069	0.038	0.015	**0.014**
STERE [22]	S_α ↑	0.906	0.828	0.76	0.86	0.904	**0.908**
	$maxF$ ↑	0.87	0.718	0.689	0.808	0.872	**0.877**
	E_ξ ↑	0.917	0.824	0.818	0.884	0.918	**0.921**
	MAE ↓	**0.041**	0.111	0.126	0.065	**0.041**	**0.041**
RGBD135 [2]	S_α ↑	**0.938**	0.882	0.834	0.899	0.931	0.932
	$maxF$ ↑	**0.911**	0.756	0.735	0.855	0.905	0.907
	E_ξ ↑	**0.974**	0.886	0.894	0.949	0.965	0.968
	MAE ↓	**0.019**	0.056	0.063	0.065	0.02	0.021
LFSD [18]	S_α ↑	**0.855**	0.787	0.714	0.815	0.85	**0.855**
	$maxF$ ↑	0.854	0.682	0.703	0.803	0.852	**0.855**
	E_ξ ↑	0.883	0.766	0.795	0.859	0.88	**0.885**
	MAE ↓	0.081	0.161	0.162	0.104	**0.078**	**0.078**
SSD [17]	S_α ↑	**0.87**	0.785	0.77	0.872	0.869	**0.87**
	$maxF$ ↑	0.825	0.678	0.682	0.825	0.821	**0.83**
	E_ξ ↑	0.897	0.798	0.805	0.894	0.896	**0.901**
	MAE ↓	0.052	0.125	0.115	0.052	**0.051**	**0.051**

other five datasets, and the edges are very inaccurate and the object boundaries are not aligned, resulting in a poor performance after using the edge-optimized loss function instead.

Effectiveness of CSF Module. From the comparison of w/o CSF and DEANet, we can see that the performance of the model will be reduced after changing CSF to channel tandem. The possible reason is that the system does not properly fuse the multimodal information in RGB and Depth well, resulting in learning only the information of RGB images, which is certainly more The results are certainly worse.

Using RGB only and Depth only. Comparing DEANet-RGB and DEANet-D shows that using the RGB for detection is better than using the Depth, which indicates that the RGB images provide more information.

5   Conclusion

In this paper, we propose a RGB-D SOD framework called DEANet. Experimental results show the effectiveness of our proposed CSF module to capture the spatial and channel dependencies between the RGB and Depth inputs from dimensional and spatial perspectives. In addition, our proposed EL function is also conferred to provide smoother edges to the predicted results. Better performance than state-of-the-art methods was demonstrated on six datasets and supported by ablation tests. In the future, we hope to be able to apply this method in the field of real production.

Acknowledgment. This work is financially supported by the National Natural Science Foundation of China (61602286, 61976127) and the Special Project on Innovative Methods (2020IM020100).

References

1. Chen, L.C., Yuille, A.L.: Deeplab: semantic image segmentation with deep convolutional nets, atrous convolution, and fully connected crfs. IEEE Trans. Pattern Anal. Mach. Intell. **40**, 834–848 (2018)
2. Cheng, Y., Cao, X.: Depth enhanced saliency detection method. In: International Conference on Internet Multimedia Computing and Service, pp. 23–27 (2014)
3. Cheng, M.-M., Hu, S.M.: Global contrast based salient region detection. IEEE Trans. Pattern Anal. Mach. Intell. **37**, 569–582 (2015)
4. Chopra, S., LeCun, Y.: Learning a similarity metric discriminatively, with application to face verification. In: International Conference on Computer Vision and Pattern Recognition, pp. 539–546 (2005)
5. Cong, R., Ling, N.: HSCS: hierarchical sparsity based co-saliency detection for RGBD images. IEEE Trans. Multimedia **21**, 1660–1671 (2019)
6. Cong, R., Hou, C.: Saliency detection for stereoscopic images based on depth confidence analysis and multiple cues fusion. IEEE Sig. Process. Lett. **23**, 819–823 (2016)
7. Fan, D.P., Borji, A.: Structure-measure: a new way to evaluate foreground maps. In: IEEE International Conference on Computer Vision, pp. 4558–4567 (2017)
8. Fan, D.P., Borji, A.: Enhanced-alignment measure for binary foreground map evaluation. In: Proceedings of the Twenty-Ninth International Joint Conference on Artificial Intelligence, pp. 698–704 (2018)
9. Fan, D.P., Cheng, M.M.: Rethinking RGB-D salient object detection: models, datasets, and large-scale benchmarks. CoRR arXiv:1907.06781 (2019)
10. Feng, D.P., McCarthy, C.: Local background enclosure for RGB-D salient object detection. In: International Conference on Computer Vision and Pattern Recognition, pp. 2343–2350 (2016)
11. Fu, K., Zhu, C.: Siamese network for RGB-D salient object detection and beyond. CoRR arXiv:2008.12134 (2020)

12. Han, J., Li, X.: CNNS-based RGB-D saliency detection via cross-view transfer and multiview fusion. IEEE Trans. Cybern. **48**, 3171–3183 (2018)
13. Hou, Q., Torr, P.H.S.: Deeply supervised salient object detection with short connections. IEEE Trans. Pattern Anal. Mach. Intell. **41**, 815–828 (2019)
14. Jiang, Z., Davis, L.S.: Submodular salient region detection. In: International Conference on Computer Vision and Pattern Recogintion, pp. 2043–2050 (2013)
15. Ju, R., Wu, G.: Depth saliency based on anisotropic center-surround difference. In: IEEE International Conference on Image Processing, pp. 1115–1119 (2014)
16. Li, G., Yu, Y.: Visual saliency based on multiscale deep features. In: International Conference on Computer Vision and Pattern Recogintion, pp. 5455–5463 (2015)
17. Li, G., Zhu, C.: A three-pathway psychobiological framework of salient object detection using stereoscopic technology. In: IEEE International Conference on Computer Vision, pp. 3008–3014 (2017)
18. Li, N., Yu, J.: Saliency detection on light field. In: IEEE Transactions on Pattern Analysis and Machine Intelligence, pp. 2806–2813 (2014)
19. Liang, F., Qing, L.: Stereoscopic saliency model using contrast and depth-guided-background prior. Neurocomputing **275**, 2227–2238 (2018)
20. Liu, N., Han, J.: Dhsnet: deep hierarchical saliency network for salient object detection. In: International Conference on Computer Vision and Pattern Recogintion, pp. 678–686 (2016)
21. Liu, N., Han, J.: Learning selective self-mutual attention for RGB-D saliency detection. In: International Conference on Computer Vision and Pattern Recognition, pp. 13753–13762 (2020)
22. Niu, Y., Liu, F.: Leveraging stereopsis for saliency analysis. In: International Conference on Computer Vision and Pattern Recogintion, pp. 454–461 (2012)
23. Peng, H., Ji, R.: Rgbd salient object detection: A benchmark and algorithms. In: IEEE International Conference on Computer Vision, pp. 92–109 (2014)
24. Piao, Y., Lu, H.: Depth-induced multi-scale recurrent attention network for saliency detection. In: IEEE International Conference on Computer Vision, pp. 7253–7262 (2019)
25. Qu, L., Yang, Q.: Rgbd salient object detection via deep fusion. IEEE Trans. Image Process. **26**, 2274–2285 (2017)
26. Quo, J., Bei, J.: Salient object detection for RGB-D image via saliency evolution. In: IEEE International Conference on Multimedia and Expo, pp. 1–6 (2016)
27. Song, H., Ren, T.: Depth-aware salient object detection and segmentation via multiscale discriminative saliency fusion and bootstrap learning. IEEE Trans. Image Process. **26**, 4204–4216 (2017)
28. Szegedy, C., Wojna, Z.: Rethinking the inception architecture for computer vision. In: International Conference on Computer Vision and Pattern Recogintion, pp. 2818–2826 (2016)
29. Wang, N., Gong, X.: Adaptive fusion for RGB-D salient object detection. IEEE Access **7**, 55277–55284 (2019)
30. Xie, S., He, K.: Aggregated residual transformations for deep neural networks. In: IEEE Conference on Computer Vision and Pattern Recognition, pp. 5987–5995 (2017)
31. Yang, C., Yang, M.H.: Saliency detection via graph-based manifold ranking. In: International Conference on Computer Vision and Pattern Recogintion, pp. 3166–3173 (2013)
32. Zhang, Z., Fan, D.P.: Bilateral attention network for RGB-D salient object detection. IEEE Trans. Image Process. **30**, 1949–1961 (2021)

33. Zhao, J., Zhang, L.: Contrast prior and fluid pyramid integration for RGBD salient object detection. In: International Conference on Computer Vision and Pattern Recogintion, pp. 3927–3936 (2019)
34. Zhu, C., Wang, R.: An innovative salient object detection using center-dark channel prior. In: IEEE International Conference on Computer Vision, pp. 1509–1515 (2017)

SynthTriplet GAN: Synthetic Query Expansion for Multimodal Retrieval

Ivona Tautkute[1,4](✉) [iD] and Tomasz Trzciński[2,3,4] [iD]

[1] Polish-Japanese Academy of Information Technology, Warsaw, Poland
s16352@pjwstk.edu.pl
[2] Warsaw University of Technology, Warszawa, Poland
tomasz.trzcinski@pw.edu.pl
[3] Jagiellonian University of Cracow, Kraków, Poland
[4] Tooploox, Wrocaw, Poland

Abstract. This paper addresses the problem of object retrieval using a multimodal query (a query that combines visual input with additional semantic information in natural language feedback). We propose a SynthTriplet GAN framework that resolves this task by expanding the multimodal query with a synthetically generated image that captures semantic information from both image and text input. We introduce a novel triplet mining method that uses a synthetic image as an anchor to directly optimize for embedding distances of generated and target images. We demonstrate that apart from the added value of retrieval illustration with a synthetic image with the focus on customization and user feedback, the proposed method greatly surpasses other multimodal generation methods and achieves state of the art results in the multimodal retrieval task. We also show that in contrast to other retrieval methods, our method provides explainable embeddings.

Keywords: Machine learning · Computer vision · Generative adversarial networks · Multimodal embeddings

1 Introduction

Many applications used by everyday Internet users rely heavily on searching through datasets of multimodal data, such as images, text snippets and videos. Given the increasing size of these databases, it becomes more important to provide more effective search methods to navigate the most popular types of data - images and text. Both textual and visual search engines reached a certain level of maturity during the last several decades [1,2]. Nevertheless, using separate search engines per each modality suffers from one significant shortcoming: it prevents the users from specifying a very natural query such as: *I want product similar to the image but in a different color.*

Current methods to address the problem of multimodal retrieval typically map image and text features to a common multimodal embedding where the search is performed [3–5]. Common embeddings, however, have a disadvantage of

© Springer Nature Switzerland AG 2021
T. Mantoro et al. (Eds.): ICONIP 2021, LNCS 13111, pp. 287–298, 2021.
https://doi.org/10.1007/978-3-030-92273-3_24

Fig. 1. Embedding interpolation in the latent space from "the same but blue" to "similar shirt in yellow" on a sample from men's shirts. Shapes and special pattern structure such as logo, graphic are preserved during color interpolation. (Color figure online)

being hard to interpret. Synthetic image provides a natural visual interpretation of the multimodal signal that can be displayed to the end user and provide additional information about the search query performed, thus improving the user experience of the retrieval system. Such visual representation allows to identify and modify the influence of individual uni-modal signals over the multimodal representation. In some examples, instead of equally represented image and text signals, user expects a search query that is biased towards one signal. Synthetic image allows user to confirm or reject (and modify) the multimodal search query. Finally, in contrast to common multimodal retrieval, synthetic query expansion helps to identify the cause of unsatisfactory multimodal retrieval results. It allows to verify whether the search failed due to misinterpretation of the multimodal query or due to a difficulty of finding similar items, *e.g.* because of the lack of such items in the dataset.

To address these shortcomings, we propose a novel method for multimodal retrieval with synthetic query expansion. By generating a synthetic image that corresponds to the semantic information provided within the query, we can simplify the multimodal retrieval process to a direct visual search. We directly optimize learned multimodal embeddings for the retrieval task by incorporating triplet loss, which helps minimize distances between the embeddings of synthetic and real target images.

The main contributions of this work are as follows:

- We propose a novel method, dubbed SynthTriplet GAN[1], for multimodal retrieval with synthetic query expansion. To the best to our knowledge, this is the first work to quantitatively evaluate generating synthetic images in multimodal retrieval setting.

---

[1] Code is publicly available at https://github.com/IvonaTau/SynthTriplet-GAN.

Fig. 2. SynthTriplet GAN multimodal retrieval with synthetic query expansion.

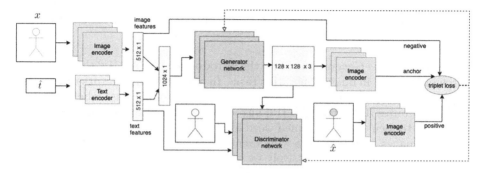

Fig. 3. Model architecture.

- We introduce a new method for triplet mining in triplet loss with a synthetically generated anchor to optimize the learned embeddings for the retrieval task.
- We demonstrate that our method provides interpretable embeddings that can be disentangled through latent traversal.

The remainder of the paper is organized in the following way: in Sect. 2 we discuss related work, in Sect. 3 we describe our proposed method, in Sect. 4 we present experimental results and perform a study of feature disentanglement in the embedding space. We finish with conclusions in Sect. 5.

2   Related Work

Multimodal Retrieval. Systems for interactive image retrieval typically use visual pre-defined attributes, including shape, texture or color [6,7]. Attribute manipulation has also been made possible [8]. However, these methods assume a fixed set of attributes. In our work, we explore the use of feedback as a relative query in natural language, which allows for more precise and more flexible descriptions.

Another line of research lies in the intersection of computer vision and natural language processing, such as visual-question answering [9] and image captioning [10]. Similar to [11], we use both image and text as queries for retrieval with text describing the desired modification to the image. Visually-grounded dialog systems [12] have been developed to perform a meaningful conversation with humans in natural language about visual content. In those systems, the user provides feedback about presented images and the agent updates the results with respect to the feedback. Recently, transformer based methods have been proposed for multimodal retrieval. Visiolinguistic Attention Learning framework [13] inserts multiple composite transformers at varying dephts to selectively preserve and transform visual features conditioned on language semantics. These systems, however, do not offer insights on multimodal embedding used to find nearest neighbors. The user is only presented with closest matches and without an understanding of which parts of the multimodal query had the most impact on the results.

Conditional Image Generation. Since the introduction of GAN [14] there has been a growing interest in image generation tasks. In particular, many works attempted to generate images using conditional variables, for example class labels [15], text [16] or attributes [17]. AttnGAN [18] introduced an attention mechanism into the generator, to focus on fine-grained word level information. DALLE [19] is able to generate images from text for a wide range of concepts. StackGAN [20] produces high-resolution images progressively by stacking multiple GANs. However, these works generate new images from random noise vectors and have limited functionality in terms of providing an image input. In contrast, our work focuses on creating a new image given both visual and textual conditional information.

Semantic Image Manipulation. Another related area of research is semantic image manipulation. The authors of TAGAN [21] propose to use a text adaptive discriminator, which consists of multiple word level local discriminators that disentangle fine grained visual attributes from text descriptions. The authors of SeqAttnGAN [22] apply a neural state tracker to encode the previous image and the textual description in each dialogue turn. In [5], the dialog based image retrieval task is formulated as a reinforcement learning problem and the dialog system rewards improving the rank of the target image during each dialog turn. On the contrary, our goal is one-shot product retrieval with a single image and text query.

3   Method

We introduce SynthTriplet GAN model which expands the multimodal query with synthetically generated images that preserve meaningful distances in the embedding space. We illustrate model architecture in Fig. 3 and multimodal retrieval mechanism is visualised in Fig. 2.

Let x denote a product image and $\hat{t}$ additional text information given by the user. The text description $\hat{t}$ provides a relative caption to target image $\hat{x}$ which is the desired result of the user's search. Given an image x and target query $\hat{t}$ our task is to generate a synthetic image $\hat{y} = G(x, \hat{t})$ (function G is the generator part of the model) which matches the text description $\hat{t}$ semantically and preserves other visual features of x. The synthetic image is then used to find the closest matches in the visual embedding space.

The input image x is encoded into a feature vector $Enc_{im}(x) = v_{im} \in \mathbb{R}^d$ using a deep convolutional neural network pre-trained on ImageNet [23] followed by a linear transformation. Words in the textual description $\hat{t}$ are represented with one-hot vectors and then embedded $Enc_{txt}(\hat{t}) = v_{txt} \in \mathbb{R}^d$ with bidirectional GRU. Finally, the image feature vector and the target description representation are concatenated to obtain the input vector, which is fed into the generator network.

Feature maps of each candidate image in the database are calculated offline and stored to be used in the online retrieval phase. At query time, $Enc_{im}(\hat{y})$ is used to search the database for the best matching item based on the Euclidean distance in the image feature space. Distances between query features and all candidates are calculated and the top-K results are returned to the user. While we use this method for accurate retrieval evaluation, using approximate nearest neighbours search library (FLANN [24]) or efficient similarity search library (FAISS [25]) improves inference time for production ready implementation.

As our goal is to learn a multimodal embedding where the distances between synthetic images generated from the multimodal query and the real target images are as small as possible, we employ triplet loss [26], a common loss function for metric learning.

We propose a novel method of triplet selection that is directly suited towards synthetic query expansion. In SynthTriplet GAN, two images are provided as input and the anchor image is synthetically generated from the source image and text query $\hat{t}$. Hence, for input image x, target image $\hat{x}$ and relative text query $\hat{t}$, the modified triplet loss is the following:

$$L_{tr}(x, \hat{x}, \hat{t}) = max(0, d(\hat{y}, \hat{x}) - d(\hat{y}, x) + m) \tag{1}$$

where $d(x, y) = ||Enc_{im}(x) - Enc_{im}(y)||_2^2$ and m is the margin. In this scenario, the anchor image is the generated image $\hat{y} = G(x, \hat{t})$, the positive image is the target image $\hat{x}$ and the negative image is the source image x. The model architecture is visualised in Fig. 3.

The SynthTriplet GAN objective consists of multimodal conditional adversarial loss and triplet loss. The network is trained by alternatively minimizing both the generator and discriminator objectives.

We perform a comprehensive study to empirically evaluate several variants of underlying GAN objectives for SynthTriplet GAN. The empirical results, comparing the retrieval values for different generator and discriminator objective functions, are presented in Sect. 4.

Firstly, we propose an image and text conditioned GAN with triplet loss with the following discriminator and generator objectives:

$$(L_D)_C = \mathop{\mathbb{E}}_{x,\hat{x},\hat{t}} - \left[logD(\hat{x}, \hat{t}) + log(1 - D(\hat{y}, \hat{t})) \right] + \lambda_D L_{tr}(x, \hat{x}, \hat{t}), \tag{2}$$

$$(L_G)_C = \mathop{\mathbb{E}}_{x,\hat{t}} log(1 - D(\hat{y}, \hat{t})) + \lambda_G L_{tr}(x, \hat{x}, \hat{t}). \tag{3}$$

Hyper-parameters λ_G and λ_D control the weights of triplet loss in the final loss function.

Going further, we analyze how adding a gradient penalty (improved Wesserstein GAN [27]) changes the results:

$$(L_D)_W = \mathbb{E}_{x,\hat{x},\hat{t}}\left[D\left(\hat{y},\hat{t}\right) - D(\hat{x},\hat{t})\right] + \lambda_W \mathbb{E}_{\bar{x},\bar{t}}\left[(\|\nabla_{\bar{x}}D(\bar{x},\bar{t})\|_2 - 1)^2\right] + \lambda_D L_{tr}(x,\hat{x},\hat{t}),$$

(4)

$$(L_G)_W = \mathbb{E}_{x,\hat{t}}[D\left(\hat{y},\hat{t}\right)] + \lambda_G L_{tr}(x,\hat{x},\hat{t}),$$

(5)

where $\bar{x},\bar{t} \sim \bar{p}_{data}$ are random samples from the training data, λ_W is the penalty coefficient, typically set to $\lambda_W = 10$ [27].

Finally, we add a text-adaptive discriminator and reconstruction loss [21]:

$$(L_D)_T = \mathbb{E}_{x,t,\hat{t}}\left[logD(x,t) + \lambda_1(logD(x,t) + log(1 - D(x,\hat{t})))\right]$$

$$+ \mathbb{E}_{x,\hat{t}}\left[log(1 - D(\hat{y}))\right] + \lambda_D L_{tr}(x,\hat{x},\hat{t}),$$

$$(L_G)_T = \mathbb{E}_{x,\hat{t}}\left[logD(x,t) + \lambda_1 logD\left(G(x,\hat{t}),\hat{t}\right)\right] + \lambda_2 L_{rec} + \lambda_G L_{tr}(x,\hat{x},\hat{t}),$$

(6)

where λ_1 and λ_2 are parameters controlling the importance of additional losses and $L_{rec} = ||x - G(x,\hat{t})||$ is the reconstruction loss [28].

4   Experiments

In this section we present the empirical results and evaluate our proposed method against baseline approaches.

4.1   Datasets

We perform experiments on Fashion Interactive Queries (Fashion IQ) dataset [3] that contains human-generated relative captions to distinguish similar image pairs and Shoes Attribute Discovery Dataset [5] introduced for the task of relative image captioning. Those two data sets are commonly used in the literature for multimodal retrieval [11,13,29,30]. The Fashion IQ database consists of more than 70 000 images and 20 000 relative captions for products in three fashion categories. Similar to baseline methods, we train a separate model for each of these three categories and evaluate them in isolation. Shoes Attribute Discovery Dataset contains 10 751 captions with one caption per pair of images.

4.2   Baseline Methods

We compare our approach with two types of baseline methods: general multimodal retrieval methods as well as generative methods. We consider the following retrieval approaches: DeepStyle [4] - multimodal retrieval method with Siamese loss, MRN [29] - multimodal residual learning component that fuses visual and textual features from CNN and RNN, FiLM [30] - feature-wise linear modulation

Fig. 4. Example retrieval results for SynthTriplet GAN model with $(L_D)_T, (L_G)_T$ loss functions.

component that contains a stack of cascaded layers, TIRG [11] - image-text composition approach with gating and residual connections for cross-modal fusion, Fashion-IQ [3] - composite text and image model for retrieval proposed in the original data set paper and VAL [13] - transformer based method with visiolinguistic attention. We also evaluate GAN based models StackGAN [20] and AttnGAN [18] which generate images in an text-to-image manner, as well as TAGAN [21] which, similarly to our work, generates images from multimodal input.

4.3   Implementation Details

We implement our method using PyTorch. We train our network for 600 epochs. For comparison with baseline methods we generate 128×128 images. It is possible to use bigger size setting in the generator architecture to generate synthetic images of higher resolution for production ready engine. For data augmentation all images are resized to 150×150, then randomly cropped to 128×128, randomly rotated by up to 10 °C and augmented with horizontal flips. For the learning rate, we follow the approach of Two Time-Scale Update Rule (TTUR), that is shown to converge to a local Nash equilibrium [31], with an Adam optimizer and learning rate of 0.0004 and 0.0001 for the discriminator and generator accordingly.

4.4   Quantitative Results

We present evaluation and baseline comparison results in Table 1. Our method strongly outperforms other GAN based models and is on par with state of the

Table 1. Comparison of recall values against baseline methods for Fashion-IQ [3] and Attribute Discovery datasets [5]. Our proposed method surpasses all evaluated generative approaches and performs on par with state of the art multimodal retrieval methods.

	Tops & Tees [3]		Dresses [3]		Shirts [3]		Shoes [5]	
	R@10	R@50	R@10	R@50	R@10	R@50	R@10	R@50
Retrieval methods:								
DeepStyle [4]	9.3	20.9	8.6	20.1	6.7	18.9	29.1	43.4
MRN [29]	18.11	36.33	12.32	32.18	15.88	34.33	41.7	67.01
FiLM [30]	17.3	37.68	14.23	33.34	15.04	34.09	38.89	68.3
TIRG [11]	7.71	23.44	8.10	23.27	11.06	28.08	45.45	69.39
Fashion-IQ [3]	11.74	31.52	13.39	35.56	11.03	29.03	–	–
VAL [13]	27.53	51.68	22.53	44.0	**22.38**	**44.15**	**51.52**	**75.83**
GAN based:								
StackGAN [20]	1.1	4.6	1.9	6.5	2.2	7.8	8.2	14.1
AttnGAN [18]	1.5	5.4	1.1	7.3	1.9	5.8	6.1	15.1
TAGAN [21]	14.2	32.1	14.6	30.7	10.7	22.0	23.01	36.78
SynthTriplet GAN	**28.01**	**52.1**	**22.6**	**45.1**	20.5	44.08	47.6	73.6

art multimodal retrieval methods. SynthTriplet GAN outperforms state of the art multimodal retrieval methods on Tops & Tees category with R@10 at 28.01 and Dresses category with R@10 at 22.6.

We also perform an ablation study to verify how adding particular components to SynthTriplet GAN helps improve a model's retrieval capabilities. First of all, we analyze variants of objective functions used in SynthTriplet GAN in Table 2 and found that adding a gradient penalty in $(L_D)_W, (L_G)_W$ improves recall when compared to conditional objectives $(L_D)_C, (L_G)_C$. Objective loss with a text-adaptive discriminator and reconstruction loss $(L_D)_T, (L_G)_T$ yields the highest recall values and is used in our final SynthTriplet GAN model.

In addition, we analyze how introducing triplet loss to the objective function improves recall. We can see from Fig. 5 that if we do not add the triplet loss to either the discriminator or generator by setting $\lambda_G = \lambda_D = 0$, the recall is lower than for positive parameter values. Also, higher recall values are slightly skewed towards higher λ_G values, which suggests that adding the triplet loss to the generator objective is more important than adding it to the discriminator objective. We find the best triplet loss weights to be $\lambda_G = 5$ and $\lambda_D = 1$ and we use them in our final SynthTriplet GAN model.

4.5   Qualitative Results

We also qualitatively examine images generated by our multimodal models. Specifically, we visualize the generated images against the target image and show the closest matches from the embedding space in terms of visual similarity

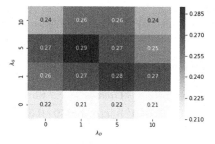

Fig. 5. Average recall for λ_D and λ_G parameter selection in the SynthTriplet GAN.

Fig. 6. Example retrieval results for the Shoes dataset [5] with synthetic image expansion.

(see Fig. 4 and 6). Generated images correspond to semantic image manipulations according to the provided text query and retrieved products are semantically close to the target image. What is more, the generated images preserve the overall structure of the input image (e.g. a packshot vs model wearing item). Visual examination illustrates why the overall performance is better on the Shoes dataset than on Fashion-IQ. The target ground truth images in the Shoes dataset are very close perceptually to the original images and only have a small number of attributes changed whereas in the Fashion-IQ data the target image might present a hogh number of attributes changed, not only those described with a text query $\hat{t}$.

4.6   Explainable Representation Learning

Multimodal representations from direct retrieval methods such as [3,4] are not interpretable. In contrast, with SynthTriplet GAN, by interpolating between representations we get meaningful results by feeding the embedding to the Generator

Table 2. Comparison of objective functions in SynthTriplet GAN. $(L_D)_C, (L_G)_C$ denote conditional loss functions for discriminator and generator, $(L_D)_W, (L_G)_W$ - loss functions with gradient penalty, $(L_D)_T, (L_G)_T$ - loss functions with text adaptive discriminators and reconstruction loss. The best recall results are achieved for SynthTriplet GAN with text-adaptive discriminator and reconstruction loss.

	Tops & Tees		Dresses		Shirts		Shoes	
Model	R@10	R@50	R@10	R@50	R@10	R@50	R@10	R@50
SynthTriplet GAN :								
$(L_D)_C, (L_G)_C$	18.0	40.9	13.4	32.9	12.6	33.3	35.8	57.9
$(L_D)_W, (L_G)_W$	25.3	47.6	17.1	38.0	17.3	39.5	40.2	61.3
$(L_D)_T, (L_G)_T$	**28.01**	**52.1**	**22.6**	**45.1**	**20.5**	**44.08**	**47.6**	**73.6**

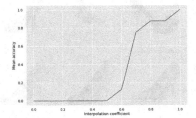 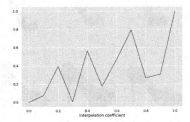

Fig. 7. Interpolation between learned embeddings gives a smooth transition between predicted attribute classes (on the left) compared to classificator predictions on baseline [4] multimodal embeddings (on the right). Illustration shows single attribute classificator (*striped*) prediction accuracy on validation set images and text query interpolation from "plain shirt" to "striped shirt".

network. To visualize this, we linearly interpolate between two sentences for the same source image. We fix the image embeddings so that differences relative to text are observed. As shown in Fig. 1, the generated images from interpolated embeddings demonstrate gradual changes in sentence meanings (e.g. from "blue shirt" to "yellow shirt"), while keeping plausible shapes and source image structure. The green color emerges halfway between "blue" and "yellow," following the natural linear interpolation of mixing color shades. By using shallow one layer neural network color attribute classifiers, (with visual features extracted from a pre-trained ResNet101 [32]), we also verify how predicted color values gradually change while interpolating between the embeddings of text queries (see Fig. 8).

In addition, we compare the results of the embedding space learned by SynthTriplet GAN to those of a baseline method not using GAN and find that the embeddings learned by our network provide a smoother surface when interpolating between embeddings (see Fig. 7).

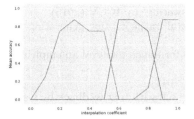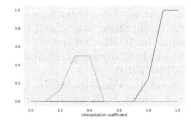

Fig. 8. Color classificator values while interpolating between embeddings of text queries "yellow" and "blue" (on the left) and from "yellow" to "red" (on the right). Classificator predictions are illustrated with respective color lines and they gradually change between classes with some new color classes emerging in between. (Color figure online)

5   Conclusions

In this paper, we address the problem of multimodal retrieval with synthetic query expansion. We propose a novel method SynthTriplet GAN based on generative adversarial networks and triplet loss, as well as a novel triplet selection method with synthetic anchor image generation and show that this helps improve the retrieval results. Finally, we demonstrate the explainability of the multimodal embedding space learned with SynthTriplet GAN.

Acknowledgment. This research was funded by Foundation for Polish Science (grant no POIR.04.04.00-00-14DE/18–00 carried out within the Team-Net program co-financed by the European Union under the European Regional Development Fund) and National Science Centre, Poland (grant no 2020/39/B/ST6/01511).

References

1. Sivic, J., Zisserman, A.: Video google: efficient visual search of videos (2006)
2. Xie, L., Wang, J., Zhang, B., Tian, Q.: Fine-grained image search. IEEE Multimedia **17**, 634–647 (2015)
3. Guo, X., Wu, H., Gao, Y., Rennie, S., Feris, R.: The fashion IQ dataset: retrieving images by combining side information and relative natural language feedback. Tech. Rep. (2019)
4. Tautkute, I., Trzcinski, T., Skorupa, A., Marasek, K., Brocki, L.: Deepstyle: multimodal search engine for fashion and interior design. IEEE Access **7**, 84613–84628 (2019)
5. Guo, X., Wu, H., Cheng, Y., Rennie, S., Tesauro, G., Feris, R.S.: Dialog-based interactive image retrieval. In: NIPS (2018)
6. Huang, J., Feris, R.S., Chen, Q., Yan, S.: Cross-domain image retrieval with a dual attribute-aware ranking network. In: ICCV (2015)
7. Hsiao, W.L., Grauman, K.: Creating capsule wardrobes from fashion images. In: CVPR (2018)
8. Zhao, B., Feng, J., Wu, X., Yan, S.: Memory-augmented attribute manipulation networks for interactive fashion search. In: CVPR (2017)

9. Antol, S., et al.: Vqa: visual question answering. In: ICCV (2015)
10. Xu, K., et al.: Show, attend and tell: neural image caption generation with visual attention. In: ICML (2015)
11. Vo, N., et al.: Composing text and image for image retrieval an empirical odyssey. In: CVPR (2019)
12. Das, A., et al.: Visual dialog. In: CVPR (2017)
13. Chen, Y., Gong, S., Bazzani, L.: Image search with text feedback by visiolinguistic attention learning. In: Proceedings of the IEEE/CVF Conference on Computer Vision and Pattern Recognition (CVPR), June 2020
14. Goodfellow, I., et al.: Generative adversarial nets. In: NIPS (2014)
15. Mirza, M., Osindero, S.: Conditional generative adversarial nets (2014)
16. Reed, S., Akata, Z., Yan, X., Logeswaran, L., Schiele, B., Lee, H.: Generative adversarial text to image synthesis. In: ICML (2016)
17. Dixit, M., Kwitt, R., Niethammer, M., Vasconcelos, N.: Aga: attribute guided augmentation. In: CVPR (2017)
18. Xu, T., et al.: AttnGAN: fine-grained text to image generation with attentional generative adversarial networks. In: CVPR (2018)
19. DALLE: creating images from text (2021). https://openai.com/blog/dall-e/,
20. Zhang, H., et al.: StackGAN: text to photo-realistic image synthesis with stacked generative adversarial networks. In: CVPR (2017)
21. Nam, S., Kim, Y., Kim, S.J.: Text-adaptive generative adversarial networks: manipulating images with natural language. In: NeurIPS (2018)
22. Cheng, Y., Gan, Z., Li, Y., Liu, J., Gao, J.: Sequential attention GAN for interactive image editing via dialogue. Tech. Rep. (2018)
23. Deng, J., Dong, W., Socher, R., Li, L.J., Li, K., Fei-Fei, L.: ImageNet: a large-scale hierarchical image database. In: CVPR (2009)
24. Muja, M., Lowe, D.: Fast approximate nearest neighbors with automatic algorithm configuration. VISAPP **1**, 331–340 (2009)
25. Johnson, J., Douze, M., Jégou, H.: Billion-scale similarity search with gpus. arXiv preprint arXiv:1702.08734 (2017)
26. Schroff, F., Kalenichenko, D., Philbin, J.: Facenet: a unified embedding for face recognition and clustering. In: CVPR (2015)
27. Gulrajani, I., Ahmed, F., Arjovsky, M., Dumoulin, V., Courville, A.: Improved training of wasserstein gans. In: Proceedings of the 31st International Conference on Neural Information Processing Systems (2017)
28. He, Z., Zuo, W., Kan, M., Shan, S., Chen, X.: Arbitrary facial attribute editing: only change what you want. arXiv preprint, arXiv:1711.10678 (2017)
29. Kim, J.H., et al.: Multimodal residual learning for visual qa. In: NeurIPS (2016)
30. Perez, E., Strub, F., Vries, H.D., Moulin, V.D., Courville, A.: Film: visual reasoning with a general conditioning layer. In: AAAI (2018)
31. Heusel, M., Ramsauer, H., Unterthiner, T., Nessler, B., Hochreiter, S.: Gans trained by a two time-scale update rule converge to a local nash equilibrium. In: NeurIPS (2017)
32. He, K., Zhang, X., Ren, S., Sun, J.: Deep residual learning for image recognition. In: CVPR (2016)

SS-CCN: Scale Self-guided Crowd Counting Network

Jinfang Zheng[1], Jinyang Xie[1], Chen Lyu[1,2], and Lei Lyu[1,2(✉)]

[1] School of Information Science and Engineering, Shandong Normal University,
250358 Jinan, China
{lvchen,lvlei}@sdnu.edu.cn
[2] Shandong Provincial Key Laboratory for Distributed Computer Software Novel
Technology, 250358 Jinan, China

Abstract. With the emergence of deep learning, many CNN-based methods have achieved competitive performance in crowd counting, in which how to effectively solve the scale variation problem plays a key role. To tackle with the problem, we present an innovative scale self-guided crowd counting network (SS-CCN) by taking full advantage of scale information in a multi-level network. The proposed SS-CCN highlights crowd information by applying scale enhancement and scale-aware attention modules in multi-level features. Moreover, semantic attention module is applied on deep layers to extract semantic information. Besides, the fine-grained residual module is proposed to further refine the crowd information. Furthermore, we pioneer a scale pyramid loss with different loss functions applied to different scales. Integrating the proposed module, our method can effectively solve the scale variation problem. Extensive experimental results on several public datasets show that our proposed SS-CCN achieves satisfactory and superior performance compared to the state-of-the-art methods.

Keywords: Crowd counting · Deep learning · Attention mechanism · Scale-aware · Scale pyramid loss

1 Introduction

As urbanization accelerates, crowds are gathering more frequently, placing higher demands on effective security monitoring, urban planning, and disaster relief. Therefore, crowd counting is quite crucial. The crowd counting task is to estimate the number and distribution of people in a crowd. In recent years, with the success of deep learning, crowd counting has achieved significant progress. However, due to the scale variation problem, it remains a daunting task, manifesting that the size of the human head varies greatly by camera view or camera position. Scale variation imposes stringent requirements on the robustness of crowd counting algorithms.

To alleviate counting errors caused by the scale variation. HA-CCN [1] applies pixel-wise attention on the feature maps. CP-CNN [2] utilizes a multi-column

© Springer Nature Switzerland AG 2021
T. Mantoro et al. (Eds.): ICONIP 2021, LNCS 13111, pp. 299–310, 2021.
https://doi.org/10.1007/978-3-030-92273-3_25

architecture to generate a high-dimensional feature map from the input image. However, scale variation is still far from being addressed. On the one hand, directly connecting all levels of feature maps without weighting their importance is not the best way to effectively fuse them. On the other hand, treating each input pixel equally ignores their specificity in scale.

Therefore, in this paper, we are committed to solving the scale variation problem. We propose a scale self-guided crowd counting network (SS-CCN) in a U-shape encoder-decoder structure. In the encoder and decoder parts, we construct a skip connection based on the scale enhancement module and scale-aware attention module. In the final part of decoding, we construct the fine-grained residual module to perform information aggregation. In addition, we design a novel scale pyramid loss to generate high-quality density maps by optimizing the structural information at multiple scales.

The main contributions can be summarized as follows:

- We propose a scale self-guided crowd counting network which can effectively utilize the scale information in a multi-level network to solve the scale variation problem in crowd scenes.
- We design a scale enhancement module and a scale-aware attention module to focus on crowd information at different scales. By using these two modules in concert to make skip connections, the crowd regions can be effectively highlighted.
- We propose a scale pyramid loss by optimizing the structural information at multiple scales to supervise the scale-dependent output.
- We propose a fine-grained residual module employing a residual module on dilated convolution to further refine the crowd information.

2   Related Work

2.1   Crowd Counting

Crowd counting from traditional methods [3,4] to CNN-based methods [1,5] has made progressive improvements. We classify CNN-based crowd counting methods into multi-column based methods and multi-level based methods, which are highly relevant to our proposed method.

Multi-Column Based Methods. The multi-column based methods adopt multi-column architectures or stack multi-branch modules to obtain rich multi-scale feature representations. MCNN [6] constructs a three-branch network with different filter sizes to capture features. Similar to MCNN, Switching-CNN [7] also uses a three-branch architecture but adds an additional classifier to select the branches to be predicted. Instead of using different filter sizes, CrowdNet [22] designs each branch with different convolution depths, and then the low-level features in the shallow branches are combined with the high-level features in the deep branches. Unlike the above methods, DADNet [8] uses four parallel columns with different dilated rates to capture multi-scale features.

Multi-Level Based Methods. The multi-level based methods learn multi-scale representations from multiple layers of the CNN and are significantly more efficient than multi-column based methods. DSSINet [9] extracts features at each level from the corresponding images in the input pyramid. AMRNet [10] introduces a scale-aware module to fully utilize multi-level features. AMSNet [11] uses a new combination of multi-scale feature extraction and fusion units by introducing NAS. CFANet [12] designs a coarse-to-fine attention mechanism using multi-level features. This kind of methods have been shown to be efficient and effective, but still fails to pay explicit attention to the scale variation problem.

2.2   Attention Based Methods

Attention based methods can perceive the scale diversity of multi-level features. Such methods have demonstrated their effectiveness in deep learning tasks. SCAR [13] uses spatial and channel attention regression networks to generate high-quality density maps. CFANet [12] adopts a multi-scale attention combination method to enhance the attention effects. SDANet [14] reduces the influence of background by an attention model based on shallow features. In this paper, we design a novel scale-aware attention module to solve the difficult scale variation problem. Unlike the above methods, our proposed attention module is focused on the level of scale in the crowd.

3   Scale Self-guided Crowd Counting Network

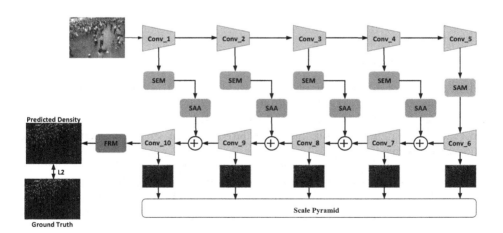

Fig. 1. The detailed structure of the proposed SS-CCN.

3.1   Overview

As shown in Fig. 1, our network consists of five main modules: the encoder module, the decoder module, scale enhancement module, scale attention module and fine-grained residual module. Specifically, in the encoder module, a pre-trained VGG-16 [15] model is chosen as the backbone network for feature extraction. In the decoder module, we perform 32-fold upsampling operations to implement information aggregation at different resolutions. Meanwhile, we use skip connections based on scale enhancement and scale attention modules between the encoder and decode modules for feature reuse and focus on crowd regions at different scales. In the end, the fine-grained residual module is followed to further accurate crowd information. In addition, to ensure that each scale-dependent output is optimized in a particular direction, we propose a scale pyramid loss. More details are explained in the following subsections.

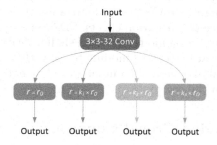

Fig. 2. Details of the scale enhancement module where $r_0 = 2$, $k_1 = 2$, $k_2 = 4$, $k_3 = 6$.

3.2   Scale Enhancement Module

Many previous works usually utilize pyramid pooling to extract multi-scale features. However, large scale pooling often results in the loss of important information. In this paper, we propose a scale enhancement module (SEM), as shown in Fig. 2, which contains four parallel dilated convolutions with dilated rate of 2, 4, 8, 12, respectively.

Specifically, for the given side feature maps f_1, f_2, f_3, f_4, f_5 generated by the encoder module, we use four dilated convolutions with the receptive field of 5×5, 9×9,17×17, 25×25 to capture multi-scale context information. Then the multi-scale contextual features are obtained $f_i^2, f_i^4, f_i^8, f_i^{12}(i = 1, 2, 3, 4, 5)$ by applying SEM to multi-level feature maps.

3.3   Scale-Aware Attention

Though multi-level features can effectively capture the global context information by adopting SEM, they contain crowd information and complex background information. Therefore, we specifically propose a scale-aware attention (SAA) module that can learn to weight the multi-scale features for highlighting the useful crowd context information.

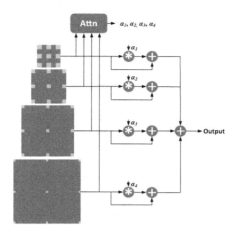

Fig. 3. Details of the scale-aware attention.

Figure 3 shows the structure of scale-aware attention module. The proposed SAA takes as input the multi-scale features from SEM. And it contains two layers, the first layer has 128 filters with kernel size 3 × 3 and the second layer has S filters with kernel size of 1 × 1 where S is the number of scales employed of 4. Formally, given a feature map $X \in R^{C \times H \times W}$, the convolutional layer CL_1 with a channel of 128 is performed first to produce $Y \in R^{C' \times H \times W}$. Then the Y passes through the convolutional layer CL_2 with a channel of 4 to produce scale-aware attention features S_c.

$$S_c = ReLU \left(CL_2(Y) \right) \tag{1}$$

where $ReLU()$ is an activation function.

Then the scale-aware attention S_a vector is generated based on S_c.

$$S_a = Sigmoid \left(S_c \right) \tag{2}$$

where $Sigmoid()$ represents the sigmoid function.

The intermediate feature X_s is generated through element-wise weighting on input X.

$$X_s = X \otimes S_a \tag{3}$$

The output X_{saa} of SAA module is then calculated in a residual block by Eq. 4.

$$X_{saa} = X + X_s \tag{4}$$

The SAA determines how much attention is given to features at different scales. It further visualizes the attention at each scale.

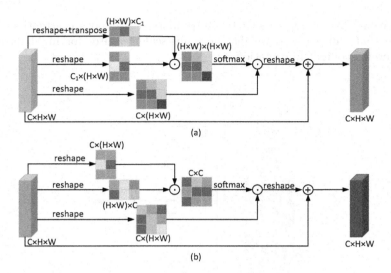

Fig. 4. The structure of the semantic attention module consisting of SA and CA. (a) SA. (b) CA.

3.4 Semantic Attention

In addition, considering that deep features have richer semantic information and less noise, we propose a Semantic Attention Module (SAM) on deep layers which contains a spatial attention (SA) module and a channel attention (CA) module.

Spatial Attention Module. The SA is shown in Fig. 4 (a). For a given feature map X with the size of $C \times H \times W$, it is fed into three different 1×1 convolutional layers. Then the three feature maps $X_1 \in R^{(HW) \times C_1}$, $X_2 \in R^{C_1 \times (HW)}$ and $X_3 \in R^{C \times (HW)}$ are attained by reshape operation. A spatial attention map S_a is generated by applying a matrix multiplication and softmax operation for X_1 and X_2.

$$SP_a = Sof\left(X_1 \odot X_2\right) \tag{5}$$

where $Sof(*)$ represents softmax operation, $\odot$ represents matrix product.

After getting SP_a, the output of X_{final} is then calculated in a residual block.

$$X_{final} = X + (SP_a \odot X_3) \tag{6}$$

Channel Attention Module. Similar to the structure of SA module, the details of CA module are shown in Fig. 4 (b). Specifically, for a given feature map X with the size of $C \times H \times W$, the feature map is reshaped as $X_4 \in R^{C \times (HW)}$ and $X_5 \in R^{(HW) \times C}$. Then a channel attention map C_a is generated by applying a matrix multiplication and softmax operation for X_4 and X_5.

$$C_a = Sof\left(X_4 \odot X_5\right) \tag{7}$$

After getting C_a, the output of X_{cfinal} is then calculated in a residual block.

$$X_{cfinal} = X + \left(X_4 \odot C_a\right) \tag{8}$$

3.5   Fine-Grained Residual Module

To further acquire accurate crowd location information, we propose a fine-grained residual module (Fig. 5) for density estimation, which approximates a conventional convolution with a filter size of $k \times k$. And a 1×1 convolution is used for feature fusion after a multi-branch convolution concatenation. In addition, We set all the convolutions to be dilated convolutions to expand the receptive field without increasing the parameters

3.6   Scale Pyramid Loss

The Euclidean distance is used to define the loss of density map.

$$L2 = \frac{1}{2\,N}\sum_{i=1}^{N}\left\|F\left(X_i;\theta\right) - D_i\right\|_2^2 \tag{9}$$

where N is the number of training images, X_i is the ith input image, $F(X_i;\theta)$ denotes the estimated density, D_i represents the ground truth density map.

Usually, this loss is only calculated between the final density map and the ground truth map, ignoring local details. In this paper, we propose a novel scale pyramid loss (SPL) to better supervise different scales to achieve pixel-level accuracy.

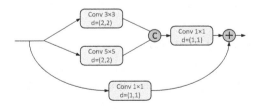

Fig. 5. Details of the fine-grained residual module.

Specifically, we feed the ground-truth G to average pooling, obtaining the ground-truth pyramid $G_i(i = 1, 2, 3, 4, 5)$ where the sizes of convolutional filters are 1, 2, 4, 8, 16, respectively. For the coarser strides 16 and 8, we use the cross-entropy loss. For the output of the finer stride 1, we use $L2$ loss. And we use the average of the cross-entropy and $L2$ losses for the intermediate strides 4 and 2. Different loss functions are applied for different strides to guide the multi-scale prediction toward its corresponding scale map for optimization.

Our SPL is computed as:

$$L = L_{CE}^{16} + L_{CE}^{8} + \frac{1}{2}\left(L_2^4 + L_{CE}^4\right) + \frac{1}{2}\left(L_2^2 + L_{CE}^2\right) + L_2^1 + L_2^0 \qquad (10)$$

where L_{CE}^{16}, L_{CE}^{8} , L_{CE}^{4} , L_{CE}^{2} denote cross-entropy loss for output strides 16, 8, 4 and 2, respectively. L_2^4, L_2^2, L_2^1 denote $L2$ loss for output strides 4, 2 and 1, respectively. L_2^0 denote $L2$ loss for final output.

4   Experiments

4.1   Training Details

We utilize the pre-trained VGG-16 to initialize the parameters of the first 13 layers of our model and use a Gaussian distribution with $\delta = 0.01$ to randomly initialize the parameters of the other convolutional layers. The network is trained end-to-end using the Adam optimizer with a learning rate of 1e-5. The batch size is set to 6. The model is trained with the loss L (Eq. (10)).

4.2   Evaluation Metrics

We use mean absolute error (MAE) and root mean square error (RMSE) as evaluation metrics.

$$MAE = \frac{1}{N}\sum_{i=1}^{N}|C_i^{ES} - C_i^{GT}|, RMSE = \sqrt{\frac{1}{N}\sum_{i=1}^{N}(C_i^{ES} - C_i^{GT})^2} \qquad (11)$$

where N is the total number of the test images, C_i^{ES} and C_i^{GT} stand for the estimated and ground-truth counts of the ith image, respectively.

4.3   Comparisons with State-of-the-Art

We compare our method with state-of-the-art methods on three challenging datasets including: the ShanghaiTech dataset [6], the UCF_CC_50 dataset [4], and the UCF-QNRF dataset [16]. The results are shown in Table 1.

ShanghaiTech Dataset. Our method achieves the best performance on both Part A and Part B, as shown in Table 1. Specifically, for the Part A with highly crowded scenes, our method reduces MAE by 1.43% and RMSE by 2.23% compared to the second-best method. For the Part B with relatively sparse scenes, compared to the second-best method, our method reduces MAE by 2.00% and RMSE by 6.08%.

Table 1. Comparisons of SS-CCN and state-of-the-art methods on three datasets.

Dataset	Part A		Part B		UCF_CC_50		UCF-QNRF	
Method	MAE	RMSE	MAE	RMSE	MAE	RMSE	MAE	RMSE
MCNN [17]	110.2	173.2	26.4	41.3	377.6	509.1	277.0	426.0
CSRNet [18]	68.2	115.0	10.6	16.0	266.1	397.5	120.3	208.5
TEDNet [19]	64.2	109.1	8.2	12.8	249.4	354.5	113	188
BL [20]	62.8	101.8	7.7	12.7	229.3	308.2	88.7	154.8
ASNet [5]	57.78	90.13	-	-	174.84	251.63	91.59	159.71
AMSNet [11]	56.7	93.4	6.7	10.2	208.4	297.3	101.8	163.2
AMRNet [10]	61.59	98.36	7.02	11.00	184.0	265.8	86.6	152.2
CFANet [12]	56.1	89.6	6.5	10.2	203.6	287.3	89.0	152.3
SS-CCN(ours)	**55.3**	**87.6**	**6.37**	**9.58**	**167.8**	**243.6**	**84.3**	**148.6**

UCF_CC_50 Dataset. We conduct five-fold cross validation on UCF_CC_50 dataset. The results are shown in Table 1. Our method surpasses all other methods especially.Compared with the second-best method, the MAE and RMSE are reduced by 4.03% and 3.19%, respectively,

UCF-QNRF Dataset. On this dataset, our method achieves the first-best values with MAE of 84.3 and RMSE of 148.6 compared with eight state-of-the-art methods, as shown in Table 1.

In summary, on the ShanghaiTech, the UCF_CC_50, and the UCF-QNRF datasets, we go beyond the current state-of-the-art methods. We also qualitatively analyze our method by visualizing density maps on the ShanghaiTech dataset. As shown in Fig. 6, our method can generate high quality density maps and perform accurate crowd counting. In addition, we also give the visualization results of CSRNet and SFCN [21]. It is worth noting that we effectively solve the problem of missing counts and redundant counts due to the scale variation.

Table 2. Ablation studies on ShanghaiTech Part A. The first five rows represent SS-CCN without SEM, SAA, SA, CA, FRM respectively. The last row represents our method SS-CCN.

Method	MAE	RMSE	SEM	SAA	SA	CA	FRM
SS-CCN-sem	62.9	105.6	-	✓	✓	✓	✓
SS-CCN-saa	63.6	106.8	✓	-	✓	✓	✓
SS-CCN-sa	61.1	100.3	✓	✓	-	✓	✓
SS-CCN-ca	60.4	101.4	✓	✓	✓	-	✓
SS-CCN-frm	57.7	91.3	✓	✓	✓	✓	-
SS-CCN(ours)	**55.3**	**87.6**	✓	✓	✓	✓	✓

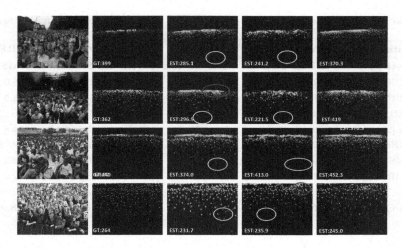

Fig. 6. Comparisons of SS-CCN with state-of-the-art methods on ShanghaiTech Part A. First column: sample images from ShanghaiTech Part A. Second column: ground-truth density maps. Third column: the results of CSRNet. Fourth column: the results of SFCN. Fifth column: the results of our SS-CCN. Yellow circles and red circles represent missing counts and redundant counts, respectively.

Table 3. Ablation study of the SPL.

Method	MAE	RMSE
Baseline + L2	59.84	104.82
Baseline + SPL	55.3	87.6

4.4   Ablation Study

On ShanghaiTech Part A dataset, we perform ablation studies to explore the roles of each component of our SS-CCN.

Table 2 shows the performance of each component used in the proposed SS-CCN. Firstly, compare with the SS-CCN, it is evident that the performance of the SS-CCN-sem deteriorates seriously, which indicates that scale enhancement is beneficial for crowd counting. Secondly, we compare the SS-CCN-saa with the SS-CCN, we can find that with SAA, the counting error is substantially reduced. Thirdly, from the comparison of the SS-CCN-sa and the SS-CCN-ca with the SS-CCN, we can see that it is useful to apply spatial attention module and channel attention module on deep layers. Finally, comparing the SS-CCN-frm with the SS-CCN, we find that although the performance gap of the two methods is tiny, the FRM plays its role and further refines the crowd information. Overall, the comparison results show that each component can be effective in improving counting performance.

Effectiveness of the SPL. To verify the effects of our SPL, we use SS-CCN for supervision with different loss functions. As shown in Table 3, the MAE and RMSE of our baseline model (SS-CCN) without SPL are 59.84 and 104.82, respectively. After integrating the SPL into the baseline model, the MAE and RMSE are 56.3 and 89.6, respectively. The relative improvement is 7.59% and 16.43%, respectively, which proves that SPL helps to supervise the scale-dependent output.

5 Conclusion

In this paper, we propose a novel Scale Self-guided Crowd Counting Network (SS-CCN) that can effectively deal with the problem of scale variation. In our method, scale enhancement module and scale-aware attention module are utilized to focus on the crowd region by taking full advantage of scale information. At the same time, we propose the semantic attention module to pay attention to semantic information on deep layers. In addition, a fine-grained residual module is specially designed at the end to refine the crowd information. Besides, we design a scale pyramid loss to reinforce the learning of scale-dependent outputs. Pixel-level accuracy is achieved by relying on local scales. Extensive experiments have shown the superior performance of our SS-CCN. In future work, we will pay more attention to how we can use scale information for more advanced crowd counting.

Acknowledgement. This work is supported by the National Natural ScienceFoundation of China (61976127).

References

1. Sindagi, V.A., Patel, V.M.: Ha-ccn: hierarchical attention-based crowd countingnetwork. IEEE Trans. Image Process **29**, 323–335 (2019)
2. Sindagi, V.A., Patel, V.M.: Generating high-quality crowd density maps usingcontextual pyramid cnns. In: Proceedings of the IEEE International Conference Oncomputer Vision, pp. 1861–1870 (2017)
3. Dollar, P., Wojek, C., Schiele, B., Perona, P.: Pedestrian detection: an evaluation ofthe state of the art. IEEE Trans. Pattern Anal. Mach. Intell. **34**(4), 743–761 (2011)
4. Idrees, H., Saleemi, I., Seibert, C., Shah, M.: Multi-source multi-scale counting inextremely dense crowd images. In: Proceedings of the IEEE Conference on Computervision and Pattern Recognition, pp. 2547–2554 (2013)
5. Jiang, X., et al.: Attention scaling for crowd counting. In: Proceedings of the IEEE/CVF Conferenceon Computer Vision and Pattern Recognition, pp. 4706–4715 (2020)
6. Zhang, Y., Zhou, D., Chen, S., Gao, S., Ma, Y.: Single-image crowd counting viamulti-column convolutional neural network. In: Proceedings of the IEEE Conferenceon Computer Vision and Pattern Recognition, pp. 589–597 (2016)

7. Sam, D.B., Surya, S., Babu, R.V.: Switching convolutional neural network forcrowd counting. In: 2017 IEEE Conference on Computer Vision and Pattern Recog-nition (CVPR), pp. 4031–4039. IEEE (2017)
8. Guo, D., Li, K., Zha, Z.J., Wang, M.: Dadnet: dilated-attention-deformable con-vnet for crowd counting. In: Proceedings of the 27th ACM International Confer-enceon Multimedia, pp. 1823–1832 (2019)
9. Liu, L., Qiu, Z., Li, G., Liu, S., Ouyang, W., Lin, L.: Crowd counting with deep-structured scale integration network. In: Proceedings of the IEEE/CVF Interna-tional Conference on Computer Vision, pp. 1774–1783 (2019)
10. Liu, X., Yang, J., Ding, W., Wang, T., Wang, Z., Xiong, J.: Adaptive mixturere-gression network with local counting map for crowd counting. In: ComputerVision - ECCV 2020–16th European Conference, pp. 241–257 (2020)
11. Hu, Y., Jiang, X., Liu, X., Zhang, B., Han, J., Cao, X., Doermann, D.S.: Nas-count:counting-by-density with neural architecture search. In: Computer Vision - ECCV2020 - 16th European Conference, pp. 747–766. Glasgow, UK 2020, Pro-ceedings, Part XXII (2020)
12. Rong, L., Li, C.: Coarse-and fine-grained attention network with background-awareloss for crowd density map estimation. In: Proceedings of the IEEE/CVF WinterConference on Applications of Computer Vision, pp. 3675–3684 (2021)
13. Gao, J., Wang, Q., Yuan, Y.: Scar: Spatial-/channel-wise attention regression net-works for crowd counting. Neurocomputing **363**, 1–8 (2019)
14. Miao, Y., Lin, Z., Ding, G., Han, J.: Shallow feature based dense attention net-work for crowd counting. In: Proceedings of the AAAI Conference on ArtificialIntelli-gence. vol. 34, pp. 11765–11772 (2020)
15. Simonyan, K., Zisserman, A.: Very deep convolutional networks for large-scaleimage recognition. In: 3rd International Conference on Learning Represen-tations, ICLR 2015, San Diego, USA, 2015, Conference Track Proceedings (2015)
16. Idrees, H., et al: Composition loss for counting, density map estimation and local-ization in densecrowds. In: Proceedings of the European Conference on Computer Vision (ECCV), pp. 532–546 (2018)
17. Zhang, C., Li, H., Wang, X., Yang, X.: Cross-scene crowd counting via deep con-volutional neural networks. In: Proceedings of the IEEE conference on computer-vision and pattern recognition, pp. 833–841 (2015)
18. Li, Y., Zhang, X., Chen, D.: Csrnet: dilated convolutional neural networks forun-derstanding the highly congested scenes. In: Proceedings of the IEEE conferenceon computer vision and pattern recognition, pp. 1091–1100 (2018)
19. Jiang, X., Xiao, Z., Zhang, B., Zhen, X., Cao, X., Doermann, D., Shao, L.: Crowd-counting and density estimation by trellis encoder-decoder networks. In: Proceed-ings of the IEEE/CVF Conference on Computer Vision and Pattern Recognition, pp. 6133–6142 (2019)
20. Ma, Z., Wei, X., Hong, X., Gong, Y.: Bayesian loss for crowd count estimation withpoint supervision. In: Proceedings of the IEEE/CVF International Conference onComputer Vision, pp. 6142–6151 (2019)
21. Wang, Q., Gao, J., Lin, W., Yuan, Y.: Learning from synthetic data for crowdcount-ing in the wild. In: Proceedings of the IEEE/CVF Conference on ComputerVision and Pattern Recognition, pp. 8198–8207 (2019)
22. Boominathan, L., Kruthiventi, S.S., Babu, R.V.: Crowdnet: a deep convolutional-network for dense crowd counting. In: Proceedings of the 24th ACM internation-alconference on Multimedia, pp. 640–644 (2016)

QS-Hyper: A Quality-Sensitive Hyper Network for the No-Reference Image Quality Assessment

Xuewen Zhang[1], Yunye Zhang[2], Wenxin Yu[1(✉)], Liang Nie[1], Ning Jiang[1], and Jun Gong[3]

[1] Southwest University of Science and Technology, Sichuan, China
yuwenxin@swust.edu.cn
[2] University of Electronic Science and Technology of China, Sichuan, China
[3] Beijing Institute of Technology, Shenzhen, China

Abstract. Blind/no-reference image quality assessment (IQA) aims to provide a quality score for a single image without references. In this context, deep learning models can capture various image artifacts, which made significant progress in this study. However, current IQA methods generally utilize the pre-trained convolution neural networks (CNNs) on classification tasks to obtain image representations, which do not perfectly represent the quality of images. In order to solve this problem, this paper uses semi-supervised representation learning to train a quality-sensitive encoder (QS-encoder), which can extract image features specifically for image quality. Intuitively, this feature is more conducive to train the IQA model than the feature used for classification tasks. Thus, QS-encoder is plunged into a carefully designed hyper network to build a quality-sensitive hyper network (QS-hyper) to solve IQA tasks in more general and complex environments. Extensive experiments on the public IQA datasets show that our method outperformed most state-of-art methods on both Pearson linear correlation coefficient (PLCC) and Spearman's rank correlation coefficient (SRCC), and it made 3% PLCC improvement and 3.9% SRCC improvement on TID2013 datasets. Therefore, it proves that our method is superior in capturing various image distortions, which meets a broader range of evaluation requirements.

Keywords: Blind image quality assessment · Representation learning · Convolution neural networks

1 Introduction

The core idea of blind image quality assessment (blind-IQA) is to capture the distortion of images and provide a quality score without any references. In the traditional task, low-quality images are general caused by compression, transmission, or improper storage, which results in some pixel-level distortion, such as white noise, blur, holes, etc. It's called degradation loss. Moreover, as people's manipulations to pictures become more complicated, the distortions of images become complex and challenging to define. In this context, any factors that

© Springer Nature Switzerland AG 2021
T. Mantoro et al. (Eds.): ICONIP 2021, LNCS 13111, pp. 311–322, 2021.
https://doi.org/10.1007/978-3-030-92273-3_26

312   X. Zhang et al.

interfere with information acquisition from images can be recognized as distortion, such as over-dark, high-brightness, ghosting, etc. In the field of IQA, these images are called distortion images in the Wild. Figure 1(a) displays the examples of degradation loss and distortion in the Wild.

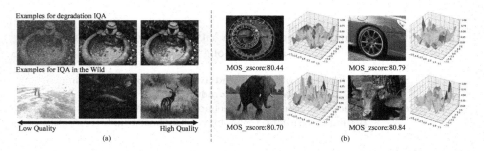

Fig. 1. (a) shows the examples of different quality of images in traditional degradation loss and image distortion in the Wild, respectively. (b) shows some images with similar quality, and a pre-trained CNN extracts the features for each of them.

Convolution neural networks (CNNs) [11] have shown great promise for dealing with IQA problems. The simplified process is that the image features extracted by CNNs are sent to fully connected layers (FCs) to map them into the latent space of image quality. However, many IQA-related datasets are too small to train a large-scale network. For example, LIVE [6] only contains 779 damaged pictures, LIVEC [6] includes 1162 pictures, etc. Therefore, pre-trained features in large-scale image datasets, such as ImageNet [5], are usually used to represent image quality. In this context, the precondition is that these features are quality-sensitive to some extent. However, these features are primarily crafted to address the classification task. We discover that the features of images with similar quality are very different (See Fig. 1(b)). These images with similar quality are all from the public IQA dataset, and z-score of the Mean Opinion Score (MOS_zscore) is the quality label. We utilized pre-trained CNNs to extract the feature of them, and features are quilt different because images are from different categories. Using these features alone may hinder the performance of the IQA model, which motivates us to propose a novel quality-sensitive encoder (QS-encoder) to obtain the representation for the image quality.

A straightforward method to obtain a QS-encoder is to train a CNN directly with enough images with quality labels. However, as mentioned above, the scale of commonly used image quality assessment datasets is small due to the high cost of producing subjective quality annotation [21]. Therefore, this paper proposes to utilize representation learning [3,4,7,9] to learn a quality-sensitive image representation without large-scale labeled datasets. In practice, we adopt a semi-supervised strategy to train a QS-encoder with large numbers of unlabeled images and a few labeled images. Experiments have shown that this encoder contributes a lot while training the image quality evaluation model, which ultimately surpasses the state-of-art methods. For this paper, the main contributions are as follows:

1. For the first time, a quality-sensitive encoder (QS-encoder) base on representation learning is proposed to obtain image quality-sensitive features without any large-scale labeled datasets.
2. We plunge QS-encode into a carefully designed hyper network to get a quality-sensitive hyper network (QS-hyper) to achieve blind image quality assessment.
3. We conduct extensive experiments on public image quality assessment datasets to prove the effectiveness of the proposed method.

2 Related Work

2.1 Blind Image Quality Assessment

Full-reference IQA methods, such as Peak Signal to Noise Ratio (PSNR) and Structural Similarity (SSIM), work by calculating the error between the image and its reference image. Reduce-reference IQA methods generally calculate the error on features level, but the reference is still indispensable. In contrast, blind/no-reference IQA can independently evaluate pictures through prior knowledge, which is more flexible and applied in broader situations. More recently, the targets and approaches of blind IQA have significantly changed.

On the one hand, studies began to focus on more complex IQA tasks. Traditional degradation distortion (such as white noise in the first row in Fig. 1(a)) is predefined and easy to capture. Recently, methods have already achieved excellent results on degradation IQA datasets [1,12–15,18,19,24]. However, these kinds of image evaluation models are limited in generalization, and general IQA in the Wild has attracted extensive studies [18,24]. The principle of IQA in the Wild tells that any factor preventing people from accessing picture information should be judged as distortion, such as high-brightness, over-darkness, ghosting, etc. IQA in the Wild is still an open problem because various and unknown distortions are difficult to capture. Besides, some particular IQA areas have also received attention, such as facial picture evaluation [16] and assessment of the generated images by generative adversarial networks (GANs) [22,23].

On the other hand, the approaches to represent the quality of image have improved a lot. Generally, blind IQA includes two fundamental steps. The primary one is to extract image features corresponding to the quality, and the next step is to learn a map from such features to quality latent space. According to investigations, IQA methods are based on hand-craft features or learning features. Previous studies base on hand-craft features, which benefit from the natural scene statistics (NSS) theory. NSS believes that high-quality natural scene pictures have a specific statistical distribution, which will be distorted when the image quality is damaged. The metrics that can describe such statistics include discrete wavelet coefficients [15], generalized Gaussian distribution (GGD)/asymmetric generalized Gaussian distribution (AGGD) [14], Weibull distribution [20], and histogram counting [19], etc. These metrics can produce many quality-aspect features, which are mapped to quality space according to machine learning methods such as support vector regression (SVR). In contrast, learning-based features include more information, which shows great promise for more complex IQA tasks. Generally, features from the pre-train CNNs are input to an elaborately designed structure to achieve excellent results. [1] divide the image into several patches to feed a quality regression model. [13] and [12] obtain comparative quality information by the Siamese network [2] and GANs, respectively. [24] starts from the problem of insufficiency of the dataset and applies meta-learning to the field of IQA. It is worth emphasizing that [18] employs a hyper network to generate an exclusive quality prediction network for each image, which improves the quality sensitivity of pre-training features. This method eventually achieves the state-of-art effect on the IQA datasets in the Wild. The mentioned learning-based methods utilized well-designed structures to solve the IQA problems, but they use category-based features that not specific to quality assessment. The difference between theirs and ours is that we aim to construct a quality-sensitive representation via representation learning to ease the mapping process from image features to quality latent space.

2.2   Representation Learning

Representation learning methods aim to discover the features that can represent the image without any label. More recently, many algorithms can achieve it, for example, the traditional clustering-based algorithm [3] and methods based on contrastive learning [4,7,9]. The core idea of contrastive learning is to attract positive pairs and repulse negative pairs. Siamese network [2] plays an essential role in representation learning, especially, [4] proposed a simple Siamese network, which used gradient stopping trick to avoid model collapse and achieved good results on low computational cost. Motivated by it, this paper makes a hypothesis that these label-free features are more likely to guide as quality-sensitive image features than pre-training features specified in the category task. Thus, a quality sensitive encoder can be trained with this strategy and a few samples with quality annotation.

3   Our Proposal

Ideally, any distortion that hinders information acquisition from pictures should be captured by the algorithm and affect quality scores. However, image features from pre-trained CNNs are category-based and not entirely suited for quality assessment. To deal with this issue, this paper plunges a quality sensitive encoder (QS-encoder) into a hyper network to obtain a quality-sensitive hyper network (QS-hyper), and Fig. 2 shows its structure.

3.1   Preliminaries

Hyper Network for Blind Image Quality Assessment. The core idea of hyper-IQA [18] is to construct an exclusive quality prediction network for each input image. These quality prediction networks have the same structure, but the semantics of each image determines its parameters. The quality score s is provided by it.

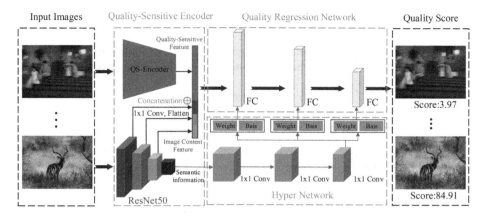

Fig. 2. The structure of the quality-sensitive hyper network (QS-hyper). Quality-sensitive encoder aims to obtain the input feature of quality regression network. The hyper network can generate parameters for the quality regression network.

$$s = f(x_{rep}; \theta) \tag{1}$$

Where $f(.)$ denotes fully connected layers (FCs), x_{rep} denotes image representation, and θ is parameter. Image representation and semantic information are determined by the backbone network, such as ResNet-50 [8]. Therefore, θ and x_{rep} are defined as follows.

$$x_{rep} = rep(x) = C(B_1(x), B_2(x), ..., B_i(x)) \tag{2}$$

$$\theta = H(B(x), \epsilon) \tag{3}$$

Where x is the input image, B is the backbone network ResNet-50, $B_i(.)$ refers to the flatten operation after 1x1 convolution on the $i-th$ feature map of B, and the $C(.)$ is concatenation operation. $H(.)$ is a hyper network that generates weight and bias for the quality prediction network f, and ϵ is the parameters of H. Eventually, the score can be expressed by the following formula.

$$s = f(rep(x), H(B(x), \epsilon)) \tag{4}$$

Simple Siamese for Representation Learning. Without any label guidance, the representation of the image can still be obtained with Siamese representation learning [4]. The specific strategy is as follows. Firstly, we input two different augmentations of the same picture into a share-parameter encoder to get the features. Secondly, the distance should be small after these two features are mapped into the similarity latent space by the same function. For each input picture x, an image pair is got by random augmentation.

$$x_1 = aug1(x), x_2 = aug2(x) \tag{5}$$

These augmentation methods are usually random combinations of some image manipulations, such as cropping, rotation, flipping, filtering, etc. Subsequently, a share-parameter encoder is employed to extract features of the pair, which are then sent to a mapping function. The loss is calculated in the similarity latent space.

$$loss_{rl} = D(p(g(x_1)), p(g(x_2))) \qquad (6)$$

Where $D(.)$ calculates the cosine similarity between two vectors, $g(.)$ is the share-parameter encoder, and $p(.)$ is the mapping function. [4] propose a trick to avoid model collapse while saving computing resources. Following their work, the final loss is defined as follows.

$$loss_{rl} = \frac{1}{2}D(p(g(x_1)), stopgrad(g(x_2))) + \frac{1}{2}D(p(g(x_2)), stopgrad(g(x_1))) \quad (7)$$

Where $stopgrad(.)$ is a gradient-stop trick to achieve the alternate reaction of the gradients in two branches.

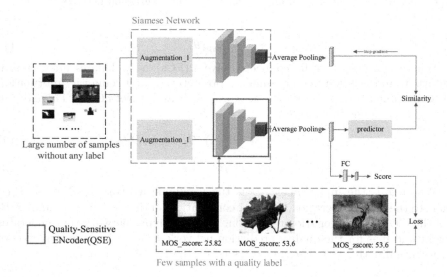

Fig. 3. Process of training the quality-sensitive encoder (QS-encoder).

3.2   Quality-Sensitive Encoder

IQA task is different from the classification task. A simple example is that the quality of two bird images may be completely different, and a bird picture may have the same quality level as a car picture. Previous IQA methods generally learn the mapping from classification features to quality scores, which limits the capabilities of the model. As shown in Fig. 3, this paper proposes a quality-sensitive encoder (QS-encoder) to obtain the representation corresponding to image quality so that the score prediction model can efficiently mapping them to quality latent space.

The body of the QS-encoder is a Siamese network with a multi-layer convolutional network. According to formula (7), it will obtain a raw encoder by minimizing $loss_{rl}$. Furthermore, this encoder can extract image features that contain more information because the training process is label-free. For example, when training a model with a category label, the model maintains the features corresponding to the image category but ignores the features about image quality. Thus, a model trained without category labels is more likely to preserve quality features. Therefore, this paper adopts a semi-supervised strategy to enforce this quality aspect. Firstly, two FCs are utilized to map the representation to the quality score, and $L1$ loss is used to optimized the model. Secondly, the raw encoder will become quality-sensitive by introducing a small number of image samples with quality labels.

$$v_r = QS\_encoder(x) \tag{8}$$

$$loss_{quality} = |t(v_r) - y| \tag{9}$$

Where $QS\_encoder(.)$ initialize with parameters of row encoder $g(.)$, $t(.)$ is a temporary mapping function to map image features to quality space. It will be withdrawn after the training process finish. y is the ground truth of quality score. Thus, a special QS-encoder for IQA tasks is obtained without the large-scale labeled datasets.

3.3 Quality-Sensitive Hyper Network

Deep feature maps of CNNs usually describe image semantic information, and these features are quite different among images with different contents, which not perfect for the IQA model. Therefore, this paper improves the hyper-IQA [18] and proposes a quality-sensitive hyper network (QS-hyper). As shown in the Fig. 2, after the target image is input to QS-encoder and ResNet-50 backbone, the content features of the image are represented by 1x1 convolution on multiple intermediate layers of the backbone. In contrast, the quality features are obtained by QS-encoder, which are input to the score prediction network after concate with content features. The output of the backbone represents the semantics of the image and is input to the hyper network to generate the parameters of the quality prediction network. The final optimization function is defined as the following formula.

$$x_{QS} = C(rep(x), QS\_encoder(x)) \tag{10}$$

$$\mathcal{L} = |f(x_{QS}, H(B(x), \epsilon)) - y| + loss_{rl} + loss_{quality} \tag{11}$$

Where quality prediction score function is as in formula (4), $C(.)$ is concatenation operation, y represents ground truth of image quality. Indeed, QS-hyper is designed for supervised learning, and QS-encoder is obtained with semi-supervised learning.

4 Experimental Results

In this section, we conducted extensive experiments to verify the effectiveness of our method, and the arrangement is as follows. Firstly, the datasets, implementation detail of our experiments, and evaluation metrics will be described. Secondly, we conduct a sufficient comparative experiment to prove the advantages of our method. Finally, further analysis and discussion will explain why QS-hyper works.

4.1 Dataset

Our experiments are conducted in two types of IQA datasets, traditional degradation images and distortion images in the Wild. According to Mean Opinion Scores (MOS), each image was viewed and rated. For the degradation images, we implement our model on LIVE [6] and TID2013 [17] which contain 779 and 3,000 images, respectively. And experiments also include IQA datasets in the Wild. LIVE-Challenge [6] contains 1,162 authentically distorted images captured from many diverse mobile devices. KonIQ-10k [10] contains 10,073 picture samples to ensure the diversity of content and distortion types. For each image sample, 120 reliable quality ratings are given by multiple workers. All datasets are divided into two parts during the training process, 80% of the samples are used for training, and 20% of the samples are used for testing.

4.2 Implementation Details

All our experiments are implemented on PyTorch with two NVIDIA 1080Ti GPUs. In terms of the QS-encoder, 15,000 distortion images without any labels are used to conduct unsupervised training to get the raw encoder. And 1,942 images with score labels are used to train QS-encoder. First, we randomly crop the images to 224×224 size and perform random flips. Next, its brightness, contrast, saturation, and hue are randomly changed according to the ratio of 0.2, and the execution probability of each operation is 80%. Finally, we set the batch size to 64 and use the Adam optimizer with a 0.9 of momentum and a 0.0005 weight decay to train 100 epochs. The hyperparameters of the hyper network follow [18]. And the input to the quality prediction network contains 50% quality-sensitive features and 50% content features, dimensions of each feature set to 1024.

4.3 Evaluation Metrics

This paper uses the Pearson linear correlation coefficient (PLCC) and Spearman's rank correlation coefficient (SRCC) to measure the correlation between the quality prediction score and ground truth. The higher the values of these two indicators, the more consistent the quality prediction is with human perception.

4.4 Comparison with Baseline

To make a comparison with the baselines, this paper selects the NSS methods with hand-craft features, such as ILNIQE [20] and BRISQUE [14]. Also, it selects the methods with learning features, such as WaDIQaM [1], metaIQA [24] and HyperIQA [18]. WaDIQam is a typical deep-learning-based method, while metaIQA and HyperIQA are the current state-of-art IQA algorithms. We keep the model parameters consistent with the original paper and unify the division of the dataset. Finally, we train the model to convergence and repeat 10 rounds to calculate the average values to reduce the error.

Table 1. Comparison results with baselines are displayed on four public IQA datasets by PLCC and SRCC.

Dataset	LIVEC		KonIQ-10K		LIVE		TID2013	
	PLCC↑	SRCC↑	PLCC↑	SRCC↑	PLCC↑	SRCC↑	PLCC↑	SRCC↑
ILNIQE [20]	54.9	51.3	53.1	50.4	90.6	91.3	64.8	52.1
BRISQUE [14]	63.2	60.7	60.9	56.9	94.2	93.6	65.1	57.3
WaDIQaM [1]	68.0	67.1	78.3	76.8	**96.3**	95.4	85.5	83.5
MetaIQA [24]	83.5	80.2	88.7	85.0	-	-	-	85.3
HyperIQA [18]	87.5	84.8	91.7	90.6	96.1	95.0	87.5	83.3
Ours	**88.5**	**87.7**	**92.5**	**90.9**	96.2	**96.0**	**90.5**	**87.2**

As shown in Table 1, our method achieved the best results in all datasets except for the LIVE. We analyze the reasons as follows. Firstly, there are only 29 pictures with different content and 5 different types of distortion in LIVE. The QS-encoder aims to enhance the model's ability to capture different kinds of distortions. Therefore, it may doesn't play a significant role in this simple dataset. The evidence lies in TID2013, this dataset is similar to LIVE but more complicated because it contains 25 different distortions and 3,000 distortion images. Our method achieves excellent results on TID2013, which means QS-hyper is superior in capturing various image distortions, which meets a broader range of evaluation requirements. Secondly, the baselines have already achieved more than 95% of PLCC and SRCC on LIVE, and the improvement room is relatively narrow. HyperIQA uses category-based pre-training features. On the contrary, our method adopts QS-encoder to extract features, which is more suitable for image quality evaluation. Holistically, the comparison experiments show that our methods achieve promising performance in common IQA datasets. To some extent, it proves that the features extracted by QS-encoder are more related to image quality than features based on classification tasks.

4.5 Examples of Results

As shown in the Fig. 4, we offer some test images and put the quality scores provided by QS-hyper below them. The images above the dotted line are from the

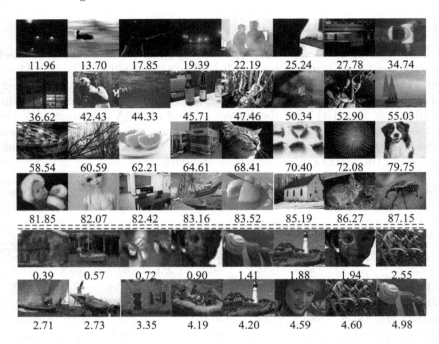

Fig. 4. It shows some test samples on KonIQ-10K (above the dotted line) and TID2013 (below the dotted line). The quality score predicted by QS-hyper is attached below the picture.

KonIQ-10K dataset, and they include various categories and distortion types. In contrast, images under the dotted line are from the TID2013 dataset, containing fewer categories and pre-defined distortion types. Overall, the prediction results on both datasets are consistent with human subjective perception. For Wild pictures, the reasons for the low score include any distortion that destroys the authenticity of the images (first row of Fig. 4), such as high-brightness, over-dark, ghosting, rotation, etc. In contrast, degradation images are relatively simple because the distortion type can be defined (fifth row of Fig. 4).

4.6　Discussion

IQA in the Wild is still an open problem, and there are two fundamental problems for CNN-based methods. Firstly, creating high-quality IQA datasets require many human resources, leading to inadequate samples to train complex models. In this context, the second problem is how to extract image features corresponding to quality without any large-scale datasets with quality labels. A simple solution is to use the pre-trained features on other datasets. However, CNNs trained on classification-task datasets (such as ImageNet) pay more attention to the image's category than quality. But it is easy to understand that two different classes of images may have the same quality. The method proposed in this paper is effective because QS-encoder simultaneously solved these two problems. Thanks to the semi-supervised strategy, it can effectively extract image quality features with a small number of labeled samples. Besides, the introduction of the QS-encoder enables the model to evaluate more complex distorted images correctly. Table 1 shows that the improvement of our method on TID2013 is more prominent than its simplified dataset LIVE, which proves that our method is more capable of general image quality assessment tasks.

5 Conclusion

After analyzing the disadvantage of category-based image representation in the IQA task, this paper proposes a quality-sensitive encoder (QS-encoder) based on representation learning to obtain features corresponding to image quality. Combined with QS-encoder, we improved the hyperIQA model to QS-hyper to achieve the blind image quality assessment in complex situations. Experiments show that our QS-hyper model surpasses most state-of-art methods and is superior in complex datasets, which meets a broader range of evaluation requirements. In future work, we will further study the representation method for image quality.

Acknowledgement. This research is supported by Sichuan Science and Technology Program (No. 2020YFS0307, No. 2020YFG0430, No. 2019YFS0146), Mianyang Science and Technology Program (2020YFZJ016).

References

1. Bosse, S., Maniry, D., Müller, K.R., Wiegand, T., Samek, W.: Deep neural networks for no-reference and full-reference image quality assessment. IEEE Trans. Image Process. **27**(1), 206–219 (2017)
2. Bromley, J., Guyon, I., LeCun, Y., Säckinger, E., Shah, R.: Signature verification using a "siamese" time delay neural network. Adv. Neural Inf. Process. Syst. **6**, 737–744 (1993)
3. Caron, M., Bojanowski, P., Joulin, A., Douze, M.: Deep clustering for unsupervised learning of visual features. In: Proceedings of the European Conference on Computer Vision (ECCV), pp. 132–149 (2018)
4. Chen, X., He, K.: Exploring simple siamese representation learning. In: Proceedings of the IEEE/CVF Conference on Computer Vision and Pattern Recognition, pp. 15750–15758 (2021)
5. Deng, J., Dong, W., Socher, R., Li, L.J., Li, K., Fei-Fei, L.: Imagenet: a large-scale hierarchical image database. In: 2009 IEEE conference on computer vision and pattern recognition, pp. 248–255. IEEE (2009)
6. Ghadiyaram, D., Bovik, A.C.: Massive online crowdsourced study of subjective and objective picture quality. IEEE Trans. Image Process. **25**(1), 372–387 (2015)
7. He, K., Fan, H., Wu, Y., Xie, S., Girshick, R.: Momentum contrast for unsupervised visual representation learning. In: Proceedings of the IEEE/CVF Conference on Computer Vision and Pattern Recognition, pp. 9729–9738 (2020)
8. He, K., Zhang, X., Ren, S., Sun, J.: Deep residual learning for image recognition. In: Proceedings of the IEEE conference on computer vision and pattern recognition, pp. 770–778 (2016)

9. Hjelm, R.D., et al.: Learning deep representations by mutual information estimation and maximization. arXiv preprint arXiv:1808.06670 (2018)
10. Hosu, V., Lin, H., Sziranyi, T., Saupe, D.: Koniq-10k: an ecologically valid database for deep learning of blind image quality assessment. IEEE Trans. Image Process. **29**, 4041–4056 (2020)
11. Krizhevsky, A., Sutskever, I., Hinton, G.E.: Imagenet classification with deep convolutional neural networks. Adv. Neural Inf. Process. Syst. **25**, 1097–1105 (2012)
12. Lin, K.Y., Wang, G.: Hallucinated-iqa: no-reference image quality assessment via adversarial learning. In: Proceedings of the IEEE Conference on Computer Vision and Pattern Recognition, pp. 732–741 (2018)
13. Liu, X., Van De Weijer, J., Bagdanov, A.D.: Rankiqa: learning from rankings for no-reference image quality assessment. In: Proceedings of the IEEE International Conference on Computer Vision, pp. 1040–1049 (2017)
14. Mittal, A., Moorthy, A.K., Bovik, A.C.: No-reference image quality assessment in the spatial domain. IEEE Transactions on Image Processing **21**(12), 4695–4708 (2012)
15. Moorthy, A.K., Bovik, A.C.: A two-step framework for constructing blind image quality indices. IEEE Signal Process. Lett. **17**(5), 513–516 (2010)
16. Ou, F.Z., et al.: Sdd-fiqa: unsupervised face image quality assessment with similarity distribution distance. In: Proceedings of the IEEE/CVF Conference on Computer Vision and Pattern Recognition, pp. 7670–7679 (2021)
17. Ponomarenko, N., et al.: Image database tid2013: peculiarities, results and perspectives. Signal Process. Image Commun. **30**, 57–77 (2015)
18. Su, S., et al.: Blindly assess image quality in the wild guided by a self-adaptive hyper network. In: Proceedings of the IEEE/CVF Conference on Computer Vision and Pattern Recognition, pp. 3667–3676 (2020)
19. Xue, W., Mou, X., Zhang, L., Bovik, A.C., Feng, X.: Blind image quality assessment using joint statistics of gradient magnitude and laplacian features. IEEE Trans. Image Process. **23**(11), 4850–4862 (2014)
20. Zhang, L., Zhang, L., Bovik, A.C.: A feature-enriched completely blind image quality evaluator. IEEE Trans. Image Process. **24**(8), 2579–2591 (2015)
21. Zhang, X., Yu, W., Jiang, N., Zhang, Y., Zhang, Z.: Sps: A subjective perception score for text-to-image synthesis. In: 2021 IEEE International Symposium on Circuits and Systems (ISCAS), pp. 1–5. IEEE (2021)
22. Zhang, X., Zhang, Y., Zhang, Z., Yu, W., Jiang, N., He, G.: Deep feature compatibility for generated images quality assessment. In: Yang, H., Pasupa, K., Leung, A.CS., Kwok, J.T., Chan, J.H., King, I. (eds.) Neural Information Processing. ICONIP 2020. Communications in Computer and Information Science, vol. 1332. Springer, Cham (2020). https://doi.org/10.1007/978-3-030-63820-7_40
23. Zhang, Y., Zhang, X., Zhang, Z., Yu, W., Jiang, N., He, G.: No-reference quality assessment based on spatial statistic for generated images. In: Yang, H., Pasupa, K., Leung, A.CS., Kwok, J.T., Chan, J.H., King, I. (eds.) Neural Information Processing. ICONIP 2020. Communications in Computer and Information Science, vol. 1332. Springer, Cham (2020). https://doi.org/10.1007/978-3-030-63820-7_57
24. Zhu, H., Li, L., Wu, J., Dong, W., Shi, G.: Metaiqa: deep meta-learning for no-reference image quality assessment. In: Proceedings of the IEEE/CVF Conference on Computer Vision and Pattern Recognition, pp. 14143–14152 (2020)

An Efficient Manifold Density Estimator for All Recommendation Systems

Jacek Dąbrowski[1], Barbara Rychalska[1,2]([envelope]), Michał Daniluk[1],
Dominika Basaj[1], Konrad Gołuchowski[1], Piotr Bąbel[1], Andrzej Michałowski[1],
and Adam Jakubowski[1]

[1] Synerise, Kraków, Poland
barbara.rychalska@synerise.com
[2] Warsaw University of Technology, Warszawa, Poland

Abstract. Most current neural recommender systems for session-based data cast recommendations as a sequential or graph traversal problem, applying recurrent networks (LSTM/GRU) or graph neural networks (GNN). This makes the systems increasingly elaborate in order to model complex user/item connection networks and results in poor scalability to large item spaces and long item view/click sequences. Instead on focusing on the sequential nature of session-based recommendation, we propose to cast it as a density estimation problem on item sets. We introduce EMDE (Efficient Manifold Density Estimator) - a method utilizing arbitrary vector representations with the property of local similarity to succinctly represent smooth probability densities on Riemannian manifolds using compressed representations we call *sketches*. Within EMDE, session behaviors are represented with weighted item sets, largely simplifying the sequential aspect of the problem. Applying EMDE to both top-k and session-based recommendation settings, we establish new state-of-the-art results on multiple open datasets in both uni-modal and multi-modal settings. EMDE has also been applied to many other tasks and areas in top machine learning competitions involving recommendations and graph processing, taking the podium in KDD Cup 2021, WSDM Challenge 2021, and SIGIR eCom Challenge 2020. We release the code at https://github.com/emde-conf/emde-session-rec.

Keywords: Recommender systems · Density estimation · Deep learning

1 Introduction

The goal of recommender systems is to suggest items which a user might find interesting, often in the setting of online stores or social media. A common problem setting in the domain of recommenders is that predictions must be made from data which is inherently sequential, representing user actions over a time-span [2,21]. Thus, the input is an ordered collection of items based on a single

---

J. Dąbrowski and B. Rychalska—Equal contribution.

© Springer Nature Switzerland AG 2021
T. Mantoro et al. (Eds.): ICONIP 2021, LNCS 13111, pp. 323–337, 2021.
https://doi.org/10.1007/978-3-030-92273-3_27

user's shopping session, and the task consists of predicting which item will be clicked or added to cart next. Many session-based recommendation (SRS) systems use methods which explicitly model sequentiality, such as recurrent neural networks (RNNs) [12,18,27] or graph neural networks (GNNs) [5,32,33]. However, these methods are known to scale poorly to growing item sets and increasing sequence size [31]. They also exhibit a number of specific efficiency-related problems, such as *neighborhood explosion* in GNNs (the number of neighbors often grows exponentially when increasing node distances are considered). Yet, as the sequential aspect of recommendation is considered vital, most efforts are focused on researching ever more complex neural network architectures in order to represent the ordered relations accurately. We propose to shift the focus from sequentiality in recommenders to an accurate representation of user behaviors understood as item sets. Our hypothesis is that the sequential aspect could be largely discarded if we manage to represent the density of aggregate user preference spaces with sufficiently high fidelity. This approach could simplify the neural architecture dramatically, as probability densities do not have a temporal nature and can be represented by approximate, fixed-size structures, serving as simple 1-d input vectors to feed-forward neural networks.

Thus, the core challenge in our setting becomes to 1) create a succinct vector representation of densities, and 2) teach a neural model to compute conditional mappings between input and output densities. To this end, we propose EMDE (Efficient Manifold Density Estimator) – a method which exploits locality sensitive hashing to create *sketches* - histogram-like structures which represent density on multidimensional manifolds. The *sketches* allow conditional mapping from one density estimate to another with simple shallow feed-forward neural networks. We show that EMDE achieves state-of-the-art results on multiple SRS datasets, going against the trend of sequential focus.

We confirm the versatility of EMDE applying it to another recommender setting - top-k recommendation task, which operates on large item collections viewed/bought over an extended time period, and achieving competitive results. Thus, we postulate that direct density estimation of item spaces is indeed a viable research pathway in the general area of recommendation. Moreover, we show that EMDE allows for easy and natural incorporation of multiple modalities, such as various types of interactions (click/purchase/add to favorites), item names or images.

Our conclusions are backed by experiments inspired by findings from [22] and [9]. They observe the *phantom progress* problem in recommender systems: carefully tuned simple heuristics (such as nearest-neighbor methods) in practice often outperform complex deep learning models, while algorithm performance is heavily dependent on the dataset and chosen performance metrics. In response to this, we use the benchmark suites from [22] and [9] to test our approach on a wide range of referential metrics and datasets, outperforming both the most advanced models and simple heuristics alike.

Apart from SRS, EMDE has also been successfully applied to travel destination recommendation (2nd place in WSDM Booking.com Challenge 2021), node classification in massive graphs (3rd place in KDD Cup 2021 Stanford

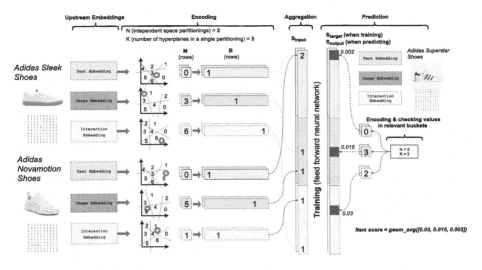

Fig. 1. EMDE recommender architecture.

MAG240M-LSC task), and cross-modal retrieval (1st place in SIGIR eCom Challenge 2020), demonstrating its ability to achieve superior results in various tasks.

2   Related Work

Neural Session-Based Recommenders. A popular branch of neural models use recurrent neural networks (RNN), suitable for data with temporal ordering. Gru4Rec [12] uses the gated recurrent unit (GRU), in a sequential setting. NARM [18] extends the approach with an item-level attention mechanism. STAMP [20] is an attention-based non-RNN model using neural memory modules to represent item long-term and short-term sequences. NextItNet [34] is based on stacked 1D dilated convolutions, instead of an RNN. SR-GNN [32] features a graph neural network (GNN) able to exploit additional paths between sessions, still focusing on sequentiality. TAGNN [33] adds a target-aware attention module to the GNN. The GNN-based models do not scale easily and are usually evaluated on small datasets (e.g. [33] evaluate on just 1/64 of the RSC15 dataset, while EMDE and most methods evaluated by [22] work on the full dataset).

Non-neural Session-Based Recommenders. Although neural recommenders are mostly regarded as state-of-the art, [22] show that simple non-neural baselines can often outperform them in practice. They propose S-KNN - a session-based nearest-neighbor technique, and its variant VS-KNN which favors recent items in sessions. AR is based on association rules, with its variant SR counting associations in item sequences. CT [23] uses context trees for reflecting possible decision pathways during sessions.

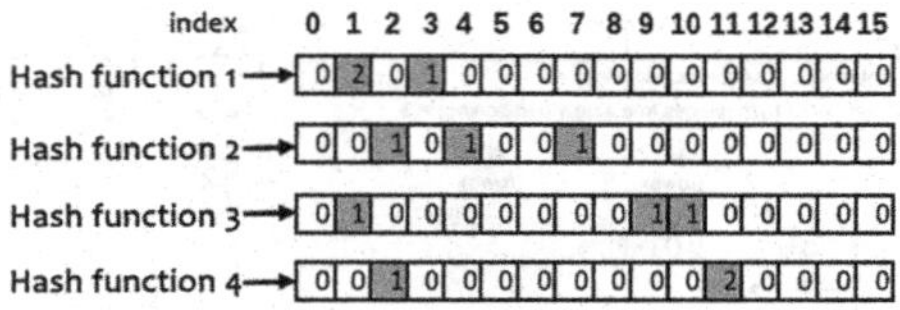

Fig. 2. An example of sketch produced by the count-min sketch algorithm. The displayed sketch stores three items, with hash collisions of two items in buckets containing the value 2.

Sketching-Based Density Estimators. [4] introduce methods for kernel density estimation (KDE) based on locality-sensitive hashing (LSH). Subsequently [29] use a sketch-based structure for a compressed representation of multiple LSH partitions for KDE. Both methods require a computation-heavy sampling procedure to arrive at density estimates. [6] introduce RACE - a LSH sketch-based method for KDE, which does not require sampling to arrive at density estimates. [7] further explores the technique of LSH sketching for approximate nearest-neighbor search on streaming data. In these methods, the considered manifold is R^n.

3   Algorithm

3.1   Preliminaries

Our solution is inspired by two algorithms: count-min sketch (CMS) [8] and locality sensitive hashing (LSH) [13].

Count-Min Sketch. CMS is a data structure used to count the number of times items appear in a data stream. Often used when the input space is too large to fit in memory, the algorithm works in sublinear space (Fig. 2). It consists of two operations: 1) incrementing item counts; 2) querying item counts by computing a minimum across hashed tables. The CMS *sketch* structure is represented by a two-dimensional array *count* with width w and depth d, representing hash functions h_d, which output a value $h_d(i_t) \in (0, .., w-1)$. Each row of the array represents a separate frequency table, and multiple such tables are introduced in order to alleviate the problem of hash conflicts. The array $count_{d \times w}$ is initialized with zeros. When an item i_t arrives, its count is updated by a value of c_t (1 by default). The procedure is expressed by the following equation:

$$count_d[h_d(i_t)] \leftarrow count_d[h_d(i_t)] + c_t.$$

The retrieval procedure of an item count consists of checking the values contained in the d respective item buckets in each row of the sketch. The minimum value of all of these is selected as the approximate item count:

$$item\_count = \min_{j=1}^{d} count_j[h_j(i_t)].$$

Locality-Sensitive Hashing. As a geometry-aware approach to hashing, LSH aims to assign input vectors to hash codes, ensuring that the probability of being in the same hash bucket is much higher for inputs which are close together in the input space, than for those which are far apart [13]. In contrast to CMS random hashing, LSH methods allow to preserve the geometric prior of the original input space when available. As we further show, CMS and LSH can be combined and adapted for compressed, geometry-aware density estimation in high dimensional spaces, which can work seamlessly with neural networks.

3.2 Efficient Manifold Density Estimator

EMDE combines weighted, compressed, geometry-aware histograms for high dimensional spaces with a neural network backbone. A typical application of EMDE consists of 4 steps: 1) computing multiple independent partitionings of the data manifold, usually done once; 2) filling the resulting structure with weighted observations, done once for each set of observations to be summarized; 3) using a feed-forward neural network to model input density into output density transformation 4) querying the output structure to obtain density estimates.

Below we describe EMDE on the example of item recommendation. The procedure is also displayed in Fig. 1. We focus on the scenario of SRS, where the data is comprised of user interaction sessions. Based on the items which have appeared in the session so far (*input chunk*), our objective is to predict the item which will be purchased/clicked next (*output chunk*). The application of EMDE to SRS proceeds in the following steps:

Obtaining Upstream Item Embeddings. First we need to precompute input embeddings using an external embedding method. EMDE can handle all sorts of embeddings, for example capturing interaction data (often interactions of different types, e.g. click, purchase, favorite), item names, attributes, or images.

Encoding. A central concept of EMDE is the data manifold $\mathbb{M}$ locally embedded in $\mathbb{R}^n$. The manifold $\mathbb{M}$ is spanned by embedding vectors computed for a particular data modality. Our objective is to perform multiple partitionings of the data manifold into regions (see *Encoding* section in Fig. 1). As such, semantically similar inputs should be assigned to the same manifold regions frequently. In a statistical interpretation, this operation corresponds to computing bucket boundaries of histograms, given samples from their input distributions. To this end, we propose a modified version of LSH algorithm we call Density-dependent LSH (DLSH). We start with choosing K random vectors r_i, then for $v \in \mathbb{M}$ we let $hash_i(v) = sgn(v \cdot r_i - b_i)$, where the bias value b_i is drawn from $Q_i(U \sim \text{Unif}[0,1])$, where Q_i is the quantile function of $\{v \cdot r_i : v \in \mathbb{M}\}$. In contrast to LSH, this scheme is density-dependent, cutting the manifold into non-empty parts, thus avoiding unutilized regions. As each hash independently divides the manifold into two parts, we treat these K binary hashcodes as bits of a K-bit integer. We thus obtain a partitioning of the manifold into 2^K disjoint regions (or $\sum_{i=0}^{n} \binom{K}{i}$ if $K > n$; we further assume $K < n$ for simplicity), which correspond to the set of all geometric intersections of regions spanned by single-bit hashes. The 2^K regions of the manifold form a single *depth* level of our sketch, analogous to a simple histogram with 2^K buckets, but in multiple dimensions.

Furthermore, we use a procedure inspired by CMS: instead of increasing the number of regions into which a manifold is partitioned, we maintain N independent partitionings, akin to different *depth* levels of a CMS. Thus, any given point lies at an intersection of all N regions it belongs to. This intersection can be extremely small, which leads to an exponential growth of the structure's resolution power.

We perform the above partitioning procedure N times independently, starting with new random vectors r_i every time, resulting in a *sketch structure* of *width* 2^K and *depth* N, named by analogy to CMS. In Fig. 1 item embeddings are encoded into a sketch of depth $N = 2$ and $K = 3$.

We apply DLSH to obtain separate partitionings for each input modality. In item recommendation context, for each item, we store N region indices (or *buckets*) in per-modality matrices $M_{n\_items \times N}$. The region indices stored in M are integers in the range $[0, 2^K - 1]$ and form a sparse item encoding, suitable for efficient storage. In Fig. 1, for item *Adidas Sleek Shoes*, its row in M is equal to $[0, 3, 6]$.

For the purposes of item-set aggregation, we one-hot encode each region index from the per-modality matrices M, obtaining per-modality matrices $B_{n\_items \times j}$, where $j \in \{1, \ldots, N \times 2^K\}$. Each row of the matrix B represents an item *sketch*, which can be interpreted as N concatenated histograms of 2^K buckets each.

Aggregation. Representations of (weighted) item multi-sets are obtained by simple elementwise (weighted) summation of individual item sketches. This follows from the additive compositionality of histograms with the same bucket ranges, or alternatively from the definition of CMS. Thanks to this property, sketches can also be constructed incrementally from data streams, which simplifies their application in industrial settings. Any subsequent normalization of sketches is performed along the *width* dimension, as every level of *depth* represents a separate, independent histogram.

For a given user and some temporal split into past and future chunks of a session, we encode each input and target item into dense sketches representation (in form of matrix B) and then we aggregate sketches of input items into single sketch S_{input} and sketches of target items into target sketch S_{target}. The aggregations are performed separately for each modality.

Model and Loss Function. We use a simple feed-forward neural network as a conditional density estimator with sketch structures for all inputs, outputs and targets - making both the model size and training time fully independent of the total number of items, original upstream embedding sizes, or the lengths of user sessions.

As a simple L_1-normalized histogram can be considered to approximate a probability mass function of a discrete distribution, sketches normalized across *width* are ensembles of such histograms for many individual distributions. We train our model to minimize mean Kullback–Leibler divergence between individual target and output probability mass functions in the ensemble. For every row in a batch, this entails: 1) L_1-normalizing the target sketch S_{target} across *width*; 2) applying the *Softmax* function to the network output logits S_{output} across *width*; 3) calculating *KL-divergence* between targets and outputs across *width*; 4) averaging the loss across *depth*. It is worth noting that our formulation bypasses the need for either: a) an extremely wide softmax layer with weight vectors for all items; b) negative sampling; both of which negatively affect stability and training time of standard methods.

To improve the stability of pre-activations in the neural network, we L_2-normalize the input *sketch* S_{input} across *width*.

Prediction. In order to produce a recommendation score for an item, we query the output sketch in a similar way to CMS queries. As the matrix M contains mappings of every item, to a single histogram bucket for all levels of sketch *depth*, a simple lookup of S_{output} at the respective indices from M is sufficient. This operation can also be efficiently realized in dense batch format amenable to GPU acceleration, as matrix multiplication $S_{output} \times B$. Both versions yield N independent probability estimates from individual elements of the depth-wise ensemble for each item. We aggregate the estimates using *geometric mean* (see *Prediction* section in Fig. 1). The difference between CMS, which uses *minimum* operation for aggregation, and our sketches stems from operating on counts (CMS) versus probabilities (EMDE). Strong theoretical arguments for optimality of *geometric mean* can be found in [10] and [14], given the interpretation of sketches as an ensemble of density estimators over manifolds. The resulting probability estimates are unnormalized i.e. don't sum to 1 across all items (normalization can be performed but is unnecessary for the recommendation setting).

4   Experiments

4.1   EMDE as a Recommender System

We report results for unimodal EMDE (no multimodal data, only basic user-item interactions found in the original datasets), and EMDE MM (configurations where selected multimodal channels are present). We evaluate all algorithms in the same framework of [22], keeping to their selected performance measures and datasets. In order to disentangle the gains induced by our method from the quality of the embeddings themselves, we use a very simple graph node embedding scheme [28], which is the same for representing both text and interaction networks. For embedding text we simply create a graph of item-token edges.

We conduct our experiments on a machine with 28 CPUs, 128 GB RAM and a commodity nVidia GeForce RTX 2080 Ti 11 GB RAM GPU card.

Table 1. Session-based recommendation results. Top 5 competitors are displayed for each dataset. * are from [22]. EMDE MM denotes multimodal configurations, while EMDE denotes non-multimodal configurations. The results are averaged over 5 data slices trained independently.

Model	MRR@20	P@20	R@20	HR@20	MAP@20	Model	MRR@20	P@20	R@20	HR@20	MAP@20
RETAIL						RSC15					
EMDE MM	**0.3664**	**0.0571**	**0.5073**	**0.6330**	**0.0309**	EMDE MM	**0.3116**	**0.0743**	0.5000	0.6680	0.0352
EMDE	**0.3524**	0.0526	**0.4709**	**0.5879**	0.0282	EMDE	**0.3104**	0.0730	0.4936	0.6619	0.0346
VS-KNN*	0.3395	**0.0531**	0.4632	0.5745	0.0278	CT [23]	0.3072	0.0654	0.471	0.6359	0.0316
S-KNN*	0.337	0.0532	0.4707	0.5788	**0.0283**	NARM	0.3047	**0.0735**	**0.5109**	**0.6751**	**0.0357**
TAGNN	0.3266	0.0463	0.4237	0.5240	0.0249	STAMP	0.3033	0.0713	0.4979	0.6654	0.0344
Gru4Rec	0.3237	0.0502	0.4559	0.5669	0.0272	SR	0.301	0.0684	0.4853	0.6506	0.0332
NARM	0.3196	0.044	0.4072	0.5549	0.0239	AR	0.2894	0.0673	0.476	0.6361	0.0325
DIGI						NOWP					
EMDE MM	0.1731	**0.0620**	**0.3849**	**0.4908**	**0.0268**	EMDE MM	*no multimodal data found*				
EMDE	0.1724	**0.0602**	**0.3753**	**0.4761**	**0.0258**	EMDE	**0.1108**	**0.0617**	**0.1847**	**0.2665**	0.0179
VS-KNN*	**0.1784**	0.0584	0.3668	0.4729	0.0249	CT	0.1094	0.0287	0.0893	0.1679	0.0065
S-KNN*	0.1714	0.0596	0.3715	0.4748	0.0255	Gru4Rec	0.1076	0.0449	0.1361	0.2261	0.0116
TAGNN	0.1697	0.0573	0.3554	0.4583	0.0249	SR [15]	0.1052	0.0466	0.1366	0.2002	0.0133
Gru4Rec	0.1644	0.0577	0.3617	0.4639	0.0247	SR-GNN	0.0981	0.0414	0.1194	0.1968	0.0101
SR-GNN	0.1551	0.0571	0.3535	0.4523	0.0240	S-KNN*	0.0687	0.0655	0.1809	0.245	**0.0186**
30MU						AOTM					
EMDE MM	**0.2703**	**0.1106**	**0.2503**	**0.4105**	**0.0331**	EMDE MM	*no multimodal data found*				
EMDE	**0.2673**	**0.1102**	**0.2502**	**0.4104**	**0.0330**	EMDE	**0.0123**	0.0083	0.0227	0.0292	0.0020
CT	0.2502	0.0308	0.0885	0.2882	0.0058	CT	0.0111	0.0043	0.0126	0.0191	0.0006
SR	0.241	0.0816	0.1937	0.3327	0.024	NARM	0.0088	0.005	0.0146	0.0202	0.0009
Gru4Rec	0.2369	0.0617	0.1529	0.3273	0.015	STAMP [18]	0.0088	0.002	0.0063	0.0128	0.0003
NARM	0.1945	0.0675	0.1486	0.2956	0.0155	SR	0.0074	0.0047	0.0134	0.0186	0.001
VS-KNN*	0.1162	0.109	0.2347	0.383	0.0309	S-KNN*	0.0054	**0.0139**	**0.039**	**0.0417**	**0.0037**

Session Based Recommendation. We conduct experiments on six popular datasets used in [22]. We reuse data preprocessing, training framework, hyperparameter search procedure and evaluation from the framework of [22][1] without introducing any changes. Within the framework, each dataset is split into five contiguous in time slices in order to minimize the risk of random effects. For each dataset we locate and use multimodal data whenever possible. We experiment on the following datasets:

- *RETAIL*: collected from a real-world e-commerce website; 212,182 actions in 59,962 sessions over 31,968 items. Contains behaviour data and item properties such as price, category, vendor, product type etc.
- *DIGI*: an e-commerce dataset shared by the company Diginetica, introduced at a CIKM 2016 challenge.
- *RSC15 (Yoochoose)*: an e-commerce dataset from 2015 ACM RecSys Challenge; 5,426,961 actions in 1,375,128 sessions over 28,582 items.
- *30Music*: music listening logs from Last.fm; 638,933 actions in 37,333 sessions over 210,633 items.
- *AOTM*: user-contributed playlists from the Art of the Mix webpage; 306,830 actions in 21,888 sessions over 91,166 items.
- *NOWP*: song playlists collected from Twitter; 271,177 actions in 27,005 sessions over 75,169 items.

[1] https://github.com/rn5l/session-rec.

Multimodal data used for each dataset are listed in Table 3. For *AOTM* and *NOWP* datasets, we were unable to find multimodal data with matching item identifiers.

Benchmarks. We compare against the benchmark methods from [22], which have been fine-tuned extensively by the benchmark's authors. We include two recent graph neural models: SR-GNN [32] and TAGNN [33], running an extensive grid search on their parameters and using the best configurations found on train/validation split from [22]. We confirm the correctness of our configurations by cross-checking against results reported in the original author papers, using their original data splits (e.g. we achieve 0.1811 MRR@20 for TAGNN on DIGI dataset with the original author train/validation split, while the metric reported by authors is 0.1803 MRR@20). We confirm that the best configurations are the same for both original author data preprocessing and preprocessing from [22]. Following [22] we skip datasets requiring more than a week to complete hyperparameter tuning. Therefore we mark TAGNN on RSC15, 30MU, NOWP and SR-GNN on 30MU, RSC15 as timeout.

Metrics. Hit rate (HR@20) and mean reciprocal rank (MRR@20) are based on measuring to what extent an algorithm is able to predict the immediate next item in a session. Precision (Precision@20), recall (Recall@20) and mean average precision (MAP@20) consider all items that appear in the currently hidden part of the session.

EMDE Configuration. Items interactions are grouped by user, artist (for music datasets) and session. Then we create a graph with those interactions, where items are graph nodes with edges between them if an interaction appears. We embed these graphs with [28]. As a result, we obtain an embedding vector for each item. We also observe that adding random sketch codes (not based on LSH) for each item improves the model performance, allowing the model to separate very similar items to differentiate their popularity. All input modalities are presented in Table 3.

We train a three layer residual feed forward neural network with 3000 neurons in each layer, with leaky ReLU activations and batch normalization. We use Adam [16] for optimization with a first momentum coefficient of 0.9 and a second momentum coefficient of 0.999^2. The initial learning rate was decayed by parameter γ after every epoch.

The input of the network consists of two width-wise L2-normalized, concatenated, separate *sketches*, one of them represents the last single item in the session, the second one all other items. The purpose of this is to amplify the importance of the last (newest) item. In order to create representation of user's behaviour for the second *sketch*, we aggregate the sketches of user's items, multiplying them with exponential time decay. Decay of sketch between time t_1 and t_2 is defined as:

$$sketch(t_2) = \alpha w^{(t_2 - t_1)} sketch(t_1) \tag{1}$$

---

[2] Standard configuration recommended by [16].

The parameters α and w define decay force.

We perform a small random search over network parameters for each dataset, which is summarized in Table 2. For all datasets we used sketches of width $K = 7$ and $w = 0.01$. We use a varied number of epochs as the framework of [21] allows this and picks the best number of epochs automatically for all tested methods.

EMDE Performance. As presentend in Table 1, EMDE outperforms competing approaches for most metric-dataset combinations, although [22] find that neural methods generally underperform compared to simple heuristics. EMDE proves superior in most cases even without the addition of multimodal data. The results with multimodal data (**EMDE MM**) are significantly better than the basic configuration in all cases. Thus, the ability to easily ingest multimodal data proves important in practical applications.

Table 2. Training hyperparameters for each SRS dataset.

Dataset	RETAIL	RETAIL MD	DIGI/DIGI MD	RSC15/RSC15 MD	NOWP	30M	30M MD	AOTM
Epochs	5	5	5	7	5	50	50	9
Batch size	256	256	512	512	256	512	512	256
lr	0.004	0.004	0.004	0.0005	0.001	0.0005	0.0005	0.0005
γ	0.5	0.5	0.5	1.0	0.75	1	1	0.9
N	10	10	10	10	10	10	9	9
α	0.95	0.9	0.97	0.9	0.9	0.9	0.9	0.9

Table 3. Input modalities of items for each SRS dataset.

Dataset	Input modalities	Dataset	Input modalities
RETAIL	Session dim 4096 iter [2,3,4,5] user dim 4096 iter [2,3,4,5] random codes	RETAIL multimodal	Session dim 1024 iter [2,4] user dim 1024 iter [3] property 6 iter 4 dim 1024 property 839 iter 4 dim 1024 property 776 iter 4 dim 1024 random codes
DIGI	Session dim 1024 iter [1,2,5] session dim 2048 iter [1,2,4,5] random codes	DIGI multimodal	session dim 1024 iter [1,2,3,4,5] purchases iter 4 dim 1024 product names iter 4 dim 1024 item in search queries iter 4 dim 1024 random codes
RSC15	Session dim 1024 iter [2,3,4] session dim 2048 iter [2,3,4] random codes	RSC15 multimodal	Session dim 1024 iter [2,3,4] session dim 2048 iter [2,3,4] purchases iter 4 dim 1024 random codes
30 M	Session dim 2048 iter [1,2,3,5] artist dim 2048 iter [2,3,4,5] user dim 2048 iter [2,3,4] random codes	30 M multimodal	Session dim 2048 iter [1,2,3,5] artist dim 2048 iter [2,3,4,5] user dim 2048 iter [2,3,4] playlist iter 4 dim 1024 random codes
NOWP	Session dim 2048 iter [1,2,3,4] artist dim 2048 iter [1,2,4,5] users dim 2048 iter [2,4, 5] random codes	AOTM	Session dim 2048 iter [1,2,3] artist dim 2048 iter[1,4,5] users dim 2048 iter [1,2,3] random codes

Top-K Recommendation. We conduct experiments on two popular, real-world, large-scale datasets: Netflix Prize [3] and MovieLens20M. The datasets contain movie ratings from viewers. We reuse the code for dataset preprocessing, training and evaluation from [9].

Benchmarks. We compare against the baselines used by [9], including a recent state-of-the-art VAE-based neural model: MultVAE [19], and a non-neural algorithm EASE [30].

EMDE Configuration. On top of EMDE, we use a simple one-hidden-layer feed-forward neural network with 12,000 neurons. We put 80% of randomly shuffled user items into the input sketch, and the remaining 20% into the output sketch to reflect train/test split ratio of items for a single user. In our multimodal configuration we include the interactions of users with disliked items (items which received a rating lower than 4). For Movielens20M, we embedded both the liked and disliked items grouped by user with [28] using dimensionality $d = 1024$ and iteration number $i = 1$. For Netflix, all embeddings likewise have $d = 1024$ and we apply iterations $i \in \{1, 2\}$ to liked items, while for disliked items $i = 1$.

Table 4. Top-k recommendation results.

Model	Recall@1	NDCG@5	Recall@5	NDCG@10	Recall@10	NDCG@20	Recall@20
MovieLens 20 M							
EMDE	**0.0529**	**0.2017**	**0.1662**	**0.2535**	**0.2493**	0.3053	0.3523
EASE [30]	0.0507	0.1990	0.1616	0.2530	0.2465	**0.3078**	**0.3542**
MultVAE [19]	0.0514	0.1955	0.1627	0.2493	0.2488	0.3052	0.3589
SLIM [24]	0.0474	0.1885	0.1533	0.2389	0.2318	0.2916	0.3350
RP3beta [25]	0.0380	0.1550	0.1279	0.2004	0.2007	0.2501	0.3018
Netflix Prize							
EMDE	**0.0328**	0.1512	0.1101	0.1876	0.1652	0.2332	0.2432
EASE [30]	0.0323	**0.1558**	**0.1120**	**0.2050**	**0.1782**	**0.2589**	**0.2677**
MultVAE [19]	0.0313	0.1485	0.1109	0.1957	0.1756	0.2483	0.2645
SLIM [24]	0.0307	0.1484	0.1062	0.1952	0.1688	0.2474	0.2552
RP3beta [25]	0.0243	0.0946	0.0595	0.1191	0.0863	0.1578	0.1390

Table 5. Results of adding multimodal data to our top-k EMDE recommenders.

Model	Recall@1	NDCG@5	Recall@5	NDCG@10	Recall@10	NDCG@20	Recall@20
MovieLens 20 M							
EMDE MM	**0.0670**	**0.2378**	**0.1963**	**0.2890**	**0.2780**	**0.3358**	**0.3710**
EMDE	0.0529	0.2017	0.1662	0.2535	0.2493	0.3053	0.3523
Netflix Prize							
EMDE MM	**0.0388**	**0.1574**	**0.1253**	**0.2155**	**0.1875**	**0.2619**	**0.2645**
EMDE	0.0328	0.1512	0.1101	0.1876	0.1652	0.2332	0.2432

EMDE Performance. The results are show in Table 4. We observe that our approach consistently and significantly outperforms the baselines for lower k

values in the top-k recommended item rankings for Movielens20M, which is consistent with CMS being a heavy-hitters estimator. In practice, the very top recommended items are key for user satisfaction as they are given the most attention by users, considering the limitation of item display capabilities and user's attention in the real world. For Netflix, we are able to outperform all competitors only on top-1 recommendation, which is probably caused by comparatively lower density estimation scores we achieve on this dataset (see Fig. 3). This is probably due to the simplistic graph embedding method we use. Table 5 presents results with added multimodal data (EMDE MM), which again are significantly higher than the unimodal case and competitors.

4.2 EMDE as a Density Estimator

Most kernel density estimation methods such as [11] are not applicable for our solution since they do not scale to high input dimensionalities or require sampling during inference, thus preventing usage as input/output for neural networks. We compare against a recent SOTA fast hashing-based estimator (HBE) method for multidimensional data [1]. This system can handle input dimensions on the scale of thousands, which is optimal for embedding systems currently in use. We repeat the Laplacian kernel testing procedure from [1] on multiple datasets: MovieLens20M and Netflix [3] (embedded with [28]), GloVe [26] and MNIST [17]. Results in Table 6 show that with optimal parameter values EMDE is a competitive density estimator despite its simplicity. Pearson correlation is used as EMDE estimates are un-normalized.

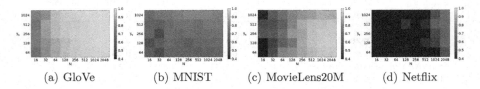

(a) GloVe   (b) MNIST   (c) MovieLens20M   (d) Netflix

Fig. 3. Density estimation quality with various N/K configurations. Metric reported is Pearson correlation coefficient against true distribution.

Table 6. Density estimation results. Metric reported is Pearson correlation coefficient against true distribution created as in [1].

Method	GloVE	MNIST	MovieLens20M	Netflix
EMDE	0.996	0.809	0.983	0.700
FastHBE	0.997	0.998	0.986	0.695

Figure 3 shows the relation between N/K parameters and estimation quality. Large values of N have an ensembling effect due to averaging of smaller regions, thus increasing N is always beneficial. With too small K the number of created regions is low and the details in data distribution are not represented. Too large K makes similar data points spread over many regions instead of being contained in one representative region and the gain from the metric prior is lost.

5   Conclusions

We present EMDE - a compact density estimator for high dimensional manifolds inspired by CMS and LSH techniques, especially amenable to treatment with neural networks optimized with KL-divergence loss. We show that both sequential and top-k recommendation problems can be cast in a simple framework of conditional density estimation. Despite simplified treatment of sequential data as weighted multi-sets, our method achieves state-of-the-art results in recommendation systems setting. Easy incorporation of multiple data modalities, combined with scalablility and the potential for incremental operation on data streams make EMDE especially suitable for industry applications. Natural extensions to sequence-aware settings, such as item pair encoding or joint encoding of item and positional vectors are promising avenues for future research.

Acknowledgements. Barbara Rychalska was supported by grant no 2018/31/ N/ST6/02273 funded by National Science Centre, Poland.

References

1. Backurs, A., Indyk, P., Wagner, T.: Space and time efficient kernel density estimation in high dimensions. In: NeurIPS (2019)
2. Ben-Shimon, D., Tsikinovsky, A., Friedmann, M., Shapira, B., Rokach, L., Hoerle, J.: Recsys challenge 2015 and the yoochoose dataset. In: RecSys (2015)
3. Bennett, J., Lanning, S., Netflix, N.: The netflix prize. In: In KDD Cup and Workshop in Conjunction with KDD (2007)
4. Charikar, M., Siminelakis, P.: Hashing-based-estimators for kernel density in high dimensions. In: 2017 IEEE 58th Annual Symposium on Foundations of Computer Science (FOCS) (2017)
5. Chen, T., Wong, R.C.W.: Handling information loss of graph neural networks for session-based recommendation (2020)
6. Coleman, B., Shrivastava, A.: Sub-linear race sketches for approximate kernel density estimation on streaming data, pp. 1739–1749, April 2020
7. Coleman, B., Shrivastava, A., Baraniuk, R.G.: Race: sub-linear memory sketches for approximate near-neighbor search on streaming data (2019)
8. Cormode, G., Muthukrishnan, S.: An improved data stream summary: the count-min sketch and its applications. In: Farach-Colton, M. (ed.) LATIN 2004: Theoretical Informatics (2004)
9. Dacrema, M.F., Cremonesi, P., Jannach, D.: Are we really making much progress? a worrying analysis of recent neural recommendation approaches. In: RecSys (2019)
10. Dognin, P., Melnyk, I., Mroueh, Y., Ross, J., Santos, C.D., Sercu, T.: Wasserstein barycenter model ensembling (2019)
11. Greengard, L., Strain, J.: The fast gauss transform (1991)

12. Hidasi, B., Karatzoglou, A.: Recurrent neural networks with top-k gains for session-based recommendations. In: CIKM (2018)
13. Indyk, P., Motwani, R.: Approximate nearest neighbors: towards removing the curse of dimensionality. In: Conference Proceedings of the Annual ACM Symposium on Theory of Computing (2000)
14. Itoh, M., Satoh, H.: Geometric mean of probability measures and geodesics of fisher information metric (2017)
15. Kamehkhosh, I., Jannach, D., Ludewig, M.: A comparison of frequent pattern techniques and a deep learning method for session-based recommendation. In: RecTemp@RecSys (2017)
16. Kingma, D.P., Ba, J.: Adam: a method for stochastic optimization. In: Bengio, Y., LeCun, Y. (eds.) ICLR (20150
17. LeCun, Y., Cortes, C.: MNIST handwritten digit database (2010). http://yann.lecun.com/exdb/mnist/
18. Li, J., Ren, P., Chen, Z., Ren, Z., Lian, T., Ma, J.: Neural attentive session-based recommendation. In: Proceedings of the 2017 ACM on Conference on Information and Knowledge Management, CIKM 2017. Association for Computing Machinery, New York (2017)
19. Liang, D., Krishnan, R.G., Hoffman, M.D., Jebara, T.: Variational autoencoders for collaborative filtering. In: WWW (2018)
20. Liu, Q., Zeng, Y., Mokhosi, R., Zhang, H.: Stamp: short-term attention/memory priority model for session-based recommendation. In: KDD (2018)
21. Ludewig, M., Jannach, D.: Evaluation of session-based recommendation algorithms. User Model. User-Adap. Inter. **28**(4–5), 331–390 (2018)
22. Ludewig, M., Mauro, N., Latifi, S., Jannach, D.: Performance comparison of neural and non-neural approaches to session-based recommendation. In: RecSys (2019)
23. Mi, F., Faltings, B.: Context tree for adaptive session-based recommendation. http://arxiv.org/abs/1806.03733
24. Ning, X., Karypis, G.: Slim: sparse linear methods for top-n recommender systems. In: ICDM (2011)
25. Paudel, B., Christoffel, F., Newell, C., Bernstein, A.: Updatable, accurate, diverse, and scalable recommendations for interactive applications. ACM Trans. Interact. Intell, Syst **7**, 1–34 (2016)
26. Pennington, J., Socher, R., Manning, C.D.: Glove: global vectors for word representation. In: Empirical Methods in Natural Language Processing (EMNLP) (2014)
27. Ruocco, M., Skrede, O.S.L., Langseth, H.: Inter-session modeling for session-based recommendation. In: DLRS (2017)
28. Rychalska, B., Bąbel, P., Gołuchowski, K., Michałowski, A., Dabrowski, J.: Cleora: a simple, strong and scalable graph embedding scheme. arXiv https://arxiv.org/abs/2102.02302 (2020)
29. Siminelakis, P., Rong, K., Bailis, P., Charikar, M., Levis, P.: Rehashing kernel evaluation in high dimensions. In: International Conference on Machine Learning (2019)
30. Steck, H.: Embarrassingly shallow autoencoders for sparse data. In: WWW (2019)
31. Tallec, C., Ollivier, Y.: Unbiasing truncated backpropagation through time. arXiv preprint arXiv:1705.08209 (2017)
32. Wu, S., Tang, Y., Zhu, Y., Wang, L., Xie, X., Tan, T.: Session-based recommendation with graph neural networks. In: AAAI (2019)

33. Yu, F., Zhu, Y., Liu, Q., Wu, S., Wang, L., Tan, T.: TAGNN: target attentive graph neural networks for session-based recommendation. association for computing machinery (2020)
34. Yuan, F., Karatzoglou, A., Arapakis, I., Jose, J.M., He, X.: A simple but hard-to-beat baseline for session-based recommendations (2018), http://arxiv.org/abs/1808.05163

Cleora: A Simple, Strong and Scalable Graph Embedding Scheme

Barbara Rychalska[1,2(✉)], Piotr Bąbel[1], Konrad Gołuchowski[1],
Andrzej Michałowski[1], Jacek Dąbrowski[1], and Przemysław Biecek[2]

[1] Synerise, Kraków, Poland
barbara.rychalska@synerise.com
[2] Warsaw University of Technology, Warszawa, Poland

Abstract. The area of graph embeddings is currently dominated by contrastive learning methods, which demand formulation of an explicit objective function and sampling of positive and negative examples. One of the leading class of models are graph convolutional networks (GCNs), which suffer from numerous performance issues. In this paper we present Cleora: a purely unsupervised and highly scalable graph embedding scheme. Cleora can be likened to a GCN stripped down to its most effective core operation - the repeated neighborhood aggregation. Cleora does not require the application of a GPU and can embed massive graphs on CPU only, beating other state-of-the-art CPU algorithms in terms of speed and quality as measured on downstream tasks. Cleora has been applied in top machine learning competitions involving recommendations and graph processing, taking the podium in KDD Cup 2021, WSDM Challenge 2021, and SIGIR eCom Challenge 2020. We open-source Cleora under the MIT license allowing commercial use under https://github.com/Synerise/cleora.

Keywords: Graph embedding · Node embedding · Graph convolutional networks

1 Introduction

Graphs are extremely useful for modeling real-life interaction structures. A graph is represented by sets of nodes and edges, where each node represents an entity from the graph domain, and each edge represents the relationship between two or more nodes. Graph structures are found for example in biology as interconnected sets of amino acids building proteins [20,34], road networks [32,37], as well as social networks [3,36], citation networks [4,25], or web data [9,26]. In most machine learning applications it is crucial to represent graph nodes as node embeddings - structures expressing node properties as an input to downstream machine learning algorithms. A simple node adjacency matrix is usually not feasible due to its large size (quadratic to the number of nodes) and lack of easily accessible representation of node properties.

© Springer Nature Switzerland AG 2021
T. Mantoro et al. (Eds.): ICONIP 2021, LNCS 13111, pp. 338–352, 2021.
https://doi.org/10.1007/978-3-030-92273-3_28

In this paper we present Cleora: an inherently simple and parallelizable CPU-based embedding scheme. Cleora is significantly faster than competitors and scales well to massive graph sizes. Our algorithm consists in multiple iterations of normalized, weighted averaging of each node's neighbor embeddings. The operation of averaging can make rapid, substantial changes to embeddings (as compared to step-wise optimization based on an objective), making the algorithm reach optimal embeddings in just four to five iterations on average.

Cleora is inspired by recent developments in research on Graph Convolutional Networks (GCNs), which find that CGNs might be unnecessarily complex. GCNs stack layers of learnable filters followed by a nonlinear activation function to compute node representations. However, it has been found that contrary to other deep learning architectures, in GCNs the nonlinearities do not contribute to performance and can be largely removed, leaving repeated aggregation operations [22,31]. With Cleora we show that this approach can be taken even further to formulate a purely unsupervised scheme without sampling of positive or negative examples. We show that in spite of simplicity, Cleora produces embeddings of competitive quality in multiple data domains.

The Cleora algorithm is implemented within a library that has its roots in our production environment, where it is used to process data from large e-commerce platforms, with graphs comprised of millions of nodes and billions of edges.

2   Related Work

The first attempts at graph embeddings were purely unsupervised, for example the classic PCA [12] or Laplacian eigenmap [6]. These methods typically exploit spectral properties of various matrix representations of graphs. Unfortunately, their complexity is at least quadratic to the number of nodes, which makes these methods far too slow for today's volumes of data. Another essential line of work is based on random walks between graph nodes. A representative of this group, the classic DeepWalk model [23] uses random walks to create a set of node sequences fed to a skip-gram model [18]. Node2vec [10] is a variation of DeepWalk where the level of random walk exploration (depth-first search) versus exploitation (breadth-first search) is controlled with parameters. Other more recent approaches make the random walk strategy more flexible at the cost of increased complexity [7,24]. LINE [29] is yet another successful approach, which aims to preserve the first-order or second-order proximity separately by the use of KL-divergence minimization. After optimizing the loss functions, it concatenates both representations. LINE is optimized to handle large graphs, but its GPU-based implementation - Graphvite [38] - cannot embed a graph when the total size of the embedding is larger than the total available GPU memory. With GPU memory size usually much smaller than available RAM, this is a serious limitation.

Another class of models - the Graph Neural Networks (GNNs), and in particular Graph Convolutional Networks (GCNs) - use multilayer aggregations of each node's neighbors' features and apply nonlinearity to each such representation. Unfortunately, GNNs usually train for a single objective, are constrained by the available GPU memory, and exhibit a number of performance issues such as the so-called *neighborhood explosion* problem [8,35].

Finally, there exists a branch of truly fast and scalable embedding methods. They often boil down to older methods implemented in parallelizable and highly efficient architectures. Pytorch BigGraph (PBG) [15] uses ideas such as adjacency matrix partitioning and reusing examples within one batch to train models analogous to successful but less scalable RESCAL [21], DistMult [33], and others, thus making these models applicable to large graphs. GOSH [2] is a GPU-based approach which trains a parallelized version of Verse [30] on a number of smaller, coarsened graphs.

3   Algorithm

3.1   Preliminaries

A graph G is a pair (V, E) where V denotes a set of nodes (also called vertices) and $E \subseteq (V \times V)$ as the set of edges connecting the nodes. An embedding of a graph $G = (V, E)$ is a $|V| \times d$ matrix T, where d is the dimension of the embedding. The i-th row of matrix T (denoted as $T_{i,*}$) corresponds to a node $i \in V$ and each value $j \in \{1, ..., d\}$ in the vector $T_{i,j}$ captures a different feature of node i.

3.2   Embedding

Given a graph $G = (V, E)$, we define the random walk transition matrix $\mathbf{M} \in \mathcal{R}^{V \times V}$ where $\mathbf{M}_{ab} = \frac{e_{ab}}{deg(v_a)}$ for $ab \in E$, where e_{ab} is the number of edges running from node a to b, and $deg(v_a)$ is the degree of node a. For ab pairs which do not exist in the graph, we set $e_{ab} = 0$. If edges have attached weights, e_{ab} is the sum of the weights of all participating edges. We randomly initialize the embedding matrix $\mathbf{T}_0 \in \mathbb{R}^{|V| \times d} \sim U(-1, 1)$, where d is the embedding dimensionality. Then for $I \in \{1, ..., i\}$ iterations, we multiply matrix $\mathbf{M}$ and T_i, and normalize rows to keep constant L_2 norm. $\mathbf{T}_I$ is our final embedding matrix.

The method can be interpreted as iterated L_2-normalized weighted averaging of neighboring nodes' representations. After just one iteration, nodes with similar 1-hop neighborhoods in the network will have similar representations. Further iterations extend the same principle to q-hop neighborhoods.

Another useful intuition is that Cleora works analogously to an ensemble of d models, as each dimension is optimized separately from others. The only operation which takes into account all dimensions (and as such, allows some information sharing) is the L_2 normalization. The normalization step ensures numeric stability, preventing the norm of embedding vectors from collapsing towards zero during repeated multiplication by the transition matrix, of which the determinant is ≤ 1.

There are a number of conditions for the algorithm to work. Most importantly, the initial vectors in matrix $\mathbf{T}_0$ need to 1) be different from each other so that the algorithm does not collapse to the same representation 2) have similar pairwise distances in order to avoid 'false friends' which are accidentally close in the embedding space. Matrix initialization from the uniform distribution creates vectors which fulfill these conditions in high dimensional space.

Note that the Cleora algorithm allows for very easy embedding of large graphs which cannot be embedded at once due to memory constraints. In such case graph chunking into smaller sub-graphs needs to be applied. After embedding each chunk separately, embeddings from each chunk can be merged by weighted averaging (simply repeating the operation which forms the backbone of Cleora). We present the full Cleora algorithm in Algorithm 1, using the example of graph embedding in chunks. Note that in the usual case of embedding a single graph, Q equals 1 and the external for loop disappears.

Data: Graph $G = (V, E)$ with set of nodes V and set of edges E, iteration number I, chunk number Q, embedding dimensionality d

Result: Embedding matrix $\mathbf{T} \in \mathbb{R}^{|V| \times d}$

Divide graph G into Q chunks. Let G_q be the q-th chunk with edge set E_q;

for q *from 1 to* Q **do**

    For graph chunk G_q compute random walk transition matrix $\mathbf{M}_q = \frac{e_{ab}}{deg(v_a)}$ for $ab \in E_q$, where e_{ab} is the number of edges running from node a to b ;

    Initialize chunk embedding matrix $\mathbf{T}_0^q \sim U(-1, 1)$;

    for i *from 1 to* I **do**

        $\mathbf{T}_i^q = \mathbf{M}_q \cdot \mathbf{T}_{i-1}^q$;

        L_2 normalize rows of $\mathbf{T}_i^q$;

    end

    $\mathbf{T}^q = \mathbf{T}_I^q$;

end

for v *from 1 to* $|V|$ **do**

    $\mathbf{T}_{v,*} = \sum_{q=1}^{Q} w_{qv} \times \mathbf{T}_{v,*}^q$ where w_{qv} is the node weight

    $w_{qv} = \frac{|n \in V_q : n = n_v|}{\sum_{k=1}^{Q} |n \in V_k : n = n_v|}$

end

Algorithm 1: Cleora algorithm. Note that chunking into Q chunks is only needed for very large graphs. Without chunking $Q = 1$ and the external for loop disappears.

Similarly, thanks to the weighted averaging approach, embedding of a new node (added to graph after the computation of full graph embedding) can be obtained by L_2-normalized weighted averaging of the node's neighbor representations.

3.3 GCN Inspiration

An analogy exists between our approach and Graph Convolutional Networks, which compute the hidden representation h_{i+1} for a node in layer $i + 1$ based on previous network layer i. The computation is done in the following way [13]:

$$h^{i+1} = \sigma(AH^iW^i)$$

where A is the normalized node adjacency matrix, H^i holds the representations of a node's neighbors and W^i is the weight matrix from layer i. [31] report that non-linearities are a possible overhead and weight matrices can be collapsed between layers, while performance results stay similar. Thus, repeated AH^i multiplications from GCN form the core operation responsible for performance of these networks. The iterative weighted averaging approach from Cleora is inspired by this mechanism. As such, Cleora can be interpreted as a form of a GCN which is stripped down to its most effective core operation.

3.4 Implementation and Complexity

Cleora is implemented in Rust in a highly parallel architecture, using multithreading and adequate data arrangement for fast CPU access. We show the application of multithreading in Fig. 1, using a very general example of multiple relations in one graph. Such multi-relation configuration is allowed within the Cleora library and will result in computation of a separate embedding matrix for each relation pair. The multi-relation capability is especially aligned for e-commerce, where various node types often appear, such as users, products, and brands.

For maximum efficiency we created a custom implementation of a sparse matrix data structure - the `SparseMatrix` struct. It follows the sparse matrix coordinate list format (COO). Its purpose is to save space by holding only the coordinates and values of nonzero entities.

Memory Consumption and Complexity. Memory consumption is linear to the number of nodes and edges. To be precise, during training we need to allocate space for the following:

- $|V|$ objects of 40 bytes to store the matrix $\mathbf{P}$;
- $2 \times |E|$ objects of 24 bytes (in undirected graphs we need to count an edge in both directions) to store the matrix $\mathbf{M}$;
- $2 \times d \times |V|$ objects of 4 bytes to store the embedding matrix $\mathbf{T}$.

As such, the total memory complexity is given by $O(|V|(1 + 2d) + 2|E|)$. The most computationally heavy operation is the multiplication of the sparse matrix $\mathbf{M}$ and dense matrix $\mathbf{T}$, which sets the computational complexity at $O(|V| * average\_node\_degree * d)$.

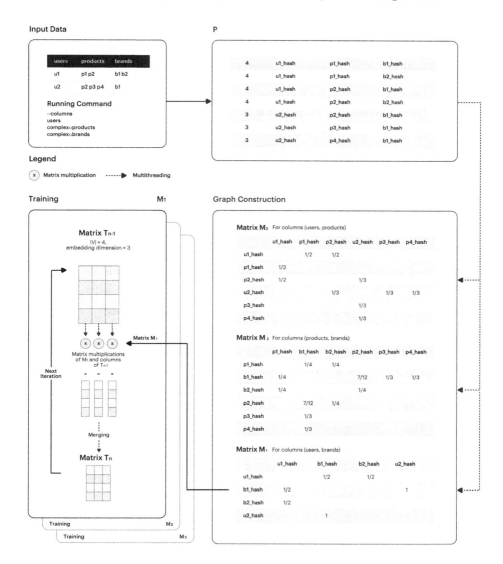

Fig. 1. Cleora architecture. Dashed lines represent parallel operations.

Table 1. Dataset characteristics.

Name	Facebook	YouTube	RoadNet	LiveJournal	Twitter
# Nodes	22,470	1,134,890	1,965,206	4,847,571	41,652,230
# Edges	171,002	2,987,624	2,766,607	68,993,773	1,468,365,182
A/Degree	12	5	3	16	36
Directed	No	No	No	Yes	Yes

Table 2. Calculation times baseline methods. For fair comparison, we include only CPU-based methods. **Total embedding time** encompasses the whole training procedure, including data loading and preprocessing. **Training time** encompasses just the training procedure itself. * - training crashed due to excessive resource consumption.

Algorithm	Facebook	YouTube	RoadNet	LiveJournal	Twitter
Total embedding time (hh:mm:ss)					
Cleora	00:00:43	00:12:07	00:24:15	01:35:40	25:34:18
PBG	00:04.33	00:54:35	00:37:41	10:38:03	-*
Deepwalk	00:36:51	28:33:52	53:29:13	*timeout*	*timeout*
Training time (hh:mm:ss)					
Cleora	00:00:25	00:11:46	00:04:14	01:31:42	17:14:01
PBG	00:02:03	00:24:15	00:31:11	07:10:00	-*

Table 3. Link prediction performance results. * - results with statistically significant differences versus Cleora.

Algo	Facebook		RoadNet		LiveJournal	
	MRR	HR@10	MRR	HR@10	MRR	HR@10
Scalable methods						
Cleora	0.072	0.176	0.924	0.943	0.608	0.667
PBG	0.082*	0.213*	0.872*	0.911*	0.567*	0.673*
GOSH	0.092*	0.232*	0.876*	0.898*	0.224*	0.401*
Non-scalable methods						
Deepwalk	0.080*	0.145*	0.963*	0.972*	*Timeout*	*Timeout*
LINE	0.075*	0.192*	0.963*	0.983*	0.566*	0.667*

Table 4. Classification accuracy - comparison with Graph Convolutional Networks.

Algorithm	Cora	CiteSeer	PubMed
AS-GCN	0.874	0.797	0.906
Cleora	0.868	0.757	0.802
AdaGCN	0.855	0.762	0.798
N-GCN	0.830	0.722	0.795
GCN	0.815	0.703	0.790

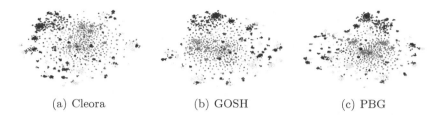

(a) Cleora   (b) GOSH   (c) PBG

Fig. 2. t-SNE projections of embeddings learned on Facebook dataset, colored by class assignment.

4 Experiments

To evaluate the quality of Cleora embeddings, we study their performance on two popular tasks: link prediction [17] and node classification. As competitors we consider recent state-of-the-art methods designed for big data: PBG [15] and GOSH [2], as well as classic models: Deepwalk [23] and LINE [29]. We divide the algorithms into 2 categories: scalable (Cleora, PBG, GOSH) an unscalable (Deepwalk, LINE). We deem LINE unscalable as its implementation cannot embed a graph when the total size of the embedding is larger than the total available GPU memory.

For each competitor, we use its original author's implementation. We train each model with the best parameter configurations reported in their original papers or repositories per each dataset. If such configuration does not exist, we run grid searches to find the optimal configurations.

Datasets. We use 5 popular datasets of various sizes and domains, summarized in Table 1. For each experiment we randomly sample out 80% of the edges found in each dataset as trainset (both for the embeddings and the proceeding proxy tasks) and the rest serves as validation/test dataset.

- **Facebook** [27]. In this graph, the nodes represent official Facebook pages while the links are mutual likes between sites.
- **Youtube** [19]. This graph represents mutual friendships in the Youtube social networks.
- **RoadNet** [16]. A road network of California. Intersections and endpoints are represented by nodes and the roads connecting these intersections or road endpoints are represented by edges.
- **LiveJournal** [5]. LiveJournal is a free online community with almost 10 million members. The graph represents friendships among members.
- **Twitter** [14]. A subset of the Twitter network with directed follower-following social network.

Hardware Configuration. We conduct all experiments on two machines: 1) Standard E32s v3 Azure (32 vCPUs/16 cores) and 256 GB RAM for CPU-based methods, and 2) 128 GB RAM, 14 core (28 HT threads) Intel Core i9-9940X 3.30GHz CPUs and GeForce RTX 2080 Ti 11GB GPU for GPU-based methods.

4.1 Embedding Computation

We use the following configurations for each of the models:

- **Cleora**: all embeddings have dimensionality $d = 1024$. We embed Facebook dataset with iteration number $i = 5$ and the other datasets with $i = 4$.
- **PBG** [15]: We use the following parameter configurations which we find to give the best results:

  - LiveJournal dataset: we reuse the original configuration from the author repository.
  - Facebook, Roadnet, Youtube: we run a grid search over all parameters and find individual best configurations for each dataset.

- **LINE** [29]: We use the configuration for Youtube dataset from author repository for embedding this dataset. We reuse this configuration for other datasets with epoch number $e = 4000$. We concatenate the base embeddings with context embeddings as recommended by the authors.
- **GOSH** [2]: The model is trained with learning rate $lr = 0.045$ and epochs $e = 1000$, defined in the original paper as the optimal configuration for our graph sizes (without any graph coarsening for maximum accuracy).
- **Deepwalk** [23]: We reuse the optimal configuration from the original paper.

Embedding Speed. Embedding training times are displayed in Table 2. We include only CPU-based methods for fair comparison. PBG is the fastest high-performing CPU-based method we are aware of, and Deepwalk serves as a baseline example of the non-scalable methods. Cleora is shown to be significantly faster than PBG in each case. Training is up to 5 times faster than PBG and over 200 times faster than Deepwalk.

We face technical difficulties with training the embeddings on the Twitter graph. Both GOSH and PBG crash during or just after loading the data into memory due to exhausting the available hardware resources. This demonstrates that Cleora can be trained on hardware which fails for other fast methods (note, though, that our hardware configuration is not small but rather standard). As a consequence, the only model we evaluate on Twitter is Cleora.

Interestingly, although the methods are very different conceptually, in Fig. 2 we can see that Cleora learns an essentially similar data abstraction as the competitors.

4.2 Link Prediction

Link prediction is one of the most common proxy tasks for embedding quality evaluation [17]. It consists in determining whether two nodes should be connected with an edge.

We collect the embeddings for all positive pairs (real edges) and for each such pair we generate a negative pair with random sampling. We compute the Hadamard product for each pair, which is a standard procedure observed to work well for performance comparison [10]. Then, we feed the products to a Logistic

Regression classifier which predicts the existence of edges. As the graphs we use are mostly large-scale, we resort to step-wise training with the `SGDClassifier` module from `scikit-learn` with a Logistic Regression solver. We reuse the evaluation setting from [15]: for each positive node pair, we pick 10,000 most popular graph nodes, which are then paired with the start node of each positive pair to create negative examples. We rank the pairs, noting the position of the real pair in the ranked list of 10,001 total examples.

In this setting we compute popular ranking-based metrics:

- MRR (mean reciprocal rank). This is the average of the reciprocals of the ranks of all positives. The standard formulation of MRR requires that only the single highest rank be summed for each example i (denoted as $rank_i$) from the whole query set Q:

$$MRR = \frac{1}{|Q|} \sum_{i=1}^{|Q|} \frac{1}{rank_i}.$$

  As we consider all edge pairs separately, this is true by default in our setting. Higher score is better, the best is 1.0.
- HitRate@10. This gives the percentage of valid end nodes which rank in top 10 predictions among their negatives. Higher score is better, the best score is 1.0.

Metrics. We use two metrics: MRR (mean reciprocal rank) - the average of the reciprocals of the ranks of all positives, and HitRate@10, which gives the percentage of valid end nodes which rank in top 10 predictions among their negatives.

Results. As shown in Table 3, the quality of Cleora embeddings is generally on par with the scalable competitors, and sometimes better than other fast algorithms aligned for big data - PBG and GOSH. Cleora performs worse than the competitors on the smallest graph - Facebook, but gets better with increasing graph size. Cleora performs especially well in the MRR metric, which means that it positions the correct node pair high enough in the result list as to avoid punishment with the harmonically declining scores.

We are unable to compare our results on the Twitter graph to competitors, thus presenting the results only for Cleora in Table 3. Due to large size of the graph and the computed embedding file (over 500 GB, far exceeding our available memory size), we train the link prediction classifier on a large connected component of the graph, containing 4,182,829 nodes and 8,197,949 edges.

4.3   Node Classification

Since Cleora shares its basic operation with GCNs, we study the performance of multiple recent GCN approaches on smaller-scale classification datasets on which these methods were originally evaluated. The datasets are: Cora (2708 nodes/5429 edges/7 classes), CiteSeer (3327 nodes/4732 edges/6 classes), PubMed (19717 nodes/ 44338 edges/3 classes). The total embedding time for

Cleora is between 3.32 s (Cora) and 27 s (PubMed), for iteration number $i = 4$ and dimensionality $d = 2048$. As baselines we evaluate the original GCN [13], N-GCN [1]: a GCN enhanced with random walks, AdaGCN [28]: a GCN with integrated AdaBoost for exploitation of higher-order neighbors, and AS-GCN [11]: a GCN with adaptive sampling for variance reduction. The results in Table 4 show that Cleora gives significantly better results than vanilla GCN and in many cases better than even more advanced approaches such as GCN-T and AdaGCN. This confirms the findings from [31].

4.4   Node Reconstruction (Inductivity)

We also evaluate the quality of embeddings of new nodes which are added to the graph after the computation of the full graph embedding table. To this end, we split the Facebook and Youtube datasets into a 'seen node' set comprised of 30% of each dataset, and 'new node' set comprised of the remaining 70% of each dataset. This setting is challenging as the vast majority of nodes will need to be reconstructed. At the same time, it gives us enough data to study embedding quality of two kinds of reconstruction: **1-hop reconstruction**, where a new node embedding is created based on 'seen node' embeddings, which have been learned directly from interaction data, and **2-hop reconstruction**, where a new node embedding is created based on reconstructed node embeddings. 2-hop reconstruction is a much harder task, as errors from previous reconstruction step will be accumulated.

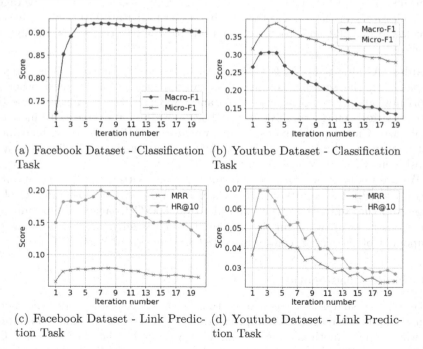

(a) Facebook Dataset - Classification Task

(b) Youtube Dataset - Classification Task

(c) Facebook Dataset - Link Prediction Task

(d) Youtube Dataset - Link Prediction Task

Fig. 3. The influence of iteration number on embedding quality.

Table 5 shows the results of the reconstruction quality check. We use the previous performance measures, also taking into account the MR (Mean Rank) measure, which is a simple average of obtained ranks in the Link Prediction task. The measure is a simplified abstraction of the MRR and HR metrics. 1-hop and 2-hop reconstruction results are computed on the reconstructed embeddings only.

We observe that the task of classification on Facebook dataset notes only a 5% micro-F1 drop in 1-hop node generation, and a 14.5% micro-F1 drop in 2-hop node generation. Youtube faced a stronger drop of 18% and 40%, respectively. A reversed tendency is observed for link prediction: the MR drops are severe for Facebook (MR falling by a half when reconstructed), while being very mild for Youtube (absolute difference in MR being only 266). This suggests that quality of reconstruction is heavily dependent on dataset. Even with 2-hop reconstruction, it is possible to obtain embeddings of high relative quality.

Table 5. Quality check of reconstructed nodes in a challenging setting where only 30% of all nodes are learned directly and 70% are reconstructed. 1-hop reconstruction nodes are computed from original nodes. 2-hop reconstruction nodes are computed from 1-hop reconstruction nodes.

Reco mode	Facebook			YouTube		
	Micro-F1	Macro-F1	MR	Micro-F1	Macro-F1	MR
Original	0.9190	0.9191	457	0.3673	0.3032	3677
1-hop	0.8718	0.8586	704	0.3013	0.2046	3751
2-hop	0.7856	0.7664	1552	0.2195	0.1136	3943

5   Optimal Iteration Number

The iteration number defines the depth of neighborhood on which a single node is averaged: iteration number i means that nodes with similar i-hop neighborhoods will have similar representations. We show the influence of i on classification performance in Fig. 3.

The iteration number is related to the concept of average path length from the area of graph topology. The average path length is defined as the average number of steps along the shortest paths for all possible pairs of network nodes. If the iteration number reaches the average path length, an average node will likely have access to all other nodes. Thus, iteration number slightly exceeding the average path length can be deemed optimal. For example, the average path length for the Facebook graph equals 5.18 and the best i is found to be 5–7 according to Fig. 3. In practice however the computation of average path length is significantly slower than the computation of Cleora embeddings. An optimal solution to determining the iteration number is to verify it empirically on the target downstream task.

Too large iteration number will make all embeddings gradually more similar to each other, eventually collapsing to an exact same representation. This behavior might be either slow or abrupt after passing the optimal point depending on the dataset, as evidenced in Fig. 3.

6   Conclusions

In this work we have presented Cleora - a simple, purely unsupervised embedding algorithm which learns representations analogous to contrastive methods. Cleora is much faster than other CPU-based methods and has useful extra properties, such as node embedding inductivity and additivity. We open-source Cleora to the community in order to aid reproducibility and allow a wide use of our method, including commercial use.

Acknowledgements. Barbara Rychalska was supported by grant no 2018/31/N/ ST6/02273 funded by National Science Centre, Poland.

References

1. Abu-El-Haija, S., Perozzi, B., Kapoor, A., Lee, J.: N-gcn: multi-scale graph convolution for semi-supervised node classification. In: UAI (2019)
2. Akyildiz, T.A., Aljundi, A.A., Kaya, K.: Gosh: embedding big graphs on small hardware. In: ICPP (2020)
3. Aletras, N., Chamberlain, B.P.: Predicting twitter user socioeconomic attributes with network and language information. In: Proceedings of the 29th on Hypertext and Social Media (2018)
4. Asatani, K., Mori, J., Ochi, M., Sakata, I.: Detecting trends in academic research from a citation network using network representation learning. PloS one **13**, e0197260 (2018)
5. Backstrom, L., Huttenlocher, D., Kleinberg, J., Lan, X.: Group formation in large social networks: membership, growth, and evolution. In: KDD (2006)
6. Belkin, M., Niyogi, P.: Laplacian eigenmaps and spectral techniques for embedding and clustering. In: Advances in Neural Information Processing Systems (2002)
7. Chen, H., Perozzi, B., Hu, Y., Skiena, S.: Harp: Hierarchical representation learning for networks. In: Proceedings of the Thirty-Second AAAI Conference on Artificial Intelligence. AAAI Press (2018)
8. Chen, J., Zhu, J., Song, L.: Stochastic training of graph convolutional networks with variance reduction. In: ICML
9. Cochez, M., Ristoski, P., Ponzetto, S.P., Paulheim, H.: Biased graph walks for rdf graph embeddings. In: WIMS (2017)
10. Grover, A., Leskovec, J.: Node2vec: scalable feature learning for networks. In: Proceedings of the 22nd ACM SIGKDD International Conference on Knowledge Discovery and Data Mining (2016)
11. Huang, W., Zhang, T., Rong, Y., Huang, J.: Adaptive sampling towards fast graph representation learning. In: NIPS (2018)
12. Jolliffe, I.T.: Principal Component Analysis and Factor Analysis. Springer, New York (1986)

13. Kipf, T.N., Welling, M.: Semi-supervised classification with graph convolutional networks. In: ICLR (2017)
14. Kwak, H., Lee, C., Park, H., Moon, S.: What is Twitter, a social network or a news media? In: WWW (2010)
15. Lerer, A., Wu, L., Shen, J., Lacroix, T., Wehrstedt, L., Bose, A., Peysakhovich, A.: PyTorch-BigGraph: a large-scale graph embedding system. In: SysML (2019)
16. Leskovec, J., Lang, K., Dasgupta, A., Mahoney, M.: Community structure in large networks: natural cluster sizes and the absence of large well-defined clusters. Internet Math. **6**29–123 (2008)
17. Liben-Nowell, D., Kleinberg, J.: The link-prediction problem for social networks. J. Am. Soc. Inf. Sci. Technol. **58**, 1019–1031 (2007)
18. Mikolov, T., Sutskever, I., Chen, K., Corrado, G.S., Dean, J.: Distributed representations of words and phrases and their compositionality. In: Advances in Neural Information Processing Systems (2013)
19. Mislove, A., Marcon, M., Gummadi, K.P., Druschel, P., Bhattacharjee, B.: Measurement and analysis of online social networks. In: Proceedings of the 5th ACM/Usenix Internet Measurement Conference (IMC 2007) (2007)
20. Mohamed, S.K., Nováček, V., Nounu, A.: Discovering protein drug targets using knowledge graph embeddings. Bioinf. **36**, 603–610 (2019)
21. Nickel, M., Tresp, V., Kriegel, H.P.: A three-way model for collective learning on multi-relational data. In: Proceedings of the 28th International Conference on International Conference on Machine Learning. ICML (2011)
22. Oono, K., Suzuki, T.: Graph neural networks exponentially lose expressive power for node classification. In: ICLR (2020)
23. Perozzi, B., Al-Rfou, R., Skiena, S.: Deepwalk: online learning of social representations. In: KDD (2014)
24. Perozzi, B., Kulkarni, V., Chen, H., Skiena, S.: Don't walk, skip! online learning of multi-scale network embeddings. In: ASONAM (2017)
25. Pornprasit, C., Liu, X., Kertkeidkachorn, N., Kim, K.S., Noraset, T., Tuarob, S.: Convcn: a cnn-based citation network embedding algorithm towards citation recommendation. In: Proceedings of the ACM/IEEE Joint Conference on Digital Libraries in 2020 (2020)
26. Ristoski, P., Paulheim, H.: Rdf2vec: rdf graph embeddings for data mining. In: International Semantic Web Conference (2016)
27. Rozemberczki, B., Allen, C., Sarkar, R.: Multi-scale attributed node embedding (2019)
28. Sun, K., Lin, Z., Zhu, Z.: Adagcn: adaboosting graph convolutional networks into deep models. In: ICLR (2021)
29. Tang, J., Qu, M., Wang, M., Zhang, M., Yan, J., Mei, Q.: Line: Large-scale information network embedding. In: WWW (2015)
30. Tsitsulin, A., Mottin, D., Karras, P., Müller, E.: Verse: Versatile graph embeddings from similarity measures (2018). https://doi.org/10.1145/3178876.3186120
31. Wu, F., Souza, A., Zhang, T., Fifty, C., Yu, T., Weinberger, K.: Simplifying graph convolutional networks. In: ICML (2019)
32. Wu, N., Zhao, X.W., Wang, J., Pan, D.: Learning effective road network representation with hierarchical graph neural networks. In: KDD (2020)
33. Yang, B., Yih, W.t., He, X., Gao, J., Deng, L.: Embedding entities and relations for learning and inference in knowledge bases. arXiv preprint arXiv:1412.6575 (2014)
34. Yue, X., et al.: Graph embedding on biomedical networks: methods, applications and evaluations. Bioinf. **36**, 1241–1251 (2020)

35. Zeng, H., Zhou, H., Srivastava, A., Kannan, R., Prasanna, V.: Accurate, efficient and scalable training of graph neural networks. J. Parallel Distrib. Comput.
36. Zhang, Y., Lyu, T., Zhang, Y.: Cosine: Community-preserving social network embedding from information diffusion cascades. In: AAAI (2018)
37. Zheng, C., Fan, X., Wang, C., Qi, J.: Gman: a graph multi-attention network for traffic prediction. In: AAAI (2020)
38. Zhu, Z., Xu, S., Qu, M., Tang, J.: Graphvite: a high-performance cpu-gpu hybrid system for node embedding. In: The World Wide Web Conference (2019)

STA3DCNN: Spatial-Temporal Attention 3D Convolutional Neural Network for Citywide Crowd Flow Prediction

Gaozhong Tang(ID), Zhiheng Zhou, and Bo Li$^{(\boxtimes)}$(ID)

School of Electronic and Information Engineering, South China University of Technology, Guangzhou 510640, China
eegztang@mail.scut.edu.cn, {zhouzh,leebo}@scut.edu.cn

Abstract. Crowd flow prediction is of great significance to the construction of smart cities, and recently became a research hot-spot. As road conditions are constantly changing, the forecasting crowd flows accurately and efficiently is a challenging task. One of the key factors to accomplish this prediction task is how to temporally and spatially model the evolution trend of crowd flows. In previous works, capturing features is carried out mainly by utilizing the structure based on a recurrent neural network which is effective to capture temporal features from time sequence. However, it is inefficient for capturing spatial-temporal features which is critical for the prediction task. In this paper, we develop an elementary module, a 3D convolution layer based on the self-attention mechanism (3DAM), which can extract spatial features and temporal correlation simultaneously. Our proposed spatial-temporal attention 3D convolution prediction network (STA3DCNN) is composed of 3DAMs. Finally, we conduct comparative and self-studying experiments to evaluate the performance of our model on two benchmark datasets. The experimental results demonstrate that the proposed model performs effectively, and outperforms 9 representative methods.

Keywords: Crowd flow prediction · Spatial-temporal features · 3D convolution neural networks · Self-attention mechanism

1 Introduction

Crowd flow prediction is of great significance for developing modern intelligent transportation system (ITS) in smart cities. It aims to predict the changes of crowd distribution in a certain period of time in cities according to the historical distribution of crowds. Accurate and real-time prediction of crowds plays a guiding role in planning the vehicle trajectory, alleviating the crowd congestion, and providing an assistant reference for road construction planning. However, it is still a challenging task due to the difficulty of efficiently fitting the nonlinear characteristics caused by the dynamic temporal and spatial changes of crowd flow.

© Springer Nature Switzerland AG 2021
T. Mantoro et al. (Eds.): ICONIP 2021, LNCS 13111, pp. 353–365, 2021.
https://doi.org/10.1007/978-3-030-92273-3_29

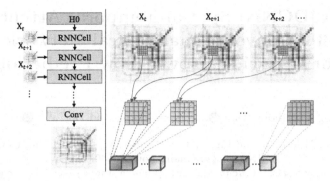

Fig. 1. The left part of the vertical line shows the structure based on RNN, while the right part is the 3DCNN diagram. 3DCNN is able to draw information by sliding convolutional kernels along the time dimension.

In the past few years, many works have been presented on the task of crowd flow prediction. Some traditional time series prediction algorithms and machine learning algorithms have been applied, such as ARIMA [16], linear regression [19], support vector regression [21], and Bayesian Analysis [20]. These models are simple and convenient to be deployed in the task, however, they are not suitable for solving the problem possessing the nonlinear characteristic, *e.g.* crowd flow prediction. With the rising of deep learning, those methods based on deep neural networks (DNNs) with outstanding nonlinear fitting capability were applied to the task of time sequence analysis. Recurrent neural network (RNN) [7] is specially designed for time sequence prediction, and the networks are able to achieve satisfying performance on processing sequential tasks [9,10,12,25]. However, the instability of crowd-flow data caused by dynamic changes in time and space is difficult to be fully fitted by the RNN-based models. Moreover, the said model is at the risk of vanishing gradient, which makes models hard to be trained and converge. RNNs are implemented with a serial structure that is appropriate to capture timing features via step-by-step iterations (as shown on the left part of the vertical line in Fig. 1) whereas the serial structure is short in the computational efficiency.

In our work, a 3D convolutional neural network (3DCNN) based on the self-attention mechanism (SAM) is introduced to remedy the defect mentioned above. As shown on the right part of the vertical line in Fig. 1, 3DCNN can extract temporal features by sliding convolution kernel along the time dimension, while the spatial feature can also be aggregated by the receptive field of convolution kernels. It is more efficient to extract the spatial feature and the temporal features simultaneously from dynamic crowd flows. In addition, 3DCNN can extract features of the entire input time series using a short network connection, which is utilized to alleviate the problem of vanishing gradient. Relying on the self-attention mechanism, our model can build a spatial connection between two regions at a long distance, meanwhile, the temporal feature of the entire input time sequence can be captured.

In this paper, we propose a spatial-temporal attention network based on a 3D convolutional neural network (STA3DCNN) to predicting crowd flows. The specific works of this paper include: i) We introduce 3DCNN and SAM to solve the problem of crowd flow prediction. 3D convolution layer and SAM are cascaded together as an elementary ingredient, 3DAM, which will be used to form modules to extract the spatial-temporal feature from various scales. ii) In order to capture the temporal feature sufficiently, we consider the feature in two modes including the high correlation features of adjacent time and cyclical pattern features in crowd flows. Then, we implement a network with two branches by employing 3DAM, which aims to automatically capture the spatial-temporal evolution features and the stable spatial-temporal cycle pattern features hidden in crowd flows, respectively. iii) We implement a bi-modal fusion module (BFM) to fuse evolution features and cyclical pattern features, and to accomplish the final prediction. The results of the experiments prove that our fusion method performs better than the baseline fusion method.

In summary, the main contributions of our work can be summarized as below:

1) We introduce 3DCNN and self-attention mechanism into the crowd flow prediction framework. Our model can efficiently extract spatial-temporal features.
2) We model crowd-flow data based on the time correlation and the cyclical pattern, while a bi-mode features fusion module is designed to merge spatial-temporal features of different modes.
3) We propose a crowd flow prediction model, STA3DCNN, and conduct experiments on two benchmark datasets to demonstrate that our model is feasible, efficient, and accurate on predicting the trend of crowd flows.

2   Related Work

In the past few years, a lot of works have been proposed on the task of crowd flow prediction. Traditional prediction methods, including linear regression [19], support vector regression [21], ARIMA [5], Bayesian model [20], are easily implemented. However, the prediction accuracy of these models is hard to satisfy the expectation, due to these models is not well fitted the nonlinear characteristic of crowd-flow data.

In recent years, deep learning shows an outstanding ability to fit nonlinear data and has the capacity on digging the latent information from data. Methods built on deep learning have been successfully utilized in time series forecasting tasks. LSTM [14] and GRU [3] have been used to extract temporal features for crowd flow prediction. By modifying the LSTM cell, Liu et al. [11] introduced the attention mechanism into the method and implemented an attentive crowd flow machine (ACFM) which can adaptively exploit diverse factors affecting changes in crowd flows. Do et al. [4] employed the attention mechanism to design a new model which consists of an encoder and a decoder based on GRU. Inspired by densely connected networks, Xu *et al.* [22] used historically dense structures to analyze historical data, and then used two serial LSTM units for the temporal feature extraction and prediction.

The spatial feature is vital for predicting the trend of crowd flows. Graph neural network (GNN) is a popular way to extract spatial features of crowd flows [1,23,27]. In previous works, the transportation network can be considered as a graph composed of nodes (areas) and edges (roads). For example, Zhao *et al.* [27] integrated the graph convolution operation into GRU cells, and extracted spatial information while performing time-dependent extraction.

Although many impressive works have been presented in the literature, there is still a challenge to capture the dynamic temporal and spatial characteristics of crowd flows regarding balance effectiveness and efficiency. In our work, we propose a crowd flow prediction method based on DNNs, STA3DCNN, which can capture spatial-temporal features effectively and efficiently.

3   Preliminary

In this section, we briefly introduce the data processing methods, preliminary concepts, and the definition of the problem of crowd flow prediction.

Region Partition. Crowds may move from one area to another along the road in a city, such as from residential areas to central business districts. Because the city may contain hundreds of thousands of road links, modeling the changes of crowd flow based on road links is too complicated to accomplish. Then, the city can be partitioned into grids, and we analyze the crowd-traffic flow in each grid. Similar to previous study [26], we divide a city's road map into $h \times w$ small areas along the longitude and the latitude, by which data can be easily processed by models. We make a compromise between the calculation amount and the prediction granularity in city partition, so that the regional crowd flow density can be better modeled.

Crowd Flow Prediction Problem. We count the flow of people entering and leaving each area within a period of time as the research object. $X_t^d \in R^{2 \times h \times w}$ denotes the change of crowd distribution at the time period t on day d, where the 1st channel represents the inflow, and the 2nd one represents the outflow. The task of crowd flow prediction is to estimate the quantity of crowd flows which will enter and leave an area according to historical crowd-flow data. Then, the problem of crowd flow prediction can be transformed into the below problem: Given sequence $[X_{t-k}^d, X_{t-k+1}^d, \ldots, X_{t-1}^d]$ of previous k time slots, to predict the crowd-flow map X_t^d at the t_{th} time interval of d_{th} day.

4   Methodology

Figure 2 shows the architecture of STA3DCNN which is designed from 3 perspectives: 1) Regarding dynamic spatial-temporal features, we implement an elementary module, 3DAM, which is comprised of a 3D convolutional layer and SAM.

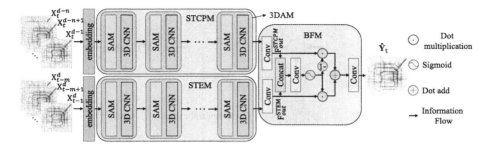

Fig. 2. Overview of the spatial-temporal 3D convolutional neural network (STA3DCNN).

3DAM can make the model pay more attention to the temporal feature among closely correlated time steps and the spatial dependence hidden in highly relevant regions. 2) 3DAM is used to form two modules which are the spatial-temporal evolution feature extraction module (STEM) and the spatial-temporal cyclical patterns feature extraction module (STCPM). The two modules work in a parallel way to extract evolution features and cyclical pattern features, respectively. It should be noticed that the spatial information can be implanted in features due to the operation characteristics of 3DAM. 3) A bi-modal feature fusion and prediction module (BFM) is implemented to merge the spatial-temporal evolution feature and spatial-temporal cyclical patterns feature by BFM and accomplish the final prediction.

4.1 3D Convolutional Neural Networks Combining with Self-Attention Mechanism

3DAM aims to fully capture the temporal feature and the spatial features of crowd flow. As shown in Fig. 3, 3DAM is composed of SAM and a 3D convolutional layer. Different from RNNs which can learn the sequence information according to the order of feeding data, the 3D convolutional network can not completely model the sequential relationship implied in the whole input time series. All of the temporal features are calculated within the receptive field of the convolution kernel in parallel, however, the model is hard to distinguish the temporal relationship between different feature channels. Hence, we implement SAM to extract the feature of the sequential relationship. In addition, the spatial feature between distant regions can be captured simultaneously by the module.

Here, SAM is expressed as

$$F_{out}^{seq} = F_{in}^{seq} \cdot f_{sig}(f_{up}(f_{pool}(F_{in}^{seq} * w_1))) \tag{1}$$

where F_{in}^{seq} denotes the input of SAM, F_{out}^{seq} denotes the output of SAM, w_1 denotes parameters of convolution kernel with kernel size 3×3 followed by an activation unit (ReLU), f_{sig} denotes a sigmoid operation, and f_{up} and f_{pool} respectively denote up-sampling operation and pooling operation with kernel

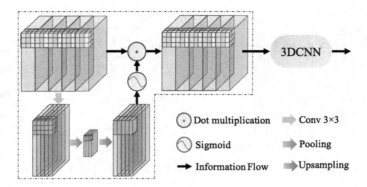

Fig. 3. Overview of our elementary module 3DAM. The part surrounded with dash line is the SAM, while the part 3DCNN accomplish the extraction of the spatial-temporal feature.

size 4×4. By updating weights of the above structure, the spatial-temporal can be captured, so as to extract effective information for crowd flow prediction.

Combining with a 3D convolutional layer, the module can be used to fully extract the spatial-temporal features. 3DCNN can extract the dependence of adjacent time through sliding convolution kernels along the time dimension. By adjusting the size of the convolution kernel, the receptive field in the time dimension is also changed. Then, with the 3D convolution kernel sliding along the time dimension with various strides, we can extract features of different time scales. The size of the convolution kernel in spatial dimension determines its spatial receptive field which can promote the capability of 3DCNN to extract spatial features by setting spatial receptive field. Thus, 3DAM can simultaneously capture temporal features and spatial features of crowd flows. We set the 3D convolutional layer with kernel size $2 \times 3 \times 3$.

4.2 Spatial-Temporal Feature Extraction

As shown in Fig. 2, STEM and STCPM are utilized to extract the spatial-temporal features. The two modules can model the change of crowd flow from two various perspectives. The closer the data is in the time dimension, the stronger the correlation is between the data. Then, STEM is designed to capture such trends in short-term and features with high correlation. Moreover, people follow a relatively fixed travel schedule during the day in urban. For example, crowd flow has two traffic peaks in the morning and evening, corresponding to the beginning and the ending of production activities. The distribution of crowd flow can be guided by the changes of crowd flow in the same period dating back to the past few days due to the cyclical change. STCPM can extract the pattern features of this cyclical change, which can provide varying perspectives for prediction.

STEM. This module is implemented to extract evolution features of crowd flow in a short period of time. Regarding the change of crowd flows is continuously evolving with time, we use the crowd-flow data of several past and adjacent moments as inputs of STEM. We utilize a series of stacked 3DAMs to capture the evolutionary change. Crowd-flow data is firstly encoded by the embedding module into 96 channels aiming to improve the diversity of feature expression. Then, the dynamic spatial-temporal features of crowd flows are extracted by the cascaded 3DAMs. The features of different time intervals have different implicit associations with the current time features, and the self-attention module in 3DAM can aggregate features from the hidden relationship. Then, 3DCNN layers are employed for spatial-temporal features extraction. The output of STEM, $F_{out}^{STEM} \in R^{96 \times h \times w}$, encodes the spatial-temporal evolution features of crowd-flow data.

STCPM. The module is used to extract cyclical patterns of crowd flows. Due to the change of producing activities and daily life in the city, the spatial and temporal distribution of people's travel trajectory often exhibit a certain regularity and periodicity. Therefore, we set weeks as the cycle of the cyclical pattern, and we acquire data at the same period of each day which is selected from the past more than a week. The data can provide enough information for our model to capture the cyclical pattern which varies from day to day within a cycle. The historical data of the same period is firstly encoded by the embedding module aiming to enlarge the amount of channels. We pass the encoded features through SAM to automatically emphasize those features with higher similarity. Then, 3DCNN in 3DAM fulfills the extraction of spatial-temporal features from crowd-flow data. The outputs of STCPM is denoted as $F_{out}^{STCPM} \in R^{96 \times h \times w}$ which encodes the cyclical patterns of crowd flow, and will be fused with F_{out}^{STEM} in the subsequent bi-mode fusion module for the final prediction.

4.3 Bi-Modal Fusion Module

After we obtained the two features, the temporal evolution, and the cyclical pattern, we can generate the final prediction by fusing features. As shown in Fig. 2, the bi-modal fusion module (BFM) is implemented to merge the two features and accomplish the final prediction. We use the self-weighting method to automatically learn the weights of the features extracted from the two modules. Specifically, we calculate the weights by concatenating F_{out}^{STEM} and F_{out}^{STCPM} together, and pass the feature through a convolution layer and a sigmoid function. BFM can be represented as:

$$F = f_{sig}(w_2 * [F_{out}^{STEM}, F_{out}^{STCPM}]), \tag{2a}$$

$$Y = w_3 * (F_{out}^{STEM} \odot F + F_{out}^{STCPM} \odot (1 - F)) \tag{2b}$$

where Y denotes the final crowd flow prediction, w_2 and w_3 denote the weights of the convolutional layer, f_{sig} denotes the sigmoid function, and '$\odot$' denotes dot multiplication. Processed by BFM, the features of temporal evolution and cyclical pattern are fully integrated, which can enhance the performance of the prediction network.

5   Experiments

We comprehensively evaluate STA3DCNN in three perspectives: performance evaluation, efficiency evaluation, and self-studying tests. We adopt PyTorch [13] toolbox to implement the proposed method. Our model is compared with 9 representative methods presented in recent years, including 3 traditional time-series analysis models, and 6 deep learning-based methods, in which two GNN-based prediction methods are included. The performance evaluation we made is the next-step prediction. The efficiency evaluation is performed on estimating the RAM (random access memory) consumption and the operating efficiency. Via self-studying experiments, we analyze the effectiveness of each component of the proposed model.

5.1   Datasets and Evaluation Criteria

Datasets. Our method has been evaluated on two public benchmark datasets: TaxiBJ dataset [25] and BikeNYC dataset [26]. The crowd-flow maps are generated from the trajectory data in the two datasets by the method presented in Sect. 3. Similar to previous works, we use the last four weeks in TaxiBJ and the last ten days in BikeNYC as a test set, while the rest data of the two datasets are used for training models.

Evaluation Criteria. We evaluate the performance of the proposed method by two popular evaluation metrics: Root Mean Square Error (RMSE) and Mean Absolute Error (MAE). Specifically, their definitions are respectively shown as below:

$$\text{RMSE} = \sqrt{\frac{1}{n} \sum_{i=1}^{n} \left(\widehat{Y}_i - Y_i \right)^2}, \tag{3a}$$

$$\text{MAE} = \frac{1}{n} \sum_{i=1}^{n} \left| \widehat{Y}_i - Y_i \right| \tag{3b}$$

where $\widehat{Y}_i$ and Y_i respectively represent the predicted crowd-flow map and its ground truth, and n denotes the number of crowd-flow maps used for validation.

5.2   Experimental Setup

In our work, the length of sequence inputted into the entire model is 16, while the length of sequence fed into STEM and STCPM are set to 8, respectively. The size of one minibatch is set to 128, and the initial learning rate in our model is

10^{-3}. Weights of all convolutional layers are initialized according to Kaiming's work [6]. We optimize the parameters of our network via Adam optimization [15] by minimizing mean square error loss with a GTX Titan Xp GPU in an end-to-end manner.

5.3   Experiment Results and Analysis

Evaluation on Crowd Flow Prediction. We apply STA3DCNN to predict the next-step crowd flow, meanwhile we make a comparison with 9 representative methods: Historical Average (HA) [18], Auto-Regressive Integrated Moving Average (ARIMA) [16], XGBoost [2], Convolution LSTM (ConvLSTM) [17], Spatio-temporal graph convolutional neural network (STGCN) [24], Spatial-Temporal Dynamic Network (STDN) [23], Context-Aware Spatial-Temporal Neural Network (DeepSTN+) [10], Spatial-temporal Graph to Sequence Model (STG2Seq) [1], and Dual Path Network (DPN) [8].

Table 1 shows the performance of our method and the 9 representative methods on the two benchmark datasets. The first 3 methods in Table 1 are traditional time series prediction methods, and the rest are deep learning-based models. Compared with models based on deep learning, the traditional models are hard to achieve satisfactory performance, because the traditional models are inadequate to fit nonlinear data. Among the deep learning-based models, our STA3DCNN achieves the best results on both two datasets. Specifically, compared with the best performing method, RMSE of our model is respectively decreased by 3.04% and 3.47% on the two datasets, while MAE is decreased by 5.45% and 0.88%, respectively. It is should be noticed that STGCN and STG2Seq

Table 1. Evaluation of crowd flow prediction on TaixBJ and BikeNYC datasets. The top-2 results are highlighted in red and blue, respectively.

Models	TaxiBJ		BikeNYC		Number of Para.	Infer. Time
	RMSE	MAE	RMSE	MAE	(Megabytes)	(Sec.)
HA [18]	57.79	-	21.57	-	-	0.04
ARIMA [16]	22.78	-	10.07	-	-	110
XGBoost [2]	22.93	-	6.91	-	-	3.45
ConvLSTM [17]	18.79	11.46	6.6	2.44	0.76	7.74
STGCN [24]	19.10	11.57	4.76	2.44	6	3.10
STDN [23]	17.83	**9.90**	5.79	2.41	37.8	1.49
DeepSTN+ [10]	17.65	10.03	4.96	2.31	1074	4.84
STG2Seq [1]	17.60	10.47	**4.61**	**2.28**	23.04	13.84
DPN [8]	**16.80**	-	-	-	-	-
STA3DCNN	16.29	9.36	4.45	2.26	**3.1**	**1.28**

are built upon GNN for spatial feature extraction. Comparatively, STA3DCNN employing 3DCNNs to extract spatial features is more effective.

Computational Efficiency of STA3DCNN. The efficiency evaluation is fulfilled in two perspectives: calculating the RAM (random access memory) consumption and estimating the operating efficiency. The former one is evaluated by counting the parameter of models, while the latter one is evaluated by estimating how long it is needed to infer and generate the final prediction. The experimental results are shown in the last two columns of Table 1.

We evaluate the model based on deep learning only due to, generally, the model built upon deep learning contains massive parameters. From the penultimate column of Table 1, it can be observed that the amount of parameters of ConvLSTM, STGCN, and our method are far less than the rest three models. Although ConvLSTM has the fewest parameters, our model surpasses a large margin in operating efficiency. In all models, the operating efficiency of HA is best, while our model is the most efficient among deep learning-based models. The inference time of STDN is slightly higher than our model, whereas the parameter quantity of STDN is more than ten times that of our model. Although the performance of STA3DCNN on the two efficiency criteria is not the best, the comprehensive performance is higher than the rest models.

Table 2. Evaluation of each component composing STA3DCNN. 'w/o' in each sub-test means 'without'.

Module	TaxiBJ		BikeNYC	
	RMSE	MAE	RMSE	MAE
STA3DCNN-w/o-STEM	43.23	21.40	7.04	3.24
STA3DCNN-w/o-STCPM	17.88	9.93	4.69	2.52
STA3DCNN-w/o-BFM	16.89	9.81	4.52	2.35
STA3DCNN-w/o-Att	16.45	9.49	4.50	2.31
STA3DCNN	16.29	9.36	4.45	2.26

Ablation Study. We verify the effectiveness of each component forming STA3DCNN by self-studying. The model is comprised of 4 key components: 3DAM, STEM, STCPM, and BFM. Among them, STEM and STCPM are two spatio-temporal feature extraction branches. Therefore, we verify each component via 4 sub-tests: 1) STA3DCNN-w/o-STEM: Verifying the cyclical patterns feature captured by STCPM to predict crowd flow without evolution features; 2) STA3DCNN-w/o-STCPM: Evaluating the evolution features captured by STEM without cyclical patterns; 3) STA3DCNN-w/o-BFM: Verifying BFM by fusing the features extracted by STEM and STCPM with the same weight; 4) STA3DCNN-w/o-att: Verifying the self-attention module in 3DAM.

The results of ablation tests on each component are shown in Table 2, from which we can observe: 1) Both STEM and STCPM are effective on this prediction task, which proves the effectiveness of evolution features and cyclical pattern features. Satisfactory performance is hard to be achieved by only using one of the two features. Besides, the contribution of evolution features to the task is greater than that of cyclical patterns features. 2) Compared with the fusion pattern via simply averaging, BFM can integrate features more effectively. Specifically, BFM can reduce RMSE by 3.55% and MAE by 4.59% on the TaxiBJ dataset, while RMSE and MAE are respectively decreased by 1.57% and 3.83% on the BikeNYC dataset. 3) The result of the STA3DCNN-w/o-att test demonstrates that SAM in our 3DAM module can effectively capture temporal and spatial features.

6   Conclusion

In this paper, we propose a spatial-temporal attention 3D convolutional neural network for the task of crowd flow prediction. Instead of utilizing RNN structure to extract features, our work introduces a more effective and efficient structure based on 3DCNN and the self-attention mechanism. We firstly implement the 3DAM module which served as an elementary module. Then, by using 3DAM, we implement the extraction module for the evolution features of the crowd flow and the cyclical pattern features. Finally, a feature fusion module is implemented to fuse features. The experimental results demonstrate that our method is effective and efficient in predicting crowd flows, and performs better than 9 representative models. The results of the ablation study demonstrate that the modules forming STA3DCNN are effective, and can incrementally improve the performance of the proposed model. In the future, we will explore the interpretability of spatio-temporal features from the actual physical meaning of the region for further improving the performance of the method.

Acknowledgment. This research was supported by National Key R&D Program of China (No. 2017YFC0806000), National Natural Science Foundation of China (No. 11627802, 51678249, 61871188), State Key Lab of Subtropical Building Science, South China University of Technology (2018ZB33), and the State Scholar- ship Fund of China Scholarship Council (201806155022).

References

1. Bai, L., Yao, L., Kanhere, S.S., Wang, X., Sheng, Q.Z.: Stg2seq: spatial-temporal graph to sequence model for multi-step passenger demand forecasting. In: IJCAI 2019 (2019)
2. Chen, T., Guestrin, C.: Xgboost: a scalable tree boosting system. In: Proceedings of the 22nd ACM SIGKDD International Conference on Knowledge Discovery and Data Mining, pp. 785–794 (2016)
3. Chung, J., Gulcehre, C., Cho, K., Bengio, Y.: Empirical evaluation of gated recurrent neural networks on sequence modeling. In: NIPS 2014 Workshop on Deep Learning, December 2014 (2014)

4. Do, L.N., Vu, H.L., Vo, B.Q., Liu, Z., Phung, D.: An effective spatial-temporal attention based neural network for traffic flow prediction. Transp. Res. Part C Emerg. Technol. **108**, 12–28 (2019)
5. Hamed, M.M., Al-Masaeid, H.R., Said, Z.M.B.: Short-term prediction of traffic volume in urban arterials. J. Transp. Eng. **121**(3), 249–254 (1995)
6. He, K., Zhang, X., Ren, S., Sun, J.: Delving deep into rectifiers: surpassing human-level performance on imagenet classification. In: 2015 IEEE International Conference on Computer Vision (ICCV), pp. 1026–1034 (2015). https://doi.org/10.1109/ICCV.2015.123
7. Jain, L.C., Medsker, L.R.: Recurrent Neural Networks: Design and Applications, 1st edn. CRC Press Inc, USA (1999)
8. Li, H., Liu, X., Kang, Y., Zhang, Y., Bu, R.: Urban traffic flow forecast based on dual path network. In: Journal of Physics: Conference Series, vol. 1453, p. 012162 (2020)
9. Li, W., Wang, J., Fan, R., Zhang, Y., Guo, Q., Siddique, C., Ban, X.J.: Short-term traffic state prediction from latent structures: accuracy vs. efficiency. Transp. Res. Part C Emerg. Technol. **111**, 72–90 (2020). https://doi.org/10.1016/j.trc.2019.12.007
10. Lin, Z., Feng, J., Lu, Z., Li, Y., Jin, D.: Deepstn+: context-aware spatial-temporal neural network for crowd flow prediction in metropolis. In: Proceedings of the AAAI Conference on Artificial Intelligence, vol. 33, pp. 1020–1027 (2019)
11. Liu, L., et al.: Dynamic spatial-temporal representation learning for traffic flow prediction. IEEE Trans. Intell. Transp. Syst. **22**, 7169–7183 (2020)
12. Liu, Y., Blandin, S., Samaranayake, S.: Stochastic on-time arrival problem in transit networks. Transp. Res. Part B Method. **119**, 122–138 (2019). https://doi.org/10.1016/j.trb.2018.11.013
13. Paszke, A., et al.: Pytorch: an imperative style, high-performance deep learning library. In: Advances in Neural Information Processing Systems, pp. 8026–8037 (2019)
14. Sak, H., Senior, A., Beaufays, F.: Long short-term memory recurrent neural network architectures for large scale acoustic modeling. Comput. Sci. **29**, 338–342 (2014)
15. Sharma, M., Pachori, R., Rajendra, A.: Adam: a method for stochastic optimization. Pattern Recogn. Lett. **94**, 172–179 (2017)
16. Shekhar, S., Williams, B.M.: Adaptive seasonal time series models for forecasting short-term traffic flow. Transp. Res. Rec. **2024**(1), 116–125 (2007)
17. Shi, X., Chen, Z., Wang, H., Yeung, D.Y., kin Wong, W., chun Woo, W.: Convolutional lstm network: a machine learning approach for precipitation nowcasting. In: NIPS 2015 Proceedings of the 28th International Conference on Neural Information Processing Systems - Volume 1, vol. 28, pp. 802–810 (2015)
18. Smith, B.L., Demetsky, M.J.: Traffic flow forecasting: comparison of modeling approaches. J. Transp. Eng. **123**(4), 261–266 (1997)
19. Sun, H., Liu, H.X., Xiao, H., He, R.R., Ran, B.: Use of local linear regression model for short-term traffic forecasting. Transp. Res. Rec. **1836**(1836), 143–150 (2003)
20. Wang, J., Deng, W., Guo, Y.: New bayesian combination method for short-term traffic flow forecasting. Transp. Res. Part C Emerg. Technol. **43**, 79–94 (2014)
21. Wu, C.H., Ho, J.M., Lee, D.: Travel-time prediction with support vector regression. IEEE Trans. Intell. Transp. Syst. **5**(4), 276–281 (2004)
22. Xu, L., Chen, X., Xu, Y., Chen, W., Wang, T.: ST-DCN: a spatial-temporal densely connected networks for crowd flow prediction. In: Shao, J., Yiu, M.L., Toyoda, M., Zhang, D., Wang, W., Cui, B. (eds.) APWeb-WAIM 2019. LNCS, vol. 11642, pp. 111–118. Springer, Cham (2019). https://doi.org/10.1007/978-3-030-26075-0_9

23. Yao, H., Tang, X., Wei, H., Zheng, G., Li, Z.: Revisiting spatial-temporal similarity: a deep learning framework for traffic prediction. In: Proceedings of the AAAI Conference on Artificial Intelligence, vol. 33, pp. 5668–5675 (2019)
24. Yu, B., Yin, H., Zhu, Z.: Spatio-temporal graph convolutional networks: a deep learning framework for traffic forecasting. In: Twenty-Seventh International Joint Conference on Artificial Intelligence IJCAI-18 (2018)
25. Zhang, J., Zheng, Y., Qi, D.: Deep spatio-temporal residual networks for citywide crowd flows prediction. In: Thirty-First AAAI Conference on Artificial Intelligence (2017)
26. Zhang, J., Zheng, Y., Qi, D., Li, R., Yi, X.: Dnn-based prediction model for spatio-temporal data. In: Proceedings of the 24th ACM SIGSPATIAL International Conference on Advances in Geographic Information Systems, pp. 1–4 (2016)
27. Zhao, L., et al.: T-GCN: a temporal graph convolutional network for traffic prediction. IEEE Trans. Intell. Transp. Syst. **21**, 3848–3858 (2019)

Learning Pre-grasp Pushing Manipulation of Wide and Flat Objects Using Binary Masks

Jiaxi Wu[1,2], Shanlin Zhong[1,2], and Yinlin Li[1(✉)]

[1] The State Key Laboratory for Management and Control of Complex Systems, Institute of Automation, Chinese Academy of Sciences, Beijing 100190, China
yinlin.li@ia.ac.cn
[2] The School of Artificial Intelligence, University of Chinese Academy of Sciences, Beijing 100049, China

Abstract. For wide and flat objects, such as books and package boxes, the robot arm cannot grasp directly because of the limit of the gripper width. Therefore, pre-grasp manipulation is needed to make them graspable, e.g., pushing it to the table side and grasp from the side. In this paper, we propose a novel method to learn the pre-grasp manipulation based on deep reinforcement learning. Instead of directly feeding the raw images, we generate the binary masks as states according to the shape and current position of the object and table. Meanwhile, we use adaptive resets to accelerate the training process, i.e., adaptively reset the initial states to demonstration states. After training on a large scale of automatically generated objects and tables of different shapes, our proposed method achieves a 97.6% success rate on novel objects. The detailed experimental videos are available at https://sites.google.com/view/pre-grasp.

Keywords: Pre-grasp manipulation · Deep reinforcement learning · Adaptive resets

1 Introduction

When wide and flat objects whose widths exceed the limit of the gripper, such as books and packing boxes, are placed flat on the table, the robot arm cannot pick directly because there is no direct vertical grasping point and they can only be picked from the side. Special grippers were designed in [1] [2] to shovel them up and make them graspable. However, such methods require the additional design of grippers, and the grippers need to be replaced when grasping different objects.

Another strategy is to push or slide the flat object to the table edge and then picked from its side [3]. This kind of manipulation before grasping is called "pre-grasp" [4]. However, the above method need pre-designed trajectories and

This work is partly supported by the Open Fund of Science and Technology on Thermal Energy and Power Laboratory (No. TPL2020C02), Wuhan 2nd Ship Design and Research Institute, Wuhan, P.R. China.

© Springer Nature Switzerland AG 2021
T. Mantoro et al. (Eds.): ICONIP 2021, LNCS 13111, pp. 366–377, 2021.
https://doi.org/10.1007/978-3-030-92273-3_30

only suitable for fixed physical parameters and cannot deal with different shapes of objects.

In recent years, with the development of deep learning, data-driven grasping methods have shown many excellent performances, which are helpful to solve the above problems. When facing multiple objects close together, QT-Opt will separate one of them from other blocks and then pick up it [5]. Dex-Net shows strong adaptability to different types of objects [6]. With the help of dynamics randomization, the policy can generalize to the real world without any training on the physical system [7]. However, those kinds of research mainly focus on the small objects that can be grasped vertically by the gripper and do not consider how to pick wide and flat objects that can only be picked from the side.

In this paper, we focus on the pre-grasp manipulation of wide and flat objects and propose a novel method based on deep reinforcement learning to achieve the pre-grasp manipulation and make the object graspable. Instead of directly feeding raw images into the networks, we use the binary masks of objects and tables as states, significantly improving policy performance. The binary masks make it easier for the policy to extract information without losing valid features, so the network can converge more quickly and achieve a higher success rate. Moreover, we adaptively reset the environment to the states in the demonstration trajectories according to the current success rate. By training on automatically generated objects and tables with different shapes, our method can achieve the pre-grasp manipulation under arbitrary shapes of objects and tables, even if it has never seen the object or the table before. In this paper, we expand the categories of objects in robotic grasping, so that the robot can better complete the autonomous grasping task in the open environment.

2   Related Work

Grasping is one of the most fundamental problems in robotic manipulation. And there are many works in this field [5,6]. However, they all assume that objects are graspable from at least one suitable position, and they do not consider how to deal with the ungraspable objects. For example, when a book is flat on the table, its width has exceeded the maximum width of the gripper, so it cannot be directly picked. In this situation, one possible solution is to push the book to the edge of the table, making it graspable, and pick it from the side [4]. This manipulation method is called "pre-grasp" [4].

Pushing [8], sliding [9], and rolling [10] are all used to reconfigure the posture of an object, making it easier to pick. However, it is hard to generalize those approaches to novel objects, especially when they are based on human demonstration and object classification.

Hang et al. proposed a motion planner based on CBiRRT, generating a suitable trajectory to slide the object to the table side [11]. However, to ensure stable contact with the object and keep its posture unchanged in the moving process, they used an underactuated gripper to slide the object from its top, which simplified the problem. In this paper, the fully driven gripper is used to push the object from its side. Objects can move freely, so the policy is more complicated, which is a challengeable problem for analysis-based approaches [12].

Sun et al. used reinforcement learning to make objects graspable through pushing and lifting [13]. They first pushed the object against a support surface and then lifted it by pivoting. However, two robot arms are required to achieve the grasping task, one for lifting the object and one for grasping, while our method only needs one. Moreover, the policy in [13] does not know the shape of the object, which makes it unable to select a suitable desired position when its graspable position changes with the environment. However, we use the binary masks as states to ensure that the policy can make decisions according to the shapes of objects and tables.

3   Background

3.1   Reinforcement Learning (RL)

A Markov Decision Process (MDP) can be denoted by a tuple (S, A, p, r, γ), where S is the set of states, A is the set of actions, p is the state transition probability function, r is the reward function, and $\gamma \in [0, 1]$ is the discount factor.

Reinforcement learning aims to maximize the expected return, which can be defined as the discounted sum of rewards $R_t = \sum_{i=t}^{T} \gamma^{i-t} r_i$. The agent's goal is to learn a policy π_θ, parameterized by θ, which performs the return-maximizing behavior. Various reinforcement learning algorithm has been proposed to solve this problem, e.g. DDPG [14], A3C [15], and PPO [16].

3.2   Reset from Demonstration

In sparse reward problems, the agent can only get rewards when the task is achieved successfully. It is difficult for the agent to learn an effective policy to solve the problems, especially facing long-horizon tasks. Restarts from demonstration states can expose the agent to easier states which need fewer steps to achieve the tasks [17]. When the agent has learned how to achieve those simpler tasks, it becomes easier for the agent to learn how to achieve the task under normal resets.

4   Methods

4.1   Procedural Generation of Objects and Tables

In order to learn a general pre-grasp policy, which can deal with different shapes of objects and tables, we first generate large-scale object and table datasets. All the generated objects are wide and flat, which exceed the limit of the gripper width. Therefore, the objects need to be pushed to the table side and picked from the side.

The generated objects can be divided into three categories: polygons, round-ness, and irregular shapes, as shown in Fig. 1. The polygons, including square, rectangle, and hexagon, are all regular and convex. The roundness, including cir-cle, eight-shape, and bee-shape, all have curved edges. In contrast, the irregular shapes are non-convex, which are composed of two rectangles joined together.

The tables we use in this paper can be divided into four categories: full-shape, arc-shape, gap-shape, and diagonal-shape. Considering the restraint of the robot arm's workspace, the object can only be picked from the right side of the table. Therefore, we only change the shapes on the right side of the table. The agent needs to consider the different table edges and choose different graspable postures for the objects.

Specifically, we use different shapes of objects and tables and randomize them in height and size to increase the robustness of the pre-grasp policy.

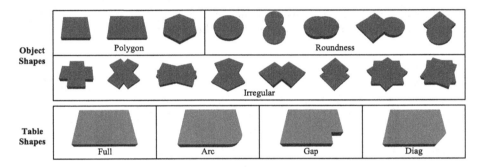

Fig. 1. Examples of objects and tables. The first two lines are examples of objects with different contours. And the last line is the examples of tables with different edges.

4.2 Learning Pre-grasp Manipulation Policy

The pre-grasp policy needs to know the shape features of objects and tables in order to work on arbitrary shapes and sizes. However, if we feed the raw image directly into the network, it is hard to learn a suitable policy, considering the information incompleteness due to the situation such as object occlusion. Besides, the simulated image inputs will increase the difficulty of sim-to-real transfer [18].

Therefore, instead of raw images, we use the binary masks of the object and table as the policy's states. Through the binary masks, the policy can extract the shape features and the relative posture of the object and table. Then, it can choose a suitable posture for the object and push it to make it graspable.

The binary masks we use includes three images: object mask I_o, table mask I_t, and their xor mask I_x, which is defined as

$$I_x = \mathrm{AND}(\mathrm{XOR}(I_o, I_t), I_o). \tag{1}$$

An example for the binary masks is shown on the left column of Fig. 2. Since the tables are different only in the lower right, the masks I_t show only this part of the tables. At the beginning of each episode, we collect the initial masks of the object and table. The binary masks for the rest step in the episode is calculated based on the initial masks and the object's current posture. Therefore, even if the robot arm is blocking the object, we can still get their entire masks.

The reinforcement learning algorithm used in this paper is twin delayed deep deterministic policy gradient (TD3) [19], a variant of DDPG [14]. The network structure is shown in Fig. 2. In the actor network, the state s includes three binary masks, the height of the object and the table, and the posture and velocity of the end effector. Moreover, the action a is the linear velocity of the end effector. Specifically, we add some auxiliary outputs to help the convolution layers converge faster, which has been used in [20]. The auxiliary outputs include the 2D coordinates of the object, the table, their relative position, and a signal to indicate if the object is graspable. The critic network is similar to the actor network, whereas there is no auxiliary output. Moreover, its state is richer than the actor network to help the critic evaluate the policy better.

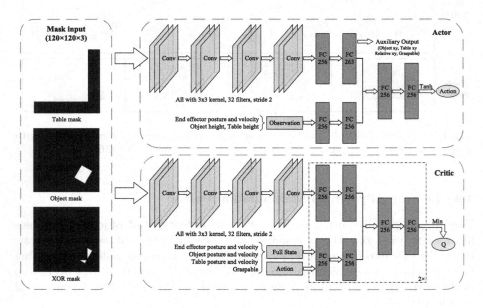

Fig. 2. The network structure.

The reward function is essential for the reinforcement learning. However, it is difficult to design a complex reward function that is easy to maximize and obtains the desired behavior after optimization. Therefore, we use the binary reward for the pre-grasp task, whose policy is more robust than hand-designed reward functions [21].

$$r_t = \begin{cases} 0, & \text{the object is graspable} \\ -1, & \text{otherwise.} \end{cases} \tag{2}$$

As described in [11], there are three requirements to make the object graspable: 1) the object must be on the table; 2) there is enough portion of the object outside the table to grasp; 3) the grasping point is reachable for the robot arm. Considering the complex shapes of the objects, these three conditions are difficult to determine from the relative position of the object and the table. However, with the help of our previous definition of the masks I_o, I_t, and I_x, it is more convenient to determine if the object is graspable and get the grasping point g.

4.3 RL with Adaptive Resets

Since we use sparse rewards, it is difficult for reinforcement learning algorithms to learn effective policy. However, reset from demonstration states can accelerate the training process of the reinforcement learning and help the agent to learn a policy with better performance [17].

Therefore, we reset the environment for two cases. When the agent does not know how to achieve the task, the state is reset to the demonstration states. It helps the agent to learn to achieve the simpler subtasks, which need fewer steps to achieve those tasks. Then, when the agent knows how to achieve the task, the state is reset normally, making the agent learn how to achieve the task during various initial situations. The choice of two reset method is determined by the current success rate sr [22], i.e.,

$$p_d = \text{clip}(1 - sr/\alpha, \epsilon_1, \epsilon_2) \tag{3}$$
$$p_n = 1 - p_d \tag{4}$$

where p_d is the probability to reset from demonstration state, p_n is the probability to reset normally, and ϵ_1 and ϵ_2 are the minimum and maximum probabilities of p_d respectively. $\alpha \in (0, 1]$ is a coefficient that adjusts the practical scope of reset from demonstration states. When $sr > \alpha$, only a small probability ϵ_1 is maintained to reset from demonstration; otherwise it is reset normally.

Correspondingly, we divide the replay buffer into the demonstration buffer and the train buffer. The demonstration buffer stores the demonstration data, which is used to sample the demonstration states. The train buffer stores the episodes which reset from the normal and demonstration states. Meanwhile, the demonstration data is used for policy training to accelerate network convergence. The entire algorithm is illustrated in Algorithm 1.

Meanwhile, when the gripper pokes the object or the table, the robot arm will stop abruptly, causing the task to fail. Therefore, we add some action restrictions on the action space to prevent those cases. With the help of the mask I_o and I_t, the gripper height can be restricted into a suitable value.

$$h = \max(h, h_t + h_o + \delta), \; if \; I_o(x, y) > 0 \tag{5}$$
$$h = \max(h, h_t + \delta), \; if \; I_t(x, y) > 0 \tag{6}$$

Algorithm 1: RL with Adaptive Resets

Initialize one RL algorithm, e.g. TD3;
Initialize train buffer $\mathcal{B}_t$ and demo buffer $\mathcal{B}_d$;
Save demo data in demo buffer $\mathcal{B}_d$;
for epi $= 1, M$ **do**
    if $p < p_d$ **then** // p is uniformly sampled in $[0,1]$
        reset from demo states ;   // sampling from demo buffer $\mathcal{B}_d$
        rollout and save in train buffer $\mathcal{B}_t$;
    else
        reset normally;
        rollout and save in train buffer $\mathcal{B}_t$;
    end
    Update success rate sr by the latest k samples of normal resets;
    for $t = 1, N$ **do**
        Sample a minibatch B_m from $\mathcal{B}_t$, $\mathcal{B}_d$;
        Perform one step optimization;
    end
end

---

where h is the gripper height, h_t and h_o are the height of the object and table, respectively, and δ is a small margin between the gripper and the object/table.

Dynamics randomization has been proved in [7] that it can help overcome the reality gap and transfer the simulated policy to the real world. Therefore, we randomize some physical parameters at the beginning of each episode, as shown in Table 1.

Table 1. Random physical parameters. The shapes, sizes, and heights of the objects and tables are also randomly initialized, which are not listed in the table.

Parameters	Default	Min	Max
Object Mass (kg)	0.288	0.1	0.5
Friction Coefficient	0.5	0.2	0.8
Damp Coefficient	0.01	0.001	0.5
Object Position (m)	$(-0.05, 0.3)$	$(-0.07, 0.25)$	$(-0.02, 0.3)$
Object Orientation (rad)	0	$-\pi$	π
Table Position (m)	$(-0.05, 0.3)$	$(-0.07, 0.25)$	$(-0.02, 0.3)$

5   Experiments

5.1   Experimental Setting

A 6-axis UR3 robot arm with Robotiq85 gripper is used to perform the pre-grasp manipulation in this paper, as shown in Fig. 3. And they are implemented in

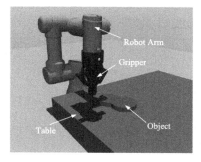

Fig. 3. Simulation environment in MuJoCo [23]. The robot arm needs to push the object to the right side of the table, making it graspable.

MuJoCo [23]. The agent's task is to perform the pre-grasp manipulation (pushing the object to the table side) to make the object graspable.

At the beginning of each episode, we first choose a table and an object randomly and get their masks through a virtual camera on top of the table. Then we randomize the physical parameters in Table 1. If the state is chosen from demonstration states, the shape, size, height, position of the object and table are initialized according to the sampled state. However, the other physical parameters are still initialized randomly.

We limit the maximum step of each episode to 75 steps, and each simulation step costs 40 ms. For our method with mask inputs, it takes approximately 3.1 h to run 5000 episodes on one GeForce GTX 1660 Ti, and achieves a 97.6% success rate on novel objects.

5.2   Simulated Results

Contrast Experiments. We compare our method with two baselines on the pre-grasp manipulation task to verify the effectiveness of our method.

Ours: Our method with binary mask inputs and adaptive resets.

Full State: Feed full state into the network, instead of the binary masks and observations in Fig. 2, like the method in [13], and we add adaptive resets to improve its performance.

Raw Image: Directly feed raw images into the network in Fig. 2, like the method in [20], and we use RL with adaptive resets for better comparison.

The experimental results are shown in Fig. 4. Our method exceeds baselines' performance and achieves the highest success rate. When using one-dimensional full states as input, the shape features of objects and tables are lost. It results in the policy's inability to know the suitable posture of the object to make it graspable, causing the task failure. When the raw images are directly input into the network, more samples are needed to make the network converge because of its rich information. Therefore, it still keeps a low success rate when the other

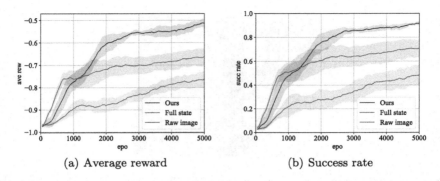

(a) Average reward   (b) Success rate

Fig. 4. Contrast experiments with two baselines. The rewards and success rates, which is the average of 100 episodes, are tested every 50 training episodes. The solid lines are the mean of 5 seeds and the shaded lines are their standard deviations.

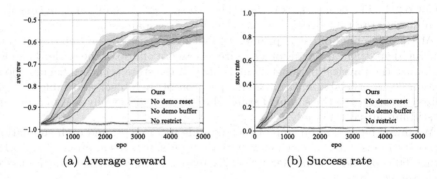

(a) Average reward   (b) Success rate

Fig. 5. Ablation study. The rewards and success rates, which is the average of 100 episodes, are tested every 50 training episodes. The solid lines are the mean of 5 seeds and the shaded lines are their standard deviations.

two methods have converged. However, through feeding the pre-extracted masks, we overcome the above shortcomings and achieve the highest success rate.

Ablation Study. Meanwhile, we perform ablation study on our algorithm to prove the effectiveness of each part. For better comparison, the following methods all feed the binary masks into the network, as described in Fig. 2.

Ours: Our method with binary mask inputs and adaptive resets.

No Demo Reset: We do not reset the initial state to the demonstration states, but we still retain the demo buffer for training.

No Demo Buffer: We do not use the demonstration data for training, but we reset the initial states to them.

No Restrict: We do not restrict the policy's action, i.e., (5) and (6).

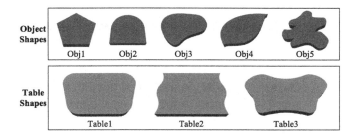

Fig. 6. Examples of novel objects and tables used in Sect. 5.3.

Table 2. Generalization of new object. For each object, we perform 100 trials on each table in Fig. 6. The physical parameters of objects and tables are randomly initialized according to Table 1.

	Obj1	Obj2	Obj3	Obj4	Obj5	All
Ours	**0.973**	**0.997**	**0.973**	**0.957**	**0.980**	**0.976**
Full state	0.580	0.633	0.610	0.580	0.653	0.611
Raw image	0.190	0.410	0.343	0.330	0.387	0.332

The experimental results are shown in Fig. 5. When not reset from the demonstration states, the policy continues to receive no reward, so its success rates remain around 2% (the object is directly initialized to a graspable position). Meanwhile, the demonstration samples can accelerate the training and make the network converge faster. Additionally, the relative position of the gripper, the object, and the table can improve the success rate of our method. This is because the restriction prevents the gripper from poking the object or table, thereby preventing the task failure. Moreover, it is helpful to future real-world experiments by avoiding the most likely failure scenario.

5.3   Generalize to Novel Objects

In this section, we use 5 novel objects (first line in Fig. 6) and 3 novel tables (second line in Fig. 6) to evaluate the generalization of our methods. We compare our method with two baselines in terms of success rates, and the results are shown in Table 2 and 3. When faced with novel objects and tables, our method can still maintain > 95% success rates, while the baselines have low success rates. This proves that our method can be generalized to novel objects and realize the pre-grasp manipulation of unseen objects. Specifically, the policy's success rates of our method on novel objects are even higher than its success rates on seen objects (Table 1). This is because the novel objects we choose are regular sizes and do not include extreme cases.

Table 3. Generalization of new tables. For each table, we perform 100 trials on each object in Fig. 6. The physical parameters of objects and tables are randomly initialized according to Table 1.

	Table 1	Table 2	Table 3	All
Ours	**0.972**	**0.986**	**0.970**	**0.976**
Full state	0.650	0.582	0.602	0.611
Raw image	0.440	0.530	0.026	0.332

6   Conclusion

In this paper, we propose a novel method based on deep reinforcement learning to achieve the pre-grasp manipulation, i.e., push the object to the table side, making it graspable. We leverage a physics simulator that allows a robot arm to autonomously perform pre-grasp trials, with the shapes and sizes of the objects and tables changing every episode. Meanwhile, adaptive resets to demonstration states are used to accelerate policy learning. Our experimental results illustrate that our method can make the novel objects graspable by pre-grasp manipulation, even if the policy has never seen such objects and tables.

In the future, we will transfer our trained policy to the real world and deploy it on physical robots. The action restrictions are proposed in this paper to improve the trained policy's performance, which effectively overcome the reality gap. Meanwhile, other methods are required to improve the effectiveness and robustness for a better sim-to-real transfer. Another research topic is how to perform the pre-grasp manipulation on non-flat tables with obstacles, where the policy is more complex, considering the 3D shape of the table and the obstacle distribution.

References

1. Babin, V., St-Onge, D., Gosselin, C.: Stable and repeatable grasping of flat objects on hard surfaces using passive and epicyclic mechanisms. Rob. Comput. Integr. Manuf. **55**(Part A), 1–10 (2019)
2. Tong, Z., He, T., Kim, C.H., Ng, Y.H., Xu, Q., Seo, J.: Picking thin objects by tilt-and-pivot manipulation and its application to bin picking. In: 2020 IEEE International Conference on Robotics and Automation, pp. 9932–9938. IEEE (2020)
3. Kappler, D., Chang, L.Y., Pollard, N.S., Asfour, T., Dillmann, R.: Templates for pre-grasp sliding interactions. Robot. Auton. Syst. **60**(3), 411–423 (2012)
4. Chang, L.Y., Srinivasa, S.S., Pollard, N.S.: Planning pre-grasp manipulation for transport tasks. In: 2010 IEEE International Conference on Robotics and Automation, pp. 2697–2704. IEEE (2010)
5. Kalashnikov, et al.: QT-OPT: scalable deep reinforcement learning for vision-based robotic manipulation. arXiv preprint arXiv:1806.10293 (2018)
6. Mahler, J., et al.: Dex-Net 2.0: deep learning to plan robust grasps with synthetic point clouds and analytic grasp metrics. arXiv preprint arXiv:1703.09312 (2017)

7. Peng, X.B., Andrychowicz, M., Zaremba, W., Abbeel, P.: Sim-to-real transfer of robotic control with dynamics randomization. In: 2018 IEEE International Conference on Robotics and Automation, pp. 3803–3810. IEEE (2018)
8. Dogar, M.R., Srinivasa, S.S.: Push-grasping with dexterous hands: Mechanics and a method. In: 2010 IEEE/RSJ International Conference on Intelligent Robots and Systems, pp. 2123–2130. IEEE (2010)
9. King, J.E., et al.: Pregrasp manipulation as trajectory optimization. In: Robotics: Science and Systems, Berlin (2013)
10. Chang, L.Y., Zeglin, G.J., Pollard, N.S.: Preparatory object rotation as a human-inspired grasping strategy. In: Humanoids 2008–8th IEEE-RAS International Conference on Humanoid Robots. pp. 527–534. IEEE (2008)
11. Hang, K., Morgan, A.S., Dollar, A.M.: Pre-grasp sliding manipulation of thin objects using soft, compliant, or underactuated hands. IEEE Rob. Autom. Lett. 4(2), 662–669 (2019)
12. Stüber, J., Zito, C., Stolkin, R.: Let's push things forward: a survey on robot pushing. Frontiers Rob. AI 7, 8 (2020)
13. Sun, Z., Yuan, K., Hu, W., Yang, C., Li, Z.: Learning pregrasp manipulation of objects from ungraspable poses. In: 2020 IEEE International Conference on Robotics and Automation, pp. 9917–9923. IEEE (2020)
14. Lillicrap, T.P., et al.: Continuous control with deep reinforcement learning. arXiv preprint arXiv:1509.02971 (2015)
15. Mnih, V., et al.: Asynchronous methods for deep reinforcement learning. In: International Conference on Machine Learning, pp. 1928–1937. PMLR (2016)
16. Schulman, J., Wolski, F., Dhariwal, P., Radford, A., Klimov, O.: Proximal policy optimization algorithms. arXiv preprint arXiv:1707.06347 (2017)
17. Vecerik, M., et al.: Leveraging demonstrations for deep reinforcement learning on robotics problems with sparse rewards. arXiv preprint arXiv:1707.08817 (2017)
18. Tobin, J., Fong, R., Ray, A., Schneider, J., Zaremba, W., Abbeel, P.: Domain randomization for transferring deep neural networks from simulation to the real world. In: 2017 IEEE/RSJ International Conference on Intelligent Robots and Systems, pp. 23–30. IEEE (2017)
19. Fujimoto, S., Hoof, H., Meger, D.: Addressing function approximation error in actor-critic methods. In: International Conference on Machine Learning, pp. 1587–1596. PMLR (2018)
20. Matas, J., James, S., Davison, A.J.: Sim-to-real reinforcement learning for deformable object manipulation. In: Conference on Robot Learning, pp. 734–743. PMLR (2018)
21. Popov, I., et al.: Data-efficient deep reinforcement learning for dexterous manipulation. arXiv preprint arXiv:1704.03073 (2017)
22. Hermann, L., Argus, M., Eitel, A., Amiranashvili, A., Burgard, W., Brox, T.: Adaptive curriculum generation from demonstrations for sim-to-real visuomotor control. In: 2020 IEEE International Conference on Robotics and Automation, pp. 6498–6505. IEEE (2020)
23. Todorov, E., Erez, T., Tassa, Y.: MuJoCo: a physics engine for model-based control. In: 2012 IEEE/RSJ International Conference on Intelligent Robots and Systems, pp. 5026–5033. IEEE (2012)

Multi-DIP: A General Framework for Unsupervised Multi-degraded Image Restoration

Qiansong Wang[1], Xiao Hu[2], Haiying Wang[1], Aidong Men[1],
and Zhuqing Jiang[1(✉)]

[1] Beijing University of Posts and Telecommunications, Beijing 100876, China
{wangqs97,why,menad,jiangzhuqing}@bupt.edu.cn
[2] National Radio and Television Administration, Beijing 100045, China

Abstract. Most existing image restoration algorithms only perform a single task. But in the real world, the degradation pattern could be much more complex, such as blurred images that have been smudged or images with haze that have been blurred, and we call it multi-degradation. Many of these degenerations are coupled with each other, making it impossible to restore images by merely stacking the algorithms. In this paper, we propose Multi-DIP that uses DIP networks to solve the multi-degradation problem. We integrate multiple image restoration tasks into a unified framework. However, multi-degradation can cause difficulties for DIP networks to extract image priors. To alleviate this problem, we design a multi-scale structure to stabilize and improve the quality of generated images. We implement two image restoration tasks with the proposed DIP framework: *deblur + inpainting* and *dehaze + deblur*. Extensive experiments show that our proposed method achieves promising results for restoring multi-degraded images.

Keywords: Deep image prior · Multi-scale · Image restoration · Multi-degradation

1 Introduction

There are various low-level tasks in computer vision. In image inpainting, the task is to fill in the image's missing part through the context information [21]. The goal of blind deblur is to reconstruct the blurred image into a clear image when the blur kernel is unknown [8,12]. The task of image dehazing is to remove the image's underlying haze layer and generate the image without haze [3,9]. Supervised learning has achieved good results in the above fields, and one of the most important reasons is that the neural network structure can extract the

This work is sponsored by the National Key Research and Development Program under Grant (2018YFB0505200), National Natural Science Funding (No. 62002026) and MoE-CMCC "Artificial Intelligence" Project under Grant MCM20190701.

T. Mantoro et al. (Eds.): ICONIP 2021, LNCS 13111, pp. 378–389, 2021.
https://doi.org/10.1007/978-3-030-92273-3_31

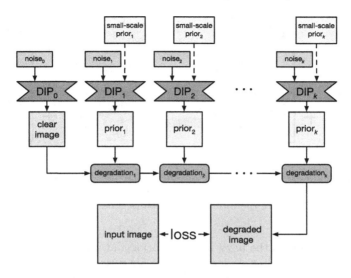

Fig. 1. The structure of our Multi-DIP. It's unsupervised and the restored image is directly generated by DIP_0. One or several DIP networks simulate a degradation process of an image, and the pipeline models the image multi-degradation. DIP networks use noise as the input, and uses small-scale prior to constrain the generated results.

priors from massive datasets. However, testing the model on image domains that varied from datasets leads to significant degradation of the performance [7,25]. Therefore, multi-degradation restoration rises at the horizon, aiming to solve the degradation of multiple modes with one model simultaneously.

Also, the coupling of different degradation leads to the shift in image domains, and the existing methods are not flexible in this scope. They are either the traditional algorithms of manual modeling or the supervised end-to-end deep learning for specific tasks. In Wang et al. [20], an end-to-end convolutional neural network is used to restore images with noise and atmospheric degradation based on the atmospheric scattering model. Zhang et al. [24] also use an end-to-end network to achieve super-resolution and deblurring of degraded images through a predetermined blur kernel. Once the task is changed, it is required to redesign the dataset and network with the condition of network convergency. The challenge of generalizations to other tasks is the primary obstacle for supervised learning in this field.

However, unsupervised learning saves the external training set, and naturally is free from the cross-domain problem described above. Deep image prior (DIP) [19] is a representative unsupervised learning method for image restoration. There are also corresponding DIP solutions for several of the computer vision tasks mentioned above. For image inpainting, DIP [19] uses an encoder-decoder to capture the image priors and directly generate the restored image. For image blind deblurring, Self-Deblur [16] uses two DIP networks to generate the restored image and the blur kernel respectively. Double-DIP [5] uses the

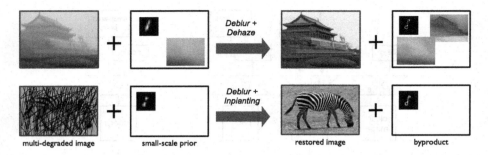

Fig. 2. Multi-degraded image restoration using Multi-DIP. Two tasks follow the similar pipeline. The small-scale prior generated by small-scale images provides constraints for restoration. Byproducts are the intermediate results generated by DIP networks.

ground truth airlight of the hazy image as prior and post-process the transmission map with guided-filter. Using DIP only for a single task fails to utilize its full potential. As long as the image degradation is modeled, it is theoretically feasible to restore arbitrary degradation using DIP.

In this paper, we propose a Multi-DIP framework capable of restoring multi-degraded images. We input different noise images to different DIP networks, and then the degradation equation uses the intermediate results generated by these DIP networks to model image restoration. To stabilize the restoration of multi-degraded images, we use a multi-scale approach. The results generated from the small-scale images are processed and then used as the prior to initialize the large-scale DIP network. The errors caused by small-scale images can be fine-tuned by subsequent large-scale images, which is a classic *coarse-to-fine* manner and has achieved good results in many tasks [15,26]. The overall structure is shown in Fig. 1, and the tasks we implement with Multi-DIP are shown in Fig. 2.

Our contributions are summarized as follows:

- We introduce a general pipeline of restoring multi-degraded images. We redesign the dehazing part to show how to integrate a complex restoration task with our Multi-DIP framework.
- We initialize the large-scale image with the prior generated in restoring the small-scale image for multi-degraded images. This multi-scale approach stabilizes and improves the performance of our DIP framework.
- We propose a new dataset, syn-Set14, for *inpainting + deblur*. Because there are few datasets in this field, we conduct qualitative and quantitative experiments on this dataset to prove the effectiveness of our method.

2   Deblur + Inpainting

2.1   Coupled Degradation

As illustrated in the previous section, when a blurred picture is smudged, we need to perform a joint task of deblurring and dehazing. In this task, the blur

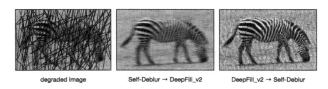

degraded image   Self-Deblur → DeepFill_v2   DeepFill_v2 → Self-Deblur

Fig. 3. Different combinations of *stacked* algorithms.

kernel and the occluded mask are coupled with each other. If we use a *stacked* algorithms to solve this problem, we will find that the incomplete and blurred image corrupts the image prior required for deblurring and inpainting tasks respectively.

To show the influence of coupled problems more intuitively on the image reconstruction process, we have carried out experiments in two practices: deblur first and then inpainting, and inpainting first and then deblur. For the fairness of the experiment, the same as our method based on Multi-DIP, the inpainting method needs a pre-given occluded mask, and the deblur method does not need to be given blur kernel in advance. Specifically, DeepFill v2 [22] are used for inpainting tasks, while Self-Deblur is used for deblur tasks. Results are shown in Fig. 3. In the multiple degradation problem, wrong reconstruction results will be obtained no matter which stacking combination is adopted.

2.2   Network Structure

We denote the degraded image $I(x)$ under this task as:

$$I(x) = (k(x) \otimes y(x)) \odot m(x) \tag{1}$$

where $k(x)$ is the unknown blur kernel, $m(x)$ is the pre-given inpainting mask, $\otimes$ is the two-dimensional convolution operation, $\odot$ is Hadamard product, and $y(x)$ represents the restored image. We use the DIP framework (shown in Fig. 4) to solve this problem by simply simulating the image's degradation process (Eq. 1). In our approach, the blur operation directly impacts the clear image restored by the network, and the smudge operation acts directly on the blurred image. This is consistent with the image degradation pipeline under this task and does not excavate prior directly from the corrupt image.

2.3   Optimization Detail

In this task, the inpainting mask has been given, so the DIP framework aims to reconstruct the blur kernel, fill the content under the mask, and the clear image is generated during this process. The effectiveness of multi-scale blur kernels generation has been shown in [13,14], so we use the blur kernel generated from small-scale images to initialize that of large-scale images. Specifically, the blur

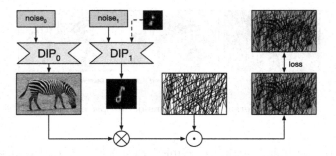

Fig. 4. Slove *deblur + inpainting* task with Multi-DIP.

kernel's noise is purged, and then we center and upsample this kernel to fit the large-scale images. As shown in Fig. 4, after obtaining the blur kernel for initialization, parameters of DIP_1 are first fixed, and this blur kernel is used to optimize DIP_0 for a few iterations. The parameters of DIP_0 are then fixed, and DIP_1 is optimized using the restored images generated by DIP_0. Finally, after the two networks are fully initialized, the joint optimization begins.

2.4 Dataset

The combination of different multi-degradation is quite diverse, resulting in many tasks without a complete dataset. Our experiment only needs test sets, so we consider adding different degrees of degradation to the existing complete test sets to thoroughly verify our model's performance with qualitative and quantitative experiments.

Set14 [23] is one of the most used test sets in super-resolution. Its details and diversity are very suitable for the *inpainting + deblur* task. We add two different sizes of blur kernels to each image in Set14, and each size contains three distinct types of blur kernels. Then, we add three different degrees of occluded masks to each generated image. The specific blur kernel and mask are shown in Fig. 5. Since the image size is not identical, we use the bilinear interpolation to scale each mask to the target image resolution. Finally, we obtain 252 multi-degraded images for the *inpainting + deblur* task.

2.5 Experiment

We use syn-Set14 for our experiment. Due to the influence of network randomly initialized parameters and random input noise, the quantitative results of each experiment will fluctuate. To alleviate this problem, we calculate the average of three restoration results of each image. For this new dataset, we do a detailed test on the quantitative evaluation of 14 sets of images and thoroughly analyze the performance of Multi-DIP under different degradation conditions.

Performance on Different Degradation Categoreis. Table 1 report the quantitative results on syn-Set14. The table shows that a larger kernel size means

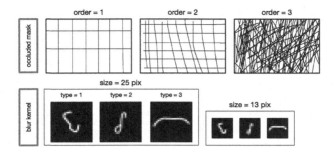

Fig. 5. Degradations in the syn-Set14 dataset.

Fig. 6. Visual results on syn-Set14 in *inpainting + deblur* task. Comparison of single-scale and multi-scale initialization are shown in second and third row.

lower PSNR of the restored image. The average PSNR of restored images with a small blur kernel is 0.61dB higher than that with a large blur kernel. The result is intuitive because the degradation level of images increases with a larger kernel size, and the task becomes more challenging for Multi-DIP. This further proves the necessity of multi-scale initialization. In addition, the performance of *pepper* is identical on both kernel sizes. These images with relatively simple structures lack complex texture, so different degrees of degradation have little impact on the restoration process. The restoration performance of the same image varies on different types of kernels. However, the degradation process involves the interaction between image content and blur kernel, so there is no pattern to follow in kernel type. The last degradation category is the degraded order of the occluded mask. Most images get the highest PSNR results when the degraded order is the smallest. The average PSNR of restored images with *order2* mask is 0.11dB lower than that with *order1* mask, and *order3* mask is 1.12dB lower than that with *order2* mask. A few images get the highest PSNR with *order2* mask because there are not many differences between *order1* and *order2* mask. The restoration performance based on DIP is fluctuated, resulting in better performance on the image with larger degradation order. The degradation of *order3* mask

Table 1. The quantitative experiment (PSNR) on syn-Set14. The bold number indicates the best result of each image in each category.

Degradation category	Type	Pictures													
		Baboon	Barbara	Bridge	Coastguard	Comic	Face	Flowers	Foreman	Lenna	Man	Monarch	Pepper	ppt	Zebra
Kernel size	13	**20.35**	**23.46**	**25.24**	25.84	**22.94**	29.12	**22.92**	29.05	23.36	**27.37**	24.11	22.49	**24.05**	24.46
	25	19.63	23.02	23.60	24.35	22.09	28.49	22.75	27.41	23.18	27.00	24.02	**22.49**	23.94	24.29
Kernel type	1	**20.11**	23.35	24.21	24.37	**22.65**	28.97	22.96	**28.53**	**23.44**	27.58	24.16	**22.52**	24.31	24.50
	2	19.81	**23.44**	**24.96**	23.88	22.25	28.75	22.58	28.05	23.40	26.93	23.93	22.45	23.67	24.21
	3	20.06	22.95	24.10	**26.87**	22.63	28.71	**22.97**	28.11	22.97	27.03	24.11	22.51	24.00	24.42
Mask order	1	**20.57**	23.56	**25.52**	25.07	**23.24**	**29.14**	**23.25**	**28.44**	**23.48**	**28.15**	**24.35**	22.56	24.48	**24.93**
	2	20.21	**23.73**	24.57	**25.70**	23.12	29.01	23.15	28.29	23.41	27.88	24.22	**22.57**	**24.53**	24.80
	3	19.21	22.45	23.18	24.36	21.17	28.27	22.11	27.97	22.93	25.52	23.63	22.35	22.97	23.40

Table 2. The quantitative comparison (PSNR) of single-scale and multi-scale initialization in *inpainting + deblur* task. The bold number indicates the best result of each image in each category.

	Pictures													
	Baboon	Barbara	Bridge	Coastguard	Comic	Face	Flowers	Foreman	Lenna	Man	Monarch	Pepper	Ppt	Zebra
Multi-scale	**20.00**	**23.25**	**24.43**	**25.04**	**22.51**	28.81	**22.84**	**28.23**	**23.27**	**27.18**	**24.07**	**22.49**	**24.10**	**24.38**
Single-scale	19.10	22.23	22.59	22.02	21.87	**28.86**	22.82	27.28	22.67	26.52	23.99	**22.49**	23.99	23.91
Diff	+0.90	+1.02	+1.84	+3.02	+0.64	-0.05	+0.02	+0.95	+0.60	+0.66	+0.08	+0.00	+0.11	+0.47

is significantly higher than that of the former two. While results show that the restoration performance under *order3* mask is the lowest, the results are very stable according to Table 1, which further confirms the ability of Multi-DIP to restore complex degraded images.

Performance of Multi-scale and Single-Scale. The experiments above are based on multi-scale initialization. We further compare multi-scale and single-scale manner, reported in Table 2 and Fig. 6. We observe that the average PSNR of images restored with multi-scale initialization is 0.72dB higher than that with a single-scale manner, which indicates Multi-DIP framework provides a much more stable restoration process.

3   Deblur + Dehaze

Referring to the atmospheric scattering model [6], the dehazing task can be denoted as:

$$I(x) = t(x)J(x) + (1 - t(x))A(x) \tag{2}$$

Where $I(x)$ is the hazy image, $t(x)$ is the transmission map, $J(x)$ is the clear image, and $A(x)$ represents the airlight map. Double-DIP implements the dehazing function, but it does not fully use the DIP network's ability to excavate priors from images in its specific implementation. In the following, we explain the difference between the dehazing algorithm based on Multi-DIP and Double-DIP. The detailed experiment is carried out on the HSTS dataset.

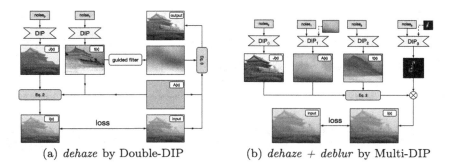

(a) *dehaze* by Double-DIP   (b) *dehaze + deblur* by Multi-DIP

Fig. 7. The network structure for two different tasks and methods.

3.1 Double-DIP in Dehaze

Double-DIP implements a variety of computer vision tasks by separating multiple layers of a single image. In dehaze, it separates a hazy image into its underlying haze-free image and the obscuring haze layers. Double-DIP wants to use multiple DIP networks as generators to obtain these unknown variables. The atmospheric scattering model simulated by the DIP network can generate hazy images and finally obtain haze-free images $J(x)$ in the intermediate result. However, its specific implementation differs somewhat from this idea.

First, Double-DIP uses the real airlight values provided in [1] to initialize the DIP network. Although we use the pre-given mask in the inpainting task in Sect. 3, this mask can be easily obtained by manual labeling. Double-DIP tries to use the method provided in [6] to get the prior of airlight value, but the result is not satisfactory. It ends up using the pre-given real data directly, which are not so easy to obtain. Secondly, the clear image restored by Double-DIP is not the $J(x)$ generated by the DIP network; the transmission map generated by the DIP network is processed with a guided-filter. The $J(x)$ is deduced by the atmospheric scattering model using the provided airlight value. Image $y(x)$ restored by Double-DIP can be denoted as:

$$y(x) = \frac{1}{t(x)} \times (I(x) - (1 - t(x)A(x))) \tag{3}$$

The transmission map is processed very blurred, resulting in little difference between the final clear images obtained on 100 iterations and 10000 iterations. It can be said that the optimization of this network is not directly reflected in the restored images. The specific network structure of Double-DIP dehazing is shown in Fig. 7(a).

3.2 Multi-DIP in Dehaze + Deblur

To integrate the dehazing function into the DIP framework, this part of the DIP network should use as few post-processing methods as possible. Each DIP net-

Table 3. The qualitative comparison of dehazing methods on HSTS Dataset.

	Tarel et al. [18]	He et al. [6]	Meng et al. [11]	Berman et al. [2]	Chen et al. [4]	Ren et al. [17]	Ours
PSNR	14.50	14.84	15.08	17.42	18.54	18.64	19.81
SSIM	0.7600	0.7609	0.7382	0.7917	0.8184	0.8168	0.8227

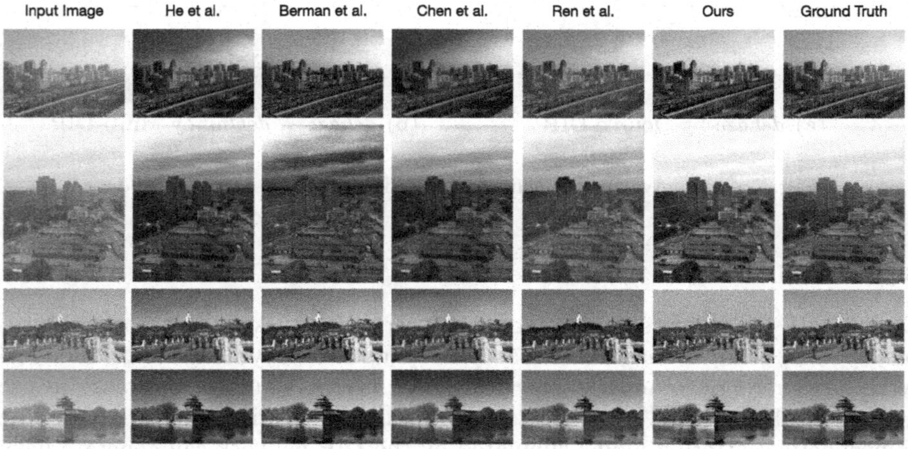

Fig. 8. Visual results of dehazing methods on HSTS Dataset.

work should produce meaningful outputs (e.g., blur kernel, airlight map, transmission map, restored images). Also, to ensure practicality, hard-to-obtain priors (e.g., real airlight values) should not be used.

We improve the dehazing method proposed by Double-DIP. Three DIP networks generate the airlight map, the transmission map, and the clear image without any post-processing and external prior. DIP [19] states that the neural network is used as the image prior and generates images through a hand-selected network structure. That is, we can make the networks accomplish different tasks by modifying their structures. For the deblurring task, we choose a fully connected network because the generated blur kernel does not have natural image features suitable for using a convolutional network [16]. As for the dehazing task, we need three DIP networks. If they are not distinguished by network structure, it is easy to produce undesired results, which is the shortage of Double-DIP. We designed different DIP structures for different tasks based on their complexity. For example, the task for the DIP network responsible for restoring the haze-free image is relatively challenging, so we use the encoder-decoder with deeper depth and more feature maps.

Three DIP networks can directly represent the degradation process of haze images, but no constraint is given to the restored image during the optimization. For the *inpainting + deblur* task, the pixel value is not directly added or subtracted in the whole process, which means that the restored image will not suffer from color distortion. However, according to [6], the *dehaze + deblur* task has

Fig. 9. Blurred real-world hazy images restored by our Multi-DIP. Images at the bottom are airlight maps, transmission maps, and blur kernels respectively.

an operation of subtracting airlight. If this process is not supervised, it is likely to produce unsatisfactory results. In order to solve this problem, Double-DIP introduces the real airlight value to its network, but obviously, this is not an elegant solution. Our Multi-DIP use the field-depth prior [10] as constraint. The field-depth of a clear image is positively correlated to the difference between its brightness and saturation. For haze images, a deeper field signifies a higher haze level, so we use the airlight map to strip the haze in these areas. The prior is recast in the following:

$$\mathcal{L}_{reg} = \frac{1}{m \times n} \sum_{i=0}^{m-1} \sum_{j=0}^{n-1} \|V_G(i,j) - S_G(i,j)\|^2 \tag{4}$$

where V_G and S_G denote the brightness and saturation of restored images respectively.

We narrow the differences between brightness and saturation of restored images and let the network that generates the airlight map represent the region's illumination. The restored image in this pipeline is not a haze-free image, but Multi-DIP only needs the airlight map generated in the first stage as initialization. This procedure shows the flexibility of our framework. Results compared with other unsupervised dehazing algorithms are shown in Table 3 and Fig. 8.

For *Dehaze + Deblur* task, the degraded image $I(x)$ can be modeled as the following equation:

$$I(x) = (t(x)J(x) + (1 - t(x))A(x)) \otimes k(x) \tag{5}$$

In an end-to-end manner, the network (as shown in Fig. 7(b)) in our dehazing and deblurring DIP framework only needs to generate clear images which are in line with [19]. We take the airlight map and the blur kernel as the initialization, where the blur kernel is initialized as the way in Sect. 3. We upsample the airlight map generated from the small-scale image. At the early stage of training, the MSE loss is calculated with the generated airlight map, and this restriction is removed after a certain number of iterations. Results are shown in Fig. 9.

4 Conclusions

In this paper, we propose a novel Multi-DIP framework to solve the multi-degradation problem. Our framework can effectively decouple the combination of multiple degradation modes. We use a multi-scale approach to initialize the large-scale DIP framework with the prior generated by the small-scale DIP. Meanwhile, we use the dehazing task as an example to show how to integrate the existing network into the Multi-DIP framework. For quantitative and qualitative experiments, we design a dataset for *deblur + inpainting*. Extensive experiments show that our multi-scale initialization method can effectively help the DIP network converge correctly.

References

1. Bahat, Y., Irani, M.: Blind dehazing using internal patch recurrence. In: 2016 IEEE International Conference on Computational Photography (ICCP), pp. 1–9. IEEE (2016)
2. Berman, D., Avidan, S., et al.: Non-local image dehazing. In: Proceedings of the IEEE Conference on Computer Vision and Pattern Recognition, pp. 1674–1682 (2016)
3. Cai, B., Xu, X., Jia, K., Qing, C., Tao, D.: DehazeNet: an end-to-end system for single image haze removal. IEEE Trans. Image Process. **25**(11), 5187–5198 (2016)
4. Chen, C., Do, M.N., Wang, J.: Robust image and video dehazing with visual artifact suppression via gradient residual minimization. In: Leibe, B., Matas, J., Sebe, N., Welling, M. (eds.) ECCV 2016. LNCS, vol. 9906, pp. 576–591. Springer, Cham (2016). https://doi.org/10.1007/978-3-319-46475-6_36
5. Gandelsman, Y., Shocher, A., Irani, M.: "Double-dip": unsupervised image decomposition via coupled deep-image-priors. In: The IEEE Conference on Computer Vision and Pattern Recognition (CVPR), vol. 6, p. 2 (2019)
6. He, K., Sun, J., Tang, X.: Single image haze removal using dark channel prior. IEEE Trans. Pattern Anal. Mach. Intell. **33**(12), 2341–2353 (2010)
7. Ji, X., Cao, Y., Tai, Y., Wang, C., Li, J., Huang, F.: Real-world super-resolution via kernel estimation and noise injection. In: Proceedings of the IEEE/CVF Conference on Computer Vision and Pattern Recognition Workshops, pp. 466–467 (2020)
8. Kupyn, O., Budzan, V., Mykhailych, M., Mishkin, D., Matas, J.: DeblurGAN: blind motion deblurring using conditional adversarial networks. In: Proceedings of the IEEE Conference on Computer Vision and Pattern Recognition, pp. 8183–8192 (2018)
9. Li, B., Peng, X., Wang, Z., Xu, J., Feng, D.: An all-in-one network for dehazing and beyond. arXiv preprint arXiv:1707.06543 (2017)
10. Li, B., Gou, Y., Gu, S., Liu, J.Z., Zhou, J.T., Peng, X.: You only look yourself: unsupervised and untrained single image dehazing neural network. Int. J. Comput. Vis., 1–14 (2021)

11. Meng, G., Wang, Y., Duan, J., Xiang, S., Pan, C.: Efficient image dehazing with boundary constraint and contextual regularization. In: Proceedings of the IEEE International Conference on Computer Vision, pp. 617–624 (2013)
12. Nah, S., Hyun Kim, T., Mu Lee, K.: Deep multi-scale convolutional neural network for dynamic scene deblurring. In: Proceedings of the IEEE Conference on Computer Vision and Pattern Recognition, pp. 3883–3891 (2017)
13. Pan, J., Hu, Z., Su, Z., Yang, M.H.: Deblurring text images via l0-regularized intensity and gradient prior. In: Proceedings of the IEEE Conference on Computer Vision and Pattern Recognition, pp. 2901–2908 (2014)
14. Pan, J., Sun, D., Pfister, H., Yang, M.H.: Blind image deblurring using dark channel prior. In: Proceedings of the IEEE Conference on Computer Vision and Pattern Recognition, pp. 1628–1636 (2016)
15. Pavlakos, G., Zhou, X., Derpanis, K.G., Daniilidis, K.: Coarse-to-fine volumetric prediction for single-image 3d human pose. In: Proceedings of the IEEE Conference on Computer Vision and Pattern Recognition, pp. 7025–7034 (2017)
16. Ren, D., Zhang, K., Wang, Q., Hu, Q., Zuo, W.: Neural blind deconvolution using deep priors. In: Proceedings of the IEEE/CVF Conference on Computer Vision and Pattern Recognition, pp. 3341–3350 (2020)
17. Ren, W., Liu, S., Zhang, H., Pan, J., Cao, X., Yang, M.-H.: Single image dehazing via multi-scale convolutional neural networks. In: Leibe, B., Matas, J., Sebe, N., Welling, M. (eds.) ECCV 2016. LNCS, vol. 9906, pp. 154–169. Springer, Cham (2016). https://doi.org/10.1007/978-3-319-46475-6_10
18. Tarel, J.P., Hautiere, N.: Fast visibility restoration from a single color or gray level image. In: 2009 IEEE 12th International Conference on Computer Vision, pp. 2201–2208. IEEE (2009)
19. Ulyanov, D., Vedaldi, A., Lempitsky, V.: Deep image prior. In: Proceedings of the IEEE Conference on Computer Vision and Pattern Recognition, pp. 9446–9454 (2018)
20. Wang, K., Zhuo, L., Li, J., Jia, T., Zhang, J.: Learning an enhancement convolutional neural network for multi-degraded images. Sens. Imaging 21, 1–15 (2020)
21. Yang, C., Lu, X., Lin, Z., Shechtman, E., Wang, O., Li, H.: High-resolution image inpainting using multi-scale neural patch synthesis. In: Proceedings of the IEEE Conference on Computer Vision and Pattern Recognition, pp. 6721–6729 (2017)
22. Yu, J., Lin, Z., Yang, J., Shen, X., Lu, X., Huang, T.S.: Free-form image inpainting with gated convolution. In: Proceedings of the IEEE/CVF International Conference on Computer Vision, pp. 4471–4480 (2019)
23. Zeyde, R., Elad, M., Protter, M., et al.: On single image scale-up using sparse-representations. In: Boissonnat, J.-D. (ed.) Curves and Surfaces 2010. LNCS, vol. 6920, pp. 711–730. Springer, Heidelberg (2012). https://doi.org/10.1007/978-3-642-27413-8_47
24. Zhang, K., Gool, L.V., Timofte, R.: Deep unfolding network for image super-resolution. In: Proceedings of the IEEE/CVF Conference on Computer Vision and Pattern Recognition, pp. 3217–3226 (2020)
25. Zheng, Y., Huang, D., Liu, S., Wang, Y.: Cross-domain object detection through coarse-to-fine feature adaptation. In: Proceedings of the IEEE/CVF Conference on Computer Vision and Pattern Recognition, pp. 13766–13775 (2020)
26. Zhou, E., Fan, H., Cao, Z., Jiang, Y., Yin, Q.: Extensive facial landmark localization with coarse-to-fine convolutional network cascade. In: Proceedings of the IEEE International Conference on Computer Vision Workshops, pp. 386–391 (2013)

Multi-Attention Network for Arbitrary Style Transfer

Sihui Hua and Dongdong Zhang(✉)

Department of Computer Science and Technology, Tongji University, Shanghai, China
{16hsh,ddzhang}@tongji.edu.cn

Abstract. Arbitrary style transfer task is to synthesize a new image with the content of an image and the style of another image. With the development of deep learning, the effect and efficiency of arbitrary style transfer have been greatly improved. Although the existing methods have made good progress, there are still limitations in the preservation of salient content structure and detailed style patterns. In this paper, we propose Multi-Attention Network for Arbitrary Style Transfer (MANet). In details, we utilize the multi-attention mechanism to extract the salient structure of the content image and the detailed texture of the style image, and transfer the rich style patterns in the art works into the content image. Moreover, we design a novel attention loss to preserve the significant information of the content. The experimental results show that our model can efficiently generate more high-quality stylized images than those generated by the state-of-the-art (SOTA) methods.

Keywords: Style transfer · Attention mechanism · Deep learning

1 Introduction

With the development of deep learning, recent years have witnessed the continuous progress of image style transfer. Especially with the success of convolutional neural network (CNN), it has become the main research method of image style transfer. Gatys et al. [1] first showed that the content information could be extracted from natural images and the style information could be obtained from artworks through a pre-trained VGG network [12], and proposed an image reconstruction algorithm to realize the stylization. However, this algorithm is restricted by low efficiency. In order to reduce the computational cost, several methods [3,6,14] based on feed-forward networks have been developed, which can effectively generate stylized images, but they are limited to a fixed style or lack of visual quality.

For arbitrary style transfer, several approaches have been proposed. For instance, AdaIN [2] is the first method realize effective real-time style transfer, which only adjusts the mean and variance values of content image to match those values of style image. However, this method is too simple to affect the output quality. WCT [7] matches content features with style features through

© Springer Nature Switzerland AG 2021
T. Mantoro et al. (Eds.): ICONIP 2021, LNCS 13111, pp. 390–401, 2021.
https://doi.org/10.1007/978-3-030-92273-3_32

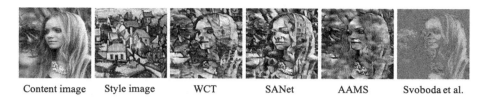

Content image   Style image   WCT   SANet   AAMS   Svoboda et al.

Fig. 1. The existing methods do not well maintain the original semantics of content and transfer the fine texture of style. The output images of WCT [7] and SANet [9] lack part of the woman's outline in the content image. While for AAMS [16] and Svoboda et al. [13], the extraction of style is insufficient.

the whitening and coloring process of covariance replacing variance, and then the stylized features are embedded in the pre-trained encoder-decoder to synthesize stylized images. Nevertheless, the increase of feature dimension will greatly increase the calculation of complexity. Avatar-Net [11] is a style decoration method based on image blocks. It maps the features of content and style while maintaining the content structure to get better quality. Xing et al. [15] proposed a portrait-aware method, which applied fine-grained and coarse-grained style transfer to the background and the entire image, respectively. Jung et al. [4] proposed Graph Instance Normalization (GrIN), which made the style transfer approach more robust by taking into account similar information shared between instances. Svoboda et al. [13] employed a two-stage peer-regularization layer that used graph convolutions to reorganize style and content in latent space.

Recently, with the introduction of the attention mechanism, great breakthroughs have been made in style transfer. Yao et al. [16] applied the self-attention mechanism to style transfer model and added multi-stroke control. In addition, Park et al. [9] proposed a style-attentional network which matched style features with content features.

Although the above methods have achieved good results, there are still some limitations. First of all, these methods do not take into account the original semantic structure of content image comprehensively. Moreover, the existing methods do not reflect the detailed texture of the style image, making the style of output deviate. As shown in Fig. 1, some algorithms lack part of the outline of the content image, while some algorithms do not extract the style patterns enough. These seriously reduce the quality of stylized images.

To address these limitations, we propose Multi-Attention Network for Arbitrary Style Transfer (MANet). It employs multi-attention mechanism to preserve the salient structure of content image and the detailed texture of style image, and renders the rich style patterns of art works into the generated result. The proposed MANet includes unary content attention module (UA), pairwise style attention module (PA) and fusion attention module (FA). The UA module and PA module model the salient boundaries of content and learn within-region relationships of style through the unary self-attention mechanism and the pairwise self-attention mechanism respectively, so as to retain the main content features and vivid style patterns. Then, we integrate the enhanced content and style features through FA module to achieve stylized result. In addition, we propose a novel attention loss. When content image and style image generate stylized result, we design the attention loss to minimize the difference of attention between content image and stylized result, which ensures that the salient semantic information of the content image can be preserved in the process of style transfer. To summarize, our main contributions are as follows:

- We propose an efficient multi-attention network (MANet) for arbitrary style transfer, including UA module, PA module and FA module.
- We propose a novel attention loss function to enhance the salient features of the content, which can retain the salient structure of the original content image.
- Various experiments show that our method can preserve the salient structure of content images and detailed texture of style images, and combine content features and style features flexibly.

2 Related Work

In order to realize arbitrary style transfer efficiently, some methods have been proposed. Huang et al. [2] proposed AdaIN, which transferred the statistics of the mean and variance of the channel in the feature space for style transfer. Li et al. [7] proposed WCT, which integrated whitening and coloring transforms to match the statistical distribution and correlation between content and style features to achieve style transfer. AdaIn and WCT holistically adjust the content features to match the second-order statistics of style features. Svoboda et al. [13] proposed a two-stage peer-regularization layer that used graph convolutions to reorganize style and content in latent space.

Recently, several approaches introduced self-attention mechanism to obtain high-quality stylized images. Park et al. [9] proposed a style-attentional network, which flexibly matched the semantically nearest style features to the content features. It slightly modified the self-attention mechanism (such as the number of input data) to learn the mapping between the content and style features. Yao et al. [16] adapted the self-attention to introduce a residual feature map to catch salient characteristics within content images, and then generated stylized images with multiple stroke patterns.

However, the above methods cannot effectively preserve salient content structure and capture detailed style patterns. The disadvantages of these methods can be observed in Sect. 4.2. To this end, we propose an arbitrary style transfer network, named multi-attention network, and we design a new attention loss to enhance salient content features. In this way, the method can naturally integrate style and content while maintaining the original structure of content and detailed texture of style.

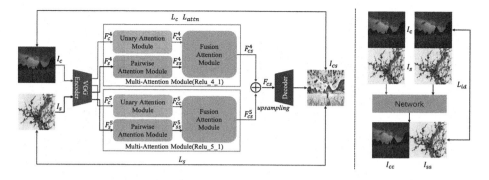

Fig. 2. The overall framework of our network.

3 Methodology

For the purpose of achieving arbitrary style transfer, the proposed network consists of an encoder-decoder module and a multi-attention module. Figure 2 shows the overall framework. A pre-trained VGG19 network [12] is used as an encoder and a symmetric decoder to extract deep features. Inputting a content image I_c and an arbitrary style image I_s, we can extract their respective feature maps $F_c^i = E(I_c)$ and $F_s^i = E(I_s)$ (i is the number of a certain layer). To consider both the overall style distribution and local styles, we extract the features of two layers ($Relu\_4\_1$ and $Relu\_5\_1$) in the encoder, and combine the final results. Meanwhile, considering that the use of a public encoder can only extract features in a few specific fields, it lacks attention to the salient structural parts of the content and the internal pixel relationship of the style. Therefore, we propose a multi-attention module that can learn salient boundaries of content and learn within-region relationship of style separately, and can integrate content and style features appropriately in each position to obtain the stylized features F_{cs}. The multi-attention module is described in detail in Sect. 3.1. The decoder follows the setting of [2] and gets the stylized result $I_{cs} = D(F_{cs})$. We design a new attention loss to preserve the salient structure of the content. Section 3.2 describes the four loss functions we used to train the model.

3.1 Multi-Attention Module

As shown in Fig. 3, the multi-attention module includes three parts: unary content attention module, pairwise style attention module and fusion attention module. With content/style feature $F_c^i(F_s^i)$ through the content/style attention module, we can get $F_{cc}^i(F_{ss}^i)$ that retain salient features. Then the fusion attention module appropriately embeds style features in the content feature maps.

Unary Content Attention Module. The semantic information of content should be preserved during the style transfer to keep the structure consistent

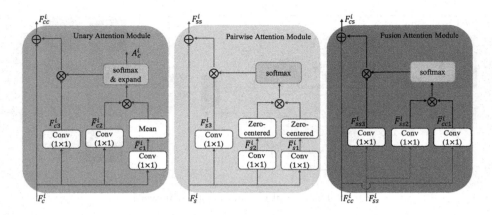

Fig. 3. The framework of Multi-Attention Module.

before and after stylization. Following [17], we design the Unary Content Attention module (UA) to model the salient boundaries. The content feature map F_c^i from the encoder is normalized and fed to two convolutional layers to obtain new feature maps $\bar{F}_{c1}^i$ and $\bar{F}_{c2}^i$. At the same time, we feed the unnormalized F_c^i to another convolutional layer to obtain the feature map F_{c3}^i. Unary content attention map is A_c^i is formulated as follows:

$$A_c^i = expand(softmax(\mu(\bar{F}_{c1}^i)^T \otimes \bar{F}_{c2}^i)) \tag{1}$$

where $expand(\cdot)$ represents to expand the size, $\otimes$ represents the matrix multiplication and $\mu(\cdot)$ denotes the mean of features. Then we get the optimized content features F_{cc}^i:

$$F_{cc}^i = F_{c3}^i \otimes A_c^i + F_c^i \tag{2}$$

Pairwise Style Attention Module. It is necessary to learn the main style patterns of the style image, and render the style appropriately to the content image in the process of style transfer. For a certain style, it contains many elements. So we design the Pairwise Style Attention module (PA) to learn pixel relationships within the same category region in the style image following [17]. Thus to strengthen the components and highlight the expressiveness of the style and to extract the detailed texture. The style feature map F_s^i is normalized and fed to two convolutional layers to obtain new feature maps $\bar{F}_{s1}^i$ and $\bar{F}_{s2}^i$, and then they are subtracted the mean. At the same time, F_s^i is fed to another convolutional layer to obtain the feature map F_{s3}^i. The pairwise style attention map A_s^i is formulated as follows:

$$A_s^i = softmax((\bar{F}_{s1}^i - \mu(\bar{F}_{s1}^i))^T \otimes (\bar{F}_{s2}^i - \mu(\bar{F}_{s2}^i))) \tag{3}$$

Then, we get the enhanced style features F_{ss}^i:

$$F_{ss}^i = F_{s3}^i \otimes A_s^{i\,T} + F_s^i \tag{4}$$

Fusion Attention Module. Through UA and PA modules, we obtain the enhanced content and style features. Similar to [9], we add FA module to appropriately integrate content and style features. Figure 3 shows the FA process. The enhanced content features F_{cc}^i and style features F_{ss}^i are normalized to obtain $\bar{F}_{cc}^i$ and $\bar{F}_{ss}^i$. Then we feed $\bar{F}_{cc}^i$, $\bar{F}_{ss}^i$ and F_{ss}^i to three convolutional layers to generate three new feature maps $\bar{F}_{cc1}^i$, $\bar{F}_{ss2}^i$ and F_{ss3}^i. The correlation map A_{cs}^i is formulated as follows:

$$A_{cs}^i = softmax(\bar{F}_{cc1}^i{}^T \otimes \bar{F}_{ss2}^i) \tag{5}$$

where A_{cs}^i maps the correspondence between the enhanced content features F_{cc}^i and the enhanced style features F_{ss}^i. Then, we can calculate the stylized feature map of each layer ($Relu\_4\_1$ and $Relu\_5\_1$) as follows:

$$F_{cs}^i = F_{ss3}^i \otimes A_{cs}^i{}^T + F_{cc}^i \tag{6}$$

Finally, we get the final stylized feature map F_{cs} from the two MANets:

$$F_{cs} = F_{cs}^4 + upsampling(F_{cs}^5) \tag{7}$$

3.2   Loss Function

Our model contains 4 loss functions during training.

Content Loss. Similar to AdaIN [2], the content loss is computed using the pre-trained encoder. The content loss L_c is utilized to make the stylized image close to the content image in content, as follows:

$$L_c = \sum_{i=4}^{5} \|\phi_i(I_{cs}) - \phi_i(I_c)\|_2 \tag{8}$$

where ϕ_i represents the feature map extracted from i-th layer in the encoder.

Attention Loss. The stylized image should preserve the salient characteristics of the original content image. Therefore, we propose a new attention loss to minimize the difference in attention between content image and stylized result, taking into account the insufficiency that the salient information in content may be distorted. In addition, it helps to make the visual effect of the generated image better. The attention loss L_{attn} is as follows:

$$L_{attn} = \sum_{i=4}^{5} \|A_c^i(I_{cs}) - A_c^i(I_c)\|_2 \tag{9}$$

where $A_c^i(\cdot)$ represents the attention map obtained by feeding the features extracted from i-th layer in the encoder to the content attention module.

Style Loss. We apply the style loss in AdaIN [2], and L_s is used to make the generated image close to the style image in style:

$$L_s = \sum_{i=1}^{5} \|\mu(\phi_i(I_{cs})) - \mu(\phi_i(I_s))\|_2 + \|\sigma(\phi_i(I_{cs})) - \sigma(\phi_i(I_s))\|_2 \quad (10)$$

where $\sigma(\cdot)$ represents the variance of features.

Identity Loss. Similar to [9], we introduce the identity loss to consider both the global statistics and the local mapping relation between content and style features. The identity loss is formulated as follows:

$$L_{id} = \lambda_{id1}(\|I_{cc} - I_c\|_2 + \|I_{ss} - I_s\|_2)$$
$$+ \lambda_{id2} \sum_{i=1}^{5}(\|\phi_i(I_{cc}) - \phi_i(I_c)\|_2 + \|\phi_i(I_{ss}) - \phi_i(I_s)\|_2) \quad (11)$$

where $I_{cc}(I_{ss})$ denotes the generated result by using two same content (style) images as content and style images simultaneously. λ_{id1} and λ_{id2} denote the weight of identity loss. Our total loss function formula is as follows:

$$L = \lambda_c L_c + \lambda_{attn} L_{attn} + \lambda_s L_s + L_{id} \quad (12)$$

where λ_c, λ_{attn} and λ_s are weighting parameters.

4   Experiments

4.1   Implementation Details

When we trained the network, we used MS-COCO [8] as content dataset, and WikiArt [10] as style dataset, both of which contain approximately $80,000$ training images. In the training process, we used the Adam optimizer [5] with a learning rate of 0.0001 and a batch size of five content-style image pairs, and we randomly cropped the 256×256 pixels area of both images. In the testing stage, any input size can be supported. The weights λ_c, λ_{attn}, λ_s, λ_{id1}, and λ_{id2} are set to 3, 5, 3, 50, and 1 to balance each loss.

4.2   Comparison with Prior Methods

Qualitative Evaluation. We show the style transfer results of five SOTA technologies: AdaIN [2], WCT [7], SANet [9], AAMS [16] and Svoboda et al. [13], as shown in Fig. 4. AdaIN only needs to adjust the mean and variance of content features. However, due to the oversimplification of this method, its output quality is affected, and the color distribution of some content is often preserved (e.g., the preserved complexion of content in row 1 and the missing eyes and eyebrows in row 5 in Fig. 4). WCT synthesizes stylized images through whitening and coloring

| Content | Style | Ours | AdaIN | WCT | SANet | AAMS | Svoboda et al. |

Fig. 4. Example results for comparisons

transformations, but sometimes has content distortion (e.g., the distorted faces and objects in Fig. 4). SANet uses the style-attentional network to match the semantically closest style feature to the content feature, retaining the global style and local style. However, sometimes the salient features of the content image are distorted (e.g., the blurred face in rows 3, 7 and the unclear main structure in rows 4,6). AAMS also introduces a self-attention mechanism to increase multi-stroke control. However, the content and style are not well integrated and the stylized image is blurry. The content structure is not obvious, and the texture information of the style is not displayed (rows 2, 3, 4, 6, and 8 in Fig. 4). Svoboda et al. introduces a fixpoint triplet style loss and a two-stage peer-regularization layer. But because it learns the overall artist style, the correlation between the stylization result and the style image is very limited, and it cannot be controlled and reflect the main mode of the style (rows 1, 3, 4, 5, 6, and 7). In contrast, our

Table 1. Quantitative comparison over different methods.

	AdaIN	WCT	SANet	AAMS	Svoboda et al.	Ours
Preference/%	15.1	10.6	19.7	13.8	7.9	32.9
L_c (content)	10.96	13.29	14.41	12.26	12.54	11.93
L_s (style)	14.92	15.30	14.90	15.19	15.74	12.57

algorithm can adapt to multiple style and preserve the structural information of the content, as shown in Fig. 4.

Different from the above methods, our multi-attention network can further retain the salient information of content and the detailed texture of style. In addition, our method can effectively integrate content and style by learning the relationship between content and style features, so that the generated result not only retains the semantic information of the content, but also contains rich colors and textures of the style.

Quantitative Evaluation. To compare our visual performance with the above-mentioned SOTA methods further, we conducted a user study. For each method, we used 18 content images and 20 style images to generate 360 results. We selected 20 content and style combinations, showing the generated images of six methods to 50 participants to choose their favorite result for each combination. We collect 1,000 votes in total, and the preference results are shown in the second row of Table 1. The results show that our method can obtain preferred results.

Evaluating the results of style transfer is very subjective. For quantitative evaluation, we also made two comparisons. They are reported in the last two rows of Table 1. We compared different methods through content and style loss. The evaluation metrics include content and style terms used in previous methods (AdaIn [2]). The results were obtained by calculating the average content and style loss of 100 images in 512×512 scale. It can be seen that our method does not directly minimize content and style loss, because we use a total of four loss types. Nevertheless, the style loss obtained by our method is the lowest among all methods, and the content loss is only slightly higher than that of AdaIN. It indicates that our method favors fully stylized results rather than results with high content fidelity.

4.3   Ablation Study

Attention Loss Analysis. We compare the styled results with and without attention loss to verify the effect of attention loss in this section. As shown in Fig. 5, compared with the stylized results without attention loss, using attention loss can retain the salient features of the original content image and more visible content structure. With attention loss, the stylized results take into account that

| Content | Style | Ours | w/o L_{attn} | W_m | Two NL | Relu_4_1 | Relu_5_1 |

Fig. 5. Ablation study.

| content | $\alpha = 0.25$ | $\alpha = 0.50$ | $\alpha = 0.75$ | $\alpha = 1.00$ | style |

Fig. 6. Content-style trade-off.

the salient information in the content image may be distorted, and preserve the significant information of content.

Multi-Attention Module Analysis. In this section, we will try to reveal the effectiveness of the multi-attention module. In [17], the transformation in unary non-local (NL) neural networks was changed to use independent 1×1 convolution transformation W_m. But only one convolution is not enough to extract the salient information of the content in style transfer. Figure 5 shows the result of using W_m. It can be seen that the salient structure of the content is not clear enough. We also compared the results of using two NL [17] instead of UA and PA modules. As illustrated, this method cannot extract effective features for content and style separately, and the result is not good enough in reflecting content and style.

In addition, Fig. 5 shows two stylized outputs obtained from $Relu\_4\_1$ and $Relu\_5\_1$, respectively. The content structure is good when only $Relu\_4\_1$ is used for style transfer. But the partial styles are not displayed well. On the contrary, $Relu\_5\_1$ obtains a detailed style mode, but the content structure is distorted. In our work, we integrates two layers to obtain a completely stylized result while preserving the salient information of the content.

4.4   Runtime Controls

Content-Style Trade-Off. During training, to control the degree of stylization, we can adjust the style weight λ_s in Eq. 12. During test time, the degree of stylization can be controlled by changing α:

$$I_{cs} = D(\alpha F_{cs} + (1 - \alpha)F_c) \tag{13}$$

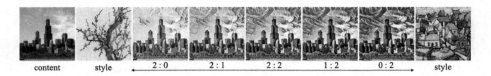

content   style   2 : 0   2 : 1   2 : 2   1 : 2   0 : 2   style

Fig. 7. Style interpolation.

α can be adjusted between 0 and 1. When $\alpha = 0$, the original content image is obtained, and when $\alpha = 1$, we obtain the most stylized image. Figure 6 presents the examples.

Style Interpolation. In order to obtain multi-style results, feature maps from different styles can be fed into the decoder, thereby combining multiple style images into one generated result. Figure 7 shows the results.

5   Conclusions

In this paper, we propose a multi-attention network to extract the salient structure of the content image and the detailed texture of the style image, and appropriately combine the content and style. Furthermore, we propose a new attention loss to consider the deficiencies that the salient information in the content image may be distorted, and to ensure that the significant semantic information of the content image is preserved in the style transfer process. Sufficient experiments show that our network can consider the salient content structure and detailed style patterns to synthesize better results.

References

1. Gatys, L.A., Ecker, A.S., Bethge, M.: Image style transfer using convolutional neural networks. In: Proceedings of the IEEE Conference on Computer Vision and Pattern Recognition, pp. 2414–2423 (2016)
2. Huang, X., Belongie, S.: Arbitrary style transfer in real-time with adaptive instance normalization. In: Proceedings of the IEEE International Conference on Computer Vision, pp. 1501–1510 (2017)
3. Johnson, J., Alahi, A., Fei-Fei, L.: Perceptual losses for real-time style transfer and super-resolution. In: Leibe, B., Matas, J., Sebe, N., Welling, M. (eds.) ECCV 2016. LNCS, vol. 9906, pp. 694–711. Springer, Cham (2016). https://doi.org/10.1007/978-3-319-46475-6_43
4. Jung, D., Yang, S., Choi, J., Kim, C.: Arbitrary style transfer using graph instance normalization. In: 2020 IEEE International Conference on Image Processing (ICIP), pp. 1596–1600. IEEE (2020)
5. Kingma, D.P., Ba, J.: Adam: a method for stochastic optimization. arXiv preprint arXiv:1412.6980 (2014)

6. Li, C., Wand, M.: Precomputed real-time texture synthesis with Markovian generative adversarial networks. In: Leibe, B., Matas, J., Sebe, N., Welling, M. (eds.) ECCV 2016. LNCS, vol. 9907, pp. 702–716. Springer, Cham (2016). https://doi.org/10.1007/978-3-319-46487-9_43
7. Li, Y., Fang, C., Yang, J., Wang, Z., Lu, X., Yang, M.H.: Universal style transfer via feature transforms. arXiv preprint arXiv:1705.08086 (2017)
8. Lin, T.-Y., et al.: Microsoft COCO: common objects in context. In: Fleet, D., Pajdla, T., Schiele, B., Tuytelaars, T. (eds.) ECCV 2014. LNCS, vol. 8693, pp. 740–755. Springer, Cham (2014). https://doi.org/10.1007/978-3-319-10602-1_48
9. Park, D.Y., Lee, K.H.: Arbitrary style transfer with style-attentional networks. In: Proceedings of the IEEE/CVF Conference on Computer Vision and Pattern Recognition, pp. 5880–5888 (2019)
10. Phillips, F., Mackintosh, B.: Wiki art gallery, inc.: a case for critical thinking. Issues Account. Educ. **26**(3), 593–608 (2011)
11. Sheng, L., Lin, Z., Shao, J., Wang, X.: Avatar-net: multi-scale zero-shot style transfer by feature decoration. In: Proceedings of the IEEE Conference on Computer Vision and Pattern Recognition, pp. 8242–8250 (2018)
12. Simonyan, K., Zisserman, A.: Very deep convolutional networks for large-scale image recognition. arXiv preprint arXiv:1409.1556 (2014)
13. Svoboda, J., Anoosheh, A., Osendorfer, C., Masci, J.: Two-stage peer-regularized feature recombination for arbitrary image style transfer. In: Proceedings of the IEEE/CVF Conference on Computer Vision and Pattern Recognition, pp. 13816–13825 (2020)
14. Ulyanov, D., Lebedev, V., Vedaldi, A., Lempitsky, V.S.: Texture networks: feed-forward synthesis of textures and stylized images. In: ICML, vol. 1, p. 4 (2016)
15. Xing, Y., Li, J., Dai, T., Tang, Q., Niu, L., Xia, S.T.: Portrait-aware artistic style transfer. In: 2018 25th IEEE International Conference on Image Processing (ICIP), pp. 2117–2121. IEEE (2018)
16. Yao, Y., Ren, J., Xie, X., Liu, W., Liu, Y.J., Wang, J.: Attention-aware multi-stroke style transfer. In: Proceedings of the IEEE/CVF Conference on Computer Vision and Pattern Recognition, pp. 1467–1475 (2019)
17. Yin, M., et al.: Disentangled non-local neural networks. In: Vedaldi, A., Bischof, H., Brox, T., Frahm, J.-M. (eds.) ECCV 2020. LNCS, vol. 12360, pp. 191–207. Springer, Cham (2020). https://doi.org/10.1007/978-3-030-58555-6_12

Image Brightness Adjustment
with Unpaired Training

Chaojian Liu[1]([✉]), Hong Chen[2], and Aidong Men[1]

[1] Beijing University of Posts and Telecommunications, Beijing 100876, China
{liuchaojian,menad}@bupt.edu.cn
[2] China Mobile Research Institute, Beijing 100053, China
chenhongyj@chinamobile.com

Abstract. In camera-based imaging, exposure correction is an important issue. Wrong exposures include overexposure and underexposure, while prior works mainly focus on underexposed images or general image enhancement. However, it is challenging to collect images of different brightness levels in practice. This paper proposes a network structure based on Generative Adversarial Network (GAN) trained on unpaired image datasets. Instead of using ground truth data to supervise learning, we adopt information extracted from the input to regular unpaired training. Our method uses style transfer for reference to separate the content space from the brightness space, realizing the conversion of an image of arbitrary brightness into images of different brightness. A large number of experiments demonstrate that our method realizes the conversion of different brightness. Our work can restore the overexposed and underexposed images of different levels and enhance low-illuminance images effectively. We organize a dataset with different exposure levels based on the existing dataset as our training dataset.

Keywords: Brightness adjustment · Generative adversarial network · Unpaired learning

1 Introduction

Overexposure and underexposure errors are common in photography, which lead to poor image quality. There are many reasons for exposure errors, such as the measurement error of the scene light during automatic exposure, the error of manually adjusting the exposure, and hard lighting conditions. The problems mentioned above caused by shooting are difficult to correct directly after complicated camera image signal processing (ISP). Images generated by wrong exposure have low contrast, poor visual quality and affect further image processing (such as image segmentation, target recognition).

Previous methods mainly focused on correcting underexposure errors [6,11, 13,14,23] or general image quality enhancement [4,8]. A recent work [1] begins to pay attention to this problem, restoring both over- and underexposure images to the image with correct exposure. However, in practice, we need a model that

© Springer Nature Switzerland AG 2021
T. Mantoro et al. (Eds.): ICONIP 2021, LNCS 13111, pp. 402–414, 2021.
https://doi.org/10.1007/978-3-030-92273-3_33

can obtain images of different brightness levels, instead of a fixed correct expo-sure value. In addition, the method [1] is based on paired datasets for training. However, work based on damaged and clean image pairs for training has some shortcomings: 1) high cost of capturing images; 2) unreal synthetic data; 3) poor model generalization. Therefore, our work aims to solve the problem of conver-sion between different brightness levels by unpaired training.   Motivated by

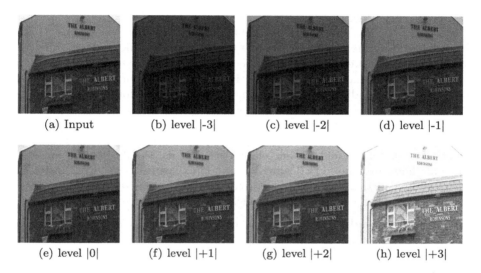

(a) Input   (b) level |-3| (c) level |-2| (d) level |-1|

(e) level |0| (f) level |+1| (g) level |+2| (h) level |+3|

Fig. 1. This method aims to adjust the brightness level. Picture (a) is an input image. Pictures (b~h) are images after adjusting the brightness, from underexposure to over-exposure.

unsupervised cross-domain image-to-image translation [12,19], we adopt gener-ative adversarial networks (GANs) to transform the brightness of images with unpaired training. According to the hypothesis of [24], we fit the brightness code into a Gaussian distribution to convert from one brightness level to another (see Fig. 1). Our method can also realize the correction of wrong exposure and can be applied to different datasets and real-world images. The main contributions of this paper are summarized as follows:

1. Our proposed method is the first multi-level exposure adjustment method based on unpaired training. Our work can process both underexposed and overexposed images and convert images between different brightness levels. Since the work does not require paired datasets, it can reduce the cost of data collection and simplify training.
2. The proposed model encodes the image into content space and brightness space for learning. The brightness code is fitted to a Gaussian distribu-tion, and the labels correspond to different Gaussian distributions in order

to realize conversion between different brightness levels. We use the self-regularization of the image features to design the loss to make up for the unpaired training.
3. Extensive experiments demonstrate the effectiveness of our method. Moreover, it generalizes better and is suitable for various datasets and real-world images because of unpaired training.

2   Related Work

Image Enhancement and Exposure Correction. Traditional exposure correction and contrast enhancement methods mostly utilize histogram equalization to improve image quality [9,26]. Alternatively, some works correct the image with exposure error by adjusting the tone curve. Plenty of previous works adopt the Retinex theory [17], assuming that one image could be separated into reflectance and illumination. Therefore, these methods obtain the illumination map to restore a well-exposed target image. Representative methods based on Retinex theory include [11,21] and the deep learning methods [15,23]. However, most of these methods are limited to dealing with underexposure errors [6,11,13–15,23]. [1] is the first method to definitely correct both overexposed and underexposed images with a single deep-learning model.

Generative Models. The generative model captures a real data distribution through the training data and then uses the learned model and distribution to create new data. In recent years, common deep generative models include Variational Auto-encoder (VAE), Generative Adversarial Network (GAN), Autoregression, and Flow-based model. **VAE**[16] is a generative network based on Variational Bayes (VB) inference. The generated samples are usually blurred due to injected noise and imperfect measurement methods (such as square error), which is a shortcoming of VAE. **GAN**[10] is another popular generative model. It includes two models trained simultaneously: a generative model to generate samples, and a discriminative model to distinguish between natural samples and generated samples. However, the GAN model is challenging to converge in the training stage, and the samples generated by GAN are often far away from natural samples. Therefore, many methods [2,5,25] are devoted to improving the quality of generated samples. **CVAE-GAN**[22] models images as a combination of labels and latent attributes in a probabilistic model. CVAE-GAN can use randomly extracted values on the latent attribute vector to generate images of a specific category, by changing the fine-grained category labels input to the generation model. The structure of our method is based on CVAE-GAN, with a decoder (generator), a discriminator and a classifier (category label assistance), but the difference is that ours has two separate encoders. **UNIT**[19] believes that different datasets can share the same hidden space. Furthermore, **MUNIT**[12] believes that the space they can share is called content space, and they should have a different space called style space. Our method draws on the assumptions of MUNIT. We divide the image into content and brightness for encoding and convert the brightness code into Gaussian distribution. With the help of these designs for training, it is possible to sample the Gaussian distribution corresponding to different brightness levels as the brightness and then reconstruct the image with the content.

Exposure dataset. The SICE dataset [3] includes a multi-exposure sequence of 589 scenes and their corresponding high-quality reference images. Each sequence has multiple images with different exposure levels. [1] establishes a dataset based on the MIT-Adobe FiveK dataset and each image uses a different relative exposure values (EVs) for rendering. We reorganize these two datasets as our experimental datasets.

3   Method

The purpose of our model is to change the image brightness level. We follow the assumption of [12] and decouple brightness and content. As shown in Fig. 2, our framework follows [2] and consists of five parts: 1) The content encoder network E_c, which encodes content space. 2) The brightness encoder network E_z, which encodes brightness space. 3) The generative network G, which generates images based on content code and brightness code. 4) The discriminative network D, which distinguishes real/fake images. 5) The classifier network C, which determines the class of images. We introduce the assumptions on which the method is based in Sect. 3.1. The network structure and the designed loss function are proposed respectively in Sect. 3.2 and 3.3.

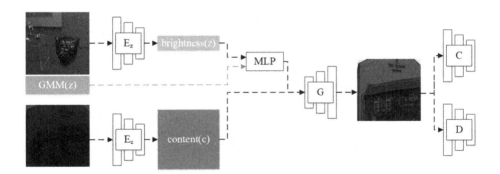

Fig. 2. The network architecture of our method. The image providing the content generates the content code through the encoder E_c. The brightness code can be generated from the reference image through the encoder E_z (yellow dotted line) or directly sampled from a Gaussian distribution (green dotted line). Finally, the content code and the brightness code are recombined through the generation network G to generate a new image. The classifier C determines whether the current brightness is correct. The discriminator D distinguishes whether the image is real. (Color figure online)

3.1 Assumption

Following works [12,19], our model assumes that each image can be decoupled in a domain-invariant content space and a domain-specific attribute space. We aim to adjust brightness, so the latent attribute feature is limited to brightness in our model; that is, different attributes correspond to different brightness levels. We use a content encoder to model content features, while we use a brightness encoder to express brightness features by mixing Gaussian components. Formally and similarly to GMM-UNIT [24], we use a K-component d-dimensional Gaussian Mixture Model (GMM) to model the latent brightness space z:

$$p(z) = \sum_{k=1}^{K} \varphi_k N\left(z; \mu^k, \Sigma^k\right) \tag{1}$$

where z denotes a random brightness vector sample, φ_k, μ^k and Σ^k denote respectively the weight, mean vector, and covariance matrix of the k-th GMM component ($\varphi_k \geq 0$, $\sum_{k=1}^{K} \varphi_k = 1$). According to the setting of CVAE-GAN [2], we let each brightness level k (category Y in [2]) correspond to an exclusive mean μ^k(variance is identity matrix I), where μ^k is trained by the model. In this case, there are as many Gaussian distributions as there are classes. When generating, we can control the category of the generated image by controlling the mean. Therefore, we model each brightness domain corresponding to a GMM component. In other words, different brightness levels correspond to Gaussian distributions with different mean values. Thus, for an image x (i.e.,$p \in \chi^k$) from the domain χ^k corresponding to the brightness level k, its latent variable z is assumed to follow the k-th Gaussian component: $z^k \sim N\left(z; \mu^k, I\right)$. Our goal is to transform the image x from the domain χ^k to the domain χ^ℓ, where $k, \ell \in \{1, \ldots, K\}$.

3.2 Network Architecture

Our network structure is shown in Fig. 2, consisting of a content encoder, a brightness encoder, a decoder (generator), a discriminator, and a classifier. The overall network complies with end-to-end training, and each part is composed of convolutional neural networks.

Encoder. For an input image x, we first decompose it into two parts. The content encoder E_c obtains the latent content code $c \in C$ that is shared by both domains; the brightness encoder E_z obtains the latent brightness code $z \in Z$ that is specific to the individual domain (i.e., $c = E_c(x)$, $z = E_z(x)$. In particular, for the brightness component, we fit it to a Gaussian distribution with different means. For each sample, the brightness encoder network outputs the mean and covariance of the latent vector z, i.e., μ and σ. According to the reparameterization trick, sampling a z from $N(\mu, \sigma^2)$ is equivalent to sampling an ε from $N(0, I)$, and then let $z = \mu + \varepsilon \times \sigma$. In order to achieve the control of different brightness levels, we make the distribution generated by the encoder E_z approximate the Gaussian distribution of a specific mean and unit variance.

The content encoder is composed of several convolutional layers and residual blocks for downsampling and feature extraction. Instance Normalization (IN) is used after the convolutional layer. The brightness encoder includes several convolutional layers, followed by a global pooling layer and a fully connected layer. We do not use IN to retain the original feature mean and variance.

Decoder (Generator). After obtaining the mapping from x to c and z, we employ the network G to get the generated image x', $x' = G(c, z)$. z may be a Gaussian distribution encoded by E_z, also may be randomly sampled from a Gaussian distribution. Specifically, it processes the content code through several residual blocks and finally generates a reconstructed image through several upsampling and convolutional layers. Motivated by work [12], the residual block uses Adaptive Instance Normalization (AdaIN) to align the mean and variance of the content image features to the mean and variance of the brightness image. The parameters of AdaIN are generated dynamically from the brightness code by a multilayer perceptron (MLP):

$$\text{AdaIN}(c, \gamma, \beta) = \gamma \left(\frac{c - \mu(c)}{\sigma(c)} \right) + \beta \tag{2}$$

where c is content code, $\mu(c)$ and $\sigma(c)$ respectively represent the mean value and standard deviation of the content image's features, γ and β correspond to the brightness image are parameters generated by the MLP. Thus, the content image is first standardized, multiplied by the standard deviation of the brightness image, and then added to its mean value. So that the standard deviation and mean value of the original content feature map are the same as the brightness feature map, achieving brightness conversion.

Discriminator. The patchGAN [25] is adopted by the discriminator D to determine whether the image x' is "real" or "fake". This mechanism combines local image features with global image features.

Classifier. We use vanilla GAN as a classifier C to classify the image's brightness and determine the current generated image's brightness level (label).

3.3 Loss Function

Reconstruction Losses. The following losses are designed to keep the reconstructed image consistent with the original image. We use the regularization of the image features to design the loss, which can be divided into three kinds of restrictions on the image, content, and brightness. The first is for the reconstructed image. In addition to calculating the L_1 loss for the reconstructed image x' and the original image x, we introduce the structural similarity (SSIM) loss. SSIM is sensitive to the structure but not sensitive to brightness and contrast. It is an evaluation metric that conforms to human subjective perception [22]. We use $(1 - \text{SSIM})$ as a loss item. In addition, we add the perceptual loss of style transfer [7]. If $c_x = E_c(x), z_x = E_z(x)$ and $x' = G(c_x, z_x)$:

$$L_1 = \|x' - x\|_1 \tag{3}$$

Given images x and x', the structural similarity of the two images can be calculated as follows [22]:

$$\text{SSIM} = \frac{(2\mu_x\mu_{x'} + C_1)(2\sigma_{xx'} + C_2)}{(\mu_x^2 + \mu_{x'}^2 + C_1)(\sigma_x^2 + \sigma_{x'}^2 + C_2)} \tag{4}$$

where μ_x, $\mu_{x'}$, μ_x^2, $\mu_{x'}^2$ and $\sigma_{xx'}$ are the mean, variance and covariance of x and x'. C_1, C_2 are constants used to maintain stability. The loss of structure based on style transfer is as follows:

$$L_p = \frac{1}{W_{i,j}H_{i,j}} \sum_{x=1}^{W_{i,j}} \sum_{x'=1}^{H_{i,j}} (\phi_{i,j}(x) - \phi_{i,j}(x'))^2 \tag{5}$$

where $\phi_{i,j}$ denotes the feature map extracted from a VGG-16 model pre-trained on ImageNet. $W_{(i,j)}$ and $H_{(i,j)}$ are the dimensions. i represents its i-th max pooling, and j represents its j-th convolutional layer after i-th max pooling layer. In this paper, we set $i = 5, j = 3$. The *reconstruction loss* of the image can be expressed as:

$$L_{rec\_x} = L_1 + (1 - \text{SSIM}) + L_p \tag{6}$$

The *content and brightness reconstruction losses* measure the code between the original image and the reconstructed image:

$$L_{rec\_c} = \mathbb{E}_{x\sim p_{\chi^k}, z\sim N(\mu^\ell, I)} \left[\|E_c(G(c_x, z)) - c_x\|_1 \right] \tag{7}$$

$$L_{rec\_z} = \mathbb{E}_{x\sim p_{\chi^k}} \left[\|E_z(G(c_x, z_x)) - z_x\|_1 \right] \tag{8}$$

The **distribution consistency loss** is based on the Kullback-Leibler (KL) divergence, which measures the gap between the z_x encoded by the original image and its corresponding Gaussian distribution. Thus, the hypothesis that the brightness code is approximately Gaussian distribution is established. We modify the KL loss:

$$L_{KL} = \mathbb{E}_{x\sim p_{\chi^k}} \left[D_{KL}(z_x \| N(\mu^k, I)) \right] \tag{9}$$

where $D_{KL}(p\|q) = -\int p(t)\log p(t)/q(t)dt$.

Classification and Discrimination Losses. L_C measures whether the image belongs to the label (brightness level) corresponding to the current image. L_C^G measures whether the image belongs to the label corresponding to the converted image. L_D measures whether the current image and the converted image are real. L_D^G measures whether the converted image are real.

$$L_C = \mathbb{E}_{x\sim p_{\chi^k}, d_{\chi^k}} \left[\log C(d_{\chi^k} \mid x) \right] \tag{10}$$

$$L_C^G = \mathbb{E}_{x\sim p_{\chi^k}, d_{\chi^\ell}, z\sim N(\mu^\ell, I)} \left[\log C\left(d_{\chi^\ell} \mid G(c_x, z)\right) \right] \tag{11}$$

$$L_D^G = \mathbb{E}_{x\sim p_{\chi^k}, z\sim N(\mu^\ell, I)} \left[D\left(G(c_x, z)\right)^2 \right] \tag{12}$$

$$L_D = \mathbb{E}_{x\sim p_{\chi^k}} \left[D(x)^2 \right] + \mathbb{E}_{x\sim p_{\chi^k}, z\sim N(\mu^\ell, I)} \left[(1 - D(G(c_x, z)))^2 \right] \tag{13}$$

where d_{χ^k} is the label of k-th level, d_{χ^ℓ} is the label of ℓ-th level. The *full objective function* of our network is:

$$L = L_C + L_D + L_G$$
$$L_G = \lambda_x L_{rec\_x} + \lambda_c L_{rec\_c} + \lambda_z L_{rec\_z} + \lambda_{KL} L_{KL} + L_C^G + L_D^G \tag{14}$$

We empirically set $\lambda_x = 5$, $\lambda_c = 1$, $\lambda_z = 1$ and $\lambda_{KL} = 0.5$.

4   Experiment

In this section, we conduct extensive experiments to evaluate the performance of our method. In Sect. 4.1, we present the implementation details of our method . Then, we compare our method with some state-of-the-art (SOTA) methods by quantitative and qualitative experiments in Sect. 4.2. Finally, a simple ablation study is shown in Sect. 4.3.

4.1   Implementation Details

We train on a reorganized SICE dataset [3]. The SICE dataset includes Part1 and Part2, containing 360 and 229 sequences with different exposures, respectively. According to the SICE dataset description, images at the same position in the sequence correspond to the same EV value. We select seven images in the middle of each sequence, and the images that have the same brightness compose a subset. All the images are resized to 128×128. We choose the restructured Part1 as the training dataset and choose different test datasets according to the comparison experiment. We train our method for 1000 epochs with PyTorch on an NVIDIA 2080Ti GPU. Since the discrimination network is more complex than the generation network, different learning rates are set, $\mathrm{lr}_g = \mathrm{lr}_c = 1e^{-4}$, $\mathrm{lr}_d = 2\mathrm{lr}_g$, and update the generation network every five iterations. We use the Adam optimizer in the training and set the batch size to 8.

4.2   Comparison with State-of-the-Arts

Evaluation Metrics. We employ Peak Signal to Noise Ratio (PSNR) and Structure SIMilarity index (SSIM) as the Full-Reference Image Quality Assessment (FR-IQA) metrics in the experiment. In addition, Natural Image Quality Evaluator (NIQE) is adopted as the No-Reference Image Quality Assessment (NR-IQA) metric. The higher the PSNR and SSIM or the smaller the NIQE score, the better the image quality is considered.

We compare our method with existing methods in this section: LIME [11], DPED [13], RetinexNet [23], EnlightenGAN [14], Zero-DCE [6], the deep self-regularized low-light image enhancement (Jiang et al. [15]), and the multi-scale photo exposure correction(Afifi M et al. [1]). All the images are resized to 512 × 512.

First, the experiment is conducted on the reorganized dataset of the paper [1] (similar to the processing of SICE). Some values in Table 1 come from the reference [1]. In the table, we measure the conversion of images from different exposure levels (different EV values) to standard brightness levels. The dataset [1] is a paired dataset with ground truth. The ground truth is used as the standard brightness image in the test. It can be obtained from Table 1 that our method is close to SOTA methods. Method [1] adopts its proposed dataset with paired training, while our method trains with unpaired training on the SICE dataset, which is unfair to us. However, our performance is still excellent, which shows that we have good generalization ability. Since [1] does not provide the code, we compare DPED with our method in Fig. 3. As shown in Fig. 3, we can restore the underexposed and overexposed images and be closer to the ground truth.

Then, we test on the Part2 of the SICE dataset (reorganized). The results are shown in Fig. 1 and Table 2. The data in the first six rows in Table 2 comes from [15]. Since most methods are solely for underexposed images, the results will be poor if applied to overexposed images. Except for the data from [15] and our results, we show the scores of overexposed images using EnlightenGAN. Our method uses the same dataset as [6,15], which is fair as a comparative experiment. We performed best among all comparison methods. Similar to [6, 14,15], we compare NiQE scores on DCIM [18] , Lime[11], MEF [20], NPE [21], and SICE datasets due to unpaired training. The results are shown in Table 3, proving our excellent performance. Figure 4 qualitatively performs some different methods on different datasets. Our results have a good visual display.

Table 1. FR-IQA scores of different methods on the dataset of [1]. The best and suboptimal results are marked in red and blue respectively.

Method	PSNR					SSIM				
	−1.5	−1	+0	+1	+1.5	−1.5	−1	+0	+1	+1.5
LIME [11]	14.643		10.487			0.671		0.582		
DPED [13]	19.858		13.883			0.685		0.591		
RetinexNet [23]	12.494		11.059			0.619		0.600		
Zero-DCE [6]	14.9642		11.0206			0.5936		0.5196		
Afifi M et al. [1]	19.646		19.198			0.737		0.728		
Ours	18.051	19.522	24.703	19.468	16.673	0.822	0.861	0.924	0.878	0.828
	18.7863		20.2814			0.8416		0.8764		

Table 2. FR-IQA scores of different methods on the SICE dataset. The best and suboptimal results are marked in red and blue respectively.

Method	PSNR(SSIM)						
	-3	-2	-1	0	$+1$	$+2$	$+3$
LIME [11]	14.77(0.51)			–			
RetinexNet [23]	16.15(0.50)			–			
EnlightenGAN [14]	15.87(0.55)			13.38 (0.72)	11.45 (0.65)	9.53 (0.57)	7.84 (0.49)
Zero-DCE [6]	16.28(0.52)			–			
Jiang et al. [15]	17.06(0.53)			–			
Ours	18.13 (0.65)	19.10 (0.68)	20.24 (0.71)	22.49 (0.84)	19.17 (0.80)	14.97 (0.71)	11.81 (0.62)
	19.15(0.68)			17.11(0.74)			

Table 3. NR-IQA scores of different methods on different datasets. The best and suboptimal results are marked in red and blue respectively.

Method	DICM [18]	LIME [11]	MEF [20]	NPE [21]	SICE [3]
LIME [11]	3.0316	4.1586	4.5548	3.635	4.9279
RetinexNet [23]	4.7121	4.9085	5.6314	4.1107	5.7429
EnlightenGAN [14]	2.7586	3.3763	3.211	3.274	4.4353
Zero-DCE [6]	2.6963	3.7891	4.0411	3.7571	4.5748
Jiang et al. [15]	2.5392	3.691	3.8238	3.3379	4.4703
Afifi M et al. [1]	2.5	3.76	–	3.18	–
Ours	3.0463	3.2452	3.4175	3.2326	2.7326

4.3 Ablation Studies

We compare the scores without image reconstruction loss L_{rec_x}. The results prove the effectiveness of our loss in Table 4.

Fig. 3. Visual comparisons with different methods on the datasets of [1] respectively. Two rows respectively show the restoration of under- and overexposed images (i.e., ±1.5EV to 0).

Table 4. Ablation studies.

Method	PSNR	SSIM
Baseline	17.98	0.71
L_{rec_x} w/o	15.40	0.57

Fig. 4. Visual comparisons with different methods on LIME and NPE datasets respectively.

5   Conclusion

In this paper, we propose a novel method to change the brightness level of an image. Our model is established in the recent image-to-image translation work, which uses unpaired images and models brightness through Gaussian distribution. We can generate the image corresponding to the specified brightness through the label or generate the image of the reference image brightness. We train the network to extract the content code and brightness code and change the brightness level by changing the brightness code. Our proposed method is the first multi-level exposure adjustment method based on unpaired training. Extensive experiments demonstrate that the proposed method can restore both over- and underexposed images, which is competitive with the SOTA image enhancement methods. In future work, in addition to continuing to improve the structure to improve performance, we try to use this method to generate a data set as a training set for adaptive adjustment of different brightness to the target brightness.

Acknowledgements. This work was supported by National Key Research and Development Program under Grant 2019YFC1511404, National Natural Science Funding (No. 62002026) and MoE-CMCC "Artificial Intelligence" Project under Grant MCM20190701.

References

1. Afifi, M., Derpanis, G.K., Ommer, B., Brown, S.M.: Learning multi-scale photo exposure correction. CVPR, pp. 9157–9167 (2021)
2. Bao, J., Chen, D., Wen, F., Li, H., Hua, G.: Cvae-gan: Fine-grained image generation through asymmetric training. ICCV, pp. 2764–2773 (2017)
3. Cai, J., Gu, S., Zhang, L.: Learning a deep single image contrast enhancer from multi-exposure images. IEEE Trans. Image Process., 2049–2062 (2018)
4. Chen, Y.S., Wang, Y.C., Kao, M.H., Chuang, Y.Y.: Deep photo enhancer: unpaired learning for image enhancement from photographs with GANs. In: 2018 IEEE/CVF Conference on Computer Vision and Pattern Recognition, pp. 6306–6314 (2018). https://doi.org/10.1109/CVPR.2018.00660
5. Choi, Y., Choi, M., Kim, M., Ha, J.-W., Kim, S., Choo, J.: StarGAN: unified generative adversarial networks for multi-domain image-to-image translation. In: 2018 IEEE/CVF Conference on Computer Vision and Pattern Recognition, pp. 8789–8797 (2018). https://doi.org/10.1109/CVPR.2018.00916
6. Chunle, G., et al.: Zero-reference deep curve estimation for low-light image enhancement. CVPR, pp. 1777–1786 (2020)
7. Gatys, A.L., Ecker, S.A., Bethge, M.: Image style transfer using convolutional neural networks. CVPR, pp. 2414–2423 (2016)
8. Gharbi, M., Chen, J., Barron, T.J., Hasinoff, W.S., Durand, F.: Deep bilateral learning for real-time image enhancement. ACM Trans. Graphics (TOG) (2017)
9. Gonzalez, C.R., Woods, E.R.: Digital image processing. Digital Image Process., pp. 242–243 (2002)
10. Goodfellow, J.I., et al.: Generative adversarial nets. Adv. Neural Inf. Process. Syst. **27**, 2672–2680 (2014)

11. Guo, X., Li, Y., Ling, H.: Lime: low-light image enhancement via illumination map estimation. IEEE Trans. Image Process., 982–993 (2018)
12. Huang, X., Liu, M.Y., Belongie, J.S., Kautz, J.: Multimodal unsupervised image-to-image translation. ECCV, pp. 179–196 (2018)
13. Ignatov, A., Kobyshev, N., Vanhoey, K., Timofte, R., Gool, V.L.: Dslr-quality photos on mobile devices with deep convolutional networks. ICCV (2017)
14. Jiang, Y., et al.: EnlightenGAN: deep light enhancement without paired supervision. IEEE Trans. Image Process. **30**, 2340–2349 (2021). https://doi.org/10.1109/TIP.2021.3051462
15. Jiang, Z., Li, H., Liu, L., Men, A., Wang, H.: A switched view of retinex: deep self-regularized low-light image enhancement. Neurocomputing **454**, 361–372 (2021)
16. Kingma, P.D., Welling, M.: Auto-encoding variational bayes. CoRR (2014)
17. Land, H.E.: The retinex theory of color vision. Sci. Am. **237**(6), 108–129 (1977)
18. Lee, C., Lee, C., Kim, C.S.: Contrast enhancement based on layered difference representation. ICIP, pp. 965–968 (2012)
19. Liu, M.Y., Breuel, T., Kautz, J.: Unsupervised image-to-image translation networks. Adv. Neural Inf. Process. Syst. **30**, 700–708 (2018)
20. Ma, K., K., Z., Wang, Z.: Perceptual quality assessment for multi-exposure image fusion. Image Process. IEEE Trans. (2015)
21. Wang, S., Zheng, J., Hu, H.M., Li, B.: Naturalness preserved enhancement algorithm for non-uniform illumination images. IEEE Trans. Image Process. **22**(9), 3538–3548 (2013). https://doi.org/10.1109/TIP.2013.2261309
22. Wang, Z., Bovik, A.C., Sheikh, H.R., Simoncelli, E.P.: Image quality assessment: from error visibility to structural similarity. IEEE Trans. Image Process. **13**(4), 600–612 (2004). https://doi.org/10.1109/TIP.2003.819861
23. Wei, C., Wang, W., Yang, W., Liu, J.: Deep retinex decomposition for low-light enhancement. BMVC (2018)
24. Yahui, L., Marco, N.D., Jian, Y., Nicu, S., Bruno, L., Xavier, A.P.: Gmm-unit: unsupervised multi-domain and multi-modal image-to-image translation via attribute gaussian mixture modeling (2020)
25. Zhu, J.Y., Park, T., Isola, P., Efros, A.A.: Unpaired image-to-image translation using cycle-consistent adversarial networks. In: 2017 IEEE International Conference on Computer Vision (ICCV), pp. 2242–2251 (2018). https://doi.org/10.1109/ICCV.2017.244
26. Zuiderveld, K.: Contrast limited adaptive histogram equalization. In: Graphics Gems IV, pp. 474–485. Academic Press Professional, Inc., USA (1994)

Self-supervised Image-to-Text and Text-to-Image Synthesis

Anindya Sundar Das[✉] and Sriparna Saha

Department of Computer Science and Engineering, Indian Institute of Technology Patna, Patna, India

Abstract. A comprehensive understanding of vision and language and their interrelation are crucial to realize the underlying similarities and differences between these modalities and to learn more generalized, meaningful representations. In recent years, most of the works related to Text-to-Image synthesis and Image-to-Text generation, focused on supervised generative deep architectures to solve the problems, where very little interest was placed on learning the similarities between the embedding spaces across modalities. In this paper, we propose a novel self-supervised deep learning based approach towards learning the cross-modal embedding spaces; for both image to text and text to image generations. In our approach, we first obtain dense vector representations of images using StackGAN-based autoencoder model and also dense vector representations on sentence-level utilizing LSTM based text-autoencoder; then we study the mapping from embedding space of one modality to embedding space of the other modality utilizing GAN and maximum mean discrepancy based generative networks. We, also demonstrate that our model learns to generate textual description from image data as well as images from textual data both qualitatively and quantitatively.

Keywords: Cross-modal · Semantic space · Embedding space · Maximum mean discrepancy · Mapping networks

1 Introduction

The web contains a multitude of images; most of the content images are unannotated. Describing the content of an image automatically using proper natural languages is a vital task, relevant to the area of both Natural Language Processing and Computer Vision, the impact of which could be significant, for example, it will help visually impáired people to have a better understanding of the content of images on the web using existing text-to-speech systems. It has many other important applications such as semantic visual search [6], or visual intelligence in chatbots [4]. The reverse problem is the generation of realistic images from human-written descriptions. Although notable progress has been made in generating visually realistic images, those are still far from this goal. The Generative Adversarial Network (GAN) [7] based models showed promising results by

© Springer Nature Switzerland AG 2021
T. Mantoro et al. (Eds.): ICONIP 2021, LNCS 13111, pp. 415–426, 2021.
https://doi.org/10.1007/978-3-030-92273-3_34

generating many probable visual representations of a given textual description [22,23,31].

However, one major problem in both text to image synthesis and image to text generation is that recent state-of-the-art deep models are supervised learning-based that require annotated data. Most of the available web data is unlabeled and requires expensive human annotations. Similar problems have been addressed in machine translation where unsupervised machine translation [13] attains astounding results even in cases of low-resource languages and also performs reasonably well in the case of distant languages [14]. Motivated by the recent success in machine translation, we aim to investigate whether it is possible to learn the cross-modal embedding spaces between text and visual data in a self-supervised fashion.

*The major contributions of this paper can be summarized as follows: **i.** To the best of our knowledge, the current work is the first attempt in developing a self-supervised or unsupervised way of generating images from texts and texts from images. **ii.** Firstly a generative deep image autoencoder setup is developed for generating compelling image vector semantic space as per the reconstructions are concerned. Secondly, a recurrent neural network based autoencoder is developed which embeds sentences in textual semantic space. Finally, the mapping between cross-modal semantic spaces is established using both GANs and Maximum Mean Discrepancy (MMD) [32] based generative networks [16] which utilize the adversarial kernel learning technique. **iii.** Results on Caltech-UCSD Birds-200-2011 and Oxford-102 datasets illustrate that self-supervised Image-to-Text and Text-to-Image generation techniques can generate one modality given the other modality.*

2   Related Works

Caption generation using neural networks was first proposed in [12] which used a multimodal log-bi-linear model. In the paper [27], the authors used deep convolution neural networks (CNN) as an image encoder while RNN as a decoder that generates captions. The authors of [29], introduced an attention-based approach for image caption generation which uses convolutional networks for image feature extraction and attention-based RNN as decoder for caption generation. A deep visual semantic captioning model is proposed in [26] that takes the advantage of external sources and exploits the semantic information to generate captions and can describe the objects not present in image-caption datasets. A caption generation model that is based on the dependencies between caption words, image regions, and RNN language model has been proposed in [20]. The authors [15] showed in their work, that the meaningful style representation which is not well-described in text, but present in the images can be learned in an unsupervised manner. There have been several works on the generation of text for a given image, but there are also the ones that generate an image for a given text. Generative Adversarial Networks (GANs) [7] are proven to be useful in generating photo-realistic images [22,30]. For text to image task, StackGAN-v2 [31] employs a tree-like structure comprising of multiple generators and discriminators. It generates images at multiple scales at different branches of the tree.

Our work is as closely related to machine translation as it is related to image-caption generation. Recent work in unsupervised machine translation [13] uses a shared encoder-decoder architecture and maps the sentences from two different languages into common latent space. A work, related to unsupervised learning [16] that employs maximum mean discrepancy (MMD) [32] based on two-sample tests, minimizes the MMD distance between the two distributions to obtain the mapping. Building on the ideas and advances in these previous related works, we propose a novel architecture for cross-modal generations that utilizes GAN and MMD GANs [16] for unsupervised learning.

3   Methods

Our proposed self-supervised framework comprises of three sub-modules: 1) A deep StackGAN [31] based image autoencoder 2) LSTM-based Sequence-to-Sequence text autoencoder model 3) A cross-modal embedding space mapper that maps embedding from one semantic space to the other. We make our code publicly available[1].

3.1   StackGAN Based Image Autoencoder

Our proposed model for image autoencoder is StackGAN based. StackGAN-v2 [31] takes a text embedding vector as input and produces images of increasing resolution at different branches of the network. We modified the architecture to make it an encoder-decoder based network as shown in Fig. 1, where an encoder takes an image, extracts different features at different layers of the deep network to obtain an image embedding; this image embedding subsequently is fed as input to the original conditional StackGAN decoder model which reconstructs the image at the output of the conditional StackGAN thus working as an image autoencoder. For the encoder part of the autoencoder, we have used the pretrained ResNet-50 [9]. We have redefined the last layer of ResNet-50 to obtain 1024 dimensional image embedding.

On the decoder side, the generated image is conditioned on the image-embedding vector. As described in Fig. 1, firstly the ResNet encoder encodes image i into image embedding ψ_i. Then Conditional Augmentation technique [31] is applied on image embedding ψ_i to produce continuous latent space, yielding condition variable $\hat{c} \sim \mathcal{N}(\mu(\psi_i), \sigma(\psi_i))$. The following Kullback-Leibler (KL) divergence loss term is optimized during generator training which acts as regularization that ensures the smoothness of the conditioning variable distribution:

$$D_{KL}(\mathcal{N}(\mu(\psi_i), \sigma(\psi_i))\|\|\mathcal{N}(0, 1)) \tag{1}$$

For each generator, G_i, at different branches of the tree, the hidden feature, h_i, at i-th branch is computed as $h_0 = Fn_0(c, z)$ and $h_i = Fn_i(h_{i-1}, c)$ where Fn_i is

---

[1] https://github.com/anindyasdas/SelfSupervisedImageText.

neural network, $i = 0, 1, ..., n-1$; n is the total number of branches. Generators at different stages produce images $u_i = G_i(hi)$ from low-to-high resolutions gradually adding more details. Both conditional loss and unconditional loss are being optimized while training the discriminator, D_i:

$$Loss_{D_i} = -\mathbb{E}_{x_i \sim p_{data_i}}[\log(D_i(x_i)] - \mathbb{E}_{u_i \sim p_{G_i}}[\log(1 - D_i(u_i)]$$
$$- \mathbb{E}_{x_i \sim p_{data_i}}[\log(D_i(x_i, c)] - \mathbb{E}_{u_i \sim p_{G_i}}[\log(1 - D_i(u_i, c)] \quad (2)$$

The unconditional loss dictates whether the image at discriminator input is fake or real; the conditional loss decides whether the generated image corresponds to the respective conditioning variable (Fig. 1). During the training of the generators, the following loss function is being optimized:

$$Loss_{G_i} = -\mathbb{E}_{u_i \sim p_{G_i}}[\log(D_i(u_i)] - \mathbb{E}_{u_i \sim p_{G_i}}[\log(D_i(u_i, c)] \quad (3)$$

The final loss function for training the generators is given by

$$Loss_G = \sum_{0}^{n-1} Loss_{G_i} \quad (4)$$

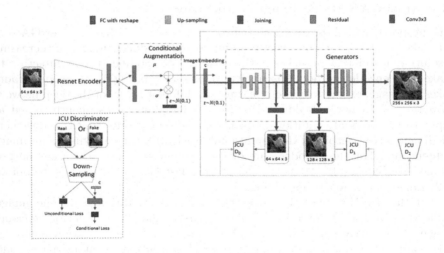

Fig. 1. Image autoencoder architecture: StackGAN Image Autoencoder. c is conditioning variable

3.2 LSTM-Based Sequence-to-Sequence Text Autoencoder Model

We have used a single-layer LSTM encoder and decoder in our text autoencoder as a sequence-to-sequence model. The encoder is bidirectional LSTM with hidden dimension 50, while the decoder is unidirectional with hidden size 100. The text encoder takes the word embedding vectors at each time step as inputs and generates corresponding hidden vectors. In this paper, we have considered all the hidden vectors to obtain the sentence embedding by max-pooling over all the hidden vectors. This latent vector is used to initialize the decoder LSTM network which regenerates the text description at the output.

3.3   Cross-modal Embedding Space Mapping Networks

Cross-modal embedding space mapping networks map from one modality embedding space to the other modality embedding space. The images and texts need not be paired, as both the networks minimize the distance between the two semantic distributions. We have employed two different architectures: One is GAN-based, and the other utilizes MMD-based generative networks.

GAN-Based Cross-Modal Embedding Space Mapping Networks
In this architecture, simple GAN models are used, for both image-to-text and text-to-image conversions. The generator translates one modality embedding into the other modality embedding, and the discriminator determines whether two embedding distributions match or not.

MMD GAN-Based Cross-Modal Embedding Space Mapping Networks
Maximum Mean Discrepancy (MMD) is a distance measure on the embedding probability space in Reproducing Kernel Hilbert Space (RKHS) [2]. Given two probability distributions P and Q and a continuous positive definite real-valued kernel k ($\mathcal{H}$ to be corresponding RKHS); the corresponding kernel means be defined as $\mu_p = \int k(.,x)dP(x)$ and $\mu_q = \int k(.,y)dQ(y)$, the distance $MMD(P,Q) = \|\mu_p - \mu_q\|$ measures the similarity between the two distributions, is known as MMD [8]. In this paper, we propose a mapping network based on MMD-GAN [16] that trains the generator g_θ to minimize MMD distance between two distributions, i.e. $\min_\theta M_k(\mathbb{P}_\mathcal{X}, \mathbb{P}_\theta)$, hence passes the hypothesis test.

Here real data $x \sim \mathbb{P}_\mathcal{X}$, generator distribution $g_\theta(z) \sim \mathbb{P}_\theta$ and $\mathbb{P}_\mathcal{Z}$ is the base distribution such that $z \sim \mathbb{P}_\mathcal{Z}$ and M_k is the square of MMD distances :

$$
\begin{aligned}
M_k(\mathbb{P}_\mathcal{X}, \mathbb{P}_\theta) &= \|\mu_{\mathbb{P}_\mathcal{X}} - \mu_{\mathbb{P}_\theta}\|^2 \\
&= \mathbb{E}_{\mathbb{P}_\mathcal{X}}\{k(x,x')\} + \mathbb{E}_{\mathbb{P}_\theta}\{k(g_\theta(z), g_\theta(z'))\} \\
&\quad - 2\mathbb{E}_{\mathbb{P}_\mathcal{X},\mathbb{P}_\theta}\{k(x, g_\theta(z))\} \quad (5)
\end{aligned}
$$

4   Experiment

We have compared our MMD-based Cross-modal mapping network with a GAN-based mapping network, in which the generator generates a mapping from one

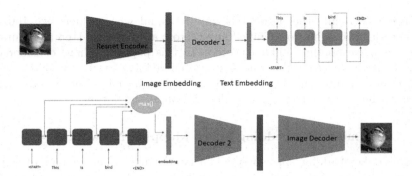

Fig. 2. End-to-end networks: self-supervised image-to-text generator and self-supervised text-to-image generator

embedding space to another, and the discriminator is a simple network to distinguish real and fake embeddings.

We first trained our image autoencoder (Sect. 3.1) for 600 epochs. We used pre-trained ResNet-50 encoder [9], the last layer of ResNet is re-defined as a fully connected layer with output dimension 1024, which is also our image vector dimension. During the training of the entire autoencoder, the weight of the ResNet, except the last layer, is kept fixed, while the parameters of the remaining network, are set as trainable. As the ResNet model is pre-trained on Imagenet dataset [5], we resized images to 224×224 and normalized images of our dataset using the mean and standard deviation of the Imagenet dataset.

Next, we pre-train our LSTM-based text autoencoder (Sect. 3.2) on 1 million sentences extracted from One Billion Word Benchmark dataset [3]. For initialization of our text autoencoder model, we have used top 50k 100-dimensional Glove embeddings [21] along with Glove embeddings of other unique words in caption datasets. The model was pre-trained for 50 epochs; this pre-trained model worked as an initializer; the model was then trained on all the captions of train sets. We have used Cross-Entropy between the generated and target sentences as the loss function.

After we trained both our autoencoders, the GAN-based Mapping Networks (Sect. 3.3) and the MMD-GAN Mapping Networks (Sect. 3.3) are trained separately using the unpaired image and text data, for both the image-to-text and the text-to-image conversions (Fig. 2). The weights of the trained autoencoders are kept fixed while we train the mapping networks. In image-to-text setup, first, the image encoder encodes an input image into image embedding, which is then used as input to image-to-text embedding mapping networks, that generate corresponding text embedding, the batch of generated text embeddings are used as fake text embeddings while the text embeddings obtained directly from text encoder act as true text embeddings; fake embeddings and true embeddings are then used to train the generative networks. Likewise, the text-to-image setup is trained.

Baselines: We have compared our StackGAN image autoencoder with the following baselines:

ResNet autoencoder: In this architecture we fine tuned ResNet-50 as encoder and the decoder comprises of several layers of upsampling followed by deconvolution layer as used in [30]. The latent dimension is set to 1024.

Com-Rec autoencoder: This model is based on [11] which is completely CNN based. We added linear layers in the bottleneck to obtain dense vector (dimension 1024) latent space.

Compressive autoencoder: This architecture is based on model as discussed in the paper [25] which comprises of an encoder, a decoder and a probabilistic model. We have added a linear layer in the bottleneck to obtain dense 1024-dimensional vector embeddings.

For Mapping Networks, as this is a novel self-supervised approach with no existing baselines available for comparisons, we define the following baselines to evaluate the performance:

GAN-based Cross-modal Mapping Network: In this architecture simple GAN models are used for both the image-to-text and text-to-image conversions. The generator translates one modality embedding into the other modality embedding and the discriminator determines whether two embedding distributions match or not.

MMD GAN-based Cross-modal Mapping Network: This is statistics based network that uses MMD [8] as objective function (Sect. 3.3).

Dataset: For the task, we have used publicly available standard Caltech-UCSD Birds-200-2011 Dataset [28] and Oxford-102 Flower Dataset. The CUB-200-2011 contains a total of 11,788 images of 200 bird species, with multiple annotations per image. All attributes are visual; mostly related to the shape, color, or pattern of the particular part. We split the dataset into train set (8,855 images, 88540 captions, 150 classes) and test set (2,933 images, 29330 captions, 50 classes) such that the respective classes do not overlap. The object-image size ratio in the dataset is less than 0.5 for 80% of the images, so we pre-processed the images to maintain the size ratio at values greater than 0.75.

The Oxford-102 dataset contains a total of 8,189 images of 102 categories of flowers. The dataset is split into train set (7,034 images, 70340 captions, 82 classes) and test set (1,155 images, 11,550 captions, 20 classes).

Evaluation Metrics: Inception score (IS) [24] and Fréchet Inception distance (FID) [10] to evaluate our generative image autoencoder model quantitatively.

We have used four standard metrics for the performance evaluation of our LSTM-based text autoencoder. These metrics are BLEU [19], METEOR [1], ROUGEL [17], CIDEr [18] to quantify the similarity between the ground reference sentence and autoencoder generated sentence. The official MSCOCO caption evaluation scripts[2] are used for evaluation.

The following evaluation metrics are used to assess the performance of our mapping networks:

---

[2] https://github.com/tylin/coco-caption.

1. **Human Score:** We conducted user studies for evaluation of our end-to-end text-to-image and image-to-text systems. We sampled 2000 samples for each of the text-to-image and image-to-text cases, assigned 5 different users (excluding any of the authors) to score the results. Generated samples are evaluated on a 4.0 scale, 1.0 being the lowest (worst case) and 4.0 being the highest (best case). Point 4.0 is awarded when the text description matches completely the image without any errors. Point 3.0 is awarded when the text description partially matches the image with minor errors. Point 2.0 is awarded when there is somewhat matching between text and image. Point 1.0 is awarded when the image and text are unrelated.

2. **Class Accuracy:** The CUB-200-2011 dataset has 150 train classes and 50 test classes and the Oxford-102 dataset has 82 and 20 train and test classes, respectively. Classes define different species for birds. Birds in the same class are from the same species, have identical features and descriptions. It is logical to expect that when one modality embedding maps into the other modality embedding, they are mapped to the same class. We first obtain the embeddings of one modality (say modality **A**) call it **true embeddings in modality A**. Then we obtain the embeddings of other modality (say modality **B**) and use them to feed into the **"Modality B-To-Modality A" mapping network** to obtain the **fake embeddings in modality A**. Then the cosine similarity between the true embeddings and fake embeddings are computed and we do an *argmax* to determine the class of fake embedding based on the highest cosine similarity scores. Then we calculate the class accuracy based on class labels of the true embeddings and predicted class labels of the fake embeddings.

5   Result and Analysis

The Inception score and FID of the StackGAN autoencoder model have been reported and compared with the baselines in Table 1. All the reported results are statistically significant. Results clearly illustrate the best performance by StackGAN autoencoder.

Table 1. Inception scores, Fréchet Inception distance (FID) (computed for 256 × 256 images)

Dataset	Model	Inception score ↑	FID ↓
CUB	**ResNet autoencoder with latent dimension 1024**	1.08 ± 0.03	275.71
CUB	**Com-Rec autoencoder with latent dimension 1024**	1.15 ± 0.02	248.95
CUB	**Compressive autoencoder with latent dimension 1024**	1.09 ± 0.08	283.64
CUB	**StackGAN autoencoder**	$\mathbf{3.66 \pm 0.09}$	**21.58**
Oxford-102	**StackGAN autoencoder**	$\mathbf{3.23 \pm 0.14}$	**57.96**

The scores for LSTM-based text autoencoder model are reported as: on CUB dataset (BLEU-1: 87.52, BLEU-4: 72.55, METEOR: 49.89, ROUGE-L: 89.04,

CIDEr: 7.04) and on Oxford-102 (BLEU-1: 85.35, BLEU-4: 70.61, METEOR: 48.06, ROUGE-L: 86.69, CIDEr: 6.59).

The sample outputs of the End-To-End Image-To-Text synthesis are shown in Fig. 4; Fig. 3 depicts the sample outputs for Text-to-Image synthesis network. Evaluation metric scores are reported in Table 2 for GAN-based end-to-end networks and MMD-based networks.

The human score indicates that there exist some correlations between the two modalities of Image-to-Text and Text-to-Image synthesis systems. However, **Class Accuracy** score is indicative of a low semantic correlation between the two modalities for both GAN based and MMD based Image-to-Text and Text-to-Image systems. The scores at Table 2 imply similar performances by both the GAN-based system and the MMD-based system.

Table 2. Human Score, class accuracy of gan-based and mmd-based image-to-text and text-to-image end-to-end systems on CUB and Oxford-102 datasets. (* means the values reported are in percentage).

Model	Metric	CUB-200-2011		Oxford-102	
		Image-to-text	Text-to-image	Image-to-text	Text-to-image
GAN-based	Human score	**2.3**	**2.5**	**2.5**	**2.4**
	Class accuracy*	**2.3**	**2.8**	**6.6**	**4.5**
MMD-based	Human score	2.1	2.4	2.2	2.3
	Class accuracy*	2.0	2.5	5.6	4.1

this bird is smaller, short beaked, yellow superciliary has shades of light brown to dark brown on the wings

a tiny bird, with a tiny head and bill, brown coverts, white secondaries, a black back, grey outer retices, and a white breast

the build of the bird is chubby

the bird has a small black bill that is somewhat curved

Fig. 3. End-to-end network output for birds: text-to-image synthesis

6 Error Analysis

A thorough analysis revealed scenarios for possible reasons for errors. The strength of the end-to-end model is dependant on strength of the individual

the flowers has thin
lavender petals

this small yellow flower has
overlapping pointed around
white pistils

the flower shown has
smooth petals that are
fused and separately
arranged orangish in region

this flower has large purple
petals petals, with pointed
edges

Fig. 4. End-to-end network output for flowers: image-to-text synthesis

components, as models are trained separately; so error in each component has a cumulative impact on the end-to-end network. The autoencoders are trained separately without sharing weights or information, as a result, the latent spaces are disjoint, which further makes it harder for the mapping networks to align learned embedding spaces on the semantic level.

7   Conclusion

In this paper, we proposed a novel self-supervised approach that performs the cross-modal translation from image to text and text to image. We showed that our Text-to-Image and Image-to-Text synthesis networks learn to map the semantic space of one modality to the semantic space of the other modality in an unsupervised fashion. However, we figure out while learning the mapping, the semantic correlation across the modalities is low. Though the current end-to-end network depicts low cross-modal semantic alignments, as part of the future work, these learned network weights can be used as initialization for the synthesis networks and the entire network can be fine-tuned till the embeddings of the two modalities semantically align in the latent space.

Acknowledgments. Dr. Sriparna Saha gratefully acknowledges the Young Faculty Research Fellowship (YFRF) Award, supported by Visvesvaraya Ph.D. Scheme for Electronics and IT, Ministry of Electronics and Information Technology (MeitY), Government of India, being implemented by Digital India Corporation (formerly Media Lab Asia) for carrying out this research.

References

1. Banerjee, S., Lavie, A.: Meteor: an automatic metric for MT evaluation with improved correlation with human judgments. In: Proceedings of the ACL Workshop on Intrinsic and Extrinsic Evaluation (2005)
2. Berlinet, A., Thomas-Agnan, C.: Reproducing Kernel Hilbert Spaces in Probability and Statistics. Springer, Heidelberg (2011). https://doi.org/10.1007/978-1-4419-9096-9

3. Chelba, C., et al.: One billion word benchmark for measuring progress in statistical language modeling. arXiv preprint arXiv:1312.3005 (2013)
4. Das, A., et al.: Visual dialog. In: Proceedings of the IEEE Conference on Computer Vision and Pattern Recognition, pp. 326–335 (2017)
5. Deng, J., Dong, W., Socher, R., Li, L.-J., Li, K., Fei-Fei, L.: Imagenet: a large-scale hierarchical image database. In: 2009 IEEE Conference on Computer Vision and Pattern Recognition, pp. 248–255 (2009)
6. Fan, L.: Semantic visual search engine. In: US Patent 7,865,492 (2017). Gehring, J., Auli, M., Grangier, D., Yarats, D., Dauphin, Y.N.: Convolutional sequence to sequence learning. arXiv preprint arXiv:1705.03122 (2011)
7. Goodfellow, I., et al.: Generative adversarial nets. In: Advances in Neural Information Processing Systems, pp. 2672–2680 (2014)
8. Gretton, A., Borgwardt, K.M., Rasch, M.J., Schölkopf, B., Smola, A.: A kernel two-sample test. J. Mach. Learn. Res. **13**, 723–773 (2012a)
9. He, K., Zhang, X., Ren, S., Sun, J.: Deep residual learning for image recognition. In: Proceedings of the IEEE Conference on Computer Vision and Pattern Recognition, pp. 770–778 (2016)
10. Heusel, M., Ramsauer, H., Unterthiner, T., Nessler, B., Hochreiter, S.: GANs trained by a two time-scale update rule converge to a local nash equilibrium. In: Advances in Neural Information Processing Systems, pp. 6626–6637 (2017)
11. Jiang, F., Tao, W., Liu, S., Ren, J., Guo, X., Zhao, D.: An end-to-end compression framework based on convolutional neural networks. IEEE Trans. Circuits Syst. Video Technol. **28**, 3007–3018 (2017)
12. Kiros, R., Salakhutdinov, R., Zemel, R.: Multimodal neural language models. In: International Conference on Machine Learning, pp. 595–603 (2014)
13. Lample, G., Conneau, A., Denoyer, L., Ranzato, M.: Unsupervised machine translation using monolingual corpora only. arXiv preprint arXiv:1711.00043 (2017)
14. Lample, G., Ott, M., Conneau, A., Denoyer, L., Ranzato, M.: Phrase-based & neural unsupervised machine translation. arXiv preprint arXiv:1804.07755 (2018)
15. Lao, Q., Havaei, M., Pesaranghader, A., Dutil, F., Jorio, L.D., Fevens, T.: Dual adversarial inference for text-to-image synthesis. In: Proceedings of the IEEE International Conference on Computer Vision, pp. 7567–7576 (2019)
16. Li, C.-L., Chang, W.-C., Cheng, Y., Yang, Y., Póczos, B.: MMD GAN: towards deeper understanding of moment matching network. In: Advances in Neural Information Processing Systems, pp. 2203–2213 (2017)
17. Lin, C.-Y. (2004). ROUGE: A package for automatic evaluation of summaries. In Text Summarization Branches Out (pp. 74–81). In: Barcelona, Spain: Association for Computational Linguistics. https://www.aclweb.org/anthology/W04-1013
18. Vedantam, R., Lawrence Zitnick, C., Parikh, D.: Cider: consensus based image description evaluation. In: Proceedings of the IEEE Conference on Computer Vision and Pattern Recognition, pp. 4566–4575 (2015)
19. Papineni, K., Roukos, S., Ward, T., Zhu, W.-J.: Bleu: a method for automatic evaluation of machine translation. In: Proceedings of the 40th Annual Meeting on Association for Computational Linguistics, pp. 311–318. Association for Computational Linguistics (2002)
20. Pedersoli, M., Lucas, T., Schmid, C., Verbeek, J.: Areas of attention for image captioning. In: Proceedings of the IEEE International Conference on Computer Vision, pp. 1242–1250 (2017)
21. Pennington, J., Socher, R., Manning, C.D.: Glove: global vectors for word representation. In: Proceedings of the 2014 Conference on Empirical Methods in Natural Language Processing (EMNLP), pp. 1532–1543 (2014)

22. Reed, S., Akata, Z., Yan, X., Logeswaran, L., Schiele, B., Lee, H.: Generative adversarial text to image synthesis. arXiv preprint arXiv:1605.05396 (2016a)
23. Reed, S.E., Akata, Z., Mohan, S., Tenka, S., Schiele, B., Lee, H.: Learning what and where to draw. In: Advances in Neural Information Processing Systems, pp. 217–225 (2016b)
24. Salimans, T., Goodfellow, I., Zaremba, W., Cheung, V., Radford, A., Chen, X.: Improved techniques for training GANs. In: Advances in Neural Information Processing Systems, pp. 2234–2242 (2016)
25. Theis, L., Shi, W., Cunningham, A., Huszár, F.: Lossy image compression with compressive autoencoders. arXiv preprint arXiv:1703.00395 (2017)
26. Venugopalan, S., Anne Hendricks, L., Rohrbach, M., Mooney, R., Darrell, T., Saenko, K.: Captioning images with diverse objects. In: Proceedings of the IEEE Conference on Computer Vision and Pattern Recognition, pp. 5753–5761 (2017)
27. Vinyals, O., Toshev, A., Bengio, S., Erhan, D.: Show and tell: a neural image caption generator. In: Proceedings of the IEEE Conference on Computer Vision and Pattern Recognition, pp. 3156–3164 (2015)
28. Wah, C., Branson, S., Welinder, P., Perona, P., Belongie, S.: The Caltech-UCSD Birds-200-2011 Dataset. Technical report CNS-TR-2011-001, California Institute of Technology (2011)
29. Xu, K., et al.: Show, attend and tell: neural image caption generation with visual attention. In: International Conference on Machine Learning, pp. 2048–2057 (2015)
30. Zhang, H., et al.: StackGAN: text to photo-realistic image synthesis with stacked generative adversarial networks. In: Proceedings of the IEEE International Conference on Computer Vision, pp. 5907–5915 (2017)
31. Zhang, H., et al.: StackGAN++: realistic image synthesis with stacked generative adversarial networks. IEEE Trans. Pattern Anal. Mach. Intell. 41, 1947–1962 (2018)
32. Tolstikhin, I.O., Sriperumbudur, B.K., Schölkopf, B.: Minimax estimation of maximum mean discrepancy with radial kernels. In: Advances in Neural Information Processing Systems, pp. 1930–1938 (2016)

TextCut: A Multi-region Replacement Data Augmentation Approach for Text Imbalance Classification

Wanrong Jiang, Ya Chen, Hao Fu, and Guiquan Liu[✉]

School of Computer Science and Technology, University of Science and Technology of China, Hefei, China
{jwr,chenya88,hfu}@mail.ustc.edu.cn, gqliu@ustc.edu.cn

Abstract. In the practical applications of text classification, data imbalance problems occur frequently, which typically leads to prejudice of a classifier against the majority group. Therefore, how to handle imbalanced text datasets to alleviate the skew distribution is a crucial task. Existing mainstream methods tackle it by utilizing interpolation-based augmentation strategies to synthesize new texts according to minority class texts. However, it may mess up the syntactic and semantic information of the original texts, which makes it challenging to model the new texts. We propose a novel data augmentation method based on paired samples, called TextCut, to overcome the above problem. For a minority class text and its paired text, TextCut samples multiple small square regions of the minority text in the hidden space and replaces them with corresponding regions cutout from the paired text. We build TextCut upon the BERT model to better capture the features of minority class texts. We verify that TextCut can further improve the classification performance of the minority and entire categories, and effectively alleviate the imbalanced problem on three benchmark imbalanced text datasets.

Keywords: Data imbalance · Data augmentation · Text classification

1 Introduction

The data imbalance problem is a crucial issue for the text classification [29]. In the binary classification task, the class with smaller size is called minority class, and the other one is called majority class [8]. However, the classification results obtained by traditional classifiers tend to be biased towards the majority class, resulting in a low classification accuracy of the minority class [14]. Existing methods of dealing with data imbalance in the text are mainly divided into data-level and algorithm-level methods [20]. In this paper, we focus on data-level methods. Data-level methods are represented by undersampling majority classes or oversampling minority classes [13]. Actually, traditional oversampling methods cause some samples to appear repeatedly, and the trained model has overfitting problems. And undersampling methods discard a large amount of samples,

© Springer Nature Switzerland AG 2021
T. Mantoro et al. (Eds.): ICONIP 2021, LNCS 13111, pp. 427–439, 2021.
https://doi.org/10.1007/978-3-030-92273-3_35

which leads the model only to learn part of the overall pattern. Nevertheless, as an improved oversampling method, data augmentation can avoid these problems by synthesizing new samples from the minority class samples [21,23]. So it has become one of the effective techniques to solve the data imbalance problem.

Mixup [31] currently is a widely used data augmentation strategy in Computer Vision (CV), which linearly combines paired samples and their labels in the input space. Due to its effectiveness, Mixup is applied to Natural Language Processing (NLP) tasks in the hidden space [12]. However, the samples synthesized by Mixup are inclined to be unnatural, which manifests as confusing the original syntactic and semantic information of them. CutMix [30] is also a data augmentation strategy in CV and extends from Mixup, which generating a new image by replacing corresponding region of the original image with a chosen single region from another training image to settle the matter in Mixup. We argue that CutMix can not be directly applicable to NLP tasks on account of discrete input space. Besides, if it is applied in hidden space like Mixup, these single replacement regions may easily involve nonsense regions which is padding regions caused by the texts being zero padded to the max length. As a result, the synthesized texts may be incredible. In order to overcome aforementioned shortcomings, we propose a novel data augmentation strategy called TextCut. We build TextCut upon the BERT [7] model to better model minority class texts. In the hidden space, the replacement regions are composed of multiple small square regions in TextCut instead of a single large region like CutMix, which allows the replacement regions to cover a wider range, thereby reducing the proportion of the padding regions in the replacement regions. Our main contributions in this article are as follows:

- To our knowledge, we are the first to introduce CutMix into NLP task. Based on it, we propose a muti-regional replacement data augmentation method to alleviate imbalanced problem by generating new texts for minority classes.
- We implement TextCut on the BERT model to better capture the features of minority class texts, and propose to perform it after one of the hidden layers to obtain more syntactic and semantic information that helps classification.
- We evaluate the proposed method on three imbalanced text datasets. It outperforms other state-of-the-art data augmentation methods and can effectively alleviate the bias problem of the text classifier.

2   Related Works

2.1   Methods Handling Text Imbalance Problem

Prior research has proposed methods that process the data imbalance problem contain data-level and algorithm-level methods [20].

Data-level method such as Synthetic Minority Oversampling Technique (SMOTE) [3] utilizes the observations of minority class samples to compound new samples by linear interpolation. On account of the great success of word vector models such as GLOVE [22] and Word2Vec [2], some studies have tend to apply SMOTE and its variants to text data in feature space [21,23]. Recently, deep learning networks have been applied to imbalanced data, with Generative Adversarial Nets(GAN) [6,10] as the representative to generate diverse samples for minority classes [25].

Correspondingly, the basic idea of algorithm-level methods [17] is to increase the weights of minority class samples and decrease that of majority class samples, which can be achieved by a cost matrix to concentrate on minority classes [9]. In addition, modifying the loss function is also one of effective techniques, such as in the case of Focal Loss [19], which introduces two hyperparameters on the basis of Cross Entropy to balance data distribution and makes the model focus on the hard-to-separate samples. GHM [18] is a modified version of Focal Loss, which proposes to design a gradient equalization mechanism to make model training more efficient and robust.

2.2   Data Augmentation in Text

Data augmentation allows limited data to produce the value equivalent to more data without substantially adding data. In fact, it seems inadvisable to augment text data due to the complex sentence structure in the text. Even so, Wei et al. [28] propose four simple operations to expand text data, namely Synonyms Replace, Randomly Insert, Randomly Swap, Randomly Delete. Chen et al. [4] apply back translation [24] and word substitution to obtain new texts. Andreas [1] creates new texts by switching subsections that occur in similar contexts. Furthermore, Guo et al. [12] are the first to introduce Mixup [31] into NLP tasks. Different variants of Mixup in text include Nonlinear Mixup [11], which uses a matrix as the coefficient of interpolation to expand the space of the synthesized texts, TMix [5], which performs linear interpolation in the hidden space of the neural model, and SeqMix [32], which performs token-level interpolation in the embedding space. Unlike previous applications of these data augmentation methods, which focus on expanding all classes, we apply data augmentation on minority classes to address the data imbalance problem.

3   Proposed Approach

In this section, we firstly illustrate the main idea of TextCut by given an example. Then, we built TextCut on BERT, and introduce the overall classification framework in detail.

3.1   TextCut

In this paper, we extend a variant of CutMix [30] to text modeling, which is a data augmentation strategy based on region-level replacement for images. The main idea of the variant, named TextCut, is to create a virtual training sample by giving two training labeled samples (x_1, y_1) and (x_2, y_2), where x is the training sample and y is the one-hot representation of the label. Since the text is

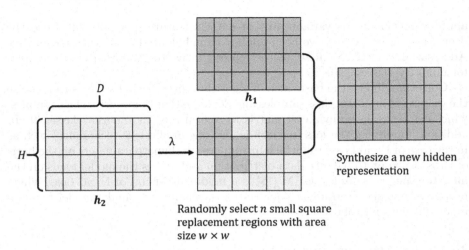

Fig. 1. An illustrative representation of proposed TextCut.

composed of discrete tokens in the input space [32], we choose to apply TextCut within the hidden space. Similar to CutMix, we define this combining operation as follows:

$$\tilde{\mathbf{h}} = (1 - \mathbf{B}) \odot \mathbf{h}_1 + \mathbf{B} \odot \mathbf{h}_2$$
$$\tilde{\mathbf{y}} = (1 - \lambda)\mathbf{y}_1 + \lambda\mathbf{y}_2 \tag{1}$$

where $\mathbf{B} \in \{0,1\}^{H \times D}$ denotes a binary mask matrix indicating which parts to drop out and fill in from two samples, H and D indicate respectively the max sentence length and the hidden representation dimension, $\mathbf{1}$ is a binary mask matrix filled with ones and $\odot$ is element-wise multiplication. Here, $\mathbf{h}_1 \in \mathbb{R}^{H \times D}$ and $\mathbf{h}_2 \in \mathbb{R}^{H \times D}$ denote the representation of x_1 and x_2 in the hidden space, and λ is the ratio of the area of all replacement regions to the total region area.

We first set the value of $\lambda \in (0, 1/2]$, which determine the proportion of a single large replacement region, and then segment it into multiple small square regions with w representing the side length of each square region. Hence, the number of them can be computed as $n = \lambda \times H \times D \mathbin{//} (w \times w)$, where $\mathbin{//}$ is the aliquot operation. We then randomly select n regions with area size $w \times w$ from $\mathbf{h}_2$ back to the original sample $\mathbf{h}_1$. Later, we will present parameter studies on λ and w.

From the above description, we realize that the binary mask matrix $\mathbf{B}$ contains multiple diminutive square matrices filled with ones. To sample these matrices, we set a bounding box coordinate $S = (b_x, b_y, b_w, b_h)$ to represent a cropping diminutive square region, where b_x and b_y indicates the position of the point in the left bottom corner, b_w and b_h indicates width and height of S. The box S is uniformly sampled according to:

$$b_x \sim Unif(w-1,\ H),\quad b_y \sim Unif(0,\ D-w+1)$$
$$b_w = w,\quad b_h = w \tag{2}$$

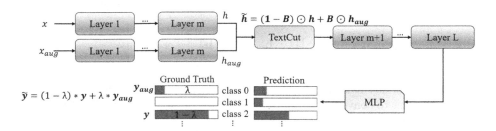

Fig. 2. The block diagram of text classification model based on BERT.

Then, we randomly sample n square mask matrices, and all the cropping regions are obtained. For this binary mask matrix $\mathbf{B}$, the elements in these bounding boxes are all 1, and the other parts are all 0.

Figure 1 shows an illustrative representation of our method, where the hidden representation size is 4×6, λ and w are set to $1/2$ and 2, respectively, then n evaluates to 3. Moreover, what calls for our attention is that the selected regions may overlap in TextCut. Considering that the dimension of the hidden layer is generally large, which is set to 768 for bert-base-uncased model, the probability of coincidence tends to be low. Thus, we ignore this problem.

3.2   Framework of Text Classification

Previous research have shown that large models tend to perform better in imbalanced settings [15]. BERT [7], as a sentence encoder, has evolved into large language model with a wide range of applications in NLP. Therefore, we build TextCut upon the BERT model. For the BERT with L layer, we intend to execute TextCut on the m-th layer, where $m \in [1, L]$. Figure 2 shows the overall framework of the text classification model. To implement the model framework, the process is divided into the following four steps:

Step 1: Select a pair of input samples x and x_{aug}. We set a sampling ratio r according to the Imbalance Ratio (IR) of the class that x belongs to, which is obtained dividing the size of the majority class with the largest size by that of the class that x belongs to [26]. Then, we randomly sample r samples from training set for x, where x_{aug} is one of them, to form r pairs of samples. Particularly, for x_1 in majority classes, no new samples are required and $x_{aug} = x_1$.

Step 2: Compute the hidden representation of the pair of input samples at the bottom layers. The bottom layers refer to these layers from 1 to m. Here, the hidden representations of x and x_{aug} in layer $[1, m]$ can be compute by $f_l(.;\theta)$, which denotes the encoding function of layer l, as follows:

$$\mathbf{h}_l = f_l(\mathbf{h}_{l-1};\theta),\ l = 1,\ 2,\ \dots, m$$
$$\mathbf{h}_l^{aug} = f_l(\mathbf{h}_{l-1}^{aug};\theta),\ l = 1,\ 2,\ \dots, m \tag{3}$$

Step 3: Synthesize a new hidden representation and feed it to the top layers. The top layers refer to these layers from $m + 1$ to L. According to formula (1), $\mathbf{h}$ and $\mathbf{h}^{aug}$ are merged into a new hidden representation, and their ground truth labels are also mixed proportionally. Then it is fed into the top layer. The whole process is formally defined as:

$$\tilde{\mathbf{h}}_m = (1 - \mathbf{B}) \odot \mathbf{h}_m + \mathbf{B} \odot \mathbf{h}_m^{aug}$$
$$\tilde{\mathbf{h}}_l = f_l(\tilde{\mathbf{h}}_{l-1}; \theta), \ l = m + 1, \ m + 2, \ ... \ , L \qquad (4)$$

Step 4: Classify samples. In our work, a one-layer MLP network is adopted as the classifier to convert the hidden representation of the last layer into a probability vector. We minimize Cross Entropy function between the mixed labels and the probability from the classifier, and jointly optimize over all parameters to train the whole model.

4   Experiments

4.1   Datasets

In this section, we adopt three benchmark imbalanced text datasets to perform experiments: Reuters-21578 (R8) [26], Cade12 [26] and Twitter Hate Speech (THS) [27]. The first two datasets use the original training set and test set as our training set and test set, and the last dataset is split into train and test sets at a ratio of 7:3. The details of the datasets are presented in Table 1.

Table 1. Details of benchmark datasets.

DataSet	Class	Train	Test	IR
R8	earn	2840	1083	–
	acq	1596	696	1.780
	crude	253	121	11.225
	trade	251	75	11.315
	money-fx	206	87	13.786
	interest	190	81	14.947
	ship	108	36	26.296
	grain	41	10	69.268
Cade12	servicos	5627	2846	–
	sociedade	4935	2428	1.140
	lazer	3698	1892	1.522
	internet	1585	792	3.550
	noticias	701	381	8.027
	compras-online	423	202	13.303
THS	0	20794	8915	–
	1	1571	670	13.236

4.2   Baselines

To demonstrate the effectiveness of our method, we compare it with three recent text data augmentation methods, which are also executed on BERT [7].

- **EDA** [28]: Easy Data Augmentation is a text augmentation method that relies on rules instead of feature representation. It includes Synonym Replacement (SR), Random Insertion (RI), Random Swap (RS), and Random Deletion (RD) with considerable effects on some small English datasets.
- **TMix** [5]: It is also a text augmentation technology extended from Mixup [31]. Based on the fact that a new sentence created by interpolation of two hidden vectors can mix the meaning of the original sentences, it performs linear interpolation in the hidden space of the text rather than in the input space.
- **SeqMix** [32]: It is another variant of Mixup. The difference is that SeqMix performs token-level interpolation in the embedding space, and then selects the token that is closest to the mixed embedding as the new token to get a corresponding new sentence.

4.3   Experiment Settings

We choose bert-base-uncased tokenizer to tokenize the text, choose bert-base-uncased model and a one-layer MLP as text encoder and classifier respectively. The classifier predicts labels through a hidden layer whose size is the total number of categories and softmax for multi-classification or sigmoid for binary classification as its activation function. The learning rate is 1e−5. The mixed layer set M is set as $\{7, 9, 12\}$ and the batch size is 16. For each batch, a certain layer is randomly selected from M as the mixed layer. In our experiments, in terms of different datasets, the max sentence length, the proportion of a single large replacement region λ and the side length w of the small regions are not quite consistent. We set them as 128, 1/4, 2 for R8, 150, 1/2, 5 for Cade12, and 50, 1/2, 2 for THS. For TMix and SeqMix, we set $\alpha = 6$ to sample mixed coefficient from $Beta(\alpha, \alpha)$. All models are implemented with Pytorch framework.

4.4   Experimental Results

In the section, we use Precision (%), Recall (%), and macro-F1 (%) to objectively evaluate baselines and our proposed method on these imbalanced text datasets.

Performance Comparison with Entire Categories. Table 2 shows the experimental results with entire categories on different datasets. TextCut(large) expresses that the replacement region is a single large region. We can draw the following conclusions: (1) Basically all models applying data augmentation technologies show better performance in all metrics than BERT itself. (2) TextCut outperforms TextCut(large) in all metrics, which verifies effectiveness of the strategy sampling multiple small square replacement regions rather than a single large replacement region. (3) TextCut is superior to TMix, SeqMix, EDA basically in all metrics. We hold on the point that the first two augmentation methods may mess up the meaning of the original texts and the last one has more disturbing to the text.

Table 2. Experimental results with entire categories.

Model	R8			Cade12			THS		
	Precision	Recall	F1	Precision	Recall	F1	Precision	Recall	F1
BERT	95.3	95.8	95.5	59.6	56.4	58.0	91.0	85.9	88.4
EDA	96.3	96.1	96.2	61.5	57.7	59.3	91.2	**88.4**	89.8
TMix	95.9	96.4	96.1	62.1	57.8	59.9	92.9	86.1	89.4
SeqMix	95.7	96.0	95.8	62.3	57.3	59.7	92.4	86.1	89.1
TextCut(large)	96.0	96.3	96.2	62.0	**58.0**	59.9	91.8	86.7	89.2
TextCut	**96.8**	**97.0**	**96.9**	**62.8**	**58.0**	**60.3**	**93.7**	87.3	**90.4**

Table 3. Experimental results on R8 with each category.

Model	earn	acq	crude	trade	money-fx	interest	ship	grain
BERT	98.9	98.1	98.3	94.8	90	86.9	97.2	100
EDA	99.1	**99.1**	98.3	96.7	88.3	91.1	97.1	100
TMix	**99.4**	97.3	**99.2**	96.7	87.1	92.2	97.2	100
SeqMix	99	98.6	97.5	95.5	**90.7**	88.9	97.2	94.7
TextCut(large)	97.9	99.0	**99.2**	96.7	89.9	90.4	95.9	100
TextCut	99.2	98.6	98.7	**96.8**	90.5	**92.2**	**98.6**	100

Performance Comparison with Each Category. In order to explore the impact of TextCut on different imbalance level, we augment each category until the size is equal to the one with the largest size. The IR of each category in all datasets is presented in Table 1. Table 3, Table 4 and Table 5 show F1 comparison of each category in the datasets. We can observe that: (1) BERT shows that the substantial performance decreases with a deterioration in class imbalance level. This is because the classifier will be biased toward the majority group. (2) TextCut has a more significant improvement for severe imbalanced categories in terms of F1. However, F1 of TextCut has a slight decrease for the categories with smaller IR among compared methods. It is natural since the concentration of TextCut is more on the minority categories than other methods when the datasets tend to trade off.

4.5   Parameter Studies

The Proportion of a Single Large Replacement Region λ. From our perspectives, λ directly affects the mixing of sample feature representations and labels. We vary the value of λ in $\{1/16, 1/8, 1/4, 1/2\}$, and the result is shown in Fig. 3. Specially, the mixed layer set M is set to $\{7,9,12\}$. It can be seen that the model shows better F1 improvement with $\lambda \geq 1/4$. For all datasets, the best F1 is about 1.0% higher than F1 at $\lambda = 1/16$. This result shows that the model is more inclined to create newer samples. The new samples and the parent samples have further distance, thus the model introduces more diversified generation.

Table 4. Experimental results on Cade12 with each category.

Model	Servicos	Sociedade	Lazer	Internet	Noticias	Compras-online
BERT	67.4	**67.5**	**70.5**	62.5	39.6	38.3
EDA	68.5	64.9	69.9	58.2	47.0	46.3
TMix	**73.1**	64.2	65.3	61.5	48.0	45.8
SeqMix	70.9	66.1	62.1	**66.4**	45.1	44.0
TextCut(large)	72.7	63.5	62.3	61.1	48.1	47.5
TextCut	72.9	63.5	64.1	61.0	**49.4**	**48.0**

Table 5. Experimental results on THS with each category.

Model	0	1
BERT	97.3	79.3
EDA	96.1	83.5
TMix	97.2	81.1
SeqMix	**97.4**	80.5
TextCut(large)	96.9	81.3
TextCut	96.2	**84.4**

The Side Length of Small Region w. We show the performance comparison of different values of w in Fig. 4, where w takes the value in $\{2, 3, 4, 5\}$. The mixed layer set M is set to $\{7, 9, 12\}$. On R8 and Cade12, F1 gets the best value with $w = 2$ for both. However, the best value is when $w = 5$ on THS. This result shows that when the max sequence length of text is relatively small, the value of w should be larger. The possible reason is that the grammatical and semantic information among tokens in the short text is closely related. When the value of w is larger, and the relevance of these information in the original sample is relatively intact.

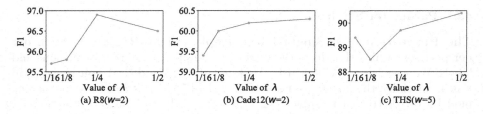

Fig. 3. F1 comparison with different value of λ on the datasets.

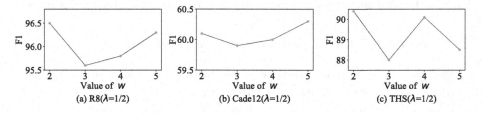

Fig. 4. F1 comparison with different value of w on the datasets.

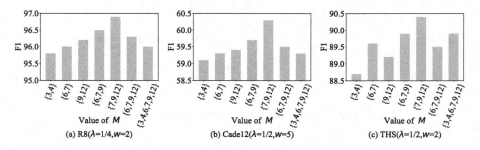

Fig. 5. F1 comparison with different value of M on the datasets.

Mixed Layer Set M. The work [5] explores that the subset $\{7, 9, 12\}$ of $\{3, 4, 6, 7, 9, 12\}$, which contains richer different types of information on BERT [16], involves useful syntactic and semantic information for classification. Similarly, with the purpose of exploring the optimal solution of M, we choose to use different subset of $\{3, 4, 6, 7, 9, 12\}$ to mix the samples. As shown in Fig. 5, We observe that $M = \{3, 4\}$ has the least performance improvement, because $\{3, 4\}$ mainly encodes surface information, which contributes less to text classification. Moreover, the model with $M = \{7, 9, 12\}$ is better than $\{6, 7, 9\}$ and $\{6, 7, 9, 12\}$. It shows that the 6th layer cannot help much in terms of classification either, while 12th layer is conducive to text classification. Our model also reaches the optimal value at $\{7, 9, 12\}$.

5   Conclusion

To alleviate the problem of class imbalance in text classification, we propose a simple but effective data augmentation method at data-level. This method, called TextCut, which samples multiple small square regions of the text in the hidden space and replaces them with regions cutout from the other text to synthesize new texts based on minority class texts. We verify the effectiveness of our proposed method through experiments evaluation on three imbalanced text datasets. The results show that TextCut has better performance on the overall and minority categories, compared with other state-of-the-art text data augmentation methods.

Acknowledgements. This paper has been supported by the National Key Research and Development Program of China (No. 2018YFB1801105).

References

1. Andreas, J.: Good-enough compositional data augmentation. In: Proceedings of the 58th Annual Meeting of the Association for Computational Linguistics, pp. 7556–7566 (2020)
2. Bojanowski, P., Grave, E., Joulin, A., Mikolov, T.: Enriching word vectors with subword information. Trans. Assoc. Comput. Linguist. **5**, 135–146 (2017)
3. Chawla, N.V., Bowyer, K.W., Hall, L.O., Kegelmeyer, W.P.: Smote: synthetic minority over-sampling technique. J. Artif. Intell. Res. **16**, 321–357 (2002)
4. Chen, J., Wu, Y., Yang, D.: Semi-supervised models via data augmentation for classifying interactive affective responses. In: AffCon@ AAAI (2020)
5. Chen, J., Yang, Z., Yang, D.: Mixtext: linguistically-informed interpolation of hidden space for semi-supervised text classification. In: ACL (2020)
6. Croce, D., Castellucci, G., Basili, R.: GAN-BERT: generative adversarial learning for robust text classification with a bunch of labeled examples. In: Proceedings of the 58th Annual Meeting of the Association for Computational Linguistics, pp. 2114–2119 (2020)
7. Devlin, J., Chang, M.W., Lee, K., Toutanova, K.: BERT: pre-training of deep bidirectional transformers for language understanding. In: Proceedings of the 2019 Conference of the North American Chapter of the Association for Computational Linguistics: Human Language Technologies, vol. 1 (Long and Short Papers), pp. 4171–4186 (2019)
8. Estabrooks, A., Jo, T., Japkowicz, N.: A multiple resampling method for learning from imbalanced data sets. Comput. Intell. **20**(1), 18–36 (2004)
9. Fernando, C., et al.: Pathnet: evolution channels gradient descent in super neural networks. arXiv preprint arXiv:1701.08734 (2017)
10. Goodfellow, I.J., et al.: Generative adversarial nets. In: NIPS (2014)
11. Guo, H.: Nonlinear Mixup: out-of-manifold data augmentation for text classification. In: Proceedings of the AAAI Conference on Artificial Intelligence, vol. 34, pp. 4044–4051 (2020)
12. Guo, H., Mao, Y., Zhang, R.: Augmenting data with Mixup for sentence classification: an empirical study. arXiv preprint arXiv:1905.08941 (2019)

13. Haixiang, G., Yijing, L., Shang, J., Mingyun, G., Yuanyue, H., Bing, G.: Learning from class-imbalanced data: review of methods and applications. Expert Syst. Appl. **73**, 220–239 (2017)
14. He, H., Garcia, E.A.: Learning from imbalanced data. IEEE Trans. Knowl. Data Eng. **21**(9), 1263–1284 (2009)
15. Jang, J., Kim, Y., Choi, K., Suh, S.: Sequential targeting: a continual learning approach for data imbalance in text classification. Expert Syst. Appl. **179**, 115067 (2021)
16. Jawahar, G., Sagot, B., Seddah, D.: What does BERT learn about the structure of language? In: ACL 2019–57th Annual Meeting of the Association for Computational Linguistics (2019)
17. Khan, S.H., Hayat, M., Bennamoun, M., Sohel, F.A., Togneri, R.: Cost-sensitive learning of deep feature representations from imbalanced data. IEEE Trans. Neural Netw. Learn. Syst. **29**(8), 3573–3587 (2017)
18. Li, B., Liu, Y., Wang, X.: Gradient harmonized single-stage detector. In: Proceedings of the AAAI Conference on Artificial Intelligence, vol. 33, pp. 8577–8584 (2019)
19. Lin, T.Y., Goyal, P., Girshick, R., He, K., Dollár, P.: Focal loss for dense object detection. In: Proceedings of the IEEE International Conference on Computer Vision, pp. 2980–2988 (2017)
20. Moreo, A., Esuli, A., Sebastiani, F.: Distributional random oversampling for imbalanced text classification. In: Proceedings of the 39th International ACM SIGIR Conference on Research and Development in Information Retrieval, pp. 805–808 (2016)
21. Padurariu, C., Breaban, M.E.: Dealing with data imbalance in text classification. Procedia Comput. Sci. **159**, 736–745 (2019)
22. Pennington, J., Socher, R., Manning, C.D.: GLOVE: global vectors for word representation. In: Proceedings of the 2014 Conference on Empirical Methods in Natural Language Processing (EMNLP), pp. 1532–1543 (2014)
23. Satriaji, W., Kusumaningrum, R.: Effect of synthetic minority oversampling technique (smote), feature representation, and classification algorithm on imbalanced sentiment analysis. In: 2018 2nd International Conference on Informatics and Computational Sciences (ICICoS), pp. 1–5. IEEE (2018)
24. Sennrich, R., Haddow, B., Birch, A.: Improving neural machine translation models with monolingual data. In: ACL (1) (2016)
25. Suh, S., Lee, H., Jo, J., Lukowicz, P., Lee, Y.O.: Generative oversampling method for imbalanced data on bearing fault detection and diagnosis. Appl. Sci. **9**(4), 746 (2019)
26. Tian, J., Chen, S., Zhang, X., Feng, Z.: A graph-based measurement for text imbalance classification. In: ECAI 2020, pp. 2188–2195. IOS Press (2020)
27. Waseem, Z., Hovy, D.: Hateful symbols or hateful people? Predictive features for hate speech detection on Twitter. In: Proceedings of the NAACL Student Research Workshop, pp. 88–93 (2016)
28. Wei, J., Zou, K.: EDA: easy data augmentation techniques for boosting performance on text classification tasks. In: Proceedings of the 2019 Conference on Empirical Methods in Natural Language Processing and the 9th International Joint Conference on Natural Language Processing (EMNLP-IJCNLP), pp. 6383–6389 (2019)

29. Yang, W., Li, J., Fukumoto, F., Ye, Y.: MSCNN: a monomeric-Siamese convolutional neural network for extremely imbalanced multi-label text classification. In: Proceedings of the 2020 Conference on Empirical Methods in Natural Language Processing (EMNLP), pp. 6716–6722 (2020)
30. Yun, S., Han, D., Oh, S.J., Chun, S., Choe, J., Yoo, Y.: CutMix: regularization strategy to train strong classifiers with localizable features. In: Proceedings of the IEEE/CVF International Conference on Computer Vision, pp. 6023–6032 (2019)
31. Zhang, H., Cisse, M., Dauphin, Y.N., Lopez-Paz, D.: Mixup: beyond empirical risk minimization. arXiv preprint arXiv:1710.09412 (2017)
32. Zhang, R., Yu, Y., Zhang, C.: SeqMix: augmenting active sequence labeling via sequence Mixup. In: Proceedings of the 2020 Conference on Empirical Methods in Natural Language Processing (EMNLP), pp. 8566–8579 (2020)

A Multi-task Model for Sentiment Aided Cyberbullying Detection in Code-Mixed Indian Languages

Krishanu Maity[(✉)] and Sriparna Saha

Department of Computer Science and Engineering, Indian Institute of Technology,
Patna, India
{krishanu_2021cs19,sriparna}@iitp.ac.in

Abstract. With the expansion of digital sphere and advancement of technology, cyberbullying has become increasingly common, especially among teenagers. In this work, we have created a benchmark Hindi-English code-mixed corpus called *BullySent*, annotated with bully and sentiment labels for investigating how sentiment label information helps to identify cyberbully in a better way. For a vast portion of India, both of these languages constitute the primary means of communication, and language mixing is common in everyday speech. A multi-task framework called *MT-BERT+VecMap* based on two different embedding schemes for the efficient representations of code-mixed data, has been developed. Our proposed multi-task framework outperforms all the single-task baselines with the highest accuracy values of $81.12(+/-1.65)\%$ and $77.46(+/-0.99)\%$ for the cyberbully detection task and sentiment analysis task, respectively.

Keywords: Cyberbullying · MuRIL BERT · Code-Mixed (Hindi+English) · VecMap · Deep multi-task learning

1 Introduction

The proliferation of mobile gadgets has become an increasing pandemic, especially among youth. While the Internet used by most adolescents is innocuous and the rewards of digital media are clear, one of the main risks is the freedom and anonymity enjoyed online, leaving young people vulnerable to cyberbullying. Intentional, conscious, and repetitive acts of cruelty of an individual to another by posting harmful posts, messages through various digital technologies are known as cyberbullying [16]. According to the National Crime Records Bureau data, incidents of cyberbullying against women or children in India surged by 36% from 2017 to 2018[1]. Cyberbullying results might vary from sadness, anxiety, transient fear to suicidal thinking. Cyberbullies need to be automatically detected at the beginning stage as an essential step in preventing their results.

---

[1] https://ncrb.gov.in/en/crime-india-2018-0.

© Springer Nature Switzerland AG 2021
T. Mantoro et al. (Eds.): ICONIP 2021, LNCS 13111, pp. 440–451, 2021.
https://doi.org/10.1007/978-3-030-92273-3_36

The process of fluidly switching between two or more languages in a discussion is known as code-mixing(CM) [12]. Hindi is one of India's official languages, with about 691 million native speakers[2]. So in India, the bulk of text exchanges on social networking platforms are in Hindi, English, or Hinglish. The depiction of the Hindi language in the Roman script is known as Hinglish. Rapidly using Hinglish words in social media may produce various spelling variations, making NLP tasks much more challenging on code mixed text. While relevant research has been carried out independently, cyberbullying detection is not substantially studied due to the lack of code-mixed datasets.

There are several works in the literature where sentiment analysis (SA) acts as a secondary task to boost the performance of primary task (like sarcasm detection [5], Complaint Identification [15]) in a multi-task (MT) framework. Till date, cyberbullying detection has been identified as a standalone problem. Sentiment analysis [13] attempts to automatically extract subjective information from user-written textual content and classify it into one of the three predefined classes, e.g., positive, negative, or neutral. When working on related tasks, multi-task learning has been beneficial [4]. The use of domain-specific knowledge in associated tasks improves the overall learning processes.

This paper aims to design a multi-task framework for cyberbullying detection in Hindi-English code-mixed data where sentiment analysis acts as a secondary task to increase the performance of primary task, i.e., cyberbullying detection. The main idea behind this work is to utilize the strong correlation between cyberbullying and sentiment. It is a very well-known fact that a sentence marked as bully generally indicates negative sentiment.

To the best of our knowledge, there are no publicly available Hindi-English code-mixed corpora with cyberbullying and sentiment labels. So to achieve our goal, we produced a code-mixed annotated dataset in Hindi and English, namely *BullySent*, for solving two tasks, i.e., cyberbullying detection (bully/Non-bully) and sentiment analysis (Positive/Neutral/Negative) concurrently.

We have developed a deep learning-based end-to-end multi-task framework for cyberbullying detection (primary task) and sentiment analysis (secondary task). Our developed model *MT-BERT+VecMap* utilizes two approaches for an efficient representation of the code mixed data. The first approach uses the BERT language model [7]. MuRIL BERT[3] (Multilingual Representations for Indian Languages), which was pre-trained on 17 Indian languages and their transliterated equivalents, was employed. The second approach uses VecMap, a bilingual word embedding mapping technique developed by Mikel Artetxe et al. [1]. The underlying idea is to separately train the embeddings of source and target languages using monolingual corpora and then, using a linear transformation matrix, align them to a shared vector space where similar words are placed together.

---

[2] https://en.wikipedia.org/wiki/List_of_languages_by_number_of_native_speakers_in_India.

[3] https://tfhub.dev/google/MuRIL/1.

The following are the primary contributions of this work:

1. We have created a new code-mixed corpus called *BullySent* of tweets annotated with bully and sentiment labels. We believe this dataset will help for further research on sentiment-aware cyberbully detection.
2. We have addressed the need for considering the sentiment label information of the tweets while identifying cyberbully.
3. We propose a multi-task framework called *MT-BERT+VecMap* for sentiment-aided cyberbullying detection. Furthermore, we have also incorporated two different embedding schemes for the efficient representations of code-mixed data.
4. We have considered some well-known machine learning models(support vector machine(SVM), logistic regression(LR)), and deep neural network models as baselines and our proposed multi-task model outperforms all the baselines with a significant margin.
5. To the best of our knowledge, this is the first work where a multi-task framework is proposed for simultaneously solving the tasks of cyberbully detection and sentiment analysis.[4]

2   Related Works

With the evolution of NLP, a significant number of studies on cyberbullying detection have been undertaken on the English language as opposed to other languages. There are some code mixed datasets available for tasks like hate speech detection, entity extraction, language identification, sentiment analysis etc.

Dinakar et al. [8] presented a cyberbullying detection algorithm based on machine learning and trained on a corpus of YouTube comments. The overall accuracies of the Naive Bayes(NB) and SVM classifiers are 63% and 66.70%, respectively. With the help of the Weka toolkit, Reynolds et al. [14] trained the C4.5 decision tree algorithm on data collected from the Formspring.me website for cyberbullying detection, and achieved 78.5% accuracy. Badjatiya et al. [2] used a dataset of 16K annotated tweets with three labels to conduct their research. They created a deep learning model using gradient boosted decision trees that has an F1 score of 0.93.

Bohra et al. [3] developed a hate speech dataset containing 4575 tweets coded in Hindi and English. When character n-grams, word n-grams, punctuations, negation words, and hate lexicons were used as feature vectors, the SVM classifier obtained a score of 71.7% accuracy. Gupta et al. [10] developed a deep GRU architecture for entity extraction in code-mixed (English-Hindi and English-Tamil) Indian languages.

Some earlier studies have considered the sentiment classification task as one of the secondary tasks to solve a primary task. In 2020, Chauhan et al. [5] proposed a multi-task framework based on two attention mechanisms (Inter-segment and Intra-segment) to examine the impact of sentiment and emotion on

---

[4] Code available at https://github.com/MaityKrishanu/Bully_Sentiment.

the sarcasm detection task. They manually annotated multi-modal MUStARD sarcasm dataset with sentiment and emotion labels. In 2021, Singh et al. [15] developed a deep multi-task framework for complaint identification and sentiment analysis (secondary task). The developed multi-task model attained 83.73% and 69.01% accuracy for the complaint identification task and sentiment analysis task, respectively, by adding Affective Space as a commonsense knowledge.

From the literature review, we have concluded that till now, cyberbullying detection is considered as a stand-alone problem and there is no publicly available dataset for sentiment-aided cyberbullying detection in code-mixed Indian languages. Therefore, in this paper attempts have been made in this direction.

3 Code-Mixed BullySent-Annotated Corpora Development

We have scraped raw tweets from Twitter with the help of the Twitter Search API[5]. It provides a platform to crawl historical tweets based on specific keywords. Between November 2020 and March 2021, we have scraped 50K+ tweets based on some keywords written in Hinglish related to cyberbullying, like Rendi, Chuthiya, Kamini, etc.

3.1 Data Preprocessing

Data preprocessing is essential for any NLP task as language is a high source of ambiguity. Raw data comprises numerous tweets that are irrelevant. For making the annotation task more convenient, we have designed a filter to remove irrelevant tweets based on the following criteria: (i) If a tweet is duplicate; (ii) If only the URL is used in a tweet; (iii) Every tweet but the Hindi, English or Hinglish tweets; (iv) If the length of the tweet is below ten characters; (v) If only a few user references are used in a tweet.

3.2 Data Annotation

Manual data annotation has been done by three annotators having a linguistic background and proficiency in both Hindi and English. Based on the context of tweets, annotators assigned two labels for each tweet, one for the cyberbully class (Non-bully/Bully) and another for the sentiment class (Positive/Neutral/Negative). For better understanding, we have provided some tweets to the annotator with gold labels and explanations. Annotators were also instructed to annotate the tweet without being biased towards any specific demographic area, religion, etc. In Table 1, there are some examples of annotated tweets. Conflicts between annotators are resolved using a majority voting policy when we finalize the annotation label of each tweet. We calculated the inter-annotator agreement (IAA) using Cohen's Kappa score to verify the quality of annotation. The data has a Kappa value of 0.81, indicating that it is of acceptable quality.

---

[5] https://developer.twitter.com/en/docs/twitter-api.

3.3   Dataset Statistics

We always emphasize that data balancing should be fair during selection of tweets from unprocessed scraped raw data. 3,034 tweets out of the 6,084 tweets in our corpus were categorized as nonbully, while the remaining 3,050 were labeled as bullies. The percentages of non-bully and bully tweets in our corpus are 49.86% and 50.14%, respectively. Dataset statistics based on bully and sentiment classes are shown in Fig. 1a and 1b, respectively.

Table 1. Samples from annotated dataset

Tweet	Sentiment Class	Bully Class
T1: smitaparikh2 Usse bhi sabse hard punishment milni chahiye kisne right diya hai usse kuch bhi likhane ka **Translation**: Smitaparikh2 should be punished heavily, who has given her the right to write anything	Negative	Bully
T2: Pubg ban kue kiya bhosdike. Tera kya jata tha mad*rch*d Sale suor khud to maje leta hai par ham logo ko marta hain **Translation**: Why have you banned Pubg. Whats was your problem mo*herf*cker pigs. You are all enjoying but we are suffering	Negative	Bully
T3: Mtlb mai dono condition mai shocked hi raha, chalo gi good ho gaya **Translation**: I mean, I was surprised by both the conditions; however, something good happens to me	Positive	Non-bully
T4: sir gi muzaffarpur Bihar se Kolkata Ka Train chalo karo **Translation**: Sir, kindly operate trains from Muzaffarpur, Bihar to Kolkata	Neutral	Non-bully

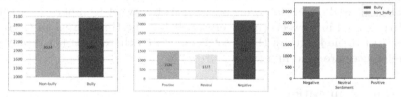

(a) Cyberbully statistics. (b) Sentiment statistics. (c) Bully Vs. Sentiment.

Fig. 1. Class wise statistics and correlation between Bully vs. Sentiment

Our corpus has 3,221 data samples with Negative sentiment labels, whereas the number of tweets having Positive and Neutral sentiment labels are 1,536 and 1,327, respectively. If we observe Fig. 1c, we could find strong correlations between the bully and negative sentiment classes, i.e., a tweet with the bully label is more likely to have a negative sentiment.

4   Methodology for Cyberbullying Detection

This section describes the end-to-end deep multi-task framework we have developed to identify cyberbully. Figure 2 depicts the overall architecture of our proposed *MT-BERT+VecMap* model.

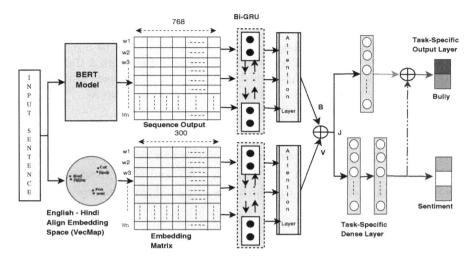

Fig. 2. Multi-task BERT+VecMap architecture.

4.1 BERT

BERT [7] is a Transformer-based [17] language model. Fine-tuning BERT has led to a decent improvement in solving several Natural Language Processing (NLP) tasks like text classification, question answering, machine translation etc. We choose the MuRIL BERT since it has been trained on 17 Indian languages, including Hindi and English, as well as their transliterated equivalents. The model uses a BERT based architecture pre-trained by the Wikipedia and Popular Crawl, along with PMINDIA and Dakshina Corpora for getting the translated and transliterated data.

4.2 VecMap

VecMap is a self learning bilingual word embedding mapping technique developed by Mikel Artetxe et al. [1]. The main advantage of the VecMap technique is that it is based on a self-learning approach that reduces the need of large bilingual dictionary as an input. We have considered Fasttext [9] Hindi and English word embeddings as inputs of VecMap. Fasttext model was trained using CBOW technique and it returns a 300 dense vector for each token. As there is no existing pre-trained embedding available for Hinglish words, we transliterated Hinglish to Devanagari-Hindi by using the dictionary provided by Khapra et al. [11]. Using the VecMap technique, at first we have created a Hindi-English align embedding vector space. Then, we have used it to create a pre-trained embedding matrix of dimension $vocab\_size \times 300$ and passed it as one of the inputs of embedding layers of CNN. The total number of unique words in the training data is $vocab\_size$.

4.3 Bi-directional GRU Layer

To learn the contextual information of input tweet from both the directions, the word vectors from both BERT and VecMap are passed through a Bidirectional GRU [6] layer. To capture long-term dependencies in the tweet, bi-directional GRU sequentially encodes these feature map into hidden states as,

$$\overrightarrow{h}_t^i = \overrightarrow{GRU}(w_t^i, h_{t-1}^i) \ , \ \overleftarrow{h}_t^i = \overleftarrow{GRU}(w_t^i, h_{t+1}^i) \tag{1}$$

where each word vector w_t^i of sentence i is mapped to a forward hidden state $\overrightarrow{h}_t^i$ and backward hidden state $\overleftarrow{h}_t^i$ by invoking $\overrightarrow{GRU}$ and $\overleftarrow{GRU}$, respectively. $\overrightarrow{h}_t^i$ and $\overleftarrow{h}_t^i$ are combined to form h_t^i, which is a single hidden state representation.

$$\left[h_t^i = \overrightarrow{h}_t^i, \overleftarrow{h}_t^i\right] \tag{2}$$

4.4 Attention Layer

The basic principle behind the attention mechanism [18] is to give greater weight to the words that contribute the most to the meaning of the phrase. To produce an attended sentence vector, we leverage the attention mechanism on the Bi-GRU layer's output. Specifically,

$$u_t^i = tanh(W_w h_t^i + b_w) \tag{3}$$

$$\sigma_t^i = \frac{exp(u_t^{i\ T} u_w)}{\sum_t exp(u_t^{i\ T} u_w))} \tag{4}$$

$$S_i = \sum_t (\sigma_t^i * h_t^i) \tag{5}$$

where u_t^i is the hidden representation of h_t^i and u_w is the context vector. S_i is the output generated by Attention layer and attention weight for a particular word is σ_t^i .

4.5 Loss Function

As a loss function, we have used categorical cross-entropy $L(\hat{y}, y)$ to train the parameters of the network.

$$L_{CE}(\hat{y}, y) = -\frac{1}{N} \sum_{j=1}^{M} \sum_{i=1}^{N} y_i^j log(\hat{y}_i^j) \tag{6}$$

Where $\hat{y}_i^j$ is predicted label and y_i^j is true label. M and N represents the number of classes, and the number of tweets, respectively.

4.6   BERT-VecMap Multi-task Framework

Let $(X_k, b_k, s_k)_{k=1}^N$ be a set of N tweets where $b_p \in B$ (Bully Classes) and $s_p \in S$ (Sentiment Classes). b_k, s_k represents the bully and sentiment labels corresponding to X_k^{th} tweet, respectively. This $MT\text{-}BERT\text{+}VecMap$ Framework aims to learn a function that maps an unknown instance X_k to its appropriate bully label b_p and sentiment label s_p.

Let the input sentence $X = \{x_1, x_2, \ldots x_n\}$ be a sequence of n input tokens, where n is the maximum length of a sentence. The input text X is fed into both the BERT and VecMap models. BERT generates two types of outputs: a pooled output of shape $[batch\ size, 768]$ that represents the whole input sequences, and a sequence output of shape $[batch\ size, max\ seq\ length, 768]$ for each input token. Let $W_B \in \mathbb{R}^{n \times D_B}$ be the embedding matrix obtained from the BERT model for input X where $D_B = 768$ is the embedding dimension of each token. On the other hand, VecMap generates an embedding matrix $W_V \in \mathbb{R}^{n \times D_V}$, where $D_V = 300$. Outputs from both BERT and VecMap are passed through Bi-GRU (128 hidden units) followed by an Attention layer to learn the contextual information and to assign more weightages on the relevant words. The outputs B and V returned by the Attention layers placed on the top of BERT+GRU and VecMap+GRU are concatenated to make a joint representation J of the input tweet X. Till now, the layers are being shared by two tasks that allow sharing of task-specific information among them. The concatenated feature vector J is passed through two separate task-specific fully connected layers (bully channel $[FC_B^1(100\ neurons)]$, sentiment channel $[FC_S^1(100\ neurons) + FC_S^2(100\ neurons)]$) followed by their corresponding output layers. The outputs from FC_S^2 of the sentiment channel are concatenated with the FC_B^1 of the bully channel for finding sentiment-aided bully feature, which helps to enhance the performance of primary task, i.e., cyberbully detection.

The final loss function L is dependent on the two task-specific individual losses as follows:

$$L = p * (L_{CE}^S) + q * (L_{CE}^B \mid L_{CE}^S) \tag{7}$$

Equation 7 implies that the loss for the cyberbully detection task L_{CE}^B is dependent on sentiment classification loss L_{CE}^S. The variables p and q, which range from 0 to 1, define the loss weights that characterise the per task loss-share to the total loss.

5   Experimental Results and Analysis

This section shows the results of different baseline models and our proposed model, evaluated on our proposed Hindi-English code-mixed corpus. The dataset and codes will be made publicly available on the associated repository. We performed stratified 10-fold cross-validation on our dataset and reported the mean metrics scores.

5.1   Baselines Setup

Following baselines are introduced for comparison with our proposed approach.

1. **MuRIL BERT Embedding + LR (Baseline-1)**: Input tweets are passing through MuRIL BERT followed by LR classifier. We have considered pooled output from BERT with dimension 768.
2. **MuRIL BERT Embedding + SVM (Baseline-2)**: Same as Baseline-1 with one modification: LR is replaced by an SVM classifier.
3. **VecMap + SVM (Baseline-3)**: VecMap generated Hindi-English aligned embedding vector space has been used to generate word embedding of each input token. Then we have utilized the SVM classifier for the prediction of the input sentence.
4. **VecMap + LR (Baseline-4)**: Input representation is the same as Baseline-3, the only difference is that we have considered Logistic Regression (LR) as the classifier instead of SVM.
5. **Single-task(ST)+ BERT (Baseline-5)**: VecMap generated word vectors are passed through BiGRU with Attention layer. Output from Attention layer is then passed to task specific fully connected layers[FC1(100) + FC2(100)] followed by output Softmax layer.
6. **ST+VecMap (Baseline-6)**: Same as baseline 5, the only difference is that input is passed through BERT instead of VecMap.
7. **MT+ BERT (Baseline-7)**: This is identical to our model, but the input is passed through only the BERT.
8. **MT+VecMap (Baseline-8)**: This is identical to our MT-BERT+VecMap, but the input is passed through only the VecMap.
9. **ST- BERT+VecMap (Baseline-9)**: Almost the same as our MT- BERT+ VecMap model, but it has only one output layer instead of two. So it can handle one task at a time.

5.2   Results and Discussion

Table 2 presents the results in terms of accuracy, precision, recall, and F1-score for all the baselines and the proposed model. From the result table, we can conclude that all the multi-task variants outperform the single-task classifiers for the cyberbully and sentiment tasks. Moreover, our proposed *MT-BERT+VecMap* performs better than the ST-BERT+VecMap with the accuracy improvements of 1.15% and 1.93% for both tasks, respectively. The results imply that sentiment knowledge enhances the performance of the cyberbully detection task.

Out of four machine learning-based baselines, VecMap+SVM (Baseline-3) achieves higher accuracy (75.32%) for cyberbully task, while for the sentiment task VecMap+LR (Baseline-4) attains the best accuracy (72.27%). multi-task-VecMap (Baseline-8) performs better compared to the other three deep learning-based baselines. MT+VecMap (Baseline-8) achieves 1.08% and 0.46%, respectively, improvements in accuracy values for cyberbully and sentiment tasks over the ST+VecMap. On the other hand, MT+ BERT (Baseline-7) attains the

Table 2. Experimental results based on 10-fold cross-validation

Model	Task	Accuracy	Precision	Recall	macro F1
Machine learning Baselines					
BERT+LR	Bully	74.41(+/−1.57)	74.24	74.17	74.36(+/−1.57)
	Sentiment	70.27(+/−2.12)	68.43	69.07	69.88(+/−2.12)
BERT+SVM	Bully	73.80(+/−2.28)	74.58	74.38	73.70(+/−2.34)
	Sentiment	69.58(+/−1.66)	71.52	68.09	70.28(+/−1.54)
VecMap+SVM	Bully	75.32(+/−0.81)	75.62	75.32	75.26(+/−0.79)
	Sentiment	69.74(+/−1.69)	72.38	69.07	70.41(+/−1.66)
VecMap+LR	Bully	73.50(+/−1.84)	73.84	73.84	73.49(+/−1.84)
	Sentiment	72.27(+/−1.51)	72.23	71.87	72.23(+/−1.51)
Deep learning Baselines					
ST+ BERT	Bully	76.97(+/−1.11)	77.59	76.80	76.89(+/−1.12)
	Sentiment	73.51(+/−1.17)	74.23	73.51	73.67(+/−1.09)
ST+VecMap	Bully	78.52(+/−2.01)	78.26	77.63	78.43(+/−2.06)
	Sentiment	75.64(+/−1.50)	75.69	75.86	75.12(+/−1.65)
MT+ BERT	Bully	78.75(+/−2.04)	77.38	78.28	78.40(+/−2.23)
	Sentiment	74.20(+/−1.65)	76.79	74.17	74.17(+/−1.47)
MT+VecMap	Bully	79.60(+/−0.95)	80.06	77.70	79.65(+/−1.42)
	Sentiment	76.10(+/−1.45)	76.37	77.13	75.62(+/−1.58)
ST- BERT+VecMap	Bully	79.97(+/−1.23)	79.34	81.31	80.13(+/−1.59)
	Sentiment	75.53(+/−1.76)	76.36	76.97	75.38(+/−1.72)
Proposed Approach					
MT-BERT+VecMap	Bully	**81.12(+/−1.65)**	82.82	80.65	**81.50(+/−1.41)**
	Sentiment	**77.46(+/−0.99)**	76.89	77.46	**76.95(+/−1.38)**

improvements in accuracy values for two tasks over the ST- BERT as 1.78% and 0.69%, respectively. Machine learning based baseline VecMap+SVM outperforms BERT+SVM with accuracy values of 1.52% and 0.16%, respectively, for two tasks. We have also examined that for all the baselines excluding Baseline-4 (VecMap+LR) when embedded with VecMap performs better than the one embedded with BERT. The superior performance of our proposed MT-BERT+VecMap model with accuracy values of 81.12% and 77.46% for each of the two tasks, respectively, validates that the joint representation of word vectors using BERT and VecMap can handle code-mixed data in a better way compared to a single representation.

Experimental results of this work demonstrate that concurrent execution of two tasks: cyberbully detection and sentiment analysis, improves the performance of the main task. Furthermore, multi-task frameworks are less time-consuming than single-task frameworks since they tackle both tasks at the same time.

6   Conclusion and Future Work

In this study, we built *BullySent*, a benchmark Hindi-English code-mixed corpus annotated with bully and sentiment labels to see if sentiment label information may assist identify cyberbully more accurately. We collected Hindi-English code-mixed tweets from Twitter and manually annotated 6084 tweets with the bully and sentiment labels. We introduced the *MT-BERT+VecMap* multi-task framework for sentiment-aided cyberbullying detection based on two different embedding techniques (BERT and VecMap) for efficient representations of code-mixed data. The developed *MT-BERT+VecMap* framework outperforms all single task models, with the accuracy improvements of 1.15% and 1.93%, for the cyberbully detection (primary task) and sentiment analysis (secondary task), respectively. The superior performance of our proposed approach, which achieved accuracy values of 81.12% and 77.46% for two tasks, respectively, confirms that the combined representation of word vectors using BERT and VecMap can handle code-mixed data better than a single representation. Experimental results of this work suggest that sentiment knowledge improves the cyberbully detection task's performance.

In the future, we would like to develop a multi-task multimodel framework for cyberbullying detection, where we will incorporate image data as another modality.

Acknowledgement. The Authors would like to acknowledge the support of Ministry of Home Affairs (MHA), India for conducting this research.

References

1. Artetxe, M., Labaka, G., Agirre, E.: Learning bilingual word embeddings with (almost) no bilingual data. In: Proceedings of the 55th Annual Meeting of the Association for Computational Linguistics (Volume 1: Long Papers), pp. 451–462 (2017)
2. Badjatiya, P., Gupta, S., Gupta, M., Varma, V.: Deep learning for hate speech detection in tweets. In: Proceedings of the 26th International Conference on World Wide Web Companion, pp. 759–760 (2017)
3. Bohra, A., Vijay, D., Singh, V., Akhtar, S.S., Shrivastava, M.: A dataset of hindi-english code-mixed social media text for hate speech detection. In: Proceedings of the Second Workshop on Computational Modeling of People's Opinions, Personality, and Emotions in Social Media, pp. 36–41 (2018)
4. Caruana, R.: Multitask learning. Mach. Learn. **28**(1), 41–75 (1997)
5. Chauhan, D.S., Dhanush, S., Ekbal, A., Bhattacharyya, P.: Sentiment and emotion help sarcasm? a multi-task learning framework for multi-modal sarcasm, sentiment and emotion analysis. In: Proceedings of the 58th Annual Meeting of the Association for Computational Linguistics, pp. 4351–4360 (2020)
6. Cho, K., Van Merriënboer, B., Bahdanau, D., Bengio, Y.: On the properties of neural machine translation: Encoder-decoder approaches. arXiv preprint arXiv:1409.1259 (2014)

7. Devlin, J., Chang, M.W., Lee, K., Toutanova, K.: Bert: Pre-training of deep bidirectional transformers for language understanding. arXiv preprint arXiv:1810.04805 (2018)
8. Dinakar, K., Reichart, R., Lieberman, H.: Modeling the detection of textual cyberbullying. In: Proceedings of the International Conference on Weblog and Social Media 2011. Citeseer (2011)
9. Grave, E., Bojanowski, P., Gupta, P., Joulin, A., Mikolov, T.: Learning word vectors for 157 languages. arXiv preprint arXiv:1802.06893 (2018)
10. Gupta, D., Ekbal, A., Bhattacharyya, P.: A deep neural network based approach for entity extraction in code-mixed indian social media text. In: Proceedings of the Eleventh International Conference on Language Resources and Evaluation (LREC 2018) (2018)
11. Khapra, M.M., Ramanathan, A., Kunchukuttan, A., Visweswariah, K., Bhattacharyya, P.: When transliteration met crowdsourcing: an empirical study of transliteration via crowdsourcing using efficient, non-redundant and fair quality control. In: LREC, pp. 196–202. Citeseer (2014)
12. Myers-Scotton, C.: Duelling Languages: Grammatical Structure in Codeswitching. Oxford University Press, Oxford (1997)
13. Pang, B., Lee, L.: Seeing stars: Exploiting class relationships for sentiment categorization with respect to rating scales. arXiv preprint cs/0506075 (2005)
14. Reynolds, K., Kontostathis, A., Edwards, L.: Using machine learning to detect cyberbullying. In: 2011 10th International Conference on Machine Learning and Applications and Workshops, vol. 2, pp. 241–244. IEEE (2011)
15. Singh, A., Saha, S., Hasanuzzaman, M., Dey, K.: Multitask learning for complaint identification and sentiment analysis. Cognitive Computation, pp. 1–16 (2021)
16. Smith, P.K., Mahdavi, J., Carvalho, M., Fisher, S., Russell, S., Tippett, N.: Cyberbullying: its nature and impact in secondary school pupils. J. Child Psychol. Psychiatry **49**(4), 376–385 (2008)
17. Vaswani, A., et al.: Attention is all you need. In: Advances in Neural Information Processing Systems, pp. 5998–6008 (2017)
18. Yang, Z., Yang, D., Dyer, C., He, X., Smola, A., Hovy, E.: Hierarchical attention networks for document classification. In: Proceedings of the 2016 Conference of the North American Chapter of the Association for Computational Linguistics: Human Language Technologies, pp. 1480–1489 (2016)

A Transformer-Based Model
for Low-Resource Event Detection

Yanxia Qin, Jingjing Ding, Yiping Sun, and Xiangwu Ding[✉]

School of Computer Science and Technology, Donghua University, Shanghai, China
{yxqin,dingxw}@dhu.edu.cn, {2191960,171310626}@mail.dhu.edu.cn

Abstract. Event detection is an important task in natural language processing, which identifies event trigger words in a given sentence. Previous work use traditional RNN/CNN based text encoders, failing to remember long-range dependencies within the sentence. This paper proposes a Transformer-based event detection model, utilizing the self-attention technique of a Transformer encoder to capture long-range dependencies. However, existing labelled event detection datasets such as ACE2005 are in small scale, being insufficient to train a deep neural model. This paper expands the scale of training data with an event trigger-aware back-translation based data augmentation technique. In addition, a multi-instance learning strategy is adopted to alleviate noises in the generated data in training. Experiments on two event detection datasets in different languages verify the effectiveness of the proposed model (The code is released at https://github.com/gitofding/event-detection).

Keywords: Event detection · Data augmentation · Transformer

1 Introduction

Event extraction aims to identify an event happened in a given text and its type (e.g., *Attack*) and participants (e.g., *Victim*). Event extraction is very important to downstream NLP tasks, such as knowledge graph construction, trending topic detection and etc. Generally, an event is triggered by a word in the text. The task of identifying event trigger words along with their event types is defined as event detection. Event detection is the first and fundamental sub-task for event extraction. As the example shown in Fig. 1, only after identifying the trigger word *"quit"* and its event type as *"End-Position"*, we can detect arguments (i.e., participants) such as *"Vivendi Universal Entertainment"* as the *Organization*.

Most recent event detection methods utilize supervised neural models, which first represent each word in a given sentence as a vector and then classify it as a trigger or non-trigger word. Transformer is a prominent deep learning model in natural language processing tasks such as machine translation [23], dependency parsing [19], summarization [1] and etc. Transformer is firstly proposed as a sequence-to-sequence model for neural machine translation [25]. It consists

Supported by a NSFC project (No. 62006039).

Fig. 1. An event example taken from the ACE2005 corpus.

of an encoder and a decoder, in which the encoder can be used for text representation by any tasks including event detection. This paper proposes to use the Transformer encoder for event detection. The Transformer encoder benefits from multiple self-attention layers to learn rich text representation and capture long-range dependencies, which must rely on a large scale of training data. Therefore, it would be a big challenge for low-resource tasks such as event extraction to benefit from the powerful Transformer encoder.

Existing solutions for the above lack-of-data problem include manually labelling more data and automatically labelling data via distant supervision techniques. Human annotation is not considered due to the huge cost of human efforts. It would be difficult to apply distant supervision to event detection because (1) it would lead to very few instances if we take sentences containing all event arguments within one sentence as positive event instances, and (2) it would introduce too many noises if we take sentences containing only one key argument or trigger as positive instances.

This paper proposes to use data augmentation techniques to increase the scale of existing data for training the Transformer-based event detection model. Data augmentation is widely used in computer vision, in which images are rotated, cutout, color changed and etc. Data augmentation for texts aims at enriching various expressions of sentences in an original dataset and thus increasing the scale of training data. Commonly used data augmentation techniques for text include synonym replacement, random deletion/swap, back-translation and etc. A back-translation based data augmentation technique is adopted in this paper. We also use a trigger-aware alignment method to label triggers in the generated data. We use both the original data and the augmented data to train the Transformer-based event detection model. One challenge is that the augmented data contains inevitable noises from both the back-translation and trigger alignment procedures. To minimize the influences of possible noises, we adopt the multi-instance learning technique for model training.

Our contributions are summarized as follows:

- We are the first to utilize the Transformer model for event detection. We also investigate that how deep can a Transformer encoder be with existing small-scale training data for event detection.
- We utilize a trigger-aware data augmentation technique to alleviate the insufficient data problem in training the Transformer-based model.
- Experiments conducted on multiple event detection datasets in different languages (i.e., English and Chinese) verify the effectiveness of the proposed Transformer-based event detection model.

2   Transformer-Based Baseline Model

We first introduce a Transformer-based event detection model in this section. As shown in Fig. 2, our model consists of a Transformer encoder to represent each word x_i in a sentence $s = \{x_1, x_2, \cdots, x_n\}$ and an event detection classifier to identify its event type $l \in \mathcal{L}$ (O for non-trigger word).

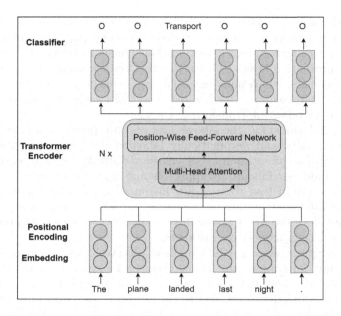

Fig. 2. Framework of a Transformer-based event detection model.

2.1   Transformer Encoder

The traditional Transformer is proposed as a sequence-to-sequence model, which consists of an encoder to represent each input sentence and a decoder to generate an output sequence. We only use the Transformer encoder for our sequence labeling task. The encoder includes N Transformer layers, each of which has two parts: a self-attention module and a position-wise feed-forward network (FFN).

The self-attention module aims to learn the representation of a sequence all by itself, in which each word is represented by a weighted sum of representations of all words within the sequence. The self-attention module also uses a multi-head attention mechanism allowing the model to jointly attend to different representation subspaces at different positions (i.e., heads). The position-wise FFN module is a fully connected layer operated on each position. The Transformer layer also incorporates the position information of the sequence by adding a positional encoding to the input embedding.

2.2   Event Detection Classifier

After representing each word x_i with a vector $h_i \in R^{d_h}$ with the Transformer encoder, we use a softmax classifier to predict its event type with the following equation:

$$p(j|x_i, \theta) = \frac{\exp(W_j^T h_i + b)}{\sum_{k=1}^{|\mathcal{L}|} \exp(W_k^T h_i + b)}, \tag{1}$$

where $p(j|x_i, \theta)$ is the probability of x_i belongs to an event type $l_j \in \mathcal{L}$, θ indicates parameters of the neural model. $W_j \in R^{d_h}$ is a weight vector, and $b \in R$ is a bias term.

To train the model, we maximize the log-likelihood of the gold event type y_i of each word x_i in the sequence:

$$J(\theta) = \sum_{i=1}^{n} log \ p(y_i|x_i, \theta). \tag{2}$$

3   Improving Transformer-Based Event Detection

Compared with other neural encoders, such as BiLSTM and CNN, a Transformer encoder can be more deeper for better text representation. However, for a low-resource task like event detection, the advantage of the Transformer may not be obvious. To further improve the Transformer-based event detection model, we utilize data augmentation to generate more training data. We use a event trigger-aware data augmentation technique in this paper. In addition, we use different strategies to train the model with two kinds of training data, namely the original training data and the automatically generated data.

3.1   Trigger-Aware Data Augmentation

As discussed in the introduction section, we utilize data augmentation to generate more training data instead of distant supervision for less noisy data. To be specific, we use a back-translation based data augmentation technique to increase expression diversity of original event detection training data. Back-translation is a process of translating sentences from a source language into a target language, and then back into the source language again. We utilize Neural Machine Translation (NMT) models for back-translation. In particular, we use the pre-trained sequence-to-sequence NMT models[1] provided by fairseq for translation. We use Germany and Russian as the target languages during back translation because there are available pre-trained NMT models in fairseq. After comparing the results of generated data via Germany, Russian and Germany+Russian, we empirically select Germany as our final target language for back-translation.

---

[1] https://github.com/pytorch/fairseq/blob/master/examples/translation/README.md.

To be noted that the performance of a downstream task does not increase as the volume of augmented data becomes larger. According to the fairseq, the performance of the English-Germany translation model is superior to English-Russian model (42.6 V.S. 36.3 on SacreBLEU scores). How these back-translation languages and models influence the performances of different downstream tasks is out of scope of this paper, but another interesting problem to investigate.

As mentioned above, event detection is defined as a word-level classification task, which means the training data needs each word's event type. Given that NMT models provide end-to-end translations, there would be no word alignment information between words in the original sentence and the generated sentence. Thus locating triggers in generated sentences would be one challenge during back translation for event detection. Thus locating the corresponding trigger word t_g in the generated sentence s_g given the trigger word t_o in the original sentence s_o would be one challenge. We assign t_g to be a word within s_g that has the largest similarity score to t_o. The event type of t_g is the same type as t_o. The word-pair similarity is calculated using cosine similarity based on a pre-trained word embedding[2]. An example of aligning trigger words is shown in Fig. 3. After manually check 200 instances, 75% of automatically aligned triggers are correct.

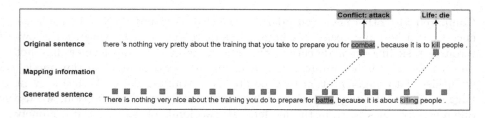

Fig. 3. An example of aligning trigger words.

3.2   Training Strategies

Training the Transformer-based event detection model with both the original data and the augmented data with different strategies lead to different performance because of inevitable noises in the automatically generated data. The first intuitive method would be mixing these two datasets together. In addition, we utilize a multi-instance learning method for training.

Multi-instance learning aims to train a model by discriminating instance bags rather than instances. Instances of a bag have the same event type. We take each word as an instance in this paper. Suppose that there are T bags of instances $\{(M_1, y_1), (M_2, y_2), \cdots, (M_T, y_T)\}$ and the i-th bag $M_i = \{m_i^1, m_i^2, \cdots, m_i^{q_i}\}$ contains q_i instances, with an event type y_i. The objective function of multi-instance learning on these T bags $J_{MIL}(\theta)$ is defined as follows:

---

[2] https://code.google.com/archive/p/word2vec/.

$$J_{MIL}(\theta) = \lambda \sum_{i=1}^{T} log p(y_i|m_i^k, \theta), \qquad (3)$$

where λ is a balancing weight, $p(y_i|m_i^k, \theta)$ is the probability of the instance m_i^k belongs to event type y_i, which can be calculated with Eq. 1. And k is constrained as follows:

$$k = \arg\max_{j} p(y_i|m_i^j, \theta). \qquad 1 \leq j \leq q_i \qquad (4)$$

Namely we select a representative instance in each bag to calculate the loss of the bag.

We alternately train the model with the objective function based on the original data and the multi-instance objective function based on the augmented data. We maximize both $J_{MIL}(\theta)$ and $J(\theta)$ through stochastic gradient descent [2] over mini-batches update rule.

4   Experiments

4.1   Settings

Data. We conduct experiments on the ACE2005 data and corresponding generated data by back-translation (BT data). For training baseline systems, we use the original ACE2005 training set. For our proposed model, we use both ACE2005 and the generated data for training. The development set of ACE2005 is used for parameter tuning and the test set is used for evaluation. Both English and Chinese ACE2005 datasets are used in this paper. Statistics of ACE2005 datasets are shown in Table 1.

Table 1. Statistics of ACE2005 datasets.

Data	Train		Dev	Test
	#Sentence	#Trigger	#Sentence	#Sentence
ACE2005-en	14780	3309	863	672
BT-en	14780	3309	–	–
ACE2005-cn	5045	1509	650	630
BT-cn	5045	1509	–	–

Hyper-parameters. Hyper-parameters are tuned on the development set. We set the batch size as 100, the learning rate as 0.4, and the maximum training epoch as 200. The dimension of word embeddings is set to 200. To avoid overfitting, a dropout mechanism [24] is adopted with the dropout rate is set to 0.5. We empirically set the weight λ in Eq. 3 as 0.04. We use Precision (P), Recall (R) and F1 value as evaluation metrics.

Baselines. We compare our model with several baseline models as follows:

- DMCNN [4] puts forward a dynamic multi-pooling CNN model to extract local sentence-level features automatically.
- JRNN [21] proposes to use a bi-directional RNN model for event extraction.
- ANN [16] utilizes event arguments information via supervised attention mechanism for event detection.
- GMLATT [13] exploits multi-lingual information for more accurate context modeling.
- GCN [14] exploits syntactic information to capture more accurate context using graph convolutional networks.

4.2   Experimental Results

The results of all the models conducted on the ACE2005 English dataset are shown in Table 2. Comparing the results of Transformer and DMCNN and JRNN (69.3% VS 69.1% and 69.3%), we can observe that the Transformer baseline performs comparably with traditional CNN/RNN encoders. After using the generated data by data augmentation and multi-instance learning training strategy, our model performs the best out of all baseline methods[3].

Table 2. Experimental results on ACE2005(en). † indicates results adopted from original papers.

Model	Trigger identification			Trigger classification		
	P(%)	R(%)	F1(%)	P(%)	R(%)	F1(%)
DMCNN† [4]	80.4	67.7	73.5	75.6	63.6	69.1
JRNN† [21]	68.5	75.7	71.9	66.0	73.0	69.3
ANN† [16]	N/A	N/A	N/A	78.0	66.3	71.7
GMLATT† [13]	N/A	N/A	N/A	78.9	66.9	72.4
GCN† [14]	N/A	N/A	N/A	77.9	68.8	73.1
Transformer	68.2	75.5	71.6	65.9	73.0	69.3
Our Model	78.0	75.3	76.6	74.7	72.1	**73.4**

Ablation Tests. Experimental results of an ablation test conducted on the ACE2005 English dataset are shown in Table 3. Results show the effectiveness of the trigger-aware data augmentation method (69.26%→71.87%) and the multi-instance learning strategy (71.87%→73.39%).

Parameter Tuning. We also conduct some parameter tuning experiments for the Transformer-based event detection model. We show the results (F1 value) of Transformer baseline and our method (i.e., improved Transformer with data

---

[3] For fairness, we do not compare with models using pre-trained language models such as ELMo and BERT.

Table 3. Ablation tests with ACE2005(en).

Model	Trigger identification			Trigger classification		
	P(%)	R(%)	F1(%)	P(%)	R(%)	F1(%)
Transformer	68.17	75.45	71.63	65.91	72.95	69.26
+BT data	72.98	77.03	74.95	69.98	73.86	71.87
+BT data+MIL	78.03	75.25	76.61	74.74	72.08	73.39

augmentation) using different Transformer encoder layers N in Fig. 4. The Transformer baseline trained on the original data performs the best when we use only one Transformer layer, because there are not enough training data to support more Transformer layers. Following above assumption, additionally using generated data by data augmentation enables the Transformer encoder capable of using more Transformer layers to obtain more meaningful text representations. The result that our model performs the best with three Transformer layers verifies the assumption. In addition, we can observe better results with more data by comparing two result lines of the baseline and our method.

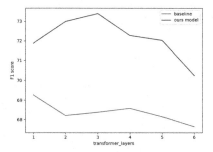

Fig. 4. Results with different transformer layers.

4.3   Influences of Different Data Augmentation Techniques

We also explore influences of different data augmentation techniques beyond back-translation such as easy data augmentation techniques [26] (EDA). The main idea of EDA techniques is randomly choosing a few words from a sentence for some specific operations such as synonym replacement, synonym insertion, position swapping, and removal. For example, the sentence "the tank **fired** the castle *last night*" is changed to "*last night* the tank **fired** the castle" with a swap operation. Compared with the original sentence, the position of time adverbial has changed, and thus increases the diversity of text structures.

To be noted, pre-processing procedures such as lower-casing and stop words removal, are conducted before using the EDA operations. In addition, we use a trigger-aware easy data augmentation method in this paper to intentionally replace and swap trigger words in the sentence. Take "*the tank **fired** the castle* *last night*" as an example, trigger-aware synonym replacement operation would lead to "*the tank attacked the castle last night*". Trigger-aware operations further increase the diversity of expressions of trigger words.

Table 4. Ablation tests with easy data augmentation technique.

Model	Trigger identification			Trigger classification		
	P(%)	R(%)	F1(%)	P(%)	R(%)	F1(%)
Transformer	68.17	75.45	71.63	65.91	72.95	69.26
+EDA	71.16	74.26	72.67	67.93	70.89	69.38
+EDA+MIL	73.52	73.66	73.59	70.16	70.30	70.23

Experimental results of the Transformer baseline, Transformer+EDA method and Transformer+EDA+MIL method are shown in Table 4. The improvements on F1 values (69.26→69.38, 69.38→70.23) further verify the effectiveness of both EDA and MIL module of the proposed method. In addition, we observe that back-translation performs better than easy data augmentation operations to event detection by comparing results of Transformer+BT+MIL and Transformer+EDA+MIL (73.39% VS 70.23%).

Table 5. Experimental results on ACE2005 Chinese dataset.

Model	Trigger identification			Trigger classification		
	P(%)	R(%)	F1(%)	P(%)	R(%)	F1(%)
DMCNN [4]	66.60	63.60	65.10	61.60	58.80	60.20
HNN† [6]	74.20	63.10	68.20	77.10	53.10	63.00
NPN† [12]	70.63	64.74	67.56	67.13	61.54	64.21
HGAT† [5]	68.20	71.47	69.80	64.22	67.30	65.73
Transformer	67.12	71.29	69.14	61.71	65.55	63.57
+BT data	69.61	67.94	68.77	66.18	64.59	65.38
+BT data+MIL	66.40	69.42	67.88	64.82	67.77	66.26

4.4 Experiments on ACE2005 Chinese Dataset

We also conduct experiments on the ACE2005 Chinese dataset to further verify the effectiveness of the Transformer-based event detection model. We use back-translation with a public translation API[4] to enrich existing training data. Experimental results of our model and several baseline methods are shown in Table 5. The Transformer baseline achieves a higher performance (63.57% VS 60.20%) than a traditional CNN model (DMCNN). It is observed that the

---

[4] https://fanyi-api.baidu.com/.

Transformer-based model performs better with more generated data by comparing Transformer and Transformer+BT data (63.57% → 65.38%). In addition, training on multiple datasets with different quality, the MIL method can further improve the model (65.38% → 66.26%), by alleviating inevitable noises in the generated data and filtering out high-quality data in each batch for model training.

5   Related Work

Event Detection. Traditional feature-driven event detection methods rely on hand-craft semantic features [7,9,10]. Neural models significantly advance event detection because of the automatic feature extraction and end-to-end learning, which can alleviate laborious feature engineering and error propagation problems. Researchers firstly use convolutional neural networks (CNN) to extract effective local information around trigger candidates for event detection [4,22]. In the same time, there are some works investigating recurrent neural networks (RNN) [11,21,27] for obtaining sequential information of sentences. Other works [6] combine both CNN and RNN for both sequential and local information. To further incorporate syntactic edges into model, researchers explore graph convolutional networks (GCN) [17,20] for event detection. This paper firstly use the Transformer model for capturing long-range dependencies in sentences for event detection.

Automatic Data Labelling. Existing methods to automatically label text data include distant supervision (DS) and data augmentation (DA). Inspired by its success in relation extraction, DS is used to build labelled event detection data from existing resources such as FrameNet [15] and Freebase [3,30]. However, there are a lot of noises in the generated data by DS because of its strong assumption that an occurrence of a trigger word indicates an occurrence of an event. Data augmentation methods, such as word-level replacement by synonym [26] or similar words [8] and sentence-level paraphrasing [29], can generate labelled data to ensure the generated data are in similar data distribution with the original data. Inspired by DA in other NLP tasks, some works apply DA for event detection. Yang et al. [28] proposed to rewrite non-trigger words with the cloze task of BERT and replace arguments with similar phrases. Lu et al. [18] proposed to paraphrase labeled sentences with an English resource grammar and compress sentences to filter out unimportant non-trigger words. In contrast, we propose a trigger-aware back-translation based data augmentation method to train the Transformer-based event detection model.

6   Conclusion

This paper firstly proposes a Transformer-based neural model for event detection. With existing insufficient labelled data, the Transformer-based encoder shows no advantages over traditional CNN/RNN encoders. With the help of automatically generated data with an event trigger-aware data augmentation method, the performances of the Transformer-based event detection model on two datasets obtain a great gain by using more Transformer layers. The future work include investigating how many data is needed to further improve the performance of a deep neural mdoel and how does the quality of the generated data influence its performance.

References

1. Angelidis, S., Amplayo, R.K., Suhara, Y., Wang, X., Lapata, M.: Extractive opinion summarization in quantized transformer spaces. Trans. ACL **9**, 277–293 (2021)
2. Bottou, L.: Stochastic gradient descent tricks. In: Montavon, G., Orr, G.B., Müller, K.-R. (eds.) Neural Networks: Tricks of the Trade. LNCS, vol. 7700, pp. 421–436. Springer, Heidelberg (2012). https://doi.org/10.1007/978-3-642-35289-8_25
3. Chen, Y., Liu, S., Zhang, X., Liu, K., Zhao, J.: Automatically labeled data generation for large scale event extraction. In: Proceedings of the 55th ACL, pp. 409–419. Vancouver, Canada, July 2017
4. Chen, Y., Xu, L., Liu, K., Zeng, D., Zhao, J.: Event extraction via dy namicmulti-pooling convolutional neural networks. In: Proceedings of the 53rd ACL, pp. 167–176. Beijing, China, July 2015
5. Cui, S., Yu, B., Cong, X., Liu, T., Li, Q., Shi, J.: Label enhanced event detection with heterogeneous graph attention networks. arXiv preprint arXiv:2012.01878 (2020)
6. Feng, X., Huang, L., Tang, D., Ji, H., Qin, B., Liu, T.: A language-independent neural network for event detection. In: Proceedings of the 54th ACL, pp. 66–71. Berlin, Germany, August 2016
7. Hong, Y., Zhang, J., Ma, B., Yao, J., Zhou, G., Zhu, Q.: Using cross-entity inference to improve event extraction. In: Proceedings of the 49th ACL, pp. 1127–1136. Portland, Oregon, USA, June 2011
8. Kobayashi, S.: Contextual augmentation: data augmentation by words with paradigmatic relations. In: Proceedings of the 2018 Conference of NAACL, pp. 452–457. New Orleans, Louisiana, June 2018
9. Li, P., Zhou, G., Zhu, Q., Hou, L.: Employing compositional semantics and discourse consistency in Chinese event extraction. In: Proceedings of the 2012 Joint Conference on EMNLP and CoNLL, pp. 1006–1016. Jeju Island, Korea, July 2012
10. Li, Q., Ji, H., Huang, L.: Joint event extraction via structured prediction with global features. In: Proceedings of the 51st ACL, pp. 73–82. Sofia, Bulgaria, August 2013
11. Lin, H., Lu, Y., Han, X., Sun, L.: Adaptive scaling for sparse detection in information extraction. In: Proceedings of the 56th ACL, pp. 1033–1043. Melbourne, Australia, July 2018
12. Lin, H., Lu, Y., Han, X., Sun, L.: Nugget proposal networks for Chinese event detection. In: Proceedings of the 56th ACL, pp. 1565–1574. Melbourne, Australia, July 2018
13. Liu, J., Chen, Y., Liu, K., Zhao, J.: Event detection via gated multilingual attention mechanism. In: Proceedings of the AAAI Conference on Artificial Intelligence, vol. 32 (2018)
14. Liu, S., Cheng, R., Yu, X., Cheng, X.: Exploiting contextual information via dynamic memory network for event detection. arXiv preprint arXiv:1810.03449 (2018)

15. Liu, S., Chen, Y., He, S., Liu, K., Zhao, J.: Leveraging FrameNet to improve automatic event detection. In: Proceedings of the 54th ACL, pp. 2134–2143. Berlin, Germany, August 2016

16. Liu, S., Chen, Y., Liu, K., Zhao, J.: Exploiting argument information to improve event detection via supervised attention mechanisms. In: Proceedings of the 55th ACL, pp. 1789–1798 (2017)

17. Liu, X., Luo, Z., Huang, H.: Jointly multiple events extraction via attention-based graph information aggregation. In: Proceedings of the 2018 Conference on EMNLP, pp. 1247–1256. Brussels, Belgium, Oct-Nov 2018

18. Lu, Y., Lin, H., Han, X., Sun, L.: Linguistic perturbation based data augmentation for event detection. Chin. J. Inform. **33**(7), 110–117 (2019)

19. Mohammadshahi, A., Henderson, J.: Recursive non-autoregressive graph-to-graph transformer for dependency parsing with iterative refinement. Trans. ACL **9**, 120–138 (2021)

20. Nguyen, T., Grishman, R.: Graph convolutional networks with argument-aware pooling for event detection. In: Proceedings of the AAAI Conference on Artificial Intelligence (2018)

21. Nguyen, T.H., Cho, K., Grishman, R.: Joint event extraction via recurrent neural networks. In: Proceedings of the 2016 Conference of NAACL, pp. 300–309. San Diego, California, June 2016

22. Nguyen, T.H., Grishman, R.: Event detection and domain adaptation with convolutional neural networks. In: Proceedings of the 53rd ACL, pp. 365–371. Beijing, China, July 2015

23. Popel, M., et al.: Transforming machine translation: a deep learning system reaches news translation quality comparable to human professionals. Nat. Commun. **11**(1), 1–15 (2020)

24. Srivastava, N., Hinton, G., Krizhevsky, A., Sutskever, I., Salakhutdinov, R.: Dropout: a simple way to prevent neural networks from overfitting. J. Mach. Learn. Res. **15**(1), 1929–1958 (2014)

25. Vaswani, A., et al.: Attention is all you need, pp. 5998–6008, December 2017

26. Wei, J., Zou, K.: EDA: Easy data augmentation techniques for boosting performance on text classification tasks. In: Proceedings of the 2019 Conference on EMNLP and the 9th International Joint Conference on Natural Language Processing (EMNLP-IJCNLP), pp. 6382–6388. Hong Kong, China, November 2019

27. Yang, B., Mitchell, T.: Leveraging knowledge bases in LSTMs for improving machine reading. In: Proceedings of the 55th ACL, pp. 1436–1446. Vancouver, Canada, July 2017

28. Yang, S., Feng, D., Qiao, L., Kan, Z., Li, D.: Exploring pre-trained language models for event extraction and generation. In: Proceedings of the 57th ACL, pp. 5284–5294. Florence, Italy, July 2019

29. Yu, J., Zhu, T., Chen, W., Zhang, W., Zhang, M.: Improving relation extraction with relational paraphrase sentences. In: Proceedings of the 28th COLING, pp. 1687–1698. Barcelona, Spain (Online), December 2020

30. Zeng, Y., et al.: Scale up event extraction learning via automatic training data generation. In: Proceedings of the AAAI Conference on Artificial Intelligence, pp. 5887–5897. New Orleans, Louisiana (2018)

Malicious Domain Detection on Imbalanced Data with Deep Reinforcement Learning

Fangfang Yuan[1], Teng Tian[1,2], Yanmin Shang[1], Yuhai Lu[1], Yanbing Liu[1,2(✉)], and Jianlong Tan[1]

[1] Institute of Information Engineering, Chinese Academy of Sciences, Beijing, China
{yuanfangfang,tianteng,shangyanmin,luyuhai,liuyanbing,
tanjianlong}@iie.ac.cn
[2] University of Chinese Academy of Sciences, Beijing, China

Abstract. Domain name system (DNS) is the key infrastructure of the Internet, yet has been deliberately abused by cyber attackers. Previous works detect malicious domain mainly based on the statistical features or the association features, which ignore the serialization impact and pay little attention to the imbalanced data problem. To address these problems, we propose a deep reinforcement learning based malicious domain detection model. We consider the malicious domain detection as a sequential decision process and employ Double Deep Q Network (DDQN) to address it. Furthermore, we devise a specific reward function to adapt to the imbalanced classification task. The specific reward function will guide the agent to learn the optimal classification policy. Extensive experiments are carried out on the real-world dataset, and experimental results demonstrate the effectiveness of our proposed method in detecting malicious domain in imbalanced DNS traffic.

Keywords: Malicious domain detection · Imbalanced classification · Deep reinforcement learning

1 Introduction

Domain name system is one of the most important infrastructure of the Internet. It provides services for mapping domain names to IP addresses, allowing people to easily identify devices, services, and other resources in the network. However, while the domain name system provides normal resolution services, it has also become one of the major attack vectors used in various illegal activities. More and more attackers are abusing domain name system to achieve malicious purposes, often causing information theft, system disruption and economic loss. Therefore, how to effectively detect and find malicious domains has become a hot and difficult issue in cyberspace security.

Existing malicious domain detection methods can be generally divided into two categories: the feature-based methods and the association-based methods.

T. Mantoro et al. (Eds.): ICONIP 2021, LNCS 13111, pp. 464–476, 2021.
https://doi.org/10.1007/978-3-030-92273-3_38

The former category [1–4] analyses the DNS traffic and extracts the features (e.g. the length of domain names, the number of distinct IP addresses, etc.) from the DNS traffic, then builds a machine learning based classifier to identify malicious domains. The latter category [5–7] utilizes association between domains to detect malicious domains. These methods are based on the intuition that a domain which is strongly associated with a malicious domain is likely to be malicious. Some researchers use the DNS-related data to construct the domain relationship graph (e.g. the domain-IP resolution graph, the client-domain graph) and employ the graph mining algorithm to infer the malicious probability of graph nodes.

These existing malicious domain detection methods have achieved excellent results to some extent. However, they have two drawbacks: (i) they ignore that the malicious domains are associated and the correctly classified domain samples have a positive impact on subsequent classification; (ii) they pay little attention to the problem of data imbalance which affects the effectiveness of detection.

In order to address these problems, we propose an imbalanced malicious domain detection model. In our model, we use the deep reinforcement learning to model serialization impact. In addition, we devise a specific reward function to solve the data imbalance problem. Specifically, at each time, the agent takes an action on a domain sample and a reward is returned to the agent to adjust its policy. The reward from the malicious domain sample is higher than that of the benign domain sample. The agent aims to maximize cumulative rewards, that is to say, to correctly classify as many domain samples as possible.

To sum up, the main contributions of our paper are as below:

(1) We regard the malicious domain detection problem as a sequential decision process and employ the Double Deep Q Network to address it.
(2) We design the DDQN based malicious domain detection model, in which a specific reward function is designed to adapt to imbalanced classification.
(3) Extensive experiments are conducted on the real-world dataset and the results demonstrate the effectiveness of our proposed method.

The rest of this paper is organized as follows. In Sect. 2, we introduce the related work. In Sect. 3, we describe our proposed model in detail. We elaborate the experimental results in Sect. 4. In Sect. 5, we summarize the work of the paper.

2   Related Work

2.1   Malicious Domain Detection

Malicious domain detection has received considerable attention from academic and industrial community. A lot of approaches have been proposed to detect malicious domain. We roughly divide them into two categories: the feature-based methods and the association-based methods.

In the feature-based methods, researchers extracted statistical features of various malicious domains and applied machine learning algorithms to detect malicious domains. Antonakakis et al. [1] proposed the Notos system and utilized the network and zone features of domains to compute a reputation score for a new domain. However, Notos requires large amounts of historical maliciousness data and a lot of training time. To partially solve the limitations of Notos, Bilge et al. [2] introduced Exposure, a malicious domain detection system based on 15 behavioral features that can automatically identify unknown malicious domains. Antonakakis et al. [3] proposed Kopis system which collected DNS traffic at the upper DNS hierarchy and can detect malicious domains from the global perspective. Schüppen et al. [4] extracted a large number of domain string statistical features for non-existent domain (NXDomain) and identified DGA-related malicious domains.

For the association-based methods, researchers define the malicious domain detection problem as the task of node classification in graphs. Manadhata et al. [5] built a host-domain bipartite graph by analyzing DNS query logs and applied Belief Propagation algorithm to find unknown malicious domains. Khalil et al. [6] constructed the domain resolution graph and used the path reasoning to find unknown malicious domains. Sun et al. [7] proposed HinDom and modeled the DNS scene as a Heterogeneous Information Network with clients, domains, IP addresses. It designed six meta-paths to evaluate domain similarity and utilized the transductive classification method to find malicious domains.

The feature-based and association-based methods have achieved good results. However, these methods mentioned pay little attention to the imbalanced data problem and does not consider the impact of all currently correctly classified domain names on subsequent classifications.

2.2 Classification on Imbalanced Data

Generally, there are two ways to handle the imbalanced classification problem. The first one is from the data level, which changes the class distribution of the data by resampling the imbalanced data. The resampling approaches consist of undersampling and oversampling. However, oversampling may lead to overfitting while undersampling can discard certain important samples. The second one is from the algorithm level, which adapts the classification algorithm to increase bias towards the minority class, such as cost-sensitive learning and ensemble learning.

Recently, deep learning has achieved great success in many fields and brought new insights into imbalanced classification. Wang et al. [8] used loss functions to train deep neural network on imbalanced datasets. Khan et al. [9] introduced cost-sensitive deep neural networks for imbalanced classification problems. Inspired by the works mentioned above, we formulate the problem of malicious domain detection as the sequential decision process and apply the DDQN model to solve it. Especially, we devise a specific reward function and it allows the agent to find out an optimal classification policy.

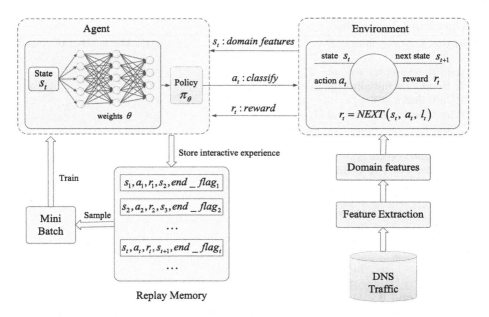

Fig. 1. Overview of the proposed model

3   The Proposed Method

3.1   Problem Formalization: Malicious Domain Detection as a Markov Decision Process

Let $D = \{(d_1, l_1), (d_2, l_2), \dots, (d_T, l_T)\}$ represents the set of imbalanced training data, where d_t is the t-th domain sample and l_t is the label of the t-th domain sample. The task of malicious domain detection is to identify the domain samples whose labels are malicious.

In this work, we regard the malicious domain detection task as a markov decision process in which the agent interacts with the environment through a series of steps, as shown in Fig. 1. In specific, the agent takes a domain sample as input and determines whether the domain sample is malicious. Then, it gets a reward from the environment. The agent gets a positive reward when it correctly classifies the domain sample, otherwise it gets a negative reward. When the agent finds out an optimal classification policy, it can correctly classify as many domain samples as possible.

A 5-tuple $(\mathcal{S}, \mathcal{A}, \mathcal{P}, \mathcal{R}, \gamma)$ is often used to define the markov decision process where: $\mathcal{S}$ is the set of all states, $\mathcal{A}$ is the set of all actions that the agent can take, $\mathcal{P} : \mathcal{S} \times \mathcal{A} \longrightarrow P(\mathcal{S})$ denotes the state transition probability function, $\mathcal{R} : \mathcal{S} \times \mathcal{A} \longrightarrow P(\mathcal{R})$ is the reward function, and $\gamma \in [0, 1]$ is a discount factor that balances the importance of immediate and future rewards. In what follows,

Algorithm 1. Training

Input: Training dataset $D = \{(d_1, l_1), (d_2, l_2), \ldots, (d_T, l_T)\}$; The number of episode K;

1: Initialize replay memory M
2: Randomly initialize the parameters θ
3: Initialize $\theta' = \theta$
4: Initialize update round G
5: **for** $k = 1$ to K **do**
6:     Shuffle D
7:     Initial state $s_1 = d_1$
8:     **for** $t = 1$ to T **do**
9:         $a_t = \pi_\theta(s_t)$
10:        $r_t = NEXT(s_t, a_t, l_t)$
11:        **if** $t = T$ **then**
12:            $end\_flag_t = True$
13:            $s_{t+1} = None$
14:        **else**
15:            $end\_flag_t = False$
16:            $s_{t+1} = d_{t+1}$
17:        **end if**
18:        add the experience $(s_t, a_t, r_t, s_{t+1}, end\_flag_t)$ to M
19:        Randomly sample $(s_i, a_i, r_i, s_{i+1}, end\_flag_i)$ from M
20:
$$\text{Set } y_i = \begin{cases} r_i, & end\_flag_i = True \\ r_i + \gamma Q'(s_{i+1}, \max_{a'} Q(s_{i+1}, a'; \theta), \theta'), & end\_flag_i = False \end{cases}$$
21:        $L(\theta) = (y_i - Q(s_i, a_i; \theta))^2$
22:        **if** $end\_flag_t = True$ **then**
23:            break
24:        **end if**
25:     **end for**
26:     **if** $k\%G = 0$ **then**
27:        $\theta' = \theta$
28:     **end if**
29: **end for**

---

we formally use the markov decision process to model malicious domain detection in imbalanced DNS data.

State $\mathcal{S}$: The state $s_t \in \mathcal{S}$ is represented as a domain sample and is denoted as a N-dimensional feature vector extracted from the DNS traffic. At the beginning of training, the first state s_1 is initialized as the first domain sample d_1. At time step t, the state s_t equals to the domain sample d_t.

Action $\mathcal{A}$: The action $a_t \in \mathcal{A}$ of the agent in our case is to determine whether a domain sample is malicious. The malicious domain detection is a binary classification problem. Hence, the actual set of actions is $\mathcal{A} = [0, 1]$, where 0 represents that the domain sample is benign and 1 represents that the domain sample is malicious.

Algorithm 2. Environment simulation

1: D_M represents the set of malicious domain samples
2: **function** $NEXT(s_t, a_t, l_t)$
3:    **if** $s_t \in D_M$ **then**
4:        **if** $a_t = l_t$ **then**
5:            Set $r_t = 1$
6:        **else**
7:            Set $r_t = -1$
8:        **end if**
9:    **else**
10:        **if** $a_t = l_t$ **then**
11:            Set $r_t = \lambda$
12:        **else**
13:            Set $r_t = -\lambda$
14:        **end if**
15:    **end if**
16: **end function**

Transition $\mathcal{P}$: The transition $p(s_{t+1}|s_t, a_t)$ is the probability that the agent takes action a_t in state s_t and moves to next state s_{t+1}. In our case, the transition probability is deterministic where the state transition follows the order of domain samples.

Reward $\mathcal{R}$: The reward r_t is used to evaluate whether an agent's action is successful. In this work, the number of malicious domain samples is smaller than that of benign domain samples. Hence, we design a specific reward function to better identify the malicious domain samples. The absolute value of the reward returned by the malicious domain sample is higher than that returned by the benign domain sample. That is to say, when the agent correctly/incorrectly identifies a malicious domain, it receives a higher reward/punishment.

The policy π is a mapping function $\pi : \mathcal{S} \longrightarrow \mathcal{A}$. $\pi(a_t|s_t)$ represents the action a_t taken by the agent in state s_t. In this work, π can be viewed as a classifier which classifies a domain sample as malicious or benign.

Based on the above definitions, the malicious domain detection in imbalanced DNS data can be defined as to seek an optimal classification policy $\pi^*(a_t|s_t)$ that maximized the cumulative rewards.

3.2   Reward Function for Malicious Domain Detection

It is difficult to recognize malicious domains correctly in imbalanced DNS data. In order to better identify malicious domains, we devise a specific reward function which is more sensitive to the malicious domains. The reward function is defined as follows:

$$R(s_t, a_t, l_t) = \begin{cases} 1, & \text{if } a_t = l_t \text{ and } s_t \in D_M \\ -1, & \text{if } a_t \neq l_t \text{ and } s_t \in D_M \\ \lambda, & \text{if } a_t = l_t \text{ and } s_t \in D_B \\ -\lambda, & \text{if } a_t \neq l_t \text{ and } s_t \in D_B \end{cases} \tag{1}$$

where $\lambda \in [0, 1]$, D_M is the set of malicious domain samples, D_B is the set of benign domain samples, l_t is the label of the domain sample in state s_t. The reward value is $1/-1$ when the agent correctly/incorrectly classifies a malicious domain sample, and the reward value is $\lambda/-\lambda$ when the agent correctly/incorrectly classifies a benign domain sample. Actually, the best value of λ varies with the number of malicious samples and benign samples. When λ is the imbalance ratio ρ, our model performs best.

3.3   DDQN Based Malicious Domain Detection

Deep Q-learning. The goal of our model is to correctly classify as many domain samples as possible. When the agent correctly classifies a domain sample, it will obtain a positive reward. Hence, we can maximize the cumulative rewards to achieve the goal.

In deep reinforcement learning, the $Q(s, a)$ function represents the expectation of the cumulative rewards that the agent can obtain in the future after taking action a in state s. The agent can achieve the maximum cumulative rewards by solving an optimal $Q^*(s, a)$ function. In our task, the greedy policy under the $Q^*(s, a)$ function is the optimal classification policy. According to Bellman equation, the $Q^*(s, a)$ function is:

$$Q^*(s, a) = E_\pi[r_t + \gamma max_a Q^*(s_{t+1}, a_{t+1} | s_t = s, a_t = a)] \tag{2}$$

Generally, the Q function is solved by iterating the Bellman equation. However, in real malicious domain detection, the state space is continuous, which makes it impractical to solve the Q function. Thus, in this work, we utilize a deep neural network named Double Deep Q Network (DDQN) to approximate the Q function.

Since the correlations present in the sequence of training samples could lead to unstable learning, we use the experience replay to address this instability. The experience replay stores the agent's experiences in a replay memory M. During learning, the agent randomly samples a mini-batch of experience $(s, a, r, s') \in \mathcal{C}$ from M and carries out a gradient descent step on the DDQN model according to the following loss function:

$$L(\theta) = \sum_{s,a,r,s' \in \mathcal{C}} (y - Q(s, a; \theta))^2 \tag{3}$$

where θ represents the parameters of the DDQN model, y is learning target values of the Q function:

$$y = \begin{cases} r, & end\_flag = True \\ r + \gamma Q'(s', \max_{a'} Q(s', a'; \theta), \theta'), & end\_flag = False \end{cases} \tag{4}$$

where s' is the next state of s, a' is action taken by the agent in state s'.

The optimal Q^* function can be obtained by minimizing the loss function (3). Under the optimal classification policy (that is, the greedy policy), the optimal

Table 1. Network Architecture of DDQN

Layer	Width	Height	Depth	Kernel size	Stride
Input	6	6	1	–	–
Convolution	8	8	256	3	2
MaxPooling	4	4	256	2	2
Convolution	6	6	256	3	2
MaxPooling	3	3	256	2	2
Flatten	1	1	2304	–	–
FullyConnected	1	1	1100	–	–
FullyConnected	1	1	500	–	–
FullyConnected	1	1	2	–	–

Q^* function will get the maximum sum of rewards. Therefore, we achieve the optimal classification policy $\pi : \mathcal{S} \longrightarrow \mathcal{A}$ for malicious domain detection in imbalanced DNS traffic.

Training Details. The DDQN model consists of two convolution-pooling layers and three fully connected layers. The structure of the DDQN model is shown in Table 1. It takes as input the domain sample and outputs a two-dimensional vector. Actually, the DDQN model can be viewed as a deep neural network based classifier without the final softmax layer. The training process of the DDQN model is shown in Algorithm 1. The environment simulation is described in Algorithm 2. When the agent is well train with Algorithm 1, it learns an optimal classification policy that guides the agent to take the action with maximum sum of future rewards at each time step.

4   Experiments and Results

4.1   Dataset

We perform experiments on the DNS traffic collected from a university. We capture DNS traffic logs of two weeks from 2020.8.31 to 2020.9.13. The DNS traffic logs can be parsed to obtain detailed domain information, such as length of domain name, number of distinct IP addresses, etc. In addition, we combine the collected DNS traffic logs with DNS related external data to enrich the domain information, such as registration records, domain blacklists, etc. At last, we extract a total of 36 domain features. The full set of domain features is listed in Table 2.

Table 2. Selected domain feature set

Types	Description
Linguistic	# of vowel, # of consonant, Conversion frequency between vowels and consonants, Contains digit, # of digit, Conversion frequency between letters and digits, # of special characters, # of character types, Ratio of longest meaningful substring length
Structural	Length of domain name, Mean subdomain length, Include www as prefix, TLD is valid, Has a single character as subdomain, Has a TLD as subdomain, Digit subdomains ratio, hexadecimal digit subdomains ratio, Underscore ratio, Contains IP
Statistical	# of IP(IPv4, IPv6), # of shared IP domain names, # of MX, # of NS, Similarity of NS, # of CNAME, Whois integrity, Survival days, Statistics of TTL(mean, standard deviation, median, # of types), Statistics of size of resource records (mean, standard deviation, median, # of types)

For the benign domains, we choose domains which appear in Alexa Top 100,000 list [10] as benign ones. For the malicious domains, we collected malicious domains from Malwaredomains.com [11], phishtank [12], etc.

In our experiments, we select 60,000 benign domains and 3,000 malicious domains from the collected DNS traffic data to build an imbalanced DNS dataset. Then, we perform 5-fold cross-validation on the imbalanced DNS dataset.

4.2   Comparative Methods

We compare our method with six imbalanced classification methods from the algorithm level and the data level, including sampling methods, cost-sensitive methods, and ensemble methods. In addition, we compare our method with several deep learning methods. Specifically, we use the Convolutional Neural Network (CNN) model and the Deep Q Network (DQN) model as baseline methods. The comparison methods are shown as follows:

CNN. A method which directly trains the CNN in the imbalanced DNS dataset without any improvement strategy.

DQN. A method is very similar to DDQN. The only difference being that there is one neural network in DQN.

Random Oversampling. A resampling method to balance the imbalanced DNS dataset by randomly replicating the malicious domain samples.

SMOTE [13]. A resampling method to balance the imbalanced DNS dataset which generates new samples by interpolation between malicious domain samples.

Random Undersampling. A resampling method to balance the imbalanced DNS dataset by randomly removing the benign domain samples.

Table 3. Experimental results of different detection algorithms

Algorithms	Precision	Recall	F1
CNN	0.9335	0.8573	0.8954
DQN	0.981	0.9985	0.9904
DDQN	0.9941	0.9985	0.997

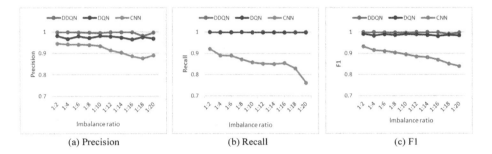

(a) Precision	(b) Recall	(c) F1

Fig. 2. Performance on different imbalance ratio

NearMiss [13]. A prototype selection method which selects the most representative samples from the benign domain samples for training.

Threshold Moving [14]. A cost sensitive method which changes the decision threshold to give preference to malicious domain samples.

EasyEnsemble [15]. An ensemble method which is the combination of undersampling and ensemble learning.

4.3   Experiment Setting and Evaluation Metrics

We use the ϵ-policy to train the DDQN model and set the exploration rate ϵ to decrease linearly from 1.0 to 0.00002. The discount factor γ is 0.9. The size of replay memory is 10,000. The optimizer is the RMSprop optimizer and the loss function is the cross entropy loss. We set the learning rate to be 0.0002. For parameters in other algorithms, the optimizer and loss function are same as the DDQN model. We utilize three metrics to evaluate the detection performance, including Precision, Recall and F-measure measures.

4.4   Results

Overall Performance: Table 3 shows the performance comparison between our model and other deep learning based detection algorithms when the imbalance ratio ρ is 0.1. From Table 3, we note that the DDQN model performs slightly better than the DQN model and both of them outperform the CNN model. This demonstrates that our method which regards malicious domain detection

Table 4. Detection results of different imbalanced classification algorithms

Algorithms	Metrics	Imbalance ratio ρ			
		50%	25%	10%	5%
Random oversampling	Precision	0.9345	0.8888	0.8406	0.7810
	Recall	0.9192	0.9085	0.9104	0.8639
	F1	0.9266	0.8979	0.8730	0.8191
SMOTE	Precision	0.9370	0.9161	0.8851	0.8237
	Recall	0.9221	0.8963	0.8913	0.8556
	F1	0.9293	0.9059	0.8869	0.8379
Random undersampling	Precision	0.9077	0.8610	0.8001	0.5362
	Recall	0.9299	0.9085	0.9212	0.9152
	F1	0.9184	0.8834	0.8543	0.6748
NearMiss	Precision	0.9387	0.9298	0.8914	0.8575
	Recall	0.9185	0.8834	0.8888	0.8074
	F1	0.9284	0.9056	0.8900	0.8311
Threshold moving	Precision	0.9408	0.9288	0.9036	0.8529
	Recall	0.9263	0.9063	0.9162	0.8623
	F1	0.9333	0.9165	0.9095	0.8526
EasyEnsemble	Precision	0.9429	0.9413	0.9042	0.8489
	Recall	0.9278	0.8949	0.9253	0.8821
	F1	0.9351	0.9171	0.9138	0.8644
DDQN	Precision	0.9985	0.9985	0.9941	0.9955
	Recall	1.0000	1.0000	0.9985	1.0000
	F1	0.9993	0.9993	0.9970	0.9978

as a sequential decision problem is useful. Besides, reinforcement learning based methods perform better than other deep learning based method.

Performance on Different Imbalance Ratio: The effect of different imbalance ratios on the detection performance is shown in Fig. 2. With the increase of data imbalance level, the performance of the CNN model shows a significant decline, but the DDQN model maintain good performance. Especially when the imbalance ratio is 5%, the DDQN model offers an improvement of around 15.86% over the CNN model for F1 evaluation metric. The reason is that the DDQN model designs a specific reward function, which allows it to perform better when DNS data is highly skewed. As for the DQN model, the DQN model performs similar to the DDQN model, but the training speed of the DQN model is much slower. Hence, the DDQN model is more suitable for malicious domain detection.

Evaluation of Different Imbalanced Classification Methods: Table 4 shows the malicious domain detection results of different imbalanced classification methods. When the imbalance ratio is 50%, 25%, 10% and 5%, our model outperforms other six imbalanced classification methods for all evaluation metrics. It demonstrates that considering the serialization impact and employing deep reinforcement learning model could improve the performance of malicious domain detection.

5   Conclusion

In this paper, we formulate the malicious domain detection problem as a sequential decision process and propose a DDQN based malicious domain detection model to solve it. Since the DNS traffic data is imbalanced, we designed a specific reward function to adapt to the imbalanced classification. When training, the environment returns a higher reward for the malicious domain sample but a low reward for the benign domain sample. After training, the agent finds an optimal classification policy which guides the agent to correctly classify the domain sample. We conduct experiments on the real-world dataset, the results show the effectiveness of our model.

Acknowledgement. This work was partly supported by the National Key Research and Development Program Grant No. 2017YFC0820700, Strategic Priority Research Program of the Chinese Academy of Sciences under Grant No.XDC02030000.

References

1. Antonakakis, M., Perdisci, R., Dagon, D., Lee, W., Feamster, N.: Building a dynamic reputation system for dns. In: USENIX Security Symposium, pp. 273–290 (2010)
2. Bilge, L., Kirda, E., Kruegel, C., Balduzzi, M.: Exposure: finding malicious domains using passive dns analysis. In: Ndss, pp. 1–17 (2011)
3. Antonakakis, M., Perdisci, R., Lee, W., Vasiloglou, N., Dagon, D.: Detecting malware domains at the upper dns hierarchy. In: USENIX Security Symposium, vol. 11, pp. 1–16 (2011)
4. Schüppen, S., Teubert, D., Herrmann, P., Meyer, U.: Feature-based automated nxdomain classification and intelligence (2018)
5. Manadhata, P.K., Yadav, S., Rao, P., Horne, W.: Detecting malicious domains via graph inference. In: Kutyłowski, M., Vaidya, J. (eds.) ESORICS 2014. LNCS, vol. 8712, pp. 1–18. Springer, Cham (2014). https://doi.org/10.1007/978-3-319-11203-9_1
6. Khalil, I., Yu, T., Guan, B.: Discovering malicious domains through passive dns data graph analysis. In: Proceedings of the 11th ACM on Asia Conference on Computer and Communications Security, pp. 663–674 (2016)
7. Sun, X., Tong, M., Yang, J., Xinran, L., Heng, L.: Hindom: A robust malicious domain detection system based on heterogeneous information network with transductive classification. In: RAID, pp. 399–412 (2019)
8. Wang, S., Liu, W., Wu, J., Cao, L., Meng, Q., Kennedy, P.J.: Training deep neural networks on imbalanced data sets. In: 2016 International Joint Conference on Neural Networks (IJCNN), pp. 4368–4374. IEEE (2016)

9. Khan, S.H., Hayat, M., Bennamoun, M., Sohel, F.A., Togneri, R.: Cost-sensitive learning of deep feature representations from imbalanced data. IEEE Trans. Neural Netw. Learn. Syst. **29**(8), 3573–3587 (2017)
10. Alexa top 1 million. https://aws.amazon.com/cn/alexa-top-sites/
11. Malware domain block list. http://www.malwaredomains.com
12. Phishtank. http://www.phishtank.com
13. Scikit-learn. https://scikit-learn.org/
14. Johnson, J.M., Khoshgoftaar, T.M.: Survey on deep learning with class imbalance. J. Big Data **6**(1), 1–54 (2019). https://doi.org/10.1186/s40537-019-0192-5
15. Liu, Z., Zeng, Y., Zhang, P., Xue, J., Zhang, J., Liu, J.: An imbalanced malicious domains detection method based on passive dns traffic analysis. Security and Communication Networks (2018)

Designing and Searching for Lightweight Monocular Depth Network

Jinfeng Liu, Lingtong Kong, and Jie Yang[✉]

Institute of Image Processing and Pattern Recognition, Department of Automation,
Shanghai Jiao Tong University, Shanghai, China
{ljf19991226,ltkong,jieyang}@sjtu.edu.cn

Abstract. Depth sensing is extremely notable in some tasks of robot and autonomous driving. Nowadays, monocular depth estimation based on deep learning becomes a research focus in computer vision. However, most of the current work is seeking for more complex models to get higher accuracy, which can not achieve real-time inference on mobile or embedded systems. Therefore, we aim to design a lightweight model in this paper. At first, we improve the state-of-the-art model, FastDepth, producing FastDepthV2, which has higher accuracy and lower latency on the NYU Depth v2 dataset. Besides, since designing artificial networks takes time and effort, we make it automatic to design lightweight models in monocular depth estimation, using neural architecture search (NAS). Further, inspired by the architecture of MobileNetV2, a factorized hierarchical search space for encoder is used in this paper. In the meanwhile, we incorporate the accuracy and multiply-add operations of a model together into the searching objective, and use gradient-based reinforcement learning algorithm in the searching iterations. The controller in the reinforcement learning framework has converged after more than 1000 searching iterations, and three network architectures with the best performance are obtained. Under the same conditions of training and testing, two of them perform better than FastDepthV2.

Keywords: Deep learning · Monocular depth estimation · Lightweight network · Neural architecture search

1 Introduction

Depth estimation is a critical function for certain tasks in robots, autonomous driving, augmented reality (AR) and some other application scenarios. Conventionally, high-accuracy depth information is mainly obtained based on active sensing techniques, such as Time-of-Flight (ToF) and LiDAR, which are still limited in application. For example, ToF is mostly suitable for indoor environments while LiDAR is too bulky and expensive to deploy. Therefore, the preferable strategy in most cases to infer the depth is based on visual information, using

This research is partly supported by NSFC, China (No: 61876107, U1803261).

T. Mantoro et al. (Eds.): ICONIP 2021, LNCS 13111, pp. 477–488, 2021.
https://doi.org/10.1007/978-3-030-92273-3_39

camera technology [1]. The most famous method among them is stereo vision [10,15], which demands two cameras spaced apart and synchronized. However, in stereo vision system, the volume of equipment can not match the deployment platform well due to the limitation of baseline length. As the emergence of deep learning causes a big trend of computer vision and artificial intelligence, monocular camera can solve all the limitations of depth estimation techniques mentioned above owing to its low cost, small volume and convenient deployment [14]. Consequently, monocular depth estimation based on deep learning becomes a research focus in computer vision.

Most previous researches in monocular depth estimation only concentrate on elevating the prediction accuracy, hence, the designed models are becoming more and more complicated [3,4,8,21,22]. A great quantity of model parameters and computation makes it difficult to deploy on mobile and embedded systems. To address the problem and attain an excellent trade-off between prediction accuracy and inference latency, we try to design a lightweight and efficient neural network model, which can quickly and accurately infer the depth information of a single RGB image on CPU devices. Besides, current well-peformed convolutional neural networks of depth estimation is basically designed by human experts. Considering the fact that model design requires relative high expert knowledge and takes a large number of repetitive experiments, this paper applies neural architecture search (NAS) [18,23] to the task of monocular depth estimation, making the design process automatic and reducing the design cost.

2   Related Work

2.1   Monocular Depth Estimation

Although multi-view depth estimation [10,15] has been studied for a long time in computer vision, obtaining depth from a single image has been considered as an ill-conditioned issue with great uncertainty until the emergence of deep learning. There are some approaches based on supervised learning [3,4,8]. Eigen et al.. [4] designed a multi-scale convolutional neural network to monocular depth estimation for the first time. Laina et al.. [8] proposed a full convolution network with residual structure to model the fuzzy mapping between monocular image and its corresponding depth map. Other approaches based on unsupervised learning have also been proposed [21,22]. Zhou et al.. [22] used an image sequence taken by a monocular camera as the training set to estimate depth information and camera pose simultaneously in an unsupervised learning way. Yin et al.. [21] improved the work in [22] together with the estimation of optical flow, and combined depth, camera motion and optical flow information for joint optimization.

Models in the methods mentioned above are more and more complicated to get higher accuracy, which are not suitable for the deployment on mobile or embedded devices. To solve this problem, some lightweight models are proposed, which can infer in real-time at the expense of a little accuracy drop [12,20]. Among them, PyDNet [12] is a pyramidal encoder-decoder structure, which can run fast on CPU due to its small size and design selection. FastDepth [20] is also an encoder-decoder model, whose encoder is the MobileNet [6], and it can infer the depth at 178 fps on one NVIDIA Jetson TX2 GPU.

2.2 Neural Architecture Search (NAS)

Traditional NAS methods rely on evolutionary algorithm [18], where the population of the network is constantly changing and architectures with poor performance are abandoned. In recent years, NAS based on reinforcement learning has achieved the most advanced results in image classification [23]. These algorithms depend on huge computing resources, and need an independent network, i.e., a controller, which samples a network architecture and receives the scalar reward after it is trained and evaluated on the target task.

Recently, several solutions are proposed to improve the efficiency of NAS. Pham *et al.* [11] expanded the computational graph of all network structures and allowed different structures to share weights. Liu *et al.* [9] adopted an incremental strategy to gradually enlarge the complexity of the network, and trained the sorted networks in parallel to predict the performance of new model. Even if these approaches make the search more efficient, they also sacrifice the expressivity of the search space, which might get suboptimal results. Nowadays, there is hardly any application of neural architecture search in monocular depth estimation.

3 Methodology

3.1 FastDepthV2

FastDepth is a fast monocular depth estimation model proposed in [20]. We firstly improve it by replacing MobileNet with MobileNetV2 [13] as the encoder, whereas the decoder still consists of 5 upsample layers of NNConv5, involving 5 × 5 depthwise separable convolution followed by nearest neighbor interpolation with a scale factor of 2, and there is also a 1 × 1 convolution at the end to get the depth map. The additive skip connections are applied between the encoder and the decoder, so the number of filter channels in the middle three NNConv5 layers should be adjusted accordingly. We depict the structure of FastDepthV2 in Fig. 1.

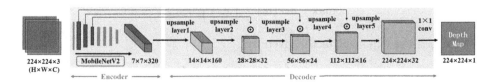

Fig. 1. The structure of FastDepthV2.

3.2   Loss Function

We illustrate the loss functions employed to train our FastDepthV2 in this part. Given the ground truth depth map $\hat{d}$ and the output of the depth estimation network d, we refer to the method in [2], formulate the total loss as the weighted sum of two loss terms:

$$L(d, \hat{d}) = \lambda_1 L_{depth}(d, \hat{d}) + \lambda_2 L_{grad}(d, \hat{d}) \qquad (1)$$

The first term L_{depth} is the point-wise L1 loss over the depth values between the prediction and ground-truth label:

$$L_{depth}(d, \hat{d}) = \frac{1}{N} \sum_i^N \left| d_i - \hat{d}_i \right| \qquad (2)$$

The second term L_{grad} is the L1 loss defined over the image gradient ∇ of the depth map:

$$L_{grad}(d, \hat{d}) = \frac{1}{N} \sum_i^N (\left| \nabla_x d_i - \nabla_x \hat{d}_i \right| + \left| \nabla_y d_i - \nabla_y \hat{d}_i \right|) \qquad (3)$$

where ∇_x and ∇_y compute the gradients in the x and y components for the depth maps of d and $\hat{d}$ respectively. It is pointed out in [2] that the weighted-sum loss function can reconstruct depth maps by minimizing the difference of the depth values and penalize the distortions of high frequency details in the depth image domain with a good compromise. In the following experiments, we empirically set $\lambda_1 = 0.1$ and $\lambda_2 = 1$.

3.3   NAS on Monocular Depth

Search Problem Formulation. In order to find architectures with high accuracy and low inference latency, we refer to the search implementation in [19] and define the search problem as a multi-objective search task, with prediction accuracy and multiply-add operations together incorporated into the searching objective. Given a model m, we use $acc(m)$ and $macs(m)$ to denote its accuracy and multiply-add operations respectively. And P is the expected target multiply-add operations, which is set as $400M$. The objective function is designed as:

$$\max_m \quad acc(m) \times \left(\frac{macs(m)}{P} \right)^\omega \qquad (4)$$

where ω is the exponent factor given by:

$$\omega = \begin{cases} \alpha & macs(m) \leq P \\ \beta & macs(m) > P \end{cases} \qquad (5)$$

where α and β are condition-specific parameters and we let $\alpha = \beta = -0.08$ in the experiment.

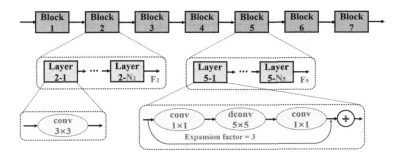

Fig. 2. The factorized hierarchical search space designed for encoder.

Search Space. A good search space is very critical in neural architecture search, which directly affects the performance and expression ability of the searched model. We use a factorized hierarchical search space similar to that of MnasNet in [19]. The difference is that our search space is designed only for the encoder. In other words, the final end-to-end model is similar to FastDepthV2, but the MobileNetV2 is replaced by the searched encoder structure and the number of filter channels in decoder layers should be adjusted accordingly. The factorized hierarchical search space, which is depicted in Fig. 2, is inspired by the 7 bottleneck blocks in MobileNetV2. It segments the model into a sequence of pre-defined blocks, with the image resolution reducing step by step. Each block is composed of identical layers, with the operations and connections determined by the search sub-space of the block. Particularly, the search sub-space of the ith block is consisted of the following items:

- Convolutional operations $ConvOp$: regular conv (Conv) with 3×3 or 5×5 kernel size, depthwise separable conv (SepDConv) with 3×3 or 5×5 kernel size, and inverted bottleneck conv (InvBConv) with various expansion factor and 3×3 or 5×5 kernel size, 8 types in total.
- Skip operations $SkipOp$: identity residual skip or no skip path, 2 types in total.
- Number of layers per block N_i: from 1 to 4, 4 types in total.
- Output filter size F_i: from 8 to 200 and a multiple of 8, 25 types in total.

In the meantime, we fix the output filter size of the last block to 320, ensuring that the model has a certain complexity.

Search Algorithm. The same as [19,23], we employ a gradient-based reinforcement learning approach for the multi-objective search problem due to its convenience. The reward $R(m)$ is the objective given by Eq. 4. Depicted in Fig. 3, the search framework of reinforcement learning consists of two components: a controller based on LSTM [5] and a trainer to get the network accuracy. We utilize the well-known sample-eval-update loop to train the controller. At each step, the controller first samples a model using its current parameters, by predicting

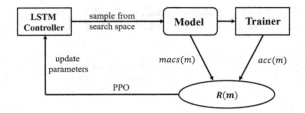

Fig. 3. The search framework of reinforcement learning.

a sequence of tokens based on the softmax logits from the LSTM. Each sampled model m is trained in the trainer to obtain its accuracy $acc(m)$, and its number of multiply-add operations $macs(m)$ is also obtained. Then the reward value $R(m)$ is calculated using Eq. 4. At the end, the parameters of the controller are updated using Proximal Policy Optimization (PPO) [16]. We repeat this process and do not stop until it converges or reaches the maximum number of iterations. Figure 4 shows an example of the controller sampling process. For simplicity, it is assumed that the number of blocks to be searched is two. It samples the structure of the two blocks in turn. And in the sampling process of each block, $ConvOp$, $SkipOp$, N_i, F_i are sampled in turn. In Fig. 4, the sampled token list is $[2, 1, 2, 0, 6, 1, 3, 1]$.

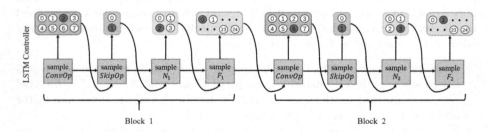

Fig. 4. An example of the controller sampling process.

4   Experimental Results

4.1   Dataset

In our experiments we use NYU depth v2 [17], which provides different indoor scene images and corresponding depth maps. It is one of the most widely used datasets in monocular depth estimation and is collected from 464 different scenes by Kinect depth camera, including 120 K training samples and 654 test samples. In this paper, a 50 K subset of training samples is used to train the model. The original resolution is 640 × 480 and we scale it to 224 × 224 to accelerate the training process and lessen the memory consumption.

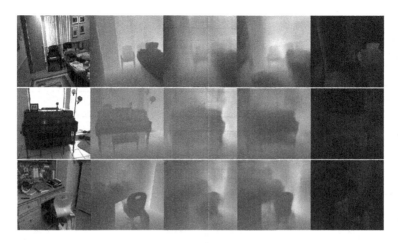

Fig. 5. Visualized results of FastDepth and FastDepthV2. Left to right columns correspond to the input RGB image, ground truth, prediction of FastDepth, prediction of FastDepthV2, and error map of FastDepthv2 respectively.

Table 1. Comparison of FastDepthV2 with prior works. For δ_1, higher is better. For all others, lower is better. Runtimes are measured on one GTX 1080Ti GPU.

Method	Input size	MACs $[G]$	rms $\downarrow$	δ_1 $\uparrow$	CPU $[ms]$	GPU $[ms]$
Eigen *et al.* [4]	228×304	2.06	0.907	0.611	307	23
Eigen *et al.* [3] (VGG)	228×304	23.4	0.641	0.769	2797	195
Laina *et al.* [8] (UpConv)	228×304	22.9	0.604	0.789	2384	237
Laina *et al.* [8] (UpProj)	228×304	42.7	**0.573**	**0.811**	3928	319
Wofk *et al.* [20] (FastDepth)	224×224	0.73	0.591	0.751	136	17
This Paper(FastDepthV2)	224×224	**0.32**	0.586	0.758	**130**	**15**

4.2   Experiment on FastDepthV2

Experiment Setup. All experiments are implemented in PyTorch with two 1080Ti GPU cards. We use a batch size of 8 and a learning rate of 0.01 in training and a batch size of 1 in evaluation. The optimizer is SGD with a momentum of 0.9 and a weight decay of 0.0001. The encoder weights are pretrained on ImageNet [7] while Gaussian initialization method is used in the decoder. Accuracy is quantified by both δ_1 (the percentage of predicted pixels where the relative error is within 25%) and rms (root mean squared error). Besides, we train FastDepth without network pruning for comparison. The two models are trained for 20 epochs.

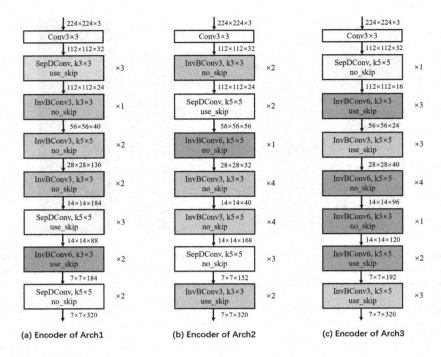

Fig. 6. The encoder structure of the optimal models.

Training and Testing. The experimental results of FastDepthV2 are compared with some previous work, including FastDepth. Table 1 gives the comparison results, which shows that FastDepthv2 and FastDepth achieve close to state-of-the-art accuracy and are faster by one order of magnitude. Besides, FastDepthV2 has higher prediction accuracy and lower inference latency than FastDepth, which is to be expected because MobileNetV2 is the improved version of MobileNet. Figure 5 shows the visualized results on the NYU depth V2 dataset. Obviously, the output depth map of FastDepthV2 has a clearer visual effect. In addition to this, an error map is also displayed, which shows the difference between the prediction of FastDepthv2 and ground truth. The brighter the pixel, the greater the corresponding depth estimation error and the error for the boundary and distant objects is larger.

4.3 Experiments of NAS

Experiment Setup. In the search experiment, the 50 K NYU depth V2 training set is divided into two disjoint sets——meta-train and meta-val, which are 48 K and 2 K respectively. The controller is a two-layer LSTM with 100 hidden units initialised from a Gaussian distribution. We use PPO with the learning rate of 0.0001 to optimize the controller. For inner trainer, the training of each sampled model is divided into two stages. At first stage, we select 8K samples as

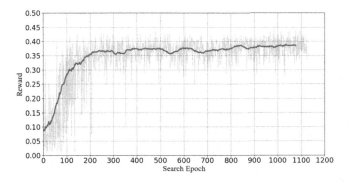

Fig. 7. Iterative curve of reward during searching.

the training set in the meta-train subset. At second stage, the whole meta-train subset is used for training, while the validation set of the two stages all uses the meta-val subset. We train the first stage for 5 epochs and train the second stage for 1 epoch. The learning rates are 0.001 and 0.003 for the encoder and the decoder respectively. And the whole architecture adopts SGD optimizer with a momentum of 0.9, a weight decay of 0.0001 and a learning rate of 0.001, using Gaussian method to initialize the weights. The search process is implemented on two 1080Ti GPU cards. In the following full training of the searched high-performance architecture, the 50 K samples are directly used as the training set, and 654 images are used as the test set. The whole encoder-decoder model uses SGD optimizer with a learning rate of 0.01, a momentum of 0.9, and a weight decay of 0.0001. We utilize Gaussian initialization method for the whole model in the training process and train the model for 20 epochs.

Search Results. After searching in monocular depth estimation on two 1080Ti GPU cards for nearly four days, nearly 1125 architectures are obtained. The iterative curve of reward in the search process is depicted in Fig. 7, which indicates that the LSTM controller has almost converged. We select three architectures called Arch1, Arch2 and Arch3 respectively that perform best in the task of monocular depth estimation during searching, and fully train them on the complete training set. The encoders of the three optimal models are shown in Fig. 6, where SepDConv denotes depth separable convolution, InvBConv3 and

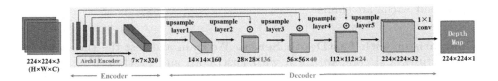

Fig. 8. The complete structure of Arch1.

Fig. 9. Visualized results of Arch1, Arch2, Arch3 and FastDepth series. Left to right columns correspond to the input RGB image, ground truth, prediction of FastDepth, prediction of FastDepthV2, prediction of Arch1, prediction of Arch2 and prediction of Arch3 respectively.

Table 2. Comparison of Arch1, Arch2, Arch3 with FastDepth and FastDepthV2. For δ_1, higher is better. For all others, lower is better. Runtimes are measured on one GTX 1080Ti GPU.

Model (without pretraining)	Parameters [M]	MACs [G]	rms ↓	δ_1 ↑	CPU [ms]	GPU [ms]
FastDepth	3.93	0.73	0.742	0.638	136	17
FastDepthV2	1.85	0.32	0.693	0.674	130	15
Arch1	**1.37**	0.39	**0.683**	**0.693**	117	**11**
Arch2	1.69	0.43	0.704	0.673	**113**	12
Arch3	1.98	**0.31**	0.692	0.684	124	14

InvBConv6 denote inverted residual block with the expansion factor of 3 and 6 respectively, k3 × 3 and k5 × 5 denote convolution kernel size, use_skip and no_skip indicate whether to use residual connection, × 1/2/3/4 indicates the number of layers per block. Note that the three architectures contain more 5 × 5 depthwise convolutions than prior lightweight models, such as MobileNet, where only 3 × 3 kernels are typically used. In fact, a 5 × 5 convolution kernel could be more efficient than two 3 × 3 convolution kernels for depthwise separable convolution. And we also give the whole architecture of Arch1 in Fig. 8, to which Arch2 and Arch3 are similar.

Comparison with FastDepth Series. We train and test the three optimal architectures and compare them with FastDepth and FastDepthV2. In order to ensure the fairness of comparison, we retrain FastDepth and FastDepthV2 with Gaussian initialization method applied to the whole end-to-end model. The visualized results are depicted in Fig. 9 and the comparison results are listed in

Table 2, which indicate that two of the best models in the searching process perform better than the artificial neural networks. And the accuracy and inference latency of the last model is very close to that of FastDepthV2. It can be considered that this result is due to the better layer diversity of the three architectures, which is good for the trade-off between accuracy and latency.

5   Conclusion

In this work, we improve the state-of-the-art fast monocular depth estimation method FastDepth by replacing its encoder with MobileNetV2 and get a model called FastDepthV2, which has higher accuracy and lower inference latency than FastDepth. Then we try to make it automatic to design lightweight models for the task of monocular depth estimation using neural architecture search approach. In order to obtain models with high accuracy and low latency, multi-objective search is adopted, with prediction accuracy and multiply-add operations together incorporated into the searching objective. We use a factorized hierarchical search space for the encoder and the search algorithm of reinforcement learning. In the end, three architectures with the best performance are obtained and two of them performs better than the two artificial networks, FastDepth and FastDepthV2. In the future, the searched encoders will be pretrained on Imagenet for further improvement.

References

1. Aleotti, F., Zaccaroni, G., Bartolomei, L., Poggi, M., Tosi, F., Mattoccia, S.: Real-time single image depth perception in the wild with handheld devices. Sensors **21**, 15 (2021)
2. Alhashim, I., Wonka, P.: High quality monocular depth estimation via transfer learning. arXiv preprint arXiv:1812.11941 (2019)
3. Eigen, D., Fergus, R.: Predicting depth, surface normals and semantic labels with a common multi-scale convolutional architecture. In: The IEEE International Conference on Computer Vision, pp. 2650–2658. IEEE Press, Santiago (2015)
4. Eigen, D., Puhrsch, C., Fergus, R.: Depth map prediction from a single image using a multi-scale deep network. In: Proceedings of the 27th International Conference on Neural Information Processing Systems, pp. 2366–2374. MIT Press, Montreal (2014)
5. Hochreiter, S., Schmidhuber, J.: Long short-term memory. Neural Comput. **9**(8), 1735–1780 (1997)
6. Howard, A.G., et al.: Mobilenets: efficient convolutional neural networks for mobile vision applications. arXiv preprint arXiv:1704.04861 (2017)
7. Jia, D., Wei, D., Socher, R., Li, L.J., Kai, L., Li, F.F.: Imagenet: a large-scale hierarchical image database. In: The IEEE Conference on Computer Vision and Pattern Recognition, pp. 248–255. IEEE Press, Miami (2009)
8. Laina, I., Rupprecht, C., Belagiannis, V., Tombari, F., Navab, N.: Deeper depth prediction with fully convolutional residual networks. In: 2016 Fourth International Conference on 3D Vision, pp. 239–248. IEEE Press, Stanford (2016)

9. Liu, C., et al.: Progressive neural architecture search. In: Ferrari, V., Hebert, M., Sminchisescu, C., Weiss, Y. (eds.) ECCV 2018. LNCS, vol. 11205, pp. 19–35. Springer, Cham (2018). https://doi.org/10.1007/978-3-030-01246-5_2

10. Marr, D., Poggio, T.: Cooperative computation of stereo disparity. Science **194**(4262), 283–287 (1976)

11. Pham, H., Guan, M.Y., Zoph, B., Le, Q.V., Dean, J.: Efficient neural architecture search via parameter sharing. In: The International Conference on Machine Learning, pp. 4095–4104. PMLR Press, Stockholm (2018)

12. Poggi, M., Aleotti, F., Tosi, F., Mattoccia, S.: Towards real-time unsupervised monocular depth estimation on cpu. In: The International Conference on Intelligent Robots and Systems, pp. 5848–5854. IEEE Press, Madrid (2018)

13. Sandler, M., Howard, A., Zhu, M., Zhmoginov, A., Chen, L.C.: Mobilenetv 2: inverted residuals and linear bottlenecks. In: The IEEE Conference on Computer Vision and Pattern Recognition, pp. 4510–4520. IEEE Press, Salt Lake City (2018)

14. Saxena, A., Sun, M., Ng, A.Y.: Make3d: learning 3d scene structure from a single still image. IEEE Trans. Pattern Anal. Mach. Intell. **31**(5), 824–840 (2009)

15. Scharstein, D., Szeliski, R.: A taxonomy and evaluation of dense two-frame stereo correspondence algorithms. Int. J. Comput. Vis. **47**(1–3), 7–42 (2002)

16. Schulman, J., Wolski, F., Dhariwal, P., Radford, A., Klimov, O.: Proximal policy optimization algorithms. arXiv preprint arXiv:1707.06347 (2017)

17. Silberman, N., Hoiem, D., Kohli, P., Fergus, R.: Indoor segmentation and support inference from RGBD images. In: Fitzgibbon, A., Lazebnik, S., Perona, P., Sato, Y., Schmid, C. (eds.) ECCV 2012. LNCS, vol. 7576, pp. 746–760. Springer, Heidelberg (2012). https://doi.org/10.1007/978-3-642-33715-4_54

18. Stanley, K., D'Ambrosio, D., Gauci, J.: A hypercube-based encoding for evolving large-scale neural networks. Artif. Life **15**(2), 185–212 (2009)

19. Tan, M., et al.: Mnasnet: platform-aware neural architecture search for mobile. In: The IEEE Conference on Computer Vision and Pattern Recognition, pp. 2815–2823. IEEE Press, Los Alamitos (2019)

20. Wofk, D., Ma, F., Yang, T.J., Karaman, S., Sze, V.: Fastdepth: fast monocular depth estimation on embedded systems. In: The International Conference on Robotics and Automation, pp. 6101–6108. IEEE Press, Montreal (2019)

21. Yin, Z., Shi, J.: Geonet: unsupervised learning of dense depth, optical flow and camera pose. In: The IEEE Conference on Computer Vision and Pattern Recognition, pp. 1983–1992. IEEE Press, Salt Lake City (2018)

22. Zhou, T., Brown, M., Snavely, N., Lowe, D.G.: Unsupervised learning of depth and ego-motion from video. In: The IEEE Conference on Computer Vision and Pattern Recognition, pp. 6612–6619. IEEE Press, Hawaii (2017)

23. Zoph, B., Vasudevan, V., Shlens, J., Le, Q.V.: Learning transferable architectures for scalable image recognition. In: The IEEE Conference on Computer Vision and Pattern Recognition, pp. 8697–8710. IEEE Press, Salt Lake City (2018)

Improving Question Answering over Knowledge Graphs Using Graph Summarization

Sirui Li[1]([✉]), Kok Wai Wong[1], Chun Che Fung[1], and Dengya Zhu[1,2]

[1] Discipline of Information Technology, Murdoch University,
South Street, Murdoch, Western Australia
{sirui.li,k.wong,l.fung,Simon.Zhu}@murdoch.edu.au
[2] Discipline of Business Information Systems, School of Management and Marketing,
Curtin University, Kent Street, Bentley, Western Australia

Abstract. Question Answering (QA) systems over Knowledge Graphs (KGs) (KGQA) automatically answer natural language questions using triples contained in a KG. The key idea is to represent questions and entities of a KG as low-dimensional embeddings. Previous KGQAs have attempted to represent entities using Knowledge Graph Embedding (KGE) and Deep Learning (DL) methods. However, KGEs are too shallow to capture the expressive features and DL methods process each triple independently. Recently, Graph Convolutional Network (GCN) has shown to be excellent in providing entity embeddings. However, using GCNs to KGQAs is inefficient because GCNs treat all relations equally when aggregating neighbourhoods. Also, a problem could occur when using previous KGQAs: in most cases, questions often have an uncertain number of answers. To address the above issues, we propose a graph summarization technique using Recurrent Convolutional Neural Network (RCNN) and GCN. The combination of GCN and RCNN ensures that the embeddings are propagated together with the relations relevant to the question, and thus better answers. The proposed graph summarization technique can be used to tackle the issue that KGQAs cannot answer questions with an uncertain number of answers. In this paper, we demonstrated the proposed technique on the most common type of questions, which is single-relation questions. Experiments have demonstrated that the proposed graph summarization technique using RCNN and GCN can provide better results when compared to the GCN. The proposed graph summarization technique significantly improves the recall of actual answers when the questions have an uncertain number of answers.

Keywords: Question answering · Knowledge graph · Graph summarization · Graph convolutional network · Recurrent convolutional neural network

© Springer Nature Switzerland AG 2021
T. Mantoro et al. (Eds.): ICONIP 2021, LNCS 13111, pp. 489–500, 2021.
https://doi.org/10.1007/978-3-030-92273-3_40

1   Introduction

Question Answering (QA) is a traditional task in Natural Language Processing (NLP). In order for the QA system to work effectively, it is necessary to precisely understand the meaning of the natural language question and select the most appropriate answers from various background information. There are two main branches in the QA system: QA over Knowledge Graphs (KGs) (KGQA) and QA over documents. Compared to QA over documents, KGQA could provide more comprehensive answers: for a given question, the answer may come from various resources in the KGQA [5]. Thereby, KGQA becomes an important topic and attracts much attention recently [4, 7, 17, 19, 20, 24]. A KG is a directed graph with real-world entities as nodes and their relations as edges [7]. In the KG, each directed edge, along with its head entity and tail entity, constitutes a triple, i.e., (head entity, relation, tail entity).

The key idea of recent KGQAs is to represent questions and entities/relations as low-dimensional vectors or embeddings [7]. Knowledge Graph Embedding (KGE) aims to learn a low-dimensional vector for each relation/entity in a KG, such that the original relation features are well preserved in the vectors [7]. These learned vectors have been employed to complete many KGQAs efficiently because they can predict missing links between entities [7, 12, 17]. However, these shallow KGEs are limited to their expressiveness [23]. Therefore, some KGQAs [12, 15, 16] have used deep learning methods, such as Long Short-Term Memory (LSTM), to represent relations/entities in a KG. Nevertheless, all these KGQAs process each triple independently, i.e., they cannot capture semantically rich neighbourhoods and hence produce low-quality embeddings [2].

Recently, Graph Convolutional Network (GCN) has been widely adopted for graph embedding due to its excellent performance and high interpretability [8]. GCN is a multi-layer neural network operating on graph-structural data. GCN models relevant information about node's neighbourhoods as a low-dimensional feature vector [8]. Unlike KGE or other deep learning methods, GCN well preserves the structural relation features and semantic neighbour features in the vectors [13]. As reported in the literature, the effectiveness of GCN is the main motivation for this paper to investigate its usage as the graph embedding technique in KGQAs.

Applying GCNs to KGQAs has three significant challenges. Firstly, simple GCNs are inefficient in KGQAs because GCNs treat all relations equally when aggregating neighbourhoods for each target node [2]. However, in most cases, it should be anticipated that the entity embeddings are propagated more along with the relations relevant to the question to provide a more relevant answer. Secondly, a relation often has various expressions in natural language questions, posing an additional challenge in question analysis [7]. For instance, the relation "person.nationality" can be expressed as "what is ...'s nationality", "which country is ... from", "where is ... from", etc. Thirdly, most current KGQAs cannot effectively answer questions with multiple entities or when there is an uncertain number of answers. They assume that a question only has one entity and could be answered by a single entity [1]. Nevertheless, a question could be *"Which films are co-acted by Vin Diesel and Paul Walker?"*. It requires the KGQA to identify two entities and return a series of films. Answering such questions requires more knowledge of the relations [1]. Some GCN-based KGQAs [19,20] answer such questions using a binary classifier, which sometimes could miss some correct answers or predict additional incorrect answers. The most popular solution is to predict answers based on the *softmax* function [4,7,24]. The softmax function assigns scores to all candidates, and then KGQAs select candidates whose scores are close to the highest score within a certain margin. The challenge here is to set a proper margin for every question because the number of answers could be uncertain.

Through analyzing the above three challenges, we propose a Graph Summarization based KGQA (GS-KGQA). GS-KGQA combines GCN with Recurrent Convolutional Neural Network (RCNN) to solve the first two challenges. RCNN has already been successfully used in text classification [9]. In our work, RCNN is used to classify a given question, and to predict the probabilities of all relations. These predicted probabilities are the relational weights used in the variant of the GCN used in this paper. This combination ensures that embeddings are propagated more along with edges relevant to the question, i.e., by propagating relations with high probabilities to ensure that the answer provided is the most relevant. The RCNN also converts the relation analysis of questions to the classification task. We propose two graph summarization algorithms to solve the third challenge; one used for questions with a single entity and another used for questions with multiple entities. Our graph summarization algorithms group candidate answers into one node prior to the softmax function.

In this paper, we demonstrated the proposed graph summarization algorithms on the most common type of questions, which is single-relation questions [7]. Single-relation questions contain only one relation. In summary, the contributions in this paper are:

1. The proposed GS-KGQA system combines GCN and RCNN to ensure that the embeddings can propagate along with the desire relations relevant to the question.
2. The proposed GS-KGQA system with the proposed graph summarization algorithms are investigated for the single-relation KGQA task and to address the issue of an uncertain number of answers. This is further investigated for single-relation questions with multiple entities.
3. Assess the effectiveness of GS-KGQA over baselines using four benchmark datasets.

2   Related Works

Among many recent deep learning tasks [6,10,11,14,25], KGQA is one of the most important area. A series of work [7,12,17] have been performed in KGE to learn the low-dimensional representations of entities and relations in a KG as follows. Huang et al. [7] jointly recovered the question's head entity, relation, and tail entity representations in the KGE spaces. Saxena et al. [17] took KGQA as a link prediction task and incorporated ComplEx, a KGE method, to help predict the answer. However, these shallow KGE models are limited to their expressiveness [23]. Later, deep learning embedding-based KGQAs [12,15,16] have been proposed to capture the expressive features with efficient parameter operators. Yunqiu et al. [16] utilized a bidirectional Gated Recurrent Unit (GRU) to project questions and relations/entities into the same space. However, they process each triple independently and produce low-quality embeddings [2].

Many GCN-based KGQAs have been proposed to capture both semantic features and structural features in entity embeddings [4,19,20,24]. Nicola et al. [4] explored the structural features of GCN to find missing links between entities. Instead of embedding the whole knowledge graph, Sun et al. [19,20] extracted question-related subgraphs and then updated node embeddings by a single-layer GCN. They selected answers based on binary classifiers. Zhang et al. [24] integrated question information into the subgraph node embedding to obtain the node presentation with question dependency. However, simple GCNs ignore the edge labels in the graph [2]. Few efforts have been given to the questions with an uncertain number of answers. It is therefore one of the objectives of this paper to investigate this challenge.

3   GS-KGQA: Proposed Method

3.1   GS-KGQA Overview

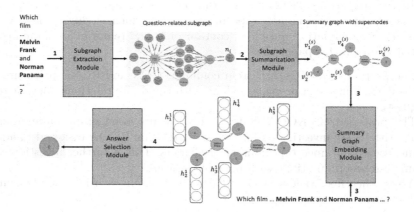

Fig. 1. The overview of GS-KGQA

The framework of the proposed GS-KGQA is illustrated in Fig. 1. It consists of four modules. They are introduced from Sect. 3.2 to Sect. 3.5.

3.2   Subgraph Extraction Module

This module finds the question-related subgraph from the KG. It identifies which entities are mentioned in a given question and links the entities to the KG. Named Entity Recognition (NER) identifies mentions in the text. After comparing some NER methods, we selected spaCy[1] for its quick and straightforward implementation. Then, all triples containing the identified entities are extracted from the movie KG to form the question-related subgraph. Note that this module could be replaced by any advanced NER methods.

3.3   Subgraph Summarization Module

The subgraph summarization module groups the question-related subgraph to a summary graph. In this paper, we highlight that single-relation questions could involve multiple entities. Different graph summarization algorithms are proposed for questions with a single entity and with multiple entities, respectively. Note that we call the entity mentioned in a given question as *question entity*; the node directly linked with a node is called *neighbour*.

The algorithm for questions with a single entity is presented in Algorithm 1. Neighbours linked with the question entity by the same relation are aggregated into one supernode. Note that one neighbour might be grouped into different supernodes.

Algorithm 1: Algorithm for questions with a single entity

Input: A question-related subgraph $G = < V, E, R >$ from the subgraph extraction module; the question entity v_c. V is the node set, E is the edge set and R is the relation set.

Output: A summary graph $G_s = < V_s, E_s, R >$

1 **for** r_i *in* R **do**
2     $supernode = \text{set}()$;
3   **for** *neighbour* v_i *of* v_c **do**
4   **if** v_i *and* v_c *is linked by* r_i **then**
5           $supernode.\text{add}(v_i)$
6   **end**
7   **end**
8     $V_s.\text{add}(supernode)$
9 **end**

The algorithm for questions with multiple entities is based on relations and intersection sets, illustrated in Fig. 2. It first categorizes neighbours of question entities based on relations. For example, it categorizes three neighbours (1, 5 and 6) of Entity C into "written_by (1, 6)" and "directed_by (1, 5)". Then, the algorithm finds the intersection node set for each relation. The intersection

---

[1] https://spacy.io/.

node set would be a supernode and the rest would be another supernodes. For example, the intersection node set for relation "written_by" is (1, 6) so Entity B has two neighbours linked by relation "written_by": (1, 6) and (4, 7). In this case, the summary graph in Fig. 2b is capable of answering questions "who directed movie A, movie B and movie C?" and "who wrote movie A, movie B and movie C?" with different entity representations. How GS-KGQA represents supernodes in the summary graph is introduced in the next section.

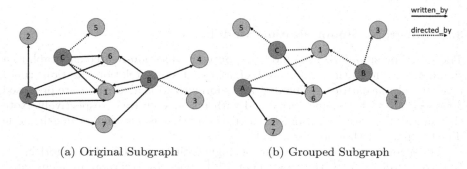

(a) Original Subgraph   (b) Grouped Subgraph

Fig. 2. An example of grouping subgroup with three question entities: A, B and C; nodes in yellow are people and green nodes are movies

3.4 Summary Graph Embedding Module

Given a question and the summary graph, this module embeds each supernode $v_i^{(s)}$ in the summary graph to a fixed dimension vector. This is done by using a single-layer variant GCN with RCNN. RCNN uses a recurrent structure to capture contextual information and a max-pooling layer to capture the key components in texts. In our work, the RCNN's input is a question, and the outputs are the probabilities of the question belonging to all relations. The probabilities are then passed to the GCN as relational weights. As a result, the final representations of supernodes take the simple form:

$$h_i^1 = \frac{h_i^0 + \sum_{j \in N_i^r} h_j^0 * w_r}{1 + |N_i^r|} \tag{1}$$

where h_i^1 represents $v_i^{(s)}$'s final representation; h_i^0 is $v_i^{(s)}$'s initialisation; w_r is the relational weight from RCNN; N_i^r contains all neighbours linked with relation r. $v_i^{(s)}$'s initialisation is:

$$h_i^0 = \frac{\sum_{n_j \in v_i^{(s)}} t_j}{|v_i^{(s)}|} \tag{2}$$

where n_j is the j-th member in the supernode $v_i^{(s)}$; t_j is n_j''s representation. To take additional semantic information into account, t_j is the word vector.

3.5   Answer Selection Module

Given a question and the summary graph embedding, the answer selection module selects one supernode that best answers the question. This is achieved by estimating probabilities of a supernode $v_i^{(s)}$ given the question embedding:

$$answer = \max_i(P(v_i^{(s)}|q)) = \max_i(softmax(\mathbf{H} \cdot LSTM(q))) \qquad (3)$$

where q is the question, $\mathbf{H}$ is a matrix whose each row represents the final representation h_i^1, $P(v_i^{(s)}|q)$ means the probability of supernode $v_i^{(s)}$ being an answer given the question q, symbol "·" is the dot product.

4   Experiments

We evaluated the effectiveness and robustness of the proposed GS-KGQA on widely adopted KGQA benchmarks. In this section, we aim to investigate the effectiveness of the proposed GS-KGQA when compared with other KGQA baselines. As the proposed GS-KGQA has two main areas: graph summarization algorithms and graph embedding, we also investigate the impact of these two proposals and how they impact the GS-KGQA system as a whole.

4.1   Datasets

We investigated four popular and publicly available KGQA datasets: WikiMovies,[2] WebQuestionsSP,[3] WC2014[4] and SimpleQuestions.[5] SimpleQuestions was abandoned because all questions only have one answer, which cannot show the effectiveness of our graph summarization algorithms. For the other three datasets, there are over 60% of questions with multiple answers. Also, entity linking for SimpleQuestions replies on the Freebase API, which is no longer available. We did not find any single-relation KGQA dataset containing questions with multiple entities, so we created a dataset called Two-Entity WikiMovies from the original WikiMovies dataset.

1. **WikiMovies** is a popular dataset of single-relation KGQA with 96k questions. Its KG is from the movie domain, including 43k entities, nine predicates, and 135k triples.
2. **WebQuestionsSP** has a smaller scale of questions but a larger scale of KG. It contains thousands of natural language questions based on Freebase,[6] which has millions of entities and triples. Its questions are either single-relation or multi-relation. We used the single-relation questions.

---

[2] https://research.fb.com/downloads/babi/.
[3] https://www.microsoft.com/en-us/download/details.aspx?id=52763.
[4] https://github.com/zmtkeke/IRN.
[5] https://github.com/davidgolub/SimpleQA/tree/master/datasets/SimpleQuestions.
[6] https://developers.google.com/freebase.

3. **WC2014** is from the football domain and based on the KG about football players participating in FIFA World Cup 2014. Its KG has 6k triples, 1k entities and ten predicates.
4. **Two-Entity WikiMovies** was created from WikiMovies. We used regular expressions to learn the question patterns from WikiMovies. It contains 14k questions and uses the same KG as WikiMovies.

4.2   Setup

GS-KGQA was implemented using Python, Pytorch and Neo4j. Neo4j is a Java-based open-source graph database. Neo4j provides query language, Cypher, to access data. All entities and predicates were initialised by self-trained word2vec vectors. We crawled the first paragraphs on Wikipedia for all entities. These paragraphs were used to train word vectors. We tuned the following hyperparameters with grid search: (1) the hidden size for LSTM ([100, 150, 200]); (2) learning rate ([0.01, 0.001, 0.0001]); (2) the word dimension ([100, 150, 200]). As a result, we set hidden size = 100, learning rate = 0.01 for the Stochastic Gradient Descent (SGD) optimizer and dimension = 150.

4.3   Effectiveness of GS-KGQA

We now answered the first research question asked at the beginning of this section, i.e., how effective is GS-KGQA. We included six KGQA baselines:

- KV-Mem (2016) [15] used the key-value memory to store knowledge and conducted QA by iteratively reading the memory. This work released Wiki-Movies.
- GRAFT-Nets (2018) [20] extracted a question-related subgraph from the entire KG with heuristics and then used variant GCN to predict the answer.
- EmbedKGQA (2020) [17] took KGQA as a link prediction task and incorporated KGE with Bert to predict the answer.
- SRN (2020) [16] was based on reinforcement learning. It leveraged beam search to reduce the number of candidates.
- TransferNet (2021) [18] computed activated scores for relations in relation analysis.
- QA2MN (2021) [12] dynamically focused on different parts of the questions in question analysis using a memory network. It used KGE to embed the KG.

As shown in the introduction above, all the baselines have taken advantage of popular techniques, such as Bert, KGE, GCN and reinforcement learning, to advance their methods. For WikiMovies and WC2014, we used their results reported in the corresponding papers or the authors' implementations. Note that we used single-relation questions in WebQuestions as introduced in Sect. 4.1; hence, we run the single-relation WebQuestions on their implementations for those that provided source codes publicly. The performances of the different methods are listed in Table 1.

Table 1. Performance of baselines on all datasets (hits@1)

Model	Dataset			
	WikiMovies	Two-Entity WikiMovies	WebQuestionsSP	WC2014
KV-Mem	93.9	–	31.3	87.0
GRAFT-Nets	96.8	–	56.2	98.5
EmbedKGQA	97.5	–	80.7	98.2
SRN	97.0	–	–	**98.9**
TransferNet	97.5	–	–	–
QA2MN	–	–	–	98.6
GS-KGQA	**98.2**	**97.6**	**84.6**	98.2

From the results in Table 1, we have three observations. First, the proposed system GS-KGQA outperforms all the baselines on WikiMovies and WebQuestionsSP. GS-KGQA achieves similar hits@1 with other baselines on WC2014. Second, most models performed badly on WebQuestionsSP because WebQuestionsSP has a relatively small number of training examples but uses a large KG. It makes the model training much harder, but GS-KGQA can still achieve a 3.9% improvement when compared to EmbedKGQA. Third, the hits@1 on Two-Entity WikiMovies demonstrates that the proposed GS-KGQA could help the QA task on questions with multi-entities, which is hardly addressed by previous works. Therefore, no comparison can be performed to other baseline techniques.

4.4 Impact of the Graph Summarization Algorithms

We now study how much could our proposed graph summarization algorithms contribute to the whole system. We found that all baselines tend to predict only one answer. It suggests that it is necessary to study questions with an uncertain number of answers. Our graph summarization algorithms were proposed to fill this gap.

We first validated the robustness of our graph summarization algorithms, i.e., if our graph summarization algorithms can group nodes correctly. Then, we wrote Cypher snippets to query the members of each supernode from the KG. Finally, we compared the members with the generated supernodes from our algorithms. All datasets achieve 100% accuracy, which is because our algorithms can be treated as a set of reliable rules.

We then conducted an ablation test and a comparison test to show the contribution of our graph summarization algorithms. We extracted questions with multiple answers (at least two answers) from all datasets and compared the hits@1 and the recall of actual answers on hits@1. The performance of GS-KGQA when not using graph summarization algorithms (denoted as GS-KGQA_noGS) and the performance of baselines when testing on questions with multiple answers are shown in Table 2. From the results, we have two major observations. First,

Table 2. This table shows the results (hits@1/recall) on questions with multiple answers

Model	WikiMovies	WC2014	WebQuestionsSP	Two-Entity WikiMovies
KV-Mem	95.1/24.5	88.1/19.7	31.0/6.2	–
GRAFT-Nets	97.2/26.0	97.6/26.3	54.8/17.8	–
EmbedKGQA	96.2/25.0	97.9/27.1	83.5/39.6	–
GS-KGQA_noGS	96.3/25.0	98.0/27.3	82.3/38.7	97.7/26.1
GS-KGQA	96.6/89.7	98.4/98.5	81.1/87.1	97.6/98.7

GS-KGQA_noGS achieves similar hits@1 to GS-KGQA. It means that other modules in GS-KGQA are robust. Second, GS-KGQA has similar hits@1 performance with other baselines, but GS-KGQA significantly outperforms the recall. It indicates that the critical role of our graph summarization algorithms is to solve the multi-answer issue, which meets one of the objectives of this paper.

In summary, our graph summarization algorithms convert a multi-label multi-class classification problem to a unary label multi-class classification. The prediction of GS-KGQA may happen to be a supernode containing all answers. Our graph summarization algorithm's robustness and the greater recall boost help GS-KGQA to answer questions with an uncertain number of answers.

4.5   Impact of the Graph Embedding

To study how much could the RCNN contribute to the proposed GS-KGQA and whether it can be done without the RCNN, we included an ablation test. The performance of GS-KGQA when not using the RCNN is denoted as GS-KGQA_noRCNN. To further validate if the variant GCN helps in the graph embedding, we replaced GCN with three scalable KGE methods in the comparison: TransE [3], TransH [22] and ComplEx [21].

From the results in Table 3, we have three major observations. First, GCN +RCNN beats KGE+RCNN in all datasets. Our variant GCN could achieve better performance than KGE because our variant GCN tends to aggregate information from direct neighbours. It is more suitable for the single-relation KGQA. Additionally, our variant GCN was initialised with semantic information. It helps GS-KGQA analyse answers based on both semantic and structural spaces; however, KGE is only in the structural space. Second, GS-KGQA_noRCNN still outperforms KGE-based GS-KGQA in some datasets. For example, GS-KGQA_noRCNN achieves 12% improvement when GS-KGQA is based on ComplEx in Two-Entity WikiMovies. It further validates the robustness of our GCN. Third, RCNN indeed could improve the performance of GS-KGQA in all datasets. GS-KGQA achieves 16%, 5.9%, 7.4%, 3.5% higher hits@1 compared to GS-KGQA_noRCNN.

In summary, the great improvement of GS-KGQA compared to GS-KGQA _noRCNN confirms that the relation analysis of the single-relation KGQA could be converted to the classification task. Moreover, assigning the classification probabilities to the GCN would enhance the embedding quality.

Table 3. Comparison among variants; the statistics are hits@1

Model	Dataset			
	WikiMovies	WebQuestionsSP	WC2014	Two-Entity WikiMovies
GS-KGQA_noRCNN	82.2	78.7	90.8	94.1
GS-KGQA	**98.2**	**84.6**	**98.2**	**97.6**
GS-KGQA_TransE	62.9	55.4	62.7	61.2
GS-KGQA_TransH	73.2	60.1	75.8	74.2
GS-KGQA_ComplEx	83.3	65.4	86.9	82.1

5 Conclusion

In this paper, a system GS-KGQA system has been proposed to answer single-relation questions. GS-KGQA combines GCN with RCNN to ensure that embeddings are propagated more along with edges relevant to the question. The RCNN converts the relation analysis of single-relation questions to the classification task. GS-KGQA utilizes graph summarization algorithms to tackle the issue that traditional KGQAs cannot answer questions with multiple entities and an uncertain number of answers. Experiment results showed GS-KGQA's effectiveness, which beats the hits@1 of all baselines by 0.7% and 3.9% on the best comparison baseline technique on WikiMovies and WebQuestionsSP, respectively. This paper also showed the importance of the use of the proposed graph summarization algorithms and the use of RCNN in the graph embedding in the proposed GS-KGQA.

References

1. Aghaebrahimian, A.: Hybrid deep open-domain question answering. In: Proceedings of the 8th Language and Technology Conference (LTC) (2017)
2. Arora, S.: A survey on graph neural networks for knowledge graph completion. arXiv preprint arXiv:2007.12374 (2020)
3. Bordes, A., Usunier, N., Garcia-Duran, A., Weston, J., Yakhnenko, O.: Translating embeddings for modeling multi-relational data. In: NIPS, pp. 1–9 (2013)
4. De Cao, N., Aziz, W., Titov, I.: Question answering by reasoning across documents with graph convolutional networks. arXiv preprint arXiv:1808.09920 (2018)
5. Deng, L., Liu, Y.: Deep Learning in Natural Language Processing. Springer, Singapore (2018). https://doi.org/10.1007/978-981-10-5209-5
6. Goh, O.S., Wong, K.W., Fung, C.C., Depickere, A.: Towards a more natural and intelligent interface with embodied conversation agent (2006)
7. Huang, X., Zhang, J., Li, D., Li, P.: Knowledge graph embedding based question answering. In: Proceedings of the Twelfth ACM International Conference on Web Search and Data Mining, pp. 105–113. ACM (2019)
8. Kipf, T.N., Welling, M.: Semi-supervised classification with graph convolutional networks. arXiv preprint arXiv:1609.02907 (2016)
9. Lai, S., Xu, L., Liu, K., Zhao, J.: Recurrent convolutional neural networks for text classification. In: Twenty-Ninth AAAI Conference on Artificial Intelligence (2015)

10. Li, D., et al.: TSPNet: hierarchical feature learning via temporal semantic pyramid for sign language translation. In: Advances in Neural Information Processing Systems, vol. 33 (2020)

11. Li, D., Yu, X., Xu, C., Petersson, L., Li, H.: Transferring cross-domain knowledge for video sign language recognition. In: Proceedings of the IEEE/CVF Conference on Computer Vision and Pattern Recognition, pp. 6205–6214 (2020)

12. Li, X., Alazab, M., Li, Q., Yu, K., Yin, Q.: Question-aware memory network for multi-hop question answering in human-robot interaction. arXiv preprint arXiv:2104.13173 (2021)

13. Li, Z., Liu, H., Zhang, Z., Liu, T., Xiong, N.N.: Learning knowledge graph embedding with heterogeneous relation attention networks. IEEE Trans. Neural Netw. Learn. Syst., 1–13 (2021). https://doi.org/10.1109/TNNLS.2021.3055147

14. Liu, Y., et al.: Invertible denoising network: a light solution for real noise removal. In: Proceedings of the IEEE/CVF Conference on Computer Vision and Pattern Recognition, pp. 13365–13374 (2021)

15. Miller, A., Fisch, A., Dodge, J., Karimi, A.H., Bordes, A., Weston, J.: Key-value memory networks for directly reading documents. arXiv preprint arXiv:1606.03126 (2016)

16. Qiu, Y., Wang, Y., Jin, X., Zhang, K.: Stepwise reasoning for multi-relation question answering over knowledge graph with weak supervision. In: Proceedings of the 13th International Conference on Web Search and Data Mining, pp. 474–482 (2020)

17. Saxena, A., Tripathi, A., Talukdar, P.: Improving multi-hop question answering over knowledge graphs using knowledge base embeddings. In: Proceedings of the 58th Annual Meeting of the Association for Computational Linguistics, pp. 4498–4507 (2020)

18. Shi, J., Cao, S., Hou, L., Li, J., Zhang, H.: TransferNet: an effective and transparent framework for multi-hop question answering over relation graph. arXiv preprint arXiv:2104.07302 (2021)

19. Sun, H., Bedrax-Weiss, T., Cohen, W.W.: PullNet: open domain question answering with iterative retrieval on knowledge bases and text. arXiv preprint arXiv:1904.09537 (2019)

20. Sun, H., Dhingra, B., Zaheer, M., Mazaitis, K., Salakhutdinov, R., Cohen, W.W.: Open domain question answering using early fusion of knowledge bases and text. arXiv preprint arXiv:1809.00782 (2018)

21. Trouillon, T., Welbl, J., Riedel, S., Gaussier, É., Bouchard, G.: Complex embeddings for simple link prediction. In: International Conference on Machine Learning, pp. 2071–2080. PMLR (2016)

22. Wang, Z., Zhang, J., Feng, J., Chen, Z.: Knowledge graph embedding by translating on hyperplanes. In: Proceedings of the AAAI Conference on Artificial Intelligence, vol. 28 (2014)

23. Xie, Z., Zhou, G., Liu, J., Huang, X.: ReInceptionE: relation-aware inception network with joint local-global structural information for knowledge graph embedding. In: Proceedings of the 58th Annual Meeting of the Association for Computational Linguistics, pp. 5929–5939 (2020)

24. Zhang, J., Pei, Z., Xiong, W., Luo, Z.: Answer extraction with graph attention network for knowledge graph question answering. In: 2020 IEEE 6th International Conference on Computer and Communications (ICCC), pp. 1645–1650. IEEE (2020)

25. Zhu, D., Wong, K.W.: An evaluation study on text categorization using automatically generated labeled dataset. Neurocomputing **249**, 321–336 (2017)

Multi-stage Hybrid Attentive Networks for Knowledge-Driven Stock Movement Prediction

Jiaying Gong and Hoda Eldardiry[✉]

Virginia Tech, Blacksburg, USA
{gjiaying,hdardiry}@vt.edu

Abstract. Stock trend prediction is challenging due to complex stock behavior including high volatility. Leveraging an additional source of information, such as social media, can improve predictions, social media data is highly unstructured. To address these challenges, we propose a Multi-Stage TCN-LSTM Hybrid Attentive Network (MSHAN), which utilizes historical stock data with selected technical indicators and weighted social media information to predict daily stock movement. MSHAN uses a multi-stage architecture and hybrid neural networks to capture long-range sequential context dependencies of time-series data and unstructured textual information. We present results using extensive experiments on the actual market public dataset StockNet and demonstrate that MSHAN outperforms other baselines and can successfully predict the directional movement of daily stock prices. The ablation study results show the effectiveness of each component of MSHAN. The market simulation analysis suggests that the application of MSHAN can enhance trading profits.

Keywords: Stock prediction · Multi-stage · Hybrid neural networks · Attention mechanism · Feature selection

1 Introduction

Stock price movement prediction is a challenging time-series forecasting problem because of the noisy and non-stationary nature of financial data [1]. Investors can make profits from correct market predictions. Therefore, an accurate and reliable forecasting model can yield great profit for investors. Conventional research focused on technical analysis by taking market time-series data as input and using statistical or machine learning models to make predictions. These conventional methods suffer from a major limiting assumption that future market behavior is based on past market behavior. Thereby, not considering external information in cases when the market reacts to new signals or sudden unexpected events.

Fundamental analysis methods that consider relations between stock data and textual information from social media, additionally leverage social media data. These methods extract factors that may influence the market using natural language processing techniques. However, existing works (Sect. 2) mainly focus on jointly learning original historical stock data (without considering other technical

© Springer Nature Switzerland AG 2021
T. Mantoro et al. (Eds.): ICONIP 2021, LNCS 13111, pp. 501–513, 2021.
https://doi.org/10.1007/978-3-030-92273-3_41

indicators) and social media data (about individual events) to predict stock price movement. These methods encode daily social media text (without considering sequential context dependencies) and combine it with the stock data to make the final predictions. Previous research on time-series prediction showed that Temporary Convolutional Networks (TCN) outperform traditional neural networks [2], fusing different neural network models outperforms single models [3,4], and multi-stage networks outperform single-stage ones [5]. Motivated by these works, we propose a Multi-Stage Hybrid Attentive Networks (MSHAN) model, a multi-stage TCN-LSTM hybrid model with an attention mechanism for stock forecasting. The TCN-LSTM further encode long-range sequential dependencies by decaying influence of older data. Further, the multi-stage TCN-BiLSTM captures several events over long-range daily event dependencies using a weighted averaged representation over several days from textual data by decaying influence of older events. The main contributions can be summarized:

- To the best of our knowledge, MSHAN is the first method to utilize multi-stage TCN-LSTM with attention mechanism for stock movement prediction. In particular, it captures long-range different event dependencies of unstructured textual information and sequential dependencies of time-series data.
- A feature selection pipeline is used to select golden technical indicators.
- Extensive experiments explore the performance of each component of MSHAN, confirming improvements over several state-of-the-art methods.

2   Related Work

Approaches to forecasting short-term stock price movement can be classified based on the information used for prediction. One approach is technical analysis (TA), relying on past stock price, volume, and related trading data. Another approach is fundamental analysis (FA), taking external unstructured data as input, such as company financial reports, news articles, tweets, etc.

Technical analysis has a long history, dating back to at least the 1930s [6]. TA typically relies only on numerical features such as past prices [7,8] and macroeconomic indicators [9,10]. A recent trend in technical analysis for stock prediction incorporates neural network approaches. For example, Recurrent Neural Networks (RNN) are used to analyze interactions and hidden patterns of dynamic stock data [11,12]. Deep Neural Networks (DNN) are also used for stock prediction [13,14]. Transfer learning is used by tuning a pre-trained model and transferring parameters to the prediction model [15]. Adversarial training addresses the stochastic challenge when only stock price is used as input features [16]. Although these approaches leverage large amounts of data, they omit potentially useful information such as rich textual data. This leads to a missed opportunity of improving forecasting by leveraging additional 'soft' information not fully represented in or extracted from quantitative trading data [17].

Fundamental analysis methods address connections between historical stock information and social media news, indicating that stock markets are highly influenced by public events, which can be extracted from multiple social media sources. Work in natural language processing (NLP) from sources such as news [18] and social media [19–22] shows the merit of FA in capturing hard-to-quantify aspects of company performance and market sentiment that TA-based methods fail to account for. With the development of attention mechanism on neural networks [23] such as Long short-term memory (LSTM) networks [24], attention layers are added to help capture important information from text [25, 26]. Powered by graph neural networks, some works use knowledge graph data to augment prediction performance with inter-stock relations [22, 27, 28]. However, such approaches do not considered multiple sequential event dependencies that differently influence stock price. In contrast, inspired by multi-stage architectures [5], where each stage features many dilated temporal convolutions to generate an initial prediction that is refined by the next stage, our proposed model can capture long-range sequential dependencies of time-series data and event relations of textual information.

3   Proposed Approach

In this section, we introduce an overview of the proposed Multi-Stage Hybrid Attentive Network (MSHAN) method. MSHAN consists of three parts: Data Preprocessing Pipeline, Stock Encoder and Social Media Information Encoder.

3.1   Problem Definition

The main objective of MSHAN is to learn relevant information jointly from both historical stock technical indicators and social media information. We formulate stock movement prediction as a binary classification problem. Thus, we formalize movement between the adjusted closing prices of stock s based on the difference of trading day d and $d - 1$ [21]. Given a stock $s \in S$, its corresponding technical indicators s_{ti} and social media information from tweets over a lookback window of size T from $[t - T, t - 1]$, we define the stock price movement of day t as:

$$Y_t = \begin{cases} 0 & p_d^c < p_{d-1}^c \\ 1 & p_d^c \geq p_{d-1}^c \end{cases} \tag{1}$$

where p_d^c indicates adjusted closing price of a given stock on day t [29]. 1 indicates the price is increasing whereas 0 indicates the price is decreasing.

3.2   Data Preprocessing

Feature Selection. Technical Analysis shows that historical stock information is a strong indicator of future trends [30]. Following Technical Analysis Library[1], we develop sixty-four additional technical indicators based on the six features (open, close, high, low, volume, adjusted close). Note that considering all technical indicators as model inputs cause noise and complexity. We implement various feature selection methods to select the gold features to reduce computational time, improve predictions and provide a better understanding of the data [31].

---

[1] https://technical-analysis-library-in-python.readthedocs.io/en/latest/.

We use L1 Regularization [32] (L1) and Model-Based Ranking (MBR) to select golden features from all technical indicators. L1 penalizes models with L1 norm as they deliver sparse solutions leading to many coefficients or weights having a value of zero. It acts as both a form of shrinkage estimator and a variable selection tool. As a result, a subset of coefficients will receive nonzero weight. MBR is a filtering method that selects features based on variable importance ranking on training data. We apply random forest (RF) classification, which fits various decision tree classifiers on different subsets of data, to select features. RF is more robust as it uses averaging to improve accuracy and avoid overfitting.

Normalization. The input of the stock encoder is set as the original six features along with selected technical indicators as shown in Table 1. Since stock movement is not determined by the absolute price value, we normalize the raw price vector by following the Offset Translation and Amplitude Scaling normalization steps:

$$p_{in} = \frac{p_i - mean(p_i)}{std(p_i)} \tag{2}$$

where $p_i \in \mathbb{R}^{d_p}$ is the price vector on day i, p_{in} is the normalized value with the same length as p_i, $mean(\cdot)$ is the mean and $std(\cdot)$ is the standard deviation.

3.3   Stock Encoder

We introduce a multi-stage TCN-LSTM hybrid model which leverages two types of network architectures. The stock encoder shown in Fig. 1 illustrates how historical stock data is encoded to capture stock price feature p_t. The input of the stock encoder is the historical stock price along with selected technical indicators shown in Table 1. Next, we introduce the single-stage TCN-LSTM hybrid model, which is the main building block of the multi-stage stock encoder.

Table 1. Selected technical indicators

Momentum	Trend	Volume and others
Relative strength index	Commodity channel index	Negative volume index
True strength index	Mass index	Cumulative return
Stochastic RSI	Average directional index (+DI)	
Stochastic oscillator	Average directional index (−DI)	
Stochastic oscillator signal		
Williams R		

Single-Stage TCN-LSTM. The single-stage TCN-LSTM consists of temporal convolutional layers and long short-term memory layers. Single-stage TCN-LSTM is built based on the TCN model [2]. The first layer of the single-stage TCN-LSTM is a convolutional layer that is included to adjusts the dimension of

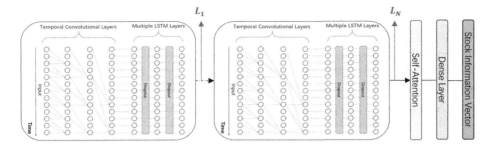

Fig. 1. An overview of the stock encoder.

the input features to match the number of feature maps. Several dilated layers with a dilation factor $d_l = 2^l$ are added after the convolutional layer.

For time-series sequence τ, that is the normalized price vector p_{in}, the dilated convolution operation on the j_{th} element is defined as:

$$D(\tau_j) = (\tau *_d F) = \sum_{m=0}^{k-1} F(m) * \tau_{\tau_j - m \cdot d}$$ (3)

where d indicates the dilation factor, k is the kernel size and $j - m \cdot d$ represents the direction of the past. Then, ReLU activation is added to the output of the previous layer. $\hat{H}_i^{(j,l)}$ and $H_i^{(j,l)}$ are results after adding the residual connection:

$$\hat{H}_i^{(j,l)} = ReLU(W_0 \cdot \hat{H}_{i-d}^{(j,l-1)} + b_0)$$ (4)

$$H_i^{(j,l)} = H_i^{(j,l-1)} + W_1 \cdot \hat{H}_i^{(j,l)} + b_1$$ (5)

where convolutions are applied over i and $i - d$, $W_n \in \mathbb{R}^{N_f \times N_f}$ denotes the weight of the dilated convolutional filters, $b_n \in \mathbb{R}^{N_f}$ is the bias vector for the residual block and N_f is the number of filters.

To further capture the sequential dependencies, we use the stacked LSTM layers on day i after the TCN layers:

$$h_i^p = LSTM^p(h_i^{(j,l)}, h_{i-1}^p) \qquad t - T \leq i \leq t$$ (6)

where $h_i^{(j,l)}$ is the output of the last layer of TCN and T is the window size.

Multi-stage TCN-LSTM. Multi-stage TCN-LSTM composes several single-stage TCN-LSTM models sequentially so that each model operates directly on the output of the previous one. The goal of stacking the single-stage TCN-LSTM models is to further refine the predictions from previous stages. In the multi-stage TCN-LSTM model, each stage takes an initial prediction from the previous stage and refines it. The input of the first stage is the normalized price vector:

$$Y^0 = p_{in}$$ (7)

$$Y^s = F(Y^{s-1}) \tag{8}$$

where Y^s is the output at stage s, and F is the single-stage TCN-LSTM discussed in Sect. 3.3. Using such a multi-stage architecture provides more sequential historical stock price information to predict the daily stock price movement.

Self Attention. The stock encoder uses an attention mechanism that is a form of additive attention [33]. The attention mechanism for processing time-series historical stock data aggregates all multi-stage TCN-LSTM hidden representations across each timestamp into an overall representation with learned adaptive weights. The self-attention mechanism context vector c_t is defined as:

$$\alpha_{t,i} = \frac{exp(score(\bar{h}_t, h_i))}{\sum_{i=1}^{T} exp(score(\bar{h}_t, h_i))} \tag{9}$$

$$c_t = \sum_i \alpha_{t,i} h_i \tag{10}$$

where $a_{t,i}$ indicates the learned attention weights for trading day i, score function can be expressed as: $\bar{h}_t \cdot W \cdot h_i$. W is the learnable parameter matrix, $\bar{h}_t$ is the concatenated hidden states of the last layer of the multi-stage TCN-LSTM.

3.4   Social Media Information Encoder

MSHAN uses a multi-stage TCN-BiLSTM encoder shown in Fig. 2 to extract social media features s_t from tweets. We first use the embedding layer to get the numerical representations of textual information. Then, we use a TCN-BiLISTM encoder to capture the weighted social media features.

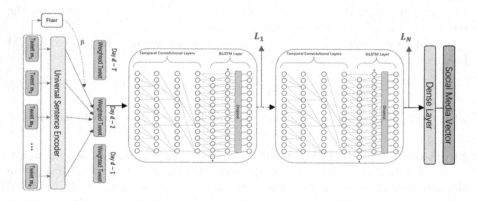

Fig. 2. An overview of the social media information encoder.

Tweet Embedding. Embeddings aim to map words from vocabulary to vectors of numerical forms. The representations are learned based on the usage of words, allowing sentences used in similar ways to result in having similar representations, naturally capturing syntactic and semantic meanings of the sentences. Previous work [22] show that sentence-level embeddings Universal Sentence Encoders (USE) [34] performs better than word-level embeddings GloVe [35] and BERT [36]. In this paper, we generate the tweet embedding vector by 512-dimension USE.

TCN-BiLSTM Encoder. There are a variable number of tweets $[t_{w1}, \cdots, t_{wk}]$ for each stock on day i. For each tweet, we first obtain a representation by Tweet Embedding layer as $[m_1, m_2, \cdots, m_k]$ where $m_j \in \mathbb{R}^D$ and k is the number of tweets per stock on day i. To get the representation of tweets for each stock within a day, we calculate the weighted average representation:

$$\bar{m}_i = \frac{\sum_{j=1}^{K} \beta \cdot m_j}{\sum \beta} \tag{11}$$

where β denotes the sentiment weight calculated by a pre-trained NLP sentiment analysis model Flair [37]. Then, we learn the social media information representation from the sequence of multiple days by the TCN-BiLSTM hybrid model. The TCN layers are same as Eqs. 3–5 The bidirectional LSTM layer is added after TCN layers to get social media information feature vector h_i^s:

$$h_i^s = BiLSTM^s(h_i^{(j,l)}, h_{i-1}^s) \qquad t - T \leq i \leq t \tag{12}$$

where $h_i^{(j,l)}$ is the output of the last layer of TCN. Similar to the stock encoder, we use a multi-stage TCN-BiLSTM to capture the dependencies between sequential events because the output of each stage is an initial prediction. Finally we blend stock features and textual information features. The output is:

$$x_t = ReLU(W \cdot (h_i^p \oplus h_i^s) + b) \tag{13}$$

where h_i^p is the stock information vector, h_i^s is social media information vector, $\oplus$ is the concatenation operation, W is the learnt weight matrix and b is the bias.

4   Experiments and Results

4.1   Dataset and Evaluation Metrics

We adopt the StockNet dataset [21] for the training and evaluation of MSHAN model. The stock data is the S&P 500 index from Yahoo Finance over a period ranging from 01/01/2014 to 01/01/2016. We use 70% of the data for training, 10% of the data for validation, and 20% of the data for testing. For social media news data, we use Twitter information provided by StockNet [21]. We align trading days by dropping samples that lack prices or tweets and further aligning the data across trading windows for related stocks. Following prior research for stock prediction [21, 22, 38], we use accuracy, F1 score, and Matthews correlation coefficient (MCC) as evaluation metrics. Compared to the F1 score, MCC is a more reliable evaluation method that produces a high score only if the prediction can obtain good results in all of the four confusion matrix categories.

4.2   Parameter Settings

We implement MSHAN with Tensorflow and optimize it with the Adam optimizer. The optimal learning rate α is selected within the range of $\{1e-4, 5e-4, 1e-5, 5e-5\}$ for minimizing the loss, the stage number s is selected from 1 to 5. The window size is 5, and the batch size is 32. The number of filters for TCN to use in the convolutional layers is 16, and the kernel size is 3. The hidden sizes of LSTM layers are 64, 32, and 16, respectively. The hidden size of BiLSTM is 16, and the USE embedding dimension is 512. We use dropout to control the capacity of neural networks to prevent overfitting and set the value to 0.3.

4.3   Baselines

We compare our proposed model MSHAN to several state-of-the-arts models. **ARIMA (TA):** Autoregressive Integrated Moving Average Model only uses historical stock prices [39]. **RNN (TA):** A general model is built on deep learning architectures using a sliding window [11]. **LSTM (TA):** A prediction model is built on the LSTM network with several TA indicators [12]. **ALSTM (TA):** A dual-stage attention-based RNN is used to make predictions by capturing the long-term temporal dependencies [40]. **Adv-ALSTM (TA):** Adversarial training is employed on neural network to improve the stock movement prediction [16]. **RandForest (FA):** Sentiment analysis and random forest classifier is applied to the tweets to study the relation between stock and tweets [19]. **TSLDA (FA):** Topic Sentiment Latent Dirichlet Allocation model is proposed to capture topics and sentiments from social media [20]. **GCN (FA):** A joint model via GCN is explored to model stock relations [27]. **StockNet (TA & FA):** StockNet uses a decoder with a variational architecture to jointly exploit price and textual information [21]. **HAN (FA):** A hybrid attention network is proposed to encode textual information in one day and across multiple days [18]. **HATS (FA):** A hierarchical attention network is proposed to weigh different relationships between stocks [28]. **MAN-SF (FA):** A multipronged attention network via GAN that jointly learns from historical price, textual information, and stock relations [22].

4.4   Results and Analysis

Model Comparison. Table 2 shows the performance of the compared methods discussed in Sect. 4.3 on the public testing dataset of StockNet. Note that the results of compared methods are reported by [16, 22] on the same StockNet dataset. They are all current state-of-the-art models. From Table 2, we observe that MSHAN achieves the best performance in Accuracy and MCC value. Compared with the strongest baseline MAN-SF, our proposed model has not used corporate relationships. However, it still achieves a better performance than MAN-SF. We conjecture that the multi-stage architecture helps capture the sequential context dependencies of both time-series data and textual information (different events). To further confirm our conjecture and explore the effect of each component, we conduct an ablation study in the following subsection.

Table 2. Results compared with other models. Best results are shown in **Bold**. TA and FA represents Technical Analysis and Fundamental Analysis, respectively.

	Model	Accuracy	F1	MCC
TA	ARIMA [39]	$0.514 \pm 1e{-}3$	$0.513 \pm 1e{-}3$	$-0.021 \pm 2e{-}3$
	RNN [11]	$0.530 \pm 5e{-}2$	$0.529 \pm 5e{-}2$	$-0.004 \pm 7e{-}2$
	LSTM [12]	$0.532 \pm 5e{-}1$	-	$0.067 \pm 5e{-}3$
	ALSTM [40]	$0.549 \pm 7e{-}1$	-	$0.104 \pm 7e{-}3$
	StockNet (TA) [21]	$0.550 \pm$ -	$0.546 \pm$ -	$0.017 \pm$ -
	Adv-ALSTM [16]	$0.572 \pm$ -	$0.570 \pm$ -	$0.148 \pm$ -
FA	RandForest [19]	$0.531 \pm 2e{-}3$	$0.527 \pm 2e{-}3$	$0.013 \pm 4e{-}3$
	TSLDA [20]	$0.541 \pm 6e{-}3$	$0.539 \pm 6e{-}3$	$0.065 \pm 7e{-}3$
	GCN [27]	$0.532 \pm 7e{-}3$	$0.530 \pm 7e{-}3$	$0.093 \pm 9e{-}3$
	StockNet (FA) [21]	$0.582 \pm$ -	$0.572 \pm$ -	$0.072 \pm$ -
	HAN [18]	$0.576 \pm 4e{-}3$	$0.572 \pm 4e{-}3$	$0.052 \pm 5e{-}3$
	HATS [28]	$0.562 \pm 2e{-}3$	$0.560 \pm 2e{-}3$	$0.117 \pm 6e{-}3$
	MAN-SF [22]	$0.608 \pm 2e{-}4$	$\mathbf{0.605 \pm 2e{-}4}$	$0.195 \pm 6e{-}4$
	MSHAN	$\mathbf{0.619 \pm 5e{-}3}$	$0.576 \pm 5e{-}3$	$\mathbf{0.223 \pm 7e{-}3}$

Ablation Study. To further illustrate the effectiveness of our proposed MSHAN, we carry out the ablation experiments in this subsection to explore the role of each module in MSHAN. The comparison results are shown in the Table 3.

From the table, we can observe that only using original features (high, low, open) gets the accuracy rate close to 50%, which is random chance. Adding all technical indicators slightly improves the performance. It is probably because that some technical indicators may not relevant to stock price movement, bringing the noise to the data. However, when feature selection is applied, the model performs much better than the model using original features or all technical indicators. We also observe that using a hybrid model (TCN-LSTM) with attention mechanism can improve performance to almost 1% of accuracy. Besides, the multi-stage architecture is effective in time-series prediction. When textual information and price signals are fused and multi-stage architecture is used to capture dependencies between sequential events, a performance gain is seen.

Table 3. Ablation study over MSHAN components.

Model component	Accuracy	F1	MCC
High + Low + Open	0.507	0.494	−0.021
All Technical Indicators	0.512	0.544	0.028
Feature Selection (FS)	0.530	0.597	0.050
FS + TCN-LSTM + Attention	0.537	0.609	0.061
FS + Multi-Stage TCN-LSTM + Attention	0.545	0.606	0.090
LSTM + Social Media Text	0.529	0.567	0.050
Multi-Stage TCN-BiLSTM + Weighted Social Media Text	0.562	0.582	0.117
MSHAN	**0.619**	0.576	**0.223**

Market Simulation. We conducted a stock market simulation following a similar simulation exercise by [41]. The analysis is intended to evaluate the potential profitability of applying our proposed model in a trading context. If the model predicts that the stock price will increase (decrease) the next day, purchase (sell short) $10,000 worth of the stock. After purchasing the stock, sell immediately if market conditions dictate that a profit of 1% ($100) or more can be made, which means we sell the stock any time when it reaches a profit of 1%. Otherwise, sell the stock at the closing price. After selling short the stock, buy it immediately if at a price 1% ($100) lower than shorted in order to cover. Otherwise, buy the stock at the closing price. Table 4 shows profit results for the best four and worst four companies' results based on daily profits. We observe that companies that make the most daily profits have higher accuracy and MCC values. Overall, investors can make more profits by using our trading method based on MSHAN.

Table 4. Market simulation performance. Due to limited space, we only report the best four and worst four companies' results based on daily profits.

	BAC	CAT	CSCO	NVS	AAPL	GE	MO	ORCL
Daily profits	2.41%	2.90%	4.67%	7.48%	−0.18%	−1.02%	−0.19%	−0.48%
Accuracy	0.633	0.643	0.622	0.571	0.571	0.588	0.548	0.588
MCC	0.327	0.154	0.231	0.249	0.175	0.147	0.091	0.105

5 Conclusion and Future Work

We propose MSHAN, multi-stage hybrid attentive networks with the attention mechanism to predict daily stock price movement. We first apply feature selection to select the most informative features as stock inputs and embedded tweets as textual information inputs. Then a multi-stage TCN-LSTM network is applied to capture long-range sequential context dependencies of unstructured textual information and time-series data. Experiments on actual market data demonstrate that our proposed model MSHAN can successfully predict directional stock price movement to an accuracy around 62%. The ablation study result shows the effectiveness (improvement on performance) of each component of multi-stage TCN-LSTM networks on stock movement prediction. A market simulation analysis suggests that the application of our method can enhance trading profit at most to 7.5% daily profits. In future work: (1) We will further use news information and company relations to capture the dynamic market better. (2) We plan to use transfer learning to implement the general model to new stocks.

References

1. Abu-Mostafa, Y.S., Atiya, A.F.: Introduction to financial forecasting. Appl. Intell. **6**, 205–213 (1996)
2. Bai, S., Kolter, J.Z., Koltun, V.: An empirical evaluation of generic convolutional and recurrent networks for sequence modeling (2018)
3. Lin, T., Guo, T., Aberer, K.: Hybrid neural networks for learning the trend in time series. In: IJCAI 2017, pp. 2273–2279 (2017)
4. Wang, J., Sun, T., Liu, B., Cao, Y., Zhu, H.: CLVSA: a convolutional LSTM based variational sequence-to-sequence model with attention for predicting trends of financial markets. Papers arXiv:2104.04041, arXiv.org, April 2021
5. Farha, Y.A., Gall, J.: MS-TCN: multi-stage temporal convolutional network for action segmentation. In: CVPR, pp. 3570–3579 (2019)
6. Cowles, A., Jones, H.E.: Some a posteriori probabilities in stock market action. Econometrica **5**(3), 280–294 (1937)
7. Kohli, P.P.S., Zargar, S., Arora, S., Gupta, P.: Stock prediction using machine learning algorithms. In: Malik, H., Srivastava, S., Sood, Y.R., Ahmad, A. (eds.) Applications of Artificial Intelligence Techniques in Engineering. AISC, vol. 698, pp. 405–414. Springer, Singapore (2019). https://doi.org/10.1007/978-981-13-1819-1_38
8. Nti, I.K., Adekoya, A., Weyori, B.: A comprehensive evaluation of ensemble learning for stock-market prediction. J. Big Data **7**, 20 (2020)
9. Dingli, A., Fournier, K.: Financial time series forecasting - a deep learning approach. Int. J. Mach. Learn. Comput. **7**(5), 118–122 (2017)
10. Hoseinzade, E., Haratizadeh, S., Khoeini, A.: U-CNNpred: a universal CNN-based predictor for stock markets (2019)
11. Selvin, S., Ravi, V., Gopalakrishnan, E., Menon, V., Kp, S.: Stock price prediction using LSTM, RNN and CNN-sliding window model, pp. 1643–1647, September 2017
12. Nelson, D., Pereira, A., de Oliveira, R.: Stock market's price movement prediction with LSTM neural networks, pp. 1419–1426, May 2017
13. Chen, H., Xiao, K., Sun, J., Wu, S.: A double-layer neural network framework for high-frequency forecasting. ACM Trans. Manage. Inf. Syst. **7**, 1–17 (2017)
14. Song, Y., Lee, J.W., Lee, J.: A study on novel filtering and relationship between input-features and target-vectors in a deep learning model for stock price prediction. Appl. Intell. **49**, 897–911 (2019)
15. Nguyen, T.-T., Yoon, S.: A novel approach to short-term stock price movement prediction using transfer learning. Appl. Sci. **9**(22), 4745 (2019)
16. Feng, F., Chen, H., He, X., Ding, J., Sun, M., Chua, T.-S.: Enhancing stock movement prediction with adversarial training. In: IJCAI (2019)

17. Tetlock, P.C., Saar-tsechansky, M., Macskassy, S.: More than words: Quantifying language to measure firms' fundamentals. J. Finan. **63**, 1437–1467 (2008)
18. Hu, Z., Liu, W., Bian, J., Liu, X., Liu, T.: Listening to chaotic whispers: a deep learning framework for news-oriented stock trend prediction. In: WSDM 2018 (2018)
19. Pagolu, V.S., Reddy, K.N., Panda, G., Majhi, B.: Sentiment analysis of twitter data for predicting stock market movements. In: SCOPES, pp. 1345–1350 (2016)
20. Nguyen, T.H., Shirai, K.: Topic modeling based sentiment analysis on social media for stock market prediction, (Beijing, China), pp. 1354–1364. ACL (2015)
21. Xu, Y., Cohen, S.B.: Stock movement prediction from tweets and historical prices, pp. 1970–1979. Association for Computational Linguistics (2018)
22. Sawhney, R., Agarwal, S., Wadhwa, A., Shah, R.R.: Deep attentive learning for stock movement prediction from social media text and company correlations. In: EMNLP. Association for Computational Linguistics, November 2020
23. Vaswani, A., et al.: Attention is all you need. CoRR, arXiv:1706.03762 (2017)
24. Hochreiter, S., Schmidhuber, J.: Long short-term memory. Neural Comput. **9**, 1735–1780 (1997)
25. Wang, Y., Li, Q., Huang, Z., Li, J.: EAN: event attention network for stock price trend prediction based on sentimental embedding. In: WebSci 2019, pp. 311–320 (2019)
26. Qiu, J., Wang, B., Zhou, C.: Forecasting stock prices with long-short term memory neural network based on attention mechanism. PLOS One **15**(1), e0227222 (2020)
27. Chen, Y., Wei, Z., Huang, X.: Incorporating corporation relationship via graph convolutional neural networks for stock price prediction. In: CIKM 2018, pp. 1655–1658 (2018)
28. Kim, R., So, C.H., Jeong, M., Lee, S., Kim, J., Kang, J.: Hats: a hierarchical graph attention network for stock movement prediction (2019)
29. Yang, L., Ng, T.L.J., Smyth, B., Dong, R.: HTML: hierarchical transformer-based multi-task learning for volatility prediction. In: WWW 2020, pp. 441–451 (2020)
30. Jeanblanc, M., Yor, M., Chesney, M.: Mathematical Methods for Financial Markets, June 2009
31. Chandrashekar, G., Sahin, F.: A survey on feature selection methods. Comput. Electr. Eng. **40**(1), 16–28 (2014)
32. Ng, A.Y.: Feature selection, l1 vs. l2 regularization, and rotational invariance. In: ICML, ICML 2004 (New York, NY, USA), p. 78 (2004)
33. Bahdanau, D., Cho, K., Bengio, Y.: Neural machine translation by jointly learning to align and translate. CoRR, arXiv:1409.0473 (2015)
34. Cer, D., et al.: Universal sentence encoder for English. In: EMNLP, pp. 169–174. ACL, November 2018
35. Pennington, J., Socher, R., Manning, C.: GloVe: global vectors for word representation. In: EMNLP, (Doha, Qatar), pp. 1532–1543. ACL, October 2014
36. Devlin, J., Chang, M.-W., Lee, K., Toutanova, K.: BERT: pre-training of deep bidirectional transformers for language understanding, pp. 4171–4186. ACL (2019)
37. Akbik, A., Blythe, D., Vollgraf, R.: Contextual string embeddings for sequence labeling. In: COLING, pp. 1638–1649 (2018)
38. Ding, X., Zhang, Y., Liu, T., Duan, J.: Knowledge-driven event embedding for stock prediction. In: COLING, (Osaka, Japan), pp. 2133–2142, December 2016
39. Brown, R.: Smoothing, Forecasting and Prediction of Discrete Time Series. Dover Phoenix Editions, Dover Publications (2004)

40. Qin, Y., Song, D., Cheng, H., Cheng, W., Jiang, G., Cottrell, G.W.: A dual-stage attention-based recurrent neural network for time series prediction. In: IJCAI 2017 (2017)
41. Lavrenko, V., Schmill, M., Lawrie, D., Ogilvie, P., Jensen, D., Allan, J.: Mining of concurrent text and time series. In: KDD, pp. 37–44 (2000)

End-to-End Edge Detection via Improved Transformer Model

Yi Gao, Chenwei Tang, Jiulin Lang, and Jiancheng Lv$^{(\boxtimes)}$

Sichuan University, Chengdu 610065, People's Republic of China
`lvjiancheng@scu.edu.cn`

Abstract. Recently, many efficient edge detection methods based on deep learning have emerged and made remarkable achievements. However, there are two fundamental challenges, i.e., the extraction and fusion of different scale features, as well as the sample imbalance, making the performance of edge detection need to be further promoted. In this paper, we propose an end-to-end edge detection method implemented by improved transformer model to promote edge detection by solving multi-scale fusion and sample imbalance. Specifically, based on the transformer model, we design a multi-scale edge extraction module, which utilizes pooling layer and dilated convolution with different rates and kernels, to realize multi-scale feature extraction and fusion. Moreover, we design an efficient loss function to guide the proposed method to fit the distribution of unbalanced positive and negative samples. Extensive experiments conducted on two benchmark data sets prove that the proposed method significantly outperforms state-of-the-art methods in edge detection.

Keywords: Edge detection · Transformer model · Multi-scale fusion · Unbalanced sample

1 Introduction

The goal of edge detection is to obtain the contours and obvious edges of objects in natural pictures. Empirically, knowing the edge information in advance will greatly improve the accuracy of many other vision tasks, e.g., object detection [13,27,29], semantic segmentation [1,7], and optical flow [18]. For example, the PAGE-Net [29] method proposes that using explicit edge information to optimize the estimation of saliency objects. The FCSN [18] method generates an edge map for each frame of the video to guide flow estimation. We have witnessed the development of edge detection from non-learning-based methods to learning-based methods. At present, the state-of-the-art edge detectors, such as DSCD [9] and BDCN [16], have surpassed humans.

This work is supported by the National Natural Science Fund for Distinguished Young Scholar (GrantNo. 61625204), and National Key Research and Development Project of China (No. 2017YFB1002201).

T. Mantoro et al. (Eds.): ICONIP 2021, LNCS 13111, pp. 514–525, 2021.
https://doi.org/10.1007/978-3-030-92273-3_42

Deep Convolutional Neural Networks (CNNs) currently dominate neural networks for most visual tasks, and edge detection is no exception. However, recent researches on visual transformer models have changed this situation. For instance, the ViT [12], DETR [5], and Swin Transformer [21] have achieved great success in image classification, object detection, and semantic segmentation. They have approached or even surpassed the performance of deep CNNs. Inspired by this, We explore the use of transformer as the backbone of an edge detector. Swin Transformer [21] proposed a transformer with shifted windows. Unlike traditional transformers, which calculates attention on the entire feature map, it divides the feature map into multiple windows and calculates attention within the windows, which can reduce the amount of calculation. The key of the method is that the windows between the two layers are interleaved to compensate for the lack of global attention information. However, it is mentioned in DETR [5] that the transformer does not work well for small objects.

Considering that edge detection is more detail-oriented than object detection, we propose a Multi-scale Edge Extraction Module (MEEM) to enhance the small target feature extraction capability of the transformer. Generally, there are far fewer edge pixels than non-edge pixels in a picture, which means that edge detection faces serious category imbalance problems. In addition, pixels near the edges are usually difficult to distinguish. To this end, we propose a loss function suitable for this kind of unbalanced and indistinguishable problem, which controls the loss value of different pixels through different dynamic weights. The main contributions of this paper are summarized as follow:

- By introducing the multi-scale edge extraction module, the proposed edge detection method is able to extract multi-scale features and obtain more semantic information.
- We design a more suitable loss function for edge detection, which handles the unbalanced and indistinguishable problems of positive and negative examples very well.
- We are the first to explore the integration of transformer into edge detection. Sufficient experiments prove that the current state-of-the-art edge detection method is defeated by our proposed method.

2 Related Work

2.1 Edge Detection

Historically, there have been three different periods of edge detection methods. The first-stage methods are for changes in color and intensity, e.g., the Canny [4] and the Sobel [17]. The first-stage edge detection methods do not require training and have a relatively fast speed. However, the edges generated by these first stage methods have no semantic information and are not accurate enough. Most of the works in the second-stage use learning-based methods for edge detection, such as Structured Edges (SE) [11]. However, these two-stage methods need to design lots of manual features, and are not an end-to-end systems. The third-stage methods are based on the end-to-end model of deep neural networks, which have now occupied the dominant position.

The HED [31] method of third-stage methods proposes an image-to-image training system and to our best knowledge, it has reached a level similar (within 2%) to that of humans for the first time on some standard data sets, such as BSDS500 [1] dataset. Furthermore, to solve the problem of category imbalance, i.e., the number of points that are not edges is far more than the number of edge points. Moreover, the HED method proposes a novel loss function, which has been adopted in many works [9,16,20]. The HED method uses the last layer of convolutional features in each stage of VGG16 [26]. In the RCF [20] method, in order to avoid losing part of the local edge, the features of all layers of convolutional features are utilized. In addition, the RCF proposes a multi-scale test method, which has been adopted by many works, e.g., LPCB [10], BDCN [16] and DSCD [9]. BDCN proposes that the supervision of each stage is generated by a bi-directional cascade model. Different from other methods, DSCD [9] proposes a step-by-step fusion edge detection system that makes training more stable.

2.2   Vision Transformer

Since the transformer was proposed in [28], it had achieved very good results in multiple tasks of Natural Language Processing (NLP). Recently, the transformer has also made a huge breakthrough in visual tasks. On the image classification task, ViT [12] proposes to input the image sequence into a pure transformer, which acquires awesome results compared to most advanced convolutional neural networks. On the object detection task, DETR [5] and Deformable DETR [34] designs an understandable object detection framework combining CNN and transformer. On the semantic segmentation task, SETR [33] only uses the transformer encoder layer combined with a simple upsampling decoder to achieve competitive results. In these works, training is more difficult than CNNs, because the transformer has quadratic complexity. More recently, inspired by ViT [12] and its follow-ups [8,15,30,32], Swin Transformer [21] proposed a key design element between consecutive self-attention layers, named shift of the window partition, which computes self-attention within local windows and allows cross-window connections. It is worth noting that Swin Transformer [21] greatly surpasses other methods in COCO, ADE20K and other data sets.

2.3   Multi-scale Representation Learning

The shallow features are suitable for expressing the information of small objects, and the deep ones are particularly suitable for expressing the information of large objects. Therefore, it is natural to think that fusing multi-scale features will improve the feature extraction of small and large targets. Multi-scale feature fusion is very efficient for a variety of visual tasks and can be divided into two directions, namely image pyramid and feature pyramid. The image pyramid is a collection of images that are arranged in a pyramid shape and are gradually reduced in resolution and are derived from the same original image. SIFT [22]

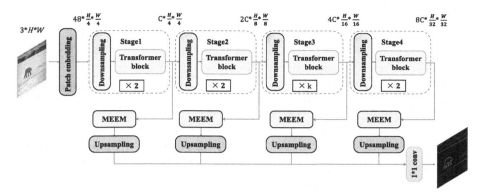

Fig. 1. Illustration of the end-to-end edge detection network based on improved transformer.

and multi-scale test mentioned above both adopt image pyramid. The feature pyramid makes full use of the features of different layers in the convolutional network or different features obtained by using different convolutions. FPN [19] leverages the architecture as a feature pyramid and makes predictions independently on each level. DeepLabV2 [6] proposed Atrous Spatial Pyramid Pooling (ASPP) which obtains multi-scale features without increasing the amount of calculation.

3 Proposed Methods

3.1 Network Architecture

In this section, We will explain the components of our proposed method named EDTR which is an end-to-end edge detection network implemented by improved transformer. Then, we described the Multi-scale Edge Extraction Module (MEEM) in detail. The network structure is shown in Fig. 1, we can see that there are four stages in the backbone, and each stage contains multiple transformers. The input of each stage is sent to the MEEM for multi-scale feature extraction, and then the output of all MEEM is fused to obtain an edge map.

The Base Swin Transformer. The backbone of our model is Swin Transformer [21] with a hierarchical structure. The author adds four sampling layers to the transformer on the basis of the experience of convolutional neural networks. The output of each stage is similar to that of a CNN, which means that the shallower layers capture local information, and the deeper layers have stronger high-level semantic information. In summary, Swin Transformer is very suitable as the backbone of visual tasks.

Multi-scale Edge Extraction Module. One difficulty of edge detection is to correctly distinguish the texture inside the object from its edge, so it is necessary to make full use of high-level semantic information to reduce false positives. In

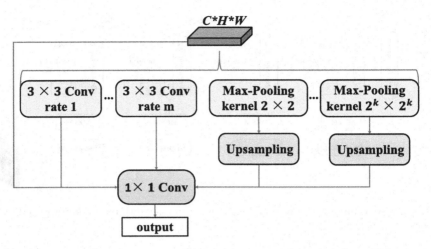

Fig. 2. The detailed architecture of MEEM. We set both m and k as 3. If they are too small, the ability to extract multi-scale features is diminished, and conversely, low-level information may be easily ignored.

general, a larger receptive field means stronger semantic information. Dilated convolution is a method to increase the receptive field, different dilation rates will lead to different receptive field. That means we can get the features of different receptive fields. Inspired by this, we use a series of dilated convolutions to better extract multi-scale features. At the same time, we use max-pooling to enhance the performance of positive examples. Figure 2 shows the structure of MEEM.

3.2   Loss Function for Unbalanced and Indistinguishable Data

The loss functions used in existing edge detection methods are mostly based on the improvement of Binary Cross Entropy (BCE) in Eq. 1. HED [31] uses two coefficients to balance positive and negative samples. Specifically, it uses a mask with the same shape as the label and sets the coefficients according to the label values at the positions corresponding to the label and the mask. HED only sets the positive samples as a larger coefficient than the negative samples but does not consider the hard-to-distinguish samples around the positive samples. Inspired by this, we set the coefficients of the hard-to-distinguish samples as positive samples as well to increase their weights in Eq. 2.

$$BCE(y, \widehat{y}) = -(y * log(\widehat{y}) + (1 - y) * log(1 - \widehat{y})), \tag{1}$$

$$IBL(y, \widehat{y}) = -(w_{positive} * y * log(\widehat{y}) + w_{negative} * (1 - y) * log(1 - \widehat{y})), \tag{2}$$

in which,

$$w_{positive} = dilate(y), \quad w_{negative} = \frac{|Y^+|}{|Y^+| + |Y^-|}, \tag{3}$$

where $\widehat{y}$, y define the predicted and ground-truth value, respectively. We use max_pool2d in PyTorch [24] to implement *dilate*. We set the kernel size to 3, which means we focus on the pixels around the positive sample that are less than 3 in distance. $|Y^+|$ and $|Y^-|$ define the number of positive and negative samples, respectively. We observe empirically that the pixels near the edge are more difficult to distinguish. After adding the positive and negative sample weights mentioned above, the model will still encounter difficulty distinguishing samples. Inspired by the focal loss, we also need to add scaling factors to reduce the weight of samples with small loss values in Eq. 4.

$$
\begin{aligned}
IBDL(y,\widehat{y}) = -\,(&w_{positive} * y * tanh(1 - \widehat{y}) * log(\widehat{y}) \\
+\,&w_{negative} * (1 - y) * tanh(\widehat{y}) * log(1 - \widehat{y})).
\end{aligned}
\tag{4}
$$

Compared to x^2 used in focal loss, The curve of $tanh$ is smoother, which is conducive to stable training, and the value near 0 changes more drastically than x^2, which can better distinguish background pixels.

When training the network, we supervised the output of each block of the network and the fusion of all outputs, Eq. 5 is our final loss function.

$$
L = \sum_{i=1}^{N}(\sum_{j=1}^{S} w_j * IBDL(y_i^j, \widehat{y}_i^j) + w_{fuse} * IBDL(y_i^{fuse}, \widehat{y}_i^{fuse})),
\tag{5}
$$

where N, S, w_j, w_{fuse} respectively define the number of network blocks, the number of pixels, the weight of the output of the j-th block, and the weight of the fusion result.

4   Experiments

In this section, We will describe the details of our experimental setup and the results on two authoritative datasets, i.e., BSDS500 [1] and NYUDv2 [25]. Our proposed EDTR method measures on three metrics, including OIS(Optimal Image Scale), ODS(F-measure at both Optimal Dataset Scale) and AP(Average Precision). All experiments are performed with Non-Maximum Suppression (NMS).

4.1   Implementation Details

We implement our network using PyTorch [24]. The default settings are the same as Swin Transformer [21]. All the experiments are conducted on four NVIDIA TITAN XP GPUs with 12 GB memory. Batch size is set to 10 for all the experiments. We choose SGD optimizer to train our network. We have also tried to use the adam optimizer, but the result is not as good as SGD. For SGD hyper-parameters, we set the initial learning rate to 1e-6 which is divided by 10 after every 10k iterations, weight decay and momentum are set to 0.9, and 2e-4 respectively.

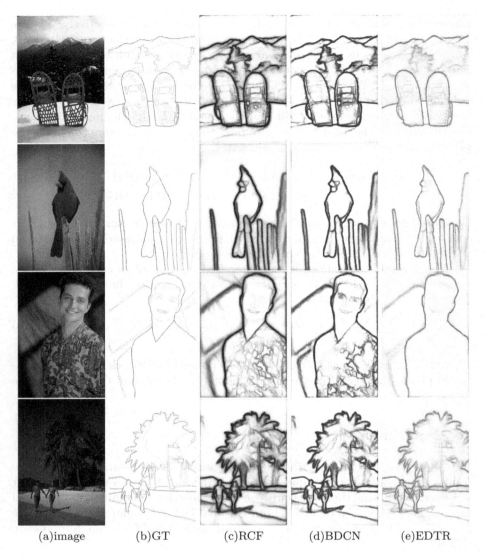

(a)image	(b)GT	(c)RCF	(d)BDCN	(e)EDTR

Fig. 3. Detection results of different methods on the BSDS500 dataset. GT means the ground-truth edge map. We do not employ Non-Maximum Suppression. Experimental results indicate that our proposed EDTR method has an effective extraction of multi-scale features leading to the capture of both coarse and fine edges. And due to the full exploitation of semantic information, EDTR can reject erroneous edges. For example, there are many textures in the clothes worn by the person in the third row. Our method can distinguish the texture from the edge of the person. In addition, our results are thinner than other methods.

4.2 BSDS500 Dataset

The BSDS500 dataset comprises 500 images, specifically, 200 images for training, 100 images for validation, and 200 images for testing. The ground truth
of images is the average of multiple individuals labeled independently. For data
augmentation, we follow the method of RCF by randomly rotating, cropping,
and flipping. We follow the RCF [20] strategy to put the training and validation
sets together for training and utilize the test set for evaluation. We also mix
the augmented data of BSDS500 with flipped PASCAL-Context dataset [23] as
training data. We show the comparison with recent works in Fig. 3, Fig. 4, and
Table 1. The performance of our proposed EDTR method is only slightly higher
than that of BDCN. This is because our proposed EDTR method focuses more
on the whole, but part of the ground truth in the BSDS500 dataset contains
textures inside the object that we believe are not edges.

Table 1. The quantitative results on
the BSDS500 [1] dataset.

Method	ODS	OIS	AP
Canny [4]	.611	.676	.580
SE [11]	.743	.763	–
MCG [2]	.744	.777	–
DeepEdge [3]	.753	.772	.807
HED [31]	.788	.808	.833
RCF [20]	.806	.833	–
RCF-MS [20]	.811	.830	–
LPCB [10]	.808	.824	–
LPCB-MS [10]	.815	.834	–
DSCD [9]	.813	.836	–
DSCD-MS [9]	.822	.859	–
BDCN [16]	.820	.838	.888
BDCN-MS [16]	.828	.844	.890
EDTR	.820	.839	.861
EDTR-MS	.830	.851	.886

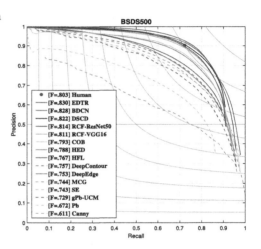

Fig. 4. The precision-recall curves of
compared works and our method on the
BSDS500 dataset [1].

4.3 NYUDv2 Dataset

The NYUDv2 dataset [25] collected 1449 pairs of aligned RGB and depth images
of interior environment, specifically, 381 images for training, 414 images for validation and 654 images for testing. We parse the in-depth information into three
dimensions: angle with gravity, horizontal deviation and height above ground.
In the evaluation, the maximum tolerance that allows the edge prediction to be

correctly matched is increased from 0.0075 to 0.011, as used in [16,20,31]. As shown in Fig. 5 and Table 2, Our proposed EDTR is superior to other works.

Table 2. The quantitative results on the NYUDv2 [25] dataset.

Method	ODS	OIS	AP
OEF-RGB [14]	.651	.667	–
SE-RGB [11]	.695	.708	.679
HED-RGB [31]	.720	.734	.734
HED-HHA [31]	.682	.695	.702
HED-RGB-HHA [31]	.741	.761	.786
LPCB-RGB [10]	.739	.754	–
LPCB-HHA [10]	.707	.719	–
LPCB-RGB-HHA [10]	.762	.778	–
RCF-RGB [20]	.743	.757	–
RCF-HHA [20]	.703	.717	–
RCF-RGB-HHA [20]	.765	.780	–
BDCN-RGB [16]	.748	.763	.770
BDCN-HHA [16]	.707	.719	.731
BDCN-RGB-HHA [16]	.767	.783	.783
EDTR-RGB	.758	.774	.778
EDTR-HHA	.709	.719	.733
EDTR-RGB-HHA	.772	.786	.799

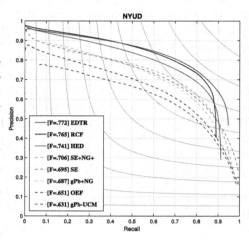

Fig. 5. The precision-recall curves of compared works and our method on the NYUDv2 dataset [25].

4.4   Ablation Study

In this section, We do a series of ablation experiments to demonstrate the effectiveness of our proposed method. The first experiment is to test the capability of our proposed loss function, our baseline is to use BCE Loss instead of our proposed loss function and to not apply the multi-scale edge extraction module(EDTR-w/o-IBDL-w/o-MEEM). Then, we trained a model only using the proposed loss function and another model using both the loss function(EDTR-w/o-IBDL) and the multi-scale enhancement module(EDTR). The quantitative results are shown in Table 3, where the numbers of blocks are set [2, 2, 6, 2]. w/o-IBDL represents our method without loss function for unbalanced and indistinguishable data, w/o-MEEM represents our method without multi-scale edge extraction module. Complete experiments prove the superiority of our method. Then we explored the impact of the number of transformer blocks on performance. A properly large number of blocks have a larger receptive field and can better capture multi-scale features. The quantitative results are shown in Table 4. Experiments show that a proper increase of blocks will improve performance.

Table 3. The ablation study of our proposed method on the BSDS500 dataset.

Method	ODS	OIS
EDTR-w/o-IBDL-w/o-MEEM	.797	.819
EDTR-w/o-IBDL	.809	.822
EDTR	.821	.833

Table 4. The ablation study of backbone. Following Swin Transformer, different numbers of blocks are set in the third stage.

Numbers of Blocks	ODS	OIS
[2, 2, 2, 2]	.806	.814
[2, 2, 6, 2]	.821	.833
[2, 2, 18, 2]	.830	.851

5 Conclusions

In this paper, we propose an end-to-end edge detection method based on an improved transformer model to promote edge detection by solving multi-scale fusion and sample imbalance. Specifically, based on the transformer model, we design a multi-scale edge extraction module, which utilizes pooling layer and dilated convolution with different rates and kernels, to realize multi-scale feature extraction and fusion. Moreover, we design an efficient loss function to guide the proposed method to fit the distribution of unbalanced positive and negative samples. The proposed method significantly outperforms other state-of-the-art edge detection methods. Through our work, we also prove the great potential of visual transformer. For future work, It is feasible to use our proposed module and loss function for computer vision tasks that require precise edges.

References

1. Arbelaez, P., Maire, M., Fowlkes, C., Malik, J.: Contour detection and hierarchical image segmentation. IEEE Trans. Pattern Anal. Mach. Intell. **33**(5), 898–916 (2010). https://doi.org/10.1109/TPAMI.2010.161
2. Arbeláez, P., Pont-Tuset, J., Barron, J.T., Marques, F., Malik, J.: Multiscale combinatorial grouping. In: Proceedings of the IEEE Conference on Computer Vision and Pattern Recognition, pp. 328–335 (2014)
3. Bertasius, G., Shi, J., Torresani, L.: DeepEdge: a multi-scale bifurcated deep network for top-down contour detection. In: Proceedings of the IEEE Conference on Computer Vision and Pattern Recognition, pp. 4380–4389 (2015)
4. Canny, J.: A computational approach to edge detection. IEEE Trans. Pattern Anal. Mach. Intell. PAMI **8**(6), 679–698 (1986). https://doi.org/10.1109/TPAMI.1986.4767851
5. Carion, N., Massa, F., Synnaeve, G., Usunier, N., Kirillov, A., Zagoruyko, S.: End-to-end object detection with transformers. In: Vedaldi, A., Bischof, H., Brox, T., Frahm, J.-M. (eds.) ECCV 2020. LNCS, vol. 12346, pp. 213–229. Springer, Cham (2020). https://doi.org/10.1007/978-3-030-58452-8_13
6. Chen, L.C., Papandreou, G., Kokkinos, I., Murphy, K., Yuille, A.L.: DeepLab: semantic image segmentation with deep convolutional nets, Atrous convolution, and fully connected CRFs. IEEE Trans. Pattern Anal. Mach. Intell. **40**(4), 834–848 (2017)

7. Cheng, M.-M., et al.: HFS: hierarchical feature selection for efficient image segmentation. In: Leibe, B., Matas, J., Sebe, N., Welling, M. (eds.) ECCV 2016. LNCS, vol. 9907, pp. 867–882. Springer, Cham (2016). https://doi.org/10.1007/978-3-319-46487-9_53

8. Chu, X., Zhang, B., Tian, Z., Wei, X., Xia, H.: Do we really need explicit position encodings for vision transformers? arXiv e-prints pp. arXiv-2102 (2021)

9. Deng, R., Liu, S.: Deep structural contour detection. In: Proceedings of the 28th ACM International Conference on Multimedia, pp. 304–312 (2020)

10. Deng, R., Shen, C., Liu, S., Wang, H., Liu, X.: Learning to predict crisp boundaries. In: Ferrari, V., Hebert, M., Sminchisescu, C., Weiss, Y. (eds.) ECCV 2018. LNCS, vol. 11210, pp. 570–586. Springer, Cham (2018). https://doi.org/10.1007/978-3-030-01231-1_35

11. Dollár, P., Zitnick, C.L.: Fast edge detection using structured forests. IEEE Trans. Pattern Anal. Mach. Intell. **37**(8), 1558–1570 (2014)

12. Dosovitskiy, A., et al.: An image is worth 16×16 words: transformers for image recognition at scale. In: International Conference on Learning Representations (2021). https://openreview.net/forum?id=YicbFdNTTy

13. Ferrari, V., Fevrier, L., Jurie, F., Schmid, C.: Groups of adjacent contour segments for object detection. IEEE Trans. Pattern Anal. Mach. Intell. **30**(1), 36–51 (2008). https://doi.org/10.1109/TPAMI.2007.1144

14. Hallman, S., Fowlkes, C.C.: Oriented edge forests for boundary detection. In: Proceedings of the IEEE Conference on Computer Vision and Pattern Recognition, pp. 1732–1740 (2015)

15. Han, K., Xiao, A., Wu, E., Guo, J., Xu, C., Wang, Y.: Transformer in transformer. arXiv preprint arXiv:2103.00112 (2021)

16. He, J., Zhang, S., Yang, M., Shan, Y., Huang, T.: BDCN: bi-directional cascade network for perceptual edge detection. IEEE Trans. Pattern Anal. Mach. Intell., 1 (2020). https://doi.org/10.1109/TPAMI.2020.3007074

17. Kittler, J.: On the accuracy of the Sobel edge detector. Image Vis. Comput. **1**(1), 37–42 (1983)

18. Lei, P., Li, F., Todorovic, S.: Boundary flow: a Siamese network that predicts boundary motion without training on motion. In: Proceedings of the IEEE Conference on Computer Vision and Pattern Recognition (CVPR), June 2018

19. Lin, T.Y., Dollar, P., Girshick, R., He, K., Hariharan, B., Belongie, S.: Feature pyramid networks for object detection. In: Proceedings of the IEEE Conference on Computer Vision and Pattern Recognition (CVPR), July 2017

20. Liu, Y., et al.: Richer convolutional features for edge detection. IEEE Trans. Pattern Anal. Mach. Intell. **41**(8), 1939–1946 (2019). https://doi.org/10.1109/TPAMI.2018.2878849

21. Liu, Z., et al.: Swin transformer: hierarchical vision transformer using shifted windows. arXiv preprint arXiv:2103.14030 (2021)

22. Lowe, D.G.: Distinctive image features from scale-invariant keypoints. Int. J. Comput. Vis. **60**(2), 91–110 (2004)

23. Mottaghi, R., et al.: The role of context for object detection and semantic segmentation in the wild. In: Proceedings of the IEEE Conference on Computer Vision and Pattern Recognition, pp. 891–898 (2014)

24. Paszke, A., et al.: Pytorch: an imperative style, high-performance deep learning library. In: Advances in Neural Information Processing Systems, vol. 32, pp. 8024–8035. Curran Associates, Inc. (2019). http://papers.neurips.cc/paper/9015-pytorch-an-imperative-style-high-performance-deep-learning-library.pdf

25. Silberman, N., Hoiem, D., Kohli, P., Fergus, R.: Indoor segmentation and support inference from RGBD images. In: Fitzgibbon, A., Lazebnik, S., Perona, P., Sato, Y., Schmid, C. (eds.) ECCV 2012. LNCS, vol. 7576, pp. 746–760. Springer, Heidelberg (2012). https://doi.org/10.1007/978-3-642-33715-4_54
26. Simonyan, K., Zisserman, A.: Very deep convolutional networks for large-scale image recognition. In: Bengio, Y., LeCun, Y. (eds.) 3rd International Conference on Learning Representations, ICLR 2015, San Diego, CA, USA, 7–9 May 2015, Conference Track Proceedings (2015). http://arxiv.org/abs/1409.1556
27. Ullman, S., Basri, R.: Recognition by linear combinations of models. IEEE Trans. Pattern Anal. Mach. Intell. **13**(10), 992–1006 (1991). https://doi.org/10.1109/34.99234
28. Vaswani, A., et al.: Attention is all you need. In: Advances in Neural Information Processing Systems 2017-Decem (Nips), pp. 5999–6009 (2017)
29. Wang, W., Zhao, S., Shen, J., Hoi, S.C., Borji, A.: Salient object detection with pyramid attention and salient edges. In: Proceedings of the IEEE/CVF Conference on Computer Vision and Pattern Recognition, pp. 1448–1457 (2019)
30. Wang, W., et al.: Pyramid vision transformer: a versatile backbone for dense prediction without convolutions. arXiv preprint arXiv:2102.12122 (2021)
31. Xie, S., Tu, Z.: Holistically-nested edge detection. In: Proceedings of the IEEE International Conference on Computer Vision, pp. 1395–1403 (2015)
32. Yuan, L., et al.: Tokens-to-Token ViT: training vision transformers from scratch on imagenet. arXiv preprint arXiv:2101.11986 (2021)
33. Zheng, S., et al.: Rethinking semantic segmentation from a sequence-to-sequence perspective with transformers. In: Proceedings of the IEEE/CVF Conference on Computer Vision and Pattern Recognition, pp. 6881–6890 (2021)
34. Zhu, X., Su, W., Lu, L., Li, B., Wang, X., Dai, J.: Deformable DETR: deformable transformers for end-to-end object detection. In: 9th International Conference on Learning Representations, ICLR 2021, Virtual Event, Austria, 3–7 May 2021. OpenReview.net (2021). https://openreview.net/forum?id=gZ9hCDWe6ke

Isn't It Ironic, Don't You Think?

Saichethan Miriyala Reddy[1] and Swati Agarwal[2](✉)

[1] University of Texas at Dallas, Richardson, USA
sxm200225@utdallas.edu
[2] BITS Pilani, Goa Campus, Goa, India
agrswati@ieee.org

Abstract. Currently, dealing with figurative language, such as irony, is one of the challenging and interesting problems in natural language processing. Because irony is so widespread in user-created content (UCC) such as social media posts, its prevalence makes it technically challenging to determine sentiments or interpret opinions. Investigating irony content is an essential problem which can be extended and leveraged for other tasks such as sentiment and opinion mining. The present work proposes a Hierarchical Attention based Neural network for identifying ironic tweets. Our method exploits the structure and semantic features like POS tagging and sentiment flow shifts. We then present our results on the Task 3 of the Semantic Evaluation 2018 workshop named "Irony Detection in English Tweets" dataset. Furthermore, we perform a comprehensive analysis over the generated results, shedding insights on future research for the irony detection task.

Keywords: Irony · Figurative language · Parts of speech · Sentiment

1 Introduction

The irony is a purposeful contrast between apparent and intended meaning in a speech or expression. The irony is a common phenomenon in human communication, and it can be found in news stories, books, websites, conversations, Tweets, sitcoms, and product evaluations, among other places. Even for humans, it is sometimes difficult to recognize the irony. Although most people have a natural sense of common sense and connotative knowledge, machine, however, struggle to execute tasks effectively that require extra-textual/contextual information. Several existing studies which employed automated model to capture irony and sentiments have revealed that classification models underperform due to the lack of essential world knowledge. On social media sites like Twitter, Reddit, and Facebook, user-generated texts frequently include the widespread usage of the creative figure of speech. Failure to detect irony can result in poor sentiment/threat analysis performance, as irony frequently causes polarity reversal [3]. Ironic text, similar to other figurative language could be metaphorical; it demands a more subtle interpretation based on interdependence or relations with the context or world knowledge.

© Springer Nature Switzerland AG 2021
T. Mantoro et al. (Eds.): ICONIP 2021, LNCS 13111, pp. 526–536, 2021.
https://doi.org/10.1007/978-3-030-92273-3_43

Thus automatic identification of ironic formulations in written text is very challenging. There is no consensual agreement in the literature on how verbal irony should be defined as a creative form of language. Only recently, irony detection has been approached from a computational perspective [11]. In many previous works, irony and sarcasm are treated interchangeably. However, since sarcasm has a target that is being ridiculed, it is essential for the natural language model to distinguish irony from sarcasm. Automatic irony detection aims to develop computational models to classify a text into positive (irony) or negative (not-irony) categories. The described problem is technically challenging due to the degree and variety of ways to express the irony. Automatic irony identification has much potential in the field of text mining, especially for applications that need context analysis, such as author profiling, online harassment detection, and sentiment analysis.

1.1 Contributions

- We apply attention mechanisms at two granular levels: word and sentence level. We enable our model to attend content differentially that are of different importance.
- To learn richer sentence representation, lexicon based sentiment scores and POS taggings are encoded to improve the accuracy of the classifier.
- To emphasise the problems, a detailed quantitative comparison was conducted with several traditional and state-of-the-art baselines, as well as an in-depth error analysis.

2 Related Work

In this Section, we briefly discuss the closely related literature to irony detection. We discuss the recently employed computational models and natural language processing based approaches for the said irony detection task. According to Joshi *et al.* [7] and Wallace *et al.* [17] described that computational irony detection models are of two types: 1) rule-based classifiers and 2) supervised systems. The problem of irony detection from text recently gained the attention of researchers. Over the last few years, several machine learning, qualitative approaches, and advanced deep learning models have been developed for addressing this problem. In this section, we first discuss the brief overview of top teams that participated in the SemEval Shared Task 3A(Irony Detection in English Tweets), then we further extend it with the recent developments in the area.

The authors of [5] suggested a Siamese neural network for irony detection that is made up of two sub-networks, each comprising an LSTM layer and an embedding layer initialized with Glove word embedding vectors. The generated weights of each LSTM layer carries the conceptual representation of its input. Intuitively, the weight difference between the output of two LSTM layers should signify representations as either incongruous to each other or not. A subtract layer is used to calculate the weight difference between two sub-networks. In [18] a densely connected LSTM network with a multi-task learning strategy developed. The POS tag features one-hot encoded and concatenated with the word embedding vectors. To capture both the semantic and grammatical information in tweets, the authors of [1] created an ensemble of two separate models. They designed a recurrent neural networks model operative at word and character levels. The WLV [13] team created an ensemble-based soft voting classifier with regression and support vector machine (SVM), as well as extra feature sets based on sentiment, semantic, and handcrafted features. Systems [9,10], and [2] were based on a collection of design features that included both syntactic and lexical features, as well as a wide range of affective-based features such as readability, incongruity, polarity, user behavior, and various aspects of sentiment and emotions. The usage of new features to exploit the affective information conveyed by emojis has been investigated.

Authors of [19] developed three attention-based models incorporating sentiment features for classifying ironic texts.

3   Dataset

In this section, we discuss the Task 3 of the SemEval 2018 workshop names "Irony Detection in English Tweets" dataset. The initial version of the dataset curated by the shared task organizers consisted of a total of 4792tweets (2396 ironic + 2396 non ironic tweets). The corpus was randomly split into a class-balanced training (80%, or 3833 cases) and test for the shared task (20 percent i.e. 958 instances). Additional ambiguous tweets, which require additional context to understand irony, are removed from the test corpus. The final test corpus contains 784 English tweets (consisting of 40% ironic tweets and remaining 60% non ironic tweets). We were able to get access to the data after registering on the shared task website. The Table 1

Table 1. Dataset statistics

	Train	Test
Number of tweets	3834	784
Mean Tweet Length	63.33	62.21
Median Tweet Length	61	58
St. Dev Tweet Length	31.00	31.58
Max Tweet Length	136	140
Min Tweet Length	2	1

3.1   Qualitative Analysis

Additionally, we have also reported a brief exploratory analysis of the dataset. To evaluate the sentiment polarity and linguistic content of ironic and non ironic tweets in the dataset, we list the statistical information based on tweet polarity in Fig. 1. For this, we utilized *Vader Sentiment Intensity Analyzer*[1]. The analysis shows that considering the entire tweet, positive or negative polarity does not correlate to irony. Word clouds have become one of the most accessible and visually appealing ways to interpret the text. They are used in a variety of scenarios to provide an overview by reducing text down to the most frequently occurring terms. The word clouds for training and test set are shown in Figs. 2 and 3, respectively. From Figs. 2 and 3 we can see training set has more diverse words with different frequencies whereas a smaller set of words with similar frequencies in the test set.

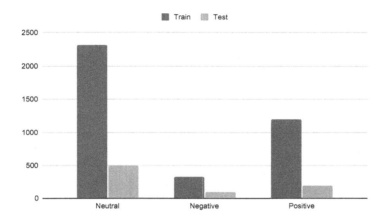

Fig. 1. Polarity of tweets when considered entire tweet as a single utterance

4   Proposed Methodology

The irony detection task is posed as a binary classification problem where tweets that are ironic are assigned 1, and remaining tweets are assigned 0. The Fig. 4 depicts the general design of our suggested model. The proposed model is a multi-step framework, including a word sequence encoder, a word level attention layer, a sentence encoder, a sentence level attention layer, POS features, and sentiment flow shifts. In the next sections, we go over the specifics of each component.

4.1   Word Encoder

Given a text sentence with words w_{it}, t ϵ [0,T], we first embed the words to vectors through an embedding matrix. W_e, $x_{ij} = W_e w_{ij}$. We obtain word annotations using a bidirectional GRU by summarizing information from both directions for words, and thus include contextual information in the annotation. The

---

[1] http://www.nltk.org/howto/sentiment.html.

Fig. 2. Word cloud of terms present in training data

Fig. 3. Word cloud of terms present in test data

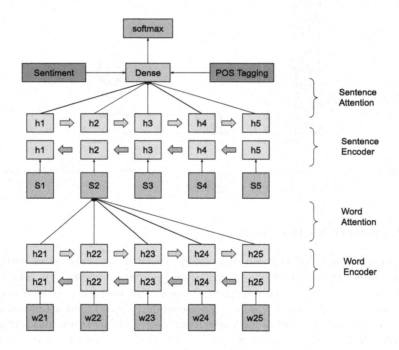

Fig. 4. Proposed architecture

bidirectional GRU contains the forward GRU $\overrightarrow{f}$ which reads the sentence s_i from w_{i1} to w_{iT} and a backward GRU $\overleftarrow{f}$ which reads from w_{iT} to w_{i1}

$$x_{it} = W_e w_{it}, t\epsilon[1, T]$$

$$\overrightarrow{h_{it}} = \overrightarrow{GRU}(x_{it}), t\epsilon[1,T]$$
$$\overleftarrow{h_{it}} = \overleftarrow{GRU}(x_{it}), t\epsilon[T,1]$$
$$h_{it} = [\overrightarrow{h_{it}}, \overleftarrow{h_{it}}]$$

We use h_{it} i.e. concatenating the forward hidden state $\overrightarrow{h_{it}}$ and backward hidden $\overleftarrow{h_{it}}$ as our representation for the word w_{it}

4.2 Word-Level Attention

As not all words contribute equally to the identification of irony, we implement the attention mechanism to extract such words that are important for differentiating and aggregate the representation of those informative words to form a sentence vector.

$$u_{it} = tanh(W_w h_{it} + b_w)$$
$$\alpha_{it} = \frac{exp(u^T{}_{it} u_w)}{\sum_t exp(u^T{}_{it} u_w)}$$
$$S_i = \sum_t \alpha_{it} h_{it}$$

4.3 Sentence Encoder

Given a sentence vectors S_i, we can use the bidirectional GRU to encode the sentence

$$\overrightarrow{h_i} = \overrightarrow{GRU}(S_i)$$
$$\overleftarrow{h_i} = \overleftarrow{GRU}(S_i)$$
$$h_i = [\overrightarrow{h_i}, \overleftarrow{h_i}]$$

Similarly, we use h_i i.e. concatenating the forward hidden state $\overrightarrow{h_i}$ and backward hidden $\overleftarrow{h_i}$ as our representation for the sentence S_i

4.4 Sentence-Level Attention

Self-attentive representations use an attention mechanism that evaluates different positions within the sequence to encode a variable length sequence into a fixed size.

$$u_i = tanh(W_s h_i + b_s)$$
$$\alpha_i = \frac{exp(u^T{}_i u_s)}{\sum_i exp(u^T{}_i u_s)}$$
$$v = \sum_i \alpha_i h_i$$

4.5   Sentiment Flow Shifts

While irony is the expression of one's meaning by using language that normally signifies the opposite, but from Fig. 1 we can see the polarity of the entire tweet does not show any correlation towards irony as itself. One of the most frequently cited irony realizations is the use of positive sentiment within a negative context or the negative sentiment within a positive context. Inspired by the work of [4], we employed the sentiment flow shifts as a feature. Conjunctions and few special symbols are used as pivotal points. Below we illustrated few examples of ironic tweets in which we can notice sentiment flow shift (negative, neutral, positive)

- **I just wrote a 13 page paper.** I was awfully tired when I was writing it and now I can't sleep.
- The most exciting way to start a Friday**: a presentation on structurally deficient bridges.**
- please note #sarcasm in last tweet before you kill yourself; many good pros including Balance Physio can show you best usage

4.6   POS Tagging

Past works [12,14] has shown that part of speech information can be beneficial for classification tasks. We used Penn Treebank [8], which has 48 tags, 36 of which are part-of-speech tags and 12 of punctuation and monetary symbols tags. The increases in the number of tags is due to a need to encode morphological information [14], as well as finer granularity (e.g., special tags for determiners, particles, modal verbs, cardinal numerals, foreign words, existential there, and so on). as part of the tags. At the same time, such a large number of tags gives more flexibility but can be redundant. So we only considered tags like Nouns, Verbs, Adjectives, Conjunctions for our experiments.

The representation of the tweet obtained from the HAN module (v) is then concatenated with the Parts of Speech vector(pos). The sentiment flow shift-vector(sfs) is passed through a fully connected layer which in turn connects it to the output channel of the classifier consisting of output neurons to identify if the tweet is ironic or not.

$$C = [v, pos, sfs]$$

$$V = relu(W_c C + b_c)$$

Where pos is Parts of Speech vector and sfs is sentiment flow shift vector. The vector V is a high level representation of the tweets.

$$\hat{y} = \sigma(V)$$

where, $\sigma(z) = \frac{1}{1+e^{-z}}$. We minimize the cross-entropy (CE) as expressed below

$$CE = y_i \cdot \log \hat{y}_i + (1 - y_i) \cdot \log (1 - \hat{y}_i)$$

where y_i is the expected class (0 or 1) and $\hat{y}_i$ is the predicted probability.

Evaluation Metrics: We follow the metrics used by the shared task organizers and previous works. We report accuracy, Precision, Recall and F1 Scores.

5 Results and Discussion

In this section, we present the experimental results obtained from the proposed classification model across a wide range of experiments. As can be seen in Table 2, that our proposed model consistently outperforms submitted system results and HAN baseline, which shows that taking sentiment and POS tagging information into account helps to produce better sentence level representations. In Table 4, we tabulated the performance of different variants of our proposed model employed on the dataset. From the table, it can be observed that *HAN+Sentiment+POS* outperforms other models with a significant margin and give higher performance than the baseline HAN by 4.2% (Table 3).

The official best system (THUNGN [18]) of the shared task obtained an F1-score of **0.705**. In Table 2, we considered the best run of the top 10 teams. Finding significant features for any non-ironic topic is hard; this is why our system includes both Sentiment flow shifts and POS Tagging along with the HAN: they aim to distinguish irony from as many different topics as possible.

Error Analysis: We discovered that several tweets had been wrongly labeled. The reason for this could be confusing entities in the tweet or a lack of context. In a few situations, our system was correct, but the incorrect tags resulted in a drop in performance evaluation. We've included a few examples below.

- A wonderful day of starting work at 6am
- really, what else can a fish be besides a fish?
- It will be impossible for me to be late if I start to dress up right now.

Statistical Significance: We have also conducted a statistical significance test to ensure that the performance boosts we saw were not due to chance. Whenever we conduct the experiments, the improvements are nearly identical.

Table 2. Comparison of our proposed approach with top 10 Official team (CodaLab) results of SemEval 2018 Task 3A ranked by the F1 score

Team	Accuracy	Precision	Recall	F_1 score
THU_NGN [18]	0735	0.630	0.801	0.705
NTUA_SLP [1]	0.732	**0.654**	0.691	0.672
WLV [13]	0.643	0.532	**0.836**	0.650
NLPRL_IITBHU [10]	0.661	0.551	0.788	0.678
NIHRIO [16]	0.702	0.609	0.691	0.648
DLUTNLP_1 [15]	0.628	0.520	0.797	0.629
ELiRF-UPV [6]	0.611	0.506	0.833	0.629
Liangxh16 [15]	0.659	0.555	0.714	0.625
CJ [15]	0.667	0.565	0.695	0.623
# NonDicevo-SulSerio [15]	0.679	0.583	0.666	0.622
Baseline	*0.635*	*0.532*	*0.659*	*0.589*
Proposed Approach	**0.761**	0.648	0.819	**0.724**

Table 3. Comparison of our proposed approach with other existing models

Model	F1-Score
LSTM	63.66
CNN	62.03
CNN-LSTM	61.16
Attention-based Bi-LSTM	64.15
Sentiment-augmented attention (AA-BiLSTM) [19]	67.86
Sentiment-supervised attention (SABi-LSTM) [19]	65.33
Sentiment transferred (STBi-LSTM) [19]	69.00
Proposed Approach	**72.49**

Table 4. Comparison between different variants of our proposed model

Model	Accuracy	Precision	Recall	F1
HAN	0.712	**0.708**	0.583	0.695
HAN+Sentiment	0.735	0.630	0.802	0.706
HAN+Sentiment+POS	0.761	0.648	**0.819**	**0.724**

6   Conclusion and Future Work

The presented work investigated the problem of irony detection on Twitter. The limited ground truth (annotated by domain experts or human annotators) is one of the major technical challenge in developing an effective automated model for irony detection. Therefore, we conducted our experiments on SemEval

2018 dataset on irony detection. We proposed several modifications to the HAN architecture and build a binary classifier model. Experiments reveal that our suggested models outperformed the baselines, which included many state-of-the-art neural models for irony detection among microposts. The proposed model obtained an F1-score of 0.725 which also outperformed the winning team on SemEval 2018 task.

As a future direction, we plan to improve our feature vectors and improve the performance of the proposed model. We plan to explore oral/gestural clues like emoticons, onomatopoeic expressions for laughter, heavy punctuation marks, quote marks, and positive/negative interjections. Since irony is one of the many figurative languages used on online social media, we also plan to develop models across other applications such as differentiating between various figurative languages and irony generation.

References

1. Baziotis, C., et al.: NTUA-SLP at SemEval-2018 task 3: tracking ironic tweets using ensembles of word and character level attentive RNNs. arXiv preprint arXiv:1804.06659 (2018)
2. Farías, D.I.H., Patti, V., Rosso, P.: Valento at semeval-2018 task 3: exploring the role of affective content for detecting irony in English tweets. In: Proceedings of the 12th International Workshop on Semantic Evaluation, pp. 643–648 (2018)
3. Farias, D.H., Rosso, P.: Irony, sarcasm, and sentiment analysis. In: Sentiment Analysis in Social Networks, pp. 113–128. Elsevier (2017)
4. Filatova, E.: Sarcasm detection using sentiment flow shifts. In: The Thirtieth International Flairs Conference (2017)
5. Ghosh, A., Veale, T.: Ironymagnet at semeval-2018 task 3: a siamese network for irony detection in social media. In: Proceedings of the 12th International Workshop on Semantic Evaluation, pp. 570–575 (2018)
6. González, J.Á., Hurtado, L.F., Pla, F.: ELiRF-UPV at SemEval-2019 task 3: snapshot ensemble of hierarchical convolutional neural networks for contextual emotion detection. In: Proceedings of the 13th International Workshop on Semantic Evaluation, pp. 195–199 (2019)
7. Joshi, A., et al.: How challenging is sarcasm versus irony classification?: a study with a dataset from English literature. In: Proceedings of the Australasian Language Technology Association Workshop 2016, pp. 123–127 (2016)
8. Marcus, M.P., Marcinkiewicz, M.A., Santorini, B.: Building a large annotated corpus of English: the Penn treebank. Comput. Linguist. **19**(2), 313–330 (1993)
9. Pamungkas, E.W., Patti, V.: # nondicevosulserio at semeval-2018 task 3: exploiting emojis and affective content for irony detection in English tweets. In: Proceedings of the 12th International Workshop on Semantic Evaluation, pp. 649–654 (2018)
10. Rangwani, H., Kulshreshtha, D., Singh, A.K.: NLPRL-IITBHU at SemEval-2018 task 3: combining linguistic features and emoji pre-trained CNN for irony detection in tweets. In: Proceedings of the 12th International Workshop on Semantic Evaluation, pp. 638–642 (2018)
11. Reyes, A., Rosso, P., Veale, T.: A multidimensional approach for detecting irony in twitter. Lang. Resour. Eval. **47**(1), 239–268 (2013)

12. Robinson, T.: Disaster tweet classification using parts-of-speech tags: a domain adaptation approach. Ph.D. thesis, Kansas State University (2016)
13. Rohanian, O., Taslimipoor, S., Evans, R., Mitkov, R.: WLV at SemEval-2018 task 3: dissecting tweets in search of irony. In: Proceedings of the 12th International Workshop on Semantic Evaluation, pp. 553–559 (2018)
14. Suman, C., Reddy, S.M., Saha, S., Bhattacharyya, P.: Why pay more? A simple and efficient named entity recognition system for tweets. Expert Syst. Appl. **167**, 114101 (2021)
15. Van Hee, C., Lefever, E., Hoste, V.: Semeval-2018 task 3: irony detection in English tweets. In: Proceedings of the 12th International Workshop on Semantic Evaluation, pp. 39–50 (2018)
16. Vu, T., Nguyen, D.Q., Vu, X.S., Nguyen, D.Q., Catt, M., Trenell, M.: NIHRIO at SemEval-2018 task 3: a simple and accurate neural network model for irony detection in twitter. arXiv preprint arXiv:1804.00520 (2018)
17. Wallace, B.C., Kertz, L., Charniak, E., et al.: Humans require context to infer ironic intent (so computers probably do, too). In: Proceedings of the 52nd Annual Meeting of the Association for Computational Linguistics (vol. 2: Short Papers), pp. 512–516 (2014)
18. Wu, C., Wu, F., Wu, S., Liu, J., Yuan, Z., Huang, Y.: THU_NGN at SemEval-2018 task 3: tweet irony detection with densely connected LSTM and multi-task learning. In: Proceedings of the 12th International Workshop on Semantic Evaluation, pp. 51–56 (2018)
19. Zhang, X., Yang, Q.: Transfer hierarchical attention network for generative dialog system. Int. J. Autom. Comput. **16**(6), 720–736 (2019)

Neural Local and Global Contexts Learning for Word Sense Disambiguation

Fumiyo Fukumoto[1]([✉]) [iD], Taishin Mishima[2] [iD], Jiyi Li[1] [iD], and Yoshimi Suzuki[1] [iD]

[1] Interdisciplinary Graduate School, University of Yamanashi, Kofu, Japan
{fukumoto,jyli,ysuzuki}@yamanashi.ac.jp
[2] Graduate School of Engineering, University of Yamanashi, Kofu, Japan
g18tk014@yamanashi.ac.jp
http://cl.cs.yamanashi.ac.jp/index_e.html

Abstract. Supervised Word Sense Disambiguation (WSD) has been one of the popular NLP topics, while how to utilize the limited volume of the sense-tagged data and interpret a diversity of contexts as relevant features remains a challenging research question. This paper focuses the problem and proposes a method for effectively leveraging a variety of contexts into a neural-based WSD model. Our model is Transformer-XL framework which is coupled with Graph Convolutional Network (GCNs). GCNs integrates different features from local contexts, i.e., full dependency structures, words with part-of-speech (POS), word order information into a model. By using hidden states obtained by GCNs, Transformer-XL learns local and global contexts simultaneously, where the global context is obtained from a document appearing with the target words. The experimental results by using a series of benchmark WSD datasets show that our method is comparable to the state-of-the-art WSD methods which utilize only the limited number of sense-tagged data, especially we verified that dependency structure and POS features contribute to performance improvement in our model through an ablation test.

Keywords: Word Sense Disambication · Graph Convolutional Network · Transformer-XL

1 Introduction

Supervised Word Sense Disambiguation (WSD) is beneficial at one level or another for most of the NLP tasks such as machine translation, information retrieval, and content analysis [9]. A well-known early attempt for WSD is based on the distributional hypothesis. The approach makes use of surrounding words and the co-occurrences within a sentence in the training data for learning sense distinctions of the target word [27]. However, supervised WSD models are hard to train because available sense-tagged data is limited.

T. Mantoro et al. (Eds.): ICONIP 2021, LNCS 13111, pp. 537–549, 2021.
https://doi.org/10.1007/978-3-030-92273-3_44

More recently, WSD based on deep learning techniques has been intensively studied. These attempts include bidirectional LSTM [13] and neural sequence learning [20]. It enables to use of not only the context of the target word itself but also its previous and next contexts which makes a learning model powerful to learn features from the training data. Despite some successes, many techniques are based on word sequence and ignore to capture different aspects of contexts simultaneously. Several attempts have utilized different representations for the same word in different contexts. One attempt is pre-trained contextualized word representations [16,19]. The attempt successfully applied to many NLP tasks including the WSD task [7], while it mainly focuses on how neural sentence encoders learn sense distinctions of the same word by utilizing a large volume of data. Another attempt is to utilize existing Lexical Knowledge Bases (LKB) such as WordNet and BableNet for contextualized sense representations [4,5,11]. Their models successfully improved the overall performance on WSD evaluation benchmarks and demonstrated that the injection of LKB can alleviate the problem of a limited number of labeled sense-tagged data. However, there are few studies that addressed the issue that how to interpret different contexts as relevant features by utilizing the limited volume of sense-tagged data.

Motivated by the previous work, we propose a method for effectively leveraging contextual features obtained from the limited volume of sense-tagged data. Consider the document from SemEval-15 WSD data:

- Kalgebra is a <u>mathematical</u> <u>calculator</u> based on content <u>markup</u> <u>MathML</u> <u>language</u>. ⋯ ⋯ Kalgebra main *window*. ⋯ ⋯ By double clicking on them you will see a dialog that lets you *change* their *values*. ⋯ ⋯

Let *window*, *change*, and *values* be a target word. We can see that the dependency relation between *change* and *values* is a good indicator to disambiguate the sense of these target words. In contrast, it is difficult to disambiguate the sense of *window* by utilizing the information within a sentence, but words such as <u>mathematical</u> <u>calculator</u> and <u>MathML</u> help to disambiguate its sense as these words are related to the topic of this document, mathematics/computing. These words are also useful to disambiguate *change* and *values*.

Our approach is based on Graph Convolutional Networks (GCNs) [10] and Transformer-XL (Trans-XL) [6]. GCNs integrates different features from local contexts, i.e., (i) full dependency structures, (ii) words with POS including the target word, and (iii) word order information into a unified framework. Besides local contexts in each sentence, our model makes use of a global context which is obtained from a whole document appearing with the target words. Following well-known early attempts on topical context and domain in WSD assuming that the sense of a word depends on the domain in which it is used [26], we focus on a document as a segment for learning global context. By utilizing hidden states obtained by GCNs, Trans-XL learns local and global contexts simultaneously. Intuitively, by sharing a variety of contextual features, the model can produce a rich representation to disambiguate word senses.

The main contributions of this work can be summarized: (1) we examine a variety of contextual features that are obtained from the limited size of sense-tagged data for the WSD task. (2) we introduce the Trans-XL framework which is coupled with GCNs for learning local and global contexts effectively. (3) through the ablation study, we verify that dependency structure and POI features contribute to performance improvement.

2 Related Work

The recent upsurge of graph neural networks such as Graph Convolutional Networks (GCNs) [10] and Relational Graph Convolutional Networks [22], which are a class of multilayer neural networks operating on graphs have been successfully applied to many NLP tasks. The attempts include semantic role labeling [15], neural machine translation [3], and pronoun resolution [25], while it has so far not been used for the WSD task. Most of these methods demonstrated that the models contributed to attaining good performance on each task, though they focused on one type of feature, i.e., syntactic information between words, and integrate them in their graph models. Vashishth et al. proposed two types of GCNs, SynGCN which utilizes the dependency context of a word, and SemGCN which incorporates semantic relations between words for learning word embedding [23]. Each GCNs learned separately which differs from our approach. We share full dependency structure, words with POS including the target word, and word order information by using the same network GCNs. It can assist GCNs to learn better information aggregations which enable our model to better capture local contexts than leveraging them independently.

Xu et al. have also attempted GCNs which make use of three types of syntactic features, i.e., word order, dependency parse, and constituency parse [25]. Their methods demonstrate that integrating several features is effective for word embeddings and semantic parsing. Their approach is similar to our work, but their objectives and network structures are different. We incorporate multiple features into the GCNs but learn the optimal number of layers corresponding to each feature. The larger number of layers can capture richer neighborhood information of a graph, but the optimal number of layers depends on the type of features. Because each feature is a different representation of the context. We believe that such architecture allows GCNs to handle meaningful context representation to disambiguate word senses.

Vaswani et al. introduced the first full-attentional architecture called Transformer [24]. Since then, the transformer has been successfully applied to many NLP tasks. It is potential for learning long-term dependency, while it is limited by a fixed-length context in the setting of language modeling. Dai et al. proposed Trans-XL that enables learning dependency beyond a fixed-length without disrupting temporal coherence [6]. Following the assumption that the sense of a word depends on the domain in which it is used, we leverage contextual features obtained by a whole document appearing the target word by utilizing the Trans-XL.

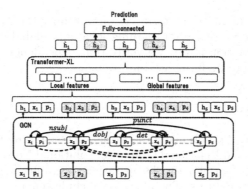

Fig. 1. NLGCL framework: GCNs integrates different features from local contexts, while Trans-XL learns local and global contexts simultaneously. "$\mathbf{x_2}$" and "$\mathbf{x_4}$" show the target word.

3   Neural Local and Global Contexts Learning

It is well-known that a proper window size of the context depends on part-of-speech information, e.g., the information within a large window is effective to disambiguate nouns but drops off dramatically for adjectives and verbs. Our method follows the insight. Figure 1 illustrates our Neural Local and Global Contexts Learning (NLGCL) framework.

3.1   Local Context Learning with GCNs

GCNs take a graph as input and apply convolution operation on each node over its local graph neighborhoods [10]. It can capture syntactic dependency structures naturally as well as word order as the information can flow in the opposite direction of edges. For instance, in Fig. 2 which illustrates the input graph of GCNs, the word "possibility" modifies the previous word "discuss". Let $G = (V, E)$ be a direct graph. Here, each $v_i \in V$ ($|V| = n$) indicates a node consisting of a word and POS information as illustrated in Fig. 1. We can define a matrix $\mathbf{A} \in \mathbb{R}^{n \times d}$. Here, each column $\mathbf{a}_i \in \mathbb{R}^d$ indicates the encoded node of v_i, i.e., we concatenate word and POS embeddings, $\mathbf{a}_i = \mathbf{x}_i \circ \mathbf{p}_i$. $(v_i, v_j, l) \in E$ refers to a labeled edge, where $l \in L$ is a relation type. In this paper, we use two types of relation which are illustrated in Fig. 2: (1) **Dependency relation** that has three information flows, i.e., from head to dependent (dep.), from dependent to head, and self-loop, and (2) **Word order:** that is created to connect each word in the chain form. To capture the forward and backward contextual information, these words are lined in two directions, i.e., from left to right and from right to left [25]. Let $\mathbf{h}_i^{(k)} \in \mathbb{R}^{d^{(k)}}$ be hidden state of node v_i in the k-th layer of the neural network and $d^{(k)}$ be the dimensionality of this layer's representations. The propagation model which calculates the forward-pass update of a node v_i in a multi-graph is given by:

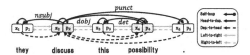

Fig. 2. Local context representation with three features. "x_i" and "p_i" refer to the i-th word embeddings and its POS embeddings, respectively. Lines denote word orders and curves indicate three types of edges with labeled syntactic relations.

$$\mathbf{h}_i^{(k+1)} = f\left(\sum_{l \in L} \sum_{j \in N_i^l} \frac{1}{c_i^l} \mathbf{W}_l^{(k)} \mathbf{h}_j^{(k)} + \mathbf{b}_l^{(k)}\right), \tag{1}$$

where N_i^l indicates the set of neighbor indices of node v_i under relation $l \in L$. c_i^l refers to a normalization constant. We set c_i^l to $|N_i^l|$. $\mathbf{W}_l^{(k)}$ stands for the weight matrix under relation $l \in L$.[1] f indicates an activation function. We used the ReLU function. In Eq. (1), we can accumulate transformed feature vectors of neighboring nodes depending on the relation type and direction of an edge through a normalized sum. On the basis of GCNs, the local context learning model is given by:

$$\mathbf{h}_i^{(k+1)} = f\left(\sum_{l \in L} \sum_{j \in N_i^l} g_{ij}^{(k)} \times \frac{1}{c_i^l}(\mathbf{W}_l^{(k)} \mathbf{h}_j^{(k)} + \mathbf{b}_l^{(k)})\right), \tag{2}$$

$$g_{ij}^{(k)} = \sigma\left(\hat{\mathbf{W}}_l^{(k)} \mathbf{h}_j^{(k)} + \hat{\mathbf{b}}_l^{(k)}\right), j \in N_i^l. \tag{3}$$

$g_{ij}^{(k)}$ is called gate mechanism [15]. It reduces the false dependency edge effects. The information from neighboring nodes may not reliable because it is often the case that the dependency relations by NLP tools are error-prone. Thus, it needs to be down-weighted. Similar to [15,25], we use the gate value obtained by Eq. (3). σ refers to the logistic sigmoid function so that the gate value ranging from 0 to 1. $\hat{\mathbf{W}}_l^{(k)} \in \mathbb{R}^{n \times d}$ and $\hat{\mathbf{b}}_l^{(k)} \in \mathbb{R}^d$ show weights and a bias for the gate, respectively. It then multiplies with the incoming message and the hidden states $\mathbf{h}_i^{(k+1)}$ are obtained as an output of the GCNs.

3.2   Local and Global Context Learning with Transformer-XL

We note that the GCN model is a special form of Laplacian smoothing which mixes the features of a node and its neighbors. The smoothing operation result is difficult to discriminate among features of nodes [25]. It is more problematic when the training data is small. Adding more layers also makes it more difficult to train [12]. Therefore, as illustrated in Fig. 1, after the hidden states $\mathbf{h}_i$

---

[1] We used 39 dependency labels provided by the Stanford CoreNLP syntactic parser for the first two types of flows, two types of word order, and self-loops which would result in having 81 ($39 \times 2 + 2 + 1$) different matrices in every layer.

of the GCNs has been learned, we concatenate them with the embeddings of word $\mathbf{x}_i$ and POS $\mathbf{p}_i$, and obtain the word representation with the local context information aggregated, i.e., $\mathbf{a}'_i = \mathbf{h}_i \circ \mathbf{x}_i \circ \mathbf{p}_i$. The concatenation operator keeps some original embeddings information. The result has a fixed length. We delete padding which makes the lengths of the sentences equal and further concatenate each sentence within the document into one sequence. On the one hand, GCNs supports the hypothesis that a sense of a word depends on the context in which it is used as it is based on the features within a sentence. On the other hand, the sense of a word, especially a polysemous noun depends on the broader contexts. To capture the long-range context in WSD, we applied the Trans-XL [6]. Trans-XL is derived from Transformers [24] and is based on the deep self-attention network. It introduces two techniques: recurrence mechanism and relative positional encoding to solve limited context-dependency and context fragmentation problems. The recurrence mechanism uses information from previous segments to capture long-term dependency. The hidden state sequence obtained by computing the previous segment is fixed and cashed. It is resued when the model processes the next new segment. This architecture allows the network with long sequences.

Another technique is relative positional encoding that utilizes the relative distance between them which solves the problem that tokens from different segments have the same positional encoding. Trans-XL has been shown very effective and achieved good performance compared to the existing language models such as Adaptive input by [2] and Deeper self-attention by [1] on five benchmark datasets including WikiText-103 [17]. Inspired by the success of neural networks capturing rich long-range contexts, we use it to learn global contexts as well as local contexts obtained by GCNs. As shown in Fig. 1, the result by concatenating each sentence within the whole document is passed to the transformer-XL. We obtain the output matrix $\mathbf{M}_{txl} \in \mathbb{R}^{n' \times 2d}$, where n' denotes the total number of words that appeared in the document.

3.3   Sense Prediction

For the result obtained by the Trans-XL, we extract each target word vector, i.e., the word which should be assigned a sense is extracted from the matrix $\mathbf{M}_{txl}$ and passed them to the fully connected layer $\mathbf{FC}_{ws}$. The weight matrix of $\mathbf{FC}_{ws}$ is referred to $\mathbf{W}_{ws} \in \mathbb{R}^{s \times 2d}$ where s is the number of senses in all of the target words. The predicted sense vector $\mathbf{y}^{(ws)}$ which is given by:

$$\mathbf{y}^{(ws)} = softmax\left(\mathbf{M}_{txl} \cdot \mathbf{W}_{ws}\right). \tag{4}$$

We obtain loss value by using $\mathbf{y}^{(ws)}$ and its true sense vector $\mathbf{t}^{(ws)}$ which is represented as a one-hot vector. The training objective is to minimize the following loss:

Table 1. Statistics of the datasets: The first line is the number of target words in each dataset. The second and thrid line refers to the average number of target words per sentence, and the average number of senses in three folds, respectively.

Dataset	SemCor	SE7	SE2	SE3	SE13	SE15
Target words	226,036	455	2,282	1,850	1,644	1,022
Target words per sent	6.1	3.4	9.4	5.3	5.4	7.4
Senses	1.6	1.1	1.2	1.2	1.1	1.1

$$L_{ws}(\theta) = \begin{cases} -\dfrac{1}{n_{ws}} \sum_{i=1}^{n_s} \sum_{w=1}^{n_w} \sum_{t=1}^{d_{ws}} t_{iwt}^{(ws)} \log(y_{iwt}^{(ws)}) & (n_{ws} \geq 1), \\ 0 & (n_{ws} = 0). \end{cases} \tag{5}$$

n_s in Eq. (5) refers to the minibatch size (the number of sentences) and n_{ws} shows the number of target words within the minibatch size. n_w denotes the number of target words within the minibatch size, and d_{ws} indicates the number of senses in all of the target words. θ refers to the parameter used in the network. $y_{iwt}^{(ws)}$ and $t_{iwt}^{(ws)}$ show the value of the t-th sense for the w-th target word in the i-th sentence within the minibatch size and its true value (1 or 0), respectively.

4 Experiments

4.1 Dataset and Model Settings

We used English all-words fine-grained WSD datasets and evaluation metric, F-score proposed by [21]. The datasets are Senseval/SemEval data consisting of Semcor training, Senseval-2 (SE2), Senseval-3 (SE3), SemEval-07 (SE7), SemEval-13 (SE13), and SemEval-15 (SE15). Similar to other related work, we choose SE7 which is the smallest test set as the development set. The data statistics on five datasets are summarized in Table 1. All the datasets are tagged by using Stanford CoreNLP Toolkit [14]. To make a fair comparison with previous work, we used GloVe as a word-embedding tool [18].

The hyperparameters which are used in our model are shown in Table 2. These hyperparameters are optimized by using Optuna[2]. They were independently determined for each dataset. In the experiments, we run three times for each model and obtained the averaged performance, F-score.

4.2 Main Results

We recall that (1) our model is based on GCNs and Trans-XL, (2) the model learns the optimal number of layers corresponding to each feature as local contexts, (3) we leveraged contextual features obtained by a whole document

[2] https://github.com/pfnet/optuna.

Table 2. Model settings for NLGCL: "m" refers to the total number of dimensions of word and POS vectors.

Hyperparameter	Value	Hyperparameter	Value
# of epoch	150	Minibatch sizes (bs)	4
Dropout range	0.5	Gradient descent	Adam
Learning rate	10^{-3}	# of dimensions of word vector	300
# of dimensions of POS vector	100	Activation function (f)	ReLU
Hyperparameter (GCN)	**Value**	**Hyperparameter (GCN)**	**Value**
# of layers (Dependency structure)	8	# of layers (Word order)	2
Activation function (σ)	Sigmoid		
Hyperparameter (Trans-XL)	**Value**	**Hyperparameter (Trans-XL)**	**Value**
# of steps to predict	64	# of steps to cache	64
# of layers	8	# of model dimensions	800
# of dimensions of embeddings ($2m$)	800	# of attention heads	20
# of dimensions of each attention head	20		

appearing the target word as global contexts. We thus examine how these methods affect the overall performance. The baselines are "with and without(w/o) GCNs" and "with and w/o Trans-XL". "With GCNs" is further classified into "with and w/o" sharing the number of parameters (P. sharing) for dependency structure and word order features. Similarly, "With Trans-XL" is divided into four types which are (i) sentence including the target word plus one surrounding sentence to the left and on to the right (1sur), (ii) all the previous sentences before the target word (previous sent), (iii) whole document (doc), and (iv) whole documents in the training data (whole docs). As a result, we compared our method to ten baselines in total. The results are summarized in Table 3.

As can be seen clearly from Table 3, combining GCNs and Trans-XL is effective for learning local and global contexts as we obtained the best results in each dataset and all five datasets. In particular, Trans-XL works well because the results by combining GCNs and Trans-XL showed a 4.5% improvement over the baseline GCNs only (w/o Trans-XL), and a 1.6% improvement over the use of Trans-XL only (w/o GCNs & doc). This is reasonable because Trans-XL learns global contexts together with local contexts trained by GCNs. The results of the NLGCL model were slightly better than those obtained by P. sharing, especially it works well for nouns and verbs. In contrast, in the baselines with only GCNs, there is no significant difference between with and without P. sharing.

The results "ALL" indicate that there is no significant difference among four ranges of global contexts in the model, Trans-XL only. However, with GCNs and Trans-XL, 1sur was worse compared with other results. This indicates that integrating GCNs with learning local contexts and Trans-XL with a more wide range of contexts are effective for disambiguating senses. In the model, Trans-XL only, it is observed that the results by "w/o GCNs & doc" were slightly better than those by "w/o GCNs & previous sent" and "w/o GCNs & 1sur"

Table 3. Main results: "*" indicates that the score is not statistically significant compared to our model (NLGCL). We tested a t-test, p-value < 0.05.

Methods	Dev	Test datasets				All test datasets				
	SE07	SE2	SE3	SE13	SE15	N	V	Adj	Adv	All
NLGCL (Ours)	63.1	72.9	**71.0**	**73.0**	71.0	**75.0**	**56.8**	78.3	80.3	**72.0**
GCNs										
P. sharing	61.8	*72.6	*69.8	71.6	*69.9	73.9	55.8	*78.0	*80.1	71.0
w/o Trans-XL	60.9	69.5	65.2	65.7	67.4	69.3	52.0	74.6	*80.0	67.0
w/o Trans-XL & P. sharing	60.0	69.4	64.6	66.1	67.5	69.1	51.9	74.6	79.2	66.9
Trans-XL										
1sur	61.5	74.1	*70.7	71.7	*70.2	74.4	*56.1	*78.3	79.6	71.6
Previous sent	**64.8**	**74.4**	*70.8	71.9	*70.4	*74.5	*56.6	*77.9	**81.7**	*71.9
Whole docs	*63.1	*72.8	*70.9	*72.6	*71.1	*74.6	*56.7	**78.9**	*80.6	*71.9
w/o GCNs & 1sur	61.7	72.2	68.7	71.2	69.6	73.7	54.5	76.7	79.6	70.4
w/o GCNs & previous sent	61.6	*72.4	68.2	71.6	69.0	73.6	54.3	76.7	*80.2	70.3
w/o GCNs & doc	61.5	*72.3	68.4	71.6	69.4	74.2	54.9	77.5	81.3	70.4
w/o GCNs & whole docs	*62.0	71.9	68.2	71.8	68.9	73.7	53.7	76.6	79.6	70.2

Table 4. Ablation results: "Dep Str" refers to Dependency structures. "*" indicates the score is not statistically significant compared to our model. We tested a t-test, p-value < 0.05.

	Dev	Test datasets				All test datasets				
	SE07	SE2	SE3	SE13	SE15	N	V	Adj	Adv	All
NLGCL (Ours)	63.1	**72.9**	**71.0**	**73.0**	**71.0**	**75.0**	**56.8**	**78.3**	80.3	**72.0**
w/o Dep Str	61.5	*72.6	68.4	71.4	70.1	73.9	54.9	76.9	79.3	70.6
w/o POS	*62.6	71.4	66.9	70.1	68.0	72.0	54.3	75.8	79.5	69.1
w/o Word order	*63.7	*72.5	69.1	71.2	69.9	73.3	*56.1	*77.6	*80.5	70.7
w/o Dep str & POS	60.6	69.6	65.5	68.8	66.9	70.4	53.2	73.8	78.0	67.7
w/o Dep str & Word order	61.5	*72.3	68.4	71.6	69.4	74.2	54.9	*77.5	**81.3**	70.4
w/o POS & Word order	*62.1	*73.4	68.7	71.6	70.0	74.0	*56.1	76.3	80.8	70.9

for all POS. However, when we use the whole training dataset, the performance for all of the POS decreased. One reason is that the datasets are collected from several domains, e.g., SE15 comes from three domains, biomedical, mathematics/computing, and social issues which deteriorate the overall performance. This indicates that a document can capture the sense of a word rather than the whole documents consisting of several domains.

4.3 Ablation Study for Local Contextual Features

We conduct two sets of ablation studies to empirically examine the impact of three types of local contextual features used in GCNs. Table 4 shows the results. Overall, we can see that dependency structures and POS information improve

Table 5. Comparative results: The four blocks show our model, MFS baseline, two supervised systems, and two pre-trained contextualized word representations.

Methods	Dev	Test datasets				All test datasets				
	SE07	SE2	SE3	SE13	SE15	N	V	Adj	Adv	All
NLGCL (Ours)	63.1	**72.9**	**71.0**	**73.0**	71.0	**75.0**	56.8	**78.3**	80.3	**72.0**
MFS	54.5	65.6	66.0	63.8	67.1	67.7	49.8	73.1	80.5	65.6
IMS [27]	61.3	70.9	69.3	65.3	69.5	70.5	55.8	75.6	82.9	68.9
IMS$_{+emb}$ [8]	62.6	72.2	70.4	65.9	71.5	71.9	56.6	75.9	**84.7**	70.1
Context2Vec [16]	61.3	71.8	69.1	65.6	**71.9**	71.2	57.4	75.2	82.7	69.6
ELMo [19]	–	71.6	69.6	66.2	71.3	–	–	–	–	69.7

the performance of our model, especially, POS information plays a crucial role in our model leading to improvement as the results on all test datasets and POS sense-tagged data decreased when we did not use it as a local context feature (w/o POS). One exception is that for adverbs, the result by using only POS information, i.e., Trans-XL only was better than our model with three features. One possible reason is that some adverbs are appearing in the document with a specific domain. But why such adverbs only affect the performance is not clear at this point. It requires further investigation to answer this question.

4.4   Comparison with Related Work

We compared our method against the best supervised and without LKB systems. These systems are: (i) IMS is a linear SVMs and utilizes a set of features of the surrounding words of the target word including POS and collocations, (ii) IMS$_{+emb}$ is an extended version of IMS with word embeddings, (iii) Context2Vec is a model which makes use of a bidirectional LSTM, and (iv) ELMo is a two-layer bidirectional LSTM language model. Both Context2Vec and ELMo evaluate WSD by using nearest neighbor matching between the test and training instance representations. Table 5 shows the results. We can see from Table 5 that NLGCL attained the best results (72.0%) on the dataset by concatenating all four test data, while no system always achieves the best performance on all the test data. Compared with two supervised systems and two pre-trained contextualized word representation systems, our model outperforms on four test datasets. This indicates that our model can capture a variety of contextual features obtained from the limited size of sense-tagged data.

We also compared our method with a pre-trained contextualized word representations model by using BERT [7], while it is difficult to make a fair comparison as our model is based on GloVe, a simple embedding method so that we can examine the contextual features obtained mainly from the sense-tagged data. The best F-score by [7] obtained by BERT linear projection was 74.1%, and it was a 2.1% improvement compared with our model. However, the result obtained by our model showed a 1.9% improvement over [7] model on SE13.

This proves that our model is especially effective for nouns as SE13 consists of only noun sense-tagged data.

5 Conclusion

We have presented a method by leveraging a variety of contexts into a neural-WSD model. The comparative results showed that our model is competitive as the improvement was 1.4% ∼ 3.1% by F-score. Moreover, we found that the dependency structure and POS features contribute to performance improvement in our model. Future work will include: (i) evaluating our model by using other Senseval/SemEval data including multilingual WSD for quantitative evaluation, and (ii) incorporating other contextual features such as relative position, coreference, and inter-sentential relations.

Acknowledgements. We are grateful to the anonymous reviewers for their comments and suggestions. This work was supported by the Grant-in-aid for JSPS, Grant Number 21K12026, and JKA through its promotion funds from KEIRIN RACE.

References

1. AI-Rfou, R., Choe, D., Constant, N., Guo, M., Jones, L.: Character-level language modeling with deeper self-attention. In: Proceedings of the Advancement of Artificial Intelligence, pp. 3159–3166 (2019)
2. Baevski, A., Auli, M.: Adaptive input representations for neural language modeling. In: Proceedings of 7th International Conference on Learning Representations (2019)
3. Bastings, J., Titov, I., Aziz, W., Marcheggiani, D., Sima'an, K.: Graph convolutional networks for text classification. In: Proceedings of the 2017 Conference on Empirical Methods in Natural Language Processing, pp. 1957–1967 (2017)
4. Bevilacqua, M., Navigli, R.: Braking through the 80% glass ceiling; raising the state of the art in word sense disambiguation by incorporating knowledge graph information. In: Proceedings of the 58th Annual Meeting of the Association for Computational Linguistics, pp. 2854–2864 (2020)
5. Blevins, T., Zettlemoyer, L.: Moving down the long tail of word sense disambiguation with gloss informed bi-encoders. In: Proceedings of the 58th Annual Meeting of the Association for Computational Linguistics, pp. 1006–1017 (2020)
6. Dai, Z., Yang, Z., Yang, Y., Carbonell, J., Le, Q.V., Salakhutdinov, R.: Transformer-XL: attentive language models beyond a fixed-length context. In: Proceedings of 30th Conference on Neural Information Processing Systems, pp. 2978–2988 (2019)
7. Hadiwinoto, C., Ng, H.T., Gan, W.C.: Improved word sense disambiguation using pre-trained contextualized word Representations. In: Proceedings of the 2019 Conference on Empirical Methods in Natural Language Processing and the 9th International Joint Conference on Natural Language Processing, pp. 5300–5309 (2019)
8. Iacobacci, I., Pilehvar, M.T., Navigli, R.: Embeddings for word sense disambiguation: an evaluation study. In: Proceedings of the 54th Annual Meeting of the Association for Computational Linguistics, pp. 897–907 (2016)

9. Ide, N., Véronis, J.: Introduction to the special issue on word sense disambiguation: the state of the art. J. Assoc. Comput. Linguist. **24**(1), 1–40 (1998)

10. Kipf, T.N., Welling, M.: SEMI-supervised classification with graph convolutional networks. In: Proceedings of the 5th International Conference on Learning Representations (2017)

11. Levine, Y., Lenz, B., Dagan, O., Ram, O., et al.: SenseBERT: driving some sense into BERT. In: Proceedings of the 58th Annual Meeting of the Association for Computational Linguistics, pp. 4656–4667 (2020)

12. Li, Q., han, Z., Wu, X.M.: Deeper insights into graph convolutional networks for semi-supervised learning. In: Proceedings of 32nd AAAI Conference on Artificial Intelligence, pp. 3538–3545 (2018)

13. Luo, F., Liu, T., Xia, Q., Chang, B., Sui, Z.: Incorporating glosses into neural word sense disambiguation. In: Proceedings of the 56th Annual Meeting of the Association for Computational Linguistics, pp. 2473–2482 (2018)

14. Manning, C.D., Surdeanu, M., Bauer, J., Finkel, J., Bethard, S.J., McClosky, D.: The stanford core NLP natural language processing toolkit. In: Proceedings of the 52nd Annual Meeting of the Association for Computational Linguistics: System Demonstrations, pp. 55–60 (2014)

15. Marcheggiani, D., Titov, I.: Encoding sentences with graph convolutional networks for semantic role labeling. In: Proceedings of the 2017 Conference on Empirical Methods in Natural Language Processing, pp. 1506–1515 (2017)

16. Melamud, O., Goldberger, J., Dagan, I.: Context2vec: learning generic context embedding with bidirectional LSTM. In: Proceedings of the 20th SIGNLL Conference on Computational Natural Language Learning, pp. 51–61 (2016)

17. Merity, S., Xiong, C., Bradbury, J., Socher, R.: Pointer sentinel mixture models. In: arXiv preprint arXiv:1609.07843 (2016)

18. Pennington, J., Socher, R., Manning, C.D.: GloVe: global vectors for word representation. In: Proceedings of the 2014 Conference on Empirical Methods in Natural Language PRocessing and the 9th International Joint Conference on Natural Language PRocessing, pp. 1532–1543 (2014)

19. Peters, M.E., et al.: Deep contextualized word representations. In: Proceedings of the 2018 Conference of the North American Chapter of the Association for Computational Linguistics: Human Language Technologies, pp. 2227–2237 (2018)

20. Raganato, A., Bovi, C.D., Navigli, R.: Neural sequence learning models for word sense disambiguation. In: Proceedings of the 2017 Conference on Empirical Methods in Natural Language Processing, pp. 1156–1167 (2017)

21. Raganato, A., Camacho-Collados, J., Navigli, R.: Word sense disambiguation; A unified evaluation framework and empirical comparison. In: Proceedings of the 15th European Chapters of the Association for Computational Linguistics, pp. 99–110 (2017)

22. Schlichtkrull, M., Kipf, T.N., Bloem, P., Berg, R.V.D., Titov, I., Welling, M.: Modeling relational data with graph convolutional networks. In: Proceedings of European Semantic Web Conference, pp. 593–607 (2018)

23. Vashishth, S., Bhandari, M., Yadav, P., Rai, P., Bhattacharyya, C., Talukdar, P.: Incorporating syntactic and semantic information in word embeddings using graph convolutional networks. In: Proceedings of the 57th Annual Meeting of the Association for Computational Linguistics, pp. 3308–3318 (2019)

24. Vaswani, A., et al.: Attention is all you need. In: Proceedings of the NIPS, pp. 6000–6010 (2017)

25. Xu, Y., Yang, J.: Look again at the syntax: Relational graph convolutional network for gendered ambiguous pronoun resolution. In: Proceedings of the 1st Workshop on Gender Bias in Natural Language Processing, pp. 99–104 (2019)
26. Yarowsky, D.: One sense per collocation. In: Proceedings of ARPA Human Language Processing Technology Workshop, pp. 266–271 (1993)
27. Zhong, Z., Ng, H.T.: It makes sense: a wide-coverage word sense disambiguation system for free text. In: Proceedings of the ACL 2010 System Demonstrations, pp. 78–83 (2010)

Towards Better Dermoscopic Image Feature Representation Learning for Melanoma Classification

ChengHui Yu[1], MingKang Tang[1], ShengGe Yang[1], MingQing Wang[1], Zhe Xu[1], JiangPeng Yan[1,2(✉)], HanMo Chen[1], Yu Yang[1], Xiao-Jun Zeng[3], and Xiu Li[1(✉)]

[1] Tsinghua Shenzhen International Graduate School, Tsinghua University, Shenzhen 518055, People's Republic of China
{ych20,tmk20,ysg20,wmq20,xu-z18,chm20,yy20}@mails.tsinghua.edu.cn,
li.xiu@sz.tsinghua.edu.cn
[2] Department of Automation, Tsinghua University, Beijing, China
yanjp17@mails.tsinghua.edu.cn
[3] Department of Computer Science, University of Manchester, Manchester, UK
x.zeng@manchester.ac.uk

Abstract. Deep learning-based melanoma classification with dermoscopic images has recently shown great potential in automatic early-stage melanoma diagnosis. However, limited by the significant data imbalance and obvious extraneous artifacts, i.e., the hair and ruler markings, discriminative feature extraction from dermoscopic images is very challenging. In this study, we seek to resolve these problems respectively towards better representation learning for lesion features. Specifically, a GAN-based data augmentation (GDA) strategy is adapted to generate synthetic melanoma-positive images, in conjunction with the proposed implicit hair denoising (IHD) strategy. Wherein the hair-related representations are implicitly disentangled via an auxiliary classifier network and reversely sent to the melanoma-feature extraction backbone for better melanoma-specific representation learning. Furthermore, to train the IHD module, the hair noises are additionally labeled on the ISIC2020 dataset, making it the first large-scale dermoscopic dataset with annotation of hair-like artifacts. Extensive experiments demonstrate the superiority of the proposed framework as well as the effectiveness of each component. The improved dataset will be publicly available after the review.

Keywords: Deep learning · Dermoscopic images · Melanoma diagnosis · Image classification

1 Introduction

Melanoma is a rare but highly fatal skin cancer, leading to nearly 75% skin cancer associated deaths [1]. Early detection and diagnosis of melanoma are crucial since

---

C. Yu and M. Tang—Equal contribution.

© Springer Nature Switzerland AG 2021
T. Mantoro et al. (Eds.): ICONIP 2021, LNCS 13111, pp. 550–561, 2021.
https://doi.org/10.1007/978-3-030-92273-3_45

the five-year survival rate will rise to 97% if identified at a curable stage [2]. However, current methods for early melanoma diagnosis highly rely on clinical judgment on dermoscopic images. Due to the rareness of melanoma and its vagueness of early symptoms, the diagnosis results are highly dependent on physicians' clinical experience and diagnostic insights [3]. Consequently, nearly half of patients are diagnosed with late-stage cancer, and therefore suffer from pain by systemic anticancer therapy and accompanying side effects, which are entirely preventable [4].

Recently, computer-aided diagnosis (CAD) has shown promising performance in the early diagnosis of cancer. With the CAD system, dermatologists are able to perform large-scale early detection of melanoma with human effort reduced. In particular, deep learning-based CAD becomes dominant on diagnostic accuracy by reason of its outstanding ability in extracting features from the input data [5–8]. To better exploit the input dermoscopic images, current melanoma classification models often rely on an ensemble strategy [9,10]. Despite their excellent performance in accuracy, such an ensemble strategy has various disadvantages, such as time consumption, resource demand, and interpretation difficulty.

In addition to the ensemble strategy, another rewarding approach towards satisfying outcomes is to make endeavors on more discriminative feature representation extraction from dermoscopic images. However, two main challenges are observed. Firstly, existing dermoscopic datasets are usually notably classimbalanced because positive samples for melanoma are fewer than negative ones. For example, positive samples only account for 1.7% of the entire ISIC2020 dataset [11]. This substantial imbalance greatly hinders the representation learning of positive features. On the other hand, dermoscopic images are often accompanied by linear-shaped obstructions, i.e., hairs, as shown in Fig. 1. To eliminate such hair-like artifacts, some efforts are made to superficially erase them from images via segmentation mask-/morphological-based inpainting [12,13]. However, this strategy may introduce other artifacts [14] or undermine the relevant lesion pixels, thus impeding the subsequent feature extraction.

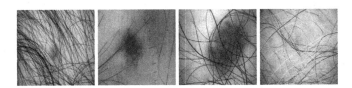

Fig. 1. Example cases with hair-like artifacts in the ISIC2020 dataset

In this study, we focus on resolving the two aforementioned challenges, i.e., data imbalance and the hair-like artifact, towards better representation learning for lesion feature. Firstly, aiming to ameliorate the data imbalance problem, we adapt a GAN-based data augmentation (GDA) strategy to generate synthetic melanoma-positive images. As for hair denoising, our initial idea stems from the decision-making process of trained dermatologists. In a dermatologist-only situation, the clinicians can identify the subtle differences in local features regardless of the presence of hair and color differences based on their experience rather than using conventional bottom-up instant image analysis fashion [15]. Correspondingly, we propose an implicit hair denoising (IHD) strategy, wherein the hair-related representations are implicitly disentangled via an auxiliary classifier network and reversely sent to the melanoma-feature extraction backbone for better melanoma-specific representation learning. Besides, in order to train the IHD module, the hair-like artifacts are additionally labeled on the ISIC2020 dataset [11], making it the first large-scale dermoscopy dataset with annotation of hair-like artifacts. Compared to the superficially inpainting-based methods [12,16], our approach focuses on the high-level feature representation without introducing other artifacts [14] to the images. Extensive experiments on multiple datasets demonstrate that our GDA and IHD strategies are effective with competitive results. The main contributions of this work are summarized as follows:

(1) To address the notable data imbalance in the melanoma classification task, we adapt a GAN-based data augmentation strategy to generate synthetic melanoma-positive images.
(2) To eliminate the impact of hair-like artifacts, we present an implicit hair denoising strategy, where the hair-related representations are implicitly disentangled, facilitating more discriminative melanoma-specific representation learning.
(3) To train the implicit hair denoising module, we provide a melanoma dataset including 33,126 cases with manually annotated hair-like artifact labels upon the ISIC2020 dataset [11], making it the first large-scale dermoscopy dataset with annotation of hair-like artifacts.

2   Methods

Figure 2 illustrates the framework of our proposed model for melanoma classification. The backbone consists of a color-constancy layer and a feature extractor to extract semantic features from dermoscopic images. Then our model classifies melanoma ONLY based on the features learned from dermoscopic images. We balance the class distribution of melanoma-positive/negative samples with the GDA strategy. Meanwhile, the hair-like artifacts would be implicitly eliminated via the IHD strategy. Details are elaborated as follows.

2.1   Backbone Setting

Our approach shares the standard backbone setting [17–19] consisting of a color constancy layer for image preprocessing and an encoder for feature extraction.

Color Constancy. Color constancy is a typical step in dermoscopic image preprocessing to reduce the environmental impact. This step could possibly simulate the neuro-physiological mechanism of color perception. Comparing several existing algorithms (e.g., Shades of Gray [20] and Max-RGB [21]), we found that Max-RGB achieved superior performance on the ISIC2020 dataset [11]. Thus, Max-RGB is adopted to adjust image colors in our study. Max-RGB assumes

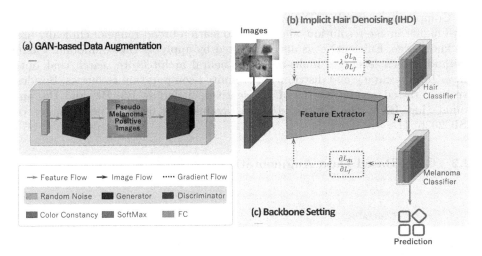

Fig. 2. The overall framework for melanoma diagnosis.

that white patches cause the maximum response of each color channel, which can be formulated as $\max_{x} f(X) = ke$, where $f(X) = [R(X), B(X), G(X)]^{\mathrm{T}}$ represents the pixel values of the original image, X is pixel coordinates, k is calibration constant, and e is illumination factor.

Feature Extraction. Feature extraction via supervised learning is widely employed in dermoscopic image classification tasks [18,19]. Following the previous work in [22], we utilizes EfficientNet-B3 [23] to extract the lesion features F_e, formulated by:

$$F_e(x_{img}; \mathbf{W}_e) = EfficientNet(x_{img}), \tag{1}$$

where $\mathbf{W}_e$ represents a parametric matrix and x_{img} denotes the input images after data enhancement (i.e., GDA and color constancy). $EfficientNet$ function indicates EfficientNet-B3. The backbone function $Backbone_m$ is parameterized by weights-biased softmax $(\mathbf{W}_m, b_m)$:

$$Backbone_m(F_e; \mathbf{W}_m, b_m) = softmax(\mathbf{W}_m F_e + b_m). \tag{2}$$

Then, the cross-entropy loss is used as the loss function in learning process:

$$\mathcal{L}_m(Backbone_m, y) = -\sum \log(Backbone_m)y, \tag{3}$$

where y represents the correct class label of input image x_{img}.

Formula (4) represents the objective function for the melanoma classifier optimization, where i indicates the i-th sample.

$$\min_{\mathbf{W}_e, \mathbf{W}_m, b_m} \left[\frac{1}{n} \sum_{i=1}^{N} \mathcal{L}_m^i(Backbone_m, y) \right], \tag{4}$$

Compared to regular CNN architecture, EfficientNet is deeper and wider with higher image resolution, allowing it to learn a broad range of clinically useful knowledge. EfficientNet is also generated by applying the compound scaling method, which leverages multi-objective neural architecture search that optimizes both accuracy and distribution of limited computation resources. Besides, we have tested several depths of EfficientNet, including B3, B4, and B6, and found that B3 is the optimized depth against the model's performance on ISIC2020 [11].

2.2   GAN-Based Data Augmentation Strategy

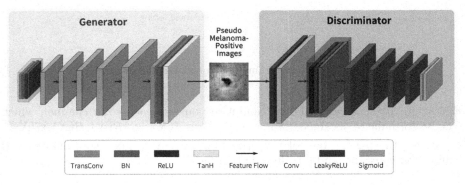

Fig. 3. The architecture of the decoupled DCGANs (Deep Convolutional Generative Adversarial Networks) used in our GAN-based data augmentation.

Due to the fact that melanoma is rare skin cancer, the positive and negative samples are severely imbalanced in the ISIC2020 dataset [11], where there are 584 positive samples out of 33,126 images (only 1.76%). Data augmentation is a promising strategy to cope with the severe data imbalance and improve the model generalizability. Inspired by [12], decoupled DCGANs (as shown in Fig. 3) is adapted to generate extra 2,000 synthetic melanoma-positive images with the upsampled resolution of 512×512. DCGAN could be formulated as $\min \mathbf{G} \max \mathbf{D} V(\mathbf{D}, \mathbf{G})$, where $\mathbf{G}$ and $\mathbf{D}$ represent Generator and Discriminator respectively. $V(\mathbf{D}, \mathbf{G})$ shows the difference between the synthetic and genuine samples. The generator minimizes the difference while the discriminator separates synthetic and genuine samples as much as possible. Specifically, the generator is trained under the supervision of the discriminator to produce images with similar distribution as the ground-truth melanoma-positive images. The distribution difference is measured by the simultaneously trained Discriminator. Then, in order to maximize data variety, the generator compares each generated image with its closest training images, in which the minimum MSE is calculated to ensure non-repeatability. Besides, the wgan loss [24] and RMSprop optimizer with a learning rate of 0.0002 are used to train both the generator and discriminator.

2.3   Implicit Hair Denoising Strategy

Hairs and other linear-shaped obstructions are usually present in dermoscopic images which result in noise in feature representation learning. Based on the fact that hair-like artifacts are often subconsciously neglected by dermatologists during diagnosis, the implicit hair denoising (IHD) strategy is proposed. Specifically, inspired by [25] which demonstrates that joint optimization will lead to both discriminativeness and domain-invariance and thus augment a new gradient reversal layer while learning features, we integrate an auxiliary classifier network to implicitly disentangle the hair-related representations, as shown in Fig. 2(b). Then, the hair-related features are feedbacked to the melanoma-feature extraction backbone for better melanoma-specific representation learning.

Formally, for EfficientNet-based features F_e after feature extractor with a parametric matrix $\mathbf{W}_e$, the reversal layer function IHD is parameterized by weights-biased softmax $(\mathbf{U}_h, v_h)$:

$$IHD(F_e; \mathbf{U}_h, v_h) = softmax(\mathbf{U}_h F_e + v_h), \tag{5}$$

Using the softmax function, each component of vector $IHD(F_e)$ represents that the neural network assigns x_{img} to the conditional probability of the corresponding class. The cross-entropy between the correct hair label y_h and IHD is adopted as the loss function for classification:

$$\mathcal{L}_h(IHD, y_h) = -\sum \log(IHD)y_h, \tag{6}$$

Formula (7) is the optimization problem on the hair classifier training under the IHD strategy, where i indicates the i-th sample.

$$\max_{\mathbf{W}_e, \mathbf{U}_h, v_h} \left[\frac{1}{n} \sum_{i=1}^{N} \mathcal{L}_h^i(IHD, y_h) \right], \tag{7}$$

3   Experiments and Results

We evaluated our approach on two public dermoscopic datasets, ISIC2020 [11] and PH2 [26]. The former was utilized to examine the feature extraction performance of our approach, while the latter was for generalization assessment of the model trained on the ISIC2020 dataset.

3.1   Datasets and Implementation Details

The experimental dataset is generated from ISIC2020 dataset [11], the largest among recent releases, originally containing 33,126 endoscopic images with patients' metadata and lesion labels. In addition, we generated another 2,000 synthetic melanoma-positive images through the GDA to balance skew classes of samples. Furthermore, we manually labeled hair-like artifacts[1] for the use of the IHD strategy. Five-folds cross-validation are adopted for model evaluation and selection after data preparation. The trained models are then fed into the dataset generated from PH2 [26] for generalization evaluation.

The proposed model was implemented based on PyTorch and trained on four NVIDIA GeForce RTX 3090 GPUs using Adam optimizer with a learning rate of $3e-5$. As suggested by Eq. (4) and Eq. (7), with the optimizer, the process of gradient descent can be formulated as follow:

$$
\begin{cases}
\theta_m \leftarrow \theta_m - \eta \dfrac{g_{m,1}}{\sqrt{g_{m,2}} + \epsilon} \\[2ex]
\theta_h \leftarrow \theta_h - \eta\lambda \dfrac{g_{h,1}}{\sqrt{g_{h,2}} + \epsilon} \\[2ex]
\theta_f \leftarrow \theta_f - \eta \left(\dfrac{g_{m,1}}{\sqrt{g_{m,2}} + \epsilon} - \lambda \dfrac{g_{h,1}}{\sqrt{g_{h,2}} + \epsilon} \right)
\end{cases}
\tag{8}
$$

where η is the learning rate, and λ is the weighted loss rate of hair-like artifacts. $g_{k,i} = \dfrac{\beta_i \theta_k + (1 - \beta_i)\frac{\partial^i L_k}{\partial \theta_k^i}}{1 - \beta_i}$ with subscript $k = \{m, h\}$ and $i = \{1, 2\}$. Also, $g_{m,i}$ and $g_{h,i}$ correspondingly represent the melanoma and hair gradient. Where β_1 and β_2 denote the exponential decay rate of first-order and second-order moments, respectively.

Moreover, we trained the IHD module without synthetic melanoma-positive images due to lack of hair-like artifact labelling. The batch size is set to 64, while input images are resized to 512×512 with 5-fold cross-validation. Color constancy is used in both the training and the inference process for image pre-processing.

3.2   Evaluation Metrics and Baselines

We used the area under the ROC curve (AUC), a widely-adopted metric to measure the performance of a classifier, as our quantitative metric. ROC curve illustrates the true-positive rate versus the false-positive rate at different classification thresholds. AUC thus measures the entire two-dimensional area underneath the whole ROC curve and is a relatively fair indicator with extreme data imbalance.

In this work, we chose four advanced melanoma classification methods as baselines to ensure validity. Table 1 includes the backbone, and performance of each baseline. The implementation details of the former three baselines followed the usual practice and derived from [27], among which we choose three models with the best performance. In addition, the lase one 'Ensemble' baseline is an ensemble of the former three baselines.

---

[1] The datasets generated and/or analyzed in this paper can be accessed from the corresponding author upon reasonable requests.

3.3 Experimental Results

Learning Ability. Here we first present the results of the experiments illustrating the learning ability of our model on the final dataset (see Sect. 3.1). As shown in Table 1, our approach outperforms all baselines by a large extent (mean AUC: about > 3.88%). Compared with the deepest baseline among non-ensemble models (SENet-based) and the ensemble (Ensemble-based) baseline: our AUC increases by 3.40% and 2.44%, respectively. Besides, our model is the lightest in terms of the number of parameters (only 10.9M). The minute increase in training parameters from the IHD (0.2M) indicates that the performance improvement does not rely on additional resource consumption. This result suggests that our proposed model is superior in learning ability in terms of accuracy and computational cheapness.

Table 1. Quantitative results on ISIC2020 dataset. 'Para': The number of learning parameters. 'BB': Our backbone. The value: mean ± standard deviation on five folds.

Backbone	Para (M)	AUC (%)	Backbone	Para (M)	AUC (%)
Inception-v4 [27]	41.2	86.86 ± 1.73	BB (EffNet-B3)	10.7	92.23 ± 0.91
SENet [27]	113.0	89.61 ± 1.32	BB+GDA	10.7	92.89 ± 0.85
PNASNet [27]	81.8	89.48 ± 1.44	BB+IHD	10.9	92.85 ± 0.82
Ensemble [27]	236.0	90.57 ± 1.67	**Proposed**	10.9	**93.01 ± 0.59**

Ablation Study. This section evaluates the effectiveness of each crafted strategy to gain a deeper understanding of our approach. Specifically, we examine the AUC of both the GDA and the IHD strategies on the final dataset (see Sect. 3.1).

As shown in Table 1, the mean AUC value on five-folds reaches 93.01%. Particularly, we observe that all the 'Backbone+' settings outperform the Backbone, indicating that both the GDA and the IHD strategies make crucial contribution to excellent model performance.

To further investigate the GDA component, we checked the AUC of the model using different number of synthetic melanoma-positive images (shown as Fig. 4) generated by the GDA. As shown in Fig. 5, with the increase of the number of synthetic images, the curve of AUC value rises, peaking when generating 2,000 images, and then falls, which illustrates the correlation between accuracy and man-made correction of data imbalance. Once the synthetic positive images greatly outnumber the genuine ones, the results could backfire, meaning that the model could be overwhelmed by synthetic information. The point where the AUC curve peaks (i.e., 2,000) is therefore picked as the optimized number of synthetic melanoma-positive images in our model.

To better understand our IHD strategy, we compared our IHD with preprocessing methods based on other denoising strategies. Note that, since segmentation mask-based hair removal preprocessing [12] requires segmented-mask as input, we adopted three morphological-based methods for comparison. Specifically, we applied each denoising approach in [13, 28, 29] on our backbone. As

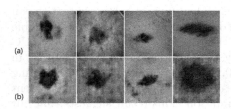

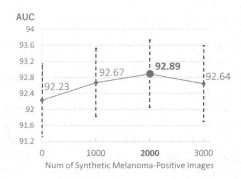

AUC

Num of Synthetic Melanoma-Positive Images

Fig. 4. Melanoma-positive samples. (a): original, (b): synthetic

Fig. 5. AUC curve with standard deviation in respect of the number of synthetic images.

shown in Table 2, we found that all morphological-based preprocessing methods impose negative effects on the backbone, while our IHD brings an improvement. This result, again, firmly suggests the superiority of our IHD strategy.

In addition, we provide visualization of some predictions as a case study. We picked out the cases where all baselines fail while only ours predicts correctly (annotated as 'Only We Succeed'), along with the cases where all the models, including ours, predict incorrectly (annotated as 'All Fail'). The results are shown in Fig. 6. Note that both images in the case of 'Only We Succeed' largely contain hair-like artifacts. This demonstrates that our approach is superior in dealing with extraneous noises and demonstrates the IHD strategy's effectiveness. As for the 'All Fail' cases, since the images are either under poor lighting or with ambiguous lesion features, this unsatisfying result could be explained by low-quality features.

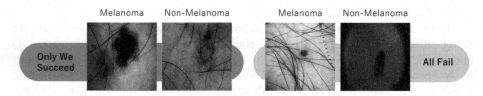

Fig. 6. The visualization case study. Only We Succeed: All other baselines failed to predict while ours predicts correctly. All Fail: All the models, including ours, failed to predict.

Generalization Capability. We evaluate the generalization of our model on the PH2 dataset [26], a small dataset with only 200 dermoscopic images wherein 20.00% are melanoma-positive and hair-like artifacts are scarce. To simulate real-world large-scale circumstances, we further augmented PH2 by adding hair noises and enlarged the PH2 to 1,000 images. The resulting dataset is annotated

Table 2. Compare to other hair removal preprocessing on ISIC 2020 dataset. The value: mean value ± standard deviation on five folds.

Methods	AUC (%)
Our Backbone (BB)	92.23 ± 0.91
BB+Hasan et al. [28]	90.85 ± 0.98
BB+Bibiloni et al. [29]	92.11 ± 0.58
BB+Calderon Ortiz et al. [13]	92.10 ± 0.67
BB+IHD (Ours)	**92.85 ± 0.82**

as PH2*. The noises are added using [30], which randomly added a different number of gray and black arcs to imitate hairs, as shown in Fig. 7.

The test results show that our model outperforms the existing advanced melanoma classifiers (see Table 3), which shows that our model, empowered by the IHD strategy, has better generalization ability despite the large existence of hair-like artifacts. This result also confirms that our model shows greater potential for clinical application in large-scale datasets, wherein images are typically with high noises and of poor quality.

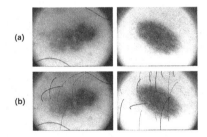

Fig. 7. The example of hair-augmented images from the PH*. (a)original (b)augmented.

Table 3. Quantitative results on inference only dataset PH2*.

Methods	AUC
Inception-v4 [27]	84.34
PNASNet [27]	82.95
SENet [27]	80.41
Ensemble [27]	85.66
Proposed	**86.48**

4   Conclusion

In this work, we focus on learning better lesion feature representations from dermoscopic images for melanoma classification. Wherein two main challenges: significant data imbalance, and surrounding artifacts, are observed. To resolve these challenges respectively, we propose the GAN-based data augmentation (GDA) and implicit hair denoising (IHD) strategy. Specifically, to balance the sample classes, a number of synthetic melanoma-positive images are generated through GDA and are used in the training process. Also, to implicitly eliminate hair-like artifacts, hair-related representations learned via an auxiliary network are feedbacked to and disentangled from the melanoma-feature extraction backbone.

Besides, to train the IHD module, we manually labeled hair-like artifacts on top of the ISIC2020 dataset, making it the first large-scale dermoscopic dataset with annotation of hair-like artifacts. Extensive experiments indicate that our approach is capable of lesion feature representation learning, showing the promising potentials for clinical applications. The improved dataset will be publicly available after the review.

Acknowledgments. This research was partly supported by the National Natural Science Foundation of China (Grant No. 41876098), the National Key R&D Program of China (Grant No. 2020AAA0108303), and Shenzhen Science and Technology Project (Grant No. JCYJ20200109143041798). Thanks to the tutors of Special Practice of Big Data Courses, who provided valuable discussions.

References

1. Jerant, A.F., Johnson, J.T., et al.: Early detection and treatment of skin cancer. Am. Fam. Physician **62**(2), 357–368 (2000)
2. Divito, S.J., Ferris, L.K.: Advances and short comings in the early diagnosis of melanoma. Melanoma Res. **20**(6), 450–458 (2010)
3. Siegel, R.L., Miller, K.D., et al.: Cancer statistics, 2020. CA: Cancer J. Clin. **70**(1), 7–30 (2020)
4. Fitzgerald, R.C.: Big data is crucial to the early detection of cancer. Nat. Med. **26**(1), 19–20 (2020)
5. Yan, J., et al.: Hierarchical attention guided framework for multi-resolution collaborative whole slide image segmentation. In: de Bruijne, M. (ed.) MICCAI 2021. LNCS, vol. 12908, pp. 153–163. Springer, Cham (2021). https://doi.org/10.1007/978-3-030-87237-3_15
6. Xu, Z., et al.: Noisy labels are treasure: mean-teacher-assisted confident learning for hepatic vessel segmentation. In: de Bruijne, M. (ed.) MICCAI 2021. LNCS, vol. 12901, pp. 3–13. Springer, Cham (2021). https://doi.org/10.1007/978-3-030-87193-2_1
7. Xu, Z., Yan, J., Luo, J., Li, X., Jagadeesan, J.: Unsupervised multimodal image registration with adaptative gradient guidance. In: IEEE International Conference on Acoustics, Speech and Signal Processing, pp. 1225–1229. IEEE (2021)
8. Xu, Z., Luo, J., Yan, J., Li, X., Jayender, J.: F3RNet: full-resolution residual registration network for deformable image registration. Int. J. Comput. Assist. Radiol. Surg. **16**(6), 923–932 (2021)
9. Ahmed, S.A.A., Yanikoğlu, B., et al.: Skin lesion classification with deep CNN ensembles. In: 2020 28th Signal Processing and Communications Applications Conference (SIU), pp. 1–4. IEEE (2020)
10. Reisinho, J., Coimbra, M., et al.: Deep convolutional neural network ensembles for multi-classification of skin lesions from dermoscopic and clinical images. In: 2020 42nd Annual International Conference of the IEEE Engineering in Medicine & Biology Society (EMBC), pp. 1940–1943. IEEE (2020)
11. Rotemberg, V., et al.: A patient-centric dataset of images and metadata for identifying melanomas using clinical context. Sci. Data **8**(1), 1–8 (2021)
12. Bisla, D., et al.: Towards automated melanoma detection with deep learning: data purification and augmentation. In: Proceedings of the IEEE/CVF Conference on Computer Vision and Pattern Recognition Workshops (2019)

13. Ortiz, J.D.C., Ticliahuanca, L.F.M., Moscol, M.E.R., Requejo, W.G.S.: Uso de algoritmos de machine learning para el diagnóstico de melanomas (2021). https:// hdl.handle.net/11042/4949
14. Xu, Z., et al.: Adversarial uni- and multi-modal stream networks for multimodal image registration. In: Martel, A.L. (ed.) MICCAI 2020. LNCS, vol. 12263, pp. 222–232. Springer, Cham (2020). https://doi.org/10.1007/978-3-030-59716-0_22
15. Croskerry, P.: Achieving quality in clinical decision making: cognitive strategies and detection of bias. Acad. Emerg. Med. $\mathbf{9}$(11), 1184–1204 (2002)
16. Khan, A.H., Iskandar, D., et al.: Classification of skin lesion with hair and artifacts removal using black-hat morphology and total variation. Int. J. Comput. Digit. Syst. $\mathbf{10}$, 597–604 (2021)
17. Ma, Z., Yin, S.: Deep attention network for melanoma detection improved by color constancy. In: 2018 9th International Conference on Information Technology in Medicine and Education (ITME), pp. 123–127. IEEE (2018)
18. Zhang, R.: Melanoma detection using convolutional neural network. In: 2021 IEEE International Conference on Consumer Electronics and Computer Engineering (ICCECE), pp. 75–78. IEEE (2021)
19. Low, K.O., Johari, A.: Skin lesion analysis for automatic melanoma detection: ISIC challenge 2019.https://challenge.isic-archive.com/leaderboards/2019. Accessed 22 June 2021
20. Finlayson, G.D., Trezzi, E.: Shades of gray and colour constancy. In: Color and Imaging Conference. vol. 1, pp. 37–41. Society for Imaging Science and Technology (2004)
21. Land, E.H.: The retinex theory of color vision. Sci. Am. $\mathbf{237}$(6), 108–129 (1977)
22. Ha, Q., Liu, B., Liu, F.: Identifying melanoma images using EfficientNet ensemble: winning solution to the SIIM-ISIC melanoma classification challenge. arXiv preprint arXiv:2010.05351 (2020)
23. Tan, M., Le, Q.: EfficientNet: rethinking model scaling for convolutional neural networks. In: International Conference on Machine Learning, pp. 6105–6114. PMLR (2019)
24. Arjovsky, M., Chintala, S., et al.: Wasserstein generative adversarial networks. In: International Conference on Machine Learning, pp. 214–223. PMLR (2017)
25. Ganin, Y., Ustinova, E., et al.: Domain-adversarial training of neural networks. J. Mach. Learn. Res. $\mathbf{17}$(1), 2096–3030 (2016)
26. Mendonça, T., Ferreira, P.M., et al.: PH^2 - a dermoscopic image database for research and benchmarking. In: 2013 35th Annual International Conference of the IEEE Engineering in Medicine and Biology Society (EMBC), pp. 5437–5440 (2013). https://doi.org/10.1109/EMBC.2013.6610779
27. Perez, F., Avila, S., et al.: Solo or ensemble? Choosing a CNN architecture for melanoma classification. In: Proceedings of the IEEE/CVF Conference on Computer Vision and Pattern Recognition Workshops, pp. 2775–2783 (2019)
28. Hasan, M., et al.: Comparative analysis of automatic skin lesion segmentation with two different implementations. arXiv preprint arXiv:1904.03075 (2019)
29. Bibiloni, P., González-Hidalgo, M., Massanet, S.: Skin hair removal in dermoscopic images using soft color morphology. In: ten Teije, A., Popow, C., Holmes, J.H., Sacchi, L. (eds.) AIME 2017. LNCS (LNAI), vol. 10259, pp. 322–326. Springer, Cham (2017). https://doi.org/10.1007/978-3-319-59758-4_37
30. Charles, P.: Maryamnadeeme (2019). https://github.com/MaryamNadeem/ fakedataproduction

Paraphrase Identification with Neural Elaboration Relation Learning

Sheng Xu[1,2] , Fumiyo Fukumoto[3(✉)] , Jiyi Li[3] , and Yoshimi Suzuki[3]

[1] School of Computer Science and Technology, Hangzhou Dianzi University,
Hangzhou, China
181050042@hdu.edu.cn
[2] Integrated Graduate School of Medicine, Engineering, Agricultural Sciences,
Faculty of Engineering, University of Yamanashi, Kofu, Japan
[3] Interdisciplinary Graduate School, University of Yamanashi, Kofu, Japan
{fukumoto,jyli,ysuzuki}@yamanashi.ac.jp
http://cl.cs.yamanashi.ac.jp/index_e.html

Abstract. Paraphrases are phrases/sentences transition preserving the same sense but using different wording. In contrast, in the case that a phrase/sentence gives more detail compared with another phrase/ sentence, it does not hold paraphrases. This paper follows the assumption and verifies how elaboration relation between phrases/sentences helps to improve the performance of the paraphrase identification task. We present a sequential transfer learning framework that utilizes contextual features learned from elaboration relation for paraphrase identification. The method learns the elaboration relation model at first until the stable and then adapts paraphrase identification. The results using the benchmark dataset, Microsoft Research Paraphrase Corpus (MRPC), show that the method attained at 1.7% accuracy improvement compared with a baseline model.

Keywords: Paraphrase identification · Elaboration relation · Transfer learning

1 Introduction

Paraphrase identification is the task to identify whether two sentences or phrases convey the same meaning or not [3,6]. The task is similar to the semantic equivalence task between two input phrases/sentences that measures the degree of semantic similarity, while it is more strict because in the case that a phrase/sentence gives more detail compared with another phrase/sentence, it does not hold paraphrases. Sentence representation learning is a core technique for capturing semantic relatedness. There have been many attempts to learn sentence representation, e.g. attempt to leverage lexical, syntactic, and semantic features [9,19], and pre-training language model with a large amount of unannotated data by transfer learning [2,7,11,14,19,20,27,32]. One such attempt is

© Springer Nature Switzerland AG 2021
T. Mantoro et al. (Eds.): ICONIP 2021, LNCS 13111, pp. 562–573, 2021.
https://doi.org/10.1007/978-3-030-92273-3_46

to utilize multi-task learning techniques [5,10,16]. The basic assumption of this approach is that it is effective for multiple tasks to be learned jointly as the knowledge learned in one task can help to improve the performance on other tasks [31]. Subramanisan et al. attempted multi-task learning for sentence representations that a single recurrent sentence encoder shared across several tasks [23]. Sun et al. proposed a multi-task learning model called ERNIE 2.0 that learns pre-training tasks incrementally [24]. Raffel et al. presented a method called Text-to-Text Transfer Transformer (T5) that treats every text processing problem including translation, question answering, and classification as a "text-to-text" problem [5]. It takes text as input and producing new text as output. The feature of this framework is to directly apply the same model, objective, training procedure, and decoding process to every task. They showed that multi-task learning improves the performance of many downstream tasks, while they do not explicitly map one task to its related/similar task in a complementing manner but handle all the tasks simultaneously.

In this paper, we propose a method for paraphrase identification by leveraging elaboration relation between sentences. Consider the sentence pairs obtained from the Microsoft Research Paraphrase Corpus (MRPC) [18,28].

(1-1) Amrozi accused his brother, whom he called "the witness", of deliberately distorting his evidence.

(1-2) Referring to him as only "the witness", Amrozi accused his brother of deliberately distorting his evidence.

(2-1) Talabani told him the Governing Council would "need UN assistance and advice in implementing the new decisions which have been taken."

(2-2) Talabani told him Iraqi leaders would "need UN assistance and advice in implementing the new decisions which have been taken" on organising an interim Iraqi government by June.

(3-1) The new companies will begin trading on Nasdaq today under the ticker symbols PLMP and PSRC.

(3-2) Also as part of the deal, PalmSource stock will begin trading on the NASDAQ stock market Wednesday under the ticker symbol: PSRC.

According to the definitions from the manual of MRPC, sentences (1-1) and (1-2) are assigned to paraphrases as they have the same meaning. In contrast, sentences (2-1) and (2-2) are no paraphrases as the sentence (2-2) mentions the information marked with the underlined that "on organising an interim Iraqi government by June" is the additional information in the sentence (2-1). Similarly, sentences (3-1) and (3-2) are non-paraphrases as the sentence (3-2) includes the information which is marked with the underlined that "Also as part of the deal, PalmSource stock" and it is a larger superset of the sentence (3-1). Moreover, "the new companies" in the sentence (3-1) is specified as "PalmSource". From these observations, we hypothesize that the contextual features learned from the elaboration identification task is possible to discriminate one sentence from another one with more detail or additional information and these contextual features help the overall performance of paraphrase identification.

Instead of training paraphrase and elaboration identification tasks with the same data, our method explicitly trains the elaboration identification model by using an existing elaboration relation training data and utilizes it for identifying paraphrases on the target data. The model has learned elaboration relation at first until the stable, and then it is transferred and learned to paraphrase identification. In this manner, the contextual features for identifying elaboration can also help the model to learn better sentence representation for paraphrase identification.

The main contribution of our work can be summarized: (1) We propose a paraphrase identification method by leveraging elaboration relation between sentences. (2) We introduce a sequential transfer learning framework that utilizes contextual features learned from elaboration identification. (3) We test our hypothesis that elaboration identification helps to improve the overall performance of the paraphrase identification task.

2   Paraphrase Identification Framework

The structure of our model for paraphrase identification is shown in Fig. 1. The learning procedure consists of two phases, learning elaboration knowledge and paraphrase identification based on elaboration knowledge. First, the model learns the elaboration knowledge to identify whether two segments (sentences) have an elaboration relation or not. Next, based on the elaboration knowledge, the transfer learning model discriminates whether two segments (sentences) are paraphrase or not.

As shown in Fig. 1, our model is based on a multi-layer bidirectional Transformer encoder [26]. The Transformer is a unified transformer model such as BERT [7], ALBERT [32], and ELECTRA [12] which generates a segment-pair representation. The input of the transformer encoder is two segments/sentences concatenated by using a special token [SEP] according to the transformer. The representation of each token consists of the corresponding token, segment, and position embeddings. The first token of each input is the special token, i.e. [CLS], and the final hidden state that corresponds to the [CLS] token is regarded as an

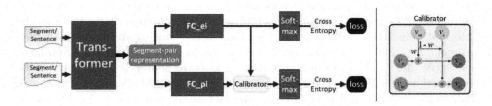

Fig. 1. Paraphrase identification framework with elaboration relation learning

Table 1. The values of **Y** and **E**, and their definition.

Name	Value	Definition
Y	1	The input two sentences are paraphrase
	0	The input two sentences are not paraphrase
E	1	One sentence is the elaboration of another
	0	Any sentence is not the elaboration of another

aggregated representation of the segment/sentence pair. We utilized the representation as the sentential encoding of two segments/sentences [7].

2.1   Learning Elaboration Relation

We hypothesize that the contextual features learned from the elaboration identification task are possible to discriminate one sentence from another one with more detail or additional information and these contextual features help the overall performance of the paraphrase identification task. As shown in Fig. 1, the vector [CLS] obtained by the transformer is passed to the fully connected layer FC_ei [7]. The size of the output layer of the FC_ei is set to two to identify the elaboration relation between two segments. Finally, the softmax function is applied to obtain probabilities of two predicted labels, elaboration or non-elaboration, in the output layer. The network is trained with the objective so that it minimizes the binary cross-entropy loss of the predicted and the actual distributions (one-hot vectors corresponding to the ground labels) by performing Adam optimization algorithm [8].

2.2   Paraphrase Identification with Sequential Transfer Learning

In the second phase, the paraphrase identification phase, the parameters of Transformer and FC_ei are transferred. During the phase, the model learns how to detect the paraphrase relation between two sentences based on the prior elaboration knowledge. Our training process for the elaboration classification has ended as the learning framework for elaboration and paraphrase is an out-domain setting, i.e. the training data for each task is different from each other.

Let probability variables **Y** and **E** denote the paraphrase relation and elaboration relation, respectively. The values of **Y** and **E**, and their definition are shown in Table 1. **Y** and **E** shown in Table 1 have two values, 1 or 0.

We recall that if two sentences form an elaboration relation, they are not paraphrases. In contrast, if two sentences do not have an elaboration relation, we cannot identify whether two sentences are paraphrase or not. This assumption is given by conditional probability distribution $P(\mathbf{Y}|\mathbf{X}, \mathbf{E})$ which is shown in Table 2. Here, the probability variable **X** denotes the input sentence pair.

The framework can effectively utilize contextual features of elaboration relation to improving the performance of paraphrase identification. According to

Table 2. The conditional probability distribution $P(\mathbf{Y}|\mathbf{X}, \mathbf{E})$. x refers to a sentence pair and p indicates unknown probability.

$\mathbf{Y} = k$	0	1
$P(\mathbf{Y} = k|\mathbf{X} = x, \mathbf{E} = 0)$	$1 - p$	p
$P(\mathbf{Y} = k|\mathbf{X} = x, \mathbf{E} = 1)$	1	0

the conditional probability distribution $P(\mathbf{Y}|\mathbf{X}, \mathbf{E})$, we update the prediction obtained by FC_pi with a calibrator.

$$v_p = v_p + w \cdot v_{ne}, \tag{1}$$

$$v_{np} = v_{np} + v_e + (1 - w) \cdot v_{ne}, \tag{2}$$

where v_p and v_{np} indicate values which are used to calculate the probabilities of paraphrase and non-paraphrase, respectively. Before updating, they have the original value obtained by FC_pi. Similarly, v_e and v_{ne} are the values obtained by FC_ei, where they represent elaboration and non-elaboration, respectively. w refers to the weight value corresponding to the conditional probability p in Table 2.

All of the values predicted by the elaboration model should be added to the value predicted by paraphrase identification because if two sentences have an elaboration relation, they should not be paraphrases. In contrast, if the relation between them is non-elaboration, whether these sentences are paraphrase is unknown. Therefore, we set a special weight to the predicted value of the non-elaboration relation. The range of the value w is from 0 to 1. After updating v_p and v_{np} by Eqs. (1) and (2), the softmax function is applied and probabilities of the final predicted labels, i.e. paraphrase, or not paraphrase are obtained. The loss function is the same as the elaboration identification task. The objective for minimizing the loss is also optimized by the Adam optimization algorithm.

3   Experiments

3.1   Experimental Setup

There are several datasets on discourse framework to learn an elaboration relation between two segments [13, 15, 17]. Among them, we chose a data for discourse coherence relation provided by Discourse Graphbank 1.0 [29][1]. The data consists of 135 documents that come from the AP Newswire, Wall Street Journal, GRE, and SAT texts. Table 3 shows corpus statistics of Discourse Graphbank 1.0.

Figure 2 illustrates an example from Discourse Graphbank 1.0 dataset. Each document is represented as a directed graph where each node shows a segment called discourse segment and labeled directed arcs indicate coherence relations.

---

[1] catalog.ldc.upenn.edu/LDC2005T08.

Table 3. Discourse Graphbank 1.0 corpus statistics

The # of words		The # of discourse segments	
Mean	545	Mean	61
Min	161	Min	6
Max	1,409	Max	143
Median	529	Median	60

(a) There is a Eurocity train on Platform 1.
(b) Its destination is Rome.
(c) There is another Eurocity on Platform 2.
(d) Its destination is Zürich.

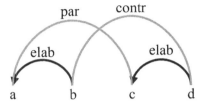

Fig. 2. An example for coherence relations in Graphbank dataset [29]

For instance, segment (b) ("Its destination is Rome.") is the elaboration of segment (a) ("There is a Eurocity train on Platform 1.").

The types of coherence consist of twelve relations: parallel, contrast, example, generalization, elaboration, explanation, violated expectation, condition, temporal sequence, attribution, same relation, and the coherence relations of each document are annotated by two annotators. Most of the segment pairs have coherence relations, while 51.2% of them have no coherence relations. The top number of coherence relations was elaboration (46.3%). We extracted a pair of segments with elaboration relation and used them as positive training data and relations other than elaboration as negative training data. The total number of elaboration and non-elaboration pairs are 3,906 and 3,267, respectively. We divide these pairs into two: 75% for training and 25% for test data. We further divided the training data into two folds, 90% for training and 10% for validation data. We used the ERECTRA_base model to train and test the elaboration data with 90.6% accuracy.

We selected benchmark dataset, MRPC [18,28] for the paraphrase identification task. MRPC contains 5,801 pairs of sentences that are extracted from news on the Internet. They are annotated to capture the equivalence of paraphrase or semantic relationship between sentences. We obtained the data from General Language Understanding Evaluation (GLUE) platform [1].

We utilized the base model for each encoding technique including BERT_base model [7] because of the environment with the restricted computational resources[2]. We used a hyperparameter optimization framework called Optuna[3] on the sets of parameters and chose the model that performed the best on the

---

[2] The experiments were conducted on Nvidia GeForce RTX 2080Ti (12 GB memory).
[3] https://github.com/pfnet/optuna.

Table 4. Accuracy on the MRPC dev set: Bold font shows the best result with each column. Bracket value refers to the improvement compared with the original five including BERT models. "∗" means that we run the model in our environment as the result obtained by the base model was not reported in [12].

Model	BERT	ALBERT	RoBERTa	XLNet	ELECTRA*
Single	86.7	90.2	90.2	90.0	90.7
Ours (w/o calibrator)	88.5 (+1.8)	90.2 (±0)	90.9 (+.7)	89.5 (-.5)	91.4 (+.7)
Ours (with calibrator)	**89.2 (+2.5)**	**91.4 (+1.2)**	**91.2 (+1.0)**	**90.4 (+.4)**	**92.4 (+1.4)**

Table 5. Accuracy and F1-score on the MRPC test set: Bold font shows the best result with each column. X and Y in X/Y refer to accuracy and F1-score, respectively. "∗" indicates that we run the model in our environment as the result obtained by the base model was not reported in each paper.

Model	BERT	ALBERT*	RoBERTa*	XLNet*	ELECTRA
Single	84.8/88.4	85.6/89.1	86.5/90.0	85.8/**89.6**	88.1/**91.2**
Ours (w/o calibrator)	**85.4**/89.2	**86.4/89.9**	86.0/89.6	84.8/88.8	87.7/91.0
Ours (with calibrator)	85.3/**89.3**	86.3/89.9	**87.6/90.7**	**85.9**/89.5	**88.2/91.2**

dev set: batch size: 16, 24, 32; learning rate: 2e-5, 3e-5, 5e-5; number of epochs: 2, 3; the weight w of calibrator: 0 to 1 with the interval of 0.1. Following by GLUE, as an evaluation metric, we used the Accuracy and/or F1-score.

3.2 Main Results

We compare our model with a baseline that has been submitted to the GLUE leaderboard and a variant of our model, i.e. (i) The single model which is paraphrase identification based on transformer encodings but without elaboration identification, and (ii) The variant model (w/o calibrator) that the training data labeled with both elaboration and paraphrase but without applying calibrator for the outputs obtained by FC_pi. The results are shown in Tables 4 and 5.

Table 4 shows the results on the MRPC dev dataset obtained by three models against five transformer models, and Table 5 shows the results on the test dataset. We can see from Table 4 that our models outperformed the baseline, a single model at a maximum of 2.5% accuracy when we utilized BERT_base model. Overall the results with the calibrator were better than those of the w/o calibrator and the best result was the ELECTRA transformer model by 92.4%. Similarly, in Table 5, the performance of our model with calibrator is better than those obtained by a single model and w/o calibrator except for BERT and ALBERT by accuracy and XLNET by F1-score. This indicates that the prediction obtained by FC_pi with a calibrator and the use of the ELECTRA transformer model contribute to the performance of paraphrase identification.

3.3   Comparison with Related Work

We compared our models with five related work which utilize BERT_base or encodings with a base model and applied it to the single task, paraphrase identification to make a fair comparison.

1. GenSen [23]
   GenSen is multi-task learning and a single recurrent sentence encoder is utilized through multiple tasks, multi-lingual NMT, NL inference, constituency parsing, and skip-thought vectors.
2. ERNIE 2.0 [24]
   Enhanced Representation through kNowledge IntEgration (ERNIE) 2.0 is a multi-task learning model. It incrementally learns pre-training tasks. The architecture is the same manner as BERT models, i.e. it consists of pre-training and fine-tuning.
3. Trans FT [2]
   Transfer Fine-Tuning is an extended model of BERT to handle phrasal paraphrase relations. Through the classification of phrasal and sentential paraphrases, the model incorporates semantic relations between a sentence pair into a pre-trained BERT model. After the training, the model can be fine-tuned in the same manner as BERT models.
4. StructBERT_base [27]
   StructBERT_base incorporates language structures into pre-training BERT_base model. The architecture utilizes a multi-layer bidirectional Transformer network. It extends the ability of the masked language model task by shuffling a certain number of tokens after token masking and predicting the right order.
5. FreeLB-BERT [4]
   The objective of Free-Large-Batch is to improve pre-trained language models such as BERT, RoBERTa, ALBERT, ELECTRA and T5 [5]. It improves the robustness in the embedding space during fine-tuning on the language understanding tasks.

The results are shown in Table 6. Table 6 indicates that our model with calibrator and ELECTRA showed a 2.1% improvement by accuracy compared with the second-best system StructBERT_Base. Similarly, our model is slightly better than the second best systems, StructBERT_Base and ERNIE as it attained at 1.3% of F1-score higher than those models.

3.4   Qualitative Analysis of Errors

We performed an error analysis by using the dataset to provide feedback for further improvement of the method. The number of false-positive and false-negative pairs of sentences obtained by our method with calibrator and ELECTRA was 133 and 78, respectively. We found that there are mainly three types of errors.

Table 6. Comparative results with related work: Bold font and underline show the best and the second results with each column, respectively.

Model	MRPC	
	Acc	F1
GenSen [23]	78.6	84.4
ERNIE 2.0 [24]	86.1	<u>89.9</u>
Trans FT [2]	–	89.2
StructBERT_base [27]	<u>86.1</u>	<u>89.9</u>
FreeLB-BERT [4]	83.5	88.1
Ours (with calibrator) and ELECTRA	**88.2**	**91.2**

1. **Inter-sentential Relations:** Two sentences which have inter-sentential relations [22,25] are difficult to identify paraphrase correctly.

   (4-1) British Airways' <u>New York-to-London</u> runs will end in October.
   (4-2) British Airways plans to retire its seven <u>Concordes</u> at the end of October.

   Sentences (4-1) and (4-2) have the same meaning, while different expressions such as "New York-to-London" and "Concordes" are used and they are co-referred entities. Identifying these sentences as "paraphrases" correctly requires capturing not only local relations within a sentence but also relations between sentences.

2. **Anaphora:** Pronouns in one sentence cannot identify a noun/noun phrase that appeared in another sentence.

   (5-1) <u>Pacific Northwest</u> has more than 800 employees, and Wells Fargo has 2,400 in Washington.
   (5-2) <u>It</u> has 800 employees, compared with Wells Fargo's 2,400.

   Sentences (5-1) and (5-2) should be paraphrases as <u>It</u> in (5-2) shows <u>Pacific Northwest</u> in (5-1). However, it is difficult to identify paraphrases because of a gap between them. One solution is that the model incorporates more linguistic information such as Co-Reference Resolution and Named Entity Recognition into the model to learn sentence representation more effectively.

3. **Equivalent content:** Two words/phrases are the same sense but cannot be identified.

   (6-1) Retail industry experts predict <u>the next five days</u> will likely make or break Christmas 2003 for many retailers.
   (6-2) As the holiday shopping season peaks, industry experts predict <u>the coming week</u> could make or break Christmas 2003 for many retailers.

   <u>the next five days</u> in (6-1) and <u>the coming week</u> in (6-2) have the same sense. The semantic equivalence of our model is based on every sentence unit as an input. It requires to capture words/phrases equivalence to identify these sentences as "paraphrases" correctly.

Apart from these observations, we recall that our model is based on a unified transformer model such as BERT, ALBERT, and ELECTRA that generates a segment-pair representation. In these pre-training models, an unsupervised method learns general, domain-independent knowledge. However, for most of the downstream tasks, there are several domain-specific data, each of which is collected from different domains/genres. For example, in the paraphrase identification task, the MRPC from news stories and QQP from the Website of Quora. It would be worth developing an effective domain-free fine-tuning method for the different domain-specific data. This is a rich space for further exploration.

4   Conclusion

We presented a method for the paraphrase identification task that utilizes the elaboration relation between two sentences auxiliary to help the semantic equivalence more accurately and thus improves the overall performance of paraphrase identification. Throughout the experiments, we showed that the prior elaboration knowledge that is learned from out-domain data is possible to help the model to classify the paraphrase relation between two sentences as the results obtained our model based on ELECTRA_base attained at the best performance, i.e. 88.2% accuracy and 91.2% F1-score on the MRPC dataset, and competitive to the five related work. The experimental result also showed that the model contributes to reducing the false positive rate. Future work will include: (i) incorporating more linguistic information or other discourse relations which are effective for further improvement on paraphrase identification, (ii) applying semi-supervised learning techniques [21,30] to improve the overall performance on the elaboration identification task, (iii) extending our model to alleviating noisy labels, and (iv) evaluating our model by using other data including QQP and STS-B GLUE dataset for quantitative evaluation.

Acknowledgements. We are grateful to the anonymous reviewers for their comments and suggestions. This work was supported by the Grant-in-aid for JSPS, Grant Number 21K12026, JKA through its promotion funds from KEIRIN RACE, and Artificial Intelligence Research Promotion Foundation.

References

1. Alex, W., Amanpreet, S., Julian, M., Felix, H., Omer H., Samuel B.R.: GLUE: a multi-task benchmark and analysis platform for natural language understanding, arXiv preprint arXiv:1804.07461 (2018)
2. Arase, Y., Tsujii, J.: Transfer fine-tuning: a BERT case study. In: Proceedings of the 2019 Conference on Empirical Methods in Natural Language Processing and the 9th International Joint Conference on Natural Language Processing, pp. 5393–5404 (2019)
3. Bhagat, R., Hovy, E.: What is a paraphrase? Assoc. Comput. Linguist. **39**(3), 463–472 (2013)

4. Chen Z., Yu, C., Zhe, G., Siqi, S., Thomas, G., Jing, L.: FreeLB: enhanced adversarial training for natural language understanding. arXiv:1909.11764 (2019)
5. Colin, R., et al.: Exploring the limits of transfer learning with a unified text-to-text transformer. arXiv preprint ArXiv: 1910.10683 (2020)
6. Dorr, N.M.B.J.: Generating phrasal and sentential paraphrases: a survey of data-driven methods. Assoc. Comput. Linguist. **36**(3), 341–387 (2010)
7. Jacob, D., Ming-Wei, C., Kenton, L., Kristina, T.: BERT: pre-training on deep bidirectional transfomers for language understanding. In: Proceedings of the 2019 Conference of the North American Chapter of the Association for Computational Linguistics: Human Language Technologies, pp. 4171–4186 (2019)
8. Kingma, D.P., Ba, J.: ADAM: a method for stochastic optimization. In: The 3rd International Conference on Learning Representations, pp. 1–15 (2015)
9. Liang, C., Paritosh, P., Rajendran, V., Forbus, K.D.: Learning paraphrase identification with structural alignment. In: Proceedings of the Twenty-Fifth International Joint Conference on Artificial Intelligence, pp. 2859–2865 (2016)
10. Liu, X., He, P., Chen, W., Gao, J.: Learning general purpose distributed sentence representations via large scale multi-task learning. In: Proceedings of the 57th Annual Meeting of the Association for Computational Linguistics, pp. 4487–4496 (2019)
11. Liu, Y., et al.: RoBERTa: A robustly optimized BERT pretraining approach. arXiv preprint ArXiv: 1907.11692 (2019)
12. Clarkand, K.C.M.T., Le, Q.V., Manning, C.D.: ELECTRA: pre-training text encoders as discriminators rather than generators. In: Proceedings of the 8th International Conference on Learning Representations (2020)
13. Mann, W.C., Thompson, S.A.: Rhetorical structure theory: toward a functional theory of text organization. Text-Interdisc. J. Study Discourse **8**(3), 243–281 (1988)
14. Matthew, P., et al.: Deep contextualized word representations. In: Proceedings of the 2018 Conference of the North American Chapter of the Association for Computational Linguistics: Human Language Technologies, pp. 2227–2237 (2018)
15. Miltsakaki, E., Prasad, R., Joshi, A., Webber, B.: The Penn discourse tree-bank. In: Proceedings of the Fourth International Conference on Language Resources and Evaluation (2004)
16. Phang, J., Fevry, T., Bowman, S.R.: Sentence encoders on STILTs: supplementary training on intermediate labeled-data tasks. arXiv preprint ArXiv: 1811.01088 (2019)
17. Prasad, R., Dinesh, N., Lee, A., Miltsakaki, E., Robaldo, L: The Penn discourse treebank 2.0. In: Proceedings of the 56th International Conference on Language Resources and Evaluation, pp. 2961–2968 (2008)
18. Quirk, C., Brockett, C., Dolan, B.: Monolingual machine translation for paraphrase generation. In: Proceedings of the 2004 Conference on Empirical Methods in Natural Language Processing, pp. 142–149 (2004)
19. Radford, A., Wu, J., Child, R., Luan, D., Amodei, D., Sutskever, I.: Language models are unsupervised multitask learners. OpenAI Blog **1**(8), 9 (2019)
20. Reimers, N., Gurevych, I.: Sentence-BERT: sentence embeddings using Siamese BERT-Networks. In: Proceedings of the 2019 Conference on Empirical Methods in Natural Language Processing and the 9th International Joint Conference on Natural Language Processing, pp. 3982–3992 (2019)
21. Sohn, K., et al.: FixMatch: simplifying semi-supervised learning with consistency and confidence. In: Proceedings of the 34th Conference on Neural Information Processing Systems (2020)

22. Stevenson, M.: Fact distribution in information extraction. In: The International Conference on Language Resources and Evaluation, pp. 183–201 (2007)
23. Subramanian, S., Trischler, A., Bengio, Y., Pal, C.J.: Learning general purpose distributed sentence representations via large scale multi-task learning. In: Proceedings of the 6th International Conference on Learning Representations (2018)
24. Sun, Y., et al.: ERNIE 2.0: a continual pre-training framework for language understanding. arXiv preprint ArXiv: 1907.12412 (2019)
25. Swampillai, K., Stevenson, M.: Inter-sentential relations in information extraction corpora. In: The International Conference on Language Resources and Evaluation, pp. 17–23 (2010)
26. Vaswani, A., et al.: Attention is all you need. In: Advances in Neural Information Processing Systems, pp. 5998–6008 (2017)
27. Wei, W., et al.: StructBERT: incorporating language structures into pre-training for deep language understanding. arXiv preprint arXiv:1908.04577 (2019)
28. William, D.B., Brockett, C.: Automatically constructing a corpus of sentential paraphrases. In: Proceedings of the Third International Workshop on Paraphrasing, pp. 9–16 (2005)
29. Wolf, F., Gibson, E., Fisher, A., Knight, M.: A procedure for collecting a database of texts annotated with coherence relations, MIT NE20-448 (2003)
30. Xie, Q., Dai, Z., Hovy, E., Luong, M.T., Le, Q.V.: unsupervised data augmentation for consistency training. In: 34th Conference on Neural Information Processing Systems (2020)
31. Zhang, Y., Yang, Q.: A survey on multi-task learning. arXiv:1707.08114 (2018)
32. Lan, Z., Chen, Z., Goodman, Z., Gimpel, K., Sharma, P., Soricut, R.: ALBERT: a lite BERT for self-supervised learning of language representations. In: Proceedings of the 8th International Conference on Learning Representations (2020)

Hybrid DE-MLP-Based Modeling Technique for Prediction of Alloying Element Proportions and Process Parameters

Ravindra V. Savangouder[(✉)], Jagdish C. Patra, and Suresh Palanisamy

Swinburne University of Technology, Melbourne, Australia
rsavangouder@swin.edu.au

Abstract. The inherent complexity in obtaining the desired microstructure in metals to achieve a specific set of mechanical properties makes the selection of an optimum level of alloy proportions and the heat treatment process parameters a challenging task. The differential evolution (DE) is a population-based evolutionary algorithm, which is capable of finding the optimal solution of non-differentiable, non-linear, and discontinuous functions. In this paper, a set of experimental data, obtained from literature, is used to train a multilayer perceptron (MLP) to predict the mechanical property (i.e., Vickers hardness number (VHN)) of austempered ductile iron (ADI), for a given set of input process parameters. A novel hybrid DE-MLP-based model is proposed to predict the input process parameters, i.e., the alloying element proportions and the heat treatment parameters, to produce ADI with a specific mechanical property. The performance of DE-MLP-based model in terms of accuracy, effect of population size, number of generations, and computational efficiency are discussed. With extensive simulation results, it is shown that the MLP model can predict VHN with a low mean absolute percent error (MAPE) of 0.21. With only 10 individuals, the DE algorithm is able to generate a feasible solution containing the input process parameters in less than 10 generations. ADI with a desired value of VHN can be produced using the alloying element proportions and heat treatment process parameters predicted by the proposed model.

Keywords: Differential evolution · Multilayer perceptron · Austempered ductile iron · Vickers hardness · Optimization

1 Introduction

In a production process of metals, it is a highly challenging task to determine the optimum value of the input processing parameters, i.e., the proportion of alloying elements and heat treatment parameters, to achieve a specific mechanical property, because of inherent complex interactions. Furthermore, the use of foundry personnel's rule of thumb and empirical models seldom results in efficient use of energy and precious alloying elements. Currently, various standards are used to produced metal components which specify a range for a given mechanical property instead of a specific value, e.g., ASTM 897M is used for manufacturing of austempered ductile iron (ADI). ADI in recent times has become an attractive material for designing machine components used

© Springer Nature Switzerland AG 2021
T. Mantoro et al. (Eds.): ICONIP 2021, LNCS 13111, pp. 574–584, 2021.
https://doi.org/10.1007/978-3-030-92273-3_47

in agricultural, locomotive, earth moving and others because of its attractive properties such as high strength, good ductility, high resistance to wear. ADI has been increasingly replacing forged and cast steel due to ease of manufacturing and comparable mechanical properties. The global annual production of ADI is estimated to be 500,000 tonnes and is expected to increase by 10% each year [5]. ADI's microstructure influences its mechanical properties and the microstructure is influenced by the proportion of the alloying elements added and the process parameters that are selected during the heat treatment process called austempering [1]. Mechanical properties such as hardness, ductility and tensile strength can be varied by altering the austempering process parameters and the proportion of the alloying elements. Any improvement in predicting the parameters and alloy proportions will help reduce the wastage of precious elements, energy, and cost.

Recently, artificial neural network (ANN) models have been used to model scientific and engineering processes that are complex in nature [3, 6, 7]. Several ANN-based models to predict mechanical properties of various materials have been proposed, however, only few studies are carried out to predict hardness of ADI using the ANN models [8, 12]. In [8], using only four parameters, a multilayer perceptron (MLP)-based modeling technique is proposed to predict VHN of ADI. Recently, using nine parameters, an ANN-based modeling scheme with improved accuracy for predicting VHN of ADI is reported [9]. R. Storn and K. V. Price, first reported differential evolution (DE) optimization algorithm in 1995 [10]. Many optimization problems, e.g., estimation of solar cells and modules parameters [4] and prediction of protein structure [11] have been solved using DE.

2 Complexity in Production of ADI and ADI Standards

In this Section, the inherent complexity in producing ADI with specified mechanical properties, the austempering process and the current practice of producing ADI are briefly described.

Many engineering materials used in the manufacturing of components for machines need to possess certain level of mechanical properties such as tensile strength, ductility and hardness to perform the intended task. These properties of materials depend on the microstructure of the material which in turn depends on the alloying elements which are added during the production of the components, their proportions and any subsequent heat treatment process. In the case of ADI, the host element is iron (Fe), with carbon (C) and silicon (Si) being the main alloying elements, which give iron its increased strength, as pure Fe is a soft material. In addition to C and Si, other alloying elements are added in various proportions to obtain the desired properties in the components. Nickel (Ni), molybdenum (Mo), copper (Cu), and manganese (Mn) are used as alloying elements which affect the hardness and other properties of ADI. Magnesium (Mg) is used to obtain ductile iron (DI) in which carbon is present in nodular form. DI components undergo austempering to obtain desired mechanical properties.

Figure 1 shows the production process of ADI. During the ADI process, the DI components are heated to an austenitizing temperature and held for a couple of hours such that the microstructure of DI is fully austenitized. Then, the components are rapidly quenched to austempering temperature ($T_{austemper}$) range (between 260 to 430 °C), and

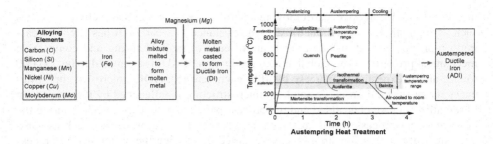

Fig. 1. ADI production process.

are heated at fixed (isothermal) temperature between 30–180 min. This time duration is called the austempering time duration ($t_{austemper}$) [1].

The physical properties of ADI are influenced by the alloying element proportions together with the austempering process parameters. In total, there are 9 parameters, $T_{austemper}$, $t_{austemper}$, C, Si, Mn, Ni, Cu, Mo and Mg which interact non-linearly that influence the final microstructure of ADI, which in turn determines its mechanical properties. Due to this inherent complexity in producing ADI as described above and due to the absence of any numerical methods to determine the optimal level of the nine parameters in order to produce ADI with a desired property, ADI production relies on the knowledge and skills of the foundry-men and their thumb rules. Currently, due to the complexity involved in obtaining desired microstructure in ADI, ADI standards, e.g., ASTM A897 and ISO17804 are used by the manufacturers of ADI. In these standards, the strength, elongation and hardness are specified as a range instead of specific value, e.g., for grade 750/500/11 of ASTM A897, the tensile strength ranges from 750–899 MPa, the yield strength ranges from 500–649 MPa and the Vickers hardness ranges from 253–318. Thus, the current method of producing ADI is prone to the wastage of precious alloying elements and energy. So, in the production of ADI and other materials, there is a need for an intelligent method through which the optimal levels of nine parameters can be determined. To solve this complexity, the authors have proposed a hybrid DE-MLP-based *inverse* model to predict the nine parameters for producing ADI for any desired VHN.

3   Hybrid DE-MLP-Based Inverse Model

The technique proposed in this paper involves two models, a forward model, in which an MLP-based model is trained using data collected from the literature that can accurately predict VHN for a given set of 9 input parameters, $T_{austemper}$, $t_{austemper}$, C, Si, Mn, Ni, Cu, Mo and Mg. The second model is the proposed novel hybrid DE-MLP-based *inverse* model, in which the DE algorithm uses the trained forward model as part of the fitness function to predict the 9 input parameters to achieve any desired VHN in ADI. Since DE is an evolutionary algorithm, more than one set of input parameters can be obtained for the desired VHN. Thus, by generating multiple set of input parameters, an optimal set of input parameters can be selected based on cost or energy used.

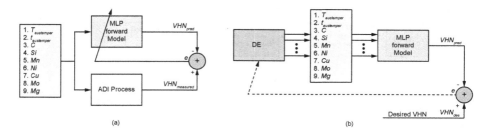

Fig. 2. (a) Schematic of MLP-based forward modeling scheme representing ADI process with nine inputs and one output and (b) Hybrid DE-MLP-based *inverse* modeling scheme representing ADI process to obtain the desired VHN.

As a system identification [7], Fig. 2a shows a schematic of the MLP-based forward modeling scheme to predict VHN of ADI. The experimental data of 9 input parameters ($T_{austemper}$, $t_{austemper}$, C, Si, Mn, Ni, Cu, Mo and Mg) are used as the input pattern and the corresponding measured VHN as the output pattern. An error is generated by comparing the VHN predicted by the MLP model and the experimentally measured VHN. Using this error, the weights of the MLP model are updated using the back propagation algorithm. The training is repeated with different parameter values and by varying the number of nodes in the hidden layer, till the mean square error (*MSE*) approaches a value near to zero. Then the testing of trained MLP model is carried out for the prediction of VHN.

The DE is a function optimization algorithm based on population which attempts to optimizes a function iteratively based on a predefined performance criteria. Computational steps in DE are similar to that in a standard evolutionary algorithm (EA). However, DE updates the members of the current generation population using scaled differences of distinct population and randomly selected members[10].

Let us consider a D-dimensional function, $f(X)$. Let $N_{individual}$, $N_{generation}$, F and C_r denote the number of individuals, number of generations, mutation scale factor and crossover rate, respectively.

Figure 3 shows the main steps in DE [2, 4]. Initially, $N_{individual}$ number of individuals are generated with a uniform probability distribution in a D-dimensional search space within predetermined limits of the parameter. Mutation step, in this step, a new individual solution called mutant vector is generated by adding the target vector and the scaled difference of two randomly selected individuals. The target vector is different to the two randomly selected vectors. In this study, "DE/rand/1/bin" was used as the mutation strategy, where "DE" represents differential evolution, "rand" represents that the target vector is chosen randomly from the current population, "1" represents that only one vector from the mutated population is used, and "bin" refers to uniform crossover using binomial distribution. Equation (1) represents the mutation step.

$$V_i^g = X_{rand}^g + F(X_{r_1}^g - X_{r_2}^g),\qquad(1)$$

where $r_1 \neq r_2 = \{1, 2, \ldots, N_{individual}\}$ are integers that are generated randomly, $X_{r_1}^g$, $X_{r_2}^g$ are randomly selected vectors from the population, X_{rand}^g is the target vector which is

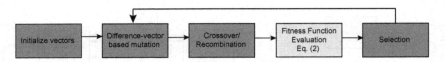

Fig. 3. Steps in DE algorithm.

randomly selected from the individuals and is different from $X_{r_1}^g$ and $X_{r_2}^g$. The amplification of the differential variation vector V_i^g is controlled by the scaling factor F.

The crossover step, in this step, a component of the mutant vector is accepted based on stochastic probability. If the random number generated is greater than C_r ($0 \leq C_r \leq$ 1), then the jth ($j = 1, 2, \ldots, D$) component of the mutant vector is accepted, otherwise, it is rejected. The crossover operation generates a trial vector. Next, the selection of the trial vector is done depending on the criteria used for selection. In a minimization problem, the fitness values of the original vector and the trial vector are compared. The trial vector is saved for the next generation if its fitness value is lower than the original vector, else, the original vector is retained. These steps are iterated through $N_{generation}$ times and the individual with least fitness value in the last generation is saved as best solution, (X_{best}).

As a system identification, the proposed hybrid DE-MLP-based *inverse* modeling scheme for predicting the nine parameters to produce ADI with desired VHN is represented in Fig. 2b. A 9-dimensional solution vector is randomly generated in every iteration. This solution vector is similar to the 9-dimensional vector used in training the forward model. The forward model uses the solution vector as input pattern to predict the VHN. This predicted VHN is termed as (VHN_{pred}). Here, the *inverse* model is used to predict the 9-dimensional solution vector for a desired VHN as required for an application. This desired VHN is denoted by VHN_{des}. An error is generated by comparing the VHN_{pred} and VHN_{des}. Therefore, the fitness function, $f(X)$ that needs to be minimized by the *inverse* model is given by

$$f(X) = |VHN_{des} - VHN_{pred}|. \tag{2}$$

Thereafter, if the trial vector's fitness function value is less than the original vector's fitness function value, then the solution is saved, else the original vector is saved as the best individual. This is repeated for a predetermined number of iterations and the best individual with the least fitness function value is saved as the best individual, (X_{best}). The 9-dimensional solution vector containing two austempering process parameters, i.e., $T_{austemper}$ and $t_{austemper}$ and the seven alloying element (C, Si, Mn, Ni, Cu, Mo and Mg) proportions is represented by X_{best} vector. Thus, this solution vector provides all the information regarding the input parameters that are required to produce ADI for VHN_{des}.

Table 1. Process parameters and alloying element proportions of eight ADI specimens [8].

Specimen #	Alloying element proportions (wt%)							Austempering	
	C	Si	Mn	Ni	Cu	Mo	Mg	Temp (°C)	Time (min)
1	3.44	2.32	0.24	1.02	0.50	0.10	0.051		
2	3.47	2.35	0.24	1.01	0.50	0.15	0.052		
3	3.42	2.32	0.24	1.00	0.51	0.21	0.048	260,	30,
4	3.42	2.33	0.23	1.02	0.50	0.25	0.049	290,	60,
5	3.46	2.41	0.25	1.00	1.00	0.10	0.053	320	90,
6	3.42	2.32	0.25	1.00	1.01	0.15	0.053		120
7	3.45	2.41	0.26	1.02	1.01	0.20	0.049		
8	3.46	2.42	0.26	1.02	1.00	0.25	0.054		
Min	3.42	2.32	0.23	1.00	0.50	0.10	0.048	260	30
Max	3.47	2.42	0.26	1.02	1.01	0.25	0.051	320	120

4   Experimental Setup

4.1   Physical Experiment Setup

The data used in this study are obtained from the literature [8]. Eight ductile iron specimens with various proportion of alloying elements have been austempered at different $T_{austemper}$ temperature and for different $t_{austemper}$ duration. All the specimen were austenitized at 900 ± 3 °C for approximately one and half hours. Then, the specimens were austempered at three different $T_{austemper}$ (260, 290 and 320 °C), each for four different $t_{austemper}$ (30, 60, 90 and 120 min). In this way, twelve samples were prepared with each of the eight specimen. Thus, in total, 96 ADI samples were prepared. Vickers hardness test was used to determine the VHN of each sample. Table 1 shows the experimental setting of the eight specimens using which the 96 samples were prepared. Each of these 96 samples has nine input parameters and a corresponding VHN value. The input parameters of all the 96 samples and the corresponding VHN values (output parameter) form the dataset used in this study.

Figure 4 illustrates the influence of austempering parameters on VHN. Figure 4a and b shows the VHN values of all the 96 samples plotted against wt% of *Si* and *Ni*, respectively. From this figure it is evident that the VHN is dependent on the alloying element proportions based on other parameter setting. The measured VHN against $t_{austemper}$ at $T_{austemper}$ = 260 °C of three specimens is shown in Fig. 4c. Here, it can be observed that for a specific proportion of alloying elements, e.g., in the case of specimen #1, when $t_{austemper}$ increases from 30 to 120 min, the VHN reduces from 525 to 500. Similarly, Fig. 4d represents the experimentally measured VHN against $T_{austemper}$ at $t_{austemper}$ = 90 min, where similar trend can be seen.

4.2   Simulation Setup

A desktop PC with Intel processor (i7 @ 3.41) GHz and 16.0 GB RAM was used to execute both the forward and *inverse* models using MATLAB software package.

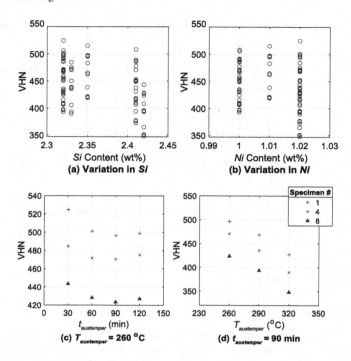

Fig. 4. Plot of measured VHN against different alloying element proportions in wt% and austempering process parameters: (a) *Si*, (b) *Ni*, (c) $t_{austemper}$ at $T_{austemper} = 260\,°C$ and (d) $T_{austemper}$ at $t_{austemper} = 90$ min.

Each of the nine input parameters was normalized between 0.0 and 1.0 for training the MLP-based forward model. The whole of the dataset with 96 samples was split into training, validation and test sets with 62, 10 and 24 samples, respectively. The model has 9 nodes in input and 1 node in output layer, respectively. The number of nodes in the hidden layer were varied between 5 and 9 and numerous experiments were conducted to obtain the best MLP learning parameters and architecture. A 3-layered MLP architecture with 7 nodes in hidden layer was obtained with *MSE* value near to zero.

The values of the first generation vectors of the DE algorithm were randomized between 0.0 to 1.0. F and C_r values were set to 0.8 and 0.5, respectively. In each run, the DE algorithm generates a 9-dimensional solution vector (X_{best}) that comprises of $T_{austemper}$, $t_{austemper}$, and wt% of C, Si, Mn, Ni, Cu, Mo and Mg for a given VHN value. VHN of all the 96 samples were chosen as VHN_{des}. In order to see the effect of the individuals on the DE algorithm, four different $N_{individual}$, ($N_{individual} = 5, 10, 15, 18$) were checked. With each $N_{individual}$, 500 independent solution vectors were generated for each of the 96 samples. In total 48,000 (96 × 500) solutions were generated with each $N_{individual}$.

5   Results and Discussions

5.1   Performance Measures

The forward model performance was measured using mean absolute percent error (*MAPE*), correlation coefficient (*CC*) and mean square error (*MSE*) and the *inverse* model performance was measured using the convergence characteristics, computation time and percent error between the experimental and the predicted solutions.

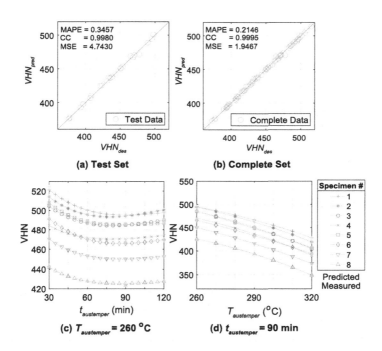

Fig. 5. Forward model performance: (a) Scatter plot for test set, (b) Scatter plot for complete set, (c) Prediction of VHN at $T_{austemper} = 260\,^{\circ}$C and (d) Prediction of VHN at $t_{austemper} = 90$ min.

5.2   Forward Model: Scatter Plots and Prediction of VHN

Figure 5 shows the performance of the forward model with the MLP architecture of {9-7-1}. A low value of MSE_{test} of 4.743 was achieved for the test set from the forward model. Figure 5a and b show scatter plot between VHN_{pred} and VHN_{des} for the test set with 24 samples and complete set with 96 samples, respectively. For these two sets, the *MAPE* was 0.3457 and 0.2146, respectively and the *CC* values were 0.9980 and 0.9995, respectively. From these values it can be observed that the forward model has successfully learnt the ADI process and can predict VHN accurately.

Figure 5c and d show that the forward model is not only able to predict VHN at measured points but also at any arbitrary $t_{austemper}$ or $T_{austemper}$ (within experimental range). The red and the blue symbols indicate the measured VHN (available from the dataset) and the predicted VHN, respectively. It can be observed that both red and the blue symbols almost overlaps indicating high prediction accuracy. In addition to this, the forward model is capable of predicting VHN values at values between the measured values of $t_{austemper}$ and $T_{austemper}$.

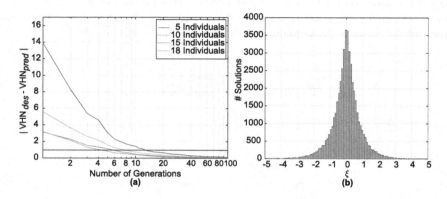

Fig. 6. (a) Convergence characteristics of the *inverse* model and (b) Distribution of ξ.

5.3   Inverse Model: Performance and Prediction of ADI Inputs Parameters

As stated in Sect. 3, the solution vector (given by the best individual vector, X_{best}) consists all the information required to produce ADI with a desired VHN. Convergence characteristics of the DE-MLP-based *inverse* model with $N_{individual} = 5, 10, 15$ and 18 is shown in Fig. 6a. Ensemble average over 100 runs was used to plot (semi-log) these convergence characteristic curves. The value of the fitness function (2) at $N_{generation} = 10$ with $N_{individual} = 5, 10, 15$ and 18 are 1.43, 0.74, 0.47 and 0.42, respectively. While, the execution times for $N_{generation} = 10$ with $N_{individual} = 5, 10, 15$ and 18 were found to be 0.31 s, 0.63 s, 0.86 s and 1.07 s, respectively. At $N_{generation} = 10$, reasonably low value of the fitness function is obtained with lower execution time.

Hence, for all the subsequent *inverse* model experiments, $N_{generation} = 10$ was selected. In Sect. 4.2 it is stated that, in the *inverse* model, 96 x 500 (= 48,000) independent solutions were obtained for each of the four selected $N_{individual}$ values. Figure 6b shows a plot of the random variable $\xi = (VHN_{des} - VHN_{pred})$ for $N_{individual} = 10$ to demonstrate how accurately the *inverse* model is able to optimize the fitness function. Ideally, the value of both, the mean, μ and the standard deviation, σ will be 0.0. The values of μ and σ for the distribution of this random variable ξ are -0.011 and 0.923, respectively. These values are near to the ideal values indicating high prediction accuracy.

In order to determine whether the *inverse* model predicted solution are feasible or not, the solutions that are in the vicinity of the experimental solution were selected. Table 2 shows four solutions predicted by the *inverse* model that are in close vicinity of the experimental data. From this Table, we can see that the *inverse* model was able to find a 9-dimensional solution for each of the four experimental data within an error of

±5%. It can be seen that the experimental and the predicted VHN values are either same or have a very small difference (about 0.1% error). This shows that the *inverse* model is indeed capable of predicting solutions that are experimentally feasible. Therefore, the solutions generated by the DE-MLP-based *inverse* model can be effectively used to produce ADI with any desired VHN.

Table 2. Hybrid DE-MLP-based inverse model predicted sample solutions that are in close vicinity of experimental solution

Sl. No.	Expt./ Predicted/ Error(%)	VHN	Solution							
			Austempering parameters		Alloying element proportion (wt%)						
			$T_{austemper}$ (°C)	$t_{austemper}$ (min)	C	Si	Mn	Ni	Cu	Mo	Mg
1	Expt.	464.9	290	60	3.47	2.35	0.24	1.01	0.50	0.15	0.052
	Predicted	465.4	300	60	3.46	2.35	0.24	1.00	1.51	0.15	0.051
	Error	0.10	-3.48	0.46	0.23	0.16	-0.65	0.61	-2.16	-0.79	2.80
2	Expt.	455.8	290	120	3.42	2.32	0.24	1.00	0.51	0.21	0.048
	Predicted	456.1	294	115	3.47	2.34	0.24	1.00	0.52	0.22	0.049
	Error	-0.07	-1.52	3.98	-1.40	-1.04	-1.61	-0.35	-1.81	-3.36	-2.83
3	Expt.	410.2	320	120	3.46	2.41	0.25	1.00	1.00	0.10	0.053
	Predicted	410.6	307	119	3.42	2.37	0.26	1.02	0.99	0.10	0.051
	Error	-0.11	3.98	1.21	1.09	1.76	-2.39	-1.93	1.10	-1.15	3.70
4	Expt.	450.6	260	90	3.45	2.41	0.26	1.02	1.01	0.20	0.049
	Predicted	450.1	271	90	3.45	2.34	0.26	1.01	0.97	0.20	0.050
	Error	0.12	-4.26	0.33	0.09	2.71	1.44	0.69	3.76	-2.42	-1.76

6   Conclusion

To overcome the inherent challenge of producing ADI with a specific microstructure which in turn affects the mechanical properties of ADI, the authors proposed a novel hybrid DE-MLP-based *inverse* modeling of the ADI process. This model can predict the austempering process parameters, i.e., austempering temperature and austempering time duration ($T_{austemper}$ and $t_{austemper}$) and the proportion of the seven alloying elements (C, Si, Mn, Ni, Cu, Mo and Mg). With only 10 individuals in the population and in less than 10 generations, the proposed DE-MLP-based model can generate a feasible solution to produce ADI with a specific VHN within 0.6 s. By using this model, several solutions can be generated for the desired hardness (VHN) value, and an optimum solution can be selected from these solutions based on cost and/or energy criteria. Besides ADI, the proposed model can be applied to any other manufacturing process for optimizing the process parameters.

References

1. Arafeh, L., Singh, H., Putatunda, S.K.: A neuro fuzzy logic approach to material processing. IEEE Trans. Syst., Man Cybern. Syst Part C **29**(3), 362–370 (1999)
2. Das, S., Suganthan, P.N.: Differential evolution: a survey of the state-of-the-art. IEEE Trans. Evol. Comput. **15**(1), 4–31 (2011)
3. Haykin, S.: Neural Networks, 2nd edn. Prentice Hall, Upper Saddle River (1999)
4. Jiang, L.L., Maskell, D.L., Patra, J.C.: Parameter estimation of solar cells and modules using an improved adaptive differential evolution algorithm. Appl. Energ. **112**, 185–193 (2013)

5. Keough, J.: Austempered Ductile Iron (ADI) - a green alternative. American Foundry Society, Schaumburg (2011). www.afsinc.org
6. Patra, J.C.: Neural network-based model for dual-junction solar cells. Prog. Photovoltaics Res. Appl. **19**(1), 33–44 (2011)
7. Patra, J.C., Kot, A.C.: Nonlinear dynamic system identification using Chebyshev functional link artificial neural networks. IEEE Trans. Syst. Man Cybern. Part B **32**(4), 505–511 (2002)
8. PourAsiabi, H., PourAsiabi, H., AmirZadeh, Z., BabaZadeh, M.: Development a multi-layer perceptron artificial neural network model to estimate the Vickers hardness of Mn-Ni-Cu-Mo austempered ductile iron. Mater. Des. **35**, 782–789 (2012)
9. Savangouder, R.V., Patra, J.C., Bornand, C.: Artificial neural network-based modeling for prediction of hardness of austempered ductile iron. In: Gedeon, T., Wong, K.W., Lee, M. (eds.) Neural Information Processing, pp. 405–413. Springer International Publishing, Cham (2019)
10. Storn, R., Price, K.: Differential evolution - simple and efficient heuristic for global optimization over continuous spaces. J. Glob. Optim. **11**(4), 341–359 (1997)
11. Varela, D., Santos, J.: A hybrid evolutionary algorithm for protein structure prediction using the face-centered cubic lattice model. In: Liu, D., Xie, S., Li, Y., Zhao, D., El-Alfy, E.S.M. (eds.) Neural Information Processing, pp. 628–638. Springer International Publishing, Cham (2017)
12. Yescas, M.A.: Prediction of the Vickers hardness in austempered ductile irons using neural networks. Int. J. Cast Met. Res. **15**(5), 513–521 (2003)

A Mutual Information-Based Disentanglement Framework for Cross-Modal Retrieval

Han Wu[1], Xiaowang Zhang[1(✉)], Jiachen Tian[1], Shaojuan Wu[1], Chunliu Dou[1], Yue Sun[2], and Zhiyong Feng[1]

[1] College of Intelligence and Computing, Tianjin University, Tianjin 300350, China
xiaowangzhang@tju.edu.cn
[2] International Engineering Institute, Tianjin University, Tianjin 300350, China

Abstract. Cross-modal retrieval essentially extracts the shared semantics of an object between two different modalities. However, "modality gap" may significantly limit the performance when analyzing from each modality sample. In this paper, to overcome the characteristics from heterogeneous data, we propose a novel mutual information-based disentanglement framework to capturing the precise shared semantics in cross-modal scenes. Firstly, we design a disentanglement framework to extract the shared parts of modalities, which can provide the basis for semantic measuring with mutual information. Secondly, we measure semantic associations from the perspective of distribution, which overcomes perturbations brought by "modality gap". Finally, we formalize our framework and theoretically prove that mutual information can obtain remarkable performance under the disentanglement framework. Sufficient experimental results evaluated on two large benchmarks demonstrate that our approach can obtain significant performance in cross-modal retrieval task.

Keywords: Cross-modal retrieval · Mutual information · Disentanglement

1 Introduction

The purpose of cross-modal retrieval task is to obtain relevant information of another modality [19] with one modality as the query. It is significant for users to obtain more comprehensive information about target events or topics across various modalities. For instance, when seeing a beautiful bird in the park, we can do searching by taking pictures to get relevant text or videos. Besides, this task has a variety of downstream applications including image caption [8], visual question answering [26], image recognition [24], and so on. The research of cross-modal retrieval has lasted for several decades and is progressively attractive with the speedy growth of multimodal data in our daily life.

Actually, the essence of cross-modal retrieval is to extract the shared semantics across two modalities to measure similarities. Existing works conduct similarity learning from the perspective of each sample, which pulls ground-truth

© Springer Nature Switzerland AG 2021
T. Mantoro et al. (Eds.): ICONIP 2021, LNCS 13111, pp. 585–596, 2021.
https://doi.org/10.1007/978-3-030-92273-3_48

image-text pairs closer one by one. However, multimodal data that exist in heterogeneous spaces have different types of distributions [14]. So measuring similarities among modalities is exceedingly challenging. This plight may significantly limit the performance in dealing with occasional perturbations of some modality samples [28]. So we wonder whether we can analyze it from the perspective of distribution. Fortunately, mutual information (MI) can calculate the dependence of two random variables [1] as a symmetrical measurement and we aims to introduce it.

However, some modality features are not useful for matching, which may easily cause entanglement between effective information and noise. Disentanglement, mapping distinctive aspects of data into dependent low-dimensional vector spaces [3], can significantly separate (ir)relevant parts of two semantics to extract their shared parts. Inspired by this, we design a disentanglement framework to depict the boundary to remove noise.

In this paper, we introduce a mutual information-based disentanglement framework to extract shared semantics between modalities to the greatest extent. The main contributions of this research are summarized as follows:

- We employ mutual information into the task of cross-modal retrieval and characterize semantic associations from the perspective of distribution, which overcomes perturbations brought by "modality gap".
- We design a disentanglement framework via parallel modality spaces to remove the impact of irrelevant semantics. Moreover, it can retain the maximum amount of information simultaneously.
- We theoretically prove that mutual information is a superior semantic measurement, and it can play significant performance under the disentanglement framework.

2   Method

Without losing generality, this paper focuses on cross-modal retrieval between image modality and text modality. Given an image set $M = \{m_1, m_2, ..., m_i\}$ and a text set $T = \{t_1, t_2, ..., t_j\}$, our objective is to extract the shared semantics between arbitrary m_i and t_j as an index to evaluate whether they are similar. The framework is showed in Fig. 1.

2.1   Construct Parallel Modality Spaces

As mentioned before, existing methods retain all information of different modalities, which are likely to cause the entanglement between effective information and noise. In other words, we need an explicit approach like disentanglement to extract shared semantics. However, an unequal amount of information was provided by different modalities when describing the same semantics [15]. As a result, it is hardly avoidable to cause the loss of information during mapping them into a common space by *Data processing lemma* in [1]. So, we design two parallel modality spaces to construct the cross-modal disentanglement framework:

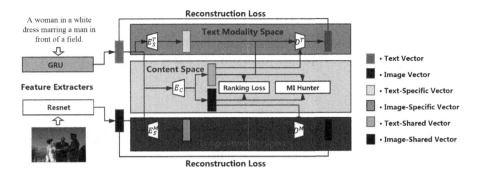

Fig. 1. The overall architecture of our framework. Especially, we construct three embedding spaces: Text Modality Space, Image Modality Space and the Content Space. The images and the text are denoted as M and T, respectively. E_s^T, E_s^M represent modality encoders and E_c is a shared content encoder. D^T, D^M are two decoders.

Let M, T represent the image samples and the text samples respectively, and S, C represent the modality space (modality-specific) and content space (modality-shared) respectively. Assume that the images and text are both described by modality-specific and modality-shared information, that is:

$$M = M_s \cup M_c, \quad T = T_s \cup T_c \tag{1}$$

As illustrated in Fig. 1, we first put individual modality into different modality encoders E_s^T, E_s^M and a shared content encoder E_c, obtaining modality vectors t_s, m_s and content vectors t_c, m_c, respectively. After that, we respectively put t_s, t_c and m_s, m_c into two decoders D^T, D^M. t and m are initial vectors from the feature extracters. Assuming that t_s, t_c can reconstruct t and m_s, m_c can reconstruct m. The two decoders perform the main task of representation learning and this process can be formulated as $\hat{t} = D^T(t_s, t_c)$ and $\hat{m} = D^M(m_s, m_c)$.

The reconstruction loss of this autoencoder structure can be formulated as follow:

$$\mathcal{L}_{rec} = ||t - D^T(t_s, t_c)|| + ||m - D^M(m_s, m_c)|| \tag{2}$$

Besides, a conventional ranking loss was employed here:

$$
\begin{aligned}
\mathcal{L}_{rank} = & \sum_i max(0, [a + dis(t_c^i, m_c^i) - \sum_j dis(t_c^i, m_c^j)]) \\
& + \sum_i max(0, [a + dis(m_c^i, t_c^i) - \sum_j dis(m_c^i, t_c^j)])
\end{aligned}
\tag{3}
$$

where $dis(t_c, m_c)$ is a distance function for t_c and m_c, and we use the Euclidean distance in our architecture. a serves as a margin parameter, encouraging positive samples to have zero penalties and negative samples to have penalties greater than a.

2.2   Mutual Information Hunter

We can cast the inference problem considered by most extant cross-modal retrieval models into the optimal framework as follows:

$$Y^* = \arg\max_{y \in \mathcal{Y}} G(X, Y) \tag{4}$$

where $x \in \mathcal{X}$ stands for a sample of one modality, *e.g.* an image. And Y^* indicates the most relevant sample from another modality Y, *e.g.* a text description. G is a measurement to quantify the similarities between the two modalities. However, available modalities are independent, which may significantly limit the performance in dealing with occasional perturbations of individual sources [28]. On the contrary, if we analyze from the perspective of distribution, the model will not be affected by the "modality gap". Therefore, we introduce mutual information (MI) and present a framework based on distribution to optimize.

MI is a crucial quantity that can calculate the dependence of two random variables from data science [1]. It is formalized in the following:

$$I(X, Y) = \sum_{x \in \mathcal{X}} \sum_{y \in \mathcal{Y}} P_{X,Y}(x, y) \log \frac{P_{X,Y}(x, y)}{P_X(x) P_Y(y)} \tag{5}$$

Intuitively, high MI means two variables are well-matched, so we need to maximize it between content information. Besides, minimize MI between modality information can also further ensure the effectiveness of removing irrelevant semantics. We use T_c, M_c, T_s and M_s to represent a batch of t_c, m_c, t_s and m_s. Therefore, the objective function of MI Hunter is defined as:

$$\mathcal{L}_{MI} = I(T_s, M_s) - I(T_c, M_c) \tag{6}$$

Each item in the above formula can be estimated by applying following formula from [2]:

$$I(X, Y) = -sp(E[-N_{P(X,Y)}]) - sp(E[e^{N_{P(X)P(Y)}}]) \tag{7}$$

$sp(z) = \log(1 + e^z)$ is the softplus function.

We define the overall loss function as follow:

$$\mathcal{L} = \mathcal{L}_{rec} + \mathcal{L}_{rank} + \mathcal{L}_{MI} \tag{8}$$

2.3   Analysis

Theorem 1. *Assume that the modality space S and content space C are independent, $H(M_c) > H(M_s)$ and $H(T_c) > H(T_s)$ (information is mainly contained in modality-shared parts). The correlations of modality-shared parts between* *images and text are far greater than modality-specific parts, that is $H_{M_c|T_c}(x|y) < H_{M_s|T_s}(x|y)$, then,*

$$D(M \parallel T) > I(M_s, T_s) - I(M_c, T_c) \tag{9}$$

where D refers to the divergence and H represents the amount of information in semantics from Information Theory in [1].

Proof. S and C are independent, so $M = M_s + M_c$, $T = T_s + T_c$. By *Refinement cannot decrease divergence* in [1], we can obtain:

$$D(M \parallel T) \geq D(M_s \parallel T_s) + D(M_c \parallel T_c) \tag{10}$$

Using the properties of KL divergence, we can get: For any two distributions M and T, $D(M\|T) \geq 0$. So,

$$D(M_c\|T_c) \geq 0, D(M_s\|T_s) \geq 0 \tag{11}$$

Combining the definition of information entropy and probability density function, we can get: $\forall\ x, y \in S$, mutual information between images and text modality-specific parts $I(M_s, T_s)$ satisfies:

$$I(M_s, T_s) = \sum_{x \in S} \sum_{y \in S} P_{M_s, T_s}(x, y) \log \frac{P_{M_s, T_s}(x, y)}{P_{M_s}(x) P_{T_s}(y)} = H(M_s) - H(M_s|T_s) \tag{12}$$

In a similar way,

$$I(M_c, T_c) = H(M_c) - H(M_c|T_c) \tag{13}$$

Further, we can obtain:

$$D(M_c\|T_c) + D(M_s\|T_s) > I(M_s, T_s) - I(M_c, T_c) \tag{14}$$

Combine (10) and (14), **Theorem** 1 holds.

3   Experiments

3.1   Dataset and Metrics

We trained and tested our framework on two large-scale multimodal benchmarks, namely MS-COCO [11] and Flickr30K [16].

MS-COCO dataset has 113,287 images for training models and 5000 for both validation and testing retrieval results. On a similar way, Flickr30K dataset consists of 29000 images for training and 1,000 for both validation and testing. We adopted the same splits as those used by state-of-the-art approaches [5].

For evaluating the accuracy of retrieval, we used the same metrics as those in [9]: R@1, R@5 and R@10, the higher, the better.

Table 1. Cross-modal results by our model and compared methods on Flickr30K.

Method	Image-to-Text			Text-to-Image		
	R@1	R@5	R@10	R@1	R@5	R@10
VSE++ [5]	52.9	80.5	87.2	39.6	70.1	79.5
DMIE [6]	57.7	–	89.2	42.9	–	79.3
SCAN [9]	67.9	89.0	94.4	43.9	74.2	82.8
CAMP [21]	68.1	89.7	95.2	51.5	77.1	85.3
PolyLoss [23]	69.4	89.9	95.4	47.5	75.5	83.1
AOQ [4]	73.2	94.5	97.0	54.0	80.3	87.7
ADAPT [22]	76.6	95.4	97.6	60.7	86.6	92.0
Ours	**78.3**	**96.5**	**98.0**	**61.2**	**87.2**	**93.1**

3.2   Model and Training Details

As in previous works [9], we used ResNet [7] as the backbone in our experiments and the dimension of the image vector was 2048. We applied a normal GRU similar to the one in [9] as our text encoder. Besides, the dimension of the embeddings that are input to the GRU was 300.

We used the Adam optimizer and trained our model for 30 epochs. We started training stage with a learning rate of 0.001 for 5 epochs. After that, we lowered it to 0.0001 for another 25 epochs. In order to make the content vector perform better, we set up a two-stage training strategy: In the first stage, we used reconstruction loss to pretrain the autoencoder structure. Besides, we warmed up the **MI hunter** to provide the ability to capture semantics. When turning to the formal training stage, we used all losses mentioned in Eq. 8. We set the margin a to 0.1 and the mini-batch size of all experiments is 128.

Note that the results were reported by two different settings on MS-COCO: one is 1K unique images averaged over 5 folds and another one is full 5K test images.

3.3   Comparisons with State-of-the-Art Methods

The efficiency of our model was evaluated by comparing to the published state-of-the-art approaches. Note that we use the experimental results given in papers and "-" indicates that the results under some specific settings are not given. Among all the baselines, only **VSE++** and **DMIE** directly use global features as their modality representations. Other methods all use the regions of images and the words of text to obtain more fine-grained local features with some attention mechanism. In order to measure cross-modal similarities, the regions and words are mapped into a common embedding space in **SCAN**, **ADAPT** and **PVSE**.

Table 2. Cross-modal results by our model and compared methods on MS-COCO.

Method	1K test images						5K test images					
	Image-to-Text			Text-to-Image			Image-to-Text			Text-to-Image		
	R@1	R@5	R@10	R@1	R@5	R@10	R@1	R@5	R@10	R@1	R@5	R@10
VSE++ [5]	64.6	90.0	95.5	52.0	79.9	92.0	41.3	71.1	81.2	30.3	59.4	72.4
DMIE [6]	68.9	–	97.0	57.3	–	94.4	43.1	–	85.9	31.8	–	74.9
PVSE [18]	69.2	91.6	96.6	55.2	86.5	93.7	45.2	74.3	84.5	32.4	63.0	75.0
CAMP [21]	72.3	94.8	98.3	58.5	87.9	95.0	50.1	82.1	89.7	39.0	68.9	80.2
SCAN [9]	72.7	94.8	98.4	58.8	88.4	94.8	50.4	82.2	90.0	38.6	69.3	80.4
PolyLoss [23]	71.1	93.7	98.2	56.8	86.7	93.0	46.9	77.7	87.6	34.4	64.2	75.9
AOQ [4]	74.1	95.2	98.5	59.8	88.6	95.0	51.2	82.5	90.1	39.4	69.7	80.4
ADAPT [22]	76.5	95.6	98.9	62.2	90.5	96.0	–	–	–	–	–	–
Ours	**78.8**	**97.4**	**98.9**	**64.5**	**91.9**	**96.7**	**58.2**	**83.5**	**92.5**	**41.6**	**74.7**	**83.6**

AOQ and **PolyLoss** both introduce a new loss function to replace traditional triplet ranking loss. Both of **DMIE** and our work mention the idea of decoupling. However, they do not use MI to measure semantics from the perspective of distribution, and the model could be affected by "modality gap".

Table 1 shows that our design surpass all the baseline approaches by large margins in all R@K metrics on Flickr30K dataset. Besides, the experimental results on MS-COCO dataset was listed in Table 2 and the comparisons with prior work also demonstrate our excellent performance. From the results, we can further obtain that our model indeed capture more precise shared semantics between modalities. Although **AOQ** and **PolyLoss** do metric learning by mining more effective negative samples to improve retrieval performance, experimental results show that our design can accomplish this task better. **CAMP** considers keeping two separate modality spaces that can avoid information loss like our model. However, it does not explicitly separate modality relevant and irrelevant semantics.

Moreover, it is noted that our model has a greater performance improvement compared to other baselines on MS-COCO dataset. We analyze it may be due to these reasons: On the one hand, categories of text in Flickr30K are relatively independent in semantics, which could learn discriminative representations easily. On the other hand, MS-COCO dataset has many different types of images and more complicated background information. Moreover, the number of targets is larger and the target size is smaller in each image. These observations prove that our model can handle more general text and more complex images due to the disentanglement framework based on MI.

Table 3. Ablation study on Flickr30K.

Method	Image-to-Text			Text-to-Image		
	R@1	R@5	R@10	R@1	R@5	R@10
C	71.2	89.6	88.5	55.2	80.2	87.3
P	72.6	92.5	92.5	57.3	84.3	90.6
C+MI	72.2	89.4	88.6	56.1	82.2	88.5
Ours (P+MI)	**78.3**	**96.5**	**98.0**	**61.2**	**87.2**	**93.1**

Query: With a boardwalk railing in the background, a man wearing jeans and a tan t-shirt leaps headfirst onto a pile of mattresses covered with sheets.

Results:

Rank1:   Rank2:   Rank3:

Query:

Results:

Rank 1: A snowboarder flying through the air doing a trick on a snowy mountain.

Rank 2: A person is flying through the air on a snowboard as the wind picks up some snow.

Rank 3: Two young girls in swimsuits and life jackets run down the beach towards some flying birds.

Fig. 2. Examples of the image-text mutual retrieval results by our model. Green denotes the ground-truth images or text. Note that our model retrieves the ground-truth images or sentences in the top-3 list of the examples we show. (Color figure online)

3.4   Ablation Study

Our carefully designed model has shown superior performance, so we carry several ablation study to verify some effective module. "**P**" represents the two parallel modality spaces. "**C**" denotes that the model maps modalities into the fully-connected layer before encoding. "**MI**" represents the use of MI hunter.

- The first component we analyze is the **parallel space** to verify the importance of retaining the maximum amount of information. As shown in Table 3, by analyzing the results about the 1st row and 2nd row (or the 3rd and 4th row), we can conclude the use of **parallel space** grants all R@K increase in mutual retrieval tasks.
- We hypothesize that our model would benefit from capturing shared semantics via **MI hunter**. As shown in Table 3, if we remove it from common space or parallel space, the differences occur between the 1st and 3rd row (or the 2nd and 4th row). These results can prove our design of **MI hunter** can successfully capture more accurate shared semantics.

In particular, the disparity between the 1st and 2nd row is smaller than that between the 3rd and 4th row. So we conclude that **parallel space** and **MI hunter** can assist each other, which fulfills our objective more effectively.

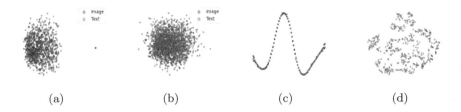

| (a) | (b) | (c) | (d) |

Fig. 3. The visualization for the samples of Flickr30K by using the t-SNE tool. (a) and (c) show the original representations of samples. (b) and (d) show the learned representations of our model.

3.5   Qualitative Results

In this part, we conduct a qualitative analysis of our framework on cross-modal retrieval. We pick a sentence to retrieve the closest images on Flickr30K and vice versa. On the left part of Fig. 2, we retrieve images based on the query sentence: "With a boardwalk railing in the background, a man wearing jeans and a tan t-shirt leaps headfirst onto a pile of mattresses covered with sheets." This sentence contains a lot of entities and rich information. It is prone to match only some entities when searching. However, our model returns the correct image at the first time, and the latter two results returned are also reasonable. Besides, the right part shows image-to-text circumstance, and the first two sentences returned by our model exactly match the query image. In general, our model can capture the comprehensive associations between images and text.

3.6   Visualization of the Learned Representations

In this section, the distributions of the representations learned from our skilled model are visualized by applying the t-SNE tool. Especially, we show 1000 sample points for each modality in Fig. 3.

- **Inter-modal Coherent.** The comparison between (a) and (b) in Fig. 3 reveals the data distributions of these two modalities are mixed and could not be distinguished. It demonstrates our disentanglement framework can indeed filter most of the noise and obtain more shared semantics.
- **Intra-modal Discriminative.** Since one image corresponding to five descriptions in datasets, the image can be regarded as the clustering label of the text. As shown in (c) and (d) from Fig. 3, our proposed model can efficiently separate text samples into several semantically discriminative clusters, further verifying our framework can help the text samples in each cluster learn more similar semantics.

4   Related Work

We can roughly divided existing cross-modal retrieval methods into two categories [14]: *common subspace learning* and *cross-modal similarity measurement.*

The first strategy always transforms the samples from different modality spaces into a common space. And then we can directly measure the similarities via distance functions. Under this category, canonical correlation analysis (CCA) [17] is a traditional linear model, mapping the different modalities from their initial spaces to a new CCA space. However, cross-modal correlations are complex, advanced and nonlinear [20], so deep neural network (DNN) methods have been used because of their powerful ability to mine nonlinear relationships [5,12]. Besides, the hash methods like [10,19] are designed to speed up the retrieval process due to the rapidly increasing multimedia data. Their purpose is to construct a hamming space and obtain the hash codes to calculate similarities.

Another category is cross-modal similarity measurement. Due to the absence of common space, cross-modal similarities cannot be computed directly by distance measuring or normal classifiers. So graph-based methods are proposed. The key idea of them is to construct one or more graphs and represent the cross-modal correlations on the level of modality instances or multimedia documents (MMDs) such as [25,27]. Another strategy belonging to this category is the neighbor analysis which finds the nearest neighbors in datasets with the queries to get the retrieval results. The co-existence relationships of data provide essential hints to bridge different modalities like [13].

5   Conclusion

In this paper, we have introduced a mutual information-based disentanglement framework to extract shared semantics between modalities, which characterizes semantic associations from the perspective of distribution. Generally speaking, our design is suitable for other scenes since we work on the level of semantics. To convey our idea simply, we mainly discuss images and text in this paper. In the future, we will generate our approach to support more complicated modalities.

Acknowledgments. This work is supported by the National Natural Science Foundation of China (NSFC) (61972455), and the Joint Project of Bayescom. Xiaowang Zhang is supported by the program of Peiyang Young Scholars in Tianjin University (2019XRX-0032).

References

1. Alajaji, F., Chen, P.-N.: An Introduction to Single-User Information Theory. SUTMT, Springer, Singapore (2018). https://doi.org/10.1007/978-981-10-8001-2
2. Belghazi, M.I., et al.: Mutual information neural estimation. In: 35th International Conference on Machine Learning, pp. 530–539. PMLR, Stockholmsmässan, Stockholm, Sweden (2018)
3. Bengio, Y., Courville, A., Vincent, P.: Representation learning: a review and new perspectives. IEEE Trans. Pattern Anal. Mach. Intell. **35**(8), 1798–1828 (2013)
4. Chen, T., Deng, J., Luo, J.: Adaptive offline quintuplet loss for image-text matching. In: Vedaldi, A., Bischof, H., Brox, T., Frahm, J.-M. (eds.) ECCV 2020. LNCS, vol. 12358, pp. 549–565. Springer, Cham (2020). https://doi.org/10.1007/978-3-030-58601-0_33

5. Faghri, F., Fleet, D. J., Kiros, J. R., Fidler, S.: VSE++: improving visual-semantic embeddings with hard negatives. In: 29th British Machine Vision Conference, Article 12. BMVA Press Newcastle, UK (2018)
6. Guo, W., Huang, H., Kong, X., He, R.: Learning disentangled representation for cross-modal retrieval with deep mutual information estimation. In: 27th ACM International Conference on Multimedia, pp. 1712–1720. ACM, Nice, France (2019)
7. He, K., Zhang, X., Ren, S., Sun, J.: Deep residual learning for image recognition. In: 26th IEEE Conference on Computer Vision and Pattern Recognition, pp. 770–778. IEEE Computer Society, Las Vegas, NV, USA (2016)
8. Karpathy, A., Fei-Fei, L.: Deep visual-semantic alignments for generating image descriptions. In: 25th IEEE Conference on Computer Vision and Pattern Recognition, pp. 3128–3137. IEEE Computer Society, Boston, MA, USA (2015)
9. Lee, K.-H., Chen, X., Hua, G., Hu, H., He, X.: Stacked cross attention for image-text matching. In: Ferrari, V., Hebert, M., Sminchisescu, C., Weiss, Y. (eds.) ECCV 2018. LNCS, vol. 11208, pp. 212–228. Springer, Cham (2018). https://doi.org/10.1007/978-3-030-01225-0_13
10. Li, C., Deng, C., Li, N., Liu, W., Gao, X., Tao, D.: Self-supervised adversarial hashing networks for cross-modal retrieval. In: 28th IEEE Conference on Computer Vision and Pattern Recognition, pp. 4242–4251. IEEE Computer Society, Salt Lake City, UT, USA (2018)
11. Lin, T.-Y., et al.: Microsoft COCO: common objects in context. In: Fleet, D., Pajdla, T., Schiele, B., Tuytelaars, T. (eds.) ECCV 2014. LNCS, vol. 8693, pp. 740–755. Springer, Cham (2014). https://doi.org/10.1007/978-3-319-10602-1_48
12. Liu, C., Mao, Z., Liu, A. A., Zhang, T., Wang, B., Zhang, Y.: Focus your attention: a bidirectional focal attention network for image-text matching. In: 27th ACM International Conference on Multimedia, pp. 3–11. ACM, Nice, France (2019)
13. Ma, D., Zhai, X., Peng, Y.: Cross-media retrieval by cluster-based correlation analysis. In: 20th IEEE International Conference on Image Processing, pp. 3986–3990. IEEE, Melbourne, Australia (2013)
14. Peng, Y., Huang, X., Zhao, Y.: An overview of cross-media retrieval: concepts, methodologies, benchmarks, and challenges. IEEE Trans. Circuits Syst. Video Technol. 28(9), 2372–2385 (2017)
15. Peng, Y., Qi, J., Yuan, Y.: Modality-specific cross-modal similarity measurement with recurrent attention network. IEEE Trans. Image Process. 27(11), 5585–5599 (2018)
16. Plummer, B.A., Wang, L., Cervantes, C.M., Caicedo, J.C., Hockenmaier, J., Lazebnik, S.: Flickr30k entities: collecting region-to-phrase correspondences for richer image-to-sentence models. In: 15th IEEE International Conference on Computer Vision, pp. 2641–2649. IEEE Computer Society, Santiago, Chile (2015)
17. Rasiwasia, N., Costa Pereira, J., Coviello, E., Doyle, G., Lanckriet, G. R., Levy, R., Vasconcelos, N.: A new approach to cross-modal multimedia retrieval. In: 18th ACM International Conference on Multimedia, pp. 251–260. ACM, Firenze, Italy (2010)
18. Song, Y., Soleymani, M.: Polysemous visual-semantic embedding for cross-modal retrieval. In: 29th IEEE Conference on Computer Vision and Pattern Recognition, pp. 1979–1988. IEEE, Long Beach, CA, USA (2019)
19. Wang, B., Yang, Y., Xu, X., Hanjalic, A., Shen, H.T.: Adversarial cross-modal retrieval. In: 25th ACM International Conference on Multimedia, pp. 154–162. ACM, Mountain View, CA, USA (2017)

20. Wang, T., Xu, X., Yang, Y., Hanjalic, A., Shen, H.T., Song, J.: Matching images and text with multi-modal tensor fusion and re-ranking. In: 27th ACM International Conference on Multimedia, pp. 12–20. ACM, Nice, France (2019)
21. Wang, Z., et al.: Camp: cross-modal adaptive message passing for text-image retrieval. In: 17th IEEE International Conference on Computer Vision, pp. 5763–5772. IEEE, Seoul, Korea (South) (2019)
22. Wehrmann, J., Kolling, C., Barros, R. C.: Adaptive cross-modal embeddings for image-text alignment. In: 32nd AAAI Conference on Artificial Intelligence, pp. 12313–12320. AAAI Press, New York, NY, USA (2020)
23. Wei, J., Xu, X., Yang, Y., Ji, Y., Wang, Z., Shen, H.T.: Universal weighting metric learning for cross-moda matching. In: 30th IEEE/CVF Conference on Computer Vision and Pattern Recognition, pp. 13002–13011. IEEE, Seattle, WA, USA (2020)
24. Wu, H., Merler, M., Uceda-Sosa, R., Smith, J. R.: Learning to make better mistakes: Semantics-aware visual food recognition. In: 24th ACM International Conference on Multimedia, pp. 172–176. ACM, Amsterdam, The Netherlands (2016)
25. Yang, Y., Xu, D., Nie, F., Luo, J., Zhuang, Y.: Ranking with local regression and global alignment for cross media retrieval. In: 17th ACM international Conference on Multimedia, pp. 175–184. ACM, Vancouver, British Columbia, Canada (2009)
26. Zhang, W., et al.: Photo stream question answer. In: 28th ACM International Conference on Multimedia, pp. 3966–3975. ACM, Virtual Event (2020)
27. Zhuang, Y.T., Yang, Y., Wu, F.: Mining semantic correlation of heterogeneous multimedia data for cross-media retrieval. IEEE Trans. Multimedia 10(2), 221–229 (2008)
28. Li, C., Zhu, C., Huang, Y., Tang, J., Wang, L.: Cross-modal ranking with soft consistency and noisy labels for robust RGB-T tracking. In: Ferrari, V., Hebert, M., Sminchisescu, C., Weiss, Y. (eds.) ECCV 2018. LNCS, vol. 11217, pp. 831–847. Springer, Cham (2018). https://doi.org/10.1007/978-3-030-01261-8_49

AGRP: A Fused Aspect-Graph Neural Network for Rating Prediction

Cong Huang, Huiping Lin$^{(\boxtimes)}$, and Yuhan Xiao

Peking University, Beijing, China
{conghuang,yuhanxiao}@pku.edu.cn, linhp@ss.pku.edu.cn

Abstract. User reviews have been widely used in rating prediction. Among rating prediction methods, the aspect-based method has proven effective because the aspects are argued as an effective expression of user preferences and item attributes. However, aspect-based methods still suffer from problems. First, the aspects are usually very sparse. Moreover, enhancing the connection between the aspects and using them to build an effective attention mechanism remains a challenge. In this paper, we propose a fused aspect-graph neural network for rating prediction (AGRP). We first extract three types of aspects, namely the user reviews aspect (URA), the item reviews aspect (IRA), and the item description aspect (IDA). We believe that these three types of aspects have different reflections on user preferences and item features. Then we propose a novel aspect graph, where the nodes represent the aspects and the edges represent the co-occurrence connection as well as the similarity connection between the aspects. The enriched aspects and connection help to address the issues of sparsity. Finally, a graph-based attention fusion method is proposed to fuse the aspect graph with the neural network through a graph attention network. The experiments show that AGRP consistently outperforms the state-of-the-art recommendation approaches on four Amazon datasets, which proves the effectiveness of our model.

Keywords: Rating prediction · Aspect graph · Graph attention network

1 Introduction

The recommendation system has been successfully applied in many applications and websites. To better provide personalized services, accurate rating prediction is important to the recommendation system.

In recent years, deep learning models based on user reviews for rating prediction have made great progress, gradually replacing matrix factorization methods. For example, the DeepCoNN [22] uses two parallel convolutional neural networks (CNNs) to encode review representation and combines the outputs of the two parallel networks through the FM layer to predict rating. Although the rating prediction algorithm has been greatly improved, due to the existence of redundant and useless information in reviews, the performance of review-based

© Springer Nature Switzerland AG 2021
T. Mantoro et al. (Eds.): ICONIP 2021, LNCS 13111, pp. 597–608, 2021.
https://doi.org/10.1007/978-3-030-92273-3_49

prediction still needs to be improved. Researchers have found that reviews are usually related to different aspects, such as price, quality and service. Thus, aspect-based rating prediction methods have been proposed [3, 21]. For example, ARP [21] proposes a Chinese review rating prediction method based on a neural aspect-aware network. It is a collaborative learning framework to jointly train review-level and multiple aspect-level rating prediction. To enrich the relationship between users and products, extracting the aspects of comments, synonyms and similarities is also considered in AARM [5].

Despite their effectiveness, aspect-based methods still suffer from disadvantages. First, the aspects are usually very sparse. Second, it is difficult to enhance the modeling of the interaction between the aspects. Moreover, the method lacks an efficient way to build attention allocation based on the correlation between the aspects.

In this paper, we propose a fused aspect-graph neural network for rating prediction (AGRP). Unlike in [5], the aspect is defined as "the word or phrases", specifically, the aspect is defined as the noun word that is extracted from the user review text and product description text. We first extract three types of aspects, namely, the user reviews aspect (URA), the item reviews aspect (IRA), and the item description aspect (IDA). Then, we build an aspect graph, where the nodes represent the aspects and the edges represent the different relations. The purpose of the aspect graph is to enhance the semantic representation learning of aspect through a fusion mechanism. Two types of relations, co-occurrence relations and similarity relations, are identified. The aspect graph provides an effective method to model the interconnection among the aspects, but also helps to address the issues of sparsity. Finally, a graph-based attention fusion method is proposed so that the aspect graph can be used by the neural network through a graph attention network (GAT) [19].

The contributions of this paper can be summarized as follows.

(1) We introduce three types of aspects into the method. We believe that these three types of aspects have different reflections on user's preference and item features. Although it introduces duplication as well, it helps greatly overcome the sparsity. Moreover, it helps identify more enriched relations between the aspects. We performed a deduplication operation on the aspect graph so that the duplication remained reasonable.

(2) We propose a novel aspect graph, which considers not only the similarity connection between the aspects, but also the co-occurrence connection, to overcome the edge sparsity in the graph. The co-occurrence connection rule allows more aspects to be associated.

(3) We propose a graph-based attention mechanism for rating prediction for the first time. We use GAT to learn the association between aspects to fuse the aspect graph with the neural network. In this way, the relatedness between user preferences and item features is learned.

(4) On four Amazon public review datasets, our model achieved state-of-the-art results compared to the most advanced models.

2   Related Work

In recent years, matrix factorization [18] has become the most popular collaborative filtering method based on rating matrix. It is proposed to solve the problem of obvious head effects and weak generalization of original collaborative filtering methods. Subsequently, many methods have been proposed to enhance matrix factorization, such as probability-based matrix factorization (PMF) [17], and non-negative matrix factorization (NMF) [12]. Although these methods have achieved good results, when the rating matrix becomes very sparse, the recommendation effect decreases significantly. Many works have used review text to improve rating prediction performance. In HFT [13], it combines latent hidden factors with latent review topics learned by document topic models such as LDA.

At present, deep learning based on neural networks has achieved great success in recommendation systems. There have been many works that use deep learning to explore review information to improve rating prediction performance, such as ConvMF [10], NCF [8], and WCN [20]. ConvMF uses CNN to learn text representations from item reviews. This method learns the local word order information through CNN and generates more accurate item representations. However, ConvMF only considers the text information of items, without the text information of users. In response to this problem, DeepCoNN [22] uses two parallel CNNs to encode reviews, and combines the outputs after encoding through the last layer of FM to perform rating prediction. NARRE [1] simultaneously takes the reviews and rating matrix as inputs. It uses the review-level attention mechanism to improve the model performance and generates useful reviews from the attention score.

Another research direction is to use the aspects in reviews for rating prediction. AARM [5] thinks that the common aspects of user and item reviews are usually sparse. To enrich the relationship between users and items, extracting the aspects of reviews, synonyms and similarities is also added. It constructs a neural attention network considering users, products and aspects simultaneously to capture users' interest in different products. A3NCF [2] captures the user's attention to various aspects of different items. Specifically, it extracts user preferences and item features from reviews. They are used to guide user and item representation learning, and capture user special attention to each aspect of the target item through the attention network.

Moreover, the above deep learning model encodes review representations using static word embedding, such as word2vec [14], and glove [16]. However, it is better to use BERT [4] to encode review text, so that the model learns contextualized word embedding.

3   Methodology

3.1   Definition

For a dataset D, the number of samples is N, where each sample (u, i, w_{ui}, r_{ui}) indicates that user u wrote a review w_{ui} with the corresponding rating r_{ui} on item i. This paper predicts the rating according to user u, item i, the user review set (removing review w_{ui}), the item review set (removing review w_{ui}), and item description text $desc_i$ to minimize the error between $\hat{r}_{ui}$ and r_{ui}. We define the concatenated user review set as the user document d_u, and the concatenated item description text and item review set are defined as the item document d_i.

3.2 Aspect Graph Construction

The construction of the proposed aspect graph is shown in Fig. 1. First, we extract aspects from user reviews, item reviews and item descriptions. Since the Amazon review text does not have corresponding aspect annotation data, we use an unsupervised method, the Latent Dirichlet Allocation (LDA) topic model, to extract the aspects. We define the topic words extracted from the LDA as aspects. In addition, we stipulate that all the parts of speech of aspects are nouns, so we filter the non-noun aspects. Then, we use the word2vec model to recall more aspects similar to the LDA extraction results.

The three types of aspects, namely, the user review aspect (URA), the item review aspect (IRA) and the item description aspect (IDA), are obtained through the aspect extractor. Table 1 shows some examples of aspects.

- URA: The aspects extracted from user reviews, which refer to user preference.
- IRA: The aspects extracted from item reviews, which are a mix of the users' preference toward the item and item attributes.
- IDA: The aspects extracted from the item description, which contains a more precise and professional description of the item.

The common aspects mentioned in user reviews and item reviews infer the similarity between user and item. However, it is not sufficient to only consider similarity. Generally, there are not enough common aspects, which leads to some isolated aspects in aspect graph. Thus, two types of connections, the co-occurrence and similarity connections, are identified according to following steps.

1. Step 1: Build the co-occurrence connection within URAs. For user reviews, if two aspects are mentioned, and both aspects belong to URA, an edge between them is built to connect them with each other (described as the red line in Fig. 1);
2. Step 2: Build the co-occurrence connection within IDAs. For an item description, if two aspects are mentioned, and both aspects belong to IDA, an edge between them is built to connect them with each other (described as the blue line in Fig. 1);
3. Step 3: Build the similarity connection between URAs and IRAs. Calculate the similarity between any URA and IRA by the word2vec model. If the cosine similarity between a URA and an IRA is greater than our predefined threshold, an edge is built to connect them with each (described as the green line in Fig. 1).
4. Step 4: Build the similarity connection between URAs and IDAs, using the same method stated in step 3.

Thus, the aspect graph, where the nodes represent the aspects and the edges represent the relations between aspects, is built through our aspect graph builder. Since there may be duplicated aspects, we performed a deduplication operation on the aspect graph.

Table 1. Some examples of the extracted aspects from Luxury_Beauty review dataset.

Category	Aspect
URA	Smell, wrinkle, hair, quality, appearance, smoothness, protein, ...
IRA	Antiperspirants, scent, fragrances, perfume, jasmine, skincare, ...
UDA	Cream, vitamin, camphor, antioxidants, fragrances, rosemary, ...

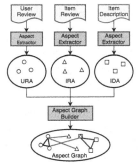

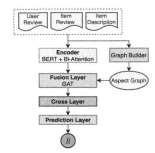

Fig. 1. The construction process of the aspect graph. (Color figure online)

Fig. 2. The AGRP model framework

3.3 Architecture

The AGRP model framework is shown in Fig. 2. The input consists of three parts: user reviews, item reviews and item descriptions. Then, the three text sets are inputted into the text preprocessing module to sort out the user documents and the item documents. They are not only used by our model but are also sent to the graph builder to obtain the aspect graph. Next, we introduce our deep recommendation model architecture, which is shown in Fig. 3.

Text Representation Layer. We input user document into BERT to obtain user document representation and item document representation. The user and item document representations are given into Bi-Attention [15], and the tensor representation of the mutual attention of the two is obtained. Bi-Attention not only causes full interaction between user representation and item representation but also reduces the dimension of features to accelerate training.

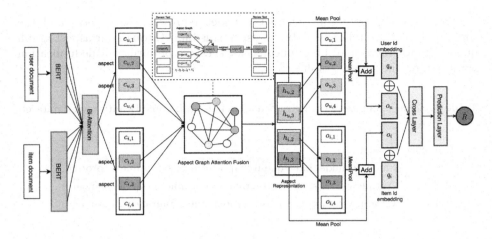

Fig. 3. AGRP model architecture.

Fusion Layer. The fusion layer of our model is the main focus of this paper. It is realized mainly by a GAT. We input user document representation, item document representation and the aspect graph into the fusion block, which is shown in Fig. 3. The main function of the fusion block is to update the representation of the aspect existing in the document, that is, for each aspect node, update its own representation according to the representation of its neighboring nodes in the aspect graph. Specifically, we use GAT to sum the representation of neighbor nodes weighted by the attention score. Suppose there is an aspect graph G, and each aspect node feature is initially represented by $\mathbf{e}_i$. The aspect feature vector is initialized as word2vec embedding. For an aspect node i, its adjacent nodes is $\mathcal{N}_i$; then, node i and adjacent nodes $j \in \mathcal{N}_i$ can calculate the attention coefficient β_{ij}:

$$\beta_{ij} = \mathbf{v}^T (\mathbf{W}[\mathbf{e}_i, \mathbf{e}_j]) \tag{1}$$

where the $\mathbf{v}, \mathbf{W}$ are trainable parameters. Therefore, the attention weight between nodes i and j is calculated with the following formula:

$$\alpha_{ij} = softmax\,(\beta_{ij}) = \frac{exp(LeakyReLU\,(\beta_{ij}))}{\sum_{k \in \mathcal{N}_i} exp(LeakyReLU(\beta_{ik}))} \tag{2}$$

The output of the GAT layer is:

$$\mathbf{h}_i = \sigma(\sum_{j \in \mathcal{N}_i} \alpha_{ij}\mathbf{e}_j) \tag{3}$$

Each node obtains the output representation of the GAT, $\mathbf{H} = [\mathbf{h}_1, \mathbf{h}_2, \ldots, \mathbf{h}_k]$. For each user document representation $\mathbf{C}_u = [\mathbf{c}_1, \mathbf{c}_2, \ldots, \mathbf{c}_m]$, we perform aspect representation fusion on the position of the aspect contained therein using element-level addition. Assuming that $token_i$ and $token_j$ in user document are aspects, and that $\mathbf{h}_1, \mathbf{h}_2$ is the corresponding aspect representation, the fused user document representation is $\mathbf{O}_u = [\mathbf{c}_1, \ldots, \mathbf{c}_i + \mathbf{h}_1, \ldots, \mathbf{c}_j + \mathbf{h}_2, \ldots, \mathbf{c}_m]$. The operation of item document is the same as above, and we obtain the new item document representation $\mathbf{O}_i$.

Cross Layer. We average pooling the fusion layer output $(\mathbf{O}_u, \mathbf{O}_i, \mathbf{H}_u, \mathbf{H}_i)$ to obtain $\mathbf{o}_u, \mathbf{o}_i$:

$$\mathbf{o}_u = MeanPooling(\mathbf{O}_u) + MeanPooling(\mathbf{H}_u) \tag{4}$$

where $\mathbf{H}_u$ is the aspect representation that appears in the user document, and $\mathbf{H}_i$ is the aspect representation that appears in item document. We also embed user id and item id to obtain $\mathbf{q}_u, \mathbf{q}_i$. Then, the formulas of the cross layer we designed are:

$$\mathbf{y}_u = Concat(\mathbf{o}_u, \mathbf{q}_u), \mathbf{y}_i = Concat(\mathbf{o}_i, \mathbf{q}_i) \tag{5}$$

$$\mathbf{y}_{u,i} = \mathbf{y}_u \odot \mathbf{y}_i + \mathbf{y}_u + \mathbf{y}_i \tag{6}$$

Prediction Layer. The output of the fusion layer is input into the prediction layer to finally obtain the prediction rating $\hat{r}_{ui}$.

$$\mathbf{y}'_{u,i} = Dropout\left(ReLU\left(Dense\left(\mathbf{y}_{u,i}\right)\right)\right) \tag{7}$$

$$\hat{r}_{u,i} = Dense\left(\mathbf{y}'_{u,i}\right) \tag{8}$$

Rating prediction is a typical regression problem. We choice the square loss objective function.

$$Loss = \sum_{u,i \in \Omega} \left(\hat{r}_{u,i} - r_{u,i}\right)^2 \tag{9}$$

where Ω represents the sample in training set, $\hat{r}_{u,i}$ is the predicted rating of user u for item i, and $r_{u,i}$ is the true rating of training set. The model parameters are optimized by backpropagation to minimize the objective function, and we use Adam [9] as the optimizer for optimization. Adam can automatically adjust the learning rate during the training process which leads to faster convergence.

4 Experiment and Analysis

4.1 Datasets and Evaluation Metric

To verify the effectiveness of our model, we use four public Amazon datasets, which are the four subcategories of Amazon 5-core [7]: Luxury_Beauty (L&B), Toys_and_Games (T&G), Kindle_Store (K&S), Movies_and_TV (M&T). These four datasets have different domains and scales, among which L&B is the smallest, containing 34256 reviews, M&T is the largest dataset, containing more than 1.6 million reviews from approximately 124 thousand users. The review rating ranges from 1 to 5. The basic statistical information of the four datasets is shown in Table 2. We use the mean square error (MSE) to evaluate the performance of all models. A lower MSE score indicates a better performance. The MSE can be defined as follows:

$$MSE = \frac{1}{N} \sum_{u,i} (\hat{r}_{u,i} - r_{u,i})^2 \tag{10}$$

where N is the number of ratings between users and items.

Table 2. Statistical details of the datasets.

	L&B	T&G	K&S	M&T
Users	3818	19412	68223	123960
Items	1581	11942	61934	50052
Ratings & reviews	34265	167597	982619	1697533

4.2 Baselines

To evaluate the performance of rating prediction, we compared AGRP with six baseline models named NMF, SVD, SVD++, HFT, DeepCoNN and NARRE. The first three models only use the rating matrix, and the last two use the deep learning method.

- NMF [12]: Non-negative matrix factorization. Its input is only the rating matrix, and the matrix after factorization must be non-negative matrix.
- SVD [6]: Singular Value Decomposition. It only uses rating matrix as input.
- SVD++ [11]: An improved algorithm based on SVD, which adds implicit feedback.
- HFT [13]: The model employs topic distributions to learn the latent factors from user or item reviews.
- DeepCoNN [22]: The deep learning model which combines user and item reviews at the same time. It uses review-based user and item representations to predict ratings.
- NARRE [1]: Introducing attention mechanism into DeepCoNN. The model uses the attention score to express the usefulness of each review.

4.3 Experimental Settings

Each dataset is randomly divided into an 80% training set, 10% validation set and 1% test set. All hyperparameters of the model are tuned on the validation set. The number of reviews per user or item cannot exceed 20. Considering that the maximum size of text tokens required by BERT should not exceed 512, we intercept the first 500 tokens. To alleviate overfitting, we turned the dropout ratio to [0.1, 0.3, 0.5, 0.7, 0.9]. Our model experiment is based on the PyTorch framework, which is a well-known deep learning library.

4.4   Performance Evaluations

Comparative Analysis of Overall Performance. The MSEs of AGRP and other comparative models on all datasets are shown in Table 3. The following conclusions can be drawn from the table:

Table 3. MSE comparison with baseline.

	L&B	T&G	K&S	M&T
NMF	1.0422	0.9553	0.7212	1.4981
SVD	0.9169	0.8858	0.5399	1.3162
SVD++	0.9053	0.8810	0.5294	1.3062
HFT	0.9042	0.8783	0.5241	1.2840
DeepCoNN	0.8957	0.8656	0.5149	1.2713
NARRE	0.8911	0.8571	0.5107	1.2654
AGRP	**0.8804**	**0.8463**	**0.4950**	**1.2517**

First, the model considering the review is better than the collaborative filtering model, which only uses the rating matrix. This is not surprising because reviews enhance the quality of hidden factors that represent users and items.

Second, deep learning methods are usually better than traditional methods without considering neural networks. To represent text semantic information, a deep learning model is usually much better than the document topic models. Deep learning represents users and items with a non-linear method, which is a limitation of the collaborative filtering method.

Third, the rating prediction performance of our model is consistently higher than the other baseline methods. The main reason for this is that AGRP is based on aspects, which effectively reflect the features of users and items. Moreover, we not only represent the embedding of a single aspect but also take advantage of the relatedness between aspects by constructing the aspect graph. The fusion of aspect graph effectively solves the problem of aspect sparsity in reviews. BERT also enhances the understanding of context semantic information.

To analyze the AGPR, we construct the following series of comparative experiments to answer the following questions:

1. The impact of using or not using aspect graph;
2. The impact of applying different aspect-graph building rules;
3. The influence of using different encoders;
4. The influence of introducing the item description into the model.

Effect of Aspect Graph. To learn whether the proposed aspect graph is effective, we further explored the model performance with the aspect graph, as shown in Fig. 4. It can be seen that if the aspect graph is removed from the model, the model effect will be reduced. On the one hand, much of the information in reviews is redundant, only some key information is useful, such as the aspects in

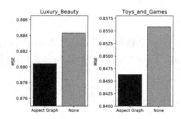

Fig. 4. Comparison of results with aspect graphs.

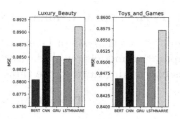

Fig. 5. MSE comparison with different encoder.

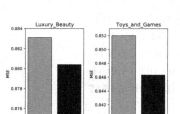

Fig. 6. Comparison with item description.

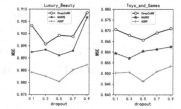

Fig. 7. Comparison of MSE with different dropout rates.

review. On the other hand, recommendation is a process of interaction between users and items, and it is not enough to focus only on the information of aspects. We need to fully correlate user preferences with product features, which is our aspect graph does.

We conducted a sensitivity analysis on the similarity threshold when building the edge between two nodes of the aspect graph. Setting a high threshold could lead to an insufficient aspect graph in which many aspects are not connected with each other. If the threshold is set too low, many unrelated aspects might be connected, causing considerable noise in the graph network. Thus, it is very important to find an adequate similarity threshold. As shown in Table 4, we carry out comparative experiments on the Luxury_Beauty dataset and determine that the threshold does have an impact on the model performance. When the similarity threshold is set to 0.5, the AGRP performs best. The performance will decrease when the threshold is set too high or too low.

Effect of Different Encoder. To verify the effectiveness of the model architecture, instead of relying solely on the effect of BERT, we conducted comparative experiments on the encoder of review text. The specific results are shown in Fig. 5. It can be seen from the figure that the effect of the CNN encoder is slightly worse, but it is also better than the NARRE model. The document modeling method we used pays more attention to the long-distance extraction of contextual features. CNN only focus on features within a specific window range, so the effect of using CNN will be slightly worse. We also use GRU and LSTM

Table 4. The impact of the threshold value of constructing the aspect graph in the Luxury_Beauty dataset. The number of aspect node in graph is 2034.

Threshold	Number of edges	MSE
0.3	270032	0.8840
0.4	190466	0.8816
0.5	151762	0.8804
0.6	135576	0.8835
0.7	129928	0.8845

to encode review text, the effect will be better than CNN, and both are better than the current optimal baseline model NARRE. According to this comparative experiment, the model architecture we proposed is still very valuable.

Effect of Item Description Text. Many models in the literature mentioned using two kinds of data as inputs, namely, user reviews and item reviews. In our method, we take the item description as an independent data source for aspect extraction and text encoding. We believe that using item descriptions is more comprehensive and effective than using redundant item reviews to extract aspects and model item representation. Figure 6 shows that using item descriptions as the input for the model improves its results.

Performances with Different Dropout Ratios. To prevent overfitting, we use the dropout technique commonly used in deep learning. In Fig. 7, setting the dropout rate to an appropriate value can improve the performance of the model. Comparing the performance of DeepCoNN, NARRE, and AGRP on the two datasets, we find that the results of our model are better, and the performance is the best when the dropout rate is equal to 0.5.

5   Conclusion

In this paper, we present an aspect-based rating prediction model called AGRP. A novel aspect graph is established to enhance the connection between the aspects. To address the challenge of aspect sparsity and aspect connection, we extract three types of aspects, namely, URA, IRA, and IDA, and define the co-occurrence connection and similarity connection between the nodes. Then, a graph-based attention fusion method is proposed so that the aspect graph could be fused by the neural network through GAT. The experiments show that AGRP consistently outperforms the state-of-the-art recommendation approaches on four Amazon datasets, which proves the effectiveness of our model.

Acknowledgement. The research is sponsored by the National Key Research and Development Project (No. 2018YFB1702900).

References

1. Chen, C., Zhang, M., Liu, Y., Ma, S.: Neural attentional rating regression with review-level explanations. In: WWW (2018)
2. Cheng, Z., et al.: A3NCF: an adaptive aspect attention model for rating prediction. IJCA I, 3748–3754 (2018)
3. Cheng, Z., Ding, Y., Zhu L., Kankanhalli, M.: Aspect-aware latent factor model: rating prediction with ratings and reviews. In: WWW, pp. 639–648 (2018)
4. Devlin, J., Chang, M.W., Lee, K., Toutanova, K.: BERT: pre-training of deep bidirectional transformers for language understanding. In: NAACL (2019)
5. Guan, X., et al.: Attentive aspect modeling for review-aware recommendation. J. ACM Trans. Inf. Syst. 37, 1–27 (2019)
6. Golub, G.H., Reinsch, C.: Singular value decomposition and least squares solutions. Numerische Mathematik 14, 403–420 (1970). https://doi.org/10.1007/BF02163027
7. He, R., McAuley, J.: Ups and downs: modeling the visual evolution of fashion trends with one-class collaborative filtering. In: WWW (2016)
8. He, X., et al.: Neural collaborative filtering. In: WWW (2017)
9. Kingma, D.P., Ba, J.L.: Adam: a method for stochastic optimization. arXiv preprint arXiv:1412.6980 (2014)
10. Kim, D., Park, C., Oh, J., Lee, S., Yu, H.: Convolutional matrix factorization for document context-aware recommendation. In: RecSys (2016)
11. Kumar, R., Verma, B.K., Rastogi, S.S.: Social popularity based SVD++ recommender system. Int. J. Comput. Appl. 87, 33–37 (2014)
12. Lee, D.D., Seung, H.S.: Algorithms for non-negative matrix factorization. In: NeurIPS (2001)
13. McAuley, J., Jure L.: Hidden factors and hidden topics: understanding rating dimensions with review text. In: RecSys (2013)
14. Mikolov T., Sutskever, I., Chen, K., Corrado, G., Dean, J.: Distributed representations of words and phrases and their compositionality. In: NeurIPS (2013)
15. Minjoon, S., Aniruddha, K., Ali, F., Hannaneh, H.: Bidirectional attention flow for machine comprehension. arXiv preprint arXiv:1611.01603 (2016)
16. Pennington, J., et al.: GloVe: global vectors for word representation. In: EMNLP(2014)
17. Salakhutdinov, R., Mnih, A.: Probabilistic matrix factorization. In: NeurIPS (2008)
18. Su, X., Khoshgoftaar, T.M.: A survey of collaborative filtering techniques. Adv. Artif. Intell. 2009(12) (2009)
19. Velickovic, P., Cucurull, G., Casanova, A., Romero, A., Lio, P., Bengio, Y.: Graph attention networks. In: ICLR (2018)
20. Wang, Q., Li, Si., Chen, G.: Word-driven and context-aware review modeling for recommendation. In: CIKM (2018)
21. Wu, C., Wu, F., Liu, J., Huang, Y., Xie, X.: ARP: aspect-aware neural review rating prediction. In: CIKM (2019)
22. Zheng, L., Noroozi, V., Yu, P.S.: Joint deep modeling of users and items using reviews for recommendation. In: WSDM (2017)

Classmates Enhanced Diversity-Self-Attention Network for Dropout Prediction in MOOCs

Dongen Wu, Pengyi Hao[✉], Yuxiang Zheng, Tianxing Han, and Cong Bai

Zhejiang University of Technology, Hangzhou, China
haopy@zjut.edu.cn

Abstract. The high dropout rate has become a major obstacle to the development of MOOCs (Massive Open Online Courses). For early detecting learners at risk to give up online learning, in this paper, from a new viewpoint of user activities and their classmates, we propose Classmates Enhanced Diversity-self-attention Network (CEDN) to predict users' dropout behavior. In CEDN, a novel model named diversity-self-attention is built for generating user-course features by utilizing diversity information (e.g. age, gender, education, course category, etc.) and the user's activity sequence. In addition, classmate relationship graphs are constructed in MOOCs according to users' course selection records. By aggregating classmates' features in the graphs, an enhanced user-course feature is built for each user with the specific course. Experiments are conducted on XuetangX dataset, a large number of experiments show that CEDN is effective in dropout prediction.

Keywords: Dropout prediction · Self-attention · MOOCs

1 Introduction

MOOCs have developed rapidly and have received great attention, providing an open and flexible learning experience for a large number of learners around the world [2]. However, there has been a problem of high dropout rates since the birth of MOOCs. According to previous research, on average, less than 10% of MOOCs registered users can actually complete these courses and obtain certification [9,13]. The high dropout rate has become a major obstacle to the further development of MOOCs, and it has also led to the waste of high-quality learning resources in MOOCs. There are many factors such as prior experience, course design, feedback, etc. that influence the dropout behavior [1]. In addition, the user's dropout behavior is also affected by the dropout behavior of other users [4]. Therefore, accurately identify potential users who may dropout can help the management to take some measures to help users.

Currently, there are some machine learning based studies for dropout prediction in MOOCs. For example, Hong et al. combined the two-level cascade classifier with three different classifiers (Random Forest (RF), Support Vector

© Springer Nature Switzerland AG 2021
T. Mantoro et al. (Eds.): ICONIP 2021, LNCS 13111, pp. 609–620, 2021.
https://doi.org/10.1007/978-3-030-92273-3_50

Machine (SVM), and MultiNomial Logistic Regression (MLR)) to achieve better prediction [7]. Youssef et al. integrated algorithms such as SVM, RF, LR, etc. to generate a powerful prediction model through selection, averaging, and stacking [18]. With the development of neural network in recent years, there are also some methods which use neural networks to solve the task of dropout prediction, for example, Qiu et al. proposed an end-to-end dropout prediction model based on a convolutional neural network and integrated feature extraction and classification into a frame work [12], Feng et al. [4] found that targeted interventions on users who may dropout can help users continue to complete their studies to a large extent. From the perspective of collective attention network, Zhang et al. analyzed the user's dropout behavior in MOOCs and found that introductory learning resources can prevent dropout and improve the accuracy of prediction [19]. By improving the LSTM, Wang et al. designed a prediction model having the ability to predict early learning behaviors at different time intervals [15]. However, the memory capacity of the LSTM unit is insufficient to maintain long-term dependence on data, so when the time series is long, the performance of LSTM will be greatly affected [16].

In this paper, we propose Classmates Enhanced Diversity-self-attention Network (CEDN) for dropout prediction in MOOCs. CEDN solves the problem of dropout prediction from two aspects. On the one hand, it fuses the relevant contextual information of the user and the course with the user's activity sequence by designing diversity-self-attention, resulting in meaningful user-course features. On the other hand, classmate relationships in MOOCs are defined in the proposed method, and classmate graphs are constructed based on the classmate relationships to enhance user-course features, resulting in accurate prediction. The proposed method is evaluated on a public real dataset. The influence of different types of activities on dropout prediction is discussed in the experiments, and the prediction is compared with several state-of-the-art methods. The main contributions can be summarized in the following three points. (1) We not only define the user activity sequences from the original activity log data but also propose a diversity-self-attention architecture, which combines diversity information and user activity sequences to generate complete user activity features with personalized characters. (2) According to the relevance of users' dropout behavior in MOOCs, we define the classmate relationship and design classmate graphs for course selection records to enhance the users' features. (3) The proposed network is an end-to-end network. Once it is well trained, all the users on their courses can be predicted at the same time.

2   Methodology

2.1   Problem Description

Given k course selection records UC formed by n users on m courses, the activity log data X_1 of users in d days of their selected courses, diversity information data X_2, including user information like age, gender, educational background, etc., and course information like category, number of course candidates, etc., it is

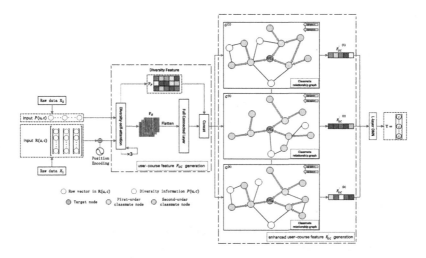

Fig. 1. The proposed CEDN for dropout prediction in MOOCs.

Table 1. Notations of the main symbols used in this paper.

Symbols	Meanings	Symbols	Meanings
$R(u_i, c_j)$	Activity sequence of user u_i on course c_j	$P(u_i, c_j)$	Diversity information of user u_i and course c_j
F_R	Activity feature	F_P	Diversity feature
UC	All course selection records	UC_t	t-th course selection records
S	All similarity relations	$G^{(t)}$	Classmate graph of UC_t
n_1, n_2	Number of node samples of first and second order	η	Size of the influence of classmate behavior
$N_1(UC_t)$	Sampled first-order classmate of UC_t	$N_2(UC_t)$	Sampled second-order classmate of UC_t
F_{UC}	User-course feature	F'_{UC}	Enhanced user-course feature

required to use X_1 and X_2 to predict whether the user will dropout from a certain course in the next period of time. For the t-th ($1 \leq t \leq k$) course selection record, it is represented by a user-course pair $(u_i, c_j) \in UC$, which is named as UC_t. By selecting the activity log data of one user on the corresponding course from X_1, it can form the user's activity sequences $R(u, c)$ for all the course selection records. The diversity information $P(u, c)$ of the user and the corresponding course from X_2 can be formed. Our goal is to input $R(u, c)$ and $P(u, c)$ into the dropout prediction model, and get the output $Y = [\hat{y}_1, \hat{y}_2, \cdots, \hat{y}_k]$ where $\hat{y}_t \in [0, 1]$, if $\hat{y}_t = 1$, the corresponding user u_i is predicted to be likely to dropout of the course c_j. The main symbols are listed in Table 1. The whole process is given in Fig. 1, which mainly consists of user-course feature generation based on diversity-self-attention module designed in Fig. 2 and enhanced user-course feature generation based on classmates graphs.

Table 2. The meaning of each value in sequence $R(u_i, c_j)$

Conditions	Meanings of $r_{a,b}$
$1 \leq a \leq d, 1 \leq b \leq 21$,	Number of activity b on day a
$1 \leq a \leq d, b = 22$	Total number of activities on day a
$1 \leq a \leq d, b = 23$	Duration of activity on day a
$a = d + 1, 1 \leq b \leq 21$	Total number of activity b in d days
$a = d + 1, b = 22$	Total number of all activities in d days
$a = d + 1, b = 23$	Total time of all activities in d days

2.2 Activity Sequence and Position Encoding

Given raw activity log data X_1, for XuetangX, there are 21 kinds of activities, which can be summarized into four types: Click, Assignment, Video, and Forum. In order to express the user's activities, an activity sequence $R(u_i, c_j) \in \mathbb{R}^{(d+1) \times 23}$ for (u_i, c_j) is established according to user's activity log within d days after starting the course. The detailed description of $R(u_i, c_j)$ is given in Table 2. For k course selection records, $R(u, c) \in \mathbb{R}^{k \times (d+1) \times 23}$ is generated, where $R(u_i, c_j)$ is given as follows,

$$R(u_i, c_j) = \begin{bmatrix} r_{1,1} & r_{1,2} & \cdots & r_{1,22} & r_{1,23} \\ r_{2,1} & r_{2,2} & \cdots & r_{2,22} & r_{2,23} \\ \vdots & & r_{a,b} & & \vdots \\ r_{d,1} & r_{d,2} & \cdots & r_{d,22} & r_{d,23} \\ r_{d+1,1} & r_{d+1,2} & \cdots & r_{d+1,22} & r_{d+1,23} \end{bmatrix}. \tag{1}$$

Due to the synchronization calculation of self-attention, there is no sequential relationship between the sequences, resulting in the loss of position information. In CEDN, position encoding [14] is utilized by alternating sine and cosine functions to supplement position information. For each row in $R(u_i, c_j)$, the position information is calculated by $PE_{pos}(2b) = sin(\frac{pos}{10000^{2b/(d+1)}})$ and $PE_{pos}(2b+1) = cos(\frac{pos}{10000^{2b/(d+1)}})$, where $b \in [0, 11]$ and $pos \in [1, d+1]$. By adding position information to $R(u_i, c_j)$ bit by bit, $R'(u_i, c_j) \in \mathbb{R}^{(d+1) \times 23}$ is obtained, then $R'(u, c)$ can be obtained for all the k course selection records.

2.3 User-Course Feature

Because of the diversity of users in MOOCs, the learning habits of different users may be different. To solve this problem, diversity-self-attention model is built in Fig. 2, which employs user activities $R'(u, c)$ and diversity information $P(u, c)$ at the same time to further describe users' activities. $P(u, c) \in \mathbb{R}^{k \times d_p}$ is constructed from X_2 for k course selection records. $P(u_i, c_j)$, a vector with d_p values of $P(u, c)$, is built with personal characteristics for (u_i, c_j), which is consisted of u_i's age, gender, educational background, the course category of c_j, and the number of users for c_j etc.

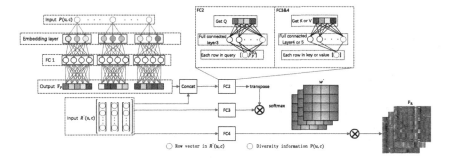

Fig. 2. Diversity-self-attention.

In the diversity-self-attention model, there is an embedding layer to map $P(u, c) \in \mathbb{R}^{k \times d_p}$ to a dense matrix $E_P \in \mathbb{R}^{k \times d_e}$. Then E_P is input into a fully connected layer to get the diversity feature $F_P = \sigma(E_P \cdot W_p + b_p)$, $F_P \in \mathbb{R}^{k \times d_v}$, $d_p < d_e < d_v$, W_p and b_p are trainable parameters. Let $F_P^{(t)}$ represent the diversity feature of $P(u_i, c_j)$, F_P can be written as $F_P = [F_P^{(1)}, \cdots, F_P^{(t)}, \cdots, F_P^{(k)}]$ for k course selection records. After that, F_P is concatenated with $R'(u, c)$ to get $query \in \mathbb{R}^{k \times (d+1) \times (23 + d_p)}$ that generates attention weights. Based on such weights, user activity features $F_R = [F_R^{(1)}, \cdots, F_R^{(t)}, \cdots, F_R^{(k)}]$ are obtained for all the k course selection records.

For a clearer description, taking the representation of the t-th user activity feature $F_R^{(t)}$ as an example. At first, $query^{(t)} \in \mathbb{R}^{(d+1) \times (23 + d_p)}$ is got as $[r'_{a,1}, \cdots, r'_{a,b}, \cdots, r'_{a,23}, F_P^{(t)}]$ for attention weight calculations, $a \in [1, d+1]$ and $b \in [1, 23]$. Let $key^{(t)} = value^{(t)} = R'(u_i, c_j) \in \mathbb{R}^{(d+1) \times 23}$. In order to enhance the feature representation ability of $query^{(t)}$, $key^{(t)}$ and $value^{(t)}$, they are mapped to a higher dimensional space with d_s dimensions by a linear layer to get $Q^{(t)}$, $K^{(t)}$ and $V^{(t)}$ respectively,

$$\begin{cases} Q^{(t)} = \sigma(query^{(t)} \cdot W_q^{(\tau)} + b_q^{(\tau)}) \\ K^{(t)} = \sigma(key^{(t)} \cdot W_k^{(\tau)} + b_k^{(\tau)}) \\ V^{(t)} = \sigma(value^{(t)} \cdot W_v^{(\tau)} + b_v^{(\tau)}) \end{cases} \tag{2}$$

where $Q^{(t)}, K^{(t)}, V^{(t)} \in \mathbb{R}^{(d+1) \times d_s}$, $W_q^{(\tau)}$, $W_k^{(\tau)}$, $W_v^{(\tau)}$, $b_q^{(\tau)}$, $b_k^{(\tau)}$ and $b_v^{(\tau)}$ are trainable parameters in τ-th diversity-self-attention. Then the attention weight $w'^{(t)} \in \mathbb{R}^{(d+1) \times (d+1)}$ is calculated by $w'^{(t)} = softmax(\frac{Q^{(t)} \cdot K^{(t)T}}{\sqrt{d_s}})$, where $K^{(t)T}$ is the transpose of $K^{(t)}$. Finally, u_i' activity feature $F_R^{(t)}$ in course c_j is got by $F_R^{(t)} = w'^{(t)} \cdot V^{(t)}$, $F_R^{(t)} \in \mathbb{R}^{(d+1) \times 23}$. For enriching the attention information and making the model pay attention to different patterns of the sequence, we set $R'(u_i, c_j) = F_R^{(t)}$ and repeat twice to increase the depth of the network.

In addition, to further represent the feature of users and their courses, the final user-course feature $F_{UC} = \sigma(\delta(F_R) \cdot W_r + b_r) \oplus F_p$ is generated by flattening and mapping to be a higher dimensional space with d_h dimensions, $F_{UC} \in \mathbb{R}^{k \times (d_h + d_p)}$. W_r and b_r are trainable parameters, $\delta(F_R)$ flattens F_R in three-dimensional space $\mathbb{R}^{k \times (d+1) \times 23}$ to two-dimensional space $\mathbb{R}^{k \times 23(d+1)}$.

2.4   Classmates Enhanced User-Course Feature

Since that the dropout behavior among users may influence each other [11], classmate graphs are established to analyze and explore the influence among users based on users' course selection records UC. Firstly, a bipartite graph including a set of user nodes and a set of course nodes based on UC is built. The edge connecting the user node and the course node represents the course selection record. Then unsupervised GraphSAGE [5] and MCNS(Markov chain Monte Carlo Negative Sampling) [17] strategy are utilized to obtain node features f in this bipartite graph, $f = [f^1, \cdots, f^i, \cdots, f^n]$, f^i represents the course selection feature of user u_i. If the cosine similarity between f^i and f^j for u_i and u_j is greater than 0.85, they are considered to be a pair of similarity relation in course selection. The set of all the similarity relations is noted as S. If $(u_i, c_j), (u_n, c_j) \in UC$ and $(u_i, u_n) \in S$, u_i and u_n are defined as classmates in course c_j.

With the above definition of classmates, for (u_i, c_j), a classmate graph $G^{(t)}$ is established. Each node in $G^{(t)}$ represents a course selection record, and the edge connecting two nodes in $G^{(t)}$ indicates that the two users have selected the same course and are classmates. Similarly, $G = \{G^{(1)}, \cdots, G^{(t)}, \cdots, G^{(k)}\}$ are constructed for all the k course selection records.

We now introduce how to express the influence of classmates through node aggregation. To clearly illustrate, $G^{(t)}$ in Fig. 1 is taken as an example. First, it is necessary to randomly sample the classmate nodes of the target node UC_t (red node in Fig. 1) with a sampling number of n_1 to obtain the set of first-order classmates $N_1(UC_t)$ (like blue nodes in Fig. 1). Let UC_{g_1} be a classmate node of $N_1(UC_t)$, for $\forall UC_{g_1} \in N_1(UC_t)$, classmate nodes are randomly sampled with the sampling number of n_2 to obtain the set of first-order classmates of UC_{g_1}: $N_1(UC_{g_1})$ (like green nodes in Fig. 1). After the above operation, the set of second-order classmates $N_2(UC_t) = \{N_1(UC_{g_1}), \forall UC_{g_1} \in N_1(UC_t)\}$ can be got.

Based on $N_1(UC_t)$ and $N_2(UC_t)$, node features are aggregated to enhance the feature of UC_t by using aggregator. Finally, the enhanced user-course feature $F'_{UC}{}^{(t)} \in \mathbb{R}^{d_h + d_p}$ is obtained based on Algorithm 1 for UC_t. So, enhanced user-course features $F'_{UC} = [F'_{UC}{}^{(1)}, \cdots, F'_{UC}{}^{(t)}, \cdots, F'_{UC}{}^{(k)}]$ are got from G.

2.5   Prediction

Now enhanced user-course features F'_{UC} are fed into an L-layer deep neural network (DNN) for dropout prediction. Let $D^{(0)} = F'_{UC}$, and each hidden layer can be formulated as $D^{(l+1)} = \sigma(D^{(l)} \cdot W_d^{(l)} + b_d^{(l)})$, where $0 \leq l \leq L - 1$ is the layer depth, $W_d^{(l)}$ and $b_d^{(l)}$ are both trainable parameters in l-layer. The sigmoid function is used in the final layer to estimate the dropout probability $Y = [\hat{y}_1, \cdots, \hat{y}_t, \cdots, \hat{y}_k]$ of k course selection records, $\hat{y}_t \in [0, 1]$ denotes the

---

Algorithm 1: Aggregate classmate features in G

Input: sampling numbers n_1, n_2 ;
the enhanced user-course feature F_{UC}.
Output: The final behavior feature F_{UC}
for $t=1:k$ **do**

    get $N_1(UC_t)$ with sampling number n_1 according to neighborhoods of UC_t;
    set $N_2(UC_t) = \{\}$;
    for $UC_{g_1} \in N_1(UC_t)$ **do**

        get $N_1(UC_{g_1})$ with sampling number n_2 according to neighborhoods of UC_{g_1};
        add $N_1(UC_{g_1})$ to $N_2(UC_t)$;
        $h^{(g_1)} \leftarrow Aggregate(\{F_{UC}^{(g_2)}, \forall UC_{g_2} \in N_1(UC_{g_1})\})$;
        $v^{g_1} \leftarrow \sigma(W_c \cdot ADD(F_{UC}^{(g_1)}, \eta \times h^{(g_1)})))$

    end

    $h^{(t)} \leftarrow Aggregate(\{v^{(g_1)}, \forall UC_{g_1} \in N_1(UC_t)\})$;
    ${F'_{UC}}^{(t)} \leftarrow \sigma(W_c \cdot ADD(F_{UC}^{(t)}, \eta \times h^{(t)}))$;

end

$F'_{UC} \leftarrow {F'_{UC}}^{(t)}, \forall t \in [1, k]$

---

probability of user u_i dropping out from course c_j, W_s and b_s are both trainable parameters. All the parameters in CEDN can be trained by minimizing the follow objective function,

$$Loss(\Theta) = \sum_{t \in [1,k]} [y_t log(\hat{y}_t) + (1 - y_t)log(1 - \hat{y}_t)] \tag{3}$$

where Θ denotes the set of model parameters, y_t is the corresponding ground truth of user u_i in course c_j.

3 Experiments

3.1 Dataset, Implementation, Measurement

XuetangX is one of the largest MOOCs platforms in China [4]. It contains 42,110,397 activity records including 24,951,551 *Video* records, 10,892,499 *Click* records, 6,205,478 *Assignment* records, and 60,869 *Forum* records from 225,642 course selection records formed by 77,083 users in 247 courses from June 2015 to June 2017. The dataset records the user's activities during the 36 days after the course started and whether the user dropout in the next 10 days. In our experiments, we divide data into training set and test set. Among them, the training set contains 157,943 course selection records, of which 119,817 records are marked as dropouts. The test set contains 67,699 course selection records, of which 51,316 records are marked as dropouts.

Our proposed method CEDN is implemented with TensorFlow and trained by Adam [8] optimizer with an initial learning rate of 1×10^{-3}. Rectified Linear

Table 3. Evaluation of user-course feature extraction.

Method	AUC (%)	F1 (%)
RNN	86.66	90.84
GRU	87.03	90.85
LSTM	87.12	90.93
Diversity-self-attention	**87.68**	**90.94**

Table 4. Evaluations on three commonly used feature aggregators.

Aggregator	AUC (%)	F1 (%)
LSTM Aggregator	87.78	91.09
Mean Aggregator	87.86	91.04
MaxPool Aggregator	**87.92**	**91.16**

Unit (Relu [10]) is adopted as the activation function. L_2 regularization is applied on the weight matrices to avoid overfitting.

Due to the uneven distribution of data, we adopt Area Under the ROC Curve (AUC) and F1 score (F1) that can reasonably judge the prediction ability of the model. AUC calculates the score based on the closeness of the output probability value of each sample to the real label. If the output probability is closer to the real label, the AUC score is higher and the prediction of the model is better. F1 makes a balance between accuracy and recall.

3.2 Evaluation of Diversity-Self-Attention

The effect of our proposed diversity-self-attention is evaluated by comparing its ability of generating user-course feature with RNN (Recurrent Neural Network), LSTM (Long Short-Term Memory) [6] and GRU (Gated Recurrent Unit) [3]. For a fair comparison, we only replace the diversity-self-attention module in Fig. 1 with the other three methods respectively. Here classmate graphs are not constructed for enhancing user-course features. The same raw activity log X_1 and raw information data X_2 are used for each method to generate user-course features, after that, L-layer DNN is used for prediction.

As can be seen from Table 3, diversity-self-attention improves the AUC of prediction by 0.56% to 1.02% and improves the F1 score of prediction by 0.01% to 0.1%, compared to RNN, LSTM, and GRU. Since diversity-self-attention extracts the user-course features by considering the time sequence of the user's activities while also considering the internal correlation between the sequences, it enhances the relevance within sequences.

3.3 Parameters in Classmate Graphs

In classmate graphs, a suitable aggregator needs to be used to aggregate classmate features. Following GraphSAGE [5], we evaluate LSTM Aggregator, Mean

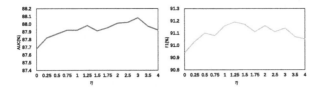

Fig. 3. The weight of classmate's influence.

Table 5. The impact of different sampling numbers.

n_1	n_2	AUC (%)	F1 (%)
1	1	87.85	91.07
3	3	87.94	91.07
5	5	87.94	91.01
10	5	87.98	**91.19**
10	10	**88.00**	91.08

Aggregator, and MaxPool Aggregator. Here, the weight of classmate's influence η is set to be 1.00, the sampling number n_1 is set to be 10, and the sampling number n_2 is set to be 5. From Table 4, it can be seen that MaxPool Aggregator performs best. Its AUC reaches to 87.92% and the F1 score reaches to 91.16%. Therefore, the next experiments use MaxPool Aggregator.

In order to analyze the impact of classmates, we discuss the value of η with Fig. 3. It can be found that the AUC increases from 87.68% to 88.08% when η increases from 0 to 3. The AUC reaches to 87.98% and F1 score reaches to 91.19% when $\eta = 1.25$. But when η is greater than 3, the prediction accuracy begins to decrease. The analysis of η shows that classmates can be effectively used to assist prediction, and the selection of appropriate η can improve the prediction accuracy to a certain extent. So $\eta = 1.25$ is used in the next experiments.

In classmate graphs, n_1 and n_2 control the number of first-order classmates and the number of second-order classmates, which affect the accuracy of prediction and algorithm complexity. As shown in Table 5, with the increase of n_1 and n_2, the prediction accuracy of CEDN is rising. When $n_1 = n_2 = 10$, the AUC reaches to 88.00%. When the number of samples is larger, the features obtained from peer nodes will be richer, but at the same time, the complexity of the model will be increased. For example, in each classmate graph, if $n_1 = n_2 = 10$, the number of first-order classmates is 10, and the number of second-order classmates is 10×10, the cost of acquiring features from classmates is expensive. Considering the balance, $n_1 = 10, n_2 = 5$ are used in the next experiments.

3.4   Importance of Different Activities

According to the four types of activities **F**orum, **A**ssignment, **V**ideo and **C**lick mentioned in Sect. 2.2, we discuss the importance and correlations of them in

Table 6. Impact of combinations of different activity types.

	With classmate		Without classmate	
	AUC (%)	F1 (%)	AUC (%)	F1 (%)
F	78.60	56.62	77.13	55.32
A	85.44	83.86	85.22	83.84
V	85.72	89.80	85.31	89.86
C	**87.23**	**90.51**	**87.00**	**90.57**
A&F	85.72	84.11	85.54	83.83
V&F	85.92	89.83	85.48	89.88
V&A	87.04	90.47	86.72	90.46
F&C	87.30	90.58	87.03	90.61
V&C	87.37	90.77	87.00	90.86
A&C	**87.80**	**90.87**	**87.50**	90.76
V&A&F	87.13	90.53	86.82	90.52
V&F&C	87.43	90.88	87.07	90.97
A&F&C	87.76	90.81	87.50	90.94
V&A&C	**87.77**	**91.00**	**87.57**	**91.09**
All	**87.98**	**91.19**	**87.68**	**90.94**

dropout prediction. As can be seen in Table 6, when only using a single activity type for prediction, the activity of *Click* performs best. Its AUC reaches to 87.00% without the enhancement of classmate graphs. It means that the activity of *Click* plays a great role in dropout prediction and makes the largest contribution to the user-course feature. *Video* and *Assignment* reflect whether a user is learning in a real scene or not, so they also achieve good results.

For the combinations of any two types of activities in dropout prediction, the combination of *Assignment* and *Click* performs best in AUC, with the help of classmate graphs, the AUC reaches to 87.80%, which is higher than the combination of *Video* and *Click*. However, in the prediction using a single type of activity, the contribution of *Video* is greater than that of *Assignment*. It shows that the internal connection between *Click* and *Assignment* is closer. Obviously, the combination of more types of activities has a better prediction. If the data is richer, the features generated are better. The combination of *Video*, *Assignment*, and *Click* reasonably perform best. When all of the four types are used, with the help of classmate graphs, AUC reaches to 87.98% and F1 score reaches to 91.19%, which is 0.3% and 0.25% higher than the predictions without classmate graphs respectively. It shows that classmate graphs can enhance user-course features, and further improve the prediction.

3.5 Comparison with Other Methods

The proposed CEDN is compared with the current state-of-the-art methods. For LR (Logistic Regression), RF(Random Forest), and GBDT(Gradient Boosting Decision Tree), we use activity sequence $R(u, c)$ extracted from the original

Table 7. Comparison with other methods.

Method	AUC (%)	F1 (%)
LR	83.25	89.12
RF	85.65	90.58
GBDT	86.05	90.41
CFIN	85.94	90.61
Ours	**88.08**	**91.13**

activity log data X_1 and $P(u,c)$ extracted from the original information data X_2 as the input. For CFIN (Context-aware Feature Interaction Network) [4], the activity features and their statistical values extracted from X_1, and the information of users and courses extracted from X_2 are used as the input. For a fair comparison, the most appropriate parameters are selected for them. For LR, L_2 regularization is used and the regularization intensity is set to be 1×10^{-5}. For RF, the number of trees in the forest is set to be 70. For GBDT, the number of boosting stages is set to be 60. For CFIN, it is trained by Adam [8] optimizer with an initial learning rate of 1×10^{-4}, and the batch size is set to be 32.

The results are given in Table 7. CEDN achieves an AUC of 88.08% and an F1 score of 91.13%, which increases by 2.03% to 4.38% and 0.55% to 2.01%, compared to LR, RF and GBDT, respectively. Compared with CFIN, CEDN increases the AUC of prediction by 2.14% and the F1 score by 0.52%. The reason is that CEDN extracts the activity sequence features of users from the original data, and enhances the user-course features by using the interaction feature of dropout behaviors among users.

4   Conclusions

In this paper, a method named classmates enhanced diversity-self-attention network (CEDN) is proposed to predict users' dropout behavior in MOOCs. Activity sequences and classmates are defined. Self-attention with diversity information is proposed to solve the problem of participants' diversities by not only employing activity sequences but also utilizing users' age, gender, education, and course category. In addition, classmate graphs are constructed according to users' course selection records, which are used to assist dropout prediction. In the experiments conducted on XuetangX dataset, the influence of classmates is analyzed, the importance of different types of users' activities on dropout prediction is discussed, and the effectiveness of CEDN is evaluated by a comparison with state-of-the-art methods. CEDN provides a way to decrease the high dropout rate in MOOCs.

Acknowledgements. This work is supported by National Natural Science Foundation of China under grants No. 61801428, U20A20196, U1908210, and Zhejiang Provincial Natural Science Foundation of China under grants No. LR21F020002.

References

1. Aldowah, H., Al-Samarraie, H., Alzahrani, A.I., Alalwan, N.: Factors affecting student dropout in MOOCs: a cause and effect decision-making model. J. Comput. High. Educ. **32**(2), 429–454 (2020)
2. Blum-Smith, S., Yurkofsky, M.M., Brennan, K.: Stepping back and stepping. In: Facilitating Learner-Centered Experiences in MOOCs. Comput. Educ. **160**, 104042 (2021)
3. Cho, K., et al.: Learning phrase representations using RNN encoder-decoder for statistical machine translation. In: Proceedings of EMNLP, pp. 1724–1734 (2014)
4. Feng, W., Tang, J., Liu, T.X.: Understanding dropouts in MOOCs. In: Proceedings of AAAI 2019, pp. 517–524 (2019)
5. Hamilton, W.L., Ying, R., Leskovec, J.: Inductive representation learning on large graphs. In: Proceedings of NIPS, pp. 1025–1035 (2017)
6. Hochreiter, S., Schmidhuber, J.: Long short-term memory. Neural Comput. **9**(8), 1735–1780 (1997)
7. Hong, B., Wei, Z., Yang, Y.: Discovering learning behavior patterns to predict dropout in MOOC. In: Proceedings of ICCSE, pp. 700–704 (2017)
8. Kingma, D.P., Ba, J.L.: Adam: a method for stochastic optimization. In: Proceedings of ICLR, pp. 1–15 (2015)
9. Li, Q., Baker, R.: The different relationships between engagement and outcomes across participant subgroups in Massive Open Online Courses. Comput. Educ. **127**, 41–65 (2018)
10. Nair, V., Hinton, G.E.: Rectified linear units improve restricted boltzmann machines. In: Proceedings of ICML (2010)
11. Qiu, J., et al.: Modeling and predicting learning behavior in MOOCs. In: WSDM, pp. 93–102 (2016)
12. Qiu, L., Liu, Y., Hu, Q., Liu, Y.: Student dropout prediction in massive open online courses by convolutional neural networks. Soft. Comput. **23**(20), 10287–10301 (2018). https://doi.org/10.1007/s00500-018-3581-3
13. Reparaz, C., Aznárez-Sanado, M., Mendoza, G.: Self-regulation of learning and MOOC retention. Comput. Hum. Behav. **111**(May), 106423 (2020)
14. Vaswani, A., et al.: Attention is all you need. In: Proceedings of NIPS (2017)
15. Wang, L., Wang, H.: Learning behavior analysis and dropout rate prediction based on MOOCs data. In: Proceedings of ITME, pp. 419–423 (2019)
16. Wang, Y., Zhang, X., Lu, M., Wang, H., Choe, Y.: Attention augmentation with multi-residual in bidirectional LSTM. Neurocomputing **385**, 340–347 (2020)
17. Yang, Z., Ding, M., Zhou, C., Yang, H., Zhou, J., Tang, J.: Understanding negative sampling in graph representation learning. In: Proceedings of ACM SIGKDD, pp. 1666–1676 (2020)
18. Youssef, M., Mohammed, S., Hamada, E.K., Wafaa, B.F.: A predictive approach based on efficient feature selection and learning algorithms' competition: case of learners' dropout in MOOCs. Educ. Inf. Technol. **24**(6), 3591–3618 (2019)
19. Zhang, J., Gao, M., Zhang, J.: The learning behaviours of dropouts in MOOCs: a collective attention network perspective. Comput. Educ. **167**, 104189 (2021)

A Hierarchical Graph-Based Neural Network for Malware Classification

Shuai Wang(ORCID), Yuran Zhao(ORCID), Gongshen Liu$^{(\boxtimes)}$(ORCID), and Bo Su(ORCID)

School of Electronic Information and Electrical Engineering, Shanghai Jiao Tong
University, Shanghai, China
{wsh1997,zyr527,lgshen,subo}@sjtu.edu.com

Abstract. In recent years, malware classification models based on
machine learning and deep learning have developed rapidly. Although
these models have yielded promising results, many of them have limited
generalization capacity for the lack of good semantic information. To
solve this problem, we start with finding an appropriate representation
of the program and convert the program to a hierarchical graph structure
composed of one Function Call Graph and many Control Flow Graphs.
Based on the graph structure, we implement a malware classification
model with better semantic representation and stronger generalization
ability by using BERT and Graph Attention Network. The results of
experiments on two different datasets demonstrate that our model outperforms other state-of-the-art models.

Keywords: Malware classification · BERT · Graph Attention Network

1 Introduction

With the development of artificial intelligence, many deep learning methods have
been applied in malware detection and classification, yielding promising results
in some malware datasets. Current methods are mainly based on statistical and
structural information of malware. However, as malware evolves continuously at
the same time, a number of techniques of bypassing detection have emerged,
such as obfuscation, polymorphism, and metamorphism, which make the malware difficult to be identified and classified by using statistical and structural
information alone [1]. To improve the model's generalization ability, it is necessary to generate a better semantic representation of the malware based on
assembly instructions.

Trying to attain the semantic meaning of programs is not a new task. Currently, numerous malware detection and classification models have used the dis-
assembly instructions and Natural Language Processing (NLP) methods to learn
the semantic information of programs. Regarding the assembly language as a natural language is plausible, but there are a lot of differences between them. As the
assembly code of a program is often extremely long, it is inappropriate to input
it directly to the network. One deficient solution is to cut off the sequence of

© Springer Nature Switzerland AG 2021
T. Mantoro et al. (Eds.): ICONIP 2021, LNCS 13111, pp. 621–633, 2021.
https://doi.org/10.1007/978-3-030-92273-3_51

instructions at a specified length [5,14], which will lead to the lack of information for big files. Besides, each program contains a throng of jump instructions and function calls, which are ignored by the sequence NLP model. Some researches [5,11] merely take the internal dependency of functions into account, neglecting the dependencies between functions. What is more, treating each instruction as a word will make the size of the vocabulary used by the language model increase dramatically, so most models only preserve the opcodes of instructions [5,14,16] or split the instruction into a fixed number of items [11], which are rough and inaccurate. There is still room for improvement.

To solve the problems mentioned above, we propose two improvement measures. First, we convert a binary program into a hierarchical graph structure rather than simply regarding it as a sequence. A program can be represented by a Function Call Graph (FCG) formed by multiple function calls, while each function can be represented by a Control Flow Graph (CFG) composed of multiple instruction blocks executed sequentially. The FCG and all CFGs constitute a hierarchical graph of the program, which keeps all instructions and information of jump instructions and function calls. Second, as instructions have different lengths, we treat each instruction as a sentence, which can preserve more information of the instructions and avoid the problem of oversized word dictionary as well.

Based on the above analysis, we propose a hierarchical graph-based malware classification model. We first design a pre-training model Inst2Vec for instruction vectorization based on CFGs and BERT [3], which is a popular pre-training language model in NLP. Then we generate the vector representations for functions and the whole program by utilizing FCGs and Graph Neural Network (GNN), which is a type of network that operates on the graph structure. Finally, we feed the program's vector representation into a feed-forward network to get the classification result. Experiments on two datasets with different classification difficulties show that our model can achieve better classification performance and have a stronger generalization ability than other state-of-the-art models. Our contributions are as follows:

1. We propose a new method utilizing the hierarchical graph structure based on CFGs and FCGs to obtain better representations for binary programs. This method not only maintains most of the information in the assembly code, but also considers execution flow information.
2. We design an unsupervised assembly language model Inst2Vec based on BERT and CFGs, which generates a more appropriate representation of instructions and provides the initial representation of functions.
3. Based on the FCG of the program, we combine Graph Attention Network (GAT) and graph pooling with our model, integrating more semantic and structural information into the representation of the whole binary program.

2   Related Work

Malware Classification. Malware classification based on deep learning can be divided into static and dynamic techniques. Static analysis takes the raw binary program into consideration, while dynamic analysis focuses on the execution flow. In this paper, we pay attention to the static methods. Malware representation plays a pivotal role in this field. At present, the most commonly used representations include two types: bytes and assembly instructions. Byte-based methods usually convert programs into images and use end-to-end models such as CNN for training [6,15], which lack the semantic information of the program. To make full use of the semantic information in the assembly instructions, instruction-based models adopt various processing methods. Solis et al. [16] presents a convolutional architecture to extract opcode n-gram from the instructions of malware. Daniel et al. [5] and Miles et al. [11] introduce hierarchical network architectures, which retain the hierarchical information of an executable. There also exist some works using CFG and FCG for malware classification, attempting to classify the malware according to the structural similarity [8].

Binary Similarity Detection. Although GNN is rarely utilized by instruction-based models in malware classification, it has already been applied in binary similarity detection. Binary code similarity detection is another essential task in computer security, aiming to detect similar binary functions by their binary code. Binary similarity detection merely take specific functions into consideration. Traditional methods are usually based on the similarity of the CFGs. Recently, some works focusing on the semantic representation of functions have been introduced. Gemini [18] generates function embeddings by an attributed CFG with manually selected features and Structure2vec network [2]. Asm2Vec [4] uses function-based CFG and Doc2Vec [10] methods to model the semantics of the function. Yu et al. [19] and PalmTree [12] proposed pre-training BERT-like models to generate the vectors for blocks and instructions, respectively.

3   Model Architecture

3.1   Overview

Our model adopts a hierarchical architecture based on the hierarchical graphs of programs, using different methods and networks to produce embeddings of instructions, functions, and the entire program respectively. H-Tran [11] and some other researches in binary similarity detection split the function into blocks and proceed to create block vectors. Although each block contains a sequence of instructions executed sequentially, it is inadequate to express a complete semantic meaning. Therefore, we skip the generation of vector representations of blocks and merely utilize the structure information of blocks to create the embeddings of functions.

The vectorization of instructions is implemented though a pre-trained model Inst2Vec, which is similar to BERT, and makes use of CFGs. The function vectorization process consists of two stages. The initial vector of function is obtained by doing Random Walk on the CFG of the function. Subsequently, all function vectors are fed into the Graph Attention Network (GAT) and fine-tuned with the program's FCG. After that, a graph pooling layer is used to combine all function representations into a program representation. Finally, the program representation is sent into a Multilayer Perceptron (MLP) to get the classification result. The overall framework of our model is shown as Fig. 1. The instruction vectors and the initial vectors of functions are directly obtained through a self-supervised model Inst2Vec. The GAT network for fine-tuning function vectors and the pooling and classification network together constitute an end-to-end supervised model. Details of the implementation for each module are shown as follows.

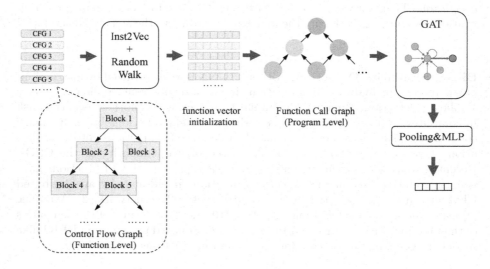

Fig. 1. Overview of our model

3.2   Inst2Vec

Inspired by Asm2Vec [4] and PalmTree [12], we construct our assembly language model Inst2Vec based on BERT and CFGs to produce embedding of instructions. Inst2Vec is a separate pre-training model, which can provide the instruction vectors directly.

As a special kind of language, each instruction in assembly language can be considered as a complete sentence while each token can be treated as a word. As there are numerous constants, it is unpractical to make the dictionary contain all of them. According to the statistics of instructions, the constants in the range of `0x00-0xff` appear more frequently. The frequency of occurrence of some constants even exceed several opcodes. Therefore, we preserve the constants in the range of `0x00-0xff` and mark other constants as `CONST`. In addition, we ignore the call information of system APIs. Specifically, given an instruction `mov ebx, dword [ecx+0x4c]`, we separate it into `mov`, `ebx`, `dword`, `[`, `ecx`, `+`, `0x4c`, and `]`.

Inst2Vec uses BERT architecture, which can learn contextual representations for tokens and proceed to produce the vector of the entire instruction. We adopt and modify the two tasks described in PalmTree [12]: Masked Language Model (MLM) and Context Instruction Prediction (CIP) to train the Inst2Vec model. Figure 2 shows the training process of Inst2Vec. When the training of Inst2Vec is finished, we use the output vector corresponding to [CLS], which is a special token added before the raw instructions, as the representation of the input instruction.

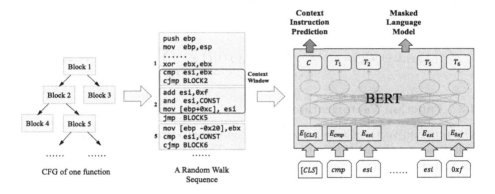

Fig. 2. Training process of Inst2Vec

Task 1: Masked Language Model. Assuming the instruction is $I = [i_1, i_2, \cdots, i_n]$ consisting of n tokens. Each token in the instruction will be replaced with a probability of 15%. If i_k is selected to be substituted, it will be masked as [MASK] in 80% of cases or randomly placed as another token in the vocabulary in 10% of cases, and it also has 10% likely to be retained. In the end, the model needs to predict the original value of i_k, which is completed through a softmax function on the top of the model:

$$p(\hat{i}_m|I) = \frac{\exp(w_m \Theta(I)_k)}{\sum_{i=1}^{N} \exp(w_i \Theta(I)_k)} \tag{1}$$

where $\hat{i}_m$ is the prediction of i_k. N is the size of the vocabulary. w_m is the weight of token m. And Θ is the parameters of Inst2Vec model, while $\Theta(I)_k$ is the corresponding vector of i_k in the last layer.

Task 2: Context Instruction Prediction. This task is designed to help Inst2Vec learn the context information of an instruction. First, we create multiple complete instruction sequences based on the CFG with the help of the Random Walk method. Then we take the instruction pairs that occur in the same context windows into consideration. Specifically, for the instruction I_{cur}, we select w instructions before I_{cur} and w instructions after I_{cur} to constitute $2w$ instruction pairs with I_{cur}, where w is the size of window. We feed these pairs into the model and a binary classification will be performed to judge whether two given instructions co-occur in the same window or not. We set $w = 2$ in our experiments. The output corresponding to [CLS] in the last layer is used to predict the relationship between two instructions:

$$p(\hat{y} = 0|I_1, I_2) = \frac{\exp(y_0\Theta(I)_{[CLS]})}{\sum_{i=0}^1 \exp(y_i\Theta(I)_{[CLS]})} \tag{2}$$

Both tasks are trained with the cross-entropy loss function. The total loss function of Inst2Vec is:

$$\mathcal{L} = \mathcal{L}_{MLM} + \mathcal{L}_{CIP} = - \sum_{i_k \in mask(I)} \log p(\hat{i}|I) - \sum_{\{I_1, I_2\} \in \mathcal{D}} \log p(\hat{y}|I_1, I_2) \tag{3}$$

3.3   Function Vectorization

The function vectorization part can be divided into two stages, namely the initialization stage and the fine-tuning stage. The initialization stage is based on the instruction vectors provided by the Inst2Vec model and the function's CFG, while the fine-tuning stage is on basis of the FCG of the entire program.

Initialization Stage. First, we obtain instruction vectors with contextual information from the Inst2Vec model introduced above. Then, we adopt the idea of Random Walk on the CFG to generate the initial function vector, which is similar to the training procedure of Inst2Vec. Every Random Walk path represents a complete instruction sequence executed sequentially in the function. For each function, we generate R Random Walk sequences and concatenate the average of all instruction vectors in each sequence to represent the function. R is set as 5 in our implementation. The initial vector of a function can be expressed as:

$$\vec{f} = \mathop{||}\limits_{r=1}^{R} \text{AvgPooling}(\text{Inst2Vec}(\text{RandomWalk}(\text{CFG}_f))) \tag{4}$$

Fine-Tuning Stage. What the function calls is an essential part of its semantic meaning. Since the relationships between functions are neglected in the initialization stage, further optimization should be taken. We utilize GAT to fine-tune the vector representation of the function.

For function node A and function node B, if function A is called by function B, there will be an edge going from A to B in FCG. Compared to ordinary FCG, the edge in our FCG has the opposite direction. Ordinary FCG focuses on the calling sequence of these functions, while our CFG considers the semantic impact between functions. In addition, the semantics of the function is also affected by its previous semantic representation, so each function also has a self-loop edge.

Since the effects on the semantic meaning of the caller function varies from function to function, we choose GAT to update the function vector. GAT can achieve adaptive matching of neighbors with different weights through the self-attention mechanism.

We use a 2-layer GAT network in our model. Here we only describe the structure of a single GAT layer for briefness. Its input is a feature set of function nodes in a program, $\mathbf{p} = \{\vec{f_1}, \vec{f_2}, \cdots, \vec{f_N}\}, \vec{f_i} \in \mathbb{R}^F$, where F is the feature dimension of the input node. The output is the feature set of function nodes updated by the GAT layer $\mathbf{p}' = \{\vec{f_1}', \vec{f_2}', \cdots, \vec{f_N}'\}, \vec{f_i}' \in \mathbb{R}^{F'}$, where F' is the feature dimension of the output node. The attention coefficient α_{ij} between function i and function j can be expressed as:

$$e_{ij} = \text{LeakyReLU}(\vec{a}^T[\mathbf{W}\vec{f_i} || \mathbf{W}\vec{f_j}]) \tag{5}$$

$$\alpha_{ij} = \text{softmax}_j(e_{ij}) = \frac{exp(e_{ij})}{\sum_{k \in \mathcal{N}_i} exp(e_{ik})} \tag{6}$$

$\mathbf{W} \in \mathbb{R}^{F' \times F}$ is the weight matrix. $\vec{a} \in \mathbb{R}^{2F'}$ is a single-layer feed-forward neural network. LeakyReLU is used for the nonlinearization process. $\mathcal{N}_i$ represents the set of function nodes called by the function node i, and $i \in \mathcal{N}_i$.

To stabilize the learning process of self-attention, we add multi-head attention and residual connection in our model. The output function node feature $\vec{f_i}'$ is:

$$\vec{f_i}' = \Big\|_{k=1}^K \sigma\Big(\sum_{j \in \mathcal{N}_i} \alpha_{ij}^k W^k \vec{f_j} \Big) + \mathbf{W_R}\vec{f_i} \tag{7}$$

$\mathbf{W_R} \in \mathbb{R}^{KF' \times F}$ is a weight matrix for residual connection. α_{ij}^k and $W^k \in \mathbb{R}^{F' \times F}$ are parameters for head k. K is the number of attention heads.

3.4   Program Vectorization and Classification

To complete the task of malware classification, it is necessary to combine all fine-tuned function representations into a program representation. In our model, we utilize the graph pooling algorithm to acquire the representation of FCG as the representation of the program. Our final choice is Average Pooling, which shows the best performance in our experiment. After the pooling layer, a MLP with softmax function is used to obtain the predicted possibility distribution of the category. In fact, the fine-tuning process of the function vector, the acquisition of the program vector and the classification process together form an end-to-end network. The whole process can be noted as:

$$\hat{y} = \text{softmax}(\text{MLP}(\text{AvgPooling}(\text{GAT}(\mathbf{p}, \text{FCG}_p)))) \qquad (8)$$

$\hat{y}$ is the predicted value of the category for program $\mathbf{p}$. We use cross-entropy loss as the loss function of the classification task.

4   Experiments

4.1   Dataset

We use a benign dataset to train the Inst2Vec model. Since programs in our malware dataset are all 32-bit PE programs, Inst2Vec model is trained with 32-bit x86 instructions. We collect more than 50,000 programs on 32-bit Window 7 and Ubuntu 16.04 operating system and finally extract about 3,250,000 instruction pairs to train our Inst2Vec model.

Samples and category information in our malware dataset are obtained from the VirusShare[1] and VirusTotal[2] websites. We use radare2[3] to generate the FCGs and CFGs of programs. After preprocessing and filtering, we create two different PE malware datasets, which are different in the amount of data and the granularity of categories. The first dataset has a total of 6,021 malware samples in 24 categories, whose labels contain both the information of type and family. The second dataset contains 27,432 samples in 11 categories. Labels of examples in the second dataset only contain the malware type, which means one category may include multiple malware families. Therefore, the second dataset is more difficult to be classified correctly compared to the first one. We note them as Dataset A and Dataset B respectively.

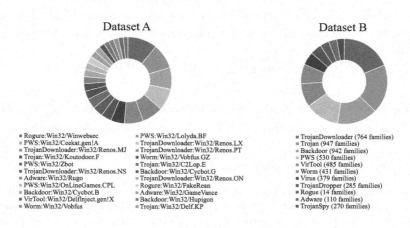

Fig. 3. Information of datasets

---

[1] https://virusshare.com.

[2] https://virustotal.com.

[3] https://rada.re/n/.

4.2 Models for Comparison

We implemented some other malware classification models for comparison, which can be divided into byte-based models and instruction-based models.

We first tested some basic models introduced in [14], which include CNN-2D, CNN-1D, BiLSTM and BiGRU. CNN-2D and CNN-1D are both based on the image generated from byte code, which use 2-dimensional and 1-dimensional images respectively. BiLSTM and BiGRU utilize the first 5,000 opcodes from each sample. We also use two Transfer Learning (TL) models described in [14], VGG19 and ResNet152, which are pre-trained and have more complex structures than other image-based models. Besides, we also take MalConv model [15] into comparison, which is a byte-based approach but not an image-based one.

Since our model is on the basis of assembly instructions, we implemented several state-of-the-art instruction-based models as well. Gibert et al. [6] proposed an instruction-based model using a CNN network with filters of various sizes, which is noted as CNN-op in our experiment. We also implemented two models that adopt the hierarchical structure, HCNN [5] and H-Tran [11]. HCNN takes the function level into consideration and accomplish a multi-layer CNN model. H-Tran uses three layers of Transformer to obtain the characteristic vectors for blocks, functions and the whole program separately. As their model is proposed for malware detection, we modify it to execute malware classification task by changing the dimensions of the output layer and replacing the logistic function in the output layer by softmax. To be fair in comparison, we do not utilize features in PE header.

4.3 Results and Analysis

We use 5-fold cross-validation to evaluate our model and other models. Table 1 shows the classification performance of each model on two datasets. Since the amount of data in each category is quite different, we focus on the weighted F1 score in the experimental results.

Results on Dataset A show that byte-based models perform slightly better than instruction-based models overall. Since Dataset A is relatively small and fine-grained, byte-based approaches, which utilize more structure information like program headers and data segments, are more suitable to complete the classification task. Given that TL models like VGG19 often have learned much prior knowledge, there is no wonder that VGG19 gets the highest scores. However, it is worth noting that there is only a tiny gap between our model's score and VGG19's, which demonstrates that merely using code segments of the program has chance to obtain comparable results with byte-based methods. Besides, our model gets at least 1.43 points higher in F1 score compared to other instruction-based models, proving the effectiveness of our representation of programs.

As classification task on Dataset B is more difficult, which needs the ability of generalization, the results are much more valuable. Instruction-based models perform better than byte-based models in general, showing the semantic information behind code segments is essential for more complex classifications.

Table 1. Performance of different deep learning models.

Model	Dataset A						Dataset B					
	Weighted Avg			Macro Avg			Weighted Avg			Macro Avg		
	P(%)	R(%)	F1(%)	P(%)	R(%)	F1(%)	P(%)	R(%)	F1(%)	P(%)	R(%)	F1(%)
Byte-based approaches												
CNN-1D	85.43	84.52	83.93	83.08	79.75	79.91	56.92	57.17	56.79	54.78	52.72	53.42
CNN-2D	89.58	88.00	88.19	85.93	85.73	85.07	58.98	58.28	57.88	60.67	53.94	56.03
MalConv	88.00	87.57	87.48	87.24	85.56	85.99	68.89	61.90	63.04	71.99	57.12	61.59
ResNet152	91.51	91.14	91.08	89.63	88.83	88.93	63.55	63.18	62.87	62.57	58.92	60.26
VGG19	**92.95**	**92.55**	**92.47**	**91.16**	89.39	89.88	69.84	69.16	68.98	70.45	65.01	66.68
Instruction-based approaches												
BiLSTM	83.77	83.92	83.54	81.72	81.21	81.08	61.46	60.96	61.14	59.39	58.90	59.09
BiGRU	85.20	85.49	85.25	83.77	83.43	83.46	62.94	62.83	62.85	59.73	60.24	59.93
HCNN	91.82	90.62	90.67	91.20	89.59	89.80	70.17	67.67	68.08	70.87	65.28	67.38
H-Tran	89.56	89.55	89.43	88.82	88.71	88.60	71.98	72.03	71.97	71.18	70.68	70.86
CNN-op	90.75	90.11	89.90	92.54	87.93	89.68	71.29	71.09	70.90	72.52	67.56	69.62
Ours	92.36	92.09	92.10	90.99	**90.96**	**90.88**	**73.83**	**73.73**	**73.73**	**72.89**	**72.14**	**72.44**

Significantly, our model gets the best results on all Precision, Recall, and F1 scores, which demonstrates that our model can adapt to more general scenes. In addition, compared with other models based on hierarchical representation, like HCNN and H-Tran, the F1 score of our model is at least 1.76 points higher, proving the importance of utilizing graph structure in the semantic representation of the whole binary programs.

We also verify the impact of each module in our model on the classification performance through experiments on Dataset A, which is displayed in Table 2.

We first test the effects of different function initialization methods. Except the method used in our model, three other methods are adopted. When random initialization is used, the model can only rely on the structure information of the program's FCG learned by GNN to predict its category. As the model only gets a precision of 26.69% under this condition, it proves the necessity of our Inst2Vec model. Asm2Vec, another unsupervised function initialization method, also yields slightly worse results than ours. What is more, we attempt to combine Inst2Vec with Doc2Vec to obtain the initial function representations, which adopts the PV-DM algorithm to modify representations generated by Inst2Vec. Its results are not as good as ours, showing the efficacy of our proposed method of averaging results of the random walk instructions set.

Besides, we examine the effect of GNN utilized in our model. We replaced GAT with several other GNNs such as GraphSAGE [7] and GCN [9]. The consequences illustrate that our GAT works best among these GNNs. Furthermore, We also test various graph pooling algorithms for comparison, including Set2Set [17], SortPooling, SumPooling, WeightAndSum, AvgPooling, and Global Attention Pooling (GAP) [13]. The results prove that AvgPooling algorithm guarantees the most significant results.

Previous works have declared the essentiality of information in data segments and program headers. Therefore, we integrate the CNN model used in

Table 2. Performance of different modules.

Model setting	Architecture	Dataset A					
		Weighted Avg			Macro Avg		
		P(%)	R(%)	F1(%)	P(%)	R(%)	F1(%)
Function Initialization (GAT+Avg)	random	26.69	28.36	26.01	25.58	25.40	22.83
	Asm2Vec	91.72	91.44	91.47	91.17	90.75	90.80
	Inst2Vec+Doc2Vec	84.54	83.64	83.25	84.97	82.45	82.53
Graph Neural Network (Inst2Vec+RW+Avg)	GraphSAGE(pool)	91.29	91.01	90.98	90.04	90.15	89.91
	GraphSAGE(lstm)	91.79	91.26	91.20	**91.68**	90.78	90.81
	GraphSAGE(gcn)	90.36	90.11	89.90	89.26	89.28	88.78
	GraphSAGE(mean)	90.89	90.77	90.66	90.30	89.70	89.83
	GCN	91.20	90.93	90.89	90.18	**90.82**	90.27
Graph Pooling (Inst2Vec+RW+GAT)	SortPooling(k = 100)	89.65	89.61	89.49	89.14	88.03	88.33
	SumPooling	90.48	90.35	90.25	89.62	88.91	89.00
	GAP	90.10	89.53	89.57	88.97	89.21	88.80
	Set2Set	91.35	91.18	91.15	90.46	90.74	90.42
	WeightAndSum	91.75	91.59	91.55	91.33	90.53	90.73
Complete (Inst2Vec+RW+GAT+Avg)	Ours	92.36	92.09	92.10	90.99	90.96	**90.88**
	Ours+CNN	**92.69**	**92.58**	**92.51**	91.00	90.77	90.73

CNN-2D, which contains non-instruction information, into our model. Experiment consequences on Dataset A show this multimodal network can improve the classification results to a certain extent, confirming the validity of previous studies. Moreover, it also proves that our model can learn features that are different from the byte-based models.

5   Conclusion

In this paper, we propose a Hierarchical Graph-based Neural Network for malware classification. We utilize CFGs and FCGs to obtain a new representation of malware programs, and then implement a classification model with BERT and GNN. Our model makes up the deficiency of neglecting the execution flow information in previous models. Experiment results indicate that our model outperforms most current state-of-the-art models and has a stronger generalization ability. Since our model only pays attention to the code segment of the program, it does not utilize other useful information in the program and is not suitable for programs that cannot be decompiled. In future work, we will explore to integrate more non-instruction information into our model to get better performance.

Acknowledgments. This research work has been funded by the National Natural Science Foundation of China (No. 61772337).

References

1. Abusitta, A., Li, M.Q., Fung, B.C.: Malware classification and composition analysis: a survey of recent developments. J. Inf. Secur. Appl. **59**, 102828 (2021)
2. Dai, H., Dai, B., Song, L.: Discriminative embeddings of latent variable models for structured data. In: International Conference on Machine Learning, pp. 2702–2711. PMLR (2016)
3. Devlin, J., Chang, M.W., Lee, K., Toutanova, K.: Bert: pre-training of deep bidirectional transformers for language understanding. arXiv preprint arXiv:1810.04805 (2018)
4. Ding, S.H., Fung, B.C., Charland, P.: Asm2vec: boosting static representation robustness for binary clone search against code obfuscation and compiler optimization. In: 2019 IEEE Symposium on Security and Privacy (SP), pp. 472–489. IEEE (2019)
5. Gibert, D., Mateu, C., Planes, J.: A hierarchical convolutional neural network for malware classification. In: 2019 International Joint Conference on Neural Networks (IJCNN), pp. 1–8. IEEE (2019)
6. Gibert, D., Mateu, C., Planes, J., Vicens, R.: Using convolutional neural networks for classification of malware represented as images. J. Comput. Virol. Hacking Tech. **15**(1), 15–28 (2018). https://doi.org/10.1007/s11416-018-0323-0
7. Hamilton, W.L., Ying, R., Leskovec, J.: Inductive representation learning on large graphs. arXiv preprint arXiv:1706.02216 (2017)
8. Hassen, M., Chan, P.K.: Scalable function call graph-based malware classification. In: Proceedings of the Seventh ACM on Conference on Data and Application Security and Privacy, pp. 239–248 (2017)
9. Kipf, T.N., Welling, M.: Semi-supervised classification with graph convolutional networks. arXiv preprint arXiv:1609.02907 (2016)
10. Le, Q., Mikolov, T.: Distributed representations of sentences and documents. In: International Conference on Machine Learning, pp. 1188–1196. PMLR (2014)
11. Li, M.Q., Fung, B., Charland, P., Ding, S.H.: I-mad: a novel interpretable malware detector using hierarchical transformer. arXiv preprint arXiv:1909.06865 (2019)
12. Li, X., Yu, Q., Yin, H.: Palmtree: learning an assembly language model for instruction embedding. arXiv preprint arXiv:2103.03809 (2021)
13. Li, Y., Tarlow, D., Brockschmidt, M., Zemel, R.: Gated graph sequence neural networks. arXiv preprint arXiv:1511.05493 (2015)
14. Prajapati, P., Stamp, M.: An empirical analysis of image-based learning techniques for malware classification. In: Stamp, M., Alazab, M., Shalaginov, A. (eds.) Malware Analysis Using Artificial Intelligence and Deep Learning, pp. 411–435. Springer, Cham (2021). https://doi.org/10.1007/978-3-030-62582-5_16
15. Raff, E., Barker, J., Sylvester, J., Brandon, R., Catanzaro, B., Nicholas, C.K.: Malware detection by eating a whole exe. In: Workshops at the Thirty-Second AAAI Conference on Artificial Intelligence (2018)
16. Solis, D., Vicens, R.: Convolutional neural networks for classification of malware assembly code. In: Recent Advances in Artificial Intelligence Research and Development: Proceedings of the 20th International Conference of the Catalan Association for Artificial Intelligence, Deltebre, Terres de L'Ebre, Spain, 25–27 October 2017, vol. 300, p. 221. IOS Press (2017)
17. Vinyals, O., Bengio, S., Kudlur, M.: Order matters: sequence to sequence for sets. arXiv preprint arXiv:1511.06391 (2015)

18. Xu, X., Liu, C., Feng, Q., Yin, H., Song, L., Song, D.: Neural network-based graph embedding for cross-platform binary code similarity detection. In: Proceedings of the 2017 ACM SIGSAC Conference on Computer and Communications Security, pp. 363–376 (2017)
19. Yu, Z., Cao, R., Tang, Q., Nie, S., Huang, J., Wu, S.: Order matters: semantic-aware neural networks for binary code similarity detection. In: Proceedings of the AAAI Conference on Artificial Intelligence, vol. 34, pp. 1145–1152 (2020)

A Visual Feature Detection Algorithm Inspired by Spatio-Temporal Properties of Visual Neurons

Eisaku Horiguchi and Hirotsugu Okuno[(✉)]

Graduate School and Faculty of Information Science and Technology,
Osaka Institute of Technology, Osaka, Japan
hirotsugu.okuno@oit.ac.jp

Abstract. Enhancing or detecting visual features related both to shape and motion is an important step in motion recognition. In the present study, we developed a spatio-temporal visual feature detection algorithm that provides information for estimating both orientation and velocity based on a physiological model of motion sensitive neurons. The algorithm consists of a low number of simple processing steps, and therefore, is suitable for circuit implementation and for edge computing. We evaluated the algorithm by using computer simulated movies and real-world movies. The results showed that the algorithm has high selectivity for motion direction and little dependence on contrast, and provides enough information for speed estimation.

Keywords: Image processing · Motion · Neuromorphic · Robot vision

1 Introduction

Enhancing or detecting spatio-temporal visual features related both to shape and motion is an important step in a wide range of applications, such as vision-based motion recognition. Many methods for vision-based recognition detect spatial or spatio-temporal visual features in the input image at the first step, and a classifier uses the features. Careful choice of features is required because they affect both the computational load and the final accuracy of classification. Even though early stages of deep neural networks (DNNs) work as a feature detector and can find moderate spatial features, it is not straightforward for DNNs to find and compute efficient spatio-temporal features.

The visual features used in the biological nervous systems can be a good example for the purpose described above because animals perform object and motion recognition efficiently. In the visual nervous system of mammals, visual features related to shape and motion are enhanced by spatio-temporal processing at an early stage. Edge enhancement starts at the retina, whose spatial input property is modeled as a difference of Gaussians [8]. The orientation selective response of the visual cortex is based on the process of the retina [5]. Starting from these simple visual feature enhancements, higher-order visual functions such as motion perception and recognition are achieved by the hierarchical visual nervous architecture.

© Springer Nature Switzerland AG 2021
T. Mantoro et al. (Eds.): ICONIP 2021, LNCS 13111, pp. 634–643, 2021.
https://doi.org/10.1007/978-3-030-92273-3_52

Using the early stage processing described above effectively, motion sensitive cortical cells that have been modeled as motion energy model respond selectively to a particular spatio-temporal feature [1], namely orientation and velocity. Based on the model, an extended model was also proposed by considering the following factors: the contribution of multiple spatial frequency components and mutual suppression from the motion detector of the opposite direction [9]. Although each step in the hierarchical neural architecture is quite simple, these neuro-inspired models provide useful visual features. And their simplicity is suitable for circuit implementation, and for practical applications to edge computing.

In the previous study, we simulated the response of the extended model in order mainly to examine the effects of the mutual suppression [3]. The results suggested that the mutual suppression of the model play an important role in increasing motion direction selectivity and in reducing contrast dependence. The model is a promising candidate for a preprocessing scheme of motion classifiers because the model provides information related both to shape and motion with little dependence on contrast in spite of its simple processing scheme.

The purpose of this study is to develop a visual feature detection algorithm that provides information for estimating orientation and velocity based on the physiological models of motion sensitive neurons [1,9]. Because the model programmed in the previous study did not provide information for estimating speed, which is an important feature in motion recognition, we equipped the model with multiple speed sensitivity without losing its simplicity and suitability for circuit implementation. And we evaluated this neuro-inspired algorithm in terms of practical applications using computer simulated movies and real-world movies. In particular, we examined the model response to motion of periodic patterns because detecting their motion is difficult for conventional motion estimation algorithms, such as Gunnar-Farneback algorithm [2], even though such patterns appear frequently in natural scenes.

2   Method

2.1   Processing Flow of the Feature Detection

Figure 1 shows the process flow of the spatio-temporal feature detection algorithm inspired by the cortical cell model with orientation and velocity selectivity [1]. The algorithm detects motions with two different speed ranges to the following four directions: upward, downward, leftward, and rightward. The flow diagram in Fig. 1 detects only leftward and rightward motion with a single speed range. The same process is applied to upward, downward and another speed range. Each step of the processing flow in Fig. 1 is simple and the number of step is low, and therefore, the algorithm is suitable for circuit implementation.

The input image is processed as follows. First, a combination of temporal filters (T_f and T_s in Fig. 1, see Sect. 2.2 for details) and two orthogonal spatial filters (E and O in Fig. 1, see Sect. 2.3 for details) makes a spatio-temporal filters that enhance either of a leftward or rightward motion (their outputs are L_E, L_O, R_E, and R_O in Fig. 1, see Sect. 2.4 for details). Letters L and R stand for leftward

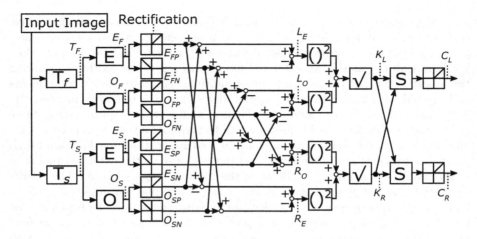

Fig. 1. Processing flow of the spatio-temporal feature detection. Blocks T_f and T_s represent temporal filters, blocks E and O represent spatial filters, block S represents mutual suppression.

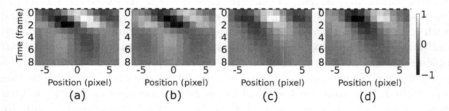

Fig. 2. Examples of spatio-temporal weights of the filters. These filters enhance left-ward motion. White and black rectangles represent weights with positive and negative values, respectively. The top row represents the weights multiplied to the current frame and lower rows represent the weights multiplied to the past frames. (a) (b) Spatio-temporal weights of the filter whose output is L_E and L_O in Fig. 1, respectively. (c) (d) Filter weights for a slow speed range detector that uses temporal filters T'_f and T'_s.

and rightward motions, respectively, indicating the direction selectivity. Another combination of temporal filters (T'_f and T'_s, see Sect. 2.2 for details) is used to detect a slower speed range. Figure 2 shows the weights of a spatio-temporal filter that enhances leftward motion with different speed sensitivity.

Next, the motion energy model output (K_L, K_R in Fig. 1) is given by the sum of the squared outputs of two orthogonal filters; this process removes the spatial phase dependence (see Sect. 2.5 for details).

A mutual suppression is applied to each motion direction detector using a nonlinear activation function (S in Fig. 1, and Eq. (7)) that is incorporated into the extended model (see Sect. 2.6 for details). This nonlinear function improves the motion direction selectivity and reduces contrast dependence [3].

2.2 Temporal Filter

Four temporal bandpass filters (T_f, T_s, T'_f and T'_s) with different temporal characteristics that simulate temporal characteristics of neurons [7] are generated as follows. The temporal characteristics of the filter are shown in Fig. 3 (a). First, infinite impulse response (IIR) temporal filters are applied to input $I(x, y)$, where (x, y) denotes the position in the image, according to the following equation:

$$T_n(x, y, t) = \alpha_n I(x, y) + (1 - \alpha_n) T_n(x, y, t - 1),$$ (1)

where t is the frame index, and $\alpha_n (n = 1, 2, 3, 4)$ is a parameter that changes the decay rate of the filter. List 1 shows values of the parameters used in this study.

Next, four temporal filters (T_f, T_s, T'_f and T'_s) are generated by the linear summation of the IIR filters. The output of T_f is expressed as:

$$T_F = l_1 T_1 + l_2 T_2 + l_3 T_3 + l_4 T_4.$$ (2)

Filtered signal T_S, which is the output of T_s, is also expressed by the same equation with a different set of α_n and l_n. Suffixes F and S represent fast and slow responding signals, respectively. As shown in Fig. 3, the output of T_f responds faster than that of T_s. Temporal filters T'_f and T'_s for slower speed range detectors are formed in the same way.

2.3 Spatial Filter

A set of Gabor-like filters are applied to the output of the two temporal filters. This spatial processing simulates the spatial characteristics of the simple cell [4], and is used to enhance edges with a particular orientation in the image. In this process, two types of Gabor-like filters whose phase difference is 90 °C are used. The two types of Gabor-like filters are hereinafter referred to as even-type and odd-type.

List 1. Parameters of the model

parameters	α_1	α_2	α_3	α_4	α	β	γ	δ	ε	ζ
values	0.77	0.55	0.33	0.11	1.0	1.0	0.01	1.0	0.01	2.0

temporal filters	T_f	T_s	T'_f	T'_s
values of (l_1, l_2, l_3, l_4)	(1,0,-1,0)	(-1,2,-1,0)	(0,1,0,-1)	(0,-1,2,-1)

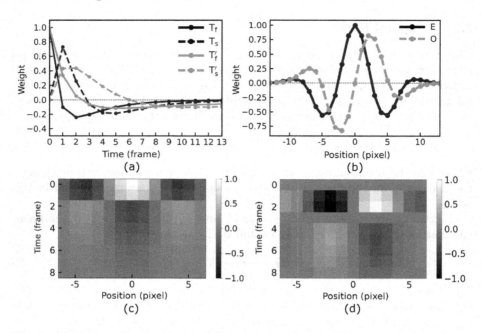

Fig. 3. (a) Temporal characteristics of the temporal filter (b) Horizontal line profile of the weight of the spatial Gabor-like filter. (c) (d) Example of a combination of a temporal filter and a spatial filter. (c) Filter weights for combination of temporal filter T_f and even-type spatial filter. (d) Filter weights for combination of temporal filter T_s and odd-type spatial filter.

Figure 3 (b) shows the horizontal line profile of the weight of the spatial Gabor-like filter. In this study, Gabor-like filters for a single frequency band were used, although the extended model [9] uses signals in multiple spatial frequency bands. The outputs of even-type and odd-type filters whose input is T_F are denoted as E_F and O_F, respectively. The outputs of even-type and odd-type filters whose input is T_S are denoted as E_S and O_S, respectively.

Next, half-wave rectifications are applied to the outputs of Gabor-like filters. This process is applied to simulate the neural signal representation, in which positive and negative signals are represented by different neurons [6], and also to correlate the positive and negative signals correctly in the latter stage. The end of the suffixes, P and N, of the output signals of the rectification in Fig. 1 represent positive and negative.

2.4   Spatio-Temporal Characteristics

Combinations of a temporal filter described in Sect. 2.2 and a spatial filter described in Sect. 2.3 form spatio-temporal filters as follows:

$$U_{fE} = T_f^T \cdot S_E \tag{3}$$

$$U_{sO} = T_s^T \cdot S_O \tag{4}$$

T_f and T_s represent the weight vectors of temporal filters T$_f$ and T$_s$, respectively. S_E and S_O represent the weight vectors of a horizontal row of the even-type and odd-type spatial filters, respectively. Although S_E and S_O are two dimensional matrices in the actual computation, vectors are used in this explanation for convenience. Figure 3(c) and (d) show the spatio-temporal weights of U_{fE} and U_{sO}, respectively. U_{fE} is a fast responding even-type filter, and U_{sO} is a slow responding odd-type filter. The simple addition of these two filters gives a spatio-temporal filter that enhances a leftward motion shown in Fig. 2(a):

$$U_{LE} = U_{fE} + U_{sO}. \tag{5}$$

The output of filter U_{LE} is L_E in Fig. 1. Filters that generate L_O, R_E, and R_O are formed by changing the combination of the temporal and spatial filters, and by changing the addition and subtraction.

2.5   Motion Energy Model

The output of the spatio-temporal filter described in Sect. 2.4 depends on the spatial phase of the input signal because of the phase dependence of the Gabor filter. The phase dependence of this detector is eliminated by summing the squares of two signals filtered by two orthogonal filters as follows:

$$K_L = \sqrt{L_E^2 + L_O^2}. \tag{6}$$

The phase-independent motion detector obtained in this way is known as the motion energy model [1]. Equation (6) describes the motion energy for leftward motion. Values of the motion energy for rightward motion (K_R), and for motions in a slower speed range (k_L and k_R), are computed in the same way.

2.6   Mutual Suppression

The output of the motion energy model has motion direction selectivity, but it still responds to motion in the opposite direction, and in some cases, the response to the opposite direction is not small enough to distinguish the direction of motion. On the other hand, the mutual suppression of the extended model used in this study [9] increases motion direction selectivity [3]. The output of the mutual suppression is expressed as

$$C_L = \alpha + \frac{\beta K_L^\zeta - \delta K_R^\zeta}{\gamma K_L^\zeta + \epsilon K_R^\zeta + 1}. \tag{7}$$

Equation (7) gives the output for leftward motion (C_L), and the output for rightward motion given by replacing K_R and K_L. Values of parameters α, β, γ, δ, ϵ, ζ are listed in List 1. This suppression process reduces the dependence on input contrast because of the term K_R and K_L in the denominator. The same processing is applied to k_R and k_L to obtain detector outputs for a slower speed range (c_R and c_L).

2.7   Velocity Estimation

In addition to motion direction, motion speed is estimated by comparing the outputs of two detectors with different speed sensitivity, such as C_R and c_R; the ratio of two detector outputs tells motion speed.

3   Experiments and Results

3.1   Simulation

We programmed the above algorithm by using Python and evaluated the output of the algorithm. For quantitative evaluation, we used computer simulated movies in which a vertical contour moves to a particular direction and a real-world movie, in which an object with a sinusoidal grating pattern moves to a particular direction; we used a linear-motion stage and a stepping motor to control the speed of the motion. For qualitative evaluation, we used a real-world movie, in which a person walks to a particular direction. In the figures showing the response of detectors, letters R, L, D and U in suffixes stand for rightward, leftward, downward, and upward motions, respectively, indicating the direction selectivity

3.2   Response to Computer Simulated Movies

Using the computer simulated movie in which a vertical contour moves to the right or the left, we investigated the contrast dependence of the models and the relationship between speed and the output. The output of the model with and without suppression was compered to verify if the reduction in contrast dependence works for the model with different speed sensitivity. We also compared the output of the models with different speed sensitivity.

In the simulated movie used to examine contrast dependence, pixel values on the right side of the moving contour was fixed to 0, and pixel values on the left side was changed from 0 to 255. The velocity of the moving contour was set to 2 pixels/frame to the right. Figure 4(a) shows contrast dependence of the models with two different speed sensitivity. The output of the model without suppression was proportional to the contrast, while the output of the model with suppression was almost constant in a certain level of contrast.

The speed-output characteristics of each model were examined by changing the velocity of the moving contour of the simulated movie. The difference of the pixel values at the contour was fixed to 100. Figure 4(b) shows the relationship between speed and output of the detectors for rightward and downward motions. The contour moves to the right or the left in the input movie and the positive value of the horizontal axis in Fig. 4(b) represents motion speed to the right. All rightward motion detectors showed a larger response to rightward motion. The detector of the model without suppression (K_R, k_R) showed a certain amount of response to leftward motion (negative speed in Fig. 4(b)), whereas the detectors of the model with suppression (C_R, c_R) showed almost no response to leftward

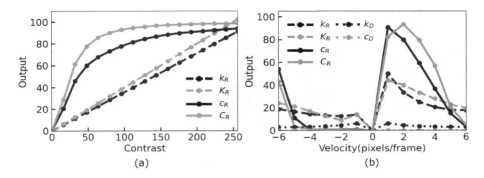

Fig. 4. Contract dependence of the models. In the simulated input movie, a contour moves to the right at 2 pixels/frame. K_R and C_R represent outputs of fast rightward motion detectors. k_R and c_R represent outputs of slow rightward motion detectors. k_D and c_D represent outputs of slow downward motion detectors. (b) Relationship between speed and output of the models. In the simulated input movie, a contour whose difference of the pixel values is 100 moves to the right.

motion. The difference of model outputs with different speed sensitivity (C_R, c_R) offers information to estimate speed. The detectors for the orthogonal direction (k_D, c_D) showed almost no response to both leftward and rightward motions.

3.3 Response to a Moving Sinusoidal Grating Pattern

We tested if the model provide information for estimating the motion direction and speed of an object with a periodic pattern by using a sinusoidal grating pattern shown in Fig. 5(a).

Figure 5(b) shows the responses of the model that detects slow rightward motion to the pattern. Figure 5(c) shows the motion direction estimated by a conventional motion estimation algorithm, Gunnar-Farnebak algorithm [2]. The estimated direction was totally different from the true direction. Figure 5(d) and (e) show the outputs of models when the pattern moved at 1 and 2 pixels/frame to the right, respectively. In both cases, detectors for rightward motion (C_R, c_R) only showed large responses, and these rightward motion detectors with different speed preference showed a larger response to their preferred speed range. In short, the response was correct and stable even if the input is a periodic pattern, whose motion is difficult to estimate for conventional motion estimate algorithms.

3.4 Response to a Walking Person

Figure 6(b)–(f) show the responses of the models to the real-world movie shown in Fig. 6(a). The results showed that the motion speed, as well as motion direction, was detected correctly; the horizontal speed (Fig. 6(d)) estimated from the ratio of the detectors for fast and slow rightward motions represents faster motion at the hand and the leg, whose actual speed is faster than that of the body.

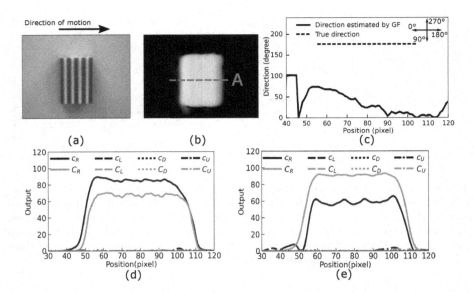

Fig. 5. Input image and output signals in which a sinusoidal grating pattern moves to the right (a) Input image acquired by an image sensor on a linear motion stage moved at a constant velocity. (b) Output of the detector for slow rightward motion. (c) Direction of motion estimated by Gunnar-Farnebak algorithm at dashed line A in (b) (d) (e) Output of detectors for four motion directions at dashed line A in (b) when the pattern moved at approximately 1 and 2 pixels/frame, respectively.

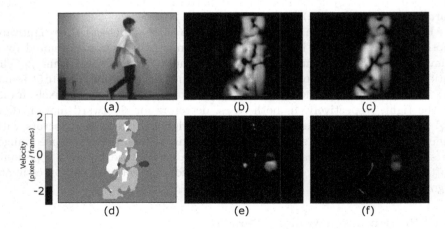

Fig. 6. Input and output images in which a person walks to the right (a) Input movie. (b) (c) Output of the detectors for slow and fast rightward motion, respectively. (d) Result of velocity estimation. The gray levels represent the estimated horizontal velocity. (e) (f) Output of the detectors for slow and fast leftward motion, respectively.

4 Conclusions

In this study, we developed a visual feature detection algorithm inspired by spatio-temporal properties of visual neurons. The results showed that the proposed algorithm provided information for estimating both orientation and velocity even though the moving object has a periodic pattern. The output of the algorithm in response to a walking person represented all the shape, the direction and the speed of motion correctly. These results suggest that the proposed algorithm is useful in terms of practical applications and that the algorithm implemented into circuits would facilitate efficient motion recognition in edge computing systems.

Acknowledgments. This work was supported by JSPS KAKENHI Grant Number 19K12916.

References

1. Adelson, E.H., Bergen, J.R.: Spatiotemporal energy models for the perception of motion. J. Opt. Soc. Am. A **2**(2), 284–299 (1985)
2. Farnebäck, G.: Two-frame motion estimation based on polynomial expansion. In: Bigun, J., Gustavsson, T. (eds.) SCIA 2003. LNCS, vol. 2749, pp. 363–370. Springer, Heidelberg (2003). https://doi.org/10.1007/3-540-45103-X_50
3. Horiguchi, E., Okuno, H.: A spatio-temporal feature extraction algorithm that simulates a physiological model of a neuron in the early visual cortex. In: The Twenty Sixth International Symposium on Artificial Life and Robotics 2021, pp. 431–436 (2021)
4. Hubel, D.H., Wiesel, T.N.: Receptive fields of single neurones in the cat's striate cortex. J. Physiol. **148**(3), 574–591 (1959)
5. Hubel, D.H., Wiesel, T.N.: Receptive fields, binocular interaction and functional architecture in the cat's visual cortex. J. Physiol. **160**(1), 106–154.2 (1962)
6. Movshon, J.A., Thompson, I.D., Tolhurst, D.J.: Spatial summation in the receptive fields of simple cells in the cat's striate cortex. J. Physiol. **283**, 53–77 (1978)
7. Okuno, H., Hasegawa, J., Sanada, T., Yagi, T.: Real-time emulator for reproducing graded potentials in vertebrate retina. IEEE Trans. Biomed. Circuits Syst. **9**(2), 284–295 (2015)
8. Rodieck, R.W.: Quantitative analysis of cat retinal ganglion cell response to visual stimuli. Vision. Res. **5**(12), 583–601 (1965)
9. Rust, N.C., Schwartz, O., Movshon, J.A., Simoncelli, E.P.: Spatiotemporal elements of macaque V1 receptive fields. Neuron **46**(6), 945–956 (2005)

Knowledge Distillation Method for Surface Defect Detection

Jiulin Lang, Chenwei Tang, Yi Gao, and Jiancheng Lv[✉]

Sichuan University, Chengdu 610065, People's Republic of China
lvjiancheng@scu.edu.cn

Abstract. In this paper, we propose a multi-scale attention mechanism-guided knowledge distillation method for surface defect detection. Enables a lighter student model to mimic the complex teacher model through the use of knowledge distillation techniques, the proposed method improves the defect detection accuracy and maintains high real-time performance, simultaneously. Specifically, we first present a multi-scale fusion-based teacher network. Owing to the fusion of two resolution scales features, the teacher network can keep high compatibility with the low-resolution student network during knowledge distillation, so as to better direct the student model. Then, in the process of knowledge distillation, attentional mechanisms were introduced with the aim of enabling the student network to more effectively mimic the foreground attention map and features of the teacher network. Finally, in order to address the imbalance of foreground and background in defect detection, we introduce a class-weighted cross entropy loss. Experiments conducted on three benchmark datasets proved the validity and efficiency of the proposed method in surface defect detection.

Keywords: Surface defect detection · Knowledge distillation · Multi-scale fusion · Attention mechanism

1 Introduction

Due to long-term operation and exposure to air, the surface of equipment in industrial production environments can develop various defects, such as corrosion, cracking, peeling off, blistering and other defects (as shown in Fig. 1). If the surface defects are not repaired promptly, these defects will have a serious impact on the use of the equipment, resulting in the reduction of the efficiency and quality of industrial production. In recent years, more and more deep learning based methods are being applied to industrial scenarios due to powerful automatic feature extraction and great achievements in numerous domains of computer vision. However, the majority of the current deep learning-based approaches need to train the models on large-scale datasets to achieve specific industrial intelligence

This work is supported by the National Natural Science Fund for Distinguished Young Scholar (GrantNo. 61625204), National Key Research and Development Project of China (No.2017YFB1002201).

T. Mantoro et al. (Eds.): ICONIP 2021, LNCS 13111, pp. 644–655, 2021.
https://doi.org/10.1007/978-3-030-92273-3_53

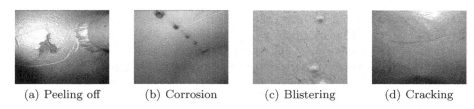

(a) Peeling off   (b) Corrosion   (c) Blistering   (d) Cracking

Fig. 1. Various defects on the surface of the equipment

applications. A large amount of computing power and memory resource consumption limit the promotion and progress of deep learning-based methods in industrial intelligent applications involving the deployment of edge devices such as mobile or embedded devices.

Most previous deep learning-based methods solve surface defect detection by training a single object detection depth neural network. However, due to the imbalance of samples, as well as the uneven data quality caused by the illumination, distance, and technique of shooting, most of the existing approaches based on depth object detection could not complete the equipment surface defect detection task well and in real time. To solve these challenges, many techniques have been proposed, including branching reduction, model compression, and so on. In this paper, we propose to utilize knowledge distillation to achieve model compression. Moreover, the proposed method, called Knowledge Distillation Method (KDM), improves the defect detection accuracy, and maintains high real-time performance, simultaneously. Our contribution could be concluded as follows:

- We propose the KDM with a multi-scale fusion based teachers network for surface defect detection. By the fusion of two resolution scales features, the teacher network can keep high compatibility with the low-resolution student network during knowledge distillation, so as to better direct the student model.
- In the process of knowledge distillation, we introduce the attention mechanism that allows student to imitate more efficiently the foreground attention map and features of the teacher network. We also introduce a class-weighted cross entropy loss to address the unbalance between background and foreground on defect detection.
- Experiments conducted on three benchmark datasets show that the proposed KDM method significantly reduces the computation and memory consumption and improves the real-time and accuracy in surface defect detection.

2   Related Work

2.1   Object Detection

Currently, object detection techniques could be divided into anchor-free and anchor-based methods. The comparison between these two lies in whether the proposals are extracted by using the anchor. Nowadays, most of the methods used in industry for surface defect detection utilize object detection methods based on the anchor mechanism, e.g., SSD [8], Faster R-CNN [11], YOLOv3 [10], etc. However, there is an obvious disadvantage of this approach, that is, the hyper-parameters related to the anchor box, like the aspect ratio and scale of the anchor box are difficult to design. In different industrial application scenarios, we need to design the scale and aspect ratio of the anchor according to our data situation, which requires strong a priori knowledge. The setting of the hyper-parameter Intersection over Union (IoU) threshold is also an issue when object category classification is based on anchor.

Since Huang et al. [5] proposed the DenseBox, object detection models of the anchor-free have been developing rapidly. In 2019, Tian et al. [15] proposed FCOS, which is a dense predictive approach to object detection similar to semantic segmentation. FCOS is a pioneering work in anchor-free methods with advantages in speed and accuracy. The teacher model and student model of our proposed KDM in this paper both use the FCOS structure, which is an innovative attempt for surface defect detection tasks.

2.2 Knowledge Distillation

In 2015, Hinton et al. [4] proposed KD, which allows the student to imitate the results of the teacher, migrating knowledge out of the complex, high-accuracy teacher model to the streamlined, low-complexity student network. The knowledge distillation provides an efficient model compression scheme for deep neural network models deployed on IoT, mobile, and other devices. In the same year, Romero et al. [12] presented FitNets, and in their approach, the intermediate feature layer of the teacher network also provides a 'hint' to direct the student model's training in their approach. In 2017, Zagoruyko et al. [18] further advanced knowledge distillation by introducing attentional mechanisms into knowledge distillation to enable the student network imitate the attention map from teacher. In the same year, a compact and fast object detection model using knowledge distillation to learn was proposed by Chen et al. [1]. In order to improve the efficiency of knowledge distillation on the object detection task, Wang et al. [16] presented a refined feature mimicking approach by having the student network imitate the teacher model near the Ground Truth (GT) of the feature map to obtain better performance.

3 Method

The KDM framework is displayed in Fig. 2, involves two components, i.e., the attention mechanism-guided student network and the teacher network. We introduce the knowledge distillation mechanism, hope to train a more concise student model through the guidance of the teacher model, and ensure a better detection performance of the student simultaneously. Considering that the input of the student is generally low-resolution image, we introduce multi-scale fusion in

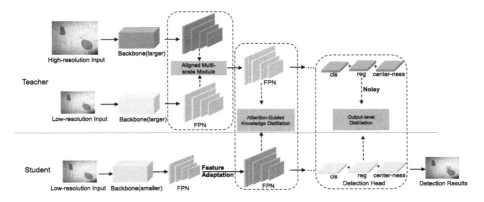

Fig. 2. Framework diagram of multi-scale attention-guided knowledge distillation based surface defect detection method.

the teacher network to ensure that the teacher network can have high compatibility when guiding the student network. In addition, we introduced an attention mechanism in the knowledge distillation, which aims to allow students to learn the capabilities of the teacher and to acquire more refined features. Furthermore, to solve the issue of foreground and background imbalance in defect detection, we also introduce a class-weighted cross entropy loss in the proposed KDM. In detail, we construct the teacher network based on multi-scale fusion and the attention mechanism-guided knowledge distillation of the proposed KDM as follow:

Teacher Network Based on Multi-scale Fusion. We training the powerful teacher network of the proposed KDM with multi-resolution inputs [9]. Specifically, we first pre-process the surface images of the equipment with defects by flipping, affine transforming (including scaling, cropping, etc.), and so on. Then, we define the pre-processed defect images as the high-resolution input data. After that, the pre-processed defect images are down-sampled with a scaling factor of 0.5, and then the down-sampled defect images are defined as low-resolution input data. As shown in Fig. 3, both low-resolution data and high-resolution data are fused and utilized as inputs to the teacher network based on multi-scale fusion. In the low- and high-resolution feature pyramids, layers with the same output size are fused. Moreover, the original low-resolution input, original high-resolution input, and the fused feature pyramid are input to the part of the Fully Convolutional One-Stage (FCOS) detection head, as well as trained together. In this way, the teacher network based on multi-scale fusion can fuse features from two input resolutions. When deploying, to achieve the real-time requirements, the student network usually inputs the low-resolution images. Therefore, this multi-scale fusion teacher network is well compatible with the low-resolution student network in the process of knowledge distillation.

Attention Mechanism-guided Knowledge Distillation. We propose an attention mechanism-guided distillation approach to allow the student network to imitate the key locations of the teacher network based on multi-scale fusion

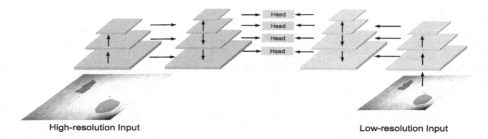

Fig. 3. Framework diagram of teacher network based on multi-scale fusion.

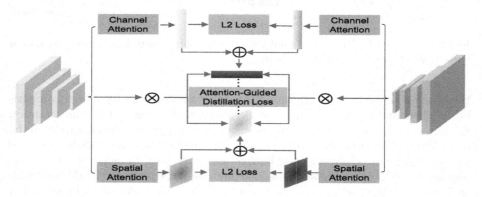

Fig. 4. Framework diagram of attention mechanism-guided knowledge distillation.

for a more fine-grained knowledge distillation. For the knowledge distillation in the classification and regression layers, we noise the output of the teacher model to achieve regularization [13]. In order to make the student more efficient in imitating the teacher at the feature layer, we conduct the knowledge distillation with different strengths of attentional guidance for different layers of the feature pyramid. The framework of knowledge distillation guided by the attention-based mechanism is shown in Fig. 4. The attention mechanism-guided knowledge distillation consists of three main components: the spatial attention knowledge distillation, the channel attention knowledge distillation, and the attention-guided feature map knowledge distillation.

We first define F^T as a feature map of a layer of the feature pyramid of the teacher after multi-scale fusion. F^S is a feature map of a layer corresponding to the feature pyramid network of the student. C^T and C^S denote the channel attention maps of F^T and F^S, respectively. The dimensions of C^T and C^S are $(C, 1, 1)$, where C is the number of channels in the feature map, calculated as shown in Eq. 1. M^T and M^S refer to the spatial attention maps of F^T and F^S, respectively. The dimensions of M^T and M^S are both $(H, W, 1)$, where W and H are the width and height of the feature, and the calculation formula is shown in Eq. 2. Then, the channel attention maps C^T and spatial attention maps M^T

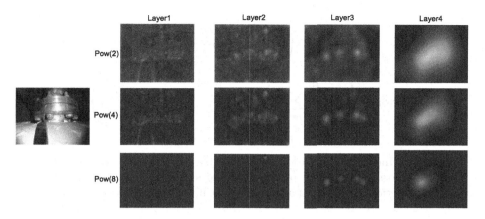

Fig. 5. Spatial attention map visualization of different nth power at different stages.

of feature map of teacher network F^T, as well as the channel attention maps C^S and spatial attention maps M^S of feature map of student network F^S are driven as follows.

$$C^T = \frac{1}{HW} \sum_{i=1}^{H} \sum_{j=1}^{W} \left| F_{i,j}^T \right|, \qquad C^S = \frac{1}{HW} \sum_{i=1}^{H} \sum_{j=1}^{W} \left| F_{i,j}^S \right|, \tag{1}$$

$$M^T = \left(\frac{1}{C} \sum_{k=1}^{C} \left| F_k^T, \right| \right)^n, \qquad M^S = \left(\frac{1}{C} \sum_{k=1}^{C} \left| F_k^S, \right| \right)^n. \tag{2}$$

Specifically, we first perform the mean-taking operation on all channels of the feature map during the various phases of the network. Then, we perform an n-th power operation on the result. After that, the feature map needs to be sampled up to the initial scale. Figure 5 visualizes the spatial attention map of different n-th power at various stages of the model network. The larger the n of n-th power operation, the higher the network will focus its attention on the part with the higher activation value. From the visualization in Fig. 5, we can see that different layers have different attention maps. In the attention maps of the lower layers, there is a higher activation value around the defect. Moreover, the activation value of the attention maps mainly corresponds to the overall part of the defect and does not pay attention to the details in the higher layers.

When the proposed KDM student was trained, we utilize the early-stop teacher regularization distillation strategy [2], i.e., stopping the distillation early when convergence is near to achieve the best distillation effect. The loss function Loss_F for attention mechanism-guided knowledge distillation in the feature layer involves three parts, i.e., Loss_c, Loss_m, and Loss_g, as shown by Eq. 3–Eq. 6.

$$\text{Loss}_c = \left(\sum_{k=1}^{C} \left(C_k^T - C_k^S \right)^2 \right)^{\frac{1}{2}}, \tag{3}$$

$$\text{Loss}_m = \left(\sum_{i=1}^{H} \sum_{j=1}^{W} \left(M_{i,j}^T - M_{i,j}^S \right)^2 \right)^{\frac{1}{2}}, \tag{4}$$

$$\text{Loss}_g = \left(\sum_{k=1}^{C} \sum_{i=1}^{H} \sum_{j=1}^{W} \left(F^T_{k,i,j} - F_{k,i,j}^S \right)^2 * C_k^T * M^T_{i,j} \right)^{\frac{1}{2}}, \tag{5}$$

$$\text{Loss}_F = \alpha \text{Loss}_c + \beta \, \text{Loss}_m + \gamma \text{Loss}_g, \tag{6}$$

where Loss_F means the total loss of knowledge distillation in the feature layer. The Loss_c, Loss_m, and Loss_g represent the loss of knowledge distillation in the channel attention map, the spatial attention map, and the feature map guided by attention, respectively. The Loss_c, Loss_m, and Loss_g all use the $L2$ loss. And α, β, γ are the weights of Loss_c, Loss_m, and Loss_g, which are set as $\alpha = 1$, $\beta = 1$, and $\gamma = 2$ in this paper.

Class-weighted Cross Entropy Loss. To solve the issue of foreground and background imbalance in surface defect detection, we introduce a class-weighted cross entropy loss [1] in the output layer of the proposed KDM. The knowledge distillation loss function Loss_{ouput} in the output layer of our proposed KDM involves three components, i.e., the loss of classification L_{cls}^S, the loss of regression L_{reg}^S, and the center_ness loss $L_{center\_ness}^S$ as as shown in Eq. 7–Eq. 10.

$$L_{cls}^S = \mu L_{\text{hard}} \left(P_{cls}^S, y_{cls} \right) + (1 - \mu) \left(- \sum w_{cls} P_{cls}^T \log P_{cls}^S \right), \tag{7}$$

$$L_{\text{reg}}^S = L_{\text{IOU}} \left(P_{\text{reg}}^S, y_{\text{reg}} \right) + v L_{\text{reg\_kd}}^S \left(P_{\text{reg}}^S, P_{\text{reg}}^T, y_{\text{reg}} \right) \tag{8}$$

$$L_{\text{center\_ness}}^S = L_{BCE} \left(P_{cn}^S, y_{cn} \right) + \lambda L_{cn\_kd}^S \left(P_{cn}^S, P_{cn}^T, y_{cn} \right) \tag{9}$$

$$Loss_{ouput} = \delta L_{cls}^S + \zeta L_{\text{reg}}^S + \eta L_{\text{center\_ness}}^S, \tag{10}$$

where Loss_{ouput} is the knowledge distillation loss function of output layer, L_{cls}^S, L_{reg}^S, $L_{center\_ness}^S$ are the knowledge distillation loss functions of classification, regression, and center_ness parts, respectively. The δ, ζ, η are the weights of L_{cls}^S, L_{reg}^S, $L_{center\_ness}^S$, which are set as $\delta = 1$, $\zeta = 1$, and $\eta = 2$ in this paper. L_{cls}^S consists of L_{hard} and class-weighted cross entropy loss function [1], w_{cls} takes 1.5 when the category is the background, and takes the 1 in other cases, and L_{hard} uses the focal loss function, which represents the hard loss. L_{reg}^S, $L_{center\_ness}^S$ both consist of two parts, one part is hard loss consisting of ground truth labels as shown in L_{IOU} and L_{BCE} in Eq. 8 and Eq. 9, and the other part is soft loss consisting of teacher output as shown in $L_{reg_kd}^S$ and $L_{cn_kd}^S$ at Eq. 8, Eq. 9, and the soft losses both use the teacher bounded regression loss [1], which is used to control students to imitate the teacher within a certain range, and no additional loss is provided once a certain range is exceeded. L_{IOU} is the IOU loss function, and L_{BCE} is the BCE loss function.

Table 1. Number of three datasets.

Dataset	Train	Test
NEU	3357	832
DAGM2007	1046	1054
RSDDs	231	84

4 Experiments

4.1 Datasets and Metrics

Table 1 shows the details of the NEU, DAGM2007, and RSDDs datasets. For the evaluation metrics, we refer to cocoapi's[1] evaluation method to evaluate our proposed approach. Where AP denotes the average accuracy across all categories and 10 IOU thresholds (0.50:0.05:0.95), AP_{50} denotes the average accuracy across all categories at an IOU of 0.5, AP_{75} denotes the average accuracy across all categories at an IOU of 0.75, and AR denotes the maximum recall across 1 detection per image as a result of all IoUs and all categories on the average.

NEU Dataset. The NEU [14] dataset is a surface defect database published by the Northeastern University, which collects six different surface defects of rolled steel strips, and each containing 300 samples.

DAGM2007 Dataset. DAGM2007 [17] is a dataset of surface defect images of various types of textures for the enhancement of algorithms for industrial optical inspection. It consists of 10 datasets, each containing 1000 images which display a defect-free background grain, as well as 150 images.

RSDDs Dataset. The RSDDs [3] contains two types of rail images, each containing at least one type of defect and with complex background interference, which is extremely challenging.

4.2 Experiment Results and Analysis

The test results of teachers, students, and YOLOv3, RetinaNet [7] and YOLOv5 [6] on different datasets are displayed in Table 2. This shows that our student network has strong detection performance after knowledge distillation. On the NEU dataset, the student outperformed RetinaNet on all metrics and outperformed YOLOv5 on AP_{75}, with AR outperforming all baseline methods. On the DAGM2007 dataset, the student outperformed YOLOv5 on AP_{75} and AR. On the RSDDs dataset, the student outperformed YOLOv3 and RetinaNet on AP, exceeded all baseline methods on AP_{75}, and outperformed YOLOv3 on AR. it shows that our proposed knowledge distillation method can be used as a feasible compression framework for defect detection models, which is enlightening for the deployment of defect detection models on edge devices. Finally, some results are given in Figs. 6, 7 and 8.

---

[1] https://cocodataset.org/#detection-eval.

Table 2. Quantitative comparison of different methods on different datasets.

	NEU	DAGM2007	RSDDs	AP	AP$_{50}$	AP$_{75}$	AR
Teacher	✓			39.16	69.97	40.2	28
Student	✓			**38.31**	**70.35**	**37.13**	**27.2**
Teacher		✓		63.08	97.97	71.45	70.8
Student		✓		**52.35**	**94.12**	**54.35**	**60.5**
Teacher			✓	43.38	88.22	32.21	36.3
Student			✓	**40.79**	**86.2**	**34.35**	**35**
YOLOv3	✓			42.28	76.7	41.2	26.5
YOLOv3		✓		63.7	98.7	72.9	69.2
YOLOv3			✓	33.9	71.4	29.7	30.6
RetinaNet	✓			29.2	61.4	24	20.4
RetinaNet		✓		58.7	96	64	65.3
RetinaNet			✓	38	80.5	28.4	36.5
YOLOv5	✓			39.2	73.1	36.3	24.9
YOLOv5		✓		54.8	90.2	58.6	60.0
YOLOv5			✓	46.3	89.9	32.4	40.2

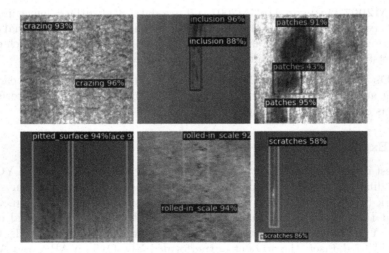

Fig. 6. Some detection results on NEU using student network.

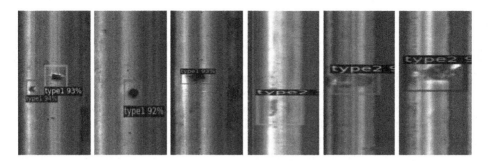

Fig. 7. Some detection results on RSDDs using student network.

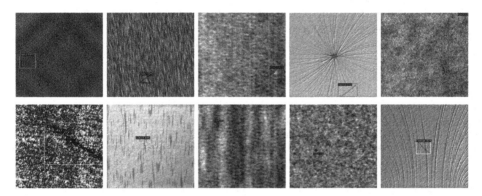

Fig. 8. Some detection results on DAGM2007 using student network.

4.3   Ablation Study

To demonstrate the effectiveness of the presented approach, we also performed ablation experiments in this paper. All these defect detection experiments were evaluated based on NEU, DAGM2007, and RSDDs dataset. The results of the ablation experiments are shown in Table 3.

Table 3. Ablation study on NEU, DAGM2007, RSDDs, and both Student and FCOS backbone networks are ResNet-50.

	NEU	DAGM2007	RSDDs	AP	AP_{50}	AP_{75}	AR
Student	✓			**38.31**	**70.35**	**37.13**	**27.2**
FCOS	✓			36.9	77.1	31.1	25.3
Student		✓		**52.35**	**94.12**	**54.35**	**60.5**
FCOS		✓		49	93.8	44.9	55.8
Student			✓	**40.79**	**86.2**	**34.35**	**35**
FCOS			✓	38.7	87.7	22.9	33.1

5   Conclusion

In this paper, we applying knowledge distillation to the domain of surface defect detection and propose a new training framework, named KDM, for industrial defect detection. By using the knowledge distillation strategy to allow a lighter student models to imitate the complex teacher network. Specifically, we first introduce a multi-scale fusion-based teacher for better guidance of the student, and then, in the process of knowledge distillation, we introduce attention mechanisms that enable the student network to more effectively mimic the foreground attention graph and features of the teacher network. Finally, in order to address the imbalance of foreground and background in defect detection, we use a class-weighted cross entropy loss. In general, the KDM greatly reduces the computational and memory consumption of deep neural networks while balancing accuracy and speed. Moreover, experiments show that the presented KDM is appropriate for industrial applications of surface defect detection.

References

1. Chen, G., Choi, W., Yu, X., Han, T., Chandraker, M.: Learning efficient object detection models with knowledge distillation. In: Proceedings of the 31st International Conference on Neural Information Processing Systems, pp. 742–751 (2017)
2. Cho, J.H., Hariharan, B.: On the efficacy of knowledge distillation. In: Proceedings of the IEEE/CVF International Conference on Computer Vision, pp. 4794–4802 (2019)
3. Gan, J., Li, Q., Wang, J., Yu, H.: A hierarchical extractor-based visual rail surface inspection system. IEEE Sens. J. **17**(23), 7935–7944 (2017). https://doi.org/10.1109/JSEN.2017.2761858
4. Hinton, G., Vinyals, O., Dean, J.: Distilling the knowledge in a neural network. arXiv preprint arXiv:1503.02531 (2015)
5. Huang, L., Yang, Y., Deng, Y., Yu, Y.: Densebox: Unifying landmark localization with end to end object detection. CoRR abs/1509.04874 (2015). http://arxiv.org/abs/1509.04874
6. Jocher, G., Nishimura, K., Mineeva, T., Vilario, R.: YOLOv5. https://github.com/ultralytics/yolov5 (2020). Accessed 10 July 2020
7. Lin, T., Goyal, P., Girshick, R.B., He, K., Dollár, P.: Focal loss for dense object detection. In: IEEE International Conference on Computer Vision, ICCV 2017, Venice, Italy, 22–29, October 2017, pp. 2999–3007. IEEE Computer Society (2017). https://doi.org/10.1109/ICCV.2017.324
8. Liu, W., et al.: SSD: single shot multibox detector. In: Leibe, B., Matas, J., Sebe, N., Welling, M. (eds.) ECCV 2016. LNCS, vol. 9905, pp. 21–37. Springer, Cham (2016). https://doi.org/10.1007/978-3-319-46448-0_2
9. Qi, L., et al.: Multi-scale aligned distillation for low-resolution detection. In: Proceedings of the IEEE/CVF Conference on Computer Vision and Pattern Recognition, pp. 14443–14453 (2021)
10. Redmon, J., Farhadi, A.: Yolov3: an incremental improvement. CoRR abs/1804.02767 (2018). http://arxiv.org/abs/1804.02767
11. Ren, S., He, K., Girshick, R.B., Sun, J.: Faster R-CNN: towards real-time object detection with region proposal networks. IEEE Trans. Pattern Anal. Mach. Intell. **39**(6), 1137–1149 (2017). https://doi.org/10.1109/TPAMI.2016.2577031

12. Romero, A., Ballas, N., Kahou, S.E., Chassang, A., Gatta, C., Bengio, Y.: Fitnets: hints for thin deep nets. arXiv preprint arXivarXiv:1412.6550 (2014)
13. Sau, B.B., Balasubramanian, V.N.: Deep model compression: distilling knowledge from noisy teachers. arXiv preprint arXiv:1610.09650 (2016)
14. Song, K., Yan, Y.: A noise robust method based on completed local binary patterns for hot-rolled steel strip surface defects. Appl. Surf. Sci. **285**, 858–864 (2013)
15. Tian, Z., Shen, C., Chen, H., He, T.: FCOS: fully convolutional one-stage object detection. In: 2019 IEEE/CVF International Conference on Computer Vision, ICCV 2019, Seoul, Korea (South), October 27 - November 2, 2019, pp. 9626–9635. IEEE (2019). https://doi.org/10.1109/ICCV.2019.00972
16. Wang, T., Yuan, L., Zhang, X., Feng, J.: Distilling object detectors with fine-grained feature imitation. In: Proceedings of the IEEE/CVF Conference on Computer Vision and Pattern Recognition, pp. 4933–4942 (2019)
17. Wieler, M., Hahn, T.: Weakly supervised learning for industrial optical inspection. In: DAGM symposium in (2007)
18. Zagoruyko, S., Komodakis, N.: Paying more attention to attention: Improving the performance of convolutional neural networks via attention transfer. arXiv preprint arXiv:1612.03928 (2016)

Adaptive Selection of Classifiers for Person Recognition by Iris Pattern and Periocular Image

Keita Ogawa[1]([✉]) and Keisuke Kameyama[2]

[1] Degree Programs in Systems and Information Engineering, Graduate School of Science and Technology, University of Tsukuba, Tsukuba, Japan
ogawa@adapt.cs.tsukuba.ac.jp
[2] Faculty of Engineering, Information and Systems, University of Tsukuba, Tsukuba, Japan

Abstract. Iris recognition is a type of biometric authentication that can achieve high authentication accuracy. However, its classification accuracy is significantly reduced when the image quality is low. In recent years, research on multi-modal authentication that uses not only the iris but also the periocular information that can be acquired together with the iris has been actively conducted. The purpose of this study is to improve the robustness of classification accuracy for degraded observed images by using iris and periocular modalities. In this paper, a method to select a classifier that is useful for authentication from the iris and periocular classifiers will be proposed for when either of the iris or the periocular image is of low quality. For the selection of the modal classifier, we propose and use the Multi Modal Selector that adaptively selects a classifier useful for classification by using parts of the outputs of the iris and periocular classifiers. In the experiment, it was shown that high classification accuracy can be maintained by adaptively selecting a useful classifier.

Keywords: Biometrics · Iris · Periocular image · Multimodal · Adaptive combination

1 Introduction

1.1 Research Background and Purpose

Iris recognition is a type of biometric authentication that uses the pattern on the iris of the eye. The iris is a ring-shaped part of the eye that corresponds to the outside of the pupil and the inside of the sclera. Iris recognition has been reported to have practically usable authentication accuracy [2]. However, the texture of the iris may be of poor quality depending on the observation conditions. When a low-quality iris image is used for iris recognition, the classification accuracy is significantly reduced [14]. On the other hand, the information of the area around the eye such as the eyelids and eyelashes that can be acquired together with the

© Springer Nature Switzerland AG 2021
T. Mantoro et al. (Eds.): ICONIP 2021, LNCS 13111, pp. 656–667, 2021.
https://doi.org/10.1007/978-3-030-92273-3_54

iris (periocular information) has been reported to be useful in personal authentication [1]. However, objects such as hair and spectacles are also observed around the eyes, and the classification accuracy is significantly reduced when such obstacles interfere [8]. The purpose of this study is to develop a method to maintain the classification accuracy even if one of the images is of low quality. As the evaluation standard, we focus on classification accuracy rather than authentication accuracy. In this study, Use of a classifier (Multi Modal Selector) obtained by supervised learning that adaptively selects the modal classifier which is useful for classification, is proposed.

1.2   Contributions of this Research

The main contributions of this research are as follows.

- The Multi Modal Selector selects a modal classifier that is useful for classification even when one of the iris or the periocular area is a low quality image, and uses the classifier with high classification accuracy. This enables that the classification accuracy as a system can be maintained high under suboptiomal observation conditions.
- The Multi Modal Selector can be implemented by a general machine learning-based classification method.

2   Related Research

2.1   Iris and Periocular Region

Figure 1 shows an example of a near-infrared periocular image used for personal recognition. The eye can be divided into three main areas. The black circular area at the center is the pupil, and the ring-shaped part around it with gray texture is called the iris. The white area outside the iris is the sclera.

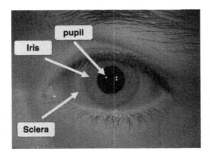

Fig. 1. A periocular image (sampled from [10]).

2.2   Iris Recognition and Periocular Recognition

For iris recognition, the periocular image is first obtained. Next, the iris is detected and the detected iris is normalized by a nonlinear coordinate transformation into a rectangular image [2] as shown in Fig. 7 (normalization). Feature extraction is performed from the normalized iris image, and authentication is performed using a classifier.

For periocular authentication, the periocular image is used directly. Features are extracted from the periocular images, and authentication is performed by recognition using a classifier based on the features.

Iris recognition and periocular images are being actively studied [2, 9].

2.3   Multimodal Authentication Using Iris and Periocular Images

In recent years, research on multi-modal authentication by fusing information of the iris and periocular images has been actively conducted in order to achieve a more robust authentication [14]. In the study of fusion of iris and periocular information, works such as fusion at the score level [12] and fusion at the functional level [14] have been conducted. Score-level fusion which is based on conducting experiments multiple times with varying weights to find the optimal weight. In the fusion of functional levels, the optimum weight is obtained by learning. Both methods use the fixed weights acquired by training, so if the observed image is degraded, the appropriate weights may not be the weights acquired during training.

2.4   Pattern Classification Method that Combines Multiple Classifiers

The combination of multiple classifiers improves the classification ability over a single classifier. For pattern recognition in general, bagging [3] is one of the ensemble learning methods [3] as a method of combining a plurality of classifiers and using them for classification. Also, the Mixture of Experts [13], which is a method of switching between multiple classifiers as local experts for the input space, is known.

2.5   Issues and the Aim of this Work

Both periocular authentication and iris authentication are practically usable authentication methods, but the classification accuracy decreases when the observed image is degraded [8, 14]. In such situations, the method of weighting and fusing the characteristics and classification results using fixed weights obtained during learning is not appropriate and may reduce the accuracy. Therefore, the aim of this study is to develop a method for adaptively selecting reliable classification results by looking at the outputs of the modal classifiers, instead of using a set of fixed weights.

3   Proposed Method

3.1   Overall Flow

Figure 2 shows the flow of the proposed method.

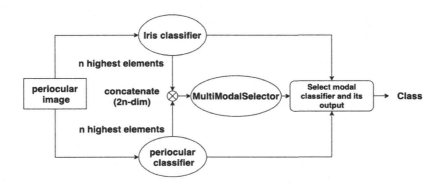

Fig. 2. Flow of the proposed method.

The classification of the input periocular image into classes corresponding to individuals using the proposed method can be broadly divided into five phases. First, the periocular image to be recognized is acquired, and the following phases 1 to 5 are processed.

1. Detect iris from the image that includes the periocular region.
2. Normalize the detected iris image.
3. Classify the normalized iris image by the iris classifier. Obtain iris class probability vector for the input image.
4. Input the periocular image to the periocular classifier. Obtain periocular class probability vector for the input image.
5. Let the Multi Modal Selector, which evaluates the reliability of the iris classifier and the periocular classifier, use the significant parts of the output vectors of both classifiers to select reliable classification results.

3.2   Iris Detection and Normalization

To detect the iris from the periocular image, the pupil is first detected, and then the iris is detected based on the center of the pupil. The iris is detected by matching with an ellipse so that the iris can be detected even when the shape of the iris is not circular or when the subject is incooperative. Then, using a coordinate transformation, a ring-shaped iris is opened and converted into a rectangle of predetermined dimensions regardless of the degree of pupil dilation to obtain a normalized iris image [2].

3.3   Iris and Periocular Classifiers

The iris classifier and periocular classifier classify the input image into one of the registered classes. Both classifiers are realized by supervised learning applied to classifiers such as convolutional neural networks (CNN). The periocular classifier uses the periocular image as an input, and the iris classifier uses the normalized iris image created in Sect. 3.2 as the input image. The output is a vector having the dimensionality of the registered number of classes, and the element corresponding to the class to which the input image belongs is trained to be the maximum. Hereinafter, the classifier in charge of each modality will be referred to as a modal classifier.

3.4   Multi Modal Selector

Multi Modal Selector (MMS) selects a useful classifier based on the output vector of the iris classifier and periocular classifier. It is considered that the output of each classifier retains not only the classification result but also the characteristic indicating the reliability of the classification result. By learning and utilizing the patterns observed in the modal classifier's outputs that reflect the reliability of the classification, we aim to maintain the final classification accuracy of the system as a whole.

In selecting a classifier, first, the outputs y_i and y_p of the iris classifier and the periocular classifier are input into the softmax function, respectively. The components of the softmax output s_i and s_p are sorted in descending order, and the vectors z_i and z_p consisting of the first n elements are extracted. Then, the $2n$-dimensional vector I that concatenates the vectors s_i and s_p is used as the input to the MMS. The output O of MMS is a scalar value indicating which modal classifier is used (Fig. 3).

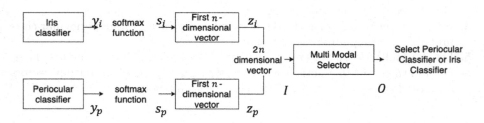

Fig. 3. Selection of a modal classifier using the Multi Modal Selector

MMS is realized by supervised learning. When learning, one of the two images input to the modal classifiers is intentionally degraded. MMS is trained to select the reliable modal classifier that received non-degraded information, by looking at the classifier's output vector. Table 1 shows the combination of deterioration of the input images. Figures 4 and 5 show the intentionally degraded modal images.

Table 1. Combination of input image degradation upon training MMS

Combination	Periocular image	Iris image
1	Degrade (Random Erase)	Non-degraded
2	Non-degraded	Degrade (Gaussian Filter)

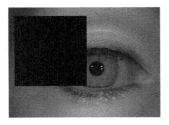

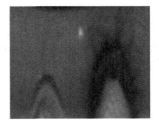

Fig. 4. Periocular image degraded by Random Erase

Fig. 5. Normalized iris image degraded by Gaussian blur

4 Experiments

4.1 Dataset

Experiments were performed using the CASIA-Iris-Lamp dataset [10], which consists of near-infrared (NIR) periocular images. The CASIA-Iris-Lamp dataset has periocular images of 411 subjects. We used periocular images of 135 people who had 19 or more images of both the left and right eyes and whose iris could be normalized correctly by the method in Sect. 3.2.

4.2 Iris Detection and Normalization

Figures 6 and 7 are the detected iris and the normalized iris images, respectively. Bicubic interpolation [6] was used as the interpolation method for coordinate transformation.

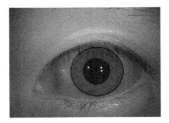

Fig. 6. Iris detection result (before normalization)

Fig. 7. Normalized iris image

4.3   Recognition by Iris and Periocular Classifier

The CNN models Neural Residual Network 18 (Resnet 18) [5] and Visual Geometry Group 16 (VGG16) [9] were used as the iris classifier and the periocular classifier, respectively. When training the classifiers, 1080 images of training data (4 images for each class) and 540 images of validation data (2 images for each class) were used. The training epoch was set to 100 times, and the loss function of the cross entropy error was used. The two classifiers fine-tune the weights that have been obtained by pre-training with the ImageNet dataset [11]. Table 2 shows the accuracy rate for the training (train), verification (val), and test (test) data of each modal classifier.

Table 2. Accuracy rates of the trained modal classifiers

Classifier type	Train	Val	Test
Iris classifier	100.00%	95.93%	93.33%
Periocular classifier	100.00%	99.63%	98.67%

4.4   Multi Modal Selector

The MMS was constructed using generic machine learning-based classification methods of Multilayer Perceptron (NN), Support Vector Machine (SVM) [7], and Random Forest (RF) classifiers [4]. MMS uses 1350 images of training data (5 images for each class) and 2700 images of test data (10 images for each class), all of which are fed to the trained modal classifiers, and portions of their outputs as described in Sect. 3.4 were used as inputs to the MMS.

4.5   Experimental Conditions

As shown in Table 3, the experiments were conducted by changing the degree of degradation of the degraded image at the time of the test in 5 stages. The "Accuracy of the classifier using the degraded images" is the approximate classification accuracy of the modal classifier when the degraded image is input. The "Classification accuracy 100%" in Experiment 1 means that images without degradation were used.

Table 3. Experiment types

Experiment number	Accuracy of the classifier using degraded images
Experiment 1	100% (no deterioration)
Experiment 2	Around 80%
Experiment 3	Around 50%
Experiment 4	Around 20%
Experiment 5	Around 1%

Figures 8 and 9 are examples of the degraded modal images used in Experiment 2. Figures 10 and 11 are examples of the degraded modal images used in Experiment 5.

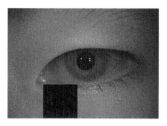

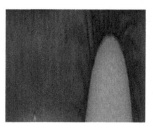

Fig. 8. Periocular image degraded due to partial occlusion (modal classification accuracy around 80%)

Fig. 9. Normalized iris image degraded by blurring (modal classification accuracy around 80%)

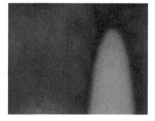

Fig. 10. Periocular image degraded due to partial occlusion (modal classification accuracy around 1%)

Fig. 11. Normalized iris image degraded by blurring (modal classification accuracy around 1%)

4.6 Evaluation Criteria

Two evaluation criteria were used in the experiments. Namely, the selection accuracy of the MMS and the overall classification accuracy. The selection accuracy P_s is defined as,

$$P_s = \frac{\text{The number of times MMS selected the classifier correctly}}{\text{Total number of classifications}} \times 100. \quad (1)$$

Classification accuracy P_c is defined as,

$$P_c = \frac{\text{Number of successful classifications}}{\text{Total number of classifications}} \times 100. \quad (2)$$

The classification methods used were compared by adding the following two methods, "random" and "selection accuracy 100%".

Random: Randomly select a classifier without using MMS.
Selection accuracy 100%: Always select the classifier that receives a non-degraded image without using MMS.

4.7   Experimental Results: Selection Accuracy

Figure 12 is a graph of the selection accuracies(P_s) of MMS (SVM, RF, NN) in Experiments 2 to 5. The horizontal axis is the classification accuracy of the modal classifier when using the deteriorated image, and the vertical axis is the selection accuracy (P_s).

MMS has high selection accuracy in experiments with severe degradation, and can correctly select a highly reliable classifier when the degradation of the other input is significant.

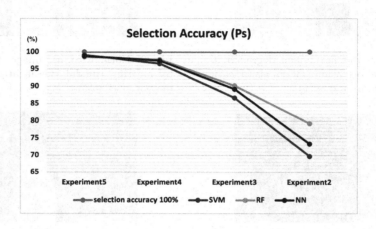

Fig. 12. Selection accuracy

4.8   Experimental Results: Classification Accuracy

Figure 13 is a graph of the selection accuracies (P_c) of MMS (SVM, RF, NN) in Experiments 1 to 5. The horizontal axis is the classification accuracy of the modal classifier when using the deteriorated image, and the vertical axis is the classification accuracy (P_c).

Due to the use of MMS realized by the general machine learning-based classification methods in Experiments 1 to 5, even when one of the iris or the periocular is significantly deteriorated, the classification accuracy is maintained to 94% or higher.

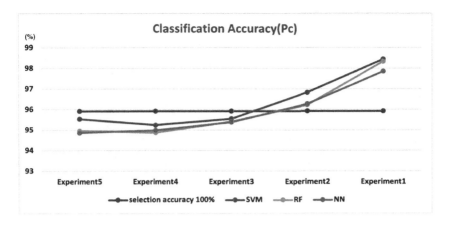

Fig. 13. Classification accuracy

4.9 Comparison of the Proposed Method and the Fusion Method

When the score level fusion [12] method in combining the results of the modal classifiers is used, the fixed weight acquired at the time of learning is used. Here, we weighted the outputs of the iris classifier and the periocular classifier by 0.7:0.3, and used the weighted output vectors of the two modal classifiers to compare with the proposed method.

Figure 14 shows the classification accuracy when the proposed MMS implemented by a k-nearest neighbor classifier (KNN) and a Multilayer perception(NN), and the fusion method (iris0.7-periocular0.3) were compared for Experiments 1–5. The experiment with the lowest classification accuracy for the proposed method and the fusion method is Experiment 4, and the experiment with the highest accuracy is Experiment 1. The decrease in accuracy in Experiment 1 and Experiment 4 of the fusion method was 4% or more, but the decrease in accuracy in the proposed method was about 3%. It was found that the Multi Modal Selector can maintain the classification accuracy without significantly losing the classification accuracy as compared with the score level fusion method, and it was found that the fluctuation of the classification accuracy due to the change in the deterioration degree of the input image was suppressed.

Since the functional level [14] fusion method uses the fixed weights acquired during training as in the score level fusion method, the classification accuracy fluctuates greatly.

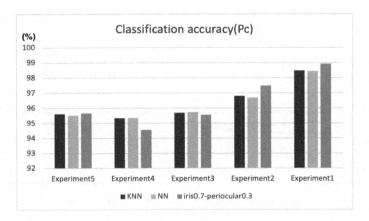

Fig. 14. Classification accuracy of using two implementations of MMS and the fusion method

5   Conclusion

The purpose of this study was to propose a Multi Modal Selector(MMS) that adaptively selects a classifier that is useful for classification from the iris classifier and the periocular classifier when either the iris or the periocular area is a deteriorated image. It also aimed to maintain the classification accuracy. MMS is trained to observe the classifier outputs indicating their confidence and select the classifier which is more reliable.

From the experimental results, it was found that MMS maintains the classification accuracy by improving the selection accuracy as the degree of deterioration increases. We also showed that MMS can be implemented with common machine learning-based classification methods. It has also been shown that MMS not only chooses a classifier that uses undegraded images, but also contributes further to improving overall classification accuracy by choosing a reliable classifier.

It was found that MMS maintains classification accuracy when compared with the score level fusion method that uses fixed weights, and suppresses fluctuations in classification accuracy due to changes in the degree of deterioration of the input image. In the score-level fusion method, it is necessary to repeat multiple experiments to derive the optimum weight, but MMS can acquire the selection rule of the classifier with single learning.

6   Future Tasks

In this study, we used the degradation by random occlusion and Gaussian blur. However, when actually using the system, there can be noises such as spectacles and hair that are not present during learning. Therefore, it is necessary to evaluate the performances under the degradation conditions of images existing in the real world. In addition, methods to maintain the authentication accuracy even when both the iris and periocular images are degraded, needs to be investigated.

Acknowledgment. This work was supported by JSPS Kakenhi grant number 19K12151.

References

1. Amani, A., Muhammad, H., Hatim, A., Aqil, A.: ConvSRC: smartphone-based periocular recognition using deep convolutional neural network and sparsity augmented collaborative representation. J. Intell. Fuzzy Syst. **38**(3), 3041–3057 (2020)
2. Daugman, J.G.: High confidence visual recognition of persons by a test of statistical independence. IEEE Trans. PAMI **15**(11), 1148–1161 (1993)
3. Gaikwad, D., Thool, R.C.: Intrusion detection system using bagging ensemble method of machine learning. In: 2015 International Conference on Computing Communication Control and Automation, pp. 291–295 (2015)
4. Ham, J., Chen, Y., Crawford, M.M.: Investigation of the random forest frame work for classification of hyperspectral data. IEEE Trans. GSS **43**(3), 492–501 (2005)
5. He, K., Zhang, X., Ren, S., Sun, J.: Deep residual learning for image recognition. In: Proceedings of the IEEE Conference on CVPR, pp. 770–778 (2016)
6. Keys, R.G.: Cubic convolution interpolation for digital image processing. IEEE Trans. ASSP **29**(6), 1153–1160 (1981)
7. Noble, W.S.: What is a support vector machine? Nat. Biotechnol. **24**, 1565–1567 (2006)
8. Park, U.: Periocular biometrics in the visible spectrum. IEEE Trans. Inf. Forensics Secur. **6**(1), 96–106 (2011)
9. Simonyan, K., Zisserman, A.: Very deep convolutional networks for large-scale image recognition. In: International Conference on Learning Representations, pp. 1–14 (2015)
10. Tan, T.: CASIA Iris image database (2010). http://biometrics.idealtest.org/
11. Umer, S., Sardar, A., Dhara, B.C., Rout, R.K., Pandey, H.M.: Person identification using fusion of iris and periocular deep features. Neural Netw. **122**, 407–419 (2020)
12. Woodard, D.L., Pundlik, S., Miller, P., Jillela, R., Ross, A.: On the fusion of periocular and iris biometrics in non-ideal imagery. In: 2010 ICPR, pp. 201–204 (2010)
13. Yuksel, S.E.: Twenty years of mixture of experts. IEEE Trans. NNLS **23**(8), 1177–1193 (2012)
14. Zhang, Q., Li, H., Sun, Z.: Deep feature fusion for iris and periocular biometrics on mobile devices. IEEE Trans. Inf. Forensics Secur. **13**(11), 2897–2912 (2018)

Multi-Perspective Interactive Model for Chinese Sentence Semantic Matching

Baoshuo Kan[1], Wenpeng Lu[1(✉)], Fangfang Li[2], Hao Wu[3], Pengyu Zhao[1], and Xu Zhang[1]

[1] School of Computer Science and Technology, Qilu University of Technology
(Shandong Academy of Sciences), Jinan, China
10431200583@stu.qlu.edu.cn, lwp@qlu.edu.cn
[2] Lendlease Digital, Sydney, Australia
fangfang.li@lendlease.com
[3] School of Computer, Beijing Institute of Technology, Beijing, China
wuhao123@bit.edu.cn

Abstract. Chinese sentence semantic matching is a fundamental task in natural language processing, which aims to distinguish whether two Chinese sentences are semantically similar or not. Originated from English semantic matching task, most existing matching methods merely focus on learning the sentence representation from word granularity, but neglect the uniqueness of Chinese characters and the semantic interactions within a sentence on different granularities, and the interactions between sentences. As a result, most existing matching methods on Chinese language only achieve very limited performance improvement. In the paper, we propose a multi-perspective interactive (MPI) model for Chinese sentence semantic matching, which first employs a multi-granularity encoding layer to transform the characters and words in sentences into their embedding representation, then devises a multi-perspective interactive layer to capture the intra-sentence interactions within a sentence but on different granularities and the inter-sentence interactions between sentences. Finally, a prediction layer takes all the captured interactions as input to estimate the matching degree. We also conduct extensive experiments on real-world data set to assess the model performance. The extensive experimental results demonstrate that our proposed model achieves significantly better performance than the compared benchmarks.

Keywords: Multi-perspective · Multi-granularity · Interactive features · Chinese sentence semantic matching

1 Introduction

Sentence semantic matching is an important task to decide if two sentences are semantically similar or not, which is the key component in many natural language processing applications, such as retrieval-based chatbots [4] and answer selection [11].

© Springer Nature Switzerland AG 2021
T. Mantoro et al. (Eds.): ICONIP 2021, LNCS 13111, pp. 668–679, 2021.
https://doi.org/10.1007/978-3-030-92273-3_55

In the recent decade, deep learning has been becoming more and more active in machine learning research, which also greatly impacts natural language processing community. Actually, deep learning has gained great success in sentence semantic matching tasks, by modeling the semantic features and learning the matching representations of sentence pairs via various neural architectures [1,20]. Most existing sentence semantic matching models focus on the English language, which try to best capture semantic features on word granularity. However, the Chinese language is unique and different from English, because the character is actually pictograph, with the same character representing special sometimes even different meanings in different scenarios. Therefore, both characters and words should be considered when modeling the semantic features of Chinese texts. That is why most existing semantic matching methods on English are normally either unsuitable or not the best for the Chinese language.

In order to solve the problem, some researchers attempt to incorporate the features on multiple granularities for modeling Chinese texts [7,21]. Usually, character and word embeddings are combined together with some simple operations, such as concatenation or summation. However, these simple combination methods are unfortunately unable to capture the abundant interactive features between different granularities, resulting in only limited performance improvement.

For the Chinese sentence semantic matching task, effectively capturing the interactive features within a sentence, and the interactions between different granularities of a sentence pair is essential for a sound matching model. Most existing matching methods usually only focus on the representation learning on each individual sentence, but ignore the interactions between sentence pairs, which leads to inferior performance [23]. To capture the more complicated semantics interactions between sentence pairs, some work based on interactive models emerges, such as stacked multi-layer convolutional networks [14], and complicated alignment mechanism [21]. However, these sophisticated architectures still fail to conquer the problems in the Chinese sentence semantic matching task because of the lacking capability to capture interactive features from multiple perspectives, including interactive features within a sentence (namely intra-sentence features), and the interactions between a sentence pair (namely inter-sentence features).

To address the challenge as above, this paper proposes a multi-perspective interactive model for Chinese sentence semantic matching. Specifically, this model first employs a multi-granularity encoding layer to transform the characters and words in sentences into their embedding representation, then devises a multi-perspective interactive layer to capture the intra-sentence interactions between different granularities within a sentence and the inter-sentence interactions between sentences. Finally, this model utilizes a prediction layer to estimate the matching degree. Extensive experimental results demonstrate that our method achieves significantly better performance than the compared benchmark methods.

This paper makes the following major contributions:

- We propose a novel neural architecture for Chinese sentence semantic matching, named multi-perspective interactive model (MPI). In contrast to the existing approaches, our model aims to capture the sophisticated intra-sentence interactions within a sentence on different granularities, and the inter-sentence interactions between a sentence pair.

- We invent a novel multi-perspective interactive layer to model the intra-sentence interactions between characters and words within a sentence and the inter-sentence interactions between sentences.
- Experiments on the real-world LCQMC dataset demonstrate that the proposed MPI model achieves better performance than the compared state-of-the-art benchmarks.[1]

2   Related Work

Deep Sentence Semantic Matching Models based on deep learning have been widely applied in sentence semantic matching task. These models normally consist of two important components: (1) learning textual representations [5,10,17] for input sentence, (2) learning complicated interactions between given sentences [2,3]. Given two input sentences, deep sentence matching models usually try to first learn the textual representation for each sentence and the complicated interactions between sentences, then utilize a similarity function or a more complicated prediction layer to estimate the similarity degree of the two sentence representations as the matching score. As one successful and broadly applied deep learning method in NLP applications, attention mechanism has been recently applied in sentence matching as well to capture interactive features between sentences, which have achieved encouraging semantic matching performance [9,22]. Although some existing methods already model the interactive features between sentences, most of these approaches still neglect to capture the fine-granularity features within a sentence. Therefore, some works have attempted to model the semantic features in Chinese sentences with multi-granularity embeddings [7,21], which simply combine the character and word embeddings together with basic operations, such as concatenation and summation. However, the simple combination of words and characters embeddings still neglects the interactive features between different granularities in a sentence, which inevitably miss key semantic information. That's actually where this paper mostly contributes to not only learning complicated intra-sentence interactions within a sentence on multiple granularities, but also learning inter-sentence interactions between sentence pairs, in Chinese sentence semantic matching task.

Pre-trained Language Models, e.g., BERT [8], have shown powerful performance in natural language processing. For Chinese sentence semantic matching, BERT takes characters as input tokens and ignores word information. Moreover, because BERT is computationally expensive in the pre-training procedure, a series of lightweight frameworks based on BERT are put forward [12]. Although the lightweight frameworks reduce the computational complexity, the performance of the original BERT model is inevitably decreased as well. How to

---

[1] Codes are available at https://github.com/baoshuo/MPI.

achieve comparable performance with BERT with fewer computational resources is another key challenge in Chinese sentence semantic matching.

3   Task Definition

A Chinese sentence semantic matching data set can be represented as $D = \{(Q, A, y)_i\}_{i=1}^{N}$, where Q and A refer to two sentences, $y \in \{0, 1\}$ denotes the matching label. If Q and A are semantically similar, y is 1, otherwise, y is 0. For the sentence Q, its character-granularity form is represented as $Q_c = \{q_{c1}, \ldots, q_{ct}\}$, where $\{q_{ci}\}_{i=1}^{t}$ are the characters and t is the number of characters. Its word-granularity form is represented as $Q_w = \{q_{w1}, \ldots, q_{wl}\}$, where $\{q_{wj}\}_{j=1}^{l}$ are the words and l is the number of words. For the sentence A, the similar symbols are defined. Our goal is to learn a matching model $g(Q, A)$ from D. For any sentence pair (Q, A), $g(Q, A)$ evaluates the matching degree between (Q, A).

4   Model

4.1   Model Overview

The overall architecture of the proposed multi-perspective interactive model for Chinese sentence semantic matching, named MPI for short, is shown in Fig. 1. MPI consists of three layers, i.e., the multi-granularity encoding layer, multi-perspective interactive layer, and prediction layer. The multi-granularity encoding layer accepts characters and words in sentences and transfers them into their embedding representations. The multi-perspective interactive layer captures the intra-sentence interactions between different granularities within a sentence and the inter-sentence interactions between sentences and generates the final representation for matching two input sentences. Finally, the prediction layer judges the matching degree of the sentence pair according to the matching representation.

4.2   Multi-Granualrity Encoding Layer

In order to fully utilize the semantic information contained in character and word granularities, the multi-granularity encoding layer first transforms characters and words into their embeddings, then employs BiLSTM (i.e., bidirectional long short-term memory [6]) components to encode the embedding matrix.

As shown in Fig. 1, for the input sentences pair Q and A, their character and word sequences are denoted as Q_c, Q_w, A_c and A_w, which are converted into their corresponding embedding representations by Word2Vec [16]. Afterwards, the representations are padded to a fixed length, which are denoted as: $\bar{\mathbf{Q}}_{\mathbf{c}} \in \mathbb{R}^{k \times d}$, $\bar{\mathbf{Q}}_{\mathbf{w}} \in \mathbb{R}^{k \times d}$, $\bar{\mathbf{A}}_{\mathbf{c}} \in \mathbb{R}^{k \times d}$ and $\bar{\mathbf{A}}_{\mathbf{w}} \in \mathbb{R}^{k \times d}$. k is the padded length, and d is the dimensionality of the embeddings. $\bar{\mathbf{Q}}_{\mathbf{c}}$, $\bar{\mathbf{Q}}_{\mathbf{w}}$, $\bar{\mathbf{A}}_{\mathbf{c}}$ and $\bar{\mathbf{A}}_{\mathbf{w}}$ are further encoded

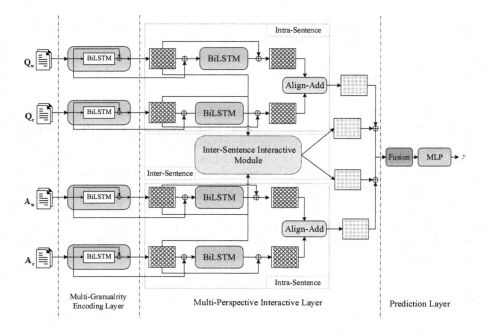

Fig. 1. Overview of our proposed MPI model

by four independent BiLSTMs, respectively. The embedding representations and
the outputs of BiLSTM are concatenated as the outputs of the multi-granularity
encoding layer, described with Eqs. (1) and (2).

$$\bar{\mathbf{Q}}_\mathbf{c}^\mathbf{B} = [\bar{\mathbf{Q}}_\mathbf{c}; \mathrm{BiLSTM}(\bar{\mathbf{Q}}_\mathbf{c})], \qquad \bar{\mathbf{Q}}_\mathbf{w}^\mathbf{B} = [\bar{\mathbf{Q}}_\mathbf{w}; \mathrm{BiLSTM}(\bar{\mathbf{Q}}_\mathbf{w})], \tag{1}$$

$$\bar{\mathbf{A}}_\mathbf{c}^\mathbf{B} = [\bar{\mathbf{A}}_\mathbf{c}; \mathrm{BiLSTM}(\bar{\mathbf{A}}_\mathbf{c})], \qquad \bar{\mathbf{A}}_\mathbf{w}^\mathbf{B} = [\bar{\mathbf{A}}_\mathbf{w}; \mathrm{BiLSTM}(\bar{\mathbf{A}}_\mathbf{w})], \tag{2}$$

where $\bar{\mathbf{Q}}_\mathbf{c}^\mathbf{B} \in \mathbb{R}^{k \times d}$, $\bar{\mathbf{Q}}_\mathbf{w}^\mathbf{B} \in \mathbb{R}^{k \times d}$, $\bar{\mathbf{A}}_\mathbf{c}^\mathbf{B} \in \mathbb{R}^{k \times d}$ and $\bar{\mathbf{A}}_\mathbf{w}^\mathbf{B} \in \mathbb{R}^{k \times d}$ are the outputs of
the multi-granularity encoding layer, which can be viewed as the initial sentence
contextual representations.

4.3   Multi-Perspective Interactive Layer

There are abundant interactive features in and between different granularities
and sentences, which can provide critical information for sentence semantic
matching. Especially, between a pair of sentences, characters and characters
(words and words) are interactive with each other; within a sentence, the words
and characters are also interactive with each other. Therefore, as shown in Fig. 1,
we devise the multi-perspective interactive layer consisting of inter-sentence and
intra-sentence interactive modules, which model the inter-sentence interactions
and the intra-sentence interactions simultaneously.

Inter-Sentence Interactive Module. Both character-level and word-level interactions of two sentences are critical for sentence semantic matching. As shown in Fig. 2, we devise inter-sentence interactive module to capture the interactive features between the pair of sentences.

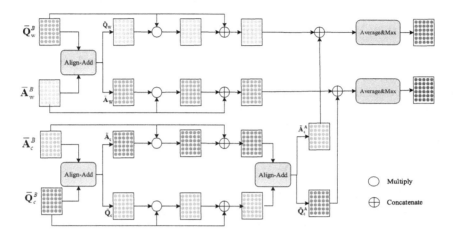

Fig. 2. Structure of inter-sentence interactive module

In order to fully explore the interaction information between two sentences at character granularity, this module first accepts the initial sentence contextual representations generated by the multi-granularity encoding layer, marked as $\bar{\mathbf{Q}}_{\mathbf{c}}^{\mathbf{B}} = \{\bar{\mathbf{q}}_{ci}^{\mathbf{B}}\}_{i=1}^{k}$ and $\bar{\mathbf{A}}_{\mathbf{c}}^{\mathbf{B}} = \{\bar{\mathbf{a}}_{cj}^{\mathbf{B}}\}_{j=1}^{k}$, then computes the attention weight between $\bar{\mathbf{q}}_{ci}^{\mathbf{B}}$ and $\bar{\mathbf{a}}_{cj}^{\mathbf{B}}$, described with Eq. (3).

$$\mathbf{e}_{i,j} = \left(\bar{\mathbf{q}}_{ci}^{\mathbf{B}}\right)^{\top} \bar{\mathbf{a}}_{cj}^{\mathbf{B}}. \tag{3}$$

Once obtaining the attention weight, we further consider to utilize the interactive information from another sentence to generate the relevant representation. For a character in the sentence Q, its relevant representation is computed with the embeddings of the characters in the sentence A, weighted by the attention $\mathbf{e}_{i,j}$, describe with Eq. (4).

$$\tilde{\mathbf{q}}_{ci} = \bar{\mathbf{a}}_{ci}^{\mathbf{B}} + \sum_{j=1}^{k} \frac{\exp\left(\mathbf{e}_{i,j}\right)}{\sum_{x=1}^{k} \exp\left(\mathbf{e}_{i,x}\right)} \bar{\mathbf{a}}_{cj}^{\mathbf{B}}, i \in \{1,\ldots,k\}, \tag{4}$$

where the characters in $\{\bar{\mathbf{a}}_{cj}^{\mathbf{B}}\}_{j=1}^{k}$ that are relevant with $\bar{\mathbf{q}}_{ci}^{\mathbf{B}}$ are selected to generate $\tilde{\mathbf{q}}_{ci}$. The same operation is performed for each character in the sentence

A to generate its relevant representation carried by the characters in the sentence Q, described with Eq. (5).

$$\tilde{\mathbf{a}}_{cj} = \bar{\mathbf{q}}^{\mathbf{B}}_{cj} + \sum_{i=1}^{k} \frac{\exp\left(\mathbf{e}_{i,j}\right)}{\sum_{x=1}^{k} \exp\left(\mathbf{e}_{x,j}\right)} \bar{\mathbf{q}}^{\mathbf{B}}_{ci}, j \in \{1,\ldots,k\}. \tag{5}$$

After that, we define $\tilde{\mathbf{Q}}_{\mathbf{c}} = \{\tilde{\mathbf{q}}_{c1},\ldots,\tilde{\mathbf{q}}_{ck}\}$ and $\tilde{\mathbf{A}}_{\mathbf{c}} = \{\tilde{\mathbf{a}}_{c1},\ldots,\tilde{\mathbf{a}}_{ck}\}$ as character-granularity relevant representations of two sentences. Besides, the same operation is performed for each word in sentences Q and A. We define $\tilde{\mathbf{Q}}_{\mathbf{w}} = \{\tilde{\mathbf{q}}_{w1},\ldots,\tilde{\mathbf{q}}_{wk}\}$ and $\tilde{\mathbf{A}}_{\mathbf{w}} = \{\tilde{\mathbf{a}}_{w1},\ldots,\tilde{\mathbf{a}}_{w_k}\}$ as word-granularity relevant representations of two sentences.

In order to simplify the aforementioned equations, we integrate them, i.e., Eqs. (3), (4) and (5), into a new uniform equation, which is defined as align-add operation, as Eq. (6). The same operation is adopted for $\tilde{\mathbf{Q}}_{\mathbf{w}}$ and $\tilde{\mathbf{A}}_{\mathbf{w}}$.

$$\tilde{\mathbf{Q}}_{\mathbf{c}}, \tilde{\mathbf{A}}_{\mathbf{c}} = \text{Align-Add}\left(\bar{\mathbf{Q}}^{\mathbf{B}}_{\mathbf{c}}, \bar{\mathbf{A}}^{\mathbf{B}}_{\mathbf{c}}\right). \tag{6}$$

In order to avoid information loss and enhance sentence representations, we employ residual connections to combine the above relevant representation and the initial contextual representations to generate the enhanced relevant representations, described as Eqs. (7) and (8).

$$\tilde{\mathbf{Q}}^{\mathbf{F}}_{\mathbf{c}} = [\tilde{\mathbf{Q}}_{\mathbf{c}}; \tilde{\mathbf{Q}}_{\mathbf{c}} \odot \bar{\mathbf{Q}}^{\mathbf{B}}_{\mathbf{c}}], \qquad \tilde{\mathbf{A}}^{\mathbf{F}}_{\mathbf{c}} = [\tilde{\mathbf{A}}_{\mathbf{c}}; \tilde{\mathbf{A}}_{\mathbf{c}} \odot \bar{\mathbf{A}}^{\mathbf{B}}_{\mathbf{c}}], \tag{7}$$

$$\tilde{\mathbf{Q}}^{\mathbf{F}}_{\mathbf{w}} = [\tilde{\mathbf{Q}}_{\mathbf{w}}; \tilde{\mathbf{Q}}_{\mathbf{w}} \odot \bar{\mathbf{Q}}^{\mathbf{B}}_{\mathbf{w}}], \qquad \tilde{\mathbf{A}}^{\mathbf{F}}_{\mathbf{w}} = [\tilde{\mathbf{A}}_{\mathbf{w}}; \tilde{\mathbf{A}}_{\mathbf{w}} \odot \bar{\mathbf{A}}^{\mathbf{B}}_{\mathbf{w}}], \tag{8}$$

where $\odot$ represents the element-wise multiplication.

Because word segmentation may be ambiguous, it may induce some noise information. Therefore, it is necessary to pay more attention to character granularity. In order to explore more semantic features on character granularity, we further apply align-add operation on it, described in Eq. (9). Its outputs are concatenated together with the enhanced relevant representations, described in Eq. (10), which are final representations of inter-sentence interaction.

$$\tilde{\mathbf{Q}}^{\mathbf{A}}_{\mathbf{c}}, \tilde{\mathbf{A}}^{\mathbf{A}}_{\mathbf{c}} = \text{Align-Add}\left(\tilde{\mathbf{Q}}^{\mathbf{F}}_{\mathbf{c}}, \tilde{\mathbf{A}}^{\mathbf{F}}_{\mathbf{c}}\right), \tag{9}$$

$$\mathbf{Q}^{\mathbf{A}} = [\tilde{\mathbf{Q}}^{\mathbf{A}}_{\mathbf{c}}; \tilde{\mathbf{Q}}^{\mathbf{F}}_{\mathbf{w}}], \qquad \mathbf{A}^{\mathbf{A}} = [\tilde{\mathbf{A}}^{\mathbf{A}}_{\mathbf{c}}; \tilde{\mathbf{A}}^{\mathbf{F}}_{\mathbf{w}}]. \tag{10}$$

Intra-Sentence Interactive Module. Within a sentence, its words and characters can represent the sentence meaning from different perspectives. The semantic information conveyed by characters and words is interactive and complementary to each other. In order to fully mine the features within a sentence, we devise the intra-sentence interactive module.

As shown in Fig. 1, we first adopt residual connections to concatenate the original embedding representations and the initial sentence contextual representations, then utilize BiLSTM to capture the temporal semantic information, described with Eqs. (11) and (12).

$$\bar{\mathbf{Q}}_{\mathbf{c}}^{\mathbf{D}} = \text{BiLSTM}([\bar{\mathbf{Q}}_{\mathbf{c}}; \bar{\mathbf{Q}}_{\mathbf{c}}^{\mathbf{B}}]), \qquad \bar{\mathbf{A}}_{\mathbf{c}}^{\mathbf{D}} = \text{BiLSTM}([\bar{\mathbf{A}}_{\mathbf{c}}; \bar{\mathbf{A}}_{\mathbf{c}}^{\mathbf{B}}]), \qquad (11)$$

$$\bar{\mathbf{Q}}_{\mathbf{w}}^{\mathbf{D}} = \text{BiLSTM}([\bar{\mathbf{Q}}_{\mathbf{w}}; \bar{\mathbf{Q}}_{\mathbf{w}}^{\mathbf{B}}]), \qquad \bar{\mathbf{A}}_{\mathbf{w}}^{\mathbf{D}} = \text{BiLSTM}([\bar{\mathbf{A}}_{\mathbf{w}}; \bar{\mathbf{A}}_{\mathbf{w}}^{\mathbf{B}}]). \qquad (12)$$

In order to further enhance the representation of temporal features in sentences, we concatenate it with the original embedding matrix together, i.e., $\tilde{\mathbf{Q}}_{\mathbf{c}}^{\mathbf{D}} = [\bar{\mathbf{Q}}_{\mathbf{c}}^{\mathbf{D}}; \bar{\mathbf{Q}}_{\mathbf{c}}]$, $\tilde{\mathbf{A}}_{\mathbf{c}}^{\mathbf{D}} = [\bar{\mathbf{A}}_{\mathbf{c}}^{\mathbf{D}}; \bar{\mathbf{A}}_{\mathbf{c}}]$, $\tilde{\mathbf{Q}}_{\mathbf{w}}^{\mathbf{D}} = [\bar{\mathbf{Q}}_{\mathbf{w}}^{\mathbf{D}}; \bar{\mathbf{Q}}_{\mathbf{w}}]$ and $\tilde{\mathbf{A}}_{\mathbf{w}}^{\mathbf{D}} = [\bar{\mathbf{A}}_{\mathbf{w}}^{\mathbf{D}}; \bar{\mathbf{A}}_{\mathbf{w}}]$.

In order to capture the interactive features between character and word granularities within the current sentence, we utilize the align-add operation to encode them to generate the intra-sentence interactive representations, described with Eq. (13).

$$\mathbf{Q}_{\mathbf{c}}^{\mathbf{D}}, \mathbf{Q}_{\mathbf{w}}^{\mathbf{D}} = \text{Align-Add}\left(\tilde{\mathbf{Q}}_{\mathbf{c}}^{\mathbf{D}}; \tilde{\mathbf{Q}}_{\mathbf{w}}^{\mathbf{D}}\right), \quad \mathbf{A}_{\mathbf{c}}^{\mathbf{D}}, \mathbf{A}_{\mathbf{w}}^{\mathbf{D}} = \text{Align-Add}\left(\tilde{\mathbf{A}}_{\mathbf{c}}^{\mathbf{D}}; \tilde{\mathbf{A}}_{\mathbf{w}}^{\mathbf{D}}\right). \quad (13)$$

So far, we have obtained the initial sentence contextual representations by the multi-granularity encoding layer, intra-sentence interactive representations and inter-sentence interactive representations by the multi-perspective interactive layer. We concatenate them together, and utilize global average and max pooling operations to extract the key features to generate the final representations of two sentences, described with Eqs. (14) and (15).

$$\mathbf{Q} = [[\bar{\mathbf{Q}}_{\mathbf{c}}^{\mathbf{B}}; \bar{\mathbf{Q}}_{\mathbf{w}}^{\mathbf{B}}; \mathbf{Q}_{\mathbf{c}}^{\mathbf{D}}; \mathbf{Q}_{\mathbf{w}}^{\mathbf{D}}]_{\max}^{avg}; [\mathbf{Q}^{\mathbf{A}}]_{\max}^{avg}], \qquad (14)$$

$$\mathbf{A} = [[\bar{\mathbf{A}}_{\mathbf{c}}^{\mathbf{B}}; \bar{\mathbf{A}}_{\mathbf{w}}^{\mathbf{B}}; \mathbf{A}_{\mathbf{c}}^{\mathbf{D}}; \mathbf{A}_{\mathbf{w}}^{\mathbf{D}}]_{\max}^{avg}; [\mathbf{A}^{\mathbf{A}}]_{\max}^{avg}], \qquad (15)$$

where $\mathbf{Q}$ and $\mathbf{A}$ contain the deep connection and difference to each other, which can be viewed as the final representations of two sentences.

4.4 Prediction Layer

After obtaining the final representations of two sentences, we investigate different fusion methods to merge them together, including weighted sum, dot-product, concatenation, and subtraction. Finally, we find that the subtraction of two sentences achieves the best performance over other operations. Our model will predict the similarity of two sentence. Therefore, the final prediction are obtained by Eq. (16).

$$\mathbf{M} = |\mathbf{Q} - \mathbf{A}|, \quad p = \text{MLP}(\mathbf{M}), \qquad (16)$$

where $\mathbf{M}$ represents the final matching representation. $\mathbf{M}$ is fed into a multi-layer perceptron (MLP) classifier with the Sigmoid activation.

The training objective $\mathcal{L}$ is to minimize the binary cross-entropy loss [18]:

$$\mathcal{L} = -\sum \lambda(y,p)(y \log p + (1-y) \log(1-p)), \qquad (17)$$

where y denotes the ground-truth label in the dataset and p represents the label predicted by the model. $\lambda(y,p)$ is computed with Eq. (18).

$$\lambda(y,p) = 1 - \theta(y-m)\theta(p-m) - \theta(1-m-y)\theta(1-m-p), \qquad (18)$$

where $\theta(\cdot)$ is the unit step function and m is the threshold.

5   Experiments

5.1   Dataset

We conduct extensive experiments on a real-world Chinese dataset for sentence semantic matching, i.e., LCQMC [13]. Each instance in LCQMC contains a pair of sentences and a binary label, which indicates whether the two sentences are semantically similar or not. The dataset consists of 260,068 instances.

5.2   Implementation Details

For the multi-granularity encoding layer, the embedding dimension and the units number of BiLSTM are set to 300 and the dropout rate is set to 0.52 for BiLSTM. In the multi-perspective interactive layer, the unit number and dropout rate of BiLSTM are the same as the multi-granularity encoding layer. For the prediction layer, the unit number of the first two dense layers is set to 600 and 50, and ReLU is employed as the activation function. The unit number of the last dense layer is set to 1 with a Sigmoid function. In the loss function, the threshold m is set as 0.7. Adam with a initial learning rate of 0.01 is utilized as the optimizer. All experiments are conducted on a single Nvidia 2080Ti GPU. Accuracy (ACC) and F_1-score are adopted as evaluation metrics.

5.3   Comparison with State-of-the-Arts

We compare our model MPI with two kinds of state-of-the-art models, i.e., representation-based and interaction-based models. The representation-based models include Text-CNN [5], BiLSTM [17], and Lattice-CNN [10]. Text-CNN is a text classification model which employs CNNs to encode sentences. BiLSTM leverages bidirectional LSTM to capture the semantic information of a sentence. Lattice-CNN takes word lattice as inputs to alleviate the problem of potential ambiguity. The interaction-based models include BiMPM [19], ESIM [3], LET [15]. BiMPM first encodes each sentence by BiLSTM to obtain the implicit feature, followed by multiple-view matching methods. ESIM consists of two BiLSTMs, where the first one is used to encode sentences and the other is employed to fuse information. LET adopts the word lattice graph instead of

Table 1. Comparison with state-of-the-art models on LCQMC dataset.

Models	Interaction	ACC	F_1-score
Text-CNN [5]	×	72.80	75.70
BiLSTM [17]	×	76.10	78.90
Lattice-CNN [10]	×	82.14	82.41
BiMPM [19]	√	83.30	84.90
ESIM [3]	√	82.58	84.49
GMN [2]	√	84.60	86.00
LET [15]	√	84.81	86.08
MPI	√	**86.29**	**86.64**

a character sequence or a single word sequence as the input to capture multi-granularity interactive information. Table 1 shows the performance comparison and some observations are as follows.

First, compared with interaction-based models with single granularity (i.e., BiMPM and ESIM), multi-granularity models (i.e., GMN, LET, and MPI) demonstrate superior performance on both ACC and F_1-score, showing that focusing on multiple granularities helps to captures rich semantic features. Second, compared with the multi-granularity model (i.e., GMN, LET), our model MPI outperforms them in terms of ACC and F_1-score. This is probably because our model captures more sophisticated interactions within and between two sentences. Third, compared with all baselines, our model achieves a better performance on all metrics. The reason may lie in that multi-perspective interactions not only in a single sentence but also across two sentences can benefit each other, which are beneficial to enhance the matching representation for the accurate prediction.

Besides, compared with the BERT [8], our model is more streamlined and computationally efficient. We adopt FLOPs (number of floating-point operations) to compare the computational complexity of different models. The larger FLOPs means the longer computational time. The experiments on LCQMC show that the FLOPs and ACC of BERT are 21,785 million, and 85.73%, while those of our model MPI are 58.2 million and 86.29%, respectively. That is, our model can beat BERT while requiring less computational time and resources.

5.4 Ablation Study

We present ablation studies by comparing the standard MPI model with five variants (baselines): (1) **del-intra**: removes the intra-sentence interactive module, and feeds the output of the BiLSTM directly into the prediction layer; (2) **del-inter**: removes most of interactions between the same granularity in inter-sentence interaction modules; (3) **char alt**: only adopts characters as its input; (4) **word alt**: only adopts words as its input; In terms of accuracy and F_1-score, the performance comparisons of ablated models are shown in Fig. 3

First, both the performances of **del-intra** and **del-inter** degrade greatly. This demonstrates that the intra-sentence and inter-sentence interactive infor-

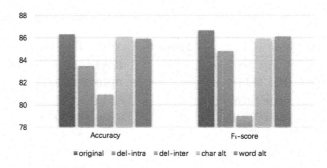

Fig. 3. Ablation study

mation are crucial for the accurate matching prediction. According to Fig. 3, the decrease of **del-inter** is more larger than that of **del-intra**, which shows that inter-sentence interactions are more important than intra-sentence interactions. Second, the performances of **char alt** and **word alt** are also inferior to the standard MPI model. This indicates that multi-granularity information is helpful to our model.

6   Conclusion

In this paper, we propose a multi-perspective interactive (MPI) model for the Chinese sentence semantic matching task, which employs a multi-granularity encoding layer to transform the characters and words in sentences into their embedding representation, and a multi-perspective interactive layer to capture the intra-sentence interactions between different granularities within a sentence and the inter-sentence interactions between sentences, followed by a prediction layer to estimate the matching degree of two input sentences. The proposed model has been evaluated on the real-world dataset LCQMC and performed the best compared to benchmark methods.

Acknowledgment. The research work is partly supported by National Key R&D Program of China under Grant No.2018YFC0830705 and No.2018YFC0831700, National Natural Science Foundation of China under Grant No.61502259, and Key Program of Science and Technology of Shandong Province under Grant No.2020CXGC010901 and No.2019JZZY020124. Wenpeng Lu is the corresponding author.

References

1. Cer, D., et al.: Universal sentence encoder for English. In: Proceedings of EMNLP, pp. 169–174 (2018)
2. Chen, L., et al.: Neural graph matching networks for Chinese short text matching. In: Proceedings of ACL, pp. 6152–6158 (2020)
3. Chen, Q., Zhu, X., Ling, Z.H., Wei, S., Jiang, H., Inkpen, D.: Enhanced LSTM for natural language inference. In: Proceedings of ACL, pp. 1657–1668 (2017)

4. Gu, J.C., et al.: Speaker-aware BERT for multi-turn response selection in retrieval-based chatbots. In: Proceedings of CIKM, pp. 2041–2044 (2020)
5. He, T., Huang, W., Qiao, Y., Yao, J.: Text-attentional convolutional neural network for scene text detection. In: Proceedings of the IEEE Transactions on Image Processing, vol. 25, no. 6, 2529–2541 (2016)
6. Hochreiter, S., Schmidhuber, J.: Long short-term memory. Neural Comput. **9**, 1735–1780 (1997)
7. Huang, J., Yao, S., Lyu, C., Ji, D.: Multi-granularity neural sentence model for measuring short text similarity. In: Candan, S., Chen, L., Pedersen, T.B., Chang, L., Hua, W. (eds.) DASFAA 2017. LNCS, vol. 10177, pp. 439–455. Springer, Cham (2017). https://doi.org/10.1007/978-3-319-55753-3_28
8. Kenton, J.D.M.W.C., Toutanova, L.K.: Bert: Pre-training of deep bidirectional transformers for language understanding. In: Proceedings of NAACL-HLT, pp. 4171–4186 (2019)
9. Kim, S., Kang, I., Kwak, N.: Semantic sentence matching with densely-connected recurrent and co-attentive information. In: Proceedings of AAAI, vol. 33, pp. 6586–6593 (2019)
10. Lai, Y., Feng, Y., Yu, X., Wang, Z., Xu, K., Zhao, D.: Lattice CNNs for matching based Chinese question answering. In: Proceedings of AAAI, vol. 33, pp. 2786–6641 (2019)
11. Laskar, M.T.R., Huang, X., Hoque, E.: Contextualized embeddings based transformer encoder for sentence similarity modeling in answer selection task. In: Proceedings of The 12th Language Resources and Evaluation Conference, pp. 5505–5514 (2020)
12. Liu, W., Zhou, P., Wang, Z., Zhao, Z., Deng, H., Ju, Q.: FastBERT: a self-distilling BERT with adaptive inference time. In: Proceedings of ACL, pp. 6035–6044 (2020)
13. Liu, X., et al.: LCQMC: A large-scale Chinese question matching corpus. In: Proceedings of the COLING, pp. 1952–1962 (2018)
14. Lu, W., Yu, R., Wang, S., Wang, C., Jian, P., Huang, H.: Sentence semantic matching based on 3D CNN for human-robot language interaction. In: Proceedings of ACM Transactions on Internet Technology (TOIT), vol. 21, no. 4, pp. 1–24 (2021)
15. Lyu, B., Chen, L., Zhu, S., Yu, K.: Let: Linguistic knowledge enhanced graph transformer for Chinese short text matching. In: Proceedings of the AAAI, vol. 35, pp. 13498–13506 (2021)
16. Mikolov, T., Chen, K., Corrado, G., Dean, J.: Efficient estimation of word representations in vector space. arXiv preprint arXiv:1301.3781 (2013)
17. Mueller, J., Thyagarajan, A.: Siamese recurrent architectures for learning sentence similarity. In: Proceedings of the AAAI, vol. 30, pp. 2786–2792 (2016)
18. Su, J.: Text emotion classification (iv): Better loss function. https://spaces.ac.cn/archives/4293
19. Sun, Y., et al.: Ernie: Enhanced representation through knowledge integration. arXiv preprint arXiv:1904.09223 (2019)
20. Wang, S., et al.: Cross-thought for sentence encoder pre-training. In: Proceedings of the EMNLP, pp. 412–421 (2020)
21. Wang, Z., Hamza, W., Florian, R.: Bilateral multi-perspective matching for natural language sentences. In: Proceedings of the IJCAI, pp. 4144–4150 (2017)
22. Yang, R., Zhang, J., Gao, X., Ji, F., Chen, H.: Simple and effective text matching with richer alignment features. In: Proceedings of ACL, pp. 4699–4709 (2019)
23. Zhang, S., Tan, H., Chen, L., Lv, B.: Enhanced text matching based on semantic transformation. IEEE Access **8**, 30897–30904 (2020)

An Effective Implicit Multi-interest Interaction Network for Recommendation

Wei Yang[1,2], Xinxin Fan[3], Yiqun Chen[1,2], Feimo Li[1,2(✉)],
and Hongxing Chang[1,2]

[1] University of Chinese Academy of Sciences, Beijing, China
[2] Institute of Automation, Chinese Academy of Sciences, Beijing, China
{yangwei2019,chenyiqun2020,lifeimo2012,hongxing.chang}@ia.ac.cn
[3] Beihang University, Beijing, China
zf1921334@buaa.edu.cn

Abstract. Data features in real industrial recommendation scenarios are high-dimensional, diverse and sparse. Rich feature interaction can improve the model effect and bring practical benefits. Factorization machines (FMs) can perform explicit second-order feature interactions, while deep neural networks (DNNs) can perform implicit non-linear feature interactions. A series of models integrating FMs and DNNs are used to perform diverse feature interactions. However, most of the previous work performed feature interaction without considering the diverse interests of users. In reality, users often have multiple preferences and interests, which are implicitly included in the features and need to be effectively extracted. In this paper, we propose an implicit multiple interest network (IMIN), taking into account the importance of interest. Specifically, the model constructs the implicit multiple interests of the user and the item through the implicit multi-interest layer, and realizes the interest alignment between the user and the item through the interest alignment layer. We further use the interest interaction and aggregation layer to construct rich interest feature interactions. In addition, we introduce an auxiliary loss in the model optimization part to ensure the difference of interest. We conducted comprehensive and rich experiments on three real-world data sets. Experimental results show that IMIN performs better than other competitive models, which proves the effectiveness of the model.

Keywords: Multiple interest · Feature interaction · Recommendation

1 Introduction

With the explosion of Internet information, recommendation systems play an important role in information matching [2], which are used in media, entertainment, e-commerce and other scenarios [16]. At the same time, the number of users and items increases exponentially, which greatly increases the difficulty of accurate recommendation. Under the scenario of large-scale recommendation system, there are rich and diverse features [6], including user attribute features, item attribute features, user history features, text features, etc. These features

© Springer Nature Switzerland AG 2021
T. Mantoro et al. (Eds.): ICONIP 2021, LNCS 13111, pp. 680–691, 2021.
https://doi.org/10.1007/978-3-030-92273-3_56

tend to be high dimensional, sparse, and diverse [18]. How to extract effective information from massive data features to provide more accurate recommendation effect is a key problem [24].

With the rise of deep learning [12], deep neural networks (DNNs) have been widely used in natural language processing, recommendation, computer vision and other fields due to its strong nonlinear fitting ability [4]. DNNs have been proved to be able to fit arbitrary functions, so it can be used for complex nonlinear feature combination. However, the implicit learning feature interaction information of DNNs is not always effective. Therefore, many fusion models use FMs to learn explicit low-order feature interaction and DNNs to learn implicit feature interaction [5,7].

However, all previous work concatenates the embedding of all features, and then uses Factorization Machine (FM) or DNNs to learn the interaction between features [3,14,20], without considering the diverse interests of users. In actual situations, users' preferences are often diverse, which means that users have a variety of different interests. For example, the user may like fashionable and luxurious items in terms of dressing, but prefer high-quality and inexpensive items in life. The multiple interests of the user can more fully reflect the characteristics of the user, which needs to be effectively modeled.

Considering the problems mentioned above, we propose an implicit multiple interest network (IMIN), taking into account the importance of interest. Specifically, the model constructs the implicit multiple interests of the user and the item through the implicit multi-interest layer, and realizes the interest alignment between the user and the item through the interest alignment layer. We further use the interest interaction and aggregation layer to construct rich interest feature interactions. In addition, we introduce an auxiliary loss in the model optimization part to ensure the difference of interest. The main contributions of this work can be summarized as follows:

- We propose an implicit multiple interest representation and interest alignment layer, which can not only construct multiple interests of users and items, but also model the matching relationship between interests.
- We propose an implicit multiple interest network (IMIN), taking into account the importance of interest. The model constructs a variety of interests, and effectively models interest information through interest alignment and interest interaction.
- We conduct extensive experiments on three real-world datasets to demonstrate the effectiveness of our model. Our model IMIN performs best when compared to other competitive networks.

2   Related Work

Traditional recommendation systems are mainly based on collaborative filtering models [19], which use the preferences of a group with similar interests and common experience to recommend information that users are interested in. It mainly includes user-based and item-based models [17]. The model based on collaborative filtering cannot solve the problem of data sparsity, so a series of models based on matrix factorization (MF) [11] appear. Matrix factorization introduces the latent factor as the implicit representation of user and item, which further improves the accuracy of model prediction. Collaborative filtering models are suitable for small-scale scenarios, but cannot be effectively applied to large-scale rich scenarios.

DNNs can effectively conduct nonlinear combination between features and model high-order complex feature interaction, which are widely used in recommendation systems [23]. A series of models fusing DNN and FM are further derived. Wide & Deep [3] learns high-order feature interactions by using multilayer perceptron (MLP), and constructs effective feature combinations based on manual feature engineering. DeepFM [5] uses FM for the low-order combination of features on the wide side, avoiding feature engineering. DCN [20] realizes low-order and high-order combination of features by using cross layer. xDeepFM [13] introduces a compressed interaction network to generate feature interactions in an explicit fashion and at the vector-wise level.

In addition to modeling directly from the perspective of feature intersection, there are models for modeling from a matching perspective. DMF [22] adds a nonlinear MLP network to the traditional MF. NCF [7] concatenates user and item embedding vectors together, and then learns high-order interactions through MLP network. In addition, Many methods based on attention mechanism have also been proposed. AFM [21] learns the importance of different feature interactions by introducing an attention network when performing feature interactions. DIN [25] applies the attention mechanism to the user's sequential behavior, and fully extracts the user's interest information contained in the historical behavior. The introduction of interest can model user characteristics more accurately.

3   Model

In this part, we introduce the various components of the model in detail. First, we introduce the presentation layer for constructing implicit multiple interests of users and items. Then we introduce the interest alignment layer to align the interest information between users and items. Then we introduce the interest interaction and aggregation layer, which is used to effectively construct the interaction between interest features. Finally, we introduce an auxiliary loss to ensure the difference between a variety of interests.

3.1   Implicit Multiple Interest Representation Layer

User features are direct expressions of user characteristics and reflect the user's personal preferences. In actual situations, users' preferences are often diverse, which means that users have a variety of different interests. For example, the user may like fashionable and luxurious items in terms of dressing, but prefer high-quality and inexpensive items in life. In order to effectively capture the user's multiple interests, we use a multi-head self-attention mechanism to implicitly construct it. First, the self-attention mechanism based on the user's feature set is as follows:

$$A_j = softmax(\frac{Q_j^T K_j}{\sqrt{d}})V_j \tag{1}$$

where $A_j \in R^{M \times d}$ represents the feature interaction of attention perception, which can be regarded as the expression of feature information under the j-th subspace. d_k refers to the matrix dimension. Q_j, K_j, V_j are defined as follows:

$$Q_j = W_j^q Z_u, K^u = W_j^k Z_u, V^u = W_j^v Z_u \tag{2}$$

where $Z_u \in R^{M \times k}$ represents the user feature matrix. M denotes the number of user fields, and k denotes the embedding dimension of each field feature. $W_j^q, W_j^k, W_j^v \in R^{k \times d}$ represents the attention parameter matrix, and d represents the mapping dimension. Further, we use the *maxpooling* operation to extract the most important feature information from A_j^u, and use *meanpooling* to propose the averaged feature information from A_j, which is defined as follows:

$$
\begin{aligned}
a_j &= [a_{j,1}; a_{j,2}] \\
a_{j,1} &= max\_pooling(A_j) \\
a_{j,2} &= mean\_pooling(A_j)
\end{aligned}
\tag{3}
$$

where $a_j \in R^{2d}$ is the user feature expression in the j-th subspace, which can be regarded as the j-th implicit interest representation of the user. Similarly, there may be multiple selected points of interest for an item. We can get $b_j \in R^{2d}$ based on the feature set of item using the above method, which represents the j-th implicit interest representation of item.

3.2   Interest Alignment Layer

The implicit multi-interest representation of user can be constructed based on user characteristics, and the implicit multi-interest representation of item can also be constructed. When a certain interest of the user matches a certain interest of the item, it means that the two have the same preference under the interest space. In order to effectively construct matching information between users' multiple interests and item multiple interests, we need to align multiple interest information. By designing user and item to perceive all the interest information of each other, information alignment can be realized, which is defined as follows:

$$
\begin{aligned}
a_i' &= \sum_{j=1}^{l_b} \frac{exp(a_i \cdot b_j)}{\sum_{k=1}^{l_b} exp(a_i \cdot b_k)} b_j \\
b_j' &= \sum_{i=1}^{l_a} \frac{exp(a_i \cdot b_j)}{\sum_{k=1}^{l_a} exp(a_k \cdot b_j)} a_i
\end{aligned}
\tag{4}
$$

where $a_i' \in R^{2d}$ represents the i-th implicit interest representation of the user who perceives the interest information of the item, and $b_i' \in R^{2d}$ represents the j-th implicit interest representation of the item that perceives the user's interest information. Further, in order to avoid losing the original interest information by only using the aligned interest, the original interest information and the aligned interest information need to be fused. We use a gated network to learn the weights of different interest, which is defined as follows:

$$\gamma_i = W_a[a_i; a_i'; a_i \odot a_i'; a_i - a_i'] + \epsilon_a$$
$$a_i^f = \gamma_i a_i + (1 - \gamma_i) a_i' \tag{5}$$

where $a_i^f \in R^{2d}$ represents the i-th fusion interest representation of the user, and γ_i represents the importance weight. $\odot$ stands for element-wise multiplication. The multiplication operator emphasizes the similarity of two vectors, and the subtraction operator emphasizes the difference between the two vectors. Further, we connect all the fusion interest representations of the user together, as the global interest representation of the user as follows:

$$h_u = mean\_pooling([a_1^f; a_2^f; \cdots ; a_{l_a}^f]) \tag{6}$$

where $h_u \in R^{2d}$ represents the global interest representation of the user. Similarly, our fusion interest representation based on item can get the item global interest representation $h_i \in R^{2d}$.

3.3   Interest Interaction Layer

The interest representation constructed based on the implicit multi-interest representation layer only reflects the feature interaction information of the user or item itself, which does not learn the feature interaction between the user and the item. In order to effectively learn rich feature information, we construct feature interactions based on user implicit multiple interest representations and item implicit multiple interest representations, which are defined as follows:

$$S_{i,j} = a_i \odot b_j \tag{7}$$

where $S_{i,j} \in R^{2d}$ represents the interaction between the i-th interest feature of the user and the j-th interest feature of the item. Considering that the importance of different feature interactions is different, we design a compressed activation network to learn the importance of feature interactions. First, we perform the mean pooling operation on feature interaction, which is designed as follows:

$$r_{i,j} = f_{sq}(S_{i,j}) = \frac{1}{2d} \sum_{k=1}^{2d} S_{i,j}^k \tag{8}$$

Then we use the extended network to learn the importance weight, which is designed as follows:

$$A_s = f_{ex}(R) = \sigma_2(W_2 \sigma_1(W_1 R)) \tag{9}$$

where $A_s \in R^{l_a \times l_b}$ represents the weight matrix, and σ_2 and σ_1 represent the activation function. We multiply the feature interaction matrix by the weight matrix, which is defined as follows:

$$S^{'} = A_s \odot S \tag{10}$$

In order to further learn the high-level interactions of features, we stitch all feature interactions together as follows:

$$s = sum\_pooling(S^{'}) \tag{11}$$

where $s \in R^{2d}$ represents the low-level feature interaction between user and item. $sum\_pooling$ means to sum the matrix $S^{'}$ into a one-dimensional vector. Further, we use residual network to learn low-order and high-order feature interactions, which is defined as follows:

$$x_{l+1} = f(W_l x_l + \epsilon_l) + x_l \tag{12}$$

where x_l denotes the feature representation of the l-th layer, x_0 is equal to s. The feature interaction finally learned through the L-layer network is denoted as x.

3.4 Information Aggregation Layer

The user global interest representation h_u and item global interest representation h_i are constructed through the interest alignment layer. The global interest representation represents the overall feature information of user and item. The low-order and high-order feature interaction x between user interest features and item interest features are constructed through the interest interaction layer, which reflects the feature interaction information. Taking into account the different importance of different information, we design a gated network to control the transmission of information, which is defined as follows:

$$\begin{aligned} h^{'} &= tanh(W_g x + U_g(\beta \odot h) + \epsilon_g) \\ q &= \alpha \odot h + (1 - \alpha) \odot h^{'} \end{aligned} \tag{13}$$

where $q \in R^k$ represents aggregate feature information, α represents update gate, and β represents reset gate. W_g, U_g, ϵ_g represent network parameters. α and β are defined as follows:

$$\begin{aligned} \alpha &= \sigma(W_\alpha x + U_\alpha h + \epsilon_\alpha) \\ \beta &= \sigma(W_\beta x + U_\beta h + \epsilon_\beta) \end{aligned} \tag{14}$$

Based on the aggregate feature q that combines global interest information and feature interaction information, the final prediction result is:

$$p = \sigma(W_p q + \epsilon_p) \tag{15}$$

where p represents the prediction result of the model. W_p and ϵ_p represent network parameters.

3.5   Training Optimization

In this paper, we mainly predict whether the user will interact with the item, which can be regarded as a classification task. We mainly optimize logloss for classification tasks, which are defined as follows:

$$Loss_1 = -y_i log(p_i) - (1 - y_i)log(1 - p_i) \tag{16}$$

where $y_i \in \{0, 1\}$ represents the label of the sample, and p_i represents the predicted probability that the user clicks on the item. In addition, we design an implicit multi-interest representation layer for learning multi-interest representations. In order to ensure the difference of different interests, we introduce regularized auxiliary loss for multi-interest generation, which is designed as follows:

$$Loss_2 = -\lambda_1 \sum_{i=1}^{l_a} \sum_{j=i+1}^{l_a} \frac{a_i \cdot a_j}{|a_i||a_j|} - \lambda_2 \sum_{i=1}^{l_b} \sum_{j=i+1}^{l_b} \frac{b_i \cdot b_j}{|b_i||b_j|} \tag{17}$$

where a_i denotes the i-th implicit interest representation of the user, and b_j represents the j-th implicit interest representation of item. λ_1 and λ_2 represent hyperparameters, which are used to control the degree of regularization. Finally, we fuse log loss and auxiliary loss to get the total loss as follows:

$$Loss = \frac{1}{N} \sum_{i=1}^{N} Loss_1 + Loss_2 \tag{18}$$

where $Loss$ represents the total loss, and N denotes the number of samples.

4   Experiment

In this section, we solve the following problems by designing different experiments:

- **Q1** How does our proposed IMIN compare to state-of-the-art models?
- **Q2** Do the various modules and strategies we propose really make sense to improve the effect of the model?

4.1   Experimental Settings

Datasets. We evaluated model performance on the following data sets:

Frappe[1] Dataset [1]. Frappe is a context-aware mobile app recommender system. Frappe dataset are composed of application logs that contain ID information, weather information, and other rich contextual information. The dataset contains 192,406 samples.

---

[1] https://www.baltrunas.info/research-menu/frappe.

MovieLens[2] Dataset [6]. It is the baseline dataset in the recommendation scenario. MovieLens contains a lot of movie recommendation data, including user information, movie information, time information and other rich features. We use the dataset of one million samples.

Criteo[3] Dataset. It is an open industry benchmark dataset used to develop models for predicting ad click-through rates, which contains 45million samples. The dataset describes the prediction of the probability of clicking on the advertisement on the page given a user and the visited page.

Evaluation Metrics. We use AUC to measure model performance. In practical scenarios, positive and negative samples are often unbalanced, and AUC can evaluate model performance well in this case. In addition, in order to visually show the improvement degree of different models compared with the benchmark model, we introduce RelaImpr [8] metric, which is defined as follows:

$$RelaImpr = (\frac{AUC(measured\_model) - 0.5}{AUC(base\_model) - 0.5} - 1) \times 100\% \qquad (19)$$

Baselines. The competitive models we compare are as follows:

- FM [15]: FM uses latent vector representation to carry out the second-order interaction between features, which fully improves the model's predictive ability. FM is a widely used benchmark model.
- DNN [4]: DNN has powerful representation and fitting capabilities, and can fully learn the implicit interactions between features. It is a benchmark model based on neural networks.
- Wide & Deep [3]: It includes both the explicit feature interaction constructed by feature engineering and the implicit feature interaction constructed by neural network. It can significantly enhance the model learning ability.
- NFM [7]: NFM first performs second-order feature interaction at the vector level, and further learns complex interactions through neural networks.
- DeepFM [5]: DeepFM combines the second-order explicit feature interaction constructed by FM and the implicit feature interaction constructed by DNN.
- DCN [20]: DCN has designed a network that explicitly constructs low-order and high-order feature interactions, which can effectively construct feature interaction information.
- xDeepFM [13]: xDeepFM introduces a compressed interaction network to generate feature interactions in an explicit fashion and at the vector-wise level. xDeepFM can learn low-order and high-order feature interactions explicitly and implicitly.
- FiBiNET [9]: FiBiNET can dynamically learn the importance of features via the Squeeze-Excitation network mechanism. It is able to effectively learn the feature interactions via bilinear function.

---

[2] https://grouplens.org/datasets/movielens/.
[3] http://labs.criteo.com/2014/02/kaggle-display-advertising-challenge-dataset/.

Parameter Settings. We take 90% of each dataset as the training set, 10% as the validation set, and 10% as the test set. The validation set is mainly used for hyperparameter selection. The embedding size is selected in [8, 16, 32, 64, 128, 256, 512]. The number of hidden layers is adjusted sequentially from 1 to 5. For model optimization, we uniformly adopt Adam [10], which is a widely used optimizer. Considering the running time and efficiency, we set the batch size to 512, and select the learning rate in [0.0005, 0.001, 0.005, 0.01, 0.05, 0.1]. Neural network models all use dropout and batch normalization strategies to prevent overfitting. The dropout rate is adjusted sequentially from 0 to 0.5. In addition, we also use an early stop strategy during the training process, and stop training when the model does not improve in 5 consecutive epochs. For simplicity, we set the embedding size and hidden layer size to be the same. For IMIN, we set the number of implicit interests of users and items to be the same, and keep the hidden layer and embedding dimensions consistent.

4.2 Performance Comparison (Q1)

To verify the effectiveness of our model, we conducted comprehensive experiments on three real datasets. The experimental results are shown in Table 1. First, we can see that compared to the second-order feature interaction model FM and the implicit high-order feature interaction model DNN, models that integrate low-order and high-order feature interactions, such as xDeepFM and DCN, perform better. Second, our model surprisingly outperforms other state-of-the-art models on all three datasets. The AUC of our IMIN on the Frappe dataset is 0.9891, which is significantly higher than that of xDeepFM (0.9858), and is 3.03% higher than that of FM on RelaImpr. Since our model takes into account various interests of users and items, the matching relationship between interests is fully established. The experimental results fully verify the effectiveness of our model.

Table 1. Performance of different models on MovieLens, Frappe and Criteo datasets.

Models	MovieLens		Frappe		Criteo	
	AUC	RelaImpr	AUC	RelaImpr	AUC	RelaImpr
FM	0.8072	0.000%	0.9795	0.00%	0.7924	0.00%
DNN	0.8082	0.33%	0.9814	0.40%	0.8004	2.74%
Wide& Deep	0.8105	1.07%	0.9838	0.90%	0.8017	3.18%
PNN	0.8113	1.34%	0.9845	1.04%	0.8028	3.56%
NFM	0.8116	1.43%	0.9844	1.02%	0.8031	3.66%
DeepFM	0.8121	1.60%	0.9847	1.08%	0.8035	3.80%
DCN	0.8118	1.49%	0.9849	1.13%	0.8042	4.04%
xDeepFM	0.8129	1.86%	0.9858	1.31%	0.8069	4.96%
FiBiNET	0.8144	2.34%	0.9872	1.61%	0.8081	5.37%
IMIN	**0.8165**	**3.03%**	**0.9891**	**2.00%**	**0.8095**	**5.85%**

4.3 Model Ablation Analysis (Q2)

In order to study whether each module is really meaningful for the improvement of the model effect, we conducted a comprehensive ablation experiment. First, we remove interest alignment layer (IAL) to explore the role of interest alignment between users and items, and then we remove the interest interaction layer (IIL) to explore the role of interest feature interactions. Second, we replaced the gating fusion mechanism with vector addition and vector connection respectively to explore the effect of the gating mechanism. We conducted experiments on the three datasets, and some of the results are shown in Fig. 1.

– we can see that the effect of the model is worse after removing interest align-ment and interaction. Although the effect of interest interaction layer is better than interest alignment, interest alignment layer can be used as supplemen-tary information to further enhance the model effect.
– Whether it is vector addition or vector connection, the performance of the model is worse. This shows that there is a gap in the feature interaction of different perspectives and cannot be integrated in a simple and direct way. The results further verify the effectiveness of our gating mechanism.

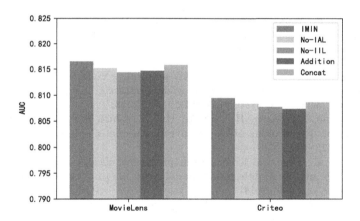

Fig. 1. Performance of different modules on MovieLens and Criteo datasets.

5 Conclusion

In this paper, we propose an implicit multiple interest network (IMIN), tak-ing into account the importance of interest. The model constructs a variety of interests, and effectively models interest information through interest alignment and interest interaction. We conduct extensive experiments on three real-world datasets to demonstrate the effectiveness of our model. Our model IMIN per-forms best when compared to other competitive networks.

There are two directions for future study. First, we consider introducing time series information to enrich interest modeling. We can expand the user's interest into long-term and short-term dynamic interest, thereby further improving the accuracy of prediction. Second, we consider the introduction of multi-modal features. By introducing modal information such as pictures, texts, etc., item features can be modeled more accurately.

Acknowledgments. This work is supported by the National Key Research and Development Program of China under Grant No. 2019YFF0301801, and the National Natural Science Foundation of China under Grant No. 61806199.

References

1. Baltrunas, L., Church, K., Karatzoglou, A., Oliver, N.: Frappe: Understanding the usage and perception of mobile app recommendations in-the-wild. arXiv preprint arXiv:1505.03014 (2015)
2. Bobadilla, J., Ortega, F., Hernando, A., Gutierrez, A.: Recommender systems survey. Knowl.-based Syst. **46**, 109–132 (2013)
3. Cheng, H.T., et al.: Wide & deep learning for recommender systems. In: Proceedings of the 1st Workshop on Deep Learning for Recommender Systems, pp. 7–10 (2016)
4. Covington, P., Adams, J., Sargin, E.: Deep neural networks for youtube recommendations. In: Proceedings of the 10th ACM Conference On Recommender Systems, pp. 191–198 (2016)
5. Guo, H., Tang, R., Ye, Y., Li, Z., He, X.: Deepfm: a factorization-machine based neural network for ctr prediction. arXiv preprint arXiv:1703.04247 (2017)
6. Harper, F.M., Konstan, J.A.: The movielens datasets: history and context. ACM Trans. Interact. Intell. Syst. (tiis) **5**(4), 1–19 (2015)
7. He, X., Liao, L., Zhang, H., Nie, L., Hu, X., Chua, T.S.: Neural collaborative filtering. In: Proceedings of the 26th International Conference on World Wide Web, pp. 173–182 (2017)
8. He, X., et al.: Practical lessons from predicting clicks on ads at facebook. In: Proceedings of the Eighth International Workshop on Data Mining for Online Advertising, pp. 1–9 (2014)
9. Huang, T., Zhang, Z., Zhang, J.: Fibinet: combining feature importance and bilinear feature interaction for click-through rate prediction. In: Proceedings of the 13th ACM Conference on Recommender Systems, pp. 169–177 (2019)
10. Kingma, D.P., Ba, J.: Adam: A method for stochastic optimization. arXiv preprint arXiv:1412.6980 (2014)
11. Koren, Y., Bell, R., Volinsky, C.: Matrix factorization techniques for recommender systems. Computer **42**(8), 30–37 (2009)
12. LeCun, Y., Bengio, Y., Hinton, G.: Deep learning. Nature **521**(7553), 436–444 (2015)
13. Lian, J., Zhou, X., Zhang, F., Chen, Z., Xie, X., Sun, G.: xdeepfm: Combining explicit and implicit feature interactions for recommender systems. In: Proceedings of the 24th ACM SIGKDD International Conference on Knowledge Discovery & Data Mining, pp. 1754–1763 (2018)

14. Qu, Y., et al.: Product-based neural networks for user response prediction. In: 2016 IEEE 16th International Conference on Data Mining (ICDM), pp. 1149–1154. IEEE (2016)
15. Rendle, S.: Factorization machines. In: 2010 IEEE International Conference on Data Mining, pp. 995–1000. IEEE (2010)
16. Ricci, F., Rokach, L., Shapira, B.: Introduction to recommender systems handbook. In: Ricci, F., Rokach, L., Shapira, B., Kantor, P.B. (eds.) Recommender Systems Handbook, pp. 1–35. Springer, Boston, MA (2011). https://doi.org/10.1007/978-0-387-85820-3_1
17. Sarwar, B., Karypis, G., Konstan, J., Riedl, J.: Item-based collaborative filtering recommendation algorithms. In: Proceedings of the 10th International Conference on World Wide Web, pp. 285–295 (2001)
18. Sarwar, B.M.: Sparsity, scalability, and distribution in recommender systems (2001)
19. Su, X., Khoshgoftaar, T.M.: A survey of collaborative filtering techniques. Advances in Artificial Intelligence 2009 (2009)
20. Wang, R., Fu, B., Fu, G., Wang, M.: Deep & cross network for ad click predictions. In: Proceedings of the ADKDD'17, pp. 1–7 (2017)
21. Xiao, J., Ye, H., He, X., Zhang, H., Wu, F., Chua, T.S.: Attentional factorization machines: Learning the weight of feature interactions via attention networks. arXiv preprint arXiv:1708.04617 (2017)
22. Xue, H.J., Dai, X., Zhang, J., Huang, S., Chen, J.: Deep matrix factorization models for recommender systems. In: IJCAI, vol. 17, pp. 3203–3209. Melbourne, Australia (2017)
23. Zhang, S., Yao, L., Sun, A., Tay, Y.: Deep learning based recommender system: a survey and new perspectives. ACM Comput. Surv. (CSUR) 52(1), 1–38 (2019)
24. Zhang, W., Du, T., Wang, J.: Deep learning over multi-field categorical Data. In: Ferro, N., et al. (eds.) ECIR 2016. LNCS, vol. 9626, pp. 45–57. Springer, Cham (2016). https://doi.org/10.1007/978-3-319-30671-1_4
25. Zhou, G., et al.: Deep interest network for click-through rate prediction. In: Proceedings of the 24th ACM SIGKDD International Conference on Knowledge Discovery & Data Mining, pp. 1059–1068 (2018)

Author Index

Agarwal, Swati 526
Ali, Fadel Muhammad 87
Arymurthy, Aniati Murni 87

Bąbel, Piotr 323, 338
Bai, Cong 609
Basaj, Dominika 323
Biecek, Przemysław 338

Cao, Xiaochun 28, 224
Chang, Hongxing 680
Chen, Chong 3
Chen, HanMo 550
Chen, Hong 402
Chen, Pan 237
Chen, Weizheng 100
Chen, Ya 427
Chen, Yiqun 680
Cheng, Yuang 138
Chi, Haoang 113
Choe, Yoonsuck 150

Dąbrowski, Jacek 212, 323, 338
Daniluk, Michał 323
Das, Anindya Sundar 415
Deng, Minghua 3
Ding, Jingjing 452
Ding, Xiangwu 452
Ding, Yue 138
Dou, Chunliu 585

Eldardiry, Hoda 501

Fan, Xinxin 680
Feng, Zhiyong 585
Foucher, Sebastien 138
Fu, Guohong 51
Fu, Hao 427
Fukumoto, Fumiyo 537, 562
Fung, Chun Che 489

Gao, Yi 514, 644
Gołuchowski, Konrad 323, 338
Gong, Jiaying 501

Gong, Jun 311
Guo, Jie 75
Guo, Yuhang 3

Han, Tianxing 609
Hao, Pengyi 609
He, Qing 40
Horiguchi, Eisaku 634
Hou, Hongxu 188
Hu, Xiao 378
Hua, Sihui 390
Huang, Cong 597
Huang, Zheng 75
Hui, Hong 75

Jakubowski, Adam 323
Jiang, Ning 311
Jiang, Wanrong 427
Jiang, Zhuqing 378
Ju, Wei 3

Kameyama, Keisuke 656
Kan, Baoshuo 668
Kang, Chunmeng 274
Kim, Daesik 63
Kim, Jangho 63
Kim, Jeesoo 63
Kong, Lingtong 477
Kowalik, Szymon 15
Kwak, Nojun 63

Lang, Jiulin 514, 644
Lee, Sang-Heon 150
Li, Bo 353
Li, Fangfang 668
Li, Feimo 680
Li, Jiyi 537, 562
Li, Qinbo 150
Li, Sirui 489
Li, Tao 3
Li, Xiangyu 100
Li, Xiu 550
Li, Yinlin 366
Li, Zuoyan 175

Liang, Tianyou   250
Lin, Huiping   597
Lin, Shaohui   237
Liu, Chaojian   402
Liu, Gongshen   621
Liu, Guanqun   200
Liu, Guiquan   427
Liu, Jinfeng   477
Liu, Lingbo   262
Liu, Ruixin   175
Liu, Shaolei   162
Liu, Yanbing   464
Lu, Wenpeng   668
Lu, Yuhai   464
Luo, Jinian   75
Luo, Xiao   3
Lv, Jiancheng   514, 644
Lv, Xuerui   125
Lyu, Chen   274, 299
Lyu, Lei   274, 299

Ma, Lizhuang   237
Ma, Zeyu   3
Maity, Krishanu   440
Mańdziuk, Jacek   15
Men, Aidong   378, 402
Meng, Min   250
Michałowski, Andrzej   323, 338
Mishima, Taishin   537

Nie, Liang   311

Ogawa, Keita   656
Okuno, Hirotsugu   634

Palanisamy, Suresh   574
Pascual, Damián   138
Patra, Jagdish C.   574

Qi, Junkun   28
Qin, Yanxia   452
Qiu, Weidong   75

Reddy, Saichethan Miriyala   526
Richter, Oliver   138
Rychalska, Barbara   212, 323, 338

Saha, Sriparna   415, 440
Savangouder, Ravindra V.   574
Shang, Yanmin   464

Sheng, Xing   274
Shi, Fan   224
Si, Runxuan   113
Sinaga, Marshal Arijona   87
Song, Zhijian   162
Su, Bo   621
Sun, Shuo   188
Sun, Yang   51
Sun, Yi   40
Sun, Yiping   452
Sun, Yue   585
Suzuki, Yoshimi   537, 562

Tan, Jianlong   464
Tan, Xin   237
Tang, Chenwei   514, 644
Tang, Gaozhong   353
Tang, MingKang   550
Tang, Yuhua   113
Tautkute, Ivona   287
Tian, Jiachen   585
Tian, Teng   464
Trzciński, Tomasz   287

Volk, Martin   138

Wan, Qing   150
Wang, Chuan   28
Wang, Haiying   378
Wang, Lei   200
Wang, Manning   162
Wang, MingQing   550
Wang, Qiansong   378
Wang, Rui   28, 224
Wang, Shuai   621
Wang, Xin   200
Wattenhofer, Roger   138
Wieczorek, Mikołaj   212
Wong, Kok Wai   489
Wu, Dongen   609
Wu, Han   585
Wu, Hao   668
Wu, Jiaxi   366
Wu, Jigang   250
Wu, Nier   188
Wu, Qiong   274
Wu, Shaojuan   585

Xiao, Yuhan   597
Xie, Jinghao   250

Xie, Jinyang   299
Xu, Jiachen   237
Xu, Sheng   562
Xu, Zhe   550

Yan, JiangPeng   550
Yang, Dengjie   40
Yang, Jie   477
Yang, Shaowu   113
Yang, ShengGe   550
Yang, Wei   680
Yang, Wenyuan   175
Yang, Yu   550
Ye, Shiwei   40
Yoo, Jaeyoung   63
Yu, ChengHui   550
Yu, Nan   51
Yu, Wenxin   311
Yu, Xuehui   40
Yuan, Fangfang   464

Zeng, Xiao-Jun   550
Zha, Daren   200
Zhang, Dongdong   390

Zhang, Li   125
Zhang, Sanyi   224
Zhang, Xiaowang   585
Zhang, Xu   668
Zhang, Xuewen   311
Zhang, Yongxiang   237
Zhang, Yunye   311
Zhao, Jing   113
Zhao, Lin   200
Zhao, Pengyu   668
Zhao, Yuran   621
Zheng, Jinfang   299
Zheng, Wei   188
Zheng, Yuxiang   609
Zheng, Zhuoran   274
Zhong, Huasong   3
Zhong, Shanlin   366
Zhou, Dongzhan   262
Zhou, Xinchi   262
Zhou, Zhiheng   353
Zhu, Dengya   489
Zhu, Yuesheng   175
Zhuang, Fuzhen   40
Zhuang, Yunliang   274

Printed in the United States
by Baker & Taylor Publisher Services